Library and Book Trade Almanac™

formerly The Bowker Annual

2021 | 66th Edition

Library and Book Trade Almanac™

formerly **The Bowker Annual**

2021 | 66th Edition

Editor John B. Bryans

 Information Today, Inc.

Published by Information Today, Inc.
Copyright © 2021 Information Today, Inc.
All rights reserved

International Standard Book Number 978-1-57387-572-1
International Standard Serial Number 2150-5446
Library of Congress Catalog Card Number 55-12434

Information Today, Inc.
143 Old Marlton Pike
Medford, NJ 08055-8750
Phone: 800-300-9868 (customer service)
          800-409-4929 (editorial queries)
Fax: 609-654-4309
E-mail (orders): custserv@infotoday.com
Web Site: http://www.infotoday.com

Typesetting by Amnet Systems

Printed and bound in the United States of America

US $315.50
ISBN 13: 978-1-57387-572-1
31550>

9 781573 875721

Contents

Preface and Acknowledgments ix

Part 1
Reports from the Field

Special Reports
How the COVID-19 Pandemic Affected Libraries ... and
Vice Versa   *David Shumaker* 3
Trade Publishing in 2020: How COVID-19 and Campaigns for Justice
Changed the Book Business   *John Maher* 16
Count on Libraries: Promoting a Fair, Accurate, and Complete 2020
Census Count   *Karen Brown* 22

Federal Agency and Federal Library Reports
Library of Congress   *Carla Hayden* 29
Federal Library and Information Network   *Laurie Neider* 48
National Agricultural Library   *Paul Wester* 52
National Library of Medicine   *Jody Nurik* 62
United States Government Publishing Office   *Gary Somerset* 71
National Technical Information Service   *Wayne Strickland* 79
National Archives and Records Administration 82
National Center for Education Statistics
Christopher A. Cody, Tara Lawley, and *Maura Spiegelman* 93
Defense Technical Information Center 97
Education Resources   *Karen Tate* and *Erin Pollard* 101

National Association and Organization Reports
American Library Association   *Julius C. Jefferson, Jr.* 105
American Booksellers Association 121
Association of Research Libraries   *Kaylyn Groves* 128
The Scholarly Publishing and Academic Resources Coalition   *Heather Joseph* ..139
Council on Library and Information Resources   *Kathlin Smith* 145
Association for Library and Information Science Education   *Sandra Hirsh* 153

International Reports

International Federation of Library Associations and Institutions
Beacher Wiggins and *Susan R. Morris* 159
Library and Archives Canada   *Leslie Weir* 167
International Board on Books for Young People
Mingzhou Zhang and *Liz Page*.. 171

Part 2
Legislation, Funding, and Grants

Legislation

Legislation and Regulations Affecting Libraries in 2020: A Report from ALA's
Public Policy and Advocacy Office   *Kathi Kromer* and *Shawnda Hines*.............179

Funding Programs and Grant-Making Agencies

National Endowment for the Humanities...189
Institute of Museum and Library Services   *Crosby Kemper III*...........................201
EveryLibrary   *John Chrastka*...212

Part 3
Library / Information Science Education, Placement, and Salaries

Career Resources and Job Listings for Library and Information Professionals
Susanne Markgren 221
Placements and Salaries 2020: First Jobs Out of Library School
Suzie Allard.. 228
Accredited Master's Programs in Library and Information Studies..................... 245
Library Scholarship Sources...251
Library Scholarship and Award Recipients, 2020.. 256

Part 4
Research and Statistics

Library Research and Statistics

Number of Libraries in the United States and Canada.. 285
Highlights of IMLS Public Library Surveys.. 288
School Librarian Employment in the United States   *Debra E. Kachel* and
Keith Curry Lance 295

Library Acquisition Expenditures, 2020–2021: U.S. Public, Academic, Special, and Government Libraries 301

Year in Architecture 2020   *Emily Puckett Rodgers* and *Library Journal* Staff..310

Public Library State Rankings, 2018 322

Book Trade Research and Statistics

Prices of U.S. and Foreign Published Materials   *George Aulisio*........................331

Book Title Output and Average Prices: 2018–2020   *Constance Harbison* 371

Number of Book Outlets in the United States and Canada 385

Part 5
Reference Information

Ready Reference

How to Obtain an ISBN   *Beat Barblan* 389

The ISSN, and How to Obtain One.. 394

How to Obtain an SAN   *Beat Barblan* 397

Distinguished Books

The Year's Notable Books... 401

The Reading List... 402

The Listen List 403

Best Fiction for Young Adults 404

Quick Picks for Reluctant Young Adult Readers 407

The Alex Awards..413

Amazing Audiobooks for Young Adults 413

Outstanding International Books for Young Readers 417

Notable Children's Books 418

Notable Recordings for Children 421

Notable Children's Digital Media 424

Top Ten Book Lists, 2020 426

Literary Prizes, 2020...429

Part 6
Directory of Organizations

Directory of Library and Related Organizations

Networks, Consortia, and Other Cooperative Library Organizations.................... 461

Library and Information-Industry Associations and Organizations, U.S. and Canada.. 478

State, Provincial, and Regional Library Associations.. 540
State and Provincial Library Agencies... 554
State School Library Associations 560
International Library Associations 569
Foreign Library Associations... 576

Directory of Book Trade and Related Organizations

Book Trade Associations, United States and Canada 587
International and Foreign Book Trade Associations... 592

National Information Standards Organization (NISO).. 599
Calendar, 2021–2028.. 607
Acronyms..617
Index.. 623

Preface and Acknowledgments

This year, the staff of Information Today, Inc.'s *Library and Book Trade Almanac* presents the latest annual volume with an extra degree of gratitude. Unofficially, the 2021 installment of *LBTA* is our COVID-19 edition, and as you might imagine, the process of gathering, updating, and editing some 70 reports and datasets during a global pandemic was challenging.

Although we expected complications, we were encouraged by early responses from our contributors. When we asked them to describe the impact of COVID-19 on their work in 2020, they came through, offering a wealth of lessons learned and examples of how their people and organizations persevered and innovated successfully for the public good (and for that of employees) throughout the year. Thanks to their stories, I'm confident readers will judge this 2021 edition as a particularly strong entry in the reference series that began as *The Bowker Annual Library and Book Trade Almanac* over 65 years ago.

To a few highlights of the volume.

Special Reports by journalists David Shumaker and John Maher, writing on how the pandemic affected libraries and book publishing in 2020, respectively, are first up and not to be missed. Shumaker encapsulates the year in libraries elegantly and with insight, which will come as no surprise to those who follow his work in the information industry press. Maher, News and Digital Editor for *Publishers Weekly,* has been generous with his advice in the past, which led to his report. The theme I broached initially was "COVID-19 and book publishing;" thankfully, he brought a more expansive vision, going beyond the pandemic to cover relevant social justice issues, such as racial inequities and the lack of diversity within the publishing business.

A third timely Special Report was suggested by someone I regard as an *LBTA* secret weapon. Shawnda Hines of ALA's Office of Policy and Advocacy, who herself coauthored a Special Report in 2020 and consistently elevates our section on Legislation in Part 2 (see page 179), believed the work of libraries and librarians in support of the decennial U.S. Census was an important story. We listened, agreed, and were delighted with her introduction to Karen Brown, Ph.D., whose engaging and informative report begins on page 22.

Statistics on school librarianship have been increasingly hard to come by in recent years, as research on the subject by the National Center for Education Statistics (NCES, see page 93) and other organizations has dwindled or stalled. The paucity of research we have been able to identify and report on is disappointing, to say the least, and should alarm all who view healthy, well-staffed school libraries and media centers as crucial to our children's education and our nation's future. Happily for *LBTA* readers this year, John Chrastka of EveryLibrary (see page 212) provided an introduction to Debra E. Kachel, who along with her colleague

Keith Curry Lance helped address our coverage gap with a report entitled "School Librarian Employment in the United States." Their research is conducted for the SLIDE project—learn more about this welcome initiative beginning on page 295 and be sure to visit its website.

There are many other features to recommend this 2021/66th edition of *LBTA*—for instance, the extensive directory listings in Part 6—but given limitations of space and time I must leave you to discover them for yourself. To close, I want to acknowledge a number of talented individuals who have supported this production with skill and enthusiasm. Without repeating names seen above, special thanks go to contributors George Aulisio, Connie Harbison, Susanne Markgren, Liz Page, Kathlin Smith, Narda Tafuri, and Steve Zalusky. I also wish to recognize Meredith Schwartz, her staff and writers at *Library Journal* for the quality of their reporting and the generosity they have shown us for decades.

The *LBTA* team is an assemblage of gifted professionals who never fail to inspire me. My thanks to Joel Jones Alexander, Nan Badgett, Christine McNaull, and associate editor Sonya Manes. The opportunity to work with Owen O'Donnell, director of ITI's Reference Division, has been more rewarding than I could have ever expected, and that's saying a lot because I've known, liked, and admired Owen for more than twenty years.

To our readers, thank you for using *Library and Book Trade Almanac* in your work. Stay safe and healthy.

Part 1
Reports from the Field

Special Reports

How the COVID-19 Pandemic
Affected Libraries . . . and Vice Versa

David Shumaker

Introduction and Timeline: Is the Library Closed?

It all began with an outbreak of viral illness in Wuhan, China, in late 2019. By the end of December, Chinese specialists had identified the cause as a new variant of coronavirus. In early January 2020, reports of the new virus began to appear in American news media, and on the 21st, the first American case was identified, in Washington State. That same month, the World Health Organization (WHO) began to issue guidance on controlling the spread of the virus, which, in February, it named coronavirus disease 2019—COVID-19 for short. On March 11, WHO declared the outbreak a pandemic.

By early March, American libraries had begun to confront the pandemic's impact on their services. On the 11th, American Library Association (ALA) executive director Tracie Hall issued a statement recognizing that library actions would be driven by the decisions of parent organizations like universities, schools, and local governments (Hall 2020). Soon, ALA's executive board went further, issuing a statement on March 17 that recommended the closure of academic, public, and school libraries. By that time, many libraries around the country had already locked their doors, suspended the lending of library materials, and directed staff to work from home where possible.

Initial actions. by libraries and other institutions, were tentative and provisional. The hope persisted that resumption of in-person services could occur in a matter of a few weeks. In its March 17 statement, the ALA board reiterated its intention to hold its annual conference in person in June—a decision that was reversed just a week later. The Ohio State Library, along with other state government units, announced a three-week closure on March 13. On April 3, it extended

David Shumaker, currently retired, was formerly clinical associate professor in the Department of Library and Information Science, Catholic University of America; and manager of Information Services at the MITRE Corporation. He is the author of *The Embedded Librarian: Taking Knowledge Where It's Needed* (Information Today, 2012) and numerous professional articles. His awards and recognitions include the Special Libraries Association's Rose Vormelker Award, as well as the Ainsworth Rand Spofford and Distinguished Service awards of the District of Columbia Library Association.

the closure to May 1, and on April 30 extended it again, to June 1. Similar actions were taken in other states, and by other libraries. In all, over 3,000 library buildings were reported closed (Ashworth 2020). A May survey found that 62 percent of responding public libraries had fully closed their buildings, while 26 percent provided curbside pickup of borrowed items, and 11 percent offered limited building access to patrons. Only 1 percent of respondents reported being open with no restrictions ("Libraries Respond: COVID-19 Survey. Survey of Responses and Activities Collected May 12-18, 2020" n.d.).

As summer approached, the pandemic's severity varied among states and regions. In some areas, the number of new COVID-19 cases began to decline, and librarians began to plan for a phased reopening of buildings and restoration of services. Libraries in a single region sometimes followed very different timetables. For example, libraries in the District of Columbia began to reopen in late May, while libraries in the neighboring suburbs kept their buildings closed months longer. In Richmond, Virginia, library buildings reopened in May, only to close again in July (Zauzmer 2020). San Antonio libraries reopened with restrictions on June 16 (Crowe 2020), while in New York City—one of the earliest and most severely affected places in the country—some libraries reopened on a limited basis in July, having been closed since March 13 (Farinacci 2020). Meanwhile, academic and school libraries made contingency plans as they awaited decisions from their institutional administrators on whether campuses would open in the fall.

Nationwide, the number of new cases continued to drop through mid-September, but a second wave followed that proved much worse than the first. Local trends and the fear of new outbreaks drove many libraries that had reopened their buildings to close them again. The New York Public Library moved to Phase 2 reopening with limited in-person services on November 9, but retreated to Phase 1 with "grab and go" service just one week later (Moloney 2020). Washington, D.C., libraries reclosed in December (Brice-Sadler and Carman 2020). Similarly, some academic institutions were forced to reverse course, closing campuses, sending students home, and resuming distance learning (Dixon 2020). *Library Journal* editor Meredith Schwartz captured the situation as the end of the year approached: "Day by day I see some libraries going back into early phases of their pandemic plans, sometimes all the way to full facility closure, while others are still opening up" (2020b).

At year's end, the immediate situation remained dire, even as hope appeared on the horizon. The numbers of new cases and deaths nationwide continued to climb into the New Year, but news that vaccines had been approved and were going into production, together with new national leadership to organize their distribution, offered the prospect of defeating the disease and resuming normal life in 2021. Meanwhile, libraries continued to serve their communities with new approaches, informed by the knowledge and experience gained over nearly a full year of contending with the pandemic. As ALA president Julius Jefferson put it, "Even when our buildings are not open, libraries are never closed" (Jefferson 2021).

Challenge and Response: How Libraries Coped

When the virus first began to spread, library managers and staff were faced with an array of challenging decisions, in an exceptionally difficult environment. Little was known about the actual means of transmission. Was the virus spread by physical contact? Through the air? Could it survive on surfaces and be transmitted by contact with an object, like a book, that had been handled by an infected person? What was the risk to staff of handling materials returned by borrowers—or of working in the library buildings at all? Which jobs could be done remotely?

Libraries faced these issues in an environment of serious threats and actual reductions in their resources. Local governments began to lose tax revenue, while universities lost income from tuition and fees. The Federal CARES Act and Family First Act, or FFCRA, mitigated the losses for some, but still the impacts were severe. Public libraries in Dallas, St. Louis, Madison, Wisconsin, and San Jose, California, were among many affected by budget cuts and layoffs (Crowe 2020; Peet 2020; Reid 2020; Woudenberg 2020).

In the absence of knowledge, many government leaders, library boards, and administrators of schools and universities adopted a cautious policy. Many libraries declared themselves closed, locking their doors and putting a hold on lending, while others recognized that certain services could safely continue. They made it easy for new patrons to obtain virtual library cards. They promoted their digital resources and, if funding permitted, acquired more. They provided telephone reference services, in many cases rerouting the calls to staff members working from home. They procured videoconferencing services, often through the vendor Zoom, and began to convert in-person programs to virtual programs. Virtual storytimes for early childhood learning became a hit in many localities, relieving young children and their parents from some of the pressure of staying at home.

Library leaders established the REopening Archives, Libraries, and Museums (REALM) project (https://www.oclc.org/realm/home.html), which built a body of scientific evidence on the transmissibility of coronavirus through the sharing of library materials and spaces, and informed practices for handling items. Some library agencies, including the Maryland State Library Resource Center and Oregon State Library, developed operational guidelines based on REALM results ("Handling Materials during COVID-19" 2020; "Updated Advice on Handling Library Materials during COVID-19 Pandemic" 2020). Many libraries established contactless curbside pickup services for items requested through their websites and by phone.

As the pandemic wore on, it became clear that decisions about stopping and starting services were complicated. When buildings reopened, some libraries required that patrons make appointments and many set capacity and time limits. Librarians moved furniture, installed plastic shields at service points, and made other physical adjustments. For academic and school librarians, if the decision was to continue distance learning, they focused on creating online courses and providing virtual services to students. Where administrators chose to pursue a blended learning approach, librarians did all the above.

Virtual programming required suitable audio and video capabilities, new presentation and program-moderating skills, robust videoconferencing accounts, effective signup systems, and attention to security measures to prevent malefactors from disrupting sessions. Similarly, school and academic librarians, along with classroom teachers and subject faculty, quickly found out what those with prior distance education experience already knew: effective online pedagogy requires new approaches and styles. Teaching strategies that worked fine for in-person classes had to be radically overhauled.

There were legal considerations as well: did the libraries' public performance rights to copyrighted stories extend to digital transmission? Authors and publishers attuned to the library market responded by issuing blanket permissions for such performances, while some library advocates asserted that librarians could make a fair use case, and did not need permission (Lipinski 2020; Messner n.d.; Ostman 2020). Even the Congressional Research Service got involved, issuing its own analysis in April (Richards 2020).

Library management systems had to be modified in unanticipated ways. Some libraries discontinued fines for overdue materials; their systems then had to be reconfigured to suppress fine calculations and change or eliminate overdue notifications. For large public library systems, scheduling applications that associated a given program with a given branch library had to be modified, as virtual programs could be attended by any library user systemwide—or even beyond the library's geographic service boundary.

In June, National Public Radio reporter Thomas Wilburn reported on the jump in demand for library e-books and audiobooks. Citing data from Overdrive, he reported that "weekly library e-book lending across the country has increased by nearly 50 percent since March 9" with a doubling in demand for children's materials (2020). The importance of digital collections put new pressures on vendors and publishers to collaborate with libraries. Amazon, which has long resisted licensing its e-books to libraries, came under pressure to change its policy—though it had not done so by the end of the year (Klar 2020). Meanwhile, a *Library Journal* survey found that academic libraries were increasing their reliance on open access materials, including open educational resources (Kletter 2020). On the other hand, an Internet Archive initiative to provide a "National Emergency Library" was abandoned due to copyright challenges from publishers and the Authors Guild (Musil 2020).

Beyond Coping: How Libraries Stepped Up to Meet Community Needs

Coping with the COVID-19 pandemic to restore basic services was vital and challenging work, but dedicated, innovative librarians soon realized that it wasn't enough. The pandemic, like other natural and human-caused disasters, had created new community needs. So librarians set about reaching out to their communities and expanding their reach. We'll look at some of the important actions they took.

Meeting New Connectivity Needs

In recent years, Internet connectivity has been cited as one of the top reasons Americans visit public libraries. In the spring of 2020—when offices, universities, and schools were transitioning to work at home and distance learning—the demand for connectivity surged. Yet libraries were closing their doors, too, so going to the library was no longer an option. The solution? Library access points were left on, 24/7 in some cases, even while the lights were off inside. Libraries boosted signals and moved hotspots so that people could connect from the parking lots. They began, or expanded, lending of hotspots. They converted bookmobiles to mobile access points. A Public Library Association survey found that

93 percent of public libraries provided or planned to provide wifi access on their grounds, 44 percent had moved routers to improve access outside the building, and 23 percent were lending wifi hotspots. These efforts were rewarded with the Federal Communications Commission's Digital Opportunity Equity Recognition (DOER) award ("America's Libraries Receive Inaugural FCC Honor" 2020).

Facilitating Social Services

As with the Great Recession (2007–2009), in 2020 the COVID-19 pandemic caused widespread demand for existing social services and created some entirely new needs. Most obviously, the sudden, dramatic increases in unemployment led to expanded demands for help with unemployment applications, career advisement, and job hunting. Public librarians reported an especially strong surge in demand from people in lower-income jobs and from the over-50 age group (Fields 2020). As food banks, rental assistance, foreclosure moratoriums, and other specialized aid programs were established, librarians had to broaden and update their knowledge to provide accurate, usable information and assistance to their communities. Some provided assistance online and by phone. Others, like the Joliet (Illinois) Public Library, decided to continue with some in-person services. Megan Millen, the library's executive director, noted that "in our community, a lot of people need our close-up assistance on how to fill out a job application or an unemployment application" (Keilman 2020).

Addressing Inequality

The pandemic developed even as other events raised concerns of racism, social justice, and economic inequality in society. Librarians realized that connectivity alone was not the answer to equitable information access. For a student or job applicant without a suitable computer, wifi was meaningless. The Hawkeye Community College Library (IA) lent 143 laptops to students so that they could continue their studies ("Public Libraries Respond to COVID-19: Survey of Response & Activities" n.d.). In Alameda County, California, the library provided power outside its building, as well as wifi (Nonko and Salinas 2020). For students who had been dependent on school-provided meals, no in-person classes meant no food. And for families whose breadwinners had lost their jobs, no income and inadequate financial support programs meant hunger.

Libraries responded to these needs in ways tailored to their communities. Some, like the public library in Woodstock, Illinois, started a food pantry (Keilman 2020). In Little Rock, the Central Arkansas Library System expanded an existing partnership to provide grab-and-go meals seven days a week at branches and other locations (Schwartz 2020a). The San Francisco Public Library addressed the needs of low-income families and those with essential workers by repurposing branches into day-care facilities, while in Los Angeles the libraries served as cooling stations (Nonko and Salinas, 2020).

New Needs and New Services

Beyond connectivity and the heightened impacts of inequality, libraries pivoted to address new needs, serve new audiences, and deliver new services. Even as regular volunteer activities had to be suspended, some libraries found novel ways to engage volunteers. In Homer Glen, Illinois, the township library neatly redirected its student volunteers, giving them new ways to earn service learning hours while meeting new needs. Among the new activities were writing greeting cards for children in foster care and hospitals, and contributing to a community digital archive about the pandemic (Keilman 2020).

Some libraries made a point of reaching out to senior citizens. The AnyThink Library (Colorado) systematically called senior patrons to check on their well-being. In one case, the call resulted in the library supplying a laptop and hotspot to enable the person to connect to academic and other services (Simpson 2020). In La Crosse, Wisconsin, librarians assembled and distributed "senior activity kits" ("Area Libraries Offer Project to Safely Connect the Community with Seniors" 2020). In Virginia, the Montgomery-Floyd Regional Library partnered with the local Agency on Aging for a Senior Connection program that included activity kits (Clauson-Wicker 2021).

In Iowa City and elsewhere, public libraries extended their usual readers' advisory service and started "grab bags" or "book bundles" to mitigate patrons' inability to browse the collection. With these services, the patron fills out a form indicating their general interest, and the librarians select appropriate materials, which can be picked up curbside or in some cases, delivered (Russell 2020).

The responses of academic and school libraries depended on the teaching and learning plans of their parent institutions. At New Canaan (Connecticut) High School, students could visit the virtual library—a Google Meeting, which is left open throughout the school day—no hall pass needed. In some classes, librarians cotaught through Zoom breakout rooms, as well (Tamez-Robledo 2020). School closure meant the loss of student access to the library and thus more emphasis on access to networked digital resources. In Waco, Texas, Brooklyn, New York, the Lancaster-Lebanon (Pennsylvania) district, and many others, school and public libraries partnered to make public library e-books and e-reference resources available to all students and teachers (Fox 2020; Ishler 2020; Saegert 2020). In Brooklyn, the public library also created a new online resource guide specifically for home-schoolers and remote learners (https://www.bklynlibrary.org/online-resources/topic/remote-learning) (Fox 2020). Similarly, many academic libraries promoted open educational resources and other open access materials (Kletter 2020).

These innovations didn't always require large investments, sophisticated plans, or advanced technologies. Berkeley, California, librarians noticed that students were spending long periods outside the library, using its wifi connectivity for their schoolwork. What else might they need when spending the day there? Bathrooms! So librarians installed portable toilets (Sass 2020). Similarly, in Seattle, five library branches remained open solely to provide bathroom access (Nonko and Salinas 2020).

Confronting the Pandemic and the Infodemic

Our society actually suffered two pandemics at the same time. One was biological, caused by the novel coronavirus. The second was what WHO termed an "info-demic" (Lin and Trinkunas 2020), resulting from rampant misinformation about the health crisis.

As a first step, libraries led the fight against the infodemic by example. As exhorted by *Library Journal*'s Meredith Schwartz, they based their service policies on science, not rumor. Sometimes, they were subjected to criticism and hostility. In Weber County, Utah, the library's mask mandate and hand sanitizer requirement prompted "periodic grumbling among some" and a complaint at a county commission meeting from a community member who felt that the policies violated her rights as an American citizen ("Weber County Library System COVID-19 Rules Generate Some Ire, but Mostly Praise" 2020).

Beyond leading by example, librarians took an active role in fighting COVID-19 through information services that supported medical researchers. One effort of note was organized by Elaine Hicks, a librarian at Tulane University, together with colleagues Stacy Brody (George Washington University) and Sara Loree (St. Luke's Health System). Hicks, Brody, and Loree formed the Librarian Reserve Corps. With other volunteers, they managed the flow of research reports coming into WHO's Global Outreach Alert and Response Network (GOARN)—amounting to over 100,000 by autumn. For their crucial volunteer efforts above and beyond their regular work, the three were recognized as *Library Journal*'s 2020 Librarians of the Year (Peet 2021).

Many more librarians addressed the public information challenges of the pandemic. They pivoted their web based resources to provide accurate information in response to widespread misinformation. Academic libraries across the country published research and literature guides. Public libraries linked to county and state health departments, the Federal Centers for Disease Control, and other authoritative sources. At times they also had to refute racist complaints about the origin of the disease (Ewen 2020).

The Next Normal: The Post-pandemic Future of Library Services

Someday, we all hope, the pandemic will be over. When that day comes, it's hard to imagine that libraries will simply return to prepandemic business as usual. Instead, librarians may feel that they've been fast-forwarded to a dramatically different future yet one that displays continuity with the past.

Changes in librarianship will mirror changes in society at large, as they always do. Journalist Carlos Lozada, reviewing three books about the pandemic's effects on American society, notes a common theme: that the pandemic is accelerating changes already underway (2020). Two of the accelerating trends he cites are particularly relevant to librarians: our increasing reliance on digital technologies, and the increasing vulnerability of disadvantaged communities.

Other sources concur. In early April, a Pew Research study found that over half of Americans considered the Internet "essential for them personally during the pandemic" (Vogels et al. 2020). Geoffrey Fowler refers to the pandemic as "an inflection point for nerds and non-nerds alike" (Fowler 2020). He points out specific activities like online shopping, telework, distance learning, telemedicine, and home entertainment. In a later survey, in October, Pew found that over half of those working at home during the pandemic would like to continue doing so (Parker et al. 2020).

For librarians, the impact includes digital collections, and more. The use of digital collections, and libraries' investments in them, had already been increasing relative to physical collections in recent years. In 2020, they set new records. E-book vendor Overdrive reported a 33 percent increase, to 430 million digital items "borrowed" worldwide. It also reported rapid growth in the adoption of its Sora app for schoolchildren, to 43,000 schools worldwide ("33% Growth for Digital Books from Public Libraries and Schools in 2020 Sets Records" 2021). A similar pattern has emerged in higher education. Clemson University Library dean Christopher Cox pronounced circulating physical collections "irrelevant" (Cox 2020). While that may be an overstatement—the demise of print materials has been predicted before—the trend is consistent with the overall shift toward digital activities in our society.

The trend to all things digital also encompasses library-sponsored meetings and programs. Public librarians have learned that virtual programs can overcome transportation and distance barriers, attracting attendees from a wider geographic area than programs offered solely in-person at a single branch library. Formal education was also affected by this trend. In higher education, the trend toward distance learning has been underway for over a decade; the pandemic served to increase its exposure among students and professors.

Librarians' own professional development has been affected in much the same way. During the pandemic, online conferences and seminars attracted audiences that exceeded expectations (Shumaker 2020a, 2020b). The virtual format eliminates travel time and expense, while enabling attendees to time-shift their viewing of recorded sessions. The in-person meeting may well rebound, but will any conference organizer fail to offer some sort of digital component in the future?

One change that doesn't fit this framework is the adaptation of library spaces. Librarians that have opened their buildings have installed partitions and barriers, moved furniture to allow social distancing, and taken other steps to thwart virus transmission. Fearing a similar pandemic in the future, library architects are now designing flexible buildings that can be easily configured to keep people apart if needed. Yet this configuration runs counter to the library's mission to be a community hub where people come together. As Karen Kleckner Keefe, the executive director of the Hinsdale (Illinois) Public Library put it, "It's awful because it's the opposite of what we normally try to do. We want to be the community living room, we want everyone to stay and get comfortable. And to design service to prevent lingering and talking is so different from everything we've been working toward" (Harris, 2020).

There's one more trend undergoing a fast-forward shift, and that's the trend for librarians to redefine their relationships with their communities. With libraries of things, makerspaces, embedded librarians, teacher librarians and other innovations, librarians have been taking new approaches to engage their communities. As the pandemic has created new needs, they have stepped up with an array of new services. As our reliance on digital technologies increases, librarians will do even more. First and foremost, they are positioned to address the increasing vulnerability of disadvantaged communities. As the technology providers of last resort, as well as the "people's university" in every community, librarians will always make equal access to information and technology a top priority. As well, they are positioned to attack the infodemic—not just the one associated with

COVID-19, but the epidemic of topical mis- and disinformation that is plaguing society.

Librarians will face serious challenges. The problem of publishers limiting library access to e-books must be addressed if collections are to meet community needs. "Intellectual property" questions affecting digital programs will need to be addressed as well. An even greater concern is the availability of resources. Local government officials and university leaders are already confronting revenue shortfalls, and many library budgets are likely to feel ongoing effects. Librarians will need to continue advocating for themselves and building on their record of addressing the needs of their communities during the pandemic in order to maintain the benefits of the work they have done to cope with it, innovate to meet community needs, and contribute to society's recovery.

References

"33% Growth for Digital Books from Public Libraries and Schools in 2020 Sets Records." 2021. *Cision PR Newswire*. January 7. https://www.prnewswire.com/news-releases/33-growth-for-digital-books-from-public-libraries-and-schools-in-2020-sets-records-301202452.html.

"America's Libraries Receive Inaugural FCC Honor." 2020. *American Libraries*. December. https://americanlibrariesmagazine.org/wp-content/uploads/2020/10/1120.pdf.

"Area Libraries Offer Project to Safely Connect the Community with Seniors." 2020. *La Crosse Tribune*. December 18. https://lacrossetribune.com/community/vernonbroadcaster/news/area-libraries-offer-project-to-safely-connect-the-community-with-seniors/article_f3994539-16ff-5a0a-a198-f8c2df2872a9.html/.

Ashworth, B. 2020. "Covid-19's Impact on Libraries Goes beyond Books." *Wired*. March 25. https://www.wired.com/story/covid-19-libraries-impact-goes-beyond-books/.

Brice-Sadler, M., and T. Carman. 2020. "D.C. to Ban Indoor Dining, Close Museums, Restrict Libraries to Curbside." *Washington Post*. December 18. https://www.washingtonpost.com/local/dc-indoor-dining-ban/2020/12/18/dfa816a0-417e-11eb-8db8-395dedaaa036_story.html.

Clauson-Wicker, S. 2021. "Montgomery-Floyd Libraries Write New Chapter during the Pandemic." *Roanoke Times*. February 14. https://roanoke.com/news/local/montgomery-floyd-libraries-write-new-chapter-during-the-pandemic/article_647a3b4e-6bd0-11eb-a3d5-aff7face1d18.html.

Cox, C. 2020. "Changed, Changed Utterly." *Inside Higher Ed*. June 5. https://www.insidehighered.com/views/2020/06/05/academic-libraries-will-change-significant-ways-result-pandemic-opinion.

Crowe, C. 2020. "Libraries Get Creative about Reopening as Budget Cuts Loom." *Smart Cities Dive*. June 16. https://www.smartcitiesdive.com/news/city-library-reopening-coronavirus-budget-shortfall/579852/.

Dixon, J. A. 2020. "In Second Pandemic Wave, College Libraries Again Adjust to Shutdowns." *Library Journal*. December 1. https://www.libraryjournal.

com/?detailStory=In-Second-Pandemic-Wave-College-Libraries-Again-Adjust-to-Shutdowns.

Ewen, L. 2020. "Libraries and Pandemic Preparedness." *American Libraries.* March 5. https://americanlibrariesmagazine.org/blogs/the-scoop/covid-19-libraries-pandemic-preparedness/.

Farinacci, A. 2020. "Same Old Story No More: Reopening NYC Libraries Rethink How They Operate Amid Pandemic." *Spectrum News.* July 13. https://www.ny1.com/nyc/all-boroughs/news/2020/07/13/same-old-story-no-more--nyc-libraries-rethink-how-they-operate-amid-pandemic.

Fields, L. 2020. "Where to Get Help Finding a Job: The Virtual Library." *Forbes.* July 24. https://www.forbes.com/sites/nextavenue/2020/07/24/where-to-get-help-finding-a-job-the-virtual-library/?ss=retirement&sh=77175a3f3d25.

Fowler, G. A. 2020. "In 2020, We Reached Peak Internet. Here's What Worked—And What Flopped." *Washington Post.* December 28. https://www.washingtonpost.com/topics/road-to-recovery/2020/12/28/covid-19-tech/.

Fox, L. 2020. "Partners in Crisis." *American Libraries.* June 1. https://americanlibrariesmagazine.org/2020/06/01/partners-in-crisis-library-partnerships/.

Hall, T. D. 2020. "ALA Statement on COVID-19." *American Libraries.* March 13. https://americanlibrariesmagazine.org/blogs/the-scoop/ala-statement-covid-19/

"Handling Materials during COVID-19." 2020. Maryland State Library Resource Center, Enoch Pratt Free Library. https://www.slrc.info/uploadedFiles/slrc/home/slides/Handling%20Materials%20During%20Covid-19_10.28.2020.pdf.

Harris, E. A. 2020. "Libraries Strive to Stay 'Community Living Rooms' as They Reopen." *New York Times.* June 11. https://www.nytimes.com/2020/06/11/books/coronavirus-library-reopening.html.

Ishler, F. 2020. "Lancaster-Lebanon IU13 and Lebanon County Libraries Form Partnership to Expand Access to Ebooks for Students." *LebTown.* Dec. 9. https://lebtown.com/2020/12/09/lancaster-lebanon-iu13-and-lebanon-county-libraries-form-partnership-to-expand-access-to-ebooks-for-students/.

Jefferson, J. 2021. "A New Year of Hope." *American Libraries.* February. https://americanlibrariesmagazine.org/2021/01/04/a-new-year-of-hope/.

Keilman, J. 2020. "From Food Pantries to Parking Lot Wi-Fi, Public Libraries Evolve during COVID-19 Pandemic." *Chicago Tribune.* November 29. https://www.chicagotribune.com/coronavirus/ct-covid-coronavirus-libraries-20201129-yakvhdiiobbypmre2btu2hhwpe-story.html.

Klar, R. 2020. "Amazon under Pressure to Lift Ban on E-Book Library Sales." *Hill.* December 2. https://thehill.com/business-a-lobbying/528280-amazon-under-pressure-to-lift-ban-on-e-book-library-sales.

Kletter, M. 2020. "Library Journal Survey: Academic Library Open Access Use Up during Pandemic." *Library Journal.* December 16. https://www.libraryjournal.com/?detailStory=Library-Journal-Survey-Academic-Library-Open-Access-Use-Up-During-Pandemic-covid-19.

"Libraries Respond: COVID-19 Survey. Survey of Responses and Activities Collected May 12–18, 2020." n.d. American Library Association. http://www.ilovelibraries.org/sites/default/files/ALA-COVID-19-Survey-Results-MAY-2020-Summary-Text-Only.pdf.

Lin, H., and H. Trinkunas. 2020. "The COVID-19 Infodemic: What Can Be Done about the Infectious Spread of Misinformation and Disinformation." *Bulletin of the Atomic Scientists*. https://thebulletin.org/2020/09/the-covid-19-info demic-what-can-be-done-about-the-infectious-spread-of-misinformation-and-disinformation/.

Lipinski, T. 2020. "Do Online Storytimes Violate Copyright?" *American Libraries*. June 16. https://americanlibrariesmagazine.org/2020/06/16/do-online-storytimes-violate-copyright/.

Lozada, C. 2020. "The Great Acceleration." *Washington Post*. December 18. https://www.washingtonpost.com/outlook/2020/12/18/coronavirus-great-acceleration-changes-society/.

Messner, K. n.d. "Publisher Guidelines on Fair Use for Online Storytimes & Read-Alouds during COVID-19." https://katemessner.com/publisher-guidelines-on-fair-use-for-online-storytimes-read-alouds-during-covid-19-school-closures/.

Moloney, S. 2020. "NYPL Libraries Revert to Phase 1 Operations amid Rising COVID-19 Cases." *Norwood News*. December 13. https://www.norwoodnews.org/nypl-libraries-revert-to-phase-1-operations-amid-rising-covid-19-cases/.

Musil, S. 2020. "Internet Archive to End Temporary Free E-Book Program after Lawsuit." CNET. June 11. https://www.cnet.com/news/internet-archive-to-end-temporary-free-e-book-program-after-lawsuit/.

Nonko, E., and V. Salinas. 2020. "How Libraries Are Stepping Up as a Front Line of Resilience." *Governing*. June 10. https://www.governing.com/now/How-Libraries-Are-Stepping-Up-as-a-Front-Line-of-Resilience.html.

Ostman, S. 2020. "News: Online Story Time & Coronavirus: It's Fair Use, Folks." *Programming Librarian*. March 24. https://programminglibrarian.org/articles/online-story-time-coronavirus-it%E2%80%99s-fair-use-folks.

Parker, K., J. M. Horowitz, and R. Minkin. 2020. "How the Coronavirus Outbreak Has—and Hasn't—Changed the Way Americans Work." Pew Research Center. https://www.pewsocialtrends.org/2020/12/09/how-the-coronavirus-outbreak-has-and-hasnt-changed-the-way-americans-work/.

Peet, L. 2020. "After St. Louis County Library Lays Off 122 Workers, Employees Allege Retaliation for Activism." *Library Journal*. December 8. https://www.libraryjournal.com/?detailStory=After-St-Louis-County-Library-Lays-Off-122-Workers-Employees-Allege-Retaliation-for-Activism.

Peet, L. 2021. "Battling the Infodemic: LJ's 2021 Librarians of the Year." *Library Journal*. January 5. https://www.libraryjournal.com/?detailStory=Battling-the-Infodemic-LJs-2021-Librarians-of-the-Year-covid-19.

"Public Libraries Respond to COVID-19: Survey of Response & Activities." n.d. Public Library Association. http://www.ala.org/pla/issues/covid-19/surveyoverview.

Reid, A. 2020. "Madison Libraries Could See Hours, Staff, Branch Cuts Due to Budget Shortfalls from Coronavirus." *Channel 3000*. July 9. https://www.channel3000.com/madison-libraries-could-see-hours-staff-branch-cuts-due-to-budget-shortfalls-from-coronavirus/.

Richards, K. T. 2020. "COVID-19 and Libraries: E-Books and Intellectual Property Issues." Congressional Research Service. https://crsreports.congress.gov/product/pdf/LSB/LSB10453.

Russell, K. 2020. "In Pandemic, Libraries Come to You." *Gazette*. December 28. https://www.thegazette.com/subject/news/community/cedar-rapids-public-library-coronavirus-pandemic-policy-book-delivery-curbside-pickup-20201228.

Saegert, R. 2020. "Waco Libraries to Boost Student Access to E-Books, Databases." *Waco Tribune-Herald*. December 15. https://wacotrib.com/news/local/education/waco-libraries-to-boost-student-access-to-e-books-databases/article_71fec2d4-3c06-11eb-a5cb-6fe08c8f8d0f.html.

Sass, R. 2020. Opening Keynote. LJ Design Institute. November 18.

Schwartz, M. 2020a. "Central Arkansas Library System, Gwinnett County Library System, Union County Library System Awarded 2020 Jerry Kline Community Impact Prize Honorable Mention." *Library Journal*. October 22. https://www.libraryjournal.com/?detailStory=central-arkansas-library-system-gwinnett-county-library-system-union-county-library-system-awarded-2020-jerry-kline-community-impact-prize-honorable-mention.

Schwartz, M. 2020b. "One Step Forward | Editorial." *Library Journal*. December 8. https://www.libraryjournal.com/?detailStory=one-step-forward-editorial-covid-19.

Shumaker, D. 2020a. "Law Librarians Take Off Their Masks at Annual Conference." *Information Today* 37 (6) (September): 10.

Shumaker, D. 2020b. EveryLibrary's Library Advocacy and Funding Conference. *Information Today* 37 (8) (December): 8.

Simpson, K. 2020. "Coronavirus Temporarily Closed the Book on Colorado's Public Libraries. But They Found New Ways to Fulfill Their Mission." *Colorado Sun*. June 8. https://coloradosun.com/2020/06/08/coronavirus-colorado-libraries-their-mission/.

Tamez-Robledo, N. 2020. "COVID-19 Is Forever Changing How Students Experience Libraries." *EdSurge*. November 19. https://www.edsurge.com/news/2020-11-19-covid-19-is-forever-changing-how-students-experience-libraries/.

"Updated Advice on Handling Library Materials during COVID-19 Pandemic." 2020. State Library of Oregon.

Vogels, E. A., A. Perrin, L. Rainie, and M. Anderson. 2020. "53% of Americans Say the Internet Has Been Essential during the COVID-19 Outbreak." Pew Research Center. https://www.pewresearch.org/internet/2020/04/30/53-of-americans-say-the-internet-has-been-essential-during-the-covid-19-outbreak/.

"Weber County Library System COVID-19 Rules Generate Some Ire, but Mostly Praise." 2020. *Standard-Examiner*. November 15. https://www.standard.net/news/government/weber-county-library-system-covid-19-rules-generate-some-ire-but-mostly-praise/article_c173143e-43c0-56c6-a309-3f45e4065af2.html.

Wilburn, T. 2020. "Libraries Are Dealing with New Demand for Books and Services during the Pandemic." NPR. June 16. https://www.npr.org/2020/06/16/877651001/libraries-are-dealing-with-new-demand-for-books-and-services-during-the-pandemic.

Woudenberg, C. 2020. "San Jose Libraries Plan for Devastating $1 Million Budget Blow." Sfbay.ca: All Bay All Day. June 26. https://sfbayca.com/2020/06/26/san-jose-libraries-plan-for-devastating-1-million-budget-blow/.

Zauzmer, J. 2020. "Librarians Alarmed about Coronavirus Safety at D.C.'s Reopened Public Libraries." *Washington Post*. July 23. https://www.washingtonpost.com/dc-md-va/2020/07/23/librarians-alarmed-about-coronavirus-safety-dcs-reopened-public-libraries/.

Trade Publishing in 2020:
How COVID-19 and Campaigns for
Justice Changed the Book Business

John Maher

On December 31, 2019, news that Sonny Mehta, the head of Alfred A. Knopf for more than three decades, had died the day prior circulated throughout the book business. It was the first major trade publishing story of 2020: the loss of a titanic tastemaker before the year had even begun, followed by the uncertainty surrounding his succession at one of the American publishing industry's most venerable imprints. Mehta's passing might have been among the most prominent trade publishing stories in any other year, but by the time Little, Brown and Company named Reagan Arthur to replace him a few weeks later, one of the most difficult and dynamic chapters in publishing history was being written.

Even months into 2021, many in the book business are still trying to make heads or tails of the events of the year before. For starters, two heads of house at Big Five publishers were replaced last year after nearly a decade of stability across the board in those positions: Jonathan Karp was named CEO of Simon & Schuster (S&S) in May following the sudden death of Carolyn Reidy, while the departure of Macmillan CEO John Sargent was announced in September due to what Macmillan parent company, Holtzbrinck Publishing Group, described, in a statement, as "disagreements regarding the direction of Macmillan." Macmillan US Trade president Don Weisberg was named to succeed Sargent.

Toward the end of 2020, a number of major publishers, including Houghton Mifflin Harcourt's (HMH's) trade division and S&S, were put up for sale. HMH has yet to find a buyer, but Penguin Random House (PRH), the country's largest trade publisher, ultimately placed the winning bid to buy S&S, its third largest. While the Department of Justice is unlikely to block the acquisition on antitrust grounds, authors' groups—including the Authors Guild, the Romance Writers of America, the National Writers Union, Sisters in Crime, Western Writers of America, and the Horror Writers Association—have already asked the government to do so. The move faces significant pushback from many in the book world who are frustrated by the further consolidation of an ever-shrinking number of major trade publishers—all of which, should PRH's acquisition of S&S be completed, will be owned by non-American parent companies.

But while the seemingly inevitable consolidation of the book business has been in the works long before 2020, last year was marked by two particularly important paradigm shifts. The first began during the first few months of 2020, when a handful of major publications were affected following outcry from authors and trade-publishing workers. A few months later, a mass movement calling for civic change and justice for people of color, and especially Black people, exploded nationwide following the police killing of George Floyd in Minneapolis. Book

John Maher is news and digital editor at *Publishers Weekly* and a founding editor of The Dot and Line, a web publication of animation journalism. His work has been published by *New York* magazine, the *Los Angeles Times*, and *Esquire*, among others. Data presented in this report were sourced principally from *Publishers Weekly*, Publishers Lunch, and the *New York Times*.

business workers took up that call, demanding that publishers reckon with the book business's historic lack of diversity. These campaigns ultimately resulted in not just a renewed focus on increasing accountability and diversity in trade publishing but, arguably, a slew of entry-level salary increases and historically significant hires of people of color.

Then, of course, there was the COVID-19 pandemic, by far the year's most difficult challenge for the book business and the world. Its effects hit New York City, the center of North America's trade-publishing business and the first U.S. city to find itself confronting an outbreak of the coronavirus, in mid-March, prompting stay-at-home orders and dealing a massive blow to the national economy from which the book world was far from exempt. As a result, bookstores and libraries closed down for months, forced to resort to online sales and curbside pickup for much of the year, while publishing offices were shuttered for the foreseeable future, pushing publishers to rethink the way they do business.

Yet the pandemic's results on the book business were mixed. Despite early warning signs, sales skyrocketed overall, as vast numbers of Americans became homebound. Still, publication dates were pushed further and further back, brick-and-mortar bookstores found their sales gutted by lack of foot traffic and the challenges of a forced shift in business model, and author events, book fairs, and conferences in the United States and abroad were taken virtual or called off entirely—some of them permanently. All this change was set against the backdrop of a presidential election year, which always presents a challenge for publishers' publication schedules, and especially so in a year as politically contentious as the past four years have been.

The year 2020 was, to put it mildly, tempestuous for trade publishing. It was also, for better or for worse, transitional.

Sounding the Call: Publishing Workers Demand Social Justice

Sargent's departure was far from Macmillan's first bump in the road in 2020. That came in January, when its Flatiron Books imprint published one of its lead titles for the year, *American Dirt* by Jeanine Cummins, after a significant publicity push and to much acclaim. The book's timely story, which follows a bookseller as she attempts to escape from a Mexican drug cartel by crossing the U.S. border with her son, found vocal support from such public figures as Sandra Cisneros and Stephen King, who blurbed it, and Oprah Winfrey, who selected it for her book club. But Cummins, whose advance for the book was in the seven figures and who is neither Mexican nor an immigrant, was accused of profiting from cultural appropriation by authors—some prominent, and most of them identifying as Hispanic or Latinx—whose voices were later joined by a number of their colleagues in trade publishing. As a result, Flatiron canceled part of Cummins's book tour, apologized, and hired literary magazine and nonprofit veteran Nadxieli Nieto, who holds a seat on the board of Latinx in Publishing, as editor-at-large in April, with a focus on acquiring books by Latinx, Black, and Indigenous authors, as well as other authors of color. Nieto was promoted to executive editor within less than a year.

It was only the first of the major calls for reform in trade publishing concerning issues of diversity and social justice, many of which were led not by authors but by workers inside the houses themselves—and all of which had material results. The next was at Hachette Book Group (HBG) on March 5, when employees staged a walkout en masse in protest of the acquisition, by HBG's Grand Central Publishing division, of the memoir *Apropos of Nothing* by Woody Allen. Those who walked out cited allegations made by Allen's daughter, Dylan Farrow, that he had sexually molested her as a child—allegations that Allen denies but which are echoed by Farrow's brother, Ronan, an author at HBG's Little, Brown imprint, who issued his own condemnation of the acquisition at the time before severing his ties with the publisher. After HBG CEO Michael Pietsch initially defended the decision to publish the book, Grand Central dropped the title a day later.

In June, just weeks after the death of George Floyd at the hands of the Minneapolis Police Department, a one-two punch of collective actions over the course of three days arguably prompted the most significant change across trade publishing in the year. On June 6, author L. L. McKinney coined a hashtag for a social media campaign, #PublishingPaidMe, which encouraged writers to publicly reveal their book advances. The outpouring of tweets that followed indicated that, generally speaking, authors of color, and especially Black authors, receive lower advances than white authors.

Then, on June 8, a group of more than 1,300 workers across the book and media industries, most of whom were junior staffers, stepped off the job under the name Pub Workers for Justice. The action was taken, PW4J said, in protest of white supremacist and racist power structures and state violence, as well as in response to the statements Big Five CEOs issued to their employees following Floyd's death, which the workers considered insufficient in addressing trade publishing's complicity in upholding white supremacist power structures. Those who participated spent the day engaging in acts of community service in order, as per the group's mission, to "build a community that will protect us from the inherent exploitation and racist practices of the publishing industry."

In the following six months, publishers scrambled to address the concerns these campaigns brought to the forefront of industry discourse. On July 6, former Pulitzer Prize administrator Dana Canedy was named successor to Karp as publisher of Simon & Schuster's flagship imprint, making her the third woman and first Black person to hold the position. A little over a week later, Lisa Lucas, the first Black person and first woman to serve as executive director of the National Book Foundation, was tapped to take over as publisher of PRH imprints Pantheon and Schocken beginning in January 2021. Publishers launched a number of new imprints emphasizing works by writers of color, including Legacy Lit at HBG; the Native-focused Heartdrum at HarperCollins; Phoebe Robinson's Tiny Reparations subimprint of PRH's Dutton; and Nicola and David Yoon's Joy Revolution at Random House Children's Books.

In September, PRH and HBG each released reports on demographics within the workplace and pledged actions to diversify their workforces and the lists of books they publish. And by January each of the Big Five publishers had announced that they had raised, or would raise, entry-level salaries to $40,000 or above, depending on the publisher.

The COVID-19 Pandemic: The Good, the Bad, and the Complicated

Meanwhile, by March, the U.S. economy was facing its biggest external crisis in decades, and trade publishing seemed far from exempt.

At first, all signs pointed to economic calamity across the board for the book business, as the pandemic that would go on to kill close to 380,000 Americans by year's end took its financial toll. Bookstores and libraries closed their doors, book fairs and conferences were called off or moved online, and worries over the supply chain began to arise—especially once Amazon cut back on fulfilling book orders to focus on shipping items deemed "essential" to consumers. As early as March, publishers shuttered their offices and began producing books remotely, a trend that, for the most part, continued through the end of the year. A *Publishers Weekly* survey conducted in late November, which assessed the impact of the pandemic on work policies at trade publishers, found that 93 percent of those who responded to the survey said they worked remotely at some point in 2020, and that 96 percent of that number added that they continue to work from home.

Hundreds of publication dates, many of them major, were delayed until later in the year despite previous efforts to avoid publishing major books close to Election Day in November and in some cases were delayed into 2021. In-person book tours were canceled as nearly every tool upon which publicity and marketing teams relied to promote their products—book signings, media mixers, and even print galleys—was shelved for months, if not indefinitely. Companies including Macmillan and Scholastic implemented austerity measures that included hiring freezes, temporary reductions in pay for select employees, and even furloughs and layoffs.

By and large, however, trade publishers were among the least negatively impacted members of the book business where the financial effects of the pandemic were concerned. In-person events and sales being tangential to their primary business, trade publishers largely avoided the devastating losses suffered by physical retail outlets and events companies like Reed Exhibitions—which holds, among other events, BookExpo and BookCon, both of which Reed will be "retiring" in 2021. Printing shortages affected them, but not the way they did the country's two largest printers, Quad and LSC Communications. Both companies, especially LSC, were already dealing with financial strain before last spring, when Quad shut down its printers at three plants and LSC declared bankruptcy. (Quad sold its book printing business in the fall, while LSC's assets were purchased by private equity firm Atlas Holdings in September 2020.) In fact, the fall printing shortages publishers were forced to contend with were in part a result of what remains a surprising bright spot for trade publishing in 2020: the spike of sales in print books.

Trade publishers, indeed, sold a whole heap of books in 2020, as online sales offset plummeting sales through brick-and-mortar bookstores, through the school and library markets, through specialty retailers including airport and museum bookstores, and through gift shops. As a result, sales of print books rose 8.2 percent over 2019 at outlets that report to NPD BookScan—the largest annual increase measured by the service since 2010—while the Association of American Publishers (AAP) reported a 9.7 percent increase in net dollars for the trade segment over the year prior. (Numbers released by BookScan and AAP often show discrepancies, for a handful of reasons: BookScan collects unit sales via the point-of-sale systems of major book retailers, mass merchandisers, and bookstores and gets almost instant results, whereas publishers report their own dollar sales numbers to AAP through a survey.)

With most physical retailers hampered significantly by shutdown and social-distancing orders throughout the nation for much of the year—with the notable exception of supermarkets and such big-box stores as Walmart and Target, which for the most part remained open—online sales skyrocketed during the year. (According to AAP, publishers also benefited from a 20.2 percent decrease in returns during 2020 due to a shift toward more online sales.) Sales of print books were up at Amazon.com, unsurprisingly, after the e-tailer returned to shipping products beyond medicine and cleaning solutions and other items deemed essential. But sales also rose through Target.com and Walmart.com, and the newly launched Bookshop.org—which is partnered with a number of independent bookstores, as well as the American Booksellers Association, and whose sales are fulfilled by Ingram Content Group—sold more than $50 million in books after its launch in January 2020, enough to enable it to expand into foreign markets. Sales of e-books saw a rebound in the year as well, and sales of digital audiobooks continued their steady double-digit growth; Libro.fm, the digital audio bookseller, reported a 200 percent jump in units sold over 2019.

The bulk of the year's sales trends were dictated by current events. Sales of new titles—many of which saw their publication dates rescheduled, their marketing and promotional budgets reduced, and discoverability diminished due to limitations on browsing at physical outlets—were weak, whereas sales of backlist titles rose significantly in every major category last year; as a January 26 article in *Publishers Lunch* indicated, "2020 was the first time that backlist hardcovers (at 113.5 million units) have outsold frontlist hardcovers (at 111.5 million units)." Sales of social justice titles helped spark that rise in backlist, with two backlist social justice titles—Robin DiAngelo's *White Fragility* (Beacon Press) and Ibram X. Kendi's *How to Be an Antiracist* (One World)—landing at #9 and #14, respectively, on *Publishers Weekly*'s year-end bestseller list. Political books continued their strong showing, as did books written by authors whose surname is Obama. And sales of children's educational materials skyrocketed as schools closed and parents were forced to become teachers—although whether the publishers of those materials are considered part of the trade remains a matter of debate.

Eyes to the Horizon: What the Future Holds for Trade Publishing

Where the trade publishing business will go from here is difficult to predict; the pandemic is, after all, anything but over. Still, some changes will almost certainly stick.

Online sales will probably remain higher than they were before COVID-19, even if the discrepancy between digital and in-person sales will likely begin to even out once the bulk of the American population becomes vaccinated. Some publishers will continue to save on overhead by cutting back on business travel and entertainment budgets, including by sending fewer people to trade shows in person and by continuing to limit the production and mailing of print galleys. Virtual author events, while unlikely to permanently supplant in-person tours, will continue in significantly higher numbers than before the pandemic—especially for books with smaller publicity budgets, such as those by many midlist authors.

What most remains in question is whether trade publishers will continue to address the needs of their workers and the demand for a more diverse industry and selection of titles without public outrage and employee criticism being pegged to the news cycle. Will the gains in many major publishers' bottom lines result in more increases for entry- and mid-level workers, or will high-ranking corporate officers see the bulk of the benefit? Will publishers actively work to recruit, retain, and mentor young Black and Indigenous people and other people of color, promoting them through the ranks in an attempt to permanently transform the makeup of an industry that, according to the 2020 diversity baseline survey update released by Lee & Low Books last year, is 76 percent white? Or will the majority of diverse hires in the business going forward continue to be from outside trade publishing and at the executive level, putting a bandage on the issue without addressing its root cause?

That is: will trade publishing's decisionmakers commit to systemic change in the way they conduct their business? Or are they just hoping, after a year of upheaval, for a return to more of the same?

Count on Libraries:
Promoting a Fair, Accurate, and
Complete 2020 Census Count

Karen Brown

Importance of the Census

Completing the Census form takes only about ten minutes, but the impact of the Census count lasts for ten years. The constitutionally required decennial count of every person living in the United States has an enormous impact on political representation and the allocation of more than $1.5 trillion each year in federal funding.[1] The Census Bureau's goal for the 2020 Census was to "count everyone once, only once, and in the right place,"[2] and libraries were vital partners in promoting an accurate, fair, and complete count by raising awareness about the importance of the Census and encouraging participation in it.

The 2020 Census was a major event for libraries, but their contributions to this effort were not unique to the ongoing work that libraries do every day. As 2019 American Library Association (ALA) president Loida Garcia-Febo said in her invited remarks at a U.S. Census Bureau public briefing held one year before the start of the Census, "The Census results will have tremendous impact on funding and representation for our communities . . . ALA is committed to helping our communities achieve a complete count because libraries serve everyone."[3]

The effect of the Census on representation and funding dates back to 1787, when Congress first mandated a decennial Census count to draw congressional districts that determine the apportionment of seats in the House of Representatives and representation in the Electoral College.[4] Census results are also the basis for drawing districts for state and local offices. In addition, the Census count determines the allocation of funding for a multitude of federal programs, including K–12 and higher education, health care and hospitals, social services, highway planning and construction, and, of particular importance to libraries, Library Services & Technology Act (LSTA) grants to states. Government agencies, businesses, community organizations, and researchers rely on Census data for critical information about U.S. demographics that is used for planning and decision making.

2020 Census: Disruptions and Changes

Considering the immense undertaking of a Census count, collaboration and partnerships are critical, and libraries leveraged their connections with local groups and businesses and through their participation on Complete Count Committees (CCC).

Karen Brown, Ph.D., is a professor emerita at Dominican University in the School of Information Studies, frequently teaching in assessment, foundations of the profession, and literacy and learning. She has held positions focusing on library administration, collection development, and instruction at the University of Wisconsin, University of Maryland, Columbia University, and Bard College. She is one of the Association of College and Research Libraries' adjunct consultants and, during 2020, assisted the American Library Association's 2020 Census initiative.

CCCs are established by tribal, state, and local governments and community leaders to promote a complete Census count. When Rhonda Sewell, manager of external and governmental affairs for Toledo–Lucas County Public Library, received a letter in May 2019 from Toledo's mayor and Lucas County commissioners asking her to join a CCC, she recognized the important role the library could play. Toledo was losing population, and a complete count was critical to avoid being undercounted and not receiving needed federal funds. More than $1,800 per person was at stake in Ohio, Sewell noted.[5]

In a January 2021 MSNBC interview, Librarian of Congress Carla Hayden highlighted the community connections made by librarians, explaining, "They go to the community meetings, they go to city council meetings, or county meetings, that they are part of whatever else is going on in the community. So, they can raise their hands and say, 'Oh, we have to do the census, so maybe you could have those meetings or things in the library.'"[6] Taking on leadership roles to promote awareness of the Census and sponsoring events to encourage participation in the Census count are not new to libraries, but the 2020 Census proved to be unprecedented. Debate about the "citizenship question," the introduction of an online response option and online application for Census jobs, and, most significantly, the COVID-19 pandemic required libraries of all types to plan and deliver services in new ways.

The proposed addition of a new question to the 2020 Census form that would ask the citizenship status of every person living in each U.S. household, regardless of birthplace, sparked controversy and a contentious political debate.[7] Despite a U.S. Supreme Court ruling that struck down the measure, misinformation and confusion continued, particularly among immigrant groups that have historically been an undercounted population.[8] In Waukegan, Illinois, where 55 percent of the residents identify as Hispanic/Latinx, the Waukegan Public Library (WPL) hired a native Spanish speaker to reach out to this target population. Elizabeth Santana Andujar, a Census engagement specialist, recounted her experience. "I talked to a woman who was upset with the government, and she said she thought [the Census] would be something to harm immigrants. . . . She was so upset, but I had the opportunity to explain what the benefits are to being counted. She changed her mind a little bit, and she said, 'I'm going to talk with my husband and my family to explain how this is beneficial for us,' so I see that my work works."[9] As trusted community institutions, libraries were important sources for accurate information about the Census.

For the first time, in 2020 the Census included an online response form, and, even though paper and telephone responses were still options, the Census Bureau encouraged individuals to complete the form online. Computers and wifi access were also needed to apply for the 500,000 temporary Census jobs and to complete the online training necessary for many of the positions. Millions of Americans, however, lack broadband Internet service at home. According to the Federal Communications Commission (FCC) 2018 Internet Access Services report, 21 million American households do not have standard broadband Internet service.[10]

Many people also lack basic computer and online skills. Libraries have longed recognized the digital divide that persists in our country, and they played a critical role during the Census by providing reliable Internet access and in-person, telephone, and online assistance with completing the online Census form and applying for Census positions. They anticipated the likely surge in wifi and computer use and made sure public access computers and their Internet network could handle a higher level of use. During the Census count period, many libraries designated some computers as "Census Express" so that users could quickly complete the online response form without a library card number. Libraries also left their wifi on when the buildings were closed to facilitate access to the Internet from their parking lots and areas near their buildings.[11]

When the COVID-19 pandemic engulfed the country in early 2020, the Census effort nationwide felt the impact. The Census Bureau had to delay and adjust its operations, extending completion of the count from July 31, 2020, to October 31, 2020. New health-related protocols and requirements were put in place that required libraries—along with other organizations, agencies, and businesses—to rework plans for Census programs and activities. Most libraries were forced to close their buildings and pivot services online or outside the building. Outreach has always been a critical library service but took on added importance during the pandemic, particularly the need to reach underserved populations in the community.

Reaching Hard-to-Count Populations

Historically, certain groups of people have been undercounted disproportionately by the decennial Census. Hard-to-count populations who have often been missed in the Census count include young children, people experiencing homelessness, people of color, people with low incomes, recent immigrants, Indigenous peoples, and those who live in rural or remote areas. In the 2010 Census, for example, children under age five were the most undercounted group, with an estimated 2 million missed.[12] The undercount was especially severe among young Black and Latinx children.[13] Language and literacy barriers, fear of the government, or frequent changes in residence all contribute to challenges the Census Bureau faces when trying to locate, contact, or persuade people to participate in the Census. When individuals are undercounted, their communities are underfunded and underrepresented. During the 2020 Census, public libraries were uniquely positioned to reach out to the diverse communities they service. In fact, a public library is located within five miles of 99 percent of hard-to-count populations.[14]

The broad reach of libraries in their communities contributed to the Census Bureau's goal of a complete count. New York Public Library (NYPL), for example—which has 92 locations across the Bronx, Manhattan, and Staten Island—created the Census Navigators program. Six part-time employees with strong customer service skills and fluency in a non-English language provided information about the Census in neighborhoods that might potentially be undercounted. According to Jay Brandon, civic engagement and community partnerships manager at NYPL, "We have wide reach. . . . [The library's footprint] allows us to serve in a capacity that not only supports other community organizations but allows us to work in tandem with them to ensure that New York has a complete count."[15]

To bolster the reach of libraries to geographic and demographic communities that were at greatest risk of being undercounted, ALA provided funding for Library Census Equity Grants of $2,000 each. More than 500 libraries of all types submitted applications for the 59 mini-grants available, an indication of the profession's commitment to reducing barriers to participation in the Census.[16] Grant recipients used the funds for a variety of activities, including purchasing additional portable computers and mobile hotspots to expand access to the online response option; establishing "census corners," dedicated spaces with computer access and information in English and Spanish for completing the Census online; and equipping a bookmobile in geographically isolated communities to facilitate educational events on the Census and offer access to the online response option in locations such as country stores and senior centers.

Advocacy, Awareness, and Engagement

Throughout the 2020 Census, libraries hosted events and disseminated information to raise awareness of the Census, knowing that the more people were familiar with the Census and its impact on their lives, the more likely they would be to participate. Multiple means of information dissemination were employed. Brochures and flyers were distributed at library programs, in school packets, and at off-site events. When services for most libraries went online during the pandemic, libraries included a reminder of the Census as part of their curbside pickup, in e-mails and website announcements, and during wellness check telephone calls. They displayed Census reminders on the libraries' electronic signs and placed yard signs on their grounds. More than 60 percent of public libraries responding to a March 2020 Public Library Association (PLA) survey reported using their social media channels to promote the 2020 Census.[17]

Articles and letters in local media outlets promoted the Census and highlighted library contributions to achieving a complete count. In a joint letter to the *Tennessean* newspaper by Fabian Bedne, a planner for Nashville's mayor and a former Metro Council member, and Kent Oliver, director of the Nashville Public Library, Bedne stressed the importance of the Census to himself and the community. "I got my first elected office job thanks in part to the 2010 Census," Bedne said. "The subsequent remapping created a more accurately representative District 31, reflecting the arrival of many new Americans, and this paved the way for Nashville Metro Council's first elected immigrant: me."[18]

Youth programming provided opportunities to reach families and build awareness of the Census. Gail Borden Public Library District (Illinois), for example, sponsored a Kids Digital Art Contest, and all children from birth to five through school age (K–12) were invited to submit on social media a piece of art (e.g., a drawing, painting, video, or photograph) expressing why they count in the 2020 Census for a chance to receive a $50 gift certificate.[19] Phoenix Public Library, in collaboration with the city of Phoenix, hosted My First Census / Mi Primer Censo, a bilingual event for families with children under the age of ten that included a family photo opportunity.[20]

Both public libraries and school libraries delivered Census-themed programming, such as the Census Bureau's Statistics in Schools curriculum, which offers learning materials for pre-K, elementary, and high school students (and their families). Social studies teachers in Los Angeles and Sacramento collaborated to develop strategies for including instruction about the Census in the curriculum. "Kids need to know the structure of government," said Crissy Maher, a fifth grade teacher at Arnold Adreani Elementary in Elk Grove, California.[21] One fifth grade unit, for example, explored westward expansion and encouraged discussion about what motivated people to move west and how the Census affected the representation of Americans in these territories. "A lot of [students] were shocked by their ability, as children, to affect something that happens in the federal government—if they're counted," Maher says."[22]

Likewise, academic libraries created events to promote awareness of the Census among college students, another designated hard-to-count population. Both Catholic University of America and the University of California, Berkeley, mounted library exhibits. *Power and the People: The U.S. Census and Who Counts*—the University of California, Berkeley, exhibit (which was also available online)— addressed critical topics, including "The Power of Redistricting," "Race & Civil Rights," "Latinx & Ethnicity," "Japanese Americans in World War II & the Census," and "Incarceration." In tandem with the exhibit, the library sponsored a faculty-student panel that explored how American cultures and sociology students applied Census data in course projects.[23] These examples provide just a snapshot of the multiple ways that libraries of all types raised awareness and encouraged participation in the Census.

Libraries Recognized for Contributions to Complete Count Efforts

The results of the Census are expected to be released by September 30, 2021 (six months later than previous Census reports).[24] According to an October 2020 Census Bureau statement, 99.98 percent of all housing units and addresses nationwide were accounted for in the Census count, and the response rate was slightly higher than the 2010 Census.[25] Libraries are being recognized for mobilizing the assets of the library community and working in collaboration with others to advance complete count efforts. The *Rio Grande Guardian*, for example, praised the strategic collaboration of the Pharr-San Juan-Alamo (PSJA) Independent School District, explaining, "PSJA's Census count effort was led by the district's Census Planning Committee. This comprised leaders in various key departments such as Student Services, Communications, Parental Engagement, Data Services, Social Studies Curriculum, and Library Services. They, in turn, collaborated with the cities of Pharr, San Juan, and Alamo." As early as summer 2019 the school district was reaching out to families and staff, raising awareness of the upcoming Census.

Likewise, the Editorial Board of the *Toledo Blade* acknowledged the work of the local public library during the pandemic, stating, "Library officials seized opportunities to launch new programs specifically aimed at helping the community through the pandemic. For instance, in the fall the library hosted 'Democracy Days' to help people get the computer access they needed to register to vote and complete a 2020 Census form."[26]

Even though the 2020 Census count has been completed, libraries continue to work in their communities, helping individuals and organizations navigate and understand Census data for decision making, planning, and community engagement and economic development. ALA recently launched the Census Data Literacy project, a joint initiative of PLA and ALA's Public Policy and Advocacy Office, to increase awareness and use of Census data to reach multiple audiences, including small businesses and entrepreneurs, local historians, students, and nonprofits and government agencies.[27] Libraries know the value and importance of accurate, reliable data, and their participation in the Census counts contributes to achieving a fair and complete count that will have a significant impact for ten years and more.

Notes

1. "Counting for Dollars 2020: The Role of the Decennial Census in the Geographic Distribution of Federal Funds," Counting for Dollars 2020," GW Institute of Public Policy, George Washington University, April 29, 2020, http://gwipp.gwu.edu/counting-dollars-2020-role-decennial-census-geographic-distribution-federal-funds.

2. U.S. Census Bureau, "Why We Conduct the Decennial Census," United States Census Bureau, April 16, 2020, https://www.census.gov/programs-surveys/decennial-census/about/why.html.

3. "ALA President to Speak at U.S. Census Bureau Press Conference," American Library Association, March 27, 2019, http://www.ala.org/news/member-news/2019/03/ala-president-speak-us-census-bureau-press-conference.

4. U.S. Census Bureau, "Constitution Day," United States Census Bureau, August 20, 2020, https://www.census.gov/programs-surveys/sis/resources/constitution-day.html#:~:text=The%20framers%20of%20the%20Constitution,10%20years%20(decennial%20census).

5. Terra Dankowski, "Reaching the Hard to Count," *American Libraries Magazine*, February 28, 2020, https://americanlibrariesmagazine.org/2020/03/02/census-2020-reaching-hard-to-count/.

6. "Transcript: Carla Hayden: Palace to Knowledge," MSNBC, NBCUniversal News Group, January 27, 2021, https://www.msnbc.com/podcast/transcript-carla-hayden-palace-knowledge-n1255883.

7. Hansi Lo Wang, "Trump's Proposed Census Citizenship Question Bucks Centuries of Precedent," NPR, May 22, 2019, https://www.npr.org/2019/05/22/719159163/has-the-u-s-census-ever-asked-about-everyones-citizenship-status.

8. Robert Barnes and Ann Marimow, "Supreme Court Puts Census Citizenship Question on Hold," *Washington Post*, WP Company, June 28, 2019, https://www.washingtonpost.com/politics/courts_law/supreme-court-puts-census-citizenship-question-on-hold/2019/06/27/6b2a49cc-93cb-11e9-b570-6416efdc0803_story.html.

9. Terra Dankowski, "Reaching the Hard to Count," *American Libraries Magazine*, February 28, 2020, https://americanlibrariesmagazine.org/2020/03/02/census-2020-reaching-hard-to-count/.

10. U.S. Federal Communications Commission, "Internet Access Services: Status as of December 21, 2018," FCC, September 2020, https://docs.fcc.gov/public/attachments/DOC-366980A1.pdf.

11. Jessica D. Gilbert Redman, "The 2020 Census Starts in Two Weeks—Are Your Computers Ready?" LITA Blog, February 24, 2020, https://litablog.org/2020/02/the-2020-census-starts-in-two-weeks-are-your-computers-ready/.

12. "Hard-to-Count Communities in the 2020 Census," Georgetown Center on Poverty and Inequality, accessed March 3, 2021, https://www.georgetownpoverty.org/issues/democracy/census-2/hard-to-count/.

13. William O'Hare et al., "Research Identifies New Strategies to Reduce Undercount of Young Children in U.S. 2020 Census," Population Reference Bureau, June 12, 2019, https://www.prb.org/new-strategies-to-reduce-undercount-of-young-children-in-2020-census/.

14. Tracy Strobel, "Libraries and the 2020 Census," *American Libraries Magazine*, October 30, 2018, https://americanlibrariesmagazine.org/blogs/the-scoop/libraries-and-the-2020-census/.

15. Terra Dankowski "Reaching the Hard to Count," *American Libraries Magazine*, February 28, 2020, https://americanlibrariesmagazine.org/2020/03/02/census-2020-reaching-hard-to-count/.

16. "ALA Awards More than $100,000 to 59 Library Census Equity Fund Grantees," News and Press Center, March 2, 2020, http://www.ala.org/news/member-news/2019/12/ala-awards-more-100000-59-library-census-equity-fund-grantees.

17. "Public Libraries Launch, Expand Services during COVID-19 Pandemic," News and Press Center, April 16, 2020, http://www.ala.org/news/press-releases/2020/04/public-libraries-launch-expand-services-during-covid-19-pandemic-0.

18. Fabian Bedne and Kent Oliver, "Nashville Public Library Wants Everyone to Count in U.S. Census: Opinion," *Tennessean*, February 19, 2020, https://www.tennessean.com/story/opinion/2020/02/19/nashville-public-library-and-census-making-sure-everyone-counts/4788802002/.

19. "Census Art Contest," Gail Borden Public Library District—Elgin, Illinois," https://www.gailborden.info/uncategorized/2737-census-art-contest.

20. Karen Barr, "My First Census Brings Awareness to an Undercounted Population: Kids," *Raising Arizona Kids Magazine*, February 21, 2020, https://www.raisingarizonakids.com/2020/02/my-first-census-photo-contest-undercounted-population-kids/.

21. Grace Hwang Lynch, "Libraries Are Preparing for the 2020 Census: With Plenty at Stake, There's Still Work to Be Done," *School Library Journal*, January 21, 2020, https://www.slj.com/?detailStory=Libraries-Are-Preparing-for-the-2020-Census-With-Plenty-at-Stake-Theres-Still-Work-To-Be-Done-schools.

22. Grace Hwang Lynch, "Libraries Are Preparing for the 2020 Census: With Plenty at Stake, There's Still Work to Be Done," *School Library Journal*, January 21, 2020, https://www.slj.com/?detailStory=Libraries-Are-Preparing-for-the-2020-Census-With-Plenty-at-Stake-Theres-Still-Work-To-Be-Done-schools.

23. Ann Glusker, "Teaching, Learning and Creating Change with Data: A Census-Focused Library and American Cultures Event," UC Berkeley Library Update, December 6, 2019. https://update.lib.berkeley.edu/tag/american-cultures-program/.

24. US Census Bureau, "Census Bureau Statement on Redistricting Data Timeline," United States Census Bureau, February 12, 2021, https://www.census.gov/newsroom/press-releases/2021/statement-redistricting-data-timeline.html.

25. U.S. Census Bureau, "2020 Census Response Rate Update: 99.98% Complete Nationwide," United States Census Bureau, October 19, 2020, https://www.census.gov/newsroom/press-releases/2020/2020-census-all-states-top-99-percent.html.

26. "What the Library Gives Us," *Toledo Blade*, February 13, 2021, https://www.toledoblade.com/opinion/editorials/2021/02/13/what-the-toledo-lucas-county-public-library-gives-us/stories/20210209101.

27. "Census Data Literacy," Public Library Association (PLA), http://www.ala.org/pla/data/census.

Federal Agency and Federal Library Reports

Library of Congress

10 First Street S.E., Washington, DC 20540
202-707-5000
https://loc.gov

Carla Hayden
Librarian of Congress

The Library of Congress is the largest library in the world, with more than 171 million items in various languages, disciplines, and formats. As the world's largest repository of knowledge and creativity, the library has as its mission to engage, inspire, and inform the United States Congress and the American people with a universal and enduring source of knowledge and creativity.

The library's collections are housed in its three buildings on Capitol Hill and in climate-controlled facilities at Fort Meade, Maryland. Its audiovisual materials are held at the Packard Campus of the National Audio-Visual Conservation Center, in Culpeper, Virginia. The library also provides global access to its resources through its website, https://loc.gov.

Highlights of 2020

In fiscal year (FY) 2020 the Library of Congress

- Responded to more than 907,000 reference requests from Congress, the public, and other federal agencies[1]
- Welcomed 565,388 visitors to its Capitol Hill campus and recorded more than 174.8 million visits and 805.1 million page views on its web properties
- Through the U.S. Copyright Office, issued over 443,911 copyright registrations and recorded 7,410 documents containing 235,228 titles
- Circulated nearly 20.3 million copies of braille, audio, and large print items to patrons, via the National Library Service for the Blind and Print Disabled and its network of state and local libraries
- Circulated 359,716 items for use inside and outside the Library

[1] Direct use of Congressional Research Service reports is included in this calculation.

- Performed more than 6.8 million preservation actions on items in the Library's physical collections
- Employed 3,242 permanent staff members
- Operated with a total fiscal 2020 appropriation of $719.359 million and the additional authority to spend $55.703 million in offsetting receipts

The Library recorded a total of 171,636,507 items in its collections, including

- 25,040,975 cataloged books in the Library of Congress classification system
- 15,491,708 items in the nonclassified print collections, including books in large type and raised characters, incunabula (books printed before 1501), monographs and serials, music, bound newspapers, pamphlets, technical reports, and other print material
- 131,103,824 items in the nonclassified (special) collections, including
  - 4,171,419 audio materials
  - 74,466,487 manuscripts
  - 5,619,694 maps
  - 17,446,403 microforms
  - 1,875,476 moving images
  - 8,193,762 items of sheet music
  - 2,023,913 other (including machine-readable items)
  - 17,306,670 visual materials

Carla Hayden, longtime chief executive of the Enoch Pratt Free Library system in Baltimore and a former president of the American Library Association (ALA), began the fifth year of a renewable ten-year term as the 14th Librarian of Congress.

The Library and the COVID-19 Pandemic

When the COVID-19 pandemic struck the United States in March 2020, the Library of Congress adopted new approaches that allowed the institution to carry out its mission of serving Congress and the American public while also allowing Library employees and contractors to work in safety.

On March 12 the Library closed its doors to researchers and visitors and canceled upcoming public programs—cancellations that, for in-person programs, eventually would extend through the end of the fiscal year and beyond. The following week, the Library limited the number of employees allowed on-site at Library facilities to those performing essential tasks. At the same time, it vastly expanded its telework program, requiring staff members who could perform their work remotely to do so.

In late June and again in late July, the Library expanded the number of employees allowed on-site to facilitate the completion of priority work. Among many projects, teams cleared an estimated mail backlog of over 100,000 letters and 20,000 packages; archivists and technicians once again began processing physical collections, working to reduce arrearages; and reference librarians consulted on-site collections to answer reference questions. The Health Services Division (HSD) and the Architect of the Capitol collaborated to create a safe on-site work environment.

Congress, the Library, and COVID-19

Despite the forced the closure of many government offices across Washington, D.C., the Library continued to carry out its mission of providing support to Congress. The Congressional Research Service (CRS) furnished support throughout the legislative process and across a wide range of public policy issues. CRS launched a webpage that offered nearly 1,000 CRS products and resources related to the pandemic and transitioned in-person seminars to a webinar format.

In order to ensure congressional access to collections stored off-site, Collections Management Division (CMD) staff remained available to retrieve material from both the Fort Meade and Cabin Branch locations. CMD staff on Capitol Hill provided on-site support throughout the pandemic to ensure materials were properly charged and delivered.

The U.S. Copyright Office also worked closely with Congress on pandemic-related issues, helping address the pandemic's impact on the copyright ecosystem by assisting with the Coronavirus Aid, Relief, and Economic Security (CARES) Act.

The Library canceled all in-person meetings and events after March 13. The Congressional Relations Office (CRO) was able to maximize outreach efforts and engage members through virtual programming. CRO facilitated, organized, and staffed 37 virtual events with congressional offices and 110 calls between the Librarian and members of Congress and was able to fill all congressional requests.

CRO furnished updates to Congress and Library leadership and staff on COVID-19-response legislation. It also worked with Congress to extend contract-performance language for the agency's severable service contracts impacted by the pandemic and provide reimbursement of staff salaries at the Little Scholars Child Development Center in coordination with the Financial Services Directorate (FSD) and Office of the General Counsel (OGC). To fund the costs added by the pandemic, FSD tracked COVID-19 expenses and led three congressional reprogrammings, which allowed the purchase of additional IT equipment, licenses, and bandwidth for the remote workforce; covered additional custodial and health services; and supported salaries of revolving fund staff as their organizations' revenues dropped. Total 2020 COVID-19–related costs of approximately $18.6 million were absorbed without a supplemental appropriation.

Researcher Access

When the Library was forced to close its buildings to researchers and visitors in March, the expected date for reopening on-site facilities was unknown. By late spring, it was apparent the closure of the Library's 20 reading rooms would continue. As the Library is a major research library, the operating status of the reading rooms was of major concern, not just to Library staff but also to the community of scholars and researchers that depends on access. The Library created a special

Reading Rooms Committee (RRC) of senior executives and public service managers to make preparations for the eventual resumption of public access.

The RRC was charged with identifying new guidelines and operational requirements that would ensure the health and safety of Library staff and the public once conditions allowed for the reopening of reading rooms. The many logistical and staffing challenges, with an unknown reopening date, expanded the scope and planning complexity required to move from discussion to implementation. The RRC maintained extensive and continuous coordination with the Library's Health Service Division, the OGC, the Office of Communications, the Office of Security and Emergency Preparedness, and the Office of the Librarian.

The RRC eventually proposed a plan to reopen reading rooms in phases. Reopening would allow for services and staffing to be ramped up incrementally and for new guidelines and procedures to be assessed or modified over time. Major changes in service policies from prepandemic routines included requiring appointments in designated time slots for all researchers; significantly restricting time and occupancy limits to meet physical-distancing requirements; and adhering to new health and safety guidelines relevant to limiting contagious exposure. By the end of the fiscal year, no date had been set for reopening reading rooms, but procedures, logistics, room setup, staffing, training, and communication were planned and ready for execution.

Beginning in April, the Library required all staff and visitors to pass a health-screening review and temperature check upon entry to the buildings. Staff and visitors were required to wear masks at all times in public areas and adhere to physical-distancing guidelines. Plexiscreen barriers were installed at service desks and public service points, and expanded cleaning routines were established. Signage designed to emphasize new policies and encourage designated pathways was installed.

An initially unplanned project of the RRC was the establishment of a temporary on-site Electronic Resources Center (ERC), which opened in September to provide in-person access for researchers, by appointment, to the Library's digital collections and external subscription databases. The introduction of the ERC allowed the Library to quickly provide access to collections materials requiring minimal in-person staffing and materials handling. The ERC would continue to operate until the first phase of reading room reopenings.

Public Events and Outreach

After it closed its doors to the public in March, the Library still needed to provide public access to the institution and did so in a variety of ways, including creating new programs, reimagining existing ones, and offering both to the public online. In late March, the Library's Center for Learning, Literacy and Engagement (CLLE), working with the Office of the Chief Information Officer and the Office of Communications, launched the loc.gov/engage webpage, a centralized hub for information about Library resources, activities, and programs for adults, teens, and children suddenly removed from their normal activities.

The Library encouraged the public to explore existing virtual exhibits, invited the public to serve as virtual volunteers to help digitize collections as part of its By the People crowdsourcing effort, and, via its National Book Festival Presents series, offered virtual programs with popular authors.

When schools closed due to the pandemic, CLLE responded by creating a set of teacher webinars and a new series of informal "office hours" sessions that brought educators and general audiences together with experts from across the institution. By the end of FY 2020 CLLE had created 63 online programs attended by 3,721 people. CLLE also offered virtual workshops for student groups. Led by a Library facilitator, the workshops explored diverse topics through Library collections, ranging from Rosa Parks to comic books and mythology.

When in-person public events were canceled in March, the Music Division and the American Folklife Center (AFC) reinvented their existing concert series online. In June the Music Division premiered its Boccaccio Project, which offered ten short commissions written in response to the pandemic. AFC modified its in-person Homegrown concert series to present Homegrown at Home, a series of 19 video performances by traditional artists streamed to thousands of viewers across the country.

In September the Library took its national outreach efforts further, hosting the 20th National Book Festival entirely online for the first time. More than 22,000 visitors registered to watch presentations by over 120 authors. The three-day festival concluded with a national broadcast on PBS stations that was viewed by more than 2 million people.

Providing Copyright Services

The U.S. Copyright Office is responsible for administering a complex and dynamic set of laws and processes including copyright registration, the recordation of title and licenses, statutory licensing provisions, and other aspects of the 1976 Copyright Act and the 1998 Digital Millennium Copyright Act. During the pandemic, the Copyright Office expanded its capabilities for receiving and processing electronic submissions and applications.

This work was done against a backdrop of a broader, ongoing IT development effort to modernize the copyright registration system; during the fiscal year, Copyright held a series of virtual public events to get input on the modernization process. Amid the pandemic, the Library in September 2020 announced the appointment of a new register of copyrights, Shira Perlmutter, who entered office the following month via a virtual swearing-in ceremony with Librarian of Congress Carla Hayden.

Collecting the Pandemic

As the pandemic started, the Library quickly began collecting material, for both its physical and digital collections, that reflected the experiences of the nation and the world with COVID-19.

The Geography and Map Division, for example, mapped the pandemic and identified geospatial data and cartographic visualizations to add to its collections. The Prints and Photographs Division collected photographs via donations and collaborated with the photo-sharing website Flickr to significantly expand its documentation of American experiences with COVID-19. Photographers were invited to contribute photographic and graphic art images to the Flickr group COVID-19: American Experiences; Library curators reviewed submissions and selected images to feature in Flickr galleries and to preserve in the Library's permanent collections.

By mid-March, even before a formal collection plan was in place, the Library was already capturing web content about the pandemic through its ongoing crawling of thousands of sites in existing collections. In addition, since the Library is a member of the International Internet Preservation Consortium, there was a desire to suggest sites for its global Novel Coronavirus collection. The Library's expert staff was encouraged to nominate sites for that effort. By May that same staff had recommended a substantial number of sites to be harvested by the Library for its own collection, with more than 75 percent from outside the U.S.

The Collection Development Office (CDO) and the web-archiving team of the Digital Collection Management and Services Division developed a collecting proposal that took into account both the scope and funding of the project. The plan had three primary objectives: to fill major gaps in the Library's pandemic web collection, to determine high-priority subtopics within the U.S. for collecting, and to better identify and organize material the Library already collected. An eventual public launch of the collection, tentatively named the Coronavirus Web Archive, was also planned. Since the Library's web archives program observes a one-year embargo on harvested content, the collection will likely be made fully available during the latter half of 2021.

Digital Transformation and COVID-19

As the pandemic changed the ways Americans live, learn, and work, efforts to make the Library more digitally enabled and to throw open its treasure chest, connect with users in new ways, and invest in the future became more important than ever. The Library's digital strategy and ongoing technical transformation proved critical to serving Congress and the American people during the pandemic. Planned digital initiatives, including the LOC Collections mobile app and innovator-in-residence projects Newspaper Navigator and Citizen DJ, were accelerated, providing new ways for the public to find and use Library collections. Library events were reimagined as digital-only programs, and Library content creators experimented with new ways to engage with remote audiences.

Technology and digital programs also provided ways for Library staff to transition to telework more efficiently. A quick expansion of the By the People program allowed many Library employees whose normal duties required physical access to the collections to pivot to expanding access to Library collections by transcribing handwritten items, including thousands of pages from Theodore Roosevelt's personal papers. Virtual desktops were used to allow the Library's junior fellows to participate in a new, entirely digital summer internship program.

Library leadership encouraged staff to learn new digital skills and build consensus about the present and future of the Library's digital transformation by hosting workshops and staff-led training. Among other efforts, the Digital Strategy staff initiated a six-week program of workshops designed to expand digital literacy and provide connection points with colleagues.

By inspiring internal collaboration during this challenging time, the Library has more fully embraced and nurtured new technologies to connect and inspire Americans. While the pandemic has changed how we interact and communicate with one another, it has also made clear that the Library can and will successfully integrate its rich history with modern technology.

Serving Congress

The Library of Congress was established in 1800 to provide resources to members of Congress for use in their work. The Joint Committee on the Library—the oldest continuing joint committee of Congress—was created through legislation in 1802, providing for congressional oversight. The unique collaboration between Congress and the Library has allowed them to serve the nation together for 220 years.

In FY 2020 the Library supported members of Congress, their staffs, and constituents in a variety of ways, from providing reference, research, and analysis on key issues to supplying surplus books to congressional districts. The Library also continued to implement new technologies to make the legislative process more accessible and transparent to the public.

Legislative Support

The Congressional Research Service (CRS) in the Library serves Congress with the highest-quality research, analysis, information, and confidential consultation to support the exercise of its legislative, representational, and oversight duties in its role as a coequal branch of government. The work of CRS is authoritative, confidential, objective, nonpartisan, and timely. CRS examines pressing legislative issues facing Congress; identifies and assesses policy options; and provides analysis, consultation, and briefings to support Congress throughout the legislative process across the full range of public policy issues.

In FY 2020 CRS responded to more than 75,000 congressional requests. The CRS website for Congress, crsreports.congress.gov, drew more than 1 million views, including nearly 382,000 views of the service's reports and general distribution products.

Congress established the Law Library of Congress in 1832 with the mission of making its resources available to Congress and the U.S. Supreme Court—a mission that expanded to include other branches of government and the global legal community. Librarians and lawyers respond to congressional inquiries about U.S., foreign, comparative, and international legal and legislative research, drawing upon the world's largest collection of legal resources. The collection comprises over 5 million items, including 2.9 million print volumes and global legal materials in various formats.

The Law Library's legal reference librarians are available to assist congressional staff whenever either chamber of Congress is in session, no matter the hour. In FY 2020 the Law Library responded to 456 research requests from Congress and provided assistance to congressional offices with 671 reference questions.

Copyright Law and Policy

The U.S. Copyright Office, headed by the register of copyrights, administers the nation's copyright laws for the advancement of the public good and the benefit of authors and users of creative works. The register's duties under the Copyright Act include registering creative works, recording information about copyright ownership, and administering certain statutory licenses. The office also provides expert impartial assistance to Congress, the courts, and executive branch agencies on questions of domestic and international copyright law and policy and develops educational resources and events for the public.

In FY 2020 the Copyright Office worked closely with Congress on several fronts, including the COVID-19 pandemic, as it continued work on multiple policy studies. The office generally adjusts its fees every three to five years after conducting a study of the actual cost of providing fee-based services, and, in March 2020, a new fee schedule went into effect.

Congressional Preservation Efforts

The Library leads several major preservation initiatives at the behest of Congress to ensure America's history and culture are captured and preserved for generations to come. In its concern for preserving the nation's audiovisual heritage, Congress enacted the National Film Preservation Act of 1988 and the National Recording Preservation Act of 2000. These acts direct the Librarian of Congress to select "culturally, historically, or aesthetically" significant films and sound recordings, respectively, for preservation. To date, 775 films and 550 sound recordings have been selected for preservation.

Established by Congress in 2000, the Veterans History Project (VHP) in the Library's American Folklife Center (AFC) preserves the memories of those in our nation's armed services and others who shared America's wartime experience in the 20th and early 21st centuries. During FY 2020 the Veterans History Project received 2,304 collections, including 119 that arose from the Gold Star Family Act. VHP now holds more than 111,000 from veterans across the nation.

Supporting the Library

The president signed the Further Consolidated Appropriations Act (P.L. 116-94) on December 20, 2019, providing the Library a total budget authority of $775.062 million for FY 2020, including $719.359 million in appropriations and $55.703 million in offsetting receipts authority. In the Coronavirus Supplemental Appropriations Act (Public Law 116-136, CARES Act), the Library was provided $6 million in authority via a technical correction and $700,000 in supplemental authority to support the Little Scholars Child Development Center.

Total Library budget authority increased approximately 3 percent over FY 2019. The funding supported the Visitors Experience project, which will increase the accessibility of the Library's most-prized artifacts; raise the Library's public profile; and make the Library a destination for discovery, creating, and learning. It also supported the modernization and reconstitution of analytical capacity in the Office of the Chief Financial Officer; data center transformation and modernization; congress.gov enhancements; and National Library Service modernization expanding user access in the braille and talking book program and replacing the Braille and Audio Reading Download (BARD) website with cloud-based Internet delivery technology. The funding continued to support the VHP and the Teaching with Primary Sources program.

The 2020 enacted budget continues a multiyear strategic modernization in all areas, not just IT standardization, optimization, and modernization, but also infrastructure, business process, and targeted workforce skills to increase access and engage user-centered customer service to Congress and the American people.

Librarian of Congress Carla Hayden testified in February 2020 before the House Appropriations Subcommittee and provided written testimony to the Senate Appropriations Subcommittee (due to the pandemic) on the Library's FY 2021 budget request. The Library's request focused on expanding access and enhancing services, optimizing resources, and measuring impacts to ensure the Library's ability to support Congress and the American people. The House subcommittee also heard separate testimony from the director of the Congressional Research Service and the acting register of copyrights.

On December 27, 2020, the president signed Public Law 116-260, the Consolidated Appropriations Act, 2021, to provide the Library with $802.128 million of funding authority, including $757.346 million in appropriation and $44.782 million in offsetting collection authority. Six programmatic increases were provided in the enactment, including funding for cybersecurity enhancements, eAcquisition and contract management, compact shelving replacement, copyright royalty judges staffing, Music Modernization Act staffing, and science and technology research capacity.

The Library of Congress Trust Fund Board, created in 1925 by an act of Congress, acted as trustee of private funds invested for the benefit of the Library. Its work supports Library literacy programs, exhibitions, acquisitions, scholarly programs and fellowships, concerts, and other initiatives.

Collections

The Library of Congress is both the nation's library and the largest library in the world. The institution's vast collections encompass virtually all formats, languages, and subjects. It is perhaps the most comprehensive accumulation of human knowledge ever assembled.

In FY 2020 the Library's collections grew to more than 171 million items. The Library added close to 1.85 million items to its collections during the year through purchase, gift, exchange, or transfer from other government agencies. The U.S. Copyright Office transferred a total of 552,593 works with an estimated value of more than $45 million; more than 450,000 of the transferred items were received from publishers under the mandatory deposit provision of the law. Receipts via eDeposits included 222,641 e-books, 55,818 e-serial issues, and 7,542 newspaper eprint issues.

The Acquisitions and Bibliographic Access Directorate (ABA) acquired 1,082,791 items for the Library's collections through cost-effective methods, including purchase and exchange. In addition, ABA facilitated the acquisition of 509,925 collection items through solicited gifts to the Special Collections Directorate.

The Library's six overseas offices (located in Cairo, Islamabad, Jakarta, Nairobi, New Delhi, and Rio de Janeiro) acquired, cataloged, and preserved materials from parts of the world where the book and information industries are not well developed. In FY 2020 those offices acquired 208,247 collection items, on a cost-recovery basis, for the more than 100 U.S. libraries that participated in the Cooperative Acquisitions Program.

Collection Development

The Collection Development Office (CDO) directly supports the Library's strategic goal of acquiring and maintaining a universal collection of knowledge and the record of America's creativity to meet the needs of Congress, researchers, and the American public. It ensures that the Library's analog and digital collections reflect the breadth and depth of knowledge published in all media, languages, and regions of the world. In FY 2020 CDO took on major roles in the project to build an online tool, the Material Acquisition Request Service (MARS), to replace the paper Recommendation for Acquisition and Memorandum of Recommendation forms. MARS launched successfully at the beginning of FY 2021.

As the pandemic started, CDO distributed guidance to recommending officers on collecting COVID-19 websites. Later, CDO, with the Digital Collection Management and Services Division, created a coordinated coronavirus web collecting plan that was handed off to a team of recommending officers for implementation. Similarly, as mass protests took place across the United States and around the world after the May 25, 2020, killing of George Floyd in Minneapolis, CDO and DCMS quickly developed the parameters of a web collecting plan focused on the protests, also assigned to a recommending officers' collecting team.

Although the Library's long-term practice has been to permanently retain the materials in its collections and not to deaccession them except under specific circumstances, the practice had never been codified in a formal policy. That gap was filled as CDO consulted widely within the Library and developed, then issued, a collections retention policy.

Preservation

The Preservation Directorate is guided by the Library's mission to provide a "universal and enduring" collection that is format neutral in order to record knowledge and creativity. To that end, the directorate executes millions of preservation actions each year in support of the diverse array of preservation strategies required by the national collection. Expert staffs perform preventative and corrective treatments and transfer information from obsolete or at-risk media into new formats. They manage secure, environmentally optimized storage facilities and maintain inventory control. The directorate is a center for fundamental research and processional education, and the Library's insights and innovations set standards and enhance preservation and conservation practices worldwide.

In FY 2020 the directorate continued to assess and treat Library collections using established technologies, practices, and procedures to reduce risks to collection materials. It also engaged in scientific research to explore new approaches to preservation. The directorate performed 6.8 million preservation actions on books, serials, prints, photographs, audiovisual materials, and other items. During the fiscal year, 71,431 items were bound into new library bindings; 26,068 were treated or repaired in conservation labs; 9,148 were placed in protective containers or housings; and 97,398 book equivalents and 355,230 sheets were deacidified. Staff surveyed the preservation needs of 713,234 items from the general and special collections, monitored over 230 environmental data loggers, and continued to play a key role in the Library's security and emergency-response programs.

To protect information at risk from deterioration and ensure its informational content is available, staff members reformat original media. Digital transformation was an important focus for the year. The Library captured 5 million pages on microfilm, including 3.8 million by the Preservation Directorate and 1.2 million microfilmed by the overseas offices.

Newspapers

The Library's newspaper collection items received 2,318,651 page views and 845,209 visits in FY 2020, not including the Chronicling America website. Chronicling America recorded 7.3 million page views and 66.3 million visits. The collection now includes 2,360,347 issues of 3,263 titles from 48 states, two territories, and the District of Columbia. Jointly sponsored by the Library of Congress and the National Endowment for the Humanities, the National Digital Newspaper Program (NDNP) supports the enhancement of access to American newspapers through the site. Various partnerships and collaborations enable cultural heritage institutions to select and digitize representative newspapers from their states and territories for contribution to the collection.

Audiovisual Collections

The Packard Campus of the National Audio-Visual Conservation Center, located in Culpeper, Virginia, houses the Library's recorded sound and moving image collections—the world's largest and most comprehensive. The center launched 15 online collections in FY 2020, all of them part of the American Archive of Public Broadcasting collaboration with WGBH.

In FY 2020 the Moving Image Section acquired 61,008 analog items. The largest gift consisted of 50,000 manuscript items that were added to the Jerry Lewis Collection. In addition, the section acquired 20,637 born-digital items, including 5,631 files of the copyright collection, 2,840 via direct file transfer from the Senate, and 1,090 in the HistoryMakers Collection.

The Recorded Sound Section is committed to building and enhancing a collection of commercial and noncommercial recordings in all formats from all periods. The section acquired 16,571 physical audio recordings, 34,712 manuscript items, and 124,199 born-digital recordings in FY 2020.

National Recording Registry

On March 25, 2020, the Librarian announced the addition of 25 sound recordings to the National Recording Registry, bringing the total to 550.

"Whispering" (single), Paul Whiteman and His Orchestra (1920)

"Protesta per Sacco e Vanzetti," Compagnia Columbia; "Sacco e Vanzetti," Raoul Romito (1927)

"La Chicharronera" (single), Narciso Martinez and Santiago Almeida (1936)

Arch Oboler's Plays episode "The Bathysphere" (November 18, 1939)

"Me and My Chauffeur Blues" (single), Memphis Minnie (1941)

The 1951 National League tiebreaker: New York Giants vs. Brooklyn Dodgers— Russ Hodges, announcer (October 3, 1951)

Puccini's *Tosca* (album), Maria Callas, Giuseppe di Stefano, Tito Gobbi, Victor de Sabata, etc. (1953)

"Hello Muddah, Hello Fadduh" (single), Allan Sherman (1963)

WGBH broadcast of the Boston Symphony on the day of the John F. Kennedy assassination, Boston Symphony Orchestra (1963)

Fiddler on the Roof (album), Original Broadway cast (1964)

"Make the World Go Away" (single), Eddy Arnold (1965)

Hiromi Lorraine Sakata Collection of Afghan Traditional Music (1966–1967, 1971–1973)

"Wichita Lineman" (single), Glen Campbell (1968)

Dusty in Memphis (album), Dusty Springfield (1969)

Mister Rogers Sings 21 Favorite Songs from "Mister Rogers' Neighborhood" (album), Fred Rogers (1973)

Cheap Trick at Budokan (album), Cheap Trick (1978)

Gustav Holst: Suite No. 1 in E-flat, Suite no. 2 in F / Handel: *Music for the Royal Fireworks* / Bach: Fantasia in G (Special Edition Audiophile Pressing), Frederick Fennell and the Cleveland Symphonic Winds (1978)

"Y.M.C.A." (single), Village People (1978)

A Feather on the Breath of God (album), Gothic Voices; Christopher Page, conductor; Hildegard von Bingen, composer (1982)

Private Dancer (album), Tina Turner (1984)

Ven Conmigo (album), Selena (1990)

The Chronic (album), Dr. Dre (1992)

"I Will Always Love You" (single), Whitney Houston (1992)

Concert in the Garden (album), Maria Schneider Orchestra (2004)

Percussion Concerto (album), Colin Currie; Jennifer Higdon, composer (2008)

National Film Registry

On December 14, 2020, the Librarian of Congress named 25 films to the National Film Registry, bringing the total to 775.

The Battle of the Century (1927)
The Blues Brothers (1980)
Bread (1918)
Buena Vista Social Club (1999)
Cabin in the Sky (1943)
A Clockwork Orange (1971)
The Dark Knight (2008)
The Devil Never Sleeps (1994)
Freedom Riders (2010)
Grease (1978)
The Ground (1993–2001)

The Hurt Locker (2009)
Illusions (1982)
The Joy Luck Club (1993)
Kid Auto Races at Venice (1914)
Lilies of the Field (1963)
Losing Ground (1982)
The Man with the Golden Arm (1955)
Mauna Kea: Temple Under Siege (2006)
Outrage (1950)
Shrek (2001)
Suspense (1913)
Sweet Sweetback's Baadasssss Song (1971)
Wattstax (1973)
With Car and Camera Around the World (1929)

Access

The Library makes its multiformat collections publicly available in its multiple reading rooms and research centers on Capitol Hill and at the Packard Campus of the National Audio-Visual Conservation Center, and through its website. By cataloging its holdings in English and other languages, the Library provides bibliographic access to its vast and growing collections. Through shared and cooperative cataloging, the Library helps the nation's libraries provide better access to their collections.

Visitors to all Library buildings in FY 2020, for the months of October 2019 to March 2020, when the Library shut down its on-site operations, totaled more than 565,000. Of these, approximately 540,000 visited the Jefferson Building. In normal years, the Library's Great Hall and exhibitions remain open to the public on federal holidays with the exception of Thanksgiving, Christmas Day, and New Year's Day.

Reference Services

During FY 2020 28,549 new reader-identification cards were issued, a significant decrease over the previous fiscal year. The Library's staff responded to more than 157,493 reference requests, of which more than 76,995 were received online, including through the Ask a Librarian service. The Library circulated 244,981 physical items on-site, a decrease of 73 percent from the previous year. More than 50,805 items were circulated off-site to authorized borrowers.

Cataloging

The Library managed 52,843,642 MARC records in its Integrated Library System during the year. The Library cataloged 252,824 new works in addition to 717,384 million manuscript items on 183 bibliographic records. The Cataloging-in-Publication program cataloged 58,631 titles, and the Electronic Cataloging-in-Publication

E-book Program prepared cataloging in advance of publication for 39,871 e-books. The Library established 251,436 name and series authorities, 8,667 subject headings, and 2,320 new Library of Congress Classification numbers. The Dewey Program, which supports libraries worldwide that classify their titles in Dewey Decimal Classification (DDC), assigned DDC to 123,183 titles.

During the year, the Library's curatorial divisions created 81 new Encoded Archival Description finding aids online. As a result, researchers can now access 73.4 million archival items in the Library's collections.

Bibliographic Framework Initiative

BIBFRAME is an initiative begun in FY 2011 as a replacement for the cataloging metadata standard known as MARC 21. During 2020 progress was accelerated for BIBFRAME. More than 100 cataloging staff continued to participate in the pilot project, which tested production of BIBRAME descriptions in a simulated cataloging environment. Participants included copy catalogers and catalogers of text, maps, moving images, notated (print) music, rare books, sound recordings, and still images and moving images in 35mm film, Blu-ray, and DVD formats.

Access for the Blind and Print Disabled

In FY 2020 the National Library Service for the Blind and Print Disabled (NLS) circulated nearly 20.3 million copies of braille, audio, and large print items. NLS added 5,612 books and 1,047 magazine issues to its Braille and Audio Reading Download service (BARD) during the fiscal year, bringing the total number of available titles there to approximately 137,000 (119,000 books and 18,000 magazines). Patrons downloaded about 4.6 million books and magazines from BARD in FY 2020.

NLS took significant steps toward fulfilling its overall modernization plan. It developed and began a pilot program to test an affordable refreshable braille display, moving closer to achieving a longtime goal. It also reached a major milestone with the adoption of Duplication on Demand by more than half of its network libraries. Those libraries now can create their own talking-book cartridges on-site from NLS-produced digital files, allowing them to fill patron requests quickly and reducing costs associated with maintaining large physical collections.

The Library's Website, Congress.gov, and Social Media

The Library's website, loc.gov, provides users with access to the institution's unparalleled resources, such as its online catalogs; selected collections in various formats; copyright, legal, and legislative information; exhibitions; and videos and podcasts of events.

In FY 2020 Library web properties experienced the largest volume of traffic in Library history. Those properties (excluding the Legislative Information System, congress.gov, and copyright.gov) recorded more than 117 million visits and 647 million page views—increases of 39 percent and 58 percent, respectively. Mobile visits made up 46 percent of those visits, an increase of nine percentage points over the previous fiscal year.

Culminating over a dozen years of work, the Library was able to retire the legacy Legislative Information System from congressional use in November 2019, making congress.gov the official source for legislative information for both Congress and the public. Traffic to congress.gov increased significantly over the previous fiscal year. Visits rose 68 percent to 50.8 million, and page views increased 41 percent to 134.1 million. Mobile visits rose 124 percent to 22.9 million, accounting for 45 percent of all visits to the site.

The World Digital Library (WDL) site recorded 19.6 million visits in FY 2020, a 190 percent increase over FY 2019. The site drew 3.7 million visits on March 16 following a tweet from UNESCO advising users to take advantage of WDL resources during COVID-19 quarantines.

The Library streamed videos of concerts, lectures, and other events on YouTube and Facebook each month. Once public events were limited due to the pandemic, the Library instead premiered prerecorded videos and livestreamed events staged remotely. During FY 2020 the Library premiered 48 videos and livestreamed eight events. The premiere videos and livestreams included events featuring Pulitzer Prize–winning author Colson Whitehead; U.S. Poet Laureate Joy Harjo; Kluge Prize recipient Danielle Allen; biographers Douglas Brinkley and Jeanne Theoharis; and authors Erik Larson, Jason Reynolds, and Alice McDermott.

During FY 2020 the Library made 763 new videos available on its main YouTube channel, videos that were liked 79,381 times and viewed nearly 6.6 million times. The channel gained 40,340 subscribers during the year. The Copyright Office also made 53 new videos available on its YouTube Channel. The Library's Podcast account features selected podcasts, historical films from Library collections, and video and audio recordings from collections and of events at the Library. In FY 2020 the Library added 17 files to iTunes podcasts. The account gained over 2,296 new subscriptions and drew 65,301 visitors and 68,723 consumptions. Since the account was launched in 2009, the Library has added 4,020 files and attracted 984,078 visitors and 230,823 subscriptions, with a total consumption of 4.44 million files.

Photo enthusiasts continued to access and help identify Library photos from the early 1900s through the Library of Congress Flickr account. During the fiscal year, the Library added 2,433 photos to that account, bringing the total to 37,230. Over the account's lifetime, the Library has accumulated 72,729 followers and 379,414,576 image views. A second Flickr account, Library of Congress Life, features photos and videos of Library buildings and events. That account added 435 images during the fiscal year, which were viewed 355,979 times. Over the account's lifetime, the Library has posted 969 images and earned 606,256 views and 104 followers.

In FY 2020 the Library also launched an account on Unsplash, a website devoted to sharing free images. The Library posted 163 images, which were viewed more than 76.6 million times and downloaded 205,125 times. The Library's Instagram account continued to share images from virtual events, concerts, and exhibitions. The account added 23,215 new followers for a total of 78,944 at the end of FY 2020. It received 256,040 likes for a lifetime total of 520,673.

In addition to its main Facebook page, the Library offers Facebook pages for the Law Library, the AFC, Performing Arts, NLS, VHP, and the Library's international collections. During FY 2020 the Library posted 3,564 times on those pages, gained 29,304 followers, received 369,901 likes on posts, and received over 47.2 million impressions. Library Facebook accounts have a total of 565,256 followers, and posts have received a combined 438.5 million lifetime impressions.

In FY 2020 the Library maintained 13 public-facing Twitter accounts and two Congressional Research Service–protected Twitter accounts for use by members of Congress and congressional staff. The public-facing accounts issued 6,455 tweets during the fiscal year, gaining 93,443 retweets and 6,330 replies. The public accounts also gained 47,276 followers (for a total of 1.63 million followers) and received over 66.5 million impressions.

The Library maintains 17 blogs that serve as a vehicle for sharing collection discoveries and engaging with users. During the fiscal year, the Library published 1,405 posts, which drew over 3.9 million page views for a lifetime total of 21.2 million page views. The Library's blogs collectively drew 34 percent more visits than in FY 2019.

The Library offers 61 email alerts, including all Library and copyright-related topics for subscription. Loc.gov sent 4,378 bulletins in FY 2020 and recorded 202,723 new subscriptions. Copyright.gov sent 137 bulletins and recorded 105,221 new subscriptions.

Promoting Creativity, Scholarship, and Lifelong Learning

The Library of Congress collections chronicle centuries of human creativity—a rich, diverse, and enduring source of knowledge for the American public and scholars around the world. During the year, the Library presented hundreds of public programs that promoted creativity, scholarship, and lifelong learning. These programs included exhibitions, lectures, concerts, webinars, symposia, panel discussions, and short-term displays of collection items. Webcasts of many of these events can be viewed on the Library's website.

The Library is a catalyst for promoting scholarship through the John W. Kluge Center and AFC, which offer fellowship opportunities in various disciplines and publications that showcase the Library's unparalleled collections.

In addition to its fellowships, research services, and collections access, the Library promotes lifelong learning and literacy through its Center for Learning, Literacy, and Engagement (CLLE) and K–12 educational outreach efforts, which assist the nation's teachers in engaging students through the use of primary sources in the classroom.

Educational Outreach

Reaching educators and providing them with useful opportunities and materials were more important than ever during this year, when the pandemic forced many schools to transition to online learning. Through its Teaching with Primary Sources (TPS) program, the Library provides educators across the grade spectrum and the curriculum with high-quality professional-development programs and classroom materials. These opportunities and tools help them effectively use primary sources from the Library's digital collections in their teaching.

In FY 2020 Learning and Innovation Office staff and TPS partners engaged more than 17,000 educators nationwide in professional development presentations and activities, directly impacting the learning of hundreds of thousands of students nationally and internationally. Participants in these activities represented 98 percent of all congressional districts and hailed from 50 states, the District of Columbia, and Puerto Rico. Staff produced over 60 hours of new online educational programming presented live and made available through the archive. During the fiscal year, TPS awarded nearly $6.8 million in grants to support a wide array of projects, programs, and innovative web applications for teachers across the country.

The Teaching with the Library of Congress blog reached over 32,000 subscribers with 110 posts, and the @TeachingLC Twitter account reached more than 35,000 followers. These posts and tweets provided teaching strategies, primary sources, and insights from CLLE staff and from experts across the Library, covering topics ranging from civil rights to STEM to roadside architecture.

Celebrating Achievement

Throughout the year, the Library of Congress celebrates the achievements of the nation's creative and scholarly communities. The Library also recognizes the accomplishments of its staff members. The Library sponsors privately endowed programs that honor achievement in the humanities. Through these awards and prizes, the Library honors those who have advanced and embodied the ideals of individuality, conviction, dedication, scholarship, and lifelong learning.

Kluge Prize

The John W. Kluge Prize for Achievement in the Study of Humanity recognizes individuals whose outstanding scholarship in the humanities and social sciences has shaped public affairs and civil society. The prize comes with a $500,000 award. In June 2020 Danielle Allen was named recipient of the 2020 prize. Allen is the director of the Edmond J. Safra Center for Ethics and the James Bryant Conant University Professor at Harvard University.

Library of Congress Prize for American Fiction

The Library of Congress Prize for American Fiction honors an American literary writer whose body of work is distinguished not only for its mastery of the art but also for originality of thought and imagination. In July the Library announced Colson Whitehead as the winner of the 2020 prize. Whitehead is the author of the Pulitzer Prize–winning novels *The Nickel Boys* and *The Underground Railroad*.

The Library of Congress Lavine / Ken Burns Prize for Film

On October 16, 2020, the Library announced the award of the inaugural Library of Congress Lavine / Ken Burns Prize for Film to *Flannery*, a film directed by Elizabeth Coffman and Mark Bosco that documents the life of writer Flannery O'Connor. The prize is cosponsored with Ken Burns, the Better Angels Society, and the Lavine Foundation. It provided $200,000 to the filmmakers to complete the postproduction work on their film.

Leicester B. Holland Prize

The Leicester B. Holland Prize recognizes the best single-sheet, measured drawing of a historic building, site, or structure prepared to the standards of the Historic American Buildings Survey, the Historic American Engineering Record, or the Historic American Landscapes Survey. In November 2019 the prize was bestowed on an architectural team at Catholic University of America in Washington, D.C., for their drawing featuring the Old Dominion Bank Building, now known as the Athenaeum, built in 1851 in Alexandria, Virginia.

Literacy Awards

Created and sponsored by philanthropist and Madison Council chairman David M. Rubenstein, the Library of Congress Literacy Awards seek to reward organizations that have done exemplary, innovative, and easily replicable work over a sustained period of time to promote literacy in the United States and abroad.

David M. Rubenstein Special Response Awards ($50,000 each)

In FY 2020 three organizations received Special Response awards for their work during the COVID-19 pandemic: the National Center for Families Learning of Louisville, Kentucky, for its work to eliminate poverty through educational solutions for families; children's book publisher Pratham Books of Bengaluru, India, for its efforts to help children gain access to affordable books in multiple languages; and Room to Read, of San Francisco, which seeks to transform the lives of children in low-income communities by focusing on literacy and gender equality in education.

American Prize ($50,000)

The Immigrant Learning Center of Malden, Massachusetts, addresses the needs of low-income immigrants and refugee adults in the greater Boston area.

International Prize ($50,000)

The International Rescue Committee's Pakistan Reading Project, based in New York City, supports regional and provincial education departments to improve literacy and reading skills of public school children in grades one and two throughout Pakistan.

FEDLINK Awards

The Federal Library and Information Network (FEDLINK) serves federal libraries and information centers as their purchasing, training, and resource-sharing consortium. Each year, FEDLINK presents the winners of its national awards for federal librarianship, which recognize the innovative ways federal libraries, librarians, and library technicians fulfill the information demands of government, business, scholars, and the public. [For 2020 award winners and other details, see the Federal Library and Information Network (FEDLINK) report immediately following the Library of Congress report in this edition—*Ed.*]

Library of Congress Additional Sources of Information

Library of Congress website	loc.gov
Main phone number	202-707-5000
Reading room hours and locations	loc.gov/rr/
	202-707-6400
General reference	loc.gov/rr/askalib/
	202-707-4773
Visitor information	loc.gov/visit/
	202-707-8000
Exhibitions	loc.gov/exhibits/
	202-707-4604
Copyright information	copyright.gov
	202-707-3000
Copyright hotline (to order forms)	202-707-9100
Library catalogs	catalog.loc.gov/
Cataloging information	loc.gov/aba/
National Library Service for the Blind and Print Disabled	loc.gov/nls/
	202-707-5100
	TDD 202-707-0744
Literacy promotion	read.gov
Resources for teachers	loc.gov/teachers/
Legislative information	Congress.gov
Library of Congress Shop (credit card orders)	loc.gov/shop
	888-682-3557

Federal Library and Information Network

Laurie Neider
Executive Director

The Federal Library and Information Network (FEDLINK) is an organization of federal agencies working together to achieve optimum use of the resources and facilities of federal libraries and information centers by promoting common services, coordinating and sharing available resources, and providing continuing professional education for federal library and information staff.

FEDLINK serves as a forum for discussion of the policies, programs, procedures, and technologies that affect federal libraries and the information services they provide to their agencies, to the Congress, the federal courts, and the American people.

In spite of challenges created by the COVID-19 pandemic, during fiscal year (FY) 2020 FEDLINK continued its mission to achieve better utilization of federal library and information resources by providing the most cost-effective and efficient administrative mechanism for providing necessary services and materials to federal libraries and information centers.

FEDLINK Executive Report

FEDLINK's Advisory Board (FAB) focused its bimonthly meetings on a variety of broad federal information issues including administrative issues related to market sustainability and system updates for the FEDLINK-assisted acquisition model. At several sessions, board members reviewed current working groups and identified working group action plans and directional planning.

FEDLINK held one exposition in FY 2020. The 2019 Fall Expo, "Sharing Information among Federal Libraries," featured a keynote address by Laurie Hall, superintendent of documents, Government Publishing Office, and plenary sessions on digital collaboration tools and networking within the information professions. At the end of the fiscal year, FEDLINK sponsored a paid training called "Digital Conversion: Planning for Success."

FEDLINK Working Group Highlights

FEDLINK Awards Committee

To honor the many innovative ways federal libraries, librarians, and library technicians fulfill the information demands of government, business, research, scholarly communities, and the American public, the Awards Committee administered a series of national awards for federal librarianship.

Winners of the FY 2019 awards, announced In June 2020, were

Federal Library / Information Center of the Year

Large Library/Information Center (with a staff of 11 or more federal and/or contract employees): D'Azzo Research Library (DRL), Wright-Patterson Air Force Base, Ohio, was recognized for increasing information access and outreach to students and faculty of the Air Force Institute of Technology (AFIT), engineers and scientists of the Air Force Research Laboratory (AFRL), and the global research community. In FY 2019 the library launched its institutional repository, AFIT Scholar, a single, central, searchable database, and delivered 36,850 thesis and dissertation downloads to 2,486 institutions in 166 countries. Working with AFRL and base contracting, the organizations collaborated to purchase more than 23 databases and journal collections, saving more than $382,000. On-site, a staff of 13 responded to 5,612 reference requests and taught 36 academic research classes to 532 participants while completing a library space reconfiguration that increased visits by 8 percent.

Small Library/Information Center (with a staff of ten or fewer federal and/or contract employees): Bureau of Land Management Library (BLM), Denver, Colorado, was recognized for creativity in improving the user experience, facilitating access to research and developing solutions and virtual collections to increase library use. In FY 2019 BLM Library implemented a journal link resolver to identify sought-after resources in a growing collection of digitized documents and relevant journals and a website that includes the Library's catalog, electronic journal holdings, and digitized collections. The library spearheaded an initiative to preserve historic and rare bureau documents and created a searchable collection of 833 of its directives from 1964 to 1995—comprising more than 31,000 files and 250,000 pages—and a growing historical photo archive.

Federal Librarian of the Year

Greta Marlatt, outreach and academic support manager, Dudley Knox Library, Naval Postgraduate, Monterey, California, was recognized for furthering data science research and education in support of the combat effectiveness of the naval service. She provided instruction to Defense Analysis, National Security, the Center for Homeland Defense and Security, and the Institute for Global Security and taught a number of citation management courses and conducted bibliographic instruction. In FY 2019 Marlatt headed an important library renovation and collection relocation space-planning effort to remove barriers to collections, people, and services while creating learner-centered physical and virtual spaces. She managed $2 million in library acquisitions; curated more than 30 LibGuides in the areas of congressional information, area studies, military information, and conflict and security studies; and responded to 750 off-desk reference questions.

2019 Federal Library Technician of the Year

Gabriele Davis, library technician, U.S. Army Garrison Rheinland Pfalz Libraries, Kaiserslautern, Germany, was recognized for her strategic knowledge management, technical expertise, and dedicated customer service. In FY 2019 Davis was solely responsible for cataloging and retrospective cataloging of the library collection of the Parent & Professional Educational Resource Center collection for ten child and youth services facilities and expanded early literacy and makerspace programming at the garrison's Morale, Welfare, and Recreation (MWR) Libraries. She also supported interlibrary loan services to 16 other European Army libraries and Air Force post libraries. Unofficially known throughout MWR libraries in Europe as "the fastest cataloger in the West," Davis cataloged or modified up to 1,300 records a month while providing direct circulation desk coverage at two libraries and supporting library programming for more than 1,000 programs.

FEDLINK Working Groups Survey of Federal Library COVID-19 Responses and Reopening Plans

In response to the COVID-19 pandemic and resulting federal library closures, as early as April 2020 members of the FEDLINK Library Leadership Working Group began compiling anecdotal reports of reopening plans. As plans began to form by May, the working group made a call to its 75 agency representatives to share information about their federal library plans to reopen. At the same time, the National Science Foundation's (NSF) library program manager, a member of the FEDLINK Library Leadership Working Group, was developing an instrument for a broader survey of academic, federal, and public libraries.

After discussions of survey questions and distribution efforts, the FEDLINK Library Leadership Working Group, the FEDLINK Research and Metrics Working Group, and the NSF Library agreed to combine their questions to collaborate on a stand-alone federal library survey and produce independent reports. The FEDLINK survey asked federal libraries to share their planning and insights on responding to the challenge of offering library services while mitigating the spread of SARS-CoV-2, the virus that causes COVID-19. The federal library survey report highlighted the results of how colleagues, across a range of government agencies, planned to reopen their federal libraries in response to the COVID-19 public health challenge.

FEDLINK Publications and Education Office

FEDLINK continued to develop targeted resources to support the FEDLINK program, including governing body and educational programming support; directional, business, and customer service plans; promotional materials; and supporting materials for both exposition programs and working group projects and events. Staff supported 16 FEDLINK Marketplace demonstrations as part of its educational platform for vendor outreach. FEDLINK continued its publication program as a digital communication provider and used its website and community listservs for outreach on critical advocacy and program information to more than 2,000 electronic subscribers.

FEDLINK Contracts and Network Operations

FEDLINK provided assisted acquisition services to the federal information community by procuring publications in a wide variety of formats (print and electronic journals; print and electronic books; sound recordings; audiovisual materials; items via document delivery and interlibrary loan; and access to databases of full text, indices, abstracts, and a variety of other data) and library support services (cataloging and related technical processing services; staffing support;

information management; resource sharing; integrated library systems; digitization; digital archiving; and preservation services).

Through interagency agreements (IAAs), FEDLINK's contracts and network staff members worked on behalf of federal agencies with more than 100 vendors to conduct competitions, issue orders, and resolve issues with vendors. FEDLINK exceeded its financial goals for FY 2020 by 12 percent in revenue and 13 percent in total purchases made via FEDLINK's contracts.

National Agricultural Library

U.S. Department of Agriculture, Agricultural Research Service
Abraham Lincoln Bldg., 10301 Baltimore Ave., Beltsville, MD 20705-2351
E-mail agref@nal.usda.gov
World Wide Web https://www.nal.usda.gov

Paul Wester

Director

The U.S. Department of Agriculture's National Agricultural Library (NAL) is one of the world's largest and most accessible agricultural research libraries, offering service directly to the public either on-site in Beltsville, Maryland, or via its website, https://www.nal.usda.gov.

The library was established in 1862 at the same time as the U.S. Department of Agriculture (USDA). It became a national library in 1962, when Congress established it as the primary agricultural information resource of the United States (7 USCS § 3125a). Congress assigned to the library the responsibilities to

- Acquire, preserve, and manage information resources relating to agriculture and allied sciences
- Organize agricultural information products and services and provide them within the United States and internationally
- Plan, coordinate, and evaluate information and library needs relating to agricultural research and education
- Cooperate with and coordinate efforts toward development of a comprehensive agricultural library and information network
- Coordinate the development of specialized subject information services among the agricultural and library information communities

NAL is located in Beltsville, Maryland, near Washington, D.C., on the grounds of USDA's Henry A. Wallace Beltsville Agricultural Research Center. Its 14-story Abraham Lincoln Building is named in honor of the president who created the Department of Agriculture and signed several of the major U.S. laws affecting agriculture.

The library employs about 100 librarians, information specialists, computer specialists, administrators, and clerical personnel, supplemented by about 50 contract staff and cooperators from NAL partnering organizations.

NAL's reputation as one of the world's foremost agricultural libraries is supported and burnished by its expert staff, ongoing leadership in delivering information services, expanding collaborations with other U.S. and international agricultural research and information organizations, and extensive collection of agricultural information, searchable through AGRICOLA (AGRICultural On-Line Access), the library's bibliographic database.

In 2012 NAL reorganized to better align its functions with its overall strategic plan, which includes simplified access to all NAL content, expansion of digital content, and the integration of scientific data sets and discovery tools.

The Collection

The NAL collection dates to the congressionally approved 1839 purchase of books for the Agricultural Division of the Patent Office, predating the 1862 establishment of USDA itself. Today NAL provides access to billions of pages of agricultural information—an immense collection of scientific books, journals, audiovisuals, reports, theses, artifacts, and images—and to a widening array of digital media, as well as databases and other information resources germane to the broad reach of agriculture-related sciences.

The library's collection contains more than 8 million items, dating from the 15th century to the present, including the most complete repository of USDA publications and the world's most extensive set of materials on the history of U.S. agriculture. Publications are selected for the collection based on the National Agricultural Library Collection Development Policy.

Building the Collection

NAL is the only U.S. national library with a legislated mandate to collect in the following disciplines: plant and animal health, welfare, and production; agricultural economics, products, and education; aquaculture; forestry; rural sociology and rural life; family and consumer science; and food science, safety, and nutrition. In addition to collecting as comprehensively as possible in these core subject areas, NAL collects extensively in many related subjects, such as biology, bioinformatics, biochemistry, chemistry, entomology, environmental science, genetics, invasive species, meteorology, natural resources, physics, soil science, sustainability, water quality, and zoology. The library has primary responsibility for collecting and retaining publications issued by USDA and its agencies. As well, NAL collects publications from around the world.

Special Collections

The NAL Special Collections program emphasizes access to and preservation of rare and unique materials documenting the history of agriculture and related sciences. Items in the library's special collections include rare books, manuscripts, nursery and seed trade catalogs, posters, objects, photographs, and other rare materials documenting agricultural subjects. Materials date from the 1500s to the present and include many international sources. Detailed information about these special collections is available on the NAL website at https://specialcollections.nal.usda.gov.

Special collections of note include the following:

- The U.S. Department of Agriculture History Collection (https://special collections.nal.usda.gov/usda-history-collection-introductionindex), assembled over 80 years by USDA historians, includes letters, memoranda, reports, and papers of USDA officials, as well as photographs, oral histories, and clippings covering the activities of the department from its founding through the early 1990s.
- The U.S. Department of Agriculture Pomological Watercolor Collection (http://usdawatercolors.nal.usda.gov) includes more than 7,000 detailed,

botanically accurate watercolor illustrations of fruit and nut varieties developed by growers or introduced by USDA plant explorers. Created between 1886 and the 1940s, the watercolors served as official documentation of the work of the Office of the Pomologist and were used to create chromolithographs in publications distributed widely by the department. Although created for scientific accuracy, the works are artistic treasures in their own right. The full collection has been digitized and is now available online.

* The Henry G. Gilbert Nursery and Seed Trade Catalog Collection (https://specialcollections.nal.usda.gov/guide-collections/henry-g-gilbert-nursery-and-seed-trade-catalog-collection), begun in 1904 by USDA economic botanist Percy L. Ricker, has grown to comprise more than 200,000 U.S. and foreign catalogs. The earliest items date from the late 1700s, but the collection is strongest from the 1890s to the present. Researchers commonly use the collection to document the introduction of plants to the United States, study economic trends, and illustrate early developments in American landscape design.

* The Rare Book Collection (https://specialcollections.nal.usda.gov/guide-collections/rare-book-collection) highlights agriculture's printed historical record. It covers a wide variety of subjects but is particularly strong in botany, natural history, zoology, and entomology. International in scope, the collection documents early agricultural practices in Britain and Europe, as well as the Americas. Manuscript collections (https://specialcollections.nal.usda.gov/guide-collections/index-manuscript-collections), now numbering more than 400, document the story of American agriculture and its influence on the world.

NAL continues to digitize these and other unique materials to share them broadly via its website and has published detailed indexes to the content of many manuscript collections to improve discovery. AGRICOLA, NAL's catalog, includes bibliographic entries for special collection items, manuscripts, and rare books. The library provides in-house research and reference services for its special collections and offers fee-based duplication services.

Preservation/Digitization

NAL is committed to the preservation of its print and nonprint collections. It continues to monitor and improve the environmental quality of its stacks to extend the longevity of all materials in the collection. The library has instituted a long-term strategy to ensure the growing body of agricultural information is systematically identified, preserved, and archived.

NAL's digital conversion program has resulted in a growing digital collection of USDA publications and many non-USDA historical materials not restricted by copyright. NAL is in the midst of a large-scale project to digitize agricultural literature and provide online access to the general public. Important and distinctive items were selected from the NAL collection, with an initial focus on USDA-issued publications and nursery and seed trade catalogs. Publications are accessible at NAL's Internet Archive collection (https://archive.org/details/usdanationalagriculturallibrary) and in the National Agricultural Library Digital Collections (https://naldc.nal.usda.gov/).

Library Services

Reference Services

NAL serves the agricultural information needs of customers through a combination of web-based and traditional library services, including reference, document delivery, and information centers. The NAL website offers access to a wide variety of full-text resources, as well as online access to reference and document delivery services.

The main reading room in the library's Beltsville facility features a walk-up service desk, access to an array of digital information resources (including full-text scientific journals), current periodicals, and an on-site request service for materials from NAL's collection. Services are available 8:30 A.M. to 4:30 P.M. Monday through Friday, except federal holidays.

NAL's reference services are accessible online using the Ask a Question form on the NAL webpages; by use of e-mail addressed to agref@ars.usda.gov; by telephone at 301-504-5755; or by mail to Research Services, National Agricultural Library ARS/USDA, 10301 Baltimore Avenue, Beltsville, MD 20705. Requesters receive assistance from Research Services staff in all areas and aspects of agriculture, but staff particularly answer questions, provide research guidance, and make presentations on topics not addressed by the seven subject-focused information centers of the library.

Information Centers

NAL's seven information centers are reliable sources of comprehensive, science-based information on key aspects of U.S. agriculture, providing timely, accurate, and in-depth coverage of their specialized subject areas. Their expert staff offers extensive web-based information resources and advanced reference services:

- The Alternative Farming Systems Information Center (AFSIC) (https://www.nal.usda.gov/afsic) specializes in identifying and accessing information relating to farming methods that maintain the health and productivity of the entire farming enterprise, including natural resources. This focus includes sustainable and alternative agricultural systems, crops, and livestock.
- The Animal Welfare Information Center (AWIC) (https://www.nal.usda.gov/awic) provides scientific information and referrals to help ensure the proper care and treatment of animals used in biomedical research, testing, teaching, and exhibitions, and by animal dealers. Among its varied outreach activities, the center conducts workshops for researchers on meeting the information requirements of the Animal Welfare Act.
- The Food and Nutrition Information Center (FNIC) (https://www.nal.usda.gov/fnic) provides credible, accurate, and practical resources for nutrition and health professionals, educators, government personnel, and consumers. FNIC maintains a staff of registered dietitians who can answer questions on food and human nutrition.
- The Food Safety Research Information Office (FSRIO) (https://www.nal.usda.gov/fsrio) delivers information on publicly funded—and, to the extent possible, privately funded—food safety research initiatives. The Research

Projects Database provides more than 12,000 active food safety research projects in a searchable database of U.S. and international agencies. The Research Publications Feed offers access to real-time updates of peer-reviewed publications in food safety.

- The National Invasive Species Information Center (NISIC) (https://www. invasivespeciesinfo.gov/subject/educator) delivers accessible, accurate, referenced, up-to-date, and comprehensive information on invasive species drawn from federal, state, local, and international sources.
- The Rural Information Center (RIC) (https://www.nal.usda.gov/ric) assists local officials, organizations, businesses, and rural residents working to maintain the vitality of rural areas. It collects and disseminates information on such diverse topics as community economic development, small business development, health care, finance, housing, environment, quality of life, community leadership, and education.
- The Water and Agriculture Information Center (WAIC) (https://www.nal. usda.gov/waic) collects, organizes, and communicates scientific findings, educational methodologies, and public policy issues related to water and agriculture.

In addition to these information centers, NAL manages the popular Nutrition.gov website (http://www.nutrition.gov) in collaboration with other USDA agencies and the Department of Health and Human Services. This site provides evidence-based nutrition information for the general consumer and highlights the latest in nutrition news and tools from across federal government agencies. A team of registered dietitians at NAL's Food and Nutrition Information Center maintains Nutrition.gov and answers questions on food and nutrition issues.

Document Delivery Services

NAL's document delivery operation responds to thousands of requests each year from USDA employees and from libraries and organizations around the world. NAL uses the Relais Enterprise document request and delivery system to support document delivery. With Relais fully integrated with the Voyager library system, with DigiTop, and with other Open-URL and ISO ILL-compliant systems, NAL customers can request materials or check on the status of their requests via the web, and the needed materials can easily be delivered electronically. Document requests can also be submitted via OCLC (NAL's symbol is AGL) and DOCLINE (NAL's libid is MDUNAL). Visit https://www.nal.usda.gov/services/request.shtml for details.

Digital Products

The NAL websites, which encompass nearly all the content and services described here, collectively receive millions of page views per month from people seeking agricultural information.

AGRICOLA

AGRICOLA comprises an online catalog of NAL collections, and the article citation database delivers worldwide access to agricultural information through its searchable web interface (http://agricola.nal.usda.gov). Alternatively, users can access AGRICOLA on a fee basis through several commercial vendors, or they can subscribe to the complete AGRICOLA file, also on a fee basis, directly from the library by e-mailing AgricolaPublishers@ars.usda.gov.

The AGRICOLA database covers materials in all formats, including printed works from the 15th century onward. Its records describe publications and resources encompassing all aspects of agriculture and allied disciplines. AGRICOLA, updated daily, includes the following two components:

- NAL Public Access Catalog, containing more than 1 million citations to books, audiovisual materials, serial titles, and other materials in the NAL collection. (The catalog also contains some bibliographic records for items cataloged by other libraries but not held in the NAL collection.)
- NAL Article Citation Database, consisting of more than 6 million citations to journal articles, book chapters, reports, and reprints. NAL has implemented automated indexing / text analytics software to produce its Article Citation Database. This application combines semantic analysis, machine learning, and human rules to automatically assign subject terms to journal articles.

DigiTop

DigiTop, USDA's Digital Desktop Library, delivers the full text of 7,000+ journals and 5000+ newspapers worldwide, provides 27 agriculturally significant citation databases including AGRICOLA, BIOSIS Previews, Business Source Premier, CAB Abstracts, GEOBASE, GeoRef, Scopus, and Web of Science. DigiTop also supplies a range of digital reference resources, and offers focused, personalized services. Navigator is a component of DigiTop that allows cross-searching of multiple bibliographic databases. This discovery service includes citations from academic journals, newspapers, magazines, and nonprint sources. DigiTop is available to on-site visitors and to the entire USDA workforce worldwide—more than 100,000 people—around the clock. NAL staff provides help desk and reference services, continuous user education, and training for DigiTop users.

Ag Data Commons

The newly released Ag Data Commons' mission is to serve as USDA's single-point-of-access to open agricultural research data. Its catalog with nearly 2,000 records is a gateway to data from large ongoing USDA research programs, including those listed below. Its repository also publishes and preserves data files from many studies. Standardized records describe datasets in detail and link them with corresponding journal publications. The goal of the Ag Data Commons, https://data.nal.usda.gov, is to enable data reuse for bigger, better science and decision-making.

The Ag Data Commons uses a customized version of the open-source DKAN software, which is compliant with U.S. Project Open Data standards for federal agencies. The system includes both a catalog function describing the data and pointing to its online location, and a repository holding and publishing data not otherwise available.

Specialized data services provided by the National Agricultural Library include the following:

- USDA Food Composition Database—https://ndb.nal.usda.gov
- I5K Workspace@NAL—https://i5k.nal.usda.gov
- Life Cycle Assessment Commons (LCA Commons)—https://www.lca commons.gov
- Dr. Duke's Phytochemical and Ethnobotanical Databases—https://phytochem.nal.usda.gov
- Long-Term Agroecosystem Research (LTAR)—https://ltar.nal.usda.gov
- Geospatial Data Catalog (GeoData)—https://geodata.nal.usda.gov

NALDC

The National Agricultural Library Digital Collections (NALDC) (https://naldc.nal.usda.gov/naldc/home.xhtml) offers easy access to collection materials available in digital format. NALDC offers rich searching, browsing, and retrieval of digital materials and collections, and provides reliable, long-term online access to selected publications. NALDC includes historical publications, U.S. Department of Agriculture (USDA) research, and more.

The scope of NALDC includes items published by the U.S. Department of Agriculture (USDA) and clearly intended for public consumption, scholarly, and peer-reviewed research outcomes authored by USDA employees while working for USDA, and other items selected in accordance with the subjects identified in the NAL Collection Development Policy.

PubAg

PubAg (https://pubag.nal.usda.gov) contains full-text articles authored by USDA employees and citations to the peer-reviewed journal literature of agriculture. These citations have been enriched through subject analysis and application of terms from NALT (NAL's Agricultural Thesaurus). They also contain links to the full text at publisher websites and other locations.

PubAg was launched originally in late 2014 and was upgraded in 2017 to include the following features: a spell checker to improve users' search quality; a type-ahead feature to suggest search terms; the ability to select records for actions such as formatting citations, printing, and e-mailing records and sending them to a reference manager; filtering retrieved results by journal name, publication year, or subject term; and providing access to a publicly available Application Programming Interface (API); and an Advanced Search function.

National Agricultural Library Thesaurus (English and Spanish)

NAL is known for its expertise in developing and using a thesaurus, or controlled vocabulary, a critical component of effective digital information systems. The National Agricultural Library Thesaurus (NALT) is a hierarchical vocabulary of agricultural and biological terms organized according to 17 subject categories. It comprises primarily biological nomenclature, with additional terminology supporting the physical and social sciences.

The 2020 NALT (https://agclass.nal.usda.gov/agt.shtml), available in English and Spanish, contains 396 new definitions in the thesaurus and a separate glossary. New for 2020 is assigning a taxonomic rank to all taxon names from every biological kingdom. Many virus names were replaced and updated according to 18th report of the International Committee on Taxonomy of Viruses. Latin plant names were added and updated after taxonomic verification by the Germplasm Resources Information Network (GRIN). Other expanded subject areas are plant breeding, agricultural technology, human nutrition and diet, genetics, chemistry, enzymes, food sciences, pathology, and environmental sciences. The 2020 NALT is the 19th edition; it was originally released in 2002.

NALT continues to be available as Linked Open Data. NAL can now connect its vocabulary to other linked data vocabularies, which, in turn, will connect NALT to the larger semantic web. Such interconnections will help programmers create meaningful relationships that will make it easier to locate related content.

Associated with NALT, the NAL Glossary provides definitions of agricultural terms. The 2020 edition contains 6,333 definitions, ranging across agriculture and its many ancillary subjects, an increase of 396 definitions from last year. Most definitions are composed by NALT staff. (Suggestions for new terms or definitions can be sent by e-mail to agref@ars.usda.gov.)

NAL publishes Spanish-language versions of the thesaurus and glossary, which carry the names Tesauro Agrícola and Glosario, respectively. Both are updated concurrently with the annual release of the English-language version. The 2020 edition of the Spanish-language version of NALT contains more than 117,000 terms and 6,330 definitions.

The thesaurus and glossary are primarily used for indexing and for improving the retrieval of agricultural information, but they can also be used by students (from fifth grade up), teachers, writers, translators, and others who are seeking precise definitions of words from the agricultural sciences. Users can download all four publications—English and Spanish thesaurus and glossary—in both machine-readable (MARC, RDF-SKOS, and XML) and human-readable (DOC, PDF) formats at https://agclass.nal.usda.gov/download.shtml.

Networks of Cooperation

The NAL collection and information resources are supplemented by networks of cooperation with other institutions, including arrangements with agricultural libraries at U.S. land-grant universities, other U.S. national libraries, agricultural libraries in other countries, and libraries of the United Nations and other international organizations.

AgNIC

Agriculture Network Information Collaborative (AgNIC) is a voluntary alliance of member institutions, mostly U.S. land-grant university libraries, dedicated to enhancing collective information and services among the members and their partners for all those seeking agricultural information over the Internet.

More information about AgNIC and its activities can be found at https://www.agnic.org.

USAIN

The United States Agricultural Information Network (USAIN) is a professional membership organization that provides a forum for members to discuss food and agricultural issues, and seeks to take a leadership role in the formation of a national information policy as related to food and agriculture. Central to its mission is cooperation with and support of the National Agricultural Library.

Learn more about USAIN at https://usain.org/.

AgLaw

Agricultural Law Information Partnership (AgLaw) is a collaboration between the National Agricultural Library, National Agricultural Law Center (NALC), and the Center for Agriculture and Food Systems (CAFS) at the Vermont Law School. The Partnership supports the dissemination of agricultural and food law information to consumers, researchers, and legal professionals. Agricultural law is defined broadly to include land-based agriculture, food and fiber production and systems, aquaculture, and energy issues.

Explore the AgLaw Partnership at https://www.nal.usda.gov/aglaw/agricultural-law-information-partnership.

AGLINET

Through the Agricultural Libraries Network (AGLINET), NAL serves as the U.S. node of an international agricultural information system that brings together agricultural libraries with strong regional or country coverage and other specialized collections. NAL functions as a gateway to U.S. agricultural libraries and resources, fulfilling requests for information via reciprocal agreements with several other libraries, information centers, and consortia. As an AGLINET member, NAL agrees to provide low-cost interlibrary loan and photocopy service to other AGLINET libraries. Most materials requested through AGLINET are delivered digitally, although reproductions via fiche or photocopy are used when appropriate. AGLINET is administered by the Food and Agriculture Organization of the United Nations.

Information Management and Information Technology

Over the past quarter century, NAL has applied increasingly sophisticated information technology to support the ever more complex and demanding information needs of researchers, practitioners, policymakers, and the general public. Technological developments spearheaded by the library date back to the 1940s and 1950s, when NAL Director Ralph Shaw invented "electronic machines" such as the photo charger, rapid selector, and photo clerk. Over the years NAL has made numerous technological improvements, from automating collections information to delivering full-text and image collections digitally on the Internet.

NAL has fully implemented the Voyager integrated library management system from Ex Libris, Ltd. The system supports ordering, receiving, and invoice processing for purchases; creating and maintaining indexing and cataloging records for AGRICOLA; circulating print holdings; and providing a web-based online catalog for public searching and browsing of the collection. In addition, the system is fully integrated with an automated interlibrary loan and document delivery system by Relais International that streamlines services and provides desktop delivery of needed materials.

National Library of Medicine

8600 Rockville Pike, Bethesda, MD 20894
301-496-6308, 888-346-3656, fax 301-496-4450
E-mail publicinfo@nlm.nih.gov
World Wide Web http://www.nlm.nih.gov

Jody Nurik
Director, Office of Communications and Public Liaison

The National Library of Medicine (NLM) is a leader in biomedical and health data science research and the world's largest biomedical library. NLM's research and information services support scientific discovery, health-care delivery, and public health decision making. NLM pioneers new ways to make biomedical data and information more accessible, build tools for better data management and personal health, and help create a more diverse and data-skilled workforce. The Library's work enables researchers, clinicians, and the public to use a wealth of biomedical data to improve health. There is not a biomedical discovery, public health advance, or clinical care action in the past 30 years that has not benefited from NLM resources.

NLM's cutting-edge research and training programs—with a focus on artificial intelligence (AI), machine learning, computational biology, and biomedical informatics and health data standards—help catalyze basic biomedical science, data-driven discovery, and health-care delivery.

NLM strives to achieve key objectives of the NLM Strategic Plan—to accelerate data-powered discovery and health, reach new users in new ways, and prepare a workforce for a future of data-driven research and health—while also supporting NIH-wide efforts to answer the call to respond to national priorities, such as the COVID-19 pandemic, close the gap in health disparities, and capitalize on fundamental investments. NLM achieves its objectives through effective preservation of valued scientific and data resources, judicious investments in extramural and intramural research, informed stewardship of federal resources, and innovative partnerships to align priorities and leverage investments across HHS, the federal government, and the biomedical research community.

NLM facilitates scientific discovery by connecting data and information resources. Used by scientists across the country and the globe, NLM resources hasten the development of new approaches for COVID-19 testing, evaluate promising vaccine candidates, and demonstrate the effectiveness of innovative treatments. NLM rapidly increased access to full-text coronavirus-related scientific journal articles through its PubMed Central® (PMC) digital archive. NLM began working with the global publishing community to make tens of thousands of research publications related to coronaviruses, along with publications related to coronaviruses, freely and immediately available to the public. Publications are available in formats that support automated text mining to increase discoverability. NLM helped make an enormous collection of coronavirus-related information accessible to artificial intelligence (AI) and machine-learning researchers to accelerate discoveries about COVID-19 by collaborating with publishers, scholarly societies, and leading information technology (IT) companies. Additional information on NLM's response to the COVID-19 pandemic can be found throughout this narrative.

Leveraging its 184-year history, NLM develops and applies innovative approaches to acquire, organize, curate, and deliver current biomedical information across the United States and around the globe. NLM's advanced biomedical information services are among the most visited websites in the federal government, providing researchers, health-care professionals, and the public access to high-quality biomedical information and data, including biomedical literature, genomic data, clinical trial data, and chemical data.

NLM's Response to COVID-19

NLM has worked on multiple fronts to improve researchers' understanding of the novel coronavirus (SARS-CoV-2) and the disease it causes (COVID-19).
In 2020 activities included

- Releasing the first SARS-CoV-2 genome sequence to the public on January 12, 2020, through NLM's GenBank, the world's largest genetic sequence database. On January 25 NLM released the first genome sequence from the United States in collaboration with the Centers for Disease Control and Prevention (CDC). By the end of 2020, GenBank contained almost 50,000 SARS-CoV-2 sequences.
- Creating several special sites and services to improve access to SARS-CoV-2/COVID-19 data and to facilitate research. For example, NLM created the "Severe acute respiratory syndrome coronavirus 2 data hub," where people can search, retrieve, and analyze sequences of the virus that have been submitted to the GenBank database.
- Facilitating access to COVID data through NLM's Sequence Read Archive (SRA). COVID-focused datasets were made available through this cloud-based platform, allowing researchers to access these datasets and download them or compute on them directly in the cloud. NLM's SRA is the world's largest publicly available repository of unprocessed sequence data that can be mined for previously unrecognized pathogen sequences. Researchers may now compute across the full SRA dataset for metagenomic research on the new coronavirus in ways not previously possible. Also, NLM has recently begun a collaboration with other NIH Institutes and Centers on surveillance data for tracking of COVID-19 community spread and with the CDC to collect COVID-19 sequence data.
- Launching the NIH Preprint Pilot, to test the viability of making preprints searchable in PubMed Central (PMC) and, by extension, discoverable in PubMed, starting with approximately 1,600 COVID-19 preprints reporting NIH-supported research.
- Developing LitCovid, a curated literature hub for tracking scientific publications about the novel coronavirus. LitCovid provides centralized access to more than 94,000 relevant articles in PubMed, categorizes them by research topic and geographic location, and is updated daily. NLM worked with publishers to get the full corpus of coronavirus research into PubMed for free, immediate access, in machine-readable forms.

- Responding to scientific challenges by providing access to biomedical literature and data in a central location. To make finding resources easier, NLM developed a centralized SARS-CoV-2 webpage to facilitate access to submission interfaces and content from NLM resources, such as GenBank and SRA (sequence data), PubMed and PMC (literature), PubChem® (chemical data), and ClinicalTrials.gov.

- NLM also continued development of the COVID-19 Open Research Dataset (CORD-19), a collaborative effort between NLM and leaders across the technology sector and academia. Hosted by the Allen Institute for AI, CORD-19 is a free and growing resource that was launched with more than 29,000 scholarly articles about COVID-19 and the coronavirus family of viruses. CORD-19 represents the most extensive machine-readable coronavirus literature collection available for text mining to date. This dataset enables researchers to apply novel AI and machine learning strategies to identify new knowledge to help end the pandemic. Researchers can submit text and data-mining tools to be applied to the dataset via the Kaggle platform.

- Adding more than 88,000 COVID-19 related citations in PubMed in 2020. NLM helps users access this rapidly growing corpus by automatically expanding searches for COVID-19 to include additional key terms and PubMed Clinical Queries to include special COVID-19 filter categories, helping users retrieve comprehensive results.

- Posting over 4,300 clinical studies related to COVID-19/SARS-COV-2 on ClinicalTrials.gov in 2020. Trials were summarized by location and funding, and whether a drug or vaccine was studied, and shared on the new ClinicalTrials.gov COVID-19 Views page. ClinicalTrials.gov created a page listing 3,500 COVID-19-related studies that were registered with the World Health Organization. This provided a more comprehensive registry.

- Growing PubChem, an archive of chemical and biological data on small molecules; PubChem contained information on more than 109 million unique chemical structures and more than 1.2 million bioassays at the end of 2020. To support researchers investigating the SARS-CoV-2 virus and COVID-19, PubChem created a special, streamlined interface allowing rapid access of relevant chemical structures, bioassays, pathways, literature, patents, biological proteins, and gene targets from curated data sources that is updated weekly.

- Identifying, selecting, and archiving a remarkable volume of web and social media content documenting the COVID-19 outbreak as part of NLM's Global Health Events web archive collection. This initiative includes ongoing engagement and collaboration with international colleagues as well as colleagues across multiple federal agencies and the cultural heritage sector.

Accelerating Data-Driven Discovery and Health

In addition to the activities driven by the onset of the COVID-19 pandemic, NLM continues to advance support for professionals within and outside the field of information science. Every day, millions of scientists, health professionals, and members of the public from around the world use NLM's online information resources to translate research results into new treatments, develop new products, inform clinical decision-making, and improve public health.

NLM works to accelerate discovery and advances health through data-driven research, reach more people in more ways through enhanced dissemination and engagement, and build a workforce for data-driven research and health. Activities toward workforce building included preparing information professionals for data-driven discovery through NLM's Network of the National Library of Medicine (NNLM), which leverages more than 8,000 academic health science libraries, hospital and public libraries, and community organizations across the United States.

Dissemination and Engagement

Activities to enhance information delivery included

- Indexing approximately 1.4 million new journal articles for PubMed, NLM's most heavily used database, which contained records for over 31.5 million articles in biomedical and life sciences journals at the end of 2020.
- Growing PubMed Central, the digital archive of full-text biomedical literature, which included full text additions for a total of more than 6.6 million articles at the end of 2020.
- Expanding ClinicalTrials.gov, a database of privately and publicly funded clinical studies conducted around the world, which listed approximately 363,000 registered studies at the end of 2020. Of these studies, 47,000 had posted study results and adverse events information. NLM continued a multiyear effort to modernize ClinicalTrials.gov to deliver an improved user experience on an updated platform that will accommodate growth and enhance efficiency.
- Expanding dbGaP, a genotypes and phenotypes database, which connects individual-level genomic data with individual-level clinical information. By the end of 2020, dbGaP contained data from 1,648 studies, and more than 2,482 research papers had been published based on new analyses of these data. dbGaP allows unrestricted access to summary-level genomic results from most NIH-supported genomic studies.
- Expanding the RefSeq database by adding nearly 39 million sequence records (a 17 percent increase) to provide a comprehensive collection of sequence and gene information as well as an integrated and well-annotated view of the genetic elements contributing to the nature and behavior of all studied organisms (e.g., human, model organisms, microbes, and viruses).
- Migrating the NLM AccessGUDID data portal to the cloud. This NLM portal for the FDA's Global Unique Device Identification Database (GUDID) contains FDA unique identifiers and registration information for more than 2.7 million medical devices, supporting improvements in care and patient safety. In 2020 AccessGUDID received 31.7 million application program interface (API) calls from computer systems accessing the resource and more than 115,246 downloads of the AccessGUDID dataset.
- Expanding NLM's historical collections, including the release of 15 fully digitized manuscript collections in NLM Digital Collections, and a freely

accessible digital repository of more than 200 prints and photographs, 40 audiovisual titles, and 1,800 rare or unique books. NLM is also curating and archiving a series of virtual free History Talks by a diverse group of researchers, along with interviews, on NLM's popular blog Circulating Now.

• The research symposium "Reporting, Recording, and Remembering the 1918 Influenza Epidemic" was hosted and archived in cooperation with the National Endowment for the Humanities (NEH) Office of Digital Humanities, as part of the ongoing NLM/NEH partnership to collaborate on research, education, and career initiatives.

Promoting Public Awareness and Access to Information

NLM offers plain-language, direct-to-consumer information through its flagship consumer health website, MedlinePlus. This resource includes information about a broad variety of health topics, human genetics, medical tests, medications, dietary supplements, and healthy recipes. In 2020 MedlinePlus offered more than 1,000 health topics in English and Spanish.

Consumer health information from MedlinePlus and several other NIH Institutes and Centers is also accessible through MedlinePlus Connect. MedlinePlus Connect responds to more than 225 million requests to the MedlinePlus Connect API from health IT and EHR (Electronic Heath Record) systems requesting patient-specific delivery of consumer health information from MedlinePlus and other NIH Institutes and Centers. Genetics Home Reference was consolidated into MedlinePlus, creating a new area of the website called Medline Plus genetics. MedlinePlus Genetics provides consumer-level information on more than 1,300 genetic conditions, 1,400 genes, all the human chromosomes, and mitochondrial DNA, as well as extensive background information on human genetics.

In collaboration with other NIH Institutes and Centers, NLM continues to produce *NIH MedlinePlus magazine* in both English (print and online) and Spanish (online). In response to public health concerns surrounding print materials distribution during a pandemic, and reduced public access to public and professional spaces, the magazine shifted to digital-only publication in 2020. Increased engagement on the digital platform has resulted in a threefold increase in page views, users, new users, and sessions in 2020.

NLM's Office of Engagement and Training (OET) serves as a strategic connector between NLM and its multiple audiences throughout the U.S. and internationally. This office serves as a strategic connector between NLM and its multiple audiences. OET also engages and partners with specific populations, particularly groups experiencing health disparities, and coordinates the NNLM. In 2020 NNLM funded more than 238 outreach projects across the country to enhance awareness and access to health information and to address health literacy issues.

Research and Development for Advanced Information Systems, Standards, and Research Tools

NLM conducts advanced research and development in biomedical informatics and computational biology through its Intramural Research Program (IRP). Research includes work on health information standards and discovery; natural language processing; and image processing, as well as theoretical, analytical, and applied computational approaches to a broad range of fundamental problems in molecular biology and medicine.

In 2020 NLM

- Applied machine-learning techniques to develop a new research area, Visual Question Answering (VQA), for answering questions about images. One notable application of this automation is for visually impaired people to describe their environment. NLM is developing clinical and biomedical approaches and applications for VQA.

- Developed deep learning techniques for image analysis. In collaboration with NIH's National Eye Institute, NLM scientists are studying a set of 51,700 retinal photographs to identify and measure the size of the lesions associated with diagnosing and managing retinal diabetes and age-related macular degeneration (AMD). By leveraging cutting-edge, deep-learning techniques and repurposing "big" imaging data from two major longitudinal AMD clinical trials, the researchers developed a novel data-driven approach (based on their previous DeepSeeNet system) for automatic AMD risk prediction with performance far exceeding that of human retinal specialists.

- Conducted research and development on the representation, integration, and retrieval of molecular biology data and biomedical literature, in addition to providing an integrated genomic information resource. These databases range from data on human genetic variation and viral pathogens to information on genetic tests. NLM's development of large-scale data integration techniques with advanced information systems are key to expanding the ability to support the accelerated pace of research made possible by new technologies, such as next-generation DNA sequencing, microarrays, and small molecule screening.

- Contributed to research on genetic causes of antimicrobial resistance as part of an ongoing collaboration with the National Antimicrobial Resistance Monitoring System, a public health surveillance system that tracks changes in the antimicrobial susceptibility of foodborne pathogens. This work resulted in greater than 98 percent consistent predictions. The tool predicts the genes and proteins in the new National Database of Antibiotic Resistant Organisms, which consists of more than 400,000 pathogens and is part of the National Action Plan for Combating Antibiotic-resistant Bacteria.

NLM has been a major force in health data standards for more than 30 years. NLM supports the development, maintenance, and dissemination of health data standards and associated tools used widely in health care and research, including LOINC® (Logical Observation Identifiers Names and Codes) and SNOMED CT (Systematized Nomenclature of Medicine—Clinical Terms). Importantly, NLM's support allows key health data standards to be used free of charge in the U.S. and widely implemented in health care, public health, biomedical research, and product development.

The Unified Medical Language System (UMLS) integrates and distributes key terminology, classification and coding standards, and associated resources to promote creation of more effective and interoperable biomedical information systems and services. UMLS resources help computer programs to interpret biomedical text and health data correctly in NIH-funded research, in commercial product development, and in many electronic information services.

RxNorm is a widely used drug terminology developed by NLM and used for electronic prescription and exchange of drug information. NLM has developed a graphical user interface (RxNav) and APIs to facilitate access by researchers, industry, and the public. In 2020 these drug APIs received 1 billion queries.

NLM has been an active proponent of the Health Level Seven (HL7) Fast Healthcare Interoperability Resources (FHIR) standard that is now supported at the NIH level to support data science. Both the Office of the National Coordinator for Health IT and the Centers for Medicare and Medicaid Services (CMS) include requirements for use of FHIR in recent rulemaking related to the 21st Century Cures Act. NLM has also developed a number of software tools to facilitate use of FHIR.

In response to the COVID-19 Pandemic, NLM, CDC, FDA, and LIVD (LOINC In-Vitro Device) developed a catalog that provides guidance for reporting SARS-CoV-2 test results using LOINC, SNOMED CT, and device identifiers. The use of this mapping tool should reduce inaccuracies and time spent on the import of laboratory test results sent through laboratory information systems.

The Value Set Authority Center, in response to the COVID-19 pandemic, adapted to stakeholders' needs for timely updates of provisional codes that several standard terminologies currently produce and frequently update. NLM stewards the NIH Common Data Elements (CDE) Repository, a free, collaborative platform for sharing and discovering structured, human and machine-readable definitions of data elements, variables, and measures recommended for use in NIH-funded clinical research. In 2020 NLM began making enhancements to improve the usability of the NIH CDE Repository.

Extramural Programs

NLM funds extramural research, resource, and workforce development grants that build important foundations in biomedical informatics and data science, bringing the methods and concepts of computational, informational, quantitative, social/behavioral, and engineering sciences to bear on problems related to basic biomedical/behavioral research, health care, public health, and consumer use of health-related information.

NLM offers several types of grants within these three general categories: research grants include research projects grants, grants for small businesses, and small exploratory/developmental research projects; resource grants include scholarly works in the history of science and medicine and information resources to reduce health disparities; and workforce grants include university-based training, fellowships, and career transition grants. In 2020 NLM funded 186 awards, including 35 that were co-funded with other NIH Institutes and Centers.

Biomedical Informatics Research

NLM's research project grants (RPGs) support pioneering research and development to advance knowledge in biomedical informatics and data science.

Complementing initiatives at other Institutes and Centers at NIH, NLM research grant programs support investigator-initiated innovation in basic and applied research, ranging from small proof-of-concept projects to larger sustained collaborations, creating and testing approaches and tools that will be valuable to more than one domain of interest.

In 2020 NLM issued 28 new RPGs, including one exploratory/developmental award that reflects current and expanding investments in data science as well as investments in data science applications for patients. Several of these awards address data analytic topics, including collaborative filtering for improved information retrieval, 360-degree automated characterization of the built environment, and evidence-based communication of numbers in health. New awards in translational bioinformatics focus on reconstruction and modeling of dynamical molecular networks, inference of molecular mechanisms of complex disease, and panomic analytics for microbiome data. In support of the NIH Next Generation Researcher initiative, NLM awarded new research project support to ten early-stage investigators.

NLM sets aside funds to support small business innovation and research and technology transfer (SBIR/STTR). In 2020 NLM met its required set-aside by funding three new and one continuing SBIR/STTR awards; NLM's allocation of funds for SBIR/STTR was more than $1.5 million. The new projects center on decision support for real-time trauma resuscitation, a block-chain enabled healthcare network for population health data, and a home-based monitoring system for children with cerebral palsy.

Resource Grant Programs to Reach More People in More Ways

Eight continuing awards were made in NLM's unique Information Resources to Reduce Health Disparities program on topics such as information resources for migrant workers, support for communities at risk for Chagas disease, and environmental health literacy resources for Appalachian Kentucky. NLM encourages minority-serving organizations to apply. In the Scholarly Works resource grant program, two new and three continuing grants were awarded targeted to the interests of biomedical terminology specialists, public health officials, and clinical informaticians.

Some NLM research grants focus on developing tools and resources for consumers and patients. For example, in 2020 one new and ten continuing research awards were made through the NLM's Data Science Research Personal Health Libraries for Consumers and Patients program in areas such as Spanish-language smartphone access to health information, personalized web service for epilepsy patients, and personalized health maps for patients with diabetes.

Research Management and Support (RMS)

RMS activities provide administrative, budgetary, communications, and logistical support for NLM programs to ensure strategic planning, messaging, and evaluation; regulatory compliance; policy development; international coordination; and partnerships with other federal agencies, Congress, the private sector, and the public. NLM is streamlining its organizational and administrative structure to enhance collaborative leadership, innovation, and customer service.

Administration

The director of NLM, Patricia Flatley Brennan, R.N., Ph.D., is guided in matters of policy by a Board of Regents consisting of ten appointed and nine ex officio members.

United States Government Publishing Office

732 North Capitol St. N.W., Washington, DC 20401
World Wide Web http://www.gpo.gov

Gary Somerset
Chief Public Relations Officer
202-512-1957, e-mail gsomerset@gpo.gov

The U.S. Government Printing Office (GPO) was created when President James Buchanan signed Joint Resolution 25 on June 23, 1860. GPO opened its doors for business nine months later, on March 4, 1861, the same day Abraham Lincoln took the oath of office to become the 16th president of the United States. On that day, GPO began operation in buildings purchased by Congress, at the same address it occupies today.

A historic moment occurred for GPO in December 2014, when President Barack Obama signed into law a bill changing the agency's name to the U.S. Government Publishing Office. The new name reflects the increasingly prominent role that GPO plays in providing access to government information in digital formats through GPO's govinfo (govinfo.gov), apps, e-books, and related technologies. The information needs of Congress, federal agencies, and the public have evolved beyond only print, and GPO has transformed itself to meet its customers' needs.

Under Title 44 of the United States Code, GPO is responsible for the production and distribution of information products for all three branches of the federal government. These include the official publications of Congress, federal agencies, and the courts. Today GPO provides products in print and a variety of digital forms, all of which are born digitally. In addition, GPO produces passports for the Department of State and secure credentials for many government agencies.

As the federal government's official resource for gathering, producing, cataloging, providing access to, and preserving published information in all forms, GPO has disseminated millions of publications to the public. GPO's Superintendent of Documents and its Library Services and Content Management (LSCM) organizations administer and manage the four programs required by Title 44:

- The Federal Depository Library Program (FDLP)
- Cataloging and indexing (C&I)
- Distributing government publications to the International Exchange Service
- The By-Law Program, under which certain government publications are distributed to members of Congress and to other government agencies as mandated by law

The Federal Depository Library Program (FDLP) dates back to 1813, when Congress first authorized legislation to ensure the provision of certain congressional documents to selected universities, historical societies, and state libraries. At that time, the secretary of state was responsible for distributing publications. In 1857 the secretary of the interior assumed oversight of printing and the designation of depositories. In the Printing Act of 1895, the governance of the depository program was transferred to the Office of the Superintendent of Documents at GPO. Duties remained largely unchanged until 1993, when Public Law 103-40, the Government Printing Office Electronic Information Access Enhancement Act, amended GPO's duties to not only provide public access to printed publications but to Internet-accessible publications as well.

Two centuries after the start of FDLP, the program continues to serve a vital need of the public through the partnership with federal depository libraries located in nearly every congressional district. GPO is obviously a much different agency in the digital age than it was years ago. While its name has changed, its mission—Keeping America Informed—is as important and relevant as ever. GPO's public information programs are examples of the agency's long-standing commitment to free, permanent public access to U.S. government information.

The Superintendent of Documents and LSCM organizations support GPO's continued digital transformation through initiatives to enhance historic and current content on govinfo.gov and the Catalog of U.S. Government Publications (CGP), and through the development of free online tools and resources to help FDLP libraries manage their depository library more effectively and efficiently.

COVID-19 Guidance and Resources for FDLP Libraries

Throughout the COVID-19 pandemic, LSCM has been working to support federal depository libraries with the tools and resources they need. GPO created the COVID-19 Toolkit for FDLP libraries (https://www.fdlp.gov/promotion/covid-19-fdlp-toolkit). It includes operational information for FDLP staff, related federal information resources for library patrons, infographics for download, recorded webinars, and more. GPO also published guidance documents for FDLP libraries for handling library collections safely during COVID-19. It includes information on disinfecting versus quarantining publications, setting up a publication quarantine area, and accounting for materials in quarantine. Finally, GPO staff have been offering one-on-one consultations related to library operations and collections care throughout the pandemic.

Key Stakeholders: The Libraries in the FDLP

GPO Partnerships

Since 1997, GPO has developed strategic partnerships with federal depository libraries, federal agencies, and other institutions to increase public access to electronic U.S. government information.

GPO's partner categories are

- Preservation Steward
- Digital Preservation Steward
- Digital Content Contributor
- Digital Access Partner
- Cataloging and Metadata Contributor
- Other/Specialized

Partnering is an integral part of how GPO is "Keeping America Informed," and over the past two decades, these partnerships have grown and evolved. At the close of fiscal year (FY) 2020 there were 68 official GPO partnerships: 43 Preservation Stewards, 1 Digital Preservation Steward, 5 Digital Content Contributors, 16 Digital Access Partners, 2 Cataloging and Metadata partners, and 1 specialized partner.

During FY 2020 these libraries made the commitment to serve as Preservation Stewards for the following collections:

- Lawrence University: *American State Papers* and various 19th-century publications
- State Library of Pennsylvania: various 19th-century publications
- University of North Texas: various federal publications, including the bound Congressional Record and the Serial Set

The Donald E. Pray Law Library, College of Law at the University of Oklahoma, is also now serving as a Digital Access Partner for their resource, American Indian and Alaskan Native Documents in the Congressional Serial Set, 1817–1899.

The University Libraries, University of Washington, is now a Digital Content Contributor. Their first contribution is a Treasury publication entitled Your Path, Peace and Security.

GPO Collaborations

In FY 2020 LSCM staff contributed to and collaborated with groups in support of the FDLP and Cataloging & Indexing Programs, including

- GPO is continuing its collaboration with the Law Library of Congress to digitize and make accessible volumes of the U.S. Congressional Serial Set back to 1817. The Law Library of Congress is inventorying and digitizing the Serial Set, while GPO is focused on metadata, the development of a new govinfo collection, and seeking any replacement volumes needed by the Law Library. Digitization began in fall 2019 and will continue for some time. GPO received the first delivery of digitized content, 445 volumes, from the Law Library during summer 2020. The team is using this content to develop workflows and processes that will be used to process deliveries going forward. The team is ensuring data integrity throughout the processes, gathering and producing metadata for the serial set volumes and documents, and compiling requirements to design the Serial Set collection in govinfo.
- In a collaboration with the Law Library of Congress (LC), LSCM is cataloging Global Legal Research Directorate Reports to increase public access. In FY 2020 LSCM cataloged 503 of these reports, which are accessible through the CGP.
- Through its partnership in the Civics Renewal Network (CRN), a consortium of organizations committed to strengthening civic life in the United States by increasing the quality of civics education in our nation's schools, LSCM makes available, through the CRN website, K–12 resources that support civics education.

- LSCM continued its partnership in the Technical Report Archive & Image Library (TRAIL). LSCM and TRAIL members work together to ensure that federal technical reports are openly accessible, and participating LSCM staff members offer expertise in cataloging and other areas and participate in the exchange of information about U.S. government scientific and technical information.
- The Digital Public Library of America (DPLA) and LSCM continued their collaboration to broaden public access to the information made available via the CGP. Through the partnership, over 224,031 records from the CGP are available to the public through the DPLA website. Examples of records include the federal budget; laws; federal regulations; and congressional hearings, reports, and documents. LSCM and DPLA also partner to provide eBooks to the DPLA Exchange, making this government content even more widely accessible.
- LSCM continues to be heavily involved in cooperative cataloging and metadata activities with members of the library community. LSCM is an active participant in all components of the Program for Cooperative Cataloging (PCC), which is managed by LC, including Bibliographic Record Cooperative (BIBCO), Cooperative Online Serials (CONSER), Name Authority Cooperative (NACO), and Subject Authority Cooperative (SACO).
- GPO has been a member of OCLC since 1976 and contributes bibliographic records for U.S. government information to the international database daily.
- LSCM is part of the Electronic Cataloging in Publication Program (ECIP). ECIP provides cataloging records for books in advance of publication. The publisher then includes the record on the verso of the publication's title page. Through the Electronic Cataloging in Publication (ECIP) Program, LSCM is creating prepublication bibliographic records for publications from federal agency publishers. LSCM has been a part of ECIP since 2015 and created 21 ECIP records in FY 2020. LSCM staff have created ECIP records for GPO, the Combat Studies Institute, the Air Force Research Institute, the Smithsonian Institution Scholarly Press, USGS, and the National Gallery of Art, to name a few.
- In October 2018, in an agreement with the Library of Congress, LSCM's Library Technical Services (LTS) staff began cataloging Congressional Research Service (CRS) reports for the CGP and OCLC. Because these reports are frequently updated, GPO has cataloged each report title as an integrating resource. At the close of FY 2020 LTS staff had cataloged over 6,600 separate, unique CRS report titles, approximately 78 percent of all reports available on the site. GPO prioritized cataloging any reports concerning COVID-19 and the coronavirus, and many of those records are now available in the CGP.

FDLP National Collection Strategy Framework

The *National Collection of U.S. Government Public Information: A Strategy Framework Document* provides a long-term foundation and high-level structure to guide and inform the development of more detailed short-term strategic action plans for the Public Information Programs of the Superintendent of Documents, replacing the *National Plan for Access to U.S. Government Information.*

The broader strategic themes that will help us achieve our vision of providing government information when and where it is needed are

ENRICH   The National Collection of U.S. Government Public Information

EXPAND   Access to government information, services to depository libraries, partnerships/collaborations

ENGAGE   With depository libraries, federal agencies, the general public, and other stakeholders

FDLP Academy

The FDLP Academy (https://www.fdlp.gov/about-the-fdlp/fdlp-academy) was launched to support the FDLP community's education and training needs and to advance U.S. government information literacy.

The FDLP Academy enhances U.S. government information knowledge through events, conferences, webinars, and webcasts coordinated by GPO that cover a variety of government information topics. Many sessions are presented by GPO staff, while others are presented by staff from other federal agencies and from members of the FDLP community, as recruited and hosted by GPO.

Since its inception in 2012, the FDLP Academy has hosted over 500 webinars, with over 65,000 combined registrants and over 120 recorded webcasts. Training topics cover all aspects of government information resources and librarianship.

Enhancing Content in Govinfo

LSCM has worked closely with GPO's Office of Programs, Strategy, & Technology (PST) throughout the development and ongoing enhancement of govinfo.gov. Continuing to add to the collections currently available on govinfo is of the highest priority, with a goal of offering complete and historic holdings to its collections.

Notable additions in FY 2020 include

- Digitized volumes of the U.S. Government Manual (1935–1994)
- New submissions from Digital Content Contributors:
  - Washington State Library
  - Boise State University
  - University of Washington
- Publications related to FY 2021 federal appropriations
- Volume 2 of the Precedents of the U.S. House of Representatives (2017 series)
- Railroad Retirement Board publications
- National Institute of Standards and Technology (NIST) publications

Govinfo Certification as a Trustworthy Digital Repository

Since 2015 GPO has worked to be named as a Trustworthy Digital Repository (TDR) for government information through certification of govinfo under ISO 16363:2012.

Certification under ISO 16363 provides GPO stakeholders, including the FDLP community, assurance that govinfo is a standards-compliant digital archive in which government information shall be preserved, accessible, and usable well into the future.

Certification of govinfo validates GPO's commitment to standards-based digital preservation practices and activities across 109 criteria in the areas of

- Organizational Governance
- Digital Object Management
- Infrastructure and Security Management

Trusted Digital Repository certification has been a key GPO strategic initiative and a joint effort between GPO's LSCM and PST business units.

On December 28, 2018, GPO made history by becoming the first organization in the United States and second organization in the world to achieve ISO 16363:2012 Certification. The Primary Trustworthy Digital Repository (TDR) Authorisation Body Ltd. awarded GPO ISO 16363:2012 for govinfo and publicly announced the certificate on their website.

As of September 2020, GPO is currently the only institution in the world to hold ISO 16363 Trustworthy Repository Certification. GPO is currently undergoing a second surveillance audit to maintain certification.

FDLP LibGuides

FDLP LibGuides (https://libguides.fdlp.gov/) is a service provided by GPO for depository libraries and the public. Guides are created by LSCM staff on a variety of topics, including those requested by the FDLP community. All guides are available for free use. Libraries and agencies can also submit their own guides for inclusion on the FDLP LibGuides Community page. In an effort to provide resources that are useful to all of our libraries, LSCM staff members continue to review the site and make enhancements to the look and content.

During FY 2020 LibGuides had more than 35,000 views, which is an increase of more than 15 percent from FY 2019. Significant views increased during March–July, with views exceeding 3,000 each of those months.

Catalog of U.S. Government Publications

The Catalog of U.S. Government Publications (CGP) (catalog.gpo.gov) is the finding tool for locating publications produced by the federal government, both current and historic. Students, researchers, community leaders, and anyone who needs to find information published by the U.S. government can get help from a great online resource. You can access library catalog records on a wide range of topics including defense, citizenship, U.S. laws, health, science, and more from

CGP. There are also direct links to the documents—unless the publication exists only in print. People who need or prefer a print document can learn where to find the nearest federal depository library from the CGP. The CGP even has a feature called MetaLib, which lets you research and retrieve reports, articles, and citations by searching across multiple U.S. government databases at once. What's more, there's a collection of U.S. government eBooks from a variety of federal agencies, all free to access.

There were over 23 million (23,326,449) successful searches of the CGP in FY 2020.

A service was launched in October 2017 to provide sets of bibliographic records from the CGP free of charge on a monthly basis via the GPO's CGP on GitHub repository site. The CGP on GitHub datasets contain records produced by GPO staff according to national standards such as Resource Description and Access (RDA) and Anglo-American Cataloging Rules (AACR2) and include GPO Historic Shelflist project brief bibliographic records and other retrospective records.

LSCM recently added new collections of bibliographic records to the CGP on GitHub repository and expanded the range of the content of the record sets. LSCM also reorganized the structure of the repository to facilitate the use of the files. LSCM staff also added a collection of records for publications on COVID-19 and coronavirus.

Web Archiving and the End of Term Harvest

The FDLP Web Archive (https://www.archive-it.org/home/FDLPwebarchive) provides point-in-time captures of U.S. federal agency websites while preserving the functionality of the sites to the extent possible. The aim is to provide permanent public access to federal agency web content. GPO harvests and archives the websites with Archive-It, a subscription-based web harvesting and archiving service offered by the Internet Archive.

LSCM continues to harvest digital publications and websites in order to advance FDLP collection development efforts. Throughout FY 2020 LSCM has

- Increased the size of the FDLP Web Archive collection to 28.2 TB, with over 250,000,000 URLs
- Made available 203 website collections in the FDLP Web Archive on Archive-It and 258 records available through the CGP

LSCM is currently monitoring collections in the web archive that are releasing information about the coronavirus to ensure timely capture of these collections.

GPO is again a partner in the End of Term Web Archive, which captures U.S. government websites at the end of a presidential administration.

FDLP Distribution Facilities

At GPO's Distribution Facility in Laurel, Maryland, the GPO staff continues to distribute publications, fulfill claims, and send special mailings of tangible items to federal depository libraries and international libraries participating in the International Exchange Service.

In March 2020 shipments were suspended due to the COVID-19 pandemic and mass library closures. In July shipments resumed for libraries able to accept them, and GPO's FDLP Distribution staff began working staggered shifts with new COVID safety protocols in place.

In FY 2020 the staff distributed 2,688 titles, totaling 490,781 copies of materials, to FDLP libraries.

At GPO's Distribution Facility in Pueblo, Colorado, the staff distributes FDLP promotional items to FDLP libraries nationwide. As of the end of FY 2020 the Pueblo staff managed the inventory and dissemination of 30 different types of FDLP handouts and promotional items.

National Technical Information Service

U.S. Department of Commerce, Alexandria, VA 22312

Wayne Strickland

Acting Associate Director, Office of Program Management

The National Technical Information Service (NTIS) has long been in the forefront of information collection and retrieval. Established in 1945 as the Publication Board to collect and disseminate government-sponsored research, NTIS became the first major computerized database of scientific and technical information in 1964. In the 1990s NTIS began digitizing the full texts of the reports in its collection and in 2009 began an online subscription service to make those full text digital copies immediately downloadable.

NTIS manages the largest publicly available U.S. government-sponsored collection of technical and scientific reports, which totals more than 3 million publications. This collection is called the National Technical Reports Library (NTRL), a data dissemination program that involves a multistep process, including document acquisition, indexing, summarizing, and archiving. Through NTRL's online portal, the collection is made available for comprehensive online bibliographies, commercial database vendors, and document delivery services.

Today, almost one-third of NTRL's 3 million federal publications (approximately 990,000 documents comprising 3.2 terabytes of data) are fully digitized and available for download at no charge. The database covers a wide variety of topics, including aeronautics, artificial intelligence, chemistry, energy, environment, health care, library and information sciences, mathematics, medicine and biology, pandemics, physics, and transportation, to name some. In all there are 39 major subject categories and 375 subcategories. The database is updated weekly, and historically more than 10,000 federally funded scientific reports are added every year.

To ensure perpetual access to authentic federally funded scientific research data in a "raw" format for academia, industry, and promoting innovation, Chapter 23 of Title 15 of the United States Code (15 U.S.C. 1151–1157) codified NTIS's basic authority to operate a permanent clearinghouse of scientific and technical information. With this chapter NTIS was also given authority to charge fees for its products and services and to recover all costs through such fees "to the extent feasible."

This authority was restated in the National Technical Information Act of 1988, codified as 15 U.S.C. 3704b. That Act gave NTIS the authority to enter into joint ventures and declared the clearinghouse to be a permanent federal function that could not be eliminated or privatized without congressional approval.

The American Technology Preeminence Act of 1992 (Public Law 102-245): (1) required all costs associated with bibliographic control to be recovered by fees; (2) required agencies to make copies of their scientific and technical reports available to NTIS; and (3) directed NTIS to focus on developing new electronic methods and media for disseminating information.

In 2016 the NTRL was transitioned to be publicly accessible for free while serving active consumers who include technical professionals and librarians. Through its stewardship, NTIS recognizes the value of this digital asset and strives to provide web-friendly NTRL services, which enables straightforward access to such a unique, original, and authenticated collection of scientific, technical, and engineering information. NTIS removed its cost-recovery subscription service and began providing free public access to the entire NTRL clearinghouse. This open access for the NTRL publicly expanded the advanced search capabilities for title words, source agency, authors, publication year, and full-text availability. NTIS's Office of the Chief Information Officer (OCIO) team created the infrastructure for a metadata bibliographic database management system (MBS).

The future of NTRL will include exploring open-source publishing technologies and the development of application architecture for automated cataloging and indexing. Such technology modernization will ensure efficiencies for even greater compliance with §3704b that mandates the transfer of federal scientific and technical information through the encouragement of the head of each federal executive department or agency in a timely manner to NTIS. Ongoing efforts to upgrade the NTRL content management system has become an NTIS priority. A primary focus is to ensure that the research community and the public benefit from the eventual digitization of all tangible formatted legacy documents.

Unfortunately, due to the COVID-19 pandemic and the need to safeguard its workforce, NTIS is in maximum telework status and all handling of legacy content has been suspended. During this period, telework status does afford opportunities to collaborate with federal agency modernization strategies for the submission of future content digitally. Additionally, NTIS has begun investigating and implementing innovative options for automated cataloging and indexing of new scientific content. As science dictates, NTIS will also ensure updates to researched information categories in the NTRL.

The 21st-century goal for NTRL is to continue being at the forefront of promoting economic growth by ensuring perpetual availability to federally funded scientific research in all data formats. NTRL will comprise important information that will be readily reproducible, discoverable, and openly accessible. Establishing trusted relationships with federal labs, federal agencies, the library community, researchers, industry, and the public will highlight an economic growth pipeline for showcasing federal research, authorship, and achievement to better serve the public.

More than 300 U.S. government agencies and federal laboratories contribute to the NTIS collection, including the National Aeronautics and Space Administration; the Environmental Protection Agency; the departments of Agriculture, Commerce, Defense, Energy, Health and Human Services, Homeland Security, Interior, Labor, Treasury, Veterans Affairs, Housing and Urban Development, Education, and Transportation; and numerous other agencies.

National Technical Reports Library (NTRL) on the Web

NTIS offers web-based access to federal information and data on scientific, business and technical research products at https://ntrl.ntis.gov/NTRL/.

Since NTIS discontinued its operating cost-recovery efforts in 2016 for NTRL (which historically utilized a fee-based subscription model), NTIS has been providing the public NTRL service for free while continuously exploring alternative funding models and partnerships to minimize operating loss and modernize maintenance of this valued U.S. government–sponsored collection through automation technologies. In recent years NTIS succeeded in cost-saving efforts that helped dramatically lower operating losses. In fiscal years (FY) 2020 and 2021, NTIS will move NTRL into a cloud infrastructure to further reduce costs.

Key NTIS/NTRL Contacts

Phone

Program Assistants
800-553-6847 or
703-605-6000
8:30 A.M.–5:00 P.M. Eastern time, Monday–Friday

Mail

National Technical Information Service
5301 Shawnee Rd.
Alexandria, VA 22312

National Archives and Records Administration

700 Pennsylvania Ave. N.W., Washington, DC 20408
1-86-NARA-NARA or 1-866-272-6272
World Wide Web https://www.archives.gov

The National Archives and Records Administration (NARA), an independent federal agency, is the nation's record keeper. NARA safeguards and preserves the important records of all three branches of the federal government so that the people can discover, use, and learn from this documentary heritage. NARA ensures continuing access to records that document the rights of American citizens, the actions of government officials, and the history of the nation.

NARA carries out its mission through a national network of archives and records centers stretching from Boston to San Francisco and Atlanta to Seattle, in addition to 14 presidential libraries that document administrations back to that of Herbert Hoover—a total of 44 facilities nationwide.

The agency includes the National Historical Publications and Records Commission (NHPRC), the grant-making arm of NARA; the Office of the Federal Register, which publishes the official records of the actions of the government; the Information Security Oversight Office (ISOO), which oversees the government's classification programs; the National Declassification Center (NDC), which is streamlining the declassification process; and the Office of Government Information Services (OGIS), which reviews agencies' Freedom of Information Act (FOIA) administration and practices.

NARA also assists federal agencies, the courts, and Congress in documenting their activities by providing records storage, offering reference service, administering records management programs, scheduling records, and retiring noncurrent records to federal records centers. NARA also provides training, advice, and guidance on many issues relating to records management.

NARA's constituents and stakeholders include educators and their students at all levels, a history-minded public, family historians, the media, the archival community, and a broad spectrum of professional associations and researchers in such fields as history, political science, law, library and information services, and genealogy.

The size and breadth of NARA's holdings are staggering. NARA's electronic records holdings amount to 811 terabytes of data. This consists of records that were "born digital" and managed in a digital form throughout their life cycle.

In addition, NARA maintains traditional holdings that will be converted to digital form for preservation purposes and to ensure access to them far into the future. This, along with the ever-growing quantity of "born digital" records, creates a big data challenge for NARA and the federal government.

NARA's current traditional holdings include more than 15 billion pages and 44 million photographs. In addition, 18 Federal Records Centers (FRCs), located around the country, provide storage for about 27 million cubic feet of noncurrent records for 200 federal agencies.

NARA issued its Strategic Plan for fiscal years (FYs) 2018 through 2022, which sets its long-term objectives. It has four strategic goals: Make Access Happen, Connect with Customers, Maximize NARA's Value to the Nation, and Build

Our Future through Our People. Specific initiatives are underway at NARA to reach each goal.

Records and Access

Information Security Oversight Office

The Information Security Oversight Office (ISOO) is responsible to the president for policy and oversight of the government-wide security classification system, the National Industrial Security Program, and the emerging federal policy on "controlled unclassified information" (CUI). ISOO receives policy and program guidance from the assistant to the president for national security affairs and National Security Council staff in the Executive Office of the President.

ISOO oversees the security classification programs (classification, safeguarding, and declassification) in both government and industry. It is also responsible for exercising NARA's authorities and responsibilities as the executive agent for controlled unclassified information. ISOO contributes materially to the effective implementation of the government-wide security classification program and has a direct impact on the performance of thousands of government employees and contract personnel who work with classified national security information. For more information on ISOO, visit archives.gov/isoo.

National Declassification Center

In December 2009 Executive Order 13526 established the National Declassification Center (NDC) within the National Archives to address declassification of classified federal government records. The focus of this effort was to promote transparency and accountability of records created by the Executive Branch of the U.S. government.

NDC led a process that streamlined the declassification review processes for classified historical records and eliminated a 350-million-page backlog at the National Archives. NDC is committed to completing QA on all accessioned classified records no later than one year after they have been transferred to our custody. To date they have met that goal for records received annually from 2014 through 2016. To facilitate public access to these records, NDC established an "Indexing on Demand" process that allows a researcher to request priority indexing and release for eligible record series.

NDC also processes requests for classified records under the Freedom of Information Act (FOIA) and Mandatory Review Provisions of Executive Order 13526 (MDR). To respond to these requests, NDC works closely with other agencies to ensure exempted records are reviewed by the appropriate equity agency, then processes declassified and redacted records for release. For more information about NDC, go to archives.gov/declassification.

Office of Government Information Services

As the FOIA Ombudsman, OGIS educates stakeholders about the FOIA process, resolves disputes, and assesses agency compliance.

The Open Government Act of 2007 created OGIS within the National Archives. The statute requires that OGIS offer mediation services to help resolve FOIA disputes and review agency FOIA policies and procedures. FOIA also charges OGIS with identifying methods to improve compliance with the statute.

The OGIS director chairs the FOIA Federal Advisory Committee. The Committee brings together FOIA experts from inside and outside of government to identify major issues with the implementation of FOIA and develop consensus solutions. The OGIS director also serves as the co-chair of the Chief FOIA Officers Council.

For more information about OGIS, visit archives.gov/ogis or follow OGIS on Twitter @FOIA_Ombuds.

Electronic Records Archives

NARA uses the Electronic Records Archives (ERA) system to take in and store electronic records from the White House, Congress, and agencies across the federal government. In addition, since 2012, NARA has required all federal agencies to use ERA to submit records schedules to NARA for approval by the Archivist of the United States. The adoption of ERA by federal agencies and the use of ERA to support the transfer of electronic presidential records have led to the transfer of increasing volumes of electronic records to NARA for preservation and eventual access through its public access portal, the National Archives Catalog (NAC).

NARA has launched a new system, ERA 2.0, to update and enhance the agency's capabilities to meet the ever-expanding challenges in preserving born-electronic records and digitized material. ERA 2.0 uses cloud services for greater scalability in terms of storage and computer processing to increase NARA's ability to preserve and provide access to greater amounts of digital material over time.

The ERA 2.0 system consists of three major components: a digital processing environment, a digital object repository, and a business object management component. The processing component provides the capability to upload digital material of all types, gives staff a variety of software tools for verification and processing, supports the creation and editing of metadata, and allows users to submit packages of processed digital material to the repository component for preservation. The repository supports the capability to ingest processed digital material to provide for safe archival storage, delivers advanced staff search and discovery capabilities, provides digital material for further processing for preservation, and makes copies of records available for public access through the NAC. The business object management component, slated for deployment in late 2020, will provide a redesign of the online forms and approval workflows used by NARA and federal agencies to schedule and transfer records to NARA. For more information about ERA, see archives.gov/era.

Applied Research Division

NARA's Applied Research Division serves as the agency's center for advanced and applied research capabilities in the fields of computer science, engineering, and archival science. The division's staff conducts research on new technologies, both for awareness of new types of electronic record formats that will need to be preserved and to evaluate new technologies that might be incorporated into electronic records management and preservation systems at NARA to increase their effectiveness. The staff also helps NARA managers and employees acquire the knowledge and skills they need to function effectively in e-government through presentations on new technologies. For more information, visit archives.gov/applied-research.

NARA's Website

The online entrance to the National Archives is archives.gov, which provides the most widely available means of electronic access to information about and services available from NARA. Links to various sections provide help to the particular needs of researchers, including veterans and their families, educators and students, and the general public—as well as records managers, journalists, historians, and members of Congress.

The NARA website provides the following:

- Directions on how to contact NARA and conduct research at its facilities around the country
- Direct access to certain archived electronic records at archives.gov/aad
- Digital copies of selected archived documents
- A contact form, at archives.gov/contact, for customer questions, reference requests, comments, and complaints
- Electronic versions of *Federal Register* publications
- Online exhibits
- Classroom resources for students and teachers at archives.gov/education
- Online tools such as eVetRecs (archives.gov/veterans/military-service records), which allows veterans and their next-of-kin to complete and print, for mail-in submission, requests for their military service records

Public Access Projects

NARA's Office of Innovation is responsible for oversight of the digitization of NARA's holdings and for ensuring public access through the National Archives Catalog (catalog.archives.gov). The Office of Innovation is constantly developing improved tools, techniques, and workflows to accelerate access. In the coming years the Office of Innovation will continue to find new ways to improve digitization and access as we work toward our strategic goal of 500 million pages available in the catalog by the end of FY 2024 (for more information see https://www.archives.gov/about/plans-reports/strategic-plan).

Engagement with "citizen archivists" also represents a critical component to improving access. The tagging, transcribing, and commenting performed by public volunteers help to make NARA's holdings more discoverable to researchers through the addition of critical metadata and searchable text.

The History Hub (History.gov) is another tool that helps expand access to the nation's history and to NARA's holdings. After registering on the History Hub, individuals can submit questions about U.S. history; the platform allows responses from NARA staff, staff at other participating cultural heritage organizations such as the Library of Congress, and the public. This crowdsourced platform helps eliminate the silos that exist between information residing at different organizations and allows researchers, citizen historians, and archival professionals to more easily find answers to their questions.

Social Media

NARA uses multiple social media platforms to increase access to the records in its holdings, which is at the heart of its mission. The main goals of social media at NARA are to increase awareness about archival holdings and programs and to enrich the agency's relationship with the public through conversations about its services and holdings. In addition to expanding access, use of social media creates a more collaborative work environment and increases communication and knowledge sharing both within NARA and externally with other federal agencies.

The National Archives has 18 blogs, including one by the archivist of the United States. NARA also offers historical videos from its holdings and videos of recent public events on the agency's ten YouTube channels. The agency shares photographs and documents from its collections through Flickr Commons. Across the country, more than 200 NARA staff contribute actively to the agency's 130 social media accounts, including Facebook, Twitter, Tumblr, Instagram, and others.

Followers can also use Really Simple Syndication (RSS) feeds of the "Document for Today" feature, NARA news, and press releases. Several mobile apps and e-books have been developed and are available free of charge in the iTunes store and Android Market for Today's Document, DocsTeach, and recent exhibits.

Social media also allow NARA's researchers, friends, and the public to become citizen archivists by tagging, sharing, and transcribing documents. For more information, go to archives.gov/citizen-archivist.

Additional information about NARA's social media projects is available at archives.gov/social-media.

National Archives Museum

The National Archives Museum, a set of interconnected resources made possible by a public–private partnership between NARA and the National Archives Foundation, provides a variety of ways to explore the power and importance of the nation's records.

The Rotunda for the Charters of Freedom at the National Archives Building in Washington, D.C., is the centerpiece of the National Archives Museum. On display are the Declaration of Independence, the Constitution, and the Bill of Rights—known collectively as the Charters of Freedom. The Public Vaults is a 9,000-square-foot permanent exhibition that conveys the feeling of going beyond the walls of the Rotunda and into the stacks and vaults of the working archives. Dozens of individual exhibits, many of them interactive, reveal the breadth and variety of NARA's holdings.

Complementing the Public Vaults, the Lawrence F. O'Brien Gallery hosts a changing array of topical exhibits based on National Archives records. The 290-seat William G. McGowan Theater is a showplace for NARA's extensive audio-visual holdings and serves as a forum for lectures and discussions.

The David M. Rubenstein Gallery houses a permanent interactive exhibit, "Records of Rights," which documents the struggles and debates over civil rights and liberties throughout American history. The Rubenstein Gallery is also home for a 1297 copy of the Magna Carta, owned by Rubenstein.

Inside the Boeing Learning Center, the ReSource Room is an access point for teachers and parents to explore documents found in the exhibits and to use NARA records as teaching tools. The center's Constitution-in-Action Learning Lab is designed to provide an intense field trip adventure for middle and high school students that links to curriculum in the classroom.

DocsTeach (docsteach.org) is an education website designed to provide instruction to teachers in the best practices of teaching with primary sources. Using documents in NARA's holdings as teachable resources, DocsTeach strongly supports civic literacy. This tool gives all teachers access to primary sources, instruction in best practices, and opportunities to interact with their counterparts across the nation.

When developing the DocsTeach site, the agency established an online community that served as a virtual meeting place for NARA's education team and colleagues from schools, institutions, and organizations nationwide to collaborate and share innovative ideas and best practices for this online resource.

The National Archives' New York City field office is located in the Alexander Hamilton U.S. Custom House at the southern tip of Manhattan. There, NARA has a large research center as well as diverse educational and program activities offered for free in the Learning Center. The new Learning Center incorporates many of the resources and activities found in the Washington, D.C., building but also includes New York–specific offerings.

At its Kansas City, Missouri, field office at 400 West Pershing Road, NARA also has a welcome center, changing exhibitions, workshops, and other public programs.

A set of webpages now makes the National Archives Museum available anywhere. An illustrated history of the Charters of Freedom can be found there, as well as information on educational programs, special events, and current exhibits at the National Archives.

Those traveling to Washington can bypass the public line during peak tourist season by making online reservations at recreation.gov. For more information, see "The National Archives Museum" at https://museum.archives.gov. An online version of the "Records of Rights" exhibition is available at recordsofrights.org.

National Archives Research Centers

At the Robert M. Warner Research Center in the National Archives Building in Washington, D.C., and the Steny H. Hoyer Research Center at the National Archives at College Park, Maryland, researchers can consult with staff experts on federal records held in each building and submit requests to examine original documents.

The Warner Research Center holds approximately 275,000 rolls of microfilmed records, documenting military service prior to World War I, immigration into the United States, the federal census, the U.S. Congress, federal courts in the District of Columbia, the Bureau of Indian Affairs, and the Freedmen's Bureau.

The center also contains an extensive, ever-expanding system of reference reports, helping researchers conduct research in federal documents.

Executive branch records housed in the National Archives Building include those of the Bureau of Indian Affairs and of civilian agencies responsible for maritime affairs. Military records in this building include records of the Army before World War I and the Navy and Marine Corps before World War II. In addition, the National Archives Building holds many records relating to the federal government's interaction with individuals; these are often consulted for genealogical research.

The Steny H. Hoyer Research Center in College Park holds textual records of civilian agencies from 1789; investigative records and military holdings that include records from the Army and Army Air Forces dating from World War I and Navy, Marine Corps, intelligence, defense-related, and seized enemy records dating from World War II. In addition to textual records, special media records include motion pictures, still photographs and posters, sound recordings, maps, architectural drawings, aerial photographs, and electronic records. A research room for accessioned microfilm holds records of the Department of State's Berlin Document Center and other World War II–era captured documents.

Field Archives

NARA has 12 field archives where the public can do research. They are located in or near Boston, New York, Philadelphia, Atlanta, Chicago, St. Louis, Kansas City, Fort Worth, Denver, Riverside (California), San Francisco, and Seattle. Archived records of significance, as well as, in some locations, immigration records, are available for use by the public in these field archives.

Presidential Libraries

NARA operates the libraries and museums of the 14 most recent U.S. presidents, beginning with Herbert Hoover, whose library is in West Branch, Iowa, and maintains the presidential records of the Obama Administration. The others are Franklin D. Roosevelt, Hyde Park, New York; Harry S. Truman, Independence, Missouri; Dwight D. Eisenhower, Abilene, Kansas; John F. Kennedy, Boston; Lyndon Baines Johnson, Austin; Richard Nixon, Yorba Linda, California; Gerald R. Ford, Ann Arbor (library) and Grand Rapids (museum), Michigan; Jimmy Carter, Atlanta; Ronald Reagan, Simi Valley, California; George H. W. Bush, College Station, Texas; William J. Clinton, Little Rock; and George W. Bush, Dallas. Unlike other presidential libraries administered by NARA, the Barack Obama Presidential Library will be a fully digital library. After the records are digitized, NARA will store and preserve the original materials in an existing NARA facility that meets NARA's standards for archival storage. Staff at that location will be responsible for caring for the records and artifacts. Currently, the Obama Administration materials are housed in a temporary facility in Hoffman Estates, Illinois, which is not open to the public.

At archives.gov/presidential-libraries, visitors can learn about the presidential library system as a whole and link to individual library websites to learn about the lives of the presidents and the times in which they served.

Federal Records Centers Program

NARA also serves federal agencies, the courts, and Congress by providing records storage, reference service, life-cycle management, and guidance on many issues relating to records management. A network of 18 Federal Records Centers (FRCs) stores 27 million cubic feet (about 52 billion pages) of noncurrent records for 200 agencies.

The Federal Records Centers Program is nationwide. NARA has records centers in or near Atlanta; Boston; Chicago; Dayton; Denver; Fort Worth; Kansas City; Miamisburg, Ohio; Lee's Summit, Missouri; Lenexa, Kansas; Philadelphia; Pittsfield, Massachusetts; Riverside, California; St. Louis; San Francisco; Seattle; Suitland, Maryland; and Valmeyer, Illinois.

Genealogy Research

Genealogy research brings thousands of people to NARA facilities every year. In its holdings NARA has census records dating back to 1790, records dealing with immigration, land and pension records, and passenger lists from ships arriving from all over the world.

NARA is often considered the first stop in searching for one's ancestry, at its facilities in the Washington, D.C., area or one of its 12 field centers around the country. At these locations, NARA staff offers genealogy workshops to show the public how to look through documents dating back to the Revolutionary period.

NARA also offers an annual Genealogy Fair, which is now a "virtual" event at which NARA staff provides tips and techniques for researching genealogy records at the National Archives. Lectures are designed for experienced genealogy profes sionals and novices alike. Watch past Fairs online at https://www.archives.gov/calendar/genealogy-fair.

NARA also maintains close relationships with genealogical associations as well as organizations such as Ancestry.com and Fold3, which can be accessed without charge at any NARA location.

The National Archives has the census schedules on microfilm available from 1790 to 1940. (Most of the 1890 Census was destroyed in a Department of Commerce fire, although partial records are available for some states.)

Archives Library Information Center

The Archives Library Information Center (ALIC) provides access to information on American history and government, archival administration, information management, and government documents. ALIC is located in the National Archives at College Park. Customers also can visit ALIC on the Internet at archives.gov/research/alic, where they will find "Reference at Your Desk" Internet links, staff-compiled bibliographies and publications, and an online library catalog. ALIC can be reached by telephone at 301-837-3415.

Government Documents

Government publications are generally available to researchers at many of the 1,250 congressionally designated federal depository libraries throughout the nation. A record set of these publications also is part of NARA's archival holdings. Publications of the U.S. Government (Record Group 287) is a collection of selected publications of government agencies, arranged by the SuDoc classification system devised by the Office of the Superintendent of Documents, U.S. Government Publishing Office (GPO).

The core of the collection is a library established in 1895 by GPO's Public Documents Division. By 1972, when NARA acquired the library, it included official publications dating from the early years of the federal government and selected publications produced for and by federal government agencies. Since 1972 the 25,000-cubic-foot collection has been augmented periodically with accessions of government publications selected by the Office of the Superintendent of Documents as a by-product of its cataloging activity. As with the federal depository library collections, the holdings in NARA's Record Group 287 comprise only a portion of all U.S. government publications.

NARA Publications

Historically NARA has published guides and indexes to various portions of its archival holdings. Many of these are still in print, though the most up-to-date information about NARA holdings now is available almost exclusively through online searches at archives.gov. The agency also publishes informational leaflets and brochures.

Some publications appear on NARA's website, at archives.gov/publications/online, and many are available from NARA's Customer Service Center in College Park by calling 866-272-6272. The NARA website's publications homepage (archives.gov/publications) provides more detailed information about available publications and ordering.

General-interest books about NARA and its holdings that will appeal to anyone with an interest in U.S. history and facsimiles of certain documents are published by the National Archives Foundation. They are for sale at the foundation's myArchives Store in NARA's downtown Washington building and via the NARA website's eStore page at myarchivesstore.org.

Federal Register

The *Federal Register* is the daily gazette of the U.S. government, containing presidential documents, proposed and final federal regulations, and public notices of federal agencies. It is published by the Office of the Federal Register and printed and distributed by GPO. The two agencies collaborate in the same way to produce the annual revisions of the *Code of Federal Regulations* (*CFR*). Free access to the full text of the electronic version of the *Federal Register* and *CFR*, and to an unofficial, daily-updated electronic *CFR* (the *e-CFR*), is available via fdsys.gov. Federal Register documents scheduled for future publication are available for public inspection at the Office of the Federal Register (7 G Street, N.W., Suite A-734, Washington, DC 20401) or online at the electronic Public Inspection Desk (federalregister.gov/public-inspection). Federalregister.gov provides access to proposed rules, and rules published in the *Federal Register* are open for public comment (the website federalregister.gov and the multiagency website regulations.gov also provide means to comment on these documents).

The full catalog of other Federal Register publications is posted at http://www.ofr.gov and includes the *Compilation of Presidential Documents*, *Public Papers of the Presidents*, slip laws, *United States Statutes at Large*, and the *United States Government Manual*. Printed or microfiche editions of Federal Register publications also are maintained at federal depository libraries (gpo.gov/libraries).

The Public Law Electronic Notification Service (PENS) is a free subscription e-mail service for notification of recently enacted public laws. Varied subscriptions to the daily *Federal Register* are available from federalregister.gov. Additional information about Federal Register programs appears on Facebook (facebook.com/federalregister) and Twitter (@FedRegister).

The Office of the Federal Register also publishes information about its ministerial responsibilities associated with the operation of the Electoral College and ratification of constitutional amendments and provides access to related records. Publication information concerning laws, regulations, and presidential documents and services is available from the Office of the Federal Register (telephone 202-741-6070). Information on Federal Register finding aids, the Electoral College, and constitutional amendments is available through archives.gov/federal-register.

Publications can be ordered by contacting GPO at bookstore.gpo.gov, or by toll-free telephone at 866-512-1800. To submit orders by fax or by mail, see https://bookstore.gpo.gov/help-and-contact.

Grants

The National Historical Publications and Records Commission (NHPRC) is the national grants program of the National Archives. The Archivist of the United States chairs the commission and makes grants on its recommendation. NHPRC's 14 other members represent the president (two appointees), the Supreme Court, the Senate and House of Representatives, the departments of State and Defense, the Librarian of Congress, the American Association for State and Local History, the American Historical Association, the Association for Documentary Editing, the National Association of Government Archives and Records Administrators, the Organization of American Historians, and the Society of American Archivists.

The commission's mission is to provide opportunities for the American people to discover and use records that increase understanding of the nation's democracy, history, and culture. Through leadership initiatives, grants, and fostering the creation of new tools and methods, the commission connects the work of the National Archives to the work of the nation's archives. NHPRC grants help archives, universities, historical societies, professional organizations, and other nonprofit organizations to establish or strengthen archival programs, improve training and techniques, preserve and process records collections, and provide access to them through finding aids, digitization of collections, and documentary editions of the papers of significant historical figures and movements in American history. The commission works in partnership with a national network of state archives and state historical records advisory boards to develop a national archival infrastructure. For more information about the commission, visit archives.gov/nhprc. For more information about the projects it supports, go to facebook.com/nhprc.

Administration

The head of NARA is David S. Ferriero, who was appointed archivist of the United States in 2009 by President Obama. As of January 2020 the agency employed 2,597 people working at NARA locations around the country.

National Center for Education Statistics

U.S. Department of Education, Institute of Education Sciences
Potomac Center Plaza, 550 12th St. S.W., 4th fl., Washington, DC 20202

Christopher A. Cody and Tara Lawley
Academic Libraries, Integrated Postsecondary Education Data System

Maura Spiegelman
School Library Media Centers, Schools and Staffing Survey/
National Teacher and Principal Survey

In an effort to collect and disseminate more complete statistical information about libraries, the National Center for Education Statistics (NCES) initiated a formal library statistics program in 1989 that included surveys on academic libraries, school library media centers, public libraries, and state libraries. At the end of December 2006, the Public Libraries Survey and the State Library Agencies Survey were officially transferred to the Institute of Museum and Library Services (IMLS). The Academic Libraries Survey and the School Library Media Centers Survey continued to be administered and funded by NCES. However, the School Library Media Centers Survey was incorporated into the School and Staffing Survey (SASS), and the Academic Libraries Survey was incorporated into the Integrated Postsecondary Education Data System (IPEDS).

The library surveys conducted by NCES are designed to provide comprehensive nationwide data on the status of libraries. Federal, state, and local officials, professional associations, and local practitioners use these surveys for planning, evaluating, and making policy. These data are also available to researchers and educators.

Past information about elementary and secondary public school library media centers is available on the School and Staffing Survey website, http://nces.ed.gov/surveys/sass/. The Library Statistics Program's website, http://nces.ed.gov/surveys/libraries, provides links to data search tools, data files, survey definitions, and survey designs for the complete Academic Libraries Survey files from 1996 to 2012. The IPEDS Academic Libraries Information Center, http://nces.ed.gov/ipeds/Section/Alscenter, contains current survey definitions and designs, and the IPEDS Use the Data Website at https://nces.ed.gov/ipeds/Home/UseTheData contains complete data files for the Academic Libraries component beginning in 2014. The two library surveys conducted by NCES are described below.

Academic Libraries

The IPEDS Academic Libraries (AL) component provides descriptive statistics from academic libraries in the 50 states, the District of Columbia, and, if applicable, other U.S. jurisdictions (Guam, the Commonwealth of the Northern Mariana Islands, Puerto Rico, and the U.S. Virgin Islands).

NCES surveyed academic libraries on a three-year cycle between 1966 and 1988. From 1988 to 1998, AL was a component of IPEDS collected on a two-year cycle. From 2000 to 2012, the Academic Libraries Survey (ALS) separated from

IPEDS but remained on a two-year cycle as part of the Library Statistics Program. During this time period, IPEDS and ALS data were still linked by the identification codes of the postsecondary education institutions. In aggregate, these data provide an overview of the status of academic libraries nationally and by state. Beginning with the 2014–2015 collection cycle, AL was reintegrated back into IPEDS, and the AL component became a mandatory, annual survey for all degree-granting Title IV institutions. It was at this time that many questions from the 2012 ALS collections and services sections were removed or revised. Since 2014, the AL component has undergone many changes.

Currently, the 2020–2021 AL survey collects data on libraries in the entire universe of degree-granting Title IV postsecondary institutions using a web-based data collection system. The survey component collects the counts and the circulation/usage of books, serials, media, and databases, both in physical and electronic formats. Additionally, academic libraries report on interlibrary loan services. Also, starting 2020–2021, the AL survey began collecting again information on library staff.

Institutions with reported total library expenditures over zero or institutions that have access to a library collection are required to report collections data, while those with expenditures equal to or greater than $100,000 are required to report collections and detailed expenditures data. Academic libraries report expenditures for salaries, wages, and fringe benefits, if paid from the library budget; materials and services expenditures; operations and maintenance expenditures; and total expenditures. For the 2020–2021 Al survey, institutions were asked to report data to accurately reflect the time period corresponding with the IPEDS survey component, even if such reporting is seemingly inconsistent with prior-year reporting. NCES expects that some data reported during the 2020–2021 data collection year will vary from established prior trends due to the impacts of coronavirus pandemic. Additionally, for the AL survey, institutions were also asked to include any library-related expenses that are covered by Coronavirus Aid, Relief, and Economic Security (CARES) Act funds in the appropriate expense sections.

For the final 2012 ALS data collection, a First Look report, "Academic Libraries: 2012" (NCES 2014-038), was released on the NCES website in February 2014, as were the final data file and documentation for the 2012 ALS (NCES 2014-039). NCES also has a web-based peer analysis tool for AL called "Compare Academic Libraries" (https://nces.ed.gov/surveys/libraries/compare/) using AL 2012 data. Beginning with the 2014–2015 IPEDS collection cycle and ending with the 2017–2018 IPEDS collection cycle, the following First Look reports were released for Academic Libraries:

- "Enrollment and Employees in Postsecondary Institutions, Fall 2014; and Financial Statistics and Academic Libraries, Fiscal Year 2014" (NCES 2016-005)
- "Enrollment and Employees in Postsecondary Institutions, Fall 2015; and Financial Statistics and Academic Libraries, Fiscal Year 2015" (NCES 2017-024)
- "Enrollment and Employees in Postsecondary Institutions, Fall 2016; and Financial Statistics and Academic Libraries, Fiscal Year 2016" (NCES 2018-002)

- "Enrollment and Employees in Postsecondary Institutions, Fall 2017; and Financial Statistics and Academic Libraries, Fiscal Year 2017" (NCES 2019-021)

Beginning with the 2018–2019 IPEDS collection cycle, IPEDS no longer produces First Look reports; however, AL data, web reports, and tables from 2014 and on are available via the IPEDS Use the Data website (https://nces.ed.gov/ipeds/Home/UseTheData). Academic library statistics information can be obtained from Christopher A. Cody, Integrated Postsecondary Education Data System, e-mail IPEDS@ed.gov.

School Library Media Centers

National surveys of school library media centers in elementary and secondary schools in the United States were conducted in 1958, 1962, 1974, 1978, and 1986, 1993–1994, 1999–2000, 2003–2004, 2007–2008, and 2011–2012.

NCES, with the assistance of the U.S. Bureau of the Census, conducted the School Library Media Center Survey as part of the Schools and Staffing Survey (SASS). SASS is the nation's largest sample survey of teachers, schools, and principals in K–12 public and private schools. Data from the school library media center questionnaire provide a national picture of public school library staffing, collections, expenditures, technology, and services. Results from the 2011–2012 survey can be found in "Characteristics of Public Elementary and Secondary School Library Media Centers in the United States: Results from the 2011–2012 Schools and Staffing Survey" (NCES 2013-315).

NCES also published a historical report about school libraries titled *Fifty Years of Supporting Children's Learning: A History of Public School Libraries and Federal Legislation from 1953–2000* (NCES 2005-311). Drawn from more than 50 sources, this report gives descriptive data about public school libraries since 1953. Along with key characteristics of school libraries, the report also presents national and regional standards, and federal legislation affecting school library media centers. Data from sample surveys are provided at the national, regional, and school levels, and by state.

NCES recently redesigned the Schools and Staffing Survey as the National Teacher and Principal Survey (NTPS). NTPS focuses on teachers, principals, and the schools in which they work. The 2017–2018 survey counted the number of school library media centers; data on library media center staff were not collected but will be part of the next NTPS. For more information about the NTPS or to review data collected in the 2015–2016 and 2017–2018 school years, visit https://nces.ed.gov/surveys/ntps/.

Additional information on school library media center statistics can be obtained from Maura Spiegelman, e-mail maura.spiegelman@ed.gov.

NCES has included some library-oriented questions relevant to the library usage and skills of the parent and the teacher instruments of the new Early Childhood Longitudinal Study (ECLS). For additional information, visit http://nces.ed.gov/ecls. Library items also appear in National Household Education Survey (NHES) instruments. For more information about that survey, visit http://nces.ed.gov/nhes.

NCES included a questionnaire about high school library media centers in the Education Longitudinal Study of 2002 (ELS: 2002). This survey collected data from tenth graders about their schools, their school library media centers, their communities, and their home life. The report, "School Library Media Centers: Selected Results from the Education Longitudinal Study of 2002" (ELS: 2002) (NCES 2005-302), is available on the NCES website. For more information about this survey, visit http://nces.ed.gov/surveys/els2002.

How to Obtain Printed and Electronic Products

Reports are currently published in the First Look format. First Look reports consist of a short collection of tables presenting state and national totals, a survey description, and data highlights. NCES also publishes separate, more in-depth studies analyzing these data.

Internet Access

Many NCES publications (including out-of-print publications) and edited raw data files from the library surveys are available for viewing or downloading at no charge through the Electronic Catalog on the NCES website at http://nces.ed.gov/pubsearch.

Ordering Printed Products

Many NCES publications are also available in printed format. To order one free copy of recent NCES reports, contact the Education Publications Center (ED Pubs) at https://www.usa.gov/federal-agencies/education-publications-center-edpubs, by e-mail at edpubs@edpubs.ed.gov, by toll-free telephone at 877-4-ED-PUBS (1-877-433-7827) or TTY/TDD 877-576-7734, by fax at 703-605-6794, or by mail at ED Pubs, P.O. Box 22207, Alexandria, VA 22304.

Many publications are available through the Education Resources Information Clearinghouse (ERIC) system. For more information on services and products, visit https://eric.ed.gov.

Out-of-print publications and data files may be available through the NCES Electronic Catalog on the NCES website at http://nces.ed.gov/pubsearch or through one of the 1,250 federal depository libraries throughout the United States (see http://catalog.gpo.gov/fdlpdir/FDLPdir.jsp). Use the NCES publication number included in the citations for publications and data files to quickly locate items in the NCES Electronic Catalog. Use the GPO number to locate items in a federal depository library.

Defense Technical Information Center

Fort Belvoir, VA 22060
World Wide Web https://discover.dtic.mil/

The Defense Technical Information Center (DTIC) is a Department of Defense (DoD) field activity, under the leadership of the Office of the Under Secretary of Defense for Research and Engineering, OUSD(R&E).

DTIC's mission is to collect, disseminate, and analyze scientific and technical (S&T) information to rapidly and reliably deliver knowledge that propels development of the next generation of warfighter capabilities.

With more than 4.7 million documents, DTIC is DoD's central resource for scientific and technical information, enabling the entire DoD research community to build on the accumulated knowledge base produced from the department's multi-billion-dollar annual investment in science and technology. DTIC provides digital applications and services that facilitate search, analysis, and collaboration, making information widely available to decision makers, researchers, engineers, and scientists across the DoD.

In this capacity, DTIC has three main focus areas. "Collection" entails the gathering, preservation, and management of defense technical information. "Dissemination" involves the distribution of content across the department to facilitate collaboration and discovery. Finally, the DoD Information Analysis Centers (DoD IACs) help solve DoD's technology challenges through rapid, flexible, and low-cost research services to acquisition program managers, DoD laboratories, Program Executive Offices (PEOs), and Combatant Commands.

Ultimately, DTIC aims to maximize the availability and use of DoD-funded technical information, while balancing information sharing with information protection.

Reaching across the Federal Government

DTIC offers its capabilities to a broad user base within the federal government. Although some applications are publicly available on https://discover.dtic.mil, many are restricted to registered federal government and contracted personnel. Federal employees and contractors with a PKI card can access these sites with their credentials. More information about the benefits of and eligibility for restricted access can be found at https://discover.dtic.mil/dtic-registration-benefits/.

Who uses DTIC applications and services? Among its registered users are

- Acquisition personnel
- Active duty military personnel
- Congressional staff
- DoD contractors
- Engineers
- Faculty and students at military schools and universities
- Historians

- Information professionals/librarians
- Program analysts
- Program executive offices
- Researchers
- Science and technology advisors
- Scientists
- Security managers
- Small business owners
- Software engineers and developers

Collection

DTIC's holdings include both public and access-controlled documents. DTIC's information collection activities leverage many sources, including DoD organizations and contractors; other U.S. government organizations and their contractors; nonprofit organizations working on DoD-funded scientific, research, and engineering activities; academia; and foreign governments. DTIC primarily accepts information electronically and, when necessary, in physical print and digital formats such as CD and DVD. More information about submission and selection is available at https://discover.dtic.mil/submit-documents/.

DTIC's holdings include more than 4.7 million documents, such as technical reports on completed research; research summaries of planned and ongoing work; independent research and development summaries; defense technology transfer agreements; DoD planning documents; DoD-funded journal articles; DoD international agreements; conference proceedings; security classification guides; command histories; and special collections dating back to World War II.

Dissemination

The Research and Engineering (R&E) Gateway—accessible only to registered users via https://discover.dtic.mil/—is the entry point to DTIC's full suite of applications, some of which are also available on the public website https://www.discover.dtic.mil. In an access-controlled environment, the R&E Gateway offers access to DoD research, other scientific and technical information, and collaboration with other subject matter experts.

By providing the highest awareness of relevant information, the R&E Gateway helps the defense research community build on past work and collaborate on current projects. The broad availability of DTIC documents helps avoid duplication of effort and maximize the efficient use of DoD project funds.

Some of DTIC's applications and products are

- R&E Gateway Search—Available to registered users, Search is DTIC's principal application for discovering scientific and technical information from DTIC's repository of 4.7 million documents. With Search, users can access DoD's body of S&T knowledge to quickly find the most relevant information for their research needs.

- *Journal of DoD Research and Engineering* (JDR&E)—The JDR&E is published quarterly for registered users. An access-controlled forum, the JDR&E advances the development of DoD priority technologies through rigorous peer review of scientific research. The journal provides visibility into controlled defense research and promotes the scientific collaboration that results in new warfighter capabilities.
- PubDefense—In 2013 the White House Office of Science and Technology Policy mandated that federally funded, scholarly journal articles must be made available and free to the public following a 12-month embargo. PubDefense is DTIC's publicly accessible tool to access journal articles, conference papers, and related materials resulting from research funded by the DoD and Office of the Director of National Intelligence/Intelligence Advanced Research Projects Agency. Public datasets associated with these scholarly publications are also available through PubDefense. The application is available at https://publicaccess.dtic.mil/padf_public/#/home.
- Horizons—Horizons helps registered users understand how research and development spending and efforts flow from basic research to deployed technologies. With various search filters and graphical overviews, users can assess congressional budget report data across many fiscal years—and additional controlled research project information—to facilitate better execution and planning of investments.
- DTIC Thesaurus—Available to the public at https://discover.dtic.mil/thesaurus/, the Thesaurus provides a broad, multidisciplinary subject-term vocabulary that aids in information search and retrieval. Subject terms, called Descriptors, are organized into hierarchies, where series of narrower terms are linked to broader terms.

DoD Information Analysis Centers

The DoD Information Analysis Centers (DoD IACs) provide research and analysis services to, and develop scientific and technical information products for, the DoD S&T community in the broad domains of Cyber Security, Defense Systems, and Homeland Defense. The DoD IACs draw on the expertise of hundreds of scientists, engineers, and information specialists who provide research and analysis to customers with diverse, complex, and challenging requirements.

The DoD IACs provide a broad variety of research and analysis products and services, including customer-driven research and analysis, prototyping, answers to scientific and technical inquires, access to the S&T community's subject matter experts, technical training, and wide-ranging scientific and technical information products.

For larger research challenges requiring up to five years of effort and costing hundreds of millions of dollars, the IAC program provides access to research and development contracts populated with highly qualified, prevetted industry leaders across a broad swath of 22 technical areas of interest to the DoD.

These 22 technical focus areas are Software and Data Analysis; Cybersecurity; Modeling and Simulation; Knowledge Management and Information Sharing; Advanced Materials; Autonomous Weapon Systems; C4ISR; Directed Energy;

Energetics; Military Sensing; Non-Lethal Weapons and Information Operations; RMQSI; Survivability and Vulnerability; Weapons Systems; Homeland Defense and Security; Critical Infrastructure Protection: Weapons of Mass Destruction; CBRN Defense; Biometrics; Medical; Cultural Studies; and Alternative Energy.

Education Resources

National Library of Education

Knowledge Utilization Division
National Center for Education Evaluation and Regional Assistance
Institute of Education Sciences, U.S. Department of Education
400 Maryland Ave. S.W., Washington, DC 20202
World Wide Web https://ies.ed.gov/ncee/projects/nle

Karen Tate
Director

The U.S. Department of Education's National Library of Education (NLE), created in 1994, is the primary resource center for education information in the federal government, serving the research needs of the Department of Education, the education community, and the public. NLE resides in the National Center for Education Evaluation and Regional Assistance, Institute of Education Sciences.

NLE was created by Public Law 103-227, the Educational Research, Development, Dissemination, and Improvement Act of 1994, and reauthorized under Public Law 107-279, the Education Sciences Reform Act of 2002. The act outlines four primary functions of NLE:

- Collect and archive information, including products and publications developed through, or supported by, the Institute of Education Sciences; and other relevant and useful education-related research, statistics, and evaluation materials and other information, projects, and publications that are consistent with scientifically valid research or the priorities and mission of the institute, and developed by the department, other federal agencies, or entities
- Provide a central location within the federal government for information about education
- Provide comprehensive reference services on matters relating to education to employees of the Department of Education and its contractors and grantees, other federal employees, and the public
- Promote greater cooperation and resource sharing among providers and repositories of education information in the United States

NLE works closely with the Education Resources Information Center (ERIC). ERIC collects and archives information and provides a central location within the federal government for information about education. Because ERIC serves as the major public program, it is covered separately. [See "Education Resources Information Center" beginning on page 103—*Ed.*]

The primary responsibility of NLE is to provide information services to agency staff and contractors, the general public, other government agencies, and other libraries. Located in the agency's headquarters building in Washington, D.C., the library houses current and historical collections and archives of information on education issues, research, statistics, and policy; there is a special emphasis on agency publications and contractor reports, as well as current and historical federal education legislation.

NLE's primary customer base includes about 4,000 department staff nationwide; department contractors performing research; education organizations and media; and academic, special, and government libraries.

Collections

The focus of NLE's collection is on education issues, with an emphasis on research and policy, with some materials on related topics including law, public policy, economics, urban affairs, sociology, history, philosophy, psychology, and cognitive development. In addition to current materials, the collection has books dating from the early 19th century, including approximately 800 books on education research in the United States and more than 25,000 historical textbooks. Some of these books were donated to the library by Henry Barnard, the first U.S. commissioner of education.

NLE maintains collections of historical documents associated with its parent agency, the U.S. Department of Education, having a complete collection of ERIC microfiche; research reports reviewed by the What Works Clearinghouse and special panels; and publications of or relating to the department's predecessor agencies, including the National Institute of Education and the U.S. Office of Education in the Department of Health, Education, and Welfare. These collections include reports, studies, manuals, statistical publications, speeches, and policy papers. NLE also serves as a selective federal depository library under the U.S. Government Publishing Office program.

Services

NLE provides reference and other information services, including legislative reference and statistical information services, to department staff, to the education community at large, and to the general public, as well as offering document delivery services to department staff and interlibrary loan services to other libraries and government agencies.

Contact Information

The U.S. Department of Education Research Library can be contacted by e-mail at askalibrarian@ed.gov. The library's reference desk is available by telephone from 9 A.M. to 5 P.M. weekdays, except federal holidays, at 800-424-1616 (toll free) or 202-205-5015, and by fax at 202-401-0547. For the hearing-impaired, the toll-free number for the Federal Relay Service is 800-877-8339.

Located in the department's headquarters building at 400 Maryland Ave. S.W., the library is open to researchers by appointment from 9 A.M. to 5 P.M. weekdays, except federal holidays.

Education Resources Information Center

Knowledge Utilization Division
National Center for Education Evaluation and Regional Assistance
Institute of Education Sciences, U.S. Department of Education
550 12th St., S.W., Washington, DC 20208
https://eric.ed.gov

Erin Pollard
Program Officer, ERIC
202-245-8344, e-mail erin.pollard@ed.gov

The Education Resources Information Center (ERIC) is the world's largest and most frequently used digital library of education resources. Since its inception in 1966, ERIC has added over 1.8 million records of journal articles, reports, and other materials. Over 1 million records are for peer-reviewed work, and 440,000 records have free full text available to download from ERIC. Each ERIC bibliographic record contains an abstract of a journal article or gray literature document (for example, a technical report or conference paper), along with an abstract, audience, type of report, information on the assessment used, location where the research was conducted, and descriptors that work as keywords to guide users to relevant results.

Background

ERIC is a free, online database of education research that serves over 12 million users each year. With more than 50 years of service to the public, ERIC is one of the oldest programs in the U.S. Department of Education. As the world's largest education resource, it is distinguished by two hallmarks: free dissemination of bibliographic records, and the collection of gray literature such as research conference papers and government contractor reports.

The authorizing legislation for ERIC is part of the Education Sciences Reform Act of 2002, Public Law 107-279. This legislation envisioned ERIC subject areas or topics (previously covered by the ERIC Clearinghouses) as part of the totality of enhanced information dissemination to be conducted by the Institute of Education Sciences. In addition, information dissemination includes material on closing the achievement gap and on educational practices that improve academic achievement and promote learning.

Mission of ERIC

ERIC undertakes five major activities:

- *Pursues good sources.* ERIC reviews journal issues and publications from education-focused programs, organizations, and agencies to locate research in the field of education. A unique feature of ERIC is the inclusion of "gray literature," such as work from nonprofits, advocacy organizations, government agencies, or other sources that are typically not indexed by commercial databases. ERIC currently provides content from 1,973 sources, including 1,247 journals and 726 organizations and agencies. Ninety-nine percent of ERIC's journals are peer reviewed.

- *Works to make research publicly available.* ERIC negotiates with publishers to make as much of its content as freely available as possible. There are 102,000 full-text, peer-reviewed articles available for free download.
- *Creates records with supporting information so users know if resources are a good fit.* ERIC creates about 48,000 records per year that provide users with information about each article. Information in the record includes an abstract, audience, type of report, information on the assessment used, location where the research was conducted, and descriptors that work as keywords to guide users to relevant results. The metadata gives users the information they need to quickly see if the article will be relevant and useful to them.
- *Powers search engines with ERIC metadata to help users find good research, wherever they are searching.* ERIC shares its metadata with the public to enable search engines, academic databases, and other information providers to power their searches with ERIC data.
- *Integrates with other federally funded resources.* As applicable, ERIC records are linked with other federally funded resources, including What Works Clearinghouse study pages, Institute of Education Sciences grant abstracts, and links to federal websites. These interrelationships provide additional information and assist users in finding relevant and valuable IES resources.

Selection Standards

The selection policy provides that all materials added to the ERIC database are rigorous and relevant sources of research directly related to the field of education. The majority of journals indexed in ERIC are peer-reviewed, and peer-reviewed status is indicated for all journals indexed since 2004, when this data began to be documented by the ERIC system. The peer-review status for nonjournals is indicated for all sources with a documented peer-review process. The collection scope includes early childhood education through higher education, vocational education, and special education; it includes teacher education, education administration, assessment and evaluation, counseling, information technology, and the academic areas of reading, mathematics, science, environmental education, languages, and social studies.

To be considered for selection, all submissions must be in digital format and accompanied by author permission for dissemination. For individual document submissions, authors (copyright holders) can upload materials through a link on the ERIC website. Journal publishers, associations, and other entities with multiple documents also submit electronic content following guidance and instructions consistent with provider agreements from ERIC.

ERIC Users

About 12 million users search the ERIC website and download more than 7 million full-text documents each year from users all over the world. Approximately half of ERIC's users are driven from a commercial search engine, while 40 percent are driven from academic search engines.

ERIC can be reached at ERICRequests@ed.gov. Questions can also be transmitted via the message box on the "Contact Us" page on the ERIC website.

National Association and Organization Reports

American Library Association

225 N. Michigan Ave., Suite 1300, Chicago, IL 60601
800-545-2433
World Wide Web http://www.ala.org

Julius C. Jefferson, Jr.
President

The American Library Association (ALA) was founded in 1876 in Philadelphia and later chartered in the Commonwealth of Massachusetts. ALA has approximately 57,000 members, including librarians, library trustees, and other interested people from every state and many nations. The association serves public, state, school, and academic libraries, as well as special libraries for people working in government, prisons, and other institutions.

ALA is home to eight membership divisions, each focused on a type of library or library function. They are the American Association of School Librarians (AASL); the Association for Library Service to Children (ALSC); the Association of College and Research Libraries (ACRL); Core: Leadership, Infrastructure, Futures; the Public Library Association (PLA); the Reference and User Services Association (RUSA); United for Libraries; and the Young Adult Library Services Association (YALSA).

In June 2020, the ALA Council voted to approve Core: Leadership, Infrastructure, Futures as a new ALA division beginning September 1, 2020, and to dissolve the Association for Library Collections and Technical Services (ALCTS), the Library and Information Technology Association (LITA), and the Library Leadership and Management Association (LLAMA), effective August 31, 2020.

ALA hosts 20 roundtables for members who share interests that lie outside the scope of any of the divisions. A network of affiliates, chapters, and other organizations enables ALA to reach a broad audience.

ALA offices address the broad interests and issues of concern to ALA members. They track issues and provide information, services, and products for members and the public. Current ALA offices are the Chapter Relations Office (CRO); the Communications and Marketing Office (CMO); the Development Office; the Executive / ALA Governance Office; the Human Resources Office; the International Relations Office (IRO); the Library and Research Center (LARC); the Office for Accreditation; the Office for Diversity, Literacy and Outreach

Services (ODLOS); the Office for Human Resource Development and Recruitment (HRDR); the Office for Intellectual Freedom (OIF); the Public Policy and Advocacy Office (PPAO); the Public Programs Office (PPO); and Publishing.

With headquarters in Chicago, ALA's PPAO is based in Washington, D.C., and United for Libraries is in Exton, Pennsylvania. ALA also has an editorial office for *Choice*, a review journal for academic libraries, in Middletown, Connecticut. In 2020 the association relocated its headquarters from 50 E. Huron and 40 E. Huron to 225 N. Michigan Avenue, Chicago.

Leadership and Strategic Planning

Julius C. Jefferson, Jr., section head of the Congressional Research Service at the Library of Congress in Washington, D.C., was inaugurated as ALA president at the association's 2020 Annual Conference, held virtually. Jefferson's major initiative was "Holding Space: A national conversation series with libraries," a nationwide virtual tour to highlight the innovation and impact of a diverse range of libraries and to engage stakeholders to advocate for libraries and the communities they serve. The initiative featured town halls, roundtable discussions, and interviews with library leaders, state and local partners, and elected officials covering topics ranging from Historically Black Colleges and Universities (HBCUs) and academic libraries, to school, tribal, and public libraries—all while amplifying the concerns of each community along the route. It kicked off on July 27, 2020, from the Library of Congress and concluded on August 7, 2020. Another important initiative was ALA Connect Live, a series of monthly conversations among ALA's executive board, staff, and membership.

Patricia "Patty" M. Wong, city librarian at Santa Monica (California) Public Library, was elected 2021–2022 ALA president-elect and will be inaugurated at the association's 2021 Annual Conference, to be held virtually. Other officers are Wanda Kay Brown, immediate past-president, Winston-Salem State University; Maggie Farrell, University of Nevada, Las Vegas, treasurer; and Tracie D. Hall, who became ALA's new executive director on February 24, 2020.

Conferences and Workshops

2020 Midwinter Meeting

From January 24–28 ALA hosted its 2020 Midwinter Meeting & Exhibits in Philadelphia at the Pennsylvania Convention Center and nearby locations. The conference was attended by more than 8,000, including more than 2,600 U.S. exhibitors, and offered peers and leaders a wide variety of educational sessions, keynote presentations, and social gatherings.

The conference opened with best-selling author and social entrepreneur Wes Moore, who discussed the need for community support and how libraries have consistently sustained their communities, and his new book, *Five Days: The Fiery Reckoning of an American City*, a kaleidoscopic account of five days in the life of a city on the edge after Freddie Gray's death.

As a special guest of ALA president Wanda K. Brown, Chef Jeff Henderson shared a powerful message at the ALA President's Program. While incarcerated for drug trafficking, Henderson discovered, almost by accident, a passion for cooking while working in the prison kitchen. With fierce determination and people who believed in him, he eventually became the first African American chef at Caesars Palace in Las Vegas, which led to an executive chef position at Café Bellagio.

Artist and author Chanel Miller closed the Midwinter Meeting with an inspiring video illustrating what libraries mean to her. Miller, who stunned the world with a victim impact statement after a sexual assault on the Stanford University campus, talked about what, and who, gives her hope as she moves forward.

New at the Midwinter Meeting was the I Love My Librarian Awards. The national award recognizes the outstanding public service contributions of librarians working in public, school, college, community college, or university libraries who transform communities and improve lives. Ten winners were selected from more than 1,950 nominations submitted by library users nationwide.

Sponsored by ALA's Center for the Future of Libraries, the Symposium on the Future of Libraries featured sessions exploring the near-term trends already inspiring innovation in libraries and the longer-term trends that will help libraries adapt to the needs of their communities. For the fourth consecutive year, concurrent sessions were dedicated to education, technology, diversity and inclusion, government, and social justice.

At the 2020 Midwinter Meeting, the ALA executive board charged the ODLOS Advisory Committee with creating an Equity, Diversity, and Inclusion (EDI) Assembly. The purpose of this EDI Assembly is to provide a forum for all groups within ALA and ALA-affiliated organizations working on initiatives related to equity, diversity, and inclusion to discuss their activities, identify opportunities for collaboration and coordination, and explore new initiatives related to the association's strategic direction for equity, diversity, and inclusion.

ALA 2020 Virtual Event

ALA canceled its 2020 Annual Conference due to the pandemic, marking only the second time (the first being World War II) that the association has canceled the June meeting. In lieu of its annual conference, June 24–26 ALA held a virtual event, "Community Through Connection," which attracted 7,349 attendees and 651 exhibitors. Three months of intense planning began following the introduction of the concept on April 20, 2020. The event featured more than 50 educational sessions, including COVID-19-related information pertinent to libraries and available in an on-demand format, live-chat opportunities with authors and speakers, more than 75 publisher and exhibitor sessions on new book titles, a virtual exhibit floor with more than 600 participating exhibitors, 11 featured speakers, and a "Swag-a-Palooza" with hundreds of free items for attendees.

Through the support of event sponsors, ALA was able to offer a modest $60 registration fee and to allow library professionals who had recently been furloughed or laid off, or who were experiencing a reduction of paid work hours, to attend at no cost. ALA Virtual content remained readily accessible for a full year. Attendees could view sessions again, view those missed during the live event, or use content for training or research purposes.

The event was opened by ALA 2019–2020 president Wanda Kay Brown, who debuted a new video, *Finding Your ALA*, tied to the theme of her presidency. ALA executive director Tracie D. Hall next discussed her first four months in office—a period that coincided with the start of the COVID-19 pandemic and the global uprising against police brutality and racism.

Serial entrepreneur, nonprofit CEO, and political leader Stacey Abrams was the ALA President's Program speaker. Interviewed by executive director Hall, Abrams addressed both the effects of the pandemic and the use of deadly force by police. She described the nation as amid "two massive conversations," the first regarding the inequities that have been laid bare by COVID-19, noting that African Americans are twice as likely to contract the virus than any other community in the U.S.—despite representing only 13–14 percent of the nation's population— and the second regarding police brutality and systemic injustice.

Other highlights included daily live-chat opportunities, key sessions on COVID-19, and a session focusing on retention efforts of minority librarians in librarianship from the perspectives of early, middle, and advanced career librarians. The virtual exhibit floor provided attendees an opportunity to visit with more than 600 participating exhibitors and also offered live events. Exhibitors made themselves available through phone, social media, or video chat. At the conclusion of the conference, Wanda Kay Brown passed the gavel virtually to newly elected ALA president Julius C. Jefferson, Jr.

PLA 2020 Conference

The annual Public Library Association (PLA) Conference took place February 25–29 in Nashville, drawing more than 8,700 attendees. Over 110 sessions challenged, engaged, and inspired attendees, along with special events such as the Book Buzz, Career Center, Spark Talks, and How-To Festival. For the first time, PLA integrated its Professional Development Theory of Change into conference programming, helping attendees chart their paths to becoming data-driven leaders, community advocates, stewards of the public library and its values, and networked innovators.

Events, Celebrations, and Observances

Holding Space Tour

On Monday July 27 ALA president Julius C. Jefferson, Jr., embarked upon a 12-stop virtual tour to spotlight how libraries of all kinds across the country are addressing the needs of their diverse communities and engaging stakeholders to advocate for libraries. Jefferson's ten-day "Holding Space" tour began at the Library of Congress in Washington, D.C., and ended at the Hawaii State Library on Friday, August 7. At each stop, Jefferson met with library leaders, state and local partners, elected officials, and other community influencers to cover a vast terrain of issues facing a broad range of institutions, including libraries at HBCUs, other academic libraries, school libraries, Tribal libraries, and public libraries. Jefferson invited tour participants to join ALA's campaign urging members of Congress to support the Library Stabilization Fund Act, which would protect the jobs of more than 366,000 library workers and the services provided by 116,000 libraries.

ALA Connect Live

In times of uncertainty, connection and conversation are more important than ever. This is what inspired the March 2020 launch of "ALA Connect Live." Initially an idea of president-elect Julius C. Jefferson, Jr., to connect with members, ALA Connect Live is an opportunity to bring the library community together to discuss trending issues and challenges, and to scale knowledge and best practices. ALA Connect Live allows participants to engage in open dialog with ALA leaders and with their fellow library professionals.

ALSC Virtual Institute

On October 2–3, the Association for Library Service to Children (ALSC) held its 2020 Institute, "Dive In: Engage, Amplify, Activate," providing attendees an opportunity to develop themselves as library professionals serving children and families. Due to the pandemic, the Institute moved to a virtual environment with low-cost registration, resulting in its highest registration to date. Programming included six general sessions, with speakers ranging from nationally celebrated authors and illustrators, to thought leaders and practitioners in child development, to librarians on the front lines of working and serving communities in today's world.

Sharjah Virtual International Forum

The first Sharjah Virtual International Forum was held November 10–12, 2020. It was celebrated with the theme "Libraries and Librarians Meeting the Challenges in New Normal." Each day featured two hours of presentations from librarians from different types of libraries on how they have pivoted or what transformation needs are taking place now and for beyond the pandemic. ALA president Julius C. Jefferson Jr., delivered the keynote of the first day of the live-streamed forum "Meeting the Challenge in Times of Crisis."

Banned Books Week

The ALA Office for Intellectual Freedom (OIF) released the Top 100 Most Banned and Challenged Books from the past decade. The list's release launched Banned Books Week, September 27–October 3, ALA's annual observance that celebrates our freedom to read and highlights the harms of censorship. The 2020 Banned Books Week theme was "Censorship is a Dead End. Find Your Freedom to Read." Libraries, bookstores, universities, and organizations hosted online Banned Book Week programs and resources, and ALA itself hosted online programs and virtual activities for libraries, library workers, and the public.

Library Card Sign-up Month

During Library Card Sign-up Month, held each September, DC's Wonder Woman championed the power of a library card as Library Card Sign-up Month Honorary Chair. Wonder Woman posters, stickers, and bookmarks were made available for purchase through the ALA Store. Tools for libraries to participate were also available on the Libraries Transform website.

National Friends of Libraries Week

Friends of the Library groups around the country marked the 15th annual National Friends of Libraries Week October 18–24, 2020. Even while facing the challenges of their library buildings being closed, or open for limited hours, Friends groups continued to advocate for their libraries by promoting their groups, hosting virtual events and fundraisers, and showing appreciation for library staff and boards. Additional events in celebration of National Friends of Libraries Week are posted on Facebook and Twitter under #NationalFriendsofLibrariesWeek and #NFOLW20.

National Library Week

"Find your place at the library," the theme for National Library Week (NLW) 2020, held April 19–25, was chosen before the emergence of the global pandemic. To acknowledge the altered landscape, the event highlighted how libraries are offering virtual services and digital content their communities need now more than ever, serving as a rich pipeline for content, delivering access to e-books, movies, music, video games, virtual storytime and activities, and much more. "Find your place at the library" emphasized that everyone is welcome at the library.

Preservation Week

From April 26 to May 2 ALA celebrated the tenth anniversary of Preservation Week, a public awareness initiative that aims to promote preservation and conservation in communities with the help of libraries, institutions, and museums. Preservation Week inspires actions to preserve personal, family, and community collections in addition to library, museum, and archival materials and raises awareness of the role libraries and other cultural institutions play in providing ongoing education and outreach. The 2020 theme was "Preserving Oral History."

Highlights of the Year—ALA Initiatives, Honors, and Offices

Task Force on the UN 2030 Sustainable Development Goals

The United Nations 2030 Sustainable Development Goals (SDGs) are a call to action to end poverty, protect the planet, and improve the lives and prospects of everyone, everywhere. The 17 goals were adopted by all UN members, including the United States. In 2020 ALA president Julius C. Jefferson, Jr., created a task force charged with developing a multiyear strategic plan to increase library participation in achieving the SDGs.

Former ALA Executive Director Receives Lippincott Award

Mary W. Ghikas received the 2020 Joseph W. Lippincott Award for distinguished service to the profession of librarianship. Ghikas was honored for her many accomplishments during a long, varied, and distinguished career as a librarian, library administrator, network director, and ALA leader.

Communications and Marketing Office

Media Relations

During 2020 27,769 articles mentioned ALA, with a total circulation of 20.3 billion. (Circulation rate is calculated using the number of articles/mentions multiplied by the monthly unique visitors for each media outlet's website.)

I Love Libraries

I Love Libraries is an initiative of ALA created to spread the world about the value of today's libraries. The site promotes the value of libraries and librarians, explains key issues affecting libraries, and urges readers to support and take action for their libraries.

Libraries Transform

Libraries Transform closed out the year with more than 17,630 libraries and library advocates using the free program in all 50 states, more than 100 countries, and all 6 inhabited continents. Resources include dozens of downloadable "Because" statement graphics for print and digital media, templates and instructions for creating customized public awareness materials, and celebrity PSA videos for sharing on social media.

Governance

In March 2020 the ALA executive board recommended that libraries can and should leave their wifi networks on even when their buildings are closed wherever possible. The board stated, "In these unprecedented times, we should take whatever steps we can to leverage our resources to maximize benefit to our communities— particularly for those with the fewest resources.

In June, decrying the death of George Floyd at the hands of the Minneapolis Police Department, "the latest in a long line of recent and historical violence against Black people in the United States," the board declared that it stands with the Black Caucus of ALA (BCALA) in condemning violence and racism toward Black people and all people of color.

In October, in the weeks leading up to the November election, the board affirmed its support for libraries and urged members to "stand strong," stating, "Libraries are nonpartisan, but they are not indifferent. Libraries are one of the few places where people of diverse backgrounds, beliefs, age groups and socioeconomic levels can gather. ALA supports the right of every eligible individual to cast their ballot without the threat of intimidation or reprisal."

Office for Diversity, Literacy and Outreach Services

Libraries Respond

The ALA Office for Diversity, Literacy and Outreach Services (ODLOS) created Libraries Respond as a space for the office to keep current events in conversation with libraries' ongoing work in and commitment to equity, diversity, and inclusion. In 2020 ODLOS created three new resources: "Black Lives Matter," "Combating Xenophobia and Fake News in Light of COVID-19," and "Supporting and Protecting Transgender Staff and Patrons."

Joint Cultural Competencies Task Force

ACRL, the Association of Research Libraries (ARL), ODLOS, and PLA announced in May the formation of the Building Cultural Proficiencies for Racial Equity Framework Task Force. The group is charged to create a framework for cultural proficiencies in racial equity that can be used in public and academic libraries through conducting an environmental scan, drafting the framework, and seeking comments from stakeholders and the broader library community.

2020 Spectrum Scholars

ODLOS awarded scholarships to 61 exceptional students who are pursuing graduate degrees in library and information studies. Since 1997, ALA has awarded more than 1,240 Spectrum Scholarships.

Adapting EDI Trainings to Virtual Spaces

Since 2016 ODLOS has been facilitating in-person trainings for library audiences on such equity, diversity, and inclusion topics as implicit bias, privilege, microaggressions, and cultural competence. In response to the COVID-19 pandemic, staff adapted these trainings to a virtual format and the office has seen increased demand. In partnership with ALA's Chapter Relations Office, ODLOS provides trainings for library associations and library partners.

Welcoming New Interest Groups

On September 1, 2020, the Association of Specialized Government and Cooperative Library Agencies (ASGCLA) dissolved as a division of ALA. ODLOS welcomed a number of new groups whose purposes closely align with the office's mission:

- Bridging Deaf Culture
- Consumer Health Information Librarians
- Library Services for Dementia/Alzheimer's
- Library Services for the Incarcerated and Detained
- Library Services to Persons with Print Disabilities
- Tribal Librarians
- Universal Access

Chapter Relations Office

Extreme weather across the country damaged libraries. On August 10, a weather storm known as a derecho sent intense winds across the Midwest. The Marion Public Library in Iowa suffered significant interior and exterior damage rendering it unusable to patrons. Hurricanes Laura on August 26 and Delta on October 4 hit Louisiana hard. Through its Library Disaster Relief Fund, ALA sent $10,000 for the Marion Public Library to purchase laptops, tablets, a printer, and wifi hotspots, as they serve their community from temporary locations in the aftermath of the disaster. And $20,000 from the Fund allowed Calcasieu Public Library to acquire portable buildings to replace the three branch locations lost to the hurricanes.

The Student Organization of Library and Information Studies (SOLIS) at Old Dominion University created a new ALA student chapter, the first student chapter to be formed in Virginia and the 67th ALA student chapter.

International Relations Office

The "Croatia Linked Data International Symposium" project was the recipient of the International Relations Round Table (IRRT) Mission Enhancement Grant. This project assisted the Croatian Library Association's (CLA's) efforts in fostering the transition from current technologies rooted in Machine Readable Cataloging (MARC) to linked open data both for traditional technical services workflows and discovery.

Public Programs Office

STAR Net STEAM Equity Project

Through the STAR Net STEAM Equity Project, 12 rural public libraries each received $15,000 over four years to participate in professional development activities, support community collaborations, and purchase STEAM learning materials. In partnership with library staff and their community collaborators, the project will empower tweens and their families around equitable STEAM learning and career paths by leveraging their existing strengths, interests, and diverse cultures.

Media Literacy in the Library

In response to the need for media literacy education, ALA released a free digital guide and related webinar series. "Media Literacy in the Library: A Guide for Library Practitioners" contains information, program ideas, and conversation starters on topics like misinformation and disinformation; architecture of the Internet; civics; media landscape and economics; and media creation and engagement.

Peggy Barber Grant

Library workers were invited to apply for the inaugural Peggy Barber Tribute Grant, a programming grant named after the transformative ALA leader responsible for the creation of National Library Week and the Celebrity READ series.

Libraries Transform Communities Engagement Grant

The Milwaukee Wisconsin Public Library for Deaf Storyslam, a free community event in which deaf individuals of varying backgrounds share personal stories and experiences with the broader community, received the first $2,000 grant, part of ALA's Libraries Transforming Communities (LTC) community engagement initiative.

American Dream Grants

Sixteen grants of $5,000 each were awarded to public libraries through ALA and the Dollar General Literacy Foundation. Public libraries were eligible if they served adult English-language learners and were located within 20 miles of a Dollar General retail store, distribution center, or corporate office.

Resilient Communities: Libraries Respond to Climate Change Grants

Twenty-five libraries were selected to receive $1,000 programming grants to support in-person or virtual climate-related programs and activities; a small collection of documentaries/docudramas on DVD, with public performance rights; Climate Resilience Hub support, provided by Communities Responding to Extreme Weather (CREW) in coordination with ALA; and online training and support.

Community Connect: Digital Access at Home

Selected libraries in 14 states were selected for a program supporting digital access and financial capability for rural communities nationwide. They included Washington County Public Library, a rural four-branch system serving 3,600 people in the Florida Panhandle; Camp Verde Community Library, in a central Arizona town of 10,000 in the Verde River Valley; and Estill County Public Library in Irvine, Kentucky.

Emergency Relief

The National Endowment for the Humanities (NEH) awarded ALA $278,000 in emergency relief funds to support humanities projects, including the creation of humanities content and resources for library workers in the face of the COVID-19 global pandemic. The funding, awarded through the NEH Coronavirus Aid, Relief, and Economic Security (CARES) Act, will support the development of professional development materials to help libraries present virtual and socially distanced programming for their communities.

Office for Intellectual Freedom

ALA issued a statement opposing Missouri House Bill 2044, introduced on January 8, 2020, which proposed the creation of five-member "parental library review boards" to identify "age-inappropriate" public library materials and restrict access to those materials. The bill proposed criminal prosecution for librarians who make such materials available to minors and would deny funding to libraries that do not employ parental library review boards to restrict access to their materials.

ALA also opposed Tennessee HB 2721, which would require a parental oversight board to replace policies and library experts in the development of library collections and services. Libraries that fail to comply with the proposed law would lose local funding and incur fines, and librarians and library workers could face jail time.

Responding to health and privacy concerns during the reopening of libraries during the pandemic, the ALA Intellectual Freedom Committee (IFC) and its Privacy Subcommittee approved guidelines to assist library workers: "Guidelines for Reopening Libraries During the COVID-19 Pandemic," and "Guidelines on Contact Tracing, Health Checks, and Library Users' Privacy." In addition, the IFC Privacy Subcommittee sponsored "Protecting Privacy in a Pandemic: A Town Hall for Library and Information Workers," a webinar held in May 2020 to provide an opportunity for library and information workers to discuss their concerns and issues about privacy that are arising as libraries move to digital platforms and remote services during the pandemic.

Public Policy and Advocacy Office

Throughout 2020, as America's libraries continued to provide essential services amid the public health crisis, economic decline, social unrest, and political turmoil, ALA and its nationwide network of advocates demonstrated the value of libraries to policymakers at every level of government, advocating for COVID emergency relief, annual federal funding for libraries, and library broadband—especially for those in communities hit hardest by the pandemic—as well as voter engagement for the 2020 elections and complete count efforts in the 2020 U.S. Census. [For more information, see the report "Legislation and Regulations Affecting Libraries in 2020: A Report from ALA's Public Policy and Advocacy Office" in Part 2 of this volume—*Ed.*]

Division Highlights

American Association of School Librarians

In response to pandemic school closings and the turn to virtual learning, the American Association of School Librarians (AASL) focused on building community and best practice among school library professionals. AASL began hosting weekly town halls to give school librarians the opportunity to discuss the impact the COVID-19 pandemic had on schools, educators, and learners. Topics included innovative ways to engage students virtually and maximize collaboration with other educators.

AASL launched a series of national surveys to capture how school librarians are indispensable in their schools, districts, and states. The resulting snapshots provided insight into the school library resources and instruction school librarians were providing in physical, virtual, or hybrid settings to ensure teaching and learning. School librarians continued to serve students, other educators, parents, and the learning community through the pandemic. AASL curated resources to support teaching, learning, and safety during school closures and when schools reopened. Bloggers on AASL's Knowledge Quest website explored digital tools and resources, recommended books and resources, and highlighted ways to expand school library practice and professional learning networks.

Association for Library Service to Children

The impact of COVID-19 has played a significant role in motivating major shifts in activities, practices, and conversations among library professionals and other groups serving children and their caregivers. Several areas of interest have become discussion points within the children's library profession, as library workers pivoted workflow processes and services. In 2020 ALSC worked to ensure library professionals are equipped to lead the reimagining of youth library services and build awareness for the integral role libraries play in their communities.

To support advocacy efforts, ALSC launched #LookToLibraries in August 2020, offering free access to media mentoring tools and resources to support library professionals in all types of libraries and caregivers as they assist children with understanding and healing in challenging situations. Resources include booklists and a compilation of web resources from expert sources, such as the Centers for Disease Control and Prevention (CDC), to provide guidance on talking with children about sensitive topics, COVID-19, and managing stress, and keeping children healthy while school is out.

The Virtual Storytime Services Guide was created in response to the pandemic and the need for library staff to transition their in-person programming to virtual opportunities for their communities. ALSC worked with member volunteers and Colorado Libraries for Early Literacy to develop the comprehensive guide, which features best practices, resources, and tips on how to plan, promote, and conduct virtual storytime programming.

Seminars and Conferences

The 2020 Bill Morris Seminar: Book Evaluation Training was held during the 2020 ALA Midwinter Meeting, bringing together 56 participants, facilitators, speakers, and ALSC board members for an all-day training in book evaluation.

The 2020 Charlemae Rollins President's Program, "Telling Our Authentic Story: Connecting, Sharing, and Bridging Divides through Children's Literature," took place virtually on July 14, 2020, at the ALA Annual Conference. The panel presentation drew 300 attendees for a discussion of authenticity in children's literature.

Public Library Association

In 2020 PLA entered its 76th year to many successes but also to huge challenges due to the COVID-19 crisis. By March 2020 PLA and public libraries nationwide found themselves in uncharted waters, with great risk and huge needs, due to the coronavirus. PLA led the field in understanding and educating about COVID-19, fielding two online surveys in March and May 2020 and receiving responses from over 2,500 unique libraries. Survey findings showed that as public libraries closed their buildings to the public, staff continued to serve their communities in innovative ways, expanding access to digital resources, launching virtual programs, and coordinating services with local government agencies.

COVID-19 wasn't the only crisis libraries and communities faced in 2020, as long-standing inequalities and systemic racism came to prominence after high-profile violent acts perpetrated against the Black, Indigenous, and People of Color (BIPOC) communities. PLA issued a statement in July 2020, sharing the anger, sadness, and frustration of members and standing in solidarity with people engaging in collective action against systemic racism, oppression, and injustice. PLA followed the statement with action steps public library staff could take as well as a series of Twitter chats (#chatPLA). Near the end of 2020, PLA launched a new professional development program, PLA Leadership Lab: Embedding EDI in Library Leaders.

PLA initiatives continued to meet critical library and community needs. Thanks to grant funding from Microsoft, PLA supported rural libraries' technology needs by granting hundreds of hotspot devices, laptops, and wifi access points to increase skills and access for community members. PLA promotes skill development and access to employment though its programs like DigitalLearn and its Skilling for Employment Post COVID-19 initiative. For the third year, PLA's

Promoting Health Communities: Libraries Connecting You to Coverage initiative helped libraries promote health insurance enrollment. Also in 2020 PLA completed its project Public Libraries Respond to the Opioid Crisis with Their Communities, funded by IMLS and in partnership with OCLC. By the end of 2020, nearly 2,000 libraries had used PLA's Project Outcome to measure and analyze their program outcomes, collecting 323,261 survey responses from program participants.

Reference and User Services Association

Lost Children Archive, by Valeria Luiselli, published by Alfred A. Knopf, a division of Penguin Random House LLC, was chosen as the winner of the 2020 Andrew Carnegie Medal for Excellence in Fiction, while *Midnight in Chernobyl*, by Adam Higginbotham, published by Simon & Schuster, won the 2020 Andrew Carnegie Medal for Excellence in Nonfiction. The selections were announced at RUSA's Book and Media Awards ceremony, sponsored by NoveList, during the ALA Midwinter Meeting.

These awards, established in 2012, serve as a guide to help adults select quality reading material. They are the first single-book awards for adult books given by ALA and reflect the expert judgment and insight of library professionals and booksellers who work closely with adult readers. [See the "Distinguished Books" section of Part 5 in this volume for listings of notable and award-winning books, audiobooks, and digital media recommended by ALA and other organizations—*Ed.*]

United for Libraries

United for Libraries: The Association of Library Trustees, Friends, and Foundations, hosted its first virtual conference in August 2020. The virtual event featured four keynotes and seven programs on topics including fundraising; advocacy; planning; board development; and equity, diversity, and inclusion.

Between April and September of 2020, United for Libraries sponsored or cosponsored nine COVID-related webinars with a combined total of more than 25,000 registrations for the live events and thousands more for on-demand access. Additionally, more than 8,000 people were provided direct access to the webinars through statewide membership/training with United for Libraries.

Young Adult Library Services Association

YALSA's 2020 symposium was held virtually November 6–8, 2020, with the theme "Biggest Little Spaces: How Libraries Serve the Expanding Worlds of Teens." The Symposium included a variety of educational programs, author talks, and electronic galleys.

Also in 2020 YALSA released its recommended reading list, Outstanding Books for the College Bound (OBCB). Developed every five years as a tool for students preparing for college, educators, librarians, and parents, the OBCB is organized in five categories:

- Arts and Humanities
- History and Cultures

- Literature and Language Arts
- Science and Technology
- Social Sciences

Publishing

ALA Editions | ALA Neal-Schuman

Professional development books published by ALA in 2020 included

- *Design Thinking*, by Rachel Ivy Clarke
- *Management Basics for Information Professionals*, 4th ed., by G. Edward Evans and Stacey Greenwell
- *Law Librarianship in the Age of AI*, edited by Ellyssa Kroski
- *Gather 'Round the Table: Food Literacy Programs, Resources, and Ideas for Libraries*, by Hillary Dodge
- *Enhancing Teaching and Learning: A Leadership Guide for School Librarians*, 4th ed., by Jean Donham and Chelsea Sims
- *Cultivating Civility: Practical Ways to Improve a Dysfunctional Library*, by Jo Henry, Joe Eshleman, and Richard Moniz
- *Copyright Law for Librarians and Educators: Creative Strategies and Practical Solutions*, 4th ed., by Kenneth D. Crews
- *Linked Data for the Perplexed Librarian*, by Scott Carlson, Cory Lampert, Darnelle Melvin, and Anne Washington (published in collaboration with ALCTS)
- *Collection Management for Youth: Equity, Inclusion, and Learning*, 2nd ed., by Sandra Hughes-Hassell
- *STEAM Activities in 30 Minutes for Elementary Learners*, by Deborah Rinio (AASL)
- *The Newbery and Caldecott Awards: A Guide to the Medal and Honor Books*, 2020 ed. (ALSC)
- *Intellectual Freedom Stories from a Shifting Landscape*, edited by Valerie Nye (OIF)
- *Young Activists and the Public Library: Facilitating Democracy*, by Virginia A. Walter
- *Libraries and the Substance Abuse Crisis: Supporting Your Community*, by Cindy Grove
- *Foundations of Library and Information Science*, 5th ed., by Richard E. Rubin and Rachel G. Rubin
- *Diversity, Equity, and Inclusion in Action: Planning, Leadership, and Programming*, edited by Christine Bombaro
- *A Trauma-Informed Approach to Library Services*, by Rebecca Tolley
- *Developing and Maintaining Practical Archives: A How-To-Do-It Manual*, 3rd ed., by Gregory S. Hunter

- *Classroom Management for School Librarians*, by Hilda K. Weisburg
- *Makerspaces in Practice: Successful Models for Implementation*, edited by Ellyssa Kroski

The ALA Editions title *Law Librarianship in the Age of AI*, edited by Ellyssa Kroski, was awarded the 2020 Joseph L. Andrews Legal Literature Award by the American Association of Law Libraries (AALL). Additionally, the publications board of the Society of American Archivists (SAA) selected for its 2020/2021 "One Book, One Profession" reading initiative the ALA Neal-Schuman title *A Matter of Facts: The Value of Evidence in an Information Age*, by Laura A. Millar.

ALA Graphics

ALA Graphics, home of the iconic Celebrity READ campaign and exclusive art from award-winning children's book illustrators, is also the official source of materials for National Library Week, Library Card Sign-up Month, and Banned Books Week, among other events. In 2020, American ice-dancing duo and Olympic bronze medalists Maia Shibutani and Alex Shibutani joined the Celebrity READ campaign, as did Marley Dias, the 15-year-old founder of #1000BlackGirlBooks. And from a galaxy far, far away, "The Child" (aka Baby Yoda, or Grogu) from the Disney+ live action television series *Star Wars: The Mandalorian*, appeared on a READ poster and bookmark.

With a focus on diversity, new posters and bookmarks celebrated Black History, Women's History, and Asian/Pacific American Heritage, illustrated by Ekua Holmes, Laura Freeman, and Dan Santat, respectively. Sophie Blackall created a new poster and bookmark inspired by her 2019 Caldecott Medal–winning picture book, *Hello Lighthouse*.

Booklist

Booklist's internationally recognized, award-winning staff published 26 issues in 2020. The publication remains the most trusted collection development and readers' advisory resources in the field, publishing more than 8,000 original reviews annually. With counsel from its diverse advisory board members, *Booklist* offered more than 150 columns, essays, author interviews, lists, read-alikes, core collections, and related content in 2020. *Booklist* also publishes the popular Book Links, a quarterly supplement in print and online formats dedicated to publishing the very best literature-based resources for educators and librarians. *Booklist* is the sponsor or cosponsor of various ALA media awards, including the Andrew Carnegie Medals for Excellence in Fiction and Nonfiction, the Michael L. Printz Award, the William C. Morris Award, and the Odyssey Award.

American Libraries

American Libraries magazine is the flagship publication of ALA and its 57,000 members, covering news, trends, professional development, commentary, and product information. It is published six times per year, plus one digital-only issue and occasional supplements. In 2020, cover stories included a U.S. Census special report (March/April); Coping in the Time of COVID-19, a series on how libraries were adapting to the pandemic (June); a feature on advancing digital equity during COVID-19 (July/August); the annual Library Design Showcase (September), recognizing the architectural feats of new and renovated buildings; and a story on how patrons countered pandemic isolation with online games of Dungeons & Dragons (November/December).

Other highlights included previews and coverage for ALA's Midwinter Meeting and ALA Virtual conferences; Marshall Breeding's annual Library Systems Report (May); "The Rainbow's Arc," a collection of interviews celebrating the Rainbow Round Table's 50th anniversary (June); "Let Them Lead," a story about how libraries support teens in their activism, including those who participated in Black Lives Matter demonstrations (November/December); and interviews with politician Stacey Abrams, cookbook authors Marcus Samuelsson and Osayi Endolyn, and authors Julia Alvarez, Laurie Halse Anderson, Yaa Gyasi, and Samantha Irby.

American Libraries published its annual "The State of America's Libraries" report during National Library Week (April 4–10, 2020), in partnership with ALA's Communications and Marketing Office.

American Libraries Online

More than 212 online-only features and Scoop blog posts were published at American Libraries Online (americanlibraries.org) in 2020. Much of the year's coverage centered on how COVID-19 affected the library world, covering topics such as safety measures, library closings, digital programming, outdoor services, contact tracing, and worker furloughs. "How to Sanitize Collections in a Pandemic" was the website's most-read story of the year.

AL Direct

AL Direct is *American Libraries'* award-winning weekly e-newsletter, covering library news, activities, facilities, events, state and federal legislation, and more. It is delivered to nearly 40,000 library professionals every Wednesday. The top three AL Direct news items in 2020 were "Reclosing . . . After Reopening," a story about libraries struggling with the decision to keep buildings open or closed during the pandemic; "2020 Holiday Gift Guide for Librarians and Book Lovers"; and "Are There Exceptions to Face-Mask Requirements?," an installment of the Letters of the Law series.

Call Number Podcast

In 2020, *American Libraries* renamed its Dewey Decibel podcast "Call Number with American Libraries," to distance itself from the problematic legacy of Melvil Dewey. Call Number continues to release monthly, half-hour episodes (with occasional bonus installments) featuring conversations with librarians, authors, celebrities, and scholars on topics affecting the library world. Popular episodes in 2020 included "Libraries Respond to COVID-19"; "Patron Privacy," an episode on how COVID-19 has exacerbated privacy issues such as Zoombombing; and "Small and Rural Libraries."

American Booksellers Association

333 Westchester Ave., Suite 202, White Plains, NY 10604
915-406-7500
World Wide Web http://www.bookweb.org

Founded in 1900, the American Booksellers Association (ABA) is a national not-for-profit trade organization that celebrated its 120th anniversary in 2020 and that supports more than 2,000 independent bookstores across the country. These stores are community centers that serve a unique role in sharing a love of books, promoting the open exchange of ideas, enriching the cultural life of communities, and creating economically vibrant neighborhoods.

Recognizing the key cultural and economic role that independent bookstores play in their communities, ABA provides information, education, business tools, programs, and advocacy for local businesses, working to strengthen and expand independent bookstores throughout the country. A volunteer board of 13 booksellers governs the association. ABA is headquartered in White Plains, New York.

Beginning the Year with New Leadership and Vision

ABA began 2020 with its 15th annual Winter Institute, held January 21–24 in Baltimore, Maryland. Approximately 755 booksellers (including 292 first-timers) from 450 stores attended the four-day educational and networking event, ABA's largest ever. They were joined by more than 140 authors, 135 publisher partners, and 68 international guests who traveled from as far as the Netherlands, Colombia, Guatemala, and New Zealand.

Among the speakers at the event was incoming ABA CEO Allison K Hill. Addressing booksellers at an opening breakfast, she spoke about her trip from Los Angeles to Baltimore and the conversation she had with her seatmate on the flight, who asked her what she does for a living. "I'm a leader in a movement that changes lives every day," Hill told him. "I talked about the work that we all do: changing lives by putting the right book in someone's hand, creating communities, creating opportunities for the exchange of ideas, defending freedom of speech, publishing and celebrating underrepresented voices, boosting local economies, and contributing to culture and society."

Looking ahead to her role as CEO, Hill noted, "A change in leadership is a tremendous opportunity to reframe the conversation in our industry. I believe that this moment in time is a critical one in the industry. The measure of our success going forward isn't necessarily the number of stores but a more sustainable model, more profitable bookstores, and better wages for booksellers. That future requires a sea change and this week, for me, marks the beginning of that transformation."

In another important leadership change at ABA, Joy Dallanegra-Sanger began 2020 as ABA's COO. She had served as ABA's senior programming officer since 2011 and led the development of several association initiatives, including the Children's Institute, Indies Introduce, and ABA's preorder campaign for the indie channel. ABA president Jamie Fiocco of Flyleaf Books in Chapel Hill, North Carolina, said, "Joy has shown extraordinary leadership in her eight years at ABA, as she has forged essential relationships with our industry partners and developed

programs to help booksellers sell more books at greater profit. ABA is most fortu-
nate to have Allison and Joy heading our staff."

Dallanegra-Sanger said, "I look forward to a strong partnership with Allison and continuing my commitment to strengthening the position of independent
bookstores in the retail marketplace."

Responding to Unprecedented Challenges

Less than two months after the end of the Winter Institute, the book industry, the
nation, and the world would face an extraordinary transformation with the outbreak of COVID-19, which in March 2020 was named a global pandemic.

The health crisis triggered the most challenging business environment in the
U.S. in almost 100 years, with a significant portion of the U.S. facing mandated
business closures and social distancing beginning in March. Independent bookstores are unique centers of their communities, places that are especially valued
because they offer opportunities to gather together and connect. The necessary
health steps of social distancing and, in some communities, temporary closures hit
indie bookstores particularly hard.

Responding quickly, ABA, with the help of HarperCollins, ran a full-page,
full-color ad in the *Wall Street Journal* on March 20 to encourage the support of
all local businesses. The publisher generously donated the ad space to ABA and
coordinated its inclusion. The ad, which encourages consumers to "Support local
now, enjoy local later," identified six ways to help out small businesses, including buying a gift card, placing orders online, and sharing with followers on social
media how they've supported local businesses.

But that was just the beginning of the story. Independent bookstores rose to
the challenge, achieving extraordinary growth in online sales in the independent
bookstore channel in 2020. Bookstores that prior to the pandemic were doing less
than 1 percent of their sales online saw the number jump to 80 to 100 percent,
the critical factor being whether their store was open for limited browsing and
in-store shopping or closed to the public. The stores that ABA tracks showed a
680 percent increase in online sales during the year, though in most cases the
increase still couldn't make up for lost in-store sales. As the pandemic continues
in 2021, there's too much uncertainty to make a long-term forecast beyond noting
that online sales are unlikely to ever return to prepandemic levels for most stores.

Beyond online sales, booksellers responded to the crisis with numerous innovations. Independent bookstores are staffed by booksellers with decades of experience, who can help customers find their next great read in a way unmatched by any
algorithm, and booksellers have found numerous virtual ways to help book buyers
discover titles and connect with authors in a post-COVID-19 world. In 2020 many
began offering Instagram Live storytimes for kids; Zoom debut author interviews;
Facebook Live book group meetings; opportunities to FaceTime with bookstore
staff to shop or get recommendations; online book "mixers," where authors, booksellers, and reps are invited to have a drink and talk books; and virtual writing
workshops. Many stores now offer curbside and/or home delivery, including delivering books by bicycle in some communities.

Despite these and many other efforts, U.S. bookstores sales declined overall
in 2020. During the year, 78 ABA member bookstores closed, an average of one
per week after the pandemic began in March.

Following the outbreak, ABA expanded its communications with and outreach to member bookstores. CEO Allison Hill began a daily e-mail update; a weekly COVID-related issue of the association newsletter, *BTW*; twice weekly virtual "coffee breaks" for members, offering support, information, and resources; frequent online marketing and technology meetups; and timely legal webinars and advocacy sessions.

While ABA's initial efforts focused on advocacy, education, communication, community, and helping members dramatically ramp up their e-commerce operations, the association also recognized that members needed financial relief as well. ABA waived membership dues for four months; waived fees for member stores for the association's IndieCommerce and IndieLite ecommerce platforms; waived most of IndieCommerce support fees for the eight weeks of sales generated from April 13 to June 7; and donated $100,000 to the Book Industry Charitable Foundation (Binc) to support booksellers.

In addition, ABA help lead the industrywide campaign #SaveIndieBookstores to support all bookstores nationwide, which launched in April with a $500,000 donation from James Patterson. The bestselling author partnered with Binc and ABA to promote the campaign, and he and other prominent authors called upon writers, readers, and booklovers to contribute. Booksellers were encouraged to access a variety of digital assets at the campaign's website to promote the effort, including logos and social media images. At its close on May 5 the #SaveIndieBookstores campaign had raised a total of $1,239,595 to support independent booksellers across the country, with immediate funding to offset business lost due to the COVID-19 crisis. More than 1,800 donors contributed to the cause.

As COVID relief legislation was being crafted in Washington, D.C., ABA's advocacy team communicated member needs and concerns about government financial assistance with the staffs of the House and Senate Small Business Committees; worked with other trade organizations and built coalitions; and regularly provided member bookstores with key information about state and federal financial assistance and new IRS regulations, answering members' questions via e-mail, webinars, and twice-weekly member virtual "coffee break" meetings. The ABA member website, BookWeb.org, provided convenient access to an extensive range of content outlining and explaining business-related relief benefits and options for members.

Also in 2020, ABA implemented new advocacy software that allowed the Advocacy team to more efficiently stay on top of key legislative and regulatory updates. The software has a database of key contact information for federal and state lawmakers and allows ABA members to contact their lawmakers using a one-click tool.

Going into the 2020 holiday season, there were concerns that potential breakdowns in the supply chain might prevent bookstores from quickly restocking popular titles. An additional concern was the USPS's ability to deliver gifts shipped from stores in a timely manner. With these and other likely disruptions in mind as booksellers entered the fourth-quarter sales season, ABA created a range of DIY images and designs that stores employed to encourage readers to shop early. These promotions, which featured the motto "October is the new December" and the message "buy early, buy local," appeared in retailer newsletters, on websites, in stores, and across social media throughout the fourth quarter.

To address the threat of closure facing many ABA member bookstores, in October the association launched a campaign designed to promote indie bookstores nationally and speak to the critical choice between shopping indie and shopping Amazon. The #BoxedOut campaign, timed to coincide with Amazon's Prime Day, debuted with six indie bookstore installations and a national social media effort that all ABA member booksellers were invited to join. "Boxed Out" was designed by DCX Growth Accelerator, the agency behind Payless Shoes' "Palessi" prank, which received the Silver Agency of the Year award from *AdAge*.

To tangibly demonstrate how the U.S. has been overtaken by the ubiquitous cardboard Amazon boxes, DCX created bespoke cardboard coverings to dominate each storefront. Piles of cardboard boxes spilled out of the now-cardboard buildings, stamped with such messages as "If you want Amazon to be the world's only retailer, keep shopping there." Cardboard books further brought the campaign message to life, with "titles" like *To Kill a Locally Owned Bookstore*.

The campaign's signature "Boxed Out" installations were located in New York at McNally Jackson in Manhattan; Cafe con Libros, Community Bookstore, and Greenlight Bookstore in Brooklyn; Book Soup in West Hollywood; and Solid State in Washington, D.C. To help member bookstores nationwide participate, ABA provided materials that included social media assets and materials such as posters and graphics for creating an in-store installation, as well as a sample press release and talking points to share with local media.

At the campaign's launch, ABA CEO Allison K Hill said, "People may not realize the cost and consequences of 'convenience' shopping until it's too late. More than one indie bookstore a week has closed since the COVID-19 crisis began. At the same time, a report forecasts that Amazon will generate $10 billion in revenue on October 13 and 14 during its Prime Day promotion. Connecting these dots, it's clear to see convenience has a cost and a consequence. Closed indie bookstores represent the loss of local jobs and local tax dollars; the loss of community centers; and the loss of opportunities for readers to discover books and connect with other readers in a meaningful face-to-face way."

"Boxed Out" garnered widespread national media attention, with coverage from, among others, *PBS NewsHour*, the *New York Times*, the *Boston Globe*, *Adweek*, AP, and Vox. The campaign quickly went viral, and within two weeks had reached more than 427 million viewers of bookstore-related content.

Also in the fourth quarter, author, journalist, and former national evening news anchor Dan Rather served as the 2020 spokesperson for Indies First, ABA's national campaign in support of independent bookstores that takes place annually on Small Business Saturday. Utilizing a range of social media assets and accompanying text created to promote Indies First, Rather encouraged readers of all ages to visit their local indie bookstores on November 28 in honor of Indies First / Small Business Saturday. In the days leading up to the celebration, Rather tweeted in support of independent bookstores, as well as throughout the day on Small Business Saturday. In addition, a national Zoom event featuring Rather took place on December 2.

Association and Governance

The results of balloting by the bookstore members of ABA to elect directors to serve on the ABA board were announced in May 2020. Elected to three-year terms (2020–2023) as directors were Kenny Brechner of Devaney, Doak & Garrett

Booksellers in Farmington, Maine; Christine Onorati of WORD in Brooklyn, New York, and Jersey City, New Jersey; and Tegan Tigani of Queen Anne Book Company in Seattle, Washington. Brechner and Onorati are coming to the end of their first three-year terms on the board, while Tigani was serving the unexpired period of what would have been ABA president Jamie Fiocco's term as a board member and was now eligible for a full term.

Continuing on the 11-member board are ABA president Jamie Fiocco of Flyleaf Books in Chapel Hill, North Carolina, and ABA vice president Bradley Graham of Politics and Prose Bookstore in Washington, D.C., as well as board directors Jenny Cohen of Waucoma Bookstore in Hood River, Oregon; Kelly Estep of Carmichael's Bookstore in Louisville, Kentucky; Kris Kleindienst of Left Bank Books in St. Louis, Missouri; Chris Morrow of Northshire Bookstore in Manchester Center, Vermont, and Saratoga Springs, New York; Pete Mulvihill of Green Apple Books in San Francisco, California; and Angela Maria Spring of Duende District Books in Washington, D.C., and Albuquerque, New Mexico.

ABA members also voted in favor of association bylaws changes in 2020. Importantly, in July, member stores approved bylaws changes that increased the number of ABA board members from 11 to 13 and stipulated that the board will include at least four booksellers who are Black, Indigenous, or People of Color, at least two of whom are Black. Following the approval of that bylaws change, the board welcomed two new board members, Jake Cumsky-Whitlock of Solid State Books in Washington, D.C., and Melanie Knight of Books Inc. in San Francisco, California.

On Thursday, June 11, 2020, ABA hosted a virtual version of its Town Hall, where booksellers were invited to share their thoughts about the association and the book industry at large. The meeting was facilitated by ABA president Jamie Fiocco. Fiocco was joined by ABA CEO Allison Hill, ABA VP Bradley Graham, and fellow board members.

The Town Hall saw a number of discussions surrounding diversity, antiracism, inclusion, and free speech, with some members challenging the association to take steps to ensure that all members are represented and heard from, are part of the ABA governance process, and feel safe at association events. During the Town Hall, Angela Maria Spring of Duende District Bookstore said, "Everyone, including the board and ABA . . . We need to be listening to the Black community and other minority communities, and hearing what they need before we can incorporate it. That goes across the board for every industry, for anything that anybody does."

ABA took several steps during 2020 to respond to the challenges of more fully meeting the needs of its Black, Indigenous, and People of Color (BIPOC) members and increasing diversity, equity, and inclusion. In addition to the board bylaws change, ABA continued to waive fees for new BIPOC members and to conduct outreach to Black-owned bookstores and BIPOC-owned bookstores in general; instituted monthly BIPOC meetups and periodic surveys about the needs of participants; began conducting quarterly BIPOC forums to hear directly about BIPOC member needs and concerns and offer support; and revised the ABA member application to include demographic data in order to better represent and support bookstore members.

In addition, ABA created a resource page for Black Lives Matter and a Diversity resource page on the association website, Bookweb.org. ABA staff participated in an antiracism training session, and follow-up staff meetings offered the opportunity to discuss matters related to the important issue and to share materials for discussion. The ABA staff committee focusing on equity and access has informed and assisted ABA's outreach to Black-owned bookstores. More than 35 Black-owned bookstores joined ABA in 2020.

Education throughout the Year

The realities of the pandemic in 2020 meant that ABA could not offer its annual in-person conferences or participate in other in-person regional industry events. In response, however, the association moved events online and modified schedules so that virtual programming was offered on an ongoing basis to members.

In July ABA hosted a Virtual Children's Institute. Nearly 400 independent booksellers came together for the event, and highlights included a keynote with author Isaac Fitzgerald; a conversation between Newbery Award–winning authors Kwame Alexander and Jerry Craft; and education sessions on store voice and profitability as well as representation of Black girls in middle grade and young adult science fiction and fantasy titles.

Throughout the year, ABA produced and distributed a wide range of ongoing educational and professional development content to its members virtually. This included hosting two webinars on the importance of reporting aggregate numbers on stores' sales and an eight-part webinar series on preparing for the critical fourth-quarter holiday sales season. And each month the association hosted ABA Meetups for members that focused on marketing and technology topics. The meetups are an opportunity to socialize and learn from fellow booksellers on a range of relevant topics in a friendly, welcoming atmosphere. Also scheduled throughout the year are ABA Coffee Breaks, live forums hosted by ABA where booksellers can talk with one another about any bookselling-related topics. Five Coffee Breaks are scheduled each month, and the sessions are an open forum.

In addition, the ABA Children's Group hosted the first event in its Virtual Reading Series for educators and students in October with a four-part series featuring authors Ibi Zoboi and Yusef Salaam presenting their young adult novel, *Punching the Air*. In November ABA offered the second installment of the consumer-focused reading series with a two-part program featuring Black Lives Matter founder and author Patrisse Khan-Cullors. The session was moderated by Hannah Oliver Depp, owner of Loyalty Bookstores in Washington, D.C., and Silver Spring, Maryland, and focused on the young readers edition of *When They Call You a Terrorist: A Story of Black Lives Matter and the Power to Change the World*.

Member Support—Health Care

In 2020, the Book Industry Health Insurance Partnership (BIHIP), a coalition of 11 organizations, including ABA, announced a partnership with Lighthouse Insurance Group (LIG) Solutions to provide members with a choice of health insurance options. The goal of the initiative was to find a company that could provide coalition members with extensive knowledge of the health insurance market to help members navigate the wide array of insurance options. Additionally, the coalition wanted to ensure that the program would benefit all stores and employees, including individual members and their immediate family; business owners and their W2 employees; 1099-employees / independent contractors; association volunteers; and association staff and immediate family.

In support of this effort, ABA sponsored webinars and offered ongoing information updates to assist members through open enrollment and Affordable Care Act health coverage periods.

Association of Research Libraries

21 Dupont Circle NW, Washington, DC 20036
202-296-2296, email webmgr@arl.org
World Wide Web http://www.arl.org

Kaylyn Groves
Senior Writer and Editor

The Association of Research Libraries (ARL) is a nonprofit organization of 125 research libraries in Canada and the United States whose mission is to advance research, learning, and scholarly communication. The Association fosters the open exchange of ideas and expertise; advances diversity, equity, and inclusion; and pursues advocacy and public policy efforts that reflect the values of the library, scholarly, and higher education communities. ARL forges partnerships and catalyzes the collective efforts of research libraries to enable knowledge creation and to achieve enduring and barrier-free access to information.

Following are highlights of ARL's achievements in 2020, many of which were undertaken in partnership with member libraries or other organizations. For more details, please visit https://www.arl.org/annualreport2020/.

2020 Highlights

During 2020 ARL navigated major societal and institutional challenges by prioritizing the opportunities and addressing the core concerns of research libraries and archives. The COVID-19 pandemic dominated our members' lives in 2020. ARL provided a venue for our members to learn from one another as events unfolded, as well as to highlight their actions to address the crisis, such as supporting research and documenting the present for the future. We used our collective voice to support open access to digital content under the current conditions, including supporting controlled digital lending. We accelerated our commitment to advancing open science, particularly as it relates to research data, copyright, and open monographs.

The nationwide protests against police brutality toward Black people in the U.S. were a stark reminder of the urgent need to dismantle systemic racism and to act on our principles of diversity, equity, and inclusion within our profession. Our public statements made our position clear. We redesigned our flagship Leadership Fellows program to prepare leaders for a world of continual opportunities and challenges, and to lead with diversity, equity, and inclusion at the center of all they do. We created two new positions, one for the senior director of Leadership and Organizational Development and the other for the senior director of Diversity, Equity, and Inclusion. Both positions focus on ensuring we deliver opportunities for diverse and underrepresented individuals in our profession, and that all leaders have the competencies and support they need to create diverse and equitable organizations.

2020 by the Numbers

Member Engagement

- 124 member institutions
- 14 new member representatives welcomed
- 87 percent of member representatives actively engaged in the work of the Association

Representation

- 10 partner boards and steering committees (AGU, BRDI, Dryad, IARLA, OA Working Group, ROR, SCOSS, SocArXiv, SPARC, U.S. National Committee for CODATA)
- With the Library Copyright Alliance, 2 testimonies and 3 comments
- 239 online media mentions

Expertise and Thought Leadership

- 20 publications
- 3 presentations
- 13 statements on enduring, equitable access to information, and on diversity, equity, and inclusion
- 37 blog posts

Events

- 78 organizations, including 30 ARL members, participated in Fair Use Week
- 13 Peer-to-Peer Confabs for ARL directors and AULs
- 3 Library Assessment Conference sessions with 881 participants
- 2 Association Meetings: Spring Meeting with 154 registrants, Fall Meeting with 168 registrants
- 1 ARL Fall Forum with 427 participants
- 1 TOME Meeting with 107 registered

Educational Programs

- $639,000+ invested in fellows and scholars programs, including sponsorships
- 24 Leadership & Career Development Program (LDCP) Fellows accepted with 24 career coaches recruited
- 20 webinars for LCDP and the ARL Fellowship for Digital & Inclusive Excellence (AFDIE)
- 18 Kaleidoscope Diversity Scholars accepted with 18 mentors recruited
- 16 virtual sessions for LCDP Fellows and Kaleidoscope Program Scholars with 314 participants

- 5 member sessions with 211 participants
- 3 *On the Edge* sessions with 161 participants

Resources and Tools

- 599,778 pageviews on ARL.org
- 11.5k Twitter followers, a gain of 11.6 percent
- 8,965 unique views on the Member Resources website
- 5,413 Facebook fans, a gain of 1.2 percent
- 2,756 subscribers to the weekly *ARL News* e-mail
- 1,014 subscribers to the *Day in Review* e-mail (introduced July 17, 2020)
- 66 Instagram followers on new account (introduced October 19, 2020)
- 21 institutions who conducted the LibQUAL+ survey
- 13 briefings for member representatives on public policy and higher education, a gain of 3.4 percent

Advocate for Public Policies in Support of Our Mission and Shared Objective

Our priority is to advocate and advance law and policy that safeguard and further the interests of researchers and learners by ensuring that libraries can acquire, share, lend, reformat, and preserve content with maximum digital affordances. ARL partners with the Canadian Association of Research Libraries (CARL) on Canadian public policy issues and works in coalition with the International Alliance of Research Library Associations (IARLA) on global policy development.

Ensure an Environment That Supports Accessible, Sustainable, Equitable, Barrier-Free Scholarship, with User Privacy

ARL is the collective voice for research libraries and archives on public policy in the U.S. and internationally. The Association leads on policy and legal issues that advance sustainable, equitable, and barrier-free access to information and culture while protecting core values of privacy and freedom of expression. We do much of this work through the Library Copyright Alliance (LCA), whose membership includes ARL, the American Library Association (ALA), and the Association of College & Research Libraries (ACRL).

Accessibility

The ARL–CARL Joint Task Force on Implementation of the Marrakesh Treaty began meeting in September 2020. In 2019, the United States joined the Marrakesh Treaty, the goal of which is to facilitate access to print works for visually impaired persons and persons with print disabilities across international borders. An estimated 7 percent of published works are available in formats accessible to people with print disabilities, a problem known as the global book famine. With the legal framework around the Marrakesh Treaty established—in the United States, this included amendments to Section 121 of the Copyright Act—the ARL-CARL task force will support an interinstitutional pilot project to test cross-border lending.

Copyright and Fair Use

LCA filed an amicus brief in support of Google in an ongoing case against Oracle, in which Google claims its use of Oracle application programming interfaces (APIs) to develop new software is a fair use. In the brief, LCA asks that the U.S. Supreme Court consider implications on the settled state of fair use law in its deliberation and determination. A ruling on this case is expected in 2021.

In response to a request by the U.S. Copyright Office for comments on state sovereign immunity, LCA submitted comments reiterating many of the points in its 2019 amicus brief in the related Supreme Court case *Allen* v. *Cooper*. In *Allen* v. *Cooper*, the Supreme Court dismissed a copyright infringement claim against North Carolina, ruling that Congress lacks the authority to abrogate state sovereign immunity and that the Copyright Remedy Clarification Act is unconstitutional.

Throughout the year, LCA submitted testimony, comments, letters, and petitions supporting the Digital Millennium Copyright Act (DMCA) as an appropriate and powerful tool to address copyright infringement and arguing that any change to DMCA will impact the library community's ability to achieve the constitutional aim of promoting the progress of science and the useful arts. Without the DMCA's exemptions for such work as text- and data-mining research, knowledge about newer works that are still under copyright, and that are more likely to be by or about women and people of color, is precluded.

ARL signed the "Position Statement on Controlled Digital Lending" and issued a statement urging publishers to end their lawsuit against the Internet Archive. Controlled digital lending (CDL) is rooted in the fair use doctrine of U.S. copyright law, and circumstances like the COVID-19 emergency are not part of the test that U.S. courts apply in considering whether a use is fair. However, the urgency of the moment has increased interest in the CDL model and legal theory.

ARL published a commissioned white paper, *Modern Interlibrary Loan Practices: Moving beyond the CONTU Guidelines*, meant to guide libraries in developing standards for interlibrary loan (ILL) practices and copyright payments based on the current research and publishing environment. The original Commission on New Technological Uses of Copyrighted Works (CONTU) guidelines were based on outdated journal pricing, scholarly publishing, and library acquisitions practices from the 1970s, and have not been reevaluated or adjusted as intended.

Higher Education

ARL issued a statement calling on the White House to withdraw its executive order on "Combating Race and Sex Stereotyping," which would disallow agencies from receiving federal grants if federal funds were used for "race or sex stereotyping or any form of race or sex scapegoating." At a time when research libraries and archives are working to acknowledge and address structural racism, ARL's Board expressed deep concern that the executive order would stifle the training that is necessary to provide equitable and meaningful employment opportunities for Black, Indigenous, and other People of Color (BIPOC) in the research library community. A federal judge in California issued a preliminary nationwide injunction halting the executive order. The Biden-Harris Administration will repeal this executive order.

ARL and 69 other higher education associations joined an amicus brief by the American Council on Education (ACE) on behalf of Harvard and MIT, arguing for preliminary injunctive relief to the Department of Homeland Security's 2020 Student Exchange Visitor Program directive. Under the directive, students attending schools that were operating entirely online would not have been allowed to "take a full online course load and remain in the United States," and those institutions that decided to go virtual to protect the health and safety of students, staff, and faculty would subject their international students to deportation. The U.S. government ultimately reversed the directive.

In its work as a member of the Washington Higher Education Secretariat, ARL signed on to letters to the federal government regarding COVID-19 relief funding for higher education, international students, Title XI, and freedom of speech.

Privacy

With several partners ARL filed an amicus brief in the Supreme Court case *Ahmad* v. *University of Michigan* concerning a public record request circumventing a deed of gift. The brief supported the University of Michigan's position that donated papers should be subject to the terms of their negotiated contracts. ARL's concern in this case is that a decision against the university could adversely impact libraries and archives, which rely on deeds of gift to preserve original papers, and ultimately make them accessible. Negating these agreements or determining that donated papers are preempted by public information laws could mean fewer donations of original documents that are necessary to preserve the cultural and historical record.

Catalyze Collective Efforts to Achieve Enduring and Barrier-Free Access to Information

Our priority is to align library strategy, staffing, and spending to advance the principles and practices of open scholarship. Through collective action, ARL works to increase the amount of high-quality scholarship that is openly available and to support and position our members to lead on "open science by design" within their own institutions. Much of this work is done in partnership—with organizations and groups ranging from individual libraries, to peer associations, to disciplinary communities. In 2020, ARL organized a new staff unit of Scholarship and Policy and successfully recruited new directors for both Information Policy and Scholars & Scholarship.

Increase the Amount of Openly Available Scholarship

From shaping and influencing public and institutional policy to enable greater access to scholarship, to specific initiatives to support open monographs, ARL and its member libraries are increasing the amount of scholarship that is openly available. In March 2020 universities and other research institutions closed their physical facilities due to COVID-19, and at the same time saw dire predictions about budget cuts due to lost institutional revenue. The uncertainty of this environment and its time horizon led ARL to sign the International Coalition of Library Consortia (ICOLC) "Statement on the Global COVID-19 Pandemic and Its Impact on Library Services and Resources" and collaborate with the International Alliance of Research Library Associations (IARLA) to amplify the ICOLC statement. Additionally, with the Oberlin Group and the Association of College & Research Libraries (ACRL), ARL urged publishers to continue providing free emergency access and to hold subscription prices steady.

Consistent with the objectives laid out in its 2020 Budget Narrative, ARL also submitted comments on the "Draft NIH Policy for Data Management and Sharing," responded to the U.S. Office of Science and Technology Policy request for comments on "Desirable Characteristics of Repositories," and prepared a prospectus with the Knowledge Futures Group for the National Academies Board of Research Data and Information on the importance of shared open infrastructure to advance university-based publishing. ARL commended cOAlition S on its Rights Retention Strategy for authors and institutions, and participated in the Plan S Rights Retention Strategy Summit. ARL participated on the board of the Global Sustainability Coalition for Open Science Services (SCOSS) and promoted community calls of Invest in Open Infrastructure (IOI) to shape its agenda as a new organization and represent the interests of research libraries.

With our strong partnership with the Association of University Presses (AUPresses), ARL convened virtual meetings of the press and library community (P2L) and TOME (Toward an Open Monograph Ecosystem), which also includes the Association of American Universities (AAU). Both meetings took advantage of the virtual setting to be more inclusive in both presenters and participants, and both used the opportunity to provide new directions and agenda-setting for the respective partnerships.

Advance Open Science by Design

"Open science by design" is a strategy to remove barriers and move toward widespread open access to scientific data, research, and publications. The strategy is based on the principle that research conducted openly and transparently leads to better science as well as more equitable access to knowledge. ARL strengthens research library partnerships within the greater research ecosystem to advance this priority and set of objectives. In 2020 our focus was on research data and the importance of library leadership and participation within institutional and other alliances on data management, sharing, and stewardship.

ARL and CARL launched a Joint Task Force on Research Data Services. The task force will conclude its work in spring 2021 with a report and tools for addressing institutional strategies, national and international data policy, and resilient partnerships.

With funding from the National Science Foundation (NSF) and the National Institutes of Health (NIH), the Association of American Universities (AAU) and Association of Public and Land-grant Universities (APLU) convened a "National Summit on Accelerating Public Access to Research Data." Eleven ARL member representatives attended the summit, along with strong representation from the ARL data librarian community, including members of the ARL-CARL Joint Task Force on Research Data Services. The summit deliverable will be a guide for institutions.

ARL—with partners AAU, APLU, and the California Digital Library— concluded its NSF-funded project Implementing Effective Data Practices, with the publication of a final set of community-vetted recommendations and a toolkit for implementing them within individual institutions.

Create Diverse, Equitable, Inclusive, and Accessible Services, Collections, and Work Environments

At the outset of 2020 our focus shifted to include helping research libraries to both recruit a diverse workforce and develop and maintain inclusive organizations. Our decisions and actions were even more urgent given the continued police brutality against Black people in the United States and the disproportionate impact of COVID-19 on BIPOC communities, which highlighted continuing structural racial inequities. These issues elevated the need for internal reflection about our own structural equity and antiracism practices.

Better Equip ARL Members to Develop and Sustain Diverse and Inclusive Organizations

In a year of historical proportions, we used our voice to condemn systemic racism and violence against Black people and other communities of color and to stand against the executive order on "Combating Race and Sex Stereotyping."

The 2020 ARL Fall Forum "Leading Libraries toward Anti-racism in a Changing World" brought together over 400 attendees. The Julia C. Blixrud Memorial Lecture "New Paradigms of Justice: How Librarians Can Respond to the Knowledge Crisis" was presented by Safiya Noble. We celebrated Nix Mendy, winner of the Blixrud Scholarship, whose "ARL Views" blog post provides a summary of the forum.

We focused on ARL diversity scholars and fellows, and on raising awareness of how institutions can create more diverse and inclusive cultures. The cohorts starting in 2020 include 24 fellows in the Leadership and Career Development Program, 18 scholars in the Kaleidoscope Program, and 5 fellows participating in the ARL/SAA Mosaic Program. With these programs beginning in a time of turmoil, member representatives continued to provide mentorship for fellows, and the Association staff and visiting program officers reenvisioned the mentoring and coaching needed—including providing coaches for the mentors. The final ARL Fellowship for Digital and Inclusive Excellence Program cohort of 12 fellows concluded in June 2020.

In reflecting ARL's guiding principles and commitment to diversity, equity, and inclusion, the Association began a review of its policies, starting with committee membership. Our Association seeks to better reflect our profession and to increase opportunities for our member representatives and their staff in shaping it.

Develop a Framework for DEI Competencies

The latest issue of *Research Libraries Issues* explores diversity, equity, and inclusion (DEI) in research libraries, providing insights based on theory and practice. It includes research on competency frameworks in DEI, as well as training and experiences that libraries and other industries have been implementing on a local level.

This work informs the Joint Task Force on Building Cultural Proficiencies for Racial Equity Framework, formed by the Association of College & Research Libraries (ACRL), Association of Research Libraries (ARL), the American Library Association (ALA) Office for Diversity, Literacy, and Outreach Services (ODLOS), and the Public Library Association (PLA). The framework will be a foundational resource to help academic and public libraries build inclusive cultures. It will offer guidelines on development and implementation of organizational policies, as well as best practices to support diverse workforces.

The Racial Equity Framework will also inform the design of a new ARL Diversity, Equity, and Inclusion Institute. In 2020 the Institute of Museum and Library Services (IMLS) awarded ARL a grant to fund the research and design of this institute. As an urgent priority, the DEI Institute will include a curriculum framework and assessment metrics for training content that will be piloted by ARL following the funding period. The audience for the institute will be staff members in cultural heritage and information organizations who want to build inclusive and equitable organizations and advance broader systemic change.

Provide Data and Analytics on Research Library Practices, Effectiveness, and Impact

ARL's Research and Analytics program conducts data collection, analysis, and reporting on several aspects of research libraries and archives. This was a year of transition for the Research and Analytics program at ARL as the Association welcomed new staff to the team, and saw others move on to exciting new opportunities. In 2020 the program focused much of its attention on making improvements to its assessment tools and website. These modifications provide a foundation on which the Association will be able to build its Research and Analytics program toward measuring impacts and outcomes, and more active and dynamic data reporting.

Provide Leading Research Library Assessment Instruments

We continued ARL's practice of collecting, processing, and publishing data from the annual statistics and salary surveys while also implementing changes to improve our data products. The Salary Survey Task Force formed in 2019 issued its final report, which included several recommendations to enhance Salary Survey data collection and reporting. The ARL executive director accepted the recommendations, and we completed implementation for the 2020 survey cycle data collection. These changes benefit members with a more streamlined, clear, and well-documented Salary Survey instrument.

Extending from 2019 market analysis work, we continued our survey improvement efforts by beginning work on upgrading the LibQUAL+ instrument. The goal of this effort is to enhance the user experience and usability of the survey. Much of 2020 was spent conducting research, outreach, and initial user testing. We look forward to more extensive user testing and introducing a revised product later in 2021.

Communicate the Impact and Relevance of Research Libraries and Archives

Beginning in March 2020, the unforeseen COVID-19 crisis interrupted the Research Library Impact Framework initiative. The crisis forced a number of the project and practice brief teams to put their activities on hold while the teams dealt with the transitions to remote working and remote library services. Throughout this time, the ARL visiting program officers (VPOs) were in regular contact with library teams to reassure them that it was important for members to address their local issues. A virtual meeting in the spring with the team members included a discussion of how colleagues were managing in this time of deep uncertainty and change. As a result of these discussions, and in consultation with the initiative advisory group, ARL requested and received a no-cost extension from this initiative's funder, IMLS, until June 2022.

The ARL deputy executive director and VPOs completed a review with each team to ascertain the status of projects and to identify any additional assistance that might be useful. A virtual meeting in the fall with the project and practice brief teams highlighted that teams were beginning to return to their projects. Several practice briefs will be published in early 2021.

Shape and Inform Leadership Practice throughout Research Libraries

The ARL Academy is a crucial resource for advancing professional development for library leaders as partners in the research enterprise. The unified suite of programs empowers ARL libraries and archives staff with the tools necessary to meet the current and future needs of users. Offerings focus on leadership and skills development; diversity, equity, and inclusion; and the challenges of organizational change.

Develop Library Staff as Partners in the Research Enterprise

Academy Research Project

The Academy Research Project was designed to comprehend and identify the gap between current and future executive leadership roles, express what is changing in the value proposition of libraries as a result of changing roles for deans/directors, identify ways to engage campus leadership about how the dean/director could play new and/or different roles, and identify executive skill-development needs and discussion opportunities to inform ARL programming and strategic priorities. In addition, the project added to its initial scope: identifying themes, impact, and projections regarding COVID-related consequences to higher education broadly and academic libraries specifically.

Leadership Fellows Program

The ARL Leadership Fellows program provides opportunities for leadership growth by combining (1) a curriculum designed for library leadership and (2) enriching relationships with members of a peer cohort and with established, practicing leaders in the research and learning ecosystem. In 2020, following an external program review and subsequent recommendations and approval from the Board of Directors, the Leadership Fellows program was completely redesigned. New structure and new content that include a greater emphasis on diversity, equity, and inclusion were launched in the design and development phase of the program.

AUL/Senior Leadership Institute

The ARL Academy AUL Leadership Institute Task Force served as part of the ARL Academy Advisory Committee and was charged with advising the committee on the design of a high-caliber program for senior library leaders. The task force produced a program plan that refined draft goals and outcomes for the program; recommended professional development needs for senior library leaders; refined draft programmatic elements, learning outcomes, and program evaluation criteria based on the needs of research libraries and attendees; and recommended experts for programmatic elements. The recommendations and design suggestions from the task force will be taken up by the 2020–2021 ARL Academy Advisory Committee.

On the Edge

The ARL Academy presented three *On the Edge* virtual sessions for member representatives and staff in 2020: Torsten Reimer of the British Library led a discussion on research libraries in 2030; Clifford Lynch of the Coalition for Networked Information (CNI) led a session on a series of conversations CNI convened with IT and library leaders; and Lynn Bufka of the American Psychological Association led a discussion on well-being and stress management for senior leaders.

Deepen and Expand Understanding of Research Library Impact

Our commitment is to deepen and expand the understanding of the research library's value and brand identity, particularly in terms of its impact in the research enterprise and more broadly. The societal issues of 2020, including the COVID-19 pandemic and protests against police brutality, solidified the need to place greater emphasis on understanding the role of research libraries and archives in the research community and in institutions, as well as in society at large. We especially emphasized research libraries' role as strongholds of democracy to combat the rise of disinformation. We promoted the work of member libraries, showcased research library expertise, and publicly supported policies and initiatives that further the missions and goals of the research enterprise.

Foster a Culture of Engagement and Collaboration among ARL Members

At the onset of the COVID-19 pandemic, ARL Communications launched a number of initiatives focused on promoting the work of member libraries, emphasizing the expertise and necessity of research libraries. Our strategy focused on member benefits and centering the needs of members through the rise of the pandemic. Members received COVID-19 update webpages that began as daily status updates on individual research libraries. As it became evident that longer-term changes would become more widespread, we sent members weekly updates, including news and resource pages from member libraries. Member library communications teams were provided a submission form to share stories about their initiatives and resources concerning COVID-19. ARL published the stories in a series of blog posts.

We launched the *Day in Review* to highlight news stories and resources relating to the research enterprise. The *Day in Review* quickly became an enjoyed asset, now reaching more than 1,000 daily recipients by e-mail. On social media, ARL shares articles and news from member libraries and strategic partners.

We launched the *ARL Views* blog in order to increase storytelling concerning the work of ARL members, using the blog to promote research library trends.

We engaged with members through interviews, submission forms, and the ARL Communicators Google Group.

Near the end of 2020, we conducted a survey of member library communications staff that will help us assess additional needs that help toward building a culture of engagement and collaboration.

Increase Reach within the Research and Learning Community, Higher Education, and Public Affairs

ARL Communications staff used the events of 2020 as opportunities to promote our members' work and connect how their work impacts institutions and society as a whole. We published news releases and statements that spoke to the societal issues of our time and also uplifted research libraries as democratic institutions committed to barrier-free access to information, intellectual freedom, diversity, equity, inclusion, and antiracism.

Statements published on ARL.org as well as posts on the "ARL Views" blog highlighted ARL's mission and goals. We branded the "ARL Views" blog so it could function as a noticeable key resource for storytelling and information. We also merged past "ARL Policy Notes" blog posts into the new blog to make them readily available and easy to find.

We received positive public response to our statements and blog posts, exemplified by interviews, citations, and media mentions.

The Scholarly Publishing and Academic Resources Coalition

Heather Joseph

Executive Director

1201 Connecticut Ave. NW, #608, Washington, DC 20036
202-630-5090, sparc@sparcopen.org
https://www.sparcopen.org

Background and Mission

The Scholarly Publishing and Academic Resources Coalition (SPARC), is a global coalition committed to making Open the default for research and education. SPARC promotes the faster and wider sharing of research outputs and educational materials to increase the impact of research, fuel the advancement of knowledge, and increase the return on research and education investments. SPARC staunchly supports efforts to promote diversity, inclusion, equity, and social justice in and through the library community.

SPARC is a catalyst for action. Supported by 230 members primarily in the United States and Canada, and with international affiliates active in Africa, Europe, and Japan, its pragmatic agenda focuses on collaborating with stakeholders in the global community to encourage new norms, practices, and policies that promote equitable access, sharing, and use of scholarship.

Responding to COVID-19

As the global pandemic unfolded, SPARC and its members scrambled to understand how it would affect operations. Fortunately, SPARC is designed to be agile and was able to quickly review programming priorities and supporting resources. The organization was already structured to function largely as a virtual organization, having moved away from large in-person meetings to more targeted regional and virtual events, so operational disruption was minimal. Additionally, SPARC's key focus areas, providing open access to research articles and data, as well as promoting Open Educational Resources, proved to be central to enabling higher education's continuity of operations during the pandemic. SPARC also set up a COVID-19 resource to equip members with tools to help them quickly pivot to address new circumstances on their campuses.

Strategy

To promote the changes in both infrastructure and culture needed to make Open the default in research and education, SPARC's strategy centers on

1 Advocating for policies that enable Open practices throughout research and education

2 Educating stakeholders on opportunities to change the scholarly communication system
3 Incubating projects that promote new models for sharing research outputs
and developing educational materials that support the needs of scholars
and society

SPARC works to identify shared values and opportunities for action between its
library members and stakeholders in the global research and education environment,
including faculty and administration, public and private research funders, and the
public. SPARC places a premium on empowering students and early career professionals, and actively incorporates collaboration with them across all program areas.

Priorities

SPARC's work focuses on Open Access, Open Data, Open Education, Open Infrastructure, and Realigning Incentives to support Open Research. Additionally, to
maximize progress, SPARC supports efforts that champion intellectual freedom, a
free and open Internet, privacy, confidentiality, and equitable copyright and intellectual property policies.

The following were key priorities in 2020:

Conducting Policy Advocacy

SPARC's top priority continued to be to advance policies that promote Open
Access to research outputs (including articles and data) and educational materials
at the institutional, state, national, and international levels. SPARC has advanced
this priority by

- Educating key policymakers (including Executive Branch, U.S. Congress,
  and others) on SPARC's core policy priorities. Proactively working with
  regulators and legislators to educate them on issues in the scholarly pub-
  lishing market, and to initiate interventions where necessary.
- Developing proactive strategies to extend/expand policy progress in the
  United States and Canada, and globally, as well as defend against threats
  to existing policies.
- Leveraging stakeholder communities to accelerate policy progress.
- Working with the media to promote public awareness of the benefits of
  Open policies.
- Working with private funders by convening the Open Research Funders
  Group to create and implement Open policies in the United States and
  globally.

Educating Leaders on Retaining Control of Scholarly Communications Infrastructure and Data

SPARC concentrated its work on leveraging resources to sustain crucial infrastructure underpinning the scholarly communications ecosystem. That work included

- Leading research and development efforts on new economic and organizational models for the collective provisioning of Open resources and infrastructure, including support for targeted new investment instruments, and actively collaborating with community efforts to accelerate progress, including funding and staffing of the new Investing in Open Infrastructure (IOI) organization
- Developing plans for multistakeholder approaches to collectively fund open resources
- Advising nonprofit publishers and other resource providers on designing effective open business models

Promoting Culture Change through Realigning Incentives

SPARC actively promoted strategies for the realignment of existing reward and incentive structures to advance Open as the default in research and education. SPARC's work to further this priority included

- Leveraging the leadership of research funders and higher education leaders at the university president/provost level to serve as champions and peer-influencers to promote incentive realignment
- Serving as organizers, in partnership with the National Academy of Sciences, Engineering and Medicine (NASEM) Roundtable on Realigning Incentives, comprised of research funders and higher education leaders promoting peer-to-peer discussion and development of strategies to promote adoption of practices and policies rewarding open sharing of research outputs and educational resources
- Supporting the activities of the Roundtable's six working groups and together creating a toolkit for national use by institutions and funders
- Encouraging inclusion of rewards/recognition for Open behaviors in all relevant funder and institutional documents including orientation materials, funding solicitations, and job postings in addition to evaluation and promotion guidelines
- Promoting exemplars that have made demonstrable progress toward realigning rewards
- Supporting research into current evaluation, reward, and incentive structures
- Leveraging the OpenCon community to promote culture change within the next generation

Providing Resources to Support Campus Action

SPARC produced and promoted resources that enable its members to take timely and informed actions. SPARC's work to advance this priority included

- Providing members up-to-the-moment updates and analyses of key policy and scholarly communications–related trends and developments
- Issuing action alerts and other opportunities for timely member library participation in advocacy, education, and partnership initiatives

- Delivering tools and resources to support member campus advocacy and education activities)
- Providing free member campus consultation by the SPARC team to promote awareness, education, and advocacy for key program areas
- Growing SPARC's Negotiation Community of Practice to support libraries in reevaluating their relationships with commercial vendors, preparing to reduce their subscription spend, and aligning financial investments with library values

Continuing Priorities

Global Collaboration. SPARC continued to reflect and support the global nature of scholarly communications by

- Advocating for better global representation in the leadership of open and scholarly communications–related initiatives
- Drawing attention to the need for more globally inclusive business models for the communication of research results
- Coordinating and promoting International Open Access Week as a catalyst for action across the community
- Identifying new opportunities and establishing partnerships with key stakeholders in other global regions

Supporting Students and Early Career Researchers. SPARC promoted the inclusion of students and early career academic professionals in all areas of Open Access by

- Supporting the OpenCon community for students and early career academic professionals
- Continuing joint advocacy efforts to leverage community presence on Open Access, Open Data, and Open Education, and for related issues
- Maintaining relationships with key national and international organizations representing students and early career academic professionals

Program Activities and Outcomes 2020

Policy and Advocacy

- SPARC regularly represents the community in policy forums and consultations in the United States as well as internationally. Its strong SPARC affiliates in Africa, Europe, and Japan provide it with a network of colleagues and collaborators that strengthens its advocacy presence and reach.
- SPARC led an effort to secure the continued funding for an Open Textbook pilot grant program at the U.S. Department of Education. In 2021, the program will be renewed for $7 million, to expand the use of open textbooks at colleges and universities, which is expected to save students multiple

times the original investment. This brings total funding for the program to $24 million over four fiscal years.

- Supported by pro-bono legal counsel, SPARC led successful opposition that blocked a proposed merger between textbook publishers Cengage and McGraw-Hill.
- SPARC supported the UNESCO consultation on Open Science, providing detailed recommendations and draft language.
- SPARC released an updated State OER Policy Playbook and disseminated recommendations on how state governments and institutions could leverage U.S. federal COVID-19 relief funds to support improved remote learning through OER strategies.
- SPARC provided competitive analyses and recommendations for concrete actions that institutions can take to retain control of infrastructure and data, including the 2020 Update to the SPARC Landscape Analysis and Roadmap for Action.
- SPARC continues to convene the "Open Research Funders Group," whose members include the Gates, Sloan, Arnold, Arcadia, and Soros Foundations, among others, and provides the group with a forum for regular discussion and opportunities for collaboration in strengthening the Open research environment.
- SPARC promoted a full overhaul of the 2013 White House Memorandum on Public Access to Publicly Funded Research Outputs and participated in in-person stakeholder meetings as well as written consultations.

Campus Education

- SPARC's annual International Open Access Week, a partnership with the international Open Access community, continues to grow in popularity and participation. This year's theme was "Open with Purpose: Taking to Build Structural Equity and Inclusion."
- SPARC supported members' local campus efforts by providing free consultations by SPARC staff to member campuses, SPARC-sponsored speakers for events, practical guides, talking points, templates, and expert counsel on campus Open Access and Open Education issues.
- SPARC continued to expand online programs to cover hot topics of interest to members and conduct regular community calls to advance member institutions' efforts in a variety of different topic areas.
- SPARC launched the fourth cohort of its Open Education Leadership Program, for the first time expanding the program to include both librarians and other professionals working in the open education field.
- SPARC served as the operations lead for the 2020 Open Education Conference, supporting a community-driven organizing process that successfully flipped this 17-year-old annual event to virtual for the first time, drawing more than 1,500 participants from 70 countries. SPARC produced a monthly newsletter for members summarizing key happenings and hosted webcasts on important topics, including rapid reaction events to address breaking news.

Communication and Media

SPARC is regularly consulted and quoted as an expert source on topics relating to scholarly communications. Its programs have been featured in both the national and trade press by such outlets as *Bloomberg,* the *New York Times, Nature, Inside Higher Ed, Scientific American,* and *Diverse Issues in Higher Education.*

Through its website, SPARC highlighted the work of Open Access champions. SPARC honored OpenStax with a 2020 Innovator Award. SPARC regularly produced news stories about model policies, emerging trends, initiatives, and impact stories that demonstrate how operating in Open is making a difference in advancing knowledge discovery.

SPARC-ACRL Forums

A major component of SPARC's community outreach occurs at meetings of the American Library Association (ALA), where SPARC works with the Association of College and Research Libraries (ACRL) and its scholarly communication committee to bring current issues to the attention of the community.

In January 2020 the SPARC-ACRL Midwinter Forum in Philadelphia focused on the work and strategic planning that needs to happen before a big deal or journal package negotiation.

In August, the online Forum explored how different institutions are reevaluating their relationships with vendors, seeking to align their spending with their values, and keeping an eye on the long-term consequences of urgent decisions that need to be made in the short term.

Governance

SPARC is guided by a steering committee. The committee members are Gwen Bird (Simon Fraser University), Chris Bourg (Massachusetts Institute of Technology), H. Austin Booth (New York University), Talia Chung (University of Ottawa), Christopher Cox (Clemson University), Karen Estlund (Colorado State University), Scarlet Galvan (Grand Valley State University), Carrie Gits (Austin Community College), Jennifer Grayburn (Union College), Rachel Harding (University of Toronto), Joy Kirchner (York University), Beth McNeil (Purdue University), Carmelita Pickett (University of Virginia), Judy Ruttenberg (Association of Research Libraries), Steven Escar Smith (University of Tennessee–Knoxville), Virginia Steel (University of California–Los Angeles), and Elaine Thornton (University of Arkansas).

Council on Library and Information Resources

211 North Union Street, Suite 100-PMB1027, Alexandria, VA 22314
World Wide Web http://www.clir.org
Twitter @CLIRNews

Kathlin Smith
Director of Communications

The Council on Library and Information Resources (CLIR) is an independent, nonprofit organization that forges strategies to enhance research, teaching, and learning environments in collaboration with academic and cultural institutions, scholars, specialists, and practitioners. CLIR President Charles Henry leads the 20-member staff and works in close liaison with seven CLIR Distinguished Presidential Fellows.

CLIR is supported by fees from sponsoring institutions, grants from public and private foundations, contracts with federal agencies, and donations from individuals. A list of current sponsors, members, and funders is available at https.//www.clir.org/about/current-sponsors-and-funders/.

CLIR's board establishes policy, oversees the investment of funds, sets goals, and approves strategies for their achievement. A full listing of CLIR board members is available at https://www.clir.org/about/governance/.

Responding to the COVID-19 Pandemic

As the COVID-19 virus surged in early spring 2020, CLIR was forced to rethink plans and program administration. Because the organization had already transitioned to a virtual, distributed office in April 2019, staff were accustomed to working remotely and functioning as a team through the use of online collaborative tools. This allowed CLIR to quickly focus on two primary challenges: first, rethinking all of its scheduled conferences, meetings, and workshops; and second, devising responses to the needs and challenges of its grantees and fellows. The following overview of CLIR's activity describes the organization's responses to the challenges of 2020.

Fellowships and Grants

Digitizing Hidden Special Collections and Archives

Digitizing Hidden Special Collections and Archives is a national grant competition administered by CLIR for digitizing rare and unique content in collecting institutions. Supported by the Andrew W. Mellon Foundation, the program is built on the model of CLIR's Cataloging Hidden Special Collections and Archives program, which ran from 2008 to 2014.

Since 2015 Digitizing Hidden Collections has awarded about $4 million annually to institutions holding collections of high value for research, teaching, and learning. A review panel, comprising experts from a range of scholarly and technical disciplines, evaluates proposals and recommends award recipients. Awards range from $50,000 to $250,000 for single-institution projects and $50,000 to $500,000 for collaborative projects.

The COVID-19 crisis has affected the program in three primary ways. First, in response to disruptions at cultural and educational institutions nationwide, CLIR extended the 2020 application and review deadlines by about two months. Grant awards were therefore not announced by the end of 2020 but will become public in late winter 2021. Second, CLIR created a COVID-19 Emergency Relief Fund for recipients of Digitizing Hidden Collections grants whose activities had been impeded or delayed by the pandemic. CLIR awarded $122,280 in emergency funds to support the completion of previously approved primary grant activities. Finally, the Digitizing Hidden Collections Symposium, which was to be held in Baltimore in November 2020, was rescheduled for 2022. To mark five years of funded projects, the grants team instead organized a one-day virtual event in November for grant recipients, reviewers, and program staff.

More information about the Digitizing Hidden Collections program, including a list of funded projects, is available at https://www.clir.org/hiddencollections/.

Recordings at Risk

Launched in 2017 with funding from the Andrew W. Mellon Foundation, Recordings at Risk is a national regranting program to support the preservation of rare and unique audio and audiovisual content of high scholarly value through digital reformatting. It is intended to encourage professionals who may be constrained by limited resources or technical expertise to take action against the threats of media degradation and obsolescence. The program helps institutions identify priorities and develop practical strategies for digital reformatting, build relationships with partners, and raise awareness of best practices.

Grants range from $10,000 to $50,000 and cover costs of preservation reformatting for audio or audiovisual content by qualified external service providers. In May 2020 CLIR announced awards for 20 projects, totaling more than $650,000. The eighth call for proposals opened in November 2020, with applications due in January 2021. To date the program has awarded $3.3 million.

CLIR extended the grant terms of newly funded projects to 18 rather than 12 months and granted project and reporting extensions for other active grants on an as-needed basis. Instead of opening a new grant cycle in May 2020, as had been scheduled, staff decided to delay the next open application period to November 2020. Stay-at-home-orders issued in the spring slowed work at applicant and recipient institutions as well as at digitization service providers, affecting applicants' abilities to present competitive proposals to the program.

The COVID-19 Emergency Relief Fund, noted in the previous section, was also made available for recipients of Recordings at Risk grants, and $20,991 in relief funds were distributed to support the completion of previously approved primary grant activities that had been impeded or delayed by the pandemic.

More information about the program, including a list of funded projects, is available at https://www.clir.org/recordings-at-risk/.

Postdoctoral Fellowship Program

CLIR's Postdoctoral Fellowship Program, now in its seventeenth year, offers recent Ph.D. graduates an opportunity to work on projects that strengthen connections among library collections and services, promote the effective use of collections and technologies, and curate and preserve the products of current research. Launched in 2004, the program has supported 215 fellows at 93 host institutions across the United States, Canada, and overseas. Fellowships are typically for two years.

In July CLIR named eight postdoctoral fellows to the 2020–2022 cohort. Fellows are working in data curation for African American and African Studies, funded by the Andrew W. Mellon Foundation; in data curation for energy social science, supported by the Alfred P. Sloan Foundation; and in digital humanities and digital scholarship, funded by individual host institutions. The new fellows began the program with an introductory online seminar in late July; the typical multiday group orientation could not be held because of the pandemic.

The COVID-19 pandemic has had a significant impact on three cohorts of fellows. Recruitment of the 2020 fellows was challenging because many institutions initiated hiring freezes in spring 2020, and because of concerns around being able to support fellows once hired. The eight fellowship recipients started work remotely, though some were able to take a hybrid approach depending on their needs and the host institution's policies on remote and in-person work.

Fellows in the 2018 and 2019 cohorts lost many months of their fellowship experience because of closures starting in March 2020. The 2019 cohort was barely five months into their fellowships, and fellows in the 2018 cohort were still months short of completing their work. In response, CLIR staff worked with hosts, funders, and fellows to reallocate funds to extend some of the 2018 fellowships. Three of that cohort's fellows received extensions of six to twelve months. CLIR also requested and received funding from the Andrew W. Mellon Foundation to provide an additional two years of support for each of the ten fellows in Data Curation for African American and African Studies.

In-person cohort meetings were moved online, along with one microgrant-supported symposium, "Capacity Assessment of Latin American and Caribbean Partners: A Symposium about Open Access, Technological Needs, and Institutional Sustainability." Recommendations from the symposium will be published in five languages early in 2021.

Additional information about the postdoctoral fellowship program, including a list of current and former fellows, is available at https://www.clir.org/fellow ships/postdoc/.

Mellon Dissertation Fellowships

Since 2002, with funding from the Andrew W. Mellon Foundation, CLIR has awarded 257 fellowships to support dissertation research in the humanities or related social sciences using original sources.

CLIR did not award new Mellon Fellowships for Dissertation Research in Original Sources in 2020. Instead, funds remaining in the program grant were reallocated to extend fellowships for the 16 fellows in the field whose work had been disrupted by the pandemic. Funds will be disbursed in accordance with revised research schedules between November 2020 and August 2021. CLIR also relaxed program guidelines to allow fellows to work with digitized original sources, given the many restrictions on travel and the indefinite closure of many libraries and archives. In October 2020 CLIR held an online meeting for the current cohort to enable fellows to share anecdotes from their time in the field and to discuss the impact of COVID-19 on their research and the repositories upon which they rely.

More information on the fellowship program, including a list of fellowship recipients, is available at https://www.clir.org/fellowships/mellon/fellowship recipients/.

Initiatives and Partnerships

Digital Library Federation

A program of CLIR, the Digital Library Federation (DLF) is a community of practitioners who advance research, learning, social justice, and the public good through the creative design and wise application of digital library technologies. DLF connects CLIR's vision and research agenda to a network of practitioners working in digital libraries, archives, labs, museums, and elsewhere. DLF promotes work on standards and best practices; research and data management; practices that open new opportunities for research, teaching, and learning; professional development; the social contexts and impact of digital library work; and community-driven frameworks for policy advocacy.

DLF at 25

In 2020 DLF marked its 25th anniversary with the release of a yearlong program review conducted by Joanne Kossuth, founding director of 1MountainRoad consultancy. Kossuth's review draws on hundreds of responses collected from interviews and written exchanges with CLIR and DLF staff, representatives of member institutions, DLF advisory committee and working group members, and Forum participants. The review, available at https://www.clir.org/wp-content/uploads/sites/6/2020/05/DLF-Review-Report.pdf, has informed the search for the next DLF senior program officer, who will be named in 2021.

DLF Forum

DLF's annual signature event, the Forum, is open to digital library practitioners from member institutions and the broader community. The Forum provides an opportunity for DLF's advisory committee, working groups, and community members to conduct business and present their work; it also enables community members to share experiences and practices with one another and support a broader level of information sharing among professional staff. The Forum allows DLF to continually review and assess its progress with input from the community at large.

The largest and most complex task of 2020 was moving the DLF Fall Forum and associated events online, a decision made in response to the risks of holding an in-person event during the pandemic. The virtual Forum took place November 9–10 and was followed by two affiliated events: "NDSA Digital Preservation 2020: Get Active with Digital Preservation" on November 12, and "5 for 5: Conversations on Five Years of Digitizing Hidden Collections" on November 13. All events were free of charge and drew nearly 2,200 registrants representing all 50 states and 36 countries—by far the broadest geographical representation to date. Recordings and transcripts of the Forum presentations are available at https://2020clirevents.aviaryplatform.com/collections/1172.

The 2021 Fall Forum is planned for November 7–11 in St. Louis, Missouri. CLIR will continue to monitor public health conditions and by spring 2021 will decide on the feasibility of an in-person meeting.

Working Groups

DLF hosts 12 working groups, which collaborate virtually and are typically informal, volunteer-led efforts. Highlights of 2020 included the following:

- Release of the Born-Digital Access Working Group's publication, *Levels of Born-Digital Access*, which won the Software Sustainability Institute (SSI) Award for Research and Innovation, presented as part of the Digital Preservation Coalition's 2020 Digital Preservation Awards in early November. The publication also received a 2020 NDSA Innovation Award.
- Release of a white paper, *Survey of Benchmarks in Metadata Quality: Initial Findings*, by the Assessment Interest Group's Metadata Working Group, in May 2020.
- Webinars on user experience and service design, and working remotely during a global pandemic, presented by the Project Managers Group.
- Webinars on privacy in practice and engaging student perspectives in library learning analytics, presented by the Privacy and Ethics in Technology Working Group.

A webinar on inclusive design and accessible exhibits, presented by the Digital Accessibility Working Group.

Working groups are open to all interested professionals. A full list of DLF groups is available at https://www.diglib.org/groups/.

Authenticity Project Fellowship Program

In 2019, DLF and the HBCU Library Alliance launched the Authenticity Project, an IMLS-funded mentoring and professional development program for early-to-mid-career library staff from Historically Black Colleges and Universities (HBCUs), along with opportunities for building authentic connections and promoting genuine exchange among participants from HBCUs and predominantly white institutions.

The initial plan was that in each of the project's three years, fifteen fellows would be matched with two experienced library professionals: an established mentor from an HBCU Library Alliance library or with a strong background in HBCUs, and a "conversation partner" working in an area of the fellow's interest from a predominantly white institution. In 2019 fellows worked with their mentors and conversation partners on topics ranging from grant writing and project management to self-care and interinstitutional collaboration.

Because of the COVID-19 pandemic, the program took a hiatus in 2020. The program will continue in 2021 with support from faculty with expertise in online mentoring and community building. Fellows will receive funding to attend the next in-person DLF Forum and Learn@DLF workshops and have access to online discussion spaces and networking opportunities. They will also participate in regular facilitated, online networking and discussion sessions.

Additional information is available at https://www.diglib.org/opportunities/authenticity-project/.

National Digital Stewardship Alliance (NDSA)

DLF serves as the host institution for the NDSA, a consortium of 225 partnering organizations, including universities, professional associations, businesses, government agencies, and nonprofit organizations committed to the long-term preservation of digital information. NDSA activities are organized by three interest groups (Content, Infrastructure, and Standards and Practices), out of which smaller working groups often emerge. NDSA hosts the annual Digital Preservation conference, which, since 2016, has followed the DLF Forum and—like the Forum—was held virtually in November 2020. More information about NDSA is available at https://ndsa.org/.

Digital Library of the Middle East

In June 2020 CLIR launched the Digital Library of the Middle East (DLME) (dlmenetwork.org/library) platform. Developed by an engineering team from CLIR and Stanford University Libraries, and in collaboration with Qatar National Library, the new platform offers free and open access to the rich cultural legacy of the Middle East and North Africa (MENA) region by bringing together collections from cultural heritage institutions worldwide. The platform enables search of more than 133,000 artifacts from 90 collections and provides descriptions and images, along with information about the objects' history and provenance. It can be searched in English or Arabic.

In collaboration with partners and curators in the MENA region, the DLME will continue to seek new contributions including text, video, photographs, archives, manuscripts, 3-D data, and maps illuminating the region's history over 12 millennia.

Iraqi-Jewish Archives Exhibitions

In 2003 a U.S. Army team found a collection of more than 2,700 books and tens of thousands of documents recording centuries of Jewish life in Iraq in a flooded basement of the Iraqi intelligence headquarters. To ensure the survival and accessibility of the materials, the U.S. National Archives and Records Administration and its partners preserved, cataloged, and digitized the books and documents. An online exhibit at https://ijarchive.org/exhibit-pages/discovery-recovery.html describes the collection and its discovery. Traveling exhibits were also initiated, though they have been paused until additional resources and support are secured.

In October 2020 CLIR signed a memorandum of understanding with the State Department's Bureau of Near Eastern Affairs to collaborate in seeking support for exhibits of the material, as well as for potential meetings, conferences, and symposia.

Kurdish Heritage Institute Digitizing Initiative

In late 2020 phase one of CLIR's digitization project at the Kurdish Heritage Institute (KHI) in Sulaimani, in the Kurdistan Federal Region of Iraq, concluded. In phase one, CLIR trained a four-person team in digitization, data management, and record keeping; project collaborators then digitized and created records for thousands of books from the KHI's collection. A new round of funding from the U.S. Embassy in Baghdad provides money for the ongoing migration of those records to the KHI website for public use. This will make the KHI the first fully functional digital library in Iraq. The project co-directors are Peter Herdrich and Amed Demirhan.

HBCU Library Alliance Partnership

In October 2020, CLIR and the HBCU Library Alliance received a $75,000 planning grant from the Andrew W. Mellon Foundation to identify common barriers and shared visions for creating access to historic collections held by libraries at Historically Black Colleges and Universities (HBCUs). The rare and unique collections in the care of HBCUs, from historic documents to photographic prints and audiovisual media, contain a wealth of information about African American history, culture, and lives. However, many of these materials are inaccessible. The project, which runs through March 2022, will involve focus group conversations and formal assessments of the current technical capacity of HBCU libraries. The findings will enable the HBCU Library Alliance to envision how its 76 member institutions can work together to preserve, describe, and digitize the unique collections they steward. This collaboration advances the primary goals of the CLIR-HBCU Library Alliance Partnership, announced in July 2019 (https://www.clir.org/2019/07/clir-and-hbcu-library-alliance-form-national-partnership/).

Leading Change Institute

The 2020 Leading Change Institute, hosted by CLIR and EDUCAUSE and initially scheduled for June, was postponed because of COVID-19. Current plans call for the 2020 cohort to meet in Washington, D.C., in summer 2021. In the meantime, the Institute's deans, Joanne Kossuth and Elliott Shore, have hosted weekly program chats for the participants and program alumni.

LCI, which marked its 20th anniversary in 2020, aims to prepare and develop the next generation of leaders in libraries, information services, and higher education by engaging those who seek to further develop their skills for the benefit of higher education. Since the Institute's inception as the Frye Leadership Institute, 793 people have participated, representing a broad range of both domestic and international institutions of higher learning. A list of participants is available at https://leadingchangeinstitute.org/alumni/.

Chief Information Officers Group

Since 2002 CLIR has facilitated a semiannual forum of directors of organizations that have merged their library and information technology units on the campuses of liberal arts colleges and small universities. Because of COVID-19, both in-person meetings were canceled. Instead, the group held one virtual meeting June 16–17.

At their meetings and through a listserv, members discuss library and computing issues as an integrated whole. They have explored such topics as organizational models for optimizing success; governance structures; fostering diversity, equity, and inclusion in merged organizations; data security and privacy; and digital scholarship. A list of current members is available at https://www.clir. org/initiatives-partnerships/cios/.

Affiliates

Affiliates are institutions or consortia with which CLIR has forged a supportive alliance in pursuit of common goals; these include facilitating the integration of services, tools, platforms, and expertise in ways that will reduce costs and create greater efficiencies for the benefit of all. In most cases CLIR serves as a host institution or fiscal manager for an affiliate organization. CLIR currently has six affiliates, including two that joined in 2020: the Institute for Liberal Arts Digital Scholarship (ILiADS), and *Weave: Journal of Library User Experience*. A full listing of current affiliates is available at https://www.clir.org/initiatives-partnerships/ clir-affiliates/.

Publications

COVID (Re)Collections. In March 2020 CLIR launched a blog series, "COVID (Re)Collections," exploring responses to the COVID-19 pandemic by the library, cultural heritage, and information community. From April through September, 15 pieces were posted by individuals at institutions around the country. The series is available at https://www.clir.org/covid-recollections/.

Material Memory: Podcast. Launched in November 2019, CLIR's podcast completed its first season, celebrating the UN-designated Year of Indigenous Languages, in March 2020. Season two, focusing on cultural memory and the climate crisis, launched in November 2020. The season takes a critical look at the role of information and cultural heritage professionals in responding to the climate crisis and considers how different approaches to preservation can help or harm affected communities. Host Nicole Kang Ferraiolo, director of strategic initiatives at CLIR, speaks with guests about what's at stake at the intersection of climate and memory, and where to go from here. Episodes are available through major podcast apps, as well as at https://material-memory.clir.org/.

CLIR Issues 133–138. CLIR's bimonthly newsletter is available at https://www. clir.org/pubs/issues/.

Association for Library and Information Science Education

ALISE Headquarters, 4 Lan Drive, Suite 310 Westford, MA 01886
978-674-6190, e-mail office@alise.org
World Wide Web http://www.alise.org

Sandra Hirsh
President 2020–2021

The Association for Library and Information Science Education (ALISE) is an independent, nonprofit professional association, founded in 1915 as the Association of American Library Schools (AALS). It changed to its current name in 1983 to reflect more accurately the mission, goals, and membership of the association. Its mission is to promote innovative, high-quality education for the information professions internationally through engagement, advocacy, and research.

Membership

Membership is open to individuals and institutions. Personal members can include anyone interested in the objectives of the association, with categories including full-time (faculty member, administrator, librarian, researcher, or other interested individual); emerging professional (doctoral students as they transition to faculty member status, maximum of three years); part-time/retired (part-time or adjunct faculty, or retired professionals); and student (doctoral or other students, maximum of six years). Institutional members include schools with programs that offer a graduate degree in library and information science or a cognate field. International affiliate institutional membership is open to any school outside the United States or Canada that offers an educational program in library and information science at the professional level as defined or accepted by the country in which the school is located. Associate institutional membership status is accorded to libraries and organizations other than schools of library and information science.

Structure and Governance

ALISE is constituted of operational groups, including the board of directors; committees; the council of deans, directors, and program chairs; school representatives; and special interest groups (SIGs). The association has been managed since October 2018 by McKenna Management, Inc., in Westford, Massachusetts, with Cambria Happ as executive director. The board of directors is composed of seven elected officers serving three-year terms. Officers for 2020–2021 were Sandra Hirsh (San José State University), president; Lisa O'Connor (University of North Carolina, Greensboro), vice-president/president-elect; Stephen Bajjaly (Wayne State University), past president; Heather Moulaison Sandy (University of Missouri), secretary/treasurer; Denice Adkins (University of Missouri), director for membership; Lilia Pavlovsky (Rutgers University), director for community building; and Mega Subramaniam (University of Maryland), director for programming.

At the end of the Annual Conference in September 2021, Bajjaly, Moulaison Sandy, and Pavlovsky will conclude their terms of service and three newly elected officers will join the board: a new vice-president/president-elect, a new director for community building, and a new secretary/treasurer.

The board establishes policy, sets goals and strategic directions, and provides oversight for the management of the association. Face-to-face meetings are held in conjunction with the Annual Conference to focus on policy, planning, programming, and other matters. For the remainder of the year, business is conducted through teleconferences, an online collaborative work platform, and e-mail.

Committees play a vital role in carrying out the work of the association. Since fall 2008, an open call for volunteers to serve on committees has been used to ensure broader participation in committee service, with members for the coming year appointed by the vice-president/president-elect for most committees. Principal areas of activity include awards, conference program planning, governance, nominations, research competitions, and tellers. Four new standing committees were established in October 2020: advancement, community building, membership, and programming. (See https://www.alise.org/alise-committees for a full list.) Each committee is given an ongoing term of reference to guide its work as well as the specific charges for the year. Task forces can be charged to carry out tasks outside the scope of the existing standing committees.

The ALISE Council of Deans, Directors, and Program Chairs consists of the chief executive officers of each ALISE institutional member school. The group convenes at the Annual Conference and discusses issues via e-mail in the interim. Jim Elmborg (University of Alabama) and Kimiz Dalkir (McGill University) serve as the 2020–2021 co-chairs.

Within each institutional member school, a school representative is named to serve as a direct link between the membership and the ALISE board. These individuals communicate to the faculty of their school about ALISE and the association's events and initiatives and provide input on membership issues to the ALISE board.

Special interest groups (SIGs) enable members with shared interests to communicate and collaborate, with a particular emphasis on programs at the Annual Conference. New SIGs are established as areas of interest emerge. Ongoing SIGs, grouped by thematic clusters, are

- *Roles and Responsibilities:* Doctoral Students; Part-Time and Adjunct Faculty
- *Teaching and Learning:* Curriculum; Innovative Pedagogies
- *Topics and Courses:* Archival/Preservation Education; Disabilities in LIS; Equity and Social Justice; Gender Issues; Health; Historical Perspectives; Information Ethics; Information Policy; International Library Education; School Library Media; Technical Services Education; Youth Services

Communication

Announcements, notifications, and membership updates are posted to the ALISE membership listserv. News and events are published on ALISE's official website (http://www.alise.org). The organization has been actively using its social media accounts, including Twitter (@alisehq) and Facebook (https://www.facebook.com/ALISEHQ/) to connect with its members and communities, as well as to post announcements and ALISE-related events in a timely manner.

Publications

The ALISE publications program has four components:

- The *Journal of Education for Library and Information Science* (*JELIS*) is a peer-reviewed quarterly journal edited by John Budd and Denice Adkins. The journal is a scholarly forum for discussion and presentation of research and issues within the field of library and information science (LIS) education. The University of Toronto Press began to serve as the publisher of *JELIS* in 2018. The journal is open access at a green level. It is indexed in Elsevier's Scopus, among other indexing sources.
- The *ALISE Library and Information Science Education Statistical Report* publishes data collected annually from its institutional members on their curriculum, faculty, students, and income and expenditures. Members can gain free access to existing reports by logging in to the members-only area of the ALISE website.
- The ALISE Book Series, published by Rowman & Littlefield, addresses issues critical to Library and Information Science education and research through the publication of epistemologically grounded scholarly texts that are inclusive of regional and national contexts around the world. The series editors are Jaya Raju (University of Cape Town) and Dietmar Wolfram (University of Wisconsin–Milwaukee). The first two books in this book series were published in 2020: *The Information Literacy Framework: Case Studies of Successful Implementation* and *E.J. Josey: Transformational Leader of the Modern Library Profession*.
- The ALISE website is the public face of the association and provides information about the association and news of activities and opportunities of interest to members. It provides login access to the MemberClicks system, where members can access members-only benefits (reports, member directory, etc.), renew membership, register for the conference and webinars, and access other services. The ALISE website was completely redesigned in 2020.

Annual Conference

The 2021 annual conference will be held in Milwaukee, Wisconsin, on September 21–23, 2021. The conference theme is "Crafting a Resilient Future: Leadership, Education, & Inspiration." Program co-chairs Sue Alman (San José State University) and Kim Thompson (University of South Carolina), with President Hirsh, are planning the ALISE conference. The conference will offer presentations, poster sessions, and networking and placement opportunities, along with the unCommons—a gathering place to share, debate, brainstorm, and network. The ALISE

Academy will close out the conference. Conference proceedings are housed by the IDEALS repository (https://www.ideals.illinois.edu/handle/2142/98928).

Professional Development

ALISE offers regular webinars free to members to facilitate virtual engagement with research and other membership interests during the year between conferences. Recent webinar offerings have included "Developing & Leading Virtual Teams," "Higher Education and Research Community Responses to the COVID-19 Pandemic," and "Navigating Difficult Conversations." Persons who are interested in offering a webinar may submit a proposal through the webinar submission web page (http://www.alise.org/webinar-proposals).

The ALISE Leadership Academy was offered for the second time January 30–21, 2020, in Palm Desert, California. Based on feedback from LIS program leaders and past participants, the theme for this year's Leadership Academy was "Vision 2020: Leading in a Constantly Changing World." ALISE initiated the Leadership Academy to create communities within library and information science for the exploration of leadership roles as chairs, directors, and deans. We aim to build interest in leadership and to build the confidence of prospective leaders. The Academy also provides prior attendees a forum to reconvene, to reflect on their learnings from the past year, and to gain new insights to deploy in the future. In 2021, the ALISE Leadership Academy will be held virtually through a series of webinars.

Grants and Awards

ALISE supports research and recognizes accomplishments through its grants and awards programs. Research competitions include the ALISE Research Grant Competition, the ALISE / Bohdan S. Wynar Research Paper Competition, the ALISE/ProQuest Methodology Paper Competition, the ALISE / Eugene Garfield Doctoral Dissertation Competition, and the ALISE Community conn@ CT Mini-Grants. Support for conference participation is provided by the University of Washington Information School Youth Services Graduate Student Travel Award, the Doctoral Student to ALISE Award, the ALISE/Jean Tague Sutcliffe Doctoral Student Research Poster Competition, and the ALISE Diversity Travel Award to the ALISE Annual Conference. This last award was created in collaboration with the ALA Office for Diversity Spectrum Scholarship Program, which created a parallel award, the ALA/ALISE Spectrum Travel Award to ALISE, partially funded by ALISE.

Awards recognizing outstanding accomplishments include the ALISE/ Norman Horrocks Leadership Award (for early-career leadership), the ALISE / Pratt-Severn Faculty Innovation Award, the ALISE Service Award, the ALISE Award for Professional Contribution, the ALISE/Connie Van Fleet Award for Research Excellence in Public Library Services to Adults, and the ALISE Excellence in Teaching Award. Winners are recognized at an awards luncheon at the Annual Conference. (For a list of award winners, see http://www.alise.org/awards-grants.)

Collaboration with Other Organizations

ALISE seeks to collaborate with other organizations on activities of mutual interest. ALISE members also serve on committees for various national organizations, including ALA committees.

ALISE continues to build its international connections, with members serving on the International Federation of Library Associations (IFLA) Standing Committees that address education and research. ALISE has been expanding its collaborations with peer organizations including the Association for Information Science and Technology (ASIS&T) and the iSchools Organization; the partnership of these three organizations is called the iFederation.

Impact of COVID-19

ALISE moved quickly to organize a webinar to help instructors convert their course content to online delivery in a webinar called "Yes You Can! Tips for Moving Online at Short Notice" in March 2020; this was a very popular webinar that attracted a large audience. ALISE issued the document "Statement about COVID-19 and the Library and Information Science Community." ALISE also developed a list of COVID-19 resources (https://www.alise.org/covid-19-resources).

Due to the COVID-19 pandemic in 2020, ALISE held its 2020 annual conference virtually rather than as planned in Pittsburgh, Pennsylvania. The virtual conference was well attended, and more people from outside the United States and Canada were able to participate. Many presentations, posters, and discussions focused on the pandemic, for example, "LIS Education in a Pandemic Era: Innovative Teaching Methods, Strategies, & Technologies" and "Crisis Management, COVID-19, and Libraries: Implications for LIS Education." The 2021 annual conference theme, "Crafting a Resilient Future," is also pandemic related. Going forward, ALISE will continue to explore ways to offer ALISE members more enriching content virtually and to provide ALISE members with opportunities to engage with each other in virtual formats.

Conclusion

ALISE is guided by its strategic plan. In 2020, the 2017–2020 strategic plan was closed out, and the association underwent a significant strategic process that resulted in a completely updated strategic plan for 2021–2025 (https://www.alise.org/history-strategic-direction-). The association looks forward to continuing its leading role in LIS education and research.

International Reports

International Federation of Library Associations and Institutions

Postal Address: P.O. Box 95312, 2509 CH Den Haag, Netherlands
Visiting Address: Prins Willem-Alexanderhof 5, 2595 BE The Hague, Netherlands
Tel. +31 70 3140884, fax +31 70 3834827, e-mail ifla@ifla.org
World Wide Web http://www.ifla.org

Beacher Wiggins

Director for Acquisitions and Bibliographic Access, Library of Congress
Secretary, IFLA Standing Committee on Acquisition and Collection Development, 2019–2023

Susan R. Morris

Special Assistant to the Director for Acquisitions and Bibliographic Access, Library of Congress
Member, IFLA Standing Committee on Cataloguing, 2019–2023

The International Federation of Library Associations and Institutions (IFLA) is the preeminent international organization representing librarians, other information professionals, and library users. The Federation's major work in 2020 fell into three areas: reconceptualizing the annual conference; designing a new governance structure to support the IFLA Vision and Strategy; and optimizing the IFLA website, http://www.ifla.org, as a resource for planning, assessment, and advocacy. Carrying out these major projects during the global COVID-19 pandemic, IFLA proved itself both idealistic and realistic in promoting its four core values: freedom of access to information and expression, as stated in Article 19 of the Universal Declaration of Human Rights; the belief that such access must be universal and equitable to support human well-being; delivery of high-quality library and information services in support of that access; and the commitment to enabling all members of IFLA to participate without regard to citizenship, disability, ethnic origin, gender, geographical location, political philosophy, race, or religion.

World Library and Information Congress (WLIC): Cancellation and Redesign

In the face of the deadly pandemic that was rapidly spreading around the world, the IFLA Governing Board announced in April that the 2020 World Library and Information Congress was cancelled. The WLIC had been planned for Dublin, Ireland, in August 2020 and would have been the 86th annual congress. The annual

General Assembly, usually held during the WLIC, was held virtually in November, in compliance with Dutch laws of incorporation.

The 2021 World Library and Information Congress had been planned for Rotterdam, Netherlands, but the IFLA Governing Board and headquarters staff announced in September 2020 that the WLIC would instead be a virtual event in 2021, with support from the Dutch National Committee for the Congress. At the same time, IFLA announced plans to design a new, hybrid virtual-physical format for future congresses, with a view to facilitating participation in all countries, for all who wish to attend. The conference exhibitor fees and registration fees are higher than for most conferences in the library community, but revenue from the WLIC historically has not loomed large in IFLA's funding model; in fact, the 2019 WLIC in Athens, Greece, ran a deficit of €46,152, or more than U.S.$50,000. The custom of convening all registered participants in opening and closing ceremonies limits the number of potential host cities to those with conference halls seating at least 3,000 people. In response to members' concerns about expense and inconvenience, IFLA live-streamed eleven key sessions at the Athens WLIC for audiences around the world and made them available free of charge on the WLIC website and the IFLA YouTube channel. The IFLA Governing Board is committed to improving both the conference experience for participants and the financial security of the organization. A survey of members in October showed that participants desire a conference experience that is affordable, inclusive, and creative, with sessions that are shorter than conventional in-person WLIC sessions. Headquarters staff began analyzing the survey responses closely to design the first online WLIC, which will most likely take place in August 2021. The General Assembly at its November 2020 meeting voted to propose to the Governing Board that in the future, IFLA should hold the WLIC in person only once every three years. If accepted by the Governing Board, this proposal could take effect in 2024 at the earliest, because IFLA has contractual obligations to hold the WLIC in Dublin in 2022 and in Rotterdam in 2024.

IFLA Global Vision and IFLA Strategy 2019–2024

The IFLA Strategy 2019–2024 developed from the IFLA Global Vision that President Glòria Pérez-Salmerón launched in March 2018. Pérez-Salmerón, and Secretary General Gerald Leitner unveiled the new IFLA Strategy 2019–2024 at the Athens WLIC. The IFLA Strategy presents four strategic directions: strengthen the global voice of libraries; inspire and enhance professional practice; connect and empower the field; optimize the organization. Each strategic direction is supported by four key initiatives, forming a call to action for all libraries to inspire, engage, enable, and connect with their societies.

Most of 2020 was devoted to reexamining IFLA's organization and governance the better to support IFLA's strategy and strengthen its participatory and inclusive identity. The IFLA Governing Board and headquarters staff adopted the slogan "no decisions about you without you." The review began with a Board workshop, December 10–11, 2019. After an initial draft was issued on June 19, 2020, a survey and a series of virtual workshops over the summer sought feedback from individuals. A final proposal for a new governance structure and revised

IFLA Statutes was accepted by the General Assembly in November, and approval by the Governing Board was expected by February 2021.

The new governance structure would streamline the Governing Board from 19 members to 11, eliminating the need for an Executive Committee. A new Regional Council would guide, support, and set priorities for IFLA's advocacy work in each of six regions of the world. Six new regional divisions would report to the Regional Council: Asia and Oceania; North Africa and the Middle East, to include countries of Western Asia; Latin America and the Caribbean; Africa; Europe; and North America. The six regional divisions would follow the United Nations pattern of political divisions, with the result that the North America regional division would include only Canada and the United States, with Mexico assigned to the Latin America and Caribbean. The establishment of regional divisions, in contrast to the three regional sections that currently exist under a single division, will provide greater visibility to IFLA's regional advocacy work and foster greater participation in countries with developing economies. The other 41 sections that are currently assigned to five divisions would continue as "professional units" but would be organized in more divisions, reporting to a Professional Council. The chair of each professional unit's standing committee would be authorized to appoint five additional members, to ensure that each region of the world was represented on the standing committee. Four strategic programs would be replaced by Advisory Committees reporting to the Governing Board: the Committee on Standards; the Cultural Heritage Programme; Copyright and Legal Matters; and Freedom of Access to Information and Free Expression. In contrast to the current structure, the advisory committee chairs would not automatically have seats on the Professional Council. The new structure allows sections or divisions to sponsor special interest groups, short-term working groups focusing on a specific topic or issue, and networks or crosscutting matrixes to enable individuals to communicate with each other and the governance structure on enduring interests.

Standards

In the current 2016–2021 Strategic Plan, key initiative 1.4, "Promoting IFLA Standards to support libraries in the provision of services to their communities," is tied to the strategic direction for "libraries in society," rather than the strategic direction for "information and knowledge." The definition of "IFLA standard" is quite broad and encompasses conceptual models, formatting codes, rules, guidelines, and best practices, ranging from the Statement of International Cataloguing Principles (ICP) to IFLA Guidelines for Library Services to People Experiencing Homelessness. The ICP and Library Reference Model (LRM) are the foundation of many national and international cataloging codes, such as *RDA: Resource Description & Access* in the Anglo-heritage and Germanic library communities. In 2020, a translation of the LRM into Chinese was completed and published on the IFLA website, which also includes the LRM in Catalan, English, German (portions only), Hungarian, Italian, Korean, Lithuanian, Portuguese, Spanish, and Ukrainian.

IFLA has liaison relationships with several technical committees of the International Standardization Organization (ISO); representation on the European

Committee for Standardization (CEN) Technical Committee—Conservation of Cultural Heritage; and an ex officio position on the International ISBN Agency Board.

Copyright and Libraries

IFLA advocates vigorously for open access to digital content and for the right of libraries to benefit from fair use and exemptions from copyright restrictions. Its Copyright and Other Legal Matters (CLM) strategic program is managed by an advisory committee working with IFLA headquarters. The CLM Advisory Committee represents IFLA on the Standing Committee on Copyright and Related Rights (SCCR) of WIPO, the World Intellectual Property Organization.

Cultural Heritage Disaster Reconstruction

IFLA's strategic direction recognizes culture as a basic human need and calls for sustained effort to preserve cultural heritage. In 1996 IFLA was a founding member of the International Committee of the Blue Shield and its successor, the Blue Shield, to protect cultural property in the event of natural and human disasters. Its current Blue Shield partners are the International Council on Archives, the International Council on Monuments and Sites, and the International Council of Museums. Since 2016, IFLA has maintained a Risk Register for Documentary Cultural Heritage, a confidential repository of information about unique documentary heritage assets, including indigenous languages and digital cultural heritage resources, deemed to be at risk from natural or human-caused disasters. In 2020, IFLA participated in efforts to protect cultural heritage in the disputed South Caucasus territory of Nagorno-Karabakh.

Grants and Awards

The Federation continues to work with corporate partners and national libraries to maintain programs and opportunities that would otherwise not be possible, especially for librarians and libraries in developing countries. For the first time in 20 years, OCLC did not name a cohort of Jay Jordan IFLA/OCLC Early Career Development Fellows, following its decision in 2019 to evaluate new directions for the program.

The IFLA PressReader International Marketing Award was presented in 2020 to the Foshan Library in Foshan, Guangdong, China, for its program "N[eighborhood]-Library: To Forge a Closer Community of Shared Future" through a system of 818 public mini-libraries serving this city of 7.2 million residents. (The International Marketing Award was sponsored by the Emerald Group from 2008 through 2014 and, after a hiatus in 2015, by the French library systems and services vendor Bib-Libre from 2016 through 2018. PressReader became the sponsor in 2019.) The award usually includes a cash stipend and support for travel to the WLIC. For 2020, the Foshan Library instead received funding to purchase technology.

Numerous awards and travel grants were cancelled for 2020 and 2021 but are expected to continue when in-person congresses resume. Such awards include the Standing Committee for the IFLA Academic and Research Libraries Section travel grants, co-sponsored by Sage and Ex Libris since 2015; registration awards for 40 first-time conference attendees through IFLA WLIC Participation Grants, including the Bersekowski Awards; the IFLA New Professionals WLIC Attendance Grants; and the Dr. Shawky Salem Conference Grant.

Other IFLA awards recognize exemplary libraries or librarians. The IFLA Green Library Award, established in 2015, recognizes a green or sustainable library project. Sponsored by De Gruyter, the award was designed by the IFLA Environment, Sustainability, and Libraries Special Interest Group. In 2020, the recipient was the Ranjit University Library, Thailand.

The IFLA/Systematic Award recognizes a library that best combines innovative architecture with information technology solutions, accounting for digital developments and local culture. The winning library must operate in a building that is newly built or newly repurposed as a library. With an award of $5,000 from Systematic, this is one of IFLA's most generous awards. No award was made in 2020 because of pandemic disruptions, but library buildings completed in both 2019 and 2020 may be nominated in 2021.

The IFLA Dynamic Unit and Impact Award was not presented in 2020 but will be announced in 2021.

The IFLA Honorary Fellowships, IFLA Medal, and IFLA Scroll of Appreciation recognize service to IFLA by individuals. At the November 2020 General Assembly meeting, five individuals received the IFLA Scroll of Appreciation, including Evelyn Woodberry of Australia and Victoria Owens of Canada, who were recognized for their important advocacy for libraries and library users in relation to copyright law. Guy Berthiaume, Librarian and Archivist of Canada Emeritus, and Inga Lundén of Sweden, a longtime leader in IFLA, received the IFLA Medal.

Membership and Finances

IFLA has more than 1,500 members in more than 150 countries all over the world, including 300 American members. As of November 2020, members included 136 national and international library associations. Initially established at a conference in Edinburgh, Scotland, in 1927, it has been registered in Netherlands since 1971 and has headquarters facilities at the Koninklijke Bibliotheek (Royal Library) in The Hague. Although IFLA did not hold a General Conference outside Europe and North America until 1980, there has since been steadily increasing participation from Asia, Africa, South America, and Australia. The Federation maintains regional offices for Africa (in Pretoria, South Africa); Asia and Oceania (in Singapore); and Latin America and the Caribbean (in Buenos Aires, Argentina; formerly in Mexico City, Mexico, and Rio de Janeiro, Brazil). The organization has seven official working languages—Arabic, Chinese, English, French, German, Russian and Spanish. It maintains four language centers: for Arabic, in Alexandria, Egypt; for Chinese, in Beijing, China; for the French-speaking communities of Africa, in Dakar, Senegal; and for Russian, in Moscow, Russia. The language centers contribute to more effective communication with their respective language communities by providing translations of IFLA publications and becoming involved in local or regional professional events.

IFLA offers a range of membership categories: international library associations, national library associations, other associations (generally regional or special library associations), institutions, institutional subunits, one-person libraries, school libraries, national association affiliates (limited to three consecutive years and open only to national associations with operating budgets of €10,000 or less, to encourage membership in countries with developing economies), personal affiliates, student affiliates, new graduate members, and nonsalaried personal members. Association and institution members have voting rights in the IFLA General Council and IFLA elections and may nominate candidates for IFLA offices. Institutional subunits, one-person libraries, and school libraries have limited voting rights for section elections; association affiliates and personal members do not have voting rights but may submit nominations for any IFLA office, and individuals may run for office themselves. Except for affiliates, membership fees are keyed to the UNESCO Scale of Assessment and the United Nations List of Least Developed Countries, to encourage participation regardless of economic circumstances. Membership dues are quite low, ranging from €51 per year for individual students, recent graduates, and retirees to more than €25,000 per year for the largest national library associations.

UNESCO has given IFLA formal associate relations status, the highest level of relationship accorded to nongovernmental organizations by UNESCO. In addition, IFLA has observer status with the United Nations, WIPO, the International Organization for Standardization (ISO), and the World Trade Organization, and associate status with the International Council of Scientific Unions. IFLA participates in the Internet Governance Forum, under UN auspices.

Leading corporations in the information industry have formed working relationships with IFLA as Corporate Partners. The Corporate Partners provide financial and in-kind support and in turn gain the opportunity to convey information about their products and services to IFLA members and others who pay attention to IFLA's publications and activities. Several levels of corporate partnership are available. Most prominently, since 2014 OCLC has been IFLA's first and sole Platinum Partner, providing extraordinary support that continued in 2020. Other corporate partners choose to support IFLA at three exceptional levels—gold, silver, or bronze. Gold Corporate Partners in 2020 were Emerald and Sage Publications. Silver Partners were De Gruyter Saur, Elsevier, and Sabinet; and Bronze Partners were Otto Harrassowitz GmbH and Zeutschel GmbH. The Federation's Associate Supporters were Annual Reviews and NDB Biblion.

The IFLA Foundation (Stichting IFLA) was established in 2007. The Foundation accepts private donations and bequests and also is funded by other IFLA income. It gives funding priority to proposals and projects that promise to have a long-term impact in developing and strengthening IFLA; are clearly related to at least one of IFLA's strategic priorities; and are not likely to be funded by other bodies. The Foundation also occasionally makes grants for attendance at the World Library and Information Conference; the grants are administered by the IFLA headquarters and governance structure rather than directly by the Foundation. The Foundation's Board of Trustees does not respond directly to requests for Foundation grants, which are considered by IFLA headquarters and other appropriate IFLA units. A related foundation, Stichting IFLA Global Libraries, was established in November 2016 with generous funding from the Bill and Melinda

Gates Foundation. The secretary general of Stichting IFLA Global Libraries is Gerald Leitner, and its chair is Pérez-Salmerón. Its trustees are IFLA president Mackenzie and two appointed trustees, currently Deborah Jacobs and Lundén; the Gates Foundation has the right to appoint one trustee but is not obligated to do so. Stichting IFLA Global Libraries focuses on strengthening the library field and empowering public libraries.

Personnel, Structure, and Governance

The secretary general of IFLA is Gerald Leitner. His e-mail address is iflasg@ifla. org. Helen Mandl is the deputy secretary general and the manager for member services. Her e-mail address is helen.mandl@ifla.org. In addition, IFLA headquarters has 21 staff members.

The editor of the peer-reviewed quarterly *IFLA Journal* is Steven W. Witt of the University of Illinois at Urbana-Champaign. The journal has a 12-member editorial committee, chaired by Shali Zhang of Auburn University and reporting to the IFLA Professional Committee. The journal is published by SAGE.

Christine Mackenzie of Melbourne, Australia, is IFLA's president for 2019–2021. She is a past treasurer of IFLA and served as president-elect in 2017–2019. She chose "Let's work together" as her presidential theme, highlighting the unity and inclusiveness that the IFLA Strategy 2019–2024 stresses.

The president-elect is Barbara Lison, director of the Stadtbibliothek Bremen, Germany. The new treasurer is Antonia Arahova, director of the Presidential Library of Greece. The past president is Glòria Pérez-Salmerón, past president of FESABID (Federación Española de Sociedades de Archivística, Biblioteconomía, Documentación y Museística) and president of IFLA, 2017–2019.

Under the 2008 IFLA Statutes, which were in effect throughout 2020, the 19 members of the Governing Board (plus the secretary general, ex officio) are responsible for the Federation's general policies, management, and finance. Additionally, the Board represents the Federation in legal and other formal proceedings. Currently the only American member of the Governing Board is Michael Dowling, director for chapter relations and international relations for the American Library Association.

Two long-standing IFLA projects are the IFLA website and the IFLA Voucher Scheme. The Voucher Scheme enables libraries to pay for international interlibrary loan requests using vouchers purchased from IFLA rather than actual currency or credit accounts. Since 2019, IFLA has charged a handling fee in addition to the voucher cost, but by eliminating bank charges and invoices for each transaction, the voucher scheme continues to reduce the administrative costs of international library loans and allows libraries to plan budgets with less regard to short-term fluctuations in the value of different national currencies. The voucher scheme has also encouraged participating libraries to voluntarily standardize their charges for loans.

The IFLA website has evolved from a straightforward repository of press releases and committee rosters into an invaluable resource for library advocacy and research. To support advocacy, the website features the periodic IFLA Trend Report, an environmental scan of the international library community, and the IFLA Ideas Store, which preserves the comments and survey responses that informed the new governance proposal. A major addition in 2020 was the Library Map of the World, a graphic compendium of statistics about libraries in every country. Work on the Map began in 2018 to assist countries in updating their profiles for the United Nations 2030 Sustainable Development Goals.

The IFLA Data Protection Policy complies with the General Data Protection Regulation (GDPR) of the European Union. Under the revised policy, IFLA can publish contact details of its officers, staff, standing committee members, and special interest group conveners on its website and in section newsletters and the *IFLA Journal*. Consent from individuals is gathered on a data protection registration form. IFLA does not sell contact information for individuals.

Library and Archives Canada

Leslie Weir
Librarian and Archivist of Canada

Library and Archives Canada (LAC) had placed a strong emphasis on collaboration and its role in the community when, in 2020, the global pandemic took the institution into uncharted territory. With the health and safety of our staff a top priority, we worked together to continue providing as much access as possible to our users.

Service Point Closures

On March 14, 2020, LAC officially closed all its service points (Vancouver, Winnipeg, Ottawa, and Halifax), and staff were told to work from home. Inevitably, the closures impacted a number of our services, including onsite research, copy services, DigiLab (self-serve mass digitization service), tours, workshops, public programming, general Access to Information and Privacy (ATIP) responses, exhibitions, online content, and social media promotion.

As health restrictions began to relax over the summer and businesses started to reopen, we continued to assess and adapt all of our facilities and services to ensure the health and safety of our employees and clients. In August a limited number of LAC staff began to return to physical worksites to start offering more services gradually, and we resumed copy services (online orders) and responses to ATIP requests, though at a reduced capacity. We also began to provide enhanced reference services (research support).

Due to the fluctuation in COVID-19 numbers across Canada, the reopening of our service locations has been an in-flux process since September 2020. Our research rooms and service points across the country reopened, in accordance with directions from provincial health bodies, between September and November. Some of the protocols we introduced over the months include quarantining archives and books for three days (72 hours) after being handled. We also limited the number of staff and visitors authorized onsite to ensure physical distance; all visits, in all locations, continue to require a booking in advance. The presence of suspected, potential, or confirmed COVID-19 cases at any of LAC's locations may impact our operations and prompt the temporary closure of our rooms. We know that things can change quickly, so we remain ready and adaptable; however, the majority of service points have since closed again in light of a rise in cases.

In order to inform LAC's regular clients and future visitors about our most up-to-date service offerings, the communications team developed a webpage that pulled together all relevant information. Before reopening our facilities to the public, we wanted to ensure that our clients were aware of any and all health and safety measures we were taking. To inform them, we produced a short video that was promoted on social media. We also created a user-friendly, online, step-by-step process for our clients to book appointments with staff and in our consultation rooms.

To strengthen communications with LAC users and all Canadians, the social media team has also been working with the government of Canada to create their priority messaging around COVID-19 and public health messages. LAC helped to produce social media content that used material from our collection to reference historical situations in which Canadians had to pull together for a common cause. This content was used to promote the government's COVID-19 alert app and, later, to communicate information about the vaccine.

Digital Services

Despite the pandemic's impact on LAC's services, we have a strong online service component to our work and, though business could not continue as usual, LAC staff stayed connected to our users as much as possible. Since the beginning of the pandemic, LAC never stopped providing research support and orientation services. We continued to help users find online content or analog documents that could be digitized on demand via our Copy Services, and oriented them to the service or programs specific to users' needs. Reference archivists and librarians, genealogy consultants, and archival and orientation technicians also came onsite, whenever possible, to access the collection on behalf of our users in order to provide enhanced reference services when our consultation and reference rooms were still closed.

A number of services were able to continue, almost as normal, despite the closures. These services continued because they had always been conducted online (or remotely) or because they are considered critical to Canadians, including online client registration, remote research support (by phone, e-mail, correspondence, videoconference), responses to urgent ATIP requests that required onsite consultation of records (clients in failing health), responses to ATIP requests that could be completed in a remote working environment, and review of the historical document collections related to class action lawsuits.

Work also continued, with minimal interruption, on developing and enhancing LAC's digital services. In September LAC launched an updated version of Collection Search powered by a new search engine. Collection Search is a tool that searches over 22 databases, representing 30 percent of the described collection at LAC, including the largest databases such as Collections and Fonds. This tool will eventually search more than 100 stand-alone databases currently available on our website from a single search box. Throughout the pandemic, we continued to make regular improvements to Collection Search to address feedback from clients and to fix bugs.

Beginning in July LAC was also able to continue the development of its podcasts, blogs, Flickr, and Co-lab "challenges." Co-lab is an online tool that the public can use to transcribe, tag, translate, and describe digitized images in LAC's collection. The more material that people transcribe, tag, translate, or describe in Co-lab, the more accessible and usable our digital collection becomes for all Canadians. During 2020 LAC released two Co-lab challenges, with three more planned through March 2021.

The COVID-19 pandemic demonstrated that web archiving is one of the few immediate actions information professionals, digital librarians, and archivists can take to preserve primary resources related to an extended crisis. From the beginning of the COVID-19 pandemic, LAC was fully engaged in documenting the evolution of the pandemic and its effects on Canadian society. The team curated a diverse collection that includes websites from government and nongovernment sources, as well as social media relating to the pandemic's impact on life in Canada. So far, we have collected approximately eight terabytes of website data and captured 722,280 tweets related to COVID-19. The digital information harvested will be used for future research and will help tomorrow's Canadians understand what it was like for those living through the crisis. Having this information preserved will provide future leaders with important background, data, and experiences to help guide their decisions.

Online Public Programming

LAC also reached audiences through public programming activities that were adapted to be offered online. LAC hosted online roundtables, information sessions about collections and how to do research at LAC, subject-oriented lectures, webinars, and virtual tours of 395 Wellington, LAC Winnipeg, and LAC Vancouver. This online programming was paired with virtual tools such as videos, quizzes, and games.

One of our most popular events was a workshop and webinar via LAC's Facebook page called "In the Trenches: Digitized Records of the First World War." LAC also collaborated with the Vancouver Public Library to pilot a virtual version of its weekly "Connection to Kith and Kin" (Indigenous genealogy café) via Zoom. We also hosted a number of online conversations, as part of our Signatures Interview Series, with well-known Canadians featured in our collection. Some of our interviewees of note were Beverley McLachlin, Canada's first female chief justice of the Supreme Court of Canada, and Adrienne Clarkson, Canada's 26th governor general. These interviews were a unique opportunity to see behind-the-scenes photographs and documents with personal commentary from the public figure themselves.

Our online programming also included collaborative events with other institutions, both local and international. A highlight of our online public programming for 2020 was the Ottawa International Writers Festival, which we cohosted with the Ottawa Public Library. The German National Library and LAC are collaborating to present a four-part series of conversations between October 2020 and October 2021 to explore the effects of digitization on our respective institutions and priorities. Our virtual programming has been a massive success and has kept us connected to our users and a diversity of communities.

Acquisition and Description

LAC's Published Heritage Branch responded to the COVID-19 pandemic by modifying existing workflows, reassigning tasks in support of priority digital initiatives, and proactively building digital capacity amongst staff for the benefit of researchers, publishing and library clients, and LAC staff. LAC Acquisitions staff, who are usually tasked with processing analog materials, were retrained to process digital materials. This change of focus for Acquisitions staff ended up significantly reducing LAC's backlog of digital processing and has built new digital capacity across the team. By assigning analog staff to work on digital tasks, we increased the volume of digital processing by 205 percent compared to the same period of the previous fiscal year. As well as chipping away at our backlog and developing new skills, the Acquisitions staff also completed a significant data cleanup. This cleanup involved making corrections to bibliographic records in order to improve discoverability of items in LAC's catalog.

During the initial lockdown in March 2020, staff of the Description Division of the Published Heritage Branch started describing digital material from home. Working remotely allowed us to maintain nearly the same output as normal, simply by describing more digital than analog titles. Some core functions in the Description Division, such as systems support and library standards development, made a seamless shift to remote work. In other cases, such as with ISSN (International Standard Serial Number) and CIP (Cataloguing in Publication), our work processes were revised to become completely digital. This transition happened in the first few weeks of the lockdown, and these functions can now be carried out wholly at a distance. Some work processes have been adapted to minimize the need to move physical material, which has reduced the risk for staff onsite and created efficiencies by not necessitating multiple quarantine periods for the material.

In September the Description Division launched a pilot project to allow catalogers to check out published material and describe the material from home. Participating catalogers come onsite weekly to pick up a new box that they can describe from home. This process allows division staff to continue to describe physical material while having a minimal number of staff working in the office.

Looking Ahead

Recent virtual events, such as the Ministerial Roundtable on Libraries and Archives cohosted by LAC and Canadian Heritage, have allowed us to discuss the impacts of COVID-19 on our sector and reflect together on sustainable solutions to a variety of issues faced by culture and heritage institutions in Canada. In order to continue this crucial dialog within our community, LAC will host a Galleries, Libraries, Archives, and Museums (GLAM) Think Tank during winter 2021, which will further explore the ways in which COVID-19 has challenged how we deliver our services, our employees' ability to carry out their work, and the finite institutional resources and capacities we possess. The Think Tank will bring together key players from the Canadian GLAM community in order to discuss the themes of enhancing the digital presence of GLAMs, promoting GLAMs' social value in a post-COVID-19 landscape, demonstrating GLAMs' relevance in a crisis context, building capacity at the local level, and ways in which GLAMs can reinvent themselves.

The year 2020 was challenging, and, even into 2021, we continue to wait and see how COVID-19 will affect our lives. Despite the uncertainty, LAC continues to focus on its staff and on doing our best to provide Canadians with access to our collection and services. As we go through the health crisis as a community and as an institution, we are adapting and learning with a hopeful eye to the future.

International Board on Books for Young People

Nonnenweg 12, Postfach, CH-4009 Basel, Switzerland
E-mail ibby@ibby.org
World Wide Web http://www.ibby.org

Mingzhou Zhang
President, 2018–2022

Liz Page
Executive Director

The founding of the International Board on Books for Young People (IBBY) was the result of the visionary commitment of Jella Lepman (1891–1970). Born in Stuttgart, Germany, she became a politically active journalist. In 1936 she emigrated with her son and daughter from Nazi Germany to London and became a British citizen, working for the British Foreign Office and the BBC during World War II and, beginning in 1941, for the American Broadcasting Station in Europe.

When the war ended, Lepman was engaged at the American headquarters in Germany as adviser for questions relating to children and young people. Despite a lack of funds, she organized an exhibition of children's illustrations and children's books from 20 countries in Munich in 1946. Three years later, with initial funding from the Rockefeller Foundation, she established the International Youth Library in Munich and was its director until 1957.

In the postwar years, individuals actively engaged in the field of children's literature in many countries became aware of the importance of children's books as a means for promoting international understanding and peace. They realized that children everywhere should have access to books with high literary and artistic standards and thus become enthusiastic and informed readers.

With this vision in mind, Lepman organized a meeting in Munich under the title "International Understanding through Children's Books" in November 1951. The goal of the meeting was the foundation of an international organization to promote children's books. The speeches and discussions at this conference were covered by news media worldwide. The meeting resulted in the establishment of a committee to form the International Board on Books for Young People—IBBY.

The committee met in Munich in 1952 and made a formal declaration of intent. The meeting was chaired by Swiss publisher Hans Sauerländer, and the effort was international in character from the beginning; the meeting included representatives from Austria, Germany, the Netherlands, Norway, Sweden, and Switzerland.

The success of this preparatory work resulted in the establishment of IBBY, which was registered as a nonprofit organization in Switzerland when the new organization's first General Assembly and Congress were held at the Swiss Federal Institute for Technology (ETHZ) in Zurich in October 1953. The congress brought together founding members including the authors Erich Kästner, Lisa Tetzner, Astrid Lindgren, Jo Tenfjord, Fritz Brunner, and Pamela Travers; the Swiss illustrators Alois Carigiet and Hans Fischer; the publishers Hans Sauerländer and Bettina Hürlimann; and specialists in reading research including Richard Bamberger.

The initial capital for the founding of IBBY was donated by the Swiss foundation Pro Juventute, and its secretary general, Otto Binder, was elected as IBBY's first president. In the early years IBBY also received support from the International Youth Library. However, the dues from the ten national sections that had joined IBBY by 1956 were not sufficient to establish a permanent office, and IBBY's activities were mainly carried out through donations and voluntary work. The organization of the administration was the task of the acting presidents who served for two-year terms during the first decade. Succeeding Otto Binder were Swedish publisher Hans Rabén (1956–1958), Italian professor of education Enzo Petrini (1958–1960), and Lepman (1960–1962).

A notable professionalization of IBBY and an extension of membership were achieved during the presidency of Bamberger (1962–1966). In addition, the publication of IBBY's quarterly journal, *Bookbird*, edited by Lepman, Bamberger, and Lucia Binder, became a permanent activity at this time. During the presidencies of Slovenian publisher Zorka Persic (1966–1970) and Finnish school principal Niilo Visapää (1970–1974), IBBY grew so large that it was no longer possible to rely entirely on voluntary work. In 1974 a permanent office, the IBBY Secretariat, was established in Basel. Leena Maissen was appointed its director and remained in that post until her retirement in 2003. Currently the post is held by Liz Page.

IBBY is a nonprofit organization that represents an international network of people who are committed to bringing books and children together. The annual dues from the national sections are IBBY's only source of regular income; projects are supported by sponsors. IBBY cooperates with many international organizations and children's book institutions around the world and exhibits at the International Children's Book Fair in Bologna and other international book fairs.

The biennial IBBY Congresses, which have taken place in 26 countries, have become increasingly important meeting points for the worldwide membership, now comprising 81 national sections, to share information and experiences.

Mission and Programs

IBBY's mission is

- To promote international understanding through children's books
- To give children everywhere the opportunity to have access to books with high literary and artistic standards
- To encourage the publication and distribution of quality children's books, especially in developing countries
- To provide support and training for those involved with children and children's literature
- To stimulate research and scholarly works in the field of children's literature
- To protect and uphold children's rights as outlined in the United Nations Convention on the Rights of the Child

As part of its mission, IBBY administers three major international awards: the Hans Christian Andersen Award, which is presented to an author and illustrator whose body of work has made lasting contributions to children's literature; the IBBY-Asahi Reading Promotion Award, which is given to a group or an institution whose activities are judged to be making a lasting contribution to reading promotion programs for children and young people; and the IBBY-iRead Outstanding Reading Promoter Award, which recognizes outstanding individuals who are working to promote the expansion and development of children's reading. All three awards are given biennially and presented at the IBBY congresses; the next awards will be presented at the 37th IBBY Congress in Moscow, Russia, in 2021.

The IBBY Honour List is a biennial selection of outstanding recently published books, honoring writers, illustrators, and translators from IBBY member countries. An annotated catalog is published for each Honour List selection.

The IBBY Collection for Young People with Disabilities offers information and documentation services for organizations, research workers, teachers, students, librarians, publishers, authors, illustrators, policymakers, and the media who work with young people with special needs. The IBBY Selection of Outstanding Books for Young People with Disabilities is prepared biennially and presented in an annotated catalog. The collection is based at the North York Central Library Branch of the Toronto Public Library in Canada.

Traveling exhibitions of the IBBY Honour List and the Outstanding Books for Young People with Disabilities selections can be booked from IBBY. Detailed information can be found on the IBBY website (http://www.ibby.org).

IBBY established International Children's Book Day in 1967 to inspire a love of reading and to call attention to children's books. Each year the day is sponsored by an IBBY national section and is celebrated on or around Hans Christian Andersen's birthday, April 2.

The IBBY Yamada workshop and project program relies on its international network to help produce and develop book cultures for children within regions that have special needs and lack support.

IBBY established its Children in Crisis program to provide support for children whose lives have been disrupted by war, civil disorder, or natural disaster. The two main activities supported are the therapeutic use of books and storytelling in the form of bibliotherapy, and the creation or replacement of collections of selected books that are appropriate to the situation. The Sharjah/IBBY Fund for Children in Crisis was active from 2012 to 2016. The fund supported projects in Afghanistan, Iran, Lebanon, Palestine, Pakistan, and Tunisia.

In response to the waves of refugees from Africa and the Middle East arriving on the Italian island Lampedusa, IBBY launched the project "Silent Books, from the world to Lampedusa and back" in 2012. The project involved creating the first library on Lampedusa to be used by local and immigrant children. The second part required creating a collection of silent books (wordless picture books) that could be understood and enjoyed by children regardless of language. These books were collected from IBBY National Sections. The books are deposited at the documentation and research archive in Rome (Palazzo della Esposizioni), while a second set is deposited at the library in Lampedusa and a third makes a traveling exhibition for the IBBY network.

Congresses

IBBY's biennial World Congresses, hosted by different national sections, bring together IBBY members and other people involved in children's books and reading development from all over the world. In addition to lectures, panel discussions, seminars, and book exhibitions, the IBBY Membership Assembly takes place. The presentation of the Hans Christian Andersen Awards, the IBBY-Asahi Reading Promotion Award, the IBBY-iRead Reading Promoter Award, and the IBBY Honour List are highlights of the biennial congresses. The 37th IBBY Congress was postponed from 2020 because of the coronavirus pandemic and is now scheduled for September 10–12, 2021 in Moscow. The 38th IBBY Congress will be in Putrajaya, Malaysia, in 2022.

IBBY national sections also organize regional conferences to improve communication, networking, and professional exchange, and to strengthen ties of friendship and cooperation between the sections in the region.

Bookbird: A Journal of International Children's Literature is a refereed quarterly journal published by IBBY and is open to any topic in the field of international children's literature. *Bookbird* also has occasional themed issues. Calls for manuscripts are posted on the IBBY website. Regular features include coverage of children's literature studies, IBBY activities, and children's literature awards around the world. *Bookbird* also pays special attention to reading promotion projects worldwide. Its editor works in cooperation with an international editorial review board, guest reviewers, and correspondents who are nominated by IBBY national sections.

IBBY cooperates with several international organizations, including the International Federation of Library Associations and Institutions (IFLA), the International Publishers Association (IPA), and the International Literacy Association (ILA).

IBBY and the Pandemic

Twenty twenty was quite a year, with virtually every aspect of our lives disrupted by the pandemic. Unable to travel to meetings, book fairs, and conferences, we all needed to go digital—fortunately, we had the technology to do it. Children still needed books and stories, and librarians wanted to reach out and support struggling schools and families. IBBY members around the world set an inspiring example. They designed and hosted online workshops and storytelling events, and shared do-it-yourself books, among other projects designed to help ameliorate the impact of the health crisis. Four examples follow.

First, IBBY's Lithuania Section devised the project Tiny Books to the Rescue. The section invited authors and illustrators to create books folded from one sheet of A4-sized paper. The project team included the Vaikų žemė (Children's World) reading promotion program, the Child Psychology Centre, the Lithuanian IBBY Section, and the Lithuanian Culture Institute. Nine tiny books were translated into English and are available to download at https://www.ibbylietuva.lt/content/uploads/2020/07/TINY-BOOKS-TO-THE-RESCUE.pdf

Second, IBBY Palestine has long struggled to address serious challenges at the two libraries in Gaza, and the pandemic exacerbated the problems. Hospitals struggled to cope, and the IBBY section could not reach the children who most needed support during this time. With perseverance, IBBY Palestine and its partners found ways to get drawing and writing materials into the hands of many of the children.

Relatively few Palestinian families have access to the Internet, so online storytelling was not an ideal solution for these children. Eventually, they were able to visit the libraries in small groups that could be socially distanced; masks and hand sanitizer were provided. The section used some of its limited funds to provide food coupons and, in severe cases, winter clothing to the children's families. The distribution of stationery has continued, allowing children to write, draw, and share their stories.

Third, during the pandemic, IBBY Indonesia has been running webinars to promote reading. One successful event, a webinar on how to make reading promotion materials, targeted grandparents—frequently children's principal caregivers in times of crisis. The section also produced online video storytelling sessions by local legends, which proved very popular.

Fourth, in El Salvador, the IBBY section is based at San Salvador's Biblioteca de los Sueños. Although the library and schools have been closed since the start of the pandemic, librarians were able to set up a home-delivery book system. The area is dangerous, not only because of the rampant spread of the virus, but also due to the high levels of violence that children encounter almost daily. The libraries in Gaza and El Salvador serve as refuges of peace and safety for the children, and IBBY will continue to support them for as long as possible.

IBBY's U.S. National Section

The United States Board on Books for Young People (USBBY) is the U.S. national section of IBBY. It is a nonprofit organization devoted to building bridges of international understanding through children's and young adult books. The Friends of IBBY in the United States was founded in 1976 and became a national section of IBBY in 1984. Membership in USBBY is open to individuals and organizations interested in its mission

A volunteer board includes USBBY's president, president-elect, past president, recording secretary, treasurer, and 12 directors, four elected and eight appointed, representing the membership as well as the patron organizations that support USBBY, such as ILA, the Children's Book Council (CBC), the American Library Association (ALA), and the National Council of Teachers of English (NCTE).

USBBY offers a forum for those interested in national and international activities relating to children's literature. It publishes a semiannual newsletter for its members, creates an annual list of the most outstanding international literature published or distributed in the United States for children and young adults, maintains an active website, sponsors a biennial regional conference that features speakers of international interest, and cosponsors sessions held at annual conferences of ALA, ILA, and NCTE.

USBBY sponsors the publication of a series of annotated bibliographies of outstanding international literature for young people, the Bridges to Understanding series, published by Scarecrow Press.

It also sponsors the creation of an annual USBBY Outstanding International Books (OIB) list, published yearly in *School Library Journal*, and a bookmark listing the selected titles is distributed via the USBBY website, https://www.usbby.org/outstanding-international-books-list.html, and at meetings and conferences throughout the year. [Find the 2020 list on page 417 of this volume—*Ed.*]

The OIB committee selects international books that are deemed most outstanding of those published during the calendar year. Books selected for the list represent the best of children's literature from other countries; introduce American readers to outstanding authors and illustrators from other countries; help American children see the world from other points of view; provide a perspective or address a topic otherwise missing from children's literature in the United States; exhibit a distinct cultural flavor; and are accessible to American readers. Committee members judge the books based on artistic and literary merit, originality or creativity of approach, distinctiveness of topic, uniqueness of origin, and qualities that engage and appeal to children.

USBBY also submits nominations for the Hans Christian Andersen Award and prepares a biennial selection of outstanding recently published books for the IBBY Honour List, the Silent Books project, and the IBBY list of Outstanding Books for Young People with Disabilities. In addition, it nominates programs for the IBBY-Asahi Reading Promotion Award and the IBBY-iRead Reading Promoter Award.

USBBY's Bridge to Understanding Award formally acknowledges the work of adults who use books to promote international understanding among children. The award was established in memory of Arlene Pillar, an educator who served USBBY as newsletter editor from 1984 until her death in 1990. Organizations eligible for this award include schools, libraries, Scout troops, clubs, and bookstores. The winning program may be a one-time event or an ongoing series that serves children ranging in age from kindergarten through tenth grade. The award carries a prize of $1,000 and a certificate. Recent winners included "Promoting Global Awareness in Second Graders," a project in the Madeira City School District in Cincinnati that involved four second-grade teachers as well as the elementary art, music, library, gym, and computer teachers. The project was described as helping students to "make personal connections to the characters of the books, develop empathy, and relate to other children of the world through literature."

Other USBBY activities include support of IBBY's Hands across the Sea Fund, which gives assistance to underfunded IBBY sections.

USBBY has an active twinning relationship with four other IBBY national sections, allowing USBBY members to know and work closely with specific countries and to internationalize USBBY perspectives. Specific initiatives within the twinning program may include payment of IBBY dues for underfunded national sections; provision of funding to purchase books or other needed resources for classrooms and libraries; providing funding or training for writers, illustrators, editors, librarians, and publishers; facilitating fellowships for writers, illustrators, editors, librarians, and publishers, or persons who want to study children's literature; supporting cultural exchange and visits between members of USBBY and twinning national sections; developing reciprocal website postings of newsletters, information about projects, lists of children's books published in each country, and relevant websites; and including news about twinning partners in "Global Partnerships," a regular column in the USBBY newsletter, Bridges. Current USBBY twinning partners are Haiti, Lebanon, Palestine, and El Salvador.

The USBBY Secretariat is at the Center for Teaching through Children's Books at National Louis University, 5202 Old Orchard Road, Suite 300, Skokie, IL 60077. It can be reached by telephone at 224-233-2798, and its e-mail is secretariat@usbby.org, website: http://www.usbby.org. USBBY's executive director is V. Ellis Vance, 5503 N. El Adobe Drive, Fresno, CA 93711-2363, e-mail executive.director@usbby.org.

Part 2
Legislation, Funding, and Grants

Legislation

Legislation and Regulations Affecting Libraries in 2020: A Report from ALA's Public Policy and Advocacy Office

Kathi Kromer
Associate Executive Director

Shawnda Hines
Assistant Director, Communications

American Library Association
Public Policy and Advocacy Office

The COVID-19 pandemic ushered in a year like no other as libraries, along with other community institutions, businesses, and the government were forced to transform their normal operations to accommodate the ongoing public health crisis. The push to conduct work, school, and socializing online exacerbated already-existing digital divides. At the same time, connectivity safety nets—including public and school libraries—could not provide services as usual as buildings closed. These factors led to an intensive year in the policy space as the American Library Association led advocacy for library interests in the proposed pandemic relief funding bills, including support for library digital inclusion work.

Beyond these extraordinary events, several other notable legislative and regulatory issues of importance to libraries arose in 2020, including Tribal library access to the federal E-Rate program, a review of the Digital Millennium Copyright Act, a continued push for access to digital content, support for a complete count in the 2020 United States Census, and efforts to engage voters in the November 2020 elections.

Federal (Emergency) Funding for Libraries

For the fourth year in a row, the president sent Congress a budget request recommending elimination of more than $220 million in direct library funding and millions more in library-eligible programs. The Trump White House again proposed eliminating the Institute of Museum and Library Services (IMLS), along with its Library Services and Technology Act (LSTA), Innovative Approaches for Literacy (for school libraries), and other programs. ALA launched a successful grassroots campaign to urge ALA members to contact their representatives and senators to ask them to sign the annual "Dear Appropriator" letters supporting LSTA and the Innovative Approaches to Literacy (IAL) program. ALA members en masse carried the message to Congress that elimination of LSTA and IAL would have devastating effects on some of the nation's most vulnerable populations: children in low-income communities, families who cannot afford home broadband, and veterans transitioning to civilian life, as well as rural and Tribal residents with limited access to important resources.

Thanks to the work of ALA advocates, FY 2021 federal library funding ultimately received increased support from Congress when the annual spending bill passed in late December as part of the Consolidated Appropriations Act of 2020. IMLS funding increased by $5 million (to a total of $257 million), including $2 million for the LSTA directed to the Grants to States program. The IAL program also saw a $1 million increase (to a total of $28 million), with at least half of this funding dedicated to school libraries.

As the pandemic unfolded over the course of 2020, ALA pivoted and, in addition to annual federal advocacy campaigns, simultaneously engaged its members and Congress to secure the inclusion of library funding in the largest economic stimulus package in history—the Coronavirus Aid, Relief, and Economic Security Act (CARES) Act. The $2.2 trillion economic stimulus bill was passed in March. Specifically, ALA quickly acted to bolster two bipartisan congressional letters supporting $2 billion in library funding. Rep. Andy Levin (D-Mich.) and Senator Jack Reed (D-R.I.) circulated letters supporting library funding in the House and Senate. With just a few days to act, ALA launched a grassroots campaign to build momentum for these letters and worked with coalition partners to support CARES Act funding that would benefit libraries.

Early, decisive action by library advocates led to $50 million for IMLS to prevent, prepare for, and respond to the coronavirus pandemic. This included work to expand digital network access, purchase Internet-capable devices, and provide technical support services to communities. Also included was more than $30 billion in relief for schools and colleges, plus billions more for state and local governments and nonprofit organizations. Following passage of the CARES Act, the Public Policy and Advocacy Office worked to educate ALA members about the funding resources available and provided guidance for state library associations on petitioning governors to prioritize support for libraries when distributing CARES Act funding for their respective states.

As congressional efforts to pass other COVID-19 relief packages emerged, including House Democrats' unsuccessful HEROES Act (H.R. 6800), ALA ensured that libraries were included at every opportunity. While federal appropriations, both COVID-19 emergency funding and regular appropriations, stalled over the summer months, ALA worked with congressional champions to introduce a library relief package. Rep. Levin and Senator Reed introduced the Library Stabilization Fund Act (S. 4181 and H.R. 7486) in the House and the Senate, respectively, to establish a $2 billion fund for library stabilization, addressing the significant financial losses libraries were facing due to the economic impact of the pandemic. By the end of the 116th Congress, advocates had secured 68 cosponsors to the House bill and 17 to the Senate, as well as the endorsement of 23 national organizations.

Finally, in December 2020, the Build America's Libraries Act (S. 5071) was introduced by Senator Reed. The legislation called for $5 billion to repair and construct modern library facilities nationwide in underserved and disadvantaged communities. The same provisions were included as part of the Economic Justice Act (S. 5065), also introduced in December. Provisions of the Economic Justice Act could have improved school and academic library facilities, provided $12 billion in E-rate funds for libraries and schools to provide home Internet connectivity, and ensured eligibility for Tribal libraries to participate in the E-rate program.

The Year of Broadband

The novel coronavirus brought long-overdue attention to the digital inequity that cuts across rural, urban, Tribal, and suburban communities, and libraries played a critical role in plugging gaps in the nation's grossly inadequate broadband infrastructure. As momentum increased in both the House and Senate for the federal government to address the desperate need for home Internet access, ALA ensured libraries were part of the relief and recovery proposals. As a result, both chambers introduced numerous bills that included provisions to ensure libraries were equipped to address the digital needs of their communities, and ALA worked with congressional staff and coalition partners to shape legislation. In the Moving Forward Act (H.R. 2), a $1.5 billion infrastructure bill passed in the House in June, ALA successfully called on Congress to create opportunities for libraries, including provisions that would establish two grant programs to support digital literacy training, requisite devices, and community partnerships to increase broadband adoption. The bill also provided funding for hotspot and device lending by libraries as an additional means to address the lack of home Internet access.

On the Senate side, Sens. Joe Manchin (D-W.Va.) and Susan Collins (R-Maine) introduced the HOTSPOTS Act, which would have provided $160 million to IMLS for a hotspot pilot program, with funding going to state library agencies. The bill, endorsed by ALA, included a guaranteed minimum for small states and earmarks for Tribes and territories and organizations that primarily serve Native Hawaiians. ALA also endorsed the bipartisan Accelerating Connected Care and Education Support Services on the Internet Act (ACCESS the Internet Act) introduced by Senators Manchin and John Cornyn (R-Tex.). The $2 billion legislation addressed immediate gaps in Internet access necessary for distance learning and telehealth. The distance learning provision included a two-year, $200 million hotspot pilot program for libraries to be administered by IMLS with a minimum allotment of $1.6 million per state, allowing Tribes and territories to purchase and distribute Internet-connected devices to libraries in low-income and rural areas.

Advocacy efforts that started over the summer to push for library broadband funding in the next COVID relief package intensified in the last quarter of 2020, culminating in a race against the clock as Congress rushed to pass a relief bill during the lame-duck session following the November elections. ALA's goal was to keep the pressure on lawmakers to provide $200 million to IMLS for libraries to expand Internet access through boosting wifi signals or loaning Internet-capable devices such as hotspots. Libraries were also to be eligible for $3.2 billion in funding slated for the FCC's E-rate program for similar purposes to support students and library patrons without home Internet access. ALA supported several versions of these provisions included in a bipartisan, bicameral COVID Relief Framework and subsequent Act, a $908 billion package led by Senator Manchin. Unfortunately, the provisions ALA supported did not get included in the Consolidated Appropriations Act, which was signed into law on December 27.

ALA's efforts to influence broadband policy were successful, particularly with respect to increasing support for broadband in Tribal communities. ALA renewed support for the Tribal Connect Act, bipartisan and bicameral legislation first introduced in 2017 and reintroduced in the summer of 2020 (H.R. 7973 and S. 4529). Building on endorsement for the legislation, ALA released a new Policy Perspectives paper, "Built by E-Rate: A Case Study of Two Tribally-Owned Fiber Networks and the Role of Libraries in Making It Happen" in September 2020. The paper details Tribal libraries' role in creating two broadband consortia that are owned, operated by, and serving Tribal communities in northern New Mexico. The two multi-million-dollar networks were funded through the Federal Communications Commission's E-rate program, specifically as a result of program changes that ALA advocated for during the 2013–2014 proceeding to modernize the program. Established in 1998, E-rate provides billions of dollars in discounts to assist libraries and public schools in obtaining high-speed Internet access and advanced telecommunications services at affordable rates. While the Tribal Connect Act itself did not pass, ALA's efforts to showcase the needs of Tribal libraries was key in redefining "Tribal library" to eventually expand Tribal eligibility for E-rate funding.

Libraries' critical contributions in filling connectivity gaps throughout the pandemic were recognized by the FCC in October. ALA nominated "America's libraries" for the inaugural Digital Opportunity Equity Recognition (DOER) Awards created by FCC Commissioner Geoffrey Starks. ALA President (2020–2021) Julius C. Jefferson, Jr., attended a virtual reception hosted by Commissioner Starks to receive a DOER Award on behalf of "America's libraries" in recognition of the tireless efforts of all the nation's libraries in addressing the digital divide, especially during the COVID-19 pandemic.

Copyright

As librarians and educators across the country faced challenges when taking class courses online due to "shelter in place" orders, copyright was a major concern. Library copyright experts responded to hundreds of questions, prepared educational documents, and participated in educational webinars on issues ranging from reading aloud online for digital storytimes to navigating potential copyright issues involved in sharing video content with students as a part of online learning.

At the federal level, copyright policy developments continued at prepandemic levels. Senate Judiciary Subcommittee on Intellectual Property chairman Tom Tillis (R-N.C.) made good on his 2019 announcement that the subcommittee would undertake a yearlong review of the Digital Millennium Copyright Act (DMCA). The review eventually resulted in the December 2020 release of a discussion draft of the Digital Copyright Act of 2021. The Library Copyright Alliance voiced serious concerns with the draft, which proposed sweeping changes to the safe harbors for online service providers contained in Section 512 of the DMCA. The proposed changes would threaten libraries' ability to provide public Internet access by requiring increased filtering, which would limit free speech and fair use rights. It would change the current Section 512 liability protection for service providers (including libraries) by enforcing a "notice and stay down" regime over a "notice and take down" regime.

Among numerous troubling provisions, the draft of the Digital Copyright Act of 2021 also included the relocation of the Copyright Office from the Library of Congress to the Department of Commerce, a move that would vastly increase the Copyright Office's regulatory authority. The Register of Copyrights would become a presidential appointment, removing hiring and all other authority from the Librarian of Congress. With new party leadership and Senator Tillis no longer chair of the Subcommittee, strong interest in pursuing the controversial draft in 2021 appears less likely.

The Copyright Office underwent leadership changes of its own at the outset of 2020, when Copyright Register Karyn Temple resigned. In September Librarian of Congress Carla Hayden appointed Shira Perlmutter as the next register of copyrights and director of the U.S. Copyright Office. Perlmutter previously worked at the United States Patent and Trade Office as a chief policy officer and director for international affairs as well as in the Copyright Office. Among other things, she led the interagency group that prepared the Marrakesh Treaty Implementation Act. (A decade-long effort by library advocates, the legislation passed in 2018, thereby increasing the availability of accessible content for the print disabled as well as implementing cross-border sharing of accessible content.) ALA anticipates the new register will make modernization of the Copyright Office a top priority and balance the interests of content creators, rights holders, and the public in copyright policy.

A balanced approach is the best that can be hoped for in a problematic new small claims tribunal to be established in the Copyright Office. The Copyright Alternatives in Small-Claims Enforcement ("CASE") Act, opposed by the Library Copyright Alliance since the idea was introduced in 2013, was surreptitiously included in the Consolidated Appropriations Act of 2020 and signed into law. Fortunately, two provisions protect libraries from infringement claims—to an extent. First, claims cannot be brought against state government entities. Most public colleges and universities, and their libraries, are state government entities and thus are excluded. Second, a "preemptive opt-out" for libraries and archives would exempt public libraries run by state and municipal entities and permanently exempt libraries that opt out of the tribunal when a notice is filed. However, these protections do not help library users, students, or university faculty, who would still be subject to claims.

ALA and other library groups will need to educate library users that filing a notice to opt out of the small claims tribunal would generally be in their interest because under the CASE Act, defendants do not have the advantages they would have in a federal court: full discovery, the option of a jury trial, the opportunity to appeal, or protection from statutory damages of $7,500 per work—even when the work has not been registered with the Copyright Office. The U.S. Copyright Office has one year to implement CASE, and the Library Copyright Alliance will be involved in providing comment throughout any public rulemaking.

Another chapter closed in 2020 when, after 12 years of litigation, U.S. District Court judge Evans issued a long-awaited ruling in the Georgia State (GSU) e-reserves case, *Cambridge University Press, et al.* v. *Georgia State University*.

The initial court filings in 2008 argued that GSU was practicing "systematic, widespread, and unauthorized copying and distribution of a vast amount of copyrighted works" through a system called "e-reserves" in which controlled access is provided to digital content for students in a given course. As instructed by the federal appeals court, Judge Evans reassessed her fair ruling determinations of the 48 alleged infringements and decided that 37 were fair uses. She also ruled that the existence of a licensing market was not determinative, as some uses were ruled fair even when a license was available. Thus, *Georgia State* demonstrates that fair use carefully applied can permit e-reserves. In November 2020 the Association of American Publishers (AAP) and the Copyright Clearance Center announced their decision to forgo an appeal, bringing an end to the case.

E-book Access

The conversation around e-book pricing and access continued to unfold in 2020, especially at the state level. In March library advocates in New York sent 10,000 letters to state lawmakers as part of a public campaign in response to efforts to limit library access to e-books. The letters, encouraged by the New York Library Association in partnership with ALA, were in support of legislation that would require publishers who offer e-books to the consumer market to extend licenses to libraries within the state without discrimination. On the same day, the Rhode Island Library Association (RILA), ALA, local library workers, patrons, and elected officials gathered to speak against "Big Publishing's" practices that limit libraries' ability to provide full access to new publications.

Weeks later, Macmillan Publishers announced that, in the context of the COVID-19 pandemic, the publisher would cancel its embargo on sales of new e-book titles to libraries. Under the company's nascent policy, which took effect on October 1, 2019, only a single copy of an e-book was allowed per library system for the first eight weeks after a title's release. Notably, Macmillan CEO John Sargent departed Macmillan at the end of 2020 over disagreements regarding the direction of the publisher.

In June e-book lending was again in the spotlight after John Wiley & Sons, Hachette Book Group, Penguin Random House, and HarperCollins filed suit against the Internet Archive, a move supported by AAP. In response to the pandemic, the Internet Archive had created a "National Emergency Library," temporarily suspending wait lists to borrow e-books and allowing multiple users to read one digital copy simultaneously. The publishers argued that the Internet Archive is engaging in copyright infringement for its practice of controlled digital lending generally as well as for the particular instance of the National Emergency Library. In a statement issued in response to the development, ALA asserted that "the complaint of the Plaintiffs against the Internet Archive is strongly indicative that the current system of library e-book lending is broken. Libraries often pay $60 for one copy of an eBook as compared to typical price of $14 for consumer retail and the library gets only two years of access—and then libraries must pay again for an additional two years, and so on. The current inequitable system opens the door for organizations such as the Internet Archive to develop alternatives that provide affordable access to libraries."

At the federal level, ALA continued to engage with members of the House Judiciary Subcommittee on Antitrust, Commercial, and Administrative Law on equitable access to information and library e-book issues. Advocacy for library e-book lending was focused on the highly anticipated report from the House Judiciary Committee, based on its yearlong investigation of competition in digital markets. At the request of Subcommittee chairman David Cicilline (D-R.I.), ALA submitted a report in 2019 on unfair practices in digital markets. The Subcommittee released its report in fall 2020, and ALA and the library community are formulating proposals for how to leverage it toward legislative solutions to the e-book problem.

2020 Census: Libraries Step Up

Following extensive preparations to support a complete count in the decennial Census, ALA and libraries across the nation began the year by hosting in-person and online programs in the lead-up to the Census self-response drive, which started in March 2020. As the COVID-19 pandemic unfolded and libraries discontinued in-person services, libraries adapted Census activities appropriately. Scrapping plans for community outreach events, libraries answered questions related to the Census by phone, sent direct emails to patrons and Friends groups, and held virtual events geared to promote Census participation. More than 60 percent of respondents to an April survey from the Public Library Association (PLA) reported using social media to promote participation in the 2020 Census. Libraries' complete count efforts came to a close when the 2020 Census data collection ended on October 15. [For more about libraries, ALA, and the 2020 Census, see the Special Report by Karen Brown in Part 1 of this volume—*Ed.*]

With the 2020 Census completed, ALA and PLA have initiated a new grant-funded project to advance Census data literacy skills in the profession and the communities that libraries serve. Development is underway for a series of webinar trainings and online resources that will increase library staff knowledge, skills, and confidence to use Census data to plan and implement services that best meet the needs of diverse local communities. The trainings also will empower library staff to provide inclusive patron training in key areas, particularly related to local business and economic development, nonprofit and government planning, and student and community research.

Libraries Build Business

While the pandemic-challenged environment devastated many businesses, it also presented new opportunities. Just as COVID-19 took hold in March, ALA selected a cohort of 13 libraries to participate in Libraries Build Business, a national initiative supported by Google.org to partner with libraries across the country to develop and expand services to aspiring and existing small business owners and entrepreneurs from low-income and underrepresented backgrounds. Projects ranged from the Successful Street Vending program at Los Angeles Public Library to the New Start Entrepreneurship Incubator for returning citizens at Gwinnett County (Georgia) Public Library.

Libraries Build Business showcased libraries' role as catalysts for equitable opportunity, just when it was needed most. Serving a mix of urban, suburban, rural, and tribal communities around the country, the 13 libraries adjusted to execute their projects virtually and/or in compliance with health and safety guidelines.

The project will share promising practices and library-led models with the field. Through program evaluations, Libraries Build Business will glean what is replicable and adaptable for small business and entrepreneur programs nationally. Upon the initiative's completion in 2021, Libraries Build Business evaluation materials developed in collaboration with the cohort will also be available to the field.

In November, ALA released a new Policy Perspectives paper, *Open to Change: Libraries Catalyze Small Business Adaption to COVID-19*. Drawing on experiences of the Libraries Build Business cohort, the paper provides practical perspective on the COVID-19 challenge for small businesses, highlights some innovative ways that small businesses and entrepreneurs are pivoting, and contains ideas for libraries to support small business communities as they continue to respond to the impacts of the pandemic.

2020 Elections

Throughout the last half of 2020, libraries registered, informed, and engaged voters before the November election. A record number of voters cast their ballots before the historic 2020 elections, and in states where they are eligible and selected by their local election offices to do so, many libraries served as ballot drop-off points and/or early or election day polling locations.

In then president-elect Joe Biden's victory speech, he told educators that they will "have one of your own" in the White House, referring to his wife Dr. Jill Biden's long career as a teacher. Based on campaign pledges, the Biden-Harris Administration will be more favorable to education investment and the values of equity, diversity, and inclusion. President Biden's cabinet selections indicate a significant shift in policy around education, telecommunications, and workforce issues, among many others.

The change of leadership in the White House does not, however, automatically translate into wins for libraries. Votes cast further down the ballot will have an even bigger impact on the decision making in the next, and very divided, Congress. More than half of the newly elected members of Congress come from state and local elected offices, which illustrates the potentially national impact of local leadership and the exponential value of local library advocacy.

Looking Forward to 2021

The country continues to grapple with the COVID-19 pandemic and related challenges, including digital inclusion. The new Biden-Harris Administration and democratic majorities in both the House and Senate make it more promising that additional relief funding will materialize in their first 100 days. ALA anticipates working with Sen. Reed to reintroduce the Build America's Libraries Act. Still, the realities of the ongoing pandemic, the trillions already spent for emergency relief, and many other long-neglected domestic priorities will necessitate that library advocates remain vigilant in fighting for funding. Moving forward, advocates cannot assume library, education, infrastructure, and workforce spending will be any easier.

The hard work of library advocates throughout 2020, along with ALA's aggressive engagement with Congress during the intensive negotiations on COVID-19 relief funding at the end of the year, have solidified libraries' place at the policy negotiating table on behalf of the people they serve—especially those hardest hit. As the pandemic recedes, it will be important to maintain the visibility of libraries by showcasing how libraries are key providers of programs and services needed to advance economic recovery.

Funding Programs and Grant-Making Agencies

National Endowment for the Humanities

400 7th St. S.W., Washington, DC 20506
202-606-8400, 800-634-1121
TDD (hearing impaired) 202-606-8282 or 866-372-2930 (toll free)
E-mail info@neh.gov, World Wide Web http://neh.gov

The National Endowment for the Humanities (NEH) is an independent federal agency created in 1965. It is one of the largest funders of humanities programs in the United States.

Because democracy demands wisdom, NEH promotes excellence in the humanities and conveys the lessons of history to all Americans, seeking to develop educated and thoughtful citizens. It accomplishes this mission by providing grants for high-quality humanities projects in six funding areas: education, preservation and access, public programs, research, challenge grants, and digital humanities.

Grants from NEH enrich classroom learning, create and preserve knowledge, and bring ideas to life through public television, radio, new technologies, museum exhibitions, and programs in libraries and other community places. Recipients typically are cultural institutions, such as museums, archives, libraries, colleges and universities, and public television and radio stations, as well as individual scholars. The grants

- Strengthen teaching and learning in the humanities in schools and colleges
- Preserve and provide access to cultural and educational resources
- Provide opportunities for lifelong learning
- Facilitate research and original scholarship
- Strengthen the institutional base of the humanities

For more than a half century, NEH has reached millions of people with projects and programs that preserve and study the nation's culture and history while providing a foundation for the future.

The endowment's mission is to enrich cultural life by promoting the study of the humanities. According to the National Foundation on the Arts and the Humanities Act, "The term 'humanities' includes, but is not limited to, the study of the following: language, both modern and classical; linguistics; literature; history; jurisprudence; philosophy; archaeology; comparative religion; ethics; the history, criticism, and theory of the arts; those aspects of social sciences which have humanistic content and employ humanistic methods; and the study and application of the humanities to the human environment with particular attention to reflecting our diverse heritage, traditions, and history and to the relevance of the humanities to the current conditions of national life."

The act, adopted by Congress in 1965, provided for the establishment of the National Foundation on the Arts and the Humanities in order to promote progress and scholarship in the humanities and the arts in the United States. The act included the following findings:

- The arts and the humanities belong to all the people of the United States.
- The encouragement and support of national progress and scholarship in the humanities and the arts, while primarily matters for private and local initiative, are also appropriate matters of concern to the federal government.
- An advanced civilization must not limit its efforts to science and technology alone but must give full value and support to the other great branches of scholarly and cultural activity in order to achieve a better understanding of the past, a better analysis of the present, and a better view of the future.
- Democracy demands wisdom and vision in its citizens. It must therefore foster and support a form of education, and access to the arts and the humanities, designed to make people of all backgrounds and wherever located masters of technology and not its unthinking servants.
- It is necessary and appropriate for the federal government to complement, assist, and add to programs for the advancement of the humanities and the arts by local, state, regional, and private agencies and their organizations. In doing so, the government must be sensitive to the nature of public sponsorship. Public funding of the arts and humanities is subject to the conditions that traditionally govern the use of public money. Such funding should contribute to public support and confidence in the use of taxpayer funds. Public funds provided by the federal government ultimately must serve public purposes the Congress defines.
- The arts and the humanities reflect the high place accorded by the American people to the nation's rich culture and history and to the fostering of mutual respect for the diverse beliefs and values of all persons and groups.

What NEH Grants Accomplish

Since its founding, NEH has awarded more than 70,000 competitive grants.

Interpretive Exhibitions

Interpretive exhibitions provide opportunities for lifelong learning in the humanities for millions of Americans. Since 1967 NEH has awarded approximately $310 million in grants for interpretive exhibitions, catalogs, and public programs, which are among the most highly visible activities supported by the endowment. NEH support finances exhibitions; reading, viewing, and discussion programs; web-based programs; and other public education programs at venues across the country.

Renewing Teaching

Over NEH's history, more than 100,000 high school and college teachers have deepened their knowledge of the humanities through intensive summer study supported by the endowment; tens of thousands of students benefit from these better-educated teachers every year.

Reading and Discussion Programs

Since 1982 NEH has supported reading and discussion programs in the nation's libraries, bringing people together to discuss works of literature and history. Scholars in the humanities provide thematic direction for the discussion programs. Using selected texts and such themes as "Work," "Family," "Diversity," and "Not for Children Only," these programs have attracted more than 2 million Americans to read and talk about what they've read. Funded programs have ranged from veterans' reading groups focused on classic Greek and Roman texts about the experience of war, to community reading and discussion programs examining 200 years of Maine state history and humanities-focused reading and discussion programs for at-risk youth. Most recently, NEH supported a national "Lift Every Voice" reading and discussion program on African American poetic traditions based around the Library of America anthology *African American Poetry: 250 Years of Struggle & Song*.

Chronicling America

NEH's National Digital Newspaper Program is supporting projects to convert microfilm of historically important U.S. newspapers into fully searchable digital files. Developed in partnership with the Library of Congress, this long-term project ultimately will make more than 30 million pages of newspapers accessible online. For more on this project, visit http://chroniclingamerica.loc.gov.

Stimulating Private Support

About $2 billion in humanities support has been generated by NEH challenge grants, which require grant recipients to match federal funds. NEH Infrastructure and Capacity Building Challenge grants leverage federal funding to spur private investment in capital projects and infrastructure upgrades to ensure the long-term health of our cultural institutions.

Presidential Papers

Ten presidential papers projects, from Washington to Eisenhower, have received support from NEH. Matching grants for the ten projects have leveraged millions of dollars in nonfederal contributions.

New Scholarship

NEH grants enable scholars to do in-depth study. Jack Rakove explored the making of the Constitution in his Original Meanings, and James McPherson chronicled the Civil War in his *Battle Cry of Freedom*. NEH grants have led to the publication of some 7,000 books, 16 of which have received Pulitzer Prizes, and 20 Bancroft Prizes.

History on Screen

Since 1967 NEH has awarded approximately $310 million to support the production of films for broad public distribution, including the Emmy Award–winning series *The Civil War*, the Oscar-nominated films *Brooklyn Bridge, The Restless Conscience,* and *Freedom on My Mind,* and film biographies of John and Abigail Adams, Eugene O'Neill, and Ernest Hemingway. Over seven successive nights on PBS, more than 33 million people watched Ken Burns's *The Roosevelts* (2014), which chronicles the lives of Teddy, Eleanor, and Franklin. The NEH-funded series *The Vietnam War* (2018), by Ken Burns and Lynn Novick, was seen by 39 million viewers. Other recent NEH-supported films include *The Vote*, on the women's suffrage movement; *Chasing the Moon*, on the U.S. Space Race; Stanley Nelson's *Freedom Riders* and *Freedom Summer* documentaries; and *Worlds of Ursula K. Le Guin.*

American Voices

NEH support for scholarly editions makes the writings of prominent and influential Americans accessible. Ten presidents are included, along with such key figures as Martin Luther King, Jr., George C. Marshall, and Eleanor Roosevelt. Papers of prominent writers—among them Emily Dickinson, Walt Whitman, Mark Twain, and Robert Frost—are also available.

Library of America

Millions of books have been sold as part of the Library of America series, a collection of the riches of the nation's literature. Begun with NEH seed money, the 303 volumes published to date include the works of such figures as Henry Adams, Edith Wharton, William James, Eudora Welty, and W. E. B. Du Bois.

The Library of America also received a $150,000 grant for the publication of *American Poetry: The Seventeenth and Eighteenth Centuries* (two volumes) and an expanded volume of selected works by Captain John Smith—a key figure in the establishment of the first permanent English settlement in North America, at Jamestown, Virginia—and other early exploration narratives.

Technical Innovation

NEH support for the digital humanities is fueling innovation and new tools for research in the humanities. Modern 3D technology allows students to visit sites ranging from ancient Egypt to the 1964–1965 New York World's Fair. Spectral imaging was used to create an online critical edition of explorer David Livingstone's previously unreadable field diary of 1871.

Science and the Humanities

The scientific past is being preserved with NEH-supported editions of the letters of Charles Darwin, the works of Albert Einstein, and the 14-volume papers of

Thomas Edison. Additionally, NEH and the National Science Foundation have joined forces in Documenting Endangered Languages (DEL), a multiyear effort to preserve records of key languages that are in danger of becoming extinct.

EDSITEment

EDSITEment (http://edsitement.neh.gov) assembles the best humanities resources on the web, drawing over 400,000 visitors each month. Incorporating these Internet resources, particularly primary documents, from more than 350 peer-reviewed websites, EDSITEment features more than 500 online lesson plans in all areas of the humanities. Teachers use EDSITEment's resources to enhance lessons and to engage students through interactive technology tools that hone critical-thinking skills.

COVID Emergency Relief

In 2020, NEH distributed $75 million appropriated to the agency under the CARES Act to aid cultural institutions affected by the coronavirus pandemic. NEH CARES grants helped preserve humanities jobs and provided emergency funding to continue essential operations at more than 300 humanities institutions across the country. This funding allowed museums to shift exhibitions and public programs online, supported historic sites in planning to welcome visitors with social distancing protocols in place, enabled the creation of online educational resources and virtual field trips for educators, and underwrote research and publication activities at archives, colleges, libraries, and university presses.

Federal-State Partnership

The Office of Federal-State Partnership links NEH with the nationwide network of 56 humanities councils, which are located in each state, the District of Columbia, Puerto Rico, the U.S. Virgin Islands, the Northern Mariana Islands, American Samoa, and Guam. Each council funds humanities programs in its own jurisdiction.

Directory of State Humanities Councils

Alabama

Alabama Humanities Foundation
1100 Ireland Way, Suite 202
Birmingham, AL 35205-7001
205-558-3980, fax 205-558-3981
http://www.alabamahumanities.org

Alaska

Alaska Humanities Forum
421 W. 1st Ave., Suite 200
Anchorage, AK 99501
907-272-5341, fax 907-272-3979
http://www.akhf.org

Arizona

Arizona Humanities Council
Ellis-Shackelford House
1242 N. Central Ave.
Phoenix, AZ 85004-1887
602-257-0335, fax 602-257-0392
http://www.azhumanities.org

Arkansas

Arkansas Humanities Council
407 President Clinton Ave., Suite 201
Little Rock, AR 72201
501-320-5761, fax 501-537-4550
http://www.arkansashumanitiescouncil.org

California

Cal Humanities
538 9th St., #210
Oakland, CA 94607
415-391-1474, fax 415-391-1312
http://www.calhum.org

Colorado

Colorado Humanities
7935 E. Prentice Ave., Suite 450
Greenwood Village, CO 80111
303-894-7951, fax 303-864-9361
http://www.coloradohumanities.org

Connecticut

Connecticut Humanities Council
100 Riverview Center, Suite 270
292 Main Street
Middletown, CT 06457
860-685-2260, fax 860-685-7597
http://cthumanities.org

Delaware

Delaware Humanities
100 W. Tenth St., Suite 509
Wilmington, DE 19801
302-657-0650, fax 302-657-0655
http://dehumanities.org

District of Columbia

Humanities D.C.
925 U St. N.W.
Washington, DC 20001
202-387-8393, fax 202-387-8149
http://wdchumanities.org

Florida

Florida Humanities Council
599 Second St. S.
St. Petersburg, FL 33701-5005
727-873-2000, fax 727-873-2014
http://www.floridahumanities.org

Georgia

Georgia Humanities Council
50 Hurt Plaza S.E., Suite 595
Atlanta, GA 30303-2915
404-523-6220, fax 404-523-5702
http://www.georgiahumanities.org

Hawaii

Hawai'i Council for the Humanities
First Hawaiian Bank Bldg.
3599 Waialae Ave., Room 25
Honolulu, HI 96816
808-732-5402, fax 808-732-5432
http://www.hihumanities.org

Idaho

Idaho Humanities Council
217 W. State St.
Boise, ID 83702
208-345-5346, fax 208-345-5347
http://www.idahohumanities.org

Illinois

Illinois Humanities Council
125 S. Church St., Suite 650
Chicago, IL 60603-5200
312-422-5580, fax 312-422-5588
http://www.ilhumanities.org

Indiana

Indiana Humanities
1500 N. Delaware St.
Indianapolis, IN 46202
317-638-1500, fax 317-634-9503
http://www.indianahumanities.org

Iowa

Iowa Department of Cultural Affairs
State Historical Building
600 E. Locust Street
Des Moines, IA 50319
515-281-3223
www.Iowaculture.gov

Kansas

Kansas Humanities Council
112 S.W. 6th Ave., Suite 400
Topeka, KS 66603-3895
785-357-0359, fax 785-357-1723
https://www.humanitieskansas.org

Kentucky

Kentucky Humanities
206 E. Maxwell St.
Lexington, KY 40508
859-257-5932, fax 859-257-5933
http://www.kyhumanities.org

Louisiana

Louisiana Endowment for the Humanities
938 Lafayette St., Suite 300
New Orleans, LA 70113-1782
504-523-4352, fax 504-529-2358
http://www.leh.org

Maine

Maine Humanities Council
674 Brighton Ave.
Portland, ME 04102-1012
207-773-5051, fax 207-773-2416
http://www.mainehumanities.org

Maryland

Maryland Humanities Council
108 W. Centre St.
Baltimore, MD 21201-4565
410-685-0095, fax 410-685-0795
http://www.mdhumanities.org

Massachusetts

Mass Humanities
66 Bridge St.
Northampton, MA 01060
413-584-8440, fax 413-584-8454
http://www.masshumanities.org

Michigan

Michigan Humanities Council
119 Pere Marquette Drive, Suite 3B
Lansing, MI 48912-1270
517-372-7770, fax 517-372-0027
http://michiganhumanities.org

Minnesota

Minnesota Humanities Center
987 Ivy Ave. E.
St. Paul, MN 55106-2046

651-774-0105, fax 651-774-0205
http://www.mnhum.org

Mississippi

Mississippi Humanities Council
3825 Ridgewood Rd., Room 311
Jackson, MS 39211
601-432-6752, fax 601-432-6750
http://www.mshumanities.org

Missouri

Missouri Humanities Council
The Grand Central Building at Union Station
415 South 18th St., Suite 100
St. Louis, MO 63103
Toll free: 1-800-357-0909
314-781-9660, fax 314-781-9681
http://www.mohumanities.org

Montana

Humanities Montana
311 Brantly
Missoula, MT 59812-7848
406-243-6022, fax 406-243-4836
http://www.humanitiesmontana.org

Nebraska

Nebraska Humanities Council
215 Centennial Mall South, Suite 330
Lincoln, NE 68508
402-474-2131, fax 402-474-4852
http://www.humanitiesnebraska.org

Nevada

Nevada Humanities
1670-200 N. Virginia St.
P.O. Box 8029
Reno, NV 89507-8029
775-784-6587, fax 775-784-6527
http://www.nevadahumanities.org

New Hampshire

New Hampshire Humanities
117 Pleasant St.
Concord, NH 03301-3852
603-224-4071, fax 603-224-4072
http://www.nhhc.org

New Jersey

New Jersey Council for the Humanities
28 W. State St., Suite 6
Trenton, NJ 08608
609-695-4838, fax 609-695-4929
http://www.njhumanities.org

New Mexico

New Mexico Humanities Council
4115 Silver Ave. S.E.
Albuquerque, NM 87108
505-633-7370, fax 505-633-7377
http://www.nmhum.org

New York

Humanities New York
150 Broadway, Suite 1700
New York, NY 10038
212-233-1131, fax 212-233-4607
http://www.humanitiesny.org

North Carolina

North Carolina Humanities Council
320 East 9th St., Suite 414
Charlotte, NC 28202
704-687-1520, fax 704-687-1550
http://www.nchumanities.org

North Dakota

Humanities North Dakota
418 E. Broadway, Suite 8
Bismarck, ND 58501
701-255-3360, fax 701-223-8724
http://www.humanitiesnd.org

Ohio

Ohio Humanities Council
471 E. Broad St., Suite 1620
Columbus, OH 43215-3857
614-461-7802, fax 614-461-4651
http://www.ohiohumanities.org

Oklahoma

Oklahoma Humanities
424 Concord Dr., Suite E
Oklahoma City, OK 73102
405-235-0280, fax 405-235-0289
http://www.okhumanities.org

Oregon

Oregon Council for the Humanities
921 S.W. Washington St., #150
Portland, OR 97205
503-241-0543, fax 503-241-0024
http://www.oregonhumanities.org

Pennsylvania

Pennsylvania Humanities Council
325 Chestnut St., Suite 715
Philadelphia, PA 19106-2607
215-925-1005, fax 215-925-3054
http://www.pahumanities.org

Rhode Island

Rhode Island Council for the Humanities
131 Washington St., Suite 210
Providence, RI 02903
401-273-2250, fax 401-454-4872
http://www.rihumanities.org

South Carolina

South Carolina Humanities
2711 Middleburg Drive, Suite 203
P.O. Box 5287
Columbia, SC 29254
803-771-2477, fax 803-771-2487
http://www.schumanities.org

South Dakota

South Dakota Humanities Council
1215 Trail Ridge Rd., Suite A
Brookings, SD 57006
605-688-6113, fax 605-688-4531
http://sdhumanities.org

Tennessee

Humanities Tennessee
807 Main Street, Suite B
Nashville, TN 37201
615-770-0006, fax 615-770-0007
http://www.humanitiestennessee.org

Texas

Humanities Texas
1410 Rio Grande St.
Austin, TX 78701
512-440-1991, fax 512-440-0115
http://www.humanitiestexas.org

Utah

Utah Humanities
202 W. 300 North
Salt Lake City, UT 84103
801-359-9670, fax 801-531-7869
http://www.utahhumanities.org

Vermont

Vermont Humanities
11 Loomis St.
Montpelier, VT 05602
802-262-2626, fax 802-262-2620
http://www.vermonthumanities.org

Virginia

Virginia Foundation for the Humanities
145 Ednam Drive
Charlottesville, VA 22903-4629
434-924-3296, fax 434-296-4714
http://www.virginiahumanities.org

Washington

Humanities Washington
130 Nickerson St., Suite 304
Seattle, WA 98109
206-682-1770, fax 206-682-4158
http://www.humanities.org

West Virginia

West Virginia Humanities Council
1310 Kanawha Blvd. East
Charleston, WV 25301
304-346-8500, fax 304-346-8504
http://wvhumanities.org/

Wisconsin

Wisconsin Humanities Council
3801 Regent St.
Madison, WI 53705

608-262-0706, fax 608-263-7970
http://www.wisconsinhumanities.org

Wyoming

Wyoming Humanities Council
1315 E. Lewis St.
Laramie, WY 82072-3459
307-721-9243, fax 307-742-4914
http://www.thinkwy.org

American Samoa

Amerika Samoa Humanities Council
P.O. Box 5800
Pago Pago, AS 96799
684-633-4870, fax 684-633-4873
http://ashcouncil.org

Guam

Humanities Guahan
222 Chalan Santo Papa
Reflection Center, Suite 106
Hagåtña, Guam 96910
671-472-4460, fax 671-472-4465
http://www.humanitiesguahan.org

Northern Marianas Islands

Northern Marianas Humanities Council
P.O. Box 506437
Saipan, MP 96950
670-235-4785, fax 670-235-4786
http://www.nmhcouncil.org/

Puerto Rico

Fundación Puertorriqueña de las Humanidades
109 San José St., 3rd floor
Box 9023920
San Juan, PR 00902-3920
787-721-2087, fax 787-721-2684
http://www.fphpr.org

NEH Overview

Division of Education Programs

Through grants to educational institutions and professional development programs for scholars and teachers, this division is designed to support study of the humanities at all levels of education.

Grants support the development of curricula and materials, faculty study programs, and conferences and networks of educational institutions.

Contact: 202-606-8500, e-mail education@neh.gov.

Seminars and Institutes

Grants support summer seminars and institutes in the humanities for college and school teachers. These faculty-development activities are conducted at colleges and universities in the United States. Those wishing to participate in seminars should submit their seminar applications to the seminar director.

Contact: 202-606-8471, e-mail sem-inst@neh.gov.

Landmarks of American History and Culture

Grants for Landmarks workshops provide support to teachers and community college faculty. These professional development workshops are conducted at or near sites important to American history and culture (such as presidential residences or libraries, colonial-era settlements, major battlefields, historic districts, and sites associated with major writers or artists) to address central themes and issues in American history, government, literature, art history, and related subjects in the humanities.

Contact: 202-606-8463, e-mail landmarks@neh.gov.

Division of Preservation and Access

Grants are made for projects that will create, preserve, and increase the availability of resources important for research, education, and public programming in the humanities.

Support may be sought to preserve the intellectual content and aid bibliographic control of collections; to compile bibliographies, descriptive catalogs, and guides to cultural holdings; and to create dictionaries, encyclopedias, databases, and electronic archives. Applications also may be submitted for education and training projects dealing with issues of preservation or access; for research and development leading to improved preservation and access standards, practices, and tools; and for projects to digitize historic U.S. newspapers and to document endangered languages. Grants are also made to help smaller cultural repositories preserve and care for their humanities collections. Proposals may combine preservation and access activities within a single project.

Contact: 202-606-8570, e-mail preservation@neh.gov.

Division of Public Programs

Public humanities programs promote lifelong learning in American and world history, literature, comparative religion, philosophy, and other fields of the humanities. They offer new insights into familiar subjects and invite conversation about important humanities ideas and questions.

The Division of Public Programs supports an array of public humanities programs that reach large and diverse public audiences through a variety of program formats, including interpretive exhibitions, radio and television broadcasts, lectures, symposia, interpretive multimedia projects, printed materials, and reading and discussion programs.

Grants support the development and production of television, radio, and digital media programs; the planning and implementation of museum exhibitions, the interpretation of historic sites, the production of related publications, multimedia components, and educational programs; and the planning and implementation of reading and discussion programs, lectures, symposia, and interpretive exhibitions of books, manuscripts, and other library resources.

Contact: 202-606-8269, e-mail publicpgms@neh.gov.

Division of Research Programs

Through fellowships to individual scholars and grants to support complex, frequently collaborative research, the Division of Research Programs contributes to the creation of knowledge in the humanities.

Fellowships and Stipends

Grants provide support for scholars to undertake full-time independent research and writing in the humanities. Grants are available for a maximum of one year and a minimum of two months of summer study.

Contact: 202-606-8200, e-mail (fellowships) fellowships@neh.gov, (summer stipends) stipends@neh.gov.

Research

Grants provide up to three years of support for collaborative research in the preparation for publication of editions, translations, and other important works in the humanities, and in the conduct of large or complex interpretive studies, including archaeology projects and humanities studies of science and technology. Grants also support research opportunities offered through independent research centers and international research organizations.

Contact: 202-606-8200, e-mail research@neh.gov.

Office of Challenge Grants

Nonprofit institutions interested in developing new sources of long-term support for educational, scholarly, preservation, and public programs in the humanities can be assisted in these efforts by an NEH Infrastructure and Capacity Building Challenge Grant. Grantees are required to raise nonfederal donations to match federal funds. Both federal and nonfederal funds may be used for infrastructure upgrades and other capital projects to ensure the long-term health of cultural institutions.

Contact: 202-606-8309, e-mail challenge@neh.gov.

Office of Digital Humanities

The Office of Digital Humanities encourages and supports projects that utilize or study the impact of digital technology on research, education, preservation, and public programming in the humanities. Launched as an initiative in 2006, Digital Humanities was made permanent as an office within NEH in 2008.

NEH is interested in fostering the growth of digital humanities and lending support to a wide variety of projects, including those that deploy digital technologies and methods to enhance understanding of a topic or issue; those that study the impact of digital technology on the humanities; and those that digitize important materials, thereby increasing the public's ability to search and access humanities information.

The office coordinates the endowment's efforts in the area of digital scholarship. Currently NEH has numerous programs throughout the agency that are actively funding digital scholarship, including Humanities Collections and Resources, Institutes for Advanced Topics in the Digital Humanities, Digital Humanities Start-Up Grants, and many others. NEH is also actively working with other funding partners in the United States and abroad in order to better coordinate spending on digital infrastructure for the humanities.

Contact: 202-606-8401, e-mail odh@neh.gov.

A full list of NEH grants programs and deadlines is available on the endowment's website at http://www.neh.gov/grants.

Institute of Museum and Library Services

955 L'Enfant Plaza North, S.W., Suite 4000, Washington, DC 20024-2135
202-653-4657, fax 202-653-4600
http://www.imls.gov

Crosby Kemper III
Director

The Institute of Museum and Library Services (IMLS) is an independent grant-making agency and the primary source of federal support for the nation's libraries and museums.

The mission of IMLS is to advance, support, and empower America's museums, libraries, and related organizations through grant making, research, and policy development. Its vision is a nation where museums and libraries work together to transform the lives of individuals and communities.

IMLS was created with the passage of the Museum and Library Services Act of 1996, which was reauthorized on December 31, 2018. The agency has statutory authority to award financial assistance, collect data, form strategic partnerships, and advise policymakers and other federal agencies on museum, library, and information services.

The agency consolidates federal library programs dating back to 1956 with museum programs dating back to 1976.

IMLS helps to ensure that all Americans have access to museum, library, and information services. The agency invests in new and exploratory approaches, as well as proven and tested methods. IMLS funds work that advances collective knowledge, lifelong learning, and cultural and civic engagement. And the agency builds capacity within the museum and library fields to enable better service to communities and to enhance community decision-making by sharing trends and data.

IMLS has an expansive reach. The agency is the largest source of federal funding for libraries in the nation, directing population-based funding to all 50 states, the District of Columbia, the U.S. territories, and Freely Associated States through its Grants to States program. The agency's discretionary grants are selected through a highly respected and competitive peer review process, drawing on professionals located across the nation.

This work enables museums and libraries located in geographically and economically diverse areas to deliver essential services that make it possible for individuals and communities to flourish.

Strategic Goals

When IMLS was established by the Museum and Library Services Act of 1996, bringing together federal programs dating back to 1956, lawmakers recognized that U.S. libraries and museums are powerful national assets. They saw "great potential in an institute that is focused on the combined roles that libraries and museums play in our community life." The law charges IMLS with advising policymakers on library, museum, and information services and supporting a wide range of programs that improve the lives of individuals throughout the nation.

IMLS carries out this charge as the agency adapts to meet the changing needs of the nation's museums and libraries and their communities. IMLS's role—to advance, support, and empower America's museums and libraries through grant making, research, data collection, and policy development—is essential to helping these institutions navigate change and continue to improve their services.

IMLS goals and objectives are to

1 Promote Lifelong Learning. IMLS supports learning and literacy for people of all ages through museums and libraries.

2 Build Capacity. IMLS strengthens the capacity of museums and libraries to improve the well-being of their communities.

3 Increase Public Access. IMLS makes strategic investments that increase access to information, ideas, and networks through libraries and museums.

4 Achieve Excellence. IMLS strategically aligns its resources and relationships to support libraries and museums nationwide.

The agency's strategic goals and objectives are outlined in Transforming Communities, the IMLS Strategic Plan 2018–2022. The five-year plan frames how the agency envisions meeting the essential information, education, research, economic, cultural, and civic needs of the American public.

COVID-19 Response

CARES Act Grants

On March 27, 2020, the President signed the Coronavirus Aid, Relief, and Economic Security (CARES) Act. Pub. L.116-136 authorized funding for IMLS to assist states, tribes, museums, and libraries to "prevent, prepare for, and respond to coronavirus . . . expand digital network access, purchase Internet accessible devices, and provide technical support services" for the benefit of communities impacted by the public health emergency.

CARES Act Allotments to State Library Administrative Agencies

Process

Using a population-based formula, the Grants to States program awarded $30 million in CARES Act funds to the 59 State Library Administrative Agencies (SLAAs) in the 50 states, the District of Columbia, the U.S. Territories, and the Freely Associated States. IMLS distributed these awards on April 21, 2020, with funds remaining available until September 30, 2021. IMLS directed the SLAAs to prioritize (1) digital inclusion and related technical support; (2) other efforts that prevent, prepare for, and respond to COVID-19; and (3) reaching museum and tribal partners, in addition to traditionally eligible library entities, where appropriate. Apart from a waived match requirement, all other Grants to States statutory provisions applied, including the 4 percent cap for administration, reporting requirements, and compliance with provisions such as the Children's Internet Protection Act (CIPA).

Highlights

Early informal CARES Act plans from the states indicated an emphasis on connectivity, including purchasing hotspots, devices with data plans, wifi extenders and repeaters, and other equipment upgrades. In just five months after SLAAs received the CARES Act awards, a national rollup of publicly available information showed that 41 of 59 states and territories had already publicized their investments. High-level data as of September 2020 pointed to the following:

- Funds had reached at least 1,775 libraries, 80 museums, and 20 tribal entities.
- Twenty-one SLAAs were offering competitive CARES Act subawards, and some with multiple opportunities for a total of 30 programs.
- Six SLAAs were offering noncompetitive CARES Act subawards, based on formulas of need or other distribution methods.
- SLAAs had already announced over 1,750 subawards.
- SLAAs and their subrecipients had already announced the purchase of over 4,000 devices, such as hotspots, laptops, and tablets.
- Twenty SLAAs were offering statewide programs, and some with multiple offerings for a total of 32 programs.
- Connectivity efforts remained the primary CARES Act focus among the states, but 19 states had also purchased supplies to help libraries safely reopen their physical spaces.

The CARES Act grants represented a significant shift for the Grants to States program in terms of SLAAs finding creative ways to reach museums and tribes, in addition to traditionally eligible libraries. While not all SLAAs had the flexibility to do so, as of the end of September 2020, 11 states had found ways to incorporate museums into their CARES Act grant making, and 7 states had done the same for tribes. Of the more than 80 museums reached by the funds, 59 had received direct subawards of their own, which signaled a true sea change for the program.

IMLS CARES Act Grants for Native American / Native Hawaiian Museum and Library Services

IMLS established a competitive funding opportunity to support Native American tribes and organizations that primarily serve Native Hawaiians in responding to the COVID-19 pandemic. IMLS encouraged project proposals that primarily addressed digital inclusion, related technical support and training, access to information, rehiring or reskilling staff, and other needs resulting from the pandemic. A total of $1.2 million was set aside for the program, and requests could range from $10,000 to $150,000. IMLS did not require cost share, and the period of performance could range from one to two years.

Highlights

The Institute of Museum and Library Services awarded $1.2 million in IMLS CARES Act Grants to 15 organizations to fund projects assisting Native American tribes and Native Hawaiian serving organizations through their tribal libraries and cultural centers to respond to the coronavirus pandemic. Organizations receiving awards are providing $178,892 in nonfederal matching funds. Funded projects were selected from 100 applications requesting $9,772,100 in funding.

IMLS CARES Act Grants for Museums and Libraries

IMLS established a competitive funding opportunity to support libraries and museums in helping their communities respond to the COVID-19 pandemic. Based on the model of National Leadership Grants, IMLS encouraged project proposals that focused on preserving jobs, training staff, addressing the digital divide, planning for reopening, and providing technical support and capacity building for digital inclusion and engagement while prioritizing services for high-need communities. Applicants that developed projects addressing digital inclusion and related technical support were urged to define high-need communities on the basis of economic indicators such as poverty rates, Supplemental Nutrition Access Program (SNAP) participation rates, unemployment rates, and broadband availability and adoption. A total of $13.8 million was set aside for the program, and requests could range from $25,000 to $500,000. There was no cost share requirement, and the period of performance could range from one to two years.

Highlights

The Institute of Museum and Library Services awarded $13.8 million in IMLS CARES Act Grants to 68 museums and libraries to support their response to the coronavirus pandemic. Institutions receiving awards are providing $1,753,470 in nonfederal matching funds. Funded projects were selected from 1,701 applications requesting $409,251,399.

Sixty-four percent of the awards came from organizations that were designated as museum entities, and many represent projects engaging libraries as partners. Museum award recipients represented a diverse range of disciplines and institution types, including art, science, natural history, institutes of higher education, HBCUs, history, and others.

REopening Archives, Libraries, and Museums (REALM) Project

To provide information to libraries, archives, and museums about the important and existential problems facing them in the global pandemic, IMLS entered into a cooperative agreement with Online Computer Library Center (OCLC) and Battelle. The REALM project is drawing upon scientific research and Battelle laboratory work to produce, widely disseminate, and periodically update evidence-based information that can inform operational considerations for reducing the risk of transmission of COVID-19 through libraries, archives, and museums to their staffs and visitors.

IMLS exercised its fundraising authorities to carry out the project. As such, the REALM project was made possible in part with support from the Institute of Museum and Library Services, the Library of Congress, the Andrew W. Mellon Foundation, and the Carnegie Corporation of New York.

The project is conducting laboratory tests to assess the attenuation of COVID-19 on materials common in libraries, archives, and museums (LAM) and to assess emergent published research for applicable scientific information that can be applied to the LAM community risk-based decision making. More about the status of the project and its publications can be found at https://www.oclc.org/realm/home.html.

Library Services

The Museum and Library Services Act (20 U.S.C. § 9171) authorizes the Office of Library Services to

- Enhance coordination among federal programs that relate to library, education, and information services
- Promote continuous improvement in library services in all types of libraries in order to better serve the people of the United States
- Facilitate access to resources in all types of libraries for the purpose of cultivating an educated and informed citizenry
- Encourage resource sharing among all types of libraries for the purpose of achieving economical and efficient delivery of library services to the public
- Promote literacy, education, and lifelong learning, including by building learning partnerships with school libraries in the nation's schools, including tribal schools, and developing resources, capabilities, and programs in support of state, tribal, and local efforts to offer a well-rounded educational experience to all students
- Enable libraries to develop services that meet the needs of communities throughout the nation, including people of diverse geographic, cultural, and socioeconomic backgrounds; individuals with disabilities; residents of rural and urban areas; Native Americans; military families; veterans; and caregivers
- Enable libraries to serve as anchor institutions to support community revitalization through enhancing and expanding the services and resources provided by libraries, including those services and resources relating to workforce development, economic and business development, critical-thinking skills, health information, digital literacy skills, financial literacy and other types of literacy skills, and new and emerging technology
- Enhance the skills of the current library workforce and recruit future professionals, including those from diverse and underrepresented backgrounds, to the field of library and information services
- Ensure the preservation of knowledge and library collections in all formats and enable libraries to serve their communities during disasters
- Enhance the role of libraries within the information infrastructure of the United States in order to support research, education, and innovation
- Promote library services that provide users with access to information through national, state, local, regional, and international collaborations and networks
- Encourage, support, and disseminate model programs of library and museum collaboration

Grants to States

The Grants to States program awards population-based formula grants to each State Library Administrative Agency (SLAA) in the 50 states; the District of Columbia; the U.S. territories of the Commonwealth of Puerto Rico; the U.S. Virgin Islands; American Samoa; Guam; and the Commonwealth of the Northern Mariana Islands; and the Freely Associated States of the Federated States of Micronesia, the Republic of the Marshall Islands, and the Republic of Palau (20 U.S.C. § 9131). Following the passage of the 2018 Act, fiscal year (FY) 2020 was the first year that the three Freely Associated States submitted five-year plans, which IMLS approved before disseminating their allotments.

The formula consists of a minimum allotment set by law plus a supplemental amount based on population (dependent on annual appropriations). Population data are based on the information available from the U.S. Census Bureau.

The 2018 Act increased minimum allotments for states from $680,000 to $1,000,000, and for Pacific territories and Freely Associated States, from $60,000 to $100,000. Increases to the minimum allotments depend on increases to the program's overall budget, which grew by $6 million in FY 2020. Although this increase did not fully enact the new statutory minimum allotments, it did raise the base to $795,384 for states, with $60,000 for other entities. The Act limits administrative costs at the state level to 4 percent and requires a 34 percent match from nonfederal state or local funds.

Programs and services delivered by each SLAA support the purposes and priorities set forth in the Library Services and Technology Act (LSTA). SLAAs must complete five-year plans, conduct a five-year evaluation based on those plans, and report annually to IMLS on their progress in strengthening library services, which helps improve practice and inform policy. SLAAs set goals and objectives for their states regarding the use of Grants to States funds within the statutorily required five-year plan approved by IMLS. These goals and objectives are determined through a planning process that includes statewide needs assessments.

Use of Funds

States are subject to a statutory "maintenance of effort" requirement that helps ensure that federal funds do not supplant state investments. SLAAs may use their funding for

- Expanding services for learning and access to information and educational resources in a variety of formats, including new and emerging technology, in all types of libraries, for individuals of all ages, in order to support such individuals' needs for education, lifelong learning, workforce development, economic and business development, health information, critical-thinking skills, digital literacy skills, and financial literacy and other types of literacy skills

- Establishing or enhancing electronic and other linkages and improved coordination among and between libraries and entities, for the purpose of improving the quality of and access to library and information services

- Providing training and professional development, including continuing education, to enhance the skills of the current library workforce and leadership, and advance the delivery of library and information services

- Enhancing efforts to recruit future professionals, including those from diverse and underrepresented backgrounds, to the field of library and information services
- Developing public and private partnerships with other agencies, tribes, and community-based organizations
- Targeting library services to individuals of diverse geographic, cultural, and socioeconomic backgrounds, to individuals with disabilities, and to individuals with limited functional literacy or information skills
- Targeting library and information services to persons having difficulty using a library and to underserved urban and rural communities, including children from families with incomes below the poverty line
- Developing library services that provide all users access to information through local, state, regional, national, and international collaborations and networks
- Carrying out other activities as described in the state library administrative agency's plan

Support for Pacific Territories and Freely Associated States

Under the 2010 LSTA, grants to the Pacific Territories and the Freely Associated States were made pursuant to a Special Rule, 20 U.S.C. § 9131(b)(3), that established a separate grants process for the Pacific region and the U.S. Virgin Islands.

The 2018 Act modified the Special Rule, and FY 2019 was the last year of competitive funding to the Pacific Territories and Freely Associated States through this separate mechanism. To reduce administrative costs and burden, all entities that had been eligible for the program under the Special Rule received allotments through the Grants to States program in FY 2020.

Discretionary Grants

The Office of Library Services offered six funding opportunities in FY 2020: National Leadership Grants, Accelerating Promising Practices for Small Libraries, Native American Library Services Basic Grants, Native American Library Services Enhancement Grants, Native Hawaiian Library Services, and the Laura Bush 21st Century Librarian Program.

Office of Library Services Highlights

The Office of Library Services (OLS) demonstrated exceptional flexibility and adaptability in response to the pandemic. OLS successfully executed its regular grant programs and two signature events, in addition to CARES Act grant programs. OLS staff helped grantees navigate newly available COVID-19 flexibilities for their open awards by processing over 200 extensions, budget revisions, and other scope changes. Deadlines for four regular OLS grant programs were adjusted to support applicants transitioning to remote work and the delivery of library programs and services virtually.

Working remotely, OLS staff swiftly shifted to virtual delivery of its in-person events. This included review panels, the National Student Poets Program, the National Book Festival, and the Grants to States conference, which was attended by 177 representatives from the states. This was a substantial increase from the 65 representatives from states who attend the in-person conference. OLS also supported grantees that needed to adjust their projects in response to the pandemic.

Museum Services

The Museum and Library Services Act (20 U.S.C. § 9171) authorizes the Office of Museum Services to

- Encourage and support museums in carrying out their educational role, as core providers of learning and in conjunction with schools, families, and communities
- Encourage and support museums in carrying out their public service role of connecting the whole of society to the cultural, artistic, historical, natural, and scientific understandings that constitute our diverse heritage
- Encourage leadership, innovation, and applications of the most current technologies and practices to enhance museum services through international, national, regional, state, and local networks and partnership
- Assist, encourage, and support museums in carrying out their stewardship responsibilities to achieve the highest standards in conservation and care of the diverse cultural, historic, natural, and scientific heritage of the United States to benefit future generations
- Assist, encourage, and support museums in achieving the highest standards of management and service to the public, and to ease the financial burden borne by museums as they serve their communities in new and different ways
- Support resource sharing and partnerships among museums, libraries, schools, and other community organizations
- Encourage and support museums as a part of economic development and revitalization in communities
- Ensure museums of various types and sizes in diverse geographic regions of the United States are afforded attention and support
- Support efforts at the state and regional levels to leverage museum resources and maximize museum services
- Assist museums in their civic engagement efforts to ensure that every person in the United States has access to high-quality museum services

IMLS also conducts a grant program with the purpose of improving operations, care of collections, and development of professional management at African American museums, pursuant to the National Museum of African American History and Culture Act (20 U.S.C. § 80r-5).

Discretionary Grants

The Office of Museum Services offered six competitive funding opportunities in FY 2020: Museums for America (MFA), Inspire! Grants for Small

Museums, Museums Empowered, National Leadership Grants for Museums, Native American / Native Hawaiian Museum Services, and Museum Grants for African American History and Culture.

Office of Museum Services Highlights

The Office of Museum Services received 784 applications in FY 2020 and supported 32 percent of the total applications in 46 states and the District of Columbia through its discretionary grant programs. Through the appropriation for MFA, an increased amount was allocated to meet the capacity building needs of small museums through the Inspire! Grants for Small Museums program, a special initiative under MFA. IMLS launched three research and evaluation studies designed to better understand its investments, identify gaps and opportunities, and enhance its funding opportunities for the museum field.

To address the need to offer digital resources created by the pandemic in the museum community, IMLS directed funds from the FY 2020 National Leadership Grants for Museums to support three targeted projects that would make a significant difference in strengthening the digital capacity of museums.

Interagency Collaboration

The Museum and Library Services Act authorizes IMLS to enter into interagency agreements to promote or assist with the museum, library, and information services-related activities of other federal agencies (20 U.S.C. § 9103). Recognizing the role of museums and libraries as anchor institutions, the Act directs the agency to coordinate and work jointly with other federal departments and agencies on

- Initiatives, materials, technology, or research to support education, workforce development, economic and business development, and related activities and services undertaken by libraries
- Resource and policy approaches to eliminate barriers to fully leveraging the role of libraries and museums in supporting the early learning, literacy, lifelong learning, digital literacy, workforce development, and education needs of the people of the United States
- Initiatives, materials, technology, or research to support educational, cultural, historical, scientific, environmental, and other activities undertaken by museums

In addition to project support, the director of IMLS holds several statutory positions, including on the Federal Council on the Arts and the Humanities, in the American Folklife Center, and in connection with the nation's Semiquincentennial Commission.

Policy Research, Analysis, Data Collection, and Dissemination

IMLS is authorized to support and conduct policy research, data collection, analysis and modeling, evaluation, and dissemination of information to extend and improve the nation's museum, library, and information services (20 U.S.C. § 9108). The Act identifies the following objectives:

- To enhance and expand the capacity of museums, libraries, and information services to anticipate, respond to, and meet the evolving needs of communities and the public, including by identifying trends and developments that may impact the need for and delivery of services
- To provide information and data on the role, value, and impact of museum, library, and information resources, including the identification of trends and the potential gaps in the availability and use of museum and library services by their communities and the public
- To measure the effectiveness of museums, libraries, and information services throughout the United States, including the impact of federal programs authorized under the Act
- To identify indicators and outcomes that can be used to create enhancements to the efficiency and efficacy of museum, library, and information services
- To promote advancement and growth in museum, library, and information services through sharing of best practices and effective strategies in order to better serve the people of the United States
- To facilitate planning for, and building of, institutional capacity in order to improve museum, library, and information services at the national, state, local, and regional levels; and international communications and cooperative networks

In carrying out these objectives, IMLS engages with the SLAAs and networks of museums and libraries, as well as with national, state, tribal, and regional museum and library organizations.

Surveys

IMLS produces evaluations and performs data collection and analysis to inform policy decisions and support the museum and library fields of practice. These efforts identify trends, make important comparisons, and enable objective policy-making at the national and state levels. The primary data products maintained by IMLS are the Public Libraries Survey (PLS) and the State Library Administrative Agency (SLAA) Survey.

The PLS has been conducted annually since 1988 and is a definitive source on the state of public libraries in the United States. PLS data provides key information on over 9,000 public library systems and 17,000 public library outlets nationwide. Over the past year, IMLS enhanced the PLS by continuing improvements for its data collection and data utilization practices.

The SLAA Survey has been collected annually since 1994 and biennially after 2010. The survey is a definitive source on the state of state library agencies in the United States and provides key information on the state library agencies in all 50 states and the District of Columbia.

For IMLS surveys and data, visit https://www.imls.gov/research-tools/data-collection and see the report "Highlights of IMLS Public Library Surveys" beginning on page 288 of this volume.

IMLS Website and Publications

The IMLS website (www.imls.gov) provides a wealth of information on the agency's activities, including IMLS-sponsored conferences, webinars, publications, and grant programs. Through an electronic newsletter, *IMLS News*, and the blog, IMLS provides information on grant deadlines, success stories, and opportunities.

IMLS is on twitter @US_IMLS and Facebook at https://www.facebook.com/ USIMLS.

EveryLibrary

P.O. Box 406, Riverside, IL 60546
312-574-0316, e-mail info@everylibrary.org
World Wide Web http://www.everylibrary.org | action.everylibrary.org | SaveSchoolLibrarians.org

John Chrastka
Executive Director

Founded in December 2012 as a political action committee for libraries, EveryLibrary focuses on building political power for libraries at all levels of government across all types of libraries. EveryLibrary is the first and only nationwide political action committee for libraries. Its mission statement is "Building voter support for libraries." Its vision statement, and the inspiration for its name, is "Any library funding issue anywhere should matter to every library everywhere." It is chartered in the state of Illinois as a nonprofit and is designated as a 501(c)4 social welfare organization by the IRS, enabling it to raise and expend funds on political engagement, legislative and regulatory matters, and direct and indirect lobbying of elected or appointed officials.

Board and Advisors

EveryLibrary is administered by a board of directors and is run by staff. It has no members. Its 2020 board of directors were John Chrastka, president and executive director; Erica Findley, treasurer; Patrick "PC" Sweeney, board secretary and political director; and Brian D. Hart, Harmony V. Faust, Peter Bromberg, Jeannie Allen, Lori Ayers, Roberto Delgadillo, Gary Kirk, and Kathleen McEvoy, directors. In 2020, PC Sweeney was invited to become a member of the national steering committee for National Voter Registration Day, a nonpartisan movement to encourage voter participation and ballot access.

Organizational History

As a 501(c)4 organization, EveryLibrary works with library boards and staff on informational communications campaigns and with local citizen ballot committees as they conduct "Get Out the Vote" and "Vote Yes" campaigns for local library ballot measures. These library ballot campaigns are either advisory or binding and include bonds, levies, mill levies, warrant articles, parcel taxes, measures, and other referenda placed before voters by library boards, municipal councils, and petitions. EveryLibrary's support includes providing pro bono technical assistance and training to library leaders as well as early campaign financial support and pro bono consulting to campaign committees and citizen's groups. Through 2020, EveryLibrary has helped take 115 libraries to their Election Days, winning 84 percent and securing over $338 million (aggregated per annum) in stable funding for those libraries.

EveryLibrary is funded by individual donors, both monthly and annually, and corporate (vendor) donors. Being able to provide its services at no cost to libraries and committees allows EveryLibrary to focus on best practices for campaigns rather than revenue generation from direct consulting.

COVID-Informed Responses

EveryLibrary understands that funding for public libraries is tied to state and municipal budgets and that the future of school libraries is linked to the stability of education funding. In 2020, pandemic-related shutdowns seriously and negatively impacted budgets for public libraries, state libraries and state aid, academic libraries, and school libraries. This impact has been unevenly experienced across the country because of the structure of local and state tax schemes, prepandemic budgetary choices by leaders, and in-crisis management decisions. Library staff have been personally affected deeply by the pandemic. During the 2020 shutdowns, EveryLibrary took early actions and kept a consistent position that focused on the health, well-being, and financial security of library staff and librarians across all types of libraries.

Early in the pandemic, EveryLibrary called on library leaders to close libraries to public service and provide for ongoing employment and appropriate accommodations to staff. EveryLibrary supported the creation and deployment of the "Help a Library Worker Out" (HALO) mutual aid program from its companion organization the EveryLibrary Institute. The HALO Fund, as it was called, provided personal cash grants to individuals in financial need. Over $80,000 were raised and distribute to affected library workers and librarians from school, public, and academic settings. EveryLibrary also issued early guidance to library nonprofits on provisions within the CARES Act for continuity of operations and payroll protections for workers and staff. As a viable vaccine began to roll out across the country, EveryLibrary took a principled position to include library workers at public libraries and academic institutions in state or local Phase 1B or 1C vaccination plans.

As the pandemic shutdowns impacted the delivery and quality of education across the country, EveryLibrary dedicated significant funding resources to advertise the assets, collections, programs, and services from public libraries, state libraries, and school and academic libraries to the public, especially to parents and other stakeholders, through its extensive social media networks and via paid advertising on search engines. This promotional activity was focused on connecting potential users with important resources with the aim of highlighting the role and impact of libraries during the pivot to digital, online, and virtual. Since early in the pandemic, EveryLibrary has urged public libraries to consider the economic impact of their purchasing decisions on their local communities and encouraged library boards to adopt "buy local" policies.

Library Ballot Measures

In 2020 EveryLibrary supported eight public library campaigns to establish, renew, or expand funding for operations, collections, programs, services, and staffing, or to issue a bond for construction or remodeling of library facilities, and one statewide education funding coalition campaign to benefit among its provisions school library program budgets. Because of the pandemic, voting rights and ballot access were of particular concern for EveryLibrary. In 2020, EveryLibrary's ballot-focused legislative advocacy included support for S. 3529, the National Disaster Emergency Ballot Act; advocacy supporting the funding and functions of the U.S. Postal Service; and participation in the national coalitions for National Voter Registration Day and National Disability Voter Registration Week.

Library election highlights in 2020 included passing three new operating levies. These were for the New Lenox (Illinois) Public Library and the Gail Borden Public Library (Illinois), which were both sunsetting building bonds and looked to voters for approval of new operational support, and for the Morgantown (West Virginia) Public Library System, where new funding would allow for an important expansion of services. In Louisville, Ohio, and Eugene, Oregon, EveryLibrary provided financial support to the local Vote Yes committee along with campaign consulting as their communities considered and renewed the basic levy funding for their public libraries. Any disruption to their levy would have caused significant rollbacks and cuts to services, staffing, programs, and overall operations. Voters in Riverside, Illinois, passed a $1.7 million building bond to renovate and modernize the children's section of their historic library. EveryLibrary's nonprofit registration is in Riverside, making this its "hometown" library.

On the loss side, voters in McCall, Idaho, rejected a proposal from the city for a bond to expand and modernize the library facilities. In Portage County, Ohio, voters likewise declined to establish a local levy to fund the library, which currently only receives state aid for operational expenses. A local levy would allow for significant and important expansion of their work. This is the second time that EveryLibrary has worked to support the Portage County Library and the eighth time voters there have rejected a similar funding question.

Direct Political Actions for Public Libraries

EveryLibrary is uniquely focused on helping local libraries during political and funding crises, and state or national library organizational partners reach and activate the public about budgetary, legislative, or regulatory issues. Many direct actions are operationalized through its action.everylibrary.org platform. This digital advocacy and communications platform allows EveryLibrary to field petitions and e-mailing campaigns targeted at elected officials and to use social-influencing campaigns to effect positive change for libraries and their users. EveryLibrary can set up a direct action for a library in crisis in only a few hours. At the close of 2020, the EveryLibrary network of library activists included well over 200,000 individuals who had taken an active role in at least one prolibrary campaign.

Highlights include collaborative campaigns to help libraries facing a crisis in West Haven, Connecticut, Ellsworth, Maine, and Lacrosse, Wisconsin. Each of these libraries faced threats of budget cuts or defunding from their local municipal funding partners. Alongside the leadership teams, EveryLibrary employed a combination of grassroots and direct lobbying. At the state level, EveryLibrary actively opposed HB 2044 in Missouri alongside the Missouri Library Association. This bill would have removed library boards and staff from the process of evaluating materials challenges and created censorship boards of local residents. It was defeated in committee. At the federal level, President Trump's fiscal year (FY) 2021 budget again targeted the Institute of Museum and Library Services (IMLS) for defunding and elimination. EveryLibrary continued its SaveIMLS.org campaign begun at the start of the Trump Administration to empower and activate public support for this unique and important federal office. EveryLibrary continued to endorse and support the "one dollar per capita" funding request for the Library Services and Technology Act (LSTA) put forward by the Chief Officers of State Library Agencies (COSLA).

School Library and School Librarian Campaigns

Through an ongoing partnership with Follett Learning, EveryLibrary continues to support school library budgets and school librarians through its SaveSchool Librarians.org digital action site and through advocacy partnerships with state school library associations and organizations.

In January 2020, EveryLibrary supported the Pennsylvania School Librarians Association's (PSLA) "Rally to Restore School Librarians" in Philadelphia. This event was a capstone direct action event designed to highlight the lack of certified school librarians in the district alongside PSLA's legislative agenda to mandate school librarians in every school in the Commonwealth. Throughout the year and with a pandemic-influenced focus, EveryLibrary continued to support PSLA's legislative agenda through direct and grassroots lobbying. In November, PSLA and EveryLibrary partnered to create and field a questionnaire to all state legislative candidates about school library programs and education funding. This approach to partnerships and ecosystem building is a core value for EveryLibrary.

The immediate impact of the coronavirus-related shutdown for schools created significant pressures on education funding in some localities. EveryLibrary was able to respond rapidly when school librarian jobs were threatened. Important campaigns included with one the Washington, D.C., Teachers Union (WTU Local 6) in support of over 100 school librarians at the District of Columbia Public Schools. The chancellor's office there had threatened to reclassify school librarians from required to optional, which would have essentially removed all contract protections from their positions. EveryLibrary was proud to campaign alongside WTU to preserve these positions. In smaller districts like Greensburg-Salem, Pennsylvania, and Sweetwater in Chula Vista, California, pandemic-related shutdowns were used by school boards as an opportunity to cut school library funding and programs. EveryLibrary's local campaigns were aligned in support of preserving the school librarians' jobs. In Nevada, EveryLibrary assisted with public outreach and engagement in support of a policy change for the Clark County School District that ensures that certified school librarians staff library programs.

As the pandemic advanced, EveryLibrary worked to support several education funding bills and measures at the state and local level. In Arizona EveryLibrary was the digital outreach partner to the Arizona Library Association on their campaign to help pass Proposition 208, the Invest in Education Act. This statewide ballot measure will reindex state income taxes to better fund education. As it did in Pennsylvania, EveryLibrary continued to support and encourage public engagement for the Michigan Association for Media in Education's school librarian mandate bill. At the federal level, EveryLibrary fielded several education-focused direct advocacy campaigns to Congress about bills such as the Coronavirus Child Care and Education Relief Act (CCCERA), the Education Jobs Fund (H.R. 8691), and education funding provisions in the December 2020 Continuing Resolution and Pandemic Relief Bill. This focus on the education funding ecosystem is vital because all school library programs and positions are budgeted within local education agency formulas, which have been severely strained during the pandemic.

Library Advocacy and Funding Conference

EveryLibrary and the EveryLibrary Institute cohosted the inaugural Library Advocacy and Funding Conference as an online event in September 2020. The conference was uniquely positioned in the library advocacy ecosystem to connect over 1,000 attendees from the United States and abroad with more than 50 presenters from outside of libraries who focus on political action, advocacy, fundraising, organizing, and digital engagement. This conference was launched in response to the unprecedented budgetary pressures that libraries were facing during the pandemic and that all libraries should anticipate in the years to come. Attendees self-reported a high level of satisfaction with the format and content of the conference. Subsequent Library Advocacy and Funding Conferences and convenings are planned.

The EveryLibrary leadership team continued to be in high demand in 2020 at state and national online conferences, symposia, and convenings. Executive Director John Chrastka and Political Director PC Sweeney spoke at numerous events including the Design Institute and Directors Summit from *Library Journal*, the Washington Library Association Conference, the Mississippi Library Association Conference, the Kentucky Library Association Conference, and the Colorado Association of Libraries Conference. EveryLibrary leaders were panelists for National Entrepreneurship Week and National Disability Voter Registration Week events domestically, and internationally at the Chancen 2020 Conference in Hamburg, Germany, and the (virtual) International Public Library Fundraising Conference.

Organizational Agenda

EveryLibrary will continue to work in 2021 to fulfill its core mission of building voter support for libraries of all types. EveryLibrary identifies three mission-critical pandemic-influenced problems for the library funding ecosystem in 2021: austerity budgets for municipalities impacted by tax revenue shortfalls, similar severe disruptions to K–12 and higher ed budgets, and, with the end of the Trump Administration, a likely shift in focus by political and social reactionaries toward local issues and systems. By helping librarians build partnerships and join coalitions based on a shared value system, EveryLibrary hopes to continue to empower librarians in the political process.

EveryLibrary's six strategic priorities in 2021 continue to be

- To deepen its efforts to support local library communities that go on the ballot to renew or extend their basic taxpayer-approved funding and cultivate opportunities for libraries that want to enhance services and facilities through municipal budgets or voter-approved measures
- To join and support coalitions that align with the mission of libraries as institutions, that promote and extend the rights and prosperity of the people whom libraries serve, and that protect the rights, employment, and pensions of the people who work in all types of libraries
- To continue to build a unique and extensive network of Americans who believe in the power of libraries to change lives and build communities, and who are ready to become advocates and activists for libraries
- To support the role of library boards and commissions in governing libraries, making policy, and setting budgets that are responsive to diverse local priorities and create inclusive, prosperous, and vibrant communities.
- To focus its support of School Library programs as effective solutions for some of the biggest problems facing schools and districts around the country
- To be a leader and a listener in a national discussion about the role that public, academic, and school libraries have in people's lives, and to work within the profession and across civil society to find the best ways to preserve, protect, and extend everyone's right to use libraries.

Budget, Donor Transparency, and Reporting

EveryLibrary puts its donor funding to work in three ways: directly on local library campaigns—for both public libraries and school libraries; on building its national reach as an advocacy organization for libraries; and on staff and projects that run the organization. As the only national 501(c)4 for libraries, it "bundles" small donations from around the country and sends them to local Vote Yes committees where needed.

EveryLibrary is entirely supported by individual donors and library vendor donors. It does not ask for or receive any funding from grant-making, philanthropic, or charitable organizations. As an independent 501(c)4, EveryLibrary is ineligible for government grants (federal or state). EveryLibrary's operating budget allocates one-third to direct campaign expenditures, one-third to salaries and operations, and one-third to growing its organizational reach. To keep costs low, staff and interns collaborate across the country in a virtual office environment that has few fixed expenses. Its office environment is supported by G-Suite; Nation Builder hosts its public-facing webpages; and it utilizes PayPal, Stripe, and Act Blue as third-party donation processors.

EveryLibrary provides a high level of transparency about its donations and is one of only a few national political action groups that encourage donors to self-disclose. EveryLibrary voluntarily provides annual financial disclosure information to GuideStar, a large national nonprofit clearinghouse and rating service, where it currently holds a Gold Rate certification.

Part 3
Library/Information Science Education, Placement, and Salaries

Career Resources and Job Listings for Library and Information Professionals

Susanne Markgren

There are many strategies to consider when seeking employment and/or advancement in one's career, and when we find ourselves dealing with a global pandemic and all the aftermath that comes with it—our normal approaches may not prove successful. More than ever, keeping an open mind and employing creative job-seeking and career-planning strategies are needed. The jobs themselves have changed and may not ever resemble their prepandemic selves. This is a time to reevaluate goals and reassess skills; a time to stay connected with colleagues, mentors, and former teachers and employers; and a time to seek out new connections and online groups.

Coverage from *Library Journal*'s "Placements and Salaries 2020" (adapted immediately following this article) offers some mixed results from its 2019 graduate survey, with salary levels and full-time positions on the rise along with the rate of unemployment. Unlike previous years, gender salary disparity is widening, and more graduates are working in positions outside LIS. As for job satisfaction, 72 percent of graduates are satisfied with their placements (in LIS), while 80 percent of graduates working in non-LIS settings claimed the same level of satisfaction—a slight decline from last year.

The top job-seeking resources that were mentioned in the *LJ* survey are Indeed.com, ALA JobLIST, campus job boards and online discussion lists, LinkedIn, and city/state/regional websites. Half of the schools reporting attested to the need for additional support to 2020 and future graduates, which may involve virtual career guidance beyond graduation, more focus on internships and mentoring, and reenvisioning career goals.

This article identifies a variety of current (at time of publication) online resources and tools that may help students, recent graduates, and experienced library professionals navigate their way to a new, or improved, position. The resources have been curated based on popularity, longevity, and influence. All are freely available online, and as with every online information source, users should employ critical analysis and judgment to determine currency, accuracy, and bias.

The Directory of Organizations in Part 6 of this volume may also prove useful for job seekers. Many of these organizations, institutions, libraries, and associations maintain their own job sites and social media accounts where active job listings can be found.

Susanne Markgren is coauthor of the career guidance books *How to Thrive as a Library Professional: Achieving Success and Satisfaction* (Libraries Unlimited, 2019), with Linda Miles, and *Career Q&A: A Librarian's Real-Life, Practical Guide to Managing a Successful Career* (Information Today, Inc., 2013) with Tiffany Eatman Allen.

Organization of the Resources

The resources that follow are organized into four sections. The first, "Career Advice Sites and Resources," lists informational websites, useful for those seeking information and advice on specific areas of librarianship and archive work. Many of these are association sites, and some offer materials and guidance on résumé writing and preparing for interviews.

The second section lists "Podcasts" that provide listeners with current news, hot-topics, interviews, and reviews, as well as real-world examples and narratives from working library and informational professionals in various types of positions and settings. And, as a bonus, they can be highly enlightening and entertaining.

The third consists of a two-part section of "Job Listings" resources—the first specific to librarians, archivists, and information professionals; the second covering a broader range of resources. The selected sites primarily post jobs in the United States, but some also post international opportunities. It is good practice to search a variety of job sites, systematically and routinely, to get the most comprehensive and current snapshot of available positions. It is also a good idea to seek out specific libraries, companies, institutions, and associations on social media sites. Where available, Twitter handles have been included at the end of each listing.

The final section highlights a couple of "Discussion Lists" that may be useful for both discovering and disseminating job postings.

Career Advice Sites and Resources

American Association of Law Libraries (AALL)—Career Center

https://www.aallnet.org/careers/career-center
Offers information on careers in law libraries, advice on how to find a job, and access to the *AALL Salary Survey*.   @aallnet

American Association of School Librarians (AASL)—Education and Careers

http://www.ala.org/aasl/about/ed
Career and education resources for those seeking to enter or advance in the school library field. Job listings are found at ALA JobLIST.   @aasl

American Library Association (ALA) JobLIST—Career Development Resources

http://www.ala.org/educationcareers/employment/career-resources
A wealth of resources from ALA to help with the job search as well as enhance career development efforts.   @ALA_JobLIST and @alaplacement

Association of College and Research Libraries (ACRL)

http://www.ala.org/acrl
Under the heading "Professional Tools" are useful descriptions of various positions and information on recruitment and retention. Job listings are found at ALA JobLIST.   @ALA_ACRL

BCALA (Black Caucus of the American Library Association) Career Center

https://jobs.bcala.org/career-resources
Tools and resources to make your résumé stand out, ace the interview, advance your career.   @BC_ALA

Bureau of Labor Statistics, U.S. Department of Labor, Occupational Outlook Handbook, Librarians

https://www.bls.gov/ooh/education-training-and-library/librarians.htm
Provides information on librarian jobs and salaries, and insight into the growth and outlook of the profession.

Library Worklife—HR E-News for Today's Leaders

http://ala-apa.org/newsletter
Informs readers on issues such as career advancement, certification, pay equity, recruitment, research, and work/life balance.   @alaapa

Medical Library Association (MLA) Career Center

http://www.mlanet.org/p/cm/ld/fid=352
Includes information, resources, and connections for students and job seekers alike.   @MedLibAssn

MLIS SKILLS AT WORK—A Snapshot of Job Postings Spring 2020

https://ischool.sjsu.edu/sites/main/files/file-attachments/career_trends.pdf
Prepared annually by the MLIS online degree program at the San José State University (SJSU) School of Information.   @SJSUiSchool

Public Library Association (PLA)—Careers in Public Librarianship

http://www.ala.org/pla/tools/careers
Information and career advice about public librarianship from a leading ALA division. Job listings are found at ALA JobLIST.   @ALA_PLA

RBMS—Careers and Scholarships

http://rbms.info/careers-faq
Advice and resources for those interested in careers in special collections. @RBMSinfo

SAA (Society of American Archivists) Career Learning Center

https://careers.archivists.org/jobseekers/resources/blueskyLMS
Encourages an integrative career and professional development process that enhances your skill set.   @archivists_org

Skilling for Employment Post COVID-19

Public Library Association (PLA)
http://www.ala.org/pla/initiatives/digitalskilling

PLA and Microsoft are helping libraries identify tools to assist members in gaining skills for jobs that are well positioned to grow in the future.

Your Library Career: Career Q&A for Library People

http://yourlibrarycareer.com
A Q&A forum and career development archive of professional guidance and advice for librarians, library staff, and those thinking of entering the profession. Includes "How I got My First Job" interviews.

Podcasts

Call Number with American Libraries

https://americanlibrariesmagazine.org/tag/al-podcast
Each month, the podcast spotlights conversations with librarians, authors, thinkers, and scholars about topics from the library world and beyond.

Circulating Ideas: The Librarian Interview Podcast

https://circulatingideas.com
Circulating Ideas facilitates conversations about the innovative people and ideas allowing libraries to thrive in the 21st century.

Cyberpunk Librarian

https://cyberpunklibrarian.com
Join the Cyberpunk Librarian, as he talks about ideas, trends, and cool stuff for technologically minded librarians who are high tech and low budget.

FYI: The Public Libraries Podcast

http://publiclibrariesonline.org/category/media/podcast
Covers current programs and initiatives in public libraries such as serving the homeless, EDI, Imposter Syndrome, embedded librarianship, early literacy, social services, marketing, and much more.

The Librarian's Guide to Teaching

https://librariansguidetoteaching.weebly.com
Hosted by two librarians interested in sharing their experiences, discussing current trends, and having meaningful conversations about librarianship.

Library Pros

https://www.thelibrarypros.com
A librarian and information technology pro talking libraries, library tech, and everything in between.

Linking Our Libraries

https://linkingourlibraries.libsyn.com

The hosts share information with all types of libraries, archives, and other non-profit staff and leaders, working to build their skills.

School Librarians United

https://schoollibrariansunited.libsyn.com
A podcast dedicated to the nuts and bolts of running a successful school library.

T is for Training

https://tisfortraining.wordpress.com
A podcast dedicated to improvement through learning. Also, it is about training, presenting, learning, teaching, understanding, and compassion.

Job Listings for Librarians, Archivists, and Information Professionals

ALA JobLIST

http://joblist.ala.org | @ALA_JobLIST

American Association of Law Libraries (AALL) —Career Center

https://careers.aallnet.org/jobs | @aallnet

Archives Gig

https://archivesgig.wordpress.com | @archivesgig

ARLIS/NA JobList

https://www.arlisna.org/professional-resources/arlis-na-joblist | @ARLIS_NA

Association for Information Science and Technology (ASIS&T) Careers

https://asist-jobs.careerwebsite.com | @asist_org

Association of Research Libraries (ARL)—Job/Residency/Internship Listings

http://www.arl.org/leadership-recruitment/job-listings | @ARLnews

BCALA Jobs

https://jobs.bcala.org | @BC_ALA

INALJ

http://inalj.com | @INALJ (different states have their own handles)

Metropolitan New York Library Council (METRO) Jobs

https://metro.org/jobs | @mnylc

NASIG Jobs
http://nasigjobs.wordpress.com | @NASIG

Special Library Association (SLA) Jobs
https://careers.sla.org | @SLAhq

Job Listings Not Specific to Librarians, Archivists, and Information Professionals

Higher Education
Chronicle of Higher Education: Jobs
https://jobs.chronicle.com | @chronicle

EDUCAUSE Career Center
https://www.educause.edu/careers/educause-career-center | @educause

HigherEdJobs.com
http://www.higheredjobs.com | @insidehighered

Government https://jobs.educause.edu
USAJobs.gov
https://www.usajobs.gov | @USAJOBS

Interdisciplinary (mega job sites)
Glassdoor
https://www.glassdoor.com/index.htm | @Glassdoor

Handshake
https://www.joinhandshake.com | @joinHandshake

Indeed
https://www.indeed.com | @indeed

LinkedIn Jobs
https://www.linkedin.com/jobs | @LinkedIn

Monster
https://www.monster.com | @Monster

SimplyHired

https://www.simplyhired.com | @SimplyHired

Zip Recruiter

https://www.ziprecruiter.com | @ZipRecruiter

Discussion Lists

Job openings are regularly posted on electronic discussion (e-mail) lists and many schools and associations maintain their own discussion lists. The following are lists of lists, maintained by large library organizations.

ALA Electronic Discussion Lists—Index of Lists

https://lists.ala.org/sympa/lists | @ALALibrary

International Federation of Library Associations and Institutions (IFLA)—Mailing Lists

https://www.ifla.org/mailing-lists | @IFLA

Placements and Salaries 2020:
First Jobs Out of Library School

Suzie Allard

Library Journal's annual Placements and Salaries survey reports on the experiences of library and information science (LIS) students who graduated and sought their first librarian jobs in the previous year—in this case, 2019. As such, we began to collect data in March 2020, just as COVID-19 was beginning to gain speed in the United States. Naturally, addressing the professional and personal upheaval resulting from the coronavirus took priority over responding, which likely resulted in somewhat lower participation in this survey than usual by both schools and graduates.

The experience of these 2019 graduates will be very different from next year's respondents, the LIS class of 2020, whose members are graduating into an ongoing pandemic. Nonetheless, trends evident from the experience of 2019 graduates bear watching, and they both hold promise and suggest concerns.

Some highlights from the survey:

- Salary levels and the prevalence of full-time appointments continue to improve.
- However, unemployment levels for new graduates are also growing.
- Gender salary disparity is no longer narrowing; substantial disparities were evident in this year's results.
- The trend toward more graduates working in LIS institutions seems to be reversing, with the proportion of graduates working outside LIS nearly tripling.
- Continuing the trend begun last year, graduates noted that user experience/usability analysis is one of their top two primary job duties.

Table 1 / Status of 2019 Graduates

School Region	Number of Schools Reporting	Number of Graduates Responding	Employed in LIS field	Employed outside of LIS	Currently Unemployed or Continuing Education	Total Answering	Percentage Employed Full Time
Midwest	11	396	217	157	20	394	88%
Northeast	8	224	167	36	21	224	83%
South Central	7	169	134	19	16	169	86%
Southeast	5	172	112	31	29	172	93%
West (Pacific/ Mountain)	5	145	129	10	6	145	78%
Total	36	1,106	759	253	92	1,104	86%

Table based on survey responses from schools and individual graduates. Figures will not necessarily be fully consistent with some of the other data reported. Tables do not always add up, individually or collectively, since both schools and individuals omitted data in some cases.

Suzie Allard (sallard.utk.edu) is professor of information sciences and associate dean of research, University of Tennessee College of Communication and Information, Knoxville, and winner of the 2013 *Library Journal* Teaching Award.

Adapted from *Library Journal*, October, 2020. For additional information and content visit libraryjournal.com.

Table 2 / Placements and Full-Time Salaries of 2019 Graduates by Region

Placement Region	Number of Placements	No. Responding				Low Salary ($)			High Salary ($)			Average Salary ($)				Difference in Average M/F Salary†	Median Salary ($)			
		Women	Men	Non-binary*	All	Women	Men	Non-binary*	Women	Men	Non-binary*	Women	Men	Non-binary*	All		Women	Men	Non-binary*	All
Midwest	257	169	41	4	214	22,000	34,749	36,000	97,500	150,000	55,000	49,742	75,356	42,473	53,866	51.5%	48,454	72,000	36,420	50,000
Northeast	195	129	25	7	161	26,000	35,000	41,000	165,000	112,500	54,250	59,302	62,505	50,292	59,759	4.5%	56,000	58,000	51,500	55,000
Southeast	173	80	17	7	104	25,700	28,000	42,000	105,000	70,926	62,500	51,216	48,403	50,300	50,672	-5.5%	51,187	50,000	52,000	50,687
Pacific	155	92	28	6	126	32,000	53,000	31,500	137,500	200,000	137,500	79,379	103,158	87,625	85,016	30.0%	68,000	107,500	90,750	70,500
South Central	112	87	12	1	100	25,500	25,000	40,500	110,000	92,500	40,500	43,883	58,822	40,500	50,050	20.3%	46,000	55,108	40,500	46,951
Mountain	53	29	8	1	38	18,000	25,000	36,000	90,000	82,500	36,000	50,026	48,938	36,000	49,293	-2.2%	48,500	48,500	36,000	47,000
Canada/Int'l	12	8	3	—	11	23,000	50,000	—	83,700	35,644	—	46,557	67,822	—	55,069	45.6%	33,000	67,822	—	50,000
Total	957	594	134	26	754	18,000	25,000	31,500	165,000	200,000	137,500	56,337	70,132	55,384	58,703	24.4%	52,000	60,850	51,000	53,000

This table represents only salaries reported as full time. Some data were reported as aggregate without breakdown by gender or region. Comparison with other tables may show different number of placements.

*Includes nonbinary, other, and declined to answer gender.

†The minimum sample is too small to yield statistically significant results when compared to placements and salaries of other genders. Therefore, all gender comparisons shown are male to female only.

229

Unsurprisingly, LIS schools expect that 2020 graduates will face a challenging job search because of changes driven by COVID-19. Thirty-six of the 52 U.S.-based American Library Association (ALA) accredited schools participated in this survey for the 2019 calendar year. These schools reported awarding degrees to 4,263 graduates. Five fewer schools (about 12 percent fewer) participated this year, which likely accounts for the 10.5 percent decline in total graduates when compared to 2018. Nearly 26 percent of 2019 graduates shared the outcomes and experiences of their job searches by completing the questionnaire. This response rate is down 3 percent from 2018.

As in prior years, most respondents describe themselves as female (77 percent). The proportion of male graduates was similar to last year (19 percent in 2019 and 20 percent in 2018). This was the third year for which the survey offered a nonbinary gender option, representing about 3.4 percent of responding 2019 graduates, somewhat higher than for their 2018 counterparts (2.8 percent). These proportions are similar to those reported by the schools for their total number of graduates, although more people self-identified as the additional gender options than were reported by the schools. Because the nonbinary sample is too small to yield statistically significant results when compared to placements and salaries of other genders, gender comparisons shown in the tables are male-to-female only.

The 2019 graduates' self-identification of race/ethnicity presents a different profile than last year. There is greater white/non-Hispanic representation (81 percent versus 76 percent in 2018) and a very reduced representation of Asian/Pacific Islanders (3 percent in 2019 and 9 percent in 2018). There was a similar representation of Hispanic/Latinx (5 percent), Black / African American (4 percent), and biracial/multiracial respondents (4 percent). Similar to last year, less than 2 percent identified as Native Alaskan / American Indian / First Nation or another race.

The age distribution also had many similarities to last year, with over half of respondents indicating they were between 26 and 35 years old (58 percent), yielding an average age of 34. Continuing what we've seen in previous years, most graduates were 35 or under (69 percent), while 13 percent were over 45. Continuing a trend noted last year, there was a slight decline in the percentage of graduates who said that they were pursuing their first career (53 percent).

Full-Time Is Up, but So Is Unemployment

Many indicators, such as salary levels and full-time appointments, are moving in a positive direction for the class of 2019; however, there are also areas for concern, such as unemployment levels and increasing gender salary disparity.

For the seventh year in a row, there is an increase in the average full-time starting salary, with this year's average of $58,655 being a 5.9 percent increase over 2018. Another positive trend we have been following for six years continued with graduates reporting high levels of full-time employment (86 percent, up from 80 percent last year) and permanent positions (94 percent, up from 91 percent last year).

However, the increase in the percentage of full-time positions may be caused by a decrease in part-time positions available, because the percentage of graduates who reported being unemployed doubled from last year to 8 percent (also higher than the 6 percent we saw in 2017). Among those who are unemployed, the majority (79 percent) say they are currently seeking employment in the LIS field. Others are a student in another program (18 percent), taking time off for personal reasons (4 percent), and interning (2 percent). About 1 percent reported being furloughed. We cannot determine how COVID-19 affected the employment status of 2019 graduates, but we do know that many institutions were instituting hiring freezes and contemplating furloughs during this period.

Similar to last year, 14 percent of 2019 graduates report being employed part-time; however, the nature of part-time employment is different than last year, with a substantially higher percentage of people reporting having only one position (65 percent versus 54 percent in 2019), and fewer holding two jobs (28 percent in 2019 versus 36 percent in 2018), for an average of 1.4 positions.

One striking change is where 2019 graduates are employed. Last year, about nine out of ten graduates reported being employed in the LIS field. In 2019, this has decreased to about seven out of ten graduates (69 percent). Accompanying this trend is a rapid increase in graduates saying they are employed outside the LIS field (23 percent in 2019 and 9 percent in 2018).

Of those working in LIS-related positions, more than half (57 percent) report being employed in a LIS organization of some type, a sharp decline from last year. Some 12 percent say they are working in a LIS capacity but in some other type of organization, which is similar to last year.

In a decline from last year, fewer than half of employed 2019 graduates who are working said they work in either a public library (28 percent) or an academic library (19 percent). Those working in private industry (17 percent) grew by about 50 percent over last year, while those at K–12 schools decreased slightly (to 9 percent). Other graduates report working in other academic units at a college or university (5 percent), a government library (4 percent), a nonprofit, nonlibrary institution (3 percent), an archives/special collections (3 percent), a special library (3 percent), or another governmental agency (3 percent).

The majority of graduates express satisfaction with their current placement (72 percent). Continuing the pattern we saw last year, graduates working in non-library settings expressed higher satisfaction (80 percent) than those in a LIS institution (76 percent), although the difference between these two levels is not as great as last year. This year, graduates who work outside the LIS field were less likely to report being satisfied than last year (42 percent versus 53 percent).

Don't Quit Your Day Job?

Similar to last year, a substantial number of graduates (47 percent) are pursuing a second career, and nearly one in five graduates had never worked in a library before entering their LIS program.

Nonetheless, more than half the graduates (59 percent) remained with an employer or position they held prior to joining their master's program or while attending their master's program. This was particularly true for graduates working outside the LIS field. For some of these graduates, earning the master's degree while staying in an existing employment situation resulted in a raise (26 percent), a promotion (21 percent), or moving to professional staff (14 percent).

We also asked graduates if they were interested in pursuing another advanced degree in the future since a second degree can influence career trajectory. A small group were definitely planning to pursue an additional degree (7 percent), and

Table 3 / Full-Time Salaries by Type of Organization and Gender

	Total Placements				Low Salary ($)			High Salary ($)			Average Salary ($)				Median Salary ($)			
	Women	Men	Non-binary*	All	Women	Men	Non-binary*	Women	Men	Non-binary*	Women	Men	Non-binary*	All	Women	Men	Non-binary*	All
Public Libraries	120	18	5	144	23,500	35,000	36,000	75,000	73,500	54,250	47,893	52,935	43,134	48,491	47,404	52,000	36,420	48,416
College / University Libraries	125	25	7	157	23,000	25,000	40,500	83,700	107,500	62,500	52,497	56,770	52,214	53,165	53,500	56,403	52,000	53,500
School Libraries	50	6	2	58	18,000	46,000	31,500	106,000	100,000	38,000	57,902	71,536	34,750	58,514	53,750	66,608	34,750	53,750
Government Libraries	19	6	1	26	32,042	39,000	42,000	75,000	70,926	42,000	52,437	58,618	42,000	53,462	52,000	61,890	42,000	55,250
Private Industry	56	33	4	93	30,000	40,000	43,000	165,000	200,000	137,500	89,994	99,988	89,500	93,519	88,750	92,500	88,750	90,000
Special Libraries	17	1	—	18	37,000	57,500	—	71,000	57,500	—	51,403	57,500	—	51,742	52,000	57,500	—	53,000
Archives / Special Collections	14	5	—	19	35,000	34,749	—	72,000	60,700	—	48,247	48,690	—	48,363	47,396	50,000	—	48,792
Nonprofit Organizations	11	2	1	14	36,000	50,000	41,000	97,500	70,000	41,000	60,000	60,000	41,000	58,643	57,500	60,000	41,000	53,750
Other Organizations	37	6	—	43	29,000	25,000	—	125,000	85,644	—	54,044	46,357	—	52,971	48,650	39,500	—	45,000

This table represents only full-time salaries and all placements reported by type. Some individuals omitted placement information, rendering some information unusable.
*Includes nonbinary, other, and declined to answer gender.

24 percent said they were probably pursuing this. More than two-thirds said another advanced degree was not a part of their future plans.

Salaries Rising, Unevenly

2019 graduates who are working full-time have average annual earnings of $58,655, a 5.9 percent increase over last year. The median is $53,000. The average hourly rate is similar to last year at $19.87, which translates into an annual full-time salary of more than $41,000, the same as last year.

The news on gender salary disparities is not encouraging, as substantial disparities were evident in this year's results, reversing the trend toward a narrowing salary gap that had emerged in 2017. In 2019, male graduates employed full-time reported an overall average salary of $70,132, versus the average of $56,357 for female graduates, representing a differential of more than 24 percent. The overall gender differential has markedly increased from 2018 (10 percent), 2017 (12 percent), and 2016 (about 18 percent). This disparity is not just the result of one very high-paying position for a male graduate, since the differential is evident at high levels in the Midwest (51 percent), Canada/International (46 percent), Pacific (30 percent), and South Central (20 percent) regions.

Work Setting vs. Skillsets

The 2019 graduates described their work and setting very differently than what we heard in the first two years this question was asked. In both 2017 and 2018, more than two-thirds called themselves librarians working in a library, while this year, only 59 percent said they were a librarian working in a library. Similar to previous years, 4 percent said they were a librarian who wasn't working in a library. The difference was made up by a similar level of self-described "non-librarian" graduates working in a library (18 percent) or outside of one (19 percent).

Each year we ask graduates to review an array of duties in LIS and name which is the primary duty for their job. In 2019, we see some changes from 2018, which mirrored what we saw in 2017. The top of the list continued to be reference and information services (9 percent) and the 2018 newcomer, user experience/

Table 4 / Average Salary for Starting Library Positions, 2011–2019

Year	# Library Schools Represented	Avg. Full-Time Starting Salary	Difference in Avg. Salary	Percentage Change
2011	41	$44,565	$2,009	4.72%
2012	41	44,503	-62	-0.14
2013	40	45,650	1,147	2.58
2014	39	46,987	1,337	2.93
2015	39	48,371	1,384	2.95
2016	40	51,798	3,427	7.08
2017	41	52,152	354	0.68
2018	41	55,357	3,205	6.15
2019	36	58,655	3,298	5.96

Table 5 / Placements by Full-Time Salary of Reporting 2019 Graduates

Schools	Average Salary ($)				Median Salary ($)			Low Salary ($)			High Salary ($)			Placements			
	Women	Men	Non-binary**	All	Women	Men	Non-binary**	Women	Men	Non-binary**	Women	Men	Non-binary**	Women	Men	Non-binary**	Total Placements
Alabama	48,020	43,000	—	46,138	44,100	44,000	—	36,000	39,000	—	72,000	46,000	—	5	3	—	8
Albany	46,430	—	—	46,430	48,000	—	—	42,640	—	—	48,650	—	—	3	—	—	3
Arizona	37,074	34,000	—	36,306	35,000	34,000	—	30,000	34,000	—	46,223	34,000	—	3	1	—	4
Buffalo	52,500	45,500	—	49,000	55,000	46,500	—	40,000	35,000	—	60,000	54,000	—	4	4	—	8
Catholic*	54,803	65,805	—	56,098	55,000	65,805	—	35,085	59,510	—	75,000	72,100	—	15	2	—	17
Emporia State	49,786	40,000	—	49,133	45,000	40,000	—	28,000	40,000	—	110,000	40,000	—	14	1	—	15
Hawaii Manoa	57,984	50,000	—	56,387	54,468	50,000	—	40,000	50,000	—	83,000	50,000	—	4	1	—	5
Illinois–Urbana-Champaign	47,507	68,000	53,500	49,744	48,200	68,000	53,500	29,000	65,000	53,500	57,910	71,000	53,500	18	2	1	21
Indiana–Purdue	48,406	34,749	—	44,504	49,000	34,749	—	32,781	34,749	—	58,000	34,749	—	5	2	—	7
Iowa	54,000	52,134	—	53,067	52,000	56,403	—	52,000	28,000	—	58,000	72,000	—	3	3	—	6
Kent State*	38,387	42,308	—	38,714	33,280	42,308	—	22,000	42,308	—	68,000	42,308	—	11	1	—	12
Kentucky	43,101	107,667	36,420	54,102	45,309	73,000	36,420	18,000	50,000	36,420	68,000	200,000	36,420	13	3	1	17
Long Island	61,266	—	51,500	58,010	61,500	—	51,500	45,000	—	50,000	77,062	—	53,000	4	—	2	6
Maryland	50,528	50,325	—	50,477	52,250	50,800	—	40,000	39,000	—	62,000	60,700	—	12	4	—	16
Michigan*	85,121	97,516	132,500	89,960	82,500	92,500	132,500	37,000	55,000	127,500	165,000	160,000	137,500	66	31	2	99
Missouri	51,667	—	—	51,667	51,000	—	—	50,000	—	—	54,000	—	—	3	—	—	3
North Texas	45,936	48,843	40,500	46,273	49,000	49,000	40,500	23,000	25,000	40,500	65,000	70,000	40,500	21	5	1	27
Oklahoma	43,750	—	—	43,750	43,750	—	—	42,000	—	—	45,500	—	—	2	—	—	2
Pratt	59,333	57,500	—	58,875	58,000	57,500	—	54,000	57,500	—	66,000	57,500	—	3	1	—	4
Rutgers	60,085	70,711	54,250	61,774	52,500	70,000	54,250	26,000	40,000	54,250	125,000	100,000	54,250	22	5	1	28
San José*	58,376	49,917	45,833	56,430	56,000	55,500	52,000	32,000	25,000	31,500	95,000	70,000	54,000	31	6	3	41
Simmons	58,138	60,324	47,167	57,879	55,000	60,000	41,000	31,000	52,000	38,000	132,000	69,000	62,500	58	7	3	68
South Florida	39,315	—	—	39,315	41,204	—	—	35,000	—	—	41,741	—	—	3	—	—	3
Southern California	62,586	70,000	—	63,328	64,000	70,000	—	56,000	70,000	—	67,500	70,000	—	9	1	—	10

Southern Mississippi	45,405	49,890	—	45,932	45,500	49,890	—	30,000	40,000	—	65,000	59,779	—	15	2	—	17
St. Catherine	47,200	—	36,000	45,333	49,000	49,000	36,000	40,000	—	36,000	52,000	—	36,000	5	—	1	6
St. John's	46,597	61,667	42,000	52,399	51,500	53,000	42,000	32,292	52,000	42,000	56,000	80,000	42,000	3	3	1	7
Syracuse	47,934	—	43,000	47,112	49,000	—	43,000	36,672	—	43,000	59,000	—	43,000	5	—	1	6
Tennessee	48,685	—	48,685	48,685	50,000	—	—	35,000	—	—	74,000	—	—	9	—	—	9
Texas Women's	53,993	85,644	—	55,432	58,500	85,644	—	24,100	85,644	—	83,700	85,644	—	21	1	—	22
Valdosta	42,972	44,500	—	43,250	40,000	44,500	—	25,700	35,000	—	63,000	54,000	—	9	2	—	11
Washington	50,087	61,000	—	50,996	50,000	61,000	—	42,000	61,000	—	65,000	61,000	—	11	1	—	12
Wayne State	45,122	63,000	51,000	46,882	45,000	63,000	5?,000	25,000	54,000	50,000	71,000	72,000	52,000	23	2	2	27
Wisconsin–Madison	46,334	81,107	55,000	54,110	45,500	72,213	55,000	34,000	40,000	55,000	56,813	140,000	55,000	14	4	1	19
Wisconsin–Milwaukee	50,804	46,000	36,000	48,717	52,000	45,000	36,000	35,000	43,000	36,000	70,000	50,000	36,000	10	3	1	14
Average / Total	56,309	70,040	54,556	58,655	52,000	61,000	50,300	18,000	25,000	31,500	165,000	200,000	137,500	457	101	21	580

This table represents placements and salaries reported as full time. Some individuals or schools omitted information, rendering information unusable.

*Some schools conducted their own survey and provided raw data.

**Includes nonbinary, unsure, and declined to answer gender.

usability analysis (7 percent), returned in second place. However, there were some notable changes in the remaining top five: children's services (7 percent) moved up to third, archival and preservation (7 percent) moved into fourth, and administration and adult services (both just over 6 percent) tied for fifth position. While administration had been in the fifth spot in 2018, adult services was not this high on the list. In addition, school librarian / school library media specialist (just under 6 percent) dropped from third to seventh. Among graduates who identified their work as outside the LIS field, top duties were user experience/usability analysis (37 percent), data analytics (14 percent), and administration (12 percent).

Graduates were also asked to indicate all the duties that were part of their jobs, and half identified reference/information services as one of their assignments. Other frequently mentioned assignments were collection development/acquisitions (40 percent), outreach (33 percent), patron programming (32 percent), public services (31 percent), and circulation and reader's advisory (both 30 percent). Among those employed outside the LIS field, assignments seem to be more focused, since fewer items are identified by each respondent. The top assignment is administration (23 percent), followed by data analytics (18 percent), budgeting/financing (16 percent), information technology (14 percent), outreach and records management (both 13 percent), and data curation/management and communications, and PR and social media (both 12 percent). Only 10 percent of graduates feel their job is in an emerging area of LIS practice, which is lower than last year (16 percent).

Where They Come From

Prior work experiences or education may affect graduates' educational experiences and their professional placement after graduation. In prior years we asked whether they had worked in a library prior to starting their program. This year we changed the question to better understand a graduate's library work experience, so we asked if they had worked in a library prior to beginning their master's program (14 percent), while completing their master's work (29 percent), or both (39 percent). Nearly 80 percent of graduates had some library experience before they began their job search. While the change in the question means results are not directly comparable to prior years, the results do appear consistent, since the percentage of graduates who didn't work in a library or who did so while completing the program is about 46 percent, compared to about half of respondents last year.

What we learned by asking this question in a new way is that graduates who worked in the library during their degree program seem to benefit, since they also account for the largest portion of full-time placements after graduation. Another indication that gaining library work experience may be beneficial for attaining a placement after graduation is that among unemployed graduates, more than a third had no library work experience. However, library work experience does not appear as important among those who gained placements outside the LIS field, since more than half of these graduates did not work in a library before or during their graduate studies.

This year, about a quarter of the graduates held an advanced degree before they started their LIS master's program, which is similar to 2017 but below the uptick we saw last year. The 7 percent dual-enrolled in another graduate or certificate program—such as a JD, Ph.D., or second master's—while they were working on their LIS degree exhibited a similar pattern, closely matching 2017.

LIS Program Experiences

Graduates earned their degrees through many different delivery options. Online programs continue to be highly utilized. More than half (55 percent) completed their degree via fully online instruction, which was somewhat less than last year (59 percent) but still substantially higher than 2017's 49 percent. More than a third (35 percent) of graduates learned through a mix of online and on-site courses. Fully on-site instruction accounted for about 10 percent of graduates' experience.

Graduates shared the LIS master's program experiences or activities that they found most helpful when seeking job placement. The top four were unchanged from last year; gaining internship/practicum/field experience (57 percent) and technology skills (e.g., database searching, HTML coding, or other Internet-oriented skills) (48 percent) accounted for the top two positions. The next two experiences were both identified by 41 percent of graduates as being the most helpful or important: subject specialization knowledge (such as cataloging or reference) and networking with professionals working in their area of interest.

Graduates were asked whether they had participated in internships during their time as a LIS student. Most (60 percent) reported participating in one or more internships as an LIS student. Nearly a quarter completed two or more internships.

We also asked what the programs required beyond coursework. Creating an e-portfolio (47 percent) and completing an internship (37 percent) were the most common; completing a formal project (20 percent) and taking a comprehensive exam (16 percent) were also mentioned.

Soft Skills

This was the second year that graduates were asked about their access to and evaluation of soft skills training through their LIS graduate programs. Soft skills help a person interact more effectively with other people, augmenting hard skills such as disciplinary knowledge and learned skills directly related to accomplishing work duties. Employees with soft skills are often more successful in the workplace. The survey focused on six soft skills: conflict resolution, cultural competency, customer service, design thinking, ethics, and leadership.

Similar to last year, graduates noted that their LIS programs provided opportunities to learn about five of these soft skills, and levels were higher across the board: ethics (96 percent), cultural competency (83 percent), leadership (82 percent), customer service (80 percent), and design thinking (75 percent). Customer service saw the greatest increase in availability. Opportunities to learn about conflict resolution were less common than last year, dropping from nearly half to only 44 percent.

Graduates who had access to learning about each soft skill tended to rate these skills as useful at similar levels to last year: ethics (86 percent), cultural competency (76 percent), and leadership (75 percent). There was less—but still a reasonable level of—enthusiasm for customer service (67 percent) and design thinking (62 percent). There was much less enthusiasm for what they learned about conflict resolution, which, at 38 percent, was even lower than last year.

Table 6 / Full-Time Salaries of Reporting Professionals by
Primary Job Assignment

Primary Job Assignment	No. Rec'd	Percent of Total	Low Salary	High Salary	Average Salary	Median Salary
Reference/Information Services	48	9%	$32,042	$70,000	$51,385	$51,000
Administration	41	8%	30,000	110,000	53,302	51,000
School Librarian / School Library Media Specialist	40	8%	18,000	106,000	56,689	53,750
Children's Services	36	7%	25,000	74,000	46,151	46,625
User Experience / Usability Analysis	35	7%	52,500	137,500	99,560	97,500
Archival and Preservation	31	6%	25,000	72,000	49,078	50,000
Adult Services	27	5%	30,000	70,000	48,471	47,923
Metadata, Cataloging, and Taxonomy	25	5%	39,000	85,200	55,583	55,000
YA/Teen Services	20	4%	30,000	61,000	46,367	47,954
Teacher Librarian	15	3%	23,000	91,000	52,816	52,000
Training, Teaching, Instruction	15	3%	38,500	83,700	57,507	62,000
Access Services	13	3%	25,000	59,532	45,246	50,000
Data Analytics	13	3%	45,000	90,000	67,185	69,000
Collection Development / Acquisitions	12	2%	37,000	59,534	49,003	50,000
Circulation	11	2%	26,000	70,000	45,092	42,000
Technical Services	11	2%	22,000	59,779	39,151	38,000
Digital Content Management	10	2%	28,000	73,000	48,816	48,750
Solo Librarian	10	2%	38,000	64,270	45,999	44,500
Outreach	9	2%	29,000	65,000	49,450	50,000
Patron Programming	6	1%	26,000	58,000	45,167	49,500
Public Services	6	1%	28,000	85,644	51,795	48,562
Records Management	6	1%	34,000	60,500	46,358	46,325
Emerging Technologies	4	1%	52,500	60,000	55,875	55,500
Information Technology	4	1%	48,000	74,000	63,500	66,000
Market Intelligence / Business Research	4	1%	57,000	200,000	110,250	92,000
Website Design	4	1%	60,000	82,500	70,125	69,000
Data Curation and Management	3	1%	37,500	70,000	52,833	51,000
Government Documents	3	1%	42,000	75,000	55,667	50,000
Knowledge Management	3	1%	41,755	61,000	50,918	50,000
Rights and Permissions	3	1%	25,000	68,000	45,787	44,360
Systems Technology	3	1%	53,000	60,000	56,000	55,000
Budgeting/Finance	2	0%	42,000	56,000	49,000	49,000
Assessment	1	0%	52,000	52,000	52,000	52,000
Communications, PR, and Social Media	1	0%	55,000	55,000	55,000	55,000
Other	38	7%	30,000	132,000	54,199	49,000
Total Answering	515	100%	$18,000	$200,000	$55,233	$52,000

This table represents full-time placements reported by primary job assignment.

Some individuals omitted placement information; therefore comparison with other tables may show different numbers of placements and average and median salaries.

Table 7 / Did you work in a library before entering or while completing
your Master's program?

	Currently Employed			
	In Library Science Inst.	Doing Library Work outside a Library	Outside of LIS Field	Unemployed
Before Entering Master's Program	13.10%	18.60%	12.00%	17.40%
While Completing Master's Program	28.60%	30.40%	23.90%	31.90%
Both	48.10%	27.50%	10.90%	13.00%
Neither	10.10%	23.50%	53.30%	37.70%

Finding and Starting the Job

Graduates who did not return to a previous employer or a position they previously held were asked about their job search approach and experiences. On average, graduates began their job search about 5.5 months before graduation. Mirroring last year, 30 percent of job searches were initiated four to six months before graduation. Searches began one to three months before program completion for 23 percent. Similar to 2018, 13 percent began the search a year or more before graduation. Only 13 percent waited to graduate before beginning their search.

Forty-six percent of job seekers secured their new professional position before they graduated. For those who didn't find their position before graduation, there was an average of 4.2 months past graduation before placement. Just under a third of these job seekers took six months or more to find a job. These measures exhibit a slight trend, suggesting that job seekers found jobs more quickly than they did last year.

Among all graduates employed full-time (whether with a previous or new employer), only 26 percent relocated to take their position.

Each graduate was asked to list up to three resources they found helpful during job-seeking. The responses represented general employment sites (i.e., Indeed, Linked In), trusted partners (ALA job list), and other organizations' resources including professional associations (i.e., SAA), local, state and federal (i.e. USAjobs. gov) government job websites, university job sites and listservs, and HigherEdJobs. com.

The top five resources were Indeed.com (31 percent), ALA JobLIST (25 percent), campus job boards / online discussion lists (19 percent), LinkedIn (17 percent) and city/state/regional websites (12 percent). The next five resources were association job boards (11 percent), Archive Gig (10 percent), institution/employer websites (8 percent), HigherEdJobs (8 percent), and, tied for 10th place, networking/ networking events and word of mouth.

This rank order was very similar for those who were employed in a library science institution. Indeed and LinkedIn were much more important resources for those who were employed outside the LIS field and somewhat more important for those doing library work outside of a library.

School Placement Help

The specific support each LIS program offers for graduates as they build their career path varies by school, but common features include providing information about available positions and resources for conducting an effective job search. More than a quarter of the schools offer formal mentoring programs that range from pairing alumni professionals with students, to career advising staff, to semester-long extracurricular programs that help students learn about completing job applications, the interview process, and building personal networks.

On average, each school made students aware of 401 job opportunities in the last year. The most prevalent tool LIS schools use to help students become aware of job opportunities is through listserv announcements (92 percent). Half the schools also use social media. Other strategies are posting announcements on bulletin boards or in student areas and through student groups or other student activities (both 47 percent). In a decrease from last year, only 22 percent of the schools indicated that they have a formal placement service or center. Other specific strategies they use include career programming, career fairs, career support groups, university career resources, and highlighting external resources such as the ALA JobLIST and Handshake. Overall, LIS schools felt that the time it took to help with placements was the same as last year and that they did not change their use of resources.

Compared to previous years, LIS schools report that some of the job positions available were new types of positions or job titles. Particular titles they cited included head of metadata and discovery, reproducibility librarian, research metrics librarian, bioinformationist, social media librarian, data science librarian, user experience specialist, and scholarly communication for research infrastructure.

How Schools Think COVID-19 Will Affect Placements

We asked the LIS schools how they expected the pandemic to affect their ability to support their 2020 graduates' job search. Half the schools expect there to be effects, including needing to spend additional time supporting new graduates in spring 2020, as well as those who graduated in December 2019; helping graduates with searches during hiring freezes that are happening throughout the industry; extending career support for an extra year beyond the normal time frame; shifting to more virtual career support; increased focus on internship opportunities; and increasing mentor programs. As employers are forced to reimagine their businesses and institutions, schools must help graduates find creative ways to envision their career goals and their preferred work environment.

Table 8 / 2019 Total Graduates and Placements by School*

Schools	Graduates				Employed Full Time				Response	
	Women	Men	Other/Unsure	All	Women	Men	Nonbinary**	All	# Rec'd	Rate
Alabama	75	16	—	91	7	3	—	10	12	13.20%
Albany	15	4	—	19	3	—	—	3	5	26.30%
Arizona	56	13	—	69	5	1	—	6	12	17.40%
Buffalo	79	11	—	90	4	5	—	9	10	11.10%
Catholic*	32	3	—	35	20	2	—	22	25	71.40%
Emporia State	116	20	—	136	20	1	—	21	29	21.30%
Hawaii–Manoa	12	3	—	15	4	1	—	5	6	40.00%
Illinois–Urbana–Champaign	184	60	—	244	19	4	1	24	29	11.90%
Indiana–Purdue	74	18	—	92	6	2	—	8	11	12.00%
Iowa	25	7	—	32	5	4	—	9	12	37.50%
Kent State*	168	40	—	208	13	2	—	15	21	10.10%
Kentucky	61	12	—	73	18	3	1	22	23	31.50%
Long Island	81	17	—	98	6	—	2	8	11	11.20%
Maryland	65	13	—	78	16	4	1	21	29	37.20%
Michigan*	124	66	4	194	99	46	2	147	157	80.90%
Missouri	49	8	—	57	5	—	—	5	7	12.30%
NC–Chapel Hill*	78	25	—	103	—	—	—	—	95	92.20%
North Texas	273	57	—	330	24	7	1	32	43	13.00%
Oklahoma	48	9	—	57	6	1	—	7	8	14.00%
Pratt	34	12	—	46	5	1	—	6	8	17.40%
Rutgers	107	52	—	159	30	6	1	37	49	30.80%
San José*	426	89	—	515	50	10	4	70	86	16.70%

241

Table 8 / 2019 Total Graduates and Placements by School* *(cont.)*

Schools	Graduates				Employed Full Time				Response	
	Women	Men	Other/Unsure	All	Women	Men	Nonbinary**	All	# Rec'd	Rate
Simmons	247	45	3	295	71	9	4	84	112	38.00%
South Florida	65	14	—	79	4	—	1	5	8	10.10%
Southern California	41	4	—	45	10	1	—	11	19	42.20%
Southern Mississippi	44	6	—	50	21	3	—	24	27	54.00%
St. Catherine	37	3	1	41	6	1	1	8	14	34.10%
St. John's	21	8	—	29	6	3	1	10	11	37.90%
Syracuse	35	6	—	41	10	—	1	11	18	43.90%
Tennessee	63	20	—	83	9	1	—	10	20	24.10%
Texas Women's	173	11	—	184	25	2	—	27	36	19.60%
Valdosta State	65	16	—	81	12	2	—	14	15	18.50%
Washington	101	24	3	128	15	1	—	16	22	17.20%
Wayne State	108	22	—	130	32	3	3	38	56	43.10%
Wisconsin–Madison	71	11	—	82	19	6	1	26	32	39.00%
Wisconsin–Milwaukee	127	95	32	254	15	7	2	24	28	11.00%
Total	3,380	840	43	4,263	620	142	27	795	1,106	25.90%

Tables do not always add up, individually or collectively, due to omitted data from schools and/or individuals.

*Some schools conducted their own survey and provided raw data. Comparison with other tables may show different numbers of placements.

**Includes nonbinary, other, and declined to answer gender.

Table 9 / Comparison of Full-Time Salaries by Type of Organization and Placement Region

	Total Placements	Low Salary	High Salary	Average Salary	Median Salary
Public Libraries					
Northeast	37	$26,000	$70,000	$49,430	$51,000
Southeast	18	25,700	60,000	43,296	43,025
South Central	17	23,500	72,000	43,404	42,000
Midwest	44	25,000	73,500	47,182	46,500
Mountain	12	36,000	75,000	50,925	50,000
Pacific	13	46,000	74,000	60,880	60,000
Canada/Int'l	—	—	—	—	—
All Public	141	23,500	75,000	48,402	47,923
College/University					
Northeast	40	32,292	80,000	58,470	58,300
Southeast	32	32,000	71,000	49,668	51,800
South Central	18	24,100	60,000	39,909	40,000
Midwest	40	28,000	107,500	54,421	55,000
Mountain	8	34,000	65,000	48,625	48,500
Pacific	14	32,000	70,000	58,734	60,000
Canada/Int'l	2	23,000	83,700	53,350	53,350
All Academic	154	23,000	107,500	52,866	53,250
School Libraries					
Northeast	16	45,000	106,000	71,987	67,500
Southeast	3	49,826	59,000	54,109	53,500
South Central	23	36,000	73,000	54,854	58,000
Midwest	6	45,000	62,477	50,246	48,500
Mountain	3	18,000	46,223	36,691	45,850
Pacific	4	31,500	95,000	64,875	66,500
Canada/Int'l	1	50,000	50,000	50,000	50,000
All School	56	18,000	106,000	58,872	53,750
Government Libraries					
Northeast	2	64,270	69,000	66,635	66,635
Southeast	18	35,085	75,000	55,237	58,455
South Central	2	32,042	38,900	35,471	35,471
Midwest	2	46,500	52,000	49,250	49,250
Mountain	1	40,040	40,040	40,040	40,040
Pacific	1	53,000	53,000	53,000	53,000
Canada/Int'l	—	—	—	—	—
All Government	26	32,042	75,000	53,462	55,250
Private Industry					
Northeast	14	31,000	165,000	75,500	61,500
Southeast	3	43,000	92,500	71,000	77,500
South Central	9	30,000	110,000	75,667	82,500
Midwest	26	42,640	160,000	80,005	80,000
Mountain	2	82,500	90,000	86,250	86,250
Pacific	38	42,000	200,000	116,355	115,000
Canada/Int'l	—	—	—	—	—
All Private Industry	92	30,000	200,000	93,752	91,250

Table 9 / Comparison of Full-Time Salaries by Type of
Organization and Placement Region *(cont.)*

	Total Placements	Low Salary	High Salary	Average Salary	Median Salary
Special Libraries					
Northeast	4	$45,000	$62,000	$55,125	$56,750
Southeast	4	37,000	55,000	49,000	52,000
South Central	2	38,500	65,000	51,750	51,750
Midwest	4	37,000	45,000	41,750	42,500
Mountain	2	52,000	63,358	57,679	57,679
Pacific	2	58,000	71,000	64,500	64,500
Canada/Int'l	—	—	—	—	—
All Special	18	37,000	71,000	51,742	53,000
Archives / Special Collections					
Northeast	3	50,000	54,000	52,667	54,000
Southeast	5	40,000	60,700	51,140	53,000
South Central	1	42,000	42,000	42,000	42,000
Midwest	6	34,749	52,000	41,875	40,000
Mountain	1	35,000	35,000	35,000	35,000
Pacific	2	48,792	56,160	52,476	52,476
Canada/Int'l	—	—	—	—	—
All Archives / Special Collections	18	34,749	60,700	47,050	47,396
Nonprofit Organizations					
Northeast	4	41,000	97,500	67,750	66,250
Southeast	2	50,000	68,000	59,000	59,000
South Central	—	—	—	—	—
Midwest	7	36,000	70,000	52,571	50,000
Mountain	—	—	—	—	—
Pacific	1	64,000	64,000	64,000	64,000
Canada/Int'l	—	—	—	—	—
All Nonprofit	14	36,000	97,500	58,643	53,750
Other Organizations					
Northeast	11	34,000	125,000	60,832	50,000
Southeast	4	28,000	105,000	56,250	46,000
South Central	7	34,000	74,000	47,023	41,160
Midwest	6	29,000	55,000	42,060	42,000
Mountain	2	25,000	30,000	27,500	27,500
Pacific	8	44,000	94,000	62,213	55,250
Canada/Int'l	2	33,000	85,644	59,322	59,322
All Other	40	25,000	125,000	53,675	46,825

This table represents only full-time salaries and all placements reported by type. Some individuals omitted placement information, rendering some information unusable.

Accredited Master's Programs in Library and Information Studies

This list of graduate programs accredited by the American Library Association is issued by the ALA Office for Accreditation. Regular updates and additional details appear on the Office for Accreditation's website at http://www.ala.org/CFApps/lisdir/index.cfm. A total of 139 U.S. and Canadian institutions offering both accredited and nonaccredited programs in librarianship are included in the 73rd edition (2020–2021) of *American Library Directory* (Information Today, Inc.).

Northeast: Conn., D.C., Md., Mass., N.J., N.Y., Pa., R.I.

Catholic University of America, School of Arts and Sciences, Dept. of Lib. and Info. Science, 620 Michigan Ave. N.E., Washington, DC 20064. Renate Chancellor, chair. Tel. 202-319-5085, fax 319-5574, e-mail cuaslis@cua.edu, World Wide Web http://lis.cua.edu. Admissions contact: Louise Gray. Tel. 202-319-5085, fax 319-5574, e-mail grayl@cua.edu.

Clarion University of Pennsylvania, College of Business Admin. and Info Sciences, Dept. of Info. and Lib. Science, 210 Carlson Lib. Bldg., Clarion, PA 16214. Linda L. Lillard, chair. Tel. 866-272-5612, fax 814-393-2150, e-mail libsci@clarion.edu, World Wide Web http://www.clarion.edu/libsci. Admissions contact: Michelle Ritzler. Tel. 866-393-2337, e-mail gradstudies@clarion.edu.

Drexel University, College of Computing and Informatics, Dept. of Info. Science, 3141 Chestnut St., Philadelphia, PA 19104-2875. Xia Lin, dept. head. Tel. 215-895-2474, fax 215-895-2494, e-mail istinfo@drexel.edu, World Wide Web https://drexel.edu/cci/academics/graduate-programs/. Admissions contact: Matthew Lechtenburg. Tel. 215-895-1951, e-mail ml333@drexel.edu.

Long Island University, College of Education, Info. and Technology, Palmer School of Lib. and Info. Science, 720 Northern Blvd., Brookville, NY 11548-1300. Bea Baaden, dir. Tel. 516-299-3818, fax 516-299-4168, e-mail post-palmer@liu.edu, World Wide Web https://www.liu.edu/post/Academics/College-of-Education-Information-and-Technology/Palmer-School-of-Library-Information-Science/Academic-Programs/MS-Library-Information-Science. Admissions contact: Heather Ranieri. Tel. 516-299-4110, e-mail heather.ranieri@liu.edu.

Pratt Institute, School of Info. and Lib. Science, 144 W. 14 St., New York, NY 10011. Anthony Cocciolo, dean. Tel. 212-647-7682, fax 212-367-2492, e-mail si@pratt.edu, World Wide Web https://www.pratt.edu/academics/information/degrees/library-and-information-science-mslis/. Admissions contact: Quinn Lai. Tel. 212-647-7701, e-mail qlai@pratt.edu.

Queens College, Grad. School of Lib. and Info. Studies, Rm. 254, Rosenthal Lib., 65-30 Kissena Blvd., Flushing, NY 11367-1597. Kwong bor Ng, chair. Tel. 718-997-3790, fax 718-997-3797, e-mail qc_gslis@qc.cuny.edu, World Wide Web http://sites.google.com/a/qc.cuny.edu/gslis/. Admissions contact: Roberta Brody. Tel. 718-997-3790, e-mail roberta_brody@qc.edu.

Rutgers University, School of Communication and Info., Dept. of Lib. and Info. Science, New Brunswick, NJ 08901-1071. Marie Radford, chair. Tel. 848-932-7602, e-mail: mi@comminfo.rutgers.edu, World Wide Web http://comminfo.rutgers.edu. Admissions contact: Lilia Pavlovsky. Tel. 732-932-7576.

Saint John's University, College of Liberal Arts and Sciences, Div. of Library and Information Science, 8000 Utopia Parkway, Queens, NY 11439. James Vorbach, dir. Tel. 718-990-1834, fax 718-990-2071, e-mail vorbach@stjohns.edu, World Wide Web http://www.stjohns.edu/academics/programs/library-and-information-science-master-science. Admissions contact: Michael Crossfox. Tel. 718-990-6200, e-mail dlis@stjohns.edu.

Simmons University, School of Lib. and Info. Science, College of Organizational,

Computational and Info. Sci., 300 The Fenway, Boston, MA 02115. Sanda Erdelez, dir. Tel. 617-521-2800, fax 617-521-3192, e-mail slisadm@simmons.edu, World Wide Web http://simmons.edu/slis. Admissions contact: Kate Benson. Tel. 617-521-2868, e-mail slisadm@simmons.edu.

Southern Connecticut State University, College of Education, Dept. of Info. and Lib. Sci., 501 Crescent St., New Haven, CT 06515. Hak Joon Kim. Tel. 203-392-5781, fax 203-392-5780, e-mail ils@southernct.edu, World Wide Web http://inside.southernct.edu/information-and-library-science. Admissions contact: Arlene Bielefield. Tel. 203-392-5708, e-mail bielefielda1@southernct.edu.

Syracuse University, School of Info. Studies, 343 Hinds Hall, Syracuse, NY 13244. Jian Qin, MLIS program dir. Tel. 315-443-2911, fax 315-443-6886, e-mail ischool@syr.edu, World Wide Web http://ischool.syr.edu/academics/graduate/masters-degrees/ms-library-and-information-science/. Admissions contact: Blythe Bennett. Tel. 315-443-2911, e-mail mslis@syr.edu.

University at Albany, State Univ. of New York, College of Emergency Preparedness, Homeland Security and Cybersecurity, Draper 015, Albany, NY 12222. Jennifer Goodall, vice dean. Tel. 518-442-5258, fax 518-442-5632, e-mail infosci@albany.edu, World Wide Web http://www.albany.edu/cehc/programs/ms-information-science. Admissions contact: Graduate Admissions. Tel. 518-442-3980, e-mail graduate@albany.edu.

University at Buffalo, State Univ. of New York, Graduate School of Educ., Dept. of Info. Sci, 534 Baldy Hall, Buffalo, NY 14260-1020. Dan Albertson, chair. Tel. 716-645-2412, fax 716-645-3775, e-mail ub-lis@buffalo.edu, World Wide Web http://ed.buffalo.edu/information/about.html. Admissions contact: Ryan Taughrin. Tel. 716-645-2110, e-mail gse-info@buffalo.edu.

University of Maryland, College of Info. Studies, 4121 Hornbake Bldg., College Park, MD 20742. Ursula Gorham, MLIS program dir. Tel. 301-405-2039, fax 301-314-9145, e-mail ischooladmission@umd.edu, World Wide Web http://ischool.umd.edu/academics/master-of-library-and-information-science. Admissions contact: Morgan Adle.

Tel. 301-405-2039, e-mail mlisprogram@umd.edu.

University of Pittsburgh, School of Computing and Info., Info. Culture and Data Stewardship, 135 N. Bellefield Ave., Pittsburgh, PA 15260. Mary K. Biagini, chair. Tel. 412-624-5230, fax 412-648-7001, e-mail sciadmit@pitt.edu, World Wide Web http://www.sci.pitt.edu/academics/masters/mlis/. Admissions contact: Shabana Reza. Tel. 412-624-3988, e-mail shabana.reza@pitt.edu.

University of Rhode Island, Grad. School of Lib. and Info. Studies, Rodman Hall, 94 W. Alumni Ave., Kingston, RI 02881. Valerie Karno, dir. Tel. 401-874-2878, fax 401-874-4964, e-mail vkarno@uri.edu, World Wide Web http://www.uri.edu/artsci/lsc.

Southeast: Ala., Fla., Ga., Ky., La., Miss., N.C., S.C., Tenn., P.R.

East Carolina University, College of Educ., Lib. Science Degree Program, Mailstop 172, ECU, Greenville, NC 27858. Barbara Miller Marson, MLIS program dir. Tel. 252-328-2347, fax 252-328-4368, e-mail marsonb@ecu.edu, World Wide Web http://bit.ly/ECUML. Admissions contact: Camilla King. Tel. 252-328-6012, e-mail gradschool@ecu.edu.

Florida State University, College of Communication and Info., School of Info., 142 Collegiate Loop, P.O. Box 3062100, Tallahassee, FL 32306-2100. Kathleen Burnett, dir. Tel. 850-644-5775, fax 850-644-9763, e-mail jb.mitchell@cci.fsu.edu, World Wide Web http://ischool.cci.fsu.edu. Admissions tel. 850-645-3280, e-mail ischooladvising@admin.fsu.edu.

Louisiana State University, College of Human Sciences and Education, School of Lib. and Info. Science, 267 Coates Hall, Baton Rouge, LA 70803. Carol Barry, dir. Tel. 225-578-3158, fax 225-578-4581, e-mail slis@lsu.edu, World Wide Web http://slis.lsu.edu. Admissions contact: LaToya Coleman Joseph. Tel. 225-578-3150, e-mail lcjoseph@lsu.edu.

North Carolina Central University, School of Lib. and Info. Sciences, P.O. Box 19586, Durham, NC 27707. Jon P. Gant, dean. Tel.

919-530-7585, fax 919-530-6402, e-mail slisadmissions@nccu.edu, World Wide Web http://www.nccuslis.org. Admissions contact: Nina Clayton. Tel. 919-530-5184.

University of Alabama, College of Communication and Info. Sciences, School of Lib. and Info. Studies, Box 870118, Tuscaloosa, AL 35487-0252. James Elmborg, dir. Tel. 205-348-2719, fax 205-348-3746, e-mail info@slis.ua.edu, World Wide Web http://www.slis.ua.edu. Admissions tel. 205-348-4610, contact form: https://slis.ua.edu/contact-slis/.

University of Kentucky, College of Communication and Info., School of Lib. and Info. Science, 320 Little Lib., Lexington, KY 40506-0224. Jeffrey T. Huber, dir. Tel. 859-257-8876, fax 859-257-4205, e-mail ukslis@uky.edu, World Wide Web http://www.uky.edu/cis/slis. Admissions contact: Will Buntin. Tel. 859-257-3317, e-mail wjbunt0@uky.edu.

University of North Carolina at Chapel Hill, School of Info. and Lib. Science, CB 3360, 100 Manning Hall, Chapel Hill, NC 27599-3360. Gary Marchionini, dean. Tel 919-962-8366, fax 919-962-8071, e-mail info@ils.unc.edu, World Wide Web http://sils.unc.edu/programs/graduate/msls. Admissions contact: Lara Bailey.

University of North Carolina at Greensboro, School of Educ., Dept. of Lib. and Info. Studies, 446 School of Educ. Bldg., P.O. Box 26170, Greensboro, NC 27402-6170. Lisa O'Connor, chair. Tel. 336-334-3477, fax 336-334-4120, e-mail lis@uncg.edu, World Wide Web http://soe.uncg.edu/academics/departments/lis. Admissions contact: Nora Bird. Tel. 336-256-1313, e-mail njbird@uncg.edu.

University of Puerto Rico, Info. Sciences and Technologies, P.O. Box 21906, San Juan, PR 00931-1906. Noraida Domínguez-Flores, acting dir. Tel. 787-763-6199, fax 787-764-2311, e-mail egcti@uprrp.edu, World Wide Web http://egcti.upr.edu. Admissions contact: Migdalia Dávila-Pérez. Tel. 787-764-0000 ext. 3530, e-mail migdalia.davila@upr.edu.

University of South Carolina, College of Info. and Communications, School of Lib. and Info. Science, 1501 Greene St., Columbia, SC 29208. R. David Lankes,

dir. Tel. 803-777-3858, fax 803-777-7938, e-mail rdlankes@sc.edu, World Wide Web http://www.libsci.sc.edu. Admissions tel. 803-777-3887, e-mail slisss@mailbox.sc.edu.

University of South Florida, College of Arts and Sciences, School of Info., 4202 E. Fowler Ave., CIS 1040, Tampa, FL 33620. James Andrews, dir. Tel. 813-974-3520, fax 813-974-6840, e-mail si@usf.edu, World Wide Web https://www.usf.edu/arts-sciences/departments/information/programs/graduate-programs/ma-in-library-and-information-sciences/index.aspx. Admissions contact: Alexis Shinawongse. Tel. 813-974-8022.

University of Southern Mississippi, College of Educ. and Health Sciences, School of Lib. and Info. Science, 118 College Dr., No. 5146, Hattiesburg, MS 39406-0001. Theresa Welsh, dir. Tel. 601-266-4228, fax 601-266-5774, e-mail slis@usm.edu, World Wide Web http://www.usm.edu/slis. Admissions tel. 601-266-5137, e-mail graduatestudies@usm.edu.

University of Tennessee, College of Communication and Info., School of Info. Sciences, 451 Communication Bldg., Knoxville, TN 37996. Carol Tenopir, interim dir. Tel. 865-974-2148, fax 865-974-4967, e-mail sis@utk.edu, World Wide Web http://www.sis.utk.edu, Admissions tel. 865-974-2148.

Valdosta State Univ., Dept. of Lib. and Info. Studies, 1500 N. Patterson St., Odum 4600, Valdosta, GA 31698-0133. Linda R. Most, dept. head. Tel. 229-333-5966, fax 229-259-5055, e-mail mlis@valdosta.edu, World Wide Web http://www.valdosta.edu/mlis. Admissions contact: Sheila Peacock.

Midwest: Ill., Ind., Iowa, Kan., Mich., Minn., Mo., Ohio, Wis.

Chicago State University, College of Education, Department of Info. Studies, 9501 S. King Dr., Education Bldg., Room 208, Chicago, IL 60628-1598. Rae-Anne Montague, LIS program coordinator. Tel. 773-995-2598, fax 773-821-2203, e-mail montague@csu.edu, World Wide Web https://www.csu.edu/collegeofeducation/Infomediastudies. Admissions contact: Gloria Adams. Tel.

773-995-2404, e-mail graduateprograms@ csu.edu.

Dominican Univ., School of Info. Studies, 7900 W. Division St., River Forest, IL 60305. Kate Marek, dean. Tel. 708-524-6983, fax 708-524-6657, e-mail sois@dom. edu, World Wide Web http://www.dom. edu/academics/majors-programs/master-library-and-information-science. Admissions contact:Aracelis Sanchez.Tel.708-524-6456, e-mail asanche2@dom.edu.

Emporia State University, School of Lib. and Info. Management, Campus Box 4025, 1 Kellogg Circle, Emporia, KS 66801-5415. Wooseob Jeong, dean. Tel. 620-341-5203, fax 620-341-5233, e-mail sliminfo@emporia.edu, World Wide Web http://www.emporia.edu/ school-library-and-information-management/ programs-certificates-licensures/master-library-science/.Admissions contact: Kathie Buckman. Tel. 620-341-5065.

Indiana University, School of Informatics, Computing and Engineering, Info. and Lib. Science, Luddy Hall, Suite 2999C, 700 N. Woodlawn Ave., Bloomington, IN 47408. Raj Achayra, dean. Tel. 812-855-2018, fax 812-855-6166, e-mail ilsmain@indiana.edu, World Wide Web http://www.ils.indiana. edu/about/accreditation.html. Admissions contact: Michelle Dunbar-Sims. Tel. 812-855-2018, e-mail GoLuddy@iu.edu.

Indiana University–Purdue University Indianapolis, School of Informatics and Computing, Dept. of Lib. and Info. Science, 535 W. Michigan St., IT 475, Indianapolis, IN 46202. Andrea Copeland, chair. Tel. 317-278-4636, fax 317-278-7669, e-mail soicindy@iupui.edu, World Wide Web http://soic.iupui.edu/lis. Admissions e-mail soicapps@iupui.edu.

Kent State University, School of Info., P.O. Box 5190, Kent, OH 44242-0001. Meghan Harper, dir. Tel. 330-672-2782, fax 330-672-7965, e-mail ischool@kent.edu, World Wide Web http://www.kent.edu/iSchool/ master-library-information-science. Admissions contact: Cheryl Tennant.

Saint Catherine University, Graduate College, School of Business and Professional Studies, MLIS Program/Information Management Department, 2004 Randolph Ave. No. 4125, St. Paul, MN 55105. Joyce Yakawa, interim

dir. Tel. 651-690-6802, fax 651-690-8724, e-mail imdept@stkate.edu, World Wide Web https://www.stkate.edu/academics/ academic-programs/gc-library-and-information-science. Admissions contact: Ashley Wells. Tel. 612-214-0741, e-mail aewells@ stkate.edu.

University of Illinois at Urbana-Champaign, School of Info. Science, 501 E. Daniel St., Champaign, IL 61820-6211. Emily Knox, interim assoc. dean for acad. affairs. Tel. 217-333-3280, fax 217-244-3302, e-mail ischool@illinois.edu, World Wide Web http://ischool.illinois.edu. Admissions contact: Moises Orozco Villicana. Tel. 217-300-5007, e-mail orozco6@illinois. edu.

University of Iowa, Graduate College, School of Lib. and Info. Science, 3087 Main Lib., Iowa City, IA 52242-1420. David Eichmann, dir. Tel. 319-335-5707, fax 319-335-5374, e-mail slis@uiowa.edu, World Wide Web http://slis.grad.uiowa.edu. Admissions contact: Carol Ives. Tel. 319-335-5709, e-mail carol-ives@uiowa.edu.

University of Michigan, School of Info., 4322 North Quad, 105 S. State St., Ann Arbor, MI 48109-1285. Elizabeth Yakel, sr. assoc. dean. Tel. 734-763-2285, fax 734-764-2475, e-mail umsi.admissions@umich.edu, World Wide Web http://si.umich.edu/. Admissions contact: Laura Elgas.

University of Missouri, College of Educ., Info. Science and Learning Technologies, 303 Townsend Hall, Columbia, MO 65211. Jenny Bossaller, chair. Tel. 877-747-5868, fax 573-884-0122, e-mail sislt@missouri. edu, World Wide Web http://lis.missouri. edu. Admissions tel. 573-882-4546.

University of Wisconsin–Madison, College of Letters and Sciences, Info. School, 600 N. Park St., Madison, WI 53706. Kyung-Sun Kim, interim dir. Tel. 608-263-2900, fax 608-263-4849, e-mail info@ischool. wisc.edu, World Wide Web http://ischool. wisc.edu. Admissions contact: Tanya Hendricks Cobb. Tel. 608-263-2909, e-mail student-services@slis.wisc.edu.

University of Wisconsin–Milwaukee, School of Info. Studies, P.O. Box 413, Milwaukee, WI 53201. Dietmar Wolfram, senior assoc. dean. Tel. 414-229-4707, fax 414-229-6699,

e-mail soisinfo@uwm.edu, World Wide Web http://uwm.edu/informationstudies/.
Wayne State University, School of Info. Science, 106 Kresge Lib., Detroit, MI 48202. Hermina Anghelesco, interim dir. Tel. 313-577-1825, fax 313-577-7563, e-mail asklis@wayne.edu, World Wide Web http://sis.wayne.edu/mlis/index.php. Admissions contact: Matthew Fredericks. Tel. 313-577-2446, e-mail mfredericks@wayne.edu.

Southwest: Ariz., Okla., Texas

Texas Woman's University, School of Lib. and Info. Studies, P.O. Box 425769, Denton, TX 76204-5438. Ling Hwey Jeng, dir. Tel. 940-898-2602, fax 940-898-2611, e-mail slis@twu.edu, World Wide Web http://www.twu.edu/slis. Admissions contact: Mary Honard. E-mail slis@twu.edu.
University of Arizona, College of Social and Behavioral Sciences, School of Info., 1103 E. Second St., Tucson, AZ 85721. Catherine Brooks, dir. Tel. 520-621-3565, fax 520-621-3279, e-mail si-info@email.arizona.edu, World Wide Web http://ischool.arizona.edu/master-arts-library-and-information-science. Admissions contact: Barb Vandervelde. Tel. 520-621-3567, e-mail barbv@email.arizona.edu.
University of North Texas, College of Info., Dept. of Info. Science, 1155 Union Circle, No. 311068, Denton, TX 76203-5017. Jiangping Chen, chair. Tel. 940-565-2445, fax 940-369-7600, e-mail lis-chair@unt.edu, World Wide Web http://informationscience.unt.edu./master-science. Admissions contact: Caley Barnhart. Tel. 940-891-6861, e-mail ci-admissions@unt.edu.
University of Oklahoma, School of Lib. and Info. Studies, College of Arts and Sciences, 401 W. Brooks, Norman, OK 73019-6032. Susan Burke, dir. Tel. 405-325-3921, e-mail slisinfo@ou.edu, World Wide Web http://slis.ou.edu/. Admissions contact: Sarah Connelly.
University of Texas at Austin, School of Info., Suite 5.202, 1616 Guadalupe St., Austin, TX 78701-1213. Eric T. Meyer, dean. Tel. 512-471-3821, fax 512-471-3971, e-mail info@ischool.utexas.edu, World Wide Web http:// www.ischool.utexas.edu. Admissions contact: Carla Criner. Tel. 512-471-5654, e-mail criner@ischool.utexas.edu.

West: Calif., Colo., Hawaii, Wash.

San José State University, School of Info., Applied Sciences and Arts, One Washington Sq., San Jose, CA 95192-0029. Linda Main, assoc dir. Tel. 408-924-2490, fax 408-924-2476, e-mail sjsuischool@gmail.com, World Wide Web http://ischool.sjsu.edu/master-library-and-information-science. Admissions contact: Linda Main. Tel. 408-924-2494, e-mail linda.main@sjsu.edu.
University of California, Los Angeles, Graduate School of Educ. and Info. Studies, Dept. of Info. Studies, Box 951520, Los Angeles, CA 90095-1520. Jeffrey Prager, interim chair. Tel. 310-825-8799, fax 310-206-3076, e-mail info@gseis.ucla.edu, World Wide Web http://is.gseis.ucla.edu. Admissions contact: Susan Abler. Tel. 310-825-5269, e-mail abler@gseis.ucla.edu.
University of Denver, Morgridge College of Educ., Research Methods and Info. Science, 1999 E. Evans Ave., Denver, CO 80208-1700. Nicholas Cutforth, chair. Tel. 303-871-3587, fax 303-871-4456, e-mail mce@du.edu, World Wide Web http://www.du.edu/education. Admissions contact: Rachel Riley. Tel. 303-871-2508, e-mail rachel.riley@du.edu.
University of Hawaii, College of Natural Sciences, Lib. and Info. Science Program, 2550 McCarthy Mall, Honolulu, HI 96822. Rich Gazan, chair. Tel. 808-956-7321, fax 808-956-5835, e-mail slis@hawaii.edu, World Wide Web http://www.hawaii.edu/lis.
University of Southern California, Marshall School of Business, 3550 Trousdale Parkway, DML 312, Los Angeles, CA 90089-0183. Christopher Stewart. Tel. 213-640-4034, e-mail mmlis.program@marshall.usc.edu, World Wide Web http://librarysciencedegree.usc.edu. Admissions tel. 877-830-8647, e-mail info@librarysciencedegree.usc.edu.
University of Washington, The Information School, 370 Mary Gates Hall, Seattle,

WA 98195-2840. Anind Dey, dean. Tel. 206-685-9937, fax 206-616-3152, e-mail ischool@uw.edu, World Wide Web http://ischool.uw.edu. Admissions tel. 206-543-1794, e-mail mlis@uw.edu.

Canada

Dalhousie University, School of Info. Management, Kenneth C. Rowe Management Bldg., Halifax, NS B3H 4R2. Vivian Howard, interim dir. Tel. 902-494-3656, fax 902-494-2451, e-mail sim@dal.ca, World Wide Web http://www.sim.management.dal.ca. Admissions contact: JoAnn Watson. Tel. 902-494-2471, e-mail joann.watson@dal.ca.

McGill University, School of Info. Studies, 3661 Peel St., Montreal, QC H3A 1X1. Kimiz Dalkir, dir. Tel. 514-398-4204, fax 514-398-7193, e-mail sis@mcgill.ca, World Wide Web http://www.mcgill.ca/sis. Admissions contact: Kathryn Hubbard. Tel. 514-398-4204 ext. 0742, e-mail sis@mcgill.ca.

University of Alberta, School of Library and Information Studies, Faculty of Education, 7-104 Education North, Edmonton, AB T6G 2G5. Kathleen De Long, interim chair. Tel. 780-492-3932, fax 780-492-2024, e-mail slis@ualberta.ca, World Wide Web http://www.ualberta.ca/school-of-library-and-information-studies/programs. Admissions contact: Joan White. Tel. 780-492-3679, e-mail slis@ualberta.ca.

University of British Columbia, School of Information, Irving K. Barber Learning Centre, Suite 470, 1961 East Mall, Vancouver, BC V6T 1Z1. Erik Kwakkel, dir. Tel. 604-822-2404, fax 604-822-6006, e-mail ischool.info@ubc.ca, World Wide Web http://www.slais.ubc.ca. Admissions contact: Sandra Abah. Tel. 604-822-3459, e-mail ischool.program@ubc.ca.

Université de Montréal, École de bibliothéconomie et des sciences de l'information, C.P. 6128, Succursale Centre-Ville, Montreal, QC H3C 3J7. Lyne Da Sylva, acting dir. Tel. 514-343-6044, fax 514-343-5753, e-mail ebsiinfo@ebsi.umontreal.ca, World Wide Web http://www.ebsi.umontreal.ca. Admissions contact: Alain Tremblay. Tel. 514-343-6044, e-mail alain.tremblay.1@umontreal.ca.

University of Ottawa, School of Info. Studies, Desmarais Bldg., Ottawa, ON K1N 6N5. Mary Cavanagh, dir. Tel. 613-562-5130, fax 613-562-5854, e-mail esis@uOttawa.ca, World Wide Web http://arts.uottawa.ca/sis/. Admissions contact: Catherine Bernard. Tel. 613-562-5800 ext. 1324, e-mail artsgrad@uottawa.ca.

University of Toronto, Faculty of Info., 140 George St., Toronto, ON M5S 3G6. Wendy Duff, dean. Tel. 416-978-3202, fax 416-978-5762, e-mail inquire.ischool@utoronto.ca, World Wide Web http://www.ischool.utoronto.ca. Admissions contact: Barbara Brown. Tel. 416-978-8589, e-mail barb.brown@utoronto.ca.

University of Western Ontario, Grad. Programs in Lib. and Info. Science, Faculty of Info. and Media Studies, Room 240, North Campus Bldg., London, ON N6A 5B7. Grant Campbell, grad. chair. Tel. 519-661-4017, fax 519-661-3506, e-mail mlisinfo@uwo.ca, World Wide Web http://www.fims.uwo.ca. Admissions contact: Shelley Long.

Library Scholarship Sources

For a more complete list of scholarships, fellowships, and assistantships offered for library study, see *Financial Assistance for Library and Information Studies,* published annually by the American Library Association (ALA). The document is also available on the ALA website at http://www.ala.org/educationcareers/scholarships.

American Association of Law Libraries. (1) Degree Candidates Scholarships are available for individuals studying to become law librarians as either a library or law school student, or to library school graduates seeking an advanced degree in a related field. Preference is given to AALL members, but scholarships are not restricted to members. Applicants with law library experience are also given preference, but it is not required. Evidence of financial need must be submitted. (2) AALL Scholarship is awarded annually to individuals seeking a degree from an accredited library or law school, and who intend to have a career in legal information, or to a library school graduate seeking an advanced degree in a related field. (3) Lexis-Nexis John R. Johnson Memorial Scholarship is awarded annually to individuals seeking a degree from an accredited library or law school, and who intend to have a career in legal information, or to a library school graduate seeking an advanced degree in a related field. (4) George A. Strait Minority Scholarship & Fellowship is awarded annually to students enrolled in an ALA-accredited library graduate school or a law school and who are members of a minority group as defined by current U.S. guidelines, and are degree candidates in an accredited library or law school and intend to have a career in law librarianship. (5) Marcia J. Koslov Scholarship supports AALL members who work in a government law library by providing funding to attend continuing education programs. For information, write to AALL Scholarship Committee, 105 W. Adams St., Suite 3300, Chicago, IL 60603.

American Library Association. (1) ALA Century Scholarship of $2,500 that funds services or accommodation for a library school student(s) with disabilities admitted to an ALA-accredited library school. (2) David

A. Clift Scholarship of $3,000 to a U.S./Canadian citizen or permanent resident who is pursuing an MLS in an ALA-accredited program. (3) Tom and Roberta Drewes Scholarship of $3,000 to a library support-staff member who is a U.S./Canadian citizen or permanent resident and is pursuing an MLS in an ALA-accredited program. (4) deg farrelly Memorial/Alexander Street Press AMIA/FMRT Media Librarian Scholarship given once a year to a master's degree candidate in library science who intends to work professionally with media collections in libraries. (5) Mary V. Gaver Scholarship of $3,000 to a U.S./Canadian citizen or permanent resident who is pursuing an MLS specializing in youth services in an ALA-accredited program. (6) Miriam L. Hornback Scholarship of $3,000 to an ALA or library support staffer who is a U.S./Canadian citizen or permanent resident who is pursuing an MLS in an ALA-accredited program. (7) Christopher Hoy/ERT Scholarship of $5,000 to a U.S./Canadian citizen or permanent resident who is pursuing an MLS in an ALA-accredited program. (8) Julia J. Brody Public Librarian Scholarship of $4,000 to a U.S./Canadian citizen or permanent resident who is pursuing an MLS specializing in public library services in an ALA-accredited program. (9) Tony B. Leisner Scholarship of $3,000 to a library support-staff member who is a U.S./Canadian citizen or permanent resident pursuing an MLS in an ALA-accredited program. (10) Peter Lyman Memorial/SAGE Scholarship in New Media to support a student in an ALA-accredited master's program in Library and Information Studies pursuing a specialty in new media. (11) Regina U. Minudri Young Adult Scholarship of $3,000 scholarship to be given once a year to a master's degree candidate in library science who intends to work professionally with young adults in public libraries. (12) W. David Rozkuszka Scholarship of $3,000 to an individual who is currently working with government documents in a library and is working toward a master's degree in library science. (13) Spectrum Scholarship Program is ALA's national diversity and recruitment effort designed to address the specific issue of underrepresentation of critically needed ethnic librarians within the profession while serving as a model for ways to bring attention to larger diversity issues in the future. For information, write to ALA Scholarship Clearinghouse, 50 E. Huron St., Chicago, IL 60611, or see http://www.ala.org/scholarships.

ALA/Association for Library Service to Children. (1) Bound to Stay Bound Books Scholarship provides financial assistance for the education of individuals who intend to pursue an MLS or advanced degree and who plan to work in the area of library service to children. (2) Frederic G. Melcher Scholarship provides financial assistance for individuals who intend to pursue an MLS degree and who plan to work in children's librarianship. For information, write to ALA Scholarship Clearinghouse, 50 E. Huron St., Chicago, IL 60611, or see http://www.ala.org/scholarships.

ALA/Association of College and Research Libraries. The WESS-SEES De Gruyter European Librarianship Study Grant supports research in European studies with an emphasis on librarianship, the book trade, resource documentation, and similar information-science-related topics. An award of €2,500 is given to cover travel to and from Europe and transportation, room, and board in Europe, for up to 30 consecutive days. Application is electronic only. Note: The 2021 grant is temporarily on hold due to funding suspension from the sponsor and submissions are not currently being accepted.

ALA International Relations Committee. Bogle Pratt International Library Travel Fund of $1,000 is given to an ALA personal member to attend their first international conference. Applications should be submitted via e-mail to the ALA International Relations Office, intl@ala.org.

ALA/Library and Information Technology Association. (1) LITA/Christian (Chris) Larew Memorial Scholarship of $3,000 for study in an ALA-Accredited Master of Library Science (MLS) program to encourage the entry of qualified persons into the library and information technology field. (2) LITA/OCLC Spectrum Scholarship of $5,000 to a U.S. or Canadian citizen who is a qualified member of a principal minority group (American Indian or Alaskan native, Asian or Pacific Islander, African American, or Hispanic) for study in an ALA-Accredited Master of Library Science (MLS) program who has a strong commitment to the use of automated systems in libraries and plans to follow a career in the library and automation field. (3) LITA/LSSI Minority Scholarship of $2,500 to a U.S. or Canadian citizen who is a qualified member of a principal minority group (American Indian or Alaskan native, Asian or Pacific Islander, African American, or Hispanic) for study in an ALA-Accredited Master of Library Science (MLS) program who has a strong commitment to the use of automated systems in libraries and plans to follow a career in the library and automation field. For information, write to ALA Scholarship Clearinghouse, 50 E. Huron St., Chicago, IL 60611, or see http://www.ala.org/scholarships.

ALA/Public Library Association. Demco New Leaders Travel Grant of up to $1,500 for a varying number of PLA Members to enhance their professional development by making possible their attendance at major professional development activities. For information, write to PLA Awards Program, ALA/PLA, 50 E. Huron St., Chicago, IL 60611, or see http://www.ala.org/pla/about/awards.

American-Scandinavian Foundation. Fellowships (up to $23,000) and grants (up to $5,000) to pursue research, study, or creative arts projects in Denmark, Finland, Iceland, Norway, or Sweden. For information, write to Fellowships and Grants, American-Scandinavian Foundation, 58 Park Ave., New York, NY 10026, or see http://www.amscan.org/fellowships-and-grants/.

Association for Library and Information Science Education (ALISE). (1) ALISE Community conn@CT mini-grants of $750 for

ALISE members to address a library and information need of a social justice organization through community engagement (in a collaborative manner). (2) A varying number of research grants totaling $5,000 for members of ALISE. For information, write to ALISE, 4 Lan Drive, Suite 310, Westford, MA 01886.

Association of Bookmobile and Outreach Services (ABOS). (1) The Bernard Vavrek Scholarship of $1,000 to a student who is currently enrolled and has completed at least one semester in a library and/or information science graduate degree program, and who is interested in becoming an outreach/bookmobile librarian. (2) The John Philip Excellence in Outreach Award to recognize outstanding contributions and leadership by an individual in bookmobile and outreach services. (3) The Carol Hole Conference Attendance Award consisting of ten awards of free conference registration and $500 stipends for the winners' travel expenses and/or accommodations for a conference. For information, write to David Kelsey, ABOS Awards Chair, at awards@abos-outreach.com.

Association of Jewish Libraries. (1) One or two academic scholarships of $1,000 to a student enrolled or accepted in a graduate school of library and information science. Additionally, free full conference registration is included and encouraged. (2) A conference subvention award for attending the Association of Jewish Libraries annual conference. Free full conference registration, travel, and (shared) room are included. For information, see http://jewishlibraries.org/conference_support_scholarships.

Association of Seventh-Day Adventist Librarians. The D. Glenn Hilts Scholarship for a member of the Seventh-Day Adventist Church in an ALA-accredited graduate library program or, if attending outside the United States or Canada, a program recognized by the International Federation of Library Associations (IFLA). Recipient must be enrolled as a full-time student and use the scholarship only for tuition and books. For information, write to ASDAL Scholarship and Awards Committee, McKee Library, Southern Adventist University, P.O. Box 629, Collegedale, TN 37315.

Beta Phi Mu. (1) The Sarah Rebecca Reed Scholarship consisting of two $2,250 awards for individuals beginning LIS studies at an ALA-accredited school. Note: Not awarded in 2021. (2) The Frank B. Sessa Scholarship of ten $150 awards for Beta Phi Mu members' continuing education. (3) The Harold Lancour Scholarship of $1,750 for a librarian conducting foreign research. (4) The Blanche E. Woolls Scholarship for School Library Media Service of $2,250 for an individual beginning LIS studies with a concentration in School Library Media. Note: Not awarded in 2021. (5) The Eugene Garfield Doctoral Dissertation Scholarship of up to six $3,000 awards for doctoral students who are working on their dissertations in LIS and related fields. For information, write to Beta Phi Mu Honor Society, P.O. Box 42139, Philadelphia, PA 19101, or see https://www.betaphimu.org/scholarships_overview.html.

Canadian Association of Law Libraries. (1) The Diana M. Priestly Scholarship of $2,500 for a student enrolled in an approved Canadian law school or accredited Canadian library school. (2) CALL/ACBD Research Grant of up to $3,000 for research in areas of interest to members and to the association. (3) CALL/ACBD Education Reserve Fund Grants for CALL members to further their education in pursuits that do not fit the guidelines of already established scholarships. (4) The James D. Lang Memorial Scholarship to support attendance at a continuing education program. (5) The Eunice Beeson Memorial Travel Fund to assist members of the Association who wish to attend the annual meeting but, for financial reasons, are unable to do so. (6) Janine Miller Fellowship of $2,500 for one CALL member to attend the Law via the Internet Conference. For information, see https://www.callacbd.ca/Awards.

Canadian Federation of University Women. (1) The Aboriginal Women's Award of $10,000 to $25,000 for studies in specific programs of Law, Medicine, or Nurse Practitioner or a Master of Aboriginal Studies. (2) The Ruth Binnie Fellowship of $6,000 for a student in master's studies that focus on one or more aspect(s) of the field of human ecology/home economics/family and consumer sciences. (3) The Canadian Home Economics Association Fellowship of $6,000 for a student enrolled in a postgraduate program in the field of human ecology/home economics/family and consumer sciences in Canada. (4) the CFUW Memorial Fellowship of $8,000 for a student who is currently enrolled in a master's program in science, mathematics, or engineering in Canada or abroad. (5) The Bourse Georgette LeMoyne award of $5,000 for graduate study in any field at a Canadian university (the candidate must be studying in French). (6) The Elizabeth and Rachel Massey Award of $5,000 for postgraduate studies in the visual arts or in music. (7) The Margaret McWilliams Pre-Doctoral Fellowship of $11,000 for a female student who has completed at least one full year as a full-time student in doctoral-level studies. (8) The 1989 Ecole Polytechnique Commemorative Award of $7,000 for graduate studies in any field at the doctoral level and one award of $5,000 for master's study. The applicant must justify the relevance of her work to women. (9) The Linda Souter Humanities Award of $6,000 for a master's or doctoral student studying in the area of the humanities. (10) The Alice E. Wilson Award of $5,000 for four mature students returning to graduate studies in any field after at least three years. (11) CFUW 100th Anniversary Legacy Fellowship of one $5,000 award to a woman who has completed one calendar year of a doctoral program. For information, write to Fellowships Program Manager, Canadian Federation of University Women, cfuwfls@rogers.com.

Chinese American Librarians Association. (1) The Sheila Suen Lai Scholarship of $500 to a Chinese descendant who has been accepted in an ALA-accredited program. (2) The CALA Scholarship of Library and Information Science of $1,000 to a Chinese descendant who has been accepted in an ALA-accredited program. (3) The Huang Tso-ping and Wu Yao-yu Research and Scholarship awards faculty and students at the Wuhan University, China; one award is for a library school faculty member ($400) and two awards go to library school students ($200 each). For information, write to Jen Woo at jennifer.woo@sfpl.org.

Council on Library and Information Resources. Mellon Fellowships for Dissertation Research in Original Sources offers up to 15 awards of $2,000 per month for periods ranging from 9 to 12 months and an additional $1,000 upon participating in a symposium on research in original sources and submitting a report acceptable to CLIR on the research experience. For information, write to the Council on Library and Information Resources, 2221 South Clark Street, Arlington, VA 22202. Note: Not accepting applications in 2021.

Massachusetts Black Librarians' Network. $500 for students of African descent entering an ALA-accredited master's program in library science. For information, write to Massachusetts Black Librarians' Network, P.O. Box 400504, Cambridge, MA 02140.

Medical Library Association. (1) The Cunningham Memorial International Fellowship for health sciences librarians from countries other than the United States and Canada. (2) A scholarship of up to $5,000 for a person entering an ALA-accredited library program, with no more than one-half of the program yet to be completed. (3) A scholarship of up to $5,000 for a minority student studying health sciences librarianship. (4) A varying number of Research, Development, and Demonstration Project Grants of $100 to $1,000 for U.S. or Canadian citizens, preferably MLA members. (5) The Clarivate Analytics/MLA Doctoral Fellowship of $2,000 for doctoral work in medical librarianship or information science. (6) The Librarians without Borders Ursula Poland International Scholarship of $1,000 to fund an international project by a U.S. or Canadian health sciences librarian. For information, write to MLA Grants and Scholarships Coordinator, awards@mlahq.org, or see http://www.mlanet.org/page/awards.

Mountain Plains Library Association. A varying number of grants of up to $600 for applicants who are members of the association and have been for the preceding two years. For information, write to Judy Kulp, Executive Secretary, MPLA, 14293 W. Center Drive, Lakewood, SD 80228.

Society of American Archivists. (1) The F. Gerald Ham and Elsie Ham Scholarship of $10,000 for graduate students in archival education at a U.S. university that meets the society's criteria for graduate education. (2) The Mosaic Scholarship of $5,000 for up to two U.S. or Canadian minority students enrolled in a graduate program in archival administration. (3) The Josephine Foreman Scholarship of $10,000 for a U.S. citizen or permanent resident who is a minority graduate student enrolled in a program in archival administration. (4) The Oliver Wendell Holmes Travel Award of $1,000 to enable foreign students involved in archival training in the United States or Canada to attend the SAA Annual Meeting. (5) The Donald Peterson Student Travel Award of up to $1,500 to enable graduate students or recent graduates to attend the meeting. (6) The Harold T. Pinkett Student of Color Awards to enable minority students or graduate students to attend the meeting. (7) The Brenda S. Banks Travel Award to

recognize and acknowledge individuals of color who have demonstrated professional archival experience and who manifest an interest in becoming active members of the Society of American Archivists. For details, write to Rana Hutchinson Salzmann, Society of American Archivists, 17 N. State St., Suite 1425, Chicago, IL 60607, or see http://www2.archivists.org/governance/handbook/section12.

Special Libraries Association. Leadership Symposium Scholarship of $1,000 for travel expenses and registration at symposium (value $395) for members who demonstrate a desire and commitment to advance their leadership skills and abilities within SLA units. For information, write to Special Libraries Association, 7918 Jones Branch Dr., Suite 300, McLean, Virginia 22102

Library Scholarship and Award Recipients, 2020

Compiled by the staff of *Library and Book Trade Almanac*

Scholarships and awards are listed by organization.

American Association of Law Libraries (AALL)

AALL Educational Scholarships. To assist individuals studying to become law librarians with their educational expenses. *Winners:* (college graduate seeking library degree) Bailey DeSimone, Annie Leung, Nadia Montenegro; (law school graduate seeking library degree) Alex Hutchings, Natasha Landon, Michael Muehe, Christine Park; (library school graduate seeking law degree) Cynthia Bassett.

AALL Grants. To enable law librarians to participate in professional educational opportunities at the AALL Annual Meeting or to engage in original research on topics important to law librarianship. *Winners:* (annual meeting grants) Havilah Joy-Steinman Bakken, Carla Bywaters, Eugene M. Giudice, Anna C.B. Russell, Suzanne Stephenson; (annual meeting chapter registration grant) Jennine Kottwitz.

AALL Hall of Fame Award. Recognizes significant, substantial, and long-standing contributions to the profession and service to the Association. *Winners:* Steven P. Anderson, Mary Lu Linnane, Carol A. Watson, Gail Warren.

AALL Marcia J. Koslov Scholarship. To an AALL member to finance conference or seminar attendance. *Winner:* Not awarded in 2020.

AALL New Product Award. For new commercial information products that enhance or improve existing law library services or procedures or innovative products that improve access to legal information, the legal research process, or procedures for technical processing of library materials. *Winner:* LexisNexis for LexisNexis Digital Library.

AALL Spectrum Article of the Year Award. *Winner:* Rena Seidler for "Shedding Light on Legal Research Accessibility Issues for the Blind" (January/February 2019).

AALL George A. Strait Minority Scholarship & Fellowship. *Winners:* (scholarship and fellowship) Kimberly Villafuerte Barzola, Michael Muehe, Christine Park; (scholarship) Brittany Butler, Juan Andres Fuentes, Dinorah La Luz, Sophie Le, Kaia MacLeod, Rebecca Plevel, Renu Sagreiya.

Joseph L. Andrews Legal Literature Award. *Winners:* Ed Edmonds and Frank G. Houdek (co-editors) and HeinOnline for *Business and Legal Aspects of Sports Entertainment* (BLASE); Ellyssa Kroski for *Law Librarianship in the Age of AI.*

Emerging Leader Award. To recognize newer members who have made significant contributions to AALL and/or to the profession and have demonstrated the potential for leadership and continuing service. *Winners:* Lindsey Ann Carpino, Benjamin J. Keele, Sara V. Pic.

Excellence in Community Engagement Award. For outstanding achievement in public relations activities. *Winners:* Pierce County (Washington) Law Library for the Legal Research Center at Lakewood; University of Missouri-Kansas City (UMKC) School of Law, Leon E. Bloch Law Library, and Legal Aid of Western Missouri, Kansas City, Missouri, for Self-Help Clinic.

Marian Gould Gallagher Distinguished Service Award. To recognize extended and sustained service to law librarianship. *Winners:* Dr. Yvonne J. Chandler, Jolande Goldberg, Melody Lembke, Michelle M. Wu.

Innovations in Technology Award. To recognize an AALL member, special interest section, chapter, or library for innovative use of technology in the development and creation of an application or resource for law librarians or legal professionals. *Winner:* ALLStAR Advisory Board for "ALLStAR Official Survey."

Law Library Advocate Award. To an AALL member who has been a strong advocate of private law librarianship through service to an AALL special interest section, their organization, or the larger legal community and demonstrates outstanding potential for continued service and leadership within the profession. *Winner:* Hon. Daryl L. Moore.

Law Library Journal Article of the Year. *Winner:* Frederick W. Dingledy for "From Stele to Silicon: Publication of Statutes, Public Access to the Law, and the Uniform Electronic Legal Material Act."

LexisNexis Call for Papers Awards. To promote the scholarship of AALL members and of students on any subject relevant to law librarianship. *Winners:* (new member) Nicholas Mignanelli for "Legal Research and Its Discontents: A Bibliographic Essay on Critical Approaches to Legal Research"; (short form) Danyahel (Danny) Norris for "All Roads Lead to the Library: An Academic Law Library Departmental Outreach Program"; (open) Janet Sinder for "Correcting the Record: Law Journals and Scholarly Integrity in the Digital Age"; (student) Rebecca Elaine Tavares Chapman for "Protecting Our Spaces of Memory: Rediscovering the Seneca Nation Settlement Act through Archives."

LexisNexis/John R. Johnson Memorial Scholarships. *Winners:* (college graduate seeking library degree) Marissa Rydzewski; (college graduate seeking dual law/library degree) Emma Kearney; (law school graduate seeking library degree) Michael Poveromo; (library school graduate seeking law degree) Cynthia Bassett; (library school graduate seeking non-law degree) Victoria Capatosto.

LexisNexis Research Fund Grants. *Winners:* John Cannan for "The New Orthodoxy: How Congress Passes Laws Now"; Katarina Daniels for "Law Librarians Leading the AI Charge in Law Faculties and Across University Library Systems."

Minority Leadership Development Award. *Winner:* Heather Hummons, head of access services / adjunct faculty at the DePaul University College of Law Rin Law Library in Chicago, Illinois.

Robert L. Oakley Advocacy Award. To recognize an AALL member who has been an outstanding advocate and has contributed significantly to the AALL policy agenda at the federal, state, local, or international level. *Winner:* Scott G. Burgh, chief law

librarian (retired), City of Chicago Law Department, Chicago, Illinois.

Bethany J. Ochal Award for Distinguished Service to the Profession. To honor members who have made significant contributions to law librarianship and are nearing the end of their library careers or have recently retired. *Winners:* Steve Anderson, Thurgood Marshall State Law Library, Annapolis, Maryland; Donna Bausch, Norfolk (Virginia) Public Law Library; Donna Williams, California Judicial Center Law Library, San Francisco, California.

Public Access to Government Information Award. Recognizes individuals or organizations that have made significant contributions to protect and promote greater access to government information. *Winners:* Jeremy J. McCabe, research services librarian, Georgetown University Law Library, Washington, DC; Leah Prescott, associate law librarian for digital initiatives and special collections, Georgetown University Law Library, Washington, DC.

Volunteer Service Award. Honors volunteers who have made significant contributions to the work of AALL. *Winner:* Nicole P. Dyszlewski.

American Library Association (ALA)

ALA Excellence in Library Programming Award ($5,000). For a cultural/thematic library program or program series that engages the community in planning, sponsorship, and/or active participation, addresses an identified community need, and has a measurable impact. *Donor:* ALA Cultural Communities Fund. *Winner:* Alexandria (Virginia) Library for "We Are the Alexandria Library Sit-In," a yearlong celebration of the 80th anniversary of a historic protest against the city library's whites-only policy that was one of the first sit-ins of its kind in the nation.

ALA Honorary Membership. To recognize outstanding contributions of lasting importance to libraries and librarianship. *Honoree:* Not awarded in 2020.

ALA/Information Today, Inc. Library of the Future Award ($1,500). For a library, consortium, group of librarians, or support organization for innovative planning for, applications of, or development of patron training programs about information technology in a library setting. *Donors:* Information Today, Inc., and IIDA. *Winner:* Broward County (Florida) Library for "Project Welcome" to welcome English-language learners to the area, inform them of BCL resources, and support them on their journey to English literacy, economic prosperity, and belonging.

ALA Medal of Excellence. For creative leadership and professional achievement in library management, training, cataloging and classification, and the tools and techniques of librarianship. *Donor:* OCLC. *Winner:* Not awarded in 2020.

Hugh C. Atkinson Memorial Award. For outstanding achievement (including risk taking) by academic librarians that has contributed significantly to improvements in library automation, management, and/or development or research. *Offered by:* ACRL, ALCTS, LITA, and LLAMA. *Winners:* Beth Denker, George Machovec, and Rose Nelson, Colorado Alliance of Research Libraries.

Carroll Preston Baber Research Grant (up to $3,000). For innovative research that could lead to an improvement in library services to any specified group(s) of people. *Donor:* Eric R. Baber. *Winner:* Not awarded in 2020.

Beta Phi Mu Award ($1,000). For distinguished service in library education. *Donor:* Beta Phi Mu International Library and Information Science Honorary Society. *Winner:* John M. Budd, professor emeritus of the School of Information Science and Learning Technologies, University of Missouri.

Bogle-Pratt International Library Travel Fund Award ($1,000). To ALA members to attend their first international conference. *Donors:* Bogle Memorial Fund and Pratt Institute School of Information and Library Science. *Winner:* Sarah Schroeder, business and economics reference and instruction librarian, University of Washington Bothell / Cascadia College Campus Library.

W. Y. Boyd Literary Award. See "Literary Prizes, 2020" in Part 5.

David H. Clift Scholarship ($3,000). To worthy U.S. or Canadian citizens enrolled in an ALA-accredited program toward an MLS degree. *Winner:* Evan Delano.

Tom and Roberta Drewes Scholarship ($3,000). To a library support staff member pursuing a master's degree in an ALA-accredited program. *Donor:* Quality Books. *Winner:* Nicole Lewis.

EBSCO/ALA Conference Sponsorship Award ($1,000). To enable librarians to attend the ALA Annual Conference. *Donor:* EBSCO. *Winners:* Not awarded in 2020.

Equality Award ($1,000). To an individual or group for an outstanding contribution that promotes equality in the library profession. *Donor:* Rowman & Littlefield. *Winner:* Em Claire Knowles.

Elizabeth Futas Catalyst for Change Award ($1,000). A biennial award to recognize a librarian who invests time and talent to make positive change in the profession of librarianship. *Donor:* Elizabeth Futas Memorial Fund. *Winner (2020):* Nora Wiltse.

Gale, a Cengage Company, Financial Development Award ($2,500). To a library organization for a financial development project to secure new funding resources for a public or academic library. *Donor:* Gale, a Cengage Company. *Winner:* Roxbury Public Library, Succasunna, New Jersey.

Mary V. Gaver Scholarship ($3,000). To a student pursuing an MLS degree and specializing in youth services. *Winner:* Ariana Brown.

Ken Haycock Award for Promoting Librarianship ($1,000). For significant contribution to public recognition and appreciation of librarianship through professional performance, teaching, or writing. *Winner:* Lesley Farmer, California State University, Long Beach.

Miriam L. Hornback Scholarship ($3,000). To an ALA or library support staff person pursuing a master's degree in library science. *Winner:* Sara Kennedy.

Paul Howard Award for Courage ($1,000). A biennial award to a librarian, library board, library group, or an individual for exhibiting unusual courage for the benefit of library programs or services. *Donor:* Paul Howard Memorial Fund. *Winner (2019):* Tyler Magill, Alderman Library, University of Virginia.

John Ames Humphry/OCLC/Forest Press Award ($1,000). To one or more individuals for significant contributions to international librarianship. *Donor:* OCLC/Forest Press. *Winner:* Peter Lor.

Tony B. Leisner Scholarship ($3,000). To a library support staff member pursuing a master's degree. *Donor:* Tony B. Leisner. *Winner:* Melissa Wilson.

Joseph W. Lippincott Award ($1,500). For distinguished service to the library profession. *Donor:* Joseph W. Lippincott III. *Winner:* Mary Ghikas.

Peter Lyman Memorial/Sage Scholarship in New Media. To support a student seeking an MLS degree in an ALA-accredited program and pursing a specialty in new media. *Donor:* Sage Publications. *Winner:* Courtney Dalton.

James Madison Award. To recognize efforts to promote government openness. *Winner:* Not awarded in 2020.

Schneider Family Book Awards. See "Literary Prizes, 2020" in Part 5.

Scholastic Library Publishing Award ($1,000). To a librarian whose "unusual contributions to the stimulation and guidance of reading by children and young people exemplifies achievement in the profession." *Sponsor:* Scholastic Library Publishing. *Winner:* Jennifer McQuown.

Lemony Snicket Prize for Noble Librarians Faced with Adversity ($3,000 plus a $1,000 travel stipend to enable attendance at the ALA Annual Conference). To honor a librarian who has faced adversity with integrity and dignity intact. *Sponsor:* Lemony Snicket (author Daniel Handler). *Winner:* Heather Ogilvie, Bay County Public Library, Panama City, Florida.

Spectrum Scholarships ($5,000). To minority students admitted to ALA-accredited library schools. *Donors:* ALA and Institute of Museum and Library Services. *Winners:* Spectrum Initiative Scholarships ($5,000). To minority students admitted to ALA-accredited library schools. *Donors:* ALA and Institute of Museum and Library Services. *Winners:* Megdelawit Abebe, Arianna Alcaraz, Viola Allo, Alex Aspiazu, Alexandra Barlowe, Lyndon Batiste, Danielle Luz Belanger, Keyana Branch, Mitsuko Brooks, Arun Bryson, Dymond Bush, Anon Cadieux, Kahlila Chaar-Pérez, Ulises Chavez Ramirez, Monique Christian-Long, María del Carmen Cifuentes, Charlotte Cotter, Laurier Cress, Tacia Díaz, Christianne Elefante, Irmarie Fraticelli-Rodriguez, Ally Fripp, Claudio Garcia, Ramón García, Joseph Gaskin, Alexandra Genia, Rita Ghazala, Alessandra Gonzalez, Criss Guy, Amanda He, Jacquelyn Howell, Hana Kadoyama, Kyra Lee, Luisa Leija, Andrea Lemoins, Christopher Lopez, Kaia MacLeod, Krystal Madkins, Raquel Martínez, Anthony Martínez, Kaypounyers Maye, Cani McMillian, Arianna McQuillen, Angelica Mejia, Ashley Mitchell, Abigail Morales, Tannaz Motevalli, Kendra Moyer, Chinyere E. Oteh, Alice Pérez Ververa, Charles Pratt IV, Cesar Reyes, Rayyon Robinson, Mayra Rosas, Luog Saepharn, Hope Saldivar, Mimosa Shah, Alexander Soto, Julia Stone, Anders Villalta, Chaoya Yang

Sullivan Award for Public Library Administrators Supporting Services to Children. To a library supervisor/administrator who has shown exceptional understanding and support of public library services to children. *Donor:* Peggy Sullivan. *Winner:* Alice Knapp, president, Ferguson Library, Stamford, Connecticut.

H. W. Wilson Library Staff Development Grant ($3,500). To a library organization for a program to further its staff development goals and objectives. *Donor:* H. W. Wilson Company. *Winner:* Cumberland County (Pennsylvania) Library System Foundation.

American Association of School Librarians (AASL)

AASL/ABC-CLIO Leadership Grant (up to $1,750). To AASL affiliates for planning and implementing leadership programs at state, regional, or local levels. *Donor:* ABC-CLIO. *Winner:* Maryland Association of School Librarians.

AASL Collaborative School Library Award ($2,500). For expanding the role of the library in elementary and/or secondary school education. *Donor:* Scholastic Book Fairs. *Winners:* Jillian Ehlers, Metropolitan Expeditionary Learning School, Forest Hills, New York.

AASL Distinguished School Administrator Award ($2,000). For expanding the role of the library in elementary and/or secondary school education. *Donor:* ProQuest. *Winner:* Kevin Smith, Wilton (Connecticut) Public Schools.

AASL/Frances Henne Award ($1,250). To a school library media specialist with five or fewer years in the profession to attend an AASL regional conference or ALA Annual Conference for the first time. *Donor:* Libraries Unlimited. *Winner:* Andrea Trudeau.

AASL Innovative Reading Grant ($2,500). To support the planning and implementation of an innovative program for children that motivates and encourages reading, especially for struggling readers. *Sponsor:* Capstone. *Winner:* Stefanie Throndson, North Hampton (Iowa) Elementary School.

AASL President's Crystal Apple Award. To an individual, individuals, or group for a significant impact on school libraries and students. *Winner:* Not awarded in 2020.

Distinguished Service Award ($3,000). For outstanding contributions to librarianship and school library development. *Donor:* Rosen Publishing Group. *Winner:* Mona Kerby.

Intellectual Freedom Award ($2,000 plus $1,000 to the media center of the recipient's choice). To a school library media specialist and AASL member who has upheld the principles of intellectual freedom. *Donor:* ProQuest. *Winners:* Martha Hickson, North Hunterdon High School, Annandale, New Jersey; Donna Morris, Daniel Boone Elementary School, Richmond, Kentucky.

National School Library of the Year Award ($10,000). Honors school libraries exemplifying implementation of AASL's National School Library Standards for Learners, School Librarians, and School Libraries. *Donor:* Follett Library Resources. *Winner:* Mesquite (Texas) Independent School District.

Association for Library Collections and Technical Services (ALCTS)

ALCTS Presidential Citations for Outstanding Service. *Winners:* Lindsay Cronk, Erica Findley, Chelcie Rowell.

Hugh C. Atkinson Memorial Award. *See under:* American Library Association.

Ross Atkinson Lifetime Achievement Award ($3,000). To recognize the contribution of an ALCTS member and library leader who has demonstrated exceptional service to ALCTS and its areas of interest. *Donor:* EBSCO. *Winner:* Magda El-Sherbini.

Paul Banks and Carolyn Harris Preservation Award ($1,500). To recognize the contribution of a professional preservation specialist who has been active in the field of preservation and/or conservation for library and/or archival materials. *Donor:* Preservation Technologies. *Winner:* Jennifer Hain Teper.

Blackwell's Scholarship Award. *See under:* Outstanding Publication Award.

George Cunha and Susan Swartzburg Preservation Award ($1,250). To recognize cooperative preservation projects and/or individuals or groups that foster collaboration for preservation goals. *Sponsor:* Hollinger Metal Edge. *Winner:* Not awarded in 2020.

First Step Award (Wiley Professional Development Grant) ($1,500). To enable librarians new to the serials field to attend the ALA Annual Conference. *Donor:* John Wiley & Sons. *Winner:* Paromita Biswas.

Harrassowitz Award for Leadership in Library Acquisitions ($1,500). For significant contributions by an outstanding leader in the field of library acquisitions. *Donor:* Harrassowitz. *Winner:* Not awarded in 2020.

Margaret Mann Citation (includes $2,000 scholarship award to the U.S. or Canadian library school of the winner's choice). To a cataloger or classifier for achievement in the areas of cataloging or classification. *Donor:* Online Computer Library Center (OCLC). *Winner:* Julie Moore.

Outstanding Collaboration Citation. For outstanding collaborative problem-solving efforts in the areas of acquisition, access, management, preservation, or archiving of library materials. *Winner:* From Private Treasures to Global Public Access: Enabling Global Access to a Private Gift Donation through Collaboration between the University of Toronto Libraries and the French Institute of Pondicherry Tamil Studies Programme.

Outstanding Publication Award ($250). To honor the year's outstanding monograph, article, or original paper in the field of acquisitions, collection development, and related areas of resource development in libraries. *Winner:* Rachel Ivy Clarke and

Sayward Schoonmaker for "Metadata for Diversity: Identification and Implications of Potential Access Points for Diverse Library Resources" in *Journal of Documentation* (September 2019).

Esther J. Piercy Award ($1,500). To a librarian with no more than ten years' experience for contributions and leadership in the field of library collections and technical services. *Donor:* YBP Library Services. *Winner:* Maggie Dull.

ProQuest Award for Innovation ($2,000). To recognize significant and innovative contributions to electronic collections management and development practice. *Donor:* ProQuest. *Winners:* Alex Valencia, Lynn Whittenberger, Meredith Wynn.

Edward Swanson Memorial Best of *LRTS* Award ($250). To the author(s) of the year's best paper published in the division's official journal. *Winners:* Maria Savova and Jason S. Price, Ph.D. for "Redesigning the Academic Library Materials Budget for the Digital Age: Applying the Power of Faceted Classification to Acquisitions Fund Management" (April 2019)

Ulrich's Serials Librarianship Award ($1,500). For distinguished contributions to serials librarianship. *Sponsor:* ProQuest. *Winner:* Not awarded in 2020.

Association for Library Service to Children (ALSC)

ALSC/Baker & Taylor Summer Reading Program Grant ($3,000). For implementation of an outstanding public library summer reading program for children. *Donor:* Baker & Taylor. *Winner:* Homewood (Alabama) Public Library.

ALSC/Booklist/YALSA Odyssey Award. To the producer of the best audiobook for children and/or young adults available in English in the United States. See Odyssey Award in "Literary Prizes, 2020" in Part 5.

ALSC/Candlewick Press "Light the Way" Grant ($3,000). To a library conducting exemplary outreach to underserved populations. *Donor:* Candlewick Press. *Winner:* Monterey Park (California) Bruggemeyer Library.

May Hill Arbuthnot Honor Lectureship. To an author, critic, librarian, historian, or teacher of children's literature who prepares a paper considered to be a significant contribution to the field of children's literature. *Winner:* Neil Gaiman (lecture postponed).

Mildred L. Batchelder Award. See "Literary Prizes, 2020" in Part 5.

Louise Seaman Bechtel Fellowship ($4,000). For librarians with 12 or more years of professional-level work in children's library collections, to read and study at Baldwin Library, University of Florida. *Donor:* Bechtel Fund. *Winner:* Not awarded in 2020.

Pura Belpré Award. See "Literary Prizes, 2020" in Part 5.

Bound to Stay Bound Books Scholarships ($7,000). For men and women who intend to pursue an MLS or other advanced degree and who plan to work in the area of library service to children. *Donor:* Bound to Stay Bound Books. *Winners:* Emily Thomas Chambliss, Donald Giacomini, Lola Edwards Gomez, Jennifer Nicole Johnson.

Randolph Caldecott Medal. See "Literary Prizes, 2020" in Part 5.

Carnegie-Whitney Awards (up to $5,000). For the preparation of print or electronic reading lists, indexes, or other guides to library resources that promote reading or the use of library resources at any type of library. *Donors:* James Lyman Whitney and Andrew Carnegie Funds. *Winners:* Elvis Bakaitis for "Lesbian Aging Studies: A Theoretical and Cross-Cultural Approach"; Tatiana Bryant for "AfroLatinx Studies Annotated Bibliography"; Chapel Cowden for "Perspectives on Death & Dying"; Lisa Jackson for "The Ashley Bryan Project: A Resource of Children's Books and Book Art by Persons of African Descent"; Carolyn Klotzbach-Russell and Kim Plassche for "The Essential Great Lakes"; Natalia Kovalyova for "American Indian Rhetorical Traditions"; Michelle Kowalsky for "Neurodiversity Resources for Librarians and Educators"; Grace Lui for "Informed Success: A Resource Guide for Student Entrepreneurs"; April Sheppard for "Arkansas and Mississippi Delta Heritage"; Junior Tidal and Joan Jocson-Singh for "A Bibliography Exploring Extreme Music and Marginalized Communities"; Brian Watson for "50 Years On, Many Years Past: Nonfictions of Sexuality."

Century Scholarship ($2,500). For a library school student or students with disabilities admitted to an ALA-accredited library school. *Winner:* Abbie McLean.

Children's Literature Legacy Award. See "Literary Prizes, 2020," in Part 5.

Distinguished Service Award ($1,000). To recognize significant contributions to, and an impact on, library services to children and/or ALSC. *Winner:* Claudette McLinn.

Theodor Seuss Geisel Award. See "Literary Prizes, 2020" in Part 5.

Maureen Hayes Author / Illustrator Visit Award (up to $4,000). For an honorarium and travel expenses to make possible a library talk to children by a nationally known author/illustrator. *Sponsor:* Simon & Schuster Children's Publishing. *Winner:* Algonquin Area (Illinois) Public Library.

Frederic G. Melcher Scholarships ($6,000). To two students entering the field of library service to children for graduate work in an ALA-accredited program. *Winner:* Karen You-Chuan Wang.

John Newbery Medal. See "Literary Prizes, 2020" in Part 5.

Penguin Random House Young Readers Group Awards ($600). To children's librarians in school or public libraries with ten or fewer years of experience to attend the ALA Annual Conference. *Donor:* Penguin Young Readers Group and Random House Children's Books. *Winners:* Amalia Butler, Maplewood (New Jersey) Memorial Library; Carla Davis, Multnomah County (Oregon) Library; Jennifer Minehardt, New York Public Library.

Robert F. Sibert Medal. See "Literary Prizes, 2020" in Part 5.

Association of College and Research Libraries (ACRL)

ACRL Academic or Research Librarian of the Year Award ($5,000). For outstanding contribution to academic and research librarianship and library development. *Donor:* YBP Library Services. *Winner:* John E. Ulmschneider, Virginia Commonwealth University.

ACRL/CLS Innovation in College Librarianship Award ($3,000). To academic librarians who show a capacity for innovation in the areas of programs, services, and operations; or creating innovations for library colleagues that facilitate their ability to better serve the library's community. *Winners:* Brett Spencer, Sarah Hartman-Caverly, Alexandra Chisholm, Penn State University, Berks Campus.

ACRL/DLS Routledge Distance Learning Librarian Conference Sponsorship Award ($1,200). To an ACRL member working in distance-learning librarianship in higher education. *Sponsor:* Routledge/Taylor & Francis. *Winner:* Samantha (Sam) Harlow, University of North Carolina, Greensboro.

ACRL/EBSS Distinguished Education and Behavioral Sciences Librarian Award. To an academic librarian who has made an outstanding contribution as an education and/or behavioral sciences librarian through accomplishments and service to the profession. *Donor:* John Wiley & Sons. *Winner:* Cassandra Kvenild, University of Wyoming.

ACRL/STS Oberly Award for Bibliography in the Agricultural or Natural Sciences. Awarded biennially for the best English-language bibliography in the field of agriculture or a related science in the preceding two-year period. *Donor:* Eunice Rockwood Oberly. *Winners (2019):* Douglas Karlen and Lorraine Pellack for "Iowa Crop Variety Yield Testing: A History and Annotated Bibliography."

ACRL/WGSS Award for Career Achievement in Women and Gender Studies Librarianship ($750). To a distinguished academic librarian who has made outstanding contributions to women and gender studies through accomplishments and service to the profession. *Donor:* Duke University Press. *Winner:* Emily Drabinski, City University of New York.

ACRL/WGSS Award for Significant Achievement in Women and Gender Studies Librarianship ($750). To a distinguished academic librarian who has made outstanding contributions to women and gender studies through accomplishments and service to the profession. *Donor:* Duke University Press. *Winner:* Shawn(ta) Smith-Cruz, New York University.

Hugh C. Atkinson Memorial Award. *See under:* American Library Association.

CJCLS/EBSCO Community College Learning Resources Program Award ($750). Recognizes significant achievement in community college programs. *Donor:* EBSCO. *Winner:* Colorado Community College System.

Miriam Dudley Instruction Librarian Award ($1,000). For a contribution to the advancement of bibliographic instruction in a college or research institution. *Winner:* Veronica Arellano Douglas, University of Houston.

ESS De Gruyter European Librarianship Study Grant (€2,500). Supports research pertaining to European studies, librarianship, or the book trade. *Sponsor:* Walter de Gruyter Foundation for Scholarship and Research. *Winner:* Emma Popowich, University of Manitoba.

Excellence in Academic Libraries Awards ($3,000). To recognize outstanding college and university libraries. *Donor:* YBP Library Services. *Winners:* (university) University of Maryland; (college) Nevada State College; (community college) Santa Rosa (California) Junior College.

Instruction Section Innovation Award ($3,000). To librarians or project teams in recognition of a project that demonstrates creative, innovative, or unique approaches to information literacy instruction or programming. *Donor:* ProQuest. *Winners:* Sarah LeMire, Terri Pantuso, Kathy Anders, Texas A&M University, for OER Textbook for Composition and Information Literacy.

Marta Lange / Sage-CQ Press Award. To recognize an academic or law librarian for contributions to bibliography and information service in law or political science. *Donor:* Sage-CQ Press. *Winner:* Jeremy Darrington, Princeton University.

Katharine Kyes Leab and Daniel J. Leab American Book Prices Current Exhibition Catalog Awards (citations). For the best catalogs published by American or Canadian institutions in conjunction with exhibitions of books and/or manuscripts. *Sponsor:* Leab Endowment. *Winners:* (expensive) Huntington Library, Art Museum, and Botanical Gardens, San Marino, California; (moderately expensive) The University of Pennsylvania Libraries Kislak Center for Special Collections, Rare Books and Manuscripts; (inexpensive) Oakland University Art Gallery; McLaughlin Library of the University of Guelph School of Fine Art and Music and the Archives and Special Collections; (brochures) The University of Alberta Bruce Peel Special Collections; (electronic exhibitions) Northwestern University Transportation Library.

Ilene F. Rockman Instruction Publication of the Year Award ($3,000). To recognize an outstanding publication relating to instruction in a library environment. *Sponsor:* Emerald Group. *Winner:* Amanda L. Folk, for "Reframing Information Literacy as Academic Cultural Capital: A Critical and Equity-Based Foundation for Practice, Assessment, and Scholarship."

Association of Specialized Government and Cooperative Library Agencies (ASGCLA)

ASGCLA Cathleen Bourdon Service Award. To recognize an ASGCLA personal member for outstanding service and leadership to the division. *Winner:* Not awarded in 2020.

ASGCLA Exceptional Service Award. To recognize exceptional service to patients, the homebound, and inmates, and to medical, nursing, and other professional staff in hospitals. *Winner:* Nili Ness, Queens (New York) Public Library.

ASGCLA Leadership and Professional Achievement Award. To recognize leadership and achievement in the areas of consulting, multitype library cooperation, statewide service and programs, and state library development. *Winner:* Wendy Cornelisen, Georgia Public Library System.

Francis Joseph Campbell Award. For a contribution of recognized importance to library service for the blind and physically handicapped. *Winner:* Not awarded in 2020.

Federal Achievement Award. For achievement in the promotion of library and information service and the information profession in the Federal community. *Winner:* Nancy Faget, Army Research Laboratory.

Federal Rising Stars Initiative. To an ASGCLA member new to the profession in a federal or armed forces library or government information management setting. *Winner:* Not awarded in 2020.

KLAS / National Organization on Disability Award for Library Service to People with Disabilities ($1,000). To a library organization to recognize an innovative project to benefit people with disabilities.

Donor: Keystone Systems. *Winner:* Moline (Illinois) Public Library for ARTability.

Black Caucus of the American Library Association (BCALA)

Baker & Taylor Support Staff Award. For dedicated and outstanding performance by a library support staff member. *Winners:* Not awarded in 2020.

BCALA Book Literary Award. *Winners:* (first novelist) Ta-Nehisi Coates for *The Water Dancer* (Random House); (poetry) Eve L. Ewing for *1919* (Haymarket Books); (fiction) Colson Whitehead for *The Nickel Boys* (Knopf Doubleday); (nonfiction) Daniel R. Day for *Dapper Dan: Made in Harlem: A Memoir* (Random House).

BCALA Trailblazers Award. Presented once every five years in recognition of outstanding and unique contributions to librarianship. *Winners (2015):* Thomas Alford, Mary Biblo.

DEMCO/BCALA Excellence in Librarianship Award. To a librarian who has made significant contributions to promoting the status of African Americans in the library profession. *Winner:* Dr. Shaundra Walker.

E. J. Josey Scholarship Award. *Winners:* Not awarded in 2020.

Ethnic and Multicultural Information and Exchange Round Table (EMIERT)

David Cohen Multicultural Award ($300). To recognize articles of significant research and publication that increase understanding and promote multiculturalism in North American libraries. *Donor:* Routledge. *Winners:* Denice Adkins, Jenny Bossaller, Heather Moulaison Sandy, School of Information Science & Learning Technologies, University of Missouri.

EMIERT Distinguished Librarian Award. Given biennially to recognize significant accomplishments in library services that are national or international in scope and that include improving, spreading, and promoting multicultural librarianship. *Winner:* Not awarded in 2020.

Coretta Scott King Awards. See "Literary Prizes, 2020" in Part 5.

Exhibits Round Table (ERT)

Christopher J. Hoy/ERT Scholarship ($5,000). To an individual or individuals who will work toward an MLS degree in an ALA-accredited program. *Donor:* Family of Christopher Hoy. *Winner:* Amanda Toledo.

Freedom to Read Foundation

Freedom to Read Foundation Gordon M. Conable Conference Scholarship. To enable a library school student or new professional to attend the ALA Annual Conference. *Winner:* Not awarded in 2020.

Freedom to Read Foundation Roll of Honor (citation): To recognize individuals who have contributed substantially to the foundation. *Winner:* Kelley L. Allen.

Judith Krug Fund Banned Books Week Event Grants ($1,000 to $2,500). To support activities that raise awareness of intellectual freedom and censorship issues during the annual Banned Books Week celebration. *Winners:* Cambria County (Pennsylvania) Library; Center for Transformative Action (CTA) / Ithaca (New York) City of Asylum; Central Washington University Libraries, Ellensburg, Washington; Kurt Vonnegut Museum and Library, Indianapolis, Indiana; Manor (Texas) High School Library; Maricopa (Arizona) Public Library.

Gay, Lesbian, Bisexual, and Transgender Round Table (GLBTRT)

Larry Romans Mentorship Award ($1,000). To recognize librarians who, through their sustained mentoring efforts, have made a difference in our profession. *Winner:* Not awarded in 2020.

Stonewall Book Awards. See "Literary Prizes, 2020" in Part 5.

Government Documents Round Table (GODORT)

James Bennett Childs Award. To a librarian or other individual for distinguished lifetime contributions to documents librarianship. *Winner:* Not awarded in 2020.

GODORT-Sponsored ALA Emerging Leader Award. A leadership development program that enables newer library workers from across the country to participate in problem-solving work groups, network with peers, gain an inside look into ALA structure, and have an opportunity to serve the profession in a leadership capacity. *Winner:* Not awarded in 2020.

Bernadine Abbott Hoduski Founders Award. To recognize documents librarians who may not be known at the national level but who have made significant contributions to the field of local, state, federal, or international documents. *Winner:* Not awarded in 2020.

Margaret T. Lane/Virginia F. Saunders Memorial Research Award. *Winners:* Dr. Martin Halbert, Roberta Sittel, Dr. Katherine Skinner, Deborah Caldwell, Marie Concannon, James R. Jacobs, Shari Laster, and Scott Matheson for *Toward a Shared Agenda: Report on PEGI Project Activities for 2017–2019* (Educopia Institute).

NewsBank/Readex/GODORT/ALA Catharine J. Reynolds Research Grant. To documents librarians for travel and/or study in the field of documents librarianship or an area of study benefiting their performance. *Donor:* NewsBank and Readex Corporation. *Winner:* Not awarded in 2020.

ProQuest/GODORT/ALA Documents to the People Award. To an individual, library, organization, or noncommercial group that most effectively encourages or enhances the use of government documents in library services. *Winner:* Jacquelyn Daniel.

Larry Romans Mentorship Award ($1,000). To recognize librarians who, through their sustained mentoring efforts, have made a difference in our profession. *Winner:* Not awarded in 2020.

W. David Rozkuszka Scholarship ($3,000). To provide financial assistance to individuals currently working with government documents in a library while completing a master's program in library science. *Winner:* Samantha Reardon.

Intellectual Freedom Round Table (IFRT)

Gerald Hodges Intellectual Freedom Chapter Relations Award. *Winner:* Connecticut Library Association Intellectual Freedom Committee.

John Phillip Immroth Memorial Award for Intellectual Freedom ($500). For notable contribution to intellectual freedom fueled by personal courage. *Winner:* Rebecca Ginsburg.

Eli M. Oboler Memorial Award. See "Literary Prizes, 2020" in Part 5.

Library and Information Technology Association (LITA)

Hugh C. Atkinson Memorial Award. *See under:* American Library Association.

Ex Libris Student Writing Award ($1,000 and publication in *Information Technology and Libraries*). For the best unpublished manuscript on a topic in the area of libraries and information technology written by a student or students enrolled in an ALA-accredited library and information studies graduate program. *Donor:* Ex Libris. *Winner:* Samantha Grabus for "Evaluating the Impact of the Long S upon 18th-Century *Encyclopedia Britannica* Automatic Subject Metadata Generation Results."

LITA/Christian Larew Memorial Scholarship in Library and Information Technology ($3,000). To encourage the entry of qualified persons into the library and information technology field. *Sponsor:* Informata.com. *Winner:* Michael Carroll.

LITA/Library Hi Tech Award for Outstanding Communication for Continuing Education in Library and Information Science. To an individual or institution for outstanding communication in library and information technology. *Donor:* Emerald Group. *Winner:* Alison Macrina.

LITA/OCLC Frederick G. Kilgour Award for Research in Library and Information Technology ($2,000 and expense-paid attendance at the ALA Annual Conference). To bring attention to research relevant to the development of information technologies. *Donor:* OCLC. *Winner:* Jian Qin, iSchool, Syracuse University.

Library History Round Table (LHRT)

Phyllis Dain Library History Dissertation Award. Given irregularly in odd-numbered years to the author of a dissertation treating the history of books, libraries, librarianship, or information science. *Winner (2019):* Travis Ross for "History, Inc—Herbery Bancroft's History Co. and the Problem of Selling Past." (Next award in 2023.)

Donald G. Davis Article Award (certificate). Awarded biennially for the best article written in English in the field of U.S. and Canadian library history. *Winner (2020):* Laura E. Helton for "On Decimals, Catalogs, and Racial Imaginaries of Reading" (PMLA).

Eliza Atkins Gleason Book Award. Presented every third year to the author of a book in English in the field of library history. *Winner* (2019): Wayne Wiegand and Shirley Wiegand for *The Desegregation of Public Libraries in the Jim Crow South: Civil Rights and Local Activism* (Louisiana State University Press).

Justin Winsor Library History Essay Award ($500). To the author of an outstanding essay embodying original historical research on a significant subject of library history. *Winner:* Julie Park for "Infrastructure Story: The Los Angeles Central Library's Architectural History."

Library Leadership and Management Association (LLAMA)

Hugh C. Atkinson Memorial Award. *See under:* American Library Association.

John Cotton Dana Library Public Relations Awards ($10,000). To libraries or library organizations of all types for public relations programs or special projects ended during the preceding year. *Donors:* H. W. Wilson Foundation and EBSCO. *Winners:* Niles-Maine District Library, Niles, Illinois, for "Best. Deal. Ever!,"a 16-month campaign to increase library card ownership in a culturally and economically diverse service area; Bridges Library System, Waukesha, Wisconsin, for "Library Card Sign-up Month" to reach non-library users; Enoch Pratt Free Library, Baltimore, Maryland, for a public awareness campaign that kept customers informed throughout the main library's $115 million renovation process, leading up to a multi-faceted grand opening celebration; Alexandria (Virginia) Library for "We Are the Alexandria Library Sit-In," a yearlong celebration of the 80th anniversary of a historic protest against the city library's

whites-only policy that was one of the first sit-ins of its kind in the nation; Cleveland (Ohio) Public Library for the library's 150th anniversary; Milton (Ontario, Canada) Public Library for its "Be Inspired" branding to support efforts to better meet the evolving needs of its patrons; Anaheim (California) Public Library for the "OC ZineFest"; Deerfield (Illinois) Public Library for "The Fight to Integrate Deerfield: 60 Year Reflection," a months-long initiative about a significant period in the town's local history and its lasting impact.

Library Research Round Table (LRRT)

Jesse H. Shera Award for Excellence in Published Research. For a research article on library and information studies published in English during the calendar year. *Winners:* Rachel Ivy Clarke and Sayward Schoonmaker for "Metadata for Diversity: Identification and Implications of Political Access Points for Diverse Library Resources" (*Journal of Documentation*).

Jesse H. Shera Award for Support of Dissertation Research. To recognize and support dissertation research employing exemplary research design and methods. *Winner:* Bonnie Tulloch for "Do the Ends Justify the Memes? Exploring the Relationship between Youth, Internet Memes, and Digital Citizenship."

Map and Geospatial Information Round Table (MAGIRT)

MAGIRT Honors Award. To recognize outstanding achievement and major contributions to map and geospatial librarianship. *Winner:* Tsering Wangyal Shawa.

New Members Round Table (NMRT)

NMRT ALA Student Chapter of the Year Award. To an ALA student chapter for outstanding contributions to the association. *Winner:* University of Illinois at Urbana Champaign.

NMRT Annual Conference Professional Development Attendance Award (formerly the Marshall Cavendish Award) (tickets to the

ALA Annual Conference event of the winners' choice). *Winners:* Not awarded in 2020.

NMRT Professional Development Grant. To new NMRT members to encourage professional development and participation in national ALA and NMRT activities. *Winner:* Not awarded in 2020.

Shirley Olofson Memorial Award ($1,000). To an individual to help defray costs of attending the ALA Annual Conference. *Winner:* Sarah Brewer, Minnesota Genealogical Society Library, Mendota Heights, Minnesota.

Office for Diversity

Achievement in Library Diversity Research Honor. To an ALA member who has made significant contributions to diversity research in the profession. *Winner:* Not awarded in 2020.

Diversity Research Grants ($2,500). To the authors of research proposals that address critical gaps in the knowledge of diversity issues within library and information science. *Winners:* Rachel Woodbrook, University of Michigan, for "EDI Open Data for the Public Good and for Social Change", Raymond Pun, Alder Graduate School of Education, for "Exploring Library Advocacy Work by Library Workers of Color: A Qualitative Study Using Critical Race Theory"; Brittani Sterling, Brittany Paloma Fiedler, and James Cheng, University of Nevada–Las Vegas University Libraries, for "We're Still Here at Mid-Career: The Retention of Academic Librarians of Color and Our Lived Experiences."

Office for Information Technology Policy

L. Ray Patterson Copyright Award. To recognize an individual who supports the constitutional purpose of U.S. copyright law, fair use, and the public domain. *Sponsor:* Freedom to Read Foundation. *Winner:* Not awarded in 2020.

Office for Literacy and Outreach Services (OLOS)

Jean E. Coleman Library Outreach Lecture. *Sponsor:* OLOS Advisory Committee. *Lecturer:* Not awarded in 2020.

Public Library Association (PLA)

Baker & Taylor Entertainment Audio Music/Video Product Grant ($2,500 worth of audio music or video products). To help a public library to build or expand a collection of either or both formats. *Donor:* Baker & Taylor. *Winner:* McCracken County Public Library. Paducah, Kentucky.

Gordon M. Conable Award ($1,500). To a public library staff member, library trustee, or public library for demonstrating a commitment to intellectual freedom and the Library Bill of Rights. *Sponsor:* LSSI. *Winner:* Jonathan Newton.

Demco New Leaders Travel Grants (up to $1,500). To PLA members who have not attended a major PLA continuing education event in the past five years. *Winners:* Not awarded in 2020.

EBSCO Excellence in Rural Library Service Award ($1,000). Honors a library serving a population of 10,000 or fewer that demonstrates excellence of service to its community as exemplified by an overall service program or a special program of significant accomplishment. *Donor:* EBSCO. *Winner:* Astor County (Florida) Library.

Helping Communities Come Together Award recognizes a public library's ability to identify community needs specifically in times of crisis and division, and respond in creative and exemplary ways. *Donor:* The Singer Group. *Winner:* Flint (Michigan) Public Library.

John Iliff Award ($1,000). To a library worker, librarian, or library for the use of technology and innovative thinking as a tool to improve services to public library users. *Sponsor:* Innovative. *Winner:* Oscar Grady Public Library, Saukville, Wisconsin.

Allie Beth Martin Award ($3,000). To honor a public librarian who has demonstrated extraordinary range and depth of knowledge about books or other library materials and has distinguished ability to share that knowledge. *Donor:* Baker & Taylor. *Winner:* Beth Atwater, Johnson County (Kansas) Library.

PLA Innovation Award ($2,000). To recognize a public library's innovative achievement in planning and implementing a creative community service program. *Winner:* Mill Valley (California) Public Library.

Charlie Robinson Award ($1,000). To honor a public library director who, over a period of seven years, has been a risk taker, an innovator, and/or a change agent in a public library. *Donor:* Baker & Taylor. *Winner:* Rivkah Sass, Sacramento (California) Public Library.

Romance Writers of America Library Grant ($4,500). To a library to build or expand a fiction collection and/or host romance fiction programming. *Donor:* Romance Writers of America. *Winner:* Ferguson (Missouri) Municipal Public Library.

Public Programs Office

Sara Jaffarian School Library Program Award for Exemplary Humanities Programming ($4,000). To honor a K–8 school library that has conducted an outstanding humanities program or series. *Donors:* Sara Jaffarian and ALA Cultural Communities Fund. *Winner:* Batesville (Indiana) Intermediate School.

Reference and User Services Association (RUSA)

Award for Excellence in Reference and Adult Library Services ($1,500). To recognize a library or library system for developing an imaginative and unique library resource to meet patrons' reference needs. *Donor:* Reference USA. *Winner:* Jen Lemberger, City of Santa Barbara (California) Library.

BRASS Academic Business Librarianship Travel Award ($1,250). To recognize a librarian new to the field of academic business librarianship and support his or her attendance at the ALA Annual Conference. *Donor:* Business Expert Press. *Winner:* Catherine Fournier Boulianne, University of Toronto Mississauga.

BRASS Excellence in Business Librarianship Award ($4,000). For distinguished activities in the field of business librarianship *Donor:* Mergent. *Winner:* Steven Mark Cramer, University of North Carolina Greensboro.

BRASS Public Librarian Support Award ($1,250). To support attendance at the ALA Annual Conference of a public librarian who has performed outstanding business

reference service. *Donor:* Morningstar. *Winner:* Ashley Johnson.

BRASS Research Grant Award ($2,500). To an ALA member seeking support to conduct research in business librarianship. *Donor:* Emerald Publishing. *Winner:* Ash E. Faulkner, Ohio State University Libraries, for "Global Financial Literacy Study."

BRASS Student Travel Award ($1,250). To enable a student enrolled in an ALA-accredited master's program to attend the ALA Annual Conference. *Donor:* Simply Analytics. *Winner:* Daphnie Neal, Akron-Summit (Ohio) County Public Library.

Sophie Brody Medal. See "Literary Prizes, 2020" in Part 5.

CODES Zora Neale Hurston Award. To recognize the efforts of RUSA members in promoting African American literature. *Donor:* Harper Collins. *Winner:* Not awarded in 2020.

CODES Louis Shores Award (citation). To an individual, team, or organization in recognition of excellence in reviewing of books and other materials for libraries. *Winner:* NPR Books.

ETS Achievement Award. To recognize excellence in service to RUSA's Emerging Technologies Section (ETS). *Winner:* Carmen Cole, Sally W. Kalin Librarian for Learning Innovations, Penn State University.

HS Genealogy/History Achievement Award ($1,500). To encourage and commend professional achievement in historical reference and research librarianship. *Donor:* ProQuest. *Winner:* Jennifer Brannock, University of Southern Mississippi.

HS History Research and Innovation Award ($2,500). To an MLS-degreed librarian from an ALA-accredited school to facilitate and further research relating to history and history librarianship. *Donor:* Gale Cengage. *Winner:* Not awarded in 2020.

Margaret E. Monroe Library Adult Services Award ($1,250). To a librarian for his or her impact on library service to adults. *Donor:* NoveList. *Winner:* Lucy M. Lockley, St. Charles City-County (Missouri) Library.

Isadore Gilbert Mudge Award ($5,000). For distinguished contributions to reference librarianship. *Donor:* Credo Reference. *Winners:* Chris Le Beau, University of Missouri-Kansas City.

RSS Service Achievement Award. To an RSS member who has made either a sustained contribution toward attaining the goals of the Reference Services Section or a single significant contribution that has resulted in a positive impact upon the work of the section. *Winner:* Not awarded in 2020.

John Sessions Memorial Award (plaque). To a library or library system in recognition of work with the labor community. *Donor:* Department for Professional Employees, AFL/CIO. *Winner:* Labor Collections of the Archives and Special Collections of the University of Alaska Anchorage/Alaska Pacific University Consortium Library, Anchorage, Alaska.

STARS Mentoring Award ($1,250). To a library practitioner new to the field of interlibrary loan, resource sharing, or electronic reserves, to attend the ALA Annual Conference. *Donor:* Atlas Systems. *Winner:* Not awarded in 2020.

STARS Virginia Boucher Distinguished ILL Librarian Award ($2,000). To a librarian for outstanding professional achievement, leadership, and contributions to interlibrary loan and document delivery. *Winner:* Brian Miller, Big Ten Academic Alliance, Champaign, Illinois.

United for Libraries

Trustee Citation. To recognize public library trustees for individual service to library development on the local, state, regional, or national level. *Winner:* Not awarded in 2020.

United for Libraries/Baker & Taylor Awards. To recognize library friends groups for outstanding efforts to support their libraries. *Donor:* Baker & Taylor. *Winner:* Not awarded in 2020.

United for Libraries Major Benefactors Citation. To individuals, families, or corporate bodies that have made major benefactions to public libraries. *Winner:* Not awarded in 2020.

United for Libraries Public Service Award. To a legislator who has been especially supportive of libraries. *Winner:* Not awarded in 2020.

United for Libraries/Thrift Books Friends Grant ($850 plus free conference registration).

Enables one member of a Friends of the Library group at a public library to attend the ALA Annual Conference. *Donor:* Thrift Books. *Winner:* Not awarded in 2020.

Young Adult Library Services Association (YALSA)

Baker & Taylor/YALSA Collection Development Grants ($1,000). To YALSA members who represent a public library and work directly with young adults, for collection development materials for young adults. *Donor:* Book Wholesalers, Inc. *Winners:* Kristine Kreidler, Lantana (Florida) Public Library.

Baker & Taylor/YALSA Conference Scholarship Grants ($1,000). To young adult librarians in public or school libraries to attend the ALA Annual Conference for the first time. *Donor:* Baker & Taylor. *Winner:* Phyllis Magady, Muskogee (Oklahoma) Public Library.

Dorothy Broderick Student Scholarship ($1,000). To enable a graduate student to attend the ALA Conference for the first time. *Sponsor:* YALSA Leadership Endowment. *Winner:* Not awarded in 2020.

Margaret A. Edwards Award. See "Literary Prizes, 2020" in Part 5.

Great Books Giveaway (approximately 3,000 books, videos, CDs, and audiocassettes). *Winner:* Maricopa (Arizona) Public Library.

Frances Henne/YALSA Research Grant ($1,000). To provide seed money to an individual, institution, or group for a project to encourage research on library service to young adults. *Donor:* Greenwood Publishing Group. *Winner:* Not awarded in 2020.

William C. Morris YA Debut Award. See "Literary Prizes, 2020" in Part 5.

Michael L. Printz Award. See "Literary Prizes, 2020" in Part 5.

YALSA/MAE Award for Best Literature Program for Teens ($500 for the recipient plus $500 for his or her library). For an exemplary young adult reading or literature program. *Sponsor:* Margaret A. Edwards Trust. *Winner:* Dawn Abron, Zion-Benton (Illinois) Public Library.

YALSA Service to Young Adults Outstanding Achievement Award ($2,000). Biennial award to a YALSA member who has demonstrated unique and sustained devotion to young adult services. *Winner (2020):* Mega Subramaniam, College of Information Studies (iSchool), University of Maryland.

Art Libraries Society of North America (ARLIS/NA)

ARLIS/NA Distinguished Service Award. To honor an individual whose exemplary service in art librarianship, visual resources curatorship, or a related field, has made an outstanding national or international contribution to art information. *Winner:* Milan Hughston.

ARLIS/NA Wolfgang M. Freitag Internship Award ($3,000). To provide financial support for students preparing for a career in art librarianship or visual resource librarianship. *Winner:* Not awarded in 2020.

Melva J. Dwyer Award. To the creators of exceptional reference or research tools relating to Canadian art and architecture. *Winner:* Kirsty Robertson for *Tear Gas Epiphanies: Protest, Culture, Museums* (McGill-Queens Press).

Gerd Muehsam Award. To one or more graduate students in library science programs to recognize excellence in a graduate paper or project. *Winner:* Not awarded in 2020.

H.W. Wilson Foundation Research Award ($3,000). For research activities by ARLIS/NA individual members in the fields of librarianship, visual resources curatorship, and the arts. *Winner:* Robert Craig Bunch for *Dreams, Visions, Other Worlds: Interviews with Texas Artists* (Texas A&M University Press).

George Wittenborn Memorial Book Awards. See "Literary Prizes, 2020" in Part 5.

Asian/Pacific Americans Libraries Association (APALA)

APALA Scholarship ($1,000). For a student of Asian or Pacific background who is enrolled in, or has been accepted into, a master's or doctoral degree program in library and/or information science at an ALA-accredited school. *Winner:* Patricia Ledesma Villon.

APALA Travel Grant ($500). To a U.S. or Canadian citizen or permanent resident enrolled in a master's or doctoral degree program in library and/or information science at an ALA-accredited school, or a professional possessing a master's degree or doctoral degree in library and/or information science, to enable attendance at the ALA Annual Conference. *Winner:* Jeneanne Ka-makana-lani Len Tai Lock.

Emerging Leaders Sponsorship. To enable newer library workers to participate in problem-solving work groups, network with peers, gain an inside look into ALA structure, and have an opportunity to serve the profession. *Winner:* Jamie Kurumaji.

Association for Information Science and Technology (ASIS&T)

ASIS&T Award of Merit. For an outstanding contribution to the field of information science. *Winner:* Diane H. Sonnenwald.

ASIS&T Best Information Science Book. *Winner:* Morgan Ames for *The Charisma Machine: The Life, Death, and Legacy of One Laptop per Child* (MIT Press).

ASIS&T ProQuest Doctoral Dissertation Award ($1,000 plus expense-paid attendance at ASIS&T Annual Meeting). *Winner:* Hussein Haruna for "Improving Sexual Health Education for Adolescent Students Using Game-Based Learning and Gamification."

ASIS&T Research in Information Science Award. For a systematic program of research in a single area at a level beyond the single study, recognizing contributions in the field of information science. *Winner:* Pertti Vakkari.

Clarivate Doctoral Dissertation Proposal Scholarship ($2,000). *Winner:* Saguna Shankar for "Caring for Information Practices: An Inquiry into Visions of Data, Digital Technologies, and Migration."

Clarivate Outstanding Information Science Teacher Award ($1,500). To recognize the unique teaching contribution of an individual as a teacher of information science. *Winner:* Jeonghyun "Annie" Kim, University of North Texas.

James M. Cretsos Leadership Award. To recognize new ASIS&T members who have demonstrated outstanding leadership qualities in professional ASIS&T activities. *Winner:* Aylin Ilhan.

Watson Davis Award for Service. For outstanding continuous contributions and dedicated service to the society. *Winner:* Nadia Caidi.

Pratt Severn Best Student Research Paper Award. To encourage student research and writing in the field of information science. *Winner:* Not awarded in 2020.

John Wiley Best *JASIST* Paper Award. *Winners:* Jianxiong Huang, Wai Fong Boh, Kim Huat Goh for "Opinion Convergence versus Polarization: Examining Opinion Distributions in Online Word-of-Mouth."

Bob Williams History Fund Research Grant Award. *Winner:* Not awarded in 2020.

Bob Williams History Fund Best Research Paper Award. *Winner:* Not awarded in 2020.

Association for Library and Information Science Education (ALISE)

ALISE Award for Professional Contribution. *Winner:* Suliman Hawamdeh, University of North Texas.

ALISE Best Conference Paper Award. Winners: Kyle Jones, and Lisa Janicke Hinchliffe for "New Methods, New Needs: Preparing Academic Library Practitioners to Address Ethical Issues Associated with Learning Analytics"; Marcia A. Mardis, Faye R. Jones, Scott M. Pickett, Denise Gomez, Curtis S. Tenney, Zoe Leonarczyk, and Samantha Nagy for "Librarians as Natural Disaster Stress Response Facilitators: Building Evidence for Trauma-informed Library Education and Practice."

ALISE Diversity Travel Award ($750 for travel expenses, complimentary registration to the ALISE annual conference, and one-year student membership). To increase diversity in LIS education/research for an individual who wishes to address issues of diversity through doctoral study or teaching. *Winner:* Tae Hee Lee, University of Wisconsin-Milwaukee.

ALISE/Eugene Garfield Doctoral Dissertation Competition. *Winner:* Eva Revitt, University of Alberta, for "The Academic Librarian as the Subaltern: An Institutional Ethnography of a Feminized Profession."

ALISE/Norman Horrocks Leadership Award. To recognize a new ALISE member who has demonstrated outstanding leadership qualities in professional ALISE activities. *Winner:* Sarah Buchanan, University of Missouri.

ALISE/Pratt-Severn Faculty Innovation Award. To recognize innovation by full-time faculty members in incorporating evolving information technologies in the curricula of accredited master's degree programs in library and information studies. *Winner:* Monica Maceli, Pratt Institute.

ALISE/ProQuest Methodology Paper Competition. *Winner:* Vanessa Kitzic, Travis Wagner, A. Nick Vera, and Jocelyn Pettigrew for "Using the World Café Methodology to Support Community-centric Research and Practice in Library and Information Science."

ALISE Research Grant Competition (one or more grants totaling $5,000). *Winner:* Jungwon Yoon and James Andrews, University of South Florida, for "Exploring Best Practices for Preparing Librarians in Adopting Artificial Intelligence Into Libraries."

ALISE Service Award. *Winner:* Not awarded in 2020.

ALISE/Jean Tague Sutcliffe Doctoral Student Research Poster Competition. *Winners:* (first place) Cameron Pierson, Victoria University of Wellington (New Zealand); (second place) Laura Ridenour, Cheryl Klimaszewski, Rutgers University, New Brunswick, New Jersey; (third place) LeRoy LaFleur, Simmons University, Boston, Massachusetts.

ALISE/University of Washington Information School Youth Services Graduate Student Travel Award. To support the costs associated with travel to and participation in the ALISE Annual Conference. *Winner:* Not awarded in 2020.

ALISE/Connie Van Fleet Award for Research Excellence in Public Library Services to Adults. To recognize LIS research concerning services to adults in public libraries. *Winners:* Lynn Silipigni Connaway, Chris Cyr, Michele Coleman, Kendra Morgan, Mercy Procaccini; Larra Clark, and Scott

Allen for "Public Libraries Respond to the Opioid Crisis With Their Communities."

ALISE/Bohdan S. Wynar Research Paper Competition. Winner: Mega Subramaniam, Natalie Pang, Shandra Morehouse, and S. Nisa Asgarali-Hoffman for "Positioning Vulnerability in Youth Digital Information Practices Scholarship: What Are We Missing or Exhausting?"

Doctoral Students to ALISE Grant. To support the attendance of one or more promising LIS doctoral students at the ALISE Annual Conference. *Sponsor:* Libraries Unlimited/ Linworth. *Winners:* Eric Ely, University of Wisconsin–Madison; Joseph Winberry, University of Tennessee–Knoxville.

Library Journal/ALISE Excellence in Teaching Award (formerly the ALISE Award for Teaching Excellence in the Field of Library and Information Science Education). *Winner:* Rachel Fleming-May, University of Tennessee-Knoxville.

Association of Jewish Libraries (AJL)

AJL Scholarships ($1,000). For students enrolled in accredited library schools who plan to work as Judaica librarians. *Winner:* Not awarded in 2020.

Fanny Goldstein Merit Award. To honor loyal and ongoing contributions to the association and to the profession of Jewish librarianship. *Winner:* Not awarded in 2020.

Life Membership Award. To recognize outstanding leadership and professional contributions to the association and to the profession of Jewish librarianship. *Winner:* Not awarded in 2020.

Association of Research Libraries

ARL Diversity Scholarships (stipend of up to $10,000). To a varying number of MLS students from underrepresented groups who are interested in careers in research libraries. *Sponsors:* ARL member libraries and the Institute of Museum and Library Services. *Winners:* Kimberly Villafuerte Barzola, Simmons University; Dymond Bush, Simmons University;

Brittany Butler, San José State University; Valeria Estefanía Dávila Gronros, University of Alabama; Laquanda M. Fields, University at Buffalo, SUNY; Ramón García, University of North Texas; Kaia MacLeod, University of Alberta; Arianna McQuillen, Simmons University; Karla Michelle Roig Blay, University of Texas at Austin; Luis Rubio, Pratt Institute; Brave Heart Sanchez, University of Arizona; Alexander Soto, University of Arizona; Jerilyn Pia Tinio, University of Illinois at Urbana-Champaign; Y Vy Truong, University of British Columbia; Hailey Vasquez, University of Illinois at Urbana-Champaign; Kelly West, Louisiana State University; Max Wiggins, University of Maryland; Alexandra Wong, University of Toronto.

Association of Seventh-Day Adventist Librarians

D. Glenn Hilts Scholarship ($1,500) for a member or members of the Seventh-Day Adventist Church who are enrolled in a graduate library program. *Winners:* Bliss Kuntz, University of Denver.

Beta Phi Mu

Beta Phi Mu Award. *See under:* American Library Association.

Eugene Garfield Doctoral Dissertation Fellowships ($3,000). *Winners:* Houda El mimouni, Drexel University, for "Robotic Telepresence in the Classroom and Values"; Jiangen He, Drexel University, for "Predictive and Visual Analytics of Scientific Development"; Wenqing Lu, Simmons University, for "Using Social Media Tools for Collaborative Learning: A Mixed-Method Study on Academic Group Work by Worldwide iSchool Students"; Lassana Magassa, University of Washington, for "'I Am Not Computer Savvy': A Look into the Everyday Digital Literacy Level of Formerly Incarcerated People Using a Novel Holistic Digital Literacy Framework"; Martin Nord, University of Western Ontario, for "Documents and the Positioning of the Moral Self: The United Church of Canada's Reconciliation Documents"; Bonnie Tulloch, University of British Columbia, for "Do the Ends Justify the Memes? Exploring the Relationship between Youth, Internet Memes, and Digital Citizenship."

Harold Lancour Scholarship for Foreign Study ($1,750). For graduate study in a country related to the applicant's work or schooling. *Winner:* Erin Eldermire, Flower-Sprecher Veterinary Library, Cornell University Library.

Sarah Rebecca Reed Scholarship ($2,250). For study at an ALA-accredited library school. *Winner:* Tobias Paul, University of Illinois at Urbana-Champaign.

Frank B. Sessa Scholarship for Continuing Professional Education ($1,500). For continuing education for a Beta Phi Mu member. *Winners:* Heather Arrington, At-Large, Wayne State University; Laurie Fuentes, Beta Lambda Chapter, Texas Woman's University; Sarah Cruz Mendoza, Beta Phi Chapter, University of South Florida; Sara Quashnie, Alpha Chapter, University of Illinois; Katy Sternberger, Beta Beta Chapter, Simmons University.

Blanche E. Woolls Scholarship ($2,250). For a beginning student in school library media services. *Winner:* Nicole Pereversoff, University of Western Ontario.

Bibliographical Society of America (BSA)

BSA Fellowships ($1,500–$6,000). For scholars involved in bibliographical inquiry and research in the history of the book trades and in publishing history. *Winners:* (BSA-ASECS Fellowship for Bibliographical Studies in the Eighteenth Century) Sarah Bramao-Ramos for "Readers of Manchu Language Books"; (BSA-St. Louis Mercantile Library Fellowship for Research in North American Bibliography) Allison Fagan for "Editorial Intimacies, Posthumous Publishing and Toni Morrison's Edition of Toni Cade Bambara's Those Bones Are Not My Child"; (BSA-Rare Book School Fellowship) Joshua Kruchten; (BSA Short Term Fellowships) Alexander Jacobson for "Tamizdat as Masquerade"; John McQuillen for "The 15th-Century Blockbook in America: A Descriptive

Census"; Yelizaveta Strakhov for "Representation of Translation by Scribes in Manuscripts of John Lydgate's and Benedict Burgh's Secrees of Olde Philosoffres"; (The Katharine Pantzer Junior Fellowship in the British Book Trades) Kate Nesbit for "Listening to Books: Reading Aloud and the Novel, 1800-1935"; (Katharine F. Pantzer Senior Fellowship in the British Book Trades) Kirk Melnikoff for "Bookselling in Early Modern England"; (BSA-Pine Tree Foundation Fellowship in Culinary Bibliography) Andrea Gutierrez for "Bibliography of the First Print Cookbooks in Tamil"; (BSA-Pine Tree Foundation Fellowship in Hispanic Bibliography) Daniela Samur Duque for "The Allure of Books: Bookstores and Printshops in Bogotá, 1850s–1920"; (Reese Fellowship for American Bibliography and the History of the Book in the Americas) Nazera Wright for "Early African American Women Writers and their Libraries" (Charles J. Tanenbaum Fellowship in Cartographical Bibliography) Jordana Dym and Carla Lois for "Bound Images: A History of Maps in Books."

William L. Mitchell Prize for Research on Early British Serials ($1,000). Awarded triennially for the best single work published in the previous three years. *Winner (2018):* Dr. Paul Tankard, *Facts and Inventions: Selections from the Journalism of James Boswell* (Yale University Press).

New Scholars Program. To promote the work of scholars who are new to the field of bibliography. *Winners:* Dr. Alison Fraser, University at Buffalo, SUNY, for "Homemade Books in Twentieth-Century Poetics: A Feminist Bibliography"; Dr. Elisa Tersigni, Folger Shakespeare Library, Washington, DC, for "Two Sides of the Same Book: The Creation and Use of Early Modern English Receipt Books"; Matthew Wills, University of California, San Diego, for "The Paper Crisis and the Scramble for Stability in Mao-Era Publishing."

St. Louis Mercantile Library Prize in American Bibliography ($2,000). Awarded triennially for outstanding scholarship in the bibliography of American history and literature. *Sponsor:* St. Louis Mercantile Library, University of Missouri, St. Louis. *Winners*

(2020): Dr. Lindsay DiCuirci for *Colonial Revivals: The Nineteenth-Century Lives of Early American Books* (University of Pennsylvania Press); Dr. Derrick R. Spires for *The Practice of Citizenship: Black Politics and Print Culture in the Early United States* (University of Pennsylvania Press).

Justin G. Schiller Prize for Bibliographical Work on Pre–20th Century Children's Books ($2,000). A triennial award to encourage scholarship in the bibliography of historical children's books. *Winner (2019): The Book and Periodical Illustrations of Arthur Hughes: A Spark of Genius 1832–1914,* by Maroussia Oakley (Oak Knoll Press & Private Libraries Association).

Catholic Library Association

Regina Medal. For continued, distinguished contribution to the field of children's literature. *Winner:* Christopher Paul Curtis.

Chinese American Librarians Association (CALA)

CALA Conference Travel Grant. *Winners:* Not awarded in 2020.

CALA Distinguished Service Award. To a librarian who has been a mentor, role model, and leader in the fields of library and information science. *Winner:* Guoying Liu.

CALA Outstanding Library Leadership Award in Memory of Dr. Margaret Chang Fung. *Winner:* Not awarded in 2020.

CALA President's Recognition Award. *Winners:* (individuals) Shu-hua Liu, Shuqin Jiao, Jia He, Jingshan Xiao, Lei Jin, Meng Qu, Anlin Yang, Vincci Kwong, Ying Liao, Ying Zhang, Sai Deng; (committees) Public Relations/Fundraising Committee, New Strategic Plan Preparing Committee, Best Book Subcommittee, Jing Liao Research Awards Subcommittee, Assessment Committee, Distinguished Services Award Subcommittee, Scholarship Committee, Annual Program Committee.

CALA Scholarship of Library and Information Science ($1,000). *Winner:* Joanne Chern.

Sheila Suen Lai Scholarship ($500). *Winner:* Richard Hoang.

Lisa Zhao Scholarship ($500). *Winner:* Xijia Jessica Peng.

Coalition for Networked Information (CNI)

Paul Evan Peters Award. Awarded biennially to recognize notable and lasting international achievements relating to high-performance networks and the creation and use of information resources and services that advance scholarship and intellectual productivity. *Sponsors:* Association of Research Libraries, CNI, EDUCAUSE. *Winner (2020):* Francine Berman, Rensselaer Polytechnic University and Radcliffe Institute, Harvard University.

Paul Evan Peters Fellowship ($5,000 a year for two years). Awarded biennially to a student or students pursuing a graduate degree in librarianship or the information sciences. *Sponsors:* Association of Research Libraries, CNI, EDUCAUSE. *Winners (2020):* Jen Liu and Jake Tompins.

Council on Library and Information Resources (CLIR)

CLIR Postdoctoral Fellowships in Scholarly Information Resources. *Current fellows:* Portia D. Hopkins, Luling Huang, Petrouchka Moise, Jennifer Ross, Synatra Smith, Francena Turner, Laura Wilson, Rebecca Pickens.

Digitizing Hidden Special Collections and Archives Awards. *Sponsor:* Andrew W. Mellon Foundation. *Winners (2019):* Asheville Art Museum Association, Inc. for "Digital Black Mountain College Collection and Interconnective Timeline"; Ball State University for "Unearthing a Half-Century of Archaeological Research in Indiana: Digitizing the Report of Investigations and Archaeological Report Series, and Associated Diagnostic Artifacts"; CUNY Television for "Uncovering the City University of New York's Audiovisual Heritage"; Law Library Microform Consortium for "The Early State Records for 26 U.S. States and Territories West of the Appalachians: a Digital Record from European Contact to Early Statehood Based on the Library of Congress' Microfilm Collection"; Michigan Technological University for "Michigan Miners at Home and Work: Digitizing, Mapping, and Sharing Employee Records"; Moravian Archives, Memorial University of Newfoundland, Nunatsiavut Government, and Moravian Church in Newfoundland and Labrador for "Uncommon Bonds: Labrador Inuit and Moravian Missionaries"; National Native American Boarding School Healing Coalition, Saginaw Chippewa Indian Tribe of Michigan, Museum of Indian Arts and Culture, and Indigenous Digital Archive project for "Digitizing the Records of U.S. Indian Boarding Schools"; San Francisco Art Institute for "Thinking Out Loud: Digitizing 80 Years of Lectures and Public Programs at the San Francisco Art Institute"; Mattress Factory, Ltd. for "The Greer Lankton Collection: Documenting the Life and Work of Transgender Artist Greer Lankton (1958–1996)"; Regents of the University of California (University of California, Berkeley) for "Land, Wealth and Power: Private Land Claims in California, ca. 1852–1892"; Regents of the University of Michigan for "Digitizing Natural History Materials from University of Michigan's Special Collections"; Regents of the University of New Mexico dba KNME-TV, New Mexico PBS, KRWG, KENW, KUNM, KANW, WGBH Educational Foundation, and Library of Congress for "New Mexico Public Media Digitization Project"; Indiana University, Saint Mary's College, Loyola University Chicago, Berea College, College of Wooster, DePauw University, Illinois Wesleyan University, Earlham College, Northern Illinois University, University of Saint Mary of the Lake, Southern Baptist Theological Seminary, Saint Olaf College, Knox College, Saint Meinrad Archabbey, Seminary, and School of Theology, Goshen College, Marquette University, Bowling Green State University, Ohio Wesleyan University, University of Dayton, Xavier University, Truman State University, and Muskegon Museum of Art for "Peripheral Manuscripts: Digitizing Medieval Manuscript Collections in the Midwest"; University of

La Verne for "Cataloging and Digitizing the Esther Funk Collection in University of La Verne's Cultural & Natural History Collections"; University of South Carolina for "New Insights on South Carolina and the American Civil Rights Movement: National Interracial Activism in the South Carolina Council on Human Relations Papers"; Virginia Polytechnic Institute and State University for "Entomo-3D: Digitizing Virginia Tech's Insect Collection"; Wichita State University, KMUW Public Radio, WGBH, Library of Congress, Kansas Public Broadcasting Council of Stations, Vietnamese Public Radio, KHCC Radio, High Plains Public Radio, KPR Radio, KRPS Radio, and KPTS TV for "The Kansas Public Media Preservation Project"; Woodson Research Center, Fondren Library, Rice University for "Digitizing Hidden Selections of Houston's African American and Jewish Heritage."

Mellon Fellowships for Dissertation Research in Original Sources. *Sponsor:* Andrew W. Mellon Foundation. *Winners (2019):* Hilary Barker, Colin Bos, Olivia Cacchione, Henry Clements, Marlena Cravens, Matthew Foreman, Anne Grasberger, Jasmin Howard, Clarissa Ibarra, Carl Kubler, Dana Landress, Xiuyuan Mi, Sauda Nabukenya, Catalina Ospina, Paloma Rodrigo Gonzales, Anna Weerasinghe.

EDUCAUSE

EDUCAUSE Community Leadership Award. *Winner:* Hilary J. Baker, vice president for information technology and CIO emeritus, California State University, Northridge.

EDUCAUSE DEI Leadership Award. To acknowledge and celebrate exemplary leadership in advancing equity, diversity, and inclusion. *Winner:* Deborah Keyek-Franssen, associate vice president and dean of online and continuing education, University of Utah.

EDUCAUSE Leadership Award. To acknowledge leadership in higher education information technology. *Winners:* Jack Suess, vice president of information technology and CIO, University of Maryland, Baltimore County.

EDUCAUSE Rising Star Award. To recognize early-career information technology professionals who demonstrate exceptional achievement in the area of information technology in higher education. *Winner:* Shannon Dunn, assistant director, University of Florida Information Technology Center for Instructional Technology and Training.

Friends of the National Library of Medicine

Michael E. DeBakey Library Services Outreach Award. To recognize outstanding service and contributions to rural and underserved communities by a practicing health sciences librarian. *Winner:* Heather K. Moberly, Medical Sciences Library, Texas A&M University.

Institute of Museum and Library Services

National Medal for Museum and Library Service. For extraordinary civic, educational, economic, environmental, and social contributions ($5,000). *Winners (2019):* Jamestown S'Klallam Tribal Library, Sequim, Washington; Inter-university Consortium for Political and Social Research, Ann Arbor, Michigan; New Haven (Connecticut) Free Public Library; Gulfport (Florida) Public Library; Meridian (Idaho) Library District; Barona Band of Mission Indians—Barona Cultural Center and Museum, Lakeside, California; New Children's Museum, San Diego, California; Orange County Regional History Center, Orlando, Florida; National Civil Rights Museum at the Lorraine Motel, Memphis, Tennessee; South Carolina Aquarium, Charleston, South Carolina.

International Association of School Librarians (IASL)

Ken Haycock Leadership Development Grant ($1,000). To enable applicants from any nation to attend their first IASL Annual Conference. *Winner:* Not awarded in 2020.

Jean Lowrie Leadership Development Grant ($1,000). To enable applicants from developing nations to attend their first IASL Annual Conference. *Winner:* Ifunanya Evangel Obim, Nigeria.

Takeshi Murofushi Research Award ($500). For funding a research project, preferably of international interest. *Winner:* Not awarded in 2020.

Diljit Singh Leadership Development Grant ($1,000). To enable applicants from developing nations to attend their first IASL conference. *Winner:* Grace Uchechi Onyebuchi, Nigeria.

International Board on Books for Young People (IBBY)

IBBY-Asahi Reading Promotion Award ($10,000). Awarded biennially to projects that are making a lasting contribution to reading promotion for young people. *Offered by:* International Board on Books for Young People. *Sponsor:* Asahi Shimbun. *Winner (2020):* Casa Cuna Cuenteros, volunteer group who carry out reading and storytelling activities in a children's hospital in Buenos Aires, Argentina.

International Federation of Library Associations and Institutions (IFLA)

International Federation of Library Associations and Institutions (IFLA) Honorary Fellowship. For distinguished service to IFLA. *Winners:* Not awarded in 2020.

IFLA Medal. To a person or organization for a distinguished contribution either to IFLA or to international librarianship. *Winners:* Guy Berthiaume and Inga Lundén.

Jay Jordan IFLA/OCLC Early Career Development Fellowships. To library and information science professionals from countries with developing economies who are in the early stages of their careers. *Winner:* Not awarded in 2020.

Dr. Shawky Salem Conference Grant (up to $1,900). To enable an expert in library and information science who is a national of an Arab country to attend the IFLA Conference for the first time. *Winner:* Not awarded in 2020.

Library Journal

DEMCO/*Library Journal* Paralibrarian of the Year Award. *Winner:* Not awarded in 2020.

Gale/*Library Journal* Library of the Year. *Sponsor:* Gale Cengage Learning. *Winner:* Seattle Public Library.

Library Journal/ALISE Excellence in Teaching Award (formerly the ALISE Award for Teaching Excellence in the Field of Library and Information Science Education). *See under:* Association for Library and Information Science Education (ALISE).

Library Journal Best Small Library in America ($20,000). To honor a public library that profoundly demonstrates outstanding service to populations of 25,000 or less. *Cosponsors: Library Journal* and the Bill and Melinda Gates Foundation. *Winner:* Not awarded in 2020.

Library Journal Librarian of the Year. *Winners:* Lauren Comito and Christian Zabriskie, Urban Librarians Unite, Brooklyn, New York.

Library of Congress

Kluge Fellowships in Digital Studies. To promote examination of the impact of the digital revolution on society, culture, and international relations using the library's collections and resources. *Fellow:* Not awarded in 2020.

Library of Congress Literacy Awards. *Sponsor:* David M. Rubenstein. *Winners:* (David M. Rubenstein Prize, $150,000, for a groundbreaking or sustained record of advancement of literacy by any individual or entity) National Center for Families Learning, Louisville, Kentucky; (American Prize, $50,000, for a project developed and implemented successfully during the past decade for combating illiteracy and/or aliteracy) The Immigrant Learning Center, Malden, Massachusetts; (International Prize, $50,000, for the work of an individual, nation, or nongovernmental organization working in a specific country or region) International Rescue Committee, New York, New York, for Pakistan Reading Project.

Library of Congress Prize for American Fiction. See "Literary Prizes, 2020" in Part 5.

Medical Library Association (MLA)

Virginia L. and William K. Beatty MLA Volunteer Service Award. To recognize a medical librarian who has demonstrated outstanding, sustained service to the Medical Library Association and the health sciences library profession. *Winner:* Margaret A. Hoogland.

Estelle Brodman Award for the Academic Medical Librarian of the Year. To honor significant achievement, potential for leadership, and continuing excellence at midcareer in the area of academic health sciences librarianship. *Winner:* Joey Nicholson.

Clarivate Analytics/Frank Bradway Rogers Information Advancement Award. To recognize outstanding contributions to the application of technology to the delivery of health science information, to the science of information, or to the facilitation of the delivery of health science information. *Sponsor:* Thomson Reuters. *Winner:* Gail Kouame.

Lois Ann Colaianni Award for Excellence and Achievement in Hospital Librarianship. To a member of MLA who has made significant contributions to the profession in the area of overall distinction or leadership in hospital librarianship. *Winner:* Barbara S. Reich.

Cunningham Memorial International Fellowships. For health sciences librarians from countries outside the United States and Canada, to provide for attendance at the MLA Annual Meeting and observation and supervised work in one or more medical libraries. *Winner:* Anar Kairatovna Dautova.

Louise Darling Medal. For distinguished achievement in collection development in the health sciences. *Winner:* Whitelist Working Group and Whitelist Reviewers, Association of Vision Science Librarians, Vision Science Caucus, Medical Library Association.

Janet Doe Lectureship. *Winner:* Chris Shaffer, AHIP, for "The Move to Open: Medical Library Leadership in Scholarly Communication."

EBSCO/MLA Annual Meeting Grants (up to $1,000). To enable four health sciences librarians to attend the MLA Annual Meeting. *Winners:* Names not released.

Ida and George Eliot Prize. To recognize a work published in the preceding calendar year that has been judged most effective in furthering medical librarianship. *Winners:* Peace Ossom Williamson, AHIP, and Christian Minter for "Exploring PubMed as a Reliable Resource for Scholarly Communications Services."

Carla J. Funk Governmental Relations Award ($500). To recognize a medical librarian who has demonstrated outstanding leadership in the area of governmental relations at the federal, state, or local level, and who has furthered the goal of providing quality information for improved health. *Sponsor:* Kent A. Smith. *Winner:* Not awarded in 2020.

Murray Gottlieb Prize. *See under:* Erich Meyerhoff Prize below.

T. Mark Hodges International Service Award. To honor outstanding achievement in promoting, enabling, or delivering improved health information internationally. *Winner:* Laura Shane Godbolt.

David A. Kronick Traveling Fellowship ($2,000). *Sponsor:* Bowden-Massey Foundation. *Winner:* Mark MacEachern.

Joseph Leiter NLM/MLA Lectureship. *Winner:* John S. Brownstein for "Digital Epidemiology and the COVID-19 Pandemic."

Donald A. B. Lindberg Research Fellowship ($10,000). To fund research aimed at expanding the research knowledge base, linking the information services provided by librarians to improved health care and advances in biomedical research. *Winners:* Antonio P. DeRosa for "Shared Decision-Making (SDM) Among Breast Cancer Patients: A Phenomenological Study and Exploration into Health Literacy Interventions."

Lucretia W. McClure Excellence in Education Award. To an outstanding educator in the field of health sciences librarianship and informatics. *Winner:* Amy Blevins.

John P. McGovern Award Lectureship. *Winner:* Esther Choo for "How Healthcare Inequities Have Been Exacerbated By COVID-19."

Medical Informatics Section Career Development Grant ($1,500). To support a career development activity that will contribute to advancement in the field of medical informatics. *Winner:* Suzanne Fricke.

Erich Meyerhoff Prize (formerly the Murray Gottlieb Prize). For the best unpublished essay on the history of medicine and allied

sciences written by a health sciences librarian. *Sponsor:* MLA History of the Health Sciences Section. *Winner:* Not awarded in 2020.

MLA Chapter Project of the Year Award. *Winner:* Pacific Northwest Chapter for "Logo Pin Design Contest."

MLA Continuing Education Grant ($100–$500). *Winner:* Marilia Y. Antunez.

MLA Scholarship (up to $5,000). For graduate study at an ALA-accredited library school. *Winner:* Samantha Kennefick Wilairat.

MLA Scholarship for Under-Represented Students (up to $5,000). For graduate study at an ALA-accredited library school. *Winner:* Christiana Julsaint.

Marcia C. Noyes Award. For an outstanding contribution to medical librarianship. *Winner:* Gerald J. Perry, AHIP, FMLA.

President's Award. To an MLA member for a notable or important contribution made during the past association year. *Winners:* Susan Lessick; Gerald J. "Jerry" Perry; and several MLA working groups that advanced and transformed the fundamental structure of the association.

Rittenhouse Award. For the best unpublished paper on medical librarianship submitted by a student enrolled in, or having been enrolled in, a course for credit in an ALA-accredited library school or a trainee in an internship program in medical librarianship. *Donor:* Rittenhouse Book Distributors. *Winner:* Sarah Clarke for "Data Sharing Barriers During Infectious Disease Outbreaks."

Music Library Association

Vincent H. Duckles Award. For the best book-length bibliography or other tool in music. *Winner:* John Gray for *Music of Sub-Saharan Africa: An International Bibliography and Resource Guide* (African Diaspora Press, 2018).

Dena Epstein Award for Archival and Library Research in American Music. To support research in archives or libraries internationally on any aspect of American music. *Winner:* Not awarded in 2020.

Kevin Freeman Travel Grants. To colleagues who are new to the profession to enable them to attend the MLA Annual Meeting. *Winners:* Linda Bagley, Adaliz Cruz, April

James; *Diversity Scholarship awardee:* Hang Nguyen.

Walter Gerboth Award. To members of the association who are in the first five years of their professional library careers, to assist research-in-progress in music or music librarianship. *Winner:* Not awarded in 2020.

Richard S. Hill Award. For the best article on music librarianship or article of a music-bibliographic nature. *Winner:* Joe C. Clark, Sheridan Stormes, and Jonathan Sauceda for "Format Preferences of Performing Arts Students: A Multi-Institution Study" in the *Journal of Academic Librarianship* 44, no. 5 (2018): 620-626.

MLA Citation. Awarded in recognition of contributions to the profession over a career. *Winner:* Michael Rogan.

Eva Judd O'Meara Award. For the best review published in *Notes. Winner:* Edward Komara for "Review of the Original Blues: The Emergence of the Blues in African American Vaudeville by Lynn Abbott and Doug Seroff" in *Notes* 74, no. 4 (2018): 658-661.

A. Ralph Papakhian Special Achievement Award. To recognize extraordinary service to the profession of music librarianship over a relatively short period of time. *Winners:* Not awarded in 2020.

National Library Service for the Blind and Print Disabled, Library of Congress

Library of the Year Awards ($1,000). *Winner:* (Regional Library of the Year) Oklahoma Library for the Blind and Physically Handicapped, Oklahoma City, Oklahoma; (Sub-regional Library/Advisory and Outreach Center of the Year) Talking Books and Braille Center of the San Francisco Public Library.

REFORMA (National Association to Promote Library and Information Services to Latinos and the Spanish-Speaking)

Elizabeth A. Martinez Lifetime Achievement Award. To recognize those who have achieved excellence in librarianship over an extended period of service and who have made significant and lasting contributions to REFORMA and the Latino community. *Winner:* Not awarded in 2020.

REFORMA scholarships (up to $1,500). To students who qualify for graduate study in library science and who are citizens or permanent residents of the United States. (Rose Trevino Memorial Scholarship) *Winner:* Patricia Lyons. (REFORMA Scholarship) *Winners:* Amanda Toledo, Hope Saldivar.

Arnulfo D. Trejo Librarian of the Year Award. To recognize a librarian who has promoted and advocated services to the Spanish-speaking and Latino communities and made outstanding contributions to REFORMA. *Winner:* Not awarded in 2020.

Society of American Archivists (SAA)

C. F. W. Coker Award for Description. To recognize creators of tools that enable archivists to produce more effective finding aids. *Winner:* Archives for Black Lives in Philadelphia (A4BLiP).

Distinguished Service Award. To recognize an archival institution, education program, nonprofit organization, or governmental organization that has given outstanding service to its public and has made an exemplary contribution to the archives profession. *Winner:* Orange County (Florida) Regional History Center.

Diversity Award. To an individual, group, or institution for outstanding contributions to advancing diversity within the archives profession, SAA, or the archival record. *Winner:* Rebecca Hankins.

Fellows' Ernst Posner Award. For an outstanding essay dealing with a facet of archival administration, history, theory, or methodology, published in *American Archivist. Winner:* Keith Pendergrass, Walker Sampson, Tessa Walsh, and Laura Alagna for "Toward Environmentally Sustainable Digital Preservation" (Spring/Summer 2019, Vol. 82.1).

Josephine Forman Scholarship ($10,000). *Sponsor:* General Commission on Archives and History of the United Methodist Church. *Winner:* Ishmael Ross, Louisiana State University.

Mark A. Greene Emerging Leader Award. To recognize early-career archivists who have completed archival work of broad merit, demonstrated significant promise of leadership, performed commendable service to the archives profession, or accomplished a combination of these requirements. *Winner:* Lydia Tang, Michigan State University.

F. Gerald Ham and Elsie Ham Scholarship ($7,500). To recognize an individual's past performance in a graduate archival studies program and his or her potential in the field. *Winner:* Elena Hinkle, Simmons University.

Philip M. Hamer and Elizabeth Hamer Kegan Award. For individuals and/or institutions that have increased public awareness of a specific body of documents. *Winner:* Laura Wagner, David M. Rubenstein Rare Book & Manuscript Library, Duke University, for Radio Haiti Archive.

Oliver Wendell Holmes Travel Award. To enable overseas archivists already in the United States or Canada for training to attend the SAA Annual Meeting. *Winner:* Klavier Jie Ying Wang.

J. Franklin Jameson Archival Advocacy Award. For individuals and/or organizations that promote greater public awareness of archival activities and programs. *Winners:* Brad Pomerance; CJ Eastman; Council of Independent Colleges' Humanities Research for the Public Good Program.

Sister M. Claude Lane, O.P., Memorial Award. For a significant contribution to the field of religious archives. *Winner:* Ellen Pierce, Dominican Sisters and other Religious Congregations.

Waldo Gifford Leland Award. To encourage and reward writing of superior excellence and usefulness in the field of archival history, theory, or practice. *Winner:* Jean-Christophe Cloutier for *Shadow Archives: The Lifecycles of African American Literature* (Columbia University Press, 2019).

Theodore Calvin Pease Award. For the best student paper ($100 and publication in *American Archivist*). *Winner:* Bridget Malley, University of Wisconsin-Milwaukee, for "Nothing About Us Without Us: Documenting Disability History in Western Pennsylvania" (Spring/Summer 2021, Vol. 84.1).

Donald Peterson Student Travel Award (up to $1,000). To enable a student or recent graduate to attend the SAA Annual Meeting.

Winner: Jeanie Pai, Queens College, City University of New York.

Harold T. Pinkett Student of Color Award. To encourage minority students to consider careers in the archival profession, and to promote minority participation in SAA. *Winners:* Carol Ng-He, San José State University.

Preservation Publication Award. To recognize an outstanding work published in North America that advances the theory or the practice of preservation in archival institutions. *Winner:* Lisa Elkin and Christopher A. Norris for *Preventive Conservation: Collection Storage* (Society for the Preservation of Natural History Collections, American Institute for Conservation, Smithsonian Institution, and George Washington University Museum Studies Program, 2019).

SAA Fellows. To a limited number of members for their outstanding contribution to the archival profession. *Honored:* Geof Huth, Lisa Mangiafico, and Michael Rush.

SAA Mosaic Scholarship ($5,000). To minority students pursuing graduate education in archival science. *Winners:* Mya Ballin, University of British Columbia.

SAA Spotlight Award. To recognize the contributions of individuals who work for the good of the profession and of archival collections, and whose work would not typically receive public recognition. *Winners:* Michelle Ganz, archives director, McDonough Innovation, Charlottesville, Virginia.

Special Libraries Association (SLA)

SLA James M. Matarazzo Rising Star Award. To SLA members in the first five years of membership who demonstrate exceptional promise of leadership. *Winners:* Dana Eckstein Berkowitz, JonLuc Christensen, Thérèse Mainville-Celso, Kelly Durkin Ruth.

SLA John Cotton Dana Award. For exceptional support and encouragement of special librarianship. *Winners:* Richard Hulser and Sharon Lenius.

SLA Fellows. *Honored:* Anne Barker, Jeff Bond, and John Coll.

SLA Hall of Fame Award. For outstanding performance and distinguished service to SLA. *Winners:* Rita Ormsby and Tom Rink.

Rose L. Vormelker Award. To SLA members for exceptional service through the education and mentoring of students and working professionals. *Winner:* Not awarded in 2020.

Theatre Library Association

Brooks McNamara Performing Arts Librarian Scholarship. *Winner:* Not awarded in 2020.

Louis Rachow Distinguished Service in Performing Arts Librarianship Award. For extraordinary contributions to performing arts. *Winner:* Nancy Friedland, School of Information, San José State University.

George Freedley Memorial Award. *Winner:* Juliane Braun, *Creole Drama: Theatre and Society in Antebellum New Orleans* (University of Virginia Press).

Richard Wall Award. See "Literary Prizes, 2020" in Part 5.

Other Awards of Distinction

Robert B. Downs Intellectual Freedom Award. To recognize individuals or groups who have furthered the cause of intellectual freedom, particularly as it affects libraries and information centers and the dissemination of ideas. *Offered by:* Graduate School of Library and Information Science, University of Illinois at Urbana-Champaign. *Sponsor:* Libraries Unlimited/ABC-CLIO. *Winner:* Not awarded in 2020.

I Love My Librarian Awards ($5,000, a plaque, and a $500 travel stipend to attend the awards ceremony). To recognize librarians for service to their communities, schools, and campuses. Winners are nominated by library patrons. *Sponsors:* Carnegie Corporation of New York and the *New York Times. Winners (2019–2020):* Jesús Alonso-Regalado, University at Albany, State University of New York; Stephanie Lynn Dannehl, Bertrand (Nebraska) Community School; Cathy Gulley Evans, James Frederick Smith Library, St. Mary's Episcopal School, Memphis, Tennessee; Melissa Glanden, Powhatan (Virginia) High School; MaryAnne Hansen, Renne Library, Montana State University, Bozeman, Montana; Homa Naficy, The American Place, Hartford (Connecticut) Public Library; Maria Papanastassiou, Arlington Heights (Illinois) Memorial Library; Leah Plocharcyzk, John D. MacArthur Campus Library, Florida Atlantic University; Janet Tom, San Francisco Public Library, Tracie Walker-Reed, H. Grady Spruce High School, Dallas, Texas.

RWA Cathie Linz Librarian of the Year. To a librarian who demonstrates outstanding support of romance authors and the romance genre. *Offered by:* Romance Writers of America. *Winner:* Not awarded in 2020.

USBBY Bridge to Understanding Award ($1,000). To acknowledge the work of adults who use books to promote international understanding among children. *Offered by:* United States Board on Books for Young People. *Winner:* To be announced.

Women's National Book Association Award. Awarded biennially to a living American woman who derives part or all of her income from books and allied arts and who has done meritorious work in the world of books. *Offered by:* Women's National Book Association (WNBA). *Winners (2019):* Lisa Lucas, executive director, National Book Foundation.

Part 4
Research and Statistics

Library Research and Statistics

Number of Libraries in the United States and Canada

Statistics are from the *American Library Directory (ALD)* 2021–2022 (Information Today, Inc., 2021). Data are exclusive of elementary and secondary school libraries.

Libraries in the United States

Public Libraries	16,905*
Public libraries, excluding branches	9,627
Main public libraries that have branches	1,429
Public library branches	7,277
Academic Libraries	3,496*
Community college	1,072
Departmental	234
Medical	5
Religious	5
University and college	2,424
Departmental	1,142
Law	193
Medical	228
Religious	245
Armed Forces Libraries	226*
Air Force	62
Medical	3
Army	104
Medical	21
Marine Corps	12
Navy	48
Law	1
Medical	9
Government Libraries	804*
Law	350
Medical	108

Special Libraries (excluding public, academic, armed forces, and government)	4,500*
Law	627
Medical	785
Religious	369
Total Special Libraries (including public, academic, armed forces, and government)	5,668
Total law	1,171
Total medical	1,159
Total religious	700
Total Libraries Counted (*)	25,931

Libraries in Regions Administered by the United States

Public Libraries	18*
Public libraries, excluding branches	9
Main public libraries that have branches	3
Public library branches	9
Academic Libraries	38*
Community college	3
Departmental	1
University and college	35
Departmental	18
Law	3
Medical	3
Religious	1
Armed Forces Libraries	2*
Air Force	1
Army	1
Government Libraries	3*
Law	1
Medical	1
Special Libraries (excluding public, academic, armed forces, and government)	5*
Law	3
Religious	1
Total Special Libraries (including public, academic, armed forces, and government)	14
Total law	7
Total medical	4
Total religious	2
Total Libraries Counted (*)	66

Libraries in Canada

Public Libraries	2,217*
Public libraries, excluding branches	799
Main public libraries that have branches	157
Public library branches	1,418
Academic Libraries	315*
Community college	74
Departmental	14
Religious	1
University and college	241
Departmental	168
Law	16
Medical	12
Religious	31
Government Libraries	158*
Law	25
Medical	4
Special Libraries (excluding public, academic, armed forces, and government)	522*
Law	86
Medical	120
Religious	20
Total Special Libraries (including public, academic, armed forces, and government)	611
Total law	127
Total medical	136
Total religious	68
Total Libraries Counted (*)	3,211

Summary

Total U.S. Libraries	25,931
Total Libraries Administered by the United States	66
Total Canadian Libraries	3,211
Grand Total of Libraries Listed	29,208

Note: Numbers followed by an asterisk are added to find "Total libraries counted" for each of the three geographic areas (United States, U.S.-administered regions, and Canada). The sum of the three totals is the "Grand total of libraries listed" in *ALD*. For details on the count of libraries, see the preface to the 74th edition of *ALD—Ed.*

Highlights of IMLS Public Library Surveys

The Institute of Museum and Library Services (IMLS) collects and disseminates statistical information about public libraries in the United States and its outlying areas. This article presents highlights from two recent IMLS surveys of public libraries and state library administrative agencies. For further information, see "Institute of Museum and Library Services" in Part 2 of this volume and visit https://www.imls.gov/research-tools/data-collection for the most current and comprehensive IMLS survey data and reports.

Public Libraries Survey

Following are highlights from the IMLS report *Public Libraries in the United States, Fiscal Year 2017*, released in 2020. Based on an annual public library survey (PLS), the report collected data from approximately 9,000 public library systems comprised of over 17,000 individual main libraries, library branches, and bookmobiles in all 50 states, the District of Columbia, and U.S. territories.

Revenues and Expenditures

- During the ten-year period from Fiscal Year (FY) 2008 to FY 2017, suburban libraries had the largest declines in revenue (10.5 percent) and expenditures (11 percent), with negligible declines in both revenue and expenditures for libraries in rural areas. Libraries in cities also saw a negligible (2.7 percent) decline in revenue but a more significant decline in expenditures (3.9 percent).
- During the same ten-year period, revenue per person decreased for libraries serving very large populations (more than 25,000 people) but increased for those serving small and medium-sized communities.
- In FY 2017 libraries serving small populations (fewer than 2,500 people) had higher per person revenue ($55.72) and expenditures ($51.00) than those serving areas with larger populations.
- State and local funds were libraries' two largest sources of revenue, with local sources contributing 85.9 percent and state sources contributing 6.7 percent of revenue per person at the national level.
- Libraries in towns received a greater share of revenue from state sources (12.2 percent), compared to local, federal, and other sources, than libraries in other locales. At the other end of the spectrum, libraries in suburbs saw the largest percentage of revenue from local sources (88.4 percent).
- Libraries that served small communities (fewer than 2,500 people) had the lowest share of funds from local sources (77.6 percent), while those that served large or very large communities both reported just over 86 percent of revenue from local sources.
- At the national level, two-thirds of expenditures were on staff, with 11.1 percent on collections. There was negligible variation in the relative percentage of expenditures on collections across libraries in different locales and for those serving communities of different sizes.

- Libraries in towns and rural areas spent less than 18 percent of their collections expenditures on electronic materials, while those in cities spent more than 31 percent on this material format.

Collections and Circulation

- From FY 2008 to FY 2017 libraries serving small communities had the largest growth in collection materials (303.4 percent), followed by libraries serving medium-sized communities (175.2 percent).
- During the same ten-year period, libraries serving very large populations (over 25,000 people) had the least decline in circulation (9.8 percent).
- FY 2017 collections and circulation per person were largest for libraries serving small communities (less than 2,500 people).
- Total collection materials per person were substantially lower in cities (3.2) than in rural areas (11.2). Collection materials in libraries in rural areas had a greater proportion of e-books (46.1 percent) than libraries in other locales.
- The relative number of collection materials differed by population size groups, with libraries serving small communities hosting a greater proportion of e-books (56.4 percent) than libraries in other locales.
- Suburban libraries had the highest total circulation per person (7.8) as well as the highest children's materials circulation per person (2.9).

Library Visits and Reference Transactions

- From FY 2008 to FY 2017 libraries in suburbs had the largest decline in per person library visits (20.3 percent).
- During the same ten-year period, libraries serving very large communities (populations over 25,000) had the largest decline in reference transactions (27.6 percent).
- During FY 2017 library visits varied only slightly across population size groups, with libraries serving small communities (fewer than 2,500 people) having the most visits per person (6.5).
- Per person library reference transactions did not vary substantially across locales or population size groups.

Program Offerings and Attendance

- From FY 2008 to FY 2017 programs offered and program attendance per 1,000 people increased substantially (48.2 percent and 35.5 percent, respectively).
- During the same ten-year period, library programming per 1,000 people increased substantially for libraries across population size groups. The largest change over the period was the 66.1 percent increase in programming per 1,000 people for libraries serving small communities (fewer than 2,500 people).

- Also during this period, city libraries had the largest increase in program attendance per 1,000 people (36.9 percent), followed closely by libraries in towns (36.0 percent).
- During FY 2017 libraries serving small communities had significantly more programs and higher program attendance per 1,000 people than libraries serving other population size groups. This pattern was consistent for children's programs and young adults' programs as well.
- The relative amount of children's programming differed by locale, although negligibly, with libraries in towns having a greater proportion of children's programming (59.1 percent) than libraries in other locales. City libraries offered fewer young adults' program per 1,000 people (1.6) than libraries in rural areas (2.0).

Internet Access

- From FY 2008 to FY 2017 the number of public-access Internet computers per 5,000 people increased (29.1 percent), while user sessions decreased (31.6 percent).
- The same ten-year period saw a 37.1 percent increase in the number of public-access Internet computers per 5,000 people for libraries in towns, followed closely by a 36.9 percent increase for libraries in cities. There was a 36.6 percent increase in the number of public-access Internet computers per stationary outlet (i.e., central and branch libraries).
- During the period, public-access Internet computer user sessions per person decreased for libraries across all locale types. The largest change by locale over the period was a 35 percent decrease in per person user sessions for libraries in suburbs.
- During FY 2017 the number of public-access Internet computers per stationary outlet varied by locale, with city libraries having more computers per stationary outlet (32.1) than libraries in other locales.
- Libraries serving small communities (fewer than 2,500 people) had the greatest number of public-access Internet computers per 5,000 people (23.5) and the greatest number of public-access Internet computer user sessions per person (1.4). However, libraries serving very large communities had significantly more public-access Internet computers per stationary outlet (24.6) than libraries serving the other population size groups.
- Public-access Internet computer user sessions per person showed little variation across locales.

Public Library Staff

- From FY 2008 to FY 2017 library staffing per 25,000 people declined by 7.8 percent, while the percentage of librarians with ALA-MLS credentials stayed nearly the same (68 percent in FY 2008 and 67.8 percent in FY 2017).
- During the same ten-year period, library staffing per 25,000 people decreased for libraries serving very large communities (more than 25,000

people) but increased for those serving the other three population size groups. The largest change over the period was the 7.9 percent increase in library staffing for large communities of 10,000–25,000 people.

- City libraries had the largest decline in library staff (5.2 percent) during the period, while rural libraries had the largest growth (6.0 percent).
- At the national level, there was a 2.5 percent decline in library staffing per 25,000 people from FY 2008 to FY 2017; however, the analyses in this section of the PLS demonstrate the importance of looking more closely at trends in public library staffing for libraries in different types of communities.
- During FY 2017 library staffing was proportionately largest for libraries in rural areas, followed by towns, suburbs, and cities.
- Libraries serving large communities (10,000–25,000 people) had more growth in library staffing (7.9 percent) than did those serving other population-size-served groups.
- The total number of library staff per 25,000 people varied slightly by locale, with libraries in rural areas having more staff than libraries in other locales. The percentage of librarians with ALA-MLS credentials varied significantly across locales, with the highest percentage (83.8 percent) employed in city libraries.
- Staffing levels varied by population size served. Libraries that serve small populations had more than twice as many total staff per 25,000 people as libraries that serve very large populations and about five times the number of librarians. Libraries that serve very large communities had a substantially higher percentage of ALA-MLS librarians (78.1 percent) than libraries serving other population-size-served groups.

State Library Administrative Agencies Survey

Following are executive summary highlights from the IMLS report *State Library Administrative Agencies Survey, Fiscal Year 2018*, released in April 2020. Based on a survey that has been conducted annually or biennially since 1994, the report collected data from State Library Administrative Agencies throughout the 50 states and the District of Columbia. For additional context and supplemental information or to read the full report, visit IMLS on the web.

Introduction

A State Library Administrative Agency (SLAA) is the official state agency charged with the extension and development of public library services throughout the state. It has the authority to administer state plans in accordance with the provisions of the federal Library Services and Technology Act (LSTA).

Across the 50 states and the District of Columbia, SLAAs are located in various state government agencies and report to different authorities. They coordinate and distribute federal funds from the IMLS Grants to States program in addressing statewide and local needs.

Although all SLAAs coordinate and distribute federal funds authorized by the administration of the LSTA, not all share the same function and role within their respective states. Most SLAAs provide important reference and information services to the state government, administer the state library or serve as the state archives, operate libraries for people who are blind or physically handicapped, and support the State Center for the Book. In some states, the SLAA also may function as the public library at large, providing library services to the general public.

Revenues and Expenditures

In FY 2018, SLAAs reported the following:

- Revenues totaled more than $1.1 billion across federal, state, and other revenue sources; 83 percent of this revenue was from states and 14 percent from federal sources.
- Expenditures also totaled over $1.1 billion, with 67 percent spent on financial assistance to libraries and 32 percent on operations.

Over the 14-year period from FY 2004 to FY 2018:

- Revenues and expenditures of funds through the Library Services Technology Act (LSTA) decreased by 20 percent.
- Per person revenues decreased from $4.66 in FY 2004 (in dollars adjusted for 2018) to $3.47 per person in FY 2012, a 26 percent decrease. The $3.38 per person revenues in FY 2018 represent a moderate decrease since FY 2012.

A closer review of SLAA revenues and expenditures over this period reveals a more nuanced picture:

- Between FY 2004 and FY 2008, SLAA expenditures increased 3 percent, with revenues decreasing less than 3 percent.
- From FY 2008 to FY 2012, which includes the Great Recession, SLAA revenues and expenditures declined sharply and continuously, falling by about 22 percent.
- Since FY 2012, SLAA revenues and expenditures have fundamentally leveled out.

The revenues and expenditures for SLAAs based on administrative structures also varied across this period:

- All four categories of administrative structures reported declines over the 14-year period, ranging from 9 percent to 14 percent.
- In the most recent two-year period, between FY 2016 and FY 2018, there was a continued decline in revenues and expenditures for SLAAs that were part of the state's Department of Education or in the "Other Agency" category.

Agency Workforce

- In FY 2018 there were 2,524 full-time equivalent (FTE) staff across all SLAAs.
- Nearly half (48 percent) of FTE staff were in library services, followed by library development (20 percent), other services (18 percent), and administration (14 percent).
- Overall, the number of FTE staff at SLAAs has declined by 27 percent over the 12-year period from FY 2006 to FY 2018.
- In the most recent two-year period between FY 2016 and FY 2018, there were no meaningful changes (i.e., less than 3 percent) in FTE per million residents for SLAAs in the eight SLAAs in the "Other Agency" category and the 20 SLAAs housed in Independent Agencies / Legislative Branch.
- During the same two-year period, there was a 22 percent increase in FTE per 1 million residents for the 10 SLAAs located in Departments of State/ Administration and a 22 percent decline for the 13 SLAAs in Departments of Education.

Services

The proportion of SLAAs providing services to libraries and library cooperatives varied in FY 2018:

- Forty-nine of the 51 SLAAs (96 percent) provided consulting services, most commonly for library management / organizational development, continuing education, and youth services.
- Thirty-six SLAAs (71 percent) provided some form of literacy support.
- Forty-two SLAAs (82 percent) reported having statewide reading programs.

Due to reorganization of the survey questionnaire in FY 2014, trend comparisons for services offered by SLAAs to libraries and library cooperatives are limited to the most recent four years, from FY 2014 through FY 2018. During this time

- The number of SLAAs providing the various types of services in FY 2018 remained largely unchanged from FY 2014.
- All SLAAs provided LSTA statewide services and almost all reported offering consulting services in FY 2014, FY 2016, and FY 2018.
- The percent of SLAAs providing LSTA statewide grant programs and administrative library system support remained relatively consistent over these four years, returning in FY 2018 to FY 2014 levels.
- The percent of SLAAs providing statewide reading programs increased from 69 percent in FY 2014 to 86 percent in FY 2016, then decreased slightly to 82 percent in FY 2018.

In FY 2018, SLAAs varied in the types of services provided to libraries and library cooperatives based on administrative structure. While nearly all SLAAs provided continuing education support, there were differences in other services provided based on a state's administrative structure, such as the following:

- Administrative library support services. While 70 percent of SLAAs in Independent Agency / Legislative Branch and Departments of State/Administration provided such services, only 50 percent or fewer of those in Departments of Education or in the "Other Agency" category did so.
- Program assistance services. While 85 percent of SLAAs in Independent/ Legislative agencies provided literacy program support, only 50 percent of those housed in Departments of Education did so.
- Coordination and integration services. About 70 percent of SLAAs in Departments of State/Administration and Departments of Education provided statewide coordination of digital programs and services, while half or fewer of those in the Independent/Legislative and the "Other Agency" category did so.

School Librarian Employment in the United States

Debra E. Kachel and Keith Curry Lance
The School Library Investigation—Decline or Evolution?

The SLIDE Project

The status of school librarianship is the subject of a three-year research project funded by a Laura Bush 21st Century Librarian grant from the Institute of Museum and Library Services (IMLS) to Antioch University Seattle. The School Librarian Investigation—Decline or Evolution? (SLIDE) began in September 2020. Debra E. Kachel (dkachel@antioch.edu) is the project director and Keith Curry Lance, Ph.D. (keithcurrylance@gmail.com), is the principal investigator.

State Conditions Impacting School Library Employment, 2020

SLIDE's first report, "Contexts of School Librarian Employment," was released in fall 2020 (Kachel and Lance 2021a). It reports the findings of a survey of all 50 states and the District of Columbia. Respondents were designated representatives from a state library association or state library or education agency. The findings informed the analysis of federal school library staffing data and will inform the interpretation of interviews of school-staffing decision makers nationwide beginning in 2022.

The survey asked the following questions:

- Has your state adopted standards or guidelines for school library programs?
- Does your state have certification requirements for school librarians?
- Does your state have any legal requirements for school librarian staffing?
- Does your state have a state government employee assigned specifically to work with school libraries?
- Does any state agency or organization regularly collect school and/or district-level data about school librarian employment?
- Does your state provide direct funding to school libraries for any purpose? (Example: New York provides $6.25 per student directly to each school library.)
- Does your state government provide access to licensed databases or other subscription-based e-resources, including e-books, to all schools in your state?
- List the institutions of higher education in your state that prepare school librarians or provide a link to such a list. Do not list completely online institutions that have no physical campus in your state.

Table 1 reports the answers to these questions state by state. These conditions—particularly the presence or lack of a legal requirement that schools employ school librarians and the number of higher education institutions that train them—help to explain why school librarians are more prevalent in some states than others.

For example, while most states have certification requirements for public school librarians, only ten states plus the District of Columbia require public schools to employ school librarians and enforce that mandate. Sixteen other states require school librarians but do not enforce the requirement. Twenty-four states have no legal requirements for schools to employ school librarians. Five states no longer have any school librarian preparation programs within their states' institutions of higher education. (For lists of higher education institutions preparing school librarians by state, refer to "Contexts of School Librarian Employment" [Kachel and Lance 2021a, 9–10].) Other conditions explored in the report that may be factors in decision making around school-staffing issues will be explored in the SLIDE project's 2022–2023 interviews with school leaders.

Table 1 / Contexts of School Librarian Employment by State, Fall 2020

State	School Library Standards, Guidelines, or Both	School Librarian Certification	State Staffing Mandate	School Library Government Official	State Collected Staffing Data	Direct State Funding *	State Funded E-Resources	Number of Institutions Preparing School Librarians
AK	N	Y	N	FT	Y	N	Y	0
AL	Y	Y	Y	FT	Y	Y	Y	6
AR	Y	Y	Y	PT	Y	YN	Y	3
AZ	N	Y	N	N	Y	N	Y	0
CA	Y	Y	YNE	PT	Y	N	Y	4
CO	Y	N	N	FT	Y	Y	N	2
CT	N	N	N	N	N	N	Y	2
DC	Y	Y	Y	N	N	Y	Y	1
DE	N	Y	N	N	N	N	Y	1
FL	N	Y	N	PT	Y	Y	N	2
GA	N	Y	YNE	PT	N	N	Y	4
HI	Y	Y	N	FT	Y	N	Y	1
IA	Y	Y	YNE	N	Y	N	Y	2
ID	N	N	N	FT	Y	N	Y	2
IL	Y	Y	N	N	N	Y	N	5
IN	Y	Y	YNE	N	N	N	Y	1
KS	Y	Y	YNE	PT	Y	N	Y	3
KY	Y	Y	Y	PT	Y	N	N	4
LA	Y	N	N	N	N	N	N	4
MA	N	Y	N	N	N	N	Y	3
MD	Y	Y	YNE	FT	Y	N	Y	4
ME	N	Y	YNE	PT	N	N	Y	1
MI	N	Y	N	PT	Y	N	Y	1
MN	Y	Y	N	PT	Y	N	Y	3
MO	Y	Y	N	N	Y	N	N	3
MS	Y	Y	Y	FT	Y	N	N	1
MT	Y	Y	Y	N	Y	N	N	2
NC	Y	Y	N	PT	Y	N	Y	5
ND	Y	Y	Y	PT	Y	N	N	2
NE	Y	Y	Y	PT	Y	N	Y	2

Table 1 / Contexts of School Librarian Employment by State, Fall 2020 *(cont.)*

State	School Library Standards, Guidelines, or Both	School Librarian Certification	State Staffing Mandate	School Library Govern-ment Official	State Collected Staffing Data	Direct State Funding *	State Funded E-Resources	Number of Institutions Preparing School Librarians
NH	N	Y	YNE	PT	N	N	N	1
NJ	N	Y	YNE	PT	Y	N	N	3
NM	Y	Y	YNE	N	N	Y	Y	0
NV	Y	Y	N	FT	N	N	Y	1
NY	Y	Y	YNE	FT	Y	Y	Y	6
OH	Y	Y	N	N	N	N	N	1
OK	Y	Y	Y	PT	Y	Y	Y	4
OR	Y	Y	YNE	PT	Y	N	Y	0
PA	Y	Y	N	PT	Y	N	Y	2
RI	N	Y	N	N	Y	N	Y	1
SC	Y	Y	Y	PT	Y	N	Y	1
SD	Y	Y	N	FT	Y	N	Y	2
TN	N	Y	YNE	N	N	Y	Y	6
TX	Y	Y	N	FT	N	N	N	8
UT	Y	Y	N	PT	N	Y	Y	1
VA	Y	Y	YNE	N	N	N	Y	3
VT	N	Y	YNE	N	Y	N	Y	1
WA	Y	Y	YNE	PT	Y	Y	Y	4
WI	Y	Y	Y	FT	Y	Y	Y	3
WV	Y	Y	N	PT	N	Y	Y	1
WY	N	Y	N	FT	Y	N	Y	0

YNE = Yes, but not enforced
DK = Don't know
PT/FT = Part-time / Full-time
* = Competitive funding from LSTA grants excluded
Source: Kachel and Lance (2021a). Contexts of school librarian employment. https://libslide.org/pubs/contexts.pdf.

Status of School Librarian Employment in 2018–2019

SLIDE's second report, "Perspectives on School Librarian Employment in the United States, 2009–10 to 2018–19," is being released in late spring 2021 (Lance and Kachel 2021d).

There were almost 42,280 school librarian full-time equivalents (FTEs) nationwide, according to National Center for Education Statistics (NCES) data for 2018–2019 (the latest available data). Notably, the number of positions represented by that FTE count is unknown. As there are almost 99,000 public schools nationwide, if those librarian FTEs were equally distributed across all schools in all states, the ratio of librarians to schools would be .43 FTE—less than a half-time librarian. Of course, in reality, school librarians are distributed very unequally across the states and across districts based on a variety of characteristics including enrollment, student poverty, per-pupil expenditures, and students' race/

ethnicity, language status, and disability status. These equity issues are a major focus of SLIDE's spring 2021 report, "Perspectives on School Librarian Employment in the United States, 2009–10 to 2018–19" (Lance and Kachel 2021d).

Table 2 presents the latest available data on state-by-state differences in the number of school librarian FTEs and the ratios of school librarian FTEs to schools, students to librarian FTEs, and teacher FTEs to librarian FTEs.

Table 2 / School Librarians in Full-Time Equivalents and Ratios to Schools, Students & Teachers, by State, 2018–2019 School Year

State	School Librarians in Full-Time Equivalents (FTEs)	Total Schools	Ratio of School Librarian FTEs to Schools	Total Student Enrollment	Ratio of Students to School Librarian FTEs	Teachers in Full-Time Equivalents (FTEs)	Ratio of Teacher FTEs to Librarian FTEs
AK	133.60	507	0.26	130,963	980	7,656.78	57
AL	1,322.28	1,528	0.87	739,716	559	42,113.64	32
AR	967.49	1,079	0.90	495,291	512	38,019.16	39
AZ	426.17	2,344	0.18	1,141,511	2,679	48,510.41	114
CA	266.13	10,434	0.03	6,272,734	23,570	271,805.20	1,021
CO	546.26	1,915	0.29	911,536	1,669	53,146.65	97
CT	733.95	1,022	0.72	526,634	718	42,827.56	58
DC	114.75	228	0.50	88,493	771	7,312.33	64
DE	110.00	225	0.49	138,405	1,258	9,623.64	87
FL	1,986.85	4,181	0.48	2,846,444	1,433	164,398.70	83
GA	2,065.00	2,309	0.89	1,767,202	856	117,159.30	57
HI	134.50	292	0.46	181,278	1,348	12,132.10	90
IA	412.46	1,316	0.31	514,833	1,248	35,618.46	86
ID	46.71	746	0.06	310,522	6,648	16,745.31	358
IL	1,444.56	4,345	0.33	1,982,327	1,372	132,423.10	92
IN	575.38	1,916	0.30	1,055,706	1,835	61,154.81	106
KS	676.40	1,314	0.51	497,733	736	36,723.89	54
KY	1,030.74	1,534	0.67	677,821	658	41,826.90	41
LA	978.39	1,383	0.71	711,783	728	38,913.16	40
MA	621.15	1,852	0.34	962,297	1,549	73,868.49	119
MD	1,148.33	1,418	0.81	896,827	781	60,698.90	53
ME	194.30	599	0.32	180,461	929	15,033.90	77
MI	483.54	3,728	0.13	1,504,194	3,111	85,015.36	176
MN	512.66	2,540	0.20	889,304	1,735	57,698.44	113
MO	1,359.63	2,427	0.56	913,441	672	68,498.46	50
MS	762.03	1,054	0.72	471,298	618	31,962.71	42
MT	365.21	823	0.44	148,844	408	10,575.24	29
NC	2,043.05	2,657	0.77	1,552,497	760	100,220.30	49
ND	189.25	522	0.36	113,845	602	9,470.08	50
NE	534.36	1,081	0.49	326,392	611	23,911.60	45
NH	333.60	494	0.68	178,515	535	14,643.50	44
NJ	1,289.97	2,573	0.50	1,400,069	1,085	116,188.60	90
NM	209.92	882	0.24	333,537	1,589	21,139.21	101
NV	257.50	722	0.36	492,640	1,913	23,240.00	90
NY	2,553.65	4,796	0.53	2,700,833	1,058	212,156.90	83
OH	785.87	3,566	0.22	1,695,762	2,158	101,739.40	129
OK	900.89	1,807	0.50	698,891	776	42,447.90	47

Table 2 / School Librarians in Full-Time Equivalents and Ratios to Schools, Students & Teachers, by State, 2018–2019 School Year *(cont.)*

State	School Librarians in Full-Time Equivalents (FTEs)	Total Schools	Ratio of School Librarian FTEs to Schools	Total Student Enrollment	Ratio of Students to School Librarian FTEs	Teachers in Full-Time Equivalents (FTEs)	Ratio of Teacher FTEs to Librarian FTEs
OR	164.73	1,256	0.13	6,09,507	3,700	30,151.69	183
PA	1,599.38	2,969	0.54	1,730,757	1,082	123,350.40	77
RI	193.86	320	0.61	143,436	740	10,749.13	55
SC	1,095.60	1,265	0.87	780,882	713	52,729.50	48
SD	96.18	697	0.14	138,975	1,445	9,865.42	103
TN	1,532.00	1,862	0.82	1,007,624	658	64,116.00	42
TX	4,604.80	8,979	0.51	5.433,471	1,180	359,575.90	78
UT	227.71	1,061	0.21	677,031	2,973	29,753.40	131
VA	1,791.53	2,115	0.85	1,289,367	720	86,973.59	49
VT	197.24	312	0.63	87,074	441	8,316.97	42
WA	1,031.83	2,445	0.42	1,123,736	1,089	61,837.41	60
WI	920.04	2,255	0.41	859,333	925	59,483.65	64
WV	223.24	721	0.31	267,976	1,200	18,911.60	85
WY	77.35	363	0.21	94,313	1,219	7,327.39	95
U.S. Total	42,279.45	98,779	0.43	50,694,061	1,199	3,169,762.14	75
State Average	829.04	1,937	0.47	994,001	1,736	62,152.20	100
State Median	575.38	1,383	0.48	698,891	1,058	42,113.64	77

Source: Lance and Kachel (2021d). "Perspectives on School Librarian Employment in the United States, 2009–10 to 2018–19." https://libslide.org/publications/.

Notes:
A major dataset for the SLIDE project is the Common Core of Data (CCD) of the National Center for Education Statistics (NCES). The data presented here are those reported by NCES for the 2018–2019 school year with some necessary adjustments.

CCD reports school librarians in FTEs at both state and district levels. It does not report school librarians at school (i.e., building) level. Like all other position titles for which it reports FTE data, NCES does not limit its librarian FTE count to state-certified individuals.

The state data file includes imputation for missing data, while the district data file does not. District-level librarian FTE data (not presented here) were adjusted as needed employing a combination of state data files, corrections from SLIDE's state intermediaries, and district-level imputation to fill one-year reporting gaps. If the state total from the district-level data file (including SLIDE adjustments) exceeded the figure NCES reported for a state, the larger district total replaced the smaller figure in the state file.

Visit SLIDE at https://libslide.org for access to both of these reports as well as unprecedented access to state and district-level data on school librarian employment and related district and demographic characteristics. The SLIDE website's interactive data tools enable users to isolate specific data of interest and display them in dynamically generated tables, charts, and maps. Visit the site regularly to stay abreast of the project's publications, presentations, and other communications and to observe how the interactive tools evolve throughout the grant period.

The SLIDE project is made possible in part by IMLS's Laura Bush 21st Century Librarian Grant Project RE-246368-OLS-20.

References and Further Reading

Kachel, Debra. E., and Keith Curry Lance. 2021a. "Contexts of School Librarian Employment." libSLIDE.org. January 26. https://libslide.org/pubs/contexts.pdf.

Kachel, Debra. E., and Keith Curry Lance. 2021b. "Requirements for School Librarian Employment: A State-by-State Summary." libSLIDE.org. January 27. https://libslide.org/pubs/requirements.pdf.

Kachel, Debra E., and Keith Curry Lance. 2021c. "Appendix to Contexts of School Librarian Employment." libSLIDE.org. Last modified February 2, 2021. https://libslide.org/pubs/contextsappendix.pdf.

Lance, Keith Curry, and Debra E. Kachel. Forthcoming, 2021d. "Perspectives on School Librarian Employment in the United States, 2009–10 to 2018–19." Spring. libSLIDE.org. https://libslide.org/publications/.

Library Acquisition Expenditures, 2020–2021: U.S. Public, Academic, Special, and Government Libraries

The information in these tables is taken from the 2021–2022 edition of *American Library Directory* (*ALD*) (Information Today, Inc.). The tables report acquisition expenditures by public, academic, special, and government libraries.

Understanding the Tables

Number of libraries includes only those U.S. libraries in *ALD* that reported annual acquisition expenditures. Libraries that reported annual income but not expenditures are not included in the count. Academic libraries include university, college, and community college libraries. Special academic libraries, such as law and medical libraries, that reported acquisition expenditures separately from the institution's main library are counted as independent libraries.

The amount in the *total acquisition expenditures* column for a given state is generally greater than the sum of the categories of expenditures. This is because the total acquisition expenditures amount also includes the expenditures of libraries that did not itemize by category.

Figures in *categories of expenditure* columns represent only those libraries that itemized expenditures. Libraries that reported a total acquisition expenditure amount but did not itemize are only represented in the total acquisition expenditures column.

Table 1 / Public Library Acquisition Expenditures

State	Number of Libraries	Total Acquisition Expenditures	Category of Expenditures (in U.S. dollars)								
			Books	Other Print Materials	Periodicals/ Serials	Manuscripts & Archives	AV Equipment	AV Materials	Microforms	Electronic Reference	Preservation
Alabama	8	2,201,492	454,706	11,091	6,087	0	4,700	15,004	0	93,541	20,000
Alaska	10	1,861,168	896,450	17,876	85,650	43,021	1,700	292,961	500	229,799	6,871
Arizona	15	16,885,282	2,500,763	88,424	93,330	575	0	1,086,144	0	374,884	0
Arkansas	6	705,549	263,433	250	21,274	500	0	39,307	0	42,186	0
California	45	74,930,748	21,924,223	131,195	1,769,682	6,500	43,417	8,147,923	39,578	17,545,020	68,161
Colorado	12	13,267,558	3,925,626	434,162	363,509	0	15,000	1,951,007	0	2,343,522	0
Connecticut	32	15,127,330	1,984,732	8,138	577,409	4,705	0	474,153	1,080	858,988	39,362
Delaware	2	71,429	40,000	0	5,000	0	0	0	0	0	0
District of Columbia	0	0	0	0	0	0	0	0	0	0	0
Florida	26	22,975,346	10,341,879	844,731	878,789	0	52,514	3,682,273	39,305	5,229,386	0
Georgia	10	2,046,769	838,643	42,253	72,331	0	2,026	252,210	1,850	231,928	198
Hawaii	1	4,242,675	2,491,491	43,698	120,461	0	0	0	43,895	1,120,394	0
Idaho	6	536,487	116,220	1,736	82	0	0	6,261	0	11,360	0
Illinois	68	86,999,801	10,034,097	120,728	447,076	3,000	38,594	2,887,469	9,049	4,501,268	4,000
Indiana	42	24,438,146	8,929,405	800	1,006,032	0	129,340	4,030,149	15,854	5,212,623	0
Iowa	41	4,729,142	1,810,408	55,884	123,293	4,000	1,840	578,892	5,757	503,778	0
Kansas	25	5,154,004	1,089,218	0	126,281	0	4,300	355,612	5,000	98,664	3,600
Kentucky	18	11,860,453	2,288,848	109,345	292,249	0	30,224	917,954	0	1,800,921	40,776
Louisiana	8	11,860,599	3,812,779	58,554	442,098	0	175,561	1,617,159	0	3,317,769	0
Maine	19	1,019,508	312,049	1,000	72,526	2,000	5,000	68,853	800	237,102	1,000
Maryland	2	7,791,058	0	0	0	0	0	0	0	0	0
Massachusetts	44	11,009,938	2,342,481	49,954	294,009	0	2,717	840,904	10,734	547,839	700
Michigan	48	25,968,649	3,507,186	176,532	307,788	0	30,000	1,141,921	10,038	1,079,835	500
Minnesota	17	78,051,055	1,738,299	64,813	20,830	0	83	323,916	3,898	415,231	516
Mississippi	5	819,046	471,781	0	80,664	0	0	28,981	26,000	149,093	2,162
Missouri	23	17,483,546	4,323,905	183,329	309,935	0	10,045	2,074,545	32,651	2,839,069	150

Montana	14	1,016,913	427,571	98,472	65,874	200	4,373	139,490	0	100,382	7,302
Nebraska	20	11,362,958	214,809	119,000	17,966	0	47	43,968	440	756,584	0
Nevada	3	374,744	127,003	0	6,621	0	0	33,388	0	20,000	894
New Hampshire	25	682,410	388,113	1,031	17,578	0	0	98,193	600	67,078	400
New Jersey	38	14,581,999	9,124,676	106,614	736,770	500	21,500	1,602,687	71,000	1,227,449	6,956
New Mexico	12	5,094,445	1,747,932	214,272	46,238	0	6,000	349,258	9,013	557,374	0
New York	75	37,666,177	12,668,417	44,236	794,656	0	219,654	2,187,500	36,653	2,057,022	3,950
North Carolina	7	5,150,057	562,438	0	34,755	0	7,000	156,285	1,040	14,705	0
North Dakota	9	1,276,975	513,503	300	25,579	0	0	97,880	2,000	95,005	1,000
Ohio	39	57,727,218	14,853,906	323,775	2,371,158	133	44,457	7,551,890	245,277	9,460,400	197,013
Oklahoma	13	13,151,317	4,830,502	4,339	858,323	0	3,500	2,311,123	4,095	1,931,596	0
Oregon	16	5,622,156	1,676,871	133,530	149,557	0	3,500	760,371	7,065	1,432,957	0
Pennsylvania	40	19,471,132	3,493,194	848,370	679,195	156,260	1,686	2,123,382	168,335	1,403,062	233,155
Rhode Island	7	9,796,968	573,670	71,214	45,579	0	0	144,170	70	861,204	650
South Carolina	9	29,828,680	2,646,583	31,426	114,500	0	0	4,858,473	0	647,398	0
South Dakota	8	1,553,245	776,440	15,756	19,216	0	16,846	222,695	0	492,833	0
Tennessee	12	469,761,775	23,731,900	276,606	720,857	1,000	2,438,770	8,658,606	0	18,428,323	12,107
Texas	70	46,232,059	4,786,658	2,814	300,330	0	15,827	964,488	11,520	1,311,992	46,700
Utah	7	3,044,276	1,211,389	0	7,000	0	0	666,678	0	326,538	0
Vermont	15	458,371	243,740	90	14,017	215	0	77,967	0	33,122	0
Virginia	21	10,291,043	3,718,398	5,037	304,027	21,260	22,043	1,134,033	16,244	2,195,738	1,336,701
Washington	12	4,498,456	812,665	65,834	60,062	0	975	209,160	622	312,082	400
West Virginia	6	1,014,244	515,558	3,000	47,100	0	0	152,366	13,500	239,356	1,500
Wisconsin	41	5,167,108	1,992,332	72,833	105,848	0	15,952	677,123	2,746	278,325	0
Wyoming	6	7,351,466	97,878	0	4,710	0	0	15,727	0	0	0
Puerto Rico	0	0	0	0	0	0	0	0	0	0	0
Total	1,058	1,204,212,970	178,174,768	4,883,042	15,101,901	243,869	3,366,691	66,050,499	836,209	93,034,725	2,036,724
Estimated % of Acquisition Expenditures			14.79	0.40	1.25	0.02	0.28	5.48	0.07	7.72	0.17

Table 2 / Academic Library Acquisition Expenditures

State	Number of Libraries	Total Acquisition Expenditures	Category of Expenditures (in U.S. dollars)								
			Books	Other Print Materials	Periodicals/ Serials	Manuscripts & Archives	AV Equipment	AV Materials	Microforms	Electronic Reference	Preservation
Alabama	7	4,558,387	330,768	5,899	2,091,716	0	0	20,322	0	1,029,810	21,307
Alaska	2	1,900,000	200,000	20,000	1,600,000	0	0	17,500	2,500	50,000	0
Arizona	3	3,070,069	20,330	0	42,850	0	0	750	0	241,924	0
Arkansas	6	9,920,924	979,276	419,834	5,626,174	34,264	2,000	28,472	426,218	511,257	6,187
California	36	70,350,355	2,915,183	548,107	5,537,721	102,199	6,772	161,477	26,433	10,498,552	122,194
Colorado	9	6,700,154	1,140,926	25,081	487,366	0	100	121,339	0	5,075,903	27,747
Connecticut	7	10,371,628	948,589	15,690	2,640,282	0	80,000	34,922	0	960,490	18,429
Delaware	2	12,839,012	0	0	0	0	0	0	0	0	0
District of Columbia	2	6,803,069	439,600	110,000	1,803,000	0	0	3,267	34,380	1,409,960	47,000
Florida	12	32,001,261	3,396,763	252,370	14,084,355	0	0	269,124	88,340	8,503,416	106,106
Georgia	10	16,802,918	496,693	0	77,733	0	98	26,300	0	1,745,558	300
Hawaii	0	0	0	0	0	0	0	0	0	0	0
Idaho	1	4,318,101	0	0	0	0	0	0	0	0	0
Illinois	23	51,285,272	1,388,334	7,648	2,969,472	0	0	73,667	20,779	2,239,493	69,337
Indiana	10	15,886,978	1,233,233	20,385	4,369,449	0	0	44,306	4,496	2,745,794	21,033
Iowa	13	22,515,257	2,069,601	391,576	5,720,004	0	6,000	53,816	30,353	2,087,613	78,527
Kansas	10	7,398,490	429,807	800	6,041,560	3,000	0	17,181	1,000	625,912	26,150
Kentucky	7	18,947,963	138,841	17,945	1,341,620	0	2,886	1,562	14,722	385,628	4,969
Louisiana	7	4,439,751	238,280	2,935	1,704,474	500	0	4,935	36,508	1,839,629	23,182
Maine	4	10,404,040	1,265,360	177,656	7,565,412	0	0	0	53,849	475,000	32,730
Maryland	13	166,359,023	1,514,628	34,648	8,361,219	12,434	0	39,469	6,642	1,368,821	49,919
Massachusetts	10	23,434,382	953,866	0	2,453,607	36,000	19,011	63,560	1,550	7,327,776	132,781
Michigan	20	22,069,589	1,932,268	65,821	9,013,833	5,203	0	144,896	1,358,172	6,331,014	41,856
Minnesota	8	5,222,234	655,240	10,000	1,694,494	8,200	53,955	79,268	18,459	1,047,655	41,311
Mississippi	1	96,040	10,000	0	2,700	0	0	0	0	83,340	0

Missouri	16	11,633,600	473,143	0	1,784,172	8,767	4,120	101,474	115,045	884,929	31,576
Montana	1	172,720	69,825	0	74,192	0	0	0	0	0	0
Nebraska	6	15,335,842	397,651	89,831	2,205,344	15,000	0	62,021	66,665	1,696,347	16,786
Nevada	0	0	0	0	0	0	0	0	0	0	0
New Hampshire	0	0	0	0	0	0	0	0	0	0	0
New Jersey	9	60,243,579	983,438	0	2,553,516	1,000	0	21,329	0	1,966,247	4,732
New Mexico	3	3,315,114	133,311	0	2,684,913	11,802	0	15,878	16,450	107,334	27,574
New York	32	39,532,249	6,670,347	251,509	10,118,948	29,596	66,463	265,080	48,644	9,373,193	242,392
North Carolina	18	70,468,015	408,217	82,542	920,541	0	1,106,546	112,551	126,798	1,026,945	13,000
North Dakota	2	2,965,537	365,806	0	2,011,935	0	0	30,752	684	539,766	16,594
Ohio	19	31,979,754	2,136,456	0	3,730,466	1,605	9,998	111,382	18,913	964,428	46,952
Oklahoma	5	4,572,162	188,784	575	2,535,231	1,000	0	2,433	0	970,780	4,986
Oregon	6	21,683,521	742,555	0	2,418,862	0	32,779	70,337	0	625,837	18,704
Pennsylvania	18	11,870,621	1,389,958	8,603	2,616,624	1,688	0	77,600	23,791	2,447,291	29,233
Rhode Island	3	1,855,603	439,983	0	925,966	5,840	0	23,270	3,000	450,870	6,674
South Carolina	6	6,381,487	1,021,816	289,130	769,178	20,000	137,300	87,153	60,264	2,450,960	47,510
South Dakota	2	4,668,885	208,108	0	1,716,517	0	718	18,515	2,816	106,460	25,180
Tennessee	8	6,345,282	266,242	0	753,668	0	0	38,858	8,900	808,346	1,613
Texas	26	53,967,619	4,353,015	228,514	15,512,669	5,050	89,327	118,719	67,935	5,004,441	111,716
Utah	3	7,930,967	449,582	0	445,188	0	5,000	35,458	0	206,205	21,249
Vermont	2	1,229,586	161,235	0	985,913	0	0	26,323	0	51,902	4,213
Virginia	10	26,546,240	3,269,091	0	6,680,183	0	0	215,634	11,903	4,570,793	57,528
Washington	7	9,821,770	1,053,338	0	5,985,979	2,000	27,400	46,173	6,000	669,491	5,000
West Virginia	7	2,611,839	140,867	57	63,386	6,750	14,300	11,792	11,017	411,206	7,500
Wisconsin	7	9,654,018	290,606	1,720	633,688	1,879	0	75,861	982	1,549,771	1,755
Wyoming	0	0	0	0	0	0	0	0	0	0	0
Puerto Rico	5	549,862	139,067	5,000	10,372,334	5,000	3,263	1,027,426	0	39,777,149	2,300
Total	444	933,030,769	48,450,027	3,083,876	164,095,454	318,777	1,668,036	3,802,152	2,714,208	133,245,236	1,615,832
Estimated % of Acquisition Expenditures			5.19	0.00	17.59	0.03	0.18	0.41	0.29	14.28	0.17

Table 3 / Special Library Acquisition Expenditures

State	Number of Libraries	Total Acquisition Expenditures	Category of Expenditures (in U.S. dollars)								
			Books	Other Print Materials	Periodicals/ Serials	Manuscripts & Archives	AV Equipment	AV Materials	Microforms	Electronic Reference	Preservation
Alabama	0	0	0	0	0	0	0	0	0	0	0
Alaska	0	0	0	0	0	0	0	0	0	0	0
Arizona	2	5,324	3,500	0	324	0	0	0	0	0	1,000
Arkansas	0	0	0	0	0	0	0	0	0	0	0
California	6	294,464	114,834	0	49,122	600	0	24,090	0	85,088	730
Colorado	0	0	0	0	0	0	0	0	0	0	0
Connecticut	1	1,000	0	0	0	0	0	0	0	0	0
Delaware	0	0	0	0	0	0	0	0	0	0	0
District of Columbia	2	71,000	48,000	0	20,000	0	0	0	2,000	0	1,000
Florida	0	0	0	0	0	0	0	0	0	0	0
Georgia	0	0	0	0	0	0	0	0	0	0	0
Hawaii	0	0	0	0	0	0	0	0	0	0	0
Idaho	0	0	0	0	0	0	0	0	0	0	0
Illinois	4	4,233,500	52,000	30,000	56,500	4,000	0	0	0	49,000	5,000
Indiana	1	95,000	0	0	0	0	0	0	0	0	0
Iowa	1	10,000	0	0	0	0	0	0	0	0	0
Kansas	1	6,000	3,000	0	3,000	0	0	0	0	0	0
Kentucky	0	0	0	0	0	0	0	0	0	0	0
Louisiana	1	18,000	5,000	0	13,000	0	0	0	0	0	0
Maine	0	0	0	0	0	0	0	0	0	0	0
Maryland	1	1,000	500	0	300	100	0	0	0	0	100
Massachusetts	0	0	0	0	0	0	0	0	0	0	0
Michigan	0	0	0	0	0	0	0	0	0	0	0
Minnesota	1	50,000	20,000	5,000	9,000	0	0	0	0	16,000	0
Mississippi	0	0	0	0	0	0	0	0	0	0	0

Missouri	0	0	0	0	0	0	0	0	0	0	0
Montana	0	0	0	0	0	0	0	0	0	0	0
Nebraska	0	0	0	0	0	0	0	0	0	0	0
Nevada	0	0	0	0	0	0	0	0	0	0	0
New Hampshire	2	92,000	16,000	10,000	5,000	20,000	0	0	0	32,000	9,000
New Jersey	2	4,200	1,000	0	0	0	0	0	0	0	200
New Mexico	1	2,500	1,000	0	1,000	0	0	0	0	0	500
New York	8	500,716	257,665	0	47,178	0	4,000	0	0	38,475	152,500
North Carolina	0	0	0	0	0	0	0	0	0	0	0
North Dakota	1	8,098	2,660	0	3,575	0	0	0	0	0	1,463
Ohio	2	572,701	10,666	0	782	1,066	0	100	0	5,832	0
Oklahoma	1	160,000	8,000	0	45,000	0	0	0	0	0	0
Oregon	0	0	0	0	0	0	0	0	0	0	0
Pennsylvania	0	0	0	0	0	0	0	0	0	0	0
Rhode Island	0	0	0	0	0	0	0	0	0	0	0
South Carolina	0	0	0	0	0	0	0	0	0	0	0
South Dakota	1	105,000	0	0	0	0	0	0	0	0	0
Tennessee	0	0	0	0	0	0	0	0	0	0	0
Texas	3	1,583,238	3,030	12,000	2,235	0	285	658	0	805,000	0
Utah	1	75,000	5,000	5,000	10,000	0	5,000	0	0	50,000	0
Vermont	0	0	0	0	0	0	0	0	0	0	0
Virginia	4	183,337	86,409	82	47,060	4,026	0	0	0	44,000	1,740
Washington	1	19,800	7,000	0	10,200	0	0	0	0	0	2,600
West Virginia	0	0	0	0	0	0	0	0	0	0	0
Wisconsin	2	85,500	4,000	0	20,000	0	0	0	0	60,000	0
Wyoming	0	0	0	0	0	0	0	0	0	0	0
Puerto Rico	0	0	0	0	0	0	0	0	0	0	0
Total	50	8,177,378	649,264	62,082	343,736	29,792	9,285	24,848	2,000	1,185,395	175,833
Estimated % of Acquisition Expenditures			7.94	0.76	4.20	0.36	0.11	0.30	0.02	14.50	2.15

Table 4 / Government Library Acquisition Expenditures

State	Number of Libraries	Total Acquisition Expenditures	Books	Other Print Materials	Periodicals/ Serials	Manuscripts & Archives	AV Equipment	AV Materials	Microforms	Electronic Reference	Preservation
Alabama	1	275,000	75,000	0	0	0	0	0	0	200,000	0
Alaska	0	0	0	0	0	0	0	0	0	0	0
Arizona	1	2,012	2,000	0	12	0	0	0	0	0	0
Arkansas	0	0	0	0	0	0	0	0	0	0	0
California	4	539,005	234,264	0	1,442	0	0	0	0	145,582	0
Colorado	0	0	0	0	0	0	0	0	0	0	0
Connecticut	0	0	0	0	0	0	0	0	0	0	0
Delaware	0	0	0	0	0	0	0	0	0	0	0
District of Columbia	0	0	0	0	0	0	0	0	0	0	0
Florida	0	0	0	0	0	0	0	0	0	0	0
Georgia	0	0	0	0	0	0	0	0	0	0	0
Hawaii	0	0	0	0	0	0	0	0	0	0	0
Idaho	0	0	0	0	0	0	0	0	0	0	0
Illinois	0	0	0	0	0	0	0	0	0	0	0
Indiana	0	0	0	0	0	0	0	0	0	0	0
Iowa	0	0	0	0	0	0	0	0	0	0	0
Kansas	1	515,260	26,852	0	396,491	0	0	0	0	85,690	6,227
Kentucky	0	0	0	0	0	0	0	0	0	0	0
Louisiana	1	1,627,826	524,121	0	11,796	0	0	0	887	221,858	8,034
Maine	1	380,116	0	0	0	0	0	0	0	0	0
Maryland	1	37,000	5,000	0	32,000	0	0	0	0	0	0
Massachusetts	0	0	0	0	0	0	0	0	0	0	0
Michigan	0	0	0	0	0	0	0	0	0	0	0
Minnesota	1	74,500	10,000	0	45,500	0	0	0	0	19,000	0

Mississippi	0	0	0	0	0	0	0	0	0	0
Missouri	0	0	0	0	0	0	0	0	0	0
Montana	0	0	0	0	0	0	0	0	0	0
Nebraska	0	0	0	0	0	0	0	0	0	0
Nevada	0	0	0	0	0	0	0	0	0	0
New Hampshire	0	0	0	0	0	0	0	0	0	0
New Jersey	0	0	0	0	0	0	0	0	0	0
New Mexico	0	0	0	0	0	0	0	0	0	0
New York	0	0	0	0	0	0	0	0	0	0
North Carolina	0	0	0	0	0	0	0	0	0	0
North Dakota	0	0	0	0	0	0	0	0	0	0
Ohio	0	0	0	0	0	0	0	0	0	0
Oklahoma	0	0	0	0	0	0	0	0	0	0
Oregon	0	0	0	0	0	0	0	0	0	0
Pennsylvania	125,000	0	0	0	0	0	0	0	1	125,000
Rhode Island	0	0	0	0	0	0	0	0	0	0
South Carolina	0	0	0	0	0	0	0	0	0	0
South Dakota	0	0	0	0	0	0	0	0	0	0
Tennessee	0	0	0	0	0	0	0	0	0	0
Texas	0	0	0	0	0	0	0	0	0	0
Utah	0	0	0	0	0	0	0	0	0	0
Vermont	0	0	0	0	0	0	0	0	0	0
Virginia	0	0	0	0	0	0	0	0	0	0
Washington	0	0	0	0	0	0	0	0	0	0
West Virginia	50,000	0	400,000	0	0	0	200,000	0	1	650,000
Wisconsin	10,000	0	0	0	0	0	0	0	1	10,000
Wyoming	0	0	0	0	0	0	0	0	0	0
Puerto Rico	0	0	0	0	0	0	0	0	0	0
Total	927,237	0	887,241	0	0	887	872,130	14,261	14	4,235,719
Estimated % of Acquisition Expenditures	21.89	0.00	20.94	0.00	0.00	0.02	20.59	0.34		

Year in Architecture 2020

Emily Puckett Rodgers and *Library Journal* staff

2020 Visions

Despite the delays and complications of the pandemic, many libraries persevered to debut new and renovated buildings this year. Playful, dynamic lighting, relaxed and inviting outdoor spaces, light-filled and visible interiors with embedded technology, and smart, sustainable infrastructure are this year's top trends. Digital screens, kitchens, short-throw projectors, haptic play spaces, and mobile displays join makerspaces and lounges to offer opportunities for synchronous and asynchronous engagement and learning. Creative uses of felted ceiling panels and wall tiles keep sightlines open but ensure sound stays put. And lush fabrics, area rugs, and artwork provide depth, texture, and comfort. Simply put, these libraries are bold, smart, and supple. They celebrate the past and envision the future through thoughtful design.

Vivacious and Vivid

With bold, backlit signage, translucent "LIBRARY" treatments emblazoned on curtain walls and windows, and color changing LED lighting, this year's libraries show how 21st-century technology can create environmentally efficient but eye-catching spaces that dynamically draw people in. The Melrose Branch Library of the Roanoke Public Libraries in Melrose, Virginia, for instance, offers neon colors that backlight the metal grate facade and complement the marquee-style sign.

Public and academic libraries alike are using suspended LED lighting to create bold, eye-catching displays that feature organic or geometric shapes and visually dialog with furniture or other colors within a room. The playful dynamic continues inside the Melrose Branch with arrow-shaped LED suspended lights offset by punchy coral accents, complementing coral and teal geometric vinyl floors. Squares of LED suspended lighting and layers of drop ceiling treatments offer acoustic balance and delineate spaces.

This kind of visual experience and invitation to delight are no longer reserved for children's areas. Yes, the Northeast Regional Branch of Louisville Free Public Library in Kentucky features a slide and reading nooks with bold red and pink shapes in the children's area. But it also features a "river of books," an all face-out display created from custom millwork, to show off new materials on a gently sloping surface that connects the library's community pavilion to the collection.

Emily Puckett Rodgers is space design and assessment librarian at the University of Michigan Library.

Originally published in *Library Journal*, November 19, 2020. Data appearing in the tables are based on *Library Journal's* survey of academic and public libraries for which new builds and renovation/addition projects were completed between July 1, 2019, and June 30, 2020. For additional information and content, visit libraryjournal.com.

Custom millwork and woodwork abound, carrying a cohesive design aesthetic throughout, from graphic motifs to wall and ceiling treatments and displays, desks, and cabinetry. At the Community Library in Ketchum, Idaho, snowflake-like accents of blond wood on the ceilings and walls carry into the children's area, where custom wooden reading nooks offer picturesque views. A whimsical but functional book ladder serves a floor-to-ceiling bookcase in the lecture hall.

At Ohio's Toledo Lucas County Public Library's main building, the historic art deco Central Court served as design inspiration for the 104,631-square-foot renovation. Designers used the art deco motifs and colors in the Court as foundation for new millwork, including displays, service desks, and other cabinetry.

Similarly, a color story provides continuity throughout the 175,656-square-foot Richland Main Library's, Columbia, South Carolina, renovation. Felt walls and ceiling coverings soften the original exposed concrete and provide acoustic balance. Rebuilt shelving, capped in ombre, is particularly captivating at night.

The Waunakee Public Library in Wisconsin is organized on an "X" axis, representing the intersection of the library and community hall. The new 40,000-square-foot building uses wood-clad ceiling, trim, and shelving and graphics to reinforce continuity across its versatile programming spaces. The playful graphics appear in a custom wall-mounted display and sound panels in the children's areas and as a translucent applique to glassed-in study and meeting rooms.

Light, Sound, and Scale

Both renovations and new buildings continue to find ways to bring light into and through the building, from truss-supported curtain walls, to clerestories, lightwells, and saw-toothed rooftop light monitors.

At the Ankeny Kirkendall Public Library in Iowa, crisp white walls and subtle wood accents on stairwells, drop ceiling features, and endcapped shelving join light brown, gray, and cool teal to frame vignettes, like the vibrant children's area. An enclave of sculptural vibrant blue, gray, and green felted ceiling panels hang above a play area with rounded poufs, built-in displays and bookshelves, and playful cutouts.

While exposed ducting, lighting, pipes, beams, and electrical spines persist, many of 2020's libraries take advantage of sculptural acoustic panels and drop ceiling panels to control sound and create intimately scaled spaces. At the Billie Jean King Main Library in Long Beach, California, the wood beam ceiling and metal ductwork are interrupted by an L-shaped white gypsum overhang featuring a built-in bookcase and pelican and seabird sculpture. The overhang shelters soft blue pouf seating and child-sized chairs and tables.

Nature and Community

Libraries continue to bring the outdoors in and extend event, seating, and other spaces into their surrounding footprint. While these educational outdoor paths, pavilions, plazas, courtyards, and colonnade covered walkways predate the COVID-19 pandemic, they are perfectly suited for a moment in which patrons cannot linger or gather indoors. Just as fireplaces, rocking chairs, and comfortable lounge-style

(text continues on page 318)

Table 1 / New Public Library Buildings, 2020

Community	Pop. ('000)	Code	Project Cost	Constr. Cost	Gross Area (Sq. Ft.)	Sq. Ft. Cost	Furniture/Equip. Cost	Architect
California								
Corona del Mar	12	B	$7,750,000	$6,730,000	10,315	$652.45	$300,000	WLC Architects
Long Beach	467	M	48,000,000	n.a.	95,720	n.a.	n.a.	Skidmore, Owings & Merrill
San Ysidro	28	B	14,000,000	10,300,000	15,000	686.67	3,700,000	SVA Architects; Turner Construction
Colorado								
Lyons	4	M	3,159,571	2,515,571	6,775	371.30	185,000	RATIO
Illinois								
Lindenhurst	40	M	25,406,475	18,485,137	66,933	276.17	1,774,198	StudioGC architecture+interiors
Indiana								
Indianapolis	13	B	7,560,455	5,027,921	14,701	342.01	592,112	Axis Architecture+Interiors; Meticulous Design+Arch.
Iowa								
Ankeny	67	M	17,602,305	13,147,888	60,710	216.57	1,649,768	OPN Architects
Kansas								
Tonganoxie	5	M	3,511,222	2,337,386	10,000	233.74	168,000	Sapp Design Architects; JE Dunn Construction
Kentucky								
Louisville	175	B	17,800,000	13,584,000	35,511	382.53	750,000	MSR Design; JRA Architects
Louisiana								
Baton Rouge	140	B	21,436,969	18,167,044	48,490	374.66	1,653,602	WHLC Architecture; Schwartz/ Silver Architects
Maryland								
Wheaton	160	M	71,060,000	45,000,000	92,000	489.13	2,600,000	Grimm + Parker Architects

Symbol Code: B—Branch Library; M—Main Library

Massachusetts								
Cambridge	105	B	$5,265,400	$4,798,000	10,077	$473.13	$467,400	William Rawn Associates; Arrowstreet Arch. and Design
Springfield	17	B	9,543,833	8,019,225	17,498	458.29	549,513	Johnson Roberts Associates
Nebraska								
Crete	10	M	6,852,067	6,030,275	20,000	301.51	400,000	BVH Architecture
Ogallala	5	M	2,570,606	2,192,735	12,990	168.81	96,903	JEO Architecture, Inc.
New Hampshire								
Madbury	2	M	1,588,079	1,462,204	3,500	417.77	10,000	Placework
Ohio								
Dayton	43	B	9,863,903	6,680,527	24,420	273.57	973,175	Levin Porter Associates Inc.
Massillon	40	B	4,893,602	3,586,578	10,547	340.06	418,285	HBM Architects
Oklahoma								
Bethany	22	B	7,400,000	6,013,099	23,000	261.44	513,472	Dewberry Architects Inc.
Norman	124	B	36,220,765	26,930,724	78,624	342.53	3,464,694	MSR Design; The McKinney Partnership Architects
South Carolina								
James Island	43	B	11,953,000	7,100,000	19,549	363.19	4,203,000	MSR Design; Cummings & McCrady, Inc
Virginia								
Henrico	61	B	28,372,496	21,367,074	44,803	476.91	5,268,956	Quinn Evans
Wisconsin								
Waunakee	17	M	14,550,000	10,660,000	39,400	270.56	900,000	OPN Architects

Symbol Code: B—Branch Library; M—Main Library

Table 2 / Public Library Buildings, Additions and Renovations, 2020

Community	Pop. ('000)	Code	Project Cost	Constr. Cost	Gross Area (Sq. Ft.)	Sq. Ft. Cost	Furniture/Equip. Cost	Architect
Colorado								
Eagle	40	B	$3,670,425	$4,334,114	6,000	$722.35	$44,665	Studiotrope
Ridgway	3	M	2,035,290	1,753,000	7,380	237.53	45,000	RATIO
Salida	10	M	1,954,000	1,753,000	7,294	240.33	45,000	RATIO
Georgia								
Atlanta	27	B	2,040,112	1,624,590	9,740	166.80	237,713	720 design; CPL Architecture, Engineering & Planning
Atlanta	23	B	2,014,715	1,427,406	10,920	130.71	285,740	720 design; CPL Architecture, Engineering & Planning
Atlanta	34	B	1,657,205	1,427,406	10,000	142.74	249,868	720 design; CPL Architecture, Engineering & Planning
Atlanta	31	B	1,511,589	1,321,613	7,500	176.22	164,850	720 design; CPL Architecture, Engineering & Planning
Atlanta	22	B	1,223,343	1,133,661	8,660	130.91	176,939	720 design; CPL Architecture, Engineering & Planning
College Park	25	B	1,425,762	1,192,042	9,000	132.45	207,866	720 design; CPL Architecture, Engineering & Planning
Idaho								
Ketchum	5	M	11,800,000	9,850,000	29,132	338.12	1,100,000	RATIO
Illinois								
Broadview	8	M	6,960,000	5,600,000	19,544	286.53	503,000	Dewberry
Carol Stream	60	M	5,420,000	4,300,000	37,000	116.22	700,000	Product Architecture + Design
Chicago	51	B	2,500,000	2,200,000	12,525	175.65	300,000	City of Chicago Dep't of Assets, Information and Services
Vernon Hills	27	B	6,750,000	5,920,000	27,750	213.33	350,000	Product Architecture + Design
Wauconda	14	M	1,200,000	1,017,000	15,000	67.80	75,000	Product Architecture + Design

Symbol Code: B—Branch Library; BS—Branch & System Headquarters; M—Main Library; MS—Main & System Headquarters; n.a.—not available

State / City		No.	1	2	3	4	5	Architect
Indiana								
Indianapolis	B	71	1,683,256	1,294,523	13,235	97.81	211,496	R and B Architects
Iowa								
Carroll	M	12	4,519,880	3,699,916	19,995	185.88	421,930	OPN Architects
Knoxville	M	7	3,915,719	3,082,339	18,230	168.62	241,994	FEH Design
Kansas								
Olathe	B	135	19,000,000	15,000,000	46,000	326.09	2,500,000	Group 4 Architecture, Research + Planning; Gould Evans
Louisiana								
Covington	MS	30	2,000,000	n.a.	4,000	n.a.	550,000	Burgdahl & Graves Architects
Metairie	B	38	1,900,157	1,673,311	10,000	167.33	227,146	Sizeler Thompson Brown Architects
Maryland								
Baltimore	M	620	119,900,000	96,200,000	290,000	331.72	5,500,000	Beyer Blinder Belle; Ayers Saint Gross; Sandra Vicchio & Assoc.
Massachusetts								
Weston	B	12	4,736,044	4,312,743	8,100	532.44	n.a.	LLB Architects
Minnesota								
Bloomington	B	83	6,350,000	4,630,000	14,423	321.02	450,000	LSE Architects
Eden Prairie	B	64	11,210,000	7,593,000	41,000	185.20	1,767,000	MSR Design
Lakeville	B	68	5,400,000	4,100,000	29,000	141.38	827,000	HGA
Minneapolis	B	37	8,500,000	6,275,000	13,186	475.88	450,000	MacDonald & Mack Architects
Minneapolis	B	50	4,400,000	2,800,000	10,000	280.00	500,000	LEO A DALY
Montana								
Sidney	M	11	1,923,241	1,782,977	10,000	178.30	44,266	SDI Architects + Design
New York								
Port Washington	M	31	224,289	178,700	11,000	16.25	36,946	Steven Zalben
Ohio								
Elyria	BS	18	2,319,447	1,406,630	8,443	166.60	149,325	CBLH Design, Inc.

Symbol Code: B—Branch Library; BS—Branch & System Headquarters; M—Main Library; MS—Main & System Headquarters; n.a.—not available

Table 2 / Public Library Buildings, Additions and Renovations, 2020 (cont.)

Community	Pop. ('000)	Code	Project Cost	Constr. Cost	Gross Area (Sq. Ft.)	Sq. Ft. Cost	Furniture/Equip. Cost	Architect
LaGrange	12	B	1,978,096	1,461,500	5,998	243.66	89,796	CBLH Design, Inc.
Medina	40	M	1,531,940	1,067,984	13,120	81.40	214,050	CBLH Design, Inc.
New Philadelphia	55	MS	5,032,907	3,776,719	27,007	139.84	621,328	HBM Architects
Toledo	428	MS	12,255,255	8,630,753	104,631	82.49	686,654	HBM Architects
Pennsylvania								
Hershey	25	M	1,379,555	1,131,875	13,530	83.66	20,000	Chris Dawson Architect
Rhode Island								
Providence	179	MS	28,000,000	24,000,000	85,000	282.35	1,100,000	designLAB architects
South Carolina								
Columbia	416	M	20,060,195	12,914,764	175,656	73.52	4,522,646	BOUDREAUX; McMillan Pazdan Smith; Margaret Sullivan Studio
Columbia	53	B	4,708,563	3,101,924	20,075	154.52	717,244	BOUDREAUX; McMillan Pazdan Smith; Margaret Sullivan Studio
Texas								
College Station	114	B	8,056,000	6,222,189	28,206	220.60	1,014,850	Komatsu Architecture
Vermont								
Shelburne	8	M	6,782,035	5,774,773	19,221	300.44	133,542	Vermont Integrated Architecture, PC
Virginia								
Melrose	100	B	4,137,242	3,022,522	13,090	230.90	217,420	Enteros Design, PC
Wisconsin								
Sauk City	6	M	2,300,000	600,000	9,600	62.50	50,000	MSA Professional Services, Inc
Wyoming								
Glenrock	5	B	1,407,560	993,060	14,339	69.26	178,500	RATIO

Symbol Code: B—Branch Library; BS—Branch & System Headquarters; M—Main Library; MS—Main & System Headquarters; n.a.—not available

Table 3 / Academic Library Buildings, Additions and Renovations, 2020

Institution	Project Cost	Gross Area (Sq. Ft.)	Sq. Ft. Cost	Constr. Cost	Furniture/ Equip. Cost	Seating Capacity	Architect
Hayden Library, Arizona State University, Tempe, Ariz.	$90,000,000	252,600	$273.16	$69,000,000	n.a.	n.a.	Ayers Saint Gross
Price Gilbert Memorial Library and Crosland Tower, Georgia Institute of Technology, Atlanta, Ga.	84,200,000	222,816	308.77	68,800,000	6,400,000	2,360	BNIM; Praxis3
Allison and Howard Lutnick Library, Haverford College, Haverford, Pa.	32,556,446	62,950	453.06	28,520,337	1,012,996	654	Perry Dean Rogers Partners Architects
Leonard Lief Library, Lehman College, Bronx, N.Y.	20,002,000	54,426	267.19	14,542,000	1,504,238	596	H2M Architects + Engineers
Pattee and Paterno Library, Penn State University, University Park, Pa.	16,750,000	29,100	474.23	13,800,000	750,000	532	WTW Architects
Moffett Library, Midwestern State University, Wichita Falls, Tex.	5,993,022	88,500	66.45	5,880,985	340,870	901	Steinberg Hart
Clifton W. Everett Library, Pitt Community College, Winterville, N.C.	3,451,888	30,000	115.06	3,451,888	n.a.	n.a.	MHAworks
The Commons at Horn Library, Babson College, Wellesley, Mass.	n.a.	35,000	514.29	18,000,000	n.a.	500	Finegold Alexander Architects

(continued from page 311)

seating have become staples of library design, so are residential elements of outdoor design. String lights, umbrellas, and picnic benches mimic backyard settings.

Meanwhile, biophilic interior design elements such as organic, moss-like carpeting and plush nature-hued fabrics soften and balance geometric and angular features. Many libraries extend building cladding, such as stone or wood, into interior spaces.

Ceiling panels in shades of green cover the length of the children's area at the Carol Stream Public Library, Illinois, spreading from a green felt-covered pillar reminiscent of a tree. Graphic wall treatments feature mostly black and gray tree trunks while carpeting features purple, yellow, and gray panels reminiscent of pebbles or lichen. The renovation also uses masonry walls to bring light into the floor plate and connect the interior to the adjacent wooded area and nature walk. String lights and picnic tables offer a casual seating experience outside.

The Northeast Regional Branch of Louisville Free Public Library in Kentucky features wide polished concrete social staircases with amphitheater-style seating to transition from collections to café. The stairs extend through the glass curtain wall, blending the interior and exterior. The new building features a community pavilion of several interconnected spaces that host a maker/active learning space, a teaching kitchen, green room, sound studio, café, meeting rooms, technology counter, and pre-function space. All connect to a covered outdoor patio and a plaza that in turn links the library to a surrounding park and walking paths.

The new Lake Villa District Library in Lindenhurst, Illinois, features a cutstone exterior facade in light shades of clay, gray, and cream. Carpet tiles and wall treatments bring the pattern and color palette of the stone into the interior of the main circulation area, anchored by crisp white walls and cool gray furnishings. Pops of bright green and blue endcapped shelving draw attention to programmed areas within the library, visible through punch out glass walls.

Balancing Act

Pavilions enable libraries to pack a programming punch into their offerings for specialized communities and activities such as life skills, early literacy, cultural learning, making, or quiet reading. Renovations and new construction alike organize activities to balance acts of creative collision and calming contemplation. High and low technology meet to offer a variety of experiences tailored to diverse communities.

At the new 44,803-square-foot Fairfield Area Library in Henrico County, Virginia, lightwells illuminate a dramatic, brightly colored seating area for caregivers in the children's area while organic reading nooks embedded in the walls offer a lush retreat for children. Between the children's and teens area sits a Family Collaboration Zone that connects the two. A Creation Classroom features durable finishes, ceiling-mounted, pull-down electrical outlets, and a kitchenette.

In Tempe, at Arizona State University, the Hayden Library's "Reinvention" maintained the mid-century modern shell and unique interior features like the wood balustrade with stainless steel inlay on the existing terrazzo central stairs while adding the technology, sustainable infrastructure, and spaces such as collaborative lounges and reading nooks that support 21st-century scholarship. The $90 million project uses a shared color palette to reinforce the connection between old and new, and glass-paneled interior walls offer views into technology-infused active learning classrooms and book arts and printmaking studios. Native landscaping and additional seating bring the library's footprint further into campus.

Allison and Howard Lutnick Library at Haverford College in Pennsylvania features vaulted ceilings in both original and renovated reading rooms, aligning past, present, and future. The original library had undergone a series of ad hoc renovations in the past, creating a disorienting sequence of spaces. The latest renovation updated and added 32,380 square feet of space, restoring the older "heritage" spaces and combining them with warm, well-lit contemporary learning ones. Plush area rugs and live edge conference tables bring a sense of warmth and liveliness.

In Baltimore, Maryland, the Enoch Pratt Free Library's 1933 Art Deco building now features a job and career center, a space dedicated to teens, and a Creative Arts Center. Historic elements, rooms, and materials were restored while updating invisible infrastructure. Black steel and glass walls delicately create new spaces in large, open areas and technology-rich rooms rise from floors to just below restored painted support beams.

Through color, form, and function, these libraries epitomize joyful expression. The palettes are lush, consistent, and expressive. By creating multifunctional, highly adaptive spaces that can tailor services and activities to distinct communities, these libraries bring a multilayered, sophisticated response to what it means to be "flexible" and "future-focused."

Table 4 / Six-Year Cost Summary

	Fiscal 2015	Fiscal 2016	Fiscal 2017	Fiscal 2018	Fiscal 2019	Fiscal 2020
Number of new buildings	38	33	26	20	29	23
Number of ARRs	54	59	44	37	49	44
Sq. ft. new buildings	896,195	831,110	616,436	775,395	799,232	760,563
Sq. ft. ARRs	1,222,795	1,297,229	1,090,370	936,894	908,624	1,293,490
New Buildings						
Construction cost	$274,900,907	$257,213,872	$207,532,385	$250,938,025	$184,280,310	$240,135,448
Equipment cost	26,895,130	37,522,113	21,316,125	28,190,468	19,425,446	30,638,078
Site cost	12,031,896	19,242,482	6,968,634	12,993,856	12,608,571	17,615,968
Other cost	68,193,630	73,601,931	41,281,588	53,008,395	33,743,217	41,936,956
Total—Project cost	360,746,279	397,152,182	309,498,732	360,630,814	445,147,544	376,340,748
ARRs—Project cost	311,990,635	237,347,021	299,877,478	193,355,042	199,979,075	347,773,822
New and ARR Project Cost	$672,736,914	$634,499,203	$609,376,210	$553,985,856	$645,126,619	$724,114,570

Symbol Code: ARR—Additions, Renovations, and Remodels

Table 5 / Funding Sources

	Fiscal 2015	Fiscal 2016	Fiscal 2017	Fiscal 2018	Fiscal 2019	Fiscal 2020
Federal, new buildings	$475,000	$350,000	$25,260,000	$500,000	$7,462,157	$1,000,000
Federal, ARRs	1,500,000	2,423,000	0	179,000	3,659,656	450,000
Federal, total	$1,975,000	$2,773,000	$25,260,000	$679,000	$11,121,813	$1,450,000
State, new buildings	$15,169,766	$15,025,234	$3,994,000	$31,590,106	$3,414,869	$14,703,915
State, ARRs	5,251,244	2,787,038	18,570,711	5,818,200	10,625,887	106,571,274
State, total	$20,421,010	$17,812,272	$22,564,711	$37,408,306	$14,040,756	$121,275,189
Local, new buildings	$331,311,400	$371,719,254	$271,148,486	$314,825,218	$154,816,713	$273,497,343
Local, ARRs	244,614,937	199,559,402	237,888,791	182,254,371	107,203,069	142,701,893
Local, total	$575,926,337	$571,278,656	$509,037,277	$497,079,589	$262,019,782	$416,199,236
Gift, new buildings	$24,430,676	$14,388,312	$10,626,623	$21,435,733	$13,611,075	$12,870,545
Gift, ARRs	63,353,240	32,636,393	43,448,173	5,549,824	30,870,546	42,630,986
Gift, total	$87,783,916	$47,024,705	$54,074,796	$26,985,557	$44,481,621	$55,501,531
Total—Funds Used	$686,106,263	$638,888,633	$610,936,784	$562,152,452	$331,663,972	$594,425,956

Symbol Code: ARR—Additions, Renovations, and Remodels

Public Library State Rankings, 2018

State	Library visits per capita[1]	Registered users per capita[1]	Total circulation[2] per capita[1]	Reference transactions per capita[1]
Alabama	43	28	46	15
Alaska	22	8	24	38
Arizona	38	41	29	49
Arkansas	37	16	40	8
California	35	24	37	47
Colorado	9	13	6	26
Connecticut	2	44	23	7
Delaware	29	51	35	44
District of Columbia	16	6	28	4
Florida	39	25	42	5
Georgia	50	47	50	18
Hawaii	51	6	48	50
Idaho	6	9	7	9
Illinois	11	46	13	11
Indiana	18	33	3	25
Iowa	10	9	15	38
Kansas	12	5	8	16
Kentucky	34	19	27	11
Louisiana	36	33	44	6
Maine	8	28	26	28
Maryland	30	14	11	1
Massachusetts	4	38	17	20
Michigan	26	41	20	11
Minnesota	32	4	12	31
Mississippi	48	31	51	46
Missouri	27	19	9	33
Montana	28	47	32	35
Nebraska	23	3	14	48
Nevada	42	43	33	41
New Hampshire	13	19	18	28
New Jersey	24	40	34	19
New Mexico	25	1	31	24
New York	18	17	30	3
North Carolina	44	19	43	22
North Dakota	41	49	38	21
Ohio	1	2	2	2
Oklahoma	31	14	18	32
Oregon	7	9	1	35
Pennsylvania	39	44	41	26
Rhode Island	14	50	36	35
South Carolina	45	32	39	33
South Dakota	21	39	21	44
Tennessee	46	33	47	41
Texas	49	25	45	38
Utah	20	19	5	10
Vermont	2	37	25	22

State	Library visits per capita[1]	Registered users per capita[1]	Total circulation[2] per capita[1]	Reference transactions per capita[1]
Virginia	33	17	22	11
Washington	17	25	4	43
West Virginia	47	33	49	51
Wisconsin	15	28	10	28
Wyoming	5	9	16	16

State	Public-access Internet computers per 5,000 population[3]	Public-access Internet computers per stationary outlet	Print materials per capita[1]	E-books per capita[1]
Alabama	24	25	37	22
Alaska	7	41	15	18
Arizona	29	2	51	34
Arkansas	28	37	29	33
California	49	13	43	44
Colorado	19	6	40	37
Connecticut	14	22	5	36
Delaware	26	4	47	42
District of Columbia	10	1	48	51
Florida	43	3	49	47
Georgia	41	9	45	49
Hawaii	51	40	31	50
Idaho	9	34	20	43
Illinois	11	14	14	12
Indiana	12	21	10	23
Iowa	3	46	7	4
Kansas	6	43	11	1
Kentucky	22	7	32	7
Louisiana	16	26	26	29
Maine	5	49	1	15
Maryland	38	5	39	45
Massachusetts	31	30	3	11
Michigan	15	17	22	27
Minnesota	30	28	28	31
Mississippi	36	39	36	46
Missouri	42	35	21	28
Montana	17	44	27	21
Nebraska	2	42	9	10
Nevada	50	27	49	48
New Hampshire	21	50	4	5
New Jersey	34	23	19	29
New Mexico	20	29	23	39
New York	27	19	13	20
North Carolina	46	18	43	35
North Dakota	25	45	17	25
Ohio	18	20	12	3
Oklahoma	32	31	34	26

State	Public-access Internet computers per 5,000 population[3]	Public-access Internet computers per stationary outlet	Print materials per capita[1]	E-books per capita[1]
Oregon	40	32	25	14
Pennsylvania	48	36	33	13
Rhode Island	13	16	16	9
South Carolina	37	11	38	39
South Dakota	7	48	8	16
Tennessee	39	12	42	8
Texas	44	8	45	41
Utah	45	24	30	32
Vermont	1	51	2	19
Virginia	33	10	35	17
Washington	35	15	41	38
West Virginia	47	47	24	6
Wisconsin	23	33	18	2
Wyoming	4	38	5	24

State	Audio physical materials per capita[1]	Audio downloadable materials per capita[1]	Video physical materials per capita[1]	Video downloadable materials per capita[1]
Alabama	38	28	42	9
Alaska	17	14	2	20
Arizona	43	25	42	22
Arkansas	38	30	29	22
California	43	43	45	27
Colorado	23	31	20	9
Connecticut	4	36	11	42
Delaware	31	45	35	36
District of Columbia	51	50	45	47
Florida	43	2	39	27
Georgia	50	49	45	42
Hawaii	31	50	49	47
Idaho	21	39	19	47
Illinois	4	18	12	13
Indiana	6	35	8	27
Iowa	10	9	6	36
Kansas	14	5	4	42
Kentucky	31	23	27	13
Louisiana	38	3	15	8
Maine	12	19	10	18
Maryland	23	36	35	13
Massachusetts	7	24	13	9
Michigan	12	26	15	6
Minnesota	23	43	33	42
Mississippi	48	45	44	36
Missouri	19	39	24	27
Montana	31	17	25	47

State	Audio physical materials per capita[1]	Audio downloadable materials per capita[1]	Video physical materials per capita[1]	Video downloadable materials per capita[1]
Nebraska	22	11	20	42
Nevada	41	48	33	27
New Hampshire	10	8	4	13
New Jersey	7	27	18	4
New Mexico	23	38	20	22
New York	17	33	14	36
North Carolina	48	47	51	36
North Dakota	23	15	29	18
Ohio	1	6	1	1
Oklahoma	35	34	35	27
Oregon	14	16	15	27
Pennsylvania	23	4	38	2
Rhode Island	23	20	20	27
South Carolina	41	32	39	22
South Dakota	19	21	27	47
Tennessee	43	12	49	6
Texas	47	41	45	36
Utah	14	22	25	22
Vermont	7	13	8	13
Virginia	35	10	39	9
Washington	30	41	29	27
West Virginia	35	1	29	3
Wisconsin	3	7	6	5
Wyoming	1	29	3	20

State	Total paid FTE staff[4] per 25,000 population[6]	Paid FTE librarians per 25,000 population[6]	Percentage of total FTE librarians with ALA-MLS[5]
Alabama	41	33	35
Alaska	28	27	28
Arizona	47	48	13
Arkansas	36	34	39
California	45	47	5
Colorado	10	28	17
Connecticut	8	4	20
Delaware	40	40	29
District of Columbia	2	23	1
Florida	43	45	10
Georgia	51	51	1
Hawaii	35	41	3
Idaho	15	31	31
Illinois	3	10	22
Indiana	4	14	24
Iowa	16	3	45
Kansas	5	8	37
Kentucky	24	7	47

State	Total paid FTE staff[4] per 25,000 population[6]	Paid FTE librarians per 25,000 population[6]	Percentage of total FTE librarians with ALA-MLS[5]
Louisiana	12	12	38
Maine	14	5	36
Maryland	18	18	32
Massachusetts	19	9	21
Michigan	27	25	19
Minnesota	34	36	25
Mississippi	48	20	51
Missouri	17	35	41
Montana	37	29	42
Nebraska	26	13	48
Nevada	49	50	12
New Hampshire	9	2	30
New Jersey	21	30	4
New Mexico	30	25	34
New York	7	17	14
North Carolina	46	49	6
North Dakota	38	22	40
Ohio	1	15	18
Oklahoma	29	11	44
Oregon	20	32	11
Pennsylvania	39	42	15
Rhode Island	13	16	7
South Carolina	32	38	16
South Dakota	31	18	49
Tennessee	44	46	33
Texas	50	44	23
Utah	33	37	27
Vermont	11	1	43
Virginia	25	39	8
Washington	22	43	9
West Virginia	42	24	50
Wisconsin	23	21	26
Wyoming	6	6	46

State	Total operating revenue[7] per capita[1]	State operating revenue per capita[1]	Local operating revenue per capita[1]	Other operating revenue per capita[1]
Alabama	46	29	46	32
Alaska	9	25	7	30
Arizona	43	41	38	50
Arkansas	38	15	40	23
California	28	36	21	29
Colorado	6	39	5	10
Connecticut	10	40	11	3
Delaware	42	9	41	38
District of Columbia	1	48	1	35
Florida	40	27	37	48

State	Total operating revenue[7] per capita[1]	State operating revenue per capita[1]	Local operating revenue per capita[1]	Other operating revenue per capita[1]
Georgia	50	10	48	46
Hawaii	44	2	51	35
Idaho	25	22	23	18
Illinois	5	13	3	17
Indiana	8	8	8	16
Iowa	23	30	19	20
Kansas	11	19	12	9
Kentucky	22	26	18	33
Louisiana	14	28	10	34
Maine	27	38	34	1
Maryland	16	3	28	8
Massachusetts	19	20	17	15
Michigan	20	22	16	23
Minnesota	26	24	25	14
Mississippi	51	12	50	39
Missouri	15	35	14	22
Montana	37	43	35	42
Nebraska	29	37	24	31
Nevada	35	4	42	41
New Hampshire	18	47	15	19
New Jersey	12	33	9	20
New Mexico	32	16	33	25
New York	2	11	4	2
North Carolina	45	21	44	47
North Dakota	39	14	38	28
Ohio	3	1	31	6
Oklahoma	30	32	26	27
Oregon	4	42	2	13
Pennsylvania	41	7	45	7
Rhode Island	17	5	29	5
South Carolina	36	17	36	49
South Dakota	34	48	30	43
Tennessee	49	46	47	45
Texas	48	48	43	51
Utah	31	33	22	44
Vermont	24	48	27	4
Virginia	33	18	32	40
Washington	7	45	6	21
West Virginia	47	6	49	35
Wisconsin	21	31	20	12
Wyoming	13	44	13	11

State	Total operating expenditures[8] per capita[1]	Salaries and benefits	Total collection expenditures[9]	Other operating expenditures[10]
Alabama	46	14	48	45
Alaska	8	40	20	1
Arizona	43	51	35	33
Arkansas	39	47	39	28
California	27	38	37	15
Colorado	9	44	2	8
Connecticut	6	4	13	14
Delaware	36	42	45	24
District of Columbia	1	3	8	4
Florida	42	49	40	26
Georgia	50	10	50	51
Hawaii	44	32	42	40
Idaho	26	39	26	17
Illinois	5	34	5	3
Indiana	10	48	4	7
Iowa	22	16	17	27
Kansas	12	43	10	6
Kentucky	32	37	22	25
Louisiana	17	46	15	10
Maine	21	20	36	20
Maryland	14	5	9	35
Massachusetts	16	9	11	31
Michigan	25	45	23	13
Minnesota	23	35	25	16
Mississippi	51	26	51	49
Missouri	20	50	6	11
Montana	41	11	41	44
Nebraska	28	27	18	30
Nevada	35	25	29	40
New Hampshire	18	2	24	34
New Jersey	13	8	21	19
New Mexico	34	36	16	39
New York	2	6	14	9
North Carolina	45	13	46	48
North Dakota	38	30	33	42
Ohio	3	41	1	5
Oklahoma	29	31	12	32
Oregon	4	28	7	2
Pennsylvania	39	22	44	37
Rhode Island	15	7	38	18
South Carolina	37	17	32	43
South Dakota	33	23	27	38
Tennessee	49	24	49	46
Texas	47	19	47	50
Utah	30	28	19	29
Vermont	19	15	30	21
Virginia	31	12	34	36
Washington	7	18	3	12

State	Total operating expenditures[8] per capita[1]	Salaries and benefits	Total collection expenditures[9]	Other operating expenditures[10]
West Virginia	48	33	43	47
Wisconsin	24	21	28	23
Wyoming	11	1	31	22

1 Per capita is based on the total unduplicated population of legal service areas. The determination of the unduplicated figure is the responsibility of the state library agency and should be based on the most recent state population figures for jurisdictions in the state.

2 Total circulation is the sum of physical materials circulation and electronic materials circulation.

3 Per 5,000 population is based on the total unduplicated population of legal service areas. The determination of the unduplicated figure is the responsibility of the state library agency and should be based on the most recent state population figures for jurisdictions in the state.

4 Paid staff were reported in FTEs. To ensure comparable data, 40 hours was set as the measure of full-time employment (for example, 60 hours per week of part-time work by employees in a staff category divided by the 40-hour measure equals 1.50 FTEs). FTE data were reported to two decimal places but rounded to one decimal place in the table.

5 ALA-MLS: A master's degree from a graduate library education program accredited by the American Library Association (ALA). Librarians with an ALA-MLS are also included in total librarians.

6 Per 25,000 population is based on the total unduplicated population of legal service areas. The determination of the unduplicated figure is the responsibility of the state library agency and should be based on the most recent state population figures for jurisdictions in the state.

7 Total revenue includes federal, state, local, and other revenue.

8 Total operating expenditures includes total staff expenditures, collection expenditures, and other operating expenditures.

9 Total collection expenditures includes expenditures for print, electronic, and other materials.

10 Other operating expenditures not included in staff or collections.

Note: The District of Columbia, although not a state, is included in the state rankings. Special care should be used in comparing its data to state data. Caution should be used in making comparisons with the state of Hawaii, as Hawaii reports only one public library for the entire state. Additional information on nonsampling error, response rates, and definitions may be found in *Data File Documentation Public Libraries Survey: Fiscal Year 2018.*

Source: IMLS, Public Libraries Survey, FY 2018. Data users who create their own estimates using data from these tables should cite the Institute of Museum and Library Services as the source of the original data only.

Book Trade Research and Statistics

Prices of U.S. and Foreign Published Materials

George Aulisio

Editor, ALA Core Library Materials Price Index Editorial Board

The Library Materials Price Index (LMPI) Editorial Board of Core, a division of the American Library Association, continues to monitor prices for a range of library materials from sources within North America and other key publishing centers around the world.

The U.S. Consumer Price Index (CPI) increased by 1.4 percent in 2020. CPI figures are obtained from the Bureau of Labor Statistics at http://www.bls.gov/.

In 2017 all tables that utilized a base index price increase had their base year reset to 2010. All indexes continue to utilize the 2010 base year. Percent changes in average prices from 2016–2020 are conveniently noted in Chart 1.

Index	Average Price Percent Change				
	2016	2017	2018	2019	2020
U.S. Consumer Price Index	2.1	2.1	1.9	2.3	1.4
U.S. Periodicals (Table 1)	7.1	5.6	5.7	6.7	6.8
Legal Serials Services (Table 2)	9.5	11.7	21.8*	10.9*	21.4
Hardcover Books (Table 3)	0.4	4.9	-11.8	0.9	-2.5
Academic Books (Table 4)	-11.6	16.6	0.0	-0.9	8.3
Academic E-Books (Table 4A)	-5.2	0.6	5.3	0.3	4.9
Academic TextBooks (Table 4B)	-3.1	0.3	-3.2	2.0	2.8
U.S. College Books (Table 5)	3.4	-2.8	-0.6	1.3	13.5
U.S. Mass market paperbacks (Table 6)	2.3	0.8	0.5	2.5	3.5
U.S. Paperbacks (Table 7)	20.3	-23.8	14.9	-15.6	-4.1
U.S. Audiobooks (Table 7A)	-16.7	29.3	14.1	1.6	0.2
U.S. E-Books (Table 7B)	-36.3	-20.3	0.7	0.4	6.5
+Serials (Table 8)	6.0	6.5	6.1*	6.1*	6.0
+Online Serials (Table 8A)	6.2	5.6	6.0*	6.4*	6.3
British academic books (Table 9)	9.9	-0.5	7.0	-1.8	-1.4

* = figures revised from previous editions based on new data

U.S. Published Materials

Tables 1 through 7B indicate average prices and price indexes for library materials published primarily in the United States. These indexes are U.S. Periodicals

(Table 1), Legal Serials Services (Table 2), U.S. Hardcover Books (Table 3), North American Academic Books (Table 4), North American Academic E-Books (Table 4A), North American Academic Textbooks (Table 4B), U.S. College Books (Table 5), U.S. Mass Market Paperback Books (Table 6), U.S. Paperbacks (Excluding Mass Market) (Table 7), U.S. Audiobooks (Table 7A), and U.S. E-Books (Table 7B).

Periodical and Serials Prices

The U.S. Periodical Price Index (USPPI) (Table 1) was reestablished in 2014 by Stephen Bosch, University of Arizona, and is here updated for 2021 using data supplied by EBSCO Information Services. This report includes 2017–2021 data indexed to the base year of 2010. Table 1 is derived from a selected set of titles that, as much as possible, will remain as the sample base for the index for future comparisons. The data in Table 1 are from a print preferred data pull, but over 52 percent of the titles in the index are based on online pricing, and only 26 percent are print only so that the data provide a strong mix of both print and online pricing, characteristic of a current academic library's serials collection. The subscription prices used are publishers' list prices, excluding publisher discount or vendor service charges. The pricing data for 2010–2014, the base years for the new USPPI, published in 2014, was created from one single report that pulled pricing information for a static set of titles for the five-year period. The pricing data for 2017–2021 is based on that same sampling of titles but is not an exact match due to changes that occur with serial titles. Some titles fell off the list due to pricing not being available, while other titles on the list for which pricing had not been available in 2014 now have pricing available.

The new USPPI treats a little more than 6,000 titles in comparison with the original title list, which covered only about 3,700 titles. The previous versions of the USPPI treated Russian translations as a separate category. Russian translations are no longer a focus of this index and are not tracked as a category. These were once seen as a major cost factor, but this is no longer the case, and therefore their inclusion in or exclusion from the index no longer makes sense. There are Russian translation titles in the index, but they are not reported separately.

The main barrier to creating this index is the difficulty of maintaining the title list and obtaining standard retail pricing for titles on the list. Changes in serials titles due to ceased publication, movement to open access, mergers, combining titles in packages, moving to direct orders, and publication delays are a few of the situations that can affect compilers' ability to obtain current pricing information. The new index retained that part of the title list from the previous index that remained viable and added new titles to that list based on data from EBSCO on the most frequently ordered serials in their system. From that list of serials, titles were selected for the new index to ensure that the distribution by subject was similar to the distribution in the original index. There are more titles in the selected title set than the number of titles that produced prices over the past six years. This should allow the current index to be sustainable into the future as titles fall off the list and pricing becomes available for titles that may have been delayed or are no longer in memberships.

The first five years of data, published in 2014, showed consistent price changes across subject areas due to the fact that the pricing data represented a historical look at the prices of the same set of journals. The data for 2017–2021 is based on the same sample list but is not the exact same list of titles as the data for 2010–2014 due to the issues mentioned above that can impact pricing availability. Across subject areas, the changes in price were significantly lower this year, reflecting the impact of the pandemic, showing an overall 2.3 percent increase. This is slightly lower than price changes seen in other pricing studies (see Table 8), which nearly all show a 3–4 percent increase. The 2.3 percent increase for 2021 is a marked decrease from the 6.7 percent increase seen in 2020. At the subject level, the sample sizes are smaller, so a few changes can cause a large swing in the overall price for that area. In 2021 price increases were consistent across subjects. There was only a variation from -3.6 to 4.3 percent as compared to the 2020 variance from 9.0 to 3.1 percent.

Direct comparisons between Table 1 and Table 8 should be avoided, especially at the subject level. Both tables show the overall rate of increase in serial prices to be around 3 percent; however, beyond that point, there is little that makes a statistically valid comparison. Table 8 has slightly higher overall average prices and higher prices in most subject areas. This is due to Table 8's larger set of data coming from a broad mix of sources including a much larger set of journals from foreign sources and a higher mix of STM titles. Table 1 is a mix of journals that attempts to reflect the journal collections in an average U.S. library, so the mix of journals contains more trade and popular titles than Table 8. Table 8 has more foreign titles and prices, which can be impacted by the strength of the U.S. dollar. Differences in the two datasets yield different results.

The most important trend seen in this data (Table 1) is that the consistent increases in prices that have averaged around 6 percent since 2010 have collapsed due to the impact of the pandemic on library budgets. Price increases for 2021 were half of what has been the norm for the past ten years. This year, titles in social science subjects (except for technology) dominate the list of areas with larger price increases but even those top out in the 3–4 percent range well below increases seen in the last decade. Average prices for journals in the science and technology area are still far higher than in other areas, and that trend continues, with the average cost of chemistry journals being $5,883.69 and of physics journals being $4,983.40.

In this price index, as with similar indexes, the accuracy of the average price percent change is closely tied to the number of titles in the sample size. Average price changes are far more volatile when utilizing small datasets. For that reason, conclusions drawn regarding price changes in subject areas with a limited number of titles will be less accurate than for large areas or the broader price index. For example, technology journal prices went up 4.1 percent this year but to conclude that all journals in the technology area will increase a similar amount in the coming year is likely incorrect. If a specific inflation figure for a small subject area were needed, it would be better to look at an average over a longer period or the overall number for the price study (2.3 percent) than to use the actual numbers year-by-year. The variation in pricing is too volatile in smaller sample sizes to be

(text continues on page 336)

Table 1 / U.S. Periodicals: Average Prices and Price Indexes, 2017–2021

Index Base 2010 = 100

Subject	LC Class	Titles	2010 Average Price	2017 Average Price	2018 Average Price	2019 Average Price	2020 Average Price	2021 Average Price	Percent Change 2020–2021	Index
Agriculture	S	241	$579.48	$986.13	$1,036.38	$1,108.28	$1,173.76	$1,216.54	3.6%	209.9
Anthropology	GN	54	373.64	534.23	567.65	604.61	632.59	652.36	3.1	174.6
Arts and Architecture	N	102	112.39	235.43	253.95	266.12	280.99	287.49	2.3	255.8
Astronomy	QB	29	1,793.08	2,600.94	2,747.68	2,873.15	3,068.11	2,956.53	-3.6	164.9
Biology	QH	420	2,053.06	3,014.94	3,181.34	3,380.48	3,554.67	3,619.48	1.8	176.3
Botany	QK	67	1,361.09	1,959.81	2,044.45	2,137.72	2,236.78	2,279.02	1.9	167.4
Business and Economics	HA-HJ	471	351.29	607.77	642.71	686.89	732.33	747.00	2.0	212.6
Chemistry	QD	156	3,396.26	4,769.18	5,052.35	5,407.17	5,789.22	5,883.69	1.6	173.2
Education	L	235	354.92	627.92	669.85	721.79	771.29	804.69	4.3	226.7
Engineering	T	567	1,244.39	2,050.37	2,178.10	2,339.61	2,517.49	2,583.59	2.6	207.6
Food Science	TX	46	356.17	785.80	874.78	918.54	995.71	1,032.36	3.7	289.9
General Science	Q	98	998.51	1,713.00	1,816.93	1,941.06	2,061.19	2,114.44	2.6	211.8
General Works	A	116	85.84	120.56	123.69	131.92	138.98	144.10	3.7	167.9
Geography	G-GF	88	670.60	1,132.40	1,200.02	1,289.83	1,383.22	1,438.81	4.0	214.6
Geology	QE	77	1,368.79	1,868.25	1,921.99	2,084.05	2,220.27	2,284.57	2.9	166.9
Health Sciences	R	911	1,009.55	1,633.56	1,728.81	1,850.41	1,996.87	2,060.95	3.2	204.1

Subject	LC Class	No.							%	
History	C,D,E,F	316	202.39	320.56	339.02	362.17	383.63	396.76	3.4	196.0
Language and Literature	P	297	168.12	254.73	267.67	283.85	302.67	304.15	0.5	180.9
Law	K	211	214.01	376.27	399.79	416.75	437.04	448.90	2.7	209.8
Library Science	Z	94	290.02	421.38	442.78	474.26	508.05	518.03	2.0	178.6
Math and Computer Science	QA	357	1,242.13	1,802.35	1,923.22	2,041.23	2,206.99	2,259.08	2.4	181.9
Military and Naval Science	U,V	27	239.90	424.95	446.69	470.03	491.04	495.94	1.0	206.7
Music	M	52	82.18	163.35	171.27	179.95	190.23	195.16	2.6	237.5
Philosophy and Religion	B-BD, BH-BX	222	232.37	360.28	371.79	391.27	414.06	419.66	1.4	180.6
Physics	QC	163	2,845.54	4,080.34	4,308.80	4,584.79	4,892.19	4,983.40	1.9	175.1
Political Science	J	97	312.76	757.30	811.92	870.38	942.64	977.55	3.7	312.6
Psychology	BF	127	648.21	1,122.35	1,198.41	1,280.58	1,379.49	1,419.77	2.9	219.0
Recreation	GV	58	69.79	189.07	202.42	215.26	226.25	233.77	3.3	335.0
Social Sciences	H	46	351.40	732.27	829.16	878.52	925.56	927.29	0.2	263.9
Sociology	HM-HX	248	482.59	851.58	906.33	972.34	1,041.51	1,073.22	3.0	222.4
Technology	TA-TT	124	535.73	964.32	1,019.73	1,095.16	1,190.00	1,238.38	4.1	231.2
Zoology	QL	134	1,454.26	2,174.22	2,287.90	2,434.67	2,512.73	2,483.11	-1.2	170.7
Total		6,251	$843.46	$1,382.31	$1,463.33	$1,561.88	$1,667.95	$1,706.92	2.3%	202.4

Compiled by Stephen Bosch, University of Arizona, based on subscription information supplied by Ebsco Information Services.

(continued from page 333)
comparable on a year-to-year basis. In a small sample size, the change in just one or two titles could easily have a large impact on the overall price for an area.

More extensive reports from the periodical price index have been published annually in the mid-April issue of *Library Journal* through 1992, in the May issue of *American Libraries* from 1993 to 2002, and in the October 2003 issue of *Library Resources and Technical Services.*

The Legal Serials Services Index (Table 2) is compiled by Ajaye Bloomstone, Louisiana State University Law Center Library, using data collected from various legal serials vendors. The base year for this index is 2010. This index presents price data covering the years 2010 through 2021.

As in past years, vendors were asked to provide cost data on particular titles with the assumption that the title or set has been held as an active subscription over a period of time by a large academic research law library. The cost recorded in the index is intended to be based on the upkeep of titles, not necessarily the cost incurred in purchasing a new set, though sometimes the cost is the same, and sometimes the cost of updates can be more expensive than purchasing a new set.

A nuance of legal publishing is that for some of the larger legal publishers, hard prices for a calendar year are not set at the beginning of the calendar year but halfway through, so only gross price estimates may be available in time for publication of this article. In addition to titles issued regularly (e.g., journals and law reviews), legal serials may also be updated throughout the year with both regular and irregular updates or releases, new editions, and new or revised volumes. If a title is updated irregularly, the price for its renewal may increase or decrease from one year to the next, depending on the publisher's plans for keeping the title current. It is noteworthy that although legal serials in print format are still produced, titles seem to be migrating, albeit slowly, to an electronic-only format.

Some prices were provided to the compiler with the caveat "no longer available for new sales." There is also a trend for titles purchased in print to come with

Table 2 / Legal Serials Services: Average Prices and Price Indexes, 2010–2021

Index Base: 2010 = 100

Year	Titles	Average Price	Percent Change	Index
2010	217	$1,714.96	3.5	100.0
2011	217	1,904.69	11.1	111.1
2012	219	2,058.66	8.1	120.0
2013	218	2,241.42	8.9	130.7
2014	219	2,473.44	10.4	144.2
2015	218	2,818.02	13.9	164.3
2016	217	3,085.34	9.5	179.9
2017	218	3,446.12	11.7	200.9
2018	185	4,195.99	21.8	244.7
2019	191	4,653.97	10.9	271.4
2020	187	5,648.39	21.4	329.4
2021	187	$6,775.64	20.0%	395.1

Compiled by Ajaye Bloomstone, Louisiana State University Law Center Library.

an electronic component. For such titles, the purchasing library may have no choice but to accept both formats even if the print is preferred. If one were able to purchase the print format without the electronic component, the cost might conceivably change. This leads one to believe that some titles may cease publication entirely.

For instance, if the publication is not to be phased out immediately, then the title might, at some point soon, no longer be available in print. In fact, more than 20 titles used to compile Table 2 ceased publication in 2019. To compensate for the loss of titles, new titles were added. The new titles were added with the intent to match the previous year's cost of the ceased publications plus the average percentage of an increase for the remainder of the titles from 2018 to 2019. Further decreases have occurred between 2019 and 2020 due to titles discontinuing print, ceasing altogether, or migrating to electronic format, though in terms of the titles tracked in this list over time, the number of titles which have ceased seems to have been curtailed, at least temporarily, for 2021.

Book Prices

U.S. Hardcover Books (Table 3), U.S. Mass Market Paperback Books (Table 6), U.S. Paperbacks (Excluding Mass Market) (Table 7), U.S. Audiobooks (Table 7A), and U.S. E-Books (Table 7B), prepared by Narda Tafuri, University of Scranton, are derived from data provided by book wholesaler Baker & Taylor. Figures for 2018 have been revised again in order to reflect additional late updates to the Baker & Taylor database. The Data for 2018 should not be considered finalized. The 2019 figures given here may be similarly revised in next year's tables and should be considered preliminary as are the 2020 figures. The figures for this edition of *Library and Book Trade Almanac* were provided by Baker & Taylor and are based on the Book Industry Study Group's BISAC categories. The BISAC juvenile category (fiction and nonfiction) is divided into children's and young adult. For more information on the BISAC categories, visit http://www.bisg.org.

List prices for hardcover books (Table 3) and U.S. paperback books (Table 7) showed declines of -2.5 percent and -4.1 percent, respectively. Mass market paperbacks (Table 6) exhibited an insignificant increase of 3.5 percent as did audiobooks (Table 7A) at 0.2 percent. E-Book prices (Table 7B) showed the largest increase in practice at 6.5 percent.

North American Academic Books (Table 4), North American Academic E-Books (Table 4A), and North American Academic Textbooks (Table 4B) are prepared by Stephen Bosch. The current version of North American Academic Books: Average Prices and Price Indexes 2018–2020 (Table 4) has been stable for the past several years, so it is a good summary of change in the academic book market since 2010. Direct comparisons with earlier versions published before 2014 show variations since the number of titles treated and their average prices have changed. This is especially true for those versions published before 2009. Data for the current indexes are supplied by ProQuest Books (formerly Ingrams Content Group–Coutts Information Services) and by GOBI Library Solutions from EBSCO (formerly YBP Library Services). Prior to ProQuest/Coutts supplying data, the book pricing data were obtained from Blackwell Book Services and YBP.

(text continues on page 346)

Table 3 / Hardcover Books: Average Prices and Price Indexes, 2017–2020

Index Base: 2010 = 100

BISAC Category	2010 Average Price	2017 Final Volumes	2017 Final Average Price	2017 Final Index	2018 Final Volumes	2018 Final Average Price	2018 Final Index	2019 Preliminary Volumes	2019 Preliminary Average Price	2019 Preliminary Index	2020 Preliminary Volumes	2020 Preliminary Average Price	2020 Preliminary Index
Antiques and collectibles	$51.44	133	$72.28	140.5	103	$72.96	141.8	100	$65.84	128.0	94	$74.28	144.4
Architecture	85.52	1,045	114.32	133.7	908	95.80	112.0	917	94.73	110.8	881	94.38	110.4
Art	71.53	2,171	83.05	116.1	2,041	75.20	105.1	2,229	73.79	103.2	2,034	81.21	113.5
Bibles	37.50	254	40.99	109.3	251	44.42	118.5	186	54.85	146.3	199	50.09	133.6
Biography and autobiography	53.41	1,830	50.20	94.0	1,727	46.09	86.3	1,555	41.22	77.2	1,537	42.32	79.2
Body, mind, and spirit	36.91	196	27.36	74.1	214	25.60	69.4	279	26.23	71.1	313	22.09	59.8
Business and economics	134.61	5,912	173.56	128.9	4,612	162.44	120.7	4,346	142.47	105.8	4,155	134.20	99.7
Children	24.63	15,062	24.36	98.9	16,782	26.30	106.8	16,223	25.00	101.5	15,364	23.77	96.5
Comics and graphic novels	31.51	669	42.17	133.8	668	43.57	138.3	683	48.51	154.0	669	46.42	147.3
Computers	138.53	1,282	176.40	127.3	1,155	179.43	129.5	1,146	163.88	118.3	1,054	156.62	113.1
Cooking	30.91	1,221	29.77	96.3	1,158	29.85	96.6	1,109	30.12	97.5	926	31.84	103.0
Crafts and hobbies	33.28	172	32.07	96.4	188	31.04	93.3	158	32.17	96.7	144	32.55	97.8
Design	76.59	369	70.43	92.0	359	66.91	87.4	367	66.65	87.0	314	68.77	89.8
Drama	42.91	80	111.54	259.9	67	85.39	199.0	84	109.33	254.8	75	102.44	238.7
Education	117.59	3,672	155.59	132.3	2,822	271.54	230.9	2,591	170.41	144.9	2,436	178.78	152.0
Family and relationships	32.24	193	48.24	149.6	223	47.90	148.6	220	46.27	143.5	214	48.33	149.9
Fiction	32.20	5,329	29.55	91.8	4,964	29.46	91.5	5,021	29.67	92.2	4,103	29.91	92.9
Foreign language study	132.47	242	130.05	98.2	277	125.96	95.1	215	124.55	94.0	224	119.30	90.1
Games and activities	52.07	138	49.25	94.6	183	44.44	85.4	143	38.18	73.3	137	40.64	78.1
Gardening	36.42	133	45.85	125.9	124	37.87	104.0	120	39.60	108.7	110	35.67	98.0
Health and fitness	48.51	418	85.49	176.2	343	69.30	142.9	389	80.60	166.1	351	80.83	166.6
History	82.65	6,260	102.13	123.6	5,866	94.37	114.2	6,207	102.49	124.0	5,606	106.55	128.9
House and home	44.61	122	42.32	94.9	123	39.01	87.4	131	41.77	93.6	115	37.75	84.6
Humor	21.94	303	22.53	102.7	349	22.89	104.4	297	19.42	88.5	247	19.86	90.5

Language arts and disciplines	117.67	1,566	156.55	133.0	1,355	143.93	122.3	1,476	137.17	116.6	1,332	129.20	109.8
Law	174.48	2,565	186.22	106.7	2,354	182.75	104.7	2,275	173.44	99.4	2,292	179.29	102.8
Literary collections	83.49	296	102.43	122.7	253	86.96	104.2	268	134.18	160.7	247	117.76	141.0
Literary criticism	117.63	2,594	131.89	112.1	2,403	127.02	108.0	2,645	121.70	103.5	2,503	124.79	106.1
Mathematics	133.23	1,400	177.63	133.3	1,037	155.50	116.7	1,012	141.48	106.2	875	134.49	100.9
Medical	171.13	3,848	199.26	116.4	3,050	185.97	108.7	3,566	174.60	102.0	2,917	183.13	107.0
Music	87.84	695	102.10	116.2	603	90.93	103.5	672	94.86	108.0	650	92.66	105.5
Nature	74.89	538	103.88	138.7	424	85.60	114.3	464	93.75	125.2	448	83.19	111.1
Performing arts	76.27	946	124.11	162.7	822	102.14	133.9	779	117.51	154.1	808	98.95	129.7
Pets	24.66	103	27.74	112.5	70	21.65	87.8	56	27.31	110.7	61	22.35	90.6
Philosophy	108.93	1,687	122.75	112.7	1,668	109.55	100.6	1,899	112.23	103.0	1,775	117.80	108.1
Photography	107.99	930	75.58	70.0	851	71.38	66.1	819	69.96	64.8	803	57.94	53.7
Poetry	40.76	320	39.58	97.1	295	37.01	90.8	306	36.60	89.8	255	35.40	86.9
Political science	110.32	3,928	124.68	113.0	3,482	114.34	103.6	5,511	126.57	114.7	3,622	110.59	100.2
Psychology	109.85	1,842	163.93	149.2	1,449	149.40	136.0	2,744	143.01	130.2	1,191	143.53	130.7
Reference	302.69	357	382.04	126.2	340	382.33	126.3	313	278.60	92.0	199	395.09	130.5
Religion	80.88	3,020	83.86	103.7	3,126	79.06	97.7	2,713	86.60	107.1	2,744	85.32	105.5
Science	192.20	4,623	206.46	107.4	3,902	177.18	92.2	4,132	186.88	97.2	3,538	181.87	94.6
Self-help	27.11	361	29.37	108.3	425	25.98	95.8	431	24.01	88.6	402	22.87	84.4
Social science	100.47	5,765	141.00	140.3	4,709	127.86	127.3	5,357	126.65	126.1	4,144	122.93	122.4
Sports and recreation	41.23	646	66.08	160.3	603	56.24	136.4	537	51.71	125.4	490	54.99	133.4
Study aids	101.54	21	112.76	111.0	14	103.31	101.7	9	174.43	171.8	29	126.25	124.3
Technology and engineering	164.66	4,061	205.86	125.0	3,155	204.94	124.5	3,000	184.80	112.2	3,225	180.33	109.5
Transportation	84.28	278	74.42	88.3	289	62.23	73.8	285	74.60	88.5	222	82.49	97.9
Travel	41.32	283	39.83	96.4	482	40.52	98.1	233	42.01	101.7	230	36.23	87.7
True crime	34.83	66	29.63	85.1	84	33.53	96.3	109	37.92	108.9	85	59.94	172.1
Young adult	35.99	2,404	40.14	111.5	2,122	35.79	99.4	2,000	37.20	103.4	1,506	29.94	83.2
Totals and Averages	$89.54	92,349	$110.77	123.7	84,934	$101.47	113.3	88,327	$98.98	110.5	77,895	$96.47	107.7

Compiled by Narda Tafuri, University of Scranton, from data supplied by Baker & Taylor.

Table 4 / North American Academic Books: Average Prices and Price Indexes, 2018–2020

Index Base: 2010 = 100

Subject Area	LC Class	2010		2018		2019		2020			
		Titles	Average Price	Titles	Average Price	Titles	Average Price	Titles	Average Price	Percent Change 2019–2020	Index
Agriculture	S	1,139	$107.44	1,586	$114.09	1,915	$115.92	1,969	$127.89	10.3%	119.0
Anthropology	GN	609	91.96	790	98.31	857	94.56	918	103.45	9.4	112.5
Botany	QK	260	125.84	337	149.82	456	136.82	525	156.64	14.5	124.5
Business and economics	H	10,916	97.31	13,354	107.07	14,431	107.54	15,110	113.58	5.6	116.7
Chemistry	QD	667	223.03	791	200.68	918	191.15	926	215.75	12.9	96.7
Education	L	4,688	86.47	6,256	92.00	7,122	93.01	7,488	102.26	9.9	118.3
Engineering and technology	T	6,913	133.45	9,392	148.15	11,202	153.75	12,737	155.18	0.9	116.3
Fine and applied arts	M-N	5,535	57.17	6,869	77.19	7,694	74.66	7,456	82.74	10.8	144.7
General works	A	80	75.60	251	109.68	290	98.42	295	103.92	5.6	137.5
Geography	G	1,144	104.98	1,612	113.22	1,900	123.05	2,005	123.77	0.6	117.9
Geology	QE	276	114.34	351	123.12	429	133.49	404	119.64	-10.4	104.6
History	C-D-E-F	10,079	65.29	13,470	78.64	15,105	73.36	14,357	85.45	16.5	130.9
Home economics	TX	812	44.35	859	60.45	1,170	63.04	901	72.68	15.3	163.9
Industrial arts	TT	265	52.60	229	62.68	297	57.59	207	77.94	35.3	148.2
Language and literature	P	19,364	57.31	27,174	62.36	30,452	58.25	30,316	66.40	14.0	115.9

										% Change	Index
Law	K	4,596	125.35	6 812	127.59	6,728	128.39	7,039	134.26	4.6	107.1
Library and information science	Z	636	90.18	926	110.28	921	99.72	912	101.49	1.8	112.5
Mathematics and computer science	QA	3,965	103.85	5 010	113.69	5,318	116.20	6,724	120.42	3.6	115.9
Medicine	R	8,679	112.66	11 147	126.05	12,452	137.62	12,982	135.98	-1.2	120.7
Military and naval science	U-V	773	79.99	1 162	79.21	1,391	78.80	1,429	78.83	0.0	98.5
Philosophy and religion	B	7,386	81.75	11 369	83.89	12,153	80.10	12,020	85.98	7.3	105.2
Physical education and recreation	GV	1,788	56.03	2 559	69.03	2,983	71.12	3,028	76.19	7.1	136.0
Physics and astronomy	QB	1,627	128.36	2 107	143.00	2,342	127.36	2,297	131.51	3.3	102.5
Political science	J	3,549	99.70	5 310	102.70	5,991	96.67	5,919	103.36	6.9	103.7
Psychology	BF	1,730	76.65	2 717	83.32	2,944	82.11	2,965	94.77	15.4	123.6
Science (general)	Q	631	108.40	954	107.42	1,175	112.86	1,696	134.16	18.9	123.8
Sociology	HM	6,666	88.75	10 276	93.29	11,518	89.35	11,870	100.38	12.3	113.1
Zoology	QH,QL-QF	3,029	140.26	3 438	133.32	3,916	133.28	3,843	137.87	3.4	98.3
Totals and Averages		107,802	$89.15	147 108	$96.73	164,070	$95.87	168,338	$103.87	8.3%	116.5

Compiled by Stephen Bosch, University of Arizona, from electronic data provided by ProQuest (formerly Ingrams Content Group–Coutts Information Services), and GOBI Library Solutions from EBSCO (formerly YBP Library Services). The data represent all titles (includes e-books, hardcover, trade, and paperback books, as well as annuals) treated for all approval plan customers serviced by the vendors. This table covers titles published or distributed in the United States and Canada during the calendar years listed. This index does include paperback editions and electronic books. The inclusion of these items does impact pricing in the index.

Table 4A / North American Academic E-Books: Average Prices and Price Indexes, 2018–2020

Index Base: 2010 = 100

Subject Area	LC Class	2010		2018		2019		2020			
		Titles	Average Price	Titles	Average Price	Titles	Average Price	Titles	Average Price	Percent Change 2019–2020	Index
Agriculture	S	697	$168.73	706	$133.99	874	$132.96	961	$146.83	10.4%	87.0
Anthropology	GN	385	109.96	364	104.30	393	103.92	435	114.52	10.2	104.1
Botany	QK	190	175.23	146	174.31	193	159.51	257	168.72	5.8	96.3
Business and economics	H	8,481	102.87	6,519	117.21	6,797	118.09	7,625	123.43	4.5	120.0
Chemistry	QD	521	232.57	388	209.77	446	186.38	499	228.23	22.5	98.1
Education	L	2,852	99.96	2,839	104.20	3,231	101.52	3,660	114.12	12.4	114.2
Engineering and technology	T	4,976	152.33	4,424	163.46	5,281	165.33	6,404	165.47	0.1	108.6
Fine and applied arts	M-N	1,493	83.35	2,213	101.64	2,338	96.52	2,822	106.81	10.7	128.1
General works	A	53	89.13	98	101.13	132	97.67	148	108.32	10.9	121.5
Geography	G	829	117.83	755	125.77	828	141.23	993	135.83	-3.8	115.3
Geology	QE	178	146.85	148	141.93	186	152.31	171	133.30	-12.5	90.8
History	C-D-E-F	5,189	89.42	5,936	92.25	6,233	87.41	6,582	94.95	8.6	106.2
Home economics	TX	211	78.08	293	86.37	435	81.29	407	92.92	14.3	119.0
Industrial arts	TT	23	46.11	53	93.52	77	66.08	77	109.80	66.2	238.2
Language and literature	P	7,664	103.12	9,657	90.07	10,276	81.88	11,922	92.77	13.3	90.0

Subject	LC	Count	Price	Count	Price	Count	Price	Count	Price	%	%
Law	K	2,433	147.66	2,786	139.62	2 650	147.22	3,256	146.01	-0.8	98.9
Library and information science	Z	387	89.43	376	119.59	378	111.23	383	113.09	1.7	126.5
Mathematics and computer science	QA	3,000	112.65	2,092	127.44	2 231	128.80	3,376	131.14	1.8	116.4
Medicine	R	6,404	134.60	5,190	142.45	5 741	164.83	6,297	153.95	-6.6	114.4
Military and naval science	U-V	487	105.07	518	89.70	598	93.88	663	89.29	-4.9	85.0
Philosophy and religion	B	4,262	110.31	5,163	96.99	5 189	94.03	5,983	96.13	2.2	87.1
Physical education and recreation	GV	791	76.57	1,161	84.05	1 257	89.00	1,437	91.84	3.2	119.9
Physics and astronomy	QB	1,288	147.50	985	166.71	1 078	145.53	1,154	148.24	1.9	100.5
Political science	J	2,638	110.10	2,690	112.97	2 738	110.76	2,944	110.09	3.0	103.6
Psychology	BF	1,062	91.35	1,343	96.84	1 342	95.97	1,460	110.12	14.7	120.6
Science (general)	Q	462	122.51	403	119.28	495	125.52	874	140.77	12.2	114.9
Sociology	HM	4,520	103.73	4,910	105.57	5 140	103.29	5,803	113.97	10.3	109.9
Zoology	QH, QL-R	2,336	164.32	1,514	149.98	1 655	152.48	1,803	160.50	5.3	97.4
Totals and Averages		63,812	$116.25	63,670	$114.61	68 212	$114.95	78,396	$120.64	4.9%	103.8

Compiled by Stephen Bosch, University of Arizona, from electronic data provided by ProQuest (formerly Ingrams Content Group–Coutts Information Services), and GOBI Library Solutions from EBSCO (formerly YBP Library Services). The data represent all e-book titles treated for all approval plan customers serviced by the vendors. This table covers titles published and distributed in the United States and Canada during the calendar years listed. It is important to note that e-books that were released in a given year may have been published in print much earlier.

343

Table 4B / North American Academic Textbooks: Average Prices and Price Indexes, 2018–2020

(Index Base: 2010 = 100)

Subject Area	LC Class	2010		2018		2019		2020			
		Titles	Average Price	Titles	Average Price	Titles	Average Price	Titles	Average Price	Percent Change 2019–2020	Index
Agriculture	S	49	$115.80	64	$136.09	65	$133.22	98	$138.63	4.1%	119.7
Anthropology	GN	35	90.65	56	91.22	54	103.15	47	99.66	-3.4	109.9
Botany	QK	11	109.52	7	77.83	8	119.10	21	143.66	20.6	131.2
Business and economics	H	694	121.36	1,070	117.33	1,058	121.32	1,073	117.37	-3.3	96.7
Chemistry	QD	94	134.59	115	151.54	109	130.15	131	157.96	21.4	117.4
Education	L	271	87.75	418	86.98	525	83.92	419	95.97	14.4	109.4
Engineering and technology	T	744	116.38	1,039	132.04	1,142	141.11	1,229	146.31	3.7	125.7
Fine and applied arts	M-N	73	93.33	119	95.92	171	104.39	142	96.90	-7.2	103.8
General works	A	0	0.00	9	77.86	6	114.52	7	109.84	-4.1	n.a.
Geography	G	78	105.21	106	108.43	127	121.51	101	128.18	5.5	121.8
Geology	QE	36	117.97	28	141.86	46	165.25	36	152.19	-7.9	129.0
History	C-D-E-F	81	81.49	219	95.69	158	91.78	133	96.79	5.5	118.8
Home economics	TX	39	89.52	38	116.56	39	145.85	35	146.18	0.2	163.3
Industrial arts	TT	14	84.72	14	116.57	6	99.87	8	87.86	-12.0	103.7
Language and literature	P	309	77.71	563	81.68	559	89.22	561	103.08	15.5	132.6

Subject	LC Class	Titles	Price	Titles	Price	Titles	Price	Titles	Price	% Change	Index
Law	K	242	102.09	484	107.95	464	120.14	393	123.34	2.7	120.8
Library and information science	Z	19	70.30	45	84.37	33	70.01	26	85.31	21.9	121.3
Mathematics and computer science	QA	683	96.11	1,072	114.87	997	117.72	1,073	119.49	1.5	124.3
Medicine	R	1512	126.75	1,340	141.32	2,153	138.65	1,832	138.27	-0.3	109.1
Military and naval science	U-V	3	122.65	29	106.12	27	138.42	25	154.76	11.8	126.2
Philosophy and religion	B	101	72.13	58	70.07	179	70.29	141	69.93	-0.5	97.0
Physical education and recreation	GV	51	79.39	06	106.38	129	96.87	98	110.60	14.2	139.3
Physics and astronomy	QB	243	107.38	397	140.64	402	131.64	390	130.44	-0.9	121.5
Political science	J	110	80.09	232	96.94	267	92.27	216	93.41	1.2	116.6
Psychology	BF	138	95.95	170	119.55	210	120.23	167	109.64	-8.8	114.3
Science (general)	Q	33	97.14	66	101.15	79	95.33	100	111.17	16.6	114.4
Sociology	HM	353	86.97	596	102.94	674	102.18	507	104.30	2.1	119.9
Zoology	QH, QL-QR	227	109.82	313	131.79	354	139.56	335	138.44	-0.8	126.1
Totals and Averages		6,243	$107.94	9,373	$117.79	10,041	$120.16	9,344	$123.49	2.8%	114.4

Compiled by Stephen Bosch, University of Arizona, from electronic data provided by ProQuest (formerly Ingrams Content Group–Coutts Information Services), and GOBI Library Solutions from EBSCO (formerly YBP Library Services). The data represent all textbock titles treated for all approval plan customers serviced by the vendors. This table covers titles published or distributed in the United States and Canada during the calendar years listed.

n.a. = not available

(continued from page 337)

Over time, the data and the data suppliers have changed due to changes in the industry. When compared with earlier versions, the North American Academic Books Price Index (NAABPI) now contains many more titles in the source data, which has affected the index considerably. ProQuest Books treats far more titles in their approval programs than the former Blackwell Book Services. For indexes published before 2009, Blackwell was a supplier of data for the index. Blackwell was purchased in 2009 by YBP, and the vendor data used to create the index changed at that time. After 2009 the data came from Ingram (Coutts) and YBP; prior to 2009 the data came from Blackwell and YBP. With recent changes at both ProQuest and GOBI, there have been changes to how the annual price data are pulled for books. Starting in 2016, each vendor supplied data in separate files for print, e-books, and textbooks. Prior to 2016, this was not the case, and this change caused large variations in the numbers of titles in the tables as well the average prices. The data for 2014 was normalized in 2016 to conform to the current sets of data, so the numbers of titles and prices have changed from those published in 2015 and previous years. In the future, this approach to gathering the data, separate data files for print, electronic, and texts, will improve the consistency of the data, especially for e-books. Another major change was made in 2017, when the base index year was moved to 2010 to provide consistency across the various indexes published by the Library Materials Price Index Committee.

The overall average price for books in the North American Academic Books Price Index (Table 4) rose by a significant 8.3 percent in 2020. This marked increase following years of relatively stable pricing was due mainly to growth in the number of e-books in the index. E-books in 2020 increased by about 10,000 titles while print titles decreased by about 4,000. A possible driver is the impact of the pandemic, as print was far less useful due to library closures and to the library market wanting online access. The overall number of titles has been volatile, going from 161,020 in 2017 to 147,108 in 2018, then jumping to 164,070 in 2019 and to 168,338 in 2020. The overall growth in available titles, as well as increasing prices, are pressure points for library budgets. The increase in price in 2020 was primarily due to a large increase in the number of titles available in the higher price ranges, as e-books are about 20 percent more expensive than print books. There were approximately 6,000 fewer titles treated in the lowest price ranges. Many of these books were print books. Since print books tend to be less expensive than e-books, the higher cost of e-books was a driver in the overall price increase. Overall, the ratio of print to electronic has been growing, with e-books comprising 43 percent of the titles in 2018, dropping slightly to 42 percent in 2019 and increasing to 47 percent in 2020.

Since 2008, two additional indexes have been available, one for e-books only (Table 4A) and another for textbooks (Table 4B). Based on users' high interest, the indexes continue to be published. In 2017 the base index was set to 2010. In the academic market, it has always been assumed that e-books are more expensive than their print counterparts. The cheaper versions of e-books available to consumers through such channels as Amazon and Google Books are not available to libraries at similar prices, if they are available at all in the library market. At best, the academic pricing will match the print price for single-user license models, with multiuser models being far more expensive than print. The e-book index points out this difference in price: the average price of an e-book in 2020 was $120.64 while the average price for all books was $103.87. The average price of a print book drops to $81.07 if the e-books are removed from the overall index. The high price for e-books is not that surprising, as most pricing models for academic e-books generally charge a higher price than the list print price for access to the e-books. Another factor is that STEM publishing has migrated more quickly to electronic formats for books, with social science and humanities slower to adopt digital publishing. STEM books have always been more expensive than other subjects, so this contributes to the higher cost for e-books. Over the past two years, it is becoming common practice for single-user licenses to be priced at the same price as print. Multiuser licenses are still significantly more expensive than print. Responding to customer demands, publishers and vendors offer e-books on multiple platforms with multiple pricing models; consequently, there can be multiple prices for the same title. For these indexes, only the first license level (normally single-user) is included in the data. Where multiple prices are available for different use models, the lowest price is included in the index. Because electronic access is a major market trend, it is appropriate to have e-books as a separate index. It is also important to note that the e-book market is rapidly changing. The approach of using the lowest price available for e-books may be artificially keeping the average price of e-books low for libraries that generally buy multiuser licenses. Taking advantage of the pandemic market, e-book prices increased just under 5 percent for 2020.

The cost of textbooks has been a hot topic on many college campuses. The index for textbooks (Table 4B) documents price changes in this area. The data show that textbooks tend to be more expensive than other types of books, with an average price of $123.49 in 2020. This represents a 4.8 percent increase. Over the past two years, the price had held flat at around $121. That was good news for students, but textbooks remain more expensive than regular print or e-books. Note that this index does not measure the impact of new programs like inclusive access for textbooks. Only changes in the publisher's retail price is measured. The flat increases in previous years seemed to be a positive trend as it seemed textbook publishers were responding to market pressure and resisting large price increases. That ended in 2020 as the pandemic market showed a close to 5 percent increase. Textbooks are expensive, and the prices are not yet dropping significantly. Pressure on the textbook market from alternative sources, like rental services for either print or electronic versions or resales of used copies, may have slowed price increases but has not resulted in an overall significant price drop. "E" versions are included in the textbook index, so migration to "e" format does not seem to be lowering costs. This is not much consolation for cash-strapped students.

The average price of North American academic books in 2020 (Table 4) increased by 8.3 percent as compared with the 2019 average price. This is mainly due to changes in the number of titles treated in the lower part of the price bands (below $30) and an increase in the most expensive books (see Figure 1). There was only modest growth in the number of titles published between 2018 and 2019 with the exception of the price bands below $60. This led to the slight decrease in pricing in 2019, but the drop in titles costing less than $30 also helped drive prices up in 2020.

Figure 1 / Number of Titles in Sample Grouped by Price

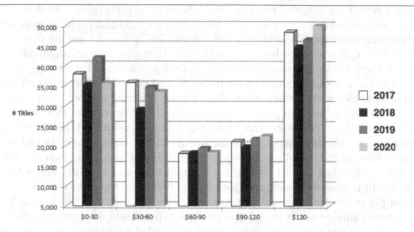

One thing that stands out when looking at the data is that the price bands at the highest end ($120 and up) continue to have a huge impact on the costs for books. The impact on pricing from the titles in the $120 and up price band is confirmed if you look at the actual dollar values in groups (sum of all prices for titles in the group). The increase at the top end of the index was the main component in the overall changes in the index for 2017–2020 as well as the minimal growth leading to no increase in 2019. In 2019 the growth in the highest range could not offset the greater growth in the lower ranges, but in 2020 the drop in the low-priced books and the increase in the most expensive books resulted in the 8.3 percent increase. Again, changes in the number of titles available is a significant driver in the increase or decrease in costs, as within the price bands the average price remains constant except for the area with prices over $120. Unlike serials, where inflation in price drives higher costs, these data show that changes in the number of titles were the primary driver in escalating costs, rather than inflationary increases in price. (See Figures 2 and 3.)

The data used for this index are derived from all titles treated by ProQuest Books (formerly Ingrams Content Group Coutts Information Services) and GOBI Library Solutions in their approval plans during the calendar years listed. The index includes e-books as well as paperback editions as supplied by these vendors, and this inclusion of paperbacks and e-books as distributed as part of the approval plans has influenced the prices reflected in the index figures. The index is inclusive of the broadest categories of materials, as that is the marketplace in which academic libraries operate, and the index attempts to chart price changes impacting that market.

Price changes vary, as always, among subject areas. This year there were several double-digit increases in subject areas, and two areas showed price decreases. The 2020 data indicate that those areas with the largest increases were not concentrated in one area but included all broad subject areas. Overall prices for books in the STM (science, technology, medicine) subjects are still higher than for

Figure 2 / Comparison of Total Costs in Sample Grouped by Price

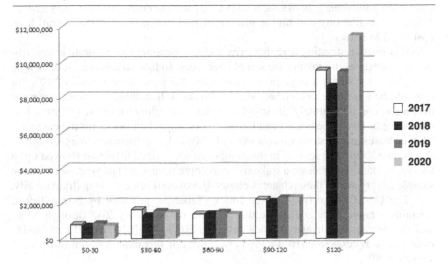

Figure 3 / Comparison of Average Price Grouped by Price Band

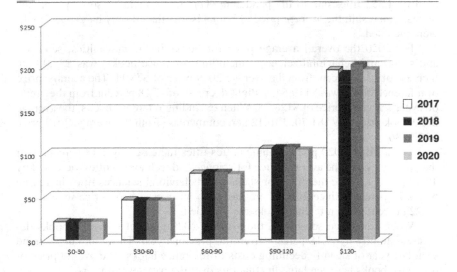

the humanities. STM publishers have tended to be early adopters of e-books and have been publishing e-books for a while. The high average prices in the sciences reflect the availability and higher pricing of e-books as well as the overall high cost of STM books.

It is worth reiterating here that price indexes become less accurate at describing price changes the smaller the sample becomes. Industrial arts is a small sample (207 titles) for which a large price change of 35.3 percent occurred in 2020, but it would be a mistake to conclude that all books in that subject area increased or decreased commensurately. In small samples, inclusion/exclusion of just a few expensive or low-priced items can have a major impact on prices for the category. The increases in industrial arts, for example, were due to increases in expensive titles coupled with a large drop in the number of low-priced titles that showed up in this year's data. This caused a spike in the average price over last year. Because the sample is very small, these changes caused the overall price to jump dramatically.

The U.S. College Books Price Index (Table 5), prepared by Narda Tafuri, contains average price and index number data for the years 2018 through 2020, and the percentage change in price between 2019 and 2020. In 2017 the index base year was reset to 2010. Previous instances of this table have an index base year of 1989.

Data for the index was compiled from 3,502 reviews of books published in *Choice* during 2020. An additional six print titles reviewed in *Choice* were omitted from the analysis due to price ($500 or more). These books were removed from the analysis so that the average prices were not skewed. The total number of books reviewed for this analysis has declined by -23.08 percent from the previous year's total of 4,553 titles due to the pandemic. This index includes some paperback prices; as a result, the average price of books is less than if only hardcover books were included.

For 2020 the overall average price for books in the humanities, sciences, and social and behavioral sciences (including reference books) was $82.98, an increase of 13.5 percent from the average 2019 price of $73.11. The average price of reference books was $119.54, a slight decrease of -7.18 percent from the previous year's average price of $128.78. When excluding reference books, the average 2020 book price was $81.70, a 16.12 percent increase from the average 2019 price of $70.36.

The average 2020 price for humanities titles increased by 2.48 percent over the previous year. The average price for science and technology titles increased by 40.19 percent, while the price for social and behavioral sciences titles increased by 17.73 percent. Since 2010, there has been an overall book price increase of 25.22 percent when reference books are included.

When calculated separately, the average 2020 price of reference books decreased slightly by -7.18 percent from the previous year. This continues a trend seen last year of steadily declining costs of reference books. The overall price of reference books has seen large fluctuations over the past several years.

Questions regarding this index may be addressed to the author at narda. tafuri@scranton.edu.

(text continues on page 362)

Table 5 / U.S. College Books: Average Prices and Price Indexes, 2018–2020

Index Base: 2010 = 100

Subject	2010		2018				2019				2020				Percent Change 2019–2020
	Titles	Average Price	Titles	Average Price	Indexed to 2010	Indexed to 2017	Titles	Average Price	Indexed to 2010	Indexed to 2018	Titles	Average Price	Indexed to 2010	Indexed to 2019	
HUMANITIES	91	$58.99	49	$71.55	121.29	103.83	47	$81.60	138.33	114.05	43	$72.40	122.73	88.73	-11.27%
Art and architecture	149	61.69	118	66.01	107.00	99.04	117	70.57	114.39	106.91	90	67.44	109.32	95.56	-4.44
Fine Arts	92	67.13	54	60.75	90.50	104.44	54	61.24	91.23	100.81	51	59.71	88.95	97.50	-2.50
Architecture	48	61.53	37	65.50	106.45	84.28	39	75.49	122.69	115.25	20	76.47	124.28	101.29	1.29
Photography	28	53.02	10	61.89	116.73	106.63	6	73.33	138.31	118.48	15	58.98	111.24	80.43	-19.57
Communication	112	59.97	83	69.52	115.92	105.30	52	72.94	121.63	104.92	48	78.05	130.15	107.01	7.01
Language and literature	94	68.66	61	87.98	128.14	114.11	82	82.60	120.30	93.88	58	84.00	122.34	101.69	1.69
African and Middle Eastern	24	62.28	12	77.33	124.17	149.60	6	64.17	103.03	82.98	8	80.49	129.24	125.43	25.43
Asian and Oceanian	24	71.99	13	76.84	106.74	86.05	17	78.53	109.08	102.20	12	70.08	97.35	89.24	-10.76
Classical	24	78.76	23	93.69	118.96	134.44	28	89.41	113.52	95.43	19	72.96	92.64	81.60	-18.40
English and American	394	61.96	201	78.96	127.44	114.34	227	80.68	130.21	102.18	167	80.17	129.39	99.37	-0.63
Germanic	22	70.36	21	81.13	115.31	108.17	21	87.55	124.43	107.91	13	84.28	119.78	96.26	-3.74
Romance	70	59.00	35	80.88	137.08	111.87	32	79.94	135.49	98.84	25	74.03	125.47	92.61	-7.39
Slavic	32	35.95	11	80.00	222.53	131.82	17	81.60	226.98	102.00	14	62.91	174.99	77.10	-22.90
Performing arts	30	61.97	9	76.88	124.06	101.25	14	84.45	136.28	109.85	8	83.74	147.14	99.16	-0.84
Film	130	64.13	85	82.03	127.91	91.82	114	89.53	139.61	109.14	73	91.18	123.34	101.84	1.34
Music	123	61.01	85	68.22	111.82	95.68	93	76.14	124.80	111.61	61	79.10	153.01	103.89	3.89
Theater and dance	45	62.38	23	75.73	121.40	85.54	44	80.01	128.26	105.65	21	93.35	146.55	116.67	16.67
Philosophy	198	63.45	186	75.81	119.48	97.72	232	74.13	116.83	97.78	119	91.42	122.47	123.32	23.32
Religion	272	57.18	196	66.42	116.16	101.19	196	69.99	122.40	105.37	150	77.71	137.83	111.03	11.03
TOTAL HUMANITIES	2,002	$61.60	1,312	$73.51	119.33	103.24	1,438	$76.90	124.84	104.61	1,015	$78.81	127.94	102.48	2.48
SCIENCE AND TECHNOLOGY	110	$58.09	82	$58.81	101.24	99.97	95	$60.44	104.05	102.77	35	$65.26	112.34	107.97	7.97
History of science and technology	78	54.10	51	58.41	107.97	85.11	59	57.41	106.12	98.29	42	74.00	136.78	128.90	28.90
Astronautics and astronomy	63	55.58	50	51.92	93.41	89.67	41	54.00	97.16	104.01	21	69.65	125.31	128.98	28.98

Table 5 / U.S. College Books: Average Prices and Price Indexes, 2018–2020 (cont.)

Index Base: 2010 = 100

Subject	2010 Titles	2010 Average Price	2018 Titles	2018 Average Price	2018 Indexed to 2010	2018 Indexed to 2017	2019 Titles	2019 Average Price	2019 Indexed to 2010	2019 Indexed to 2018	2020 Titles	2020 Average Price	2020 Indexed to 2010	2020 Indexed to 2019	Percent Change 2019–2020
Biology	151	$72.74	76	$59.55	81.87	94.30	95	$72.01	99.00	120.92	60	$98.09	134.85	136.22	36.22
Botany	85	85.09	63	59.98	70.49	85.77	70	56.79	66.74	94.68	20	94.43	110.98	166.28	66.28
Zoology	121	64.33	74	60.81	94.53	96.45	96	62.41	97.02	102.63	43	84.71	131.68	135.73	35.73
Chemistry	42	115.42	21	101.78	88.18	83.76	13	102.74	89.01	100.94	12	141.21	122.34	137.44	37.44
Earth science	102	63.33	79	66.39	104.83	93.04	68	74.46	117.57	112.16	36	78.65	124.19	105.63	5.63
Engineering	103	88.38	47	93.51	105.80	87.89	43	80.28	90.84	85.85	56	136.71	154.68	170.29	70.29
Health sciences	146	56.14	102	66.77	118.93	100.24	195	69.78	124.30	104.51	129	98.85	176.08	141.66	41.66
Information and computer science	83	73.50	59	59.41	80.83	93.08	66	77.36	105.25	130.21	45	92.86	126.34	120.04	20.04
Mathematics	108	61.97	81	77.71	125.40	100.90	74	81.00	130.71	104.23	51	94.45	152.41	116.60	16.60
Physics	50	54.74	39	69.52	127.00	85.21	39	63.49	115.98	91.33	34	127.39	232.72	200.65	100.65
Sports and physical education	67	54.06	63	55.41	102.50	79.80	87	62.40	115.43	112.62	43	71.78	132.78	115.03	15.03
TOTAL SCIENCE	1,309	$67.13	887	$65.15	97.05	91.30	1,041	$67.83	101.04	104.11	627	$95.09	141.65	140.19	40.19
SOCIAL AND BEHAVIORAL SCIENCES	129	$66.32	64	$77.53	116.90	96.35	43	$70.20	105.85	90.55	118	$83.26	125.54	118.60	18.60
Anthropology	139	63.60	85	79.38	124.81	93.44	95	89.67	140.99	112.96	117	93.06	146.32	103.78	3.78
Business management and labor	150	58.00	95	51.53	88.84	98.04	69	53.52	92.28	103.86	68	68.31	117.78	127.63	27.63
Economics	270	61.16	114	56.48	92.35	88.54	105	60.99	99.72	107.99	70	69.38	113.44	113.76	13.76
Education	158	62.56	26	74.18	118.57	102.60	43	72.74	116.27	98.06	123	82.02	131.11	112.76	12.76
History, geography and area studies	154	58.16	95	66.02	113.51	91.28	63	58.55	100.67	88.69	89	84.21	144.79	143.83	43.83
Africa	38	69.05	31	68.20	98.77	96.96	17	72.77	105.39	106.70	37	91.73	132.85	126.05	26.05
Ancient history	49	57.90	51	86.00	148.53	115.08	39	86.19	148.86	100.22	37	79.90	138.00	92.70	-7.30
Asia and Oceania	72	60.88	65	73.55	120.81	104.05	71	64.47	105.90	87.65	75	84.90	139.45	131.69	31.69

Central and Eastern Europe	56	66.53	65	76.17	114.49	107.21	31	67.21	101.02	88.24	38	80.53	121.04	119.82	19.82
Latin America and Caribbean	54	59.31	59	75.24	126.86	97.07	49	76.56	129.08	101.75	44	80.26	135.32	104.83	4.83
Middle East and North Africa	43	65.57	36	69.60	106.15	115.27	28	66.12	100.84	95.00	69	81.47	124.25	123.22	23.22
North America	444	45.50	343	54.62	120.04	108.52	245	48.96	107.60	89.64	184	58.60	128.79	119.69	19.69
United Kingdom	80	69.56	78	70.68	101.61	95.05	39	56.44	81.14	79.85	46	75.65	108.76	134.04	34.04
Western Europe	138	59.14	110	85.13	143.95	113.49	74	61.88	104.63	72.69	65	78.91	133.43	127.52	27.52
Political science	4	84.36	60	62.46	74.04	106.68	58	74.12	87.86	118.67	26	81.20	96.25	109.55	9.55
Comparative politics	183	66.34	201	67.63	101.94	104.90	115	71.06	107.11	105.07	33	89.07	134.26	125.34	25.34
International relations	213	65.64	141	61.58	93.81	99.53	91	57.20	87.14	92.89	67	98.19	149.59	171.66	71.66
Political theory	73	56.74	127	73.98	130.38	104.02	104	72.32	127.46	97.76	45	79.02	139.27	109.26	9.26
U.S. politics	253	53.03	178	63.46	119.67	103.58	125	60.62	114.31	95.52	122	61.61	116.18	101.63	1.63
Psychology	126	60.55	137	71.95	118.83	93.47	189	81.34	134.34	113.05	82	77.96	128.75	95.84	-4.16
Sociology	226	60.71	145	72.71	119.77	91.46	167	71.12	117.15	97.81	181	83.50	137.54	117.41	17.41
TOTAL BEHAVIORAL SCIENCES	3,052	$59.09	2,306	$67.28	113.86	101.05	1,360	$66.73	112.93	99.18	1,741	$78.56	132.95	117.73	17.73
TOTAL GENERAL, HUMANITIES, SCIENCE, AND SOCIAL SCIENCE (without Reference)	6,363	$61.53	4,505	$68.68	111.62	99.42	4,339	$70.36	114.35	102.45	3,383	$81.70	132.78	116.12	16.12
REFERENCE															
General	29	$61.17	19	$154.73	252.95	151.84	17	$118.52	193.76	76.60	13	$131.30	214.65	110.78	10.78
Humanities	128	117.12	70	132.66	113.27	96.97	45	104.33	89.59	79.10	32	107.96	92.18	102.89	2.89
Library and information sciences	n.a.	n.a.	n.a.	n.a.	n.a.	n.a.	32	80.48	n.a.	n.a.	21	75.32	n.a.	n.a.	-6.41
Science and technology	76	133.19	34	164.90	123.81	149.16	34	140.05	105.15	84.93	7	186.00	139.65	132.81	32.81
Social and behavioral sciences	216	152.91	90	149.17	97.55	104.40	86	156.80	102.54	105.11	46	134.35	87.86	85.68	-14.32
TOTAL REFERENCE	449	$133.44	213	$146.75	109.97	109.79	214	$128.78	96.51	87.75	119	$119.54	89.58	92.82	-7.18
GRAND TOTAL	6,812	$66.27	4,718	$72.20	108.95	99.35	4,553	$73.11	110.32	101.26	3,502	$82.98	125.22	113.50	13.5%

Compiled by Narda Tafuri, University of Scranton.

n.a. = not available

Table 6 / U.S. Mass Market Paperback Books: Average Prices and Price Indexes, 2017–2020

Index Base: 2010 = 100

BISAC Category	2010 Average Price	2017 Final Volumes	2017 Final Average Price	2017 Final Index	2018 Final Volumes	2018 Final Average Price	2018 Final Index	2019 Preliminary Volumes	2019 Preliminary Average Price	2019 Preliminary Index	2020 Preliminary Volumes	2020 Preliminary Average Price	2020 Preliminary Index
Antiques and collectibles	$8.77	n.a.	n.a.	n.a.	n.a.	n.a.	n.a.	n.a.	n.a.	n.a.	n.a.	n.a.	n.a.
Architecture	n.a.	n.a.	n.a.	n.a.	n.a.	n.a.	n.a.	n.a.	n.a.	n.a.	n.a.	n.a.	n.a.
Art	n.a.	n.a.	n.a.	n.a.	n.a.	n.a.	n.a.	n.a.	n.a.	n.a.	n.a.	n.a.	n.a.
Bibles	n.a.	n.a.	n.a.	n.a.	n.a.	n.a.	n.a.	n.a.	n.a.	n.a.	n.a.	n.a.	n.a.
Biography and autobiography	7.51	5	$9.28	123.6	8	$9.87	131.4	3	$9.99	133.0	6	$8.99	119.7
Body, mind, and spirit	7.99	n.a.	n.a.	n.a.	n.a.	n.a.	n.a.	n.a.	n.a.	n.a.	n.a.	n.a.	n.a.
Business and economics	9.32	1	8.99	96.5	3	8.99	96.5	n.a.	n.a.	n.a.	n.a.	n.a.	n.a.
Children	6.22	177	6.97	112.1	230	8.05	129.4	184	8.34	134.1	223	8.63	138.7
Comics and graphic novels	n.a.	n.a.	n.a.	n.a.	n.a.	n.a.	n.a.	n.a.	n.a.	n.a.	n.a.	n.a.	n.a.
Computers	n.a.	n.a.	n.a.	n.a.	n.a.	n.a.	n.a.	n.a.	n.a.	n.a.	n.a.	n.a.	n.a.
Cooking	n.a.	n.a.	n.a.	n.a.	n.a.	n.a.	n.a.	n.a.	n.a.	n.a.	n.a.	n.a.	n.a.
Crafts and hobbies	n.a.	n.a.	n.a.	n.a.	n.a.	n.a.	n.a.	n.a.	n.a.	n.a.	n.a.	n.a.	n.a.
Design	n.a.	n.a.	n.a.	n.a.	n.a.	n.a.	n.a.	n.a.	n.a.	n.a.	n.a.	n.a.	n.a.
Drama	6.30	n.a.	n.a.	n.a.	n.a.	n.a.	n.a.	n.a.	n.a.	n.a.	n.a.	n.a.	n.a.
Education	n.a.	n.a.	n.a.	n.a.	n.a.	n.a.	n.a.	n.a.	n.a.	n.a.	n.a.	n.a.	n.a.
Family and relationships	7.99	n.a.	n.a.	n.a.	n.a.	n.a.	n.a.	n.a.	n.a.	n.a.	1	9.99	125.0
Fiction	6.80	2,753	7.31	107.5	2,737	7.27	106.9	2,472	7.43	109.3	2,297	7.64	112.4
Foreign language study	7.08	n.a.	n.a.	n.a.	1	8.50	n.a.	n.a.	n.a.	n.a.	n.a.	n.a.	n.a.
Games and activities	n.a.	n.a.	n.a.	n.a.	n.a.	n.a.	n.a.	n.a.	n.a.	n.a.	n.a.	n.a.	n.a.
Gardening	n.a.	n.a.	n.a.	n.a.	n.a.	n.a.	n.a.	n.a.	n.a.	n.a.	n.a.	n.a.	n.a.
Health and fitness	7.92	1	9.99	126.1	3	8.66	109.3	2	10.99	138.8	n.a.	n.a.	n.a.
History	9.95	5	9.99	100.4	3	9.99	100.4	4	8.99	90.4	4	9.99	100.4
House and home	n.a.	n.a.	n.a.	n.a.	n.a.	n.a.	n.a.	n.a.	n.a.	n.a.	n.a.	n.a.	n.a.
Humor	n.a.	1	9.99	n.a.	2	12.49	n.a.	n.a.	n.a.	n.a.	n.a.	n.a.	n.a.

Subject													
Language arts and disciplines	13.25	n.a.	n.a.	n.a.	n.a.	n.a.	n.a.	1	7.99	60.3	n.a.	n.a.	n.a.
Law	n.a.	n.a.	n.a.	n.a.	n.a.	n.a.	n.a.	n.a.	n.a.	n.a.	n.a.	n.a.	n.a.
Literary collections	5.95	n.a.	n.a.	n.a.	n.a.	n.a.	n.a.	n.a.	n.a.	n.a.	n.a.	n.a.	n.a.
Literary criticism	7.99	n.a.	n.a.	n.a.	n.a.	n.a.	n.a.	n.a.	n.a.	n.a.	n.a.	n.a.	n.a.
Mathematics	n.a.	n.a.	n.a.	n.a.	n.a.	n.a.	n.a.	n.a.	n.a.	n.a.	n.a.	n.a.	n.a.
Medical	8.99	n.a.	n.a.	n.a.	n.a.	n.a.	n.a.	n.a.	n.a.	n.a.	n.a.	n.a.	n.a.
Music	n.a.	n.a.	n.a.	n.a.	n.a.	n.a.	n.a.	n.a.	n.a.	n.a.	n.a.	n.a.	n.a.
Nature	n.a.	n.a.	n.a.	n.a.	n.a.	n.a.	n.a.	n.a.	n.a.	n.a.	n.a.	n.a.	n.a.
Performing arts	9.99	n.a.	n.a.	n.a.	n.a.	n.a.	n.a.	1	8.99	90.0	n.a.	n.a.	n.a.
Pets	7.99	n.a.	n.a.	n.a.	n.a.	n.a.	n.a.	n.a.	n.a.	n.a.	n.a.	n.a.	n.a.
Philosophy	6.47	n.a.	n.a.	n.a.	n.a.	n.a.	n.a.	n.a.	n.a.	n.a.	n.a.	n.a.	n.a.
Photography	n.a.	n.a.	n.a.	n.a.	n.a.	n.a.	n.a.	n.a.	n.a.	n.a.	n.a.	n.a.	n.a.
Poetry	7.95	n.a.	n.a.	n.a.	n.a.	n.a.	n.a.	n.a.	n.a.	n.a.	n.a.	n.a.	n.a.
Political science	7.97	1	8.99	112.8	1	9.99	125.3	1	9.99	125.3	n.a.	n.a.	n.a.
Psychology	n.a.	n.a.	n.a.	n.a.	1	13.99	n.a.	1	4.99	n.a.	n.a.	n.a.	n.a.
Reference	7.99	n.a.	n.a.	n.a.	n.a.	n.a.	n.a.	n.a.	n.a.	n.a.	1	8.99	112.5
Religion	7.99	n.a.	n.a.	n.a.	n.a.	n.a.	n.a.	n.a.	n.a.	n.a.	n.a.	n.a.	n.a.
Science	n.a.	n.a.	n.a.	n.a.	n.a.	n.a.	n.a.	n.a.	n.a.	n.a.	n.a.	n.a.	n.a.
Self-help	7.99	n.a.	n.a.	n.a.	6	13.99	175.1	4	12.74	159.4	1	7.99	100.0
Social science	n.a.	n.a.	n.a.	n.a.	n.a.	n.a.	n.a.	n.a.	n.a.	n.a.	n.a.	n.a.	n.a.
Sports and recreation	7.99	n.a.	n.a.	n.a.	n.a.	n.a.	n.a.	n.a.	n.a.	n.a.	n.a.	n.a.	n.a.
Study aids	n.a.	n.a.	n.a.	n.a.	n.a.	n.a.	n.a.	n.a.	n.a.	n.a.	n.a.	n.a.	n.a.
Technology and engineering	n.a.	n.a.	n.a.	n.a.	n.a.	n.a.	n.a.	n.a.	n.a.	n.a.	n.a.	n.a.	n.a.
Transportation	n.a.	n.a.	n.a.	n.a.	n.a.	n.a.	n.a.	n.a.	n.a.	n.a.	n.a.	n.a.	n.a.
Travel	n.a.	n.a.	n.a.	n.a.	n.a.	n.a.	n.a.	n.a.	n.a.	n.a.	n.a.	n.a.	n.a.
True crime	7.64	12	8.41	110.1	7	8.42	110.2	6	8.82	115.4	8	8.62	112.8
Young adult	8.13	5	8.39	103.2	26	11.80	145.1	35	9.65	118.7	46	11.27	138.6
Totals and Averages	$6.83	2,961	$7.31	107.0	3,028	$7.40	108.3	2,714	$7.54	110.4	2,587	$7.80	114.2

Compiled by Narda Tafuri, University of Scranton, from data supplied by Baker & Taylor.

n.a. = not available

Table 7 / U.S. Paperback Books (Excluding Mass Market): Average Prices and Price Indexes, 2017–2020

Index Base: 2010 = 100

BISAC Category	2010 Average Price	2017 Final			2018 Final			2019 Preliminary			2020 Preliminary		
		Volumes	Average Price	Index	Volumes	Average Price	Index	Volumes	Average Price	Index	Volumes	Average Price	Index
Antiques and collectibles	$25.53	114	$40.67	159.3	89	$42.24	165.5	86	$40.46	158.5	77	$43.11	168.9
Architecture	45.31	762	49.39	109.0	742	49.36	108.9	899	50.41	111.3	879	46.97	103.7
Art	38.25	1,720	41.04	107.3	1,734	40.36	105.5	1,735	39.29	102.7	1,585	39.42	103.1
Bibles	38.66	714	40.54	104.9	709	45.42	117.5	630	47.69	123.4	479	56.05	145.0
Biography and autobiography	20.35	2,393	20.56	101.0	2,581	20.67	101.6	2,356	20.67	101.6	2,282	20.92	102.8
Body, mind, and spirit	18.03	689	18.24	101.2	761	18.22	101.1	805	18.94	105.0	821	18.77	104.1
Business and economics	69.30	5,956	88.76	128.1	7,064	84.06	121.3	6,624	73.45	106.0	5,993	67.95	98.1
Children	10.42	11,825	16.10	154.6	11,651	12.82	123.1	11,870	12.39	118.9	10,113	11.39	109.4
Comics and graphic novels	16.11	2,057	18.49	114.8	2,331	19.13	118.8	2,211	20.56	127.6	1,978	18.92	117.4
Computers	70.42	2,602	96.95	137.7	3,408	104.73	148.7	3,390	102.21	145.1	2,919	80.66	114.5
Cooking	19.95	934	21.35	107.0	932	21.17	106.1	828	21.85	109.5	803	21.10	105.8
Crafts and hobbies	19.34	816	20.46	105.8	693	21.54	111.4	575	22.36	115.6	580	21.73	112.3
Design	63.98	242	40.56	63.4	234	41.19	64.4	255	44.93	70.2	222	37.61	58.8
Drama	18.95	652	22.54	118.9	555	20.72	109.3	468	23.55	124.3	412	21.44	113.2
Education	42.98	4,479	58.30	135.6	4,511	63.10	146.8	4,037	60.00	139.6	3,576	80.61	187.5
Family and relationships	18.72	523	21.44	114.5	590	22.15	118.3	626	21.75	116.2	604	21.02	112.3
Fiction	17.99	10,455	16.77	93.2	10,427	17.59	97.8	9,864	17.52	97.4	8,880	17.36	96.5
Foreign language study	31.33	1,013	41.69	133.1	836	45.05	143.8	917	42.88	136.9	842	42.40	135.3
Games and activities	16.57	1,258	15.57	94.0	699	17.41	105.1	626	18.04	108.9	665	18.08	109.1
Gardening	23.45	129	23.12	98.6	120	21.39	91.2	124	22.26	94.9	101	23.37	99.6
Health and fitness	26.95	1,039	30.93	114.8	1,057	31.05	115.2	971	32.69	121.3	956	31.54	117.0
History	35.79	6,348	38.73	108.2	6,347	40.05	111.9	6,583	40.30	112.6	6,462	38.74	108.2
House and home	21.19	104	26.21	123.7	87	22.50	106.2	109	24.13	113.9	63	21.29	100.5
Humor	14.37	302	15.80	110.0	263	15.50	107.9	263	15.73	109.4	211	16.81	117.0

Language arts and disciplines	64.46	1,696	72.90	113.1	1,627	61.43	95.3	1,708	56.62	87.8	1,438	54.71	849.0
Law	72.07	3,120	83.10	115.3	3,423	90.56	125.7	3,051	84.80	117.7	3,023	81.87	113.6
Literary collections	36.42	406	27.41	75.3	440	29.88	82.1	459	24.96	63.5	415	27.23	74.8
Literary criticism	36.57	1,935	43.30	118.4	2,149	50.86	138.2	2,351	44.09	120.6	2,033	41.06	112.3
Mathematics	86.13	953	78.54	91.2	1,540	105.18	122.0	1,372	76.03	88.3	1,108	64.93	75.4
Medical	90.22	3,696	86.85	96.3	5,292	115.14	127.6	4,469	86.54	95.9	3,489	80.29	89.0
Music	22.83	1,975	29.32	128.4	1,816	27.87	122.1	1,993	30.07	131.7	2,969	24.46	107.0
Nature	37.28	565	34.67	93.0	590	45.59	122.3	665	42.08	112.9	700	35.16	94.3
Performing arts	33.53	858	38.23	114.0	948	42.79	127.6	960	37.84	112.9	843	36.01	107.4
Pets	17.34	110	18.29	105.5	113	18.71	107.9	122	20.37	117.5	100	18.60	107.3
Philosophy	52.66	1,532	42.46	80.6	1,902	52.75	100.2	1,949	41.89	79.5	1,783	41.39	78.6
Photography	31.30	416	35.12	112.2	292	34.06	108.8	318	39.93	127.6	303	36.26	115.8
Poetry	16.73	2,033	17.24	103.1	2,161	17.22	102.9	2,031	17.31	103.5	1,868	17.46	104.4
Political science	41.00	3,881	47.27	115.3	4,395	58.93	143.7	4,371	50.55	123.3	4,788	46.22	112.7
Psychology	47.98	1,949	53.42	111.3	2,058	51.04	127.2	2,130	51.14	106.6	1,795	49.51	103.2
Reference	84.85	488	189.53	223.4	425	134.68	217.7	398	129.25	152.3	247	202.40	238.5
Religion	22.08	6,776	25.74	116.6	6,753	27.36	123.9	6,684	27.92	126.5	5,554	27.06	122.5
Science	116.37	2,443	89.79	77.2	4,873	127.83	109.8	4,163	95.62	82.2	3,364	87.46	75.2
Self-help	17.84	943	17.72	99.3	1,135	17.18	96.3	1,280	17.88	100.2	1,214	17.78	99.7
Social science	45.05	4,554	48.54	107.8	5,592	60.10	133.4	5,625	49.30	109.4	6,049	46.47	103.2
Sports and recreation	22.30	1,013	26.04	116.8	913	26.52	118.9	981	27.38	122.8	854	27.12	121.6
Study aids	49.24	748	34.23	69.5	690	43.12	87.6	2,594	43.53	88.4	2,433	43.31	83.0
Technology and engineering	111.20	2,279	98.34	107.3	3,995	143.34	128.9	3,075	118.58	106.6	2,929	125.17	112.6
Transportation	36.26	523	38.89	107.3	498	34.76	95.9	398	43.91	121.1	335	34.93	96.3
Travel	20.93	1,499	21.74	103.9	1,515	21.17	101.1	1,537	21.45	102.5	932	20.82	99.5
True crime	20.94	168	20.16	96.3	221	19.96	95.3	246	19.96	95.3	203	19.55	93.4
Young adult	14.86	2,724	18.40	123.8	2,946	18.09	121.7	2,885	18.45	124.1	2,307	16.15	108.7
Totals and Averages	$42.06	106,414	$42.92	102.0	116,817	$52.81	125.6	114,667	$45.11	107.3	104,579	$43.26	102.9

Compiled by Narda Tafuri, University of Scranton, from data supplied by Baker & Taylor.

Table 7A / U.S. Audiobooks: Average Prices and Price Indexes, 2017–2020

Index Base: 2010 = 100

BISAC Category	2010 Average Price	2017 Final Volumes	2017 Final Average Price	2017 Final Index	2018 Final Volumes	2018 Final Average Price	2018 Final Index	2019 Preliminary Volumes	2019 Preliminary Average Price	2019 Preliminary Index	2020 Preliminary Volumes	2020 Preliminary Average Price	2020 Preliminary Index
Antiques and collectibles	$36.66	3	$33.32	90.9	n.a.	n.a.	n.a.	n.a.	n.a.	n.a.	3	$40.99	111.8
Architecture	41.24	10	31.49	76.4	2	$22.99	55.7	8	$33.12	80.3	5	41.99	101.8
Art	58.21	24	28.36	48.7	16	31.54	54.2	8	31.05	53.3	11	34.90	60.0
Bibles	43.28	6	49.98	115.5	2	49.99	115.5	3	76.31	176.3	12	32.17	74.3
Biography and autobiography	50.79	1,445	37.46	73.7	1,242	42.79	84.2	1,379	43.60	85.8	1,215	42.75	84.2
Body, mind, and spirit	32.98	158	29.41	89.2	147	35.88	108.8	180	35.17	106.6	163	35.81	108.6
Business and economics	49.70	883	32.32	65.0	799	35.66	71.7	656	36.87	74.2	656	40.56	81.6
Children	37.80	1,701	31.14	82.4	1,333	36.52	96.6	1,558	37.16	98.3	1,853	33.21	87.9
Comics and graphic novels	n.a.	3	8.99	n.a.	n.a.	n.a.	n.a.	66	37.57	n.a.	37	36.34	n.a.
Computers	45.00	42	29.30	65.1	27	42.32	94.0	33	38.05	84.6	12	34.73	77.2
Cooking	44.97	63	35.24	78.4	58	39.69	88.3	16	37.30	82.9	32	35.61	79.2
Crafts and hobbies	24.98	2	12.99	52.0	3	22.32	89.4	5	39.79	159.3	3	39.99	160.1
Design	n.a.	n.a.	n.a.	n.a.	6	51.31	n.a.	1	39.99	n.a.	4	41.24	n.a.
Drama	33.21	60	20.23	60.9	163	18.48	55.6	98	22.32	67.2	36	25.35	76.3
Education	45.71	39	33.89	74.1	41	33.58	73.5	39	38.20	83.6	27	39.99	87.5
Family and relationships	41.17	204	32.02	77.8	183	34.16	83.0	185	37.01	89.9	150	36.29	88.1
Fiction	50.38	11,019	34.04	67.6	9,918	39.33	78.1	11,452	40.15	79.7	12,102	40.80	81.0
Foreign language study	45.11	96	79.65	176.6	100	207.23	459.4	149	85.90	190.4	40	59.98	133.0
Games and activities	n.a.	10	40.79	n.a.	5	39.99	n.a.	2	22.49	n.a.	4	42.49	n.a.
Gardening	47.82	5	26.98	56.4	n.a.	n.a.	n.a.	1	14.99	31.3	9	37.55	78.5
Health and fitness	43.09	289	39.77	92.3	264	38.61	89.6	242	40.17	93.2	220	42.94	99.6
History	58.07	904	44.42	76.5	809	47.41	81.6	811	46.40	79.9	722	47.03	81.0
House and home	n.a.	39	41.41	n.a.	20	35.48	n.a.	13	34.45	n.a.	17	39.52	n.a.
Humor	36.62	62	29.53	80.6	93	41.75	114.0	74	35.78	97.7	75	40.51	110.6

Language arts and disciplines	38.34	39	37.71	98.3	29	34.50	90.0	47	38.01	99.1	26	42.33	110.4
Law	64.49	31	42.50	65.9	34	34.16	53.0	25	31.15	48.3	30	38.82	60.2
Literary collections	52.07	45	33.45	64.2	69	42.97	82.5	67	41.97	80.6	34	38.98	74.9
Literary criticism	42.53	32	31.68	74.5	34	41.10	96.6	27	32.61	76.7	36	34.54	81.2
Mathematics	n.a.	10	21.49	n.a.	4	26.99	n.a.	7	46.70	n.a.	2	32.49	n.a.
Medical	40.13	49	36.06	89.9	36	41.82	104.2	31	32.70	81.5	36	40.37	100.6
Music	35.67	142	28.20	79.1	61	30.91	86.6	64	41.50	116.4	49	37.84	106.1
Nature	41.20	63	31.88	77.4	53	35.10	85.2	91	41.96	101.9	107	42.63	103.5
Performing arts	40.60	72	35.41	87.2	99	40.52	99.8	116	40.91	100.8	176	42.96	105.8
Pets	38.33	46	37.77	98.5	29	38.02	99.2	13	42.38	110.6	18	37.44	97.7
Philosophy	53.05	103	23.53	44.4	54	37.87	71.4	74	34.24	64.5	53	40.57	76.5
Photography	n.a.	n.a.	n.a.	n.a.	n.a.	n.a.	n.a.	n.a.	n.a.	n.a.	1	29.99	n.a.
Poetry	33.59	46	22.24	66.2	56	27.17	80.9	106	28.89	86.0	138	30.46	90.7
Political science	48.04	324	37.68	78.4	377	39.29	81.8	369	43.08	89.7	395	45.19	94.1
Psychology	45.42	157	37.66	82.9	162	37.25	82.0	99	35.16	77.4	119	46.15	101.6
Reference	59.99	15	35.79	59.7	8	46.62	77.7	7	30.70	51.2	8	36.24	60.4
Religion	33.94	1,249	26.94	79.4	1,152	30.52	89.9	929	35.13	103.6	812	37.71	111.1
Science	51.89	158	33.96	65.4	212	38.97	75.1	168	41.25	79.5	220	40.55	78.2
Self-help	39.43	382	33.75	85.6	427	36.21	91.8	516	35.42	89.8	501	37.44	95.0
Social science	48.07	298	35.10	73.0	322	35.98	74.9	265	41.89	87.1	274	39.58	82.3
Sports and recreation	48.48	145	36.42	75.1	111	38.35	79.1	144	41.96	86.6	146	38.33	79.1
Study aids	19.41	n.a.	n.a.	n.a.	3	41.63	214.5	2	63.00	324.5	3	38.66	199.2
Technology and engineering	53.33	103	101.94	191.2	31	45.18	84.7	13	39.29	73.7	16	38.74	72.6
Transportation	46.28	9	30.21	65.3	10	45.49	100.5	2	49.99	108.0	3	46.66	100.8
Travel	50.96	39	30.91	60.7	32	43.67	85.7	49	42.32	83.0	37	40.66	79.9
True crime	52.58	182	38.99	74.2	189	36.65	69.7	193	43.11	82.0	145	45.75	87.0
Young adult	44.81	1,463	39.21	87.5	1,118	44.63	99.6	1,221	43.81	97.8	1,159	43.33	96.7
Totals and Averages	$48.00	22,269	$34.87	72.6	19,943	$39.69	82.7	21,629	$40.31	84.0	21,952	$40.38	84.1

Compiled by Narda Tafuri, University of Scranton, from data supplied by Baker & Taylor.
n.a. = not available

Table 7B / U.S. E-Books: Average Prices and Price Indexes, 2017–2020

Index Base: 2010 = 100

BISAC Category	2010 Average Price	2017 Final Volumes	2017 Final Average Price	2017 Final Index	2018 Final Volumes	2018 Final Average Price	2018 Final Index	2019 Preliminary Volumes	2019 Preliminary Average Price	2019 Preliminary Index	2020 Preliminary Volumes	2020 Preliminary Average Price	2020 Preliminary Index
Antiques and collectibles	$30.24	118	$16.64	55.0	174	$10.85	35.9	157	$10.93	36.2	111	$24.61	81.4
Architecture	66.57	818	21.98	33.0	467	48.45	72.8	494	42.44	63.8	224	40.97	61.6
Art	41.56	2,356	18.16	43.7	1,456	36.47	87.8	1,713	27.38	65.9	757	29.70	71.5
Bibles	6.11	2,148	11.88	194.4	444	10.00	163.6	304	12.00	196.5	321	16.14	264.2
Biography and autobiography	15.47	7,908	17.24	111.5	7,380	19.74	127.6	7,382	21.88	141.4	5,500	34.08	220.3
Body, mind, and spirit	13.95	2,580	11.26	80.7	3,047	11.41	81.8	3,715	12.57	90.1	3,067	17.73	127.1
Business and economics	44.82	9,248	41.29	92.1	28,520	51.31	114.5	24,760	65.94	147.1	14,690	51.22	114.3
Children	13.82	26,145	17.92	129.7	28,927	15.72	113.8	27,963	19.06	137.9	19,752	21.87	158.2
Comics and graphic novels	11.39	876	8.97	78.7	1,371	8.11	71.2	1,039	9.55	83.8	2,000	8.71	76.4
Computers	62.09	3,177	82.11	132.2	4,026	75.10	121.0	2,514	59.52	95.9	1,490	42.03	67.7
Cooking	16.79	2,691	12.13	72.2	3,228	13.35	79.5	3,232	13.38	79.7	2,377	18.99	113.1
Crafts and hobbies	17.63	1,176	11.34	64.3	652	15.07	85.5	612	15.45	87.6	556	18.77	106.5
Design	37.03	170	20.84	56.3	131	24.03	64.9	146	26.67	72.0	119	30.66	82.8
Drama	4.86	1,546	12.03	247.4	1,137	10.97	225.8	1,349	9.62	197.9	589	19.58	402.9
Education	45.95	7,660	40.50	88.1	4,578	43.77	95.3	4,372	41.11	89.5	2,407	34.58	75.3
Family and relationships	14.79	1,762	13.05	88.2	2,393	12.65	85.5	2,420	14.49	98.0	1,988	20.86	141.0
Fiction	7.06	75,766	9.84	139.3	83,090	11.26	159.5	85,595	13.65	193.3	65,371	27.94	395.8
Foreign language study	46.68	1,678	23.12	49.5	2,321	22.16	47.5	1,594	25.96	55.6	4,519	16.47	35.3
Games and activities	12.85	930	8.67	67.5	1,518	6.85	53.3	383	15.33	119.3	315	20.40	158.7
Gardening	17.41	555	12.43	71.4	339	15.12	86.8	316	15.89	91.3	313	17.83	102.4
Health and fitness	18.78	3,002	13.58	72.3	3,229	13.73	73.1	3,179	16.06	85.5	3,147	20.09	107.0
History	48.20	13,019	29.92	62.1	9,693	42.23	87.6	8,878	46.02	95.5	11,371	33.94	70.4
House and home	21.57	392	14.00	64.9	279	16.19	75.1	261	17.48	81.0	230	23.30	108.0
Humor	11.15	848	10.58	94.9	1,101	14.44	129.5	928	15.31	137.3	774	18.91	170.0

Language arts and disciplines	75.61	2,844	82.27	108.8	2,987	67.54	89.3	3,097	94.11	124.5	1,399	78.21	103.4
Law	112.19	2,657	86.63	77.2	3,121	112.45	100.2	2,825	117.69	104.9	1,507	131.28	117.0
Literary collections	20.27	2,159	15.68	77.4	1,633	14.86	73.3	6,296	4.85	23.9	1,027	17.44	86.1
Literary criticism	87.17	3,136	70.67	81.1	3,695	79.64	91.4	3,197	79.12	90.8	1,708	82.70	94.8
Mathematics	112.32	1,506	56.58	50.4	1,150	81.08	72.2	915	90.43	80.5	381	91.83	81.8
Medical	135.71	3,574	96.30	71.0	3,631	104.48	77.0	2,716	97.00	71.5	1,303	81.69	60.2
Music	32.65	2,538	20.88	64.0	3,014	16.79	51.4	1,848	23.60	72.3	1,318	29.42	90.1
Nature	59.48	806	39.73	66.8	851	27.58	46.4	793	27.61	46.4	646	30.47	51.2
Performing arts	32.17	1,879	24.11	75.0	2,125	25.84	80.3	2,008	24.52	76.2	1,022	31.53	98.0
Pets	14.50	805	10.50	72.4	451	10.52	72.5	459	13.26	91.4	322	19.12	131.9
Philosophy	71.43	3,608	34.82	48.7	2,938	48.73	68.2	2,799	43.03	60.2	2,676	31.45	44.0
Photography	27.23	514	17.08	62.7	342	18.80	69.1	285	21.96	80.6	260	20.12	73.9
Poetry	9.54	5,189	8.77	91.9	5,015	8.11	85.0	4,806	9.04	94.8	2,436	11.27	118.2
Political science	59.74	5,231	42.57	71.3	4,982	51.98	87.0	4,015	43.45	72.7	2,718	41.43	69.3
Psychology	56.42	2,720	43.12	76.4	2,157	44.82	79.4	1,955	40.00	70.9	1,958	33.63	59.6
Reference	22.92	2,999	18.62	81.2	1,083	44.46	194.0	948	65.42	285.4	623	45.94	200.4
Religion	27.81	13,497	20.67	74.3	12,123	25.91	93.2	11,062	27.40	98.5	8,501	31.64	113.8
Science	155.80	5,749	65.79	42.2	4,157	58.62	63.3	3,643	94.70	60.8	1,958	85.56	54.9
Self-help	14.06	5,351	12.17	86.5	5,229	12.69	90.2	6,871	12.41	88.3	5,717	20.12	143.1
Social science	56.83	6,985	40.93	72.0	5,355	48.42	85.2	4,342	49.07	86.3	2,802	42.69	75.1
Sports and recreation	19.22	1,920	17.26	89.8	1,668	20.77	108.1	1,501	20.84	108.4	1,136	27.21	141.6
Study aids	13.94	2,388	32.76	235.0	2,660	19.57	140.4	3,802	27.74	199.0	783	15.49	111.2
Technology and engineering	158.44	3,996	86.25	54.4	3,191	121.41	76.6	2,271	115.05	72.6	919	97.80	61.7
Transportation	33.12	271	24.87	75.1	333	27.66	33.5	278	28.47	86.0	516	25.71	77.6
Travel	15.84	2,521	14.67	92.6	2,223	16.62	104.9	3,230	12.03	76.0	1,354	21.63	136.6
True crime	10.37	411	20.53	197.9	531	21.54	207.7	612	24.57	236.9	696	28.48	274.6
Young adult	11.96	5,501	20.04	167.6	6,601	17.82	149.0	6,640	19.65	164.3	5,444	26.05	217.8
Totals and Averages	$41.61	257,324	$25.29	60.8	272,771	$29.51	70.9	266,520	$29.96	72.0	193,118	$31.90	76.7

Compiled by Narda Tafuri, University of Scranton, from data supplied by Baker & Taylor.

(continued from page 350)

Foreign Prices

As shown in the chart below, in 2020 the U.S. dollar decreased in strength against the Canadian dollar (-1.5 percent), the British pound sterling (-7.9 percent), the Japanese Yen (-3.9 percent), and the Euro (-5.0 percent).

	12/31/2016	12/31/2017	12/31/2018	12/31/2019	12/31/2020
Canada	1.35	1.26	1.36	1.30	1.28
Euro	0.95	0.83	0.87	0.89	0.82
U.K.	0.81	0.74	0.78	0.76	0.73
Japan	117.03	112.55	109.85	108.53	103.08

Data from Bureau of Fiscal Services. U.S. Treasury Department (http://www.fiscal.treasury.gov/fsreports/rpt/treasRptRateExch/treasRptRateExch_home.htm).

Serials Prices

Average Price of Serials (Table 8) and Average Price of Online Serials (Table 8A), compiled by Stephen Bosch, provide the average prices and percent increases for serials based on titles in select serials abstracting and indexing products. The serials in this price survey are published in the United States as well as overseas and are indexed in the Clarivate Analytics' (formerly ISI) Arts and Humanities Citation Index, Science Citation Index, and Social Sciences Citation Index, as well as EBSCO's Academic Search Ultimate and Masterfile Premier and Elsevier's Scopus. This is the third year where titles indexed in Scopus are included in the data. Adding Scopus expands this price survey from about 11,000 priced titles in 2015 to the current 18,239. The increase in the sample size makes the results more likely to accurately reflect pricing trends.

Tables 8 and 8A cover prices for periodicals and serials for a five-year period, 2017 through 2021. The 2021 pricing is the actual renewal pricing for serial titles indexed in the selected products. These tables were derived from pricing data supplied by EBSCO Information Services and reflect broad pricing changes aggregated from serials that are indexed in the six major products mentioned above. The U.S. Periodicals: Average Prices and Price Indexes (USPPI) (Table 1) is based on price changes seen in a static set of approximately 6,000 serial titles. The Average Price of Serials (Table 8) is based on a much broader set of titles, approximately 18,239; however, the indexed titles are not static year to year, so this pricing study does not rise to the level of a price index. The study is still useful in showing price changes for periodicals. The indexes selected for this price survey were deemed to be representative of serials that are frequently purchased in academic and public libraries. There are some foreign titles in the indexes, so the scope is broader, and this may give a better picture of the overall price pressures experienced in libraries. Table 8 contains both print and online serials pricing. Table 8A is a subset of the titles treated in Table 8 and contains only online serials pricing.

The most important trend seen in the data in Table 8 is that increases in serial prices have slowed considerably in 2021 due to the impact of the pandemic. In previous years, the price increases had remained constant since the economic recovery began in 2010. Since that time, price increases have hovered around 6 percent annually. The increase for 2021 was 3.4 percent. For titles with online availability (Table 8A), the increase for 2021 was 3.5 percent. For online serials, rates of increase in previous years had also averaged about 6 percent over the past five years. There is a difference between the average prices for print serials and online serials, so, at least for this set of data, print formats do cost less than their online counterparts. Several large publishers have made online pricing available only through custom quotes, so there is not a standard retail price, and the pricing data are not available for this survey. Consequently, the number of titles covered in the online survey (Table 8A) is less than the number of titles in Table 8, but titles with print-only pricing are now 43 percent of the overall dataset.

Another interesting trend is that the science areas do not dominate the list of subjects with the largest price increases. The subject areas that displayed large increases were quite varied. Zoology, general science, social sciences, health sciences, geology, astronomy, geography, arts and architecture, psychology, library science, recreation, physics, and sociology saw higher increases than most other areas. Some of these same areas showed the highest increases in the online table (Table 8A), as well. Average prices of journals in the science and technology areas are by far higher than average prices in other areas, and that trend continues with the average cost of chemistry and physics journals (Table 8) being $4,831.06 and $3,808.11, respectively. Online journals (Table 8A) showed similar average prices for chemistry ($5,220.25) and physics ($4,332.08).

It should again be noted that in this study, as in similar price surveys, the data become less accurate at describing price changes as the sample size becomes smaller. For that reason, analyses of price changes in subject areas with a limited number of titles will be less accurate than those for large areas or the broader price survey. Price changes are far more volatile where smaller datasets are used, as is the case with recreation, which, with just 125 titles, showed a price change of 5.3 percent in 2021—higher than most other areas. Librarians are encouraged to look at an average price change over the period or the overall number for the price study (6.0 percent) to calculate inflation. Year-to-year price changes in small subject areas are too unstable to be reliable indicators of future prices for budgeting purposes.

Foreign Book Prices

British Academic Books (Table 9), compiled by George Aulisio, University of Scranton, indicates the average prices and price indexes from 2017 through 2020. The percent of change in titles and average price are calculated for 2019 to 2020, and the index price shows the percent of change between 2020 and the base year of 2010. This index is compiled using data from GOBI Library Solutions and utilizes prices from cloth editions when available. The data also draw from select titles from continental Europe and Africa. The index does not separate more expensive reference titles. Small numbers of titles that include higher-priced reference sets may not be reliable indicators of price changes. This table does not include e-book prices.

Data in the "Totals and Averages" row include the total of the LC Classes profiled in this table, not the total of all books profiled by GOBI Library Solutions.

(text continues on page 370)

Table 8 / Average Price of Serials, Based on Titles in Select Serial Indexes, 2017–2021

Subject	LC Class	Titles	2017 Average Price	2018 Average Price	Percent Change 2017–2018	2019 Average Price	Percent Change 2018–2019	2020 Average Price	Percent Change 2019–2010	2021 Average Price	Percent Change 2020–2021
Agriculture	S	529	$990.09	$1,048.85	5.9%	$1,116.61	6.5%	$1,182.25	5.9%	$1,228.04	3.9%
Anthropology	GN	150	466.85	517.49	10.8	541.98	4.7	575.43	6.2	599.43	4.2
Arts and architecture	N	240	327.52	348.73	6.5	368.98	5.8	392.93	6.5	409.60	4.2
Astronomy	QB	72	1,906.80	1,993.89	4.6	2,093.28	5.0	2,221.71	6.1	2,164.69	-2.6
Biology	QH	1,120	2,327.70	2,464.77	5.9	2,615.57	6.1	2,746.44	5.0	2,824.66	2.8
Botany	QK	176	1,516.58	1,577.77	4.0	1,669.03	5.8	1,742.64	4.4	1,792.15	2.8
Business and economics	HA–HJ	1,344	1,223.05	1,280.73	4.7	1,347.47	5.2	1,416.76	5.1	1,469.10	3.7
Chemistry	QD	379	4,062.04	4,247.65	4.6	4,504.30	6.0	4,725.90	4.9	4,831.06	2.2
Education	L	486	683.06	728.14	6.6	782.15	7.4	832.91	6.5	872.43	4.7
Engineering	T	1,622	1,773.23	1,897.35	7.0	2,028.17	6.9	2,164.86	6.7	2,242.71	3.6
Food Science	TX	96	1,208.54	1,286.88	6.5	1,350.19	4.9	1,427.23	5.7	1,488.22	4.3
General Science	Q	222	1,270.31	1,326.02	4.4	1,406.97	6.1	1,486.83	5.7	1,527.24	2.7
General Works	A	205	235.58	245.33	4.1	263.50	7.4	278.20	5.6	289.87	4.2
Geography	G–GF	295	957.56	1,033.64	7.9	1,103.05	6.7	1,176.61	6.7	1,219.40	3.6
Geology	QE	231	1,662.51	1,761.49	6.0	1,893.41	7.5	2,011.43	6.2	2,095.30	4.2
Health Sciences	R	3,750	1,226.24	1,310.77	6.9	1,386.15	5.8	1,484.61	7.1	1,549.50	4.4
History	C,D,E,F	981	332.58	353.82	6.4	376.92	6.5	398.66	5.8	416.18	4.4
Language and literature	P	1,093	336.67	359.30	6.7	379.80	5.7	401.30	5.7	414.99	3.4

Subject	LC Class	Titles	Price	Price	%	Price	%	Price	%	Price	%
Law	K	501	412.84	436.20	5.7	459.15	5.3	482.57	5.1	502.66	4.2
Library Science	Z	179	941.63	972.52	3.3	1,019.45	4.8	1,062.22	4.2	1,110.03	4.5
Math and computer science	QA	883	1,374.66	1,463.58	6.5	1,544.14	5.5	1,645.03	6.5	1,693.79	3.0
Military and naval science	U,V	99	541.83	566.06	4.5	617.47	9.1	656.02	6.2	686.84	4.7
Music	M	171	225.00	239.51	6.5	251.85	5.2	266.71	5.9	274.58	3.0
Philosophy and religion	B-BD, BH-BX	671	329.39	347.91	5.6	363.93	4.6	379.80	4.4	393.32	3.6
Physics	QC	444	3,149.06	3,307.89	5.0	3,512.64	6.2	3,716.79	5.8	3,808.11	2.5
Political Science	J	291	577.40	620.86	7.5	664.01	6.9	707.37	6.5	736.61	4.1
Psychology	BF	333	790.78	845.72	6.9	913.75	8.6	985.32	7.2	1,014.51	3.0
Recreation	GV	125	477.90	513.47	7.4	549.50	7.0	583.52	6.2	614.46	5.3
Social sciences	H	139	728.37	769.87	5.7	812.90	5.6	860.25	5.8	870.04	1.1
Sociology	HM-HX	753	761.50	812.05	6.6	868.04	6.9	923.12	6.3	957.32	3.7
Technology	TA-TT	340	1,307.59	1,379.55	5.5	1,473.69	6.8	1,558.49	5.8	1,616.02	3.7
Zoology	QL	309	1,323.72	1,396.20	5.5	1,465.22	4.9	1,540.27	5.1	1,544.76	0.3
Totals and Averages		18,239	$1,195.68	$1,268.35	6.1%	$1,345.75	6.1%	$1,427.15	6.0%	$1,475.98	3.4%

Compiled by Stephen Bosch, University of Arizona. Data on serial pricing supplied by EBSCO and are based on titles indexed in EBSCO Academic Search Ultimate, EBSCO Masterfile Complete, Clarivate Analytics (formerly ISI) Arts and Humanities Citation Index, Clarivate Analytics Science Citation Index, Clarivate Analytics Social Sciences Citation Index, and Elsevier's Scopus.

Table 8A / Changes in the Average Price of Online Serials 2017–2021, Based on Titles in Select Serial Indexes

Subject	LC Class	Titles	2017 Average Price	2018 Average Price	Percent Change 2017–2018	2019 Average Price	Percent Change 2018–2019	2020 Average Price	Percent Change 2019–2020	2021 Average Price	Percent Change 2020–2021
Agriculture	S	227	$1,272.93	$1,338.71	5.2%	$1,438.07	7.4%	$1,521.77	5.8%	$1,590.09	4.5%
Anthropology	GN	97	606.57	651.25	7.4	691.80	6.2	739.11	6.8	770.50	4.2
Arts and Architecture	N	110	496.10	527.62	6.4	567.42	7.5	600.87	5.9	624.71	4.0
Astronomy	QB	44	2,530.63	2,646.60	4.6	2,781.66	5.1	2,968.54	6.7	2,856.43	-3.8
Biology	QH	625	2,313.03	2,448.09	5.8	2,613.85	6.8	2,734.79	4.6	2,807.95	2.7
Botany	QK	108	1,762.19	1,816.17	3.1	1,912.69	5.3	1,984.37	3.7	2,040.40	2.8
Business and Economics	HA-HJ	753	1,654.16	1,720.68	4.0	1,807.99	5.1	1,900.07	5.1	1,976.03	4.0
Chemistry	QD	209	4,280.85	4,515.18	5.5	4,838.15	7.2	5,096.33	5.3	5,220.25	2.4
Education	L	346	833.10	886.12	6.4	955.04	7.8	1,017.12	6.5	1,068.21	5.0
Engineering	T	783	1,966.86	2,116.18	7.6	2,273.36	7.4	2,432.46	7.0	2,525.15	3.8
Food Science	TX	51	1,647.49	1,750.11	6.2	1,825.95	4.3	1,929.29	5.7	2,013.91	4.4
General Science	Q	130	1,589.24	1,642.81	3.4	1,743.49	6.1	1,833.04	5.1	1,869.37	2.0
General Works	A	59	549.48	569.61	3.7	619.87	8.8	662.59	6.9	693.57	4.7
Geography	G-GF	183	909.00	980.91	7.9	1,056.86	7.7	1,133.15	7.2	1,180.41	4.2
Geology	QE	124	1,601.59	1,675.32	4.6	1,802.33	7.6	1,920.32	6.5	2,002.72	4.3
Health Sciences	R	1,657	1,415.83	1,511.20	6.7	1,588.90	5.1	1,710.90	7.7	1,779.95	4.0
History	C,D,E,F	512	449.93	478.02	6.2	514.34	7.6	547.69	6.5	574.80	4.9
Language and Literature	P	578	449.40	481.55	7.2	513.72	6.7	545.03	6.1	566.19	3.9

Subject	LC Class	No. of Titles	Price	Price	%	Price	%	Price	%	Price	%
Law	K	174	642.73	680.59	5.9	715.33	5.1	747.20	4.5	778.92	4.2
Library Science	Z	113	1,206.15	1,236.31	2.5	1,294.68	4.7	1,354.42	4.6	1,413.82	4.4
Math and Computer Science	QA	565	1,414.76	1,522.09	7.6	1,619.56	6.4	1,745.44	7.8	1,809.15	3.7
Military and Naval Science	U,V	61	667.55	697.88	4.5	765.23	9.7	815.83	6.6	859.43	5.3
Music	M	77	352.50	375.96	6.7	396.11	5.4	416.46	5.1	428.57	2.9
Philosophy and Religion	B-BD, BH-BX	308	494.66	523.76	5.9	551.29	5.3	578.89	5.0	598.38	3.4
Physics	QC	277	3,498.19	3,696.83	5.7	3,952.05	6.9	4,208.41	6.5	4,332.08	2.9
Political Science	J	193	712.89	768.36	7.8	825.35	7.4	878.11	6.4	915.32	4.2
Psychology	BF	187	932.51	994.94	6.7	1,078.97	8.4	1,169.41	8.4	1,209.20	3.4
Recreation	GV	64	706.24	758.09	7.3	814.28	7.4	863.59	6.1	906.39	5.0
Social Sciences	H	78	926.32	980.17	5.8	1,035.76	5.7	1,100.68	6.3	1,113.41	1.2
Sociology	HM-HX	511	901.54	959.52	6.4	1,028.17	7.2	1,095.89	6.6	1,137.69	3.8
Technology	TA-TT	150	1,948.04	2,054.63	5.5	2,207.29	7.4	2,345.53	6.3	2,446.73	4.3
Zoology	QL	163	1,618.67	1,695.58	4.8	1,796.97	6.0	1,904.60	6.0	1,903.34	-0.1
Totals and Averages		9,517	$1,400.15	$1,454.78	6.0%	$1,580.21	6.4%	$1,679.96	6.3%	$1,738.63	3.5%

Compiled by Stephen Bosch, University of Arizona. Data on serial pricing supplied by EBSCO and are based on titles indexed in EBSCO Academic Search Ultimate, EBSCO Masterfile Complete, Clarivate Analytics (formerly ISI) Arts and Humanities Citation Index, Clarivate Analytics Science Citation Index, Clarivate Analytics Social Sciences Citation Index, and Elsevier's Scopus.

Table 9 / British Academic Books: Average Prices and Price Indexes, 2017–2020

Index Base: 2010 = 100

Subject	LC Class	2010 Titles	2010 Average Price (£)	2017 Titles	2017 Average Price (£)	2018 Titles	2018 Average Price (£)	2019 Titles	2019 Average Price (£)	2020 Titles	2020 Average Price (£)	Percent Change 2019–2020	Index
Agriculture	S	154	£63.97	125	£79.66	142	£85.45	154	£84.11	613	£87.95	4.6%	137.5
Anthropology	GN	154	50.85	121	60.79	150	65.47	173	74.65	294	70.16	-6.0	138.0
Botany	QK	45	66.08	27	80.32	30	77.10	36	89.13	162	115.45	29.5	174.7
Business and economics	H-HJ	1,913	60.54	1,767	77.80	2,185	84.35	2,185	80.42	4,409	78.68	-2.2	130.0
Chemistry	QD	96	105.68	47	104.58	58	127.93	61	121.99	309	130.53	7.0	123.5
Education	L	558	52.21	575	78.43	723	77.96	731	78.83	2,315	69.15	-12.3	132.4
Engineering and technology	T-TS	742	61.84	692	82.39	654	86.12	693	90.24	3,845	109.15	21.0	176.5
Fine and applied arts	M, N	1,037	35.95	917	53.71	974	59.66	989	60.88	3,601	50.02	-17.8	139.1
General works	A	30	60.03	33	92.37	33	108.43	37	85.11	90	91.85	7.9	153.0
Geography	G-GF, GR-GT	276	65.69	315	87.06	317	86.29	342	81.01	798	82.65	2.0	125.8
Geology	QE	33	52.28	30	57.36	30	74.38	51	58.66	123	106.49	81.5	203.7
History	C,D,E,F	1,822	42.55	1,790	54.96	2,051	60.70	2,215	57.95	4,813	62.73	8.2	147.4
Home economics	TX	46	30.48	48	83.35	36	78.58	37	91.70	333	46.16	-49.7	151.5
Industrial arts	TT	41	28.47	25	61.26	36	53.10	23	51.59	105	55.50	7.6	194.9
Language and literature	P	3,987	31.58	2,902	50.52	3,112	55.95	3,219	55.93	7,444	47.93	-14.3	151.8

Subject	LC												
Law	K	1,153	83.10	1,207	100.34	1,276	101.89	1,313	99.48	2,050	89.98	-9.5	108.3
Library and information science	Z	100	53.58	98	62.98	93	68.03	85	79.97	269	73.66	-7.9	137.5
Mathematics and computer science	QA	207	48.29	186	71.56	195	71.84	222	78.73	2,189	77.88	-1.1	161.3
Medicine	R	1,182	55.12	859	7C.12	931	73.90	1,081	76.98	3,880	94.36	22.6	171.2
Military and naval sciences	U, V	184	40.95	127	59.93	181	65.54	155	57.91	520	55.82	-3.6	136.3
Philosophy and religion	B-BD, BH-BX	1,336	48.17	1,075	68.74	1,364	73.64	1,505	69.70	3,998	53.46	-23.3	111.0
Physics and astronomy	QB, QC	214	64.83	167	69.30	206	73.19	200	75.70	751	93.42	23.4	144.1
Political Science	J	737	71.88	802	77.93	787	87.59	1,107	77.96	1,670	73.37	-5.9	102.1
Psychology	BF	265	39.69	337	72.28	378	76.47	414	80.74	854	63.66	-21.2	160.4
Science (general)	Q	60	40.70	71	75.80	82	67.59	99	71.83	521	85.30	18.8	209.6
Sociology	HM-HX	1,169	58.24	1,358	73.25	1,649	78.65	1,685	73.91	3,367	66.26	-10.4	113.8
Sports and Recreation	GV	192	36.76	204	81.24	207	84.02	216	80.04	645	51.38	-35.8	139.8
Zoology	QH, QL-QR	382	65.79	271	73.11	262	80.40	321	85.51	1,203	101.95	19.2	155.0
Totals and Averages		18,115	£50.50	16,176	£69.11	18,142	£73.94	19,350	£72.61	51,171	£71.56	-1.4%	141.7

Compiled by George Aulisio, University of Scranton, based on information provided by GOBI Library Solutions.

(continued from page 363)

In 2020 total British academic books profiled by GOBI increased substantially to 51,171 titles. This is the fourth year the table has recorded an increase in titles. Notably, this is more than double the number of titles usually profiled.

In 2020 British academic books experienced an overall price decrease of -1.4 percent, bringing the average price for all books profiled to £71.56. The 2020 price decrease comes at a time when the United Kingdom's Consumer Price Index saw a moderate 1.0 percent inflation as of December 2020 (http://www.ons.gov.uk).

Table 9 shows how average prices have increased or decreased in comparison with the 2010 base year. For 2020 the overall index price for all LC subjects profiled in this table is at 141.7 percent. All LC classes listed are currently above their 2010 base prices. The highest increases in comparison with the 2010 base prices are science (general) (209.6 percent), geology (203.7 percent), and industrial arts (194.9 percent). There are currently no known reliable indicators for a 2020 industry forecast.

Using the Price Indexes

Librarians are encouraged to monitor publishing industry trends and changes in economic conditions when preparing budget forecasts and projections. The Library Materials Price Index (LMPI) Editorial Board endeavors to make information on publishing trends readily available by sponsoring the annual compilation and publication of price data contained in our published tables. The indexes cover newly published library materials and document prices and rates of percent changes at the national and international level. They are useful benchmarks to compare against local costs, but because they reflect retail prices in the aggregate they are not a substitute for cost data that reflect the collecting patterns of individual libraries, and they are not a substitute for specific cost studies.

Differences between local prices and those found in national indexes arise partially because the indexes exclude discounts, service charges, shipping and handling fees, and other discounts or costs that a library might see. Discrepancies may also relate to a library's subject coverage, its mix of titles purchased—including both current and backfiles—and the proportion of the library's budget expended on domestic or foreign materials. These variables can affect the average price paid by an individual library, although the individual library's rate of increase may not differ greatly from the national indexes.

Closing Note

The LMPI Editorial Board is interested in pursuing studies that would correlate a particular library's costs with the national prices. The group welcomes interested parties to its meeting at ALA Annual. The Library Materials Price Index Editorial Board consists of compilers George Aulisio, Ajaye Bloomstone, Stephen Bosch, and Narda Tafuri. George Aulisio currently serves as editor, and Rachel Fleming, University of Tennessee at Chattanooga, serves as assistant editor.

Book Title Output and Average Prices: 2018–2020

Constance Harbison

Baker & Taylor

The figures appearing in this report were provided for publication in *Library and Book Trade Almanac* by book wholesaler Baker & Taylor and are based on the Book Industry Study Group's BISAC Subject Headings. Figures for 2018 and 2019 have been revised since the previous edition was published, reflecting updates to the Baker & Taylor database. Figures for 2020 are considered preliminary at the time of this report.

Annual book title output in the United States saw a very slight uptick from 2018 to 2019, increasing by a mere .5 percent followed by a significant drop in 2020 (see Table 1). After increasing to 207,603 volumes (up from 2018's 206,591), revised total production figures for 2019 were 207,603, with preliminary 2020 results standing at 186,094. This 11.55 percent decline in output is not surprising, as the country largely entered quarantine in March 2020 when the COVID-19 outbreak was declared a pandemic. Throughout the year, publishers faced challenges as employees were furloughed and bookstores and libraries put a hold on orders due to closures and reduced capacities. Some highly popular categories including children's, fiction, and young adult experienced drops of 10–24 percent.

Typically, preliminary figures are revised upward as late-arriving materials are added to the database, suggesting that the final "total" 2020 output shown in Table 1 may increase and show less dramatic drops between 2019 and 2020.

Output and Prices by Format and Category

Overall, the output and pricing of titles peaked in 2019, with the average price of hardcover books dropping by more than 5 percent from 2018 to 2019 (Table 2). Prices increased in such categories as cooking, crafts and hobbies, and health and fitness, suggesting that publishers were raising prices on titles consumers were most interested in having while quarantined.

The average price of hardcover titles remained fairly stable from 2018 to 2019, though output fell within that period (Table 3). The period of 2018–2020 only saw a .44 percent increase in average price. The average price for hardcover fiction increased slightly in 2019 but dropped in 2020 so that it was consistent with the 2018 average. As libraries were experiencing closures, it was likely in the best interest of publishers to not increase pricing in certain categories so that consumers would instead purchase these highly circulated titles.

Mass market titles had a slight average price increase from 2018 to 2020, while preliminary 2020 figures show mass market output falling 14.6 percent over the period (Table 4). In addition to the decline in output of mass market titles, the number of categories publishing in the format fell. In 2018 mass market titles were published in 13 categories, dropping to 12 categories in 2019 and to just 9 in 2020. This trend suggests that mass market publishers are sharpening their focus on specific, proven consumer-centric categories.

(text continues on page 384)

Table 1 / American Book Production, 2018–2020

BISAC Category	2018	2019	2020
Antiques and Collectibles	192	186	171
Architecture	1,650	1,817	1,760
Art	3,785	3,981	3,624
Bibles	960	816	678
Biography and Autobiography	4,316	3,914	3,825
Body, Mind, and Spirit	975	1,084	1,134
Business and Economics	12,105	11,319	10,324
Children	28,713	28,314	25,731
Comics and Graphic Novels	2,999	2,895	2,647
Computers	4,593	4,784	4,024
Cooking	2,094	1,941	1,730
Crafts and Hobbies	890	746	742
Design	598	622	536
Drama	624	558	487
Education	7,556	6,766	6,092
Family and Relationships	815	846	820
Fiction	18,128	17,357	15,280
Foreign Language Study	1,143	1,193	1,095
Games and Activities	884	772	803
Gardening	244	244	211
Health and Fitness	1,432	1,375	1,318
History	12,298	12,880	12,107
House and Home	210	240	178
Humor	614	560	458
Language Arts and Disciplines	3,075	3,254	2,828
Law	5,926	5,425	5,419
Literary Collections	693	727	665
Literary Criticism	4,553	4,997	4,537
Mathematics	2,834	2,612	2,069
Medical	8,373	8,075	6,439
Music	2,433	2,673	3,633
Nature	1,015	1,129	1,150
Performing Arts	1,776	1,747	1,652
Pets	183	178	161
Philosophy	3,585	3,868	3,567
Photography	1,145	1,138	1,106
Poetry	2,456	2,337	2,123
Political Science	7,888	9,914	8,420
Psychology	3,602	4,949	3,030
Reference	765	712	450
Religion	9,882	9,428	8,306
Science	8,921	8,492	7,017
Self-Help	1,568	1,715	1,620
Social Science	10,400	11,041	10,251
Sports and Recreation	1,517	1,523	1,346
Study Aids	706	2,603	2,462
Technology and Engineering	7,181	6,122	6,194
Transportation	789	683	557
Travel	2,098	1,770	1,162
True Crime	312	361	296
Young Adult	5,097	4,920	3,859
Total	206,591	207,603	186,094

Table 2 / Hardcover Output and Average Per-Volume Prices, 2018–2020

BISAC Category	2018			2019			2020		
	Vols.	$ Total	Avg.	Vols.	Total	Avg.	Vols.	Total	Avg.
Antiques and Collectibles	103	$7,515.30	$72.96	100	$6,583.84	$65.84	94	$6,982.05	$74.28
Architecture	908	86,984.75	95.80	917	86,870.56	94.73	881	83,144.58	94.38
Art	2,041	153,489.40	75.20	2,229	164,469.24	73.79	2,034	165,189.00	81.21
Bibles	251	11,149.36	44.42	186	10,201.98	54.85	199	9,966.96	50.09
Biography and Autobiography	1,727	79,595.93	46.09	1,555	64,097.82	41.22	1,537	65,052.44	42.32
Body, Mind, and Spirit	214	5,478.37	25.60	279	7,317.42	26.23	313	6,912.79	22.09
Business and Economics	4,612	749,159.86	162.44	4,346	619,176.76	142.47	4,155	557,584.57	134.20
Children	16,782	441,392.83	26.30	16,223	405,531.89	25.00	15,364	365,240.62	23.77
Comics and Graphic Novels	668	29,105.91	43.57	683	33,134.20	48.51	669	31,052.33	46.42
Computers	1,155	207,241.70	179.43	1,146	187,800.99	163.88	1,054	165,073.56	156.62
Cooking	1,158	34,564.93	29.85	1,109	33,406.16	30.12	926	29,484.36	31.84
Crafts and Hobbies	188	5,835.27	31.04	158	5,083.25	32.17	144	4,687.18	32.55
Design	359	24,021.86	66.91	367	24,459.39	66.65	314	21,593.18	68.77
Drama	67	5,720.98	85.39	84	9,184.02	109.33	75	7,682.72	102.44
Education	2,822	766,276.32	271.54	2,591	441,540.10	170.41	2,436	435,512.66	178.78
Family and Relationships	223	10,681.30	47.90	220	10,179.76	46.27	214	10,342.34	48.33
Fiction	4,964	146,223.91	29.46	5,021	148,986.52	29.67	4,103	122,710.45	29.91
Foreign Language Study	277	34,889.70	125.96	215	26,778.71	124.55	224	26,723.74	119.30
Games and Activities	183	8,132.94	44.44	143	5,459.91	38.18	137	5,568.26	40.64
Gardening	124	4,696.40	37.87	120	4,752.21	39.60	110	3,924.18	35.67
Health and Fitness	343	23,771.37	69.30	389	31,351.65	80.60	351	28,372.96	80.83
History	5,866	553,559.81	94.37	6,207	636,183.94	102.49	5,606	597,346.70	106.55
House and Home	123	4,798.08	39.01	131	5,472.06	41.77	115	4,341.77	37.75
Humor	349	7,990.15	22.89	297	5,767.38	19.42	247	4,906.60	19.86
Language Arts and Disciplines	1,385	199,346.46	143.93	1,476	202,459.32	137.17	1,332	172,091.34	129.20
Law	2,384	435,671.99	182.75	2,275	394,583.33	173.44	2,292	410,923.89	179.29
Literary Collections	253	22,001.64	86.96	268	35,959.62	134.18	247	29,087.34	117.76

Table 2 / Hardcover Output and Average Per-Volume Prices, 2018–2020 (cont.)

BISAC Category	2018			2019			2020		
	Vols.	$ Total	Avg.	Vols.	$ Total	Avg.	Vols.	$ Total	Avg.
Literary Criticism	2,403	$305,226.68	$127.02	2,645	$321,883.91	$121.70	2,503	$312,355.76	$124.79
Mathematics	1,037	161,255.84	155.50	1,012	143,173.60	141.48	875	117,676.00	134.49
Medical	3,050	567,198.95	185.97	3,566	622,612.09	174.60	2,917	534,202.91	183.13
Music	603	54,831.78	90.93	672	63,749.21	94.86	650	60,230.13	92.66
Nature	424	36,294.38	85.60	464	43,498.79	93.75	448	37,267.02	83.19
Performing Arts	822	83,957.13	102.14	779	91,542.58	117.51	808	79,953.77	98.95
Pets	70	1,515.26	21.65	56	1,529.13	27.31	61	1,363.51	22.35
Philosophy	1,668	182,730.34	109.55	1,899	213,120.44	112.23	1,775	209,093.94	117.80
Photography	851	60,744.13	71.38	819	57,294.24	69.96	803	46,523.29	57.94
Poetry	295	10,916.93	37.01	306	11,200.12	36.60	255	9,028.13	35.40
Political Science	3,482	398,143.44	114.34	5,511	697,544.00	126.57	3,622	400,551.99	110.59
Psychology	1,449	216,478.64	149.40	2,744	392,424.95	143.01	1,191	170,948.15	143.53
Reference	340	129,993.85	382.33	313	87,201.59	278.60	199	78,623.85	395.09
Religion	3,126	247,128.28	79.06	2,713	234,951.39	86.60	2,744	234,111.72	85.32
Science	3,902	691,347.78	177.18	4,132	772,172.98	186.88	3,538	643,439.32	181.87
Self-Help	425	11,041.23	25.98	431	10,348.85	24.01	402	9,195.43	22.87
Social Science	4,709	602,077.95	127.86	5,357	678,447.34	126.65	4,144	509,406.39	122.93
Sports and Recreation	603	33,909.99	56.24	537	27,766.96	51.71	490	26,946.18	54.99
Study Aids	14	1,446.39	103.31	9	1,569.87	174.43	29	3,661.14	126.25
Technology and Engineering	3,155	646,584.30	204.94	3,000	554,403.15	184.80	3,225	581,565.26	180.33
Transportation	289	17,984.68	62.23	285	21,261.37	74.60	222	18,312.12	82.49
Travel	482	19,532.25	40.52	233	9,789.30	42.01	230	8,332.21	36.23
True Crime	84	2,816.25	33.53	109	4,133.22	37.92	85	5,094.65	59.94
Young Adult	2,122	75,942.05	35.79	2,000	74,408.23	37.20	1,506	45,093.03	29.94
Totals	84,934	$8,618,395.02	$101.47	88,327	$8,742,819.84	$98.98	77,895	$7,514,474.47	$96.47

Table 3 / Hardcover Output and Average Per-Volume Prices, Less than $81, 2018–2020

BISAC Category	2018			2019			2020		
	Vols.	$ Total	Avg.	Vols.	$ Total	Avg.	Vols.	$ Total	Avg.
Antiques and Collectibles	71	$2,935.46	$41.34	78	$3,662.91	$46.96	69	$3,013.06	$43.67
Architecture	554	28,443.09	51.34	498	24,511.04	49.22	517	26,411.47	51.09
Art	1,499	70,057.89	46.74	1,615	74,495.34	46.13	1,426	66,753.15	46.81
Bibles	233	8,628.49	37.03	164	6,464.13	39.42	185	8,042.06	43.47
Biography and Autobiography	1,583	48,131.05	30.40	1,435	44,339.72	30.90	1,410	43,216.96	30.65
Body, Mind, and Spirit	209	4,907.39	23.48	267	5,230.07	19.59	305	5,885.80	19.30
Business and Economics	1,427	58,664.56	41.11	1,409	58,905.69	41.81	1,500	63,668.39	42.45
Children	16,177	334,910.71	20.70	15,782	329,573.49	20.88	15,030	308,028.48	20.49
Comics and Graphic Novels	587	19,342.21	32.95	587	19,344.63	32.96	572	18,892.57	33.03
Computers	205	12,206.50	59.54	188	10,684.08	56.83	195	11,768.69	60.35
Cooking	1,139	31,865.09	27.98	1,096	30,185.21	27.54	898	24,920.84	27.75
Crafts and Hobbies	183	5,230.27	28.58	154	4,632.75	30.08	142	4,437.18	31.25
Design	260	12,123.41	46.63	271	12,239.61	45.16	218	9,628.29	44.17
Drama	30	1,397.50	46.58	27	1,395.37	51.68	26	1,286.95	49.50
Education	561	29,297.26	52.22	594	31,148.48	52.44	523	28,488.85	54.47
Family and Relationships	178	3,965.94	22.28	178	4,175.96	23.46	181	4,662.50	25.76
Fiction	4,939	142,757.39	28.90	4,991	145,431.76	29.15	4,061	117,504.57	28.93
Foreign Language Study	90	4,889.46	54.33	70	4,115.13	58.79	74	4,420.70	59.74
Games and Activities	164	5,430.02	33.11	132	4,087.02	30.96	125	3,868.31	30.95
Gardening	120	4,087.40	34.06	112	3,866.21	34.52	106	3,389.23	31.97
Health and Fitness	253	7,406.91	29.28	261	7,594.63	29.10	227	6,320.32	27.84
History	2,915	125,351.35	43.00	2,901	128,040.53	44.14	2,662	117,211.30	44.03
House and Home	119	4,448.08	37.38	125	4,927.06	39.42	111	3,976.77	35.83
Humor	346	7,005.15	20.25	296	5,617.38	18.98	245	4,661.60	19.03
Language Arts and Disciplines	236	12,853.98	54.47	275	15,459.66	56.22	241	13,976.46	57.99
Law	319	18,040.40	56.55	299	16,668.92	55.75	289	16,375.37	56.66

Table 3 / Hardcover Output and Average Per-Volume Prices, Less than $81, 2018–2020 (cont.)

BISAC Category	2018			2019			2020		
	Vols.	$ Total	Avg.	Vols.	$ Total	Avg.	Vols.	$ Total	Avg.
Literary Collections	156	$6,001.55	$38.47	130	$4,584.24	$35.26	117	$4,574.05	$39.09
Literary Criticism	682	37,787.54	55.41	698	40,201.89	57.60	667	38,698.43	58.02
Mathematics	160	8,894.77	55.59	136	8,040.95	59.12	143	8,793.33	61.49
Medical	277	15,215.86	54.93	351	19,909.63	56.72	278	15,684.50	56.42
Music	293	12,265.88	41.86	305	12,958.70	42.49	307	13,746.61	44.78
Nature	269	9,253.49	34.40	260	8,709.66	33.50	267	8,991.40	33.68
Performing Arts	257	11,192.17	43.55	290	12,644.45	43.60	260	10,918.59	41.99
Pets	70	1,515.26	21.65	53	1,234.13	23.29	60	1,258.56	20.98
Philosophy	553	29,486.85	53.32	529	27,521.16	52.02	525	26,727.08	50.91
Photography	717	32,078.34	44.74	713	32,892.67	46.13	719	33,171.49	46.14
Poetry	271	8,171.18	30.15	280	7,665.30	27.38	232	6,430.43	27.72
Political Science	1,062	49,440.85	46.55	1,171	56,411.13	48.17	1,121	50,043.80	44.64
Psychology	297	13,613.13	45.84	262	12,699.41	48.47	246	11,721.09	47.65
Reference	118	4,043.31	34.27	122	3,563.68	29.21	98	2,760.13	28.16
Religion	1,943	72,940.15	37.54	1,537	53,955.79	35.10	1,508	53,054.57	35.18
Science	609	28,590.00	46.95	631	29,637.96	46.97	570	26,161.81	45.90
Self-Help	419	10,106.28	24.12	429	9,878.90	23.03	400	8,945.43	22.36
Social Science	1,021	51,430.79	50.37	1,099	55,384.21	50.40	1,055	51,192.32	48.52
Sports and Recreation	480	15,539.70	32.37	442	13,972.65	31.61	397	13,028.91	32.82
Study Aids	8	487.75	60.97	4	197.94	49.49	21	1,136.78	54.13
Technology and Engineering	231	12,524.60	54.22	235	12,815.70	54.53	254	14,672.12	57.76
Transportation	244	10,876.28	44.57	219	9,036.67	41.26	172	8,179.19	47.55
Travel	457	15,243.31	33.36	216	7,008.35	32.45	213	6,533.31	30.67
True Crime	81	2,364.25	29.19	106	3,863.28	36.45	82	2,465.65	30.07
Young Adult	2,029	54,340.32	26.78	1,912	53,396.53	27.93	1,471	36,493.60	24.81
Totals	47,101	$1,517,780.57	$32.22	45,935	$1,495,031.76	$32.55	42,521	$1,376,193.05	$32.37

Table 4 / Mass Market Paperbacks Output and Average Per-Volume Prices, 2018–2020

BISAC Category	2018			2019			2020		
	Vols.	$ Total	Avg.	Vols.	$ Total	Avg.	Vols.	$ Total	Avg.
Biography and Autobiography	8	$78.92	$9.87	3	$29.97	$9.99	6	$53.94	$8.99
Business and Economics	3	26.97	8.99	n.a.	n.a.	n.a.	n.a.	n.a.	n.a.
Children	230	1,852.38	8.05	134	1,534.01	8.34	223	1,923.53	8.63
Family and Relationships	n.a.	n.a.	n.a.	n.a.	n.a.	n.a.	1	9.99	9.99
Fiction	2,737	19,888.77	7.27	2,472	18,362.92	7.43	2,297	17,544.63	7.64
Games and Activities	1	8.50	8.50	n.a.	n.a.	n.a.	n.a.	n.a.	n.a.
Health and Fitness	3	25.97	8.66	2	21.98	10.99	n.a.	n.a.	n.a.
History	3	29.97	9.99	4	35.96	8.99	4	39.96	9.99
Humor	2	24.98	12.49	n.a.	n.a.	n.a.	n.a.	n.a.	n.a.
Language Arts and Disciplines	n.a.	n.a.	n.a.	1	7.99	7.99	n.a.	n.a.	n.a.
Performing Arts	n.a.	n.a.	n.a.	1	8.99	8.99	n.a.	n.a.	n.a.
Political Science	1	9.99	9.99	1	9.99	9.99	n.a.	n.a.	n.a.
Psychology	1	13.99	13.99	1	4.99	4.99	n.a.	n.a.	n.a.
Reference	n.a.	n.a.	n.a.	n.a.	n.a.	n.a.	1	8.99	8.99
Self-Help	6	83.94	13.99	4	50.96	12.74	1	7.99	7.99
True Crime	7	58.93	8.42	6	52.94	8.82	8	68.92	8.62
Young Adult	26	306.70	11.80	35	337.65	9.65	46	518.51	11.27
Totals	3,028	$22,410.01	$7.40	2,714	$20,458.35	$7.54	2,587	$20,176.00	$7.80

n.a. = not available

Table 5 / Trade Paperbacks Output and Average Per-Volume Prices, 2018–2020

BISAC Category	2018			2019			2020		
	Vols.	$ Total	Avg.	Vols.	$ Total	Avg.	Vols.	$ Total	Avg.
Antiques and Collectibles	89	$3,759.55	$42.24	86	$3,479.51	$40.46	77	$3,319.43	$43.11
Architecture	742	36,623.19	49.36	899	45,319.72	50.41	879	41,288.95	46.97
Art	1,734	69,986.28	40.36	1,735	68,174.26	39.29	1,585	62,485.52	39.42
Bibles	709	32,200.73	45.42	630	30,046.78	47.69	479	26,850.19	56.05
Biography and Autobiography	2,581	53,355.20	20.67	2,356	48,709.29	20.67	2,282	47,749.68	20.92
Body, Mind, and Spirit	761	13,868.63	18.22	805	15,243.68	18.94	821	15,406.09	18.77
Business and Economics	7,064	593,799.32	84.06	6,624	486,560.75	73.45	5,993	407,240.11	67.95
Children	11,651	149,396.31	12.82	11,870	147,060.20	12.39	10,113	115,231.47	11.39
Comics and Graphic Novels	2,331	44,594.85	19.13	2,211	45,458.88	20.56	1,978	37,418.78	18.92
Computers	3,408	356,925.03	104.73	3,390	346,498.36	102.21	2,919	235,457.89	80.66
Cooking	932	19,726.98	21.17	828	18,088.46	21.85	803	16,945.76	21.10
Crafts and Hobbies	693	14,929.72	21.54	575	12,859.75	22.36	580	12,601.76	21.73
Design	234	9,638.31	41.19	255	11,456.09	44.93	222	8,348.61	37.61
Drama	555	11,497.62	20.72	468	11,023.56	23.55	412	8,834.80	21.44
Education	4,511	284,666.19	63.10	4,037	242,205.37	60.00	3,576	288,253.84	80.61
Family and Relationships	590	13,066.52	22.15	626	13,612.42	21.75	604	12,696.14	21.02
Fiction	10,427	183,366.82	17.59	9,864	172,768.49	17.52	8,880	154,116.96	17.36
Foreign Language Study	836	37,660.35	45.05	917	39,319.31	42.88	842	35,696.60	42.40
Games and Activities	699	12,170.35	17.41	626	11,292.64	18.04	665	12,024.99	18.08
Gardening	120	2,566.31	21.39	124	2,760.69	22.26	101	2,360.06	23.37
Health and Fitness	1,057	32,815.54	31.05	971	31,742.72	32.69	956	30,156.63	31.54
History	6,347	254,176.71	40.05	6,583	265,284.17	40.30	6,462	250,348.04	38.74
House and Home	87	1,957.31	22.50	109	2,630.48	24.13	63	1,341.47	21.29
Humor	263	4,077.31	15.50	263	4,135.68	15.73	211	3,547.38	16.81
Language Arts and Disciplines	1,627	99,946.14	61.43	1,708	96,713.03	56.62	1,438	78,672.48	54.71

Law	3,423	309,993.44	90.56	3,051	258,720.07	84.80	3,023	247,482.78	81.87
Literary Collections	440	13,148.75	29.88	459	11,456.08	24.96	415	11,298.62	27.23
Literary Criticism	2,149	108,644.38	50.56	2,351	103,649.51	44.09	2,033	83,477.75	41.06
Mathematics	1,540	161,880.27	105.12	1,372	104,311.87	76.03	1,108	71,944.42	64.93
Medical	5,282	608,194.33	115.14	4,469	386,730.04	86.54	3,489	280,125.61	80.29
Music	1,816	50,619.53	27.87	1,993	59,928.07	30.07	2,969	72,608.71	24.46
Nature	590	26,900.79	45.59	665	27,983.81	42.08	700	24,613.74	35.16
Performing Arts	948	40,568.08	42.79	960	36,327.83	37.84	843	30,360.31	36.01
Pets	113	2,114.04	18.71	122	2,485.27	20.37	100	1,860.31	18.60
Philosophy	1,902	100,334.13	52.75	1,949	81,643.39	41.89	1,783	73,803.17	41.39
Photography	292	9,946.24	34.06	318	12,697.19	39.93	303	10,986.72	36.26
Poetry	2,161	37,202.76	17.22	2,031	35,151.92	17.31	1,868	32,621.99	17.46
Political Science	4,395	258,989.07	58.93	4,371	220,974.81	50.55	4,788	221,302.28	46.22
Psychology	2,058	125,624.03	61.04	2,130	108,929.57	51.14	1,795	88,873.75	49.51
Reference	425	78,491.11	184.68	398	51,440.24	129.25	247	49,992.47	202.40
Religion	6,753	184,773.36	27.36	6,684	186,626.69	27.92	5,554	150,280.91	27.36
Science	4,873	622,918.59	127.83	4,163	395,084.39	95.62	3,364	294,199.42	87.46
Self-Help	1,136	19,518.15	17.18	1,280	22,882.86	17.88	1,214	21,586.90	17.78
Social Science	5,592	336,069.17	60.10	5,625	277,322.92	49.30	6,049	281,121.02	46.47
Sports and Recreation	913	24,213.19	26.52	981	26,855.78	27.38	854	23,160.12	27.12
Study Aids	690	29,753.36	43.12	2,594	112,923.13	43.53	2,433	105,381.38	43.31
Technology and Engineering	3,995	572,636.16	143.34	3,075	364,633.33	118.58	2,929	366,624.79	125.17
Transportation	498	17,309.38	34.76	398	17,475.14	43.91	335	11,702.93	34.93
Travel	1,615	34,182.49	21.17	1,537	32,972.22	21.45	932	19,403.56	20.82
True Crime	221	4,410.07	19.96	246	4,910.08	19.96	203	3,968.54	19.55
Young Adult	2,949	53,337.44	18.09	2,885	53,224.26	18.45	2,307	37,261.58	16.15
Totals	116,817	$6,168,543.58	$52.81	114,667	$5,172,784.76	$45.11	104,579	$4,524,437.41	$43.26

Table 6 / Audiobook Output and Average Per-Volume Prices, 2018–2020

BISAC Category	2018			2019			2020		
	Vols.	$ Total	Avg.	Vols.	$ Total	Avg.	Vols.	$ Total	Avg.
Antiques and Collectibles	n.a.	n.a.	n.a.	n.a.	n.a.	n.a.	3	$122.97	$40.99
Architecture	2	$45.98	$22.99	8	$264.92	$33.12	5	209.95	$41.99
Art	16	504.70	31.54	8	248.43	31.05	11	383.89	34.90
Bibles	2	99.98	49.99	3	228.94	76.31	12	386.00	32.17
Biography and Autobiography	1,242	53,143.03	42.79	1,379	60,117.57	43.60	1,215	51,941.72	42.75
Body, Mind, and Spirit	147	5,275.09	35.88	180	6,330.91	35.17	163	5,837.55	35.81
Business and Economics	799	28,488.36	35.66	656	24,186.05	36.87	656	26,609.86	40.56
Children	1,333	48,683.71	36.52	1,558	57,902.78	37.16	1,853	61,545.22	33.21
Comics and Graphic Novels	n.a.	n.a.	n.a.	66	2,479.34	37.57	37	1,344.63	36.34
Computers	27	1,142.60	42.32	33	1,255.59	38.05	12	416.74	34.73
Cooking	58	2,302.06	39.69	16	596.84	37.30	32	1,139.53	35.61
Crafts and Hobbies	3	66.97	22.32	5	198.96	39.79	3	119.97	39.99
Design	6	307.87	51.31	1	39.99	39.99	4	164.96	41.24
Drama	163	3,011.81	18.48	98	2,187.60	22.32	36	912.54	25.35
Education	41	1,376.81	33.58	39	1,489.67	38.20	27	1,079.64	39.99
Family and Relationships	183	6,251.14	34.16	185	6,846.41	37.01	150	5,442.96	36.29
Fiction	9,918	390,095.28	39.33	11,452	459,755.01	40.15	12,102	493,770.14	40.80
Foreign Language Study	100	20,722.97	207.23	149	12,799.16	85.90	40	2,399.34	59.98
Games and Activities	5	199.95	39.99	2	44.98	22.49	4	169.96	42.49
Gardening	n.a.	n.a.	n.a.	1	14.99	14.99	9	337.91	37.55
Health and Fitness	264	10,193.90	38.61	242	9,720.66	40.17	220	9,445.74	42.94
History	809	38,355.88	47.41	811	37,631.72	46.40	722	33,952.84	47.03
House and Home	20	709.54	35.48	13	447.85	34.45	17	671.82	39.52
Humor	93	3,882.78	41.75	74	2,648.06	35.78	75	3,037.94	40.51
Language Arts and Disciplines	29	1,000.56	34.50	47	1,786.29	38.01	26	1,100.70	42.33

Law	34	1,161.54	34.16	25	778.68	31.15	30	1,164.57	38.82
Literary Collections	69	2,964.76	42.97	67	2,811.89	41.97	34	1,325.45	38.98
Literary Criticism	34	1,397.44	41.10	27	880.59	32.61	36	1,243.50	34.54
Mathematics	4	107.96	26.99	7	326.87	46.70	2	64.98	32.49
Medical	36	1,505.54	41.82	31	1,013.62	32.70	36	1,453.43	40.37
Music	61	1,885.27	30.91	64	2,656.28	41.50	49	1,854.02	37.84
Nature	53	1,860.18	35.10	91	3,818.78	41.96	107	4,561.15	42.63
Performing Arts	99	4,011.92	40.52	116	4,745.81	40.91	176	7,561.34	42.96
Pets	29	1,102.51	38.02	18	762.78	42.38	18	673.83	37.44
Philosophy	54	2,044.98	37.87	74	2,533.89	34.24	53	2,150.38	40.57
Photography	n.a.	n.a.	n.a.	n.a.	n.a.	n.a.	1	29.99	29.99
Poetry	56	1,521.58	27.17	106	3,062.75	28.89	138	4,203.06	30.46
Political Science	377	14,812.56	39.29	369	15,895.82	43.08	395	17,849.29	45.19
Psychology	162	6,033.85	37.25	99	3,480.81	35.16	119	5,491.33	46.15
Reference	8	372.93	46.62	7	214.91	30.70	8	289.93	36.24
Religion	1,152	35,163.38	30.52	929	32,658.52	35.15	812	30,619.70	37.71
Science	212	8,261.87	38.97	168	6,930.04	41.25	220	8,921.98	40.55
Self-Help	427	15,463.58	36.21	516	18,276.20	35.42	501	18,756.89	37.44
Social Science	322	11,586.12	35.98	265	11,101.54	41.89	274	10,844.15	39.58
Sports and Recreation	111	4,256.85	38.35	144	6,042.57	41.96	146	5,595.46	38.33
Study Aids	3	124.90	41.63	2	125.39	63.00	3	115.97	38.66
Technology and Engineering	31	1,400.49	45.18	13	510.30	39.29	16	619.77	38.74
Transportation	10	464.91	46.49	2	99.98	49.99	3	139.97	46.66
Travel	32	1,397.54	43.67	49	2,073.45	42.32	37	1,504.57	40.66
True Crime	189	6,926.53	36.65	193	8,321.18	43.11	145	6,633.79	45.75
Young Adult	1,118	49,891.37	44.63	1,221	53,490.76	43.31	1,159	50,225.22	43.33
Totals	19,943	$791,581.53	$39.69	21,629	$871,837.23	$40.31	21,952	$886,438.24	$40.38

n.a. = not available

Table 7 / E-Book Output and Average Per-Volume Prices, 2018–2020

BISAC Category	2018			2019			2020		
	Vols.	$ Total	Avg.	Vols.	$ Total	Avg.	Vols.	$ Total	Avg.
Antiques and Collectibles	174	$1,888.50	$10.85	157	$1,716.70	$10.93	111	$2,732.12	$24.61
Architecture	467	22,623.87	48.45	494	20,965.20	42.44	224	9,178.35	40.97
Art	1,456	53,106.93	36.47	1,713	46,900.80	27.38	757	22,481.16	29.70
Bibles	444	4,439.08	10.00	304	3,649.18	12.00	321	5,182.44	16.14
Biography and Autobiography	7,380	145,658.62	19.74	7,382	161,489.29	21.88	5,500	187,418.75	34.08
Body, Mind, and Spirit	3,047	34,765.76	11.41	3,715	46,691.47	12.57	3,067	54,379.64	17.73
Business and Economics	28,520	1,463,311.03	51.31	24,760	1,632,785.10	65.94	14,690	752,426.89	51.22
Children	28,927	454,771.79	15.72	27,963	533,034.11	19.06	19,752	431,954.08	21.87
Comics and Graphic Novels	1,371	11,124.35	8.11	1,039	9,921.37	9.55	2,000	17,413.19	8.71
Computers	4,026	302,359.01	75.10	2,514	149,623.03	59.52	1,490	62,619.14	42.03
Cooking	3,228	43,104.21	13.35	3,232	43,239.44	13.38	2,377	45,127.99	18.99
Crafts and Hobbies	652	9,824.24	15.07	612	9,454.96	15.45	556	10,435.99	18.77
Design	131	3,147.66	24.03	146	3,894.38	26.67	119	3,649.01	30.66
Drama	1,137	12,477.46	10.97	1,349	12,972.99	9.62	589	11,534.50	19.58
Education	4,578	200,373.92	43.77	4,372	179,716.68	41.11	2,407	83,243.59	34.58
Family and Relationships	2,393	30,259.81	12.65	2,420	35,072.80	14.49	1,988	41,469.37	20.86
Fiction	83,090	935,469.96	11.26	85,595	1,168,389.56	13.65	65,371	1,826,700.49	27.94
Foreign Language Study	2,321	51,434.67	22.16	1,594	41,381.39	25.96	4,519	74,436.17	16.47
Games and Activities	1,518	10,394.95	6.85	383	5,871.29	15.33	315	6,425.70	20.40
Gardening	339	5,124.57	15.12	316	5,021.98	15.89	313	5,580.80	17.83
Health and Fitness	3,229	44,326.74	13.73	3,179	51,061.83	16.06	3,147	63,219.19	20.09
History	9,693	409,325.39	42.23	8,878	408,580.00	46.02	11,371	385,906.40	33.94
House and Home	279	4,517.44	16.19	261	4,562.29	17.48	230	5,358.68	23.30
Humor	1,101	15,903.31	14.44	928	14,208.81	15.31	774	14,635.58	18.91
Language Arts and Disciplines	2,987	201,750.37	67.54	3,097	291,452.48	94.11	1,399	109,409.29	78.21

Law	3,121	350,970.77	112.45	2,825	332,475.93	117.69	1,507	197,837.96	131.28
Literary Collections	1,633	24,266.12	14.86	6,296	30,534.65	4.85	1,027	17,913.59	17.44
Literary Criticism	3,895	310,185.35	79.64	3,197	252,942.45	79.12	1,708	141,216.90	82.68
Mathematics	1,150	93,236.66	81.08	915	82,746.50	90.43	381	34,985.79	91.83
Medical	3,631	379,384.24	104.48	2,716	263,458.40	97.00	1,303	106,439.73	81.69
Music	3,014	50,597.35	16.79	1,848	43,612.10	23.60	1,318	38,770.71	29.42
Nature	891	24,573.53	27.58	793	21,896.39	27.61	646	19,681.85	30.47
Performing Arts	2,125	54,907.80	25.84	2,008	49,231.72	24.52	1,022	32,220.11	31.53
Pets	451	4,742.86	10.52	459	6,084.90	13.26	322	6,156.18	19.12
Philosophy	2,938	143,156.25	48.73	2,799	120,445.82	43.03	2,676	84,167.65	31.45
Photography	342	6,431.20	18.80	285	6,257.72	21.96	260	5,230.54	20.12
Poetry	5,015	40,653.07	8.11	4,806	43,453.78	9.04	2,436	27,459.18	11.27
Political Science	4,982	258,949.15	51.98	4,015	174,437.85	43.45	2,718	112,597.38	41.43
Psychology	2,157	96,682.30	44.82	1,955	78,200.89	40.00	1,958	65,855.55	33.63
Reference	1,083	48,150.07	44.46	948	62,014.60	65.42	623	28,621.19	45.94
Religion	12,123	314,094.62	25.91	1,062	303,130.45	27.40	8,501	268,983.28	31.64
Science	4,197	413,900.00	98.62	3,643	345,000.58	94.70	1,958	167,530.71	85.56
Self-Help	5,229	66,349.76	12.69	6,871	85,263.26	12.41	5,717	115,013.28	20.12
Social Science	5,095	246,703.68	48.42	4,342	213,050.63	49.07	2,802	119,618.01	42.69
Sports and Recreation	1,669	34,669.67	20.77	1,501	31,273.96	20.84	1,136	30,912.05	27.21
Study Aids	2,660	52,057.40	19.57	3,802	105,454.58	27.74	783	12,132.31	15.49
Technology and Engineering	3,191	387,418.36	121.41	2,271	261,277.22	115.05	919	89,879.79	97.80
Transportation	333	9,211.69	27.66	278	7,914.55	28.47	516	13,266.58	25.71
Travel	2,223	36,944.94	16.62	3,230	38,860.79	12.03	1,354	29,291.21	21.63
True Crime	534	11,503.51	21.54	512	15,033.88	24.57	696	19,819.16	28.48
Young Adult	6,601	117,628.13	17.82	6,640	130,488.18	19.65	5,444	141,831.05	26.05
Totals	272,771	$8,048,852.12	$29.51	266,520	$7,986,198.96	$29.96	193,118	$6,160,350.25	$31.90

(continued from page 371)

Trade paperbacks also saw a decrease in output from 2018 to 2020 (Table 5), though at 10.5 percent the decline was smaller than that for mass market. The average trade paperback price decreased by 18 percent, likely correlating to title output, which decreased during the period in 40 of the 51 subject categories. Certain categories, including architecture and photography, experienced an unexpected increase, suggesting that publishers see value in producing a greater number of paperback editions within these traditionally hardcover genres.

Physically packaged audiobook output reached a highwater mark in 2016, when more than 32,000 volumes were produced; since then, total annual output for the format has remained in the 20,000 range. Prices had been on the rise, but showed a smaller increase in 2020 than in previous years (Table 6). As the available number of streaming sources for audiobooks increases, we are unlikely to see sharp increases in physical audio pricing; still, demand for the format should continue for as long as automobiles—the top listening "space" for audiobook fans—are equipped with CD players.

Average e-book pricing has increased slightly from 2018 to 2020 (Table 7), but for the longer view required to reliably identify pricing trends over time, for any format, readers are encouraged to refer to this report in previous annual editions of *Library and Book Trade Almanac*.

Children's books are the dominant category represented in Table 1 and, commensurately, this category ranks highly in most of the individual publication formats. Production held steady from 2017 to 2019 but dipped in 2020 in step with the market overall, likely resulting from the pandemic. The young adult category has followed a similar production pattern. Print and audio pricing has remained relatively stable for both children's and young adult titles, but e-book prices have been going up since 2018.

Fiction, a major category across all publication formats, on the whole has experienced reduced output in recent years, with preliminary 2020 hardcover figures continuing to demonstrate this trend. Hardcover fiction prices have held remarkably steady since at least 2017. Mass market fiction output has continued to erode, with small price increases seen each year. In the trade paperback format, fiction output has continued to decline annually, with little variation in pricing. Audiobook fiction pricing shows signs of stabilizing, with modest production increases occurring since 2018. E-book fiction output, which has been robust in recent years, dipped slightly in 2020; prices in the category remain on the rise.

Year after year, multiple categories combine to make nonfiction overall the largest part of the U.S. publication mix. Categories that stand out in print for 2020 include business and economics, history, religion, political science, and social science. History is in particularly high demand, perhaps from a public seeking context, lessons for our own time, and reassurance that life goes on—if not also for the sake of nostalgia.

Number of Book Outlets in the United States and Canada

The *American Book Trade Directory* (Information Today, Inc.) has been published since 1915. Revised annually, it features lists of booksellers, wholesalers, periodicals, reference tools, and other information about the U.S. and Canadian book markets. The data shown in Table 1, the most current available, are from the 2021–2022 edition of the directory.

The 10,872 stores of various types shown are located throughout the United States, Canada, and regions administered by the United States. "General" bookstores stock trade books and children's books in a general variety of subjects. "College" stores (both general and specified) carry college-level textbooks. "Educational" outlets handle school textbooks up to and including the high school level. "Mail order" outlets (both general and specified) sell general trade books by mail and are not book clubs; all others operating by mail are classified according to the kinds of books carried.

"Antiquarian" dealers sell old and rare books. Stores handling secondhand books are classified as "used." "Paperback" stores have more than 80 percent of their stock in paperbound books. Stores with paperback departments are listed under the appropriate major classification ("general," "department store," "stationer," and so forth). Bookstores with at least 50 percent of their stock on a particular subject are classified by subject.

Table 1 / Bookstores in the United States and Canada, 2020

Category	United States	Canada
Antiquarian General	384	38
Antiquarian Mail Order	122	5
Antiquarian Specialized	76	1
Art Supply Store	12	1
College General	1,727	116
College Specialized	92	5
Comics	183	23
Computer Software	2	0
Cooking	209	7
Department Store	218	17
Educational	109	13
Federal Sites	304	1
Foreign Language	11	2
General	2,067	411
Gift Shop	78	6
Juvenile	45	11
Mail Order General	38	4
Mail Order Specialized	147	7

Table 1 / Bookstores in the United States and Canada, 2020
(cont.)

Category	United States	Canada
Metaphysics, New Age and Occult	94	13
Museum Store and Art Gallery	372	26
Nature and Natural History	27	5
Newsdealer	9	1
Office Supply	6	1
Other	2,151	296
Paperback	18	1
Religious	791	71
Self Help/Development	11	4
Stationer	3	2
Toy Store	31	74
Used	330	43
Totals	9,667	1,205

Part 5
Reference Information

Ready Reference

How to Obtain an ISBN

Beat Barblan

United States ISBN/SAN Agency

The International Standard Book Numbering (ISBN) system was introduced into the United Kingdom by J. Whitaker & Sons Ltd. in 1967 and into the United States in 1968 by R. R. Bowker. The Technical Committee on Documentation of the International Organization for Standardization (ISO TC 46) is responsible for the international standard.

The purpose of this standard is to "establish the specifications for the International Standard Book Number (ISBN) as a unique international identification system for each product form or edition of a monographic publication published or produced by a specific publisher." The standard specifies the construction of an ISBN, the rules for assignment and use of an ISBN, and all metadata associated with the allocation of an ISBN.

Types of monographic publications to which an ISBN may be assigned include printed books and pamphlets (in various product formats); electronic publications (either on the Internet or on physical carriers such as CD-ROMs or diskettes); educational/instructional films, videos, and transparencies; educational/instructional software; audiobooks on cassette or CD or DVD; braille publications; and microform publications.

Serial publications, printed music, and musical sound recordings are excluded from the ISBN standard as they are covered by other identification systems.

The ISBN is used by publishers, distributors, wholesalers, bookstores, and libraries, among others, in more than 200 countries and territories as an ordering and inventory system. It expedites the collection of data on new and forthcoming editions of monographic publications for print and electronic directories used by the book trade. Its use also facilitates rights management and the monitoring of sales data for the publishing industry.

As of January 1, 2007, a revision to the ISBN standard substantially increased the numbering capacity of the system. The 10-digit ISBN identifier (ISBN-10) was replaced by the ISBN 13-digit identifier (ISBN-13). All facets of book publishing are now expected to use the ISBN-13, and the ISBN agencies throughout the world are now issuing only ISBN-13s to publishers. Publishers with existing ISBN-10s need to convert their ISBNs to ISBN-13s by the addition of the EAN prefix 978 and recalculation of the new check digit:

ISBN-10: 0-8352-8235-X
ISBN-13: 978-0-8352-8235-2

As the inventory of 978 prefixes has started to exhaust, ISBN agencies have begun assigning ISBN-13s with the "979" prefix. There is no 10-digit equivalent for 979 ISBNs.

Construction of an ISBN

An ISBN currently consists of 13 digits separated into the following parts:

1 A prefix of "978" for an ISBN-10 converted to an ISBN-13 and a prefix of "979" for ISBN-13s without a 10-digit equivalent

2 Group or country identifier, which identifies a national or geographic grouping of publishers

3 Publisher identifier, which identifies a particular publisher within a group

4 Title identifier, which identifies a particular title or edition of a title

5 Check digit, the single digit at the end of the ISBN that validates the ISBN-13

For more information regarding ISBN-13 conversion services provided by the U.S. ISBN Agency at R. R. Bowker, LLC, visit the ISBN Agency website at http://www.isbn.org, or contact the U.S. ISBN Agency at isbn-san@bowker.com.

Publishers requiring their ISBNs to be converted from the ISBN-10 to ISBN-13 format can use the U.S. ISBN Agency's free ISBN-13 online converter at http://isbn.org/converterpub.asp. Publishers can also view their ISBNs online by accessing their personal account at http://www.myidentifiers.com.

Displaying the ISBN on a Product or Publication

When an ISBN is written or printed, it should be preceded by the letters ISBN, and each part should be separated by a space or hyphen. In the United States, the hyphen is used for separation, as in the following example: ISBN 978-0-8352-8235-2. In this example, 978 is the prefix that precedes the ISBN-13, 0 is the group identifier, 8352 is the publisher identifier, 8235 is the title identifier, and 2 is the check digit. The group of English-speaking countries, which includes the United States, Australia, Canada, New Zealand, and the United Kingdom, uses the group identifiers 0 and 1. The 979 assignments by the United States ISBN Agency will start with 979-8. The 8 will be unique to the United States. Of course, as with the 978-0 and 978-1, an ISBN starting with 979-8 will allow U.S. publishers and self-publishers to market their books anywhere in the world.

The ISBN Organization

The administration of the ISBN system is carried out at three levels—through the International ISBN Agency in the United Kingdom, through the national agencies, and through the publishing houses themselves. The International ISBN Agency, which is responsible for assigning country prefixes and for coordinating the worldwide implementation of the system, has an advisory panel that represents the

International Organization for Standardization (ISO), publishers, and libraries. The International ISBN Agency publishes the *Publishers International ISBN Directory,* which is a listing of all national agencies' publishers with their assigned ISBN publisher prefixes. R. R. Bowker, as the publisher of *Books in Print,* with its extensive and varied database of publishers' addresses, was the obvious place to initiate the ISBN system and to provide the service to the U.S. publishing industry. To date, the U.S. ISBN Agency has entered more than 450,000 publishers into the system.

ISBN Assignment Procedure

Assignment of ISBNs is a shared endeavor between the U.S. ISBN Agency and the publisher. Publishers can apply online through the ISBN Agency's website www.myidentifiers.com. Once the order is processed, an e-mail confirmation will be sent with instructions for managing the account. The publisher then has the responsibility of assigning an ISBN to each title, keeping an accurate record of each number assigned, and registering each title in the *Books in Print* database at www.myidentifiers.com. It is the responsibility of the ISBN Agency to validate assigned ISBNs and keep a record of all ISBN publisher prefixes in circulation.

ISBN implementation is very much market-driven. Major distributors, wholesalers, retailers, and so forth recognize the necessity of the ISBN system and request that publishers register with the ISBN Agency. Also, the ISBN is a mandatory bibliographic element in the International Standard Bibliographical Description (ISBD). The Library of Congress Cataloging in Publication (CIP) Division directs publishers to the agency to obtain their ISBN prefixes.

Location and Display of the ISBN

On books, pamphlets, and other printed material, the ISBN shall be printed on the verso of the title leaf or, if this is not possible, at the foot of the title leaf itself. It should also appear on the outside back cover or on the back of the jacket if the book has one (the lower right-hand corner is recommended). The ISBN shall also appear on any accompanying promotional materials following the provisions for location according to the format of the material.

On other monographic publications, the ISBN shall appear on the title or credit frames and any labels permanently affixed to the publication. If the publication is issued in a container that is an integral part of the publication, the ISBN shall be displayed on the label. If it is not possible to place the ISBN on the item or its label, then the number should be displayed on the bottom or the back of the container, box, sleeve, or frame. It should also appear on any accompanying material, including each component of a multitype publication.

Printing of ISBN in Machine-Readable Coding

All books should carry ISBNs in the EAN-13 bar code machine-readable format. All ISBN EAN-13 bar codes start with the EAN prefixes 978 and 979 for books. As of January 1, 2007, all EAN bar codes should have the ISBN-13 appearing immediately above the bar code in eye-readable format, preceded by the acronym

"ISBN." The recommended location of the EAN-13 bar code for books is in the lower right-hand corner of the back cover (see Figure 1).

Figure 1 / Printing the ISBN in Bookland/EAN Symbology

ISBN 978-0-8352-0000-4

9 780835 200004

Five-Digit Add-On Code

In the United States, a five-digit add-on code is used for additional information. In the publishing industry, this code is used for price information. The lead digit of the five-digit add-on has been designated a currency identifier, when the add-on is used for price. Number 5 is the code for the U.S. dollar, while 6 denotes the Canadian dollar. Publishers that do not want to indicate price in the add-on should print the code 90000 (see Figure 2).

Figure 2 / Printing the ISBN Bookland/EAN Number in Bar Code with the Five-Digit Add-On Code

ISBN 978-0-8352-0000-4

5 2 4 9 9

9 780835 200004

978 = ISBN Bookland/EAN prefix   90000 means no information
5 = Code for U.S. $ in the add-on code
2499 = $24.99

Reporting the Title and the ISBN

After the publisher reports a title to the ISBN Agency, the number is validated and the title is listed in the many R. R. Bowker hard-copy and electronic publications, including *Books in Print*; *Forthcoming Books*; *Paperbound Books in Print*; *Books in Print Supplement*; *Books Out of Print*; *Books in Print Online*; *Books in Print Plus-CD ROM*; *Children's Books in Print*; *Subject Guide to Children's Books in*

Print; *Books Out Loud: Bowker's Guide to AudioBooks*; *Bowker's Complete Video Directory*; *Software Encyclopedia*; *Software for Schools*; and other specialized publications.

For an ISBN application and information, visit the ISBN Agency website at www.myidentifiers.com, call the toll-free number 877-310-7333, fax 908-795-3518, or write to the United States ISBN Agency, 630 Central Ave., New Providence, NJ 07974.

The ISSN, and How to Obtain One

U.S. ISSN Center
Library of Congress

In the early 1970s the rapid increase in the production and dissemination of information and an intensified desire to exchange information about serials in computerized form among different systems and organizations made it increasingly clear that a means to identify serial publications at an international level was needed. The International Standard Serial Number (ISSN) was developed and became the internationally accepted code for identifying serial publications.

The ISSN is an international standard. ISO 3297:2020, the sixth edition of the standard, was published in 2020. This edition expands on the role of the ISSN for digital resources, provides detailed information on implementing the standard in various technical environments, and explains the concept of "cluster ISSNs."

The scope of the ISSN is "continuing resources," a concept that was introduced with the 2007 edition. Continuing resources include not only serials such as journals, magazines, open-ended series, and blogs but also open-ended publications such as updating databases, updating loose-leaf services, and certain types of updating websites.

The number itself has no significance other than as a brief, unique, and unambiguous identifier. The ISSN consists of eight digits in the Arabic numerals 0 to 9, except for the last ("check") digit, which is calculated using Modulus 11 and uses an "X" in place of the numeral 10 to maintain the ISSN at 8 digits. The numbers appear as two groups of four digits separated by a hyphen and preceded by the letters ISSN—for example, ISSN 1234-5679.

The ISSN is not self-assigned by publishers. Administration of the ISSN is coordinated through the ISSN Network, an intergovernmental organization within the UNESCO/UNISIST program. The ISSN Network consists of national ISSN centers, coordinated by the ISSN International Centre, located in Paris. National ISSN Centers are responsible for registering serials published in their respective countries. Responsibility for the assignment of ISSN to titles from multinational publishers is allocated among the ISSN Centers in which the publisher has offices. A list of these publishers and the corresponding ISSN centers is located on the ISSN International Centre's website, http://www.issn.org.

The ISSN International Centre handles ISSN assignments for international organizations and for countries that do not have a national center. It also maintains and distributes the ISSN Register and makes it available in a variety of products, most commonly via the ISSN Portal, an online subscription database containing full metadata records for each ISSN as well as other features and functionality. In January 2018, a new ISSN Portal was released that includes free look-up and access to a subset of ISSN metadata. The ISSN Register is also available via Z39.50 access, and as a data file. Selected ISSN data can also be obtained in customized files or database extracts that can be used, for example, to check the accuracy or completeness of a requestor's list of titles and ISSN. Another available ISSN service is OAI-PMH, a customizable "harvesting" protocol through which external applications can automatically and regularly gather new and updated metadata on a defined schedule. The ISSN Register contains bibliographic records corresponding to each ISSN assignment as reported by national ISSN centers. The database contains records for more than 2.5 million ISSNs.

The ISSN is used all over the world by serials publishers to identify their serials and to distinguish their titles from others that are the same or similar. It is used by subscription services and libraries to manage files for orders, claims, and back issues. It is used in automated check-in systems by libraries that wish to process receipts more quickly. Copyright centers use the ISSN as a means to collect and disseminate royalties. It is also used as an identification code by postal services and legal deposit services. The ISSN is included as a verification element in interlibrary lending activities and for union catalogs as a collocating device. The ISSN is also incorporated into bar codes for optical recognition of serial publication identification and metadata and into the standards for the identification of issues and articles in serial publications. A key use of the ISSN is as an identifier in online systems, where it can serve to connect catalog records or citations in abstracting and indexing databases with full-text journal content via OpenURL resolvers or reference linking services, and as an identifier and link in archives of electronic and print serials.

Because serials are generally known and cited by title, assignment of the ISSN is inseparably linked to the key title, a standardized form of the title derived from information in the serial issue. Only one ISSN can be assigned to a title in a particular medium. For titles issued in multiple media—e.g., print, online, CD-ROM—a separate ISSN is assigned to each medium version. If a major title change occurs or the medium changes, a new ISSN must be assigned. Centers responsible for assigning ISSNs also construct the key title and create an associated bibliographic record.

A significant new feature of the 2007 ISSN standard was the Linking ISSN (ISSN-L), a mechanism that enables collocation or linking among different media versions of a continuing resource. The Linking ISSN allows a unique designation (one of the existing ISSNs) to be applied to all media versions of a continuing resource while retaining the separate ISSN that pertains to each version. When an ISSN is functioning as a Linking ISSN, the eight digits of the base ISSN are prefixed with the designation "ISSN-L." The Linking ISSN facilitates search, retrieval, and delivery across all medium versions of a serial or other continuing resource for improved ISSN functionality in OpenURL linking, search engines, library catalogs, and knowledge bases.

The ISSN standard also supports interoperability by specifying the use of ISSN and ISSN-L with other systems such as DOI, OpenURL, URN, and EAN bar codes. ISSN-L was implemented in the ISSN Register in 2008. To help ISSN users implement the ISSN-L in their databases, two free tables are available from the ISSN International Centre's home page: one lists each ISSN and its corresponding ISSN-L; the other lists each ISSN-L and its corresponding ISSNs. The Linking ISSN is the first example of a cluster ISSN; in 2020, the sixth edition of the standard introduced the potential for additional cluster ISSNs.

In the United States, the U.S. ISSN Center at the Library of Congress is responsible for assigning and maintaining the ISSNs for all U.S. serial and other continuing resource publications. Publishers wishing to have an ISSN assigned should follow the instructions on the U.S. ISSN Center's website. Although some of the more than 90 ISSN centers worldwide charge for ISSNs, ISSN assignment by the U.S. ISSN Center is free.

To obtain an ISSN for a U.S. publication by using the new application system, ISSN Uplink, or for more information about ISSNs in the United States, libraries, publishers, and other ISSN users should visit the U.S. ISSN Center's website, http://www.loc.gov/issn, or contact the U.S. ISSN Center, U.S. Programs, Law, and Literature, Library of Congress, 101 Independence Ave. S.E., Washington, DC 20540-4284; e-mail issn@loc.gov.

For information about ISSN products and services, and for application procedures that non-U.S. parties should use to apply for an ISSN, visit the ISSN International Centre's website, http://www.issn.org, or contact the International Centre at 45 rue de Turbigo, 75003 Paris, France (telephone 33-1-44-88-22-20, e-mail issnic@issn.org).

How to Obtain an SAN

Beat Barblan

United States ISBN/SAN Agency

SAN stands for Standard Address Number. The SAN system, an American National Standards Institute (ANSI) standard, assigns a unique identification number that is used to positively identify specific addresses of organizations in order to facilitate buying and selling transactions within the industry. It is recognized as the identification code for electronic communication within the industry.

For purposes of this standard, the book industry includes book publishers, book wholesalers, book distributors, book retailers, college bookstores, libraries, library binders, and serial vendors. Schools, school systems, technical institutes, and colleges and universities are not members of this industry, but are served by it and therefore included in the SAN system.

The purpose of the SAN is to ease communications among these organizations, of which there are several hundreds of thousands that engage in a large volume of separate transactions with one another. These transactions include purchases of books by book dealers, wholesalers, schools, colleges, and libraries from publishers and wholesalers; payments for all such purchases; and other communications between participants. The objective of this standard is to establish an identification code system by assigning each address within the industry a unique code to be used for positive identification for all book and serial buying and selling transactions.

Many organizations have similar names and multiple addresses, making identification of the correct contact point difficult and subject to error. In many cases, the physical movement of materials takes place between addresses that differ from the addresses to be used for the financial transactions. In such instances, there is ample opportunity for confusion and errors. Without identification by SAN, a complex record-keeping system would have to be instituted to avoid introducing errors. In addition, problems with the current numbering system—such as errors in billing, shipping, payments, and returns—are significantly reduced by using the SAN system. The SAN also eliminates one step in the order fulfillment process: the "look-up procedure" used to assign account numbers. Previously a store or library dealing with 50 different publishers was assigned a different account number by each of the suppliers. The SAN solved this problem. If a publisher prints its SAN on its stationery and ordering documents, vendors to whom it sends transactions do not have to look up the account number, but can proceed immediately to process orders by SAN.

Libraries are involved in many of the same transactions as book dealers, such as ordering and paying for books and charging and paying for various services to other libraries. Keeping records of transactions—whether these involve buying, selling, lending, or donations—entails operations suited to SAN use. SAN stationery speeds up order fulfillment and eliminate errors in shipping, billing, and crediting; this, in turn, means savings in both time and money.

History

Development of the Standard Address Number began in 1968, when Russell Reynolds, general manager of the National Association of College Stores (NACS), approached R. R. Bowker and suggested that a "Standard Account Number" system be implemented in the book industry. The first draft of a standard was prepared by an American National Standards Institute (ANSI) Committee Z39 subcommittee, which was co-chaired by Reynolds and Emery Koltay of Bowker. After Z39 members proposed changes, the current version of the standard was approved by NACS on December 17, 1979.

Format

The SAN consists of six digits plus a seventh *Modulus 11* check digit; a hyphen follows the third digit (XXX-XXXX) to facilitate transcription. The hyphen is to be used in print form, but need not be entered or retained in computer systems. Printed on documents, the Standard Address Number should be preceded by the identifier "SAN" to avoid confusion with other numerical codes (SAN XXXXXXX).

Check Digit Calculation

The check digit is based on *Modulus 11,* and can be derived as follows:

1. Write the digits of the basic number.   2 3 4 5 6 7
2. Write the constant weighting factors associated with each position by the basic number.   7 6 5 4 3 2
3. Multiply each digit by its associated weighting factor.   14 18 20 20 18 14
4. Add the products of the multiplications.   14 + 18 + 20 + 20 + 18 + 14 = 104
5. Divide the sum by Modulus 11 to find the remainder.   104 ÷ 11 = 9 plus a remainder of 5
6. Subtract the remainder from the Modulus 11 to generate the required check digit. If there is no remainder, generate a check digit of zero. If the check digit is 10, generate a check digit of X to represent 10, since the use of 10 would require an extra digit.   11 − 5 = 6
7. Append the check digit to create the standard seven-digit Standard Address Number.   SAN 234-5676

SAN Assignment

R. R. Bowker accepted responsibility for being the central administrative agency for SAN, and in that capacity assigns SANs to identify uniquely the addresses of organizations. No SANs can be reassigned; in the event that an organization should cease to exist, for example, its SAN would cease to be in circulation entirely. If an organization using an SAN should move or change its name with no change in ownership, its SAN would remain the same, and only the name or address would be updated to reflect the change.

The SAN should be used in all transactions; it is recommended that the SAN be imprinted on stationery, letterheads, order and invoice forms, checks, and all other documents used in executing various book transactions. The SAN should always be printed on a separate line above the name and address of the organization, preferably in the upper left-hand corner of the stationery to avoid confusion with other numerical codes pertaining to the organization, such as telephone number, zip code, and the like.

SAN Functions

The SAN is strictly a Standard Address Number, becoming functional only in applications determined by the user; these may include activities such as purchasing, billing, shipping, receiving, paying, crediting, and refunding. It is the method used by Pubnet and PubEasy systems and is required in all electronic data interchange communications using the Book Industry Systems Advisory Committee (BISAC) EDI formats. Every department that has an independent function within an organization could have an SAN for its own identification.

For additional information or to make suggestions, write to ISBN/SAN Agency, R. R. Bowker, LLC, 630 Central Ave., New Providence, NJ 07974, call 877 310-7333, or fax 908-795-3518. The e-mail address is san@bowker.com. An SAN can be ordered online through the website www.myidentifiers.com, or an application can be requested by e-mail through san@bowker.com.

Distinguished Books

The Year's Notable Books

The Notable Books Council of the Reference and User Services Association (RUSA), a division of the American Library Association (ALA), released its annual list of notable books on February 4, 2021. These titles were selected for their significant contribution to the expansion of knowledge or for the pleasure they can provide to adult readers.

Fiction

Leave the World Behind by Rumaan Alam (Ecco, an imprint of HarperCollins Publishers).

The Vanishing Half by Brit Bennett (Riverhead Books, an imprint of Penguin Random House).

Piranesi by Susanna Clarke (Bloomsbury Publishing).

The Office of Historical Corrections: A Novella and Stories by Danielle Evans (Riverhead Books, an imprint of Penguin Random House).

Breasts and Eggs by Mieko Kawakami, translated from the Japanese by Sam Bett and David Boyd (Europa Editions).

Temporary by Hilary Leichter (Coffee House Press).

Deacon King Kong by James McBride (Riverhead Books, an imprint of Penguin Random House).

Hamnet: A Novel of the Plague by Maggie O'Farrell (Knopf Doubleday Publishing Group).

Little Eyes by Samanta Schweblin, translated by Megan McDowell (Riverhead Books, an imprint of Penguin Random House).

Shuggie Bain by Douglas Stuart (Grove Press, an imprint of Grove Atlantic).

Run Me To Earth by Paul Yoon (Simon & Schuster).

Nonfiction

A Knock at Midnight: A Story of Hope, Justice and Freedom by Brittany K. Barnett (Crown, an imprint of Random House, a division of Penguin Random House).

Carville's Cure: Leprosy, Stigma and the Fight for Justice by Pam Fessler (Liveright Publishing Corporation, a division of W. W. Norton & Company).

Children of the Land: A Memoir by Marcelo Hernandez Castillo (Harper, an imprint of HarperCollins Publishers).

Hidden Valley Road: Inside the Mind of an American Family by Robert Kolker (Doubleday, a division of Penguin Random House).

Just Us: An American Conversation by Claudia Rankine (Graywolf Press).

Oak Flat: A Fight for Sacred Land in the American West by Lauren Redniss (Random House, a division of Penguin Random House).

Becoming Wild: How Animal Cultures Raise Families, Create Beauty, and Achieve Peace by Carl Safina (Henry Holt and Company).

We Have Been Harmonized: Life in China's Surveillance State by Kai Strittmatter (Custom House).

Memorial Drive: A Daughter's Memoir by Natasha Trethewey (Ecco, an imprint of HarperCollins Publishers).

Caste: The Origins of Our Discontents by Isabel Wilkerson (Random House, a division of Penguin Random House).

Wilmington's Lie: The Murderous Coup of 1898 and the Rise of White Supremacy by David Zucchino (Grove Press, an imprint of Grove Atlantic).

Poetry

Owed by Joshua Bennett (Penguin Books, a division of Penguin Random House).

Postcolonial Love Poem by Natalie Diaz (Graywolf Press).

Kontemporary Amerikan Poetry by John Murillo (Four Way Books).

The Reading List

Established in 2007 by the Reference and User Services Association (RUSA), a division of the American Library Association, this list highlights outstanding genre fiction that merits special attention by general adult readers and the librarians who work with them.

The winners were selected by the Reading List Council, whose members include eleven expert readers' advisory and collection development librarians. The eight genres currently included in the Council's considerations are adrenaline, fantasy, historical fiction, horror, mystery, relationship fiction, romance, and science fiction.

The RUSA website provides additional detail on each of the winning titles along with shortlists of "Readalikes" and runners up.

Adrenaline

The Holdout: A Novel by Graham Moore (Random House, an imprint and division of Penguin Random House LLC).

Fantasy

The House in the Cerulean Sea by TJ Klune (A Tor Book Published by Tom Doherty Associates).

Historical Fiction

Conjure Women: A Novel by Afia Atakora (Random House, an imprint and division of Penguin Random House LLC).

Horror

The Only Good Indians: A Novel by Stephen Graham Jones (Saga Press, an imprint of Simon & Schuster, Inc.).

Mystery

Fortune Favors the Dead: A Novel by Stephen Spotswood (Doubleday, a division of Penguin Random House LLC).

Relationship

Oona Out of Order by Margarita Montimore (Flatiron Books).

Romance

The Duke Who Didn't by Courtney Milan (Courtney Milan).

Science Fiction

The Space between Worlds by Micaiah Johnson (Del Rey, an imprint of Random House, a division of Penguin Random House LLC).

The Listen List

Established in 2010 by the CODES section of Reference and User Services Association (RUSA), the annual Listen List highlights outstanding audiobooks that merit special attention by general adult listeners and the librarians who work with them. RUSA's Listen List Council selects a dozen audiobooks that may include fiction, nonfiction, poetry, and plays. The council consists of seven librarians who are experts in readers' advisory and collection development. To be eligible, titles must be available for purchase and circulation by libraries.

An annotated version of the list on the RUSA website includes more information on each choice and lists additional audiobooks of interest.

Bear Necessity by James Gould-Bourn, narrated by Rupert Holliday-Evans (Simon & Schuster Audio).

A Burning: A Novel by Megha Majumdar, narrated by Vikas Adam, Priya Ayyar, Deepti Gupta, Soneela Nankani, Neil Shah, and Ulka Simone Mohanty (Books on Tape).

The Girl with the Louding Voice: A Novel by Abi Daré, narrated by Adjoa Andoh (Books on Tape).

Homie: Poems by Danez Smith, narrated by Danez Smith (HighBridge Audio).

Make Me Rain: Poems and Prose by Nikki Giovanni, narrated by Nikki Giovanni (HarperAudio).

Me & Patsy Kickin' Up Dust: My Friendship with Patsy Cline by Loretta Lynn, narrated by Patsy Lynn Russell (Hachette Audio).

My Dark Vanessa: A Novel by Kate Elizabeth Russell, narrated by Grace Gummer (Harper Audio).

The Only Good Indians by Stephen Graham Jones, narrated by Shaun Taylor-Corbett (Simon & Schuster Audio).

Tiny Imperfections by Alli Frank and Asha Youmans, narrated by Bahni Turpin (Books on Tape).

The Trial of the Chicago 7: The Official Transcript edited by Mark L. Levine, George C. McNamee, and Daniel Greenberg, narrated by J. K. Simmons, Jeff Daniels, Chris Jackson, John Hawkes, Chris Chalk, Luke Kirby, Corey Stoll, Norbert Leo Butz, George Newbern, and an ensemble cast (Simon & Schuster Audio).

The Vanishing Half: A Novel by Brit Bennett, narrated by Shayna Small (Books on Tape).

Wow, No Thank You: Essays by Samantha Irby, narrated by the author (Audible).

Best Fiction for Young Adults

Each year a committee of the Young Adult Library Services Association (YALSA), a division of the American Library Association, compiles a list of the best fiction appropriate for young adults ages 12 to 18. Selected on the basis of each book's proven or potential appeal and value to young adults, the titles span a variety of subjects as well as a broad range of reading levels. An asterisk denotes the title was selected as a top ten.

Agnes at the End of the World by Kelly McWilliams (Little, Brown and Company Books for Young Readers/Hachette). 978-0316487337.

All These Monsters by Amy Tintera (Houghton Mifflin Harcourt Books for Young Readers). 978-0358012405.

All-American Muslim Girl by Nadine Jolie Courtney (Farrar, Straus and Giroux Books for Young Readers/Macmillan). 978-0374309527.

Ashlords by Scott Reintgen (Crown Books for Young Readers/Penguin Random House). 978-0593119174.

*Be Not Far from Me by Mindy McGinnis (Katherine Tegen Books/HarperCollins). 978-0062561626.

Before the Ever After by Jacqueline Woodson (Nancy Paulsen Books/Penguin Random House). 978-0399545436.

The Black Flamingo by Dean Atta (Balzer+Bray/HarperCollins). 978-0062990297.

Black Girl Unlimited: The Remarkable Story of a Teenage Wizard by Echo Brown (Christy Ottaviano Books/Macmillan). 978-1250309853.

The Black Kids by Christina Hammonds Reed (Simon & Schuster Books for Young Readers). 978-1534462724.

Blood Moon by Lucy Cuthew (Walker Books/Candlewick Press). 978-1536215038.

Break the Fall by Jennifer Iacopelli (Razorbill/Penguin Random House). 978-0593114179.

Burn Our Bodies Down by Rory Power (Delacorte Press/Penguin Random House). 978-0525645627.

Call Down the Hawk by Maggie Stiefvater (Scholastic Press). 978-1338188325.

*Cemetery Boys by Aiden Thomas (Swoon Reads/Macmillan). 978-1250250469.

Charming as a Verb by Ben Philippe (Balzer+Bray/HarperCollins). 978-0062824141.

*Clap When You Land by Elizabeth Acevedo (HarperTeen/HarperCollins). 978-0062882769.

The Cousins by Karen M. McManus (Delacorte Press/Penguin Random House). 978-0525708001.

Darius the Great Deserves Better by Adib Khorram (Dial Books/Penguin Random House). 978-0593108239.

Dear Haiti, Love Alaine by Maika Moulite and Maritza Moulite (Inkyard Press/Harlequin). 978-1335777096.

Dear Justyce by Nic Stone (Crown Books for Young Readers/Penguin Random House). 978-1984829665.

*Deeplight by Frances Hardinge (Amulet Books/ABRAMS). 978-1419743207.

Don't Read the Comments by Eric Smith (Inkyard Press/Harlequin). 978-1335016027.

Early Departures by Justin A. Reynolds (Katherine Tegen Books/HarperCollins). 978-0062748409.

Elatsoe by Darcie Little Badger (Levine Querido). 978-1646140053.

The Enigma Game by Elizabeth Wein (Little, Brown Books for Young Readers/Hachette). 978-1368012584.

Fable by Adrienne Young (Wednesday Books/Macmillan). 978-1250254368.

The Faithless Hawk by Margaret Owen (Henry Holt and Co. Books for Young Readers/Macmillan). 978-1250191946.

The Falling in Love Montage by Ciara Smyth (HarperTeen/HarperCollins). 978-0062957115.

Felix Ever After by Kacen Callender (Balzer+Bray/HarperCollins). 978-0062820259.

Furia by Yamile Saied Méndez (Algonquin Young Readers/Workman Publishing). 978-1616209919.

Ghost Wood Song by Erica Waters (HarperTeen/HarperCollins). 978-0062894229.

Girl, Serpent, Thorn by Melissa Bashardoust (Flatiron Books/Macmillan). 978-1250196149.

Girl, Unframed by Deb Caletti (Simon Pulse/ Simon & Schuster). 978-1534426979.

Girls Save the World in This One by Ash Parsons (Philomel Books/Penguin Random House). 978-0525515326.

Golden Arm by Carl Deuker (Houghton Mifflin Harcourt Books for Young Readers). 978-0358012429.

*Grown by Tiffany D. Jackson (Katherine Tegen Books/HarperCollins). 978-0062840356.

He Must Like You by Danielle Younge-Ullman (Viking Books for Young Readers/Penguin Random House). 978-1984835710.

The Henna Wars by Adiba Jaigirdar (Page Street Kids/Page Street Publishing). 978-1624149689.

Here the Whole Time by Vitor Martins, translation by Larissa Helena (Scholastic Press). 978-1338620825.

Horrid by Katrina Leno (Little Brown Books for Young Readers/Hachette). 978-0316537247.

The How and the Why by Cynthia Hand (HarperTeen/HarperCollins). 978-0062693167.

I'll Be the One by Lyla Lee (Katherine Tegen Books/HarperCollins). 978-0062936929.

The Inheritance Games by Jennifer Lynn Barnes (Little, Brown Books for Young Readers/Hachette). 978-1368052405.

Kent State by Deborah Wiles (Scholastic Press). 978-1338356281.

King and the Dragonflies by Kacen Callender (Scholastic Press). 978-1338129335.

Kingdom of Souls by Rena Barron (HarperTeen/HarperCollins). 978-0062870957.

The Last True Poets of the Sea by Julia Drake (Little, Brown Books for Young Readers/Hachette). 978-1368048088.

The Left-Handed Booksellers of London by Garth Nix (Katherine Tegen Books/HarperCollins). 978-0062683250.

Legendborn by Tracy Deonn (Simon Pulse/ Simon & Schuster). 978-1534441606.

The Life and (Medieval) Times of Kit Sweetly by Jamie Pacton (Page Street Kids/Page Street Publishing). 978-1624149528.

Light It Up by Kekla Magoon (Henry Holt and Co. Books for Young Readers/Macmillan). 978-1250128898.

Lobizona by Romina Garber (Wednesday Books/Macmillan). 978-1250239129.

The Loop by Ben Oliver (Chicken House/ Scholastic Press). 978-133859306.

The Love Curse of Melody McIntyre by Robin Talley (HarperTeen/HarperCollins). 978-0062409263.

Mad, Bad & Dangerous to Know by Samira Ahmed (Soho Teen/Soho Press). 978-1616959890.

Miss Meteor by Tehlor Kay Mejia and Anna-Marie McLemore (HarperTeen/ HarperCollins). 978-0062869913.

*More Than Just a Pretty Face by Syed M. Masood (Little, Brown Books for Young Readers/Hachette). 978-0316492355.

My Calamity Jane by Cynthia Hand, Brodi Ashton, and Jodi Meadows (HarperTeen/ HarperCollins). 978-0062652812.

The New David Espinoza by Fred Aceves (HarperTeen/HarperCollins). 978-0062489883.

A Phoenix First Must Burn: Sixteen Stories of Black Girl Magic, Resistance, and Hope edited by Patrice Caldwell (Viking Books for Young Readers/Penguin Random House). 978-1984835659.

Poisoned by Jennifer Donnelly (Scholastic Press). 978-1338268492.

Punching the Air by Ibi Zoboi and Yusef Salaam (Balzer+Bray/HarperCollins). 978-0062996480.

*Raybearer by Jordan Ifueko (Amulet Books/ ABRAMS). 978-1419739828.

Sanctuary by Paola Mendoza and Abby Sher (G.P. Putnam's Sons/Penguin Random House). 978-1984815712.

The Snow Fell Three Graves Deep: Voices from the Donner Party by Allan Wolf (Candlewick Press). 978-0763663247.

A Song of Wraiths and Ruin by Roseanne A. Brown (Balzer+Bray/HarperCollins). 978-0062891495.

Super Fake Love Song by David Yoon (G.P. Putnam's Sons/Penguin Random House). 978-1984812230.

These Violent Delights by Chloe Gong (Simon Pulse/Simon & Schuster). 978-1534457690.

They Went Left by Monica Hesse (Little, Brown Books for Young Readers/Hachette). 978-0316490573.

*This Is My America by Kim Johnson (Random House Books for Young Readers). 978-0593118764.

Three Things I Know Are True by Betty Culley (HarperTeen/HarperCollins). 978-0062908025.

Tigers, Not Daughters by Samantha Mabry (Algonquin Books for Young Readers/ Workman Publishing). 978-1616208967.

Today Tonight Tomorrow by Rachel Lynn Solomon (Simon Pulse/Simon & Schuster). 978-1534440241.

Tweet Cute by Emma Lord (Wednesday Books/ Macmillan). 978-1250237323.

Unscripted by Nicole Kronzer (Amulet Books/ ABRAMS). 978-1419740848.

The Voting Booth by Brandy Colbert (Hyperion/Disney Book Group). 978-1368053297.

Watch Over Me by Nina LaCour (Dutton Books for Young Readers/Penguin Random House). 978-0593108970.

We Are Not Free by Traci Chee (Houghton Mifflin Harcourt Books for Young Readers). 978-0358131434.

We Are Not from Here by Jenny Torres Sanchez (Philomel Books/Penguin Random House). 978-1984812261.

What I Carry by Jennifer Longo (Random House Books for Young Readers). 978-0553537710.

When You Were Everything by Ashley Woodfolk (Delacorte Press/Penguin Random House). 978-1524715915.

The Year of the Witching by Alexis Henderson (Ace/Penguin Random House). 978-0593099605.

Yes No Maybe So by Becky Albertalli and Aisha Saeed (Balzer+Bray/HarperCollins). 978-0062937049.

You Know I'm No Good by Jessie Ann Foley (Quill Tree Books/HarperCollins). 978-0062957085.

You Should See Me in a Crown by Leah Johnson (Scholastic Press). 978-1338503265.

Quick Picks for Reluctant Young Adult Readers

The Young Adult Library Services Association (YALSA), a division of the American Library Association, annually chooses a list of outstanding titles that may stimulate the interest of reluctant teen readers. The list is intended to attract teens who are not inclined to read, for whatever reason.

This year's list includes 64 fiction and nonfiction titles published from late 2019 through 2020. An asterisk denotes the title was selected as a top ten.

Nonfiction

All Thirteen: The Incredible Cave Rescue of the Thai Boys' Soccer Team by Christine Soontornvat. Candlewick Press. 2020. $24.99. ISBN: 9781536209457. In June 2018, twelve boys and their coach took a break from soccer practice to explore a cave system in Thailand. Trapped by heavy rains, the team spent 17 days underground. This is the true story of their survival, and the heroic efforts of those who came to the rescue.

Almost American Girl by Robin Ha. Balzer+Bray. 2020. $22.99. ISBN: 9780062685100. Up through eighth grade Robin lived with her mom in South Korea, but when Mom takes Robin on a "vacation" to the U.S. and then abruptly announces they are staying in America permanently, Robin is forced to assimilate into American culture.

Dragon Hoops by Gene Luen Yang. First Second. 2020. $24.99. ISBN: 9781626720794. Award-winning graphic novelist, Gene Luen Yang, tells the story of the varsity boy's basketball team's quest for a state championship at the high school he taught at before becoming a writer full time.

Free Lunch by Rex Ogle. Norton Young Readers. 2019. $16.95. ISBN: 9781324003601. Sixth grader Rex tries to fit in at school while battling deep shame about living in poverty as well as suffering physical and emotional abuse at home.

Games of Deception: The True Story of the First U.S. Olympic Basketball Team at the 1936 Olympics in Hitler's Germany by Andrew Maraniss. Calkins Creek. 2019. $18.99. ISBN: 9781629794389. Berlin, Germany, 1936. Adolf Hitler and his Nazi regime are the hosts of the summer Olympic Games.

Basketball, a relatively new sport, will be officially included for the first time. Politics, anti-Semitism, and racism take center court, veiled by the propaganda-driven Nazis, yet hinting at the atrocities to come.

Girls Who Run the World: 31 CEOs Who Mean Business by Diana Kapp. Illustrated by Bijou Kerman. Delacorte Press. 2019. $19.99. ISBN: 9781984893055. Short chapters introduce the background and successful careers of 31 contemporary women entrepreneurs in fields from food and fashion to science, apps/tech, and media.

They Called Us Enemy by George Takei, Justin Eisinger, and Steven Scott. Art by Harmony Becker. Top Shelf Productions. 2019. $19.99. ISBN: 9781603094504. A graphic novel by George Takei, actor and activist, tells the story of his childhood shaped by his family's detention and internment when he was just five years old.

When Stars Are Scattered by Victoria Jamieson and Omar Mohamed. Dial Books. 2020. $12.99. ISBN: 9780525553908. This graphic memoir details the life of a young Somali boy, Omar, and his disabled brother in the Dadaab refugee camp. While Omar feels an obligation to watch over Hassan, he is pulled by the lure of school and a distant hope to one day be resettled in America.

Fiction

All Eyes on Her by L. E. Flynn. Imprint. 2020. $18.99. ISBN: 9781250158178. When small-town golden boy Mike Forrester is found dead after a hike with his girlfriend, Tabitha Cousins, 17, everyone has their own theory about what happened. Chapters from the perspectives of Tabby and Mike's friends, family, and classmates are interspersed with articles and blog posts detailing the unfolding criminal case.

Ashlords by Scott Reintgen. Crown Books for Young Readers. 2020. $17.99. ISBN: 9780593119174. The Races. Where the ruling-class Ashlords race their divine phoenix horses for fame and glory. This time, though, will be different. This time, social-media sensation Imelda Beru, the impoverished Dividian known as "The Alchemist," will show what it looks like to fight to be Champion, against all odds.

*Be Not Far From Me by Mindy McGinnis. Katherine Tegen Books. 2020. $18.99. ISBN: 9780062561626. After finding her boyfriend cheating on her during a party in the woods, Ashley takes off in anger and ends up lost, with a serious injury to her foot, and with only her wits and some survival skills to help her make it out alive.

Black Brother, Black Brother by Jewell Parker Rhodes. Little, Brown Books for Young Readers. 2020. $16.99. 9780316493802. After getting suspended from Middlefield Prep, Donte takes up fencing in order to beat the ringleader of the racist bullying against him.

The Black Flamingo by Dean Atta. Balzer+Bray. 2020. $18.99. ISBN: 9780062990297. Michael is a mixed-race, gay teenager in London, struggling to find his place in the world. Follow him from childhood through his first year of university, where he is introduced to drag society, and thanks to the support of fellow members, performs as the Black Flamingo.

Blood Sport by Tash McAdam. Orca Soundings. 2020. $9.95. ISBN: 9781459824362. When his older sister dies of a supposed drug overdose, trans teen Jason knows that something doesn't add up—his sister didn't do drugs. After uncovering a box of suspicious photos, he traces the clues to a boxing gym and takes up the sport in order to investigate more closely.

Bloom by Kenneth Oppel. Alfred A Knopf. 2020. $16.99. ISBN: 9781524773007. Strange rain unleashes an invasion of black vines that overrun and devour everything from crops to buildings, and their pollen causes severe allergic reactions. Even more ominous, the vines can trap and consume humans. Three teens discover they are immune to these noxious plants and band together to fight them.

Cinderella Is Dead by Kalynn Bayron. Bloomsbury YA. 2020. $18.99. ISBN: 9781547603879. In Mersailles, teen girls are required to attend an Annual Ball, and those not selected for marriage are "forfeit," never to be seen again. Rejected by her childhood love, Erin, Sophia escapes the Ball and searches for a way to end the King's toxic patriarchal rule forever.

Class Act by Jerry Craft. Quill Tree Books. 2020. $22.99. ISBN: 9780062885517. In this companion book to *New Kid,* Drew (Jordan's friend) is another Black student at the same mostly white private school. Through Drew's story, we see issues about growing up, evolving friendships, identity, race and class differences, and acceptance, portrayed in a graphic novel that is honest and relatable, smart, and funny.

Clean Getaway by Nic Stone. Crown Books for Young Readers. 2020. $16.99. ISBN: 9781984892973. William, nicknamed "Scoob" by his Grandmother, G'ma, joins her for an RV road trip across the South returning to locations in the "Traveler's Green Book" she and his grandfather visited in 1968 as a biracial couple. On the road, they share adventures and Scoob learns more about family, including G'ma.

Clown in a Cornfield by Adam Cesare. HarperTeen. 2020. $17.99. ISBN: 9780062854599. Quinn and her father move to Kettle Springs looking for a fresh start. What she finds is the creepy clown mascot of the old corn syrup factory. And when the clown turns homicidal, Quinn resorts to desperate measures to survive.

Cracking the Bell by Geoff Herbach. Katherine Tegen Books. 2019. $17.99. ISBN: 9780062453167. Football is the thing that turned Isaiah's life around, but after he suffers a potentially dangerous concussion, will he continue to risk his life in order to have the future that football offers him?

Dear Justyce by Nic Stone. Crown. 2020. $18.99. ISBN: 9781984829665. In this follow-up to Nic Stone's Dear Martin, readers meet 17-year-old Quan, who processes his own pain and conflict while incarcerated by writing letters to Justyce, a boy from his own neighborhood whom he feels both connected to and worlds apart from.

Felix Ever After by Kacen Callender. Balzer+Bray. 2020. $18.99. ISBN: 9780062820273. High school senior Felix wants to fall in love, but secretly worries that being queer, Black, and trans makes him too complicated to love. When an arts program classmate displays a gallery of his pre-transition photos that includes his deadname, Felix sets up a catfishing scheme to get revenge.

Find Layla by Meg Elison. Skyscape. 2020. $16.99. ISBN: 9781542019804. 14-year-old Layla is an aspiring scientist who struggles to keep her brother safe in a home environment of extreme neglect. When Layla's video for a biome project at school goes viral, it exposes the toxic mold, fungi, and maggots in their apartment and draws the attention of Child Protective Services.

Found by Joseph Bruchac. 7th Generation. 2020. $9.95. ISBN: 9781939053237. After a Native American teen witnesses a murder on a train, he's thrown down a ravine and left for dead. Will his wilderness survival skills and his grandfather's wisdom be enough to help him outwit the men hunting him?

Full Disclosure by Camryn Garrett. Knopf Books for Young Readers. 2019. $18.99. ISBN: 9781984829962. 17-year-old Simone doesn't know how to tell her new boyfriend that she's HIV-positive. When an anonymous note in her locker threatens to expose her status unless she dumps him, she fears a repeat of the bullying and public hysteria she faced at her last school.

The Girl in the White Van by April Henry. Henry Holt. 2020. $17.99. ISBN: 9781250157591. When Savannah is kidnapped, at first everyone assumes she's run away. Only Daniel doesn't believe she's a runaway, and he's determined to find her before something terrible happens. In the meantime, Savannah must team up with another kidnapped girl to try to escape her attacker.

Girl on the Run by Abigail Johnson. Underlined. 2020. $9.99. ISBN: 9780593179819. Katelyn's plan to surprise her widowed mother with an online dating profile goes awry when they're attacked and chased from their home. Separated from her mom

and on the run, Katelyn and her companion, Malcolm, try to unravel the mysteries of her mom's past, as well as her present whereabouts.

A Good Girl's Guide to Murder by Holly Jackson. Delacorte Press. 2020. $17.99. ISBN: 9781984896360. Five years ago, Sal Singh killed his girlfriend, Andie Bell, and then committed suicide. Or did he? Pippi Fitz-Amobi isn't so sure, and she's determined to review the case for her senior project.

Golden Arm by Carl Deuker. HMH Books for Young Readers. 2020. $17.99. ISBN: 9780358012429. When Lazarus's school baseball team is disbanded, he is given the opportunity to pitch for ritzy Laurelhurt, across town and a world away from the soon-to-be-demolished trailer park where his family lives. Rising star Laz aspires to the major league draft, but his brother's drug-dealing threatens Laz's chances of success.

Grown by Tiffany D. Jackson. Katherine Tegen. 2020. $17.99. ISBN: 9780062840356. Enchanted Jones dreams of a music career, but falls prey to master seducer and much older R&B mega-star Korey Fields. After Korey is found murdered, she must acknowledge the truth about what happened to her and help reveal the monster he truly was.

Hard Wired by Len Vlahos. Bloomsbury. 2020. $17.99. ISBN: 9781681190372. Fifteen-year-old Quinn's average life implodes when he discovers that he is the first sentient artificial intelligence and that his entire existence has been a 45-minute simulation. Subject to cruel experiments in a lab, Quinn fights for the recognition of his rights and plots his escape.

Harrow Lake by Kat Ellis. Dial Books. 2020. $17.99. ISBN: 9781984814531. The daughter of a celebrated horror director, Lola is shipped off to stay with her grandmother in the eerie small town where her father filmed the cult classic Nightjar. Local legend tells of a cannibalistic monster called Mr. Jitters, whom Lola senses while exploring the mystery of her mother's disappearance.

Heartstopper Vol. 1. by Alice Oseman. Graphix. 2020. $14.00. ISBN: 9781338617443. This graphic novel recounts the story of Charlie and Nick's growing friendship and camaraderie. Charlie feels more than friendship for Nick. Nick is trying to figure out what he feels for Charlie.

How It All Blew Up by Arvin Ahmadi. Viking. 2020. $17.99. ISBN: 9780593202876. On the eve of his high school graduation, 18-year-old Amir runs off to Italy in order to avoid coming out to his Persian family. Over the summer, he finds himself in a gay community in Rome, coming to terms with himself and how to approach his family, who is desperate to reconnect with him.

I Hope You're Listening by Tom Ryan. AW Teen. 2020. $17.99. ISBN: 9780807535080. After witnessing her best friend's abduction while they were young children, Dee is now the (secret) host of the true-crime podcast Radio Silent, which investigates missing-persons cases. When another little girl disappears from their street under similar circumstances, she risks her anonymity and attempts to solve both cases.

I Know You Remember by Jennifer Donaldson. Razorbill. 2019. $18.99. ISBN: 9781595148544. Ruthie returns to Anchorage to find her former and beloved-by-all best friend Zahra missing. As the investigation narrows in on what happened, Ruthie is determined to get to the bottom of it all. Who can be trusted?

I'll Be the One by Lyla Lee. Katherine Tegen Books. 2020. $17.99. ISBN: 9780062936943. Used to being told that "fat girls can't dance," Korean-American Skye Shin auditions for a K-Pop reality show to prove everyone wrong. Once cast, Skye struggles to retain her confidence as fat-phobic judges tell her to lose weight and a budding romance with an influential competitor leads to online bullying.

The Inheritance Games by Jennifer Lynn Barnes. Little, Brown and Company. 2020. $17.99. ISBN: 9781368052405. Shocked and confused, Avery Grambs is pulled from class and whisked away to the reading of billionaire Tobias Hawthorne's will—a man she's never met—and inherits his fortune. Moving into his mansion filled with puzzles, secret passageways, and disinherited family members, Avery tries to understand why she has become Tobias's heir.

Jane Anonymous by Laurie Faria Stolarz. Wednesday Books. 2019. $17.99. ISBN: 9781250303707. "Jane" was kidnapped and held captive in a locked basement for seven months. Once free of the monster who imprisoned her, Jane must battle other demons as she tries to reconstruct her life. Who was her captor and why was she taken? What happened to her friend and fellow captive, Mason?

The Last Witness by Claire McFall. Sourcebooks Fire. 2020. $10.99. ISBN: 9781728200248. Five friends head off on a camping trip along the remote Scottish coast. While hiking, Heather removes a talisman from an old burial site, and a malevolent force descends on the group. One by one, they vanish. In now/then segments, Heather unravels the aftermath from a psychiatric hospital.

Layoverland by Gabby Noone. Razorbill. 2020. $17.99. ISBN: 9781984836120. Beatrice (Bea) Fox is dead. Stuck in purgatory (which looks a lot like an airport), Bea has been assigned to work in the Memory Experience Department, helping other souls move on to heaven. Her job gets complicated, however, when she's assigned to assist Caleb, the boy who caused her death.

Long Way Down: The Graphic Novel by Jason Reynolds. Illustrated by Danica Novgorodoff. Atheneum/Caitlyn Dlouhy Books. 2020. $19.99. ISBN: 9781534444959. The Rules. #1 Don't Cry. #2 Don't Snitch. #3 Revenge. When Will's older brother, Shawn, is shot and killed, Will plans to follow rule #3. Taking the elevator, he encounters a ghost from the past at each floor. Stories are told, memories surface, and the gun Will carries is heavy.

The Loop by Ben Oliver. Chicken House. 2020. $18.99. ISBN: 9781338589306. In a near-future dystopia, 16-year-old Luka Kane has spent 736 days in the juvenile prison known as "the Loop," enduring torture and medical experimentation in exchange for a delayed execution date. When war breaks out, Luka and fellow prisoners escape and are hunted through the fallen city by dangerous foes.

Lucky Caller by Emma Mills. Henry Holt. 2020. $17.99. ISBN: 9781250179654. Nina's senior year begins with a journey into radio broadcasting, new family dynamics, and first love in this charming romantic comedy.

Lux: The New Girl by Ashley Woodfolk. Workshop. 2020. $15.99. ISBN: 9780593096024. When Lux is kicked out of yet another school, she has one more chance to fit in and make things work at Harlem's Augusta Savage School of the Arts. Starting over with new friends (even if they're as cool as the Flyy Girls) is harder than she thought.

Manning Up by Bee Walsh. West 44 Books. 2019. $9.95. ISBN: 9781538382677. Jack faces pressure on the football field and with himself, as he battles an eating disorder that he exacerbates by taking steroids.

A Match Made in Mehendi by Nandini Bajpai. Little, Brown Books for Young Readers. 2019. $17.99. ISBN: 9780316522588. New Jersey sophomore Simi comes from a long line of Punjabi matchmakers. After reluctantly acknowledging her own talent for matchmaking, she and her best friend create an app to set up students at their school. The app makes them instantly popular, but the unlikely matches it generates leads to controversy.

#NoEscape by Gretchen McNeil. Freeform. 2020. $17.99. ISBN: 9781368026260. Persey solves an unbeatable escape room and gets invited to an escape room competition where the winner can walk away with ten million dollars. However, when she and seven other contestants start playing the game they realize not everything is as it seems especially when things get deadly.

Not Hungry by Kate Karyus Quinn. West 44 Books. 2019. $9.95. ISBN: 9781538382707. June is starving but says she's not hungry. She also secretly binges and purges. When a popular athlete catches June purging in the bushes, they begin an unlikely & secret relationship. Is this yet another unhealthy choice for June?

Nowhere on Earth by Nike Lake. Knopf Books for Young Readers. 2020. ISBN: 9781984896445. After a bush plane crash leaves them stranded in the Alaskan wilderness, teen ballerina Emily Perez will do whatever it takes to protect her little brother Aidan. But the unforgiving natural world isn't the only threat—heavily armed men are in pursuit, intent on capturing her brother and exposing dangerous secrets.

Only Mostly Devastated by Sophie Gonzales. Wednesday Books. 2020. $17.99. ISBN: 9781250315892. Ollie's senior year begins in North Carolina and it also turns out that his summer crush, Will, attends the same school. While Ollie is excited to see where things go, he must contend with the fact that Will isn't willing to reveal his sexuality.

Punching the Air by Ibi Zoboi and Yusef Salaam. Blazer + Bray. 2020. $18.99. ISBN: 9780062996480. Convicted of a crime he did not commit and incarcerated, Amal Shahid deals with the injustice of it all with support from his mother and his art.

Rules for Being a Girl by Candace Bushnell and Katie Cotungo. Balzer+Bray. 2020. $19.99. ISBN: 9780062803375. Marin is confused and angry when her favorite teacher, Mr. Beckett, tries to kiss her. Upon reporting his bad behavior, Marin is further harassed and ostracized by classmates, even her best friend Chloe. Marin begins to fight back against these unfair rules for girls, but will others join her crusade?

Shuri: A Black Panther Novel by Nic Stone. Scholastic Inc.. 2020. $17.99. ISBN: 9781338585476. Princess Shuri must race to figure out what is happening to the Heart Shaped Herb (the source for the Black Panther's powers) before her brother's rule as the Black Panther and Wakanda itself are threatened.

Snapdragon by Kat Leyh. First Second Books. 2020. $12.99. ISBN: 9781250171115. Magic happens when Snapdragon (Snap) befriends Jacks, the town witch. They bond over their shared love of animals, but soon discover their lives are intertwined in ways they could not have imagined. This is a sweet graphic novel that combines magical realism with stories of self-acceptance.

These Vengeful Hearts by Katherine Laurin. Inkyard Press. 2020. ISBN: 9781335145871. After years molding herself into the perfect candidate, Ember Williams is finally invited to be a member of the dangerous and exclusive favor-trading secret society: the Red Court. Her ultimate goal? To implode the group once and for all, exacting vengeance and ending the Red Court's reign over Heller High.

Three Things I Know Are True by Betty Culley. HarperTeen. 2019. $18.99. ISBN: 9780062908025. Liv's world is shattered when her older brother, Jonah, accidentally shoots himself with a neighbor's gun. Life in small-town Maine is hard enough, but now Liv must navigate school, friendships, and a blossoming romance under the shadow of Jonah's traumatic brain injury and a trial that has divided the community.

Throw Like a Girl by Sarah Henning. Little, Brown Books for Young Readers. 2020. $17.99. ISBN: 9780316529501. Liv Rodinsky is a star softball player until after one wrong move she loses her scholarship and has to transfer to another school. With her future as a college softball player on the line, Liv has to convince Northland's softball coach to put her on the team.

The Truth App by Jack Heath. Simon & Schuster BFYR. 2020. $17.99. ISBN: 9781534449862. High school student Jarli creates an app that tells you when people are lying and releases it for beta testing. His app goes viral, but before he can even understand how that will affect his life, someone tries to kill him.

The Upside of Falling by Alex Light. Harper Teen. 2020. $17.99. ISBN: 9781534449862. Brett is a popular jock and all around nice guy with a seemingly perfect life. Becca is a smart, quiet, hardworking girl who flies under the radar. The two start a fake relationship that evolves into the real deal.

The Voting Booth by Brandy Colbert. Disney-Hyperion. 2020. $18.99. ISBN: 9781368053297. Duke and Marva "meet cute" when Duke is turned away from his polling place and Marva rescues him when his car won't start. Told in alternating chapters during one chaotic day, they talk about activism, voting rights, police brutality, gun violence, family, citizenship, racism, relationships, and cute cat memes.

What Unbreakable Looks Life by Kate McLaughlin. Wednesday Books. 2020. $18.99. ISBN: 9781250173805. After being freed from human trafficking, Lex heals from her trauma with the help of her family and a new love while also seeking justice for what happened to her.

You Should See Me in a Crown by Leah Johnson. Scholastic. 2020. $17.99. ISBN: 9781338503265. Liz feels different as a poor, Black, queer, awkward, not part of the in-crowd senior in high school. In order to get a scholarship she needs to attend college and fulfill her dreams, she must step far out of her comfort zone...so she runs for prom queen!

Wonder Woman: Tempest Tossed by Laurie Halse Anderson. Illustrated by Leila Del Duca. DC Comics. 2020. $16.99. ISBN: 9781401286453. While rescuing refugees off the coast of her homeland, Diana of Themyscira accidentally becomes one herself. Eventually landing in New York, Diana is angered by the social injustices she witnesses. Working to support her neighbors, she uncovers a human trafficking ring that only a wonder woman can defeat.

The Alex Awards

The Young Adult Library Services Association (YALSA), a division of the American Library Association, has selected ten adult books with special appeal to teen readers to receive the 2021 Alex Awards. The award is sponsored by the Margaret A. Edwards Trust.

Black Sun by Rebecca Roanhorse (Saga Press/ Gallery Books, an imprint of Simon & Schuster).

The House in the Cerulean Sea by TJ Klune (Tor Books, an imprint of Tom Doherty Associates, a division of Macmillan).

The Impossible First: From Fire to Ice—Crossing Antarctica Alone by Colin O'Brady (Scribner, an imprint of Simon & Schuster).

Kent State: Four Dead in Ohio by Derf Backderf (Abrams Comicarts).

The Kids Are Gonna Ask by Gretchen Anthony (Park Row Books, an imprint of Harlequin, a division of HarperCollins Publishers).

The Only Good Indians by Stephen Graham Jones (Saga Press/Gallery Books, an imprint of Simon & Schuster).

Plain Bad Heroines by Emily M. Danforth (William Morrow, an imprint of Harper-Collins).

Riot Baby by Tochi Onyebuchi (Tordotcom, an imprint of Tom Doherty Associates, a division of Macmillan).

Solutions and Other Problems by Allie Brosh (Gallery Books, an imprint of Simon & Schuster).

We Ride upon Sticks: A Novel by Quan Barry (Pantheon Books, a division of Penguin Random House).

Amazing Audiobooks for Young Adults

Each year, the Amazing Audiobooks Blogging Team of the Young Adult Library Services Association (YALSA), a division of the American Library Association, selects and annotates a list of notable audio recordings significant to young adults from among those released in the past two years. This year's list comprises 81 titles selected from among 149 nominations that were posted and discussed on YALSA's teen collection blog, The Hub.

While the list as a whole addresses the interests and needs of young adults, individual titles need not appeal to this entire age range but rather to parts of it. An asterisk denotes the title was selected as a top ten.

145th Street: Short Stories by Walter Dean Meyers, narration by Brandon Gill, Almarie Guerra, Johnny Heller, Dominic Hoffman, Sullivan Jones, JaQwan J. Kelly, Adenrele Ojo, Paula Parker, Heather Alicia Simms, and Bahni Turpin (Listening Library).

All Boys Aren't Blue: A Memoir-Manifesto by George M. Johnson, narration by George M. Johnson (Macmillan Young Listeners).

All the Things We Never Knew by Liara Tamani, narration by Preston Butler III and Joniece Abbott-Pratt (HarperAudio).

All-American Muslim Girl by Nadine Jolie Courtney, narration by Priya Ayyar (Dreamscape Media, LLC).

Allies by Alan Gratz, narration by Jamie Cline, Vaneh Assadourian, PJ Ochlan, Matthew Frow, Mar A. Samuel, and Norah Hunter (Scholastic Audio).

Be Not Far from Me by Mindy McGinnis, narration by Brittany Pressley (Harper-Audio).

Before the Ever After by Jacqueline Woodson, narration by Guy Lockard (Listening Library).

Beverly, Right Here: Three Rancheros, Book 3 by Kate DiCamillo, narration by Jorjeana Marie (Listening Library).

Black Brother, Black Brother by Jewell Parker Rhodes, narration by Barrie Buckner (Little, Brown Young Readers).

The Black Flamingo by Dean Atta, narration by Dean Atta (HarperAudio).

The Bone Houses by Emily Lloyd-Jones, narration by Moira Quirk (Little, Brown Young Readers).

The Bridge by Bill Konigsberg, narration by Marin Ireland (Scholastic Audio).

Burn by Patric Ness, narration by Joniece Abbott-Pratt (HarperAudio).

Call Down the Hawk: The Dreamer Trilogy, Book 1 by Maggie Stiefvater, narration by Will Patton (Scholastic Audio).

*Cemetery Boys by Aiden Thomas, narration by Avi Roque (Macmillan Young Listeners).

Charming as a Verb by Ben Philippe, narration by James Fouhey (HarperAudio).

*Clap When You Land by Elizabeth Acevedo, narration by Melania-Luisa Marte and Elizabeth Acevedo (Quill Tree Books).

Clean Getaway by Nic Stone, narration by Dion Graham (Listening Library).

A Deadly Education: The Scholomance #1 by Naomi Novik, narration by Abidjan Dadia (Random House Audio).

Dear Justyce by Nic Stone, narration by Dion Graham (Listening Library).

Don't Ask Me Where I'm From by Jennifer De Leon, narration by Inés del Castillo (Simon & Schuster Audio).

Early Departures by Justin A. Reynolds, narration by A. J. Beckles and Preston Butler III (HarperAudio).

The Extraordinaries by TJ Klune, narration by Michael Lesley (Macmillan Young Listeners).

Fable by Adrienne Young, narration by Emma Lysy (Macmillan Young Listeners).

Fighting Words by Kimberly Brubaker Bradley, narration by Bahni Turpin (Listening Library).

Flyy Girls (#1 and #2) by Ashley Woodfolk. narration by Joniece Abbott-Pratt and Imani Parks (Listening Library).

From the Desk of Zoe Washington by Janae Marks, narration by Bahni Turpin (HarperAudio).

Furious Thing by Jenny Downham, narration by Jenny Downham (Scholastic Audio).

Genesis Begins Again by Alicia D. Williams, narration by Alicia D. Williams (Simon & Schuster Audio).

*A Good Girl's Guide to Murder, Book 1 by Holly Jackson, narration by Bailey Carr, Melissa Calin, Michael Crouch, Gopal Divan, Robert Fass, Kevin R. Free, Sean Patrick Hopkins, Carol Monda, Patricia Santomasso, Shezi Sardar and Amanda Thickpenny (Listening Library).

Grown by Tiffany D. Jackson, narration by Joniece Abbot-Pratt (HarperAudio).

The Guinevere Deception by Kiersten White, narration by Elizabeth Knowelden (Listening Library).

Hood Feminism: Notes from the Women that a Movement Forgot by Mikki Kendall, narration by Mikki Kendall (Books on Tape).

The House in the Cerulean Sea by TJ Klune, narration by Daniel Henning (Macmillan Audio. 2020).

How It All Blew Up by Arvin Ahmadi, narration by Vikas Adam, Ali Afkhami, Nikki Massoud and Nazanin Nour (Listening Library).

I Killed Zoe Spanos by Kit Frick, narration by Dan Bittner, Inés del Castillo, Jonathan Davis, Gibson Frazier, Madeleine Maby, Soneela Nankani, Jackie Sanders, Candace Thaxton, Jesse Vilinsky, Jenni Barber, and Jayme Mattler (Simon & Schuster Audio).

I'll Be the One by Lyla Lee, narration by Greta Jung (HarperAudio).

Jackpot by Nic Stone, narration by Nic Stone (Listening Library).

Jane against the World: Roe v. Wade and the Fight for Reproductive Rights by Karen Blumenthal, narration by Maggi-Meg Reed (Listening Library).

*Kent State by Deborah Wiles, narration by Christopher Gebauer, Lauren Ezzo, Christina Delaine, Johnny Heller, Roger Wayne, Korey Jackson, and David de Vries (Scholastic Audio).

King of Crows by Libba Bray, narration by January LaVoy (Listening Library).

The Left-Handed Booksellers of London by Garth Nix, narration by Marisa Calin (Listening Library).

*Legendborn by Tracy Deonn, narration by Joniece Abbott-Pratt (Simon & Schuster Audio).

Lifting as We Climb: Black Women's Battle for the Ballot Box by Evette Dionne, narration by Karen Chilton (Recorded Books).

Light It Up by Kekla Magoon, narration by Landon Woodson, Karen Chilton, Cherise Booth, Eevin Hartsough, Christopher Carley, Peter Jay Fernandez, T. Ryder Smith, Julian Thomas, Kevin R. Free, and Korey Jackson (Recorded Books).

Lobizona: Wolves of No World, Book 1 by Romina Garber, narration by Sol Madariaga (Macmillan Young Listeners).

The Locked Tomb (Gideon the Ninth; Harrow the Ninth) by Tamsyn Muir, narration by Moira Quirk (Recorded Books).

Look Both Ways: A Tale Told in Ten Blocks by Jason Reynolds, narration by Jason Reynolds, Heather Alicia Simms, Chris Chalk, Bahni Turpin, Adrenle Ojo, Kevin R.Free, J. D. Jackson, Guy Lockard, January LeVoy and David Sazdin (Simon and Schuster Audio).

Mad, Bad and Dangerous to Know by Samira Ahmed, narration by Soneela Nankani and Leila Buck (Recorded Books).

Not So Pure and Simple by Lamar Giles, narration by Korey Jackson (Quill Tree Books).

The Other Side: Stories of Central American Teen Refugees Who Dream of Crossing the Border by Juan Pablo Villalobos, narration by Tim Andres Pabon and Adriana Sananes (Dreamscape Media, LLC).

Parachutes by Kelly Yang, narration by Cassie Simone and Karissa Vacker (HarperAudio).

A Peculiar Peril: The Misadventures of Jonathan Lambshead by Jeff VanderMeer, narration by Raphael Corkhill (Macmillan Young Listeners).

Pocket Change Collective (four titles) by Alok Vaid-Menon, Xiuhtezcatl Martinez, Adam Eli and Kimberly Drew, narration by the authors (Listening Library).

*Raybearer by Jordan Ifueko, narration by Joniece Abbott-Pratt (Blackstone Publishing).

Red Hood by Elana K. Arnold, narration by January LaVoy (HarperAudio).

The Rise and Fall of Charles Lindbergh by Candace Fleming, narration by Kirsten Potter (Listening Library).

Rules for Vanishing by Kate Alice Marshall, narration by Jesse Vilinsky, Robbie Daymond, and Rob Shapiro (Listening Library).

Sanctuary by Paola Mendoza, Abby Sher, narration by Paola Mendoza (Listening Library).

Say Her Name by Zetta Elliott, narration by Lauren Irwin (Recorded Books).

The Shadows between Us by Tricia Levenseller, narration by Caitlin Davies (Macmillan Young Listeners).

Shuri: A Black Panther Novel by Nic Stone, narration by Anika Noni Rose (Scholastic Audio).

Sigh, Gone: A Misfit's Memoir of Great Books, Punk Rock, and the Fight to Fit In by Phuc Tran, narration by Phuc Tran (Macmillan Audio).

A Song below Water by Bethany C. Morrow, narration by Andrea Laing and Jennifer Haralson (Macmillan Young Listeners).

A Song of Wraiths and Ruin by Roseanne A. Brown, narration by Jordan Cobb and A. J. Beckles (HarperAudio).

*The Snow Fell Three Graves Deep: Voices from the Donner Party by Allan Wolf, narration by Bahni Turpin, Whitney Dykhouse, Teri Schnaubelt, Tim Gerard Reynolds, Lauren Ezzo, Eric G. Dove, Ramón de Ocampo, and Shaun Taylor-Corbett (Candlewick on Brilliance Audio).

*Stamped: Racism, Antiracism, and You: A Remix of the National Book Award Winning Stamped from the Beginning by Jason Reynolds and Ibram X. Kendi, narration by Jason Reynolds with an introduction by Ibram X. Kendi (Little, Brown Young Readers).

Stay Gold by Tobly McSmith, narration by Theo Germaine and Phoebe Strole (HarperAudio).

The Talk: Conversations about Race, Love & Truth by Selina Alko, Tracey Baptiste, Derrick Barnes, Natacha Bustos, Cozbi A. Cabrera, Raúl Colón, Adam Gidwitz, Nikki Grimes, Rudy Gutierrez, April Harrison, Wade Hudson, Gordon C. James, Minh Lê, E. B. Lewis, Grace Lin, Torrey Maldonado, Meg Medina, Christopher Myers, Daniel Nayeri, Zeke Peña, Peter H. Reynolds, Erin K. Robinson, Traci Sorell, Shadra Strickland, Don Tate, MaryBeth Timothy, Duncan Tonatiuh, Renée Watson, Valerie Wilson Wesley, and Sharon Dennis Wyeth, narration by Fajer Al-Kaisi, Feodor Chin, Gisela Chípe, Michael Crouch, Janina Edwards, James Fouhey, Renata Friedman, Catherine

Ho, Nicole Lewis, Omar Leyva, Guy Lockard, Jesus E. Martinez and Lisa Renee Pitts (Listening Library).

They Went Left by Monica Hesse, narration by Caitlin Davies (Little, Brown Young Readers).

This Is My America by Kim Johnson, narration by Bahni Turpin (Listening Library).

A Time to Dance by Padma Venkatraman, narration by Padma Venkatraman (Listening Library).

Tristan Strong Punches a Hole in the Sky by Kwame Mbalia narration by Amir Abdullah (Listening Library).

Watch over Me by Nina LaCour, narration by Jorjeana Marie (Listening Library).

We Are Not Free by Traci Chee, narration by Scott Keiji Takeda, Dan Woren, Ryan Potter, Ali Fumiko, Sophie Oda, Andrew Kishino, Christopher Naoki Lee, Grace Rolek, Erika Aishii, Brittany Ishibashi, Kurt Sanchez Kanazawa, and Terry Kitagawa (Houghton Mifflin Harcourt).

We Had to Be Brave: Escaping the Nazis on the Kindertransport by Deborah Hopkinson, narration by Lauren Irwin (Scholastic Audio).

When Stars Are Scattered by Victoria Jamieson and Omar Mohamed, narration by Full Cast (Listening Library).

When They Call You a Terrorist (Young Adult Edition): A Story of Black Lives Matter and the Power to Change the World by Patrisse Khan-Cullors, asha bandele and Benee Knauer, narration by Patrisse Khan-Cullors and Angela Davis (Macmillan Young Listeners).

When You Were Everything by Ashley Woodfolk, narration by Imani Parks (Listening Library).

Where We Go from Here by Lucas Rocha, translated by Larissa Helena, narration by Christian Barillas, Anthony Lee Medina, and Luis Selgas (Scholastic Audio).

You Should See Me in a Crown by Leah Johnson, narration by Alaska Jackson (Scholastic Audio).

Outstanding International Books for Young Readers

Since 2006, the United States Board on Books for Young People (USBBY) has selected an annual honor list of international books for young people. The 42 titles on this year's Outstanding International Books (OIB) list, all published or released in 2020, have been identified as significant for both their exceptional quality and globe-spanning origins.

Preschool to Grade 2

Ahmed, Sufiya. *Under the Great Plum Tree.* Illus. by Reza Dalvand. Tiny Owl. UK.

Atinuke. *Catch that Chicken!* Illus. by Angela Brooksbank. Candlewick. UK / set in West Africa.

Berry, James. *A Story About Afiya.* Illus. by Anna Cunha. Lantana. UK.

Cotter, Sacha. *Cannonball.* Illus. by Josh Morgan. Sourcebooks/Sourcebooks Jabberwocky. New Zealand.

David, Gauthier. *Letters from Bear.* Trans. from French by Sarah Ardizzone. Illus. by Marie Caudry. Eerdmans Books for Young Readers. Belgium.

Frankel, Yael. *The Elevator.* Trans. from Spanish by Kit Maude. Tapioca Stories. Argentina.

Hrab, Naseem. *Weekend Dad.* Illus. by Frank Viva. Groundwood. Canada.

Júnior, Otávio. *From My Window.* Trans. from Portuguese by Beatriz C. Dias. Illus. by Vanina Starkoff. Barefoot Books. Brazil.

Maclear, Kyo. *Story Boat.* Illus. by Rashin Kheiriyeh. Tundra. Canada.

Stinson, Kathy. *The Lady with the Books: A Story Inspired by the Remarkable Work of Jella Lepman.* Illus. by Marie Lafrance. Kids Can Press. Canada.

Van de Vendel, Edward. *Little Fox.* Trans. from Dutch by David Colmer. Illus. by Marije Tolman. Levine Querido/Em Querido. Netherlands.

Weightman, Magnus. *All Along the River.* Trans. from Dutch by the author. Illus. by the author. Clavis Publishing. Belgium.

Wernicke, María. *Some Days.* Trans. from Spanish by Lawrence Schimel. Illus. by the author. Amazon Crossing Kids. Argentina.

Yoshitake, Shinsuke. *There Must Be More Than That!* Ed. by Naomi Kirsten from translation. Illus. by the author. Chronicle Books. Japan.

Grades 3 to 5

Almond, David. *War Is Over.* Illus. by David Litchfield. Candlewick. UK.

Ferrada, María José. *Mexique: A Refugee Story from the Spanish Civil War.* Trans. from Spanish by Elisa Amado. Illus. by Ana Penyas. Eerdmans Books for Young Readers. Mexico.

Järvinen, Aino. *1,001 Creatures.* Trans. from Finnish by Emily Jeremiah. Illus. by Laura Merz. Restless Books. Finland.

Krone, Bridget. *Small Mercies.* Illus. by Karen Vermeulen. Catalyst Press. South Africa.

Lam, Thao. *The Paper Boat: A Refugee Story.* Illus. by the author. Owlkids Books. Canada/Vietnam.

McKay, Hilary. *The Time of Green Magic.* Simon & Schuster/McElderry Books. UK.

McLachlan, Jenny. *The Land of Roar.* Illus. by Ben Mantle. HarperCollins/Harper. UK.

Mian, Zanib. *Planet Omar: Accidental Trouble Magnet.* Illus. by Nasaya Mafaridik. Penguin/G.P. Putnam's Sons. UK.

Nilsson, Ulf. *All the Dear Little Animals.* Trans. from Swedish by Julia Marshall. Illus. by Eva Eriksson. Gecko Press. Sweden.

Romanyshyn, Romana & Lesiv, Andriy. *Sound: Shhh...Bang...POP... BOOM!* Trans. from Ukrainian by Vitaly Chernetsky. Illus. by the authors. Chronicle/Handprint. Ukraine.

Roskifte, Kristin. *Everybody Counts: A Counting Story from 0 to 7.5 Billion.* Trans. from Norwegian by Siân Mackie. Illus. by the author. The Quarto Group/Wide Eyed Editions. Norway.

Utkin, Alexander. *Gamayun Tales I.* Trans. From Russian by Lada Morozova. Illus. by the author. Nobrow. UK/Russia.

Yabouza, Adrienne. *The Magic Doll: A Children's Book Inspired by African Art.* Trans. from French by Paul Kelly. Illus. by Élodie

Nouhen. Prestel. France / set in Central African Republic.

Grades 6 to 8

Aung Thin, Michelle. *Crossing the Farak River*. Annick Press. Australia / set in Myanmar.

Billet, Julia. *Catherine's War*. Trans. from French by Ivanka Hahnenberger. Illus. by Claire Fauvel. HarperCollins/HarperAlley. France.

Fagan, Cary. *Maurice and His Dictionary: A True Story*. Illus. by Enzo Lord Mariano. Owlkids Books. Canada.

Kadarusman, Michelle. *Music for Tigers*. Pajama Press. Canada / set in Australia.

Pêgo, Ana & Martins, Isabel Minhós. *Plasticus Maritimus: An Invasive Species*. Trans. from Portuguese by Jane Springer. Illus. by Bernardo P. Carvalho. Greystone Books/ Greystone Kids in partnership with the David Suzuki Institute. Portugal.

Robertson, David A. *The Barren Grounds*. Illus. by Natasha Donovan. Penguin Random House Canada Young Readers/Puffin. Canada.

Van den Ende, Peter. *The Wanderer*. Illus. by the author. Levine Querido/Em Querido. Netherlands.

Watanabe, Issa. *Migrants*. Illus. by the author. Gecko Press. Mexico.

Grades 9 to 12

Bhathena, Tanaz. *Hunted by the Sky*. Macmillan/Farrar Straus Giroux. US.

Cuthew, Lucy. *Blood Moon*. Candlewick/ Walker. UK.

Hardinge, Frances. *Deeplight*. Abrams/ Amulet. UK.

Kaito. *Blue Flag, Vol. 1*. Trans. from Japanese by Adrienne Beck. Illus. by the author. VIZ Media. Japan.

Thakur, Sophia. *Somebody Give This Heart a Pen*. Candlewick/Walker. UK.

Zhiying, Yu. *The Ode to the Goddess of the Luo River*. Adapted and trans. from Chinese by the author. Illus. by Ye Luying. minedition. China.

Notable Children's Books

Each year a committee of the Association for Library Service to Children (ALSC) identifies the best of the best in children's books. According to the Notables Criteria, "notable" is defined as: Worthy of note or notice, important, distinguished, outstanding. As applied to children's books, notable should be thought to include books of especially commendable quality, books that exhibit venturesome creativity, and books of fiction, information, poetry, and pictures for all age levels (birth through age 14) that reflect and encourage children's interests in exemplary ways. [See "Literary Prizes, 2020" later in Part 5 for Caldecott, Newbery, and other award winners—*Ed.*]

Younger Readers

Above the Rim: How Elgin Baylor Changed Basketball by Jen Bryant. Illus. by Frank Morrison. Abrams.

All Because You Matter by Tami Charles. Illus. by Bryan Collier. Orchard.

The Bear in My Family by Maya Tatsukawa. Illus. by the author. Dial.

Black Is a Rainbow Color by Angela Joy. Illus. by Ekua Holmes. Roaring Brook.

The Camping Trip by Jennifer K. Mann. Illus. by the author. Candlewick.

Cat Dog Dog: The Story of a Blended Family by Nelly Buchet. Illus. by Andrea Zuill. Schwartz & Wade.

The Cat Man of Aleppo by Irene Latham & Karim Shamsi-Basha. Illus. by Yuko Shimizu. Putnam.

Crossings: Extraordinary Structures for Extraordinary Animals by Katy S. Duffield.

Illus. by Mike Orodán. Simon & Schuster/ Beach Lane.

Digging for Words: José Alberto Gutiérrez and the Library He Built by Angela Burke Kunkel. Illus. by Paola Escobar. Schwartz & Wade.

Evelyn Del Rey Is Moving Away by Meg Medina. Illus. by Sonia Sánchez. Candlewick.

Home Base: A Mother-Daughter Story by Nikki Tate. Illus. by Katie Kath. Holiday.

Honeybee: The Busy Life of Apis Mellifera by Candace Fleming. Illus. by Eric Rohmann. Holiday/Neal Porter.

I Am Every Good Thing by Derrick Barnes. Illus. by Gordon C. James. Penguin/Nancy Paulsen.

I Talk Like a River by Jordan Scott. Illus. by Sydney Smith. Holiday/Neal Porter.

If You Take Away the Otter by Susannah Buhrman-Deever. Illus. by Matthew Trueman. Candlewick.

Julián at the Wedding by Jessica Love. Illus. by the author. Candlewick.

Khalil and Mr. Hagerty and the Backyard Treasures by Tricia Springstubb. Illus. by Elaheh Taherian. Candlewick.

Lift by Minh Lê. Illus. by Dan Santat. Little, Brown.

Me & Mama by Cozbi A. Cabrera. Illus. by the author. Simon & Schuster/Denene Millner.

The Most Beautiful Thing by Kao Kalia Yang. Illus. by Khoa Le. Carolrhoda/Lerner.

Nana Akua Goes to School by Tricia Elam Walker. Illus. by April Harrison. Schwartz & Wade.

'Ohana Means Family by Ilima Loomis. Illus. by Kenard Pak. Holiday/Neal Porter.

The Oldest Student: How Mary Walker Learned to Read by Rita Lorraine Hubbard. Illus. by Oge Mora. Schwartz & Wade.

One Little Bag: An Amazing Journey by Henry Cole. Illus. by the author. Scholastic.

Our Friend Hedgehog: The Story of Us by Lauren Castillo. Illus. by the author. Knopf.

Outside In by Deborah Underwood. Illus. by Cindy Derby. HMH.

Overground Railroad by Lesa Cline-Ransome. Illus. by James E. Ransome. Holiday.

A Polar Bear in the Snow by Mac Barnett. Illus. by Shawn Harris. Candlewick.

Prairie Days by Patricia MacLachlan. Illus. by Micha Archer. Simon & Schuster/Margaret K. McElderry.

Ruth Objects: The Life of Ruth Bader Ginsburg by Doreen Rappaport. Illus. by Eric Velasquez. Little, Brown.

Salma the Syrian Chef by Danny Ramadan. Illus. by Anna Bron. Annick.

See the Cat: Three Stories About a Dog by David LaRochelle. Illus. by Mike Wohnoutka. Candlewick.

Snail Crossing by Corey R. Tabor. Illus. by the author. HarperCollins/Balzer+Bray.

Southwest Sunrise by Nikki Grimes. Illus. by Wendell Minor. Bloomsbury.

Sugar in Milk by Thrity Umrigar. Illus. by Khoa Le. Running Press Kids.

Swashby and the Sea by Beth Ferry. Illus. by Juana Martinez-Neal. HMH.

Telephone Tales by Gianni Rodari. Illus. by Valerio Vidali. Tr. by Antony Shugaar. Enchanted Lion.

The Three Billy Goats Buenos by Susan Middleton Elya. Illus. by Miguel Ordóñez. Putnam.

Ty's Travels: Zip, Zoom! by Kelly Starling Lyons. Illus. by Nina Mata. Harper.

¡Vamos! Let's Go Eat by Raúl Gonzalez. Illus. by the author. HMH/Versify.

A Way with Wild Things by Larissa Theule. Illus. by Sara Palacios. Bloomsbury.

We Are Water Protectors by Carole Lindstrom. Illus. by Michaela Goade. Roaring Brook.

What About Worms!? by Ryan T. Higgins. Illus. by the author. Disney/Hyperion.

Where's Baby? by Anne Hunter. Illus. by the author. Tundra.

Middle Readers

Becoming Muhammad Ali by James Patterson & Kwame Alexander. Illus. by Dawud Anyabwile. Little, Brown/JIMMY Patterson.

Black Brother, Black Brother by Jewell Parker Rhodes. Little, Brown.

The Blackbird Girls by Anne Blankman. Viking.

Catherine's War by Julia Billet. Illus. by Claire Fauvel. Tr. by Ivanka Hahnenberger. Harper/ HarperAlley.

Echo Mountain by Lauren Wolk. Dutton.

Efrén Divided by Ernesto Cisneros. Harper/ Quill Tree.

From the Desk of Zoe Washington by Janae Marks. Illus. by Mirelle Ortega. Harper-Collins/Katherine Tegen.

King and the Dragonflies by Kacen Callender. Scholastic.

Letters from Cuba by Ruth Behar. Penguin/Nancy Paulsen.

Lupe Wong Won't Dance by Donna Barba Higuera. Levine Querido.

Mañanaland by Pam Muñoz Ryan. Scholastic.

Once Upon an Eid: Stories of Hope and Joy by 15 Muslim Voices ed. by S. K. Ali and Aisha Saeed. Illus. by Sara Alfageeh. Abrams/Amulet.

The Only Black Girls in Town by Brandy Colbert. Little, Brown.

Prairie Lotus by Linda Sue Park. HMH.

Santiago's Road Home by Alexandra Diaz. Simon & Schuster/Paula Wiseman.

Sharuko: El Arqueólogo Peruano/Peruvian Archaeologist Julio C. Tello by Monica Brown. Illus. by Elisa Chavarri. Lee & Low/Children's Book Press.

Show Me a Sign by Ann Clare LeZotte. Scholastic.

Three Keys (A Front Desk Novel) by Kelly Yang. Scholastic.

The Total Eclipse of Nestor Lopez by Adrianna Cuevas. Farrar.

We Dream of Space by Erin Entrada Kelly. Illus. by the author and Celia Krampien. Greenwillow.

What Stars Are Made Of by Sarah Allen. Farrar.

When Stars Are Scattered by Victoria Jamieson & Omar Mohamed. Illus. by Victoria Jamieson and Iman Geddy. Dial.

When You Trap a Tiger by Tae Keller. Random.

Wink by Rob Harrell. Illus. by the author. Dial.

A Wish in the Dark by Christina Soontornvat. Candlewick.

Your Place in the Universe by Jason Chin. Illus. by the author. Holiday/Neal Porter.

Older Readers

All Thirteen: The Incredible Cave Rescue of the Thai Boys' Soccer Team by Christina Soontornvat. Illus. Candlewick.

Almost American Girl: An Illustrated Memoir by Robin Ha. Illus. by the author. Harper-Collins/Balzer+Bray

Before the Ever After by Jacqueline Woodson. Penguin/Nancy Paulsen.

Brother's Keeper by Julie Lee. Holiday.

Dragon Hoops by Gene Luen Yang. Illus. by the author. First Second.

Elatsoe by Darcie Little Badger. Illus. by Rovina Cai. Levine Querido.

Fighting Words by Kimberly Brubaker Bradley. Dial.

Go with the Flow by Lily Williams and Karen Schneemann. Illus. by Lily Williams. First Second.

How We Got to the Moon: The People, Technology, and Daring Feats of Science Behind Humanity's Greatest Adventure by John Rocco. Illus. by the author. Crown.

Land of the Cranes by Aida Salazar. Scholastic.

The Magic Fish by Trung Le Nguyen. Illus. by the author. Random/RH Graphic.

Poisoned Water: How the Citizens of Flint, Michigan, Fought for Their Lives and Warned the Nation by Candy J. Cooper and Marc Aronson. Bloomsbury.

Raybearer by Jordan Ifueko. Abrams/Amulet.

Snapdragon by Kat Leyh. Illus. by the author. First Second.

Stamped: Racism, Antiracism, and You: A Remix of the National Book Award-winning Stamped from the Beginning by Jason Reynolds and Ibram X. Kendi. Little, Brown.

Superman Smashes the Klan by Gene Luen Yang. Illus. by Gurihiru. DC.

This Light Between Us: A Novel of World War II by Andrew Fukuda. Tor Teen.

All Ages

Box: Henry Brown Mails Himself to Freedom by Carole Boston Weatherford. Illus. by Michele Wood. Candlewick.

Exquisite: The Poetry and Life of Gwendolyn Brooks by Suzanne Slade. Illus. by Cozbi A. Cabrera. Abrams.

A Place Inside of Me: A Poem to Heal the Heart by Zetta Elliott. Illus. by Noa Denmon. Farrar.

Notable Recordings for Children

This annual listing of notable compact disc (CD) and digital download (DD) recordings for children 14 years and younger is produced by the Association for Library Service to Children (ALSC), a division of the American Library Association (ALA). Chosen by children's librarians and educators, the list includes recordings deemed to be of especially commendable quality that demonstrate respect for young people's intelligence and imagination, exhibit venturesome creativity, and reflect and encourage the interests of children and young adolescents in exemplary ways.

Ahimsa by Supriya Kelkar. Read by Zehra Jane Naqvi. Tantor Media, DD. Gr. 3–6. Zehra Jane Naqvi skillfully voices ten-year-old Anjali as she lives through, and becomes involved in, the 1940s Indian freedom movement.

Bear Came Along by Richard T. Morris. Read by Joshua Manning. Hachette Audio, DD. Gr. PreS–1. Inspired sound effects, music, and a lively reading by Joshua Manning add magic to this story of Bear and his new friends as they venture down the river.

The Best of Iggy by Annie Barrows. Read by Kate Reinders. Listening Library, DD. Gr. 1–3. This hilarious performance by Kate Reinders brings high-energy, always-in-trouble Iggy to life in the first of a new series.

Cats Sit on You by Story Pirates. Face Cake Records, CD. Gr. PreS–3. Based on stories written by children, this upbeat and diverse mix of songs is full of harmonious fun.

Clap When You Land by Elizabeth Acevedo. Read by Elizabeth Acevedo and Melania-Luisa Marte. HarperAudio, DD. Gr. 8+. This is a novel in verse about two sisters who learn about each other after their father's death. Listeners experience the pain and joy of the sisters as they reconcile and share their family stories.

Concrete Kids by Amyra León. Read by Amyra León. Listening Library, DD. Gr. 8+. Amyra León's narration of her autobiographical poetry collection draws listeners into the beauty, joy, and pain of her childhood and adolescence as a foster child in New York City's East Harlem.

Cozy by Jan Brett. Read by René Ruiz. Listening Library, DD. Gr. PreS–2. Subtle yet blustery sound effects create a wintry mood to accompany the friendly voices of a community of animals seeking shelter with a muskox named Cozy.

D.a.D. by Pierce Freelon. Blackspace, CD. Gr. PreS–3. Hip-hop, soul, and electronic beats meet playful and genuine lyrics in Pierce Freelon's creative family album chronicling family, fatherhood, and life.

Fart Quest by Aaron Reynolds. Read by Jonathan Myles. Macmillan Young Listeners, DD. Gr. 2–5. Jonathan Myles's narration beautifully captures the hilarious adventures of three magical apprentices facing their first quest and the opportunity to become heroes.

Fiesta Global by Flor Bromley. Flor Bromley, CD. Gr. PreS–3. Listeners join the party in Flor Bromley's celebration of the richness and diversity of music throughout the Americas, with lyrics combining Spanish and English.

Fighting Words by Kimberly Brubaker Bradley. Read by Bahni Turpin and Kimberly Brubaker Bradley. Listening Library, DD, CD. Gr. 4–8. Bahni Turpin's exemplary narration is emotionally moving in this powerful story about addiction, child sexual abuse, and the loving bond between two sisters.

From the Desk of Zoe Washington by Janae Marks. Read by Bahni Turpin. Harper-Audio, DD. Gr. 4–8. With skill and compelling realism, Bahni Turpin gives voice to aspiring pastry chef Zoe Washington as she sets out to try to prove the innocence of her incarcerated father.

Going Down Home with Daddy by Kelly Starling Lyons. Read by Daxton Edwards. Dreamscape Media, DD. Gr. K–3. Daxton Edwards's stellar narration captures the essence of a family reunion, while atmospheric sound effects celebrate farm life and family traditions.

Here We Are by Oliver Jeffers. Read by Oliver Jeffers. Listening Library, DD. Gr. PreS–2. Patiently illuminating the intricacies of life on earth, Oliver Jeffers, aided by evocative sound effects, provides a joyful reading that mirrors a lullaby appropriate for even the youngest listeners.

HotDog! by Anh Do. Read by full cast. Scholastic Audio, DD. Gr. K–3. Energetic narration, sound effects, and music capture the lively adventure of HotDog and friends.

Kent State by Deborah Wiles. Read by Christopher Gebauer, Lauren Ezzo, Christina Delaine, Johnny Heller, Roger Wayne, Korey Jackson, and David de Vries. Scholastic Audio, CD, DD. Gr. 8+. Alternating voices convey the experiences behind the shootings at Kent State University on May 4, 1970. Original music and vivid sound effects combine with the narration to create an immersive, thought-provoking experience for any listener.

The List of Things That Will Not Change by Rebecca Stead. Read by Rachel L. Jacobs. Listening Library, DD, CD. Gr. 3–6. Rachel L. Jacobs sensitively voices young Bea with appropriate emotion, anger, and joy as she settles into a life where some things are new, but others will not change.

The Madre de Aguas of Cuba by Adam Gidwitz and Emma Otheguy. Read by Rebecca Soler. Listening Library, DD. Gr. 2–4. Through dynamic narration, Rebecca Soler takes listeners on a magical adventure exploring the complexities of Cuban culture, the importance of water to the island nation, and the mystery of the Madre de Aguas.

¡Muévete!: Songs for a Healthy Mind in a Healthy Body by José-Luis Orozco. Smithsonian Folkways Recordings, CD. Gr. PreS–3. José-Luis Orozco brings traditional Mexican musicality to these songs—in both Spanish and English—encouraging young children to get their bodies in motion.

Overground Railroad by Lesa Cline-Ransome. Read by Shayna Small and Dion Graham. Live Oak Media, CD and book. Gr. 1–5. A soundscape painted with the bustle of a train, chatter of passengers, and the poetic voice of Shayna Small moves listeners through a train journey north amidst the Great Migration.

Punching the Air by Ibi Zoboi and Yusef Salaam. Read by Ethan Herisse. HarperAudio, DD. Gr. 7+. Ethan Herisse gives poetic voice to the frustrations, fears, and hopes of a young Black teen wrongfully incarcerated.

Say Her Name by Zetta Elliott. Read by Channie Waites. Recorded Books, DD. Gr. 6+. Channie Waites's narration fills these poems with resilience and courage, singing praise to Black women and girls through subtle pacing, shifting tones, well-placed pauses, and the effective use of song.

Stamped: Racism, Antiracism, and You by Jason Reynolds and Ibram X. Kendi. Read by Jason Reynolds. Hachette Audio, DD. Gr. 6+. Jason Reynolds's engaging, conversational narration empowers listeners of this essential work to discuss and disrupt their roles within the ongoing history of racism and antiracism in America.

Stepping Stones by Lucy Knisley. Read by Lauren Fortgang, Sarah Mollo-Christensen, Patricia Santomasso, Kristen DiMercurio, Bailey Carr, James Fouhey, Neil Hellegers, Sean Patrick Hopkins, Joshua Kane, Amy Landon and Barrett Leddy. Listening Library, DD. Gr. 2–4. The ups and downs of Jen's move from NYC to the country are brought to life through stellar voicing and sound effects in this full cast performance.

The Thing about Bees: A Love Letter by Shabazz Larkin. Read by Shabazz Larkin, with Legend, Royal, and Ashley Larkin. Live Oak Media, CD and book, CD. Gr. PreS–2. The author and his family give a charming and lively performance in this engaging and beautiful tribute to bees.

Tristan Strong Destroys the World by Kwame Mbalia. Read by Amir Abdullah. Listening Library, DD. Gr. 4–8. Amir Abdullah's excellent and nimble characterization captures Tristan Strong's storytelling prowess and a wide-ranging cast of characters as they return to Alke in a battle to save Tristan's loved ones from a powerful evil force.

The Very Impatient Caterpillar by Ross Burach. Read by Matt Braver and Sisi Aisha Johnson. Weston Woods Studio, CD and book. Gr. PreS–2. Playful music, engaging sound effects, and dynamic narration enhance this humorous story about a caterpillar struggling to learn patience on his journey to becoming a butterfly.

We Are Not Free by Traci Chee. Read by full cast. Houghton Mifflin Harcourt Audio, DD,

CD. Gr. 8+. The unique personalities of 14 characters are fully realized in this gripping and powerful tale of the Japanese American experience during World War II.

When Stars Are Scattered by Victoria Jamieson and Omar Mohamed. Read by full cast. Listening Library, DD. Gr. 4–8. Faysal Ahmed skillfully leads an ensemble performance that brings authenticity and emotion to Omar's personal story and experiences in a refugee camp.

Wink by Rob Harrell. Read by Michael Crouch and Marc Thompson. Listening Library, DD. Gr. 4–8. Earnest and humorous, Michael Crouch effectively voices Ross as he undergoes treatment for an eye cancer, while Marc Thompson's sound-effect-laden delivery of the comic adventures of BatPig helps drive the story forward.

The Wizards of Once: Knock Three Times by Cressida Cowell. Read by David Tennant. Hachette Audio, DD, CD. Gr. 3–6. David Tennant's dazzling narration captures every magical moment and unique character, as a prince and princess from two kingdoms must join together to save their homes from certain destruction in the third book in this bestselling series.

Notable Children's Digital Media

The Association for Library Service to Children (ALSC), a division of the American Library Association, produces this annual list covering a diverse array of digital media for children 14 and younger. The Notable Children's Digital Media list recognizes real-time, dynamic, and interactive media content that enables and encourages active engagement and social interaction while informing, educating, and entertaining in exemplary ways. This list represents the titles selected by the committee for the first half of 2020, and titles added in January 2021.

The Creature Garden by Tinybop. iOS. Elementary. Imagine and create real or original fantastic animals by hatching eggs, adding animal qualities, and testing their skills. Children can name their animal creations, feed and groom them, and have their different creations race each other. Available in English.

Droplets: Drops for Kids. iOS/Android. Elementary, Middle School. With this language-learning app created specifically for families, parents can make Kid Profiles for multiple children of varying skill levels. Users can choose from over 30 languages to learn vocabulary, spelling, and word recognition. Available in multiple languages.

How It Works? iOS/Android. Elementary. Interactive animations and texts read aloud teach kids how natural phenomena work. Kids learn about energy, the water cycle, the parts of a plant, the Earth, earthquakes, and volcanos. Each lesson includes experiment and demonstration ideas for hands-on learning, as well as puzzles, sorting games, and drawing activities. Available in multiple languages.

JigSpace. iOS. Elementary, Middle School, and or Parent/Teacher/Caregiver. Curious seekers of all ages can explore dozens of interactive 3D educational presentations, or "Jigs." This simple and easy-to-use app uses augmented reality (AR) to bring hands-on learning through step-by-step instructions on a variety of topics and concepts. Available in English.

Knowin: Learn Coding. iOS. Elementary, Middle School. Children will learn basic coding knowledge at their own pace with this app that has the user tapping their answers instead of typing. Easy to navigate and no prior knowledge of coding required. Available in English.

Krystopia: A Puzzle Journey. iOS/Android/Steam. Middle School and Up. In this science fiction puzzle game, help Nova Dune explore and learn about a civilization on the planet Krystopia, where all the people have vanished. Available in multiple languages.

Learn Chess with Dr. Wolf. iOS/Android. Elementary and Up. Learn to play chess with Dr. Wolf, the coach who teaches, points out strategic ideas, and helps with mistakes. Players who subscribe to paid coaching receive some additional individualized coaching (acknowledgment of application of skills) and receive unlimited access to twenty-five lessons. Best for beginners and intermediate players. Available in English.

Lego Duplo World. iOS/Android/Amazon. Pre–K, Early Elementary. Based on the popular real world Duplo Legos; young children are invited to explore, discover, pretend, and create. Multi-touch functionality allows parent and child to engage together in side-by-side play. Children from all backgrounds will see themselves represented in this open-ended, play-based game. Free, but with paid add-ons. Available in multiple languages.

Math Land. iOS/Android, Nintendo Switch. Pre–K, Elementary, Middle School and/or Parent/Teacher/Caregiver. Kids and adults can practice math, everything from simple addition and subtraction equations to more complex equations, with the use of different strategies in a pirate game setting. Available in multiple languages.

Mathigon. iOS/Android/Website. Elementary and Up. This free app for mathematics makes learning fun. Available in English only, the interactive platform offers a captivating narrative along with animation and colorful illustrations. From multiplication flashcards, and fractals, to prime and Fibonacci numbers, this "Textbook of the Future" allows students to explore math in a new and exciting way. Best used as supplemental learning.

Open Ocean: Marine Migration. Website. Elementary and Up. Learn about Earth's oceans, scientific research, and equipment through immersive 360-degree videos, maps, and infographics. Users can explore by visiting the free Ocean School website or by downloading their app to gain a more augmented/virtual reality experience. Available in English and French.

Play and Learn Engineering by PBS Kids. iOS/Android/Amazon. Pre–K and Elementary. This free, user-friendly app builds kids' engineering skills as they solve puzzle challenges. The challenges vary in difficulty, but all reward logic and experimentation. Reading proficiency is not necessary; brief, vocalized instructions and clear examples demonstrate the tasks clearly. Available in English and Spanish.

Pocket Build. iOS/Android. Elementary, Middle School. Children can build their own worlds in this sandbox building app. Use survival mode to mine resources and earn new developments, or use sandbox mode for unlimited creativity. Available in multiple languages.

Prodigy Math Game. iOS/Android/Website. Elementary. Math practice becomes a magical quest in this simple multiplayer game. Students can choose their grade level, then customize an avatar to engage in spell battles/math problems, collecting coins, accessories, and pets for every correct answer. Available in English.

Scribbles & Ink. Website. Pre–K, Elementary. Children draw along with characters Scribbles and Ink, either following interactive prompts or creating independently. Printable activity sheets and how-to-draw videos are also provided. The drawing tools are clear and easy to use. This is a simple but elegant drawing program for young learners. Available in English.

Sky. iOS/Android. Middle School and Up. Explore this expansive and ever-changing world with friends and family through cooperative play and exploration. Your challenge is to restore light to the constellations by solving puzzles, helping others, building friendships, and finding collectibles throughout the seven realms. Available in English and Japanese.

Swift Playgrounds. iOS. Pre–K and Up. Swift Playgrounds uses puzzles and challenges to teach coding. This app is useful for all ages, both to beginners seeking to gain the basics of coding, and those with some experience seeking to advance their skills before moving on to more difficult coding used by developers. Available in multiple languages.

Women Who Changed the World. iOS/Android. Elementary and Up. Travel through history to meet the trailblazing women who have made notable contributions to politics, the arts, and sciences. Multiple choice questions and games guide reflection of narrated and written stories with animations, complemented by factual information and quotations. Available in multiple languages.

Top Ten Book Lists, 2020

Sources included in this roundup of 2020's bestselling and most popular books are *Publishers Weekly*, *USA Today*, Barnes and Noble, Amazon, and Goodreads for print titles; and Amazon and Apple for Kindle and Apple Books digital titles, respectively. Library-centric lists include the top ten adult print book checkouts reported by two major U.S. public library systems—New York Public Library and San Diego County Library—and the ten most popular library e-books and audio-books as reported by OverDrive. [Due to varying selection criteria among the sources, apples-to-apples comparisons are not practicable—*Ed.*]

Print Bestsellers

Publishers Weekly

1. *A Promised Land*. Barack Obama.
2. *Midnight Sun*. Stephanie Meyer.
3. *Dog Man: Grime and Punishment*. Dav Pilkey.
4. *Too Much and Never Enough*. Mary L. Trump.
5. *The Ballad of Songbirds and Snakes*. Suzanne Collins.
6. *Where the Crawdads Sing*. Delia Owens.
7. *Untamed*. Glennon Doyle.
8. *The Deep End*. Jeff Kinney.
9. *White Fragility*. Robin DiAngelo.
10. *The Boy, the Mole, the Fox and the Horse*. Charlie Mackesy.

USA Today

1. *A Promised Land*. Barack Obama.
2. *Midnight Sun*. Stephanie Meyer.
3. *Too Much and Never Enough*. Mary L. Trump.
4. *Where the Crawdads Sing*. Delia Owens.
5. *The Ballad of Songbirds and Snakes*. Suzanne Collins.
6. *Untamed*. Glennon Doyle.
7. *Dog Man: Grime and Punishment*. Dav Pilkey.
8. *White Fragility*. Robin DiAngelo.
9. *Little Fires Everywhere*. Celeste Ng.
10. *American Dirt*. Jeanine Cummins.

Barnes and Noble

1. *A Promised Land*. Barack Obama.
2. *Too Much and Never Enough*. Mary Trump.

3. *Midnight Sun*. Stephenie Meyer.
4. *The Ballad of Songbirds and Snakes*. Suzanne Collins.
5. *World of Wonders*. Aimee Nezhukumatathil.
6. *The Room Where It Happened*. John Bolton.
7. *Caste: The Origins of Our Discontents*. Isabel Wilkerson.
8. *A Time for Mercy*. John Grisham.
9. *Untamed*. Glennon Doyle.
10. *Rage*. Bob Woodward.

Amazon

1. *A Promised Land*. Barack Obama.
2. *Too Much and Never Enough*. Mary L. Trump.
3. *Where the Crawdads Sing*. Delia Owens.
4. *My First Learn-to-Write Workbook*. Crystal Radke.
5. *Midnight Sun*. Stephanie Meyer.
6. *Untamed*. Glennon Doyle.
7. *If Animals Kissed Good Night*. Ann Whitford Paul.
8. *White Fragility*. Robin DiAngelo.
9. *Big Preschool Workbook, Ages 3–5*. Joan Hoffman.
10. *The Room Where It Happened*. John Bolton.

Goodreads Most Popular Books Added by Readers

1. *The Vanishing Half*. Brit Bennett.
2. *The Invisible Life of Addie LaRue*. V. E. Schwab.
3. *American Dirt*. Jeanine Cummins.

4. *The Ballad of Songbirds and Snakes.*
   Suzanne Collins.
5. *Untamed.* Glennon Doyle.
6. *The Guest List.* Lucy Foley.
7. *House of Earth and Blood.* Sarah J. Maas.
8. *Mexican Gothic.* Silvia Moreno-Garcia.
9. *In Five Years.* Rebecca Serle.
10. *Beach Read.* Emily Henry.

Digital Bestsellers

Amazon Kindle

1. *If You Tell.* Greg Olsen.
2. *When We Believed in Mermaids.*
   Barbara O'Neal.
3. *Harry Potter and the Sorcerer's Stone.*
   J. K. Rowling.
4. *In an Instant.* Suzanne Redfearn.
5. *The Bad Seed.* Jory John.
6. *Last Day.* Luanne Rice.
7. *Thief River Falls.* Brian Freeman.
8. *SpongeBob Goes to the Doctor.*
   Nickelodeon Publishing.
9. *The Last of the Moon Girls.* Barbara
   Davis.
10. *The 7 Habits of Highly Effective People.*
   Stephen R. Covey.

Apple Books*

Fiction

1. *Midnight Sun.* Stephanie Meyer.
2. *American Dirt.* Jeanine Cummins.
3. *The Guest List.* Lucy Foley.
4. *Walk the Wire.* David Baldacci.
5. *Camino Winds.* John Grisham.
6. *A Time for Mercy.* John Grisham.
7. *28 Summers.* Elin Hilderbrand.
8. *The Vanishing Half.* Brit Bennett.
9. *The Order.* Daniel Silva.
10. *The Sentinel.* Lee Child & Andrew
   Child.

Nonfiction

1. *Too Much and Never Enough.*
   Mary L. Trump.
2. *Untamed.* Glennon Doyle.
3. *A Promised Land.* Barack Obama.
4. *The Splendid and the Vile.* Erik Larson.
5. *The Room Where It Happened.*
   John Bolton.
6. *Open Book.* Jessica Simpson.

7. *Rage.* Bob Woodward.
8. *Caste: The Origins of Our Discontents.*
   Isabel Wilkerson.
9. *Hidden Valley Road.* Robert Kolker.
10. *Disloyal: A Memoir.* Michael Cohen.

* Apple does not release a unified list of best-selling adult fiction and nonfiction in the Apple Books format.

Top Print, Digital, and Audiobook Titles from the Library

New York Public Library Top Ten Print Checkouts System-wide†

1. *The Vanishing Half.* Brit Bennett.
2. *White Fragility.* Robin DiAngelo.
3. *The Glass Hotel.* Emily St. John Mandel.
4. *Where the Crawdads Sing.* Delia Owens.
5. *The Dutch House.* Ann Patchett.
6. *The Nickel Boys.* Colson Whitehead.
7. *Educated.* Tara Westover.
8. *Becoming.* Michelle Obama.
9. *Normal People.* Sally Rooney.
10. *Maybe You Should Talk to Someone.*
   Lori Gottlieb.

San Diego County Library Top Ten Print Checkouts System-wide†

1. *Where the Crawdads Sing.* Delia Owens.
2. *One Good Deed.* David Baldacci.
3. *Blue Moon.* Lee Child.
4. *Educated.* Tara Westover.
5. *The Guardians.* John Grisham.
6. *A Minute to Midnight.* David Baldacci.
7. *The Night Fire.* Michael Connelly.
8. *The Dutch House.* Ann Patchett.
9. *Redemption.* David Baldacci.
10. *The Silent Patient.* Alex Michaelides.

† Lists include adult fiction and nonfiction checkouts only.

OverDrive's Top Ten Most Popular Library Ebooks and Audio Books

Ebooks

1. *Where the Crawdads Sing.* Delia Owens.
2. *Becoming.* Michelle Obama.
3. *Educated.* Tara Westover.
4. *Little Fires Everywhere.* Celeste Ng.
5. *The Giver of Stars.* Jojo Moyes.

6. *White Fragility*. Robin DiAngelo.
7. *The Dutch House*. Ann Patchett.
8. *The Silent Patient*. Alex Michaelides.
9. *The Guardians*. John Grisham.
10. *Blue Moon*. Lee Child.

Audiobooks

1. *Harry Potter and the Sorcerer's Stone*. J. K. Rowling.
2. *Becoming*. Michelle Obama.
3. *Where the Crawdads Sing*. Delia Owens.
4. *Talking to Strangers.* Malcolm Gladwell.
5. *Educated*. Tara Westover.
6. *The Subtle Art of Not Giving a F*ck*. Mark Manson.
7. *So You Want to Talk about Race*. Ijeoma Oluo.
8. *White Fragility*. Robin DiAngelo.
9. *The Giver of Stars*. Jojo Moyes.
10. *The Silent Patient*. Alex Michaelides.

Literary Prizes, 2020

Compiled by the staff of *Library and Book Trade Almanac*

Academy of American Poets Fellowship ($25,000). For outstanding poetic achievement. *Offered by:* Academy of American Poets. *Winner:* Carmen Gimenez Smith.

Academy of American Poets Laureate Fellowships ($50,000 each). Honey Bell-Bey, Poet Laureate of Cuyahoga County, Ohio; Tina Cane, Poet Laureate of Rhode Island; Tina Chang, Poet Laureate of Brooklyn, New York; Nnamdi O. Chukwuocha, Twin Poets Laureate of Delaware; Rosemarie Dombrowski, Poet Laureate of Phoenix, Arizona; Beth Ann Fennelly, Poet Laureate of Mississippi; Angelo Geter, Poet Laureate of Rock Hill, South Carolina; Margaret Gibson, Poet Laureate of Connecticut; Rodney Gomez, Poet Laureate of McAllen, Texas; Elizabeth Jacobson, Poet Laureate of Santa Fe, New Mexico; Stuart Kestenbaum, Poet Laureate of Maine; Susan Landgraf, Poet Laureate of Auburn, Washington; Maria Lisella, Poet Laureate of Queens, New York; Porsha Olayiwola, Poet Laureate of Boston, Massachusetts; Alexandria Peary, Poet Laureate of New Hampshire; Emmy Pérez, Poet Laureate of Texas; Mary Ruefle, Poet Laureate of Vermont; Janice Lobo Sapigao, Poet Laureate of Santa Clara County, California; John Warner Smith, Poet Laureate of Louisiana; Laura Tohe, Poet Laureate of the Navajo Nation; Amie Whittemore, Poet Laureate of Murfreesboro, Tennessee; Assétou Xango, Poet Laureate of Aurora, Colorado.

Jane Addams Children's Book Awards. For children's books that effectively promote the cause of peace, social justice, world community, and equality. *Offered by:* Jane Addams Peace Association. *Winners:* (younger children) Carole Lindstrom for *We Are Water Protectors*, illustrated by Michaela Goade (Roaring Books Press); (older children) Christina Soontornvat for *A Wish in the Dark* (Candlewick Press).

Aesop Prize. For outstanding illustrated children's publications utilizing folkloric themes. *Offered by:* American Folklore Society. *Winner:* Ian Lendler for *The Fabled Life of Aesop*, illustrated by Pamela Zagaresnki (Houghton Mifflin Harcourt).

Agatha Awards. For mystery writing in the method exemplified by author Agatha Christie. *Offered by:* Malice Domestic Ltd. *Winners:* (contemporary novel) Ann Cleeves for *The Long Call* (Minotaur); (first novel) Tara Laskowski for *One Night Gone* (Graydon House, a division of Harlequin); (historical) Edith Maxwell for *Charity's Burden* (Midnight Ink); (young adult) Frances Schoonmaker for *The Last Crystal* (Auctus Press); (nonfiction) Mo Moulton for *The Mutual Admiration Society: How Dorothy L. Sayers and Her Oxford Circle Remade the World for Women* (Basic Books); (short story) Shawn Reilly Simmons for "The Last Word" in *Malice Domestic 14: Mystery Most Edible* (Wildside Press).

Ambroggio Prize ($1,000 and publication by Bilingual Press/Editorial Bilingüe). *Offered by:* Academy of American Poets. For a book-length poetry manuscript originally written in Spanish and with an English translation. *Winner:* Mara Pastor for *Deuda Natal / Natal Debt*.

American Academy of Arts and Letters Award of Merit ($25,000). Given annually, in rotation, for the short story, sculpture, novel, poetry, drama, and painting. *Offered by:* American Academy of Arts and Letters. *Winner:* Jessica Jackson Hutchins (sculpture).

American Academy of Arts and Letters Awards in Literature ($10,000 each). To honor eight writers for exceptional accomplishment in any genre. *Offered by:* American Academy of Arts and Letters. *Winners:* Marie Arana, Joel Harrington, Jeremy O. Harris, Wayne Koestenbaum, Sandra Lim, Megan McDowell, Maaza Mengiste, Viet Thanh Nguyen.

American Academy of Arts and Letters Blake-Dodd Prize ($25,000). Triennial prize to a nonfiction writer. *Offered by:* American Academy of Arts and Letters. *Winner (2020):* Janine Di Giovanni.

American Academy of Arts and Letters Benjamin H. Danks Award ($20,000). Given annually, in rotation, to a composer of ensemble works, a playwright, and a writer. *Offered by:* American Academy of Arts and Letters. *Winner:* Hanya Yanagihara (writing).

American Academy of Arts and Letters E. M. Forster Award ($20,000). To a young writer from the United Kingdom or Ireland for a stay in the United States. *Offered by:* American Academy of Arts and Letters. *Winner:* Stephen Sexton.

American Academy of Arts and Letters Gold Medal in History. For distinguished achievement. *Offered by:* American Academy of Arts and Letters. *Winner:* David W. Blight.

American Academy of Arts and Letters William Dean Howells Medal. Given once every five years in recognition of the most distinguished American novel published during that period. *Offered by:* American Academy of Arts and Letters. *Winner (2020):* Richard Powers for *The Overstory* (W.W. Norton & Company).

American Academy of Arts and Letters Sue Kaufman Prize for First Fiction ($5,000). For a work of first fiction (novel or short stories). *Offered by:* American Academy of Arts and Letters. *Winner:* Isabella Hammad for *The Parisian* (Grove Press).

American Academy of Arts and Letters Addison M. Metcalf Award ($10,000). Given biennially to a young writer of fiction, nonfiction, drama, or poetry. *Offered by:* American Academy of Arts and Letters. *Winner (2019):* Aracelis Girmay.

American Academy of Arts and Letters Katherine Anne Porter Award ($20,000). Awarded biennially to a prose writer of demonstrated achievement. *Offered by:* American Academy of Arts and Letters. *Winner (2020):* Christine Schutt.

American Academy of Arts and Letters Arthur Rense Poetry Prize ($20,000). Triennial prize to an exceptional poet. *Offered by:* American Academy of Arts and Letters. *Winner (2020):* Mary Ruefle.

American Academy of Arts and Letters Rosenthal Family Foundation Award ($10,000). To a young writer of considerable literary talent for a work of fiction. *Offered by:* American Academy of Arts and Letters. *Winner:* Valeria Luiselli for *Lost Children Archive* (Knopf).

American Academy of Arts and Letters John Updike Award ($10,000). Biennial prize to a writer in midcareer whose work has demonstrated consistent excellence. *Offered by:* American Academy of Arts and Letters. *Winner (2019):* D. A. Powell.

American Academy of Arts and Letters Harold D. Vursell Memorial Award ($20,000). To a writer whose work merits recognition for the quality of its prose style. *Offered by:* American Academy of Arts and Letters. *Winner:* Alex Kotlowitz.

American Academy of Arts and Letters Christopher Lightfoot Walker Award ($100,000). Biennial award to a writer of fiction or nonfiction who has made a significant contribution to American literature. *Offered by:* American Academy of Arts and Letters. *Winner (2020):* Leslie Marmon Silko.

American Academy of Arts and Letters E. B. White Award ($10,000). Biennial award to a writer for achievement in children's literature. *Offered by:* American Academy of Arts and Letters. *Winner (2019):* Katherine Patterson.

American Book Awards. For literary achievement by people of various ethnic backgrounds. *Offered by:* Before Columbus Foundation. *Winners:* Reginald Dwayne Betts for *Felon: Poems* (W.W. Norton & Company); Sara Borjas for *Heart Like a Window, Mouth Like a Cliff* (Noemi Press); Neeli Cherkovski, Raymond Foye, and Tate Swindell (eds.) for *Collected Poems of Bob Kaufman* (City Lights); Staceyann Chin for *Crossfire: A Litany for Survival* (Haymarket Books); Kali Fajardo-Anstine for *Sabrina & Corina: Stories* (One World); Tara Fickle for *The Race Card: From Gaming Technologies to Model Minorities* (New York University Press); Erika Lee for *America for Americans: A History of Xenophobia in the United States* (Basic Books); Yoko Ogawa, *The Memory Police* (Pantheon Books); Jake Skeets for *Eyes Bottle Dark with a Mouthful of Flowers* (Milkweed Editions); George Takei, Justin Eisinger, and Steven Scott for *They Called Us Enemy,* illustrated by Harmony Becker (Top Shelf Productions); Ocean Vuong for *On Earth We're Briefly Gorgeous* (Penguin Press); De'Shawn Charles Winslow for *In West Mills* (Bloomsbury Publishing); Albert Woodfox with Leslie George for *Solitary: My Story of Transformation and Hope* (Grove Press); (lifetime achievement) Eleanor W. Traylor;

(editor award) *The Panopticon Review*, Kofi Natambu, editor; (publisher award) Commune Editions, Jasper Bernes, Joshua Clover, and Juliana Spahr, editors; (oral literature award) Amalia Leticia Ortiz; (Walter & Lillian Lowenfels Criticism Award) *Appalachian Reckoning: A Region Responds to Hillbilly Elegy*, edited by Anthony Harkins and Meredith McCarroll (West Virginia University Press).

American Indian Youth Literature Awards. Offered biennially to recognize excellence in books by and about American Indians. *Offered by:* American Indian Library Association. *Winners (2020):* (picture book) Brenda J. Child (author), Gordon Jourdain (translator), and Jonathan Thunder (illustrator) for *Bowwow Powwow: Bagosenjige-niimi'idim* (Minnesota Historical Society Press); (middle school) Charlene Willing McManis with Traci Sorell for *Indian No More* (Tu Books); (young adult) Cynthia Leitich Smith for *Hearts Unbroken* (Candlewick Press).

American Poetry Review / Honickman First Book Prize in Poetry ($3,000 and publication of the book). To encourage excellence in poetry and to provide a wide readership for a deserving first book of poems. *Winner:* Chessy Normile for *Great Exodus, Great Wall, Great Party* (Copper Canyon Press).

Américas Book Award for Children's and Young Adult Literature. To recognize U.S. works of fiction, poetry, folklore, or selected nonfiction that authentically and engagingly portray Latin America, the Caribbean, or Latinos in the United States. *Sponsor:* Consortium of Latin American Studies Programs (CLASP). *Winners:* Tony Johnston and Maria Elena Fontanot De Rhoads for *Beast Rider* (Amulet Books); Mitali Perkins for *Between Us and Abuela*, illustrated by Sara Palacios (Farrar, Straus and Giroux).

Hans Christian Andersen Literature Award (500,000 Danish kroner, about $90,000). Biennial prize to a writer whose work can be compared with that of Andersen. *Offered by:* Hans Christian Andersen Literary Committee. *Winner (2020):* Karl Ove Knausgård.

Anthony Awards. For superior mystery writing. *Offered by:* Boucheron World Mystery Convention. *Winners:* (novel) Hank Phillippi Ryan for *The Murder List* (Forge Books); (first novel) Tara Laskowski for *One Night*

Gone (Graydon House); (paperback original) Gigi Pandian for *The Alchemist's Illusion* (Midnight Ink); (short story) Alex Segura for "The Red Zone" in *¡Pa'que Tu Lo Sepas!: Stories to Benefit the People of Puerto Rico* (Down & Out); (critical/biographical) Mo Moulton for *The Mutual Admiration Society: How Dorothy L. Sayers and Her Oxford Circle Remade the World for Women* (Basic Books); (young adult) Jen Conley for *Seven Ways to Get Rid of Harry* (Down & Out); (anthology / collection) Verena Rose, Rita Owen, and Shawn Reilly Simmons (editors) for *Malice Domestic 14: Mystery Most Edible* (Wildside Press).

Asian / Pacific American Awards for Literature. For books that promote Asian / Pacific American culture and heritage. *Sponsor:* Asian / Pacific American Librarians Association (APALA). Winners: (adult fiction) Devi Laskar for *The Atlas of Reds and Blues* (Counterpoint Press); (adult nonfiction) Gordon H. Chang for *Ghosts of Gold Mountain: The Epic Story of the Chinese Who Built the Transcontinental Railroad* (Houghton Mifflin Harcourt); (young adult) George Takei, Justin Eisinger, and Steven Scott for *They Called Us Enemy*, illustrated by Harmony Becker (Top Shelf Productions); (children's) Jen Wang for *Stargazing* (First Second / Roaring Books Press); (picture book) Teresa Robeson for *Queen of Physics: How Wu Chien Shiung Helped Unlock the Secrets of the Atom*, illustrated by Rebecca Huang (Sterling Children's Books).

Astounding Award for Best New Writer (formerly the John W. Campbell Award for Best New Writer). For the best new science fiction or fantasy writer whose first work of science fiction or fantasy was published in a professional publication in the previous two years. *Offered by:* Dell Magazines. *Winner:* R. F. Kuang for *The Poppy War* (Harper Voyager).

Audio Publishers Association Awards (Audies). To recognize excellence in audiobooks. *Winners:* (audiobook of the year) *The Only Plane in the Sky: An Oral History of 9/11* by Garrett M. Graff, narrated by a 45-person cast with Holter Graham (Simon & Schuster Audio); (drama) *Angels in America* by Tony Kushner, performed by Andrew Garfield, Nathan Lane, Susan Brown, Denise Gough, and a full cast (Penguin Random House Audio); (autobiography / memoir) *Becoming* written and narrated by Michelle Obama (Penguin Random House Audio); (best female narrator) *Nothing to See Here* by Kevin Wilson, narrated by Marin Ireland (HarperAudio); (best male narrator) *Kingdom of the Blind* by Louise Penny, narrated by Robert Bathurst (Macmillan Audio); (business / personal development) *So You Want to Start a Podcast?* written and narrated by Kristen Meinzer (HarperAudio); (faith-based fiction and nonfiction) *How the Light Gets In* by Jolina Petersheim, narrated by Tavia Gilbert (Oasis Audio); (fantasy) *The Ten Thousand Doors of January* by Alix E. Harrow, narrated by January LaVoy (Hachette Audio); (fiction) *City of Girls* by Elizabeth Gilbert, narrated by Blair Brown (Penguin Random House Audio); (history / biography) *American Moonshot* by Douglas Brinkley, narrated by Stephen Graybill (HarperAudio); (humor) *More Bedtime Stories for Cynics* by Kirsten Kearse, Gretchen Enders, Aparna Nancherla, Cirocco Dunlap, Dave Hill, narrated by Nick Offerman, Patrick Stewart, Alia Shawkat, Ellen Page, Jane Lynch, John Waters, Anjelica Huston, Wendell Pierce, Mike Birbiglia, Rachel Dratch, Matt Walsh, Nicole Byer, Harry Goaz, Aisling Bea, and Gary Anthony Williams (Audible Studios); (literary fiction and classics) *The Water Dancer* by Ta-Nehisi Coates, narrated by Joe Morton (Penguin Random House Audio); (middle grade) *Charlotte's Web* by E. B. White, narrated by Meryl Streep and a full cast (Penguin Random House Audio); (multi-voiced performance) *The Only Plane in the Sky: An Oral History of 9/11* by Garrett M. Graff, narrated by a 45-person cast with Holter Graham (Simon & Schuster Audio); (mystery) *The Chestnut Man* by Søren Sveistrup, narrated by Peter Noble (published by HarperAudio); (narration by the author) *With the Fire on High* written and narrated by Elizabeth Acevedo (HarperAudio); (nonfiction) *Grace Will Lead Us Home* by Jennifer Berry Hawes, narrated by Karen Chilton and Jennifer Berry Hawes (Macmillan Audio); (original work) *Evil Eye* by Madhuri Shekar, narrated by Nick Choksi, Harsh Nayaar, Annapurna Sriram, Bernard White, and Rita Wolf (Audible

Studios); (romance) *Devil's Daughter* by Lisa Kleypas, narrated by Mary Jane Wells (HarperAudio); (science fiction) *Emergency Skin* by N. K. Jemisin, narrated by Jason Isaacs (Brilliance Publishing); (short stories / collections) *Full Throttle* by Joe Hill, narrated by Zachary Quinto, Wil Wheaton, Kate Mulgrew, Neil Gaiman, Ashleigh Cummings, Joe Hill, Laysla De Oliveira, Nate Corddry, Connor Jessup, Stephen Lang, and George Guidall (HarperAudio); (thriller / suspense) *The Institute* by Stephen King, narrated by Santino Fontana (Simon & Schuster Audio); (young adult) *Hey, Kiddo* by Jarrett J. Krosoczka, narrated by Jarrett J. Krosoczka, Jeanne Birdsall, Richard Ferrone, Jenna Lamia, and a full cast (Scholastic Audio); (young listeners up to age eight) *The Pigeon Has to Go to School!* written and narrated by Mo Willems (Weston Woods).

Bad Sex in Fiction Award (United Kingdom). To "draw attention to the crude, badly written, often perfunctory use of redundant passages of sexual description in the modern novel, and to discourage it." *Sponsor: Literary Review. Winner:* Not awarded in 2020.

Bailey's Women's Prize for Fiction. See Women's Prize for Fiction.

Bancroft Prizes ($10,000). For books of exceptional merit and distinction in American history, American diplomacy, and the international relations of the United States. *Offered by:* Columbia University. *Winners:* Lizabeth Cohen for *Saving America's Cities: Ed Logue and the Struggle to Renew Urban America in the Suburban Age* (Farrar, Straus and Giroux); Joseph P. Reidy for *Illusions of Emancipation: The Pursuit of Freedom and Equality in the Twilight of Slavery* (University of North Carolina Press).

Barnes & Noble Book of the Year. To honor the book that B&N booksellers nominate as the book they are most proud to sell. *Offered by:* Barnes & Noble. *Winner:* Aimee Nezhukumatathil for *World of Wonders: In Praise of Fireflies, Whale Sharks, and Other Astonishments* (Milkweed Editions).

Mildred L. Batchelder Award. To the American publisher of a children's book originally published in a language other than English and subsequently published in English in the United States. *Offered by:* American Library Association, Association for Library Service to Children. *Winner:* Enchanted Lion Books for *Brown*, written by Håkon Øvreås, illustrated by Øyvind Torseter, and translated by Kari Dickson.

BBC National Short Story Award (United Kingdom) (£15,000). *Winner:* Sarah Hall for "The Grotesques."

Pura Belpré Awards. To a Latino / Latina writer and illustrator whose work portrays, affirms, and celebrates the Latino cultural experience in an outstanding work of literature for children and youth. *Offered by:* American Library Association, Association for Library Service to Children. *Winners:* (narrative) Carlos Hernandez for *Sal and Gabi Break the Universe* (Disney Hyperion / Disney Book Group); (illustration) Rafael López for *Dancing Hands: How Teresa Carreño Played the Piano for President Lincoln*, written by Margarita Engle (Atheneum Books for Young Readers / Simon & Schuster).

Helen B. Bernstein Book Award for Excellence in Journalism ($15,000). To a journalist who has written at book length about an issue of contemporary concern. *Offered by:* New York Public Library. *Winner:* Rachel Louise Snyder for *No Visible Bruises: What We Don't Know About Domestic Violence Can Kill Us* (Bloomsbury USA).

Black Caucus of the American Library Association (BCALA) Literary Awards. *Winners:* (first novelist) Ta-Nehisi Coates for *The Water Dancer* (Random House); (poetry) Eve L. Ewing for *1919* (Haymarket Books); (fiction) Colson Whitehead for *The Nickel Boys* (Knopf Doubleday); (nonfiction) Daniel R. Day for *Dapper Dan: Made in Harlem: A Memoir* (Random House); (outstanding contribution to publishing) Donald Bogle for *Hollywood Black: The Stars, the Films, the Filmmakers* (Running Press).

Irma Simonton Black and James H. Black Award for Excellence in Children's Literature. To a book for young children in which the text and illustrations work together to create an outstanding whole. *Offered by:* Bank Street College of Education. *Winner:* Natascha Biebow for *The Crayon Man: The True Story of the Invention of Crayola Crayons* (Houghton Mifflin Harcourt).

James Tait Black Memorial Prize (United Kingdom) (£10,000). To recognize literary excellence in fiction and biography. *Offered by:* University of Edinburgh. *Winners:* (fiction) Lucy Ellmann for *Ducks, Newburyport* (Galley Beggar Press); (biography) George Szirtes for *The Photographer at Sixteen* (MacLehose Press).

James Tait Black Prize for Drama (United Kingdom) (£10,000). *Offered by:* University of Edinburgh in partnership with the National Theatre of Scotland and in association with the Traverse Theatre. *Winner:* Yasmin Joseph for *J'Ouvert.*

Blue Peter Book of the Year (United Kingdom). To recognize excellence in children's books. Winners are chosen by a jury of viewers, ages 8–12, of the BBC television children's program *Blue Peter. Winners:* (best story) Vashti Hardy for *Wildspark* (Scholastic); (best book with facts) Amanda Li for *Rise Up: Ordinary Kids with Extraordinary Stories*, illustrated by Amy Blackwell, designed by Kim Hankinson and Jack Clucas (Buster Books).

Rebekah Johnson Bobbitt National Prize for Poetry ($10,000). A biennial prize for the most distinguished book of poetry written by an American and published during the preceding two years. *Offered by:* Library of Congress. *Donor:* Family of Rebekah Johnson Bobbitt. *Winners (2020):* Terrance Hayes for *American Sonnets for My Past and Future Assassin* (Penguin Books); (lifetime achievement) Natasha Trethewey.

Booker Prize for Fiction (United Kingdom) (£50,000). For the best English language novel. *Offered by:* Crankstart. *Winner:* Douglas Stuart for *Shuggie Bain* (Picador / Pan Macmillan).

Bookseller / Diagram Prize for Oddest Title of the Year. *Sponsor: The Bookseller* magazine. *Winner:* Gregory Forth for *A Dog Pissing at the Edge of a Path: Animal Metaphors in Eastern Indonesian Society* (McGill-Queen's University Press).

Boston Globe / Horn Book Awards. For excellence in children's literature. *Winners:* (fiction and poetry) Kacen Callender for *King and the Dragonflies* (Scholastic Press); (nonfiction) Ashley Bryan for *Infinite Hope: A Black Artist's Journey from World War II to Peace* (Caitlyn Dlouhy Books / Atheneum / Simon & Schuster); (picture book) Oge Mora for *Saturday* (Little, Brown).

W. Y. Boyd Literary Award for Excellence in Military Fiction ($5,000). For a military novel that honors the service of American veterans during a time of war. *Offered by:* American Library Association. *Donor:* W. Y. Boyd II. *Winner:* Ralph Peterson for *Darkness at Chancellorsville* (Forge Books).

Branford Boase Award (United Kingdom). To the author and editor of an outstanding novel for young readers by a first-time writer. *Winners:* Liz Hyder (author) and Sarah Odedina (editor) for *Bearmouth* (Pushkin Children's Books).

Bridport International Creative Writing Prizes (United Kingdom). For poetry and short stories. *Offered by:* Bridport Arts Centre. *Winners:* (poetry, £5,000) Michael Lavers for "Low Tide"; (short story, £5,000) Debra Waters for "Oh, Hululu"; (flash fiction, 250-word maximum, £1,000) Rowena Warwick for "Mum Died"; (Peggy Chapman-Andrews Award for a First Novel) Joseph Pierson for *Helen and the Fires*.

British Book Awards (aka the Nibbies) (United Kingdom). *Offered by: The Bookseller. Winners:* (book of the year) Candice Carty-Williams for *Queenie* (Trapeze); (fiction) Bernardine Evaristo for *Girl, Woman, Other* (Hamish Hamilton); (debut) Leila Slimani for *Lullaby, translated by Sam Taylor* (Simon & Schuster); (crime & thriller) Oyinkan Braithwaite for *My Sister, the Serial Killer* (Atlantic Books); (children's fiction) Holly Jackson for *A Good Girl's Guide to Murder* (Electric Monkey); (children's nonfiction & illustrated) Julia Donaldson for *The Smeds and The Smoos*, illustrated by Axel Scheffler (Alison Green Books); (nonfiction) Lisa Taddeo for *Three Women* (Bloomsbury Circus); (lifestyle) Kay Featherstone and Kate Allinson for *Pinch of Nom* (Bluebird); (audio) Penguin Random House UK Audio for *The Testaments* by Margaret Atwood, narrated by Bryce Dallas Howard, Ann Dowd, and Mae Whitman; (illustrator of the year) David McKee; (author of the year) Bernardine Evaristo.

British Fantasy Awards. *Offered by:* British Fantasy Society. *Winners:* (Karl Edward Wagner Award) Craig Lockley; (Sydney J Bounds Award for a newcomer) Ta-Nehisi Coates for *The Water Dancer* (One World); (magazine / periodical) *Fiyah*; (nonfiction)

Ebony Elizabeth Thomas for *The Dark Fantastic: Race and the Imagination from Harry Potter to the Hunger Games* (New York University Press); (comic / graphic novel) Kieron Gillen and Stephanie Hans for *Die* (Image); (independent press) Rebellion; (artist) Ben Baldwin; (anthology) Nisi Shawl (ed.) for *New Suns: Original Speculative Fiction for People of Color* (Solaris); (collection) Laura Mauro for *Sing Your Sadness Deep* (Undertow); (film / television production) *Us*, written and directed by Jordan Peele (Universal Pictures); (audio) *PodCastle* (podcast); (novella) Priya Sharma for *Ormeshadow* (Tor.com Publishing); (short story) Laura Mauro for "The Pain-Eater's Daughter" in *Sing Your Sadness Deep* (Undertow); (August Derleth Award for horror novel) Adam Nevill for *The Reddening* (Ritual Limited); (Robert Holdstock Award for fantasy novel) RJ Barker for *The Bone Ships* (Orbit).

Sophie Brody Medal. For the U.S. author of the most distinguished contribution to Jewish literature for adults, published in the preceding year. *Donors:* Sophie and Arthur Brody Foundation. *Offered by:* American Library Association, Reference and User Services Association. *Winner:* Thomas Wolf for *The Nightingale's Sonata: The Musical Odyssey of Lea Luboshutz* (Pegasus Books).

AKO Caine Prize for African Writing (£10,000). For a short story by an African writer, published in English. *Winner:* Irenosen Okojie for "Grace Jones" in *Nudibranch* (Dialogue Books).

Randolph Caldecott Medal. For the artist of the most distinguished picture book. *Offered by:* American Library Association, Association for Library Service to Children. *Winner:* Kadir Nelson for *The Undefeated*, written by Kwame Alexander (Houghton Mifflin Harcourt).

California Book Awards. To California residents to honor books of fiction, nonfiction, and poetry published in the previous year. *Offered by:* Commonwealth Club of California. *Winners:* (fiction) Steph Cha for *Your House Will Pay* (Ecco); (first fiction) Xuan Juliana Wang for *Home Remedies* (Hogarth Press); (nonfiction) David Treuer for *The Heartbeat of Wounded Knee* (Riverhead Books); (poetry) Morgan Parker for

Magical Negro (Tin House Books); (juvenile) Cynthia Kadohata for *A Place to Belong* (Atheneum); (young adult) David Yoon for *Frankly in Love* (G.P. Putnam's Sons); (contribution to publishing) Jim Marshall for *Jim Marshall: Show Me the Picture* (Chronicle Books); (Californiana) Mark Arax for *The Dreamt Land* (Knopf).

Eleanor Cameron Notable Middle Grade Books List. See LITA Excellence in Children's and Young Adult Science Fiction.

John W. Campbell Award. See *Astounding Award for Best New Writer.*

John W. Campbell Memorial Award. For science fiction writing. *Offered by:* Gunn Center for the Study of Science Fiction. *Winner:* Not awarded in 2020.

Andrew Carnegie Medal for Excellence in Fiction and Nonfiction. For adult books published during the previous year in the United States. *Sponsors:* Carnegie Corporation of New York, ALA / RUSA, and *Booklist.* *Winners:* (fiction) Valeria Luiselli for *Lost Children Archive* (Alfred A. Knopf); (nonfiction) Adam Higginbotham for *Midnight in Chernobyl: The Untold Story of the World's Greatest Nuclear Disaster* (Simon & Schuster).

Carnegie Medal (United Kingdom). See CILIP Carnegie Medal.

Center for Fiction First Novel Prize ($10,000). *Offered by:* Center for Fiction, Mercantile Library of New York. *Winner:* Raven Leilani for *Luster* (Farrar, Straus and Giroux / Macmillan).

Chicago Folklore Prize. For the year's best folklore book. *Offered by:* American Folklore Society. *Winners:* Simon Bronner for *The Practice of Folklore: Essays Toward a Theory of Tradition* (University Press of Mississippi); Andrea Kitta for *The Kiss of Death: Contagion, Contamination, and Folklore* (Utah State University Press).

Chicago Tribune Nelson Algren Short Story Award ($3,500). For unpublished short fiction. *Offered by: Chicago Tribune. Winner:* Edward Hamlin for "Haddad: A Requiem."

Chicago Tribune Heartland Prize for Fiction ($7,500). *Offered by: Chicago Tribune. Winner:* Not awarded in 2020.

Chicago Tribune Heartland Prize for Nonfiction ($7,500). *Offered by: Chicago Tribune. Winner:* Not awarded in 2020.

Chicago Tribune Literary Award. To recognize lifetime achievement of a prominent writer, usually someone with strong connections to the Midwest. *Winner:* Not awarded in 2020.

Chicago Tribune Young Adult Literary Prize. To recognize a distinguished literary career. *Winner:* Not awarded in 2020.

Children's Africana Book Awards. To recognize and encourage excellence in children's books about Africa. *Offered by:* Africa Access, African Studies Association. *Winners:* (young readers) Adrienne Wright for *Hector: A Boy, a Protest, and the Photograph That Changed Apartheid* (Page Street Kids / Macmillan); (older readers) Kwame Mbalia for *Tristan Strong Punches a Hole in the Sky* (Disney Hyperion); (new adult) Kwei Quartey for *Gold of Our Fathers* (Soho Press).

Children's Literature Legacy Award (formerly the Laura Ingalls Wilder Award). Awarded to an author or illustrator whose books have made a substantial and lasting contribution to children's literature. *Offered by:* American Library Association, Association for Library Service to Children. *Winner:* Kevin Henkes.

Cholmondeley Awards for Poets (United Kingdom) (£1,500). For a poet's body of work and contribution to poetry. *Winners:* Bhanu Kapil, Alec Finlay, Linda France, Hannah Lowe, Rod Mengham.

CILIP Carnegie Medal (United Kingdom). For the outstanding children's book of the year. *Offered by:* CILIP: The Chartered Institute of Library and Information Professionals. *Winner:* Anthony McGowan for *Lark* (Barrington Stoke).

CILIP Kate Greenaway Medal and Colin Mears Award (United Kingdom) (£5,000 plus £500 worth of books donated to a library of the winner's choice). For children's book illustration. *Offered by:* CILIP: The Chartered Institute of Library and Information Professionals. *Winner:* Shaun Tan for *Tales from the Inner City* (Walker Books).

Arthur C. Clarke Award. For the best science fiction novel published in the United Kingdom. *Offered by:* British Science Fiction Association. *Winner:* Namwali Serpell for *The Old Drift* (Hogarth Press).

Hal Clement Notable Young Adult Books List. See LITA Excellence in Children's and Young Adult Science Fiction.

David Cohen Prize for Literature (United Kingdom) (£40,000). Awarded biennially to a living British writer, novelist, poet, essayist, or dramatist in recognition of an entire body of work written in the English language. *Offered by:* David Cohen Family Charitable Trust. *Winner (2019):* Edna O'Brien.

Matt Cohen Award: In Celebration of a Writing Life (C$20,000). To a Canadian author whose life has been dedicated to writing as a primary pursuit, for a body of work. *Offered by:* Writers' Trust of Canada. *Sponsors:* Marla and David Lehberg. *Winner:* Dennis Lee.

Commonwealth Short Story Prize (United Kingdom) (£5,000 for overall winner; £2,500 for each regional winner). To reward and encourage new short fiction by Commonwealth writers. *Offered by:* Commonwealth Institute. *Winners:* (regional winner, Africa) Innocent Chizaram Ilo (Nigeria) for "When a Woman Renounces Motherhood"; (regional winner, Asia, and overall winner) Kritika Pandey (India) for "The Great Indian Tee and Snakes"; (regional winner, Canada and Europe) Reyah Martin (United Kingdom) for "Wherever Mister Jensen Went"; (regional winner, Caribbean) Brian S. Heap (Jamaica) for "Mafootoo"; (regional winner, Pacific) Harley Hern (New Zealand) for "Screaming."

Costa Book Awards (United Kingdom) (£5,000 plus an additional £25,000 for Book of the Year). For literature of merit that is readable on a wide scale. *Offered by:* Booksellers Association of Great Britain and Costa Coffee. *Winners:* (biography) Lee Lawrence for *The Louder I Will Sing* (Sphere); (novel, and Book of the Year) Monique Roffey for *The Mermaid of Black Conch: A Love Story* (Peepal Tree Press); (first novel) Ingrid Persaud for *Love After Love* (Faber & Faber); (children's) Natasha Farrant for *Voyage of the Sparrowhawk* (Norton Young Readers); (poetry) Eavan Boland for *The Historians* (W.W. Norton & Company).

Costa Short Story Award (United Kingdom). *Winners:* (first place, £3,500) Tessa Sheridan for "The Person Who Serves, Serves Again."

Crime Writers' Association (CWA) Dagger Awards (United Kingdom). *Winners:* (diamond dagger, for significant contribution to crime writing) Martin Edwards; (gold dagger, for best novel) Michael Robotham for *Good Girl, Bad Girl* (Sphere); (gold dagger, for nonfiction) Casey Cep for *Furious Hours: Murder, Fraud and the Last Trial of Harper Lee* (William Heinemann); (Ian Fleming steel dagger, for best thriller) Lou Berney for *November Road* (Harper Fiction); (John Creasey dagger, for best debut crime novel) Trevor Wood for *The Man on the Street* (Quercus); (CWA historical dagger, for the best historical crime novel) Abir Mukherjee for *Death in the East* (Harvill Secker); (CWA short story dagger) Lauren Henderson for "#Me Too" in *Invisible Blood: Seventeen New Stories of Murder and Mystery*, edited by Maxim Jakubowski (Titan Books); (international dagger, for a work translated into English) Hannelore Cayre for *The Godmother International*, translated by Stephanie Smee (Old Street Publishing); (CWA Dagger in the Library, for a body of work) Christopher Brookmyre; (debut dagger, for a previously unpublished crime writer) Josephine Moulds for *Revolution Never Lies.*

Benjamin H. Danks Award ($20,000). Given annually, in rotation, to a composer of ensemble works, a playwright, and a writer. *Offered by:* American Academy of Arts and Letters. *Winner:* Hanya Yanagihara (writing).

Dartmouth Medal. For creating current reference works of outstanding quality and significance. *Donor:* Dartmouth College. *Offered by:* American Library Association, Reference and User Services Division. *Winner:* Howard Chaing (editor) for *Global Encyclopedia of Lesbian, Gay, Bisexual, Transgender, and Queer (LGBTQ) History* (Gale, a Cengage Company).

Derringer Awards. To recognize excellence in short crime and mystery fiction. *Sponsor:* Short Mystery Fiction Society. *Winners:* (flash story, up to 1,000 words) Josh Pachter for "The Two-Body Problem" in *Mystery Weekly Magazine* (October 2019); (short story, 1,001–4,000 words) John Floyd for "On the Road with Mary Jo" in *Ellery Queen's Mystery Magazine* (January / February 2019); (long story, 4,001–8,000 words) Sandra Murphy for "Lucy's Tree" in *The Eyes of Texas: Private Eyes from the Panhandle to the Piney Woods*, edited by Michael Bracken (Down & Out Books); (novelette, 8,001–20,000 words) Brendan Dubois for *His Sister's Secrets* in *Ellery Queen's Mystery Magazine* (July / August 2019).

Diagram Prize for Oddest Title of the Year. See Bookseller / Diagram Prize for Oddest Title of the Year.

Philip K. Dick Award. For a distinguished science fiction paperback published in the United States. *Sponsor:* Philadelphia Science Fiction Society and the Philip K. Dick Trust. *Winner:* Sarah Pinsker for *Sooner or Later Everything Falls into the Sea: Stories* (Small Beer Press)

Digital Book Awards. To recognize high-quality digital content available to readers as e-books and enhanced digital books. *Sponsor:* Digital Book World. *Winners:* (publisher of the year) Hachette; (publishing executive of the year) Michael Pietsch; (Maric Dutton Brown Medal for Leadership in Diversity) Regina Brooks; (DAISY Consortium Award for Accessibility in Publishing) Department of Canadian Heritage; (DBW Outstanding Achievement Awards) Nosy Crow for *Coronavirus: A Book for Children* by Elizabeth Jenner, Kate Wilson, and Nia Roberts, illustrated by Axel Scheffler; Bookshop; CNN; (best publishing technology) Bookshop; (best use of podcasting in publishing) *The Creative Penn*; (best publishing commentator of the year) Mike Shatzkin; (best fiction) Simone St. James for *The Sun Down Motel* (Berkley); (best nonfiction) John F. Marszalek III for *Coming Out of the Magnolia Closet: Same-Sex Couples in Mississippi* (University of Mississippi Press); (best book published by a university press) University of Mississippi Press for *Coming Out of the Magnolia Closet: Same-Sex Couples in Mississippi* by John F. Marszalek III.

DSC Prize for South Asian Literature ($50,000). To recognize outstanding literature from or about the South Asian region and raise awareness of South Asian culture around the world. *Sponsor:* DSC Limited. *Winner:* Not awarded in 2020.

Dublin Literary Award (Ireland) (€100,000). For a book of high literary merit, written in English or translated into English; if translated, the author receives €75,000 and the translator €25,000. *Offered by:* City of Dublin. *Winner:* Anna Burns for *Milkman* (Faber & Faber).

Dundee Picture Book Award (Scotland) (£1,000). To recognize excellence in story-telling for children. The winner is chosen by the schoolchildren of Dundee. *Winner:* Not awarded in 2020.

Edgar Awards. For outstanding mystery, suspense, and crime writing. *Offered by:* Mystery Writers of America. *Winners:* (novel) Elly Griffiths for *The Stranger Diaries* (Houghton Mifflin Harcourt); (first novel) Angie Kim for *Miracle Creek* (Sarah Crichton Books / Farrar, Straus and Giroux); (paperback original) Adam O'Fallon Price for *The Hotel Neversink* (Tin House Books); (fact crime) Axton Betz-Hamilton for *The Less People Know About Us: A Mystery of Betrayal, Family Secrets, and Stolen Identity* (Grand Central Publishing); (critical / biographical) John Billheimer for *Hitchcock and the Censors* (University Press of Kentucky); (short story) Livia Llewellyn for "One of These Nights" in *Cutting Edge: New Stories of Mystery and Crime by Women Writers* (Akashic Books); (juvenile) Susan Vaught for *Me and Sam-Sam Handle the Apocalypse* (Paula Wiseman Books / Simon & Schuster Children's Books); (young adult) Naomi Kritzer for *Catfishing on CatNet* (Tom Doherty Associates / Tor Teen); (television episode) Jed Mercurio (teleplay) for season 5, episode 4 of *Line of Duty* (Acorn TV); (Robert L. Fish Memorial Award) Derrick Harriell for "There's a Riot Goin' On" in *Milwaukee Noir* (Akashic Books); (grand master) Barbara Neely; (Raven Award) Left Coast Crime; (Ellery Queen Award) Kelley Ragland; (Mary Higgins Clark Award) Carol Goodman for *The Night Visitors* (William Morrow); (Sue Grafton Memorial Award) Tracy Clark for *Borrowed Time* (Kensington Publishing).

Educational Writers' Award (United Kingdom) (£2,000). For noteworthy educational non-fiction for children. *Offered by:* Authors' Licensing and Collecting Society. *Winner:* Robin Walker for *Black History Matters: The Story of Black History, From African Kingdoms to Black Lives Matter* (Franklin Watts).

Margaret A. Edwards Award ($2,000). To an author whose book or books have provided young adults with a window through which they can view their world and which will help them to grow and to understand themselves and their role in society. *Donor: School Library Journal. Winner:* Steve Sheinkin for *Bomb: The Race to Build—and Steal—the World's Most Dangerous Weapon* (Flash Point / Roaring Brook Press), *The Port Chicago 50: Disaster, Mutiny, and the Fight for Civil Rights* (Roaring Brook Press), and *The Notorious Benedict Arnold: A True Story of Adventure, Heroism, & Treachery* (Flash Point / Roaring Brook Press).

T. S. Eliot Prize for Poetry (United Kingdom) (£20,000). *Offered by:* Poetry Book Society. *Winner:* Bhanu Kapil for *How to Wash a Heart* (Liverpool University Press).

Encore Award (United Kingdom) (£10,000). Awarded for the best second novel. *Offered by:* Royal Society of Literature. *Winner:* Patrick McGuinness for *Throw Me To The Wolves* (Jonathan Cape).

European Union Prize for Literature (€5,000). To recognize outstanding European writing. *Sponsors:* European Commission, European Booksellers Federation, European Writers' Council, Federation of European Publishers. *Winners:* Nathalie Skowronek (Belgium), Lana Bastašić (Bosnia And Herzegovina), Maša Kolanović (Croatia) Stavros Christodoulou (Cyprus), Asta Olivia Nordenhof (Denmark), Mudlum, aka Made Luiga (Estonia), Matthias Nawrat (Germany), Shpëtim Selmani (Kosovo), Francis Kirps (Luxembourg), Stefan Bošković (Montenegro), Petar Andonovski (North Macedonia), Maria Navarro Skaranger (Norway), Irene Solà (Spain).

FIL Literary Award in Romance Languages (formerly the Juan Rulfo International Latin American and Caribbean Prize) (Mexico) ($150,000). For lifetime achievement in any literary genre. *Offered by:* Juan Rulfo International Latin American and Caribbean Prize Committee. *Winner:* Lidia Jorge.

Financial Times and McKinsey Business Book of the Year Award (£30,000). To recognize books that provide compelling and enjoyable insight into modern business issues. *Winner:* Sarah Frier for *No Filter: The Inside Story of Instagram* (Random House Business).

Sid Fleischman Award for Humor. See Golden Kite Awards.

ForeWord Reviews Book of the Year Awards ($1,500). For independently published books. *Offered by: ForeWord Reviews* magazine. *Winners:* (editor's choice prize, fiction) Sheila O'Connor for *Evidence of V* (Rose Metal Press); (editor's choice prize, nonfiction) Behrouz Boochanifor *No Friend But the Mountains: Writing from Manus Prison,* translated by Omid Tofighian (House of Anansi).

E. M. Forster Award ($20,000). To a young writer from the United Kingdom or Ireland for a stay in the United States. *Offered by:* American Academy of Arts and Letters. *Winner:* Stephen Sexton.

Forward Prizes (United Kingdom). For poetry. *Offered by: The Forward. Winners:* (best collection, £10,000) Caroline Bird for *The Air Year* (Carcanet); (Felix Dennis Prize for best first collection, £5,000) Will Harris for *RENDANG* (Granta Poetry); (best single poem, £1,000) Malika Booker for "The Little Miracles" (Magma).

Josette Frank Award. For a work of fiction in which children or young people deal in a positive and realistic way with difficulties in their world and grow emotionally and morally. *Offered by:* Bank Street College of Education and the Florence M. Miller Memorial Fund. *Winner:* Malla Nunn for *When the Ground Is Hard* (G.P. Putnam's Sons Books for Young Readers).

George Freedley Memorial Award. For the best English-language work about live theater published in the United States. *Offered by:* Theatre Library Association. *Winner:* Juliane Braun for *Creole Drama: Theatre and Society in Antebellum New Orleans* (University of Virginia Press).

French-American Foundation Translation Prize ($10,000). For a translation or translations from French into English of works of fiction and nonfiction. *Offered by:* French-American Foundation. *Donor:* Florence Gould Foundation. *Winners:* (fiction) Alyson Waters for her translation of *A King Alone* by Jean Giono (New York Review Books); (nonfiction) Michael Loriaux and Jacob Levi for their co-translation of *Murderous Consent: On the Accommodation of Violent Death* by Marc Crépon (Fordham University Press).

Frost Medal. To recognize achievement in poetry over a lifetime. *Offered by:* Poetry Society of America. *Winner:* Toi Derricotte.

Lewis Galantière Award. Awarded biennially for a literary translation into English from any language other than German. *Offered by:* American Translators Association. *Winner (2020):* Michael Meigs for his translation of *All This I Will Give to You* by Dolores Redondo (Amazon Crossing).

Theodor Seuss Geisel Award. For the best book for beginning readers. *Offered by:* American Library Association, Association for Library Service to Children. *Winner:* James Yang for *Stop! Bot!* (Viking/Penguin).

Atwood Gibson Writers' Trust Prize for Fiction (C$60,000) (Canada). *Offered by:* Writers' Trust of Canada. *Winner:* Gil Adamson for *Ridgerunner* (House of Anansi).

Giller Prize (Canada). See Scotiabank Giller Prize.

Gival Press Novel Award ($3,000 and publication by Gival Press). Given biennially. *Winner (2020):* Jordan Silversmith for *Redshift, Blueshift.*

Gival Press Oscar Wilde Award ($500 and publication by Gival Press). Given annually to an original, unpublished poem that relates LGBTQ life by a poet who is 18 or older. *Winner:* George Klawitter for *Twenty.*

Gival Press Poetry Award ($1,000 and publication by Gival Press). Given biennially. *Winner (2019):* Matthew Pennock for *The Miracle Machine.*

Gival Press Short Story Award ($1,000 and publication by Gival Press). Given annually. *Winner:* Vikram Ramakrishnan for *Jackson Heights.*

Giverny Award. For an outstanding children's science picture book. *Offered by:* 15 Degree Laboratory. *Winner:* Brendan Wenzel for *They All Saw a Cat* (Chronicle Books).

Alexander Gode Medal. To an individual or institution for outstanding service to the translation and interpreting professions. *Offered by:* American Translators Association. *Winner:* Sue Ellen Wright.

Golden Duck Notable Picture Books List. See LITA Excellence in Children's and Young Adult Science Fiction.

Golden Kite Awards. For children's books. *Offered by:* Society of Children's Book Writers and Illustrators. *Winners:* (young reader and middle grade fiction) Padma Venkatraman for *The Bridge Home* (Nancy Paulsen Books); (young adult fiction) Julie Berry for *Lovely War* (Viking Books for Young Readers); (nonfiction text for younger readers) Elizabeth Rusch for *Mario and the Hole in the Sky: How a Chemist Saved Our Planet,* illustrated by Teresa Martinez (Charlesbridge); (nonfiction text for older readers) Deborah Heiligman for *Torpedoed: The True Story of the World War II Sinking of "The Children's Ship"* (Henry Holt and Co.); (picture book illustration) Hyewon Yum for *Clever Little Witch,* written by Muon Thi Van (Margaret K. McElderry Books); (picture book text) Ashley Benham Yazdani for *A Green Place to Be: The Creation of Central Park* (Candlewick Press); (Sid Fleischman Award) Remy Lai for *Pie in the Sky* (Henry Holt).

Governor General's Literary Awards (Canada) (C$25,000, plus C$3,000 to the publisher). For works, in English and French, of fiction, nonfiction, and poetry, and for translation. *Offered by:* Canada Council for the Arts. *Winners (2020):* To be announced.

Dolly Gray Children's Literature Awards. Presented biennially for fiction or biographical children's books with positive portrayals of individuals with developmental disabilities. *Offered by:* Council for Exceptional Children, Division on Autism and Developmental Disabilities. *Winner (2020):* Gill Lewis for *Scarlet Ibis* (Simon & Schuster).

Kate Greenaway Medal and Colin Mears Award. See CILIP Kate Greenaway Medal and Colin Mears Award.

Eric Gregory Awards (United Kingdom) (£4,000). For a published or unpublished collection by poets under the age of 30. *Winners:* Susannah Dickey, Natalie Linh Bolderston, Roseanne Watt, Kadish Morris, Amina Jama.

Griffin Poetry Prizes (Canada) (C$65,000). To a living Canadian poet or translator and a living poet or translator from any country, which may include Canada. *Offered by:* Griffin Trust. *Winners:* (international) Sarah Riggs for her translation of *Time* by Etel Adnan (Nightboat Books); (Canadian) Kaie

Kellough for *Magnetic Equator* (McClelland & Stewart).

Gryphon Award ($1,000). To recognize a noteworthy work of fiction or nonfiction for younger children. *Offered by:* the Center for Children's Books. *Winners:* Drew Daywalt (author) and Olivier Tallec (illustrator) for *This Is My Fort!* (Orchard Books).

Dashiell Hammett Prize. For a work of literary excellence in the field of crime writing by a U.S. or Canadian writer. *Offered by:* North American Branch, International Association of Crime Writers. *Winner (2020):* To be announced. *Winner (2019):* Jane Stanton Hitchcock for *Bluff* (Poison Pen).

R. R. Hawkins Award. For the outstanding professional / scholarly work of the year. *Offered by:* Association of American Publishers. *Winner:* Yale University Press for *Leonardo da Vinci Rediscovered* by Carmen C. Bambach.

Anthony Hecht Poetry Prize ($3,000 and publication by Waywiser Press). For an unpublished first or second book-length poetry collection. *Winner (2020):* To be announced.

Drue Heinz Literature Prize ($15,000 and publication by University of Pittsburgh Press). For short fiction. *Winner:* Caroline Kim for *The Prince of Mournful Thoughts and Other Stories.*

O. Henry Awards. See PEN / O. Henry Prize.

William Dean Howells Medal. Given once every five years in recognition of the most distinguished American novel published during that period. *Offered by:* American Academy of Arts and Letters. *Winner (2020):* Richard Powers for *The Overstory* (W.W. Norton & Company).

Hugo Awards. For outstanding science fiction writing. *Offered by:* World Science Fiction Convention. *Winners:* (novel) Arkady Martine for *A Memory Called Empire* (Tor); (novella) Amal El-Mohtar and Max Gladstone for *This Is How You Lose the Time War* (Saga Press); (novelette) N. K. Jemisin for *Emergency Skin* (Forward Collection / Amazon); (short story) S. L. Huang for "As the Last I May Know" (Tor.com, October 23, 2019); (series) James S. A. Corey for *The Expanse* (Orbit US); (related work) Jeannette Ng for "2019 John W. Campbell Award Acceptance Speech"; (graphic story or comic) Nnedi Okorafor (author), Tana

Ford (art), and James Devlin (colors) for *LaGuardia* (Berger Books); (dramatic presentation, long form) Neil Gaiman (screenplay) and Douglas Mackinnon (director) for *Good Omens* (Amazon Studios / BBC Studios / Narrativia / The Blank Corporation); (dramatic presentation, short form) Daniel Schofield (writer) and Valeria Migliassi Collins (director) for *The Good Place*: "The Answer" (Fremulon/3 Arts Entertainment/ Universal Television); (Lodestar Award for Best Young Adult Book) Naomi Kritzer for *Catfishing on CatNet* (Tor Teen).

ILA Children's and Young Adults' Book Awards. For first or second books in any language published for children or young adults. *Offered by:* International Literacy Association. *Winners:* (primary fiction) Susan Edwards Richmond (author) and Stephanie Fizer Coleman (illustrator) for *Bird Count* (Peachtree Publishing); (primary nonfiction) Ashley Benham Yazdani for *A Green Place to Be: The Creation of Central Park* (Candlewick Press); (intermediate fiction) Gillian McDunn for *Caterpillar Summer* (Bloomsbury Children's Books); (intermediate nonfiction) Not awarded in 2020; (young adult fiction) Kimberly Gabriel for *Every Stolen Breath* (Blink); (young adult nonfiction) Victoria Ortiz for *Dissenter on the Bench: Ruth Bader Ginsburg's Life & Work* (Clarion Books).

Independent Publisher Book Awards (IPPY). Created to recognize exemplary independent, university, and self-published titles across a wide spectrum of genres. *Sponsor:* Jenkins Group / Independent Publisher Online. *Winners:* (fine art) *Human: The Art of Beth Cavener* by Garth Clark (foreword) and Ezra Shales and Lauren Redding (essays) (Fresco Books); (performing arts) Jill S. Tietjen and Barbara Bridges for *Hollywood Her Story: An Illustrated History of Women and the Movies* (Lyons Press); (photography) Sue & Patrick Cunningham for *Spirit of the Amazon: The Indigenous Tribes of the Xingu* (Papadakis); (architecture) Boyce Thompson for *Designing for Disaster* (Schiffer Publishing); (coffee table books) William Fields for *The Four Directions: A Southwestern Journey* (William Fields Art Photography); (popular fiction) Jeff Bond for *The Pinebox Vendetta* (Jeff Bond Books);

(literary fiction) Cynthia Newberry Martin for *Tidal Flats* (Yellow Pear Press); (short story fiction) Emily W. Pease for *Let Me Out Here* (Hub City Press); (poetry—standard) (tie) Dennis J. Bernstein for *Five Oceans in a Teaspoon*, visualizations by Warren Lehrer (Paper Crown Books); Kim Dower for *Sunbathing on Tyrone Power's Grave* (Red Hen Press); (poetry—specialty) B. A. Van Sise for *Children of Grass: A Portrait of American Poetry* (Schaffner Press): (anthologies) (tie) *Stand in the Light: Native Voices Illuminated by Edward S. Curtis*, compiled by Thomas F. Voight (Rio Nuevo); *The Chimpanzee Chronicles: Stories of Heartbreak and Hope from Behind the Bars*, collection by Debra Rosenman (Wild Soul Press); (juvenile fiction) Libby Carty McNamee for *Susanna's Midnight Ride: The Girl Who Won the Revolutionary War* (Sagebrush Publishing); (young adult fiction) Lisa Braver Moss for *Shrug* (She Writes Press); (fantasy) Amanda K. King and Michael R. Swanson for *Things They Buried* (Ismae Books); (science fiction) Robert Sells for *Revelations* (self-published); (LGBT+ fiction) Gary Eldon Peter for *Oranges* (New Rivers Press); (erotica) *Laid Bare: A Collection of Erotic Lesbian Stories*, edited by Astrid Ohletz and Jae (Ylva Publishing); (historical fiction) Amy Trueblood for *Across a Broken Shore* (North Star Editions); (military / wartime fiction) Ryan Byrnes for *Royal Beauty Bright* (Amphorae Publishing Group); (horror) London Clarke for *The Meadows* (Carfax Abbey Publishing); (multicultural fiction) Sonia Saikaley for *The Allspice Bath* (Inanna Publications); (multicultural fiction—juvenile / young adult) Pierre Jarawan for *The Storyteller*, translated by Sinéad Crowe and Rachel McNicholl (World Editions); (mystery) Connie Berry for *A Dream of Death* (Crooked Lane); (suspense / thriller) Amy River for *All the Broken People* (Compathy Press); (religious fiction) Carolyn Astfalk for *All in Good Time* (Multa Verba Publishing); (romance) Sara Furlong Burr for *When Time Stands Still* (self-published); (urban fiction) Vernard Dorsey for *Silent Hero: A Homeless Success Story* (Vdor Innovations); (visionary / new age fiction) Andrew Himmel for *The Reluctant Healer* (Greenleaf Book Group Press); (true crime) Vanessa

Brown for *The Forest City Killer: A Serial Murderer, a Cold-Case Sleuth, and a Search for Justice* (ECW Press); (graphic novel / drawn book) Gina Siciliano for *I Know What I Am: The Life and Times of Artemisia Gentileschi* (Fantagraphics Books); (humor) Leland Cheuk for *No Good Very Bad Asian* (C & R Press); (children's picture book—age seven and under) Jessica M. Boehman for *The Lions at Night:* A Wordless Picture Book (Roadrunner Press); (children's picture book—all ages) Larry Issa for *Get Back in the Book!*, illustrated by Emma Chadwick (Kalamus); (children's interactive) Matthew Reinhart for *Star Wars: The Ultimate Pop-Up Galaxy*, illustrated by Kevin M. Wilson (Insight Editions).

Indies Choice Book Awards. Chosen by owners and staff of American Booksellers Association member bookstores. *Winner:* Not awarded in 2020.

International Booker Prize (United Kingdom) (£50,000). To the author and translator of a work translated into English. *Offered by:* Crankstart. *Winner:* Marieke Lucas Rijneveld for *The Discomfort of Evening*, translated by Michele Hutchison (Faber & Faber).

International Prize for Arabic Fiction ($50,000 and publication in English). To reward excellence in contemporary Arabic creative writing. *Sponsors:* Booker Prize Foundation, Emirates Foundation for Philanthropy. *Winner:* Abdelouahab Aissaoui (Algeria) for *The Spartan Court* (Dar Min).

Rona Jaffe Foundation Writers' Awards ($30,000 each). To identify and support women writers of exceptional talent in the early stages of their careers. *Offered by:* Rona Jaffe Foundation. *Winners:* (nonfiction) Hannah Bae; (fiction) Mari Christmas, Yalitza Ferreras, Temim Fruchter; (poetry) Elisa Gonzalez, Charleen McClure.

Jerusalem Prize (Israel). Awarded biennially to a writer whose works best express the theme of freedom of the individual in society. *Offered by:* Jerusalem International Book Fair. *Winner (2019):* Joyce Carol Oates.

Jewish Book Council Awards. *Winners:* (Jewish Book of the Year) Jonathan Sacks for *Morality: Restoring the Common Good in Divided Times* (Basic Books); (American Jewish studies) Laura Arnold Leibman for

The Art of the Jewish Family: A History of Women in Early New York in Five Objects (Bard Graduate Center); (autobiography and memoir) Ariana Neumann for When Time Stopped: A Memoir of My Father's War and What Remains (Scribner); (biography) Nancy Sinkoff for From Left to Right: Lucy S. Dawidowicz, the New York Intellectuals, and the Politics of Jewish History (Wayne State University Press); (book club award) Max Gross for The Lost Shtetl (HarperVia); (children's picture book) Lesléa Newman for Welcoming Elijah: A Passover Tale with a Tail, illustrated by Susan Gal (Charlesbridge); (contemporary Jewish life and practice) Arthur Green for Judaism for the World: Reflections on God, Life, and Love (Yale University Press); (debut fiction) Rachel Beanland for Florence Adler Swims Forever (Simon & Schuster); (education and Jewish identity) Sarah Bunin Benor, Jonathan B. Krasner, and Sharon Avni for Hebrew Infusion: Language and Community at American Jewish Summer Camps (Rutgers University Press); (fiction) Colum McCann for Apeirogon (Random House); (food writing and cookbooks) Monday Morning Cooking Club for Now for Something Sweet (HarperCollins); (history) Laura Arnold Leibman for The Art of the Jewish Family: A History of Women in Early New York in Five Objects (Bard Graduate Center); (Holocaust) Faris Cassell for The Unanswered Letter: One Holocaust Family's Desperate Plea for Help (Regnery Publishing); (middle grade literature) Anne Blankman for The Blackbird Girls (Viking Books for Young Readers); (modern Jewish thought and experience) Jonathan Sacks for Morality: Restoring the Common Good in Divided Times (Basic Books); (poetry) Lisa Richter for Nautilus and Bone (Frontenac House); (scholarship) Sarit Kattan Gribetz for Time and Difference in Rabbinic Judaism (Princeton University Press); (Sephardic culture) Devi Mays for Forging Ties, Forging Passports: Migration and the Modern Sephardi Diaspora (Stanford University Press); (women's studies) Laura Arnold Leibman for The Art of the Jewish Family: A History of Women in Early New York in Five Objects (Bard Graduate Center); (writing based on archival material) Magda Teter for Blood

Libel: On the Trail of an Antisemitic Myth (Harvard University Press); (young adult literature) Gavriel Savit for The Way Back (Knopf Books for Young Readers).

Sue Kaufman Prize for First Fiction ($5,000). For a work of first fiction (novel or short stories). Offered by: American Academy of Arts and Letters. Winner: Isabella Hammad for The Parisian (Grove Press).

Ezra Jack Keats Awards. For children's picture books. Offered by: New York Public Library and the Ezra Jack Keats Foundation. Winners: (writer award) Sydney Smith for Small in the City (Neal Porter Books / Holiday House Publishing); (illustrator award) Ashleigh Corrin for Layla's Happiness, written by Mariahdessa Ekere Tallie (Enchanted Lion Books).

Kerlan Award. To recognize singular attainments in the creation of children's literature and in appreciation for generous donation of unique resources to the Kerlan Collection for the study of children's literature. Offered by: Kerlan Children's Literature Research Collections, University of Minnesota. Winner: Jon Scieszka.

Coretta Scott King Book Awards ($1,000). To an African American author and illustrator of outstanding books for children and young adults. Offered by: American Library Association, Ethnic and Multicultural Exchange Round Table (EMIERT). Winners: (author) Jerry Craft for New Kid (HarperCollins Children's Books); (illustrator) Kadir Nelson for The Undefeated, written by Kwame Alexander (Versity / Houghton Mifflin Harcourt).

Coretta Scott King/Virginia Hamilton Award for Lifetime Achievement. Given in even-numbered years to an African American author, illustrator, or author / illustrator for a body of books for children or young adults. In odd-numbered years, the award honors substantial contributions through active engagement with youth, using award-winning African American literature for children or young adults. Winner: Mildred D. Taylor.

Coretta Scott King/John Steptoe Award for New Talent. To offer visibility to a writer and illustrator at the beginning of their careers. Sponsor: Coretta Scott King Book Award Committee. Winners: (author) Alicia

D. Williams for *Genesis Begins Again* (Atheneum Books for Young Readers); (illustrator) April Harrison for *What Is Given from the Heart*, written by Patricia C. McKissack (Schwartz & Wade Books).

Kirkus Prize ($50,000). For outstanding fiction, nonfiction, and young readers literature. *Offered by: Kirkus Reviews. Winners:* (fiction) Raven Leilani for *Luster* (Farrar, Straus and Giroux); (nonfiction) Mychal Denzel Smith for *Stakes Is High: Life After the American Dream* (Bold Type Books); (young readers) Derrick Barnes (author) and Gordon C. James (illustrator) for *I Am Every Good Thing* (Nancy Paulsen Books).

Lambda Literary Awards. To honor outstanding lesbian, gay, bisexual, and transgender (LGBT) literature. *Offered by:* Lambda Literary Foundation. *Winners:* (lesbian fiction) Nicole Dennis-Benn for *Patsy* (Liveright Publishing); (gay fiction) Bryan Washington for *Lot* (Riverhead Books); (bisexual fiction) Fiona Alison Duncan for *Exquisite Mariposa* (Soft Skull Press); (transgender fiction) Hazel Jane Plante for *Little Blue Encyclopedia (for Vivian)* (Metonymy Press); (bisexual nonfiction) Trisha Low for *Socialist Realism* (Coffee House Press); (transgender nonfiction) Ellis Martin and Zach Ozma for *We Both Laughed in Pleasure: The Selected Diaries of Lou Sullivan* (Nightboat Books); (LGBTQ nonfiction) Carmen Maria Machado for *In the Dream House* (Graywolf Press); (lesbian poetry) t'ai freedom ford for *& more black* (Augury Books); (gay poetry) Cyrée Jarelle Johnson for *SLINGSHOT* (Nightboat Books); (bisexual poetry) Stephanie Young for *Pet Sounds* (Nightboat Books); (transgender poetry) Xandria Phillips for *HULL* (Nightboat Books); (lesbian mystery) Ann McMan for *Galileo* (Bywater Books); (gay mystery) Michael Nava for *Carved in Bone: A Henry Rios Novel* (Persigo Press); (lesbian memoir / biography) Samra Habib for *We Have Always Been Here: A Queer Muslim Memoir* (Viking Canada); (gay memoir / biography) Saeed Jones for *How We Fight for Our Lives* (Simon & Schuster); (lesbian romance) Emily Noon for *Aurora's Angel: A Dark Fantasy Romance* (Bluefire Books); (gay romance) James Lovejoy for *Joseph Chapman: My Molly Life*

(self-published); (LGBTQ anthology) (tie) Aishah Shahidah Simmons (editor) for *Love WITH Accountability: Digging Up the Roots of Child Sexual Abuse* (AK Press) and Noam Sienna for *A Rainbow Thread: An Anthology of Queer Jewish Texts from the First Century to 1969* (Print-O-Craft); (children's / middle grade) Lisa Jenn Bigelow for *Hazel's Theory of Evolution* (HarperCollins); (young adult) Alexandra Villasante for *The Grief Keeper* (G.P. Putnam's Sons Books for Young Readers); (comics) Kelsey Wroten for *Cannonball* (Uncivilized Books); (drama) Michael R. Jackson for *A Strange Loop* (Theatre Communications Group, produced by Playwrights Horizons and Page 73); (erotica) LA Warman for *Whore Foods* (Inpatient Press); (science fiction / fantasy / horror) Rivers Solomon with Davced Diggs, William Hutson, and Jonathan Snipes for *The Deep* (Gallery / Saga Press); (studies) Emily L. Thuma for *All Our Trials: Prisons, Policing, and the Feminist Fight to End Violence* (University of Illinois Press).

Harold Morton Landon Translation Award ($1,000). For a book of verse translated into English. *Offered by:* Academy of American Poets. *Winner:* Rajiv Mohabir for *I Even Regret Night: Holi Songs of Demerara* by Lalbihari Sharma (Kaya Press).

David J. Langum, Sr. Prize in American Historical Fiction ($1,000). To honor a book of historical fiction published in the previous year. *Offered by:* Langum Foundation. *Winner:* Not awarded in 2020.

David J. Langum, Sr. Prize in American Legal History or Biography ($1,000). For a university press book that is accessible to the educated general public, rooted in sound scholarship, with themes that touch upon matters of general concern. *Offered by:* Langum Foundation. *Winner:* Not awarded in 2020.

Latner Writers' Trust Poetry Prize (C$25,000) (Canada). To a writer with an exceptional body of work in the field of poetry. *Offered by:* Writers' Trust of Canada. *Sponsor:* Latner Family Foundation. *Winner:* Armand Garnet Ruffo.

James Laughlin Award ($5,000). To commend and support a second book of poetry. *Offered by:* Academy of American Poets.

Winner: Chet'la Sebree for *Field Study* (FSG Originals).

Library of Congress Prize for American Fiction. To an author for a body of extraordinary work. *Winner:* Colson Whitehead.

Claudia Lewis Award. For the best poetry book. *Offered by:* Bank Street College of Education. *Winner:* David Elliott for *Voices: The Final Hours of Joan of Arc* (Houghton Mifflin Harcourt Books for Young Readers).

Ruth Lilly and Dorothy Sargent Rosenberg Poetry Fellowships ($25,800). To emerging poets to support their continued study and writing of poetry. *Offered by:* The Poetry Foundation. *Winners:* Isabella Borgeson, Luther Hughes, Cyrée Jarelle Johnson, Darius Simpson, and Khaty Xiong.

Ruth Lilly Poetry Prize ($100,000). To a U.S. poet in recognition of lifetime achievement. *Offered by:* The Poetry Foundation. *Winner:* Marilyn Chin.

Astrid Lindgren Memorial Award (Sweden) (5 million kroner, more than $575,000). In memory of children's author Astrid Lindgren, to honor outstanding children's literature and efforts to promote it. *Offered by:* Government of Sweden and the Swedish Arts Council. *Winner:* Baek Heena.

LITA Excellence in Children's and Young Adult Science Fiction. *Sponsor:* Library and Information Technology Association. *Winners:* (Golden Duck Notable Picture Books List) John Hare for *Field Trip to the Moon* (Margaret Ferguson Books); Aiko Ikegami for *Hello* (Creston Books); Viviane Schwarz for *How to Be on the Moon* (Candlewick Press); Tom Sullivan for *Out There* (Balzer + Bray); Stephen Savage for *The Babysitter from Another Planet* (Neal Porter Books); Brian Biggs for *The Space Walk* (Dial Books for Young Readers); Josh Schneider for *Ultrabot's First Playdate* (Clarion Books); Sergio Ruzzier for *Good Boy* (Atheneum Books); Jonathan Stutzman (author) and Heather Fox (illustrator) for *Llama Destroys the World* (Henry Holt & Co.). (Eleanor Cameron Notable Middle Grade Books List) Justin Dean for *Awesome Dog 5000* (Random House Books for Young Readers); Greg van Eekhout for *Cog* (HarperCollins); Molly Brooks for *Field Trip* (Sanity and Tallulah #2) (Disney Hyperion); M. M. Vaughan for *Friendroid* (Margaret K. McElderry Books);

Johnny Marciano and Emily Chenoweth for *Klawde: Evil Alien Warlord Cat* (Penguin Workshop); Angie Sage for *Maximillian Fly* (Katherine Tegen Books); Ronald L. Smith for *The Owls Have Come to Take Us Away* (Clarion Books); Margaret Peterson Haddix for *The Greystone Secrets #1: The Strangers* (Katherine Tegen Books); Geoff Rodkey for *We're Not from Here* (Crown Books for Young Readers); Eliot Sappingfield for *The Unspeakable Unknown* (G.P. Putnam's Sons Books for Young Readers); Joshua S. Levy for *Seventh Grade vs the Galaxy* (Carolrhoda Books). (Hal Clement Notable Young Adult Books List) Mira Grant for *Alien: Echo* (Imprint); Amie Kaufman and Jay Kristoff for *Aurora Rising* (Knopf Books for Young Readers); Suzanne Young for *Girls with Sharp Sticks* (Simon Pulse); Barry Lyga and Morgan Baden for *The Hive* (Kids Can Press); Bridget Tyler for *The Pioneer* (HarperTeen); Alexander Yates for *How We Became Wicked* (Atheneum / Caitlyn Dlouhy Books); S. E. Grove for *The Waning Age* (Viking Books for Young Readers); Victoria Lee for *The Fever King* (Skyscape); Tochi Onyebuchi for *War Girls* (Razorbill); Farah Rishi for *I Hope You Get This Message* (HarperTeen); Rachel Caine and Ann Aguirre for *Honor Bound* (Katherine Tegen Books).

Locus Awards. For science fiction writing. *Offered by:* Locus Publications. *Winners:* (science fiction) Charlie Jane Anders for *The City in the Middle of the Night* (Tor / Titan); (fantasy) Seanan McGuire for *Middlegame* (Tor.com Publishing); (horror) Marlon James for *Black Leopard, Red Wolf* (Riverhead Books / Hamish Hamilton); (young adult) Yoon Ha Lee for *Dragon Pearl* (Disney Hyperion); (first novel) Tamsyn Muir for *Gideon the Ninth* (Tor.com Publishing); (novella) Amal El-Mohtar and Max Gladstone for *This Is How You Lose the Time War* (Saga Press); (novelette) Ted Chiang for "Omphalos" in *Exhalation: Stories* (Knopf / Picador); (short story) Charlie Jane Anders for "The Bookstore at the End of America" in *A People's Future of the United States: Speculative Fiction from 25 Extraordinary Writers* (One World); (anthology) Nisi Shawl (ed.) for *New Suns: Original Speculative Fiction by People of*

Color (Solaris); (collection) Ted Chiang for *Exhalation: Stories* (Knopf / Picador); (nonfiction) Lisa Kröger and Melanie R. Anderson for *Monster, She Wrote: The Women Who Pioneered Horror and Speculative Fiction* (Quirk); (art book) John Fleskes (ed.) for *Spectrum 26: The Best in Contemporary Fantastic Art* (Flesk).
Lodestar Award for Best Young Adult Book). See Hugo Awards.
Elizabeth Longford Prize for Historical Biography (United Kingdom) (£5,000). *Sponsors:* Flora Fraser and Peter Soros. *Winner:* D.W. Hayton for *Conservative Revolutionary: The Lives of Lewis Namier* (Manchester University Press).
Los Angeles Times Book Prizes. To honor literary excellence. *Offered by: Los Angeles Times. Winners:* (Art Seidenbaum Award for First Fiction) Namwali Serpell for *The Old Drift* (Hogarth); (biography) George Packer for *Our Man: Richard Holbrooke and the End of the American Century* (Knopf); (Christopher Isherwood Prize for Autobiographical Prose) Emily Bernard for *Black Is the Body: Stories from My Grandmother's Time, My Mother's Time, and Mine* (Knopf); (current interest) Emily Bazelon for *Charged: The New Movement to Transform American Prosecution and End Mass Incarceration* (Random House); (fiction) Ben Lerner for *The Topeka School* (Farrar, Straus and Giroux); (graphic novel / comics) Eleanor Davis for *The Hard Tomorrow* (Drawn & Quarterly); (history) Stephanie E. Jones-Rogers for *They Were Her Property: White Women as Slave Owners in the American South* (Yale University Press); (mystery / thriller) Steph Cha for *Your House Will Pay* (Ecco); (poetry) Ilya Kaminsky for *Deaf Republic* (Graywolf Press); (Ray Bradbury Prize for Science Fiction, Fantasy & Speculative Fiction) Marlon James for *Black Leopard, Red Wolf* (Riverhead Books); (science & technology) Maria Popova for *Figuring* (Knopf); (young adult literature) Malla Nunn for *When the Ground Is Hard* (G.P. Putnam's Sons Books for Young Readers).
Amy Lowell Poetry Traveling Scholarship. For one or two U.S. poets to spend one year outside North America in a country the recipients feel will most advance their work.

Offered by: Amy Lowell Poetry Traveling Scholarship. *Winner:* Austin Smith.
Walter & Lillian Lowenfels Criticism Award. *Offered by:* Before Columbus Foundation. *Winner: Appalachian Reckoning: A Region Responds to Hillbilly Elegy*, edited by Anthony Harkins and Meredith McCarroll (West Virginia University Press).
J. Anthony Lukas Awards. For nonfiction writing that demonstrates literary grace, serious research, and concern for an important aspect of American social or political life. *Offered by:* Columbia University Graduate School of Journalism and the Nieman Foundation for Journalism at Harvard. *Winners:* (Lukas Book Prize, $10,000) Alex Kotlowitz for *An American Summer: Love and Death in Chicago* (Nan A. Talese / Doubleday); (Mark Lynton History Prize, $10,000) Kerri K. Greenidge for *Black Radical: The Life and Times of William Monroe Trotter* (Liveright); (Work-in-Progress Award, two prizes of $25,000 each) Bartow J. Elmore for *Seed Money: Monsanto's Past and the Future of Food* (W.W. Norton & Company) and Shahan Mufti for *American Caliph: The True Story of the Hanafi Siege, America's First Homegrown Islamic Terror Attack* (Farrar, Straus and Giroux).
Macavity Awards. For excellence in mystery writing. *Offered by:* Mystery Readers International. *Winners:* (mystery novel) Adrian McKinty for *The Chain* (Mulholland); (first mystery) Tara Laskowski for *One Night Gone* (Graydon House); (nonfiction / critical) John Billheimer for *Hitchcock and the Censors* (University Press of Kentucky); (short story) Art Taylor for "Better Days" in *Ellery Queen's Mystery Magazine* (May / June 2019); (Sue Feder Historical Mystery Award) Lara Prescott for *The Secrets We Kept* (Vintage).
McKitterick Prize (United Kingdom) (£4,000). To an author over the age of 40 for a first novel, published or unpublished. *Winner:* Claire Adam for *Golden Child* (Faber and Faber).
Man Booker International Prize (United Kingdom). See International Booker Prize.
Man Booker Prize for Fiction (United Kingdom). See Booker Prize for Fiction.
Lenore Marshall Poetry Prize ($25,000). For an outstanding book of poems published in the

United States. *Offered by:* Academy of American Poets. *Winner:* Hanif Abdurraqib for *A Fortune for Your Disaster* (Tin House).

Somerset Maugham Awards (United Kingdom) (£2,500). For works in any genre except drama by a writer under the age of 35, to enable young writers to enrich their work by gaining experience of foreign countries. *Winners:* Alex Allison for *The Art of the Body* (Dialogue Books/Little, Brown); Oliver Soden for *Michael Tippet: The Biography* (Weidenfeld and Nicholson/Orion); Roseanne Watt for *Moder Dy* (Birlinn/Polygon); Amrou Al-Kadhi for *My Life as a Unicorn* (4th Estate).

Addison M. Metcalf Award in Literature ($2,000). Awarded biennially in alternation with the Addison M. Metcalf Award in Art. *Winner (2019):* Aracelis Girmay.

Vicky Metcalf Award for Literature for Young People (C$25,000) (Canada). To a Canadian writer of children's literature for a body of work. *Offered by:* Writers' Trust of Canada. *Sponsor:* Metcalf Foundation. *Winner:* Marianne Dubuc.

Midwest Booksellers Choice Awards. *Offered by:* Midwest Independent Booksellers Association. *Winners:* (arts / photography / coffee table) Jeff Morrison for *Guardians of Detroit: Architectural Sculpture in the Motor City* (Wayne State University Press); (autobiography / memoir) Marra B. Gad for *The Color of Love* (Agate Bolden); (business) John Schuler for *Measure Their Feet* (Nodin Press); (children's fiction) Martha Simpson for *Esther's Gragger* (Wisdom Tales Press); (children's nonfiction) Pamela Cameron for *Sport: Ship of the Great Lakes* (Wisconsin Historical Society Press); (children's picture) Bridget Reistad for *Hundredth Day Disaster* (Beaver's Pond Press); (education / learning) (tie) Katherine Quie for *Raising Will* (Wise Ink Creative Publishing) and Rae Pica for *Acting Out! Avoid Behavior Challenges with Active Learning Games and Activities* (Redleaf Press); (family / parenting) Judy Stoffel for *#Lookup: A Parenting Guide to Screen Use* (Wise Ink Creative Publishing); (fantasy / sci-fi / horror / paranormal fiction) Loren Niemi for *What Haunts Us* (Moonfire Publishing); (literary / contemporary / historical fiction) Norman Gautreau for *The Light from the Dark Side of the Moon* (Amphorae Publishing); (mystery / thriller fiction) (tie) Leonard Krishtalka for *Death Spoke* (Anamcara Press) and Jeff Nania for *Figure Eight: A Northern Lakes Mystery* (Little Creek Press); (romance fiction) Frank Weber for *Last Call* (North Star Press); (short story / anthology fiction) Lisa Lenzo for *Unblinking* (Wayne State University Press); (young adult fiction) Ann Dallman for *Cady and the Bear Necklace* (Henschel Haus); (health) Chelsie Knight for *Not Another Breastfeeding Book* (Beaver's Pond Press); (history) Jon Lauck for *The Interior Borderlands* (Center for Western Studies); (regional history) Denise Lajimodiere for *Stringing Rosaries* (North Dakota State University Press); (humor) James Aylott for *Tales from the Beach House* (Beautiful Arch); (inspiration) Kelly Radi for *Wonder-Full: Activate Your Inner Superpowers* (Beaver's Pond Press); (nature) Stephanie Anderson for *One Size Fits None* (University of Nebraska Press); (poetry) Klecko for *Hitman-Baker-Casketmaker* (Paris Morning Publications); (debut poetry) Michelle Lewis for *Animal / Flame* (Conduit Books & Ephemera); (regional poetry) (tie) Laurie Allmann for *An Hour From Now* (Nodin Press) and Todd Davis for *Native Species* (Michigan State University Press); (recreation / sports / travel) Steve Hannah for *Dairylandia* (University of Wisconsin Press); (religion / philosophy) Rebecca Bender for *Still* (North Dakota University Press); (social science / political science / culture) R. Richard Wagner for *We've Been Here All Along* (Wisconsin Historical Society Press)..

William C. Morris YA Debut Award. To honor a debut book published by a first-time author writing for teens and celebrating impressive new voices in young adult literature. *Offered by:* American Library Association, Young Adult Library Services Association. *Donor:* William C. Morris Endowment. *Winner:* Ben Philippe for The Field Guide to the North American Teenager (Balzer + Bray).

Mythopoeic Fantasy Awards. To recognize fantasy or mythic literature for children and adults that best exemplifies the spirit of the Inklings, a group of fantasy writers that includes J. R. R. Tolkien, C. S. Lewis, and Charles Williams. *Offered by:* Mythopoeic

Society. *Winners:* (adult literature) Theodora Goss for *Snow White Learns Witchcraft* (Mythic Delirium); (children's literature) Yoon Ha Lee for *Dragon Pearl* (Disney-Hyperion); (Mythopoeic Scholarship Award in Inklings Studies) Amy Amendt-Raduege for *"The Sweet and the Bitter": Death and Dying in J.R.R. Tolkien's The Lord of the Rings* (Kent State University Press); (Mythopoeic Scholarship Award in Myth and Fantasy Studies) James Gifford for *A Modernist Fantasy: Modernism, Anarchism, and the Radical Fantastic* (ELS).

National Book Awards. To celebrate the best in American literature. *Offered by:* National Book Foundation. *Winners:* (fiction) Charles Yu for *Interior Chinatown* (Pantheon); (nonfiction) Les Payne and Tamara Payne, *The Dead Are Arising: The Life of Malcolm X* (W.W. Norton & Company); (poetry) Don Mee Choi for *DMZ Colony* (Wave Books); (translated literature) Yu Miri for *Tokyo Ueno Station*, translated by Morgan Giles (Riverhead Books); (young people's literature) Kacen Callender for *King of the Fireflies* (Scholastic Press).

National Book Critics Circle Awards. For literary excellence. *Offered by:* National Book Critics Circle. *Winners:* (fiction) Maggie O'Farrell for *Hamnet* (Knopf); (nonfiction) Tom Zoellner for *Island on Fire: The Revolt That Ended Slavery in the British Empire* (Harvard University Press); (biography) Amy Stanley for *Stranger in the Shogun's City: A Japanese Woman and Her World* (Scribner); (autobiography) Cathy Park Hong for *Minor Feelings: An Asian American Reckoning* (One World); (poetry) francine j. harris for *Here Is the Sweet Hand* (Farrar, Straus and Giroux); (criticism) Nicole R. Fleetwood for *Marking Time: Art in the Age of Mass Incarceration* (Harvard University Press); (John Leonard Prize) Raven Leilani for *Luster* (Farrar, Straus and Giroux); (Nona Balakian Citation for Excellence in Reviewing) Jo Livingstone; (Ivan Sandrof Lifetime Achievement Award) The Feminist Press at the City University of New York.

National Book Foundation Literarian Award for Outstanding Service to the American Literary Community. *Offered by:* National Book Foundation. *Winner:* Carolyn Reidy.

National Book Foundation Medal for Distinguished Contribution to American Letters ($10,000). To a person who has enriched the nation's literary heritage over a life of service or corpus of work. *Offered by:* National Book Foundation. *Winner:* Walter Mosley.

National Translation Awards ($5,000). To honor translators whose work has made a valuable contribution to literary translation into English. *Offered by:* American Literary Translators Association. *Winners:* (prose) Jordan Stump, translator from French, for *The Cheffe: A Cook's Novel* by Marie NDiaye (Knopf); (poetry) Jake Levine, Soeun Seo, and Hedgie Choi, translators from Korean, for *Hysteria* by Kim Yideum (Action Books).

Nebula Awards. For science fiction writing. *Offered by:* Science Fiction and Fantasy Writers of America (SFWA). *Winners:* (novel) Sarah Pinsker for *A Song for a New Day* (Berkley); (novella) Amal El-Mohtar and Max Gladstone for *This Is How You Lose the Time War* (Saga Press); (novelette) Cat Rambo for *Carpe Glitter* (Meerkat Shorts, LLC); (short story) A. T. Greenblatt for "Give the Family My Love" (published in *Clarkesworld*); (Ray Bradbury Award for dramatic presentation) Neil Gaiman for "Hard Times" episode of *Good Omens* (Amazon Studios and BBC Studios); (Andre Norton Award for young adult science fiction and fantasy) Fran Wilde for *Riverland* (Harry N. Abrams).

John Newbery Medal. For the most distinguished contribution to literature for children. *Offered by:* American Library Association, Association for Library Service to Children. *Winner:* Jerry Craft for *New Kid* (HarperCollins Children's Books).

Nibbies (United Kingdom). See British Book Awards.

Nimrod Literary Awards ($2,000 plus publication). *Offered by:* Nimrod International Journal of Prose and Poetry. *Winners:* (Pablo Neruda Prize in Poetry) Rebecca Foust for "Blackout" and other poems; (Katherine Anne Porter Prize in Fiction) Mohit Manohar for "This Has Not Been Enough."

Nobel Prize in Literature (Sweden). For the total literary output of a distinguished career. *Offered by:* Swedish Academy. *Winner:* Louise Glück.

Eli M. Oboler Memorial Award. Given biennially to an author of a published work in English or in English translation dealing with issues, events, questions, or controversies in the area of intellectual freedom. *Offered by:* Intellectual Freedom Round Table, American Library Association. *Winner (2020):* Henry Reichman for *The Future of Academic Freedom* (Johns Hopkins University Press).

Flannery O'Connor Awards for Short Fiction. For collections of short fiction. *Offered by:* University of Georgia Press. *Winner:* Kate McIntyre for *Mad Prairie* (University of Georgia Press).

Oddest Book Title of the Year Award. See Bookseller / Diagram Prize for Oddest Title of the Year.

Scott O'Dell Award for Historical Fiction ($5,000). *Offered by: Bulletin of the Center for Children's Books,* University of Chicago. *Winner:* Thanhhà Lại for *Butterfly Yellow* (HarperCollins).

Odyssey Award. To the producer of the best audiobook for children and / or young adults available in English in the United States. *Sponsors:* American Library Association, ALSC/Booklist/YALSA. *Winner:* Scholastic Audiobooks for *Hey, Kiddo: How I Lost My Mother, Found My Father, and Dealt with Family Addiction* by Jarrett J. Krosoczka, narrated by Jarrett J. Krosoczka, Jeanne Birdsall, Jenna Lamia, Richard Ferrone, and a full cast.

Seán Ó Faoláin Short Story Competition (€2,000 and publication in the literary journal *Southword). Offered by:* Munster Literature Centre, Cork, Ireland. *Winner:* Ben Fergusson for "A Navigable River."

Dayne Ogilvie Prize (C$4,000) (Canada). To an emerging Canadian writer from the LGBT community who demonstrates promise through a body of quality work. *Offered by:* Writers' Trust of Canada. *Winner:* Arielle Twist.

Orbis Pictus Award for Outstanding Nonfiction for Children. *Offered by:* National Council of Teachers of English. *Winner:* Barry Wittenstein for *A Place to Land: Martin Luther King Jr. and the Speech That Inspired a Nation,* illustrated by Jerry Pinkney (Holiday House).

Oxford-Weidenfeld Translation Prize. *Winner:* David Hackston for his translation from Finnish of *Crossing* by Pajtim Statovci (Pushkin Press).

PEN Award for Poetry in Translation ($3,000). For a book-length translation of poetry from any language into English, published in the United States. *Offered by:* PEN American Center. *Winners:* Kristin Dykstra and Nancy Gates Madsen for their translation from Spanish of *The Winter Garden Photograph* by Reina María Rodríguez (Ugly Duckling Presse).

PEN / Saul Bellow Award for Achievement in American Fiction ($25,000). Awarded biennially to a distinguished living American author of fiction. *Offered by:* PEN American Center. *Winner (2020):* To be announced.

PEN/ Bellwether Prize for Socially Engaged Fiction ($25,000). Awarded biennially to the author of a previously unpublished novel that addresses issues of social justice and the impact of culture and politics on human relationships. *Founder:* Barbara Kingsolver. *Winner (2019):* Katherine Seligman for *At the Edge of the Haight* (Algonquin).

PEN Beyond Margins Awards. See PEN Open Book Awards.

PEN / Robert W. Bingham Prize ($25,000). To a writer whose first novel or short story collection represents distinguished literary achievement and suggests great promise. *Offered by:* PEN American Center. *Winner:* Mimi Lok for *Last of Her Name* (Kaya Press).

PEN /Robert J. Dau Short Story Prize for Emerging Writers ($2,000 to 12 writers). To recognize 12 emerging fiction writers for their debut short stories. *Offered by:* PEN American Center. *Winners:* Damitri Martinez for "Bat Outta Hell" in *Foglifter Journal*; Valerie Hegarty for "Cats vs. Cancer" in *New England Review*; Sena Moon for "Dog Dreams" in *Quarterly West*; Matthew Jeffrey Vegari for "Don't Go to Strangers" in *Zyzzyva*; Ani Sison Cooney for "Evangelina Concepcion" in *Epiphany*; Willa Richards for "Failure to Thrive" in *The Paris Review*; Kristen Sahaana Surya for "Gauri Kalyanam" in *The Rumpus*; Mbozi Haimbe for "Madam's Sister" in *Granta*; Mohit Manohar for "Summertime" in *Michigan Quarterly Review*; Shannon Sanders for "The Good, Good Men" in *Puerto del Sol*, Black Voices Series; David Kelly Lawrence for "The Other Child" in *The Threepenny Review*; Kikuko Tsumura for "The Water Tower and the Turtle," translated by Polly Barton, in *Granta*.

PEN / Diamonstein-Spielvogel Award for the Art of the Essay ($10,000). For a book of essays by a single author that best exemplifies the dignity and esteem of the essay form. *Winner:* Deborah Fleming for *Resurrection of the Wild: Meditations on Ohio's Natural Landscape* (Kent State University Press).

PEN / ESPN Award for Literary Sports Writing. To honor a nonfiction book on the subject of sports. Award discontinued.

PEN/ ESPN Lifetime Achievement Award for Literary Sports Writing. For a writer whose body of work represents an exceptional contribution to the field. Award discontinued.

PEN /Faulkner Award for Fiction ($15,000). To honor the year's best work of fiction published by an American. *Winner:* Chloe Aridjis for *Sea Monsters* (Catapult).

PEN /John Kenneth Galbraith Award for Nonfiction ($10,000). Given biennially for a distinguished book of general nonfiction. *Offered by:* PEN American Center. *Winner (2019):* Bernice Yeung for *In a Day's Work* (The New Press).

PEN Grant for the English Translation of Italian Literature ($5,000). *Winner:* Minna Zallman Proctor for her translation of *The Renegade: Natalia Ginzburg, Her Life and Writing* by Sandra Petrignani.

PEN / Heim Translation Fund Grants ($2,000–$4,000). To support the translation of book-length works of fiction, creative nonfiction, poetry, or drama that have not previously appeared in English or have appeared only in an egregiously flawed translation. *Winners:* Curtis Bauer, Fiona Bell, Kevin Gerry Dunn, Dawn Fulton, Anton Hur, Yarri Kamara, Johnny Lorenz, Shabnam Nadiya, Quyen Nguyen Hoang, Jacob Rogers, Minna Zallman Proctor.

PEN /Ernest Hemingway Foundation Award. For a distinguished work of first fiction by an American. *Offered by:* PEN New England. *Winner:* Ruchika Tomar for *A Prayer for Travelers* (Riverhead Books).

PEN /O. Henry Prize. For short stories of exceptional merit, in English, published in U.S. and Canadian magazines. *Winners:* Tessa Hadley for "Funny Little Snake" in *The New Yorker*;

John Keeble for "Synchronicity" in *Harper's Magazine*; Moira McCavana for "No Spanish" in *Harvard Review*; Rachel Kondo for "Girl of Few Seasons" in *Ploughshares Solos*; Sarah Shun-lien Bynum for "Julia and Sunny" in *Ploughshares*; Stephanie Reents for "Unstuck" in *Witness*; Alexia Arthurs for "Mermaid River" in *The Sewanee Review*; Valerie O'Riordan for "Bad Girl" in *LitMag*; Patricia Engel for "Aguacero" in *Kenyon Review*; Kenan Orhan for "Soma" in *The Massachusetts Review*; Sarah Hall for "Goodnight Nobody" in *One Story*; Bryan Washington for "610 North, 610 West" in *Tin House*; Isabella Hammad for "Mr. Can'aan" in *The Paris Review*; Weike Wang for "Omakase" in *The New Yorker*; Caoilinn Hughes for "Prime" in *Granta.com*; Souvankham Thammavongsa for "Slingshot" in *Harper's Magazine*; Liza Ward for "The Shrew Tree" in *Zyzzyva*; Doua Thao for "Flowers for America" in *Fiction*; Alexander MacLeod for "Lagomorph" in *Granta*; John Edgar Wideman for "Maps and Ledgers" in *Harper's Magazine*.

PEN / Nora Magid Award ($2,500). Awarded biennially to honor a magazine editor who has contributed significantly to the excellence of the publication he or she edits. *Winner (2019):* Alexandra Watson for *Apogee*.

PEN /Malamud Award. To recognize a body of work that demonstrates excellence in the art of short fiction. *Winner:* Lydia Davis.

PEN / Ralph Manheim Medal for Translation. Given triennially to a translator whose career has demonstrated a commitment to excellence. *Winner (2018):* Barbara Harshav.

PEN /Nabokov Award for Achievement in International Literature ($50,000). To a writer of any genre and of any nationality for their exceptional body of work. *Winner:* M. Nourbese Philip.

PEN / Phyllis Naylor Working Writer Fellowship ($5,000). To a published author of children's or young adult fiction to aid in completing a book-length work in progress. *Offered by:* PEN American Center. *Winner:* Tiffany Parks for *Saving Caravaggio* (work-in-progress).

PEN / Mike Nichols Writing for Performance Award ($25,000). To a writer whose work exemplifies excellence and influence in the world of theater, television, or film. *Winner:* Tom Stoppard.

PEN Open Book Award (formerly PEN Beyond Margins Award) ($5,000). For book-length writings by authors of color, published in the United States during the current calendar year. *Offered by:* PEN American Center. *Winner:* Brandon Shimoda for *The Grave on the Wall* (City Lights Books).

PEN / Joyce Osterweil Award for Poetry ($5,000). A biennial award given in odd-numbered years to recognize a new and emerging American poet. *Offered by:* PEN American Center. *Winner (2019):* Jonah Mixon-Webster.

PEN /Laura Pels International Foundation for Theater Award. To a playwright working at the highest level of achievement in midcareer. *Offered by:* PEN American Center. *Winner:* Tanya Barfield.

PEN / Jean Stein Book Award ($75,000). To recognize a book-length work of any genre for its originality, merit, and impact. *Winner:* Yiyun Li for *Where Reasons End* (Random House).

PEN / Jean Stein Grant for Literary Oral History ($10,000). For a literary work of nonfiction that uses oral history to illuminate an event, individual, place, or movement. *Winner:* Sharony Green for *The Baa Haas* (work-in-progress).

PEN Translation Prize ($3,000). To promote the publication and reception of translated world literature in English. *Winner:* Allison Markin Powell for her translation from Japanese of *The Ten Loves of Nishino* by Hiromi Kawakami (Europa Editions).

PEN / Edward and Lily Tuck Award for Paraguayan Literature ($3,000 author and $3,000 to translator). Given in even-numbered years to the living author of a major work of Paraguayan literature. *Winner (2020):* Liz Haedo for *Pieles de Papel* (Arandura).

PEN /Voelcker Award for Poetry. Given in even-numbered years to an American poet at the height of his or her powers. *Offered by:* PEN American Center. *Winner (2020):* Rigoberto González.

PEN / Jacqueline Bograd Weld Award for Biography ($5,000). To the author of a distinguished biography published in the United States during the previous calendar year. *Offered by:* PEN American Center. *Winner:* Jacquelyn Dowd Hall for *Sisters and Rebels: A Struggle for the Soul of America* (W.W. Norton & Company).

PEN / E. O. Wilson Literary Science Writing Award ($10,000). For a book of literary nonfiction on the subject of the physical and biological sciences. *Winner:* Frans de Waal for *Mama's Last Hug: Animal Emotions and What They Tell Us about Ourselves* (W.W. Norton & Company).

Maxwell E. Perkins Award. To honor an editor, publisher, or agent who has discovered, nurtured, and championed writers of fiction in the United States. *Offered by:* Center for Fiction, Mercantile Library of New York. *Winner:* Lynn Nesbit.

Aliki Perroti and Seth Frank Most Promising Young Poet Award ($1,000). For a student poet 23 years old or younger. *Offered by:* Academy of American Poets. *Winner:* Ira Goga for "The Kitchen, Indexed."

Phoenix Awards. To the authors of English-language children's books that failed to win a major award at the time of publication 20 years earlier. *Winner:* Carolyn Coman for *Many Stones* (Namelos).

Edgar Allan Poe Awards. See Edgar Awards.

Poets Out Loud Prize ($1,000 and publication by Fordham University Press). For a book-length poetry collection. *Sponsor:* Fordham University. *Winners:* Sarah Mangold for *Her Wilderness Will Be Her Manners* (Fordham Press); (editor's prize) Stephanie Ellis Schlaifer for *Well Waiting Room* (Fordham Press).

Katherine Anne Porter Award. See American Academy of Arts and Letters Katherine Anne Porter Award.

Michael L. Printz Award. For excellence in literature for young adults. *Offered by:* American Library Association, Young Adult Library Services Association. *Winner:* A. S. King for *Dig* (Dutton Books for Young Readers).

V. S. Pritchett Short Story Prize (United Kingdom) (£1,000). For a previously unpublished short story. *Offered by:* Royal Society of Literature. *Winner:* Kate Lockwood Jefford for "Picasso's Face."

Pritzker Military Library Literature Award ($100,000). To recognize a living author for a body of work that has profoundly enriched the public understanding of American military history. *Sponsor:* Tawani Foundation. *Winner:* Col. David M. Glantz.

Prix Aurora Awards (Canada). For science fiction. *Offered by:* Canadian SF & Fantasy Association. *Winners:* (novel) Julie E. Czerneda for *The Gossamer Mage* (DAW Books); (young adult novel) Susan Forest for *Bursts of Fire* (Laksa Media Groups); (short fiction) Amal El-Mohtar and Max Gladstone for *This Is How You Lose the Time War* (Saga Press); (related work) Diane L. Walton (managing ed.) for *On Spec* magazine; (graphic novel) S. M. Beiko for *Krampus Is My Boyfriend!* (Webcomic); (poem / song) (tie) Swati Chavda for "At the Edge of Space and Time" in *Love at the Speed of Light* (Ancient Hound Books) and Sora for "Bursts of Fire"; (artist) Dan O'Driscoll; (visual presentation) Steve Blackman for *The Umbrella Academy* (Dark Horse Entertainment)

Prix Goncourt (France). For "the best imaginary prose work of the year." *Offered by:* Société des Gens des Lettres. *Winner:* Hervé Le Tellier for *L'Anomalie* (Gallimard).

PROSE Awards. For outstanding professional and scholarly works. *Offered by:* Association of American Publishers. *Winners:* (biological and life sciences) Oxford University Press for *Clinical Psychopharmacology: Principles and Practice* by S. Nassir Ghaemi; (humanities) Yale University Press for *Leonardo da Vinci Rediscovered* by Carmen C. Bambach; (physical sciences and mathematics) Princeton University Press for *99 Variations on a Proof* by Philip Ording; (reference works) Cambridge University Press for *Roman Architecture and Urbanism: From the Origins to Late Antiquity* by Fikret Yegül and Diane Favro; (social sciences) Stanford University Press for *The Cult of the Constitution* by Mary Anne Franks.

Pulitzer Prizes in Letters ($10,000). To honor distinguished work dealing preferably with American themes. *Offered by:* Columbia University Graduate School of Journalism. *Winners:* (fiction) Colson Whitehead for *The Nickel Boys* (Doubleday); (drama) Michael R. Jackson for *A Strange Loop*; (history) W. Caleb McDaniel for *Sweet Taste of Liberty: A True Story of Slavery and Restitution in America* (Oxford University Press); (biography / autobiography) Benjamin Moser for *Sontag: Her Life and Work* (Ecco); (poetry) Jericho Brown for *The Tradition* (Copper Canyon Press); (general nonfiction) (tie) Greg Grandin for *The End of the Myth: From the Frontier to the Border Wall in the Mind of America* (Metropolitan Books) and Anne Boyer for *The Undying: Pain, Vulnerability, Mortality, Medicine, Art, Time, Dreams, Data, Exhaustion, Cancer, and Care* (Farrar, Straus and Giroux).

Raiziss / De Palchi Translation Award ($10,000 book award and a $25,000 fellowship, awarded in alternate years). For a translation into English of a significant work of modern Italian poetry by a living translator. *Offered by:* Academy of American Poets. *Winner:* (book) Geoffrey Brock for his translation of *Last Dream* by Giovanni Pascoli (World Poetry Books).

RBC Bronwen Wallace Award for Emerging Writers (C$10,000) (Canada). For writers under the age of 35 who are unpublished in book form. *Offered by:* Writers' Trust of Canada. *Sponsor:* Royal Bank of Canada. *Winner:* (short story) Leah Mol for "Six Things My Father Taught Me About Bears" (poetry) Alexa Winik for "Selections from Winter Stars Visible in December."

Arthur Rense Poetry Prize ($20,000). Awarded triennially to an exceptional poet. *Offered by:* American Academy of Arts and Letters. *Winner (2020):* Mary Ruefle.

Harold U. Ribalow Prize. For Jewish fiction published in English. *Sponsor:* Hadassah magazine. *Winner:* Not awarded in 2020.

Rita Awards. *Offered by:* Romance Writers of America. Award postponed.

Rita Golden Heart Awards. For worthy unpublished romance manuscripts. *Offered by:* Romance Writers of America. Award discontinued.

Sami Rohr Prize for Jewish Literature ($100,000). For emerging writers of Jewish literature. *Offered by:* Family of Sami Rohr. *Winner:* Benjamin Balint for *Kafka's Last Trial* (W.W. Norton & Company).

Rosenthal Family Foundation Award ($10,000). To a young writer of considerable literary talent for a work of fiction. *Offered by:* American Academy of Arts and Letters. *Winner:* Valeria Luiselli for *Lost Children Archive* (Knopf).

Royal Society of Literature Benson Medal (United Kingdom). To recognize meritorious works in poetry, fiction, history and belles letters, honoring an entire career. The recipient may be someone who is not a writer but has done conspicuous service to literature. *Winner:* Boyd Tonkin.

Royal Society of Literature Giles St Aubyn Awards for Non-Fiction (United Kingdom). For first-time writers of nonfiction. *Offered by:* Royal Society of Literature. *Winners:* (£10,000) Doreen Cunningham for *Soundings: A Journey with Whales* (Virago); (£5,000) Alice Sherwood for *The Authenticity Playbook* (Harper Collins); (£2,500) Danny Lavelle for *Down and Out: A Journey Through Homelessness* (Wildfire).

Royal Society of Literature Ondaatje Prize (United Kingdom) (£10,000). For a distinguished work of fiction, nonfiction, or poetry evoking the spirit of a place. *Offered by:* Royal Society of Literature. *Winner:* Roger Robinson for *A Portable Paradise* (Peepal Tree Press).

Saltire Society Scotland Literary Awards. To recognize noteworthy work by writers of Scottish descent or living in Scotland, or by anyone who deals with the work or life of a Scot or with a Scottish problem, event, or situation. *Offered by:* Saltire Society. Award postponed.

Carl Sandburg Literary Awards. *Sponsor:* Chicago Public Library Foundation. *Winner:* Isabel Wilkerson; (21st Century Award, for an early career author with ties to Chicago) Nate Marshall.

Schneider Family Book Awards ($5,000). To honor authors and illustrators for books that embody artistic expressions of the disability experience of children and adolescents. *Offered by:* American Library Association. *Donor:* Katherine Schneider. *Winners:* (young children) Sonia Sotomayor (author) and Rafael López (illustrator) for *Just Ask! Be Different, Be Brave, Be You* (Philomel Books); (middle school) Kelly Lynne for *Song for a Whale* (Delacorte Books for Young Readers); (teen) Karol Ruth Silverstein for *Cursed* (Charlesbridge Teen).

Scotiabank Giller Prize (Canada) (C$100,000 first place, C$10,000 to each of the finalists). For the best Canadian novel or short story collection written in English. *Offered by:* Giller Prize Foundation and Scotiabank. *Winner:* Souvankham Thammavongsa for *How to Pronounce Knife* (McClelland & Stewart); (finalists) Gil Adamson for *Ridgerunner* (House of Anansi); David Bergen for *Here the Dark* (Biblioasis); Shani Mootoo for *Polar Vortex* (Book*hug Press); Emily St. John Mandel for *The Glass Hotel* (HarperCollins Publishers Ltd.).

Shamus Awards. To honor mysteries featuring independent private investigators. *Offered by:* Private Eye Writers of America. *Winners:* (hardcover novel) Matt Coyle for *Lost Tomorrows* (Oceanview); (original paperback) James DF Hannah for *Behind the Wall of Sleep* (self-published); (short story) O'Neil De Noux for "Sac-A-Lait Man" in *Ellery Queen's Mystery Magazine* (September / October 2019).

Shelley Memorial Award ($6,000 to $9,000). To a poet or poets living in the United States, chosen on the basis of genius and need. *Offered by:* Poetry Society of America. *Winner:* Rick Barot.

Robert F. Sibert Medal. For the most distinguished informational book for children. *Offered by:* American Library Association, Association for Library Service to Children. *Winners:* Kevin Noble Maillard (author) and Juana Martinez-Neal (illustrator) for *Fry Bread: A Native American Family Story* (Roaring Brook / Holtzbrinck).

Society of Authors Traveling Scholarships (United Kingdom) (£1,600). *Winners:* Luke Brown, Inua Ellams, Georgina Lawton, Neil Rollinson, Ahdaf Soueif.

Spur Awards. *Offered by:* Western Writers of America. *Winners:* (contemporary novel) Shannon Pufahl for *On Swift Horses* (Riverhead Books); (historical novel) Sheldon Russell for *A Forgotten Evil* (Cennan Books / Cynren Press); (traditional novel) Margaret Verble for *Cherokee America* (Houghton Mifflin Harcourt); (historical nonfiction) Pekka Hämäläinen for *Lakota America: A New History of Indigenous Power* (Yale University Press); (contemporary nonfiction) Dayton Duncan and Ken Burns for *Country Music: An Illustrated History* (Alfred A. Knopf); (biography) Diana Allen Kouris for *Nighthawk Rising: A Biography of Accused Cattle Rustler Queen Ann Bassett of Brown's Park* (High Plains Press); (original mass market paperback novel) Reavis Z. Wortham for *Hawke's Target* (Pinnacle / Kensington); (romance novel) C. K. Crigger for *The Yeggman's Apprentice* (Wolfpack Publishing); (juvenile fiction) Sandra Dallas for *Someplace to Call Home* (Sleeping Bear Press); (juvenile nonfiction) David Heska Wanbli Weiden for *Spotted Tail* (Reycraft Books); (storyteller—illustrated children's book) Vaunda Micheaux Nelson (author) and Gordon C. James (illustrator) for *Let 'Er Buck: George Fletcher, the People's Champion* (Carolrhoda Books / Lerner Publishing Group); (short fiction) Michael Zimmer for "The Medicine Robe" in *Contention and Other Frontier Stories* (Five Star Publishing); (short nonfiction) Flannery Burke for "'Worry, USA': Dude Ranch Advertising Looks East, 1915–1945" (*Montana: The Magazine of Western History*); (poem) Mark Sanders for "Three Kinds of Pleasure" in *In a Good Time: Poems by Mark Sanders* (WSC Press); (documentary script) Dayton Duncan for *Country Music: Episode Two: Hard Times (1933–1945)* (WETA-TV / PBS); (drama script) John Fusco for *The Highwaymen* (Netflix); (first nonfiction book) David Crow for *The Pale-Faced Lie: A True Story* (Sandra Jonas Publishing); (first novel) Shannon Pufahl for *On Swift Horses* (Riverhead Books).

Wallace Stevens Award ($100,000). To recognize outstanding and proven mastery in the art of poetry. *Offered by:* Academy of American Poets. *Winner:* Nikky Finney.

Bram Stoker Awards. For superior horror writing. *Offered by:* Horror Writers Association. *Winners (2020):* To be announced. *Winners (2019):* (novel) Owl Goingback for *Coyote Rage* (Independent Legions Publishing); (first novel) Sarah Read for *The Bone Weaver's Orchard* (Trepidatio Publishing); (young adult novel) Nzondi for *Oware Mosaic* (Omnium Gatherum); (graphic novel) Colleen Doran and Neil Gaiman for *Neil Gaiman's Snow, Glass, Apples* (Dark Horse Books); (long fiction) Victor LaValle for *Up from Slavery* in *Weird Tales Magazine* #363 (Weird Tales Inc.); (short fiction) Gwendolyn Kiste for "The Eight People Who Murdered Me (Excerpt from Lucy Westenra's Diary)" in *Nightmare Magazine* (November 2019, Issue 86); (fiction collection) Paul

Tremblay for *Growing Things and Other Stories* (William Morrow); (screenplay) Jordan Peele for *Us* (Monkeypaw Productions, Perfect World Pictures, Dentsu, Fuji Television Network, Universal Pictures); (anthology) Ellen Datlow for *Echoes: The Saga Anthology of Ghost Stories* (Gallery / Saga Press); (nonfiction) Lisa Kröger and Melanie R. Anderson for *Monster, She Wrote: The Women Who Pioneered Horror and Speculative Fiction* (Quirk Books); (short nonfiction) Gwendolyn Kiste for "Magic, Madness, and Women Who Creep: The Power of Individuality in the Work of Charlotte Perkins Gilman" in *Vastarien: A Literary Journal*, Vol. 2, Issue 1; (poetry collection) Linda D. Addison and Alessandro Manzetti for *The Place of Broken Things* (Crystal Lake Publishing).

Stonewall Book Awards. *Offered by:* Gay, Lesbian, Bisexual, and Transgender Round Table, American Library Association. *Winners:* (Barbara Gittings Literature Award) Carolina De Robertis for *Cantoras* (Alfred A. Knopf); (Israel Fishman Nonfiction Award) Saeed Jones for *How We Fight for Our Lives: A Memoir* (Simon & Schuster); (Mike Morgan and Larry Romans Children's and Young Adult Literature Award) Kyle Lukoff (author) and Kaylani Juanita (illustrator) for *When Aidan Became a Brother* (Lee & Low Books Inc.); Dean Atta (author) and Anshika Khullar (illustrator) for *The Black Flamingo* (Hodder Children's Books / Hachette Children's Group).

Story Prize ($20,000). For a collection of short fiction. *Offered by:* Story magazine. *Winner:* Deesha Philyaw for *The Secret Lives of Church Ladies* (West Virginia University Press).

Flora Stieglitz Straus Awards. For nonfiction books that serve as an inspiration to young readers. *Offered by:* Bank Street College of Education and the Florence M. Miller Memorial Fund. *Winners:* (older readers) Andrea Warren for *Enemy Child: The Story of Norman Mineta, A Boy Imprisoned in a Japanese American Internment Camp During World War II* (Margaret Ferguson Books); (younger readers) Ashley Bryan for *Infinite Hope: A Black Artist's Journey from World War II to Peace* (Atheneum / Caitlyn Dlouhy Books).

454 / Distinguished Books

Theodore Sturgeon Memorial Award. For the year's best short science fiction. *Offered by:* Gunn Center for the Study of Science Fiction. *Winner:* Suzanne Palmer for "Waterlines" in *Asimov's Science Fiction* (July / August 2019).

Sunburst Awards for Canadian Literature of the Fantastic (C$1,000). *Winners:* (adult) Silvia Moreno-Garcia for *Gods of Jade and Shadow* (Del Rey); (young adult) Allison Mills for *The Ghost Collector* (Annick Press); (short story) Rebecca Campbell for "The Fourth Trimester Is the Strangest" in *The Magazine of Fantasy and Science Fiction*, May / June 2019.

Sunday Times Audible Short Story Award (United Kingdom) (£30,000). To an author from any country for an English-language story of 6,000 words or less. *Winner:* Niamh Campbell for "Love Many."

Sunday Times Young Writer Award (United Kingdom) (£5,000). For a full-length published or self-published (in book or e-book formats) work of fiction, nonfiction or poetry, by a British or Irish author aged 18–35 years. *Winner:* Jay Bernard for *Surge* (Chatto & Windus).

Tanizaki Prize (Japan) (1 million yen, approximately $8,450). For a full-length work of fiction or drama by a professional writer. *Offered by:* Chuokoron-Shinsha, Inc. *Winner (2020):* To be announced. *Winner (2019):* Kiyoko Murata for *Hizoku*.

RBC Taylor Prize (formerly the Charles Taylor Prize for Literary Nonfiction) (Canada) (C$25,000). To honor a book of creative nonfiction widely available in Canada and written by a Canadian citizen or landed immigrant. *Offered by:* Charles Taylor Foundation. *Winner:* Mark Bourrie for *Bush Runner* (Biblioasis).

Sydney Taylor Book Awards. For a distinguished contribution to Jewish children's literature. *Offered by:* Association of Jewish Libraries. *Winners:* (picture book) Sue Macy (author) and Stacy Innerst (illustrator) for *The Book Rescuer: How a Mensch from Massachusetts Saved Yiddish Literature for Generations to Come* (Paula Wiseman Books / Simon & Schuster Children's Books); (middle grade) R. J. Palacio for *White Bird: A Wonder Story* (Knopf Books for Young Readers); (young adult) Rachel

DeWoskin for *Someday We Will Fly* (Viking / Penguin Young Readers).

Sydney Taylor Manuscript Award ($1,000). For the best fiction manuscript appropriate for readers ages 8–13, both Jewish and non-Jewish, revealing positive aspects of Jewish life, and written by an unpublished author. *Winner:* Not awarded in 2020.

Theatre Library Association Award. See Richard Wall Memorial Award.

Dylan Thomas Prize (United Kingdom) (£30,000). For a published or produced literary work in the English language, written by an author under 30. *Offered by:* Swansea University. *Winner:* Bryan Washington for *Lot* (Atlantic Books).

Henry David Thoreau Prize for Literary Excellence in Nature Writing. *Offered by:* Thoreau Society of Concord. *Winner:* George Schaller.

Thriller Awards. *Offered by:* International Thriller Writers. *Winners:* (hardcover novel) Adrian McKinty for *The Chain* (Mulholland Books); (first novel) Angie Kim for Miracle Creek (Farrar, Straus and Giroux); (paperback original) Dervla McTiernan for *The Scholar* (Penguin Books); (short story) Tara Laskowski for "The Long-Term Tenant" in *Ellery Queen's Mystery Magazine* (July / August 2019); (young adult) Tom Ryan for *Keep This to Yourself* (Albert Whitman & Company); (e-book original novel) Kerry Wilkinson for *Close to You* (Bookouture).

Thurber Prize for American Humor ($5,000). For a humorous book of fiction or nonfiction. *Offered by:* Thurber House. *Winner (2020):* To be announced.

Tom-Gallon Trust Award (United Kingdom) (£1,000). For a short story. *Offered by:* Society of Authors. *Sponsor:* Authors' Licensing and Collecting Society. *Winner:* Wendy Riley for "Eva at the End of the World."

Paul Torday Memorial Prize (United Kingdom) (£1,000). For a first novel by an author aged 60 or over. *Offered by:* Society of Authors. *Winner:* Donald S Murray for *As the Women Lay Dreaming* (Saraband).

Betty Trask Prize and Awards (United Kingdom). To Commonwealth writers under the age of 35 for "romantic or traditional" first novels. *Offered by:* Society of Authors. *Winners:* (Betty Trask Prize, £10,000) Kathryn Hind for *Hitch* (Hamish Hamilton); (Betty

Trask Awards, £2,700) Stacey Halls for *The Familiars* (Zaffre, Bonnier Books UK); Isabella Hammad for *The Parisian* (Jonathan Cape / Vintage); Okeychukwu Nzelu for *The Private Joys of Nnenna Maloney* (Dialogue Books).

Kate Tufts Discovery Award ($10,000). For a first or very early book of poetry by an emerging poet. *Offered by:* Claremont Graduate University. *Winner:* Tiana Clark for *I Can't Talk About the Trees Without the Blood* (University of Pittsburg Press).

Kingsley Tufts Poetry Award ($100,000). For a book of poetry by a midcareer poet. *Offered by:* Claremont Graduate School. *Winner:* Ariana Reines for *A Sand Book* (Tin House Books).

21st Century Award. See Carl Sandburg Literary Awards.

UKLA Children's Book Awards (United Kingdom). *Sponsor:* United Kingdom Literacy Association. *Winners:* (ages 3–6+) Arree Chung for *Mixed* (Macmillan); (ages 7–10+) Alyssa Hollingsworth for *The Eleventh Trade* (Piccadilly Press); (ages 11–14+) Susin Nielsen for *No Fixed Address* (Andersen Press); (information, ages 3–14+) Helaine Becker (author) and Dow Phumiruk (illustrator) for *Counting on Katherine* (Macmillan).

Ungar German Translation Award ($1,000). Awarded biennially for a distinguished literary translation from German into English that has been published in the United States. *Offered by:* American Translators Association. *Winner (2019):* Tim Mohr for his translation of *Sand* by Wolfgang Herrndorf (New York Review Books Classics).

John Updike Award ($10,000). Biennial prize to a writer in midcareer whose work has demonstrated consistent excellence. *Offered by:* American Academy of Arts and Letters. *Winner (2019):* D. A. Powell.

VCU / Cabell First Novelist Award ($5,000). For a first novel published in the previous year. *Offered by:* Virginia Commonwealth University. *Winner:* John Englehardt for *Bloomland* (Dzanc Books).

Harold D. Vursell Memorial Award ($20,000). To a writer whose work merits recognition for the quality of its prose style. *Offered by:* American Academy of Arts and Letters. *Winner:* Alex Kotlowitz.

Amelia Elizabeth Walden Award ($5,000). To honor a book relevant to adolescents that has enjoyed a wide teenage audience. *Sponsor:* Assembly on Literature for Adolescents, National Council of Teachers of English. *Winner:* Julie Berry for *Lovely War* (Viking Books for Young Readers);.

Richard Wall Memorial Award (formerly the Theatre Library Association Award). To honor an English-language book of exceptional scholarship in the field of recorded performance, including motion pictures, television, and radio. *Offered by:* Theatre Library Association. *Winner:* Ian Christie for *Robert Paul and the Origins of British Cinema* (University of Chicago Press).

George Washington Book Prize ($50,000). To recognize an important new book about America's founding era. *Offered by:* Washington College and the Gilder Lehrman Institute of American History. *Winner:* Rick Atkinson for *The British Are Coming: The War for America, Lexington to Princeton, 1775–1777* (Henry Holt).

Hilary Weston Writers' Trust Prize for Nonfiction (C$60,000) (Canada). *Offered by:* Writers' Trust of Canada. *Winner:* Jessica J. Lee for *Two Trees Make a Forest: In Search of My Family's Past Among Taiwan's Mountains and Coasts* (Penguin).

E. B. White Award. See American Academy of Arts and Letters E. B. White Award.

E. B. White Read-Aloud Awards. For children's books with particular appeal as read-aloud books. *Offered by:* American Booksellers Association / Association of Booksellers for Children. *Winners:* Not awarded in 2020.

Whiting Writers' Awards ($50,000). For emerging writers of exceptional talent and promise. *Offered by:* Mrs. Giles Whiting Foundation. *Winners:* (poetry) Aria Aber, Diannely Antigua, Jake Skeets, Genya Turovskaya; (fiction) Andrea Lawlor, Ling Ma, Genevieve Sly Crane; (nonfiction) Jaquira Díaz, Jia Tolentino; (drama) Will Arbery.

Walt Whitman Award ($5,000). To a U.S. poet who has not published a book of poems in a standard edition. *Offered by:* Academy of American Poets. *Winner:* Threa Almontaser for *The Wild Fox of Yemen* (Graywolf Press).

Richard Wilbur Award ($1,000 and publication by University of Evansville Press). For a book-length poetry collection. *Winner:* Aaron Poochigian for "American Divine."

Laura Ingalls Wilder Award. See Children's Literature Legacy Award.

Thornton Wilder Prize for Translation ($20,000). To a practitioner, scholar, or patron who has made a significant contribution to the art of literary translation. *Offered by:* American Academy of Arts and Letters. *Winner (2020):* Linda Asher.

Robert H. Winner Memorial Award ($2,500). To a midcareer poet over 40 who has published no more than one book of poetry. *Offered by:* Poetry Society of America. *Winner:* Teri Ellen Cross Davis.

George Wittenborn Memorial Book Awards. To North American art publications that represent the highest standards of content, documentation, layout, and format. *Offered by:* Art Libraries Society of North America (ARLIS / NA). *Winner (2020):* To be announced. *Winner (2019):* Karen Patterson (ed.) for *Lenore Tawney: Mirror of the Universe* (John Michael Kohler Arts Center / University of Chicago Press).

Thomas Wolfe Fiction Prize ($1,000). For a short story that honors Thomas Wolfe. *Offered by:* North Carolina Writers Network. *Winner:* Rachel Taube for "The Gentle Clack of a Fox's Teeth."

Thomas Wolfe Prize and Lecture. To honor writers with distinguished bodies of work. *Offered by:* Thomas Wolfe Society and University of North Carolina at Chapel Hill. *Winner:* Michael Parker.

Helen and Kurt Wolff Translator's Prize ($10,000). For an outstanding translation from German into English, published in the United States. *Offered by:* Goethe Institut Inter Nationes, New York. *Winner:* Philip Boehm for *The Fox and Dr. Shimamura* by Christine Wunnicke (New Directions).

Women's Prize for Fiction (United Kingdom) (formerly the Bailey's Women's Prize for Fiction) (£30,000). For the best novel written by a woman and published in the United Kingdom. *Winner:* Maggie O'Farrell for *Hamnet* (Tinder Press).

World Fantasy Awards. For outstanding fantasy writing. *Offered by:* World Fantasy Convention. *Winners:* (novel) Kacen Callender for *Queen of the Conquered* (Orbit); (novella) Emily Tesh for *Silver in the Wood* (Tor.com);

(short fiction) Maria Dahvana Headley for "Read After Burning" in *A People's Future of the United States* (One World); (anthology) Nisi Shawl (editor) for *New Suns: Original Speculative Fiction by People of Color* (Solaris); (collection) Brian Evenson for *Song for the Unraveling of the World: Stories* (Coffee House Press); (best artist) Kathleen Jennings; (special award, professional) Ebony Elizabeth Thomas for *The Dark Fantastic: Race and the Imagination from Harry Potter to the Hunger Games* (New York University Press); (special award, nonprofessional) Bodhisattva Chattopadhyay, Laura E. Goodin, and Esko Suoranta for *Fafnir—Nordic Journal of Science Fiction and Fantasy Research*; (lifetime achievement) Rowena Morrill; Karen Joy Fowler.

Writers' Trust Engel / Findley Award (C$25,000) (Canada). To a Canadian writer predominantly of fiction, for a body of work. *Offered by:* Writers' Trust of Canada. *Sponsors:* Writers' Trust Board of Directors, Pitblado Family Foundation, and Michael Griesdorf Fund. *Winner:* Kerri Sakamoto.

Writers' Trust Fiction Prize. See Atwood Gibson Writers' Trust Fiction Prize.

Writers' Trust / McClelland & Stewart Journey Prize (C$10,000) (Canada). To a new, developing Canadian author for a short story first published in a Canadian literary journal during the previous year. *Offered by:* Writers' Trust of Canada. *Sponsor:* McClelland & Stewart. *Winner:* Jessica Johns for "Bad Cree" in *Grain*.

Writers' Trust Shaughnessy Cohen Prize for Political Writing (C$25,000) (Canada). For literary nonfiction that captures a political subject of relevance to Canadian readers. *Offered by:* Writers' Trust of Canada. *Winner (2020):* To be announced. *Winner (2019):* Beverley McLachlin for Truth Be Told: My Journey Through Life and the Law (Simon & Schuster Canada).

YALSA Award for Excellence in Nonfiction. For a work of nonfiction published for young adults (ages 12–18). *Offered by:* American Library Association, Young Adult Library Services Association. *Winner:* Rex Ogle for *Free Lunch* (Norton Young Readers).

Young Lions Fiction Award ($10,000). For a novel or collection of short stories by an American under the age of 35. *Offered by:* Young Lions of the New York Public Library. *Winner:* Bryan Washington for *Lot* (Riverhead Books).

Young People's Poet Laureate ($25,000). For lifetime achievement in poetry for children. Honoree holds the title for two years. *Offered by:* Poetry Foundation. *Winner (2019):* Naomi Shihab Nye.

Morton Dauwen Zabel Award ($10,000). Awarded biennially, in rotation, to a progressive and experimental poet, writer of fiction, or critic. *Offered by:* American Academy of Arts and Letters. *Winner (2020):* Brenda Hillman (poetry).

Zoetrope Short Fiction Prizes. *Offered by: Zoetrope: All-Story. Winners:* (first, $1,000) Deborah Forbes for "Meet Me at the Edge"; (second, $500) Lucy Neave for "Darling"; (third, $250) Kimberly Wei Wang for "Parents."

Charlotte Zolotow Award. For outstanding writing in a picture book published in the United States in the previous year *Offered by:* Cooperative Children's Book Center, University of Wisconsin–Madison. *Winners:* Cheryl Minnema (author) and Julie Flett (illustrator) for *Johnny's Pheasant* (University of Minnesota Press).

Part 6
Directory of Organizations

Directory of Library and Related Organizations

Networks, Consortia, and Other Cooperative Library Organizations

This list is taken from the current edition of *American Library Directory* (Information Today, Inc.), which includes additional information on member libraries and primary functions of each organization.

United States

Alabama

Alabama Health Libraries Assn., Inc. (ALHeLa), Lister Hill Lib., Univ. of Alabama, Birmingham 35294-0013. SAN 372-8218. Tel. 205-975-8313, fax 205-934-2230. *Pres.* Justin Robertson.

Library Management Network, Inc. (LMN), 1405 Plaza St. S.E., Ste 309, Decatur 35603. SAN 322-3906. Tel. 256-822-2371. *Syst. Coord.* Charlotte Moncrief.

Marine Environmental Sciences Consortium, Dauphin Island Sea Laboratory, 101 Bienville Blvd., Dauphin Island 36528. SAN 322-0001. Tel. 251-861-2141, fax 251-861-4646, e-mail disl@disl.org. *Exec. Dir.* John Valentine.

Network of Alabama Academic Libraries, c/o Alabama Commission on Higher Education, 100 N. Union St., Montgomery 36104. SAN 322-4570. Tel. 334-242-2211, fax 334-242-0270. *Exec. Dir.* Sheila Snow-Croft.

Alaska

Alaska Library Network (ALN), P.O. Box 230051, Anchorage 99523-0051. SAN 371-0688. Tel. 907-205-5362, e-mail info@aklib.net. *Exec. Dir.* Steve Rollins.

Arkansas

Northeast Arkansas Hospital Library Consortium, 223 E. Jackson, Jonesboro 72401. SAN 329-529X. Tel. 870-972-1290, fax 870-931-0839. *Dir.* Karen Crosser.

California

49-99 Cooperative Library System, c/o Southern California Lib. Cooperative, 254 N. Lake Ave., Suite 874, Pasadena 91101. SAN 301-6218. Tel. 626-359-6111, fax 626-283-5949. *Exec. Dir.* Diane Bednarski.

Bay Area Library and Information Network (BayNet), 1462 Cedar St., Berkeley 94702. SAN 371-0610. Tel. 415-355-2826, e-mail infobay@baynetlibs.org. *Pres.* Vacant.

Califa, 330 Townsend St., Ste. 133, San Francisco 94107. Tel. 888-239-2289, fax 415-520-0434, e-mail califa@califa.org. *Exec. Dir.* Paula MacKinnon.

Gold Coast Library Network, 3437 Empresa Dr., Suite C, San Luis Obispo 93401-7355. Tel. 805-543-6082, fax 805-543-9487. *Admin. Dir.* Maureen Theobald.

National Network of Libraries of Medicine–Pacific Southwest Region (NN/LM-PSR), Louise M. Darling Biomedical Lib., 12-077 Center for Health Science, Box 951798, Los Angeles 90095-1798. SAN 372-8234. Tel. 310-825-1200, fax 310-825-5389, e-mail psr-nnlm@library.ucla.edu. *Dir.* Judy Consales.

Nevada Medical Library Group (NMLG), Barton Memorial Hospital Lib., 2170 South Ave., South Lake Tahoe 96150. SAN 370-0445. Tel. 530-543-5844, fax 530-541-4697. *Senior Exec. Coord.* Laurie Anton.

Northern California Assn. of Law Libraries (NOCALL), P.O. Box 26417, San Francisco, CA 94126. E-mail admin@nocall.org. *Pres.* Sarah Lin.

Northern and Central California Psychology Libraries (NCCPL), 2040 Gough St., San Francisco 94109. SAN 371-9006. Tel. 415-771-8055. *Pres.* Scott Hines.

OCLC Research Library Partnership, 155 Bovet Rd., Ste. 500, San Mateo 94402. Tel. 614-764-6000. Exec. Dir. Rachel Frick.

Peninsula Libraries Automated Network (PLAN), 2471 Flores St., San Mateo 94403-4000. SAN 371-5035. Tel. 650-349-5538, fax 650-349-5089. *Dir., Information Technology* Monica Schultz.

San Bernardino, Inyo, Riverside Counties United Library Services (SIRCULS), 555 W. 6th St., San Bernardino 92410. Tel. 909-381-8257, fax 909-888-3171, e-mail ils@inlandlib.org. *Exec. Dir.* Vera Skop.

San Francisco Biomedical Library Network (SFBLN), San Francisco General Hospital UCSF/Barnett-Briggs Medical Lib., 1001 Potrero Ave., Bldg. 30, 1st Fl., San Francisco 94110. SAN 371-2125. Tel. 415-206-6639, e-mail fishbon@ucsfmedctr.org. *Lib. Dir.* Stephen Kiyoi.

Santa Clarita Interlibrary Network (SCIL-NET), Powell Lib., Santa Clarita 91321. SAN 371-8964. Tel. 661-362-2271, fax 661-362-2719. *Libn.* John Stone.

Serra Cooperative Library System, Serra c/o SCLC, 254 N. Lake Ave., Suite 874, Pasadena 91101. SAN 301-3510. Tel. 626-283-5949. *Dir.* Diane Bednarski.

Southern California Library Cooperative (SCLC), 254 N. Lake Ave., Suite 874, Pasadena 91101. SAN 371-3865. Tel. 626-283-5949. *Dir.* Diane Bednarski.

Colorado

Colorado Alliance of Research Libraries, 3801 E. Florida Ave., Suite 515, Denver 80210. SAN 322-3760. Tel. 303-759-3399, fax 303-759-3363. *Exec. Dir.* George Machovec.

Colorado Assn. of Law Libraries, P.O. Box 13363, Denver 80201. SAN 322-4325. Tel. 303-492-7535, fax 303-492-2707. *Pres.* Diane Forge Bauersfeld.

Colorado Council of Medical Librarians (CCML), c/o CU Strauss Health Sciences Library, 12950 E. Montview Blvd. A003, Aurora 80045. SAN 370-0755. Tel. 303-724-2124, fax 303-724-2154. *Pres.* Ben Harnke.

Colorado Library Consortium (CLiC), 7400 E. Arapahoe Rd., Suite 75, Centennial 80112. SAN 371-3970. Tel. 303-422-1150, fax 303-431-9752. *Exec. Dir.* Jim Duncan.

Connecticut

Bibliomation, 24 Wooster Ave., Waterbury 06708. Tel. 203-577-4070. *Exec. Dir.* Carl DeMilia.

Connecticut Library Consortium, 234 Court St., Middletown 06457-3304. SAN 322-0389. Tel. 860-344-8777, fax 860-344-9199, e-mail clc@ctlibrarians.org. *Exec. Dir.* Jennifer Keohane.

Council of State Library Agencies in the Northeast (COSLINE), Connecticut State Lib., 231 Capitol Ave., Hartford 06106. SAN 322-0451. Tel. 860-757-6510, fax 860-757-6503. *Exec. Dir.* Timothy Cherubini.

CTW Library Consortium, Olin Memorial Lib., Middletown 06459-6065. SAN 329-4587. Tel. 860-685-3887, fax 860-685-2661. *Libn. for Collaborative Projects* Lorri Huddy.

Hartford Consortium for Higher Education, 31 Pratt St., 4th Fl., Hartford 06103. SAN 322-0443. Tel. 860-702-3801, fax 860-241-1130. *Exec. Dir.* Martin Estey.

Libraries Online, Inc. (LION), 100 Riverview Center, Suite 252, Middletown 06457. SAN 322-3922. Tel. 860-347-1704, fax 860-346-3707. *Exec. Dir.* Alan Hagyard.

Library Connection, Inc., 599 Matianuck Ave., Windsor 06095-3567. Tel. 860-937-8261, fax 860-298-5328. *Exec. Dir.* George Christian.

District of Columbia

Association of Research Libraries, 21 Dupont Circle N.W., Suite 800, Washington 20036. Tel. 202-296-2296, fax 202-872-0884. *Exec. Dir.* Mary Lee Kennedy.

Council for Christian Colleges and Universities, 321 8th St. N.E., Washington 20002.

SAN 322-0524. Tel. 202-546-8713, fax 202-546-8913, e-mail council@cccu.org. *Pres.* Shirley V. Hoogstra.
FEDLINK/Federal Library and Information Network, c/o Federal Lib. and Info. Center Committee, 101 Independence Ave. S.E., Washington 20540-4935. SAN 322-0761. Tel. 202-707-4800, fax 202-707-4818, e-mail flicc@loc.gov. *Exec. Dir.* Laurie Neider.
Washington Theological Consortium, 487 Michigan Ave. N.E., Washington 20017-1585. SAN 322-0842. Tel. 202-832-2675, fax 202-526-0818, e-mail wtc@washtheocon.org. *Exec. Dir.* Larry Golemon.

Florida

Florida Academic Library Services Cooperative (FALSC), 1753 W Paul Dirac Dr., Tallahassee 32310. Tel. 850-922-6044, fax 850-922-4869. *Exec. Dir.* Elijah Scott
Florida Library Information Network, R. A. Gray Bldg., State Library and Archives of Florida, Tallahassee 32399-0250. SAN 322-0869. Tel. 850-245-6600, fax 850-245-6744, e-mail library@dos.myflorida.com. *Bureau Chief* Cathy Moloney.
Library and Information Resources Network, 7855 126th Ave. N., Largo 33773. Tel. 727-536-0214, fax 727-530-3126.
Midwest Archives Conference (MAC), 2598 E Sunrise Blvd., Suite 2104, Fort Lauderdale 33304. E-mail membership@midwestarchives.org. *Pres.* Erik Moore.
Northeast Florida Library Information Network (NEFLIN), 2233 Park Ave., Suite 402, Orange Park 32073. Tel. 904-278-5620, fax 904-278-5625, e-mail office@neflin.org. *Exec. Dir.* Brad Ward.
Panhandle Library Access Network (PLAN), Five Miracle Strip Loop, Suite 8, Panama City Beach 32407-3850. SAN 370-047X. Tel. 850-233-9051, fax 850-235-2286. *Exec. Dir.* Charles Mayberry.
SEFLIN/Southeast Florida Library Information Network, Inc, Wimberly Lib., Office 452, Florida Atlantic Univ., 777 Glades Rd., Boca Raton 33431. SAN 370-0666. Tel. 561-208-0984, fax 561-208-0995. *Exec. Dir.* Jennifer Pratt.
Southwest Florida Library Network (SWFLN), 13120 Westlinks Terrace, Unit 3, Fort Myers 33913. Tel. 239-313-6338, fax 239-313-6329. *Exec. Dir.* Luly Castro.

Tampa Bay Library Consortium, Inc., 4042 Park Oaks Blvd., Suite 430, Tampa 33619. SAN 322-371X. Tel. 813-622-8252, fax 813-628-4425. *Exec. Dir.* Jim Walther.
Tampa Bay Medical Library Network, Medical Lib., Department 7660, 501 Sixth Ave. South, Saint Petersburg 33701. SAN 322-0885. Tel. 727-767-8557. *Chair* Susan Sharpe.
Three Rivers Regional Library Consortium, 176 S.W. Community Cir., Mayo 32066. Tel. 386-294-3858, e-mail hello@3riverslibrary.com. *Dir.* Dale Collum.

Georgia

Association of Southeastern Research Libraries (ASERL), c/o Robert W. Woodruff Library, 540 Asbury Circle, Suite 316, Atlanta 30322-1006. SAN 322-1555. Tel. 404-727-0137. *Exec. Dir.* John Burger.
Atlanta Health Science Libraries Consortium, Fran Golding Medical Lib. at Scottish Rite, 1001 Johnson Ferry Rd. N.E., Atlanta 30342-1600. Tel. 404-785-2157, fax 404-785-2155. *Pres.* Kate Daniels.
Atlanta Regional Council for Higher Education (ARCHE), 141 E. College Ave., Box 1084, Decatur 30030. SAN 322-0990. Tel. 404-651-2668, fax 404-880-9816, e-mail arche@atlantahighered.org. *Exec. Dir.* Tracey Brantley.
Consortium of Southern Biomedical Libraries (CONBLS), Robert B. Greenblatt, MD Library, 1439 Laney Walker Blvd., Augusta, 30912. SAN 370-7717. Tel. 843-792-8839. *Chair* Brenda Seago.
Georgia Interactive Network for Medical Information (GAIN), c/o Mercer Univ. School of Medicine, 1550 College St., Macon 31207. SAN 370-0577. Tel. 478-301-2515, fax 478-301-2051, e-mail gain.info@gain.mercer.edu.
GOLD Georgia Resource Sharing for Georgia's Libraries (GOLD), c/o Georgia Public Lib. Service, 1800 Century Pl. N.E., Suite 150, Atlanta 30345-4304. SAN 322-094X. Tel. 404-235-7128, fax 404-235-7201. *Project Mgr.* Elaine Hardy.
LYRASIS, 1438 W. Peachtree St. N.W., Suite 150, Atlanta 30309. SAN 322-0974. Tel. 800-999-8558, fax 404-892-7879. *CEO* Robert Miller.

Public Information Network for Electronic Services (PINES), 2872 Woodcock Blvd., Suite 250, Atlanta 30341. Tel. 404-235-7200. *Prog. Mgr.* Terran McCanna.

Hawaii

Hawaii-Pacific Chapter, Medical Library Assn. (HPC-MLA), Health Sciences Lib., Honolulu 96813. SAN 371-3946. Tel. 808-692-0810, fax 808-692-1244. *Chair* Kris Anderson.

Idaho

Canyon Owyhee Library Group (COLG), 203 E. Owyhee Ave., Homedale 83628. Tel. 208-337-4613, fax 208-337-4933.

Cooperative Information Network (CIN), 8385 N. Government Way, Hayden 83835-9280. SAN 323-7656. Tel. 208-772-5612, fax 208-772-2498.

Library Consortium of Eastern Idaho (LCEI), 113 S. Garfield, Pocatello 83204-3235. SAN 323-7699. Tel. 208-237-2192. *Pres.* Marilyn Kamoe.

LYNX Consortium, c/o Boise Public Lib., 715 S. Capitol Ave., Boise 83702-7195. SAN 375-0086. Tel. 208-384-4238, fax 208-384-4025. *Dir.* Kevin Booe.

Illinois

Assn. of Chicago Theological Schools (ACTS), Univ. of St. Mary of the Lake, 1000 E. Maple Ave., Mundelein 60060-1174. SAN 370-0658. Tel. 847-566-6401. *Coord.* Jennifer Ould.

Big Ten Academic Alliance (formerly Committee on Institutional Cooperation), 1819 S. Neil St., Suite D, Champaign 61820-7271. Tel. 217-333-8475, fax 217-244-7127, e-mail btaa@staff.cic.net. *Exec. Dir.* Keith A. Marshall.

Center for Research Libraries, 6050 S. Kenwood, Chicago 60637-2804. SAN 322-1032. Tel. 773-955-4545, fax 773-955-4339. *Pres.* Gregory Eow.

Chicago Area Museum Libraries (CAML), c/o Lib., Field Museum, Chicago 60605-2496. SAN 371-392X. Tel. 312-665-7970, fax 312-665-7893. *Museum Libn.* Christine Giannoni.

Consortium of Academic and Research Libraries in Illinois (CARLI), 100 Trade Center Dr., Suite 303, Champaign 61820. SAN 322-3736. Tel. 217-244-4664, fax 217-244-7596, e-mail support@carli.illinois.edu. *Chair* Taran Ley.

Council of Directors of State University Libraries in Illinois (CODSULI), Southern Illinois Univ. School of Medicine Lib., 801 N. Rutledge, Springfield 62702-4910. SAN 322-1083. Tel. 217-545-0994, fax 217-545-0988.

East Central Illinois Consortium (ECIC), c/o CARLE Foundation Hospital, 611 W. Park St., Urbana 61801. SAN 322-1040. Tel. 217-383-3311, 217-383-4513. *Coord.* Frances Drone-Silvers.

Heart of Illinois Library Consortium, 511 N.E. Greenleaf, Peoria 61603. SAN 322-1113. *Chair* Leslie Menz.

Illinois Heartland Library System, 1704 W. Interstate Dr., Champaign 61822. Tel. 217-352-0047. *Exec. Dir.* Leslie Bednar.

Illinois Library and Information Network (IL-LINET), c/o Illinois State Lib., Gwendolyn Brooks Bldg. 300 S. Second St., Springfield 62701-1796. SAN 322-1148. Tel. 217-785-5600. *Dir.* Greg McCormick.

LIBRAS, Inc., North Park Univ., 3225 W. Foster Ave., Chicago 60625-4895. SAN 322-1172. Tel. 773-244-5584, fax 773-244-4891. *Pres.* Estevon Montano.

Metropolitan Consortium of Chicago, Chicago School of Professional Psychology, 325 N. Wells St., Chicago 60610. SAN 322-1180. Tel. 312-329-6630, fax 312-644-6075. *Coord.* Margaret White.

Network of Illinois Learning Resources in Community Colleges (NILRC), P.O. Box 120, Blanchardville, WI 53516-0120. Tel. 608-523-4094, fax 608-523-4072. *Bus. Mgr.* Lisa Sikora.

System Wide Automated Network (SWAN), 800 Quail Ridge Dr., Westmont 60559. Tel. 844-792-6542. *Exec. Dir.* Aaron Skog.

Indiana

Central Indiana Health Science Libraries Consortium, Indiana Univ. School of Medicine Lib., Indianapolis 46202. SAN 322-1245. Tel. 317-274-8358, fax 317-274-4056.

Consortium of College and University Media Centers (CCUMC), Indiana Univ., 306 N. Union St., Bloomington 47405-3888. SAN 322-1091. Tel. 812-855-6049, fax 812-855-2103, e-mail ccumc@ccumc.org. *Exec. Dir.* Aileen Scales.

Evergreen Indiana Consortium, Indiana State Lib., 315 W. Ohio St., Indianapolis 46202. Tel. 317-234-6624, fax 317-232-0002. *Coord.* Anna Goben.

Iowa

National Network of Libraries of Medicine–Greater Midwest Region (NN/LM-GMR), c/o Hardin Library for the Health Sciences, 600 Newton Road, Iowa City, 52242. SAN 322-1202. Tel. 319-353-4479. *Dir.* Linda Walton.

Polk County Biomedical Consortium, c/o Broadlawns Medical Center Lib., Des Moines 50314. SAN 322-1431. Tel. 515-282-2394, fax 515-282-5634. *Treas.* Elaine Hughes.

Quad City Area Biomedical Consortium, Great River Medical Center Lib., West Burlington 52655. SAN 322-435X, Tel. 319-768-4075, fax 319-768-4080. *Coord.* Judy Hawk.

Sioux City Library Cooperative (SCLC), c/o Sioux City Public Lib., Sioux City 51101-1203. SAN 329-4722. Tel. 712-255-2933 ext. 255, fax 712-279-6432. *Chair* Betsy Thompson.

State of Iowa Libraries Online (SILO), State Lib. of Iowa, Des Moines 50319. SAN 322-1415. Tel. 515-281-4105, fax 515-281-6191. *State Libn.* Michael Scott.

Kansas

Dodge City Library Consortium, c/o Comanche Intermediate Center, 1601 First Ave., Dodge City 67801. SAN 322-4368. Tel. 620-227-1609, fax 620-227-4862.

State Library of Kansas / Statewide Resource Sharing Div., 300 S.W. 10 Ave., Room 312-N., Topeka 66612-1593. SAN 329-5621. Tel. 785-296-3296, fax 785-368-7291. *Dir.* Jeff Hixon.

Kentucky

Assn. for Rural and Small Libraries, 201 E. Main St., Suite 1405, Lexington 40507. Tel. 859-514-9178, e-mail szach@amrms.com. *Pres.* Andrea Berstler.

Assn. of Independent Kentucky Colleges and Universities (AIKCU), 484 Chenault Rd., Frankfort 40601. SAN 322-1490. Tel. 502-695-5007, fax 502-695-5057. *Pres.* Gary S. Cox.

Eastern Kentucky Health Science Information Network (EKHSIN), c/o Camden-Carroll Lib., Morehead 40351. SAN 370-0631. Tel. 606-783-6860, fax 606-784-2178. *Lib. Dir.* Tammy Jenkins.

Kentuckiana Metroversity, Inc., 200 W. Broadway, Suite 800, Louisville 40202. SAN 322-1504. Tel. 502-897-3374, fax 502-895-1647.

Kentucky Medical Library Assn., University of Louisville Bldg. D, Rm 110A, 500 S. Preston St., Louisville 40292. SAN 370-0623. Tel. 502-852-8530. *Contact* Tiffney Gipson.

Theological Education Assn. of Mid America (TEAM-A), Southern Baptist Theological Seminary, Louisville 40280. SAN 377-5038. Tel. 502-897-4807, fax 502-897-4600. *Dir., Info. Resources* Ken Boyd

Louisiana

Health Sciences Library Assn. of Louisiana (HSLAL), 433 Bolivar St., New Orleans 70112. SAN 375-0035. Tel. 504-568-5550. *Pres.* Rebecca Bealer.

Loan SHARK, State Lib. of Louisiana, 701 N. Fourth St., Baton Rouge 70802. SAN 371-6880. Tel. 225-342-4918, fax 225-219-4725, e-mail ill@state.lib.la.us. *Admin.* Kytara Christophe.

Louisiana Library Network (LOUIS), 1201 N. Third St., Suite 6-200, Baton Rouge 70802. E-mail louisresources@regents.la.gov. *Exec. Dir.* Terri Gallaway.

New Orleans Educational Telecommunications Consortium, 2045 Lakeshore Dr., Suite 541, New Orleans 70122. Tel. 504-524-0350, e-mail noetc@noetc.org. *Dir.* Michael Adler.

Southeastern Chapter of the American Assn. of Law Libraries (SEAALL), c/o Supreme Court of Louisiana, New Orleans 70130-2104. Tel. 504-310-2405, fax 504-310-2419. *Pres.* Michelle Cosby.

Maryland

Maryland Interlibrary Loan Organization (MILO), c/o Enoch Pratt Free Lib., Baltimore 21201-4484. SAN 343-8600. Tel. 410-396-5498, fax 410-396-5837, e-mail milo@prattlibrary.org. *Mgr.* Emma E. Beaven.

National Network of Libraries of Medicine (NNLM), National Lib. of Medicine, Bldg. 38, 8600 Rockville Pike, Room B1-E03,

Bethesda 20894. SAN 373-0905. Tel. 301-496-4777, fax 301-480-1467. *Head, National Network Coordinating Office* Amanda J. Wilson.

National Network of Libraries of Medicine–Southeastern Atlantic Region (NN/LM-SEA), Univ. of Maryland Health Sciences and Human Services Lib., 601 W. Lombard S., Baltimore 21201-1512. SAN 322-1644. Tel. 410-706-2855, fax 410-706-0099, e-mail hshsl-nlmsea@hshsl.umaryland.edu. *Dir.* Mary Tooey.

U.S. National Library of Medicine (NLM), 8600 Rockville Pike, Bethesda 20894. SAN 322-1652. Tel. 301-594-5983, fax 301-402-1384, e-mail custserv@nlm.nih.gov. *Coord.* Martha Fishel.

Washington Research Library Consortium (WRLC), 901 Commerce Dr., Upper Marlboro 20774. SAN 373-0883. Tel. 301-390-2000, fax 301-390-2020. *Exec. Dir.* Mark Jacobs.

Massachusetts

Boston Library Consortium, Inc., 401 Edgewater Place, Suite 600, Wakefield 01880. SAN 322-1733. Tel. 781-876-8859, fax 781-623-8460, e-mail admin@blc.org. *Exec. Dir.* Susan Stearns.

Boston Theological Interreligious Consortium, P.O. Box 391069, Cambridge 02139. Tel. 207-370-5275, e-mail btioffice@bostontheo logical.org. *Exec. Dir.* Stephanie Edwards.

Cape Libraries Automated Materials Sharing Network (CLAMS), 270 Communication Way, Unit 4E, Hyannis 02601. SAN 370-579X. Tel. 508-790-4399, fax 508-771-4533. *Exec. Dir.* Gayle Simundza.

Central and Western Massachusetts Automated Resource Sharing (C/W MARS), 67 Millbrook St., Suite 201, Worcester 01606. SAN 322-3973. Tel. 508-755-3323 ext. 30, fax 508-755-3721.

Cooperating Libraries of Greater Springfield (CLGS), Springfield Technical Community College, Springfield 01102. SAN 322-1768. Tel. 413-755-4565, fax 413-755-6315, e-mail lcoakley@stcc.edu.

Fenway Libraries Online, Inc. (FLO), c/o Wentworth Institute of Technology, 550 Huntington Ave., Boston 02115. SAN 373-9112. Tel. 617-989-5032. *Exec. Dir.* Walter Stein.

Massachusetts Health Sciences Libraries Network (MAHSLIN), Lamar Soutter Lib., Univ. of Massachusetts Medical School, Worcester 01655. SAN 372-8293. http://nahsl.libguides.com/mahslin/home. *Pres.* Stephanie Friree Ford.

Merrimack Valley Library Consortium, 4 High St., North Andover 01845. SAN 322-4384. Tel. 978-557-1050, fax 978-557-8101. *Exec. Dir.* Eric C. Graham.

Minuteman Library Network, 10 Strathmore Rd., Natick 01760-2419. SAN 322-4252. Tel. 508-655-8008, fax 508-655-1507. *Exec. Dir.* Susan McAlister.

National Network of Libraries of Medicine–New England Region (NN/LM-NER), Univ. of Massachusetts Medical School, 55 Lake Ave. N., Room S4-241, Worcester 01655. SAN 372-5448. Tel. 800-338-7657, fax 508-856-5977. *Dir.* Elaine Martin.

North Atlantic Health Sciences Libraries, Inc. (NAHSL), Hirsh Health Sciences Lib., 145 Harrison Ave., Boston 02111. SAN 371-0599. Tel. 617-636-3638, fax 617-636-3805. *Chair* Debra Berlanstein.

North of Boston Library Exchange, Inc. (NOBLE), 42-A Cherry Hill Drive, Danvers 01923. SAN 322-4023. Tel. 978-777-8844, fax 978-750-8472, e-mail staff@noblenet. org. *Exec. Dir.* Ronald A. Gagnon.

Northeast Consortium of Colleges and Universities in Massachusetts (NECCUM), Merrimack College, 315 Turnpike St., North Andover 01845. SAN 371-0602. Tel. 978-556-3400, fax 978-556-3738. *Pres.* Richard Santagati.

Northeastern Consortium for Health Information (NECHI), Lowell General Hospital Health Science Lib., 295 Varnum Ave., Lowell 01854. SAN 322-1857. Tel. 978-937-6247, fax 978-937-6855. *Libn.* Donna Beales.

SAILS Library Network, 10 Riverside Dr., Suite 102, Lakeville 02347. SAN 378-0058. Tel. 508-946-8600, fax 508-946-8605, e-mail support@sailsinc.org. *Exec. Dir.* Deborah K. Conrad.

Southeastern Massachusetts Consortium of Health Science (SEMCO), Wilkens Lib., 2240 Iyannough Rd., West Barnstable 02668. SAN 322-1873. *Pub. Serv. Coord.* Tim Gerolami.

Western Massachusetts Health Information Consortium, Baystate Medical Center

Health Sciences Lib., Springfield 01199. SAN 329-4579. Tel. 413-794-1865, fax 413-794-1974. *Pres.* Susan La Forter.

Michigan

Detroit Area Consortium of Catholic Colleges, c/o Wayne State Univ., Detroit 48202. SAN 329-482X. Tel. 313-883-8500, fax 313-883-8594. *Dir.* Chris Spilker.

Detroit Area Library Network (DALNET), 5150 Anthony Wayne Dr., Detroit 48202. Tel. 313-577-6789, fax 313-577-1231, info@dalnet. org. *Exec. Dir.* John E. Sterbenz, Jr.

Lakeland Library Cooperative, 4138 Three Mile Rd. N.W., Grand Rapids 49534-1134. SAN 308-132X. Tel. 616-559-5253, fax 616-559-4329. *Dir.* Carol Dawe.

The Library Network (TLN), 41365 Vincenti Ct., Novi 48375. SAN 370-596X. Tel. 248-536-3100, fax 248-536-3099. *Dir.* Steven Bowers.

Michigan Health Sciences Libraries Assn. (MHSLA), 1407 Rensen St., Suite 4, Lansing 48910. SAN 323-987X. Tel. 517-394-2774, fax 517-394-2675. *Pres.* Jill Turner.

Mideastern Michigan Library Cooperative, 503 S. Saginaw St., Suite 839, Flint 48502. SAN 346-5187. Tel. 810-232-7119, fax 810-232-6639. *Dir.* Eric Palmer.

Mid-Michigan Library League, 201 N Mitchell, Suite 302, Cadillac 49601-1835. SAN 307-9325. Tel. 231-775-3037, fax 231-775-1749. *Dir.* Sheryl L. Mase.

Midwest Collaborative for Library Services, 1407 Rensen St., Suite 1, Lansing 48910. Tel. 800-530-9019, fax 517-492-3878. *Exec. Dir.* Scott Garrison.

Southeastern Michigan League of Libraries (SEMLOL), Lawrence Technological Univ., 21000 W. Ten Mile Rd., Southfield 48075. SAN 322-4481. Tel. 810-766-4070, fax 248-204-3005. *Treas.* Gary Cocozzoli.

Southwest Michigan Library Cooperative, 401 Wix St., Ostego 49078. SAN 308-2156. Tel. 269-657-3800, e-mail aestelle@otsego library.org. *Dir.* Andrea Estelle.

Suburban Library Cooperative (SLC), 44750 Delco Blvd., Sterling Heights 48313. SAN 373-9082. Tel. 586-685-5750, fax 586-685-5750. *Dir.* Tammy Turgeon.

Upper Peninsula of Michigan Health Sciences Library Consortium, c/o Marquette Health System Hospital, 580 W. College Ave.,

Marquette 49855. SAN 329-4803. Tel. 906-225-3429, fax 906-225-3524. *Lib. Mgr.* Janis Lubenow.

Upper Peninsula Region of Library Cooperation, Inc., 1615 Presque Isle Ave., Marquette 49855. SAN 329-5540. Tel. 906-228-7697, fax 906-228-5627. *Treas.* Suzanne Dees.

Valley Library Consortium, 3210 Davenport Ave., Saginaw 48602-3495. Tel. 989-497-0925, fax 989-497-0918. *Exec. Dir.* Randall Martin.

Minnesota

Capital Area Library Consortium (CALCO), c/o Minnesota Dept. of Transportation, Lib. MS155, 395 John Ireland Blvd., Saint Paul 55155. SAN 374-6127. Tel. 651-296-5272, fax 651-297-2354. *Libn.* Shirley Sherkow.

Central Minnesota Libraries Exchange (CMLE), Miller Center, Room 130-D, Saint Cloud 56301-4498. SAN 322-3779. Tel. 320-308-2950, fax 320-654-5131, e-mail cmle@stcloudstate.edu. *Exec. Dir.* Mary Wilkins-Jordan.

Cooperating Libraries in Consortium (CLIC), 1619 Dayton Ave., Suite 204, Saint Paul 55104. SAN 322-1970. Tel. 651-644-3878. *Exec. Dir.* Ruth Dukelow.

Metronet, 1619 Dayton Ave., Suite 314, Saint Paul 55104. SAN 322-1989. Tel. 651-646-0475, fax 651-649-3169, e-mail information@ metrolibraries.net. *Exec. Dir.* Ann Walker Smalley.

Metropolitan Library Service Agency (MELSA), 1619 Dayton Ave., No. 314, Saint Paul 55104-6206. SAN 371-5124. Tel. 651-645-5731, fax 651-649-3169, e-mail melsa@ melsa.org. *Exec. Dir.* Ken Behringer.

MINITEX, Univ. of Minnesota–Twin Cities, 60 Wilson Library, 309 19th Ave. S., Minneapolis 55455-0439. SAN 322-1997. Tel. 612-624-4002, fax 612-624-4508. *Dir.* Valerie Horton.

Minnesota Library Information Network (MnLINK), Univ. of Minnesota–Twin Cities, Minneapolis 55455-0439. Tel. 800-462-5348, fax 612-624-4508. *Info. Specialist* Nick Banitt.

Minnesota Theological Library Assn. (MTLA), Luther Seminary Lib., 2375 Como Ave., Saint Paul 55108. SAN 322-1962. Tel. 651-641-3447. *Exec. Dir.* Sandra Oslund.

MNPALS, Minnesota State Univ. Mankato, 3022 Memorial Library, Mankato 56001. Tel. 507-389-2000, fax 507-389-5488. *Exec. Dir.* Johnna Horton.

Northern Lights Library Network (NLLN), 1104 7th Ave. S., Box 136, Moorhead 56563. SAN 322-2004. Tel. 218-477-2934. *Exec. Dir.* Kathy Brock Enger.

Prairielands Library Exchange, 109 S. 5th St., Marshall 56258. SAN 322-2039. Tel. 507-532-9013, fax 507-532-2039, e-mail info@ sammie.org. *Exec. Dir.* Shelly Grace.

Southeastern Libraries Cooperating (SELCO), 2600 19th St. N.W., Rochester 55901-0767. SAN 308-7417. Tel. 507-288-5513, fax 507-288-8697. *Exec. Dir.* Ann Hutton.

Twin Cities Biomedical Consortium (TCBC), c/o Fairview Univ. Medical Center, 2450 Riverside Ave., Minneapolis 55455. SAN 322-2055. Tel. 612-273-6595, fax 612-273-2675. *Mgr.* Colleen Olsen.

Mississippi

Central Mississippi Library Council (CMLC), c/o Millsaps College Lib., 1701 N. State St., Jackson 39210. SAN 372-8250. Tel. 601-974-1070, fax 601-974-1082. *Chair* Justin Huckaby.

Mississippi Electronic Libraries Online (MELO), Mississippi State Board for Community and Junior Colleges, Jackson 39211. Tel. 601-432-6518, fax 601-432-6363, e-mail melo@colin.edu. *Dir.* Audra Kimball.

Missouri

Greater Western Library Alliance (GWLA), 5109 Cherry St., Kansas City 64110. Tel. 816-926-8765, fax 816-926-8790. *Exec. Dir.* Joni Blake.

Health Sciences Library Network of Kansas City (HSLNKC), Univ. of Missouri–Kansas City Health Sciences Lib., 2411 Holmes St., Kansas City 64108-2792. SAN 322-2098. Tel. 816-235-1880, fax 816-235-6570. *Pres.* Cindi Kerns.

Kansas City Library Service Program (KC-LSP), 14 W. 10 St., Kansas City 64105. Tel. 816-701-3520, fax 816-701-3401, e-mail kc-lspsupport@kclibrary.org. *Lib. Systems and Service Prog. Mgr.* Melissa Carle.

Mid-America Law Library Consortium (MALLCO), 800 N. Harvey Ave., Oklahoma City 73102. Tel. 405-208-5393, e-mail mallcoexecutivedirector@gmail.com. *Exec. Dir.* Susan Urban.

Mid-America Library Alliance/Kansas City Metropolitan Library and Information Network, 15624 E. 24 Hwy., Independence 64050. SAN 322-2101. Tel. 816-521-7257, fax 816-461-0966. *Exec. Dir.* Mickey Coalwell.

Mobius, 111 E. Broadway, Suite 220, Columbia 65203. Tel. 877-366-2487, fax 541-264-7006. *Exec. Dir.* Donna Bacon.

Saint Louis Regional Library Network, 1190 Meramec Station Rd., Suite 207, Ballwin 63021. SAN 322-2209. Tel. 800-843-8482, fax 636-529-1396, e-mail slrln@amigos.org. *Pres.* Nina O'Daniels.

Western Council of State Libraries, 1190 Meramec Station Rd., Suite 207, Ballwin 63021-6902. Tel. 972-851-8000, fax 636-529-1396.

Montana

Treasure State Academic Information and Library Services (TRAILS), Montana State Univ., P.O. Box 173320, Bozeman 59717. Tel. 406-994-4432, fax 406-994-2851. *Coord.* Pamela Benjamin.

Nebraska

ICON Library Consortium, McGoogan Lib. of Medicine, Univ. of Nebraska, Omaha 68198-6705. Tel. 402-559-7099, fax 402-559-5498. *Exec. Secy.* Cindy Perkins.

Nevada

Desert States Law Library Consortium, Wiener-Rogers Law Lib., William S. Boyd School of Law, 4505 Maryland Pkwy., Las Vegas 89154-1080. Tel. 702-895-2400, fax 702-895-2416. *Dir.* Jean Price.

Information Nevada, Interlibrary Loan Dept., Nevada State Lib. and Archives, 100 N. Stewart St., Carson City 89701-4285. SAN 322-2276. Tel. 775-684-3360, fax 775-684-3330. *Asst. Admin., Lib. and Development Svcs.* Tammy Westergard.

New Hampshire

GMILCS, Inc., 31 Mount Saint Mary's Way, Hooksett 03106. Tel. 603-485-4286, fax 603-485-4246, e-mail helpdesk@gmilcs.org. *Systems Admin.* Marilyn Borgendale.

Health Sciences Libraries of New Hampshire and Vermont, Breene Memorial Lib., 36 Clinton St., New Hampshire Hospital, Concord 03246. SAN 371-6864. Tel. 603-527-2837, fax 603-527-7197. *Admin. Coord.* Anne Conner.

Librarians of the Upper Valley Coop. (LUV Coop), c/o Converse Free Library, 38 Union St., Lyme 03768. SAN 371-6856. Tel. 603-795-4622. *Coord.* Judith G. Russell.

Merri-Hill-Rock Library Cooperative, c/o Sandown Public Lib., 305 Main St., P.O. Box 580, Sandown 03873. SAN 329-5338. E-mail director@sandownlibrary.us. *Chair* Deborah Hoadley.

New Hampshire College and University Council, 3 Barrell Court, Suite 100, Concord 03301-8543. SAN 322-2322. Tel. 603-225-4199, fax 603-225-8108. *Pres.* Thomas R. Horgan.

Nubanusit Library Cooperative, c/o Frost Free Lib., 28 Jaffrey Rd., Marlborough 03455. SAN 322-4600. *Chair* Kristin Readel.

Rochester Area Librarians, c/o Milton Free Public Lib., 13 Main St., Milton Mills 03852. E-mail mfpl@metrocast.net *Dir.* Betsy Baker.

New Jersey

Basic Health Sciences Library Network (BHSL), Overlook Hospital Health Science Lib., 99 Beauvoir Ave., Summit 07902. SAN 371-4888. Tel. 908-522-2886, fax 908-522-2274. *Coord.* Pat Regenberg.

Bergen County Cooperative Library System (BCCLS), 21-00 Route 208 S., Ste. 130, Fair Lawn 07410. Tel. 201-498-7300, fax 201-489-4215, e-mail bccls@bccls.org. *Exec. Dir.* David Hanson.

Burlington Libraries Information Consortium (BLINC), 5 Pioneer Blvd., Westampton 08060. Tel. 609-267-9660, fax 609-267-4091, e-mail hq@bcls.lib.nj.us. *Dir.* Ranjna Das.

Health Sciences Library Association of New Jersey (HSLANJ), P.O. Box 12606, Wilmington, DE 19850-2606. Tel. 570-856-5952, fax 888-619-4432, e-mail communications@hslanj.org. *Exec. Dir.* Robb Mackes.

Libraries of Middlesex Automation Consortium (LMxAC), 27 Mayfield Ave., Edison 08837. SAN 329-448X. Tel. 732-750-2525, fax 732-750-9392. *Exec. Dir.* Eileen M. Palmer.

LibraryLinkNJ, New Jersey Library Cooperative, 44 Stelton Rd., Suite 330, Piscataway 08854. SAN 371-5116. Tel. 732-752-7720, fax 732-752-7785. *Exec. Dir.* Susanne Sacchetti.

Morris Automated Information Network (MAIN), 16 Wing Dr., Suite 212, Cedar Knolls 07927. SAN 322-4058. Tel. 973-862-4606, fax 973-512-2122. *Exec. Dir.* Phillip Berg.

Morris-Union Federation, 214 Main St., Chatham 07928. SAN 310-2629. Tel. 973-635-0603, fax 973-635-7827. *Exec. Dir.* Karen Brodsky.

New Jersey Health Sciences Library Network (NJHSN), Overlook Hospital Lib., 99 Beauvoir Ave., Summit 07902. SAN 371-4829. Tel. 908-522-2886, fax 908-522-2274. *Lib. Mgr.* Patricia Regenberg.

New Jersey Library Network, Lib. Development Bureau, 185 W. State St., Trenton 08608. SAN 372-8161. Tel. 609-278-2640 ext. 152, fax 609-278-2650. *Admin.* Ruth Pallante.

Virtual Academic Library Environment (VALE), NJEdge/NJIT, 218 Central Ave., GITC 3902, Newark 07102-1982, Tel. 855 832 3343, *Prog. Mgr.* Melissa Lena.

New Mexico

Estacado Library Information Network (ELIN), 509 N. Shipp, Hobbs 88240. Tel. 505-397-9328, fax 505-397-1508.

New Mexico Consortium of Academic Libraries, c/o Donnelly Library, 802 National Ave., Las Vegas. SAN 371-6872. *Pres.* Poppy Johnson-Renval.

New Mexico Consortium of Biomedical and Hospital Libraries, c/o Presbyterian Hospital, Robert Shafer Library, 1100 Central Ave., S.E., Santa Fe 87505. SAN 322-449X. Tel. 505-820-5218, fax 505-989-6478. *Pres.* Amanda Okandan.

New York

Academic Libraries of Brooklyn, Long Island Univ. Lib. LLC 517, One University Plaza, Brooklyn 11201. SAN 322-2411. Tel. 718-488-1081, fax 718-780-4057. *Dir.* Ingrid Wang.

Associated Colleges of the Saint Lawrence Valley, SUNY Potsdam, 288 Van Housen Extension, Potsdam 13676-2299. SAN 322-242X. Tel. 315-267-3331, fax 315-267-2389. *Admin. Coord.* Ben Dixon.

Brooklyn–Queens–Staten Island–Manhattan–Bronx Health Sciences Libns. (BQSIMB), 150 55th St., Brooklyn 11220. Tel. 718-630-7200, fax 718-630-8918. *Pres.* Sheryl Ramer Gesoff.

Capital District Library Council (CDLC), 28 Essex St., Albany 12206. SAN 322-2446. Tel. 518-438-2500, fax 518-438-2872. *Exec. Dir.* Kathleen Gundrum.

Central New York Library Resources Council (CLRC), 5710 Commons Park Dr., East Syracuse 13057. SAN 322-2454. Tel. 315-446-5446, fax 315-446-5590. *Exec. Dir.* Marc Wildman.

CONNECTNY, Inc., 6721 U.S. Highway 11, Potsdam 13676. Tel. 716-930-7752. *Exec. Dir.* Pamela Jones.

Consortium of Foundation Libraries, 32 Old Slip, 24th Fl., New York 10005-3500. SAN 322-2462. Tel. 212-620-4230, e-mail foundation libraries@gmail.com. *Chair* Susan Shiroma.

Library Assn. of Rockland County (LARC), P.O. Box 917, New City 10956-0917. Tel. 845-359-3877, e-mail president@rockland libraries.com.

Library Consortium of Health Institutions in Buffalo (LCHIB), Abbott Hall, SUNY at Buffalo, 3435 Main St., Buffalo 14214. SAN 329-367X. Tel. 716-829-3900 ext. 143, fax 716-829-2211, e-mail hubnet@buffalo. edu; ulb-lchib@buffalo.edu. *Exec. Dir.* Martin E. Mutka.

Long Island Library Resources Council (LIL-RC), 627 N. Sunrise Service Rd., Bellport 11713. SAN 322-2489. Tel. 631-675-1570. *Dir.* Tim Spindler.

Medical and Scientific Libraries of Long Island (MEDLI), c/o Palmer School of Lib. and Info. Science, Brookville 11548. SAN 322-4309. Tel. 516-299-2866, fax 516-299-4168. *Pres.* Claire Joseph.

Metropolitan New York Library Council (METRO), 599 Eleventh Ave., 8th Fl., New York 10036. SAN 322-2500. Tel. 212-228-2320, fax 212-228-2598, e-mail info@ metro.org. *Exec. Dir.* Nate Hill.

New England Law Library Consortium (NEL-LCO), 756 Madison Ave., Suite 102, Albany 12208. SAN 322-4244. Tel. 518-694-3025, fax 518-694-3027. *Exec. Dir.* Corie Dugas.

Northern New York Library Network, 6721 U.S. Hwy. 11, Potsdam 13676. SAN 322-2527. Tel. 315-265-1119, fax 315-265-1881, e-mail info@nnyln.org. *Exec. Dir.* Meg Backus.

Rochester Regional Library Council, 3445 Winton Pl., Ste. 204, Rochester 14623. SAN 322-2535. Tel. 585-223-7570, fax 585-223-7712, e-mail rrlc@rrlc.org. *Exec. Dir.* Laura Ousterhout.

South Central Regional Library Council, 108 N. Cayuga St., Clinton Hall, 3rd Floor, Ithaca 14850. SAN 322-2543. Tel. 607-273-9106, fax 607-272-0740, e-mail scrlc@ scrlc.org. *Exec. Dir.* Mary-Carol Lindbloom.

Southeastern New York Library Resources Council (SENYLRC), 21 S. Elting Corners Rd., Highland 12528-2805. SAN 322-2551. Tel. 845-883-9065, fax 845-883-9483. *Exec. Dir.* Tessa Killian.

SUNYConnect, Office of Lib. and Info. Services, Office of Library & Information Services, SUNY Administration Plaza, 353 Broadway, Albany 12246. Tel. 518-443-5577, fax 518-443-5358. *Asst. Provost for Lib. and Info. Svcs.* Carey Hatch.

United Nations System Electronic Information Acquisitions Consortium (UNSEIAC), c/o United Nations Lib., New York 10017. SAN 377-855X. Tel. 212-963-3000, fax 212-963-2608, e-mail unseiac@un.org. *Coord.* Amy Herridge.

Western New York Library Resources Council, 4950 Genesee St., Buffalo 14225. SAN 322-2578. Tel. 716-633-0705, fax 716-633-1736. *Exec. Dir.* Sheryl Knab.

North Carolina

North Carolina Community College System, 200 W. Jones St., Raleigh 27603-1379. SAN 322-2594. Tel. 919-807-7100, fax 919-807-7165. *Pres.* Peter Hans.

Northwest AHEC Library at Hickory, Catawba Medical Ctr., 810 Fairgrove Church Rd., Hickory 28602. SAN 322-4708. Tel. 828-326-3662, fax 828-326-3484. *Dir.* Karen Lee Martinez.

Northwest AHEC Library Information Network, Wake Forest Univ. School of Medicine, Medical Center Blvd., Winston-Salem 27157-1060. SAN 322-4716. Tel. 336-713-7700, fax 336-713-7701.

Triangle Research Libraries Network, Wilson Lib., CB No. 3940, Chapel Hill 27514-8890. SAN 329-5362. Tel. 919-962-8022, fax 919-962-4452. *Exec. Dir.* Lisa Croucher.

Western North Carolina Library Network (WNCLN), c/o Appalachian State Univ., 218 College St., Boone 28608. SAN 376-7205. Tel. 828-262-2774, fax 828-262-3001. *Libn.* Ben Shirley.

North Dakota

Central Dakota Library Network, Morton Mandan Public Lib., Mandan 58554-3149. SAN 373-1391. Tel. 701-667-5365, e-mail mortonmandanlibrary@cdln.info.

Ohio

Assn. of Christian Librarians (ACL), P.O. Box 4, Cedarville 45314. Tel. 937-766-2255, fax 937-766-5499, e-mail info@acl.org. *Pres.* Leslie Starasta.

Christian Library Consortium (CLC), c/o ACL, P.O. Box 4, Cedarville 45314. Tel. 937-766-2255, fax 937-766-5499, e-mail info@acl.org. *Coord.* Beth Purtee.

Consortium of Ohio Libraries, P.O. Box 38, Cardington 43315-1116 E-mail Info@into.cool-cat.org. *Chair* Lisa Murray.

Consortium of Popular Culture Collections in the Midwest (CPCCM), c/o Popular Culture Lib., Bowling Green 43403-0600. SAN 370-5811. Tel. 419-372-2450, fax 419-372-7996. *Head Libn.* Nancy Down.

Five Colleges of Ohio, 173 West Lorain Street, Room 208, Oberlin College, Oberlin 44074. Tel. 440-775-5500, e-mail info@ohio5.com. *Exec. Dir.* Sarah Stone.

Northeast Ohio Regional Library System (NEO-RLS), 1737 Georgetown Rd., Ste. B, Hudson 44236. SAN 322-2713. Tel. 330-655-0531, fax 330-655-0568. *Exec. Dir.* Betsy Lantz.

NORWELD (formerly Northwest Regional Library System), 181½ S. Main St., Bowling Green 43402. SAN 322-273X. Tel. 419-352-2903, fax 419-353-8310. *Exec. Dir.* Arline V. Radden.

OCLC Online Computer Library Center, Inc., 6565 Kilgour Place, Dublin 43017-3395. SAN 322-2748. Tel. 614-764-6000, fax 614-718-1017, e-mail oclc@oclc.org. *Pres./CEO* Skip Pritchard.

Ohio Health Sciences Library Assn. (OHSLA), Medical Lib., South Pointe Hospital, Warrensville Heights 44122. Tel. 216-491-7454, fax 216-491-7650. *Pres.* Mary Pat Harnegie.

Ohio Library and Information Network (Ohio-LINK), 1224 Kinnear Rd., Columbus 43215. SAN 374-8014. Tel. 614-485-6722, fax 614-228-1807, e-mail info@ohiolink.edu. *Exec. Dir.* Amy Pawlowski.

OHIONET, 1500 W. Lane Ave., Columbus 43221-3975. SAN 322-2764. Tel. 614-486-2966, fax 614-486-1527. *Exec. Officer* Nancy S. Kirkpatrick.

Ohio Network of American History Research Centers, Ohio Historical Society Archives–Lib., Columbus 43211-2497. SAN 323-9624. Tel. 614-297-2510, fax 614-297-2546, e-mail reference@ohiohistory.org. *Exec. Dir.* Jackie Barton.

Ohio Public Library Information Network (OPLIN), 2323 W. 5 Ave., Suite 130, Columbus 43204. Tel. 614-728-5252, fax 614-728-5256, e-mail support@oplin.org. *Exec. Dir.* Don Yarman.

Serving Every Ohioan Library Center, SEO, 40780 Marietta Rd., Caldwell 43724. SAN 356-4606. Tel. 740-783-5705, fax 800-446-4804. *Dir.* John Stewart.

Southeast Ohio and Neighboring Libraries (SWON), 10250 Alliance Rd., Suite 112, Cincinnati 45242. SAN 322-2675. Tel. 513-751-4422, fax 513-751-0463, e-mail info@swonlibraries.org. *Exec. Dir.* Cassondra Vick.

Southeast Regional Library System (SERLS), 252 W. 13 St., Wellston 45692. SAN 322-2756. Tel. 740-384-2103, fax 740-384-2106. *Dir.* Jay Burton.

Southwestern Ohio Council for Higher Education (SOCHE), Miami Valley Research Park, 3155 Research Blvd., Suite 204, Dayton 45420-4015. SAN 322-2659. Tel. 937-258-8890, fax 937-258-8899, e-mail soche@soche.org. *Exec. Dir.* Cassie Barlow.

State Assisted Academic Library Council of Kentucky (SAALCK), 12031 Southwick Lane, Cincinnati 45241. SAN 371-2222. Tel. 800-771-1972, e-mail saalck@saalck.org. *Exec. Dir.* Anne Abate.

Theological Consortium of Greater Columbus (TCGC), Trinity Lutheran Seminary, Columbus 43209-2334. Tel. 614-384-4646, fax 614-238-0263. *Lib. Systems Mgr.* Ray Olson.

Oklahoma

Mid-America Law Library Consortium (MALLCO), 800 N. Harvey Ave., Oklahoma City 73102. Tel. 405-208-5393, e-mail mallcoexecutivedirector@gmail.com. *Exec. Dir.* Susan Urban.

Oklahoma Health Sciences Library Assn. (OHSLA), HSC Bird Health Science Lib., Univ. of Oklahoma, Oklahoma City 73190. SAN 375-0051. Tel. 405-271-2285 ext. 48755, fax 405-271-3297. *Exec. Dir.* Joy Summers-Ables.

Oregon

Chemeketa Cooperative Regional Library Service, 4000 Lancaster Dr. N.E., Rm. 9/136, Salem 97305-1453. SAN 322-2837. Tel. 503-399-5165, fax 503-399-7316, e-mail contact@cclrs.org. *Dir.* John Goodyear.

Library Information Network of Clackamas County (LINCC), 1810 Red Soils Court, #110, Oregon City 97045. SAN 322-2845. Tel. 503-723-4888, fax 503-794-8238. *Lib. Network Mgr.* Kathryn Kohl.

Orbis Cascade Alliance, 2300 Oakmont Way, Eugene 97401. SAN 377-8096. Tel. 541-246-2470. *Exec. Dir.* Kim Armstrong.

Oregon Health Sciences Libraries Assn. (OHSLA), Oregon Health and Science Univ. Lib., 3181 S.W. Sam Jackson Park Rd., Portland 97239-3098. SAN 371-2176. Tel. 503-494-3462, fax 503-494-3322, e-mail library@ohsu.edu. *Pres.* Jackie Wirz.

Washington County Cooperative Library Services, 111 N.E. Lincoln St., MS No. 58, Hillsboro 97124-3036. SAN 322-287X. Tel. 503-846-3222, fax 503-846-3220.

Pennsylvania

Berks County Library Assn. (BCLA), c/o Berks County Public Libraries, 1040 Berks Rd., Leesport 19533. SAN 371-0866. Tel. 610-478-9035, 610-655-6350. *Pres.* Amy Resh.

Central Pennsylvania Consortium (CPC), c/o Franklin & Marshall College, Goethean Hall 101, Lancaster 17604. SAN 322-2896. Tel. 717-358-2896, fax 717-358-4455, e-mail cpc@dickinson.edu. *Exec. Asst.* Kathy Missildine.

Central Pennsylvania Health Sciences Library Assn. (CPHSLA), Office for Research Protections, Pennsylvania State Univ., 212 Kern Graduate Bldg., University Park 16802. SAN 375-5290. Fax 814-865-1775. *Pres.* Helen Houpt.

Eastern Mennonite Associated Libraries and Archives (EMALA), 2215 Millstream Rd., Lancaster 17602. SAN 372-8226. Tel. 717-393-9745, fax 717-393-8751. *Chair* John Weber.

Greater Philadelphia Law Library Assn. (GPLLA), P.O. Box 335, Philadelphia 19105. SAN 373-1375. *Pres.* Lori Strickler Corso.

HSLC/Access PA (Health Science Libraries Consortium), 3600 Market St., Suite 550, Philadelphia 19104-2646. SAN 323-9780. Tel. 215-222-1532, fax 215-222-0416, e-mail support@hslc.org. *Exec. Dir.* Maryam Phillips.

Interlibrary Delivery Service of Pennsylvania (IDS), c/o Bucks County IU, No. 22, 705 N Shady Retreat Rd., Doylestown 18901. SAN 322-2942. Tel. 215-348-2940 ext. 1625, fax 215-348-8315, e-mail ids@bucksiu.org. *Admin. Dir.* Pamela Dinan.

Keystone Library Network, 1871 Old Main Drive, Shippensburg 17257. Tel. 717-720-4088, fax 717-720-4211. *Interim Coord.* Ed Zimmerman.

Lehigh Valley Assn. of Independent Colleges, 1309 Main St., Bethlehem 18018. SAN 322-2969. Tel. 610-625-7888, fax 610-625-7891. *Exec. Dir.* Diane Dimitroff.

Montgomery County Library and Information Network Consortium (MCLINC), 301 Lafayette St., 2nd Fl., Conshohocken 19428. Tel. 610-238-0580, fax 610-238-0581, e-mail webmaster@mclinc.org. *Exec. Dir.* Sharon Moreland-Sender.

National Network of Libraries of Medicine–Middle Atlantic Region (NN/LM-MAR), Univ. of Pittsburgh, 3550 Terrace St., 200 Scaife Hall, Pittsburgh 15261. Tel. 412-684-2065, fax 412-648-1515, e-mail nnlmmar@pitt.edu. *Exec. Dir.* Renae Barger.

Northeastern Pennsylvania Library Network, c/o Marywood Univ. Lib., 2300 Adams Ave., Scranton 18509-1598. SAN 322-2993. Tel. 570-348-6260, fax 570-961-4769. *Exec. Dir.* Catherine H. Schappert.

Northwest Interlibrary Cooperative of Pennsylvania (NICOP), Mercyhurst College Lib., 501 E. 38th St., Erie 16546. SAN 370-5862. Tel. 814-824-2190, fax 814-824-2219. *Archivist/Libn.* Earleen Glaser.

Pennsylvania Academic Library Consortium, 1005 Pontiac Rd., Suite 330, Drexel Hill 19026. Tel. 215-567-1755. *Exec. Dir.* Jill Morris.

Pennsylvania Library Assn., 220 Cumberland Pkwy, Suite 10, Mechanicsburg 17055. Tel. 717-766-7663, fax 717-766-5440. *Exec. Dir.* Christi Buker.

Philadelphia Area Consortium of Special Collections Libraries (PACSCL), P.O. Box 22642, Philadelphia 19110-2642. Tel. 215-985-1445, fax 215-985-1446, e-mail lblanchard@pacscl.org. *Exec. Dir.* Laura Blanchard.

Southeastern Pennsylvania Theological Library Assn. (SEPTLA), c/o Biblical Seminary, 200 N. Main St., Hatfield 19440. SAN 371-0793. Tel. 215-368-5000 ext. 234. *Pres.* Patrick Milas.

State System of Higher Education Library Cooperative (SSHELCO), c/o Bailey Lib., Slippery Rock 16057. Tel. 724-738-2630, fax 724-738-2661. *Coord.* Mary Lou Sowden.

Susquehanna Library Cooperative (SLC), Stevenson Lib., Lock Haven Univ., 401 N. Fairview St., Lock Haven 17745. SAN 322-3051. Tel. 570-484-2310, fax 570-484-2506. *Interim Dir. of Lib. and Info. Svcs.* Joby Topper.

Tri-State College Library Cooperative (TCLC), c/o Rosemont College Lib., 1400 Montgomery Ave., Rosemont 19010-1699. SAN 322-3078. Tel. 610-525-0796, e-mail office@tclclibs.org. *Coord.* Mary Maguire.

Rhode Island

Ocean State Libraries (OSL), 300 Centerville Rd., Suite 103S, Warwick 02886-0226. SAN 329-4560. Tel. 401-738-2200, e-mail support@oslri.net. *Exec. Dir.* Stephen Spohn.

RILINK, 317 Market St., Warren 02885. SAN 371-6821. Tel. 401-245-4998. *Exec. Dir.* Dorothy Frechette.

South Carolina

Charleston Academic Libraries Consortium (CALC), P.O. Box 118067, Charleston 29423-8067. SAN 371-0769. Tel. 843-574-6088, fax 843-574-6484. *Chair* Charnette Singleton.

Partnership Among South Carolina Academic Libraries (PASCAL), 1122 Lady Street, Suite 300, Columbia 29201. Tel. 803-734-0900, fax 803-734-0901. *Exec. Dir.* Rick Moul.

South Carolina AHEC, c/o Medical University of South Carolina, 1 South Park Circle, Suite 203, Charleston 29407. SAN 329-3998. Tel. 843-792-4431, fax 843-792-4430. *Exec. Dir.* David Garr.

South Dakota

South Dakota Library Network (SDLN), 1200 University, Unit 9672, Spearfish 57799-9672. SAN 371-2117. Tel. 605-642-6835, fax 605-642-6472. *Dir.* Warren Wilson.

Tennessee

Appalachian College Assn., 7216 Jewel Bell Lane, Bristol 40475. Tel. 859-986-4584, fax 859-986-9549. *Pres.* Beth Rushing.

Knoxville Area Health Sciences Library Consortium (KAHSLC), Univ. of Tennessee Preston Medical Lib., 1924 Alcoa Hwy., Knoxville 37920. SAN 371-0556. Tel. 865-305-9525, fax 865-305-9527. *Pres.* Cynthia Vaughn.

Tennessee Health Science Library Assn. (THeSLA), Holston Valley Medical Center Health Sciences Lib., 130 W. Ravine Rd., Kingsport 37660. SAN 371-0726. Tel. 423-224-6870, fax 423-224-6014. *Pres.* Sandy Oelschlegel.

Tenn Share, P.O. Box 331871, Nashville 37203-7517. Tel. 615-669-8670, e-mail execdir@tenn-share.org. *Exec. Dir.* Jenifer Grady.

Tri-Cities Area Health Sciences Libraries Consortium (TCAHSLC), James H. Quillen College of Medicine, East Tennessee State Univ., Johnson City 37614. SAN 329-4099. Tel. 423-439-6252, fax 423-439-7025. *Dir.* Biddanda Ponnappa.

Texas

Abilene Library Consortium, 3305 N. 3 St., Suite 301, Abilene 79603. SAN 322-4694. Tel. 325-672-7081, fax 325-672-7082. *Exec. Dir.* Edward J. Smith.

Amigos Library Services, Inc., 4901 LBJ Freeway, Suite 150, Dallas 75244-6179. SAN 322-3191. Tel. 972-851-8000, fax 972-991-6061, e-mail amigos@amigos.org. *Chief Prog. Officer* Tracy Byerly.

Council of Research and Academic Libraries (CORAL), P.O. Box 6733, San Antonio 78212. SAN 322-3213. Tel. 210-710-4475. *Pres.* Michelea Mason.

Del Norte Biosciences Library Consortium, El Paso Community College, El Paso 79998.

SAN 322-3302. Tel. 915-831-4149, fax 915-831-4639. *Coord.* Becky Perales.

Harrington Library Consortium, 413 E. 4 Ave., Amarillo 79101. SAN 329-546X. Tel. 806-378-6037, fax 806-378-6038. *Dir.* Amanda Barrera.

Health Libraries Information Network (Health LINE), 3500 Camp Bowie Blvd. LIB-222, Fort Worth 76107-2699. SAN 322-3299. E-mail dfwhealthline@gmail.com. *Pres.* Michele Whitehead.

Houston Area Library Automated Network (HALAN), Houston Public Lib., 500 McKinney Ave., Houston 77002. Tel. 832-393-1411, fax 832-393-1427, e-mail website@hpl.lib.tx.us. *Chief* Judith Hiott.

Houston Area Research Library Consortium (HARLiC), c/o Univ. of Houston Libs., 114 University Libraries, Houston 77204-2000. SAN 322-3329. Tel. 713-743-9807, fax 713-743-9811. *Pres.* Dana Rooks.

National Network of Libraries of Medicine–South Central Region (NN/LM-SCR), c/o UNT Health Science Center, Gibson D. Lewis Library, Room 310, 3500 Camp Bowie Blvd., Fort Worth 76107. SAN 322-3353. Tel. 713-799-7880, fax 713-790-7030, e-mail nnlm-scr@exch.library.tmc.edu. *Dir.* Brian Leaf.

South Central Academic Medical Libraries Consortium (SCAMeL), c/o Lewis Lib.-UNTHSC, 3500 Camp Bowie Blvd., Fort Worth 76107. SAN 372-8269. Tel. 817-735-2380, fax 817-735-5158. *Chair* Kelly Gonzalez.

Texas Council of Academic Libraries (TCAL), VC/UHV Lib., 2602 N. Ben Jordan, Victoria 77901. SAN 322-337X. Tel. 361-570-4150, fax 361-570-4155. *Chair* Cate Rudowsky.

TEXSHARE—Texas State Library and Archives Commission, 1201 Brazos St., Austin 78701. Tel. 512-463-5455, fax 512-936-2306, e-mail texshare@tsl.texas.gov. *Dir. and State Libn.* Mark Smith.

Utah

National Network of Libraries of Medicine–MidContinental Region (NN/LM-MCR), Spencer S. Eccles Health Sciences Lib., Univ. of Utah, Salt Lake City 84112-5890. SAN 322-225X. Tel. 801-587-3650, fax 801-581-3632. *Dir.* Catherine Soehner.

Utah Academic Library Consortium (UALC), Univ. of Utah, Salt Lake City 84112. SAN 322-3418. Tel. 801-581-7701, 801-581-3852, fax 801-585-7185, e-mail UALCmail@library.utah.edu. *Chair* Wendy Holliday.

Vermont

Catamount Library Network, 43 Main St., Springfield 05156. *Mailing Address:* Ten Court St., Rutland 05701-4058. *Pres.* Amy Howlett.

Vermont Resource Sharing Network, c/o Vermont Dept. of Libs., 109 State St., Montpelier 05609-0601. SAN 322-3426. Tel. 802-828-3261, fax 802-828-1481. *Ref. Libn.* April Shaw.

Virginia

American Indian Higher Education Consortium (AIHEC), 121 Oronoco St., Alexandria 22314. SAN 329-4056. Tel. 703-838-0400, fax 703-838-0388, e-mail info@aihec.org. *Pres./CEO* Carrie Billy.

Lynchburg Area Library Cooperative, c/o Sweet Briar College Lib., P.O. Box 1200, Sweet Briar 24595. SAN 322-3450. Tel. 434-381-6315, fax 434-381-6173. *Dir.* Nan B. Carmack.

Lynchburg Information Online Network (LION), 2315 Memorial Ave., Lynchburg 24503. SAN 374-6097. Tel. 434-381-6311, fax 434-381-6173. *Systems Admin.* Lisa Broughman.

NASA Libraries Information System—NASA Galaxie, NASA Langley Research Ctr., MS 185-Technical Library, 2 W. Durand St., Hampton 23681-2199. SAN 322-0788. Tel. 757-864-2356, fax 757-864-2375. *Branch Mgr.*, Hope R. Venus.

Richmond Academic Library Consortium (RALC), James Branch Cabell Lib., Virginia Commonwealth Univ., 901 Park Ave., Richmond 23284. SAN 322-3469. Tel. 804-828-1110, fax 804-828-1105. *Pres.* Christopher Richardson.

Southside Virginia Library Network (SVLN), Longwood Univ., 201 High St., Farmville 23909-1897. SAN 372-8242. Tel. 434-395-2431, 434-395-2433, fax 434-395-2453. *Dean of Lib.* Suzy Szasz Palmer.

Southwestern Virginia Health Information Librarians, Sentara RMH Virginia Funkhouser

Health Sciences Library, 2010 Health Campus Dr., Harrisonburg 22801. SAN 323-9527. Tel. 540-689-1772, fax 540-689-1770, e-mail mdkhamph@sentara.com. *Libn.* Megan Khamphavong.

Virginia Independent College and University Library Assn., c/o Elizabeth G. McClenney, Roanoke College—Fintel Library, 220 High St., Salem 24153. SAN 374-6089. Tel. 540-375-2508. *Chair* Elizabeth G. McClenney.

Virginia Tidewater Consortium for Higher Education (VTC), 4900 Powhatan Ave., Norfolk 23529. SAN 329-5486. Tel. 757-683-3183, fax 757-683-4515, e-mail lgdotolo@aol.com. *Pres.* Lawrence G. Dotolo.

Virtual Library of Virginia (VIVA), George Mason Univ., 4400 University Dr., Fenwick 5100, Fairfax 22030. Tel. 703-993-4652, fax 703-993-4662. *Dir.* Anne Osterman.

Washington

National Network of Libraries of Medicine–Pacific Northwest Region (NN/LM-PNR), T-344 Health Sciences Bldg., Univ. of Washington, Seattle 98195. SAN 322-3485. Tel. 206-543-8262, fax 206-543-2469, e-mail nnlm@u.washington.edu. *Assoc. Dir.* Catherine Burroughs.

WIN Library Network, Gonzaga Univ., 502 E. Boone Ave., AD 95, Spokane 99258. Tel. 509-313-6545, fax 509-313-5904, e-mail winsupport@gonzaga.edu. *Pres.* Kathleen Allen.

West Virginia

Mid-Atlantic Law Library Cooperative (MALLCO), College of Law Lib., West Virginia Univ., Morgantown 26506-6135. SAN 371-0645. Tel. 304-293-7641, fax 304-293-6020. *Lib. Dir.* Lynn Maxwell.

Wisconsin

Fox River Valley Area Library Consortium (FRVALC), c/o Polk Lib., Univ. of Wisconsin–Oshkosh, 800 Algoma Blvd., Oshkosh 54901. SAN 322-3531. Tel. 920-424-3348, 920-424-4333, fax 920-424-2175. *Coord.* Holly Egebo.

Fox Valley Library Council, c/o OWLS, 225 N. Oneida St., Appleton 54911. SAN 323-9640. Tel. 920-832-6190, fax 920-832-6422. *Pres.* Pat Exarhos.

NorthEast Wisconsin Intertype Libraries, Inc. (NEWIL), c/o Nicolet Federated Library System, 1595 Alloucz Ave. Suite 4, Green Bay 54311. SAN 322-3574. Tel. 920-448-4410, fax 920-448-4420. *Coord.* Jamie Matczak.

Southeastern Wisconsin Health Science Library Consortium, Veterans Admin. Center Medical Lib., Milwaukee 53295. SAN 322-3582. Tel. 414-384-2000 ext. 42342, fax 414-382-5334. *Coord.* Kathy Strube.

Southeastern Wisconsin Information Technology Exchange, Inc. (SWITCH), 6801 North Yates Rd., Milwaukee 53217. Tel. 414-382-6710. *Coord.* Jennifer Schmidt.

Wisconsin Library Services (WILS), 1360 Regent St., No. 121, Madison 53715-1255. Tel. 608-216-8399, e-mail information@wils.org. *Dir.* Stef Morrill.

Wisconsin Public Library Consortium (WPLC), c/o WILS, 1360 Regent St., No. 121, Madison 53715-1255. Tel. 608-216-8399, e-mail information@wils.org. *Dir.* Stef Morrill.

Wisconsin Valley Library Service (WVLS), 300 N. 1 St., Wausau 54403. SAN 371-3911. Tel. 715-261-7250, fax 715-261-7259. *Dir.* Marla Rae Sepnafski.

WISPALS Library Consortium, c/o Gateway Technical College, 3520 30th Ave., Kenosha 53144-1690. Tel. 262-564-2602, fax 262-564-2787. *Chair* Scott Vrieze.

Wyoming

WYLD Network, c/o Wyoming State Lib., 2800 Central Ave., Cheyenne 82002-0060. SAN 371-0661. Tel. 307-777-6333, e-mail support@wyldnetwork.com. *State Libn.* Jamie Marcus.

Canada

Alberta

The Alberta Library (TAL), 623 Seven Sir Winston Churchill Sq. N.W., Edmonton T5J 2V5. Tel. 780-414-0805, fax 780-414-0806, e-mail admin@thealbertalibrary.ab.ca. *CEO* Grant Chaney.

Council of Prairie and Pacific University Libraries (COPPUL), c/o High Density Library, University of Calgary, 150 B – 11711 85th St. N.W., Calgary T3R 1J3. Tel. 403-220-2414. *Exec. Dir.* Vivian Stieda.

NEOS Library Consortium, Cameron Lib., 5th Fl., Edmonton T6G 2J8. Tel. 780-492-0075, fax 780-492-8302. *Mgr.* Anne Carr-Wiggin.

British Columbia

British Columbia Electronic Library Network (BCELN), WAC Bennett Lib., 7th Fl., Simon Fraser Univ., Burnaby V5A 1S6. Tel. 778-782-7003, fax 778-782-3023, e-mail office@eln.bc.ca. *Exec. Dir.* Anita Cocchia.

Center for Accessible Post-Secondary Education Resources, Langara College Library, 100 W. 49th Ave., Vancouver V5Y 2Z6. SAN 329-6970. Tel. 604-323-5639, fax 604-323-5544, e-mail caperbc@langara.bc.ca. *Dir.* Patricia Cia.

Electronic Health Library of British Columbia (e-HLbc), c/o Bennett Lib., 8888 University Dr., Burnaby V5A 1S6. Tel. 778-782-5440, fax 778-782-3023, e-mail info@ehlbc.ca. *Exec. Dir.* Anita Cocchia.

Northwest Library Federation, 12495 Budds Rd., Prince George V2N 6K7. Tel. 250-988-1860, e-mail director@nwlf.ca. *Dir.* Anna Babluck.

Public Library InterLINK, 5489 Byrne Rd., No 158, Burnaby V5J 3J1. SAN 318-8272. Tel. 604-517-8441, fax 604-517-8410, e-mail info@interlinklibraries.ca. *Exec. Dir.* Michael Burris.

Manitoba

Manitoba Library Consortium, Inc. (MLCI), c/o Lib. Admin., Univ. of Winnipeg, 515 Portage Ave., Winnipeg R3B 2E9. SAN 372-820X. Tel. 204-786-9801, fax 204-783-8910. *Chair* Heather Brydon.

Nova Scotia

Maritimes Health Libraries Assn. (MHLA-ABSM), W. K. Kellogg Health Sciences Lib., Halifax B3H 1X5. SAN 370-0836. Tel. 902-494-2483, fax 902-494-3750. *Libn.* Shelley McKibbon.

NOVANET, The Consortium of Nova Scotia Academic Libraries, 120 Western Pkwy., No. 202, Bedford B4B 0V2. SAN 372-4050. Tel. 902-453-2470, fax 902-453-2369, e-mail office@novanet.ca. *Mgr.* Bill Slauenwhite.

Ontario

Canadian Assn. of Research Libraries (Association des Bibliothèques de Recherche du Canada), 203-309 Cooper St., Ottawa K2P 0G5. SAN 323-9721. Tel. 613-482-9344, fax 613-562-5297, e-mail info@carl-abrc. ca. *Exec. Dir.* Susan Haigh.

Canadian Health Libraries Assn. (CHLA-ABSC), 468 Queen St. E., LL-02, Toronto M5A 1T7. SAN 370-0720. Tel. 416-646-1600, fax 416-646-9460, e-mail info@chla-absc.ca. *Exec. Dir.* Perry Ruehlen.

Canadian Heritage Information Network, 1030 Innes Rd., Ottawa K1B 4S7. SAN 329-3076. Tel. 613-998-3721, fax 613-998-4721, e-mail pch.rcip-chin.pch@canada.ca. *Dir.* Charlie Costain.

Canadian Research Knowledge Network (CRKN), 11 Holland Ave., Suite 301, Ottawa K1Y 4S1. Tel. 613-907-7040, fax 866-903-9094. *Exec. Dir.* Clare Appavoo.

Hamilton and District Health Library Network, 100 King Street W., Hamilton L8P 1A2. SAN 370-5846. Tel. 905-521-2100, fax 905-540-6504. *Coord.* Karen Dearness.

Health Science Information Consortium of Toronto, c/o Gerstein Science Info. Center, Univ. of Toronto, 9 King's College Circle, Toronto M5S 1A5. SAN 370-5080. Tel. 416-978-6359, fax 416-971-2637. *Exec. Dir.* Lori Anne Oja.

Ontario Council of University Libraries (OCUL), 130 Saint George St., Toronto M5S 1A5. Tel. 416-946-0578, fax 416-978-6755. *Exec. Dir.* John Barnett.

Ontario Library Consortium (OLC), c/o Brant Public Lib., 12 William St., Paris M3L 1K7. *Pres.* Kelly Bernstein.

Perth County Information Network (PCIN), c/o Stratford Public Lib., 19 St. Andrew St., Stratford N5A 1A2. Tel. 519-271-0220, fax 519-271-3843, e-mail webmaster@pcin.on. ca. *CEO* Sam Coglin.

Southwestern Ontario Health Libraries and Information Network (SOHLIN), London Health Sciences Centre, London N6A 5W9. Tel. 519-685-8500 ext. 56038. *Pres.* Jill McTavish.

Toronto Health Libraries Assn. (THLA), 3409 Yonge St., Toronto M4N 2L0. SAN 323-9853. Tel. 416-485-0377, fax 416-485-6877, e-mail medinfoserv@rogers.com. *Pres.* Zack Osborne.

Woodstock Hospital Regional Library Services, Woodstock General Hospital, 310 Juliana Dr., Woodstock N4V 0A4. SAN 323-9500. Tel. 519-421-4233 ext. 2735, fax 519-421-4236. *Contact* Bailey Urso.

Quebec

Assn. des Bibliothèques de la Santé Affiliées a l'Université de Montréal (ABSAUM), c/o Health Lib., Univ. of Montreal, Montreal H3C 3J7. SAN 370-5838. Tel. 514-343-6826, fax 514-343-2350. *Dir.* Monique St-Jean.

Federal Libraries Consortium (FLC), 550 de la Cité Blvd., Gatineau K1A 0N4. Tel. 613-410-9752, fax 819-934-7539, e-mail fed librariesconsortium.LAC@canada.ca.

Réseau BIBLIO de l'Ouatouais, 2295 Saint-Louis St., Gatineau, Quebec J8T 5L8. SAN 319-6526. Tel. 819-561-6008. *Exec. Gen.* Sylvie Thibault.

Saskatchewan

Consortium of Academic and Special Libraries of Saskatchewan (CASLS), Courthouse, 2425 Victoria Ave., Regina S4P 3M3. *Mailing address:* P.O. Box 5032, Regina S4P 3M3. *Chair* Melanie Hodges Neufeld.

Library and Information-Industry Associations and Organizations, U.S. and Canada

AIIM—The Association for Information and Image Management

Chair, Martin Birch
President and CEO, Peggy Winton
8403 Colesville Rd., Suite 1100, Silver Spring, MD 20910
800-477-2446, 301-587-8202, fax 301-587-2711, e-mail hello@aiim.org
World Wide Web http://www.aiim.org
European Office: Broomhall Business Centre, Lower Broomhall Farm, Broomhall Ln., Worcester WR5 2NT, UK
Tel. 44-1905-727600, fax 44-1905-727609, e-mail info@aiim.org

Objective

AIIM is an international authority on enterprise content management, the tools and technologies that capture, manage, store, preserve, and deliver content in support of business processes. Founded in 1943.

Officers (2021)

Chair Martin Birch, ibml; *V.Chair* Dave Jones, Instinctive Solutions; *Treas.* Kramer Reeves, IBM; *Past Chair* Ian Story, Microsoft.

Board Members

Ron Cameron, Rikkert Engels, Karen Hobert, Shukra Kichambare, Stephen Ludlow, Riley McIntosh, Rand Wacker.

Publication

The AIIM Blog.

American Association of Law Libraries

Executive Director, Vani Ungapen
105 W. Adams St., Suite 3300, Chicago, IL 60603
312-939-4764, fax 312-431-1097, e-mail vungapen@aall.org
World Wide Web http://www.aallnet.org

Our Mission

The American Association of Law Libraries advances the profession of law librarianship and supports the professional growth of its members through leadership and advocacy in the field of legal information and information policy.

Membership

4,000 members. For law librarians and other legal information professionals of any professional sector. Dues (Indiv.) $270; (Ret.) $67; (Student) $67. Year. June–May.

Officers (2020–2021)

Pres. Emily Florio; *V.P.* Diane Rodriguez; *Secy.* Mary Jenkins; *Treas.* Cornell H. Winston; *Past Pres.* Michelle Cosby.

Board of Directors

Susan David Demaine, Stacy Etheredge, Emily M. Janoski-Haehlen, June Hsiao Liebert; Karen Selden; Jason R. Sowards.

Publications

AALL EBriefing.
AALL ENewsletter (mo.).
AALL Weekly ENewsletter.

AALL Spectrum (bi-mo.; free; digital only starting 2021).
AALL State of the Profession Report (print, digital, or print-digital bundle).
Law Library Journal (q.; digital; free).
AALL Biennial Salary Survey and Organizational Characteristics (biennial; memb. only online; print e-mail orders@aall.org).
Index to Foreign Legal Periodicals (print or online).
AALL White Papers (digital).
Guide to Fair Practices for Legal Publishers.
KnowItAALL (memb. only; digital; free).
LegalTrac.
Principles and Practices for Licensing Electronic Sources.
Universal Citation Guide.

American Indian Library Association

Executive Director, Heather Devine-Hardy (Eastern Shawnee)
E-mail hhdevine@gmail.com
World Wide Web https://ailanet.org

Objective

To improve library and information services for American Indians. Founded in 1979; affiliated with American Library Association in 1985.

Membership

Any person, library, or other organization interested in working to improve library and information services for American Indians may become a member. Dues (Inst.) $40; (Indiv.) $20; (Student) $10.

Officers (2020–2021)

Pres. Cindy Hohl; *Pres. Elect* Aaron LaFromboise; *Secy.* Rhiannon Sorrell (Diné); *Treas.* Liana Juliano; *Past Pres.* George Gottschalk (Muscogee [Creek] Nation); *Memb.-at-Large* Carla Davis-Castro (Chippewa-Cree), Stacy Wells, Mary Kunesh-Podein.

Publication

AILA Newsletter (bi-ann.; memb. and non-memb.: electronic; print: memb. only). *Ed.* George Gottschalk.

American Library Association

Executive Director, Tracie D. Hall
225 N. Michigan Ave, Suite 1300
Chicago, IL 60601
312-944-6780, 800-545-2433, fax 312-440-9374, e-mail ala@ala.org
World Wide Web http://www.ala.org

Objective

The object of the American Library Association shall be to promote library service and librarianship. The mission of the American Library Association (ALA) is to provide leadership for the development, promotion, and improvement of library and information services and the profession of librarianship in order to enhance learning and ensure access to information for all. Founded 1876.

Membership

Memb. (Indiv.) 51,842; (Inst.) 5,189; (Corporate) 146; (Total) 57,177. Any person, library, or other organization interested in library service and librarians. Dues (Indiv.) 1st year, $74; 2nd year, $112; 3rd year and later, $148; (Trustee and Assoc. Memb.) $67; (Lib. Support Staff) $53; (Student) $39; (Foreign Indiv.) $89; (Nonsalaried/Unemployed/Ret.) $53; (Inst.) $175 and up, depending on operating expenses of institution.

Divisions

See the separate entries that follow: American Assn. of School Libns.; Assn. for Lib. Service to Children; Assn. of College and Research Libs; Core: Leadership, Infrastructure, Futures; Public Lib. Assn.; Reference and User Services Assn.; United for Libraries; Young Adult Lib. Services Assn.

Officers (2020–2021)

Pres. Julius C. Jefferson, Jr., Private Citizen, Washington, DC; *Pres.-Elect* Patricia Patricia "Patty" M. Wong, Santa Monica Public Library, Santa Monica, CA 90401; *Treas.* Maggie Farrell. Univ. of Nevada, Las Vegas, Las Vegas, NV

89001; *Past Pres.* Wanda Kay Brown, Winston-Salem State University, Winston-Salem, NC 27110.

Board Members

Tamika Barnes *(2018–2021)*; Latrice Booker *(2020–2023)*; Ed Garcia *(2018–2021)*; Eboni M. Henry *(2019–2022)*; Maria McCauley, Ph.D. *(2018–2021)*; Larry Neal *(2020–2023)*; Alexandra Rivera *(2020–2023)*; Karen G. Schneider *(2019–2022)*.

Round Table Chairs

Ethnic and Multicultural Information Exchange (EMIERT). Dr. Andrea Jamison.
Exhibits (ERT). David Lysinger.
Film and Media (FMRT). Steven Dennis Milewski.
Games and Gaming Round Table (GameRT). Jessica Parij.
Government Documents Round Table (GODORT). Lynda Kellam.
Graphic Novel and Comics (GNCRT). Alea Perez.
Intellectual Freedom (IFRT). Wanda Mae Huffaker.
International Relations (IRRT). Alexandra H. Humphreys.
Learning Round Table (LearnRT, formerly CLENERT). Kimberly A. Brown-Harden.
Library History (LHRT). Bernadette A. Lear.
Library Instruction (LIRT). Jennifer Hunter.
Library Research (LRRT). Abigail Phillips.
Library Support Staff Interests (LSSIRT). Nina Manning.
Map and Geospatial Information (MAGIRT). Sierra Laddusaw.
New Members (NMRT). Jennifer Wilhelm.
Rainbow Round Table (RRT) Rae-Anne Montague.
Retired Members (RMRT). Nancy M. Bolt.

Social Responsibilities (SRRT). April Sheppard.
Staff Organization (SORT). Danielle M. Ponton.
Sustainability. Laura A. Ploenzke.

Committee Chairs

Accreditation. Rachel A. Applegate.
ALA-Children's Book Council Joint. Esmerelda Majors.
American Libraries Advisory. Susan H. Polos.
Awards. Jos N. Holman.
Budget Analysis and Review. Peter Hepburn.
Chapter Relations. Amy Spence Lappin
Committee on Appointments. None listed
Committee on Committees. Ms. Patty M. Wong
Conference. Robin Kear.
Constitution and Bylaws. Dr. Ann Dutton Ewbank
Council Orientation. Rodney Lippard.
Diversity. Valerie Bell.
Diversity, Literacy, and Outreach Services Advisory. Elizabeth Jean Brumfield
Education. Dr. Karen E. Downing.
Election. No current roster.
Human Resource Development and Recruitment Advisory. Libby Holtmann
Information Technology Advisory. Gina Seymour.
Information Technology Policy Advisory. James K. Teliha
Intellectual Freedom. Erin Berman.
International Relations. Dr. Ismail Abdullahi.
Legislation. Joseph A. Thompson, Jr.
Library Advocacy. Justin Paul De La Cruz.
Literacy. Tiffeni J. Fontno.
Membership. Christina Rodrigues.
Membership Meetings. Michael Golrick.

Nominations. Madeline Ivette Pena.
Organization. James Neal.
Policy Monitoring. Edward Sanchez.
Professional Ethics. Stephen L. Matthews.
Public and Cultural Programs Advisory. Dr. Nicole A. Cooke.
Public Awareness. Erin Barnthouse.
Publishing. Christine Korytnyk Dulaney.
Research and Statistics. Dr. Leslie Campbell Hime.
Resolutions. Mike Marlin.
Rural, Native, and Tribal Libraries of All Kinds. John Sandstrom.
Scholarships and Study Grants. Bradley J. Kuykendall.
Status of Women in Leadership. Loida A. Garcia-Febo.
Training, Orientation, and Leadership Development. Dr. Alyse Jordan.

Publications

American Libraries (6 a year; memb., organizations in U.S., Canada, and Mexico $74; elsewhere $84; single copy $7.50).
Booklist (22 a year, with digital edition access to current and past issues of *Book Links* and 24/7 access to *Booklist Online*; U.S. and Canada $169.50; foreign $188).
Library Studies, Issues and Trends report.
Library Technology Reports (8 a year, online and print $340, non-U.S. $385).
Smart Libraries Newsletter (mo., online, and print $101, non-U.S. $111).

American Library Association
American Association of School Librarians

Executive Director, Sylvia Knight Norton (ex officio)
225 N. Michigan Ave., Ste. 1300, Chicago, IL 60601
312-280-4382, 800-545-2433 ext. 4382, fax (312) 280-5276, e-mail snorton@ala.org
World Wide Web http://www.aasl.org, e-mail aasl@ala.org

Objective

The American Association of School Librarians (AASL) empowers leaders to transform teaching and learning. Established in 1951 as a separate division of the American Library Association, AASL understands the current realities and evolving dynamics of the professional environment and is positioned to help members achieve universal recognition of school librarians as indispensable educational leaders. AASL publishes standards for the profession *National School Library Standards for Learners, School Librarians, and School Libraries* (2018, its latest), providing a comprehensive approach through integrated frameworks consisting of four domains (Think, Create, Share, Grow) and six Shared Foundations (Inquire, Include, Collaborate, Curate, Explore, Engage).

Membership

Memb. 5,900+. Open to all school librarians, librarians, libraries, interested individuals, and business firms, with requisite membership in ALA.

Board of Directors (2020–2021)

Pres. Kathy Carroll, Westwood HS, Lead Lib. Media Specialist, SC; *Pres.-Elect* Jennisen Lucas, Park County School District #6, District Librarian, WY; *Treas.* Erika Long, Thurgood Marshall Middle School, School Libn., TN; *Past Pres.* Mary Keeling, Newport News Public Schools, Supervisor Lib. Services, VA; *Div. Councilor* Diane R. Chen, Stratford STEM School, School Libn.,TN; Maria Cahill, Becky Calzada, Anita Cellucci, Sylvia Knight Norton, Heather Thore.

Section Leadership

AASL/ESLS. Daniella Smith, Elizabeth Burns, Angela Branyon, Joyce Valenza.

AASL/ISS. Bianca N. Spurlock, Anna Brannin, Jenna Nemec-Loise, Elizabeth Nelson.

AASL/SPVS. Christina Shepard Norman, Susan Gauthier, Jennifer Sturge, Jenny Takeda.

(Subcommittees may be found on section websites.)

Committee Chairs

AASL/ALSC/YALSA Joint Committee on School/Public Library Cooperation. Sylvia Knight Norton (SL).

Annual Conference. Allison Cline (staff liaison/SL).

Association of American University Presses Book Selection. Dona Helmer, Stephanie Book (SL).

Awards. Allison Cline (SL).

Budget and Finance. Erika Long.

Bylaws and Organization. Robbie Leah Nickel. Sylvia Knight Norton (SL).

CAEP Coordinating Committee. Sylvia Knight Norton (SL)

Chapter Delegates. Catherine M. Fuhrman.

Knowledge Quest. Sarah Searles, Meg Featheringham.

Leadership Development. Mary Keeling. Sylvia Knight Norton (SL).

Legacy. Cassandra Barnett. Allison Cline (SL).

Member Engagement. Courtney Lewis. Allison Cline (SL).

National Conference. Allison Cline (SL).

Practice. Lori Donovan. Allison Cline (SL). Sylvia Knight Norton (SL).

Professional Learning. Buffy Edwards. Jennifer Habley (SL).

Publications. Stephanie Book (SL).

School Library Event Promotion Committee. Chelsea Brantley, Jennifer Habley (SL).

School Library Research. Audrey Church, Elizabeth Burns, Meg Featheringham (SL).

School Librarian Preparation National Recognition. Judy T. Bevins.

School / Public Library Cooperation. ALSC, Sylvia Knight Norton (SL).

Social Media. Jennifer Habley (SL).

Standards. Ann Vickman, Sylvia Knight Norton (SL).

Editorial Board Chairs

Knowledge Quest Editorial Board. Sarah Searles. Meg Featheringham (editor/SL).

School Library Research Editorial Board. Audrey Church, Elizabeth Burns. Meg Featheringham (editor/SL).

Social Media Editorial Board. Jennifer Habley (SL).

Task Force Chairs

ASCD Task Force. Allison Cline (SL).

Labeling Position Statement Task Force. Jen Habley (SL).

School Library Supervisor Position Statement. Allison Cline (SL).

Awards Committee Chairs

ABC-CLIO Leadership Grant. Michael-Brian Ogawa.

Best Digital Tools for Teaching and Learning. Mary Morgan Ryan.

Chapter of the Year Award. Nicole Ballard-Long.

Collaborative School Library Award. Jennifer Powell.

Distinguished School Administrator Award. Susan Hess.

Frances Henne Award. Martha Pangburn.

Innovative Reading Grant. Alexa Lalejini.

Inspire Collection Development Grant. Nicolle Mazzola.

Inspire Special Event Grant. Zandra Lopez.

Intellectual Freedom Award. Valerie Ayer.

National School Library of the Year Award. Lisa Brakel.

Research Grant. TBD, Allison Cline (SL).

Roald Dahl Miss Honey Social Justice Award. Karen Egger.

(Allison Cline is staff liaison for all awards committees.)

Publications

Knowledge Quest (bi-mo.; memb.; nonmemb. $50 per year; outside US $60 per year; https://knowledgequest.aasl.org/subscription). *Ed.* Meg Featheringham. E-mail mfeatheringham@ala.org.

School Library Research (electronic, free, at http://www.ala.org/aasl/slr). *Ed.* Meg Featheringham. E-mail mfeatheringham@ala.org.

American Library Association
Association for Library Service to Children

Executive Director, Aimee Strittmatter
225 N. Michigan Ave., Suite 1300

Chicago, IL 60601
800-545-2433 ext. 2163, alsc@ala.org
World Wide Web http://www.ala.org/alsc/

Objective

The Association for Library Service to Children (ALSC) develops and supports the profession of children's librarianship by enabling and encouraging its practitioners to provide the best library service to our nation's children.

The Association for Library Service to Children is interested in the improvement and extension of library services to children in all types of libraries. It is responsible for the evaluation and selection of book and nonbook library materials and for the improvement of techniques of library service to children from preschool through the eighth grade of junior high school age, when such materials and techniques are intended for use in more than one type of library. ALSC has specific responsibility for the following:

1. Continuous study and critical review of activities assigned to the division.
2. Conduct of activities and carrying on of projects within its area of responsibility.
3. Cooperation with all units of ALA whose interests and activities have a relationship to library service to children.
4. Interpretation of library materials for children and of methods of using such materials with children, to parents, teachers, and other adults, and representation of librarians' concern for the production and effective use of good children's books to groups outside the profession.
5. Stimulation of the professional growth of its members and encouragement of participation in appropriate type-of-library divisions.
6. Planning and development of programs of study and research in the area of selection and use of library materials for children for the total profession.

7. Development, evaluation, and promotion of professional materials in its area of responsibility. Founded in 1901.

Membership

Memb. 3,797. Open to anyone interested in library services to children. Dues in addition to ALA membership (Regular) $50; (Student) $20; (Nonsalaried/Ret.) $35; (Associate) $25.

Address correspondence to the ALSC Office, http://www.ala.org/alsc/aboutalsc/contact.

Officers (2020–2021)

Pres. Kirby McCurtis. E-mail kirbyalsc@gmail.com; *V.P.* Lucia Martinez Gonzalez; *Past Pres.* Cecilia P. McGowan. E-mail nmcgowanalsc@gmail.com; *Div. Councilor* Kimberly Anne Patton; *Fiscal Officer* Amber Lea Creger.

Board Members

Elisa Gall; Africa S. Hands, Maggie Jacobs; Sujei Lugo; April Mazza; Soraya Anne-Machel Silverman-Montano; Meredith C. Steiner. Aimee Strittmatter (ex officio).

Committee Chairs

AASL/ALSC/YALSA Interdivisional Committee on School/Public Library Cooperation. Sam Bloom.
Advocacy and Legislation. Cassie Chenoweth, Erica M. Ruscio.
BIOPC (Black, Indigenous and/or People of Color) Discussion Group. Alia R. Jones, Hanna Lee.

Budget. Robin Ellis Friedman.

Children and Libraries Editorial Advisory. Jennifer Knight, Judy Zuckerman.

Children and Technology. Kimba M. Azore, Deidre Winterhalter.

Children's Collections Management Discussion Group. Liv Anne Hanson. Lisa R. Nabel.

Children's Literature Lecture Award Committee 2021. Gloria Repolesk.

Early Childhood Programs and Services. Darla R. Salva Cruz, Stephanie Joan Smallwood.

Early and Family Literacy. Lori Romero, Joanna Ward.

Education. Edith Campbell, Tony A. Carmack.

Excellence for Early Learning Digital Media. Celeste Swanson.

Intellectual Freedom. Dr. Elizabeth J. Hartnett, Dr. Allison G. Kaplan.

Library Service to Underserved Children and Their Caregivers. Jaime Lee Eastman, Joe Joseph Prince

Local Arrangements. John Danneker.

Managing Children's Services. Krista D. Riggs, Michael A. Rogalla

Membership. Amy Seto Forrester, Tanya A. Prax.

Nominating and Leadership Development– 2021. Nina Lindsay

Nominating and Leadership Development– 2022. Paula Holmes

Notable Children's Books. Alexandra Bell.

Notable Children's Digital Media. Robin J. Howe, Brittany A. Tavernaro.

Notable Children's Recordings. Jillian C. Frasher.

Organizational Effectiveness. Naphtali Faris, Jennal Friebel.

Preschool Services Discussion Group. Lisa Gangemi Kropp.

Program Coordinating. Michael P. Santangelo, Tara Phethean.

Public Awareness. Cassie Chenoweth, Erica M. Ruscio.

Quicklists Consulting. Kristen Rocha Aldrich, Kit Ballenger.

Scholarships. Megan Alleyn Egbert, Bina S. Williams.

School-age Programs and Service. Kimberly Probert Grad, Sierra McKenzie.

Storytelling Discussion Group. Vicky Smith.

Task Force Chairs

Diversifying Revenue Streams Task Force. Amy E. Koester.

Equity, Diversity, and Inclusion (EDI) within ALSC Implementation. Danielle Jones, Sophie Kenney.

National Institute Planning. Sarah Polen (SL)

Research Agenda. Melody R. Frese.

Summer/Out-of-School-Time Learning. Elizabeth McChesney.

Awards Committee Chairs

Mildred L. Batchelder Award 2021. Susanne Myers Harold.

Mildred L. Batchelder Award 2022. Dr. Marie A. LeJeune.

Children's Literature Legacy Award Selection Committee–2021. Junko Yokota.

Children's Literature Legacy Award Selection Committee–2022. Brian E. Wilson.

Pura Belpré Award 2021. Jessica Agudelo.

Pura Belpré Award 2022. Shelly Marie Diaz.

Pura Belpre 25th Anniversary Planning Task Force. Ramona Caponegro, Oscar Giurcovich.

Pura Belpre Expansion Task Force. Ayn Reyes Frazee, Ana-Elba Pavon.

Randolph Caldecott Award 2021. Anisha Jeffries.

Randolph Caldecott Award 2022. Dr. Claudette S. McLin.

Theodor Seuss Geisel Award 2021. Lori Coffey Hancock.

Theodor Seuss Geisel Award 2022. Eboni R. Njoku.

John Newbery Award 2021. Dr. Jonda C. McNair.

John Newbery Award 2022. Thaddeus Andracki.

Odyssey Award 2022. Pat Toney.

Professional Recognition and Scholarships. Megan Alleyn Egbert, Bina S. Williams

Programs and Services Recognition. Erin Lovelace, Jacqueline J. Partch.

Robert F. Sibert Informational Book Award 2021. Brandy Sanchez.

Robert F. Sibert Informational Book Award 2022. Catherine Potter.

Excellence in Early Learning Digital Media. Celeste Swanson.

Award Manual Revision Working Group. Caitlin D. Jacobson, Carol K. Phillips.

Publications

ALSC Matters! (q., electronic; open access).

Children and Libraries: The Journal of the Association for Library Service to Children (q.; print and online; memb.; nonmemb. $50; intl. $60).

American Library Association
Association of College and Research Libraries

Interim Executive Director, Kara Malenfant (ex officio)
225 N. Michigan Ave, Suite 1300, Chicago, IL 60601
312-280-2523, 800-545-2433 ext. 2523, fax 312-280-2520, e-mail acrl@ala.org
World Wide Web http://www.ala.org/acrl

Objective

The Association is a forum for and an advocate of academic and research librarians and library personnel. The object of the Association is to provide leadership for the development, promotion, and improvement of academic and research library resources and services, and to advance learning, research, and scholarly communication. Founded 1940.

Membership

Memb. 9,108. For information on dues, see ALA entry.

Officers (2020–2021)

Pres. Jon E. Cawthorne, Ph.D; *Vice Pres.* Julie Ann Garrison; *Past Pres.* Karen Munro.

Board of Directors

Toni Anaya, Jessica Brangiel, Faye A. Chadwell, Kim Copenhaver, April D. Cunningham, Jeanne R. Davidson, Cinthya Ippoliti, Kelly Gordon Jacobsma, Carolyn Henderson Allen, Kara Malenfant (ex officio).

Committee Chairs

ACRL 2021 Coordinating. Beth McNeil.
ACRL 2021 Colleagues. Julia M. Gelfand, Damon E. Jaggars.
ACRL 2021 Contributed Papers. Faye A. Chadwell, Clara Llebot Lorente.
ACRL 2021 Innovations. Toni Anaya, Leila June Rod-Welch.
ACRL 2021 Invited Presentations. Erla P. Heyns, Willie Miller.
ACRL 2021 Keynote Speakers. John P. Culshaw, Janice D. Welburn.
ACRL 2021 Lightning Talks. Sarah Bankston, Heidi Steiner Burkhardt.
ACRL 2021 Local Arrangements. John Danneker, Christie J. Flynn.
ACRL 2021 Panel Sessions. Merinda Kaye Hensley, LeRoy Jason LaFleur.
ACRL 2021 Poster Sessions. Trevor A. Dawes, Martin L. Garnar.
ACRL 2021 Preconference Coordinating. Bill Gillis, Federico Martinez-Garcia, Jr.
ACRL 2021 Roundtable Discussions Committee. Amanda K. Nida, Kathy A. Parsons.
ACRL 2021 Scholarships. Twanna K. Hodge, Lisa M. Stillwell.
ACRL 2021 TechConnect Presentations. Shawn P. Calhoun, Adriene I. Lim.
ACRL 2021 Virtual Conference. Rachel Besara, Paul A. Sharpe.
ACRL 2021 Workshop Programs. Anne Marie Casey, Alexia Hudson-Ward.
ACRL/CORE Interdivisional Academic Library Facilities. Anne Marie Casey, Eric A. Kidwell.
Appointments. Robert H. McDonald.
Budget and Finance. Carolyn Henderson Allen.
Chapters Council. Alison Marie Larson.
Communities of Practice Assembly. Susan Garrison. Constance M. Wade.
Conference Colleagues. Julia M. Gelfand, Damon E. Jaggars.
Equity, Diversity, and Inclusion. Mary Beth Lock

(Dr. E. J.) Josey Spectrum Scholar Mentor. Aubrey Iglesias.

External Liaisons. Rachel M. Minkin.

Liaisons Assembly. Christine Ruotolo.

Government Relations. Dr. Kevin Walker.

Immersion Program. Dr. Karen Sobel.

Leadership Recruitment and Nomination. Steven M. Adams.

Lightning Talks. Sarah Bankston, Heidi Steiner Burkhardt.

Membership. Dr. Monica D.T. Rysavy, Ph.D, Ed.D.

Section Membership. Shauna Borger Edson.

New Roles and Changing Landscapes. Erin T. Smith.

Professional Development. Rachel Besara

2021 President's Program Planning. Jennifer Garrett, Jersome Offord, Jr.

2022 President's Program Planning. Julie Ann Garrison. Megan R. Griffin

Professional Values. Dr. Tracy Elliot.

Publications Coordinating. Julia M. Gelfand.

Research Planning and Review. Ginny Boehme.

Research and Scholarly Environment. Charlotte Roh.

Standards. Dr. Jennifer E. Steele

Information Literacy Frameworks and Standards. Caitlin Elizabeth Plovnick.

Student Learning and Information Literacy. Alex R. Hodges.

Value of Academic Libraries. Dr. Amanda L. Folk.

Editorial Board Chairs

Academic Library Trends and Statistics Survey. Adrian K. Ho.

ACRL/LLAMA Interdivisional Academic Library Facilities Survey. Anne Marie Casey, Eric A. Kidwell.

Choice. Diane G. Klare.

College & Research Libraries. Wendi Arant Kaspar, Emily Drabinski.

College & Research Libraries News. Heidi Steiner Burkhardt.

New Publications Advisory. Courtney McDonald.

Project Outcome for Academic Libraries. Tiffany Garrett.

Publications in Librarianship. Daniel Clark Mack.

RBM: A Journal of Rare Books, Manuscripts, and Cultural Heritage. Richard Saunders.

Resources for College Libraries. Tammera M. Race.

Task Force Chairs

Academic Librarians Standards and Guidelines Review. Faye A. Chadwell.

ACRL/ALA/ARL IPEDS. Robert E. Dugan, Erik Mitchell.

ACRL/ARL/ODLOS/PLA Building Cultural Proficiencies for Racial Equity Framework. Jennifer Garrett.

ACRL/RBMS-ARLIS/NA-SAA Joint Task Force on Development of the Art and Rare Materials BIBFRAME Ontology Extension. Jason Kovari.

Awards. Merinda Kaye Hensley, Erin T. Smith.

Diversity Alliance. Dr. Jose A. Aguinaga, Annie Belanger.

National Survey of Student Engagement (NSSE) Information Literacy Module Review. Merinda Kaye Hensley.

Discussion Group Conveners

Assessment. Nancy B. Turner.

Balancing Baby and Book. Laura Bornella.

Copyright. Sandra Enimil, April Hathcock.

First-Year Experience. Charissa Powell.

Heads of Public Services. William H. Weare, Jr.

Hip Hop Librarian Consortium. Craig E. Arthur.

Human Resources and Organizational Development. Agnes K. Bradshaw, Julie Brewer.

International Perspectives on Academic and Research Libraries. John Hickock.

Language and Linguistics. Katie E. Gibson, Dan Mandeville.

Leadership. Russell S. Michalak, Monica D. T. Rysavy.

Learning Commons. Diane M. Fulkerson.

Librarians from Very Small Academic Institutions. Linda M. Kramer.

Librarianship in For-Profit Educational Institutions. Mary A. Snyder.

Media Resources. Gisele Genevieve Tanasse.

Philosophical, Religious, and Theological Studies. Frederick Charles Carey, Megan Welsh.

Scholarly Communication. Erin Elizabeth Owens.
Student Retention. Nicole Helregel.
Undergraduate Librarians. Chris Davidson.

Interest Group Conveners

Academic Library Services to Graduate Students. Geoffrey Johnson, Jessica Hagman.
Academic Library Services to International Students. Meredith Knoff, Allison Sharp, Mihoko Hosoi.
Access Services. Susan Garrison, Constance M. Wade, Renise Johnson, Joanna Messer Kemmitt.
African-American Studies Librarians. Tahirah Z. Akbar-Williams.
Asian, African, and Middle Eastern Studies. Deepa Banerjee, Triveni S. Kuchi.
Contemplative Pedagogy. Nancy Snyder Gibson, Madeleine Charney.
Digital Badges. Emily L. Rimland, Wendy G. Pothier.
Health Sciences. Annie Zeidman-Karpinski, Anna Ferri.
History Librarians. Kaitlyn L. Tanis, Rebecca Ann Lloyd.
Image Resources. Maggie Murphy, Jacqueline K. Fleming.
Librarianship in For-Profit Educational Institutions. Mary A. Snyder.
Library Marketing and Outreach. Sara DeSantis, Leila June Rod-Welch, Jillian Christine Eslami, Tori Golden.
Research Assessment and Metrics. Laura Bowering Mullen.
Residency. Sheila A. Garcia, Jessica Dai.
Systematic Reviews and Related Methods. Kate Ghezzi-Kopel, Sarah Young.
Technical Services. Marina Morgan, David A. Van Kleeck.
Universal Accessibility. Meredith Knoff, Maya Hobscheid.
Virtual Worlds. Alyse M. Dunavant-Jones, Breiana Theodore.

Awards Committee Chairs

Academic/Research Librarian of the Year Award. Dennis Clark, Adrian Morales.

Hugh C. Atkinson Memorial Award. Angela M. Gooden, Rebecca L. Mugridge, Dale Poulter.
Excellence in Academic Libraries Awards. Lauren Pressley, Karen Munro.

Publications / Editorial Board Chairs

Academic Library Trends and Statistics Survey. Adrian K. Ho, Devin Savage.
ACRL/Core Interdivisional Academic Library Facilities Survey. Anne Marie Casey, Eric A. Kidwell.
C&RL. Emily Drabinski, Wendi Arant Kaspar.
C&RL News. Heidi Steiner Burkhardt.
Choice. Diane G. Klare.
New Publications Advisory Board. Courtney Greene McDonald.
Project Outcome for Academic Libraries. Tiffany Garrett, Jennifer Arnold.
Publications in Librarianship. Daniel Clark Mack.
RBM. Richard Saunders, Jennifer Karr Sheehan.
Resources for College Libraries. Tammera M. Race.

Section Chairs

Anthropology and Sociology (ANSS). Juliann Couture.
Arts Section. Mackenzie Salisbury.
College Libraries Section (CLS). Mary Mallery.
Community and Junior College Libraries Section (CJCLS). Robin Brown.
Digital Scholarship Section. Kristen Grace Totleben.
Distance and Online Learning Section (DOLS). Amanda L. W. Ziegler.
Education and Behavioral Sciences Section (EBSS). April Hines.
European Studies Section (ESS). Thomas Francis Keenan.
Instruction Section (IS). Nikhat J. Ghouse.
Literatures in English Section (LES). Brian Flota.
Politics, Policy and International Relations Section (PPIRS). Erin Ackerman.
Rare Books and Manuscripts (RBMS). Petrina D. Jackson.

Science and Technology Section (STS). Rachel Borchardt.

University Libraries Section (ULS). Michelle Demeter.

Women and Gender Studies Section (WGSS). Sharon Ladenson.

Publications

Choice (12 a year; $513; Canada and Mexico $551; other international $660). Ed. Mark Cummings. Tel. 860-347-6933 ext. 119, e-mail mcummings@ala-choice.org.

Choice Reviews-on-Cards (requires subscription to *Choice* or *Choice Reviews* $576; Canada and Mexico $618; other international $713).

College & Research Libraries (*C&RL*) (6 a year; open access online-only). Ed. Wendi Arant Kaspar. E-mail warant@tamu.edu.

College & Research Libraries News (*C&RL News*) (11 a year; memb.; nonmemb. $58; Canada and other PUAS countries $63; other international $68). Ed. David Free Tel. 312-280-2517, e-mail dfree@ala.org.

RBM: A Journal of Rare Books, Manuscripts, and Cultural Heritage (s. ann.; $52; Canada and other PUAS countries $58; other international $69). Ed. Richard Saunders. Southern Utah Univ., 351 W. University Blvd. Gerrald R. Sherratt Lib., Cedar City, UT 84720-2415. Tel. 435-865-7947, fax 435-865-8152, e-mail rsaunders@suu.edu.

American Library Association CORE: Leadership, Infrastructure, Futures

Executive Director, Kerry Ward
225 N. Michigan Ave, Suite 1300, Chicago, IL 60601
800-535-2433, e-mail core@ala.org
World Wide Web http://www.ala.org/core/

Vision

Core members play a central role in every library, shaping the future of the profession through community building, advocacy, and learning.

Mission

To cultivate and amplify the collective expertise of library workers in core functions through building, advocacy, and learning.

Membership

Memb. 5,931. For information on dues, see ALA entry.

Officers (2020–2022)

Pres. Christopher J. Cronin; *Pres.-Elect* Lindsay Anne Cronk; *Past Pres.* Jennifer B. Bowen; *Div. Councilor* Jodie Gambill; *Chair of Org.* Anne Cooper Moore; *Chair of Budget* Miranda Henry Bennett.

Board of Directors

Galen Charlton, Tabatha Farney, Hong Ma, Mary E. Miller, Karen Neurohr, Lori P. Robare, Berika Williams; Tyler Dzuba, Evviva R. Weinraub Lajoie (ex officio).

Committee Chairs

Advocacy Coordination Committee. Brooke Morris Chott (SL).

Preservation Outreach Committee. Katherine Risseeuw.

Appointments Committee. SL Kerry Ward (SL).

Awards and Scholarships Coordination. Jennifer B. Bowen.

Bylaws and Organization. Anne Cooper Moore.

Budget and Finance. Miranda Henry Bennett.
Committee Recognizing Excellence in Children's and Young Adult Science Fiction. Jodie Purcell.
Communications Coordination. Chrishelle M. Thomas (SL).
Competencies Development. Nancy A. Cunningham.
Conference Program Coordination. Richard R. Guajardo, Sarah Wallbank.
Content Coordination. Jenny Levine (SL).
Continuing Education Coordination. Jeremy J. Myntti, Amanda A. Stone.
Diversity and Inclusion. Amber Billey, Ashley Ruth Lierman.
Exchange Planning. Julie Reese (SL).
Forum Planning. Julie Reese (SL).
Fundraising and Sponsorships. Kerry Ward (SL).
International Relations. Aubrey Iglesias.
Interest Group Coordination. Jenny Levine (SL).
Leadership Development and Mentoring. Julie Reese (SL).
Member Engagement Coordination. Anne M. Pepitone.
Nominating Committee. Kerry Ward (SL).
Publications Coordination. Susan E. Thomas.
Standards. Brooke Morris-Chott (SL).
Top Technology Trends. Thomas Lamanna II.

Awards Committees

ALA John Cotton Dana library Public Relations Award. Jenny Levine (SL).
Awards for Buildings and Interiors Subcommittee. Jenny Levine (SL).
Christian Larew Memorial Scholarship. Harriet Wintermute.
CORE/OCLC Frederick G. Kilgour Award for Research in library and Information technology. Steven D. Yates.
Hugh C. Atkinson Memorial Award. See ACRL.

Editorial Boards

ITAL. Ken Varnum.
LL&M. Elizabeth Nelson.
LMPI. George Aulisio.
LRTS. Mary Beth Weber.

Interest Group Chairs

Artificial Intelligence and Machine Learning in Libraries. Jay Forrest, John W. Hessler.
Authority Control. Melanie Polutta.
Bibliographic Conceptual Models. Lizzy Ellen Baus, Thomas M. Dousa.
Book and Paper. Carrie Beyer, Kim Knox Norman.
Cartographic Resources Cataloging (Core/MAGIRT). Maggie Long.
Cataloging Form and Function. Bela Gupta, Jim Hahn.
Catalog Management. Elizabeth Miraglia. Jianying Shou.
Cataloging and Classification Research. Nerissa Lindsey, Yukari Sugiyama.
Cataloging Norms. Susan Martin, Alexander Whelan.
Chief Collection Development Officers of Large Research Libraries. Karla L. Strieb.
Collection Development Issues for the Practitioner. Jessica Russell.
Collection Evaluation and Assessment. Stephanie Church, Anne Koeing.
Collection Management in Public Libraries. Jessica Russell.
Competencies and Education for a Career in Cataloging. Emily Baldoni, Karen Snow.
Consortium Management. Tracy Byerly.
Copy Cataloging. Nerissa Lindsey, Tachtorn Meier.
Creative Ideas in Technical Services. Sarah E. Hovde, Susan Martin.
Dialogue with Directors. Sheila C. Crosby.
Digital Conversation. Roger Smith.
Ebooks. Stephen H. Spohn, Jr.
Electronic Resources. Abigail Sparling, Kerry R. Walton.
Faceted Subject Access. Nerissa Lindsey, Lana Soglasnova.
Heads of Library Technology. Bohyun Kim.
Imagineering. Athina Livanos-Propst.
Instructional Technologies. Breanne Ariel Kirsch.
Library Consulting. Martha Kyrillidou.
Library Facilities and Interiors. Gili Meerovitch.
Library Storage. Jay Forrest.
Linked Data. Annamarie C. Klose, Benjamin M. Riesenberg.
Maker Technology. Rhonda Asarch, Erik Carlson.
MARC Formats. Brian Patrick Clark.

Metadata. Darnelle O. Melvin, Anne M. Washington.

Middle Managers. Jeffrey Scott Bullington, Carissa Ann Tomlinson.

New Directors. Erik Nordberg.

New Members. Narine H. Bournoutain, Laura C. Haynes.

Newspaper. Errol S. Somay.

Open Access. Emma Molls.

Open-Source Systems. James Mitchell, Robert T. Wilson.

Preservation Administration. Beth Doyle, Sabrena Johnson.

Project Management. Kristen Clark, Anastasia G. Guimaraes.

Promoting Preservation. Mark Coulbourne.

Public Libraries Technical Services. Yu-Lan Margaret Chou, Michael P. Santangelo.

Publisher-Vendor-Library Relations. Ellen Amatangelo, Ajaye Bloomstone, Beverly D. Charlot, Carolyn Morris.

Role of the Professional Librarian in Technical Services. Christine Davidian, Sai Deng.

Solo Practitioners. Rebecca Morin.

Technical Services Managers in Academic Libraries. Lauren Elise DeVoe.

Technical Services Workflow Efficiency. Sarah Faith Cruz, Jesse A. Lambertson.

WebServices4Lib.

Women, Non-Binary, and Trans Administrators. Jennifer Steinford.

Women, Non-Binary and Trans Workers in Library Technology. Melissa A. Hofmann, Sharon M. Whitfield.

Publications

Information Technologies and Libraries (4 a year). Ed. Ken Varnum.

Library Leadership and Management (4 a year). Ed. Elizabeth Nelson.

Library Resources and Technical Services

American Library Association
Public Library Association

Interim Executive Director, Mary Hirsh
225 N. Michigan Ave., Suite 1300, Chicago, IL 60601
312-280-5752, 800-545-2433 ext. 5752, fax 312-280-5029, e-mail pla@ala.org
World Wide Web http://www.pla.org

The Public Library Association (PLA) has specific responsibility for

1. Conducting and sponsoring research about how the public library can respond to changing social needs and technical developments

2. Developing and disseminating materials useful to public libraries in interpreting public library services and needs

3. Conducting continuing education for public librarians by programming at national and regional conferences, by publications such as the newsletter, and by other delivery means

4. Establishing, evaluating, and promoting goals, guidelines, and standards for public libraries

5. Maintaining liaison with relevant national agencies and organizations engaged in public administration and human services, such as the National Association of Counties, the Municipal League, and the Commission on Postsecondary Education

6. Maintaining liaison with other divisions and units of ALA and other library organizations, such as the Association for Library and Information Science Education and the Urban Libraries Council

7. Defining the role of the public library in service to a wide range of user and potential user groups

8. Promoting and interpreting the public library to a changing society through legislative programs and other appropriate means

9. Identifying legislation to improve and to equalize support of public libraries

PLA enhances the development and effectiveness of public librarians and public library services. This mission positions PLA to

- Focus its efforts on serving the needs of its members
- Address issues that affect public libraries
- Commit to quality public library services that benefit the general public

The goals of PLA are

- Advocacy and Awareness: PLA is an essential partner in public library advocacy.
- Leadership and Transformation: PLA is the leading source for learning opportunities to advance transformation of public libraries.
- Literate Nation: PLA will be a leader and valued partner of public libraries' initiatives to create a literate nation.
- Organizational Excellence: PLA is positioned to sustain and grow its resources to advance the work of the association.

Membership

Memb. 8,800+. Open to all ALA members interested in the improvement and expansion of public library services to all ages in various types of communities.

Officers (2020–2021)

Pres. Michelle Jeske, City Libn., Denver, Co; *Pres.-Elect* Melanie Huggins; Exec. Director, Richland Library, Columbia, SC; *Past Pres.* Ramiro S. Salazar, Director, San Antonio Public Library, San Antonio, TX; ALA *Div. Councilor* Stephanie Chase, Hillsboro Public Lib; *Fiscal Officer* Clara Nalli Bohrer, West Bloomfield Township Public Lib; Mary Hirsh (ex officio).

Board of Directors

Cindy Fesemyer, Toby Greenwalt, Richard Kong, Amita Kaur Lonial, Brandy A. McNeil, Dara Hanke Schmidt, Kelvin Watson.

Committee Chairs

Advocacy and Strategic Partnerships. Susan Hempstead.

Annual Conference 2021 Program. Anthanasia Fitos.
Budget and Finance. Clara Nalli Bohrer.
Committee on Equity, Diversity, Inclusion and Social Justice. Christina Fuller-Gregory, Lois Langer Thompson.
Continuing Education Advisory Group. Sarah Campbell Tansley.
Digital Literacy. Brandy A. McNeil.
Leadership Development. Elizabeth M. Joseph.
Measurement, Evaluation and Assessment. Linda Hofschire.
Membership Advisory Group. Kim DeNero-Ackroyd.
Nominating. Monique Le Conge Ziesenhenne.
PLA 2021 Annual Conference Program Subcommittee. Athanasia Fitos.
Public Libraries Advisory. Kimberly Bray Knight.
Technology. Anastasia Diamond-Ortiz.
Web Content Working Group. Steven Hofmann (SL), Megan Stewart (SL).

Task Force Chairs

2020 Census Library Outreach and Education Task Force. Larra Clark, Gavin Baker.
Family Engagement. Ashley Janet Brown, Jo Giudice.
Social Worker. Debra Walsh Keane, Patrick Lloyd, Tiffany Russell.
Task Force on Equity, Diversity, Inclusion and Social Justice. Christina Fuller-Gregory, Lois Langer Thompson.

Advisory Group Staff Liaisons

Continuing Education. Sarah Campbell Tansley.
Membership. Kim DeNero-Ackroyd, Amiya P. Hutson. Megan Stewart (SL)
Public Libraries. Kimberly Bray Knight. Megan Stewart (SL)

Publication

Public Libraries (6 a year; memb.; nonmemb. $65; Canada and Mexico $75; Int'l. $100). *Ed.* Kathleen Hughes, PLA, 50 E. Huron St., Chicago, IL 60611. E-mail khughes@ala.org.

American Library Association
Reference and User Services Association

Executive Director, Bill Ladewski
225 N. Michigan Ave, Suite 1300, Chicago, IL 60601
800-545-2433 ext. 4395, 312-280-4395, fax 312-280-5273, e-mail bladewski@
ala.org or rusa@ala.org
World Wide Web http://www.ala.org/rusa

Objective

The Reference and User Services Association (RUSA) is responsible for stimulating and supporting excellence in the delivery of general library services and materials, and the provision of reference and information services, collection development, readers' advisory, and resource sharing for all ages, in every type of library.

The specific responsibilities of RUSA are

1. Conduct of activities and projects within the association's areas of responsibility

2. Encouragement of the development of librarians engaged in these activities, and stimulation of participation by members of appropriate type-of-library divisions

3. Synthesis of the activities of all units within the American Library Association that have a bearing on the type of activities represented by the association

4. Representation and interpretation of the association's activities in contacts outside the profession

5. Planning and development of programs of study and research in these areas for the total profession

6. Continuous study and review of the association's activities

Membership

Memb. 2,600+

Officers (2020–2021)

Pres. Courtney McDonald; *Pres.-Elect* Christina Pryor. *Secy.* Jenny Presnell.; *Past Pres.* Beth German.

Board of Directors

Alesia McManus, Jessica Anne Bower, Rachael Anne Cohen, Kelly Anne McCusker, Kathy Shields, Ilana Stonebraker, Magan Szwarek, M. Kathleen Kern.

Committee Chairs

Access to Information.
Accessibility Assembly. Reed W. Strege.
AFL-CIO/ALA Labor. Jane Billinger, Benjamin Scott Blake.
Budget and Finance. Christina Pryor.
Conference Program Coordinating. Barry Trott.
Leadership Council. Courtney Greene McDonald.
Membership Engagement. Candice Townsend.
Nominating. Ann K. G. Brown.
President's Program Planning. Bill Ladewski.
Professional Competencies for Reference and User Services Librarians.
Professional Development. Tatiana Pashkova-Balkenhol.
Professional Resources. Hilary M. Kraus, William H. Weare, Jr.
Volunteer Development. Lori Lysiak, Geoffrey W. Morse.

RUSA Sections

Business Reference and Services Section (BRASS). http://www.ala.org/rusa/sections/brass/committees.
Collection Development and Evaluation Section (CODES). http://www.ala.org/rusa/sections/codes/committees.
Emerging Technologies Section (ETS). http://www.ala.org/rusa/sections/ets/committees.
History Section (HS). http://www.ala.org/rusa/sections/history/committees.

Reference Services Section (RSS). http://www.ala.org/rusa/sections/rss.

Sharing and Transforming Access to Resources Section (STARS). http://www.ala.org/rusa/sections/stars/section/starscomcharges.

(Subcommittees may be found on section websites.)

Isadore Gilbert Mudge Award. Chris Le Beau.

Gail Schlachter Memorial Research Grant. Chris Le Beau.

John Sessions Memorial Award. Bobray J. Bordelon, Jr.

Margaret E. Monroe Library Adult Services Award.

Awards Committee Chairs

Achievement Award. Chris Le Beau.

Andrew Carnegie Medal for Excellence in Fiction and Nonfiction. William Kelly

Awards Coordinating Committee. Nanette Wargo Donohue.

Excellence in Reference and Adult Services Award. Chris Le Beau.

Publications

Reference & User Services Quarterly (online only at http://journals.ala.org/index.php/rusq) (memb.). Ed. M. Kathleen Kern, Miller Learning Ctr., Univ. of Georgia.

RUSA Update (q., online newsletter, at http://www.rusaupdate.org). Ed. Carol Schuetz.

American Library Association
United for Libraries: Association of Library Trustees, Advocates, Friends, and Foundations

Executive Director, Beth Nawalinski
600 Eagleview Blvd., Suite 300, Exton, PA 19341
800-545-2433, ext. 2161, fax 215-545-3821, e-mail bnawalinski@ala.org or united@ala.org
World Wide Web http://www.ala.org/united

Objective

United for Libraries was founded in 1890 as the American Library Trustee Association (ALTA). It was the only division of the American Library Association (ALA) dedicated to promoting and ensuring outstanding library service through educational programs that develop excellence in trusteeship and promote citizen involvement in the support of libraries. ALTA became an ALA division in 1961. In 2008 the members of ALTA voted to expand the division to more aggressively address the needs of friends of libraries and library foundations, and through a merger with Friends of Libraries USA (FOLUSA) became the Association of Library Trustees, Advocates, Friends and Foundations (ALTAFF). In 2012 members voted to add "United for Libraries" to its title.

Memb. 5,000. Open to all interested persons and organizations. Dues (prorated to match ALA membership expiration) $55; (student with ALA membership) $20.

Officers (2020–2021)

Pres. David Paige; *V.P./Pres.-Elect* Charity Tyler; *Secy.* Kathleen McEvoy; *Past Pres.* Peter Pearson; *Div. Councilor* Luis Herrera; *Fiscal Officer* Amandeep Kochar.

Board of Directors

Veronda Pitchford, Christ Chanyasulkit, Gordon Baker, Nicolle Davies, Patricia Hofmann, Ned Davis, Andrea Lapsley, Kristi Pearson, Rocco Staino, Brenda Langstraat, Lauren Trujillo, Gary Kirk, Steve Laird, Skip Dye, Dick Waters, Mark Smith, Maura Deedy, Mark Miller, Alan Fishel, Deborah Doyle, Pat Schuman.

Committee and Task Force Chairs

Advocacy. Skip Dye.
Awards. Kristi J. Pearson.
Baby Boomer Access. No Active Chair.
Corporate Sponsorship Task Force. Skip Dye.
Governance Task Force. Skip Dye, Charity Tyler.
Literary Landmarks Task Force. Rocco A. Staino.
Nominating. Peter D. Pearson.
Program. Maura Deedy, Charity Tyler.

Publications

The Good, The Great, and the Unfriendly: A Librarian's Guide to Working with Friends Groups.
The Complete Library Trustee Handbook.
Even More Great Ideas for Libraries and Friends.
A Library Board's Practical Guide to Self-Evaluation.
A Library Board's Practical Guide to Hiring Outside Experts.
Getting Grants in Your Community.
Making Our Voices Heard: Citizens Speak Out for Libraries.

American Library Association
Young Adult Library Services Association

Executive Director, Tammy Dillard-Steels
225 N. Michigan Ave, Chicago, IL 60601
312-280-4390, 800-545-2433 ext. 4390, fax 312-280-5276, e-mail yalsa@ala.org
World Wide Web http://www.ala.org/yalsa
YALSA blog http://yalsa.ala.org/blog, The Hub http://yalsa.ala.org/thehub,
Wiki http://wikis.ala.org/yalsa, Twitter http://twitter.com/yalsa
Facebook http://www.facebook.com/YALSA

Objective

In every library in the nation, high-quality library service to young adults is provided by a staff that understands and respects the unique informational, educational, and recreational needs of teenagers. Equal access to information, services, and materials is recognized as a right, not a privilege. Young adults are actively involved in the library decision-making process. The library staff collaborates and cooperates with other youth-serving agencies to provide a holistic, community-wide network of activities and services that support healthy youth development.

To ensure that this vision becomes a reality, the Young Adult Library Services Association (YALSA)

1. Advocates extensive and developmentally appropriate library and information services for young adults ages 12 to 18
2. Promotes reading and supports the literacy movement

3. Advocates the use of information and digital technologies to provide effective library service
4. Supports equality of access to the full range of library materials and services, including existing and emerging information and digital technologies, for young adults
5. Provides education and professional development to enable its members to serve as effective advocates for young people
6. Fosters collaboration and partnerships among its individual members with the library community and other groups involved in providing library and information services to young adults
7. Influences public policy by demonstrating the importance of providing library and information services that meet the unique needs and interests of young adults
8. Encourages research and is in the vanguard of new thinking concerning the

provision of library and information services for youth

Membership

Memb. 3,600+. Open to anyone interested in library services for and with young adults. For information on dues, see ALA entry.

Officers (2020–2021)

Pres. Amanda Barnhart; *Pres.-Elect* Kelly Czarnecki; *Div. Councilor* Abigail Leigh Phillips; *Fiscal Officer* Kate Denier; *Secy.* Josephine Watanabe; *Past Pres.* Todd Krueger.

Board of Directors

Susannah Goldstein, Karen Lemmons, Melissa McBride, Dawn Kirkpatrick, Charli Osborne, Colleen Seisser, Valeric Tagoe. Ex officio: Tammy Dillard-Steels, Franklin Escobedo, Traci Glass, Stacey Shapiro.

Committee Chairs

AASL/ALSC/YALSA Committee on School and Public Library Cooperation. Cynthia Zervos (AASL).
Advocacy and Activism. Josephine Watanabe.
Annual Conference Marketing and Local Arrangements. Heather Beverley.
Board Development. Todd Krueger.
Division and Membership Promotion. Ruby Smart.
Editorial Advisory Board (*YALS* and YALSAblog). Tess Wilson.
Education Advisory. Sarah Evans.
Executive Committee. Amanda Barnhart.
Financial Advancement. Traci Glass.
Fund and Partner Development. Colleen Seisser.
Hub Advisory Board. Sarah Beth Coffman.
Leading the Transformation of Teen Services. Vacant
Organization and Bylaws Committee. Franklin Escobedo.
Research Committee. Adrienne Strock.

Research Journal Advisory Board. Charlie Gluck.
Selection List Oversight Committee. Celeste Swanson.
Teens' Top Ten. Jessica Lorentz Smith.
YALS/YALSAblog Editorial Advisory. Yolanda Hood, Tess Wilson.

Task Force Chairs

Advocacy Resources Community Listening Taskforce. Kerry Townsend.
Amazing Audiobooks Blogging Team. Catherine Outten.
Best Fiction Blogging Team. Allie Stevens.
Graphic Novel Selection Blogging Team. Crystal Chen.
President's Implementation Taskforce. Amanda Barnhart.
Quick Pick Blogging Team. Molly Dettmann.
Social Media Marketing Taskforce. Christine Pyles.
Teen Programming HQ. Dawn Abron.
YA Symposium Planning and Marketing Task Force. Scot Smith.

Awards Committee Chairs

ALSC/Booklist/YALSA Odyssey Award Committee 2022. Pat Toney (ALSC)
Alex Award Committee. Michael Fleming
Book Awards Committees' Oversight Committee. Kim Dare.
Margaret Edwards Committee 2022. Craig Santiago.
Michael L. Printz Award 2022. Janet Hilbun.
Morris Award Committee 2022. Patty Ramirez.
Nonfiction Award 2022. Alicia Abdul.

Publications

Journal of Research on Libraries and Young Adults (q.) (online, open source, peer-reviewed). *Ed.* Dr. Robin Moeller. E-mail yalsaresearch@gmail.com.
Young Adult Library Services (*YALS*) (q.) (online only; member; nonmember $70; foreign $70). *Ed.* Yolanda Hood. E-mail: yalseditor @gmail.com.

ARMA International

CEO, Mona Buckley
312 SW Greenwich Dr, Suite 515

Lee's Summit, MO 64082
913-444-9174, 844-565-2120, fax 913-257-3855, e-mail headquarters@armaintl.org
World Wide Web http://www.arma.org

Objective

To be the driving force that enables organizations to harness the strategic power of information, empowering the community of information professionals to advance their careers, organizations, and the profession. ARMA International is committed to finding innovative ways to provide our personal and professional communities with guidance, learning, development, and opportunity. We value the open exchange of ideas, good governance, free flow of information, and thought leadership by seeking diversity, inclusivity, and equity in all its form. The membership of ARMA International has reached a consensus that the association's most unique value to the information community is derived from the following: (a) Professional standard-setting and best practice frameworks; (b) current news, events, and industry trends; (c) network of local chapters providing opportunities for in-person training and leadership development; (d) certification preparation and continuing education

Membership

More than 6,000 in over 30 countries besides its U.S. base. Annual dues (Professional) $175; (Assoc.) $95. Chapter dues vary.

Officers

Pres. Jason C. Stearns, Citadel. E-mail jasonstearns.arma@gmail.com; *Pres.-Elect* Michael Haley, Cohasset Associates. E-mail michaelhaley.arma@gmail.com; *Treas.* Michael Landau, Veritas Technologies. E-mail michaelhaley.arma@gmail.com; *Past Pres.* Bill Bradford, Regional Transportation District (Denver). E-mail bill.bradford@armaintl.org.

Board of Directors

Tyrene Bada, John J. Jablonski, Michelle Kirk, Wendy McLain.

Publications

Implementing the Generally Accepted Recordkeeping Principles (PDF).
inDEPTH newsletter (bi-mo. memb.).
INFORMATION: The Comprehensive Overview of the Information Profession (PDF).
Information Management (IM) (bi-mo., memb., e-magazine https://magazine.arma.org). *Ed.* Nick Inglis. Tel. 913-312-5567, e-mail nick.inglis@armaintl.org.
Records and Information Management: Fundamentals of Professional Practice, 3rd Edition (PDF).
RIM and IG Around the World (mo.).

Art Libraries Society of North America

Executive Director, Cambria Happ
4 Lan Drive, Suite 310, Westford, MA 01886
978-674-6211, 800-817-0621, fax 414-768-8001, e-mail n.short@arlisna.org
World Wide Web https://www.arlisna.org

Objective

The object of the Art Libraries Society of North America (ARLIS/NA) is to foster excellence in art librarianship and visual resources curatorship for the advancement of the visual arts. Established 1972.

Membership

Memb. 1,000+. Dues (Business Affiliate) $250; (Introductory) $50 (two-year limit); (Indiv.) $150; (Student) $25 (three-year limit); (Ret.) $75; (Unemployed/Bridge) $25. Year. Jan. 1–Dec. 31. Membership is open to all those interested in visual librarianship, whether they be professional librarians, students, library assistants, art book publishers, art book dealers, art historians, archivists, architects, slide and photograph curators, or retired associates in these fields.

Officers (2020–2021)

Pres. Amy Trendler, Ball State Univ., Muncie. Tel. 765-285-5858, e-mail aetrendler@bsu.edu; *V.P./Pres.-Elect* Rebecca Price; *Secy.* Sarah Carter; *Advancement Liaison* Lindsay King; *Chapters Liaison* Stephanie Hilles; *Treas.* Doug Litts, Ryerson and Burnham Libs., The Art Institute of Chicago. Tel. 312-443-3671, e-mail dlitts@artic.edu; *Past Pres.* Laura Schwartz, University of California, San Diego. Tel. 858-534-1267, e-mail l7schwartz@ucsd.edu.

Board Members

Stefanie Hilles, Lindsay King, Amy Furness, Heather Slania. *Editorial Dir.* Roger Lawson.

Committee Chairs

Advocacy and Public Policy. Serenity Ibsen.
Awards. Suzanne Rackover.
Cataloging Advisory. Andrea Puccio.
Development. Gregory P. J. Most.
Diversity. Natisha Harper.
Documentation. Samantha Deutch.
Finance. Matthew Gengler.
International Relations. Gabrielle Reed.
Membership. Beth Owens.
Nominating. Laurel Bliss.
Professional Development. Carol Ng-He.
Strategic Directions. Emilee Mathews.

Editorial Board Chairs

Roger Lawson.

Awards Committee Chairs

Suzanne Rackover.
Distinguished Service. Sylvia Roberts.
Book Awards. Andi Back.
Research. Jeanne-Marie Musto.
Student Advancement. Spyros Koulouris.
Travel. Marianne R. Williams.

Publications

ARLIS/NA Multimedia & Technology Reviews (bi-mo.; memb.). *Eds.* Melanie Emerson, Gabriella Karl-Johnson, Alexandra Provo. E-mail arlisna.mtr@gmail.com.
ARLIS/NA Research and Reports.
ARLIS/NA Reviews (bi-mo.; memb.). *Eds.* Rebecca Price, e-mail rpw@umich.edu; Terrie Wilson, e-mail wilso398@msu.edu.
Art Documentation (2 a year; memb., subscription). *Ed.* Judy Dyki. E-mail jdyki@cranbrook.edu.
Miscellaneous others (request current list from headquarters).

Asian/Pacific American Librarians Association

Executive Director, Lessa Kanani'opua Pelayo-Lozada
P.O. Box 1598, San Pedro, CA, 90733
310-377-9584 x237, e-mail ed@apalaweb.org
World Wide Web http://www.apalaweb.org

Objective

To provide a forum for discussing problems and concerns of Asian/Pacific American librarians; to provide a forum for the exchange of ideas by Asian/Pacific American librarians and other librarians; to support and encourage library services to Asian/Pacific American communities; to recruit and support Asian/Pacific American librarians in the library/information science professions; to seek funding for scholarships in library/information science programs for Asian/Pacific Americans; and to provide a vehicle whereby Asian/Pacific American librarians can cooperate with other associations and organizations having similar or allied interests. Founded in 1980; incorporated 1981; affiliated with American Library Association 1982.

Membership

Memb. approximately 300. Dues (Corporate) $250; (Inst.) $70; (Lib. Support Staff) $20; (Life) $400; (Personal) $35 (one-year limit); (Ret.) $20 (one-year limit); (Student) $15 (Unemployed) $20. Open to all librarians and information specialists of Asian/Pacific descent working in U.S. libraries and information centers and other related organizations, and to others who support the goals and purposes of the association. Asian/Pacific Americans are defined as people residing in North America who self-identify as Asian/Pacific American.

Officers (2020–2021)

Pres. Candice (Wing-yee) Mack; *V.P./Pres.-Elect* Ray Pun; *Secy.* Melissa Cardenas-Dow; *Treas.* Jaena Rae Cabrera; *Past Pres.* Alanna Aiko Moore; *Memb.-at-Large (2019–2021)* Michelle Lee, Camden Kimura; *(2020–2022)* Yen Tran, Anu Vedantham.

Committee Chairs

Communications and Media. Jaena Rae Cabrera, Molly Higgins.
Constitution and Bylaws. Sheila Garcia, Rebecca Martin.
Family Literacy Focus. Amy Breslin Bartko.
Finance and Fundraising. Kat Bell, Peter Spyers-Duran
Literature Awards. Dora Ho, Ven Basco, Helen Look.
Media and Publicity. Molly Higgins, Silvia Lew.
Membership. Maria (Pontillas) Shackles.
Mentorship. Alvina Lai.
Nominating. Alanna Aiko Moore.
Program Planning. Raymond Pun, Ariana Potter.
Scholarships and Awards. Jennifer Embree, Lana Mariko Wood.

Publication

APALA Newsletter (2–3 a year).

Association for Information Science and Technology

Executive Director, Lydia Middleton
8555 16th St., Suite 850, Silver Spring, MD 20910
301-495-0900, e-mail asist@asist.org
World Wide Web http://www.asist.org

Objective

The Association for Information Science and Technology (ASIS&T) provides a forum for the discussion, publication, and critical analysis of work dealing with the design, management, and use of information, information systems, and information technology. The mission of the Association is to advance research and practice in information science and technology.

Membership

Regular Memb. (Indiv.) 1,100; (Student) 500; (Student Developing) $15; Dues (Professional) $150; (Professional Developing) $25; (Early Career and Ret.) $75; (Student) $45.

Officers (2020–2021)

Pres. Brian Detlor, McMaster Univ., Hamilton, ON, Canada; *Pres.-Elect* Naresh Agarwal, Simmons University, Boston, MA; *Treas.* Ina Fourie, Univ. of Pretoria, Pretoria, South Africa; *Past Pres.* Clara Chu, Univ. of Illinois at Urbana-Champaign, Urbana, IL. E-mail cmchu@illinois.edu.

Board of Directors

Dirs.-at-large Agnes Mainka, Anna Maria Tammaro, Dan Wu; *Parliamentarian* Steve Hardin.

Committee Chairs

Awards and Honors. Joan Bartlett.
Budget and Finance. Ina Fourie.
Executive. Brian Detlor.
Governance. Joseph Bush.
History. Michael K. Buckland.
Membership. Krystyna Matusiak.
Nominations. Abebe Rorissa.
Professional Development. Hsin-Liang (Oliver) Chen.
Publications. Maria Bonn.
Research Engagement. Devon Greyson.
Standards. Mark Needleman.

Publications

Inside ASIS&T newsletter (bi-mo.).

Periodicals

Journal of the Association for Information Science and Technology. (JASIST) (mo.). Available with ASIS&T membership or from Wiley Blackwell.

Bulletin of the Association for Information Science and Technology (bi-mo.; memb.; online only).

Proceedings of the ASIS&T Annual Meeting. Available from ASIS&T.

Annual Review of Information Science & Technology (ARIST).

Association for Library and Information Science Education

Executive Director, Cambria Happ
4 Lan Dr., Suite 310, Westford, MA 01886
978-674-6190, e-mail office@alise.org
World Wide Web http://www.alise.org

Objective

The Association for Library and Information Science Education (ALISE) is an independent nonprofit professional association whose mission is to promote excellence in research, teaching, and service for library and information science education through leadership, collaboration, advocacy, and dissemination of research. Its enduring purpose is to promote research that informs the scholarship of teaching and learning for library and information science, enabling members to integrate research into teaching and learning. The association provides a forum in which to share ideas, discuss issues, address challenges, and shape the future of education for library and information science. Founded in 1915 as the Association of American Library Schools, it has had its present name since 1983.

Membership

Memb. 700+ in four categories: Personal, Institutional, International Affiliate Institutional, and Associate Institutional. Dues (Indiv. full-time) $155; (Emerging Professional/Part-Time/Ret.) $85; (Student) $40; (Inst. varies, based on school budget) $400–$2,900; (Inst. Int'l./Assoc.) $350. Personal membership is open to anyone with an interest in the association's objectives.

Officers (2020–2021)

Pres. Sandy Hirsh, San José State Univ. E-Mail sandy.hirsh@sjsu.edu; *Pres.-Elect* Lisa O'Connor, University of North Carolina Greensboro. E-mail lgoconno@uncg.edu; *Secy.-Treas.* Heather Moulaison Sandy, Univ. of Missouri. E-mail moulaisonhe@missouri.edu; *Past Pres.* Stephen Bajjaly. E-mail bajjaly@wayne.edu, Wayne State Univ.

Directors

Denice Adkins; Lilia Pavlovsky; Mega Subramaniam.

Publications

Journal of Education for Library and Information Science (JELIS) (q.; online only; memb.; nonmemb. $139 individual subscription; $360 institutional subscription). *Eds.* John M. Budd and Denice Adkins. E-mail jeliseditor@alise.org.

Library and Information Science Education Statistical Report (ann.; electronic; memb.; nonmemb. $135).

ALISE Book Series. Eds. Jaya Raju and Dietmar Wolfram. E-mail jaya.raju@uct.ac.za.

Association for Rural and Small Libraries

Executive Director, Kate Laughlin
P.O. Box 33731, Seattle, WA, 98133. Tel. 206-453-3579 e-mail info@arsl.org
World Wide Web http://www.arsl.info
Twitter @RuralLibAssoc

Objective

The Association for Rural and Small Libraries (ARSL) was established in 1978, in the Department of Library Science at Clarion University of Pennsylvania, as the Center for Study of Rural Librarianship.

ARSL is a network of people throughout the United States dedicated to the positive growth and development of libraries. ARSL believes in the value of rural and small libraries, and strives to create resources and services that address national, state, and local priorities for libraries situated in rural communities.

Its objectives are

- To organize a network of members concerned about the growth and development of useful library services in rural and small libraries
- To provide opportunities for the continuing education of members
- To provide mechanisms for members to exchange ideas and to meet on a regular basis
- To cultivate the practice of librarianship and to foster a spirit of cooperation among members of the profession, enabling them to act together for mutual goals
- To serve as a source of current information about trends, issues, and strategies
- To partner with other library and nonlibrary groups and organizations serving rural and small library communities
- To collect and disseminate information and resources that are critical to this network
- To advocate for rural and small libraries at the local, state, and national levels

Membership

Dues (Indiv. varies, based on salary) $15–$49; (Inst.) $150; (Business) $200; (Affiliate) $150.

Officers (2021)

Pres. Kathy Zappitello, Conneaut Public Lib., 304 Buffalo St., Conneaut, OH. E-mail kathy. zappitello@conneaut.lib.oh.us; *V.P./Pres.-Elect* Bailee Hutchinson, Altus Public Library, Altus, OK; *Secy.* Krist Obrist, Monmouth Public Library, Monmouth, OR; *Treas.* Lisa Lewis, Show-Low Public Lib., Show-Low, AZ. E-mail llewis@showlowaz.gov; *COSLA Appointee* Timothy Owens, North Carolina State Lib., Raleigh, NC. E-mail Timothy.Owens@ncdcr.gov; *Past Pres.* Jennifer Pearson, Marshall County Memorial Lib., Lewisburg, TN. E-mail mcmlib @bellsouth.net.

Directors

Philip Carter; Julie Elmore, Kathy Street, Nancy Tusinksi.

Committee Chairs

Advocacy and Partnerships. Beth Anderson, Lisa Shaw.
Conference. Todd Deck, Holly Mercer.
Continuing Education. Allie Stevens, Joy Worland.
Elections. Jennifer Pearson.
Finance. Lisa Lewis.
Governance. Kristi Chadwick, Mary Soucie.
Marketing and Communications. Suzanne Macaulay, Sherry Scheline.
Membership. Amy Golly, Molly Schock.
Partnership. Jennie Garner, Kelly Kreps-Depin.
Scholarship. Amanda Bundy, Shirley Vonderhaar.

Association of Academic Health Sciences Libraries

Executive Director, Louise Miller
2150 N. 107 St., Suite 205, Seattle, WA 98133
206-209-5261, fax 206-367-8777, e-mail office@aahsl.org
World Wide Web http://www.aahsl.org

Objective

The Association of Academic Health Sciences Libraries (AAHSL) comprises the libraries serving the accredited U.S. and Canadian medical schools belonging to or affiliated with the Association of American Medical Colleges. Its goals are to promote excellence in academic health science libraries and to ensure that the next generation of health practitioners is trained in information-seeking skills that enhance the quality of health care delivery, education, and research. Founded in 1977.

Membership

Memb. 150+. Full membership is available to nonprofit educational institutions operating a school of health sciences that has full or provisional accreditation by the Association of American Medical Colleges. Full members are represented by the chief administrative officer of the member institution's health sciences library. Associate membership (and nonvoting representation) is available to organizations having an interest in the purposes and activities of the association. For dues information, contact the association.

Officers (2020–2021)

Pres. Chris Shaffer, UCSF Lib., Univ. of California. Tel. 415-476-2336, e-mail chris. shaffer@ucsf.edu; *Pres.-Elect* Melissa De Santis, Strauss Health Sciences Library, University of Colorado. Tel. 303-724-2152; *Secy./Treas.* Tania Bardyn, Health Sciences Lib., Univ. of Washington. Tel. 206-543-0422, e-mail bardyn @uw.edu; *Past Pres.* Sandra Franklin, Woodruff Health Sciences Ctr. Lib., Emory Univ. Tel. 404-727-0288, e-mail librsf@emory.edu.

Board of Directors

Kelly Gonzalez, Debra Rand, Gabe Rios.

Committee Chairs

Assessment and Statistics. Matthew Wilcox.
Diversity, Equity and Inclusion. Cristina Pope.
Future Leadership. Terrie Wheeler.
New and Developing Health Sciences Libraries. Nadine Dexter.
Program and Education. Colleen Cuddy.
Research Services. Gabe Rios.
Scholarly Communication. Rikke Ogawa.

Task Force Chairs

Library Services for Associated Clinical Organizations. Melissa DeSantis, Megan Von Isenburg.
Implementation. Amy Blevins.
Osteopathic Schools. Joanne Muellenbach.

Association of Christian Librarians

Executive Director, Janelle Mazelin
P.O. Box 4, Cedarville, OH 45314
937-766-2255, fax 937-766-5499, e-mail info@acl.org
World Wide Web http://www.acl.org
Facebook https://www.facebook.com/ACLibrarians
Twitter @ACLibrarians

Objective

The mission of the Association of Christian Librarians (ACL) is to strengthen libraries through professional development of evangelical librarians, scholarship, and spiritual encouragement for service in higher education. ACL is a growing community that integrates faith, ministry, and academic librarianship through development of members, services, and scholarship.

Founded 1957.

Membership

Memb. 600+ individual and 200+ institutional members. Membership is open to those who profess the Christian faith as outlined by the association's statement of faith and are employed at an institution of higher education. Associate memberships are available for nonlibrarians who both agree with ACL's statement of faith and are interested in libraries or librarianship. Dues (Indiv. 1st Year) $40; (Ret. Libn., Lib. School Student) $35; (Varies, based on income) $40–$120.

Officers

Pres. (2020–2022) Leslie Starasta, Lincoln Christian University; *V.P. (2017–2021)* Nate Farley, Univ. of Northwestern–St. Paul; *Secy. (2020–2023)* Denise Nelson, Point Loma Nazarene Univ.; *Treas. (2019–2021)* Rodney Birch, Northwest Nazarene Univ.; *Dirs.-at-Large* Andrea Abernathy, Eric Bradley, Robert Burgess, Sarah Davis, Alison Johnson, Jeremy Labosier.

Section Chairs

Bible Core. Jim Mancuso.
Liberal Arts. Amy Bessen.
Seminary. Craig Kubic.

Publications

The Christian Librarian. (2 a year; memb.; nonmemb. $30). *Ed.* Garrett Trott.
Christian Periodical Index (q.; electronic).
Librarian's Manual (English or Spanish; electronic or print; $40).
Library Guidelines for ABHE Colleges and Universities (memb.).

Association of Independent Information Professionals

President, Jennifer Pflaumer
8550 United Plaza Blvd., Suite 1001, Baton Rouge, LA 70809
225-408-4400, e-mail office@aiip.org
World Wide Web http://www.aiip.org
Facebook https://www.facebook.com/officialaiip
Twitter @AIIP

Objective

Members of the Association of Independent Information Professionals (AIIP) are owners of firms providing such information-related services as online and manual research, document delivery, database design, library support, consulting, writing, and publishing.

The objectives of the association are

- To advance the knowledge and understanding of the information profession
- To promote and maintain high professional and ethical standards among its members
- To encourage independent information professionals to assemble to discuss common issues
- To promote the interchange of information among independent information professionals and various organizations
- To keep the public informed of the profession and of the responsibilities of the information professional

Membership

Memb. 200+. Dues (Full) $200; (Assoc.) $200; (Student) $50; (Supporting) $500; (Ret.) $75; (Emeritus) $50.

Officers (2020–2021)

Pres. Jennifer Pflaumer, Paroo; *Pres. Elect* Karen Klein, Fulcrum Information Resources; *Secy.* Phyllis Smith, ITK Vector Inc.; *Treas.* Beth Plutchak, Beth Plutchak Consulting LLC; *Past Pres.* Judith Binder, RBSC Corp., Research Group.

Directors

Membership, Edward J. Ajaeb; Professional Development, Kelly Berry; Outreach, Kirsten Smith.

Publications

AIIP Connections (blog).
Member Directory (ann.).
Professional papers series.

Association of Jewish Libraries

President, Kathleen Bloomfield
P.O. Box 1118, Teaneck, NJ 07666
201-371-3255, e-mail info@jewishlibraries.org
World Wide Web http://www.jewishlibraries.org
Facebook https://www.facebook.com/jewishlibraries
Twitter @JewishLibraries

Objective

The Association of Jewish Libraries (AJL) is an international professional organization that fosters access to information and research in all forms of media relating to all things Jewish. The association promotes Jewish literacy and scholarship and provides a community for peer support and professional development.

AJL membership is open to individuals and libraries, library workers, and library supporters. There are two divisions within AJL: RAS (Research Libraries, Archives, and Special Collections) and SSCPL (Synagogue, School Center and Public Libraries). The diverse membership includes libraries in synagogues, JCCs, day schools, yeshivot, universities, Holocaust museums, and the Library of Congress. Membership is drawn from North America and

places beyond, including China, the Czech Republic, the Netherlands, Israel, Italy, South Africa, Switzerland, and the United Kingdom.

Goals

The association's goals are to

- Maintain high professional standards for Judaica librarians and recruit qualified individuals into the profession
- Facilitate communication and exchange of information on a global scale
- Encourage quality publication in the field in all formats and media, print, digital, and so forth, and to stimulate publication of high-quality children's literature

- Facilitate and encourage establishment of Judaica library collections
- Enhance information access for all through application of advanced technologies
- Publicize the organization and its activities in all relevant venues: stimulate awareness of Judaica library services among the public at large; promote recognition of Judaica librarianship within the wider library profession; and encourage recognition of Judaica library services by other organizations and related professions
- Ensure continuity of the association through sound management, financial security, effective governance, and a dedicated and active membership

AJL conducts an annual conference in the United States or Canada in late June.

Membership

Memb. 600. Year: Oct. 1–Sept. 30. Dues (Indiv.) $77; (First-year Lib. School Student) Free; (Second/third-year Lib. School Student) $36; (Ret./unemployed) $36; (Large Inst.) (Greater than 100 FTE / includes personal membership) $118; (Small Inst.) (100 or fewer FTE / includes 1 personal membership) $90; (Corporate) $118.

Board of Directors

Pres. Kathleen Bloomfield, Seal Beach, CA 90740 e-mail kathybloomfield@gmail.com; *V.P./Pres.-Elect* Michelle Chesner, Columbia Univ.; *V.P. Development* Jackie Ben-Efraim, Ostrow Lib., American Jewish Univ., 15600 Mulholland Dr., Los Angeles, CA 90077. Tel. 818-383-9672, e-mail ajladmanager@gmail. com; *V.P. Membership* Sharon Benamou, UCLA, Hebraica/Judaica and Music Catalog Librarian. E-mail benamou@library.ucla.edu *Secy.* Eitan Kensky, Stanford Univ. E-mail kensky@stanford.edu; *Treas.* Holly Zimmerman, AARP, 601 E. St. N.W., Washington, DC 20049. E-mail hzimmerman@aarp.org; *RAS Pres.* Amalia Levi; RAS V.P. Anna Levia; SSCPL Pres. Sean Boyle; SSCPL V.P. Emily Bergman; *Past Pres.* Dina Herbert, National Archives and Records Admin., Alexandria, VA. E-mail dina.herbert@gmail.com; Parliamentarian Joy Kingsolver.

Council Members

Joseph Galron; Haim Gottschalk; Rachel Leket-Mor; Rebecca Levitan; Heidi Rabinowitz; Daniel Scheide; Anjelica Ruiz; Laura Schutzman; Sheryl Stahl; Sally Steigletz.

Committee Chairs

Accreditation. Shaindy Kurzmann.
Advertising. Jackie Ben-Efraim.
Archivist. Joy Kingsolver.
Cataloging. Neil Frau-Cortes.
Conference, Local. Rachel Kamin, Marcie Eskin.
Conference, Organization-Wide. Lisa Silverman.
Conference Support. Lenore M. Bell.
Continuing Education. Haim Gottschalk.
Librarianship and Education. Haim Gottschalk.
Member Relations. Heidi Rabinowitz.
Public Relations. Rebecca Levitan.
Publications. Laura Schutzman.
Web. Sheryl Stahl.

Editorial Board Chairs

AJL News and Reviews. Sally Stieglitz.
Judaica Librarianship. Rachel Leket-Mor.

Awards Committee Chairs

Groner-Wikler Scholarship. Sean Boyle.
Jewish Fiction Award. Laura Schutzman.
Reference and Bibliography Award. Anna Levia.
Student Scholarship. Tina Weiss.
Sydney Taylor Book Award. Martha Simpson.
Sydney Taylor Manuscript Award. Aileen Grossberg.

Publications

AJL Conference Proceedings.
AJL News and Reviews (q., digital; memb.). Ed. Sally Stieglitz. Tel. 631-6751-570 ext. 2005, e-mail sstieglitz@lilrc.org.
Judaica Librarianship (annual, digital). Ed. Rachel Leket-Mor, Arizona State Univ. Libs. E-mail rachel.leket-mor@asu.edu.

Affiliate Liaisons

American Library Association (ALA). Emily Bergman; Susan Kusel.

American Theological Library Association (ATLA). Sheryl Stahl.
Association for Jewish Studies (AJS).
Catholic Library Association (CATHLA). Daniel Stuhlman.

Association of Research Libraries

Executive Director, Mary Lee Kennedy
21 Dupont Circle N.W., Suite 800, Washington, DC 20036
202-296-2296, fax 202-872-0884, e-mail webmgr@arl.org
World Wide Web https://www.arl.org

Objective

The Association of Research Libraries (ARL) is a nonprofit organization of 125 research libraries in Canada and the United States whose mission is to advance research, learning, and scholarly communication. The Association fosters the open exchange of ideas and expertise; advances diversity, equity, and inclusion; and pursues advocacy and public policy efforts that reflect the values of the library, scholarly, and higher education communities. ARL forges partnerships and catalyzes the collective efforts of research libraries to enable knowledge creation and to achieve enduring and barrier-free access to information.

Membership

Memb. 125. Membership is institutional. Dues: $30,605 for 2021.

Officers

Pres. John Culshaw, Univ. of Iowa; *V.P./Pres.-Elect* K. Matthew Dames, Boston Univ.; *Past Pres.* Lorraine Haricombe, Univ. of Texas at Austin; *Treas.* Diane Parr Walker, Univ. of Notre Dame.

Board of Directors

John Culshaw, Univ. of Iowa; K. Matthew Dames, Boston Univ.; Trevor A. Dawes, Univ. of Delaware; Bob Fox, Univ. of Louisville; Lorraine Haricombe, Univ. of Texas at Austin; Mary Lee Kennedy (ex officio, nonvoting), ARL; Joe Lucia, Temple Univ.; Robert McDonald, Univ. of Colorado Boulder; Susan Parker, Univ. of British Columbia; Sarah Pritchard, Northwestern Univ.; Diane Parr Walker, Univ. of Notre Dame; Virginia Steel, UCLA; Tyler Walters, Virginia Tech.

Advisory Group Chairs

Advocacy and Public Policy Committee. Toby Graham, Univ. of Georgia.
ARL Academy Advisory Committee. Gale Etschmaier, Florida State Univ.
Audit Committee. Sarah Pritchard, Northwestern Univ.
Code of Conduct Committee. Catherine Steeves, Western Univ.
Diversity, Equity, and Inclusion Committee. Lisa Carter, Univ. of Wisconsin–Madison.
Finance Committee. Diane Parr Walker, Univ. of Notre Dame.
Governance Committee. Virginia Steel, UCLA.
Member Engagement and Outreach Committee. Catherine Steeves, Western Univ.
Membership Committee. Joe Lucia, Temple Univ.
Program Strategy Committee. Mary Lee Kennedy, ARL.
Research and Analytics Committee. Beth Sandore Namachchivaya, Univ. of Waterloo.
Scholars and Scholarship Committee. Kristin Antelman, UC Santa Barbara.

Publications

Annual Report (ann.)
ARL Academic Health Sciences Library Statistics (ann.).

ARL Academic Law Library Statistics (ann.).
ARL Annual Salary Survey (ann.).
ARL Statistics (ann.).
Research Library Issues (irregular).

ARL Membership

Nonuniversity Libraries

Boston Public Lib.; Center for Research Libs.; Lib. of Congress; National Agricultural Lib.; National Archives and Records Administration; National Lib. of Medicine; New York Public Lib.; Smithsonian Libs. and Archives.

University Libraries

Alabama; Albany (SUNY); Alberta; Arizona; Arizona State; Auburn; Boston College; Boston Univ.; Brigham Young; British Columbia; Brown; Buffalo (SUNY); Calgary; California, Berkeley; California, Davis; California, Irvine; California, Los Angeles; California, Riverside; California, San Diego; California, Santa Barbara; Case Western Reserve; Chicago; Cincinnati; Colorado, Boulder; Colorado State; Columbia; Connecticut; Cornell; Dartmouth; Delaware; Duke; Emory; Florida; Florida State; George Washington; Georgetown; Georgia; Georgia Inst. of Technology; Guelph; Harvard; Hawaii, Manoa; Houston; Howard; Illinois, Chicago; Illinois, Urbana-Champaign; Indiana, Bloomington; Iowa; Iowa State; Johns Hopkins; Kansas; Kent State; Kentucky; Laval; Louisiana State; Louisville; McGill; McMaster; Manitoba; Maryland; Massachusetts, Amherst; Massachusetts Inst. of Technology; Miami (Florida); Michigan; Michigan State; Minnesota; Missouri; Nebraska, Lincoln; New Mexico; New York; North Carolina, Chapel Hill; North Carolina State; Northwestern; Notre Dame; Ohio; Ohio State; Oklahoma; Oklahoma State; Oregon; Ottawa; Pennsylvania; Pennsylvania State; Pittsburgh; Princeton; Purdue; Queen's (Kingston, Ontario); Rice; Rochester; Rutgers; Saskatchewan; Simon Fraser; South Carolina; Southern California; Southern Illinois, Carbondale; Stony Brook (SUNY); Syracuse; Temple; Tennessee, Knoxville; Texas, Austin; Texas A&M; Texas State; Texas Tech; Toronto; Tulane; Utah; Vanderbilt; Virginia; Virginia Commonwealth; Virginia Tech; Washington; Washington, Saint Louis; Washington State; Waterloo; Wayne State; Western; Wisconsin, Madison; Yale; York.

Association of Vision Science Librarians

Co-Chairs Rudy Barreras, Dede Rios
World Wide Web http://www.avsl.org

Objective

To foster collective and individual acquisition and dissemination of vision science information, to improve services for all persons seeking such information, and to develop standards for libraries to which members are attached. Founded in 1968.

Membership

Memb. (Indiv.) approximately 150, (Inst.) 100+.

Leadership Team

Co-Chair Rudy Barreras, Western Univ. of Health Sciences, Pomona, CA. E-mail rbarreras@westernu.edu; *Co-Chair* Dede Rios, Rosenberg School of Optometry, Univ. of the Incarnate Word, San Antonio. E-mail dmrios1@uiwtx.edu; *Secy.* Louise Collins, Massachusetts Eye and Ear Institute, Howe Lib., Boston, MA. E-mail Louise_Collins@MEEI.HARVARD.EDU; *Archivist* Gale Oren, Univ. of Michigan Kellogg Eye Ctr., John W. Henderson Lib., Ann Arbor. E-mail goren@umich.edu.

Meetings

Spring and fall meetings are held each year. The annual fall meeting runs 3-4 days and is usually timed alongside the annual meeting of the American Academy of Optometry.

Atla

Executive Director, Brenda Bailey-Hainer
200 S. Wacker Dr., Suite 3100, Chicago, IL 60606
888-665-2852 or 312-454-5100; e-mail connect@atla.com
World Wide Web http://www.atla.com

Mission

The mission of Atla (formerly known as the American Theological Library Association) is to foster the study of theology and religion by enhancing the development of theological and religious libraries and librarianship.

Membership

Dues (Inst.) $100–$1,000; (Indiv. varies, based on income) $35–$181.50, (Student) $35; (Affiliates) $100.

Officers (2020–2021)

Pres. Stephen Sweeney, Saint John Vianney Theological Seminary, 1300 South Steele St., Denver, CO 80210-2599. E-mail stephen.sweeney@archden.org; *V.P.* Ellen Frost, Perkins School of Theology, Bridwell Lib., P.O. Box 750476, Dallas, TX 75275-0476. E-mail efrost@smu.edu; *Secy.* Christina Torbert. Univ. of Mississippi—Libs., P.O. Box 1848, University, MS 38655. E-mail ctorbert@olemiss.edu; *Treas.* Armin Siedlecki, Pitts Theological Lib., Emory Univ., 1531 Dickey Dr., Suite 560, Atlanta, GA 30322. E-mail asiedle@emory.edu.

Board of Directors

Kerrie Burn, Susan Ebertz, Leslie Engelson, Suzanne Estelle-Holmer, Jeremie LeBlanc, Shanee' Yvette Murrain, Matthew Ostercamp, Michelle Spomer, Karl Stuzman, Matthew Thiesen, Brenda Bailey-Hainer (ex officio, nonvoting).

Committee Chairs

Conference. Megan Welsh.
Diversity, Equity, and Inclusion. Yasmine Abou-El-Kheir.
Endowment. Pat Graham.
International Theological Librarianship Education. Kelly Campbell.
Professional Development. Karen Clarke.
Scholarly Communication. Melody Diehl Detar.

Publications

Theological Librarianship (open access journal) http://serials.atla.com/theolib.
Theology Cataloging Bulletin (open access journal) http://serials.atla.com/tcb/index.
Atla Annual Yearbook (online open access ann. serial) http://serials.atla.com/yearbook.
Atla Newsletter (mo.; online).
Atla Proceedings (online open access ann. serial) http://serials.atla.com/proceedings.
books@Atla Open Press (online open access monographs): https://books.atla.com/atlapress.

Beta Phi Mu
(International Library and Information Studies Honor Society)

Executive Director, Alison M. Lewis
P.O. Box 42139, Philadelphia, PA 19101
267-361-5018, e-mail executivedirector@betaphimu.org or headquarters@betaphimu.org
World Wide Web http://www.betaphimu.org

Objective

To recognize distinguished achievement in and scholarly contributions to librarianship, information studies, or library education, and to sponsor and support appropriate professional and scholarly projects relating to these fields. Founded at the University of Illinois in 1948.

Membership

Memb. 40,000. Eligibility for membership in Beta Phi Mu is by invitation of the faculty from institutions where the American Library Association, or other recognized accrediting agency approved by the Beta Phi Mu Executive Board, has accredited or recognized a professional degree program. Candidates must be graduates of a library and information science program and fulfill the following requirements: complete the course requirements leading to a master's degree with a scholastic average of 3.75 where A equals 4 points, or complete a planned program of advanced study beyond the master's degree which requires full-time study for one or more academic years with a scholastic average of 3.75 where A equals 4.0. Each chapter or approved institution is allowed to invite no more than 25 percent of the annual graduating class, and the faculty of participating library schools must attest to their initiates' professional promise.

Officers

Pres. (2019–2022) Emily Knox, School of Information Sciences, Univ. of Illinois, 501 E. Daniel St., Champaign, IL 61820. Tel. 217-300-0212, e-mail knox@illinois.edu; *V.P./ Pres.-Elect (2020–2023)* Tom Rink, 9710 So. 78th East Avenue, Tulsa, OK 74133-6952. Tel. 918-449-6457, e-mail rink@nsuok.edu. *Treas. (2020–2023)* Vicki Gregory, School of Information, Univ. of South Florida, College of Arts and Sciences, 4202 E. Fowler Ave., CIS 2036, Tampa, FL 33620. Tel. 813-974-3520, e-mail gregory@usf.edu. *Past Pres. (2018–2021)* Cecelia Brown, School of Lib. and Information Studies, Univ. of Oklahoma, 401 W. Brooks, Rm. 120, Norman, OK 73019-6032. Tel. 405-325-3921, e-mail cbrown@ou.edu; *Dirs.-at-large* Michelle Demeter, Camille McCutcheon.

Directors

Gordon N. Baker, Mirah J. Dow, Jack Fisher, Laura Saunders.

Publications

Beta Phi Mu Scholars Series. Available from Rowman & Littlefield, Publishers, 4501 Forbes Blvd., Suite 200, Lanham, MD 20706. *Ed.* Andrea Falcone. E-mail bpmseries@gmail.com.

Newsletter. *The Pipeline* (biennial; electronic only). *Ed.* Alison Lewis.

Chapters

Alpha. Univ. of Illinois at Urbana-Champaign, School of Info. Sciences; *Gamma.* Florida State Univ., College of Communication and Info.; *Epsilon.* Univ. of North Carolina at Chapel Hill, School of Info. and Lib. Science; *Theta.* c/o Pratt Inst., School of Info.; *Iota.* Catholic Univ. of America, Dept. of Lib. and Info. Science; Univ. of Maryland, College of Info. Studies; *Lambda.* Univ. of Oklahoma, School of Lib. and Info. Studies; *Xi.* Univ. of Hawaii at Manoa, Lib. and Info. Science Program; *Omicron.* Rutgers Univ., Grad. School of Communication, Info., and Lib. Studies; *Pi.* Univ. of Pittsburgh, School of Info. Sciences; *Sigma.* Drexel Univ., College of Computing and Informatics; *Psi.* Univ. of Missouri at

Columbia, School of Info. Science and Learning Technologies; *Omega.* San José State Univ., School of Info.; *Beta Beta.* Simmons Univ., School of Lib. and Info. Science; *Beta Delta.* State Univ. of New York at Buffalo, Dept. of Lib. and Info. Studies; *Beta Epsilon.* Emporia State Univ., School of Lib. and Info. Management; *Beta Zeta.* Louisiana State Univ., School of Lib. and Info. Science; *Beta Iota.* Univ. of Rhode Island, Grad. School of Lib. and Info. Studies; *Beta Kappa.* Univ. of Alabama, School of Lib. and Info. Studies; *Beta Lambda.* Texas Woman's Univ., School of Lib. and Info. Sciences; *Beta Mu.* Long Island Univ., Palmer School of Lib. and Info. Science; *Beta Nu.* St. John's Univ., Div. of Lib. and Info. Science *Beta Xi.* North Carolina Central Univ., School of Lib. and Info. Sciences; *Beta Pi.*

Univ. of Arizona, School of Info.; *Beta Rho.* Univ. of Wisconsin at Milwaukee, School of Info. Science; *Beta Phi.* Univ. of South Florida, School of Lib. and Info. Science; *Beta Psi.* Univ. of Southern Mississippi, School of Lib. and Info. Science; *Beta Omega.* Univ. of South Carolina, College of Lib. and Info. Science; *Beta Beta Epsilon.* Univ. of Wisconsin at Madison, School of Lib. and Info. Studies; *Beta Beta Theta.* Univ. of Iowa, School of Lib. and Info. Science; *Pi Lambda Sigma.* Syracuse Univ., School of Info. Studies; *Beta Beta Mu.* Valdosta State Univ., Lib. and Info. Science Program; *Beta Beta Nu.* Univ. of North Texas, College of Info.; *Beta Beta Omicron.* East Carolina Univ., Dept. of Interdisciplinary Professions; *Beta Beta Xi.* St. Catherine Univ., Master of Lib. and Info. Science Program.

Bibliographical Society of America

Executive Director, Erin McGuirl
P.O. Box 1537, Lenox Hill Station, New York, NY 10021
212-452-2710, e-mail bsa@bibsocamer.org
World Wide Web http://www.bibsocamer.org

Objective

To promote bibliographical research and to issue bibliographical publications. Organized in 1904.

Membership

Dues (Partner) $80; (Sustaining) $125; (Leadership) $250; (Advancing) $500; (Lifetime) $1,250; (Emerging bibliographers, 35 and under) $25. Year. Jan.–Dec.

Officers

Pres. Barbara A. Shailor, Yale Univ.; *V.P.* Kenneth Soehner, The Watson Lib., Metropolitan Museum of Art; *Secy.* John T. McQuillen, Morgan Museum and Lib.; *Treas.* G. Scott Clemons, Brown Brothers Harriman. E-mail scott.Clemons@bbh.com. *Delegate to the ACLS* David Vander Meulen, Univ. of Virginia.

Council

(2024) María Victoria Fernández, Thomas Goldwasser, Adam G. Hooks, Nick Wilding; *(2023)* Mary Crawford, Andrew T. Nadell, Elizabeth Ott, Douglas Pfeiffer; *(2022)* Caroline Duroselle-Melish, Mark Samuels Lasner, Alice Schreyer, Jackie Vossler.

Committee Chairs

Audit. Joan Friedman.
Development. Barbara A. Shailor.
Digital Strategy Working Group. Erin McGuirl.
Events. Sonja Drimmer.
Fellowship. Hope Mayo.
Finance. Jackie Vossler.
International Development and Collaboration Working Group. T-Kay Sangwand.
Liaisons. Catherine M. Parisian.
Membership Working Group. Kyle Triplett.
New Scholars. Barbara Heritage.
Policy and Procedures Manual Working Group. Joan Friedman.
Publications. Nicholas Wilding.

Publication

Papers of the Bibliographical Society of America (q.; memb.). *Ed.* David L. Gants, Florida State Univ. E-mail editor.pbsa@bibsocamer. org.

Bibliographical Society of Canada
(La Société Bibliographique du Canada)

President, Karen Smith
360 Bloor St. W., P.O. Box 19035, Walmer, Toronto, ON M5S 3C9
E-mail secretary@bsc-sbc.ca
World Wide Web http://www.bsc-sbc.ca

Objective

The Bibliographical Society of Canada is a bilingual (English/French) organization that has as its goal the scholarly study of the history, description, and transmission of texts in all media and formats, with a primary emphasis on Canada, and the fulfillment of this goal through the following objectives:

- To promote the study and practice of bibliography: enumerative, historical, descriptive, analytical, and textual
- To further the study, research, and publication of book history and print culture
- To publish bibliographies and studies of book history and print culture
- To encourage the publication of bibliographies, critical editions, and studies of book history and print culture
- To promote the appropriate preservation and conservation of manuscript, archival, and published materials in various formats
- To encourage the utilization and analysis of relevant manuscript and archival sources as a foundation of bibliographical scholarship and book history
- To promote the interdisciplinary nature of bibliography, and to foster relationships with other relevant organizations nationally and internationally
- To conduct the society without purpose of financial gain for its members, and to ensure that any profits or other accretions to the society shall be used in promoting its goal and objectives

Membership

The society welcomes as members all those who share its aims and wish to support and participate in bibliographical research and publication. Dues (Reg.) $80; (Student) $35; (Ret.) $50; (Inst.) $100; (Life) $1,000.

Executive Council (2020–2021)

Pres. Karen Smith. E-mail president@bsc-sbc. ca; *1st V.P.* Christopher Young. E-mail vice_president_1@bsc-sbc.ca; *2nd V.P.* Svetlana Kochkina. E-mail vice_president_2@bsc-sbc. ca; *Secy.* Andrew Stewart. E-mail secretary@ bsc-sbc.ca; *Assoc. Secy.* Marie-Claude Felton; *Treas.* Tom Vincent. E-mail treasurer@bsc-sbc. ca; *Assoc. Treas.* Meaghan Scanlon; *Past Pres.* Ruth-Ellen St. Onge.

Councilors

(2019–2022) Susan Cameron, Scott Schofield, Myra Tawik; *(2020–2023)* Christopher Lyons, Chelsea Shriver, Danielle Van Wagner.

Committee Chairs

Awards. Scott Schofield.
Communications. Svetlana Kochkina.
Fellowships. Ruth Panofsky.
Publications. Geoffrey Little.

Publications

Bulletin (s. ann). *Ed.* Ruth Panofsky.
Papers of the Bibliographical Society of Canada/Cahiers de la Société Bibliographique du Canada (s. ann.). *Ed.* Elizabeth Willson Gordon.

Black Caucus of the American Library Association

President, Shauntee Burns-Simpson
P.O. Box 174, New York, NY 10159-0174
646-721-1358
World Wide Web http://www.bcala.org

Mission

The Black Caucus of the American Library Association (BCALA) serves as an advocate for the development, promotion, and improvement of library services and resources for the nation's African American community and provides leadership for the recruitment and professional development of African American librarians. Founded in 1970.

Membership

Membership is open to any person, institution, or business interested in promoting the development of library and information services for African Americans and other people of African descent and willing to maintain good financial standing with the organization. The membership is currently composed of librarians and other information professionals, library support staff, libraries, publishers, authors, vendors, and other library-related organizations in the United States and abroad. Dues (Lifetime) $500; (Corporate) $200; (Inst.) $60; (Reg.) $45; (Library Support Staff) $20; (Student) $10; (Ret.) $25.

Officers

Pres. Shauntee Burns-Simpson; *V.P./Pres.-Elect* Nichelle M. Hayes; *Secy.* Brenda Johnson-Perkins; *Treas.* Brandy McNeil; *Past Pres.* Richard E. Ashby. Jr.

Board Members

(2020-2022) KC Boyd, Dolores Brown, Valerie Carter, Taryn Fouche, Derek Mosley, Fayrene Muhammed, Satia Orange; *(2019–2021)* Latrice Booker, Vivian Bordeaux, Rudolph Clay, James Allen Davis, Jr., Tashia Munson, Ana Ndumu, Regina Renee Ward, Shamika Simpson.

Committee Chairs

Affiliates. Tiffany Alston.
ALA Relations. Latrice Booker
Awards. John Page.
Budget and Finance. Stanton Biddie.
Constitution and Bylaws. Jos Holman.
Fundraising. Kelvin Watson.
History. Sybyl Moses.
International Relations. Eboni M. Henry, Vivian Bordeaux.
Marketing and Public Relations. Shaundra Walker.
Membership. Rudolph Clay, Jr.
National Conference. Tracey Hunter Hayes.
Nomination and Election. Richard E. Ashby.
President's Advisory. Shauntee Burns-Simpson.
Programs. Shauntee Burns-Simpson, Nichelle M. Hayes.
Publications. Nichelle Hayes.
Recruitment and Professional Development. Ana Ndumu.
Services to Children and Families of African Descent. Karen Lemmons.
Technology Advisory. Zakia Ringgold.

Awards Committee Chairs

Literary Awards. Gladys Smiley Bell.
Dr. E. J. Josey Scholarship. Sylvia Sprinkle-Hamlin.

Publication

BCALA News (3 a year; memb.). *Ed.* Nichelle M. Hayes.

Canadian Association for Information Science (L'Association Canadienne des Sciences de l'Information)

President, Philippe Mongeon
World Wide Web http://www.cais-acsi.ca

Objective

To promote the advancement of information science in Canada and encourage and facilitate the exchange of information relating to the use, access, retrieval, organization, management, and dissemination of information.

Membership

Institutions and individuals interested in information science and involved in the gathering, organization, and dissemination of information (such as information scientists, archivists, librarians, computer scientists, documentalists, economists, educators, journalists, and psychologists) and who support Canadian Association for Information Science (CAIS) objectives can become association members.

Officers (2020–2021)

Pres. Philippe Mongeon, Dalhousie Univ.; *Secy.* Fei Shu, Hangzhou Dianzi Univ.; *Treas.* Michael Ridley, Western Univ.; *Past Pres.* Heather Hill, Western Univ.; *Memb.-at-Large* Danica Pawlick Potts.

Board Members

Roger Chabot, Western Univ.; Christina Parsons, Robyn Stobbs, Univ. of Alberta; Sam A. Vander Kooy, Western Univ.

Publication

Canadian Journal of Information and Library Science. (q.; memb.; print; online). For nonmember subscription information visit https://ojs.lib.uwo.ca/index.php/cjils. *Ed.* Heather Hill, Information and Media Studies, Western Univ. E-mail cjils@cais-acsi.ca.

Canadian Association of Research Libraries (Association des Bibliothèques de Recherche du Canada)

Executive Director, Susan Haigh
309 Cooper St., Suite 203, Ottawa, ON K2P 0G5
613-482-9344 ext. 101, e-mail info@carl-abrc.ca
World Wide Web http://www.carl-abrc.ca
Twitter @carlabrc

Membership

The Canadian Association of Research Libraries (CARL), established in 1976, is the leadership organization for the Canadian research library community. The association's members are the 29 major academic research libraries across Canada together with Library and Archives Canada and the National Research Council Canada, National Science Library. Membership is institutional, open primarily to libraries of Canadian universities that have doctoral graduates in both the arts and the sciences. CARL is an associate member of the Association of Universities and Colleges of Canada (AUCC) and is incorporated as a not-for-profit organization under the Canada Corporations Act.

Mission

The association provides leadership on behalf of Canada's research libraries and enhances their capacity to advance research and higher education. It promotes effective and sustainable scholarly communication, and public policy that enables broad access to scholarly information.

Officers (2019–2022)

Pres. Jonathan Bengtson, Univ. of Victoria, Victoria, BC; *V.P.* Vivian Lewis, McMaster Univ., Hamilton, ON; *Secy.* Loubna Ghaouti, Univ. Laval, Montréal, PQ; *Treas.* Susan Cleyle, Memorial Univ., St. John's, NL.

Board of Directors

Talia Chung, Univ. of Ottawa, ON (Ontario Region Representative); Dir. Susan Parker, Univ. of British Columbia, Vancouver, BC (Western Region Representative).

Committee Chairs

Advancing Research. Catherine Steeves.
Assessment. Colleen Cook.
Policy. Carol Shepstone.
Strengthening Capacity. Brett Waytuck.

Member Institutions

National Members

Lib. and Archives Canada, National Research Council Canada

Regional Members

Univ. of Alberta, Univ. of British Columbia, Brock Univ., Univ. of Calgary, Carleton Univ., Concordia Univ., Dalhousie Univ., Univ. of Guelph, Univ. Laval, McGill Univ., McMaster Univ., Univ. of Manitoba, Memorial Univ. of Newfoundland, Univ. de Montréal, Univ. of New Brunswick, Univ. of Ottawa, Univ. du Québec à Montréal, Queen's Univ., Univ. of Regina, Ryerson Univ., Univ. of Saskatchewan, Université de Sherbrooke, Simon Fraser Univ., Univ. of Toronto, Univ. of Victoria, Univ. of Waterloo, Western Univ., Univ. of Windsor, York Univ.

Catholic Library Association

Executive Director, Melanie Talley
8550 United Plaza Blvd., Suite 1001, Baton Rouge, LA 70809
225-408-4417, e-mail cla2@cathla.org
World Wide Web http://www.cathla.org

Objective

The promotion and encouragement of Catholic literature and library work through cooperation, publications, education, and information. Founded in 1921.

Membership

Memb. 1,000. Dues $25–$500. Year. July–June.

Officers

Pres. Jack Fritts. 5700 College Rd., Lisle, IL 60532. Tel. 630-829-6060, e-mail jfritts@ben. edu; *V.P./Treas.* Kathryn Shaughnessy, e-mail shaughnk@stjohns.edu; *Past Pres.* N. Curtis LeMay. E-mail nclemay@hotmail.com.

Board Members

Eva Gonsalves, Elyse Hayes, Pat Lawton, Cortney Schraut.

Section Chairs

Academic Libraries, Archives and Library Education. Bro. Andrew J. Kosmowski, SM. High School and Young Adult Library Services. Eva Gonsalves.
Parish and Community Library Services. Phyllis Petre.

Publication

Catholic Library World (q.; memb.; nonmemb. $100 domestic, $125 international). *General Ed.* Sigrid Kelsey. E-mail sigridkelsey@gmail.com.

Chief Officers of State Library Agencies

Executive Director, Timothy Cherubini
201 E. Main St., Suite 1405, Lexington, KY 40507
859-514-9150, fax 859-514-9166, e-mail info@cosla.org
World Wide Web http://www.cosla.org
Twitter @COSLA_US

Objective

Chief Officers of State Library Agencies (COSLA) is an independent organization of the chief officers of state and territorial agencies designated as the state library administrative agency and responsible for statewide library development. Its purpose is to identify and address issues of common concern and national interest; to further state library agency relationships with federal government and national organizations; and to initiate cooperative action for the improvement of library services to the people of the United States.

COSLA's membership consists solely of these top library officers, variously designated as state librarian, director, commissioner, or executive secretary. The organization provides a continuing mechanism for dealing with the problems and challenges faced by these officers. Its work is carried on through its members, a board of directors, and committees.

Officers (2020–2022)

Pres. Jennie Stapp, State Libn., Montana State Lib. Tel. 406-444-3116, e-mail jstapp2@mt.gov;

V.P./Pres.-Elect Julie Walker, State Libn., Georgia Public Lib. Svcs. Tel. 404-406-4519, e-mail jwalker@georgialibraries.org; *Secy.* Jennifer Nelson, State Library Svcs. and Charter Ctr., Minnesota Dept. of Ed. Tel. 651-582-8791, e-mail jennifer.r.nelson@state.mn.us; *Treas.* Karen Mellor, Rhode Island Office of Lib. and Information Svcs. Tel. 401-574-9304, e-mail karen.mellor@olis.ri.gov; *Past Pres.* Stacey Aldrich, State Libn., Hawaii State Public Lib. System. Tel. 808-586-3704, e-mail stacey.aldrich@librarieshawaii.org.

Directors

Randy Riley, State Libn., Lib. of Michigan. Tel. 517-373-5860, e-mail rileyr1@michigan. gov; Jamie Ritter, State Libn., Maine State Lib. Tel. 207-287-5600, e-mail james.ritter@maine. gov.

Chinese American Librarians Association

Executive Director, Lian Ruan
E-mail lruan@illinois.edu
World Wide Web http://cala-web.org

Objective

To enhance communications among Chinese American librarians as well as between Chinese American librarians and other librarians; to serve as a forum for discussion of mutual problems and professional concerns among Chinese American librarians; to promote Sino-American librarianship and library services; and to provide a vehicle whereby Chinese American librarians can cooperate with other associations and organizations having similar or allied interests.

Membership

Memb. approximately 600. Membership is open to anyone interested in the association's goals and activities. Dues (Reg.) $30; (International/Student/Nonsalaried/Overseas) $15; (Inst.) $100; (Affiliated) $100; (Life) $300.

Officers (2020–2023)

Pres. Hong Yao. E-mail Hong.Yao@queens library.org; *V.P./Pres.-Elect* Wenli Gao. E-mail wgao5@central.uh.edu; *Treas.* Suzhen Chen. E-mail suzhen@hawaii.edu; *Past Pres.* Fu Zhuo. E-mail zhuof@umkc.edu; *Incoming V.P./Pres.-Elect.* Ray Pun. E-mail raypun101@ gmail.com.

Board of Directors

(2017–2020) Ping Fu, Leping He, Weiling Liu, *(2018–2021)* Qi Chen, Michael Huang, Yuan Li, Guoying (Grace) Liu, Minhao Jiang; *(2019–2022)* Jianye He, Hong Miao, Vincci Kwong, Xiaocan Wang.

Chapter Presidents (2020–2021)

NCA: Renee Bu; SCA: Wen Wen Zhang; GMA: Andrew Yanqing Lee; MW: Liangyu Fu; NE: Jennie Pu; SE: Jianying Shou; SW: Anna Xiong; Canada: Lei Jin.

Committee Chairs

Assessment and Evaluation. Anna Xiong, Yan He.
Awards. Leping He, Yongyi Song.
Conference Program. Ying Zhang.
Constitution and Bylaws. Xiaojie Duan.
Election. Lian Ruan.
Finance. Jennifer Zhao.
International Relations. Qinghua Zu, Yuan Li.
Leadership Training. Terry Carlson.
Membership. Jingjing Wu, Yan Liu.
Nominating. Qi Chen.
Public Relations/Fundraising. Hong Yao.
Publications. Yuan Li.
Scholarship. Jie Huang, Daniel Xiao.
Web Committee. Jingjing Wu, Minhao Jiang (CALA webmaster).

Publications

CALA Newsletter (2 a year; memb.; online). *Eds.* Xiying Mi. E-mail mixiying@gmail. com; Esther DeLeon. E-mail esther.deleon@ ttu.edu.
International Journal of Librarianship (IJoL). Ed. Grace Liu. E-mail editors@calaijol.org.

Coalition for Networked Information

Executive Director, Clifford A. Lynch
21 Dupont Circle, Suite 800, Washington, DC 20036
202-296-5098, fax 202-872-0884, e-mail clifford@cni.org
World Wide Web http://www.cni.org
Facebook https://www.facebook.com/cni.org
Twitter @cni_org
YouTube https://www.youtube.com/user/cnivideo/
Vimeo http://vimeo.com/cni

Mission

The Coalition for Networked Information (CNI) promotes the transformative promise of networked information technology for the advancement of scholarly communication and the enrichment of intellectual productivity.

Membership

Memb. 240+. Membership is institutional. Dues $8,660. Year. July–June.

Staff

Assoc. Exec. Dir. Joan K. Lippincott, 21 Dupont Cir., Suite 800, Washington, DC 20036. Tel. 202-296-5098, e-mail joan@cni.org; *Asst. Exec. Dir.* Diane Goldenberg-Hart. E-mail diane@cni.org; *Admin. Asst.* Sharon Adams. E-mail sharon@cni.org; *Systems Coord.* Maurice-Angelo F. Cruz. E-mail angelo@cni.org; *Office Mgr.* Jacqueline J. Eudell. E-mail jackie@cni.org; *Communications Coord.* Diane Goldenberg-Hart. E-mail diane@cni.org.

Steering Committee Members (2020–2021)

Kristin Antelman, Univ. of California–Santa Barbara; Daniel Cohen, Northeastern Univ.; P. Toby Graham, Univ. of Georgia; Mary Lee Kennedy (ex officio) ARL; Clifford A. Lynch (ex officio) CNI; Beth Sandore Namachchivaya, Univ. of Waterloo; John O'Brien, (ex officio) EDUCAUSE; Gina M. Siesing, Bryn Mawr College; Jenn Stringer, Univ. of California–Berkeley; Ann Thornton, Columbia Univ.; Donald J. Waters.

Publications

CNI-ANNOUNCE (https://www.cni.org/resources/follow-cni/cni-announce)

CNI Executive Roundtable Reports (https://www.cni.org/tag/executive-roundtable-report).

Council on Library and Information Resources

Chair, Buhle Mbambo-Thata
211 North Union Street, Suite 100-PMB 1027, Alexandria, VA 22314
E-mail contact@clir.org
World Wide Web http://www.clir.org
Twitter @CLIRnews

Objective

In 1997 the Council on Library Resources (CLR) and the Commission on Preservation and Access (CPA) merged and became the Council on Library and Information Resources (CLIR). CLIR is an independent, nonprofit organization that forges strategies to enhance research, teaching, and learning environments in collaboration with libraries, cultural institutions, and communities of higher learning.

CLIR promotes forward-looking collaborative solutions that transcend disciplinary, institutional, professional, and geographic boundaries in support of the public good. CLIR identifies and defines the key emerging issues relating to the welfare of libraries and the constituencies they serve, convenes the leaders who can influence change, and promotes collaboration among the institutions and organizations that can achieve change. The council's interests embrace the entire range of information resources and services from traditional library and archival materials to emerging digital formats. It assumes a particular interest in helping institutions cope with the accelerating pace of change associated with the transition into the digital environment.

While maintaining appropriate collaboration and liaison with other institutions and organizations, CLIR operates independently of any particular institutional or vested interests. Through the composition of its board, it brings the broadest possible perspective to bear upon defining and establishing the priority of the issues with which it is concerned.

Officers

Chair Buhle Mbambo-Thata, National Univ. of Lesotho; *V.Chair* Guy Berthiaume, Librarian and Archivist of Canada Emeritus; *Treas.* John Price Wilkin, Univ. of Illinois at Urbana-Champaign.

Board of Directors

Edward Ayers, Univ. of Richmond; Michele Casalini, Casalini Libri; Dan Cohen, Northeastern Univ.; Jill Cousins, Hunt Museum; Tess Davis, Antiquities Coalition; Kurt De Belder, Leiden Univ.; Kathlin Fitzpatrick, Michigan State Univ.; Fenella France, Library of Congress; Charles Henry, CLIR; Michael A. Keller, Stanford Univ.; W. Joseph King, Lyon College; Carol Mandel, New York Univ. Div. of Libs.; Max Marmor, Samuel H. Kress Fdn.; Asma Naeem, Baltimore Museum of Art; Richard Ovenden, Univ. of Oxford; Sandra Phoenix, HBCU Library Alliance; Winston Tabb, Johns Hopkins Univ.; Ben Vinson III, Case Western Reserve Univ.; Sohair Wastawy, The Information Guild.

Address correspondence to headquarters.

Publications

Annual Report.
CLIR Issues (bi-mo.; electronic).

EveryLibrary

Executive Director, John Chrastka
P.O. Box 406, 45 E. Burlington St.,
Riverside, IL 60546
312-574-5098
E-mail info@everylibrary.org
World Wide Web http://www.everylibrary.org | http://action.everylibrary.org
Facebook https://www.facebook.com/EveryLibrary
LinkedIn https://www.linkedin.com/company/3801587/
Twitter @EveryLibrary

Object

EveryLibrary is a national political action committee for libraries. Organized as a 501(c)4, the organization provides pro bono advising and consulting to libraries about their funding requests, either when it appears on a ballot or through a municipal funding partner. Its school-library-focused digital activism platform SaveSchoolLibrarians.org works to support school librarian positions and budgets for school library programs. Their national network in 2020 included over 355,000 Americans.

EveryLibrary's mission is to "build voter support for libraries" at all levels of government, and it works to fulfill that mission as a completely donor-supported organization.

Board Members

Jeannie Allen, Lori Bowen Ayer, Peter Bromberg, John Chrastka, Roberto Delgadillo, Harmony V. Faust, Erica Findley, Brian D. Hart, Gary Kirk, Kathleen McEvoy, Patrick "PC" Sweeney.

EveryLibrary Institute, NFP

Executive Director, John Chrastka
6433 Fairfield
Berwyn, IL 60402
E-mail info@everylirbaryinstitute.org
World Wide Web http://everylibraryinstitute.org
Facebook https://facebook.com/everylibraryinstitute
Twitter @ELInstituteNFP

Object

The EveryLibrary Institute, NFP is a public policy and tax policy think tank for libraries that is focused on the future of public library and school library funding in the United States and abroad. Its nonprofit 501(c)3 mission is to develop research, programmatic opportunities, trainings, fiscal sponsorships, and scholarship that advance the image and impact of libraries and librarians to the general public and policymakers. Domestically, this includes publishing its journal, supporting public outreach and education across the EveryLibrary network, and providing crowdfunding services through its FundLibraries.org platform. Internationally, it partners with CILIP, the Chartered Institute for Library and Information Professionals, to host the LibrariesDeliver.uk outreach campaign about libraries in England.

Board Members

K.C. Boyd, John Chrastka, Kyle Courtney, Trevor A. Dawes, Erica Findley, Britten Follett,

Amy Garmer, Fran Glick, Kafi Kumasi, Steve Potter, Rivkah Sass, Cal Shepard, Maureen Sullivan, Patrick "PC" Sweeney, Jill Hurst-Wahl, Lance Werner.

Publication

The Political Librarian (irreg.; open access). (Transferred from EveryLibrary in 2019.) *Ed.* Christopher Stewart.

Federal Library and Information Network

Executive Director, Laurie Neider
Library of Congress, Washington, DC 20540-4935
202-707-4801, e-mail lneider@loc.gov
World Wide Web http://www.loc.gov/flicc
Twitter @librarycongress

Objective

The Federal Library and Information Network (FEDLINK) is an organization of federal agencies working together to achieve optimum use of the resources and facilities of federal libraries and information centers by promoting common services, coordinating and sharing available resources, and providing continuing professional education for federal library and information staff. FEDLINK serves as a forum for discussion of the policies, programs, procedures, and technologies that affect federal libraries and the information services they provide to their agencies, to Congress, to the federal courts, and to the public.

Membership

The FEDLINK voting membership is composed of representatives of the following U.S. federal departments and agencies: Each of the national libraries (the Library of Congress, National Agricultural Library, National Library of Education, National Library of Medicine, and the National Transportation Library); each cabinet-level executive department, as defined in 5 U.S.C. § 101; additional departments and agencies (the Defense Technical Information Center; departments of the Air Force, Army, and Navy; Executive Office of the President, Government Accountability Office, General Services Administration, Government Printing Office, Institute of Museum and Library Services, National Aeronautics and Space Administration, National Archives and Records Administration, National Technical Information Service [Department of Commerce], Office of Management and Budget, Office of Personnel Management, Office of Scientific and Technical Information [Department of Energy], Office of the Director of National Intelligence, and the Smithsonian Institution); the U.S. Supreme Court and the Administrative Office of the U.S. Courts; the District of Columbia; and other federal independent agencies and government corporations.

Address correspondence to the executive director.

Publication

FEDLINK Bulletin (bi-wk.; electronic).

Librarians, Archivists, and Museum Professionals in the History of the Health Sciences

President, Jennifer Nieves
E-mail jks4@case.edu
World Wide Web http://iis-exhibits.library.ucla.edu/alhhs/index.html

Objective

Librarians, Archivists, and Museum Professionals in the History of the Health Sciences (LAMPHHS; formerly ALHHS/MeMA) was established exclusively for educational purposes, to serve the professional interests of librarians, archivists, and other specialists actively engaged in the librarianship of the history of the health sciences by promoting the exchange of information and by improving the standards of service.

Membership

Memb. approximately 150. Dues $15.

Officers (2020–2022)

Pres. Jennifer Nieves, Dittrick Medical History Ctr., Cleveland, OH. E-mail jks4@case.edu; *V.P.* Polina Ilieva, Archives and Special Collections, UCSF Library, San Francisco, CA. E-mail jpolinailieva@ucsf.edu; *Secy.* Jamie Rees, Clendening History of Medicine Library and Museum, University of Kansas Medical Center, Kansas City, KS. E-mail lamphhs.org@gmail.com; *Treas.* Phoebe Evans Letocha,

Alan Mason Chesney Medical Archives, Johns Hopkins Univ., Baltimore, MD. E-mail alhhs.treasurer@gmail.com; *Past Pres.* Melissa Grafe, Medical Historical Lib., Harvey Cushing / John Hay Whitney Medical Lib., Yale Univ. New Haven, CT. E-mail melissa.grafe@yale.edu. *Memb.-at-Large* Judy M. Chelnick, Joel Klein, Christine Ruggere, Melanie Sorsby.

Committee Chairs

Annual Meeting 2021 Remote Arrangements. Micaela Sullivan-Fowler.
Annual Meeting 2021 Program. Emily Gustainis.
Archivist. Jodi Koste.
Nominating 2021. Gabreille Barr.
Recruiting. Jonathan Erlen.
Website. Sara Alger, Beth DeFrancis Sun.

Awards Committee Chairs

Publications Awards 2021. Christine Ruggere.
Recognition Awards 2021. Stephen Greenberg.
Watermark (q.; memb.). *Ed.* Stephen E. Novak. Augustus C. Long Health Sciences Library, Columbia University. E-mail sen13@cumc.columbia.org.

Medical Library Association

Executive Director, Kevin Baliozian
225 West Wacker Dr., Suite 650, Chicago, IL 60606-1210
312-419-9094, fax 312-419-8950, e-mail websupport@mail.mlahq.org
World Wide Web http://www.mlanet.org
Twitter @MedLibAssn

Objective

The Medical Library Association (MLA) is a nonprofit professional education organization with nearly 4,000 health sciences information professional members and partners worldwide. MLA provides lifelong educational opportunities, supports a knowledge base of health information research, and works with a global network of partners to promote the importance of high-quality information for improved health to the healthcare community and the public.

Membership

Memb. (Inst.) 400+; (Indiv.) 3,200+, in more than 50 countries. Dues (Indiv.) $75–$225; (Student) $50; (Int'l.) $150; (Affiliate) $140; (Inst.) $325–$880. Year. Institutional members are medical and allied scientific libraries. Individual members are people who are (or were at the time membership was established) engaged in professional library or bibliographic work in medical and allied scientific libraries or people who are interested in medical or allied scientific libraries. Members can be affiliated with one or more of MLA's more than 20 special-interest sections and its regional chapters.

Officers

Pres. Lisa K. Traditi, Univ. of Colorado Anschutz Med. Campus; *Pres.-Elect*; Kristine M. Alpi, Oregon Health & Science Univ.; *Secy.* Gurpreet Kaur Rana, Taubman Health Sciences Lib., Univ. of Michigan; *Treas.* Shannon D. Jones, Med. Univ. of South Carolina; *Past Pres.* Julia Esparza, Louisiana State Univ. HSC; *Exec. Dir.* Kevin Baliozian. Med. Lib. Assn.

Board of Directors

Donna R. Berryman, Sally Gore, Heather N. Holmes, Adela V. Justice, Brenda M. Linares, J. Dale Prince, Meredith I. Solomon.

Committee Chairs

Awards. Liz Kellermeyer.
Books Panel. Erin Watson.
Bylaws. David Charles Duggar.
Credentialing. Kimberly Loper.
Diversity and Inclusion. Xan Y Goodman.
Education: Steering. Merinda McLure.
Education: Information Management Curriculum. Amy Suiter.
Education: Information Services Curriculum. Amy Chatfield.
Education: Leadership and Management Curriculum. Tony Nguyen.
Education: Research and Evidence-Based Practive Curriculum. Tara R Malone.
Finance. Shannon D Jones.
Governmental Relations. Margaret Ansell, Andy Hickner.
Grants and Scholarships. Melanie J. Norton.
Joseph Leiter NLM/MLA Lectureship. Ana D. Cleveland.
Membership. Emily J Glenn.
National Program. Tara Douglas-Williams, Neville D. Prendergast.
Nominating. Julia Esparza.
Oral History. Montie L. Dobbin.
Professional Recruitment and Retention. David Midyette.

Editorial Board Chairs

JMLA Editor-in-Chief. Katherine Goold Akers.
MLAConnect Christine Willis.

Task Force Chairs

Annual Meeting Innovation. Kevin Baliozian, Lisa K. Traditi.
Joint MLA/AAHSL Legislative. Sandra L. Bandy.

Awards Committee Chairs

Virginia L. and William K. Beatty Volunteer Service. Ryan Harris.
Estelle Brodman Award for the Academic Medical Librarian of the Year. Heather Edmonds.
Lois Ann Colaianni Award for Excellence and Achievement in Hospital Librarianship. Christi Piper.
Chapter Project of the Year. Sola Whitehead.
Consumer Health Librarian of the Year Award Jury. Elisia George.
Louise Darling Medal for Distinguished Achievement in Collection Development in the Health Sciences. Brandi Tuttle.
Janet Doe Lectureship. Barbara A. Epstein.
Ida and George Eliot Prize. Kathleen Elizabeth Phillips.
Fellows and Honorary Members. Nicole Theis-Mahon.
Carla J. Funk Governmental Relations. Elaine J. Sullo.
T. Mark Hodges International Service. Michael A. Wood.
Lucretia W. McClure Excellence in Education. Lin Wu.
Erich Meyerhoff Prize. Mark Berendsen.
Research Advancement in Health Sciences Librarianship Awards Jury. Amy Christine Studer.
Rising Stars Award. Melanie E. Sorsby.
Rittenhouse Award. Kristen DeSanto.

Grants, Scholarships, and Fellowships Juries

Ysabel Bertolucci MLA Annual Meeting Grant. Maria Lopez.
Naomi C. Broering Hispanic Heritage Grant. Ana M Macias.
Continuing Education Grant. Sarah Towner Wright.
Cunningham Memorial International Fellowship. Toluwase Victor Asuhiaro.
Financial Support Jury: Conferences and Exhibits. Michelle L. Zafron.
Financial Support Jury: CE Passports. Korey G. Brunetti.
Eugene Garfield Research Fellowship. Cecelia Vetter.
Donald A. B. Lindberg Research Fellowship. Anna A. Fleming.
MLA/Hospital Libraries Professional Development Grant. Mary Katherine Haver.
MLA Librarians Without Borders® Elsevier Foundation/Research4Life Grants. Michelle L. Zafron.
MLA Research, Development, and Demonstration Project Grant. Lisa A. Adriani.
MLA Scholarships (including for underrepresented students). Sheila R Henderson, Deedra Walton.
Research Training Institute Jury. Sandy De Groote.

Publications

Journal of the Medical Library Association (q.; electronic version, free to all through PubMed Central). *Ed.* Katherine G. Akers, Wayne State Univ. E-mail jmla@journals.pitt.edu.

Music Library Association

President, Liza Vick
1600 Aspen Commons Suite 100, Middleton, WI 53562
608-836-5825, fax 608-831-8200, e-mail mla@areditions.com
World Wide Web https://www.musiclibraryassoc.org
Facebook https://www.facebook.com/Music.Library.Association
Twitter @musiclibassoc
Vimeo https://vimeo.com/musiclibraryassoc

Objective

The Music Library Association provides a professional forum for librarians, archivists, and others who support and preserve the world's musical heritage. To achieve this mission, it

- Provides leadership for the collection and preservation of music and information about music in libraries and archives
- Develops and delivers programs that promote continuing education and professional development in music librarianship
- Ensures and enhances intellectual access to music for all by contributing to the development and revision of national and international codes, formats, and other standards for the bibliographic control of music
- Ensures and enhances access to music for all by facilitating best practices for housing, preserving, and providing access to music
- Promotes legislation that strengthens music library services and universal access to music
- Fosters information literacy and lifelong learning by promoting music reference services, library instruction programs, and publications
- Collaborates with other groups in the music and technology industries, government, and librarianship, to promote its mission and values

Membership

Memb. 1,200+. Dues (Inst.) $175; (Indiv.) $140; (Ret.) $105; (Paraprofessional) $75; (Student) $65. (Foreign, add $10.) Year. July 1–June 30.

Officers

Pres. Liza Vick. E-mail lizavick@upenn.edu; *V.P./Pres.-Elect*; *Recording Secy.* Misti Shaw. E-mail mistshaw@indiana.edu; *Past Pres.* Susannah Cleveland. E-mail Susannah.Cleveland@unt.edu.

Board of Directors

Officers; *Admin. Officer* Tracey Rudnick, *Asst. Admin. Officer* Elizabeth Hille Cribbs; *Memb.-at-Large (2020–2022)* Brian McMillan, Casey Mullin, Diane Steinhaus; *(2021-2023)* Kristi Bergland, Marci Cohen, Scott Stone.

Committee Chairs

Archives and Special Collections. Maristella J. Feustle.
Awards: Best of Chapters. Sara White.
Career Development and Services. Emma Dederick, Timothy Sestrick.
Cataloging and Metadata. Hermine Vermeij.
Development. Sara White.
Diversity. Callie Holmes.
Education. Sonia Archer-Capuzzo.
Emerging Technologies and Services. Amy S. Jackson.
Finance. Anne E. Shelley.
Legislation. Kyra Folk-Farber.
Membership. Mallory Sajewski.
Music Library Advocacy. Linda B. Fairtile.
Nominating. Melissa Moll.
Oral History. Therese Z. Dickman.
Planning. Jonathan J. Sauceda.
Preservation. Treshani Perera.
Program, 2021. Kristina L. Shanton.
Program, 2022. Peter Shirts.
Program, 2023, 2024. Rachel Smiley.
Public Libraries. Kristine E. Nelsen.

Public Services. Andrea L. Beckendorf.
Publications. Deborah A. Campana.
Resource Sharing and Collection Development. Stephanie Bonjack.
Web. Kerry C. Masteller.

Awards Committee Chairs

Lenore Coral IAML Travel Grant. Darwin F. Scott.
Diversity Scholarship. Jonathan J. Sauceda.
Dena Epstein Award for Archival and Library Research in American Music. Laurie Sampsel.
Kevin Freeman Travel Grant. Carlos E. Peña.
Walter Gerboth Award. Lena Sheahan.
Publications. Treshani Perera.

Publications

Basic Manual Series. *Series Ed.* Kathleen A. Abromeit.
Basic Music Library. *Ed.* Daniel Boomhower.
Index and Bibliography Series (irreg.; price varies). *Ed.* Maristella Feustle.
MLA *Newsletter.* (6 a year; memb.). *Ed.* Jacey Kepich.
Music Cataloging Bulletin (mo.; online subscription only, $35). *Ed.* Kirk-Evan Billet.
Notes (q.; memb.). *Ed.* Jonathan J. Sauceda.
Technical Reports and Monographs in Music Librarianship (irreg.; price varies). *Ed.* Anna E. Kijas.

NASIG

President, Betsy Appleton
Address: PMB 305, 1902 Ridge Road, West Seneca, NY 14224-3312
716-324-1859, e-mail: info@nasig.org
World Wide Web: http://www.nasig.org
Twitter: @NASIG
Facebook: https://www.facebook.com/groups/2399345882/
Instagram: https://www.instagram.com/nasig_official/
LinkedIn: https://www.linkedin.com/groups/149102/
YouTube: https://www.youtube.com/channel/UCVvnh_CzXS8YgftuvIypTiQ

Vision and Mission

Established in 1985, NASIG is an independent organization working to advance and transform the management of information resources. NASIG's goal is to facilitate and improve the distribution, acquisition, and long-term accessibility of information resources in all formats and business models. There are three key components to the organization's mission:

1. NASIG supports a dynamic community of professionals including, but not limited to, librarians, publishers, and vendors engaging in understanding one another's perspectives and improving functionality throughout the information resources lifecycle with an emphasis on scholarly communications, serials, and electronic resources.
2. NASIG provides a rich variety of conference and continuing education programming to encourage knowledge sharing among its members and to support their professional and career development.
3. NASIG promotes the development and implementation of best practices and standards for the distribution, acquisition and long-term accessibility of information resources in all formats and business models throughout their lifecycle. In addition to developing best practices, NASIG supports the development of standards by NISO, an affiliated organization.

Membership

Memb. 525. For any person, library, or organization interested in information resources and scholarly communication. Dues (Indiv. based on salary range) $75–$100; (Ret.) $25; (Student) Free; (Lifetime) $1,000/one time; (Inst.) $195.

Executive Board (2020–2021)

Pres. Betsy Appleton, University of Texas at Austin; *Pres.-Elect* Ted Westervelt, Library of Congress; *Past Pres.* Kristen Wilson, Index Data; Sec. Beth Ashmore, North Carolina State University; *Treas.* Cris Ferguson, Murray State University; *Memb.-at-Large* Keondra Bailey, Duke University Press; Michael Fernandez, Yale University; Shannon Keller, New York Public Library; Katy DiVittorio, University of Colorado Denver; Mary Ann Jones, Mississippi State University; Courtney McAllister, EBSCO; *Newsletter Editor-in-Chief* Angela Dresselhaus, ProQuest, LLC.; *Marketing and Social Media Coordinator* Chris Bulock, California State University, Northridge; *Coordinator in Training* Anu Moorthy, Duke University Medical Center.

Committee Chairs

Archivist. Peter Whiting, University of Southern Indiana.

Awards and Recognition. Vanessa Mitchell, Northwestern University.

Bylaws. Laurie Kaplan, ProQuest and Stephen Sweeney, St. John Vianney Theological Seminary. Communications. Rebecca Tatterson, East Carolina University.

Conference Coordinator. Anna Creech, University of Richmond.

Conference Planning. Lisa Martincik, University of Iowa, and Nancy Bennett, University of Wisconsin-Whitewater.

Conference Proceedings Editors. Paul Moeller, University of Colorado Boulder, Cecilia Genereux, University of Minnesota Twin Cities, Kate Moore, Indiana University Southeast.

Continuing Education. Adele Fitzgerald, St. Joseph's College New York, and Jennifer Pate, University of North Alabama.

Digital Preservation. Heather Staines, MIT Knowledge Futures Group, and Michelle Polchow, University of California, Davis.

Equity and Inclusion. Dana Sinclair, State University of New York-Westbury.

Evaluation and Assessment. Bonnie Thornton, Mississippi State University.

Membership Services. David Macaulay, University of Nebraska–Lincoln, and Cindy Shirkey, East Carolina University.

Mentoring and Student Outreach. Danielle Williams, University of Evansville.

Newsletter. Angela Dresselhaus, ProQuest, LLC.

Nominations and Elections. Xiaoyan Song, North Carolina State University.

Open Initiatives. Melissa Hart Cantrell, University of Colorado Boulder.

Program Planning. Megan Kilb, University of North Carolina-Chapel Hill.

Registrar. Mary Ann Jones, Mississippi State University.

Standards. Matthew Ragucci, Wiley.

Task Force Chairs

Vendor and Publisher Engagement. Kristy White, Duquesne University

Publications

Conference Proceedings (currently published in two issues of *Serials Librarian*).

Core Competencies for Electronic Resources Librarians.

Core Competencies for Print Serials Management.

Core Competencies for Scholarly Communication Librarians.

NASIG Newsletter.

Various NASIGuides.

NASIG Blog.

NASIG Jobs Blog.

Meetings

Annual conference held in the summer. Continuing education events and webinars throughout the year.

National Association of Government Archives and Records Administrators

Executive Director, Johnny Hadlock
444 N. Capitol Street, N.W. Suite 237, Washington, DC 20001
202-508-3800, fax 202-508-3801, e-mail info@nagara.org
World Wide Web http://www.nagara.org
Twitter @InfoNAGARA

Objective

Founded in 1984, the National Association of Government Archives and Records Administrators (NAGARA) is a nationwide association of local, state, and federal archivists and records administrators, and others interested in improved care and management of government records. NAGARA promotes public awareness of government records and archives management programs, encourages interchange of information among government archives and records management agencies, develops and implements professional standards of government records and archival administration, and encourages study and research into records management problems and issues.

Membership

Most NAGARA members are federal, state, and local archival and records management agencies. Dues (Org.) $225–$750 dependent on number of contacts; (NARA Employees Indiv.) $40; (Students/Ret.) $50; (All other Indiv.) $89.

Officers (2020–2021)

Pres. Caryn Wojcik, Michigan Records Management Svcs. E-mail wojcikc@michigan.gov; *V.P.* Jennifer Green, The City of Oklahoma, jennifer.green@okc.gov; *Pres.-Elect* Patricia C. Franks, San José State Univ. E-mail patricia.franks@sjsu.edu; *Secy.* Marissa Paron, Lib. and Archives Canada. E-mail marissa.paron@canada.ca; *Treas.* Bethany Cron, National Archives and Records Admin., Ann Arbor, MI. E-mail bethany.cron@nara.gov; *Past Pres.* Casey Coleman, U.S. Securities and Exchange Commission, Washington, DC. E-mail colemanca@sec.gov.

Board of Directors

Tara Bell, Jen Hancy Conover, Anne Frantilla, Meaghan Fukunaga, Angela Ossar, Kristopher Stenson, Kathleen Williams.

Publications

Newsletter (q.; memb.; electronic).

National Information Standards Organization

Executive Director, Todd Carpenter
3600 Clipper Mill Rd., Suite 302, Baltimore, MD 21211-1948
301-654-2512, e-mail nisohq@niso.org
World Wide Web http://www.niso.org

Objective

The National Information Standards Organization (NISO) fosters the development and maintenance of standards that facilitate the creation, persistent management, and effective interchange of information so that it can be trusted for use in research and learning. To fulfill this mission, NISO engages libraries, publishers, information aggregators, and other organizations that support learning, research, and scholarship through the creation, organization, management, and curation of knowledge. NISO works with intersecting communities of interest and across the entire lifecycle of an information standard. NISO standards apply both traditional and new technologies to the full range of information-related needs, including discovery, retrieval, repurposing, storage, metadata, business information, and preservation.

NISO also develops and publishes recommended practices, technical reports, white papers, and information publications. NISO holds regular educational programs on standards, technologies, and related topics where standards-based solutions can help solve problems. These programs include webinars, online virtual conferences, in-person forums, and teleconferences.

Experts from the information industry, libraries, systems vendors, and publishing participate in the development of NISO standards and recommended practices. The standards are approved by the consensus body of NISO's voting membership, representing libraries, publishers, vendors, government, associations, and private businesses and organizations. NISO is supported by its membership and grants.

NISO is a not-for-profit association accredited by the American National Standards Institute (ANSI) and serves as the U.S. Technical Advisory Group Administrator to ISO/TC 46 Information and Documentation as well as the secretariat for ISO/TC 46/SC 9, Identification and Description.

Membership

Voting Members: 80+. Open to any organization, association, government agency, or company willing to participate in and having substantial concern for the development of NISO standards. Library Standards Alliance Members: 60+. Open to any academic, public, special, or government-supported library interested in supporting the mission of NISO.

Officers

Chair; Peter Simon, NewsBank, Inc.; *V.Chair* Mary Sauer-Games, OCLC Inc.; *Treas.* Jabin White, ITHAKA; *Past Chair* Marian Hollingsworth, Clarivate Analytics.

Directors

Ryan Bernier, Karim Boughida, Gregory Grazevich, Allan Lu, Rebecca McCloud, Wendy Queen, Rhonda Ross, Chris Shillum, Maria Stanton, Wayne Strickland, Greg Suprock, Robert Wheeler.

Committee Chairs

Audit. Greg Suprock.
Finance. Jabin White.
Governance. Maria Stanton.
Nominating. Todd Carpenter.

Staff

Assoc. Exec. Dir. Nettie Lagace; *Dir. of Content* Jill O'Neill; *Dir. of Strategic Initiatives* Jason Griffey.

Publications

Information Standards Quarterly (back issues available in open access from the NISO website).

NISO's published standards, recommended practices, and technical reports are available free of charge as downloadable PDF files from the NISO website (http://www.niso. org). Hard-copy documents are available for sale from the website.

For additional NISO publications, see the article "NISO Standards" in this volume.

Patent and Trademark Resource Center Association

President, Rebecca M. (Missy) Murphey
Reference Department, University of Delaware Library, Newark, DE 19717-5267
World Wide Web https://ptrca.org

Objective

The Patent and Trademark Resource Center Association (PTRCA) provides a support structure for the more than 80 patent and trademark resource centers (PTRCs) affiliated with the U.S. Patent and Trademark Office (USPTO). The association's mission is to discover the interests, needs, opinions, and goals of the PTRCs and to advise USPTO in these matters for the benefit of PTRCs and their users, and to assist USPTO in planning and implementing appropriate services. Founded in 1983 as the Patent Depository Library Advisory Council; name changed to Patent and Trademark Depository Library Association in 1988; became an American Library Association affiliate in 1996. In 2011 the association was renamed the Patent and Trademark Resource Center Association.

Membership

Open to any person employed in a patent and trademark resource center library whose responsibilities include the patent and trademark collection. Affiliate membership is also available. Dues (Reg.) $65; (Student) $10.

Officers (2020–2021)

Pres. Rebecca M. (Missy) Murphey, Orlando, FL; *V.P./Pres.-Elect* Sharyl Overhiser, Philadelphia, PA; *Secy.* Sara Butts, Wichita, KS; *Treas.* Jim Miller, McKeldin Lib., Univ. of Maryland, Library Lane, College Park. Tel. 301-405-9152, e-mail jmiller2@umd.edu; *Past Pres.* Jared Hoppenfeld, College Station, TX.

Committee Chairs (2020–2021)

Bylaws. Marian Armour-Gemman.
Conferences. Rebecca (Missy) Murphey.
Database. Lisha Li.
Election. No Active Chair.
Membership and Mentoring. Sharyl Overhiser.
Publications. Suzanne Reinman.

Publication

PTRCA Journal. Electronic at https://ptrca.org/ newsletters.

Polish American Librarians Association

President, Ewa Barczyk
P.O. Box 301061, Chicago, IL 60630-1061
World Wide Web http://palalib.org

Objective

Founded in 2009, the mission of the Polish American Librarians Association (PALA) is to positively affect services provided to library patrons of Polish descent and individuals interested in Polish culture.

The organization's vision is

- To enhance professional knowledge by developing forums for discussion and networks of communication among library staff working with Polish collections and patrons of Polish origin

- To promote understanding and respect among all cultures by expanding the means to access reliable, current information about Polish and Polish American culture

- To promote Polish American librarianship
- To provide opportunities for cooperation with other library associations

Membership

Membership is open to librarians, students of library schools, library support staff, and others who support the vision of PALA. Dues $50 (one-time dues to support the goals of PALA).

Officers

Pres. Ewa Barczyk, Golda Meir Lib., Univ. of Wisconsin Milwaukee, 2311 E. Hartford Ave., Milwaukee. Tel. 414-412-5456, e-mail ewa@uwm.edu; *Secy.* Paulina Poplawska, New Ulm Public Lib., New Ulm, MN. E-mail ppoplawska@tds.lib.mn.us; *Treas.* Bernadetta Koryciarz, Niles-Maine District Lib., 6960 Oakton St., Niles, IL 60714. Tel. 847-663-6642, e-mail bkorycia@nileslibrary.org; *Past Pres.* Leonard Kniffel (dec.). *Dirs.-at-Large* Iwona Bozek, Krystyna Matusiak, Hanna Przybylski, Marianne Ryan, Ronald V. Stoch.

REFORMA (National Association to Promote Library and Information Services to Latinos and the Spanish-Speaking)

President, Oscar Beaza
P.O. Box 832, Anaheim, CA 92815-0832
E-mail info@reforma.org
World Wide Web http://www.reforma.org

Objective

Promoting library services to the Spanish-speaking for nearly 40 years, REFORMA, an affiliate of the American Library Association, works in a number of areas to advance the development of library collections that include Spanish-language and Latino-oriented materials; the recruitment of more bilingual and bicultural professionals and support staff; the development of library services and programs that meet the needs of the Latino community; the establishment of a national network among individuals who share its goals; the education of the U.S. Latino population in regard to the availability and types of library services; and lobbying efforts to preserve existing library resource centers serving the interest of Latinos.

Membership

Memb. 800+. Membership is open to any person who is supportive of the goals and objectives of REFORMA. Dues (Indiv.) $10–$50; (Int'l.) Free; (Life) $450; (Inst.) $100–$250. Year.

Executive Committee (2020–2021)

Pres. Oscar Baeza, El Paso Community College. E-mail president@reforma.org; *V.P./Pres.-Elect* Nicanor Diaz, Denver Public Library. E-mail vice-president@reforma.org; *Secy.* Alma Ramos-McDermott, Lake Trafford Elementary School. E-mail secretary@reforma.org; *Treas.* Denice Adkins, Univ. of Missouri. E-mail treasurer@reforma.org; *Past Pres.* Kenny Garcia, California State University, Monterey Bay Library. E-mail past-president@reforma.org; *Memb.-at-Large* Alda Allina Migoni, Library of Congress. E-mail at-large-rep@reforma.org; *Chapter Reps.* Manny Figueroa, Queens Lib. E-mail chapter-east-region@reforma.org; David López, OC Public Libraries. E-mail chapter-west-region@reforma.org; Esther De Leon, Texas Tech University Libraries. E-mail chapter-central-region@reforma.org.

Committee Chairs

Awards. Mary Marques.
Children and Young Adult Service Committee (CAYASC). Maria Estrella.

Education. Michele A. L. Villagran.
Finance. Kenny Garcia.
Fundraising. Cynthia Bautista, Sonia Bautista.
International Relations. Elizabeth Garcia, Tess Tobin
Legislative. Mario Ascencio, Madeleine Ildefonso.
Membership. Tess Tobin
Mentoring. Antonio Apodaca.
Nominations. Maria Kramer.
Organizational Development and New Chapters. Gloria Grover.
Program. Nicanor Diaz.
Public Relations. Celia Avila, Libbhy Romero.
Recruitment and Mentoring. Minerva Alaniz.
REFORMA National Conferences Coordinating Committee. Roxana Benavides, Abigail Morales.
Scholarship. Sandra Hernandez.

Technology. Edwin Rodarte, Madeline Pena.
Translations. Joanna Artega.

Awards Committee Chairs

Pura Belpré Award. Jessica Agudelo.
Dr. Arnulfo D. Trejo Librarian of the Year. Kenny Garcia

Publication

REFORMA (e-newsletter). *Ed.* Libbhy Romero.

Meetings

General membership and board meetings take place at the American Library Association Midwinter Meeting and Annual Conference and Exhibition.

Scholarly Publishing and Academic Resources Coalition

Executive Director, Heather Joseph
1201 Connecticut Ave. N.W., P.O. 607/608, Washington, DC 20036
202-630-5090, e-mail sparc@sparcopen.org
World Wide Web https://sparcopen.org
Twitter @SPARC_NA

Objective

SPARC, the Scholarly Publishing and Academic Resources Coalition, is a global organization that promotes expanded sharing of scholarship in the networked digital environment. It is committed to faster and wider sharing of outputs of the research process to increase the impact of research, fuel the advancement of knowledge, and increase the return on research investments.

Launched as an initiative of the Association of Research Libraries, SPARC has become a catalyst for change. Its pragmatic focus is to stimulate the emergence of new scholarly communication models that expand the dissemination of scholarly research and equip libraries for the inexorable growth in research output. Action by SPARC in collaboration with stakeholders—including authors, publishers, and libraries—builds on the unprecedented opportunities created by the networked digital

environment to advance the conduct of scholarship.

SPARC's role in stimulating change focuses on the following:

- Educating stakeholders about the problems facing scholarly communication and the opportunities for them to play a role in achieving positive change
- Advocating policy changes that advance scholarly communication and explicitly recognize that dissemination of scholarship is an essential, inseparable component of the research process
- Incubating demonstrations of new publishing and sustainability models that benefit scholarship and academe

SPARC is an advocate for changes in scholarly communication that benefit more than the academic community alone. Founded in 1997, now operating independently of ARL, SPARC has expanded to represent more than 800 academic and research libraries in North America, the United Kingdom, Europe, and Japan.

Membership

Memb. 240+ institutions. SPARC membership is open to international academic and research institutions, organizations, and consortia that share an interest in creating a more open and diverse marketplace for scholarly communication. Dues are scaled by membership type and budget. For more information, visit SPARC's website at https://sparcopen.org/become-a-member, SPARC Europe at https://sparcopen.org/people/sparc-europe/, SPARC Japan at http://www.nii.ac.jp/sparc, or SPARC Africa at https://sparcopen.org/people/sparc-africa/.

Steering Committee

H. Austin Booth, Gwen Bird, Chris Bourg, Talia Chung, Christopher Cox, Karen Estlund, Scarlet Galven, Carrie Gits, Jennifer Grayburn, Rachel Harding, Heather Joseph, Joy Kirchner, Beth McNeil, Carmelita Pickett, Judy Ruttenberg, Steven Escar Smith, Virginia Steel, Elaine Thornton.

Staff

Open Education Cdtr. Aisha Abdullah. E-mail aisha@sparcopen.org.; *Dir., Open Education* Nicole Allen. E-mail nicole@sparcopen.org; *Open Education Project Mgr.* Hailey Babb. E-mail hailey@sparcopen.org; *VPO for Negotiations* Caitlin Carter. E-mail caitlin@sparcopen.org; *Senior Consultant* Raym Crow. E-mail crow@sparcopen.org; Lese Fandel. E-mail lese@sparcopen.org; *Chief Operating Officer* Val Hollister. E-mail val@sparcopen.org; *Exec. Dir.* Heather Joseph. E-mail heather@sparcopen.org; *Programs and Operations Spclst. Asst. Dir., Right to Research Coalition* Joseph McArthur. E-mail joe@righttoresearch.org; *Community Mgr., Open Research Funders Group*, Erin McKiernan. E-mail erin@sparc.open.org; *Dir. of Programs and Engagement* Nick Shockey. E-mail nick@sparcopen.org; *Instructor, Open Educ. Leadership Program* Tanya Spilovoy. E-mail leadership@sparcopen.org; *Manager of Public Policy and Advocacy* Katie Steen. E-mail katie@sparcopen.org; *Consultant* Greg Tananbaum. E-mail greg@sparcopen.org; *Open Education Project Manager.* Winni Zhang. E-mail winni@sparcopen.org.

Publications

Open Educational Resources (OER) State Policy Playbook (2020 ed.) (https://sparcopen.org/our-work/oer-state-policy-playbook/).

SPARC Landscape Analysis and Roadmap for Action (2020 update) by Claudio Aspesi (lead author), Nicole Allen, Raym Crow, Shawn Daugherty, Heather Joseph, Joseph McArthur, and Nick Shockey. (https://infrastructure.sparcopen.org/2020-update).

Society for Scholarly Publishing

Executive Director, Melanie Dolechek
1120 Route 73, Suite 200, Mount Laurel, NJ 08054
856-439-1385, fax 856-439-0525, e-mail info@sspnet.org
World Wide Web http://www.sspnet.org
Twitter @ScholarlyPub

Objective

To draw together individuals involved in the process of scholarly publishing. This process requires successful interaction of the many functions performed within the scholarly community. The Society for Scholarly Publishing (SSP) provides the leadership for such interaction by creating opportunities for the exchange of information and opinions among scholars, editors, publishers, librarians, printers, booksellers, and all others engaged in scholarly publishing.

Membership

Memb. 1,000+. Open to all with an interest in the scholarly publishing process and dissemination of information. Dues (Indiv. Renewal) $200; (Libn.) $85; (Early Career New) $60; (Student) $40; (Supporting Organization) $2,195; (Sustaining Organization) $5,747; (Intl. Indiv.) $50; (Intl. Early Career) $25; (Intl. Libn.) $25; (Intl. Student); $10. Year. Jan.–Dec.

Officers

Pres. Lauren Kane, Morressier; *Pres.-Elect* Alice Meadows, NISO; *Secy./Treas.* Emelie Delquie, Copyright Clearance Ctr.; *Past Pres.* Angela Cochran, American Society of Civil Engineers.

Board of Directors

Membs.-at-Large Meredith Adinolfi, David Crotty, Gabe Hart, Lisa Hinchliffe, Sai Konda, Elizabeth R. Lorbeer, Rebecca McLeod, Alison Mudditt, Laura Ricci, Miranda Walker.

Committee Chairs

Annual Meeting Program. Lori Carlin, Yael Fitzpatrick, Cason Lynley.
Career Development. Kelly J. Denzer, Barrett A. Winston.
Community Engagement. Byron A. Russell.
Diversity, Equity, and Inclusion. Damita Snow, Randy Townsend.
Education. Ben Mudrak.
Finance. Ted Bakamjian.
Marketing. Marianne Calilhanna, Nicola Poser.
Nominating and Awards. Adrian Stanley.

Publication

Learned Publishing (memb.). Published by the Association of Learned and Professional Society Publishers (ALPSP) in collaboration with SSP. *Ed.* (N.A.) Lette Y. Conrad.
The Scholarly Kitchen (moderated blog). *Ed.* David Crotty.

Meetings

An annual meeting is held in late May/early June.

Society of American Archivists

Executive Director, Nancy P. Beaumont
17 N. State St., Suite 1425, Chicago, IL 60602
312-606-0722, toll-free 866-722-7858, fax 312-606-0728, e-mail saahq@archivists.org
World Wide Web https://www2.archivists.org
Twitter @archivists_org

Object

Founded in 1936, the Society of American Archivists (SAA) is North America's oldest and largest national archival professional association. Representing more than 6,000 individual and institutional members, SAA promotes the value and diversity of archives and archivists and is the preeminent source of professional resources and the principal communication hub for American archivists.

Membership

Memb. 6,200+. Dues (Indiv.) $80 to $325, graduated according to salary; (Assoc.) $115; (Ret.) $77; (Student/Bridge) $55; (Inst.) $340; (Sustaining Inst.) $595.

Officers

Pres. Margery N. Sly, Temple Univ. Libraries; *V.P.* Shamila Bhatia, National Archives at College Park; *V.P./Pres.-Elect* Courtney Chartier, Emory Univ.

Leadership

Executive Dir. Nancy Beaumont; *Dir. of Publishing* Teresa Brinati; *Dir. of Finance and Admin.* Peter Carlson; *Dir. of Ed.* Rana Hutchinson Salzmann; *Web and Info. Syst. Admin.* Matthew Black; *Governance Prog. Mgr.* Felicia Owens; *Mgr./Svc. Ctr.* Carlos L. Delgado.

SAA Council

Courtney Chartier, Eric Chin, Stephen R. Curley, Amy Fitch, Melissa Gonzales, Brenda Gunn, Petrina Jackson, Derek P. Mosley, Ricardo Punzalan, Mario Ramirez, Meg Tuomala, Rachel Vagts, Rachel E. Winston; Nancy P. Beaumont (ex officio).

Committee Chairs

Development. Sharmila Bhatia.
Finance. Amy Fitch.
Grant Review. Margery N. Sly.
NDRF Review. Miriam Meislik.
Nominating. Dennis Meissner.
AWEF Review. Jessica Chapel.

Task Force and Working Groups Chairs

Archival Compensation Task Force. Greta Pittenger.
A*CENSUS II Working Group. Elizabeth Myers.

Publications

American Archivist (s. ann.; $289). *Ed.* Amy Cooper Cary. Tel (414) 288-5901, e-mail AmericanArchivist@archivists.org; *Reviews Ed.* Bethany Anderson. Tel. (217) 333-0798, e-mail ReviewsEditor@archivists.org.
Archival Outlook (bi-mo.; memb.).
In the Loop e-newsletter (bi-wk.).

Software and Information Industry Association

President, Jeff Joseph
1090 Vermont Ave. N.W. Sixth Floor, Washington, DC 20005-4905
202-289-7442, fax 202-289-7097
World Wide Web http://www.siia.net
Twitter @SIIA

The Software and Information Industry Association (SIIA) was formed January 1, 1999, through the merger of the Software Publishers Association (SPA) and the Information Industry Association (IIA).

Membership

Memb. 800+ companies. Open to companies that develop software and digital information content. For details on membership and dues, see the SIIA website, http://www.siia.net.

Leadership

Pres. Jeff Joseph. Tel. 202-789-4440. E-mail jjoseph@siia.net; *V.P., Finance and Operations* Carl Walker; *Senior V.P. and Managing Dir., FISD* Tom Davin; *V.P. for Intellectual Property and Gnl. Cnsl.* Christopher Mohr; *Membership Dir.* Ellen Savage; *Awards Dir.* Jennifer Baranowski.

Special Libraries Association

Executive Director, Amy Lestition Burke
7918 Jones Branch Drive, Suite 300, McLean, VA 22102
703-647-4900, fax 703-506-3266, e-mail aburke@sla.org
World Wide Web https://www.sla.org
Twitter @SLAhq

Mission

The Special Libraries Association (SLA) promotes and strengthens its members through learning, advocacy, and networking initiatives.

Strategic Vision

SLA is a global association of information and knowledge professionals who are employed in every sector of the economy. Its members thrive where data, information, and knowledge intersect, and its strategic partners support SLA because they believe in the association's mission and the future of its members. SLA's goal is to support information professionals as they contribute, in their varied and evolving roles, to the opportunities and achievements of organizations, communities, and society.

Membership

Memb. 9,000+ in 75 countries. Dues (Org.) $750; (Indiv.) $100–$200; (Student/Intl./ Salary less than $18,000 income per year) $50; (Ret.) $100.

Officers (2021)

Pres. Tara Murray Grove, Pennsylvania State Univ., University Park, PA. E-mail tem10@ psu.edu; *Pres.-Elect* Catherine Lavallée-Welch, Bishop's Univ., Sherbrooke, PQ. E-mail clw@ ubishops.ca; *Treas.* Alicia Biggers, Albemarle, Charlotte, NC. E-mail alicia.biggers@albe marle.com; *Past Pres.* Hal Kirkwood, Univ. of Oxford, Oxford, UK E-mail kirkwoodhal@ gmail.com.

Directors

Hildy Dworkin, P. K. Jain, Amy Jankowski, Jim Miller.

Council and Committee Chairs

Annual Conference Advisory Council. Tiffany Lopez.
Awards and Honors. Jill Strand.
Content Advisory Council. Helen Kula, Brian McCann.
Finance. Willem Noorlander.
Governance and Strategy. Catherine Lavallée-Welch.
Leadership Advisory Council. Tara Murray Grove.
Membership Advisory Council. Kim Bloedel.
Nominating Committee. Connie Crosby, Miriam Childs.
Professional Development Advisory Council. Lateka Grays.
Public Policy Advisory Council. Kevin Adams.
Public Relations Advisory Council. Elizabeth Deegan.
Technology Advisory Council. Christine Geluk, Samuel Russell.
Workplace Preparedness and Response Advisory Council (PREP). Eric Tans.

Theatre Library Association

President, Francesca Marini
c/o New York Public Library for the Performing Arts
40 Lincoln Center Plaza, New York, NY 10023
E-mail theatrelibraryassociation@gmail.com
World Wide Web http://www.tla-online.org/
Twitter @theatrelibassn

Objective

To further the interests of collecting, preserving, and using theater, cinema, and performing arts materials in libraries, museums, and private collections. Founded in 1937.

Membership

Memb. 300. Dues (Indiv.) $50; (Student/Nonsalaried) $25; (Inst.) $75; (Sustaining) $150. Year. Jan.–Dec.

Officers

Pres. Francesca Marini, Cushing Lib., Texas A&M Univ. E-mail fmarini@library.tamu.edu; *V.P.* Diana King, Univ. of California, Los Angeles. E-mail diking@library.ucla.edu; *Treas.* Beth Kattelman, Ohio State Univ. E-mail kattelman.1@osu.edu; *Past Pres.* (ex officio) Colleen Reilly, Houston Community College. E-mail colleen.reilly@hccs.edu.

Board of Directors

(2021–2023) Kristin Dougan Johnson, Suzanne Lipkin, David Nochimson, Gloria Steinberg; *(2020–2022)* Drew Barker, William Daw, Sophie Glidden-Lyon, Karin Suni; *(2019–2021)* Matt DiCintio, Mary Huelsbeck, Rachel Smiley, Scott Stone.

Committee Chairs

Book Awards. Suzanne Lipkin, Annemarie van Roessel.
Conference Planning. Diana King.
Membership. Matt DiCintio.
Nominating. Angela Weaver.
Publications. Joseph Tally.
Strategic Planning. Diana King.
Website Editorial. Eric Colleary, William Daw.

Publications

Broadside Archive (digital back issues). *Ed.* Angela Weaver *(2008–2014).*

Performing Arts Resources (occasional) see http://www.tla-online.org/publications/performing-arts-resources/performing-arts-resources-volumes/ for links to subscription and https://www.proquest.com/products-services/iipa_ft.html for database from ProQuest.

Urban Libraries Council

President and CEO, Susan Benton
1333 H St. N.W., Suite 1000 West, Washington, DC 20005
202-750-8650, e-mail info@urbanlibraries.org
World Wide Web http://www.urbanlibraries.org
Facebook https://www.facebook.com/UrbanLibrariesCouncil/
Twitter @UrbanLibCouncil

Objective

Since 1971 the Urban Libraries Council (ULC) has worked to strengthen public libraries as an essential part of urban life. A member organization of North America's leading public library systems, ULC serves as a forum for research widely recognized and used by public- and private-sector leaders. Its members are thought leaders dedicated to leadership, innovation, and the continuous transformation of libraries to meet community needs.

ULC's work focuses on helping public libraries to identify and utilize skills and strategies that match the challenges of the 21st century.

Membership

Membership is open to public libraries and to corporate partners specializing in library-related materials and services. The organization also offers associate memberships. Annual membership dues for libraries are based on the size of a library's operating budget (local + state).

Officers (2020–2021)

Chair Richard Reyes-Gavilan; *V.Chair/Chair-Elect* Mary J. Wardell-Ghirarduzzi; *Secy./Treas.* Brandon Neal; *Past Chair* Vickery Bowles; *Memb.-at-Large* Karl Dean.

Board Members

Sarah Campbell, Janet Hutchinson, John W. Laney, Michael Meyer, C. Mary Okoye, Skye Patrick, Jesus Salas, Rebecca Stavick, Michelle VonderHaar, Roosevelt Weeks.

State, Provincial, and Regional Library Associations

The associations in this section are organized under three headings: United States, Canada, and Regional. Both the United States and Canada are represented under Regional associations.

United States

Alabama

Memb. 1,200. Publication. *ALLA COMmunicator* (q.).

Pres. Daniel Tackett, Vestavia Hills Library in the Forest. Tel. 205.978.3683, e-mail daniel. tackett@vestavialibrary.org; *Pres.-Elect* Laura Pitts, Scottsboro Public Library. Tel. 256.574.4335, e-mail, laurap@scottsboro.org; *Secy.* Paula Webb, Univ. of South Alabama, 5901 USA Dr. North, Mobile 36688. Tel. 251-461-1933, e-mail pwebb@southalabama.edu; *Treas.* Karen Preuss, Montgomery City-County Public Lib., P.O. Box 1950, Montgomery 36102-1950. Tel. 334-240-4300, e-mail kpreuss@mccpl. lib.al.us; *Memb.-at-Large* (Central Alabama) Emily Allee, Birmingham Public Library. Tel. 205.226.3720, emily.allee@cobpl.org; (North Alabama) Ashley Cummins, Russellville Public Lib. Tel. 256-332-1535, e-mail ruslib110@ yahoo.com; (South Alabama) Wendy Congairdo, Thomas B. Norton Public Lib., 221 W. 19th Ave., Gulf Shores 36542. Tel. 251-968-1176, e-mail wcongiardo@hotmail.com. *Past Pres.* Jessica Hayes, Auburn University at Montgomery. Tel. 334.244.3814, e-mail jhayes11@aum. edu; *Assn. Admin.* (ex officio) Angela Moore, Alabama Lib. Assn., 6030 Monticello Dr., Montgomery 36117. Tel. 334-414-0113, e-mail allaadmin@allanet.org.

Address correspondence to administrator. Alabama Lib. Assn., 6030 Monticello Dr., Montgomery 36117. Tel. 334-414-0113, e-mail allibraryassoc@gmail.com.

World Wide Web http://allanet.org.

Alaska

Memb. 450+. Publication. *Newspoke* (q.) (online at http://akla.org/newspoke).

Pres. Jonas Lamb; *Pres.-Elect* Rayette Sterling; *Secy.* Paul Adasiak. E-mail pfadasiak@ alaska.edu; *Treas.* Samantha Blanquart; *Conference Coords.* Deborah Rinio; Christine Osciak; *ALA Rep.* Lorelei Sterling. E-mail lsterling@alaska.edu; *PNLA Rep.* Julie Niederhauser. E-mail Julie.niederhauser@ alaska.gov; *Past Pres.* Deborah Rinio.

Address correspondence to the secretary. Alaska Lib. Assn., P.O. Box 81084, Fairbanks 99708. E-mail akla@akla.org.

World Wide Web https://akla.org.

Arizona

Memb. 1,000. Term of Office. Nov.–Nov. Publication. *AzLA Newsletter* (6x yearly).

Pres. Corey Christians; *Pres.-Elect* John Walsh; *Secy.* Amber Kent, Casa Grande Public Lib., 449 N. Drylake St., Casa Grande 85122. Tel. 520 421-8710, e-mail AKent@casagrande az.gov; *Treas.* Rene Tanner, Arizona State Univ., Tempe. Tel. 480-965-7190, e-mail rene. tanner@asu.edu; *Northern Regional Rep.* Martha Baden; *Central Regional Rep.* Rachel Martinez; *Southern Regional Rep.* Carrie Dawson; *ALA Councilor* Dan Stanton; *MPLA Rep.* Amadee Ricketts; *Past Pres.* Michelle Simon, Pima County Public Lib., 101 N. Stone Ave., Tucson 85701. Tel. 520-594-5654, e-mail michesimon54@ gmail.com.

Address correspondence to Arizona 2532 N 4th St #271, Flagstaff 86004. Tel. 928.288.2011, e-mail admin@azla.org.

World Wide Web http://www.azla.org.

Arkansas

Memb. 600. Publication. *Arkansas Libraries* (4x yearly).

Pres. Philip Shackelford, South Arkansas Community College, El Dorado 71730. Tel. 870-864-7116, e-mail pshackelford@ southark.edu; *Pres.-Elect* Rachel Shankles, 891 Hwy 7, Bismarck 71929. Tel. 501-276-4949; *Secy.* Janice Weddle, Hendrix College–Bailey Library, 1600 Washington Avenue, Conway 72032; *Treas.* Lynn Valetutti, National Park College, 101 College Dr., Hot

Springs 71913, e-mail lvaletutti@np.edu; *ALA Councilor* Lacy Wolfe, Henderson State Univ., 1100 Henderson St., Box 7541, Arkadelphia 71999. Tel. 870-230-5322, e-mail wolfel@hsu.edu; *Non-Voting: SELA State Rep.* Emily Rozario, William F. Laman Public Lib., 2801 Orange St., North Little Rock 72114. E-mail emily.rozario@lamanlibrary.org; *Past Pres.* Crystal Gates, William F. Laman Public Library System, 2801 Orange Street, North Little Rock 72114. Tel. 501-404-2919.

Address correspondence to Arkansas Lib. Assn., P.O. Box 3821, Little Rock 72203. Tel. 501-313-1398, e-mail info@arlib.org.

World Wide Web http://arlib.org.

California

Memb. 2,500.

Pres. Jayanti Addleman, Hayward Public Library. E-mail JayantiAddleman@gmail.com; *V.P./Pres.-Elect* Jené Brown, Los Angeles Public Library. E-mail jbrown@lapl.org; *Treas.* Mark Fink, Yolo County Library. E-mail dwolfgram@redwoodcity.org; *Past Pres.* Hillary Theyer, E-mail Hillarytheyer@gmail.com.

Address correspondence to California Lib. Assn., 1055 E. Colorado Blvd., 5th Floor, Pasadena 91106. Tel. 626-204-4071, e-mail info@cla-net.org.

World Wide Web http://www.cla-net.org.

Colorado

Pres. Ryan F. Buller, Univ. of Denver. E-mail Ryan.Buller@du.edu; *Pres.-Elect* Tiah Frankish, Adams 12 Five Star Schools. E-mail tfrankish@gmail.com; *Secy.* Anne Holland, Space Science Institute. E-mail aholland@spacescience.org; *Treas.* Nanette Fisher, Anythink Libs. E-mail nfisher@anythinklibraries.org; *Membs.-at-Large* Tiffanie Wick, Western Colorado Univ. E-mail twick@western.edu, Brett Wade Lear, Garfield County Libraries. E- blear@gcpld.org; *Past Pres.* Tammy Sayles, Pikes Peak Lib. District. E-mail tjsmlis@gmail.com.

Address correspondence to Colorado Assn. of Libs., P.O. Box 740905, Arvada 80006-0905. Tel. 303-463-6400, e-mail cal@cal-webs.org.

World Wide Web http://www.cal-webs.org.

Connecticut

Memb. 1,000+. Term of Office. July–June. Publication. *CLA Today* (6x yearly; online). E-mail editor@ctlibrarians.org.

Pres. Thomas Piezzo, Brainerd Memorial Lib. E-mail tpiezzo@brainerdlibrary.org; *V.P./Pres.-Elect* Colleen Balie. E-mail cbailie@westhavenlibrary.org; *Recording Secy.* Danielle Duffy Valenzano, Milford Public Lib. E-mail dvalenzano@milfordct.gov; *Treas.* Kristina Edwards, Central Connecticut State Univ. E-mail kristina.edwards@uconn.edu; *Past Pres.* Lisa Karim. E-mail lkarim@simsburylibrary.Info.

Address correspondence to Connecticut Lib. Assn., 55 North Main St., Unit 49, Belchertown 01007. Tel. 860-346-2444, e-mail mscheier@ctlibraryassociation.org.

World Wide Web http://ctlibraryassociation.org.

Delaware

Memb. 200+. Publication. *DLA Bulletin* (q.; online). E-mail Nicole.Ballance@lib.de.us

Pres. Catherine Wimberley, New Castle County Libs., 2020 W. 9th St., Wilmington 19805. Tel. 302-571-7425, e-mail catherine.wimberley@newcastlede.gov; *V.P./Conference Chair* Jen Wilson, Delaware Technical Community College. Tel. 302-573-5434, e-mail jennifer.wilson@dtcc.edu; *Secy.* Marlowe Bogino, 4755 Ogletown-Stanton Road, Newark 19718. Tel. 302-733-1164, e-mail marlowe.bogino@christianacare.org; *Treas.* Jaclyn Hale, Dover Public Lib., 35 Loockerman Plz., Dover 19901. Tel. 302-736-7185, e-mail jaclynhaledla@gmail.com; *ALA Councilor* Delaware State University, William C. Jason Library Reference and Access Services Librarian, 1200 N DuPont Highway, Dover 19901. Tel. 302-857-7886, tbeckett@desu.edu; *Delaware State Libn.* Annie Norman, Delaware Div. of Libs., 121 Martin Luther King Jr. Blvd. N., Dover 19901. Tel. 302-257-3001, fax 302-739-6787, e-mail annie.norman@state.de.us; *Pres., Friends of Delaware Libs.* Kay Bowes. E-mail kaybowes@gmail.com; *Past Pres.* Alison Wessel, University of Delaware Library, Museums and Press, 181 S. College Ave., Newark 19717. Tel. 302-831-1730, e-mail alisonwessel.dla@gmail.com.

Address correspondence to Delaware Lib. Assn., c/o Delaware Division of Libs., 121 Martin Luther King Jr. Blvd. N., Dover 19901. E-mail dla@lib.de.us.

World Wide Web http://dla.lib.de.us.

District of Columbia

Memb. 300+. Term of Office. July–June.

Pres. Meg Metcalf. E-mail president@ dcla.org; *V.P.* Maria Thurder. E-mail vice_ president@dcla.org; *Secy.* Leah Castaldi. E-mail secretary@dcla.org; *Treas.* Karen Janka. E-mail treasurer@dcla.org; *ALA Councilor* Erica Harbeson. E-mail ala_councilor@dcla.org; *Past Pres.* Tracy Sumler. E-mail past_president @dcla.org.

Address correspondence to District of Columbia Lib. Assn., Union Station, 50 Massachusetts Ave. N.E., P.O. Box 1653 Washington, DC 20002.

World Wide Web http://www.dcla.org.

Florida

Memb. (Indiv.) 1,000+. Publication. *Florida Libraries* (s. ann.).

Pres. Laura Spears, Univ. of Florida; *V.P./ Pres.-Elect* Shane Roopnarine, University of Central Florida; *Secy.* Tracey Wehking, Indian River County Library System; *Treas.* Donna Vazquez, Florida Gulf Coast Univ. E-mail devazque@fgcu.edu; *State Libn.* Amy Johnson, Division of Lib. and Info. Svcs. E-mail Amy. Johnson@dos.myflorida.com; *ALA Councilor* Sara Gonzalez, Orange County Lib. System; *Past Pres.* Sarah Hammill, Florida Intl. Univ. E-mail hammills@fiu.edu; *Exec. Dir.* Lisa O'Donnell. Tel. 850-270-9205, e-mail lisa@ flalib.org.

Address correspondence to the executive director. Florida Lib. Assn., 545 E. Tennessee St., #103, Tallahassee 32308. Tel. 850-270-9205, e-mail admin@flalib.org.

World Wide Web http://www.flalib.org.

Georgia

Memb. 800+. Publication. *Georgia Library Quarterly* (q., online). *Ed.* Virginia Feher, Univ. of North Georgia. E-mail virginia. feher@ung.edu.

Pres. Wendy Cornelisen, GPLS. E-mail wcornelisen@georgialibraries.org, president@ georgialibraryassociation.org; *1st V.P./Pres.- Elect* Karen Manning, Georgia Tech. E-mail km17@mail.gatech.edu, vicepresident@geor gialibraryassociation.org; *V.P. Membership* Janice Shipp, Savannah State Univ., 2200 Savannah State Univ., Savannah 31404. Tel. 912-358-4339, e-mail shippj@savannahstate.edu; *V.P. Marketing and Branding* Marquita Gooch, Clayton County

Public Library. E-mail mgooch@claytongalib. org, marketing@georgialibraryassociation.org; *Secy.* Jean Mead, Athens Regional Library System. E-mail jmead@athenslibrary.org, secretary@georgialibraryassociation.org; *Treas.* Ben Bryson, Marshes of Glynn Libs., 208 Gloucester St., Brunswick 31520. Tel. 912-279-3735, e-mail bbryson@glynncounty-ga.gov. *Past Pres.* Laura Burtle, Georgia State University. E-mail lburtle@gsu.edu, past president@georgialibraryassociation.org.

Address correspondence to Georgia Lib. Assn., 5329 Fayette Avenue, Madison, WI 53713. Tel. 912-376-9155, e-mail membership. gla@gmail.com.

World Wide Web http://gla.georgialibraries. org.

Hawaii

Memb. 250. Publication. *KoleKole* (3x yearly).

Pres. Joyce Tokuda, Kapi'olani Community Coll. E-mail jtokuda@hawaii.edu; *V.P./Pres.- Elect* Jenny Silbiger, State Law Librarian & Access to Justice; *Secy.* Alicia Yanagihara, Nānākuli Public Lib. E-mail alicia.yanagihara@ librarieshawaii.org; *Treas.* Joy Oehlers, Kapi'olani Community College Lib., 4303 Diamond Head Rd., Honolulu 96816. Tel. 808-734-9352, e-mail aichin@hawaii.edu; *Past Pres.* Michael Aldrich, BYU-Hawai'i. E-mail michael.aldrich@byuh.edu.

Address correspondence to Hawai'i Lib. Assn., P.O. Box 4441, Honolulu 96812-4441. E-mail hawaii.library.association@gmail.com.

World Wide Web https://www.hawaii libraryassociation.org/.

Idaho

Memb. 420. Term of Office. Oct.–Oct.

President Katherine Lovan, Middleton Public Library, Middleton. E-mail klovan@mymiddle tonlibrary.org and LeAnn Gelskey, Hailey Public Lib., Hailey. E-mail leanngelskey@gmail.com; *V.P./Pres.-Elect* Erin Downey, Boise School District. Tel. 208-854-4110, e-mail erindowney.ila@gmail.com; *Secy.* Beverley Richmond, Priest Lake Public Lib., 28769 Idaho 57, Priest Lake 83856. Tel. 208-443-2454, e-mail plplibrary@hotmail.com; *Treas.* Jane Clapp, Boise State Univ. E-mail janeclapp. ila@gmail.com; *Membership Committee Chair* Cindy Bigler, Soda Springs Public Lib. E-mail sspl@sodaspringsid.com.

Address correspondence to Idaho Lib. Assn., 4911 N. Shirley Ave., Boise 83703.

World Wide Web http://idaholibraries.org.

Illinois

Memb. 3,000. Publication. *ILA Reporter* (bi-mo.; online).

Pres. Veronica De Fazio, Plainfield Public Lib. Dist.; *V.P./Pres.-Elect* Jeanne Hamilton, Bloomington Public Library; *Treas.* Megan Millen, Joliet Public Library; *ALA Councilor* Jeannie Dilger, Palatine Public Lib. District; *Past Pres.* Molly Beestrum, Northwestern Univ. Libs; *Exec. Dir.* Diane Foote. E-mail dfoote@ila.org.

Address correspondence to the executive director. Illinois Lib. Assn., 33 W. Grand Ave., Suite 401, Chicago 60654-6799. Tel. 312 644-1896, fax 312 644-1899, e-mail ila@ila.org.

World Wide Web http://www.ila.org.

Indiana

Indiana Lib. Federation. Memb. 2,000+. Publications. *Focus on Indiana Libraries* (mo.; memb.). *Communications Mgr.* Tisa M. Davis, 941 E. 86th St., Suite 260, Indianapolis 46240. Tel. 317-257-2040 ext. 104, fax 317-257-1389, e-mail askus@ilfonline.org.

Pres. Michael Williams, Indianapolis Public Library, 40 E. Saint Clair St., Indianapolis 46204. Tel. 317-275-4302; *Secy.* Kristi Howe, Vigo County Public Lib., 1 Library Sq., Terre Haute 47807; *Treas.* June Kruer, Charlestown Clark County Public Library, 51 Clark Road, Charlestown 47111; *ALA Councilor* Jos N. Holman, Tippecanoe County Public Library, 627 South St., Lafayette 47901; *Past Pres.*

Leslie Sutherlin, South Dearborn Community Schools, 5770 Highlander Place, Aurora 47001; *Exec. Dir.* Lucinda Nord. Tel. 317-257-2040 ext. 101, e-mail exec@ilfonline.org.

Address correspondence to Indiana Lib. Federation, 941 E. 86 St., Suite 260, Indianapolis 46240. Tel. 317-257-2040, fax 317-257-1389, e-mail askus@ilfonline.org.

World Wide Web http://www.ilfonline.org.

Iowa

Memb. 1,600+. Publication. *Catalyst* (bi-mo., online).

Pres. Stacy Goodhue. E-mail sgoodhue@carlisle.lib.ia.us; *Vice-Pres./Pres.-Elect* Sarah Uthoff; *Secy.* *Parliamentarian* Jennifer Sterling; *Treas.* Michele Patrick; *ALA Councilor* Samantha Helmick, Burlington Public Lib. Tel. 319-753-1647, e-mail shelmick@burlington. lib.ia.us; *Past Pres.* Mara Strickler. E-mail mstrickler@cityofpella.com.

Address correspondence to Iowa Lib. Assn., 6919 Vista Dr., West Des Moines 50266. Tel. 515-282-8192.

World Wide Web https://www.iowalibrar-yassociation.org/.

Kansas

Kansas Lib. Assn. Memb. 1,500. Term of Office. July–June. Publication. *Kansas Libraries!* (6x yearly; online). E-mail kilbmag@gmail. com.

Pres. Meagan Zampieri-Lillipopp, Hays Public Lib.; *1st V.P.* Holly Mercer, Southwest Kansas Lib. System; *2nd V.P.* Shanna Smith-Ritterhouse; *Secy.* Bethanie O'Dell, Emporia State Univ. E-mail bodell1@emporia. edu; *Treas.* Terri Wojtalewicz, Lancing Community Library; *ALA Councilor* Heather Van Dyne, Allen Community College; *Secy.* Bethanie O'Dell, Emporia State University; *Parliamentarian* Dan Ireton, Kansas State Univ. E-mail dli6873@k-state.edu. *Past Pres.* Robin Newell, Emporia Public Lib., 110 E. Sixth Ave., Emporia 66801. Tel. 620-340-6464, e-mail newellr@emporialibrary.org.

Address correspondence to the president. Kansas Lib. Assn., Northwest Kansas Lib. System, 2 Washington Sq., Norton 67654. Tel. 785-877-5148.

World Wide Web http://www.kslibassoc.org.

Kentucky

Memb. 1,600. Publication. *Kentucky Libraries Journal* (q.). *Ed.* Robin Harris, Law Lib., Brandeis School of Law, Univ. of Louisville, Louisville, 40292-0001. Tel. 502-852-6083, e-mail robin.harris@louisville.edu.

Pres. Mark Adler; *Pres.-Elect* Adele Koch; *Secy.* Andrew Adler; *Past Pres.* Kandace Rodgers.

Address correspondence to the president. Andrew Adler. 1588 Leestown Rd., Ste. 130-310, Lexington 40511. Tel. 502-863-8405. info@kla.memberclicks.net.

World Wide Web http://www.kylibasn.org/478.cfm.

Louisiana

Memb. 1,000+. Term of Office. July–June. Publication. *Louisiana Libraries* (q.). *Ed.* Celise Reech-Harper, Assoc. Dir., Beauregard Parish Lib., 205 South Washington Ave., DeRidder 70634. Tel. 337-463-6217 ext. 22, LLAcelise@gmail.com.

Pres. Sonnet Ireland. E-mail: sonnet@sonnetireland.com; *Secy.* Erin Chesnutt. E-mail echesnut@beau.org; *ALA Councilor* Vivian McCain. Tel. 318-513-5508, e-mail straitviv@gmail.com; *Parliamentarian* Chris Achee. E-mail cachee@myapl.org; *Past Pres.* Sonnet Ireland. Tel. 504-390-6834, e-mail sonnet@sonnetireland.com; *1st V.P.* Jeremy Bolom. E-mail: jbolom@mylpl.org; *2nd V.P.* Lora Amsberryaugier. E-mail lamsberr@uno.edu.

Address correspondence to Louisiana Lib. Assn., 1190 Meramec Station Rd., Suite 207, Ballwin, MO 63021. Tel 800-969-6562 ext. 3, fax 972-991-6061, e-mail lla@amigos.org.

World Wide Web http://www.llaonline.org.

Maine

Maine Lib. Assn. Memb. 950. Publication. *MLA to Z* (q., online). E-mail jeastman@yarmouthlibrary.org.

Pres. Jennifer Alvino, Windham Public Lib., 217 Windham Center Rd., Windham 04062. Tel. 207-892-1908, e-mail jaalvino@windhammaine.us; *V.P.* Wynter Giddings, Curtis Memorial Lib., 23 Pleasant St., Brunswick 04011. Tel. 207-725-3542, e-mail giddingswynter@gmail.com; *Secy.* Matt DeLaney, Millinocket Memorial Lib., 5 Maine Avenue, Millinocket, 04462. E-mail matt@millinocketmemoriallibrary.org; *Treas.* Amy Wisehart, Ellsworth Public Lib., 20 State Street, Ellsworth, 04605. E-mail awisehart@ellsworthlibrary.net; *Membs.-at-Large* Cadence Atchinson. E-mail catchinson@une.edu, Kate Wing. E-mail katemwing@gmail.com; *ALA Councilor* Kara Reiman, Maine State Lib., 64 State House Station, Augusta, 04333. Tel. 207-287-5660, e-mail kara.reiman@maine.gov; *NELA Rep.* Michelle Sampson, York Public Lib., 15 Long Sands Rd., York 03909. Tel. 207-363-2818, e-mail msampson@york.lib.me.us.

Address correspondence to Maine Lib. Assn., c/o Windham Public Lib., 217 Windham Center Road, Windham, 04062. E-mail mainelibrary@gmail.com.

World Wide Web http://mainelibraries.org.

Maryland

Maryland Lib. Assn. Memb. 1,000+. Term of Office. July–July. Publication. *The Crab* (q., memb., online). *Ed.* Annette Haldeman. E-mail annette.haldeman@mlis.state.md.us.

Pres. Andrea Berstler, Carroll County Public Lib., 1100 Green Valley Rd., New Windsor 21776. Tel. 443-293-3136, e-mail aberstler@carr.org; *V.P./Pres.-Elect* Morgan Miller, Cecil County Public Lib. 301 Newark Ave., Elkton 21921. Tel. 410-996-1055, e-mail mmiller@ccplnet.org; *Secy.* Mary Anne Bowman, St. Mary's County Public Lib., 23250 Hollywood Rd., Leonardtown 20650. Tel. 301-475-2846 ext. 1015, fax 410-884-4415, e-mail mabowman@stmalib.org; *Treas.* Carl Olson, Towson Univ., Cook Lib., 8000 York Rd., Towson 21252. Tel. 410-704-3267, e-mail colson@towson.edu; *ALA Councilor* David Dahl, Univ. of Maryland. Tel. 301-314-0395, e-mail ddahl1@umd.edu; *Conference Dir.* Naomi Keppler, Baltimore County Public Lib., 6105 Kenwood Ave., Rosedale 21237. Tel. 410-887-0521, e-mail nkeppler@bcpl.net; *Past Pres.* Joseph Thompson, Carroll County Public Lib., 1100 Green Valley Rd., New Windsor 21776. Tel. 443-293-3131, e-mail jthompson@carr.org; *Exec. Dir.* Margaret Carty, Maryland Lib. Assn., 1401 Hollins St., Baltimore 21223. Tel. 410-947-5090, e-mail mcarty@mdlib.org.

Address correspondence to Maryland Lib. Assn., 1401 Hollins St., Baltimore 21223. Tel. 410-947-5090, fax 410-947-5089, e-mail mla@mdlib.org.

World Wide Web http://www.mdlib.org.

Massachusetts

Massachusetts Lib. Assn. Memb. (Indiv.) 1,000; (Inst.) 100.
Pres. Nora Blake, Emily Williston Memorial Lib., Easthampton. E-mail president@masslib.org; *V.P.* Joanne Lamothe, Sandwich Public Lib.–Sandwich. E-mail vicepresident@masslib.org; *Secy.* Noelle Boc, Tewksbury Lib., 300 Chandler St., Tewksbury 01876. Tel. 978-640-4490, e-mail secretary@masslib.org; *Treas.* Bernadette Rivard, Bellingham Public Lib., Bellingham. E-mail treasurer@masslib.org; *Past Pres.* Esmé E. Green, Goodnow Lib., 21 Concord Rd., Sudbury 01776. Tel. 978-440-5515, e-mail pastpresident@masslib.org. Tel. 617-698-5757, e-mail pastpresident@masslib.org.

Address correspondence to Massachusetts Lib. Assn., P.O. Box 404, Malden 02148. Tel. 781-698-7764, e-mail manager@masslib.org.

World Wide Web http://www.masslib.org.

Michigan

Memb. 1,200+.
Pres. Jennifer L. Dean, University of Detroit Mercy Libraries; *Pres. Elect* Kelly Richards, Muskegon Area District Lib.; *Treas.* Scott Duimstra, Capital Area District Libraries; *ALA Councilor* Jennifer Dean; *State Librarian* Randy Riley; *Past Pres.* Kristin Shelley, East Lansing Public Lib.; *Exec. Dir.* Deborah E. Mikula, Michigan Lib. Association. Tel. 517-394-2774 ext. 224, e-mail dmikula@milibraries.org.

Address correspondence to the executive director. Michigan Lib. Assn., 3410 Belle Chase Way, Suite 100, Lansing 48911. Tel. 517-394-2774, e-mail MLA@milibraries.org.

World Wide Web http://www.milibraries.org.

Minnesota

Memb. 1,100. Term of Office. (*Pres., Pres.-Elect*) Jan.–Dec. Publication. *Roundup* (mo., online).
Pres. Stacey Hendren, Anoka County Lib.; *Pres.-Elect* Steve Harsin, Southeastern Libraries Cooperating; *Secy.* Sara Fillbrandt, Rasmussen College; *Treas.* Sarah Ethier, Scott County Lib.; *Memb.-at-Large* Katie Sundstrom, Two Harbors Public Lib.; *ALA Chapter Councilor* Hannah Buckland, Minnesota Dept. of Education; *Past Pres.* Patti Bross, Lake City Public Lib.; *Exec. Dir.* Joy DesMarais-Lanz. E-mail office@mnlibraryassociation.org.

Address correspondence to the executive director. 1611 County Road B West, Ste 315, Saint Paul 55113. Tel. 612-294-6549, e-mail office@mnlibraryassociation.org.

World Wide Web http://www.mnlibraryassociation.org.

Mississippi

Memb. 625. Term of Office. Jan.–Dec. Publication. *Mississippi Libraries* (q.). *Ed.* Tina Harry. E-mail tharry@olemiss.edu.
Pres. Mara Polk, Central Mississippi Regional Lib. System. Tel. 601-825-0100; *V.P.* Stephen Parks, State Law Lib. of Mississippi. Tel. 601-359-3612; *Secy.* Adrienne R. McPhaul, MS Gulf Coast Community College. Tel. 228-896-2514; *Treas.* Michele Frasier-Robinson, University of Southern Mississippi, Cook Lib. Tel. 601-266-6168; *ALA Councilor* Meredith Wickham, First Regional Lib. System. Tel. 662-429-4439; *Parliamentarian* Patsy C. Brewer, Waynesboro-Wayne County Lib. Tel. 601-735-2268; *Past Pres.* Mary Beth Applin, Hinds Community College. Tel. 601-857-3380; *Admin.* Paula Bass, P.O. Box 13687, Jackson 39236-3687. Tel. 601-981-4586, e-mail info@misslib.org.

Address correspondence to the administrator. Mississippi Lib. Assn., P.O. Box 13687, Jackson 39236-3687. Tel. 601-981-4586, e-mail info@misslib.org.

World Wide Web http://www.misslib.org.

Missouri

Memb. 800+. Term of Office. Jan.–Dec. Publication. *MO INFO* (bi-mo.).
Pres. Cindy Thompson, UMKC Univ. Libs. E-mail mlapresident@molib.org; *Pres.-Elect* Claudia Cook, Missouri River Regional Lib.; *Secy. and Memb.-at-Large* Shannon Midyett, Poplar Bluff Municipal Lib.; *Treas. and Memb.-at-Large* Katie Earnhart, Cape Girardeau Public Lib.; *Treas. and Memb.-at-Large* Brent Sweany, University of Missouri-Kansas City; *Memb. Co-Chair and Memb.-at-Large* Amy Held, Jefferson County Lib. Arnold Branch; *Memb. Co-Chair and Memb.-at-Large* Diana Platt, Kansas City Public Lib.; *Memb.-at-Large* Otter Bowman, Daniel Boone Regional Lib.; *ALA Councilor* Margaret Conroy, Daniel Boone Regional Lib.; *Past Pres.* Cindy Dudenhoffer, Central Methodist Univ.

Address correspondence to the president. Missouri Lib. Assn., 1190 Meramec Station Rd., Suite 207, Ballwin, 63021-6902. E-mail mlapresident@molib.org. World Wide Web http://www.molib.org.

Montana

Memb. 600. Term of Office. July–June. Publication. *Focus* (bi-mo.). *Eds.* Star Bradley and Sarah Creech. E-mail mlaFOCUSeditor@gmail.com. *Pres.* Gavin Woltjer, Billings Public Lib., 510 North Broadway, Billings 59101; *V.P./Pres.-Elect* Kit Stephenson, Bozeman Public Lib.; *Secy./Treas.* Danielle Beuhler, Lewistown Public Lib.; *ALA Rep.* Matt Beckstrom, Lewis & Clark Lib., 120 S. Last Chance Gulch, Helena 59601; *Past Pres.* Mary Anne Hansen, MSU-Bozeman Lib., P.O. Box 173320, Bozeman 59717; *Exec. Dir.* Debbi Kramer, Montana Lib. Assn., Inc., 5176 N. Valle Dorado, Kingman, AZ 86409. Tel. 406-579-3121, e-mail debkmla@hotmail.com.

Address correspondence to the executive director. Montana Lib. Assn, 5176 N. Valle Dorado, Kingman, AZ 86409. Tel. 406-579-3121. E-mail debkmla@hotmail.com. World Wide Web http://www.mtlib.org.

Nebraska

Term of Office. Jan.–Dec. *Pres.* Laura England-Biggs. E-mail nlapresident@nebraskalibraries.org; *Pres.-Elect Secy.* Emily Nimsakont. E-mail nlapresidentelect@nebraskalibraries.org; *Treas.* Denise Harders. E-mail nlatreasurer@nebraskalibraries.org; *ALA Councilor* Brenda Ealey. E-mail nlaala@nebraskalibraries.org; *Past Pres.* Michael Straatmann. E-mail nlapastpresident@nebraskalibraries.org; *Exec. Dir.* Ginger Jelinek. E-mail nlaexecutivedirector@nebraskalibraries.org.

Address correspondence to the executive director. Nebraska Lib. Assn., P.O. Box 21756, Lincoln 68542-1756. World Wide Web https://nebraskalibraries.org.

Nevada

Memb. 450. Term of Office. Jan.–Dec. Publication. *Nevada Libraries* (q.).

Pres. Tod Colegrove, Carson City Lib., E-mail tcolegrove@carson.org; *Pres.-Elect* Marcie Smedley, Henderson Libraries. E-mail mlsmedley@hendersonlibraries.com. *Exec. Secy.* Carla Land, Las Vegas–Clark County Lib. District. E-mail bookdiva@gmail.com; *Treas.* Joy Gunn, Henderson Libs. E-mail jgunn@hendersonlibraries.com; *Finance* Morgan Tiar, Washoe County Lib. System. E-mail matiar@washoecounty.us; *State Libn.* JoVon Sotak, Acting Nevada State Lib. Administrator. E-mail jsotak@admin.nv.gov; *ALA Delegate* Amy Geddes, Lyon County Lib. District. E-mail ageddes@lyon-county.org; *Past Pres.* Forrest Lewis, North Las Vegas Lib. District. E-mail lewisf@cityofnorthlasvegas.com.

Address correspondence to the executive secretary. World Wide Web https://nevadalibraries.org/.

New Hampshire

Memb. 600+. *Pres.* Yvette Couser, Merrimack Public Lib., 470 Daniel Webster Hwy., Merrimack 03784. Tel. 603-424-5021 ext. 108, e-mail ycouser@merrimacklibrary.org; *V.P./Pres.-Elect* Denise M. van Zanten, Manchester City Lib., 405 Pine Street, Manchester 03104. Tel. 603-624-6550 ext. 3329, e-mail dvanzant@manchesternh.gov; *Secy.* Denise M. van Zanten, Manchester City Library, 405 Pine Street, Manchester 03104. Tel. 603-624-6550 ext. 3329, e-mail dvanzant@manchesternh.gov; *Treas.* Kim Gabert, Wadleigh Memorial Lib., 49 Nashua St., Milford 03055. Tel. 603-249-0645, e-mail treasurer@nhlibrarians.org; *ALA Councilor* Lori Fisher, New Hampshire State Lib., 20 Park St., Concord 03301. Tel. 603-271-2393, e-mail lori.fisher@dncr.nh.gov; *Past Pres.* Amy Lappin, Lebanon Public Libs., 80 Main St., West Lebanon 03784. Tel. 603-298-8544, e-mail president@nhlibrarians.org.

Address correspondence to New Hampshire Lib. Assn., c/o New Hampshire State Lib., 20 Park St., Concord 03301-6314. E-mail nhla executive@googlegroups.com. World Wide Web http://nhlibrarians.org.

New Jersey

Memb. 1,800. Term of Office. July–June. Publication. *New Jersey Libraries NEWSletter* (q.). E-mail newsletter_editor@njlamembers.org.

Pres. Jen Schureman, Gloucester County Lib. System. E-mail jmschureman@gmail. com; *1st V.P./Pres.-Elect* Kate Jaggers, Highland Park Public Lib. E-mail librariankatej@ gmail.com; *2nd V.P.* Allan Kleiman, Montville Township Public Lib. E-mail akleiman@mont villelibrary.org; *Secy.* Selwa Shamy, Montclair Public Library. E-mail selwashamy@gmail. com; *Treas.* Samantha McCoy, West Caldwell Public Lib. E-mail mccoy@westcaldwell.bccls. org; *ALA Councilor* Eileen Palmer, LMXAC. E-mail empalmer@lmxac.org; *Past Pres.* Leah Wagner, Monroe Township Library (Middlesex). E-mail lwagner@monroetwplibrary.org; *Exec. Dir.* Juliet Machie. E-mail jmachie@njla.org.

Address correspondence to the executive director. E-mail jmachie@mjla.org.

World Wide Web http://www.njla.org.

New Mexico

Memb. 550. Term of Office. Apr.–Apr. Publication. *NMLA Newsletter* (bi-mo., online). *Ed.* Robyn Gleasner. E-mail newsletter@nmla.org.

Pres. Melanie Templet. E-mail president@ nmla.org; *V.P./Pres.-Elect* Dean Smith. E-mail vicepresident@nmla.org; *Secy.* Sarah Obenauf. E-mail secretary@nmla.org; *Treas.* Kelli Murphy. E-mail treasurer@nmla.org; *Membs.-at-Large* Ellen Bosman. E-mail ebosman@nmsu. edu, Kate Alderete. E-mail kalderete@taosgov. com, Anne Lefkosfsky. E-mail alefkofsky@ cabq.gov, Julia Kelso. E-mail librarydirector@ vglibrary.org; *ALA-APA Councilor* Aubrey Iglesias. E-mail aiglesia@nmsu.edu.

Address correspondence to New Mexico Lib. Assn., P.O. Box 26074, Albuquerque 87125. Tel. 505-400-7309, e-mail contact@ nmla.org.

World Wide Web http://nmla.org.

New York

Memb. 4,000. Term of Office. Nov.–Nov. Publication. *The eBulletin* (6x yearly, online).

Pres. Claudia Depkin, Haverstraw King's Daughters Public Lib.; *Pres.-Elect* Beth Merkle, The Strong Museum of Play; *Treas.* Roger Reyes, Suffolk Cooperative Lib. System; *Treas.-Elect* Grace Riario, Ramapo Catskill Lib. System; *ALA Chapter Councilor* Cassie Guthrie, Greece Public Lib.; *Past Pres.* Jen Cannell, St. John Fisher College; *Exec. Dir.* Jeremy Johannesen, New York Lib. Assn., 6021

State Farm Rd., Guilderland 12084. Tel. 518-432-6952, fax 518-427-1697, e-mail director@ nyla.org.

Address correspondence to New York Lib. Assn., 6021 State Farm Rd., Guilderland 12084. Tel. 518-432-6952, fax 518-427-1697, e-mail info@nyla.org.

World Wide Web http://www.nyla.org.

North Carolina

Memb. 1,100. Term of Office. Oct.–Oct. Publication. *North Carolina Libraries* (1–2x yearly, online). *Ed.* Ralph Scott. E-mail scottr@ecu. edu.

Pres. Lorrie Russell. E-mail president@ nclaonline.org; *V.P./Pres.-Elect* Libby Stone. E-mail vicepresident@nclaonline.org; *Secy.* Julie Raynor. E-mail secretary@nclaonline. org; *Treas.* Amy Harris Houk. E-mail treasurer@ nclaonline.org; *Treas.-Elect* Lara Luck. E-mail treasurer.elect@nclaonline.org; *ALA Councilor* Siobhan Loendorf. E-mail sloendorf@ catawbacountync.gov; *State Libn.* Timothy Owens (ex officio). E-mail timothy.owens@ ncdcr.gov; *Past Pres.* Michael A. Crumpton. E-mail pastpresident@nclaonline.org.

Address correspondence to North Carolina Lib. Assn., 265 Eastchester Dr., Suite 133, #364, High Point 27262. E-mail nclaonline@ gmail.com.

World Wide Web http://www.nclaonline.org.

North Dakota

Memb. (Indiv.) 300+. Term of Office. Sept.–Sept. Publication. *The Good Stuff* (q.). *Ed.* Shannon Yarbrough. E-mail shannon.yarbrough@ und.edu.

Pres. Amy Soma, Fargo Public Schools. E-mail somaa@fargo.k12.nd.us; *Pres.-Elect* Stephanie Galeazzo. E-mail sgaleazzo@co. mckenzie.nd.us. *Treas.* Aaron Stefanich, Grand Forks Public Library. E-mail aaron.stefanich@ gflibrary.com; *ALA Councilor* Sara Westall, Fargo Public Libraries. E-mail swestall@ fargolibrary.org; *State Libn.* Mary J. Soucie, North Dakota State Lib. E-mail msoucie@ nd.gov; *Past Pres.* Traci Lund, Divide County Public Lib. E-mail dcl@nccray.net.

Address correspondence to the president. North Dakota Lib. Assn., 604 E. Boulevard Ave., Bismarck 58505.

World Wide Web http://www.ndla.info.

Ohio

Memb. 2,700+. Term of Office. Jan.–Dec. Publication. *OLC News* (online).

Chair Cheryl Kuonen, Mentor Public Lib. Tel. 440-255-8811 ext. 2323; *V.Chair/Chair-Elect* Tom Dillie, Minerva Public Lib. Tel. 330-868-4101; *Secy./Treas.* Aimee Fifarek. Tel. 330-744-8636; *Immediate Past Chair* Kacie Armstrong. Tel. 216-261-5300; *ALA Councilor,* Toledo Lucas County Public Lib. Tel. 419-259-5333; *Exec. Dir.* Michelle Francis. Tel. 614-410-8092 ext. 105, e-mail mfrancis@olc.org.

Address correspondence to the executive director. Ohio Lib. Council, 495 Metro Place South, Suite 350, Dublin 43017. Tel. 614-410-8092.

World Wide Web http://www.olc.org.

Oklahoma

Memb. 500–600. Term of Office. July–June.

Pres. Lisa Wells; *V.P./Pres.-Elect* Cathy Blackman; *Secy.* Kelly Sitzman; *Treas.* Susan Urban; *ALA Councilor* Sarah Robbins; *Past Pres.* Lisa Wells.

Address correspondence to Oklahoma Lib. Assn., 1190 Meramec Station Rd., Suite 207, Ballwin, MO 63021-6902. Tel. 800-969-6562 ext. 5, fax 636-529-1396, e-mail ola@amigos. org.

World Wide Web http://www.oklibs.org.

Oregon

Memb. (Indiv.) 1,000+. Publications. *OLA Hotline.* (bi-w.). E-mail olahotline@olaweb.org; *OLA Quarterly.* (q.) *Ed.* Charles Wood. E-mail wuchakewu@gmail.com.

Pres. Kate Lasky, Josephine Community Lib. District. E-mail olapresident@olaweb. org; *V.P./Pres.-Elect* Arlene Weible, State Lib. of Oregon. E-mail olavp@olaweb.org; *Secy.* Angela Parsons. E-mail olasecretary@olaweb. org. *Treas.* Lori Wamsley, Mt. Hood Community College Lib. E-mail olatreasurer@olaweb. org; *Memb.-at-Large* Star Khan, Driftwood Public Lib. E-mail skhan@lincolncity.org; *ALA Rep.* Kirsten Brodbeck-Kenney, Driftwood Public Lib. E-mail olachaptercouncilor@ olaweb.org; *Past Pres.* Elaine Hirsch, Lewis and Clark College, Watzek Lib. E-mail olapresident@olaweb.org.

Address correspondence to Oregon Lib. Assn., P.O. Box 3067, La Grande 97850. Tel. 541-962-5824, e-mail ola@olaweb.org.

World Wide Web http://www.olaweb.org.

Pennsylvania

Memb. 1,900+. Term of Office. Jan.–Dec. Publication. *PaLA Bulletin* (q.).

Pres. Tom Reinsfelder; *1st V.P.* Jen Knisely; *2nd V.P. (2021 Monroeville)* Nicole Henline; *2nd V.P. (2022 Harrisburg)* Brianna Crum; *3rd V.P.* Dana Barber; *Treas.* Kate Shaw; *ALA Councilor* Barbara McGary; *Past Pres.* Michele Legate; *Exec. Dir.* Christi Buker. Pennsylvania Lib. Assn., 220 Cumberland Pkwy., Suite 10, Mechanicsburg 17055. Tel. 717-766-7663, e-mail christi@palibraries.org.

Address correspondence to the executive director. Pennsylvania Lib. Assn., 220 Cumberland Parkway, Suite 10, Mechanicsburg 17055. Tel. 717-766-7663, fax 717-766-5440.

World Wide Web http://www.palibraries. org.

Rhode Island

Memb. (Indiv.) 350+; (Inst.) 50+. Term of Office. June–June. Publication. *RILA Bulletin* (6x yearly). *Ed.* Deb Estrella, Tiverton Public Lib. Tel. 401-625-6796. E-mail communications@ rilibraries.org.

Pres. Julie Holden, Cranston Public Lib. Tel. 401-943-9080 ext. 101. E-mail president@ rilibraries.org; *V.P.* Rachael Juskuv, Bryant Univ. Tel. 401-232-6299, e-mail vicepresident@ rilibraries.org; *Secy.* Celeste Dyer, Cumberland Public Lib. Tel. 401-333-2552, e-mail secretary@ rilibraries.org; *Treas.* Beatrice Pulliam, Providence Public Lib. E-mail treasurer@ rilibraries.org; *Membs.-at-Large* Bohyun Kim, Univ. of Rhode Island. Tel. 401-874-4607, e-mail bohyunkim@uri.edu, Megan Hamlin-Black, Rhode Island State Libn. Tel. 401-330-3184, e-mail mblack@sos.ri.gov; *ALA Councilor* Jack Martin, Providence Public Lib. Tel. 401-455-8100, e-mail jmartin@provlib.org; *Past Pres.* Kieran Ayton, Rhode Island College, 600 Mt. Pleasant Ave., Providence 02908. Tel. 401-456-9604, e-mail kayton@ric.edu.

Address correspondence to Rhode Island Lib. Assn., P.O. Box 6765, Providence 02940.

World Wide Web http://www.rilibraries.org.

South Carolina

Memb. 350+. Term of Office. Jan.–Dec. Publication. *South Carolina Libraries Journal* (s.-ann., online). *Eds.* April Akins, Lander Univ. Tel. 864-388-8184, e-mail aakins@lander.edu; Megan Palmer, Clemson Univ. Tel. 864-656-5179, e-mail mpalme4@clemson.edu.

Pres. Megan Palmer, Clemson Univ. Tel. 864-656-5179, e-mail mpalme4@clemson.edu; *1st V.P.* Sara DeSantis, Univ. of South Carolina–Upstate. Tel. 864-503-5006, e-mail sarabd@uscupstate.edu; *2nd V.P.* Sunny Peterson, Richland Lib. Sandhills. Tel. 803-699-9230, speterson@richlandlibrary.com; *Secy.* Jessica Kohout-Tailor, Clemson University. Tel. 864-656-4177, e-mail jkohout@clemson.edu; *Treas.* Danielle Robinson, Greenville County Public Lib. Tel. 864-430-8796, lesliedanieller@gmail.com; *ALA Councilor* Jonathan Newton, USC Upstate. E-mail jdn3@uscupstate.edu; *Past Pres.* Nathan Flowers, Francis Marion Univ. Tel. 843-661-1306, e-mail nflowers@fmarion.edu. *Exec. Sec.* Donald Wood, South Carolina Lib Association, P.O. Box 1763, Columbia, 29202. Tel. 803-252-1087, fax 803-252-0589, e-mail scla@capconsc.com.

Address correspondence to the executive secretary. South Carolina Lib. Assn., P.O. Box 1763, Columbia 29202. Tel. 803-252-1087, e-mail scla@capconsc.com.

World Wide Web http://www.scla.org.

South Dakota

Memb. (Indiv.) 450+; (Inst.) 60+. Publication. *Book Marks* (q.). *Ed.* Kelly Henkel. E-mail bookmarkssd@gmail.com.

Pres. Julie Erickson, TIE, Rapid City. E-mail jerickson@tie.net; *V.P./Pres.-Elect* Shari Theroux, HM Briggs Lib, South Dakota State University, Brookings. E-mail Shari.Theroux@sdstate.edu. *Recording Secy.* Sean Minkel, Rapid City Public Lib, Rapid City. sminkel@rcplib.org *Exec. Secy./Treas.* Krista Ohrtman, Mikkelsen Lib., Augustana University, Sioux Falls. E-mail SDLibraryAssociation@gmail.com; *ALA Councilor* Lisa Brunick, Mikkelsen Lib, Augustana University, Sioux Falls. E-mail lisa.brunick@augie.edu; *Past Pres.* Ashia Gustafson, Brookings Public Lib., Brookings. E-mail agustafson@cityofbrookings.org.

Address correspondence to the executive secretary. South Dakota Lib. Assn., Mikkelsen Lib., 2001 S. Summit Ave., Sioux Falls 57197. Tel. 605-743-0889.

World Wide Web http://www.sdlibraryassociation.org.

Tennessee

Memb. 600+. Term of Office. July–June. Publications. *Tennessee Libraries* (q.; online). *Ed.* Sharon Holderman, Tennessee Tech Univ. Lib. E-mail sholderman@tntech.edu; *TLA Newsletter* (q.; online). *Ed.* Dwight Hunter. E-mail Dwight.Hunter@chattanoogastate.edu.

Pres. Erika Long. E-mail erika.long.lib@gmail.com; *V.P./Pres.-Elect* Sharon Edwards. E-mail sharonedwards405@gmail.com; *Recording Secy.* Holly Hebert. E-mail holly.hebert@mtsu.edu; *Past Pres.* Jill Rael. E-mail tnlapresident2019@gmail.com. *Exec. Dir.* Cathy Farley. E-mail exdirtla@gmail.com.

Address correspondence to the executive director. Tennessee Lib. Assn., P.O. Box 6297, Sparta 38583. Tel. 931-607-1182, e-mail exdirtla@gmail.com.

World Wide Web http://tnla.org.

Texas

Memb. 6,000. Term of Office. Apr.–Apr. Publications. *Texas Library Journal* (q.), *Ed.* Wendy Woodland. E-mail wendyw@txla.org, *TLACast* (6–8x yearly; online).

Pres. Cecilia Barham, North Richland Hills Public Lib.; *Pres.-Elect* Christina Gola, Univ. of Houston; *Treas.* Edward Melton, Harris County Public Lib.; *ALA Councilor* Mary Woodard, Mesquite ISD; *Past Pres.* Jennifer LaBoon, Fort Worth ISD; *Exec. Dir.* Shirley Robinson, Texas Lib. Assn., 3355 Bee Cave Rd., Ste. 401, Austin 78746-6763. Tel. 512-328-1518 ext. 151, e-mail shirleyr@txla.org.

Address correspondence to the executive director. Texas Lib. Assn., 3420 Executive Center Dr., Ste. 301, Austin 78731. Tel. 512-328-1518, e-mail tla@txla.org.

World Wide Web http://www.txla.org.

Utah

Memb. 650. Publication. *Utah Libraries News* (q.; online). *Ed.* Mindy Hale. E-mail mehale@slcolibrary.org.

Pres. Christina Gola, University of Houston; *Pres.-Elect* Daniel Burgard, University of North

Texas Health Science Center; *Treas.* Dianna Morganti, Texas State University; *ALA Chapter Councilor* Mary Woodard, Mesquite ISD; *Past Pres.* Jennifer LaBoon, Infobase; *Exec. Dir.* Shirley Robinson, Texas Lib. Association.

Address correspondence to the executive director.

World Wide Web http://www.ula.org.

Vermont

Memb. 300+. Publication. *VLA News* (q.). *Ed.* Janet Clapp. E-mail vermontlibrariesnews@gmail.com.

Pres. Kevin Unrath, Pierson Lib., 5376 Shelburne Road, Shelburne 05482. Tel. 802-264-5017, e-mail kunrath@shelburnevt.org; *Secy.* Marie A. Schmukal, Warren Public Lib., 413 Main St., Warren 05674. Tel. 802-496-3913, e-mail secretary@vermontlibraries.org; *Treas.* Susan Smolinsky, Peacham Lib., 656 Bayley Hazen Rd., Peacham 05862. Tel. 802-592-3216, e-mail vermontlibrariestreasurer@gmail.com; *Past Pres.* Amy Olsen, Lanpher Memorial Lib., 141 Main St, Hyde Park, VT 05655. Tel. 802-888-4628, e-mail hydeparklibrary@yahoo.com.

Address correspondence to Vermont Lib. Assn., P.O. Box 803, Burlington 05402.

World Wide Web http://www.vermont-libraries.org.

Virginia

Memb. 950+. Term of Office. Oct.–Oct. Publication. *Virginia Libraries* (ann.). *Ed.* Julia Feerrar, Virginia Tech. E-mail feerrar@vt.edu.

Pres. Jennifer Resor-Whicker, Radford University, McConnell Lib., P.O. Box 6881, Radford 24142. Tel. 540-831-5691, e-mail jrwhicker@radford.edu; *Pres.-Elect* K. T. Vaughan, Washington & Lee University; *2nd V.P.* Regina Sierra Carter, U.S. Army; *Secy.* Maryska Connolly-Brown, Hampden-Sydney University. *Treas.* Bill Edwards-Bodmer, Suffolk Public Lib.; *ALA Councilor* Lucy Rush Wittkower, Old Dominion Univ.; *Past Pres.* Jennifer Resor-Whicker, MLIS Radford University, McConnell Lib.; *Exec. Dir.* Lisa Varga, Virginia Lib. Assn., P.O. Box 56312, Virginia Beach 23456. Tel. 757-689-0594, e-mail vla.lisav@cox.net.

Address correspondence to the executive director. Virginia Lib. Assn., P.O. Box 56312,

Virginia Beach 23456. Tel. 757-689-0594, fax 757-447-3478, e-mail vla.lisav@cox.net.

World Wide Web http://www.vla.org.

Washington

Memb. (Indiv.) 742, (Inst.) 47. Publications. *Alki: The Washington Library Association Journal* (3x yearly, online). *Ed.* Johanna Jacobsen Kiciman, Univ. of Washington. E-mail alkieditor@wla.org.

Pres. Danielle Miller, Washington Talking Book & Braille Lib. E-mail danielle.miller@sos.wa.gov; *V.P./Pres.-Elect* Ahniwa Ferrari, The Evergreen State College. E-mail ferraria@evergreen.edu; *Treas.* Muriel Wheatley, Timberland Regional Lib. E-mail mwheatley@trl.org; *ALA Councilor* Steven Bailey, King County Lib. System. E-mail sbailey@kcls.org; *Past Pres.* Emily Keller, University of Washington Libraries. E-mail emkeller@uw.edu; *Exec. Dir.* Brianna Hoffman, Washington Lib. Association. E-mail brianna@wla.org.

Address correspondence to the executive director. Washington Lib. Assn., P.O. Box 33808, Seattle 98133. Tel. 206-823-1138, e-mail info@wla.org.

World Wide Web http://www.wla.org.

West Virginia

Memb. 700+.

Pres. Breana Roach Bowen. Tel. 304-528-5700, fax 304-528-5701, e-mail breana.bowen@cabell.lib.wv.us; *1st V.P./Pres.-Elect* Alexandra Schneider; *1st V.P.* Vacant; *Treas.* Erika Connelly; *ALA Councilor* Majed Khader. Tel. 304-696-3121, fax 304-696-5219, e-mail khader@marshall.edu; *Past Pres.* Heather Campbell Shock; *Exec. Dir.* Vacant.

Address correspondence to the president.

World Wide Web http://www.wvla.org.

Wisconsin

Memb. 1,900. Term of Office. Jan.–Dec. Publication. *WLA eNewsletter* (3–4x yearly; online). *Ed.* Jill Fuller. E-mail jfuller@bridgeslibrarysystem.org.

Pres. Sherry Machones. E-mail sherry machones@gmail.com; *V.P.* Nyama Reed. E-mail n.reed@wfblibrary.org; *Secy.* Desiree Bongers, Ripon Public Lib., Ripon. E-mail dbongers@riponlibrary.org; *Treas.* Katharine Clark. E-mail kclark@beloitlibrary.org; *ALA*

Councilor Sherry Machones. E-mail sma chones@northernwaters.org; *Past Pres.* Scott Vrieze. E-mail scott@melsa.org; *Exec. Dir.* Plumer Lovelace III. E-mail lovelace@wisconsinlibraries.org.

Address correspondence to Wisconsin Lib. Assn., P.O. Box 6437, 112 Owen Rd., #6437, Monona 53716. Tel. 608-245-3640, e-mail wla@wisconsinlibraries.org.

World Wide Web http://wla.wisconsin-libraries.org.

Wyoming

Memb. 450+. Term of Office. Oct.–Oct. Publication. Newsletter (ann.; August).

Pres. Jacob Mickelsen, Carbon County Lib. System. Tel. 307-328-2623, e-mail director@carbonlibraries.org; *V.P.* Jeff Collins, Laramie County Lib. System. Tel. 307-773-7220, e-mail jcollins@lclsonline.org; *ALA Councilor* Janice Grover-Roosa, Western Wyoming Community College. Tel. 307-382-1701, e-mail librarian@westernwyoming.edu; *State Libn. (ex officio)* Jamie Markus, Wyoming State Lib. Tel. 307-777-5914, e-mail jamie.markus@wyo.gov; *Past Pres.* Abby Beaver, Wyoming State Lib. Tel. 307-777-5913, e-mail abby.beaver@wyo.gov; *Communications Advisor (ex officio)* Elizabeth Thorson, Laramie County Lib. System. Tel. 307-773-7230, e-mail ethorson@lclsonline.org.

Address correspondence to Wyoming Lib. Assn., 1190 Meramac Station Rd., Suite 207, Ballwin, MO 63201. Tel. 800-969-6562 ext. 6, e-mail wla@amigos.org

World Wide Web http://www.wyla.org.

Canada

Alberta

Memb. 800+. Term of Office. May–April.

Pres. Kirk MacLeod, Alberta Law Libraries. E-mail president@laa.ca; *1st V.P.* Vacant; *2nd V.P. (interim appt.)* Alyssa Martin, Edmonton Public Lib. E-mail 2ndvicepresident@laa.ca; *Treas.* Louisa Robison, Service Alberta. E-mail treasurer@laa.ca; *Past Pres.* Briana Ehnes, Red Deer Public Lib. E-mail pastpresident@laa.ca; *Director 1* Vacant; *Director 2 (interim appt.)* Carla Lewis, University of Calgary Lib. E-mail director3@laa.ca. *Director 3* Robert Tiessen,

University of Calgary Lib. E-mail director3@laa.ca.

Address correspondence to Lib. Assn. of Alberta, 11625 136 Street NW, Edmonton T5M 1M5. Tel. 403-284-5818, 877-522-5550.

World Wide Web http://www.laa.ca.

British Columbia

Memb. 750+. Term of Office. April–April. Publication. *BCLA Perspectives* (q.; online). E-mail perspectives@bcla.bc.ca.

Pres. Chris Middlemass, Vancouver Public Lib.; *V.P./Pres.-Elect* Todd Mundle, Kwantlen Polytechnic Univ. Lib.; *Recording Secy.* TBA; *Treas.* Adam Farrell, New Westminster Public Lib.; *Asst./Incoming Treas.* Anne O'Shea, Vancouver Island Regional Lib.; *Past Pres.* Shirley Lew, Vancouver Community College Lib.; *Exec. Dir.* Annette DeFaveri. E-mail execdir@bcla.bc.ca.

Address correspondence to the executive director. British Columbia Lib. Assn., P.O. Box 19008 Rocky Point PO, Port Moody V3H 0J1. E-mail bclaoffice@bcla.bc.ca.

World Wide Web http://www.bcla.bc.ca.

Manitoba

Memb. 500+. Term of Office. May–May.

Pres. Melanie Sucha; *Secy.* Camille Fitch-Kustcher. E-mail secretary@mla.mb.ca; *Treas.* Kelly Murray; *Past Pres.* Kerry Macdonald.

Address correspondence to Manitoba Lib. Assn., 606-100 Arthur St., Winnipeg R3B 1H3. E-mail secretary@mla.mb.ca.

World Wide Web https://mla.mb.ca/.

Ontario

Memb. 5,000+. Publications. *Open Shelf* (mo., multimedia). *Ed.* Martha Attridge Bufton; *The Teaching Librarian* (3x yearly; memb.; online). *Ed.* Caroline Freibauer. E-mail membership@accessola.com.

Pres. Andrea Cecchetto, Markham Public Lib. E-mail acecch@markham.library.on.ca; *V.P./Pres.-Elect* Sabrina Saunders, The Blue Mountains Public Lib. E-mail ssaunders@thebluemountains.ca; *Treas.* Janneka Guise, Univ. of Toronto. E-mail jan.guise@utoronto.ca; *Past Pres.* Richard Reid, Durham District

School Board. E-mail richard.reid@ddsb.ca; *Exec. Dir.* Shelagh Paterson, Ontario Lib. Assn. E-mail spaterson@accessola.com.

Address correspondence to Ontario Lib. Assn., 2 Toronto St., 3rd Floor, Toronto M5C 2B6. Tel. 416-363-3388 or 866-873-9867, fax 416-941-9581 or 800-387-1181, e-mail info@accessola.com.

World Wide Web http://www.accessola.com.

Quebec

Memb. (Indiv.) 100+. Term of Office. May–April. Publication. *ABQLA Bulletin* (3x yearly). *Ed.* Maria Ressina.

Pres. Sandy Hervieux; *V.P.* Ana-Maria Trasnea; *Treas.* Emily Mackenzie; *Past Pres.* Eamon Duffy.

Address correspondence to the president. Assn. des Bibliothecaires du Quebec/Quebec Lib. Assn., C.P. 26717, CPS Beaconsfield H9W 6G7.

World Wide Web http://www.abqla.qc.ca.

Saskatchewan

Memb. 200+.

Pres. Amy Rankin, CMP Resource Centre, P.O. Box 6500, Regina. Tel. 639-625-3537, e-mail amy.rankin@rcmp-grc.gc.ca; *V.P. Engagements and Communications* Elaina St. Onge, Campion College Lib, 3737 Wascana Parkway, Regina, S4S 0A2. Tel. 306-359-1233. E-mail: elaina.st.onge@uregina.ca; *V.P. Advocacy and Development* Vacant; *Treas.* Darrel Yates. E-mail darrel.yates@dal.ca; *Past Pres.* Alison Jantz, RCMP Resource Centre; *Exec. Dir.* Dorothea Warren Saskatchewan Lib. Assn., #15 – 2010 7th Ave, Regina S4R 1C3. Tel. 306-780-9413, fax 306-780-9447, e-mail slaexdir@sasktel.net.

Address correspondence to the executive director. Saskatchewan Lib. Assn., 10—2010 7th Ave., Regina S4R 1C3. Tel. 306-780-9413, fax 306-780-3633, e-mail slaexdir@sasktel.net.

World Wide Web http://www.saskla.ca.

Regional

Atlantic Provinces: N.B., N.L., N.S., P.E.I.

Memb. (Indiv.) 320+.

Pres. Ann Smith, Acadia University, Wolfville, Nova Scotia. E-mail president@apla.ca; *V.P./Pres.-Elect* Marc Harper, Bibliothèque Champlain, 18 avenue Antonine-Maillet (local 164), Moncton, NB E1A 3E9. Tel. 506-858-4154, e-mail president-elect@apla.ca; *V.P. Nova Scotia* Cate Carlyle. E-mail ns@apla.ca; *V.P. New Brunswick* Ruth Cox. E-mail nb@apla.ca; *V.P. Newfoundland and Labrador* Becky Smith. E-mail nl@apla.ca; *V.P. Prince Edward Island* Krystal Dionne. E-mail pe@apla.ca; *Secy.* Amy Lorencz, St. Mary's Univ. Tel. 902-420-5174, e-mail secretary@apla.ca; *Treas.* Terri Winchcombe, Patrick Power Lib., St. Mary's Univ. Halifax, NS. Tel. 902-420-5535, e-mail treasurer@apla.ca; *Past President* Trecia Schell, Pictou-Antigonish Regional Lib. E-mail past-president@apla.ca.

Address correspondence to Atlantic Provinces Lib. Assn., Dalhousie Univ., Kenneth C. Rowe Mgt. Bldg., 6100 University Ave., Suite 4010, P.O. Box 15000, Halifax, NS B3H 4R2. E-mail president@apla.ca or secretary@apla.ca.

World Wide Web http://www.apla.ca.

Mountain Plains: Ariz., Colo., Kans., Mont., Neb., Nev., N.Dak., N.Mex., Okla., S.Dak., Utah, Wyo.

Memb. 700. Term of Office. Oct.–Oct. Publications. *MPLA Newsletter* (6x yearly, online). *Ed.* Melanie Argo, Madison Public Lib., 209 E. Center, Madison, SD 57042. Tel. 605-256-7525, e-mail editor@mpla.us.

Pres. Stephen Sweeney, St. John Vianney Seminary, Cardinal Stafford Lib., 1300 South Steele St., Denver, CO 80210. Tel. 303-715-3192, fax 303-715-2037, e-mail president@mpla.us; *V.P./Pres.-Elect* Robin Newell, Emporia Public Lib., 110 E. Sixth Ave., Emporia, KS 66801. Tel. 620-340-6464, e-mail vicepresident@mpla.us; *Recording Secy.* Whitney Vitale, Oklahoma State Univ., Edmon Low Lib., Stillwater, OK 74078. Tel. 405-744-7142, e-mail secretary@mpla.us; *Past Pres.* Leslie H. Langley, Southeastern Public Lib. System, Wister Public Lib., 101 Caston Ave., Wister, OK 74966. Tel. 918-655-7654, fax 918-655-3267, e-mail president@mpla.us; *Exec. Secy.* Judy Kulp, 14293 West Center Dr., Lakewood, CO 80228. Tel. 303-985-7795, e-mail execsecretary@mpla.us.

Address correspondence to the executive secretary. Mountain Plains Lib. Assn., 14293

West Center Drive, Lakewood, Colorado 80228. Tel. 303-985-7795, e-mail execsecretary@mpla.us. World Wide Web http://www.mpla.us.

New England: Conn., Maine, Mass., N.H., R.I., Vt.

Memb. (Indiv.) 650+. Term of Office. Nov.–Oct. Publication. "NELA News" (blog).

Pres. Mike Zeller, Shrewsbury Public Lib, Shrewsbury, MA. Tel. 413-323-5925 ext. 102; *V.P.* Kimberly Usselman, Cumberland Public Lib., Cumberland, RI. Tel. 413-323-5925 ext. 103; *Secy.* Lucinda Walker, Norwich Public Lib., Norwich, VT. Tel. 413-323-5925 ext. 106; *Treas.* Bernie Prochnik, Bath Public Lib., Bath, NH. Tel. 413-323-5925 ext. 105; *Past Pres.* Jennifer Bruneau, Boylston Public Lib., Boylston, MA. Tel. 413-323-5925 ext. 104; *Admin.* Robert Scheier, NELA Office, 55 N. Main St., Unit 49, Belchertown, MA 01007. Tel. 413-323-5925 ext. 100, rscheier@nelib.org.

Address correspondence to the administrator. New England Lib. Assn., 55 N. Main St., Unit 49, Belchertown, MA 01007. Tel. 413-323-5925, e-mail rscheier@nelib.org.

World Wide Web http://www.nelib.org.

Pacific Northwest: Alaska, Idaho, Mont., Ore., Wash., Alberta, B.C.

Memb. 170+. Term of Office. Aug.–Aug. Publication. *PNLA Quarterly.* Eds. Robert Perret, Jennifer Ward. E-mail pqeditors@gmail.com.

Pres. Pam Henley, Montana State Lib., Helena (and Bozeman), MT. Tel. 406-461-9049; *Vice-Pres./Pres.-Elect* Nicole Thode, Tumwater

Timberland Lib., Thurston County, WA. *2nd V.P./Membership Chair* Ilana Kingsley, Univ. of Alaska–Fairbanks, Rasmuson Lib., Fairbanks, AK. Tel. 907-474-7518; *Secy.* Erin Hvizdak, Washington State Univ., Pullman, WA. Tel. 509-335-9514; *Treas.* Lisa Fraser, PNLA, P.O. Box 1032, Bothell WA 98041. Tel. 425-369-3458, e-mail lgfraser@kcls.org; *Past Pres.* Honore Bray, Missoula Public Lib., Missoula, MT. Tel. 406-721-2665.

Address correspondence to Pacific Northwest Lib. Assn., P.O. Box 1032, Bothell WA 98041.

World Wide Web http://www.pnla.org.

Southeastern: Ala., Ark., Fla., Ga., Ky., La., Miss., N.C., S.C., Tenn., Va., W.Va.

Memb. 500. Publication. *The Southeastern Librarian (SELn)* (q.; online, open access).

Pres. SELA President: Melissa Dennis, University of Mississippi, University, MS. E-mail president@selaonline.org; *Pres.-Elect* Crystal Gates, William F. Laman Public Lib, North Little Rock, AR. E-mail president.elect@selaonline.org; *Secy.* Kristin Rogers, University of Mississippi University, MS. E-mail secretary@selaonline.org; *Treas.* Vicki Gregory, University of South Florida (Professor Emeritus), Tampa, FL. E-mail treasurer@selaonline.org; *Archivist* Camille McCutcheon, Univ. of South Carolina Upstate, Spartanburg, SC. E-mail archivist@selaonline.org; *Past Pres.* Tim Dodge, Auburn University Libraries, Auburn, AL.

Address correspondence to Southeastern Lib. Assn., Admin. Services, P.O. Box 30703, Savannah, GA 31410. Tel. 912-999-7979, e-mail selaadminservices@selaonline.org.

World Wide Web http://selaonline.org.

State and Provincial Library Agencies

The state library administrative agency in each of the U.S. states will have the latest information on its state plan for the use of federal funds under the Library Services and Technology Act (LSTA). The directors and addresses of these state agencies are listed below.

United States

Alabama

Nancy Pack, Dir., Alabama Public Lib. Svc., 6030 Monticello Dr., Montgomery 36117. Tel. 334-213-3900, fax 334-213-3993, e-mail npack@apls.state.al.us. World Wide Web http://statelibrary.alabama.gov.

Alaska

Patience Frederiksen, Dir., Alaska State Lib., P.O. Box 110571, Juneau 99811-0571. Tel. 907-465-2911, fax 907-465-2151, e-mail patience.frederiksen@alaska.gov. World Wide Web http://library.state.ak.us.

Arizona

Holly Henley, State Libn. and Dir. of Lib. Svcs., Arizona State Lib., Archives and Public Records, 1901 W. Madison St., Phoenix 85009. Tel. 602-542-6200. World Wide Web http://www.azlibrary.gov.

Arkansas

Jennifer Chilcoat, State Libn., Arkansas State Lib., 900 W. Capitol, Suite 100, Little Rock 72201. Tel. 501-682-1526, e-mail jennifer.chilcoat@ade.arkansas.gov. World Wide Web http://www.library.arkansas.gov.

California

Greg Lucas, State Libn., California State Lib., P.O. Box 942837, Sacramento 94237-0001. Tel. 916-323-9759, fax 916-323-9768, e-mail csl-adm@library.ca.gov. World Wide Web http://www.library.ca.gov.

Colorado

Nicolle Ingui Davies, Asst. Commissioner, Colorado State Lib., 201 E. Colfax Ave., Denver 80203-1799. Tel. 303-866-6733, fax 303-866-6940, e-mail davies_n@cde.state.co.us. World Wide Web http://www.cde.state.co.us/cdelib.

Connecticut

Deborah Schander, State Libn., Connecticut State Lib., 231 Capitol Ave., Hartford 06106. Tel. 860-757-6510, fax 860-757-6503, e-mail deborah.schander@ct.gov. World Wide Web http://www.ctstatelibrary.org.

Delaware

Annie Norman, Dir., Delaware Division of Libs., 121 Martin Luther King Jr. Blvd. N., Dover 19901. Tel. 302-257-3001, fax 302-739-6787, e-mail annie.norman@delaware.gov. World Wide Web http://libraries.delaware.gov.

District of Columbia

Richard Reyes-Gavilan, Exec. Dir., District of Columbia Public Lib., 1990 K St. N.W., Washington, DC 20006. Tel. 202-727-1101, fax 202-727-1129, e-mail rrg@dc.gov. World Wide Web http://www.dclibrary.org.

Florida

Amy L. Johnson, State Libn. and Div. Dir., Division of Lib. and Info. Svcs., R.A. Gray Bldg., 500 S. Bronough St., Tallahassee 32399-0250. Tel. 850-245-6600, fax 850-245-6622, e-mail info@dos.myflorida.com. World Wide Web http://dos.myflorida.com/library-archives/.

Georgia

Julie Walker, State Libn., Georgia Public Lib. Svc., 2872 Woodcock Boulevard, Suite 250, Atlanta 30341. Tel. 404-235-7200, e-mail jwalker@georgialibraries.org. World Wide Web http://www.georgialibraries.org.

Hawaii

Stacy A. Aldrich, State Libn., Hawaii State Public Lib. System, Office of the State Libn., 44 Merchant St., Honolulu 96813. Tel. 808-586-3704, fax 808-586-3715, e-mail stlib@librarieshawaii.org. World Wide Web http://www.librarieshawaii.org.

Idaho

Stephanie Bailey-White, State Libn., Idaho Commission for Libs., 325 W. State St., Boise 83702. Tel. 208-639-4145, fax 208-334-4016, e-mail stephanie.bailey-white@libraries.idaho. gov. World Wide Web http://libraries.idaho. gov.

Illinois

Greg McCormick, Dir., Illinois State Lib., 300 S. Second St., Springfield 62701-1796. Tel. 217-785-5600, fax 217-785-4326, e-mail islinfo@ilsos.net. World Wide Web http://www.cyberdriveillinois.com/departments/library/home.html.

Indiana

Jacob Speer, State Libn., Indiana State Lib., 315 W. Ohio St., Indianapolis 46202. Tel. 317-232-3675, e-mail jspeer@library.in.gov. World Wide Web http://www.in.gov/library.

Iowa

Michael Scott, State Libn., State Lib. of Iowa, 1112 E. Grand Ave., Des Moines 50319-0233. Tel. 800-248-4483, fax 515-281-6191, e-mail Michael.Scott@iowa.gov. World Wide Web http://www.statelibraryofiowa.org.

Kansas

Eric Norris, State Libn., Kansas State Lib., Capitol Bldg., 300 S.W. 10th Ave., Rm. 312-N, Topeka 66612. Tel. 785-296-5466, e-mail eric. norris@ks.gov. World Wide Web http://www. kslib.info.

Kentucky

Terry Manuel, Commissioner, Kentucky Dept. for Libs. and Archives, 300 Coffee Tree Rd., P.O. Box 537, Frankfort 40602-0537. Tel. 502-564-8303, e-mail terry.manuel@ky.gov. World Wide Web http://www.kdla.ky.gov.

Louisiana

Rebecca Hamilton, State Libn., State Lib. of Louisiana, 701 N. 4th St., P.O. Box 131, Baton Rouge 70821-0131. Tel. 225-342-4923, fax 225-219-4804, e-mail rhamilton@crt. la.gov. World Wide Web http://www.state.lib. la.us.

Maine

James Ritter, State Libn., Maine State Lib., 64 State House Sta., Augusta 04333-0064. Tel. 207-287-5600, fax 207-287-5615, e-mail james.ritter@maine.gov. World Wide Web http://www.maine.gov/msl/.

Maryland

Irene M. Padilla, State Libn., Maryland State Lib., 25 S. Calhoun St., Baltimore 21223. Tel. 667-219-4800, fax 667-219-4798, e-mail eliza beth.fletcher@maryland.gov. World Wide Web https://www.marylandlibraries.org/.

Massachusetts

James Lonergan, Dir., Massachusetts Board of Lib. Commissioners, 98 N. Washington St., Suite 401, Boston 02114-1933. Tel. 617-725-1860, ext. 222, fax 617-725-0140, e-mail james.lonergan@state.ma.us. World Wide Web http://mblc.state.ma.us.

Michigan

Randy Riley, State Libn., Lib. of Michigan, 702 W. Kalamazoo St., P.O. Box 30007, Lansing 48909-7507. Tel. 517-335-1517, e-mail rileyr1@michigan.gov. World Wide Web http://www.michigan.gov/libraryofmichigan.

Minnesota

State Libn. and Dir. of State Lib. Svcs., Minnesota State Lib. Agency, Div. of State Lib. Svcs., MN Dept. of Educ., 1500 Hwy. 36 W., Roseville 55113. Tel. 651-582-8791, fax 651-582-8752, e-mail mde.lst@state.mn.us. World Wide Web https://education.mn.gov/MDE/dse/Lib/sls/index.htm.

Mississippi

Hulen Bivins, Exec. Dir., Mississippi Lib. Commission, 3881 Eastwood Dr., Jackson 39211. Tel. 601-432-4039, e-mail hbivins@mlc.lib.ms. us. World Wide Web http://www.mlc.lib.ms.us.

Missouri

Robin Westphal, State Libn., Missouri State Lib., 600 W. Main St., P.O. Box 387, Jefferson City 65101. Tel. 573-526-4783, e-mail robin. westphal@sos.mo.gov. World Wide Web http://www.sos.mo.gov/library.

Montana

Jennie Stapp, State Libn., Montana State Lib., 1515 E. 6th Ave., P.O. Box 201800, Helena, 59620-1800. Tel. 406-444-3116, fax 406-444-0266, e-mail jstapp2@mt.gov. World Wide Web http://msl.mt.gov.

Nebraska

Rodney G. Wagner, Dir., Nebraska Lib. Commission, 1200 N St., Suite 120, Lincoln 68508-2023. Tel. 402-471-4001, fax 402-471-2083, e-mail rod.wagner@nebraska.gov. World Wide Web http://www.nlc.nebraska.gov.

Nevada

Tammy Westergard, Admin., Nevada State Lib. and Archives, 100 N. Stewart St., Carson City 89701. Tel. 775-684-3306, fax 775-684-3311, e-mail twestergard@admin.nv.gov. World Wide Web http://nsla.nv.gov/.

New Hampshire

Michael York, State Libn., New Hampshire State Lib., 20 Park St., Concord 03301. Tel. 603-271-2397, e-mail michael.york@dncr. nh.gov. World Wide Web http://www.state. nh.us/nhsl.

New Jersey

Jennifer R. Nelson, State Libn., New Jersey State Lib., an affiliate of Thomas Edison State Univ., P.O. Box 520, Trenton 08625-0520. Tel. 609-278-2640 ext. 101, fax 609-278-2652, e-mail jnelson@njstatelib.org. World Wide Web http://www.njstatelib.org.

New Mexico

Eli Guinnee, State Libn., New Mexico State Lib., 1209 Camino Carlos Rey, Santa Fe 87507-5166. Tel. 505-476-9762, e-mail Eli. Guinnee@state.nm.us. World Wide Web http://www.nmstatelibrary.org.

New York

Lauren Moore, State Libn., New York State Lib., Cultural Educ. Ctr., 222 Madison Ave., Albany 12230. Tel. 518-474-5930, fax 518-474-5786, e-mail statelibrarian@nysed.gov. World Wide Web http://www.nysl.nysed.gov/.

North Carolina

Timothy G. Owens, State Libn., State Lib. of North Carolina, Administrative Section, 4640 Mail Svc. Ctr., Raleigh 27699-4600; 109 E. Jones St., Raleigh 27601. Tel. 919-814-6784, fax 919-733-8748, e-mail timothy.owens@ncdcr.gov. World Wide Web http://statelibrary.ncdcr.gov.

North Dakota

Mary J. Soucie, State Libn., North Dakota State Lib., 604 E. Boulevard Ave., Dept. 250, Bismarck 58505-0800. Tel. 701-328-4654, fax 701-328-2040, e-mail msoucie@nd.gov. World Wide Web http://ndsl.lib.state.nd.us/.

Ohio

Wendy Knapp, State Libn., 274 E. First Ave., Suite 100, Columbus 43201. Tel. 616-644-6843, e-mail jward@library.ohio.gov.. World Wide Web http://www.library.ohio.gov/.

Oklahoma

Melody Kellogg, Dir., Oklahoma Dept. of Libs., 200 N.E. 18th St., Oklahoma City 73105-3298. Tel. 405-521-2502, fax 405-525-7804, World Wide Web http://www.odl.state. ok.us.

Oregon

Jennifer Patterson, State Libn., State Lib. of Oregon, 250 Winter St., N.E., Salem 97301. Tel. 503-378-4367, fax 503-585-8059, e-mail jennifer.l.patterson@slo.oregon.gov. World Wide Web https://www.oregon.gov/Library.

Pennsylvania

Glenn Miller, Deputy Secy. of Educ., Commissioner of Libs., and State Libn., State Lib. of Pennsylvania, Commonwealth Keystone Bldg., Plaza Lib. (Museum Plaza Wing), 400 North St., Harrisburg, PA 17120-0211. Tel. 717-787-2646, fax 717-772-3265, e-mail ra-edocldepty secty@pa.gov. World Wide Web http://www. statelibrary.pa.gov.

Rhode Island

Karen Mellor, Chief of Lib. Services, Rhode Island Office of Lib. and Info. Svcs., One Capitol Hill, Providence 02908. Tel. 401-574-9304, fax 401-574-9320, e-mail karen.Mellor@olis. ri.gov. World Wide Web http://www.olis.ri.gov.

South Carolina

Leesa M. Aiken, Dir., South Carolina State Lib., 1500 Senate St., Columbia 29201. Tel. 803-734-8668, fax 803-734-8676, e-mail laiken@statelibrary.sc.gov. World Wide Web http://www.statelibrary.sc.gov.

South Dakota

Daria Bossman, State Libn., South Dakota State Lib., MacKay Bldg., 800 Governors Dr., Pierre 57501. Tel. 605-773-3131, option 6, fax 605-773-6962, e-mail daria.bossman@state. sd.us. World Wide Web http://library.sd.gov/.

Tennessee

Charles A. Sherrill, State Libn. and Archivist, Tennessee State Lib. and Archives, 403 7th Ave. N., Nashville 37243. Tel. 615-741-7996, fax 615-532-9293, e-mail chuck.sherrill@tn.gov. World Wide Web http://www.tennessee.gov/tsla/.

Texas

Mark Smith, Dir. and Libn., Texas State Lib. and Archives Commission, 1201 Brazos St., Austin 78701; P.O. Box 12927, Austin 78711-2927. Tel. 512-463-6856, fax 512-463-5436, e-mail msmith@tsl.state.tx.us. World Wide Web http://www.tsl.state.tx.us.

Utah

Colleen Eggett, State Libn., Utah State Lib. Div., 250 N. 1950 W., Suite A, Salt Lake City 84116-7901. Tel. 801-715-6770, fax 801-715-6767, e-mail ceggett@utah.gov. World Wide Web http://library.utah.gov/.

Vermont

Jason Broughton, State Libn., Vermont State Lib., 60 Washington St., Suite 2, Barre, VT 05641. Tel. 802-636-0040, e-mail jason. broughton@vermont.gov. World Wide Web https://libraries.vermont.gov/state_library.

Virginia

Sandra Gioia Treadway, Libn. of Virginia, Lib. of Virginia, 800 E. Broad St., Richmond 23219-8000. Tel. 804-692-3535, fax 804-692-3556, e-mail sandra.treadway@lva.virginia. gov. World Wide Web http://www.lva.virginia. gov/.

Washington

Sara Jones, State Libn., Washington State Lib., Office of the Secretary of State, Point Plaza E., 6880 Capitol Blvd., Tumwater 98501; P.O. Box 42460, Olympia 98504-2460. Tel. 360-704-5276, e-mail sara.jones@sos.wa.gov. World Wide Web http://www.sos.wa.gov/library.

West Virginia

Karen Goff, Dir./State Libn., West Virginia Lib. Commission Cultural Ctr., Bldg. 9, 1900 Kanawha Blvd. E., Charleston 25305. Tel. 304-558-2041 ext. 2084, fax 304-558-2044, e-mail karen.e.goff@wv.gov. World Wide Web http:// www.librarycommission.wv.gov/.

Wisconsin

Kurt Kiefer, Asst. State Superintendent, Div. for Libs. and Tech., Wisconsin Dept. of Public Instruction, 125 S. Webster St., Madison 53703; P.O. Box 7841, Madison 53707-7841. Tel. 608-266-2205, fax 608-267-9207, e-mail Kurt.Kiefer@dpi.wi.gov. World Wide Web http://dpi.wi.gov.

Wyoming

Jamie Markus, State Libn., Wyoming State Lib., 2800 Central Ave., Cheyenne 82002. Tel. 307-777-5914, e-mail jamie.markus@wyo. gov. World Wide Web http://library.wyo.gov/.

American Samoa

Justin H. Maga, Territorial Libn., Feleti Barstow Public Lib., Box 997687, Pago Pago 96799. Tel. 684-633-5816, fax 684-633-5823, e-mail justinmaga@gmail.com. World Wide Web https://www.feletibarstow.org/.

Federated States of Micronesia

Augustine Kohler, Ntl. Historic Preservation Officer, Office of National Archives, Culture, and Historic Preservations, PS175, Palikir, Pohnpei State 96941. Tel. 691-320-2343, fax 691-320-5632, e-mail hpo@mail.fm. World Wide Web http://www.fsmgov.org.

Guam

Sandra Stanley, Admin. Officer, Guam Public Lib. System, 254 Martyr St., Hagatna 96910-5141. Tel. 671-475-4765, fax 671-477-9777, e-mail sandra.stanley@guampls.guam.gov. World Wide Web http://gpls.guam.gov/.

Northern Mariana Islands

Erlinda Naputi, Lib. Dir., CNMI Joeten-Kiyu Public Lib., P.O. Box 501092, Saipan 96950. Tel. 670-235-7322, fax 670-235-7550, e-mail ecnaputi@gmail.com. World Wide Web http://cnmilib.org.

Palau

Sinton Soalablai, Chief, Div. of School Mgt., Palau Ministry of Educ., P.O. Box 7080, Koror 96940. Tel. 680-488-2570, fax 680-488-2380, e-mail ssoalablai@palaumoe.net. World Wide Web https://www.palaugov.pw/executive-branch/ministries/education.

Puerto Rico

Mary Jean Haver, Acting Dir., Lib. and Info. Svcs. Program, Puerto Rico Dept. of Educ., P.O. Box 190759, San Juan 00919-0759. Tel. 787 773 3570, fax 787-753-6945, e-mail haver bmj@de.pr.gov. Website not available.

Republic of the Marshall Islands

Melvin Majmeto, Exec. Dir., Alele Museum, Lib. and National Archives, P.O. Box 629, Majuro 96960. Tel. 011-692-625-3372, fax 011-692-625-3226, World Wide Web https://www.alele.org.

U.S. Virgin Islands

Arlene Pinney-Benjamin, Acting Dir., The Division of Libraries, Archives and Museums, c/o Florence Augusta Williams Public Lib., 1122 King St. Christiansted, St. Croix 00820. Tel. 340-773-5715, fax 340-773-5327, e-mail arlene.benjamin@dpnr.vi.gov. World Wide Web http://www.virginislandspubliclibraries.org/usvi/.

Canada

Alberta

Diana Davidson, Dir., Alberta Public Lib. Svcs., Municipal Affairs, 8th fl., 10405 Jasper Ave., Edmonton T5J 4R7. Tel. 780-415-0284, fax 780-415-8594, e-mail diana.davidson@gov.ab.ca or libraries@gov.ab.ca. World Wide Web http://www.municipalaffairs.alberta.ca/alberta_libraries.cfm.

British Columbia

Mari Martin, Dir., Libs. Branch, Ministry of Educ., P.O. Box 9831, Stn. Prov. Govt., Victoria V8W 9T1. Tel. 250-886-2584, fax 250-953-4985, e-mail Mari.Martin@gov.bc.ca. World Wide Web https://www2.gov.bc.ca/gov/content/governments/organizational-structure/ministries-organizations/ministries/education.

Manitoba

Trevor Surgenor, Dir., Public Lib. Services Branch, Manitoba Culture, Sport and Heritage Dept., B10 - 340 9th St., Brandon R7A 6C2. Tel. 204-726-6590, fax 204-726-6868, e-mail trevor.surgenor@gov.mb.ca. World Wide Web http://www.gov.mb.ca/chc/pls/index.html.

New Brunswick

Ella Nason, Acting Exec. Dir., New Brunswick Public Libs., Provincial Office, 570 Two Nations Crossing, Suite 2, Fredericton E3A 0X9. Tel. 506-453-2354, fax 506-444-4064, e-mail ella.nason@gnb.ca. World Wide Web http://www2.gnb.ca/content/gnb/en/departments/nbpl.html.

Newfoundland and Labrador

Andrew Hunt, Exec. Dir., Provincial Info. and Lib. Resources Board, 48 St. George's Ave., Stephenville A2N 1K9. Tel. 709-643-0900, fax 709-643-0925, e-mail ahunt@nlpl.ca. World Wide Web http://www.nlpl.ca.

Northwest Territories

Brian Dawson, Territorial Libn., Northwest Territories Public Lib. Services, 75 Woodland Dr., Hay River X0E 1G1. Tel. 867-874-6531, fax 867-874-3321, e-mail brian_dawson@gov.nt.ca. World Wide Web http://www.nwtpls.gov.nt.ca.

Nova Scotia

Lynn Somers, Dir., Provincial Lib., Nova Scotia Provincial Lib., 6016 University Ave., 5th fl., Halifax B3H 1W4. Tel. 902-424-2457, fax 902-424-0633, e-mail nspl@novascotia.ca. World Wide Web https://library.novascotia.ca.

Nunavut

Ron Knowling, Mgr., Nunavut Public Lib. Svcs., P.O. Box 270, Baker Lake X0C 0A0. Tel. 867-793-3353, fax 867-793-3360, e-mail rknowling@gov.nu.ca. World Wide Web http://www.publiclibraries.nu.ca.

Ontario

Sarah Cossette, Manager, Ontario Heritage, Tourism, and Culture Division, Programs and Services Branch, 401 Bay St., Suite 1700, Toronto M7A 0A7. Tel. 416-314-7144, fax 416-212-1802, e-mail sarah.cossette@ontario.ca. World Wide Web http://www.mtc.gov.on.ca/en/libraries/contact.shtml.

Prince Edward Island

Kathleen Simmonds, Dir., Libs. and Archives, Education and Lifelong Learning, Sullivan Bldg., 16 Fitzroy St., 1st flr., Charlottetown, PE CIA 7N8. Tel. 902 314-5523, fax 902-894-0342, e-mail kesimmonds@gov.pe.ca. World Wide Web http://www.library.pe.ca.

Quebec

Jean-Louis Roy, Chairman and CEO, Bibliothèque et Archives Nationales du Québec (BAnQ), 2275 rue Holt, Montreal H2G 3H1. Tel. 800-363-9028 or 514-873-1100, e-mail pdg@banq.qc.ca. World Wide Web http://www.banq.qc.ca/portal/dt/accueil.jsp.

Saskatchewan

Alison Hopkins, Provincial Libn./Exec. Dir., Provincial Lib. and Exec. Dir., Ministry of Educ., 409A Park St., Regina S4N 5B2. Tel. 306-787-2972, fax 306-787-2029, e-mail alison.hopkins@gov.sk.ca. World Wide Web http://www.education.gov.sk.ca/provincial-library/public-library-system.

Yukon Territory

Melissa Yu Schott, Dir., Public Libs., Community Development Div., Dept. of Community Svcs., Government of Yukon, P.O. Box 2703, Whitehorse Y1A 2C6. Tel. 867-335-8600, e-mail Melissa.YuSchott@gov.yk.ca. World Wide Web https://yukon.ca.

State School Library Associations

Alabama

Youth Services and School Libns. Div., Alabama Lib. Assn. (ALLA). Memb. 600+.

Chair Caitlin Rogers, The Altamont School. E-mail crogers@altamontschool.org; *Chair-Elect* Cristina Castor, Homewood Public Lib. E-mail cristina.castor@homewoodpubliclibrary. org.

Address correspondence to the Youth Services and School Libns. Div., ALLA, 6030 Monticello Dr., Montgomery 36117. Tel. 334-414-0113, e-mail allaadmin@allanet.org.

World Wide Web https://www.allanet.org/youth-services-and-school-library-division-yssld-.

Alaska

Alaska Assn. of School Libns. (AkASL). Memb. 100+. Publication. *The Puffin* continuing basis online at http://akasl.org/puffin-news. Submissions e-mail akasl.puffin@gmail. com.

Pres. Katie Conover Clark. E-mail akasl. presidentelect@gmail.com; *Secy.* Jessica Tonnies. E-mail akasl.secretary@gmail.com; *Treas.* Janet Madsen. E-mail janet.madsen@ alaska.gov; *Past Pres.* Pam Verfaillie (Valdez).

Address correspondence to AkASL, P.O. Box 101085, Anchorage, 99510-1085, e-mail akasl.webmaster@gmail.com.

World Wide Web http://www.akasl.org.

Arizona

Teacher-Libn. Div., Arizona Lib. Assn. (AZLA). Memb. 1,000. Term of Office. Jan.–Dec.

Co-Chair Jean Kilker, Maryvale High School, 3415 N. 59th Ave., Phoenix 85033. Tel. 602-764-2134, e-mail jkilker@phoenixunion. org; *Co-Chair* Judi Moreillon, Tel. 520-603-4868, e-mail info@storytrail.com.

Address correspondence to the chairpersons, AZLA, c/o Arizona Lib. Assn., 2532 N 4th St #271, Flagstaff 86004. Tel. 928.288.2011, e-mail admin@azla.org.

World Wide Web https://www.azla.org/page/ TLD.

Arkansas

Arkansas Assn. of School Libns. (ARASL), div. of Arkansas Lib. Assn.

Chair Rachel Shankles, 891 Hwy. 7, Bismarck 71929. Tel. 501-276-4949, e-mail arasl. chair@gmail.com; *Past Chair* Daniel Fouts II, Osceola High School, 2800 W. Semmes Ave., Osceola 72370. Tel. 870-563-1863, e-mail dfouts@glaucus.org.

Address correspondence to the chairperson via e-mail.

World Wide Web https://arasl.weebly.com.

California

California School Lib. Assn. (CSLA). Memb. 1,200+. Publications. *CSLA Journal* (2x yearly). *Ed.* Mary Ann Harlan, San José State Univ. E-mail maryann.harlan@sjsu.edu; *CSLA Newsletter* (10x yearly, memb., via e-mail).

(State Board)

Pres. Lisa Bishop, Aptos Middle School, 105 Aptos Ave., San Francisco 94127; *Secy.* Terri Brown, Fort Miller Middle, Fresno Unified School Dist., 2847 Beverly Ave., Clovis 93611. E-mail tbrown411@gmail.com; *Pres.-Elect* Nina Jackson, Franklin Classical Middle School, 540 Cerritos Ave., Long Beach 90802. E-mail njcatsandbooks@gmail.com; *Treas.* Lori Stevens, Rialto Unified School Dist. E-mail lstevens2@rialtousd.org; *Past Pres.* Katie McNamara, Kern High School Dist., Fresno Pacific Univ. E-mail Katie_McNamara@ kernhigh.org.

Address correspondence to CSLA, 6444 E. Spring St., No. 237, Long Beach 90815-1553. Tel./fax 888-655-8480, e-mail info@csla.net.

World Wide Web http://www.csla.net.

Colorado

Colorado Assn. of Libs. School Library Interest Group. Memb. 18+.

Chair Terri Brungardt, Widefield School Dist. 3. E-mail brungardtt@wsd3.org.

Address correspondence to Colorado Assn. of Libs., P.O. Box 740905, Arvada 80006-0905. Tel. 303-463-6400.

World Wide Web https://cal-webs.org/ School_Libraries_Interest_Group.

Connecticut

Connecticut Assn. of School Libns. (CASL). Memb. 500+. Term of Office. July–June.

Pres. Barbara Johnson. E-mail President@ ctcasl.org; *V.P.* Melissa Thom. E-mail Vice president@ctcasl.org; *Recording Secy.* Jenny Lussier. E-mail Secretary@ctcasl.org; *Treas.* Laura Hedenberg. E-mail treasurer@ctcasl.org.

Address correspondence to the president. CASL, 4 Wotton Lane, Burlington 06013.

World Wide Web https://casl.wildapricot.org.

Delaware

Delaware Assn. of School Libns. (DASL), div. of Delaware Lib. Assn. Memb. 100+. Publications. *DASL Newsletter* (online; irreg.); column in *DLA Bulletin* (2x yearly).

Pres. Katelynn Scott, Alfred G. Waters Middle School, 1235 Cedar Lane Rd., Middletown 19709. Tel. 302-449-3490 ext. 2134, e-mail katelynn.scott@appo.k12.de.us; *V.P./Pres.-Elect* Patty Brown, Everett Meredith Middle School, 504 S. Broad St., Middletown 19709. Tel. 302-378-5001, e-mail patricia.brown@ appo.k12.de.us; *Secy.* Patty Crilley, Old State Elementary School, 580 Tony Marchio Dr., Townsend 19734. Tel. 302-378-6720, e-mail Patricia.Crilley@appo.k12.dc.us; *Treas.* Jaclyn Hale, Dover Public Lib., 35 Loockerman Plz., Dover 19901. Tel. 302-736-7185, e-mail jaclyn haledla@gmail.com; *Past Pres.* Kim Read, St. George's Technical High School, 555 Hyatt's Corner Rd., Middletown 19709, Tel. 302-449-3360, e-mail kim.read@nccvt.k12.dc.us.

Address correspondence to the president, DASL, c/o Delaware Lib. Assn., Delaware Division of Libs., 121 Martin Luther King, Jr. Blvd. N., Dover 19901.

World Wide Web http://dla.lib.de.us/divisions/dasl/.

District of Columbia

District of Columbia Assn. of School Libns. (DCASL). Memb. 8. Publication. *Newsletter* (4x yearly).

Dir. Jill Schechter; *Assistant Dir.* Angela Falkenberg.

Address correspondence to DCASL, Union Station, 50 Massachusetts Ave. NE, P.O. Box 1653 Washington, DC 20002. Tel. 301-502-4203, e-mail contactdcasl@gmail.com.

World Wide Web https://dcla.org/School-Library-Section.

Florida

Florida Assn. for Media in Educ. (FAME). Memb. 1,400+. Term of Office. Nov.–Oct. Publication. *Florida Media Quarterly* (q.; memb.). *Ed.* Okle Miller. E-mail oklc.miller@gmail.com.

Pres. Ashlee Cornett. E-mail noblebeach@ gmail.com; *Pres.-Elect* Kristen Badger. E-mail Kristen.Badger@stjohns.k12.fl.us; *Secy.* Kathleen Daniels; *Treas.* Amelia Zukoski. E-mail Amelia.Zukoski@stjohns.k12.fl.us; *Past Pres.* Lorraine Stinson. E-mail Lorraine.Stinson@ stjohns.k12.fl.us.

Address correspondence to FAME, P.O. Box 941169, Maitland 32794-1169. Tel. 863-585-6802, e-mail FAME@floridamediaed.org.

World Wide Web http://www.floridamediaed.org.

Georgia

Georgia Lib. Media Assn. (GLMA). Memb. 700+.

Pres. Martha Bongiorno. E-mail president@ glma-inc.org; *Pres.-Elect* Amanda Lee; *Secy.* Sarah Sansbury; *Treas.* Lora Taft. E-mail treasurer@glma-inc.org; *Past Pres.* Holly Frilot.

Address correspondence to GLMA, P.O. Box 148, Waverly Hall 31831. E-mail info@ glma-inc.org.

World Wide Web http://www.glma-inc.org.

Hawaii

Hawaii Assn. of School Libns. Memb. (HASL). 145. Term of Office. June–May.

Co-Pres. Maricar Kawasaki *Co-Pres.* Danielle Fujii; *V.P. Programming* Caitlin Ramirez, Mokapu Elementary; *V.P. Membership* Laurel Oshiro, Sacred Hearts Academy; *Recording Secy.* Miko Sanico; *Treas.* Donna Takara.

Address correspondence to HASL, P.O. Box 29691 Honolulu 96820. E-mail hasl.contactus@ gmail.com.

World Wide Web https://haslhawaii.weebly.com.

Idaho

School Libs. Services and Consulting, Idaho Commission for Libs. (ICfL).

School Library Action Planning Committee: School Lib. Consultant Jeannie Standal. Tel. 208-639-4139, e-mail jeannie.standal@libraries. idaho.gov; Kit Anderson, Teton High School, Teton School Dist.; Sherrilynn Bair, Snake River School Community Lib.; Dennis Hahs, Rocky Mountain High School, Joint School Dist #2; Lynn Johnson, Mountain View School Dist.; Kiersten Kerr, Coeur d'Alene School Dist.; Susan Tabor-Boesch, Wood River Middle School.

Address correspondence to Jeannie Standal, Idaho Commission for Libs., 325 W. State St., Boise 83702. Tel. 208-334-2150, fax 208-334-4016, e-mail jeannie.standal@libraries.idaho.gov.

World Wide Web https://libraries.idaho.gov/school-libraries/.

Illinois

Assn. of Illinois School Lib. Educators (AISLE). Memb. 1,000. Term of Office. July–June. Publications. Newsletter (4x yearly). *Ed.* David P. Little. E-mail newsletter@aisled.org.

Pres. Christy Semande, Canton USD #66, Canton. E-mail president@aisled.org; *Pres.-Elect* Mary Jo Matousek. E-mail preselect@aisled.org; *Secy.* Joanna Marek, La Grange School Dist. 105. E-mail secretary@aisled.org; *Treas.* Michelle Glatt. E-mail; treasurer@aisled.org; *Past Pres.* Anna Kim, Chappell Elementary, Chicago. E-mail pastpres@aisled.org; *Exec. Secy.* Carolyn Kinsella. E-mail execsecretary@aisled.org.

Address correspondence to Assn. of Illinois School Lib. Educators. P.O. Box 110, Seneca 61360. Tel./fax 815-357-6023, e-mail execsecretary@aisled.org.

World Wide Web https://www.aisled.org.

Indiana

Assn. of Indiana School Lib. Educators (AISLE), affiliation of the Indiana Lib. Federation.

Advisory Board Michelle Houser, Bellmont Senior High School; Stacey Kern, Clark-Pleasant Middle School. Tel. 317-535-2025 ext. 6874; Ben Moore, Summit Middle School; Leslie Preddy, Perry Meridian Middle School; Diane Rogers, Ben Davis 9th Grade Ctr. Tel. 317-988-7577; Justin Stenger, Shelbyville Central Schools; Emily Wilt, Chesterton High School; April Zehr, Concord High School; *Exec. Dir. ILF* Lucinda Nord, 941 East 86th

St., Suite 260, Indianapolis 46240. Tel. 317-257-2040, ext. 101, e-mail exec@ilfonline.org.

Address correspondence to AISLE, c/o Indiana Lib. Federation, 941 E. 86 St., Suite 260, Indianapolis 46240. Tel. 317-257-2040, e-mail askus@ilfonline.org.

World Wide Web https://www.ilfonline.org/page/AISLE.

Iowa

Iowa Assn. of School Libns. (IASL), div. of the Iowa Lib. Assn. Memb. 180+. Term of Office. Jan.–Jan.

Pres. Jenahlee Chamberlain, Iowa City. E-mail iaslwebpage@gmail.com; *V.P./Pres.-Elect* Michelle Kruse, Cedar Rapids. E-mail michelle.kruse.2011@gmail.com; *Secy./Treas.* Jen Keltner. E-mail kaseyjenkeltner@gmail.com; *Membs.-at-Large* Diana Geers, Miranda Kral, Carrie Teske.

Address correspondence to the president, IASL, c/o the Iowa Lib. Assn., 6919 Vista Dr., W. Des Moines 50266. Tel. 515-282-8192.

World Wide Web http://www.iasl-ia.org.

Kansas

Kansas Assn. of School Libns. (KASL). Memb. 600.

Pres. Tonya Foster. E-mail tonya_foster@cox.net; *1st V.P.* Julie Doyen. E-mail juliedo@usd383.org; *2nd V.P.* Gail Becker E-mail gbecker@usd259.net; *Secy.* Rachel Hodges. E-mail hodgesrac@gmail.com; *Treas.* Amanda Harrison. E-mail amanda.harrison@mcpherson.com; *Past Pres.* Martha House. E-mail mhouse@cgrove417.org.

Address correspondence to the president, KASL, c/o Kansas Lib. Assn., 2 Washington Sq., Norton 67654.

World Wide Web http://www.ksschool-librarians.org.

Kentucky

Kentucky Assn. of School Libns. (KASL), section of Kentucky Lib. Assn. Memb. 600+. Publication. *KASL Blog.* (blog) http://www.kaslblog.com/.

Pres. Sam Northern. E-mail samuel.northern@simpson.kyschools.us; *Pres.-Elect* Deidra Bowling-Meade. E-mail deidra.bowlingmeade@ashland.kyschools.us; *Secy.* Jen Gilbert. E-mail jennifer.gilbert@eminence.kyschools.us; *Treas.* Fred Tilsley. E-mail ftilsley@windstream.net; *PastPres.*EmilyNorthcutt.E-mailemilynorthcutt@ shelby.kyschools.us.

Address correspondence to the president.

World Wide Web http://www.kasl.us.

Louisiana

Louisiana Assn. of School Libns. (LASL), section of the Louisiana Lib. Assn. Memb. 230. Term of Office. July–June.

Pres. Kimberly Adkins. E-mail kwadkins@ caddoschools.org; *1st V.P.* Amanda Blanco. E-mail arblanco@lpssonline.com; *2nd V.P.* Kim "Lovie" Howell. Email kim.howell@ bossierschools.or; *Secy.* Stephanie Wilkes. E-mail stephaniecwilkes@gmail.com.

Address correspondence to LASL, c/o Louisiana Lib. Assn., 1190 Meramec Station Rd., Suite 207, Ballwin, MO 63021. Tel. 1-800-969-6562 ext. 3, e-mail lla@amigos.org.

World Wide Web http://laslonline.weebly.com.

Maine

Maine Assn. of School Libs. (MASL). Memb. 200+.

Pres. Jennifer Stanbro, Skillin Elementary, South Portland; *Pres.-Elect* Heather Perkinson, Greely High School; *Secy.* Cathy Potter, Falmouth Middle School, Falmouth; *Treas.* Amy Denecker–Windham High School; *Past Pres.* Amanda Kozaka, Cape Elizabeth Middle School. E-mail akozaka@capeelizabeth schools.org.

Address correspondence to the president, MASL, c/o Maine State Lib. Assn., 64 State House Station, Augusta 04333-0064. E-mail maslibraries@gmail.com.

World Wide Web http://www.maslibraries.org.

Maryland

Maryland Assn. of School Libns (MASL). Publication. Newsletter (mo.; online).

Pres. Jen Sturge, Calvert County Public Schools. E-mail president@maslmd.org; *Pres.-Elect* Lindsey Weaver, Middletown Middle School, Frederick County Public Schools. E-mail presidentelect@maslmd.org; *Secy.* Donna Mignardi, Calvert High School, Calvert County Public Schools. E-mail secretary@maslmd.org;

Treas. Brittany Tignor, Snow Hill High School, Worcester County Public Schools. E-mail treas urer@maslmd.org; *Membs.-at-Large* Annie Cumberland, Mary Brooke Fitzpatrick, Jacob Gerding; *Delegate* Tatanisha Love, Loch Raven Technical Academy. E-mail delegate@maslmd.org; *MSDE Rep.* Laura Hicks. E-mail msde@ maslmd.org; *Past Pres.* April Wathen, G. W. Carver Elementary, St. Mary's County Public Schools. E-mail president@maslmd.org.

Address correspondence to the secretary via e-mail to secretary@maslmd.org.

World Wide Web http://maslmd.org.

Massachusetts

Massachusetts School Lib. Assn. (MSLA). Memb. 800. Publication. *MSLA Forum* (irreg.; online). *Eds.* Katherine Steiger, Reba Tierney.

Pres. Laura Luker, Pioneer Valley Chinese Immersion Charter, Hadley. E-mail lluker@ maschoolibraries.org; *Pres.-Elect* Jennifer Varney, MLKing, Jr. School, Cambridge. E-mail jvarney@maschoolibraries.org; *Secy.* Jennifer Dimmick, Newton South High School. E-mail jdimmick@maschoolibraries.org; *Treas.* Michelle Fontaine, Fenn School, Concord. E-mail mfontaine@maschoolibraries.org.

Address correspondence to Emily Kristofek, office manager, P.O. Box 336. Wayland, MA 01778. Tel. 508-276-1697, e-mail ekristofek@ maschoolibraries.org.

World Wide Web http://www.maschoolibraries.org.

Michigan

Michigan Assn. for Media in Educ. (MAME). Memb. 1,200. Publication. *Media Matters!* newsletter (mo.). *Eds.* Beverly Banks. E-mail beverlybanks@wlcsd.org and Jonathan Richards. E-mail jrichards@vanburenschools.net.

Pres. Shannon Torres, Northville Public Schools, 45700 W. Six Mile Rd., Northville 48167. E-mail torressh@mimame.org; *Pres.-Elect* Erica Trowbridge, Oakridge Public Schools, Muskegon. E-mail etrowbridge@ mimame.org; *Secy.* Kelly Hinks. E-mail khincks@mimame.org; *Treas.* Lisa Kelley, Rochester Community Schools, University Hills, 600 Croydon, Rochester Hills 48309. Tel. 248-726-4404, e-mail lkelley@mimame.org; *Past Pres.* Cat Kerns, Saginaw Township Community Schools, 3460 N. Center Rd., Saginaw

48603. Tel. 989-799-5790 ext. 8080, e-mail ckerns@mimame.org; *Exec. Secy.* Teri Belcher. E-mail tbelcher@mimame.org.

Address correspondence to MAME, 1407 Rensen, Suite 3, Lansing 48910. Tel. 517-394-2808, fax 517-492-3878, e-mail mame@mimame.org.

World Wide Web http://www.mimame.org.

Minnesota

Info. and Technology Educators of Minnesota (ITEM) (formerly Minnesota Educ. Media Organization). Memb. 400+. Term of Office. July–June.

Co-Pres. Ashley Krohn, Minneapolis Public Schools; *Co-Pres.* Dana Woods, Bemidji Public Schools; *Pres.-Elect* Marie Hydukovich, South Saint Paul Public Schools; *Secy.* Sarah Rose, Minneapolis Public Schools; *Treas.* Jenifer Shier, Saint Paul Public Schools; *Past Co-Pres.* Sara Florin, Centennial Public Schools; *Past Co-Pres.* Kim Haugo, Osseo Public Schools.

Address correspondence to ITEM, P.O. Box 130555, Roseville 55113. Tel. 651-771-8672, e-mail admin@mnitem.org.

World Wide Web http://mnitem.org.

Mississippi

School Lib. Section, Mississippi Lib. Assn. (MLA). Memb. 1,300.

School Lib. Section Chair Angela Mullins, Simpson Central School/Simpson County School Dist. Tel. 601-847-2630, e-mail angelamullins39073@gmail.com.

Address correspondence to School Lib. Section, MLA, P.O. Box 13687, Jackson 39236-3687. Tel. 601-981-4586, e-mail info@misslib.org.

World Wide Web http://www.misslib.org/page-1860236.

Missouri

Missouri Assn. of School Libns. (MASL). Memb. 1,000. Term of Office. July–June.

Pres. Kirsten Shaw, Martin Warren Elementary School, Warrensburg School Dist. E-mail kshaw@warrensburgr6.org; *1st V.P.* Kris Baughman, Eastwood Hills Elementary School, Raytown C-2 School Dist. E-mail kris.baughman@raytownschools.org; *2nd V.P.* Melissa Corey, Robidoux Middle School, St. Joseph School Dist. E-mail melissa.corey@

sjsd.k12.mo.us; *Secy.* Jill Williams, McDonald County High School, McDonald County R-1 School Dist. E-mail jwilliams@mcdonaldco.k12.mo.us; *Treas.* Becky Haynes, Cassville Middle School, Cassville R-IV School Dist. E-mail beckbeckhaynes@gmail.com; *AASL Delegate* Matt King, Discovery Elementary, Orchard Farm School Dist. E-mail mking@ofr5.com; *Past Pres.* Amy Hertzberg, Nevada Middle School, Nevada R-V School Dist. E-mail ahertzberg@nevada.k12.mo.us.

Address correspondence to MASL, P.O. Box 2107, Jefferson City 65102. Tel. 573-893-4155, fax 573-635-2858, e-mail info@maslonline.org.

World Wide Web http://www.maslonline.org.

Montana

School Lib. Div., Montana Lib. Assn. (MLA). Memb. 200+.

Co-Chair Brittany Alberson, Bozeman High School Lib., 205 N. 11th Ave, Bozeman; *Co-Chair* Vic Mortimer, Corvallis Middle School Lib.; *MLA Exec. Dir.* Debbi Kramer, 5176 N. Valle Dorado, Kingman, AZ 86409. Tel. 406-579-3121, e-mail debkmla@hotmail.com.

Address correspondence to the MLA executive director.

World Wide Web http://www.mtlib.org/governance/sld.

Nebraska

Nebraska School Libns. Assn. (NSLA). Memb. 300+. Term of Office. July–June. Publication. *NSLA News* (blog; mo.).

Pres. Angela Blankenship. E-mail NSLApres@gmail.com; *Pres.-Elect* Crys Bauermeister. E-mail cbauermeister@gmail.com; *Secy.* Kelly Kenny. E-mail kenny.kelly@westside66.net; *Treas.* Beth Eilers. E-mail beth.eilers@ops.org; *Past Pres.* Cynthia Stogdill. E-mail cynstogdill@gmail.com; *Exec. Secy.* Mandy Peterson. E-mail contactnsla@gmail.com.

Address correspondence to the executive secretary via e-mail.

World Wide Web http://www.neschoollibrarians.org.

Nevada

Nevada School and Children Libns. Section (NSCLS) of the Nevada Lib. Assn. (NLA). Memb. 120.

Chair Susan Thurnbeck, Las Vegas–Clark County Lib. Dist. E-mail susantnvlibrary@gmail.com; *Past Chair* Larry Johnson, Las Vegas–Clark County Lib. Dist.; *Exec. Secy. NLA* Carla Land, Las Vegas–Clark County Lib. District. E-mail bookdiva@gmail.com.

Address correspondence to the chair, NLA School and Children Libns. Section, via e-mail.

World Wide Web http://nevadalibraries.org/ Handbook-NSCLS.

New Hampshire

New Hampshire School Lib. Media Assn. (NSHLMA). Memb. 250+. Term of Office. July–June. Publication. *NHSLMA Newsletter* (irreg.; online).

Pres. Karen Abraham, Laconia High School. E-mail president@nhslma.org; *V.P.* Justine Thain, Hooksett School Dist., Hooksett. E-mail vice-president@nhslma.org; *Secy.* Kristin Whitworth, Dover High School. E-mail secretary@nhslma.org; *Treas.* Audra Lewis, Home Street School, Dover. E-mail treasurer@nhslma.org; *Past Pres.* Caitlin Bennett, Londonderry Middle School, Londonderry. E-mail past-president@nhslma.org.

Address correspondence to the president, NHSLMA, P.O. Box 418, Concord 03302-0418. E-mail nhslma@gmail.com.

World Wide Web http://nhslma.org.

New Jersey

New Jersey Assn. of School Libns. (NJASL). Memb. 1,000+. Term of Office. Aug. 1–July 31. Publication. *Bookmark Newsletter* (mo.; memb.). *Ed.* Casey Schaffer. E-mail bookmark@njasl.org.

Pres. Beth Thomas. E-mail president@njasl.org; *Pres.-Elect.* Amy Gazaleh. E-mail presidentelect@njasl.org; *V.P.* Ewa Dziedzic-Elliott. E-mail vp@njasl.org; *Recording Secy.* Casey Jane Schaffer. E-mail secretary@njasl.org; *Treas.* Elizabeth (Beth) Willoughby. E-mail treasurer@njasl.org; *Membs.-at-Large* Beth Raff, Steve Tetreault. E-mail membersatlarge@njasl.org; *Past Pres.* Jill Mills. E-mail pastpresident@njasl.org;

Address correspondence to the recording secretary, NASL, P.O. Box 1460, Springfield 07081.

World Wide Web http://www.njasl.org.

New York

Section of School Libns., New York Lib. Assn. (NYLA). Memb. 800+. Term of Office. Nov.–Oct. Publication. *School Library Update* (3x yearly; memb.; online).

Pres. Dawn Pressimone. E-mail dpressimone@waynecsd.org; *Pres.-Elect* Lisa Perkowski; *Secy.* Jessica Regitano. E-mail jlregitano@gmail.com; *Treas.* Anne Paulson. E-mail anneppaulson@gmail.com; *V.P. of Conferences* Annarose Foley; *V.P. of Communications* Heather Turner. E-mail hturner@fabiuspompey.org; *Past Pres.* Tara Thibault-Edmonds. E-mail tthibault-edmonds@rondout.k12.ny.us.

Address correspondence to the Section of School Libns., NYLA, 6021 State Farm Rd., Guilderland 12084. Tel. 518-432-6952, fax 518-427-1697, e-mail info@nyla.org.

World Wide Web https://www.nyla.org/4DCGI/cms/review.html?Action=CMS_Document&DocID=136&MenuKey=ssl.

North Carolina

North Carolina School Lib. Media Assn. (NCSLMA). Memb. 1,000+. Term of Office. Nov.–Oct.

Pres. Cindy Sturdivant. E-mail cindysturdivant@ncslma.org; *Pres.-Elect* Jenny Umbarger. E-mail jennyumbarger@ncslma.org; *Secy.* Jen Baker. E-mail jenbaker@ncslma.org; *Treas.* Jennifer Abel, North Henderson High School, 35 Fruitland Rd., Hendersonville 28792. Tel. 828-697-4500, e-mail jenniferabel@ncslma.org; *Past Pres.* Bitsy Griffin, Old Town Global Academy, 3930 Reynolda Rd., Winston-Salem 27106. Tel. 336-703-4283, e-mail bitsygriffin@ncslma.org.

Address correspondence to the president, NCSLMA, 151 NC Hwy. 9, Suite B-188, Black Mountain, 28711.

World Wide Web http://www.ncslma.org.

North Dakota

School Lib. and Youth Svcs. section of the North Dakota Lib. Assn. (NDLA). Memb. 100.

Chair Leslie Allan, Williston Public Schools. E-mail lesley.allan@willistonschools.org; *Chair-Elect* Sharri Mosser, North Dakota State Lib. E-mail ssandwick@nd.gov; *Secy.* Carmen Redding, North Dakota State Lib. E-mail Carmen.Redding@k12.nd.us; *Past*

Chair Carmen Redding, North Dakota State Lib. E-mail Carmen.Redding@nd.gov.

Address correspondence to the School Lib. and Youth Svcs. Section, NDLA, 604 E. Boulevard Ave., Bismarck 58505.

World Wide Web https://ndla.info/SLAYS.

Ohio

Ohio Educ. Lib. Media Assn. (OELMA). Memb. 1,000.

Pres. Karen Gedeon, Cuyahoga Falls City Schools. E-mail president@oelma.org; *V.P.* Lisa Barnes Prince, Manchester Local Schools. E-mail vicepresident@oelma.org; *Secy.* Amy Keister, Louisville City Schools. E-mail secretary@oelma.org; *Treas.* Jennifer Schwelik. E-mail treasurer@oelma.org *Past Pres.* Brandi Young, South-Western City School Dist., Westland High School. E-mail pastpresident@oelma.org.

Address correspondence to OELMA, 1737 Georgetown Rd., Suite B, Hudson 43236. Tel. 330-615-2409, fax 1-800-373-9594, e-mail OELMA@neo-rls.org.

World Wide Web http://www.oelma.org.

Oklahoma

Oklahoma School Libns. Div., Oklahoma Lib. Assn. (OLA). Memb. 200+.

Chair Ashleigh Dautermann. E-mail oksl@oklibs.org; *Chair-Elect* Teresa Lansford. E-mail tlansford@norman.k12.ok.us; *Secy.* Molly Dettmann. E-mail mdettmann@norman.k12.ok.us; *Treas.* Angela Risch. E-mail arisch@norman.k12.ok.us; *Past Chair* Amanda Kordeliski. E-mail akordelis2@norman.k12.ok.us.

Address correspondence to the chairperson, School Libns. Div., OLA, 1190 Meramec Station Rd., Suite 207, Ballwin, MO 63021-6902. Tel. 800-969-6562 ext. 5, fax 636-529-1396.

World Wide Web https://www.oklibs.org/page/OKSL.

Oregon

Oregon Assn. of School Libs. (OASL). Memb. 600. Publication. *Interchange* (3x yearly). Co-ord. Ed. Dana Berglund. E-mail interchange@oasl.olaweb.org.

Pres. Kate Weber. E-mail president@oasl.olaweb.org; *Pres.-Elect* Grace Butler. E-mail presidentelect@oasl.olaweb.org; *Secy.* Jenny Takeda. E-mail secretary@oasl.olaweb.org; *Treas.* Jennifer Maurer. E-mail treasurer@oasl.olaweb.org; *Membs.-at-Large* Ayn Frazee, Elaine Ferrell-Burns. E-mail reading@oasl.olaweb.org; *Past Pres.* Laurie Nordahl. E-mail pastpresident@oasl.olaweb.org.

Address correspondence to the president, OASL, c/o Oregon Lib. Assn., P.O. Box 3067, La Grande 97850. Tel. 541-962-5824, e-mail president@oasl.olaweb.org.

World Wide Web http://www.olaweb.org/oasl-home.

Pennsylvania

Pennsylvania School Libns. Assn. (PSLA). Memb. 800+. Publication. *PSLA Pulse* (blog).

Pres. Robin Burns, Salisbury Township School Dist. E-mail rburns@psla.org; *Pres.-Elect.* Laura Ward, Fox Chapel Area School Dist. E-mail lward@psla.org; *V.P.* Aimee Emerson. E-mail aemerson@psla.org; *Secy.* Jane Farrell, Dallastown Area School Dist. E-mail secretary@psla.org; *Treas.* Jeffrey Weiss, Bradford Area School Dist., Bradford Area High School. E-mail pslatreasurer@gmail.com; *Past Pres.* Cathi Fuhrman, Hempfield School Dist. E-mail cfuhrman@psla.org.

Address correspondence to the president, PSLA, Hershey Square #125, 1152 Mae St., Hummelstown 17036.

World Wide Web http://www.psla.org.

Rhode Island

School Libns. of Rhode Island, section of the Rhode Island Lib. Assn. (RILA). Memb. 350+. Publication. *SLRI Update* (irreg.; online).

Pres. Deanna Brooks. E-mail SLRI.prez@gmail.com; *V.P.* Joan Mouradjian. E-mail SLRI.viceprez@gmail.com; *Secy.* Lisa Casey. E-mail SLRI.secretary@gmail.com; *Treas.* Jillian Waugh. E-mail SLRI.treasurer@gmail.com; *Past Pres.* Lisa Girard.

Address correspondence to the president, School Libns. of Rhode Island, RILA, P.O. Box 6765, Providence 02940.

World Wide Web https://rilibraries.org/slri.

South Carolina

South Carolina Assn. of School Libns. (SCASL). Memb. 900. Term of Office. July–June. Publication *SCASL Messenger* (q., online, memb.). *Ed.* Anya Bonnette. E-mail anya.bonnette@ocsd5.net.

Pres. Heather Loy. E-mail president@scasl. net; *Pres.-Elect* Katherine Malmquist. E-mail president.elect@scasl.net; *Secy.* Susan Myers. E-mail secretary@scasl.net; *Treas.* Camellia Harris; *Past Pres.* Pamela Williams.

Address correspondence to SCASL, P.O. Box 2442, Columbia 29202. Tel./fax 803-492-3025.

World Wide Web http://www.scasl.net.

South Dakota

South Dakota School Lib. Media Section, South Dakota Lib. Assn. (SDLA). Memb. 140+. Term of Office. Oct.–Sept.

Chair Korey Erickson, Sioux Falls Public Schools, Sioux Falls. E-mail korey.erickson@ k12.sd.us; *Past Chair* Kimberly Darata, Douglas School Dist. E-mail kimberly.darata@k12.sd.us.

Address correspondence to the chairperson. South Dakota School Lib. Media Section, SDLA, Mikkelsen Lib., 2001 S. Summit Ave., Sioux Falls 57197. Tel. 605-743-0889.

World Wide Web http://www.sdlibraryassociation.org/page/Sections.

Tennessee

Tennessee Assn. of School Libns. (TASL). Memb. 450. Term of Office. Jan.–Dec. Publication. *TASL Talks* (wk.; blog).

Pres. Lindsey Kimery, Woodland Middle School, 1500 Volunteer Pkwy., Brentwood 37027. E-mail lindskanderson@gmail.com; *Pres.-Elect* Katie Capshaw; *Secy.* Brandi Hartsell; *Treas.* Ginny Britt, Robertson County Schools. E-mail ginny.britt@rcstn.net; *Past Pres.* Vicki Winstead, Vance Middle School, 815 Edgemont Ave., Bristol 37620. E-mail vcwinstead.tasl@gmail.com.

Address correspondence to the president, TASL, P.O. Box 2013, Goodlettsville 37072.

World Wide Web http://www.tasltn.org.

Texas

Texas Assn. of School Libns. (TASL), div. of Texas Lib. Assn. Memb. 4,500+. Term of Office. Apr.–Mar.

Chair Kristi Starr. E-mail kristi.starr@lubbockisd.org; *Chair-Elect* Jill Bellomy. E-mail jillbellomy@gmail.com; *Secy.* Linda Kay. E-mail linda_kay@roundrockisd.org; *Councilor* Nicole Cruz; *Alternate Councilor* Jen

Hampton. E-mail hamptoj@hpisd.org; *Past Chair* Richelle O'Neil. E-mail richelleoneil@ gmail.com; *TLA Exec. Dir.* Shirley Robinson. E-mail shirleyr@txla.org.

Address correspondence to the chairperson, TASL, c/o Texas Lib. Assn., 3420 Executive Center Dr., Suite 301, Austin 78731. Tel. 512-328-1518, fax 512-328-8852.

World Wide Web http://www.txla.org/groups/tasl.

Utah

Utah Educ. Lib. Media Assn. (UELMA). Memb. 500+. Publication. *UELMA Works* (q.).

Pres. Emily DeJong, Beacon Heights Elementary, Salt Lake. E-mail board@uelma. org; *Pres.-Elect* Tricia Fenton, Granite School Dist., Jim Wilson, Canyons Dist. E-mail james. wilson@canyonsdistrict.org; *Secy.* Stephanie Jones, Alpine School Dist.; *Past Pres.* Lorraine Wyness, Taylorsville High School, 5225 S. Redwood Rd., Taylorsville 84123. Tel. 385-646-8949; *Exec. Dir.* Davina Sauthoff, Granite Dist. E-mail executivedirector@uelma.org.

Address correspondence to the executive director.

World Wide Web http://www.uelma.org.

Vermont

Vermont School Lib. Assn. (VSLA) Memb. 220+. Term of Office. May–May.

Pres. Peter Langella; *Pres.-Elect* Meg Allison; *Secy.* Martine Gulick. E-mail vslasecretary@gmail.com; *Treas.* Megan Sutton. E-mail msutton@acsdvt.org; *Past Pres.* Deb Ehler-Hansen. E-mail vermonthan1@gmail.com.

Address correspondence to VSLAmembership@gmail.com.

World Wide Web https://vsla.wildapricot.org.

Virginia

Virginia Assn. of School Libns. (VAASL) (formerly Virginia Educ. Media Assn. [VEMA]). Memb. 1,200. Term of Office. Nov.–Nov. Publication. *VAASL Voice* (q.; memb.).

Pres. Jennifer Cooper. E-mail president@ vaasl.org; *Pres.-Elect* Judy Deichman. E-mail presidentelect@vaasl.org; *Secy.* Heather Balsley. E-mail secretary@vaasl.org; *Treas.* Tonia Erickson. E-mail Treasurer@vaasl.org; *Past Pres.* Patrice Lambusta. E-mail pastpresident@

vaasl.org; *Exec. Dir.* Margaret Baker. E-mail executive@vaasl.org.

Address correspondence to the executive director, VAASL, P.O. Box 2015, Staunton 24402-2015. Tel. 540-416-6109, e-mail executive@vaasl.org.

World Wide Web http://vaasl.org.

Washington

School Lib. Div., Washington Lib. Assn. (WLA). Memb. 700+. Term of Office. Apr.–Apr.

Chair Sarah Logan, Camas School Dist. E-mail sarah.logan@camas.wednet.edu; *V.Chair/Chair-Elect* Ryan Grant. E-mail RGrant@mlsd.org; *Secy.* Elizabeth Roberts. E-mail elizabeth.k.roberts@gmail.com.

Address correspondence to WLA School Lib. Div., P.O. Box 33808, Seattle 98133. Tel. 206-823-1138, e-mail info@wla.org.

World Wide Web http://www.wla.org/school-libraries.

West Virginia

School Lib. Div., West Virginia Lib. Assn. (WVLA). Memb. 50. Term of Office. Nov.–Nov.

Chair Leigh Ann Hood, East Park Elementary, 805 Pittsburgh Ave., Fairmont 26554. Tel. 304-534-0927, e-mail lahood@k12.wv.us; *Past Chair* Lynda Suzie Martin, Brookhaven Elementary, 147 Estate Dr., Morgantown 26508.

Tel. 304-282-0147, e-mail librarynbct@gmail.com.

Address correspondence to the chairperson, WVLA School Lib. Div., P.O. Box 1432, Morgantown 26507.

World Wide Web http://www.wvla.org.

Wisconsin

Wisconsin Educ. Media and Technology Assn. (WEMTA). Memb. 800+.

Pres. Raquel Rand; *Pres.-Elect* Tina Birkett; *Secy.* Dawn Totzke; *Treas.* Pamela Hansen; *Past Pres.* Micki Uppena.

Address correspondence to WEMTA, 5329 Fayette Ave., Madison 53713. Tel. 608-588-6006, e-mail wemta@wemta.org.

World Wide Web http://www.wemta.org.

Wyoming

School Lib. Interest Group, Wyoming Lib. Assn. (WLA). Memb. 100+.

Co-Chair Melissa Snider, Teton County School Dist. Tel. 307-733-3020; *Co-Chair* Megan Bietz, Campbell County School Dist. Tel. 307-682-7289; *Secy.* Maggie Unterseher, Weston County School Dist. #1. Tel. 307-629-0190.

Address correspondence to the chairperson, SLIG, c/o WLA, 1190 Meramac Station Rd., Suite 207, Ballwin MO 63201.

World Wide Web https://wyla.org/School-Library-Interest-Group.

International Library Associations

International Association of Law Libraries

Kurt Carroll, President
P.O. Box 5709, Washington, DC 20016
E-mail president@iall.org
World Wide Web http://www.iall.org

Objective

The International Association of Law Libraries (IALL) is a worldwide organization of librarians, libraries, and other persons or institutions concerned with the acquisition and use of legal information emanating from sources other than their jurisdictions and from multinational and international organizations.

IALL's purpose is to facilitate the work of librarians who acquire, process, organize, and provide access to foreign legal materials. IALL has no local chapters but maintains liaison with national law library associations in many countries and regions of the world.

Membership

More than 400 members in more than 50 countries on five continents.

Officers

Pres. Kurt Carroll, Library of Congress, Washington, DC 20550. Tel. 202-707-1494, e-mail president@iall.org; *V.P.* Kerem Kahvecioglu, Haciahment Mahellesi, Pir Hüsamettin Sokak 20, 34440 Beyoğlu, Istanbul. Tel: 90 212 311 5157, e-mail vicepresident@iall.org; *Secy.* David Gee, Institute of Advanced Legal Studies, Univ. of London, 17 Russell Sq., London. Tel. 44 (0)20 7862 5822, fax 44 (0)20 7862 5770, e-mail David.Gee@sas.ac.uk; *Treas.* Barbara Garavaglia, Univ. of Michigan Law Lib., Ann

Arbor 48109-1210. Tel. 734-764-9338, fax 734-764-5863, e-mail bvaccaro@umich.edu; *Past Pres.* Jeroen Vervliet, The Hague. Tel. 31-70-302-4242, e-mail j.vervliet@ppl.nl.

Board of Directors

Kristina J. Alayan, Howard Univ. School of Law, Washington, D.C. Tel. 202-806-8047, e-mail kristina.alayan@law.howard.edu; Rebecca J. Five Bergstrom, Univ. of Oslo Law Lib. Tel. 4722859306, e-mail r.j.f.bergstrom@ub.uio.no; Heather Casey, Georgetown Univ. Law Lib., Washington, D.C. Tel. 202-661-6573, e-mail hec29@georgetown.edu; François Desseilles, Univ. of Liège Lib., Liège (Sart-Tilman). E-mail fdesseills@uliege.be; Mark D. Engsberg, MacMillan Law Lib., Emory School of Law, Atlanta, GA. Tel. 404-727-6983, e-mail mengsbe@emory.edu; Michel Fraysse, Université Toulouse, FR. Tel. 00 33 (5) 34 61 34, e-mail michel.fraysse@ut-capitole.fr; Trung Quach, Melbourne Law School, Univ. of Melbourne, Victoria. Tel. 61 3 9035 3061, e-mail trung.quach@unimelb.edu.au; Jean M. Wenger, Chicago-Kent College of Law, Chicago, IL 60661. Tel. 312-906-5610, e-mail jwenger@kentlaw.iit.edu.

Publications

International Journal of Legal Information (*IJLI*) (3x yearly; memb.).

International Association of Music Libraries, Archives, and Documentation Centres

Anders Cato, Secretary-General
Slots- og Kulturstyrelsen, Danish Agency for Culture and Palaces, H.C. Andersens Boulevard 2,
DK-1553 Copenhagen V Denmark
Tel: +45 5376 6337, e-mail secretary@iaml.info
World Wide Web http://www.iaml.info

Objective

The objective of the International Association of Music Libraries, Archives, and Documentation Centres (IAML) is to promote the activities of music libraries, archives, and documentation centers and to strengthen the cooperation among them; to promote the availability of all publications and documents relating to music and further their bibliographical control; to encourage the development of standards in all areas that concern the association; and to support the protection and preservation of musical documents of the past and the present.

Membership

Memb. approximately 1,700 in about 40 countries worldwide.

Officers

Pres. Stanislaw Hrabia, Uniwersytet Jagiellonski, Kraków. E-mail president@iaml.info; *V.P.s* Jane Gottlieb, The Juilliard School, New York; Rupert Ridgewell, British Lib., London; Jürgen Diet, Bayerische Staatsbibliothek, Munich; Anna Pensaert, Cambridge Univ. Lib. and the Pendlebury Lib. of Music; *Secy.-Gen.* Pia Shekhter, Gothenburg Univ. Lib., Box 210, SE 405 30 Gothenburg. Tel. 46-31-786-40-57, e-mail secretary@iaml.info; *Treasurer* Thomas Kalk, Stadtbüchereien Düsseldorf. E-mail treasurer@iaml.info; *Past Pres.* Barbara Dobbs Mackenzie, *Répertoire International de Littérature Musicale (RILM)*, New York.

Publication

Fontes Artis Musicae (q.; memb.). *Ed.* James P. Cassaro, Univ. of Pittsburgh, B-30 Music Bldg., Pittsburgh, PA 15260. Tel. 412-624-4131, e-mail fontes@iaml.info.

Institutional Sections

Archives and Music Documentation Centres. *Chair* Marie Cornaz, Bibliothèque Royale de Belgique, Brussels. E-mail archives@iaml.info.

Broadcasting and Orchestra Libraries. *Chair* Sabina Benelli, Teatro alla Scala, Milan. E-mail broadcasting-orchestra@iaml.info.

Libraries in Music Teaching Institutions. *Chair* Charles Peters, William & Gayle Cook Music Lib., Indiana Univ., Bloomington. E-mail teaching@iaml.info.

Public Libraries. *Chair* Blanka Ellederová, Municipal Lib. of Prague. E-mail public-libraries@iaml.info.

Research Libraries. *Chair* Thomas Leibnitz. Musiksammlung der Österreichischen Nationalbibliothek, Vienna. E-mail research-libraries@iaml.info.

Subject Sections

Audio-Visual Materials. *Chair* Jonathan Manton, Yale University, New Haven. E-mail ajustice@usc.edu.

Bibliography. *Chair* Stefan Engl, Österreichische Nationalbibliothek, Vienna. E-mail bibliography@iaml.info.

Cataloguing and Metadata. *Chair* Frédéric Lemmers, Bibliothèque royale de Belgique, Brussels. E-mail cataloguing@iaml.info.

Service and Training. *Chair* Anna Pensaert, Cambridge Univ. Lib., Cambridge. E-mail service@iaml.info.

International Association of School Librarianship

Jill Hancock, Executive Director
P.O. Box 684, Jefferson City, MO 65102
Tel. 573-635-2173, e-mail iasl@c2pro.solutions
World Wide Web http://www.iasl-online.org

Mission and Objectives

The mission of the International Association of School Librarianship (IASL) is to provide an international forum for those interested in promoting effective school library programs as viable instruments in the education process. IASL also provides guidance and advice for the development of school library programs and the school library profession. IASL works in cooperation with other professional associations and agencies.

Membership is worldwide and includes school librarians, teachers, librarians, library advisers, consultants, education administrators, and others who are responsible for library and information services in schools. The membership also includes professors and instructors in universities and colleges where there are programs for school librarians, and students who are undertaking such programs.

The objectives of IASL are to advocate the development of school libraries throughout all countries; to encourage the integration of school library programs into the instruction and curriculum of the school; to promote the professional preparation and continuing education of school library personnel; to foster a sense of community among school librarians in all parts of the world; to foster and extend relationships between school librarians and other professionals in connection with children and youth; to foster research in the field of school librarianship and the integration of its findings with pertinent knowledge from related fields; to promote the publication and dissemination of information about successful advocacy and program initiatives in school librarianship; to share information about programs and materials for children and youth throughout the international community; and to initiate and coordinate activities, conferences, and other projects in the field of school librarianship and information services. Founded 1971.

Membership

Approximately 825.

Officers

Pres. Katy Manck, Independent Book Reviewer, Gilmer, Tex. E-mail katyroo@gmail.com or Katy.Manck@gmail.com; *V.P. Assn. Operations* Mihaela Banek Zorica, Univ. of Zagreb, Faculty of Humanities and Social Sciences, Dept. of Information Sciences, Zagreb, Croatia. E-mail mbanek@ffzg.hr; *V.P. Assn. Relations* Albert Boekhorst, Brasil, Netherlands. E-mail albertkb@gmail.com; *V.P. Advocacy and Promotion* Annie Tam, the Independent Schools Foundation Academy, Hong Kong, China. E-mail atam@isf.edu.hk; *Treas.* Jennifer Branch-Mueller, Univ. of Alberta, Canada. E-mail jbranch@ualberta.ca.

Regional Board of Directors

Jerry Mathema, Africa; Hann Chaterina George, Asia; Eleanor Duggan, East Asia; Meghan Harper, North America; Laura Vilela Rodriges Rezende, Latin America/Caribbean; Vanja Jurilj, Europe; Sevgi Arioglu, North Africa/Middle East; Susan La Marca, Oceania; Zakir Hossain, International Schools.

Publications

School Libraries Worldwide (http://www.iasl-online.org/publications/slw/index.html), the association's refereed research and professional journal (online only; 2x yearly; memb.).

IASL Newsletter (http://www.iasl-online.org/publications/newsletter.html) (print; 4x yearly; memb.).

International Association of Scientific and Technological University Libraries (IATUL)

Charles Eckman, President
World Wide Web http://www.iatul.org

Objective

The main objective of the International Association of Scientific and Technological University Libraries (IATUL) is to provide a forum where library directors and senior managers can meet to exchange views on matters of current significance and to provide an opportunity for them to develop a collaborative approach to solving problems. IATUL also welcomes into membership organizations that supply services to university libraries, if they wish to be identified with the association's activities.

Membership

260 in 60 countries.

Officers

Pres. Charles Eckman, Univ. of Miami, USA. E-mail ceckman@miami.edu; *Secy.* Anna Walek, Gdańsk Univ. of Technology, Poland.

E-mail anna.walek@pg.edu.pl; *Treas.* Donna Bourne-Tyson, Dalhousie Univ., Canada. E-mail donna.bourne-tyson@dal.ca; *Past Pres.* Anne Horn, Univ. of Sheffield, UK. E-mail a.horn@sheffield.ac.uk.

Board Members

Jill Benn, Univ. of Western Australia, Perth. E-mail jill.benn@uwa.edu.au; Teresa Chitty, Univ. of Adelaide, Australia. E-mail teresa.chitty@adelaide.edu.au; Lars Egeland, Oslo Metropolitan Univ., Norway. E-mail larse@oslomet.no; Ujala Satgoor, University of Cape Town, South Africa. E-mail ujala.satgoor@uct.ac.za; J. K. Vijaykumar, King Abdullah Univ. of Science and Technology, Saudi Arabia. E-mail janardhanan.vijaykumar@kaust.edu.sa.

Publication

IATUL Conference Proceedings (https://www.iatul.org/publications/proceedings).

International Council on Archives

Anthea Seles, Secretary-General
60 rue des Francs-Bourgeois, 75003 Paris, France
Tel. 33-1-40-27-63-06, fax 33-1-42-72-20-65, e-mail ica@ica.org
World Wide Web http://www.ica.org

Objective

The mission of the International Council on Archives (ICA) is to establish, maintain, and strengthen relations among archivists of all lands, and among all professional and other agencies or institutions concerned with the custody, organization, or administration of archives, public or private, wherever located. Established 1948.

Membership

Approximately 1,900 in nearly 200 countries and territories

Officers

Pres. David Fricker, Australia; *V.P.s* M. Normand Charbonneau, Canada; Henri Zuber, France; *Secy.-Gen.* Anthea Seles, France.

Board Members

Emma De Ramon Acevedo, Chile; Hamad Bin Mohammed Al-Dhawyani, Oman; Opeta Alefaio, Fiji; Faisal Altamimi, Saudi Arabia; Azemi Abdul Aziz, Malaysia; Françoise Banat-Berger, France; Avril Belfon, Trinidad and Tobago; Alexander Lukas Bieri, Switzerland; Caroline Brown, UK; Peter Mapiwa Choto, Botswana; Margaret Crockett, France (ex officio); Yonten Dargye, Bhutan; Abdulla A. Kareem El Reyes, UAE; Charles Farrugia, Malta; Emilie Gagnet Leumas, USA; Tim Harris, UK; Jeff James, UK; Neale Macdonald, Canada (ex officio); Gustavo Castaner Marquadt, Belgium; Matthias Massode, Benin; Jean-Paul Nenga Mukanya, Congo; Yolanda Cagigas Ocejo, Spain; Antonio González Quintana, Spain; Vilde Ronge, Norway; Wang Shaozhong, China; Fina Sola I Gasset, Spain; David Sutton, UK; Ian E. Wilson, Canada; Atakilty Assefa Asgedom, Ethiopia (ex officio).

Publications

Comma (print and online; 2x yearly, memb.).
Flash (online only; 2x yearly; memb.).
ICA e-newsletter (online only; mo.).
Conference Papers and Proceedings.

International Federation of Film Archives (Fédération Internationale des Archives du Film)

Michael Loebenstein, Secretary-General
Secretariat, 42 rue Blanche, B-1060 Brussels, Belgium
Tel. 32-2-538-30-65, fax 32-2-534-47-74, e-mail info@fiafnet.org
World Wide Web http://www.fiafnet.org

Objective

Founded in 1938, the International Federation of Film Archives (FIAF) brings together not-for-profit institutions dedicated to rescuing films and any other moving-image elements considered both as cultural heritage and as historical documents.

FIAF is a collaborative association of the world's leading film archives whose purpose has always been to ensure the proper preservation and showing of motion pictures. Almost 90 member archives in more than 50 countries collect, restore, and exhibit films and cinema documentation spanning the entire history of film.

FIAF seeks to promote film culture and facilitate historical research, to help create new archives around the world, to foster training and expertise in film preservation, to encourage the collection and preservation of documents and other cinema-related materials, to develop cooperation between archives, and to ensure the international availability of films and cinema documents.

Officers

Pres. Frédéric Maire; *Secy.-Gen.* Michael Loebensten; *Treas.* Jon Wengström. *V.P.s* Cecilia Cenciarelli, Michal Bregant, Iris Elezi.

Address correspondence to Christophe Dupin, Senior Administrator, FIAF Secretariat. E-mail c.dupin@fiafnet.org.

Publications and Databases

FIAF Bulletin Online.
FIAF Directory (print).
International Index to Film Periodicals database. (OVID, ProQuest).
Journal of Film Preservation. Ed. Elaine Burrows. E-mail jfp.editor@fiafnet.org.
Treasures from the Film Archives database.
Extensive selection of books through the FIAF Bookshop.

International Federation of Library Associations and Institutions

P.O. Box 95312, 2509 CH The Hague, Netherlands
Tel. 31-70-314-0884, fax 31-70-383-4827, e-mail ifla@ifla.org
World Wide Web http://www.ifla.org

Objective

The objective of the International Federation of Library Associations and Institutions (IFLA) is to promote international understanding, cooperation, discussion, research, and development in all fields of library activity, including bibliography, information services, and the education of library personnel, and to provide a body through which librarianship can be represented in matters of international interest. IFLA is the leading international body representing the interests of library and information services and their users. It is the global voice of the library and information profession. Founded 1927.

Officers

Pres. Christine Mackenzie, Australia; *Pres.-Elect* Barbara Lison, Stadtbibliothek Bremen, Germany; *Treas.* Antonia Arahova, Athens, Greece; *Past Pres.* Glòria Pérez-Salmerón, Federación Española de Sociedades de Archivística, Biblioteconomía, Documentación y Museística, Spain; *Secy.-Gen.* Gerald Leitner (ex officio), Netherlands.

Governing Board

Huanwen Cheng (China), Michael Dowling (USA), Marwa El Sahn (Egypt), Jonathan Hernández Pérez (Mexico), Sueli Mara Soares Pinto Ferreira (Brazil), Ai Cheng Tay (Singapore), Minna von Zansen (Finland), Knud Schulz (Denmark), plus the chairs of the IFLA Professional Committee and divisions.

Publications

IFLA Annual Report.
IFLA Journal (4x yearly).
IFLA Trend Reports.
IFLA Professional Reports.
IFLA Publications Series.
IFLA Series on Bibliographic Control.
Global Studies in Libraries and Information (irreg. series).
Access and Opportunity for All: How Libraries Contribute to the United Nations 2030 Agenda.

American Membership

Associations

American Lib. Assn., Assn. for Lib. and Info. Science Educ., Assn. of Research Libs., Chief Officers of State Lib. Agencies, Medical Lib. Assn., Special Libs. Assn., Urban Libs. Council, Chinese American Libns. Assn., Polish American Lib. Assn.

Institutional Members

More than 100 libraries and related institutions are institutional members or consultative bodies and sponsors of IFLA in the United States (out of a total of more than 1,000 globally), and more than 100 are individual affiliates (out of a total of more than 300 affiliates globally).

International Organization for Standardization

Sergio Mujica, Secretary-General
ISO Central Secretariat, Chemin de Blandonnet 8, CP 4011214 Vernier, Geneva, Switzerland
Tel. 41-22-749-01-11, fax 41-22-733-34-30, e-mail central@iso.org
World Wide Web http://www.iso.org

Objective

Founded in 1947, the International Organization for Standardization (ISO) is a worldwide federation of national standards bodies that currently comprises members from 164 countries and 785 technical committees and subcommittees working on various aspects of standards development. The objective of ISO is to promote the development of standardization and related activities in the world with a view to facilitating international exchange of goods and services, and to developing cooperation in the spheres of intellectual, scientific, technological, and economic activity. The scope of ISO covers international standardization in all fields except electrical and electronic engineering standardization, which is the responsibility of the International Electrotechnical Commission (IEC). The results of ISO technical work are published as international standards.

Officers

Pres. Eddy Njoroge, Kenya; *Pres.-Elect* Ulrika Francke, Sweden; *V.P.s* Scott Steedman, UK *(Policy)*, Sauw Kook Choy, Singapore *(Technical Management)*, Mitsuo Matsumoto, Japan *(Finance)*; *Treas.* Dominique Christin, Switzerland; *Secy.-Gen.* Sergio Mujica, Chile.

Technical Work

The technical work of ISO is carried out by groups of experts collaborating worldwide, representing every imaginable sector, from soaps to spacecraft, from MP3 to coffee. Among its technical committees are

ISO/TC 46—Information and documentation (Secretariat, Association Française de Normalization, 11 rue Francis de Pressensé, 93571 La Plaine Saint-Denis, Cedex, France). Scope: Standardization of practices relating to libraries, documentation and information centers, indexing and abstracting services, archives, information science, and publishing.

ISO/TC 37—Language and terminology (Secretariat, Standardization Administration of China, No. 9 Madian Donglu, Haidian District, Beijing 100088, China). Scope: Standardization of descriptions, resources, technologies, and services related to terminology, translation, interpreting, and other language-based activities in the multilingual information society.

ISO/IEC JTC 1—Information technology (Secretariat, American National Standards Institute, 1899 L St. NW, 11th Fl., Washington, DC 20036). Scope: Standardization in the field of information technology.

Publications

ISO Annual Report.
ISOfocus (6x yearly).
Extensive selection of titles on the ISO website (https://www.iso.org/publication-list.html).

Foreign Library Associations

The following is a list of regional and national library associations around the world. A more complete list can be found in *International Literary Market Place* (Information Today, Inc.).

Regional

Africa

Standing Conference of Eastern, Central, and Southern African Lib. and Info. Assns. (SCECSAL), c/o General-Secretary, Uganda Library and Information Association, P.O. Box 5894, Kampala, Uganda. Tel. +256-772-488937, +256-782-617623, +256-782-42204, e-mail info@ulia.or.ug, World Wide Web https://www.scecsal.org/.

The Americas

Assn. of Caribbean Univ., Research, and Institutional Libs. (ACURIL), P.O. Box 21337, San Juan, Puerto Rico 00931. Tel. 787-612-9343, e-mail executivesecretariat@acuril. org, World Wide Web https://acuril.org. *Pres.* Jeannette Lebrón Ramos; *Exec. Secy.* Elizabeth Pierre-Louis.

Seminar on the Acquisition of Latin American Lib. Materials (SALALM), c/o SALALM Secretariat, Latin American Lib., 422 Howard Tilton Memorial Lib., Tulane Univ., 7001 Freret St., New Orleans, LA 70118-5549. Tel. 504-247-1366, fax 504-247-1367, e-mail salalm@tulane.edu, World Wide Web https://salalm.org. *Exec. Dir.* Hortensia Calvo. E-mail hcalvo@tulane.edu.

Asia

Congress of Southeast Asian Libns. (CONSAL), # Razathingaha Road, Nearby Razathingaha Circle, Uottra Thiri TSP, Naypyitaw, Myanmar. Tel. 95 67 418427, fax 95 67 418426, e-mail info@consalxvii.org.

The Commonwealth

Commonwealth Lib. Assn. (COMLA), c/o University of the West Indies, Bridgetown Campus, Learning Resource Center, P.O. Box 64, Bridgetown, Barbados. Tel. 246-417-4201, fax 246-424-8944, e-mail watsone@uwichill.edu.bb, World Wide Web https://uia.org/s/or/en/1100024839.

U.K. Library and Archives Group on Africa (SCOLMA), c/o Sarah Rhodes, Bodleian Social Science Lib., Univ. of Oxford, Manor Rd. Bldg., Manor Rd., Oxford OX1 3UQ, England. Tel. 01865-277162, World Wide Web http://scolma.org. *Chair* Marion Wallace; *Secy.* Sarah Rhodes.

Europe

European Bureau of Library, Information and Documentation Associations (EBLID), c/o EBLIDA Secretariat, Koninklijke Bibliotheek (National Library of the Netherlands), Prins Willem-Alexanderhof 5, 2595 BE, The Hague. Tel. 31 (0) 70 3140137, e-mail eblida@eblida.org, World Wide Web http://www.eblida.org. *Dir.* Giuseppe Vitiello.

Ligue des Bibliothèques Européennes de Recherche (LIBER) (Assn. of European Research Libs.), P.O. Box 90407, 2509 LK The Hague, Netherlands. Tel. 31-70-314-07-67, fax 070-314-01-97, e-mail liber@kb.nl, World Wide Web http://www.libereurope. eu. *Pres.* Jeannette Frey; *V.P.* Julien Roche; *Secy.-Gen.* John MacColl; *Exec. Dir.* Astrid Verheusen.

National

Argentina

ABGRA (Asociación de Bibliotecarios Graduados de la República Argentina) (Assn. of Graduate Libns. of Argentina), Paraná 918, 2do Piso, C1017AAT Buenos Aires. Tel. 54-11-4811-0043, fax 54-11-4816-3422, e-mail info@abgra.org.ar, World Wide Web http://www.abgra.org.ar. *Pres.* Maria Silvia LaCorazza; *Secy. Gen.* Barbara Krieger.

Australia

Australian Lib. and Info. Assn., Box 6335, Kingston, ACT 2604. Tel. 61-2-6215-8222, fax 61-2-6282-2249, e-mail enquiry@alia. org.au, World Wide Web http://www.alia. org.au. *CEO* Sue McKerracher. E-mail sue. mckerracher@alia.org.au.

Australian Society of Archivists, P.O. Box 576, Crows Nest, NSW 1585. Tel. 612-9431-8644, e-mail office@archivists.org.au, World Wide Web http://www.archivists.org. au. *Pres.* Nicola Laurent; *V.P.* Jessie Lymn.

National and State Libs. Australia (NSLA), State Lib. Victoria, 328 Swanston St., Melbourne VIC 3000. Tel. 03 8664 7512, e-mail nsla@ slv.vic.gov.au, World Wide Web https://www. nsla.org.au. *Chair* Marie-Louise Ayers.

Austria

Österreichische Gesellschaft für Dokumentation und Information (Austrian Society for Documentation and Info.), c/o Österreich ische Computer Gesellschaft OCG, Wollzeile 1, 1010 Vienna. E mail office@ocgdi. at, World Wide Web http://www.ocgdi.at. *Chair* Gerhard Frohlich.

Vereinigung Österreichischer Bibliothekarinnen und Bibliothekare (VOEB) (Assn. of Austrian Libns.), Universitätsbibliothek Graz, Universitätsplatz 3, 8010 Graz. E-mail voeb@ub.tuwein.ac.at, World Wide Web http://www.univie.ac.at/voeb/php. *Interim Presidents* Pamela Stückler and Eva Ramminger. *Secy.* Markus Lackner.

Bangladesh

Bangladesh Assn. of Libns., Info. Scientists and Documentalists (BALID), House # 67/B (3rd floor), Road # 9/A, Dhanmondi, Dhaka-1209, Bangladesh. E-mail balidbd@ gmail.com, info@balidbd.org, World Wide Web https://www.balid.org. *Chair* Ms. Hazera Rahman.

Belgium

Archief- en Bibliotheekwezen in België (Belgian Assn. of Archivists and Libns.), Royal Library of Belgium, Boulevard de l'Empereur 2, 1000 Brussels. Tel. 2-519-53-93, fax 2-519-56-10, e-mail abb@kbr.be, World Wide Web http://www.archibib.be. *Pres.* Marc Libert; *Admin. Secy.* Anja Marginet

Assn. Belge de Documentation/Belgische Vereniging voor Documentatie (Belgian Assn. for Documentation), 4 Boulevard de l'Empereur, 1000 Bruxelles. Tel. 2-675-58-62, fax 2-672-74-46, e-mail abdbvd@abd-bvd. be, World Wide Web http://www.abd-bvd. be. *Pres.* Sara Decoster, e-mail sara.decoster. pro@gmail.com; *Secy. Gen.* Guy Delsaut, e-mail delsautg@gmail.com.

Association des Professionales des Bibliothèques Francophones de Belgique (APBFB), Rue Nanon 98, 5002 Namur. Tel. 32-472-94-12-05, e-mail info@apbfb.be, World Wide Web http://www.apbfb.be. *Pres.* Françoise Dury.

Association Professionnelle des Bibliothécaires et Documentalistes. See Association des Professionales des Bibliothèques Francophones de Belgique (APBFB).

Vlaamse Vereniging voor Bibliotheek-, Archief-, en Documentatiewezen (Flemish Assn. of Libns., Archivists, and Documentalists), Statiestraat 179, B-2600 Berchem, Antwerp. Tel. 3-281-44-57, e-mail vvbad@ vvbad.be, World Wide Web http://www. vvbad.be. *Coord.* Jessica Jacobs. E-mail jessica.jacobs@vvbad.be.

Bolivia

Centro Nacional de Documentación Científica y Tecnológica (National Scientific and Technological Documentation Center), Av. Mariscal Santa Cruz 1175, Esquina c Ayacucho, La Paz. Tel. 02-359-583, fax 02-359-586, e-mail iiicndct@huayna.umsa.edu.bo, World Wide Web http://www.bolivian.com/ industrial/cndct.

Bosnia and Herzegovina

Drustvo Bibliotekara Bosne i Hercegovine (Libns. Society of Bosnia and Herzegovina), Zmaja od Bosne 8B, 71000 Sarajevo. Tel. 33-275-301, e-mail nubbih@nub.ba, World Wide Web http://www.nub.ba. *Pres.* Ismet Ovcina. E-mail ured.direktora@nub.ba.

Botswana

Botswana Lib. Assn., Box 1310, Gaborone. Tel. 267-732-31047, e-mail secretary@bla.org.bw,

Pres. Lynn Jabril. E-mail president@
bla.org.bw, World Wide Web https://www.
facebook.com/BotsLibAssociation/.

Brunei Darussalam

Persatuan Perpustakaan Negara Brunei Darus-
salam (National Lib. Assn. of Brunei), c/o
Class 64 Lib., SOASC, Jalan Tengah, Bandar
Seri Begawan BS8411. Fax 2-222-330, e-mail
pobox.bla@gmail.com, World Wide Web
http://bruneilibraryassociation.wordpress.
com.

Cameroon

Assn. des Bibliothécaires, Archivistes, Documentalistes et Muséographes du Cameroun
(Assn. of Libns., Archivists, Documentalists,
and Museum Curators of Cameroon), BP
12092, Yaoundé. Tel. 237-2-22-22-28-98,
e-mail abadcameroun@gmail.com, World
Wide Web http://www.abadcam.sitew.com.
Pres. Alim Garga. E-mail a_garga@yahoo.fr.

Chile

Colegio de Bibliotecarios de Chile (Chilean Lib.
Assn.), Avda. Diagonal Paraguay 383, Torre
11, Oficina 122, 6510017 Santiago. Tel.
2-222-5652, e-mail cbc@bibliotecarios.cl,
World Wide Web http://www.bibliotecarios.
cl. *Pres.* María Angélica Fuentes Martínez.

China

China Society for Lib. Science, 33 Zhong-
guancun Nandajie, Hai Dian District, Beijing
100081. Tel. 86-10-8854-4114, fax 86-10-
6841-7815, e-mail webmaster@nlc.gov.cn,
World Wide Web http://www.nlc.cn/newen/.

Colombia

Asociación Colombiana de Bibliotecólogos
y Documentalistas (Colombian Assn. of
Libns. and Documentalists), Calle 21, No.
6-58, Oficina 404, Bogotá D.C. Tel. 1-282-
3620, fax 1-282-5487, e-mail secretaria@
ascolbi.org, World Wide Web http://www.
ascolbi.org. *Pres.* Leonardo Ramírez O.

Croatia

Hrvatsko Knjiznicarsko Drustvo (Croatian Lib.
Assn.), c/o National and Univ. Lib., Hrvatske

bratske zajednice 4, 10 000 Zagreb. Tel./
fax 1-615-93-20, e-mail hkd@nsk.hr, World
Wide Web http://www.hkdrustvo.hr. *Pres.*
Dijana Machala; *Secy.* Andreja Tominac.

Cuba

Asociación Cubana de Bibliotecarios (ASCU-
BI) (Lib. Assn. of Cuba), P.O. Box 6670,
Havana. Tel. 7-555-442, fax 7-816-224,
e-mail ascubi@bnjm.cu, World Wide Web
http://ascubi.blogspot.com/. *Chair* Margarita Bellas Vilariño. E-mail ascubi@bnjm.cu.

Cyprus

Kypriakos Synthesmos Vivliothicarion (Lib.
Assn. of Cyprus), c/o Pedagogical Academy,
P.O. Box 1039, Nicosia. E-mail kebepcy@
gmail.com, World Wide Web http://kebep.
blogspot.com.

Czech Republic

Svaz Knihovniku a Informacnich Pracovniku
Ceske Republiky (SKIP) (Assn. of Lib. and
Info. Professionals of the Czech Republic),
National Library of the Czech Republic,
Mariánské námĕstí 190/5, 110 00 Prague 1.
Tel. 420-221-663-379, fax 420-221-663-
175, e-mail skip@nkp.cz, World Wide Web
https://www.skipcr.cz/. *Chair Mgr.* Roman
Giebisch.

Denmark

Arkivforeningen (Archives Society), Ingrid
Nostberg, Vestfoldmuseene IKS, Department Vestfoldarkivet, 3205 Sandefjord. Tel.
958 21 501, e-mail post@arkivarforeningen.
no, World Wide Web http://www.arki-
varforeningen.no. *Chair* Ingrid Nostberg.
Danmarks Biblioteksforening (Danish Lib.
Assn.), Vartov, Farvergade 27D, 1463 Copenhagen K. Tel. 3325-0935, fax 3325-
7900, e-mail db@db.dk, World Wide Web
http://www.db.dk. *Chair* Steen Bording
Andersen. E-mail steen.a@aarhus.dk. *Dir.*
Michel Steen-Hansen, e-mail msh@db.dk.
Danmarks Forskningsbiblioteksforening (Danish Research Lib. Assn.), c/o University of
Southern Denmark, Studiestræde 6, 1455
Copenhagen K. Tel. 45-4220-2177, e-mail
secretariat@dfdf.dk, World Wide Web

http://www.dfdf.dk. *Chair* Karin Englev. E-mail kabe@kb.dk.
Dansk Musikbiblioteks Forening (Assn. of Danish Music Libs.), c/o Helene Olsen, Sundby Library, Jemtelandsgade 3, Copenhagen S. E-mail sekretariat@dmbf.nu, World Wide Web http://www.dmbf.nu.

Ecuador

Asociación Ecuatoriana de Bibliotecarios (Ecuadoran Lib. Assn.), c/o Casa de la Cultura Ecuatoriana, Casillas 87, Quito. E-mail asoecubiblio@gmail.com, World Wide Web http://aeb-nacional.blogspot.com/.

El Salvador

Asociación de Bibliotecarios de El Salvador (ABES) (Assn. of Salvadorian Libns.), Residencial La Cima, Avenida 7, Calle 5 house # 15G, San Salvador. Tel. 503-2212-7600, e-mail abeselsalvador@gmail.com, World Wide Web https.//bibliotecarios-de-el-salvador.webnode.es/?fbclid=IwAR3eoq4LlTGeT4yrEjNIZny whAg5RJRlldkc3TBr9NGMQBsmGE-QJF SHTeM. *Pres.* Claudia Oviedo.

Finland

Suomen Kirjastoseura (Finnish Lib. Assn.), Runeberginkatu 15 A 6, 00100 Helsinki. Tel. 44-522-2941, e-mail info@fla.fi, World Wide Web http://www.fla.fi. *Exec. V.P.* Rauha Maarno. E-mail rauha.maarno@fla.fi.

France

Association des Archivistes Français (Assn. of French Archivists), 8 rue Jean-Marie Jego, 75013 Paris. Tel. 1-46-06-39-44, fax 1-46-06-39-52, e-mail secretariat@archivistes.org, World Wide Web http://www.archivistes.org.
Association des Bibliothécaires de France (Assn. of French Libns.), 31 rue de Chabrol, F-75010 Paris. Tel. 1-55-33-10-30, fax 1-55-30-10-31, e-mail info@abf.asso.fr, World Wide Web http://www.abf.asso.fr. *Chair* Alice Bernard; *Gen. Secy.* Chantal Ferreux.
Association des Professionnels de l'Information et de la Documentation (Assn. of Info. and Documentation Professionals), 25 rue Claude Tillier, 75012 Paris. Tel. 06-81-39-82-14, e-mail adbs@adbs.fr, World Wide Web http://www.adbs.fr. *Secy. Gen.* Béa Arruabarrena.

Germany

Arbeitsgemeinschaft der Spezialbibliotheken (Assn. of Special Libs.), c/o Wissenschaftskolleg zu Berlin—Bibliothek, Wallotstr. 19, 14193 Berlin. Tel. 030-89001-144, fax 030-89001-400, e-mail geschaeftsstelle@aspb.de, World Wide Web http://aspb.de. *Chair* Kirsten Schoof. E-mail kirsten.schoof@aesthetics.mpg.de.
Berufsverband Information Bibliothek (Assn. of Info. and Lib. Professionals), ASpB Secretariat c/o German Center for Aging Issues (DZA) Library, Manfred-von-Richthofen-Str., 212101 Berlin. Tel. 7121-3491-0, fax 7121-3491-34, e-mail mail@bib-info.de, World Wide Web http://www.bib-info.de.
Deutsche Gesellschaft für Informationswissenschaft und Informationspraxis eV (German Society for Information Science and Practice eV), Windmühlstr. 3, 60329 Frankfurt-am-Main. Tel. 69-43-03-13, fax 69-490-90-96, e-mail mail@dgi-info.de, World Wide Web http://www.dgi-info.de. *Pres.* Margarita Reibel-Felten.
Deutscher Bibliotheksverband eV (German Lib. Assn.), Fritschestr. 27–28, 10585 Berlin. Tel. 30-644-98-99-10, fax 30-644-98-99-29, e-mail dbv@bibliotheksverband.de, World Wide Web http://www.bibliotheksverband.de. *Pres.* Dr. Frank Mentrup; *Dir.* Barbara Schleihagen.
VdA—Verband Deutscher Archivarinnen und Archivare (Assn. of German Archivists), Woerthstr. 3, 36037 Fulda. Tel. 661-29-109-72, fax 661-29-109-74, e-mail info@vda.archiv.net, World Wide Web http://www.vda.archiv.net. *Chair* Ralf Jacob; *Managing Dir.* Thilo Bauer.
Verein Deutscher Bibliothekare eV (Society of German Libns.), Univ. Lib. Erlangen-Nürnberg, Universitatsstrasse 4, 91054 Erlangen. Tel. 09131-85-22150, e-mail geschaeftsstelle@vdb-online.org, World Wide Web http://www.vdb-online.org. *Chair* Konstanze Söllner. E-mail chairman@vdb-online.org.

Ghana

Ghana Lib. Assn., Box GP 4105, Accra. Tel. 244-17-4930, e-mail info@gla-net.org, World Wide Web http://gla-net.org. *Pres.* Comfort Asare.

Greece

Enosis Hellinon Bibliothekarion (Association of Greek Librarians), Akadimias 84, PC 106 78, Athens. Tel./fax 210-330-2128, e-mail info-eebep@eebep.gr, World Wide Web http://www.eebep.gr. *Pres.* Dr. Anthi Katsirikou; *Gen. Secy.* Eleni Molfesi.

Guyana

Guyana Lib. Assn., c/o Department of Public Information, Area 'B' Homestretch Ave., D'Urban Park, Georgetown. Tel. 592-226-6715, fax 592-227-4052, e-mail info@dpi.gov.gy, World Wide Web https://dpi.gov.gy/tag/guyana-library-association/.

Hong Kong

Hong Kong Lib. Assn., GPO Box 10095, Hong Kong, China. E-mail hkla@hkla.org, World Wide Web http://www.hkla.org. *Pres.* Kendall Crilly. E-mail president@hkla.org. *Membership Secy.* Bernice Chan. E-mail membership@hkla.org.

Hungary

Magyar Könyvtárosok Egyesülete (Assn. of Hungarian Libns.), 1827 Budapest, Budavári Palota Building F. Tel./fax 1-311-8634, e-mail mke@oszk.hu, World Wide Web http://www.mke.info.hu. *Chair* Dr. Ágnes Hajdu; *Secy. Gen.* Judit Gerencsér.

Iceland

Upplysing—Felag bokasafns-og upplysinga-fraeoa (Information—The Icelandic Lib. and Info. Science Assn.), Mailbox 8865, 128 Reykjavík. Tel. 354-864-6220, e-mail upplysing@upplysing.is, World Wide Web http://www.upplysing.is. *Chair* Þórný Hlynsdóttir. E-mail chairman@upplysing.is.

India

Indian Assn. of Special Libs. and Info. Centres, P-291, CIT Scheme 6M, Kankurgachi, Kolkata 700-054. Tel. 33-2362-9651, e-mail iaslic@vsnl.net, World Wide Web http://www.iaslic1955.org.in. *President* Narendra Lahkar; *Gen. Secy.* Abhijit Kumar.

Indian Lib. Assn., A/40-41, Flat 201, Ansal Bldg., Mukerjee Nagar, New Delhi 110009. Tel./fax 11-2765-1743, e-mail dvs-srcc@rediffmail.com, World Wide Web http://www.ilaindia.net. *Pres.* B. D. Kumbar; *Gen. Secy.* O. N. Chaubey.

Indonesia

Ikatan Pustakawan Indonesia (Indonesian Lib. Assn.), Jl. Salemba Raya, RT.8 / RW.8, Kramat Senen, Kota Jakarta Pusat, DKI Jakarta 10430. Tel. (021) 3900944, World Wide Web http://ipi.web.id.

Ireland

Cumann Leabharlann na hEireann (Lib. Assn. of Ireland), c/o 138–144 Pearse St., Dublin 2. E-mail honsecretary@libraryassociation.ie, World Wide Web http://www.libraryassociation.ie. *Pres.* Marian Higgins. E-mail president@libraryassociation.ie. *Hon. Secy.* Niall O'Brien. E-mail honsecretary@libraryassociation.ie.

Israel

Israeli Center for Libs., 22 Baruch Hirsch St., P.O. Box 801, 51108 Bnei Brak. Tel. 03-6180151, fax 03-5798048, e-mail meida@gmail.com or icl@icl.org.il, World Wide Web http://www.icl.org.il. *Chair* Moshe Perl.

Italy

Associazione Italiana Biblioteche (Italian Lib. Assn.), Biblioteca Nazionale Centrale, Viale Castro Pretorio 105, 00185 Rome RM. Tel. 6-446-3532, fax 6-444-1139, e-mail segreteria@aib.it, World Wide Web http://www.aib.it.

Jamaica

Lib. and Info. Assn. of Jamaica, P.O. Box 125, Kingston 5. Tel./fax 876-927-1614, e-mail liajapresident@yahoo.com, World Wide Web http://www.liaja.org.jm.

Japan

Info. Science and Technology Assn., 1-11-14, Shinkawa, Chuo-ku, Tokyo 104-0033.

Tel. 81-3-6222-8506, fax 81-3-6222-8107, e-mail infosta@infosta.or.jp, World Wide Web http://www.infosta.or.jp.

Nihon Toshokan Kyokai (Japan Lib. Assn.), 1-11-14 Shinkawa, Chuo-ku, Tokyo 104 0033. Tel. 3-3523-0811, fax 3-3523-0841, e-mail info@jla.or.jp, World Wide Web http://www.jla.or.jp. *Chair* Mitsuhiro Oda.

Senmon Toshokan Kyogikai (Japan Special Libs. Assn.), c/o Japan Lib. Assn., Bldg. F6, 1-11-14 Shinkawa Chuo-ku, Tokyo 104-0033. Tel. 3-3537-8335, fax 3-3537-8336, e-mail jsla@jsla.or.jp, World Wide Web http://www.jsla.or.jp. *Co-Chairs* Akio Mimura and Ishida Toru.

Jordan

Jordan Lib and Info. Assn., P.O. Box 6289, Amman 11118. Tel./fax 00962-64629412, World Wide Web http://jlia.org/component/content/en. *Pres.* Dr. Naguib Al-Sharbaji.

Kenya

Kenya Assn. of Lib. and Info. Professionals (formerly Kenya Lib. Assn.), Buruburu, P.O. Box 49468-00100 Nairobi. Tel. 20-733-732-799, e-mail info@kenyalibraryassociation. or.ke, World Wide Web http://www.kenya libraryassociation.or.ke.

Korea (Republic of)

Korean Lib. Assn., 201 Banpo-daero (Banpo-dong), Seocho-gu, Seoul. Tel. 2-535-4868, fax 2-535-5616, e-mail license@kla.kr, World Wide Web http://www.kla.kr. *Pres.* Nam Young-joon.

Laos

Association des Bibliothécaires Laotiens (Lao Lib. Assn.), c/o Direction de la Bibliothèque Nationale, Ministry of Educ., BP 704, Vientiane. Tel. 21-21-2452, fax 21-21-2408, e-mail bailane@laotel.com.

Latvia

Latvian Libns. Assn., c/o Latvian National Lib., Mukusalas iela 3, Riga, LV-1423. Tel. 67806100, fax 67280851, e-mail lnb@ lnb.lv, World Wide Web http://www.lnb. lv. *Dir.* Andris Vilks, e-mail andris.vilks@ lnb.lv.

Lebanon

Lebanese Lib. Assn., P.O. Box 113/5367, Beirut. Tel. 1-786-456, e-mail leblibassociation@ gmail.com, World Wide Web http://www. lebaneselibraryassociation.org/. *Pres.* Fawz Abdallah. E-mail fabdallas@gmail.com.

Lithuania

Lietuvos Bibliotekininkų Draugija (Lithuanian Libns. Assn.), Gedimino pr. 51, Vilnius, LT-01504. Tel. 370-5-231-8585, e-mail lbd.sekretore@gmail.com, World Wide Web http://www.lbd.lt. *Chair* Jolita Stepho naitiene. E-mail jolita.stephonaitiene@ lnb.lt.

Luxembourg

Association Luxembourgeoise des Bibliothécaires, Archivistes, et Documentalistes (ALBAD) (Luxembourg Assn. of Libns., Archivists, and Documentalists), c/o National Lib. of Luxembourg, BP 295, L-2012 Luxembourg. Tel. 352-621-46-14-15, World Wide Web http://www.albad.lu. *Pres.* Estelle Beck. E-mail presidence@albad.lu. *Secy. Gen.* Bernard Linster. E-mail secret arie@albad.lu.

Malaysia

Persatuan Pustakawan Malaysia (Libns. Assn. of Malaysia), P.O. Box 12545, 50782 Kuala Lumpur. Tel./fax 3-2694-7390, e-mail pustakawan55@gmail.com, World Wide Web http://ppm55.org. *Pres.* Dr. Rashidah binti Bolhassan, e-mail rashidahb@sarawak. gov.my.

Mali

Association Malienne des Bibliothécaires, Archivistes et Documentalistes (Mali Assn. of Libns., Archivists, and Documentalists) (AMBAD), BP E4473, Bamako. Tel. 20-29-94-23, fax 20-29-93-76, e-mail dnambko@ afribone.net.ml.

Malta

Malta Lib. and Info. Assn. (MaLIA), c/o Univ. of Malta Lib., Msida MSD 2080. E-mail info@malia-malta.org, World Wide Web https://www.facebook.com/malia.malta/.

Mauritania

Association Mauritanienne des Bibliothécaires, Archivistes, et Documentalistes (Mauritanian Assn. of Libns., Archivists, and Documentalists), c/o Bibliothèque Nationale, BP 20, Nouakchott. Tel. 525-18-62, fax 525-18-68, e-mail bibliothequenationale@yahoo.fr.

Mauritius

Mauritius Lib. Assn., Quatre Bornes, Mauritius 230. Tel. 230 5769 7392, fax 454-9553, e-mail mauritiuslibassociation@gmail.com, World Wide Web https://www.facebook.com/Mauritius-Library-Association-MLA-142991592578201/.

Mexico

Asociación Mexicana de Bibliotecarios (Mexican Assn. of Libns.), Angel Urraza 817-A, Colonia Del Valle, Benito Juárez, Mexico DF, CP 03100. Tel. 55-55-75-33-96, e-mail correo@ambac.org.mx, World Wide Web http://www.ambac.org.mx. *Chair* Brenda Cabral Vargas; *V.P.* María Guadalupe Vega Díaz.

Myanmar

Myanmar Lib. Assn., Room 003, Diamond Jubilee Hall, Yangon University, Yangon, Myanmar. Tel. 95-9-420728446, e-mail libraryassociation@mlamyanmar.org, World Wide Web http://myanmarlibrary association.org. *Pres.* Daw Ah Win.

Namibia

Namibia Information Workers Assn., P.O. Box 308, Windhoek. Tel. 264-8148-10713, e-mail niwaassociation@gmail.com. *Contact* Ms. Namutenya Hamwaalwa, e-mail hnamutenya@gmail.com.

Nepal

Nepal Lib. Assn., KVPL, Bhrikuti Mandap, Kathmandu. Tel. 01-4221163, e-mail nepal libraryassociation@gmail.com, World Wide Web https://nla.org.np/. *Pres.* Indra Prasad Adhikari. *Gen. Secy.* Reshma Dangol.

The Netherlands

KNVI—Koninklijke Nederlandse Vereniging van Informatieprofessionals (Royal Dutch Association of Information Professionals), Ambachtsstraat 15, 3861 RH Nijkerk. Tel. 033-2473427, e-mail info@knvi.nl, World Wide Web http://knvi.nl.

New Zealand

New Zealand Lib. Assn. (LIANZA), 70 Molesworth St., Wellington 6140. Tel. 027-347-5326, e-mail officeadmin@lianza.org.nz, World Wide Web http://www.lianza.org.nz. *Pres.* Anahera Morehu.

Nicaragua

Asociación Nicaraguense de Bibliotecarios y Profesionales Afines (ANIBIPA) (Nicaraguan Assn. of Libns.), Bello Horizonte, Tope Sur de la Rotonda 1/2 cuadra abajo, J-11-57, Managua. Tel. 277-4159, e-mail anibipa@hotmail.com. World Wide Web https://www.facebook.com/ANIBIPA.

Nigeria

National Lib. of Nigeria, Plot 274 Sanusi House, Central Business District, Abuja. Tel. 09-234-6773, e-mail info@nln.gov.ng, World Wide Web https://www.nln.gov.ng/. *Chair* Prof. Lenrie Olatokunbo Aina.

Norway

Arkivar Foreningen (Assn. of Archivists), Vestfoldmuseene IKS. department Vestfoldarkivet, 3205 Sandefjord. Tel. 936 56 026, e-mail post@arkivarforeningen.no, World Wide Web http://www.arkivforeningen. no/. *Deputy Chair* Mari Arnekleiv Bækkelund.

Norsk Bibliotekforening (Norwegian Lib. Assn.), Universitetsgata 14, 0164 Oslo. Tel. 23 24 34 30, e-mail nbf@norskbibliotek forening.no, World Wide Web https://norsk bibliotekforening.no/. *Dir.* Vidar Lund. *Gen. Secy.* Ann Berit Hulthin. E-mail abh@norskbibliotekforening.no.

Panama

Asociación Panameña de Bibliotecarios (Lib. Assn. of Panama), c/o Biblioteca Interamericana Simón Bolivar, Estafeta Universitaria, Panama City. E-mail biblis2@arcon.up.ac.pa, Tel. 507-6527-1904, e-mail ocastillos@hotmail.com, World Wide Web https://www.facebook.com/asociacionpanamenabibliotecarios/info.

Paraguay

Asociación de Bibliotecarios Graduados del Paraguay (Assn. of Paraguayan Graduate Libns.), Facultad Politécnica, Universidad Nacional de Asunción, 2160 San Lorenzo. Tel. 21-585-588, e-mail abigrap@pol.una.py, World Wide Web http://www.pol.una.py/abigrap.

Peru

Asociación Peruana de Archiveros y Gestores de la Información (Peruvian Assn. of Archivists and Info. Managers), Av. Manco Capac No. 1180, Dpto 201, La Victoria, Lima. Tel. 51-934-182079, e-mail contacto@archive rosdelperu.org, World Wide Web http://archiverosdelperu.org/. Pres. Ricardo Arturo Moreau Heredia.

Philippines

Assn. of Special Libs. of the Philippines, c/o Goethe-Institut Philippinen, G/4-5/F Adamson Centre, 121 Leviste St., Salcedo Village, 1227 Makati City. Tel. 2-840-5723, e-mail aslplibrarians@gmail.com, World Wide Web https://aslplibrarians.org/home. Pres. Eugene Jose T. Espinoza.
Philippine Libns. Assn., Room 301, National Lib. Bldg., T. M. Kalaw St., 1000 Ermita, Manila. Tel. 525-9401. World Wide Web http://plai.org.ph. Pres. Emma Rey.

Poland

Stowarzyszenie Bibliotekarzy Polskich (Polish Libns. Assn.), al Niepodleglosci 213, 02-086 Warsaw. Tel. 22-608-28-24, e-mail biuro@sbp.pl, World Wide Web http://www.sbp.pl. Dir. Aldona Zawałkiewicz. E-mail a.zawalkiewicz@sbp.pl; Secy. Małgorzata Dargiel-Kowalska. E-mail m.dargiel kowalska@sbp.pl.

Portugal

Associação Portuguesa de Bibliotecários, Arquivistas e Documentalistas (Portuguese Assn. of Libns., Archivists, and Documentalists), Praça Dr. Nuno Pinheiro Torres

10-A, 15500 246 Lisbon. Tel. 21-816-19-80, fax 21-815-45-08, e-mail bad@bad.pt, World Wide Web http://www.apbad.pt.

Puerto Rico

Sociedad de Bibliotecarios de Puerto Rico (Society of Libns. of Puerto Rico), Apdo 22898, San Juan 00931-2898. Tel./fax 787-764-0000. Pres. Milady Pérez Gerana.

Russia

Rossiiskaya Bibliotechnaya Assotsiatsiya (Russian Lib. Assn.), 18 Sadovaya St., St. Petersburg 191069. Tel./fax 812-110-5861, e-mail rba@nlr.ru, World Wide Web http://www.rba.ru. Exec. Secy. Trushina Irina Aleksandrovna.

Senegal

Association Sénégalaise des Bibliothécaires, Archivistes et Documentalistes (Senegalese Assn. of Libns., Archivists, and Documentalists), BP 2006, Dakar RP, Université Cheikh Anta Diop, Dakar. Tel. 77-651 00 33, fax 33-824-23-79, e-mail asbadsn@gmail.com.

Serbia

Jugoslovenski Bibliografski Informacijski Institut, Terazije 26, 11000 Belgrade. Tel. 11-2687-836, fax 11-2687-760.

Sierra Leone

Sierra Leone Assn. of Archivists, Libns., and Info. Scientists, 7 Percival Street, Freetown. Tel. 022-220-758.

Singapore

Lib. Assn. of Singapore, National Lib. Board, 100 Victoria St., No. 14-01, Singapore 188064. Tel. 6332-3255, fax 6332-3248, e-mail lassec@las.org.sg, World Wide Web http://www.las.org.sg. Pres. Dr. Sadie-Jane Nunis. E-mail president@las.org.sg.

Slovenia

Zveza Bibliotekarskih Društev Slovenije (Union of Assns. of Slovene Libns.), Turjaöka 1, 1000 Ljubljana. Tel. 1-2001-176, fax

1-4257-293, e-mail info@zbds-zveza.si, World Wide Web http://www.zbds-zveza.si. *Pres.* Sabina Fras Popovic. E-mail sabina. fras-popovic@mb.sik.si.

South Africa

Lib. and Info. Assn. of South Africa, P.O. Box 1598, Pretoria 0001. Tel. 27 (0) 12-328-2010, 27 (0) 12-323-4912, fax 27 (0) 12-323-1033, e-mail liasa@liasa.org.za, World Wide Web http://www.liasa.org.za. *Pres.* Naziem Hardy. E-mail naziem.hardy@capetown.gov.za.

Spain

Federación Española de Archiveros, Bibliotecarios, Arqueólogos, Museólogos y Documentalistas (ANABAD) (Spanish Federation of Assns. of Archivists, Libns., Archaeologists, Museum Curators, and Documentalists), de las Huertas, 37, 28014 Madrid. Tel. 91-575-1727, fax 91-578-1615, e-mail anabad@anabad.org, World Wide Web http://www.anabad.org. *Pres.* José María Nogales Herrera.

Sri Lanka

Sri Lanka Lib. Assn., Sri Lanka Professional Centre 275/75, Stanley Wijesundara Mawatha, Colombo 7. Tel./fax 11-258-9103, e-mail slla@slltnet.lk, World Wide Web http://www.slla.org.lk. *Pres.* Ruwan Gamage, e-mail president@slla.lk; *Gen. Secy.* K R N Harshani, e-mail gs@slla.lk.

Sweden

Foreningen for Archiv & Informationsforvaltening (Society of Archives and Records Management in Sweden—FAI), c/o Foreningshuset Sedab AB, Virkesvägen 26, 120 30 Stockholm. Tel. 08-121 513 21, e-mail info@fai.nu, World Wide Web https://fai.nu. *Pres.* Katarina Ekelof.
Svensk Biblioteksförening (Swedish Lib. Assn.), Oxtorgsgrand 2, 111 57 Stockholm. Tel. 08-545-132-30, fax 8-545-132-31, e-mail info@svbib.se, World Wide Web http://www.biblioteksforeningen.se. *Secy. Gen.* Karin Linder.

Svensk Förening för Informationsspecialister (Swedish Assn. for Info. Specialists), c/o Föreningshuset Sedab, Virkesvägen 26, 120 30 Stockholm. E-mail info@sfis.nu, World Wide Web http://www.sfis.nu. *Chair* Elisabeth Hammam Lie.
Svenska Arkivsamfundet (Swedish Archival Society). See Foreningen for Archiv & Informationsforvaltening (Society of Archives and Records Management in Sweden— FAI).

Switzerland

Verein Schweizer Archivarinnen und Archivare (Assn. of Swiss Archivists), Schweizerisches Bundesarchiv, Büro Pontri GmbH, Solohurnstr. 13, Postfach CH-3322, Urtenen Schönbühl. Tel. 41-31-312-26-66, fax 41-31-312-26-68, e-mail info@vsa-aas.ch, World Wide Web http://www.vsa-aas.org. *Pres.* Alain Dubois.

Taiwan

Lib. Assn. of the Republic of China (LAROC), 20 Zhongshan South Rd., Taipei 10001. Tel. 2-2361-9132, fax 2-2370-0899, e-mail lac@msg.ncl.edu.tw, World Wide Web http://www.lac.org.tw.

Tanzania

Tanzania Lib. Assn., P.O. Box 33433, Dar es Salaam. Tel./fax 255-744-296-134, e-mail info@tla.or.tz, World Wide Web http://www.tla.or.tz.

Thailand

Thai Lib. Assn., 1346 Songkhon 5 Road (between Sri Burapha Road 8-9), Klong Chan, Bang Kapi, Bangkok 10240. Tel. 02-734-9022, fax 02-734-9021, e-mail tla2497@gmail.com, World Wide Web http://tla.or.th.

Trinidad and Tobago

Lib. Assn. of Trinidad and Tobago, P.O. Box 1275, Port of Spain. Tel. 868-687-0194, e-mail latt46@gmail.com, World Wide Web https://www.facebook.com/latt46. *Pres.* Beverly Ann Williams.

Turkey

Türk Kütüphaneciler Dernegi (Turkish Libns. Assn.), Necatibey Cad Elgun Sok 8/8, 06440 Kizilay, Ankara. Tel. 312-230-13-25, fax 312-232-04-53, e-mail tkd.dernek@gmail.com, World Wide Web http://www.kutuphaneci.org.tr. *Pres.* Ali Fuat Kartal.

Uganda

Uganda Lib. and Info. Assn., P.O. Box 25412, Kampala. Tel. 256-704-885-246, e-mail secretariat@ulia.org.ug. World Wide Web https://www.facebook.com/Uganda-Library-and-Information-Association-17999835545 8703/.

Ukraine

Ukrainian Lib. Assn., a/c 62, Kiev, 03057. Tel. 380-44-383-14-32, e-mail info@ula.org.ua, World Wide Web https://ula.org.ua/en/. *Exec. Dir.* Soshynska Yaroslava.

United Kingdom

Archives and Records Assn., UK and Ireland (formerly the Society of Archivists), Priory-field House, 20 Canon St., Taunton TA1 1SW, England. Tel. 1823-327-077, fax 1823-271-719, e-mail societyofarchivists@archives.org.uk, World Wide Web http://www.archives.org.uk. *Chief Exec.* John Chambers; *Chair* Lisa Snook.

Bibliographical Society, Institute of English Studies, Senate House, Malet St., London WC1E 7HU, England. E-mail admin@bibsoc.org.uk, World Wide Web http://www.bibsoc.org.uk. *Pres.* James Raven. E-mail president@bibsoc.org.uk.

Chartered Institute of Lib. and Info. Professionals (CILIP), 7 Ridgmount St., London WC1E 7AE, England. Tel. 20-7255-0500, fax 20-7255-0501, e-mail info@cilip.org.uk, World Wide Web http://www.cilip.org.uk. *Pres.* Paul Corney; *COO* Adam Pokun.

School Lib. Assn., 1 Pine Court, Kembrey Park, Swindon SN2 8AD, England. Tel. 1793-530-166, fax 1793-481-182, e-mail info@sla.org.uk, World Wide Web http://www.sla.org.uk. *Chair* Sue Bastone; *Chief Exec.* Allison Tarrant.

Scottish Lib. and Info. Council, 175 W. George St., Glasgow G2 2LB, Scotland. Tel. 141-202-2999, e-mail info@scottishlibraries.org, World Wide Web http://www.scottishlibraries.org. *Chair* Ian Ruthven.

Society of College, National, and Univ. Libs. (SCONUL) (formerly Standing Conference of National and Univ. Libs.), 94 Euston St., London NW1 2HA, England. Tel. 20-7387-0317, fax 20-7383-3197, e-mail info@sconul.ac.uk, World Wide Web http://www.sconul.ac.uk. *Exec. Dir.* Susan Ashworth.

Uruguay

Agrupación Bibliotecológica del Uruguay (Uruguayan Lib. and Archive Science Assn.) and Asociación de Bibliotecólogos del Uruguay (Uruguayan Libns. Assn.), Eduardo V. Haedo 2255, CP 11200, Montevideo. Tel. 2409-9989, e-mail abu@adinet.com.uy, World Wide Web http://www.abu.net.uy. *Pres.* Alicia Ocaso Ferreira.

Vietnam

Hôi Thu-Vien Viet Nam (Vietnam Lib. Assn.), National Lib. of Vietnam, 31 Trang Thi, Hoan Kiem, 10000 Hanoi. Tel. 43-9366596, e-mail info@nlv.org.vn, World Wide Web http://www.vla.org.vn.

Zambia

Lib. and Info. Assn. of Zambia, P.O. Box 50183 Ridgeway, Lusaka. Tel. 260-965-024914, e-mail liaz@zambia.co.zm, World Wide Web https://zambia.co.zm/.

Zimbabwe

Zimbabwe Lib. Assn., ZimLA Midlands Branch, P.O. Box 1521, Gweru. Tel. 263-773-568-837, e-mail information@zimla.org.zw, World Wide Web https://zimbabwereads.org/zimla/. *Chair* T.G. Bohwa.

Directory of Book Trade and Related Organizations

Book Trade Associations, United States and Canada

For more extensive information on the associations listed in this section, see the annual edition of *Literary Market Place* (Information Today, Inc.).

AIGA—The Professional Assn. for Design, 222 Broadway, New York, NY 10038. Tel. 212-807-1990, fax 212-807-1799, e-mail general@aiga.org, World Wide Web http://www.aiga.org. *Exec. Dir.* Bennie F. Johnson; *Senior Dir. of Admin.* Amy Chapman.

American Book Producers Assn. (ABPA), 23 Waverly Place, Suite 6-B, New York, NY 10003. Tel. 917-620-9440, fax 212-675-1364, e-mail office@ABPAonline.org, World Wide Web http://www.abpaonline.org. *Pres.* Richard Rothschild; *V.P./Treas.* Nancy Hall; *Admin.* Michael Centore.

American Booksellers Assn., 333 Westchester Ave. Suite S202, White Plains, NY 10604. Tel. 800-637-0037, fax 914-417-4013, e-mail info@bookweb.org, World Wide Web http://www.bookweb.org. *Pres.* Jamie Fiocco, Flyleaf Books, 752 Martin Luther King Blvd., Chapel Hill, NC 27514. Tel. 919-942-7936, e-mail jamie@flyleafbooks.com; *V.P./Secy.* Bradley Graham, Politics and Prose Bookstore, 5015 Connecticut Ave. N.W., Washington, DC 20008. E-mail bgraham@politics-prose.com. *CEO* Allison Hill. E-mail allisonhill@bookweb.org.

American Literary Translators Assn. (ALTA), University of Arizona, Esquire Building #205, 1230 N. Park Ave., Tucson, AZ 85721. World Wide Web https://literarytranslators.org/. *Exec. Dir.* Elisabeth Jaquette. E-mail elisabeth@literarytranslators.org.

American Printing History Assn., Box 4519, Grand Central Sta., New York, NY 10163-4519.

World Wide Web http://www.printinghistory.org. *Pres.* Haven Hawley; *Treas.* David Goodrich; *Board Secy.* Virginia Bartow; *Exec. Secy.* Lyndsi Barnes. E-mail secretary@printinghistory.org.

American Society for Indexing, 1628 E. Southern Ave., No. 9-223, Tempe, AZ 85282. Tel. 480-245-6750, e-mail info@asindexing.org, World Wide Web http://www.asindexing.org. *Pres.* Meghan Miller Brawley. E-mail president@asindexing.org; *V.P./Pres.-Elect.* Michelle Combs. E-mail presidentelect@asindexing.org; *Exec. Dir.* Gwen Henson. E-mail gwen@asindexing.org.

American Society of Journalists and Authors, 355 Lexington Ave., 15th Fl., New York, NY 10017-6603. Tel. 212-997-0947, fax 212-937-2315, e-mail asjaoffice@asja.org, World Wide Web http://www.asja.org. *Pres.* Laura Laing. E-mail president@asja.org; *V.P.* Emily Paulsen. E-mail vicepresident@asja.org; *Exec. Dir.* Holly Koenig.

American Society of Media Photographers, Four Embarcadero Center, Suite 1400, San Francisco, CA 94111. Tel. 877-771-2767, fax 231-946-6180, e-mail asmp@vpconnections.com, World Wide Web http://www.asmp.org. *Chair* Marianne Lee. E-mail lee@asmp.org; *V.Chair* Michael Shay. E-mail shay@asmp.org.

American Society of Picture Professionals, 201 E. 25 St., No. 11C, New York, NY 10010. Tel. 516-500-3686, e-mail director@aspp.com, World Wide Web http://aspp.com/.

Pres. Cecilia de Querol. E-mail president@aspp.com; *Exec. Dir.* Darrell Perry. E-mail director@aspp.com.

American Translators Assn., 225 Reinekers Lane, Suite 590, Alexandria, VA 22314. Tel. 703-683-6100, fax 703-683-6122, e-mail ata@atanet.org, World Wide Web http://www.atanet.org. *Pres.* Ted R. Wozniak; *Secy.* Karen Tkaczyk; *Treas.* John M. Milan; *Exec. Dir.* Walter W. Bacak, Jr. E-mail walter@atanet.org.

Antiquarian Booksellers Assn. of America, 20 W. 44 St., No. 507, New York, NY 10036-6604. Tel. 212-944-8291, fax 212-944-8293, World Wide Web http://www.abaa.org. *Pres.* Brad Johnson; *V.P.* Sheryl Jaeger; *Secy.* Elizabeth Svendsen; *Treas.* Peter Blackman; *Exec. Dir.* Susan Benne. E-mail sbenne@abaa.org.

Assn. Media and Publishing, P.O. Box 34340, Washington, DC 20043. Tel. 202-789-4475, World Wide Web https://history.siia.net/amp. *President* Diane Rusignola; *V.P.* Christopher Okenka; *Secy.* Stacy Brooks Whatley.

Assn. of American Publishers, 455 Massachusetts Ave. N.W., Suite 700, Washington, DC 20001. Tel. 202-347-3375, fax 202-347-3690, World Wide Web http://www.publishers.org. *Pres./CEO* Maria A. Pallante. E-mail ceo@publishers.org. *Chair* Brian Napack; *V.Chair* Michael Pietsch; *Treas.* Jeremy North.

Assn. of University Presses, 1412 Broadway, Suite 2135, New York, NY 10018. Tel. 212-989-1010, fax 212-989-0275, e-mail info@aupresses.org, World Wide Web https://aupresses.org/. *Pres.* Niko Pfund, Oxford Univ. Press; *Pres.-Elect* Lisa Bayer, Univ. of Georgia Press; *Treas.* Alice Ennis, Univ. of Illinois Press; *Exec. Dir.* Peter Berkery. Tel. 917-288-5594, e-mail pberkery@aupresses.org.

Assn. of Canadian Publishers, 174 Spadina Ave., Suite 306, Toronto, ON M5T 2C2. Tel. 416-487-6116, fax 416-487-8815, e-mail admin@canbook.org, World Wide Web http://www.publishers.ca. *Pres.* Melissa Pitts, University of British Columbia Press, Vancouver; *V.P.* Ruth Linka, Orca Book Publishers, Victoria; *Treas.* Katherine Boersma, OwlKids Books, Toronto; *Exec. Dir.* Kate Edwards. Tel. 416-487-6116 ext. 2340, e-mail kate_edwards@canbook.org.

Audio Publishers Assn., 333 Hudson Street Suite 503, New York, NY 10013. Tel. 646-688-3044, e-mail info@audiopub.org, World Wide Web http://www.audiopub.org. *Pres.* Ana Maria Allessi; *V.P.* Amy Metsch; *Secy.* Natalie Fedewa *Treas.* Dan Zitt; *Exec. Dir.* Michele Cobb. E-mail mcobb@audiopub.org.

Authors Guild, 31 E. 32 St., 7th Fl., New York, NY 10016. Tel. 212-563-5904, fax 212-564-5363, e-mail staff@authorsguild.org, World Wide Web http://www.authorsguild.org. *Pres.* Doug Preston; *V.P.s* Monique Truong and W. Ralph Eubanks; *Secy.* Rachel Vail; *Treas.* Peter Petre; *Exec. Dir.* Mary Rasenberger.

Book Industry Study Group, 232 Madison Ave., Suite 1400, New York, NY 10016. Tel. 646-336-7141, e-mail info@bisg.org, World Wide Web http://bisg.org. *Chair* Andrew Savikas, getAbstract; *V.Chair* Kathleen Reid, Elsevier; *Secy.* David Hetherington, knk Software; *Treas.* David Hetherington, knk Software; *Exec. Dir.* Brian O'Leary. Tel. 646-336-7141, e-mail brian@bisg.org.

Book Manufacturers' Institute (BMI), P.O. Box 731388, Ormand Beach, FL 32173. Tel. 386-986-4552, fax 386-986-4553, World Wide Web http://www.bmibook.org. *Pres.* Joseph H. Upton, Above the Treeline; *Exec. Dir./Secy.* Matthew J. Baehr; *V.P./Pres.-Elect* David McCree, LSC Communications; *Treas.* Suzanne Wiersma, Wallaceburg Bookbinding.

Bookbuilders of Boston, 115 Webster Woods Lane, North Andover, MA 01845. Tel. 781-378-1361, fax 419-821-2171, e-mail office@bbboston.org, World Wide Web http://www.bbboston.org. *Pres.* James Taylor. E-mail james.taylor@bbboston.org; *1st V.P.* Margaret Rosewitz. E-mail margaret.rosewitz@bbboston.org; *2nd V.P.* Michele DeVenuto. E-mail michelle.devenuto@bbboston.org; *Treasurer* Isabel Tran. E-mail isabel.tran@bbboston.org; *Clerk* Laura Rodriguez. E-mail laura.rodriguez@bbboston.org.

Bookbuilders West. See Publishing Professionals Network.

Canadian International Standard Numbers (ISNs) Agency, c/o Lib. and Archives Canada, 395 Wellington St., Ottawa, ON K1A 0N4. Tel. 866-578-7777 (toll-free) or 613-996-5115, World Wide Web http://www.

bac-lac.gc.ca/eng/services/isbn-canada/ Pages/isbn-canada.aspx.

Canadian Printing Industries Assn., 3-1750 The Queensway, Suite 135, Toronto, ON M9C 5H5, World Wide Web http://www.cpia aci.ca. Pres. Richard Kouwenhoven, Tel. 604-438-2456, e-mail richard@hemlock. com; Assoc. Mgr. Gerry Lacombe, e-mail admin@cpia-aci.ca; Admin. Tracey Preston, Tel. 905-602-4441, e-mail tpreston.opia@ on.aibn.com.

Children's Book Council, 54 W. 39 St., 14th Fl., New York, NY 10018. Tel. 917-890-7416, e-mail cbc.info@cbcbooks.org, World Wide Web http://www.cbcbooks.org. Chair Yolanda Scott; Vice Chair Catherine Onder; Treas. Terry Borzumato-Greenberg; Secy. Ruth Chamblee; Exec. Dir. Carl Lennertz.

Community of Literary Magazines and Presses, 154 Christopher St., Suite 3C, New York, NY 10014. Tel. 212-741-9110, e-mail info@clmp.org, World Wide Web http:// www.clmp.org. Chair Nicole Dewey; Exec. Dir. Mary Gannon. E-mail mgannon@clmp. org.

Copyright Society of the USA, 1 E. 53 St., 8th Fl., New York, NY 10022. Tel. 212-354-6401, World Wide Web http://www. csusa.org. Pres. Naomi Jane Gray; V.P./Pres.-Elect Casey Chisick; Secy. Chad Rutkowski; Treas. Theodore Cheng; Exec. Dir. Kaitland E. Kubat.

Educational Book and Media Assn., P.O. Box 3363, Warrenton, VA 20188. Tel. 540-318-7770, e-mail info@edupaperback.org, World Wide Web http://www.edupaperback.org. Pres. Lisa Maisonneuve; V.P. Ben Conn; Treas. Bryan Thompson; Secy. Marin Foster; Exec. Dir. Brain Gorg.

Evangelical Christian Publishers Assn., 9633 S. 48 St., Suite 140, Phoenix, AZ 85044. Tel. 480-966-3998, fax 480-966-1944, e-mail info@ecpa.org, World Wide Web http:// www.ecpa.org. Pres./CEO Stan Jantz; Chair Jeff Crosby; V. Chair Dan Kok; Secy. Barb Sherrill; Treas. Dan Baker.

Graphic Artists Guild, 31 West 34th St., 8th Fl., New York, NY 10001. Tel. 212-791-3400, e-mail admin@graphicartistsguild.org, World Wide Web http://www.graphicartistsguild.org. Pres. Lara Kisielewska. E-mail president@graphicartistsguild.org; Treas. Linda Secondari; Secy. Bill Morse; Admin.

Dir. Paula Hinkle. E-mail membership@ graphicartistsguild.org.

Great Lakes Independent Booksellers Assn., c/o Exec. Dir., 250 Woodstock Ave, Clarendon Hills, IL 60514. Tel. 630-841-8129, e-mail larry@gliba.org, World Wide Web http://www.gliba.org. Pres. Lynn Mooney, Women & Children First, 5233 N. Clark St., Chicago, IL 60640. Tel. 773-769-9299. Exec. Dir. Larry Law.

Guild of Book Workers, 521 Fifth Ave., New York, NY 10175. Tel. 212-292-4444, e-mail communications@guildofbookworkers.org, World Wide Web http://www.guildofbookworkers.org. Pres. Bexx Caswell. E-mail president@guildofbookworkers.org; V. Pres. Brien Beidler. E-mail vicepresident@ guildofbookworkers.org; Secy. Rebecca Smyrl. E-mail secretary@guildofbookworkers.org; Treas. Laura Bedford. E-mail treasurer@guildofbookworkers.org.

Horror Writers Assn., P.O. Box 56687, Sherman Oaks, CA 91413. E-mail hwa@horror. org, World Wide Web http://www.horror. org. Pres. John Palisano. E-mail president@ horror.org; V.P. Meghan Arcuri. E-mail vp@ horror.org; Secy. Becky Spratford. E-mail secretary@horror.org; Treas. Leslie Klinger. E-mail treasurer@horror.org; Admin. Brad Hodson. E-mail admin@horror.org.

Independent Book Publishers Assn., 1020 Manhattan Beach Blvd., Suite 204, Manhattan Beach, CA 90266. Tel. 310-546-1818, fax 310-546-3939, e-mail info@ibpa-online. org, World Wide Web http://www.ibpa-online. org. Chair Karla Olson, Patagonia Books; Treas. Richard Lena, Brattle Publishing; Secy. Kathy Strahs, Burnt Cheese Press; CEO Angela Bole. E-mail angela@ibpa-online. org.

International Standard Book Numbering U.S. Agency, 630 Central Ave., New Providence, NJ 07974. Tel. 877-310-7333, fax 908-219-0188, e-mail isbn-san@bowker.com, World Wide Web http://www.isbn.org. Dir., Identifier Svcs. Beat Barblan.

Jewish Book Council, 520 Eighth Ave., 4th Fl., New York, NY 10018. Tel. 212-201-2920, fax 212-532-4952, e-mail info@jewish books.org, World Wide Web http://www. jewishbookcouncil.org. Pres. Jane Weitzman; V.P.s Joy Greenberg, Carol Levin, Lenore J. Weitzman; Secy. Elisa Spungen

Bildner; *Treasurer* Alan Kadish; *Exec. Dir.* Naomi Firestone-Teeter.

Midwest Independent Publishers Assn. (MIPA), P.O. Box 580475, Minneapolis, MN 55458-0475. Tel. 651-917-0021, World Wide Web http://www.mipa.org. *Pres.* Suzzanne Kelley, North Dakota State Univ. Press, Tel. 701-231-6848, e-mail president@mipa.org; *V.P.* Paul Nylander, Illustrada Design. Tel. 612-325-1228, e-mail vicepresident@mipa.org; *Treas.* Nayt Rundquist, New Rivers Press. Tel. 218-477-5870, e-mail treasurer@mipa.org; *Exec. Dir.* Jennifer Baum, e-mail bookawards@mipa.org.

Miniature Book Society. Tel. 619-226-4441, e-mail member@mbs.org, World Wide Web http://www.mbs.org. *Pres.* Tony Firman; *V.P.* Ron Wood; *Secy.* Cynthia Cosgrove; *Treas.* Kim Herrick.

Minnesota Book Publishers' Roundtable. E-mail information@publishersroundtable.org, World Wide Web http://www.publishersroundtable.org. *Pres.* Kellie Hultgren, KMH Editing, e-mail president@publishersroundtable.org; *V.P.* Ashley Kuehl, e-mail ashleykuehl.mbpr@gmail.com; *Secy.* Arnold Ringstad, Red Line Editorial, e-mail a.ringstad@redlineeditorial.com; *Treas.* Cathy Broberg, Catherine Broberg Editorial Services, e-mail cathy@cathybroberg.com.

Mountains and Plains Independent Booksellers Assn., 2105 Union Drive, Lakewood, CO 80215. Tel. 720-272-0805, fax 970-484-0037, e-mail info@mountainsplains.org, World Wide Web http://www.mountainsplains.org. *Pres.* Christopher Green; *Vice Pres.* Allison Senecal; *Secy.* Stephanie Schindhelm; *Exec. Dir.* Heather Duncan. E-mail heather@mountainsplains.org.

MPA—The Assn. of Magazine Media, 757 Third Ave., 11th Fl., New York, NY 10017. Tel. 212-872-3700, e-mail mpa@magazine.org, World Wide Web http://www.magazine.org. *Chair* Tom Harty; *Vice Chair* Bonnie Kintzer; *Secy.* Monica Ray; *Treas.* Debi Chirichella; *Pres. & CEO* Brigitte Schmidt Gwyn, e-mail bsgwyn@magazine.org.

National Assn. of College Stores, 500 E. Lorain St., Oberlin, OH 44074-1294. Tel. 800-622-7498, 440-775-7777, fax 440-775-4769, e-mail info@nacs.org, World Wide Web http://www.nacs.org. *Pres. and Treas.* Steve Westenbroek; *Pres.-Elect and Secy.*

Adam Hustwitt; *CEO* Eric Schlechenmayer. E-mail eschlichenmayer@nacs.org.

National Book Foundation, 90 Broad St., Suite 604, New York, NY 10004. Tel. 212-685-0261, fax 212-213-6570, e-mail nationalbook@nationalbook.org, World Wide Web http://www.nationalbook.org. *Chair* David Steinberger, Arcadia Publishing; *V. Chair* Fiona McCrea, Graywolf Publishing; *Secy.* Calvin Sims, CNN; *Treas.* Elpidio Villarreal; *Interim Exec. Director* Jordan Smith. E-mail jsmith@nationalbook.org.

National Coalition Against Censorship (NCAC), 19 Fulton St., Suite 407, New York, NY 10038. Tel. 212-807-6222, fax 212-807-6245, e-mail ncac@ncac.org, World Wide Web http://www.ncac.org. *Dirs.* Jon Anderson, Michael Bamberger, Joan E. Bertin, Judy Blume, Susan Clare, Chris Finan, Eric M. Freedman, Robie Harris, Phil Harvey, Michael Jacobs, Randall Kennedy, Emily Knox, Chris Peterson, Julie Samuels, Larry Siems, Oren J. Teicher, Emily Whitfield; *Exec. Dir.* Chris Finan. E-mail chris@ncac.org.

New Atlantic Independent Booksellers Assn. (NAIBA), 2667 Hyacinth St., Westbury, NY 11590. Tel. 516-333-0681, fax 516-333-0689, e-mail naibabooksellers@gmail.com, World Wide Web http://www.newatlanticbooks.com. *Pres.* Rebecca Fitting, Greenlight Bookstores; *V.P.* Hannah Oliver Depp, Loyalty Bookstores; *Secy.-Treas.* Erin Matthews, Books with a Past; *Exec. Dir.* Eileen Dengler. E-mail NAIBAeileen@gmail.com.

New England Independent Booksellers Assn. (NEIBA), One Beacon Street, 15th Floor, Boston, MA 02108. Tel. 617-547-3642, fax 617-830-8768, e-mail beth@neba.org, World Wide Web http://www.newenglandbooks.org. *Pres.* Beth Wagner, Phoenix Books, Essex Junction, VT; *V.P.* Emily Russo, Print: A Bookstore, Portland, ME; *Treas.* Emily Crow, An Unlikely Story, Plainville, MA; *Exec. Dir.* Beth Ineson. E-mail beth@neba.org.

Northern California Independent Booksellers Assn., 651 Broadway, 2nd Fl., Sonoma, CA 95476. Tel. 415-561-7686, fax 415-561-7685, e-mail info@nciba.com, World Wide Web http://www.nciba.com. *Pres.* Melinda Powers; *Treas.* Bridget Schinnerer; *Secy.* Carolyn Hutton; *Exec. Dir.* Calvin Crosby. E-mail calvin@nciba.com.

PEN American Center, Div. of International PEN, 588 Broadway, Suite 303, New York, NY 10012. Tel. 212-334-1660, fax 212-334-2181, e-mail pen@pen.org, World Wide Web http://www.pen.org. *Pres.* Ayad Akhtar; *Exec. V.P.* Markus Dohle; *V.P.s* Masha Gessen, Tracy Higgins; *Treas.* Yvonne Marsh; *CEO* Susanne Nossel. E-mail snossel@pen.org.

Publishing Professionals Network (formerly Bookbuilders West), c/o Postal Annex, 274 Redwood Shores Parkway, Box 129, Redwood City, CA 94065-1173. E-mail operations@pubpronetwork.org, World Wide Web http://pubpronetwork.org. *Pres.* David Zielonka. E-mail zielonka@stanford.edu; *V.P.* Dave Peattie. E-mail dave@bookmatters.com; *Secy.* Mimi Heft. E-mail mimi.heft.design@gmail.com; *Treas.* Barbara Fuller. E-mail barbara@editcetera.com.

Romance Writers of America, 5315-B Cypress Creek Parkway, #111, Houston, TX 77069. Tel. 832-717-5200, e-mail info@rwa.org, World Wide Web http://www.rwa.org. *Pres.* LaQuette. E-mail president@rwa.org; *Secy.* C. Chilove. E-mail secretary@rwa.org; *Treasurer* Laura Alford. E-mail treasurer@rwa.org; *Exec. Dir.* Leslie Scantlebury. E-mail leslie.scantlebury@rwa.org.

Science Fiction and Fantasy Writers of America, P.O. Box 3238, Enfield, CT 06083-3238. World Wide Web http://www.sfwa.org. *Pres.* Mary Robinette Kowal. E-mail president@sfwa.org; *V.P.* Tobias S. Buckell. E-mail tobias.buckell@sfwa.org; *Secy.* Curtis C. Chen. E-mail curtis.chen@sfwa.org; *CFO* Nathan Lowell. E-mail cfo@sfwa.org.

SIBA (formerly Southern Independent Booksellers Alliance), 51 Pleasant Ridge, Asheville, NC 28805. Tel. 803-994-9530, e-mail siba@sibaweb.com, World Wide Web http://www.sibaweb.com. *Exec. Dir.* Linda-Marie Barrett, E-mail lindamarie@sibaweb.com.

Society of Children's Book Writers and Illustrators (SCBWI), 4727 Wilshire Blvd., Suite 301, Los Angeles, CA 90010. Tel. 323-782-1010, e-mail scbwi@scbwi.org, World Wide Web http://www.scbwi.org. *Exec. Dir.* Lin Oliver. E-mail linoliver@scbwi.org; *Assoc. Exec. Dir.* Sarah Baker, E-mail sarahbaker@scbwi.org.

Society of Illustrators (SI), 128 E. 63 St., New York, NY 10065. Tel. 212-838-2560, fax 212-838-2561, e-mail info@societyillustrators.org, World Wide Web http://www.societyillustrators.org. *Pres.* Tim O'Brien; *Exec. Secy.* Leslie Cober-Gentry; *Exec. Dir.* Anelle Miller. E-mail anelle@societyillustrators.org.

Southern Independent Booksellers Alliance. See SIBA.

Western Writers of America, c/o Candy Moulton, 271 CR 219, Encampment, WY 82325 Tel. 307-329-8942, e-mail wwa.moulton@gmail.com, World Wide Web http://www.westernwriters.org. *Pres.* Chris Enss; *V.P.* Phil Mills, Jr.; *Exec. Dir., Secy./Treas.* Candy Moulton.

Women's National Book Assn., P.O. Box 237, FDR Sta., New York, NY 10150. Tel. 866-610-WNBA (9622), e-mail info@wnba-books.org, World Wide Web http://www.wnba-books.org. *Pres.* Natalie Obando-Desai; e-mail nationalpresidentWNBA@gmail.com; *V.P.s* Andrea Panzeca, NC Weil; *Secy.* Linda Rosen; *Treasurer* Karen Holly.

International and Foreign Book Trade Associations

For Canadian book trade associations, see the preceding section, "Book Trade Associations, United States and Canada." For a more extensive list of book trade organizations outside the United States and Canada, with more detailed information, consult *International Literary Market Place* (Information Today, Inc.), which also provides extensive lists of major bookstores and publishers in each country.

International

African Publishers' Network, c/o Ghana Book Publishers Assn., Bureau of Ghana Languages Building, Kawukudi Culture, P.O. Box Lt 471, Laterbiokorshie, Accra, Ghana. Tel. 233-302-912764, 233-209-115191, e-mail info.africanpublishers@gmail. com, World Wide Web http://www.african-publishers.net/. *Acting Exec. Dir.* Ernest Oppong.

Afro-Asian Book Council, 212, Shahpur Jat, New Delhi 110 049, India. Tel. 91-11-26493326, fax 91-11-41752055, e-mail info@aabookcouncil.org, World Wide Web http://www.aabookcouncil.org/. *Secretary-General* Ramesh Mittal. E-mail rkmittal@dkagencies.com; *Dir.* Pranav Gupta. E-mail pgprintsindia@gmail.com.

Centro Regional para el Fomento del Libro en América Latina y el Caribe (CERLALC) (Regional Center for Book Promotion in Latin America and the Caribbean), Calle 70, No. 9-52, Bogotá, Colombia. Tel. 571-518-70-70, e-mail cerlalc@cerlalc.com, World Wide Web http://www.cerlalc.org. *Dir.* Andrés Ossa Quintero.

Federation of European Publishers, Chaussee d'Ixelles 29/35, Box 4, 1050 Brussels, Belgium. Tel. 32-2-770-11-10, fax 32-2-771-20-71, e-mail info@fep-fee.eu, World Wide Web http://www.fep-fee.eu. *Pres.* Peter Kraus; *Dir.* Anne Bergman-Tahon.

International Board on Books for Young People (IBBY), Nonnenweg 12, Postfach CH-4009, Basel, Switzerland. Tel. 41-61-272-29-17, fax 41-61-272-27-57, e-mail ibby@ibby. org, World Wide Web http://www.ibby.org. *Pres.* Mingzhou Zhang; *Exec. Dir.* Elizabeth Page.

International League of Antiquarian Booksellers (ILAB), c/o Rue Toepffer 5, Case postale 499, 1211 Geneva 12, Switzerland. E-mail secretariat@ilab.org, World Wide Web http://www.ilab.org. *Pres.* Sally Burdon; *Gen. Secy.* Stewart Bennett.

International Publishers Assn. (Union Internationale des Editeurs), 23 ave. de France, CH-1202 Geneva, Switzerland. Tel. 41-22-704-1820, fax 41-22-704-1821, e-mail info@internationalpublishers.org, World Wide Web http://www.internationalpublishers.org. *Pres.* Bodour Al Qasimi; *Secy.-Gen.* José Borghino.

STM: The International Assn. of Scientific, Technical, and Medical Publishers, Prama House, 267 Banbury Road, Oxford OX2 7HT, England. Tel. 44-0-1865-339-321, fax 44-0-1865-339-325, e-mail info@stm-assoc. org, World Wide Web http://www.stm-assoc. org. *CEO* Ian Moss.

National

Argentina

Cámara Argentina del Libro (Argentine Book Assn.), Av. Belgrano 1580, 4 piso, C1093AAQ Buenos Aires. Tel. 54-11-4381-8383, fax 54-11-4381-9253, e-mail cal@editores.org.ar, World Wide Web http://www.editores.org.ar.

Fundación El Libro (Book Foundation),Yrigoyen 1628, 5 piso, C1089AAF Buenos Aires. Tel. 54-11-4370-0600, fax 54-11-4370-0607, e-mail fundacion@el-libro.com.ar, World Wide Web http://www.el-libro.org.ar. *Pres.* Gabriel Waldhuter; *Admin. Dir.* José Gutiérrez Brianza.

Australia

Australian and New Zealand Assn. of Antiquarian Booksellers (ANZAAB), 40 Charlotte St. (Ground Floor), Brisbane, Q 4000. E-mail admin@anzaab.com, World Wide

Web http://www.anzaab.com. *Pres.* Douglas Stewart.
Australian Booksellers Assn., 828 High St., Unit 9, Kew East, Vic. 3102. Tel. 3-9859-7322, fax 3-9859-7344, e-mail mail@aba. org.au, World Wide Web http://www.booksellers.org.au. *CEO* Robbie Egan.
Australian Publishers Assn., 60/89 Jones St., Ultimo, NSW 2007. Tel. 2-9281-9788, e-mail apa@publishers.asn.au, World Wide Web http://www.publishers.asn.au. *Pres.* Lcc Walker.

Austria

Hauptverband des Österreichischen Buchhandels (Austrian Publishers and Booksellers Assn.), Grünangergasse 4, A-1010 Vienna. Tel. 43-1-512-15-35, fax 43-1-512-84-82, e-mail office@hvb.at, World Wide Web http://www.buecher.at. *Mgr.* Gustav Soucek.
Verband der Antiquare Österreichs (Austrian Antiquarian Booksellers Assn.), Grünangergasse 4, A-1010 Vienna. Tel. 1-512-1535-14, e-mail sekretariat@hvb.at, World Wide Web http://www.antiquare.at.

Belarus

National Book Chamber of Belarus, 31a V Horuzhei Str., Rm. 707, 220002 Minsk. Tel. 375-17-288-67-15, fax 375-17-283-29-60, e-mail palata@natbook.org.by, World Wide Web http://natbook.org.by. *Dir.* Elena Ivanova. E-mail elvit@natbook.org.by.

Belgium

Boek.be (formerly Vlaamse Boekverkopersbond, Flemish Booksellers Assn.), Te Buelaerlei 37, 2140 Borgerhout. Tel. 03-230-89-23, fax 3-281-22-40, World Wide Web http://www.boek.be/over-boekbe.

Brazil

Cámara Brasileira do Livro (Brazilian Book Assn.), Rua Cristiano Viana 91, Pinheiros-São Paulo-SP, CEP: 05411-000. Tel./fax 11-3069-1300, e-mail cbl@cbl.org.br, World Wide Web http://www.cbl.org.br. *Pres.* Vitor Tavares.
Sindicato Nacional dos Editores de Livros (Brazilian Publishers Assn.), Rue da Ajuda 35 / 18th Fl., 20040-000 Rio de Janeiro-RJ. Tel. 21-99472-6066, 21-2533-0399, fax 21-2533-0422, e-mail snel@snel.org.br, World Wide Web http://www.snel.org.br. *Pres.* Marcos de Veiga Pereira.

Chile

Cámara Chilena del Libro AG (Chilean Assn. of Publishers, Distributors, and Booksellers), Av. Libertador Bernardo O'Higgins 1370, Oficina 501, Santiago. Tel. 2-672-0348, fax 2-687-4271, e-mail prolibro@tie.cl, World Wide Web https://camaradellibro.cl/. *Pres.* Eduardo Castillo.

Colombia

Cámara Colombiana del Libro (Colombian Book Assn.), Calle 35, No. 5A 05, Bogotá. Tel. 57-1-323-01-11, fax 57-1-285-10-82, e-mail camlibro@camlibro.com.co, World Wide Web http://www.camlibro.com.co. *Exec. Pres.* Enrique González Villa; *Secy.-Gen.* Manuel José Sarmiento Ramírez.

Czech Republic

Svaz ceských knihkupcu a nakladatelu (Czech Publishers and Booksellers Assn.), Fugnerovo nameisti 1808/3, Prague 2, 120 00. Tel. 420-227-660-644, e-mail sckn@sckn.cz, World Wide Web http://www.sckn.cz. *Dir.* Marcela Turcčková. E-mail tureckova@sckn.cz.

Denmark

Danske Boghandlerforening (Danish Booksellers Assn.), Slotsholmsgade 1 B, 1216 Copenhagen K. Tel. 45-32-54-2255, fax 45-32-54-0041, e-mail info@boghandlerne.dk, World Wide Web http://www.boghandlerforeningen.dk. *Chair* Lone Haagerup; *Dir.* Bo Dybkær
Danske Forlæggerforening (Danish Publishers Assn.), Stock Exchange, Slotsholmsgade 1, 1217 Copenhagen K. Tel. 45-33-15-66-88, e-mail info@danskeforlag.dk, World Wide Web http://www.danskeforlag.dk. *Chair* Lars Boesgaard; *Dir.* Christine Bødtcher-Hansen.

Ecuador

Cámara Ecuatoriana del Libro, N29-61 Eloy Alfaro and England, 9th Floor, Quito. Tel.

593-2-2553311, fax 593-2-2553314, e-mail info@celibro.org.ec, World Wide Web http://celibro.org.ec. *Pres.* Oswaldo Almeida Mora.

Egypt

General Egyptian Book Organization (GEBO), P.O. Box 235, Cairo 11511. Tel. 2-257-75367, e-mail walaakotb@gebo.gov.eg, World Wide Web http://www.gebo.gov.eg/.

Estonia

Estonian Publishers Assn., Roosikrantsi 6-207, 10119 Tallinn. Telephone 372-644-9866, fax 372-617-7550, e-mail kirjastusteliit@eki.ee, World Wide Web http://www.est-book.com. *Managing Dir.* Kaidi Urmet. E-mail kirjastusteliit@eki.ee.

Finland

Kirjakauppaliitto Ry (Booksellers Association of Finland), Eteläranta 10, 00130 Helsinki. Tel. 040-689-9112, e-mail toimisto@kirjakauppaliitto.fi, World Wide Web http://www.kirjakauppaliitto.fi. *Managing Director* Laura Karlsson. E-mail laura.karlsson@kirjakauppaliitto.fi.

Suomen Kirjasaatio (Finnish Book Foundation). Eteläranta 10, FI-00130 Helsinki. Tel. 358 9 228 77 255, World Wide Web https://kustantajat.fi/. *CEO* Pasi Vainio.

France

Bureau International de l'Edition Française (BIEF) (International Bureau of French Publishing), 115 blvd. Saint-Germain, F-75006 Paris. Tel. 01-44-41-13-13, fax 01-46-34-63-83, e-mail info@bief.org, World Wide Web http://www.bief.org. *Pres.* Antoine Gallimard; *Dir. Gen.* Nicolas Roche. *New York Branch* French Publishers Agency, 30 Vandam Street, Suite 5A, New York, NY 10013. Tel./fax 212-254-4540, World Wide Web https://www.frenchrights.com/.

Cercle de la Librairie (Circle of Professionals of the Book Trade), 35 rue Grégoire-de-Tours, F-75006 Paris. Tel. 01-44-41-28-00, fax 01-44-41-28-65, e-mail support@electre.com, World Wide Web http://www.electre.com.

Syndicat de la Librairie Française, Hotel Massa, 38 rue du Faubourg Saint-Jacques, F-75014 Paris. Tel. 01-53-62-23-10, fax 01-53-62-10-45, e-mail contact@syndicat-librairie.fr, World Wide Web http://www.syndicat-librairie.fr. *Admin. Secy.* Gaëlle Sacase. E-mail g.sacase@syndicat-librairie.fr.

Syndicat National de la Librairie Ancienne et Moderne (SLAM) (National Assn. of Antiquarian and Modern Booksellers), 4 rue Gît-le-Coeur, F-75006 Paris. Tel. 01-43-29-46-38, fax 01-43-25-41-63, e-mail slam livre@wanadoo.fr, World Wide Web http://www.slam-livre.fr. *Pres.* Herve Valentin; *Secy.-Gen.* Pierre Prevost.

Syndicat National de l'Edition (SNE) (National Union of Publishers), 115 blvd. Saint-Germain, F-75006 Paris. Tel. 01-44-41-40-50, fax 01-44-41-40-77, World Wide Web http://www.sne.fr. *Pres.* Vincent Montagne.

Germany

Börsenverein des Deutschen Buchhandels e.V. (Stock Exchange of German Booksellers), Braubachstr. 16, 60311 Frankfurt-am-Main. Tel. 49-69-1306-0, fax 49-69-1306-201, e-mail info@boev.de, World Wide Web http://www.boersenverein.de. *Chair* Karin Schmidt-Friderichs.

Verband Deutscher Antiquare e.V. (German Antiquarian Booksellers Assn.), Geschäftsstelle, Seeblick 1, 56459 Elbingen. Tel. 49-0-6435-90-91-47, fax 49-0-6435-90-91-48, e-mail buch@antiquare.de, World Wide Web http://www.antiquare.de. *Chair* Sibylle Wieduwilt. E-mail s.wieduwilt@antiquare.de.

Hungary

Magyar Könyvkiadók és Könyvterjesztök Egyesülése (Assn. of Hungarian Publishers and Booksellers), Kertész u. 41. I / 4, 1073 Budapest. Tel. 06-1-343-2538, e-mail mkke@mkke.hu, World Wide Web http://www.mkke.hu. *Pres.* Katalin Gál.

Iceland

Félag Islenskra Bókaútgefenda (Icelandic Publishers Assn.), Brautarholti 8, 105 Reykjavik. Tel. 517-7200, e-mail fibut@fibut.is, World Wide Web http://www.fibut.is. *Chair* Heidar Ingi Svannsson.

India

Federation of Indian Publishers, Federation House, 18/1C Institutional Area, Aruna Asaf

Ali Marg, New Delhi 110067. Tel. 11-2696-4847, fax 11-2686-4054, e-mail fippresi dent@gmail.com, World Wide Web http://www.fiponline.org. *Exec. Dir.* Shri. Ramesh K. Mittal.

Indonesia

Ikapi (Indonesian Publisher Association), Ikapi Building, Jalan Kalipasir, No. 32, Cikini, Central Jakarta, 10340. Tel. 62 21 314 1907, e-mail sekretariat@ikapi.org, World Wide Web http://www.ikapi.org. *Chair* Arys Hilman Nugraha; *Secy.* Novi Arsianti.

Ireland

Publishing Ireland/Foilsiu Eireann (formerly CLÉ: The Irish Book Publishers' Assn.), 63 Patrick St., Dun Laoghaire, Co Dublin. Tel. 353-1-639-4868, e-mail info@publishing ireland.com, World Wide Web http://www.publishingireland.com. *Pres.* Joanna Smyth; *Gen. Mgr.* Orla McLoughlin.

Israel

Israeli Association of Book Publishers, 29 Carlebach St., 67132 Tel Aviv. Tel. 3-561-4121, fax 3-561-1996, e-mail info@tbpai.co.il, World Wide Web http://www.tbpai.co.il. *Chair* Benjamin Trivaks.

Italy

Associazione Italiana Editori (Italian Publishers Assn.), Corso di Porta Romana 108, 20122 Milan. Tel. 2-89-28-0800, fax 2-89-28-0860, e-mail info@aie.it, World Wide Web http://www.aie.it. *Pres.* Ricardo Franco Levy.

Associazione Librai Antiquari d'Italia (Antiquarian Booksellers Assn. of Italy), via Discipilini 32, Riva del Garda (TN) 38066. E-mail alai@alai.it, World Wide Web http://www.alai.it. *Pres.* Mario Giupponi.

Japan

Antiquarian Booksellers Assn. of Japan, Kokusai Hamamatsucho Bldg., 9th Floor, 1-9-18 Kaigan, Minato-ku, Tokyo, 105-0022. Tel. 81-3-6367-6070, fax 81-3-6367-6196, e-mail abaj@abaj.gr.jp, World Wide Web http://www.abaj.gr.jp. *Chair* Shoichi Takagi.

Japan Assn. of International Publications, 1-1-13-4F Kanda, Jimbocho, Chiyodak-ku, Tokyo 101-0051. Tel. 3-5479-7269, fax 3-5479-7307, e-mail office@jaip.jp, World Wide Web http://www.jaip.jp. *Exec. Dir.* Mark Gresham.

Japan Book Publishers Assn., 5th Fl., Shuppan-Club Building 1-32, Kanda-Jimbocho, Chiyoda-ku, Tokyo, 101-0051. Tel. 81-0-3-6273-7065, fax 81-0-3-6811-0959, e-mail research@jbpa.or.jp, World Wide Web http://www.jbpa.or.jp. *Pres.* Yu Onodera.

Kenya

Kenya Publishers Assn., P.O. Box 42767, Nairobi 00100. Tel. 254-020-2635498, e-mail info@kenyapublishers.org, World Wide Web http://www.kenyapublishers.org. *Chair* Lawrence Njagi.

Korea (Republic of)

Korean Publishers Assn., Publishing Culture Center, 6 Samcheong-ro (Sagan-dong), Jongno-gu, Seoul. Tel. 2-733-8402, fax 2-738-5414, e-mail webmaster@kpa21 or.kr, World Wide Web http://eng.kpa21.or.kr. *Chair* Cheolho Yoon.

Latvia

Latvian Publishers' Assn., Baznicas iela 37-3, LV-1010 Riga. Tel./fax 67-217-730, e-mail lga@gramatizdeveji.lv, World Wide Web http://www.gramatizdeveji.lv. *Pres.* Renāte Punka *Exec. Dir.* Līva Ostupe.

Lithuania

Lithuanian Publishers Assn., Vokiečių st. 18A, LT 01130, Vilnius. Tel. 370-675-75692, fax 370-670-32287, e-mail info@lla.lt, World Wide Web http://www.lla.lt. *Pres.* Remigijus Jokubauskas; *Exec. Dir.* Rūta Elijošaityte-Kaikarė.

Malaysia

Malaysian Book Publishers' Assn., No. 7-6, Block E2, Jl PJU 1/42A, Dataran Prima, 47301 Petaling Jaya, Selangor. Tel. 3-7880-5840, fax 3-7880-5841, e-mail info@mabopa.com.my, World Wide Web http://www.mabopa.com.my. *Pres.* Arief Hakim Sani Rahmat.

Mexico

Cámara Nacional de la Industria Editorial Mexicana (Mexican Publishers' Assn.), Holanda No. 13, Col. San Diego Churubusco, Deleg. Coyoacán, 04120 Mexico DF. Tel. 155-56-88-20-11, fax 155-56-04-31-47, e-mail cont acto@caniem.com, World Wide Web http://www.caniem.com. *Pres.* Juan Luis Arzoz Arbide. E-mail presidencia@caniem.com.

The Netherlands

KVB—Koninklijke Vereeniging van het Boekenvak (Royal Society for the Book Trade), P.O. Box 12040, AA Amsterdam-Zuidoost. Tel. 20-624-02-12, fax 20-620-88-71, e-mail info@kvb.nl, World Wide Web http://www.kvb.nl. *Dirs.* M. K. J. David and A. Schroën.

Nederlands Uitgeversverbond (Royal Dutch Publishers Assn.), Postbus 12040, 1100 AA Amsterdam. Tel. 20-430-9150, fax 20-430-9199, e-mail info@mediafederatie.nl, World Wide Web https://mediafederatie.nl. *Chair* Derk Haank; *Dir.* Peter Stadhouders. E-mail pstadhouders@mediafederatie.nl.

Nederlandsche Vereeniging van Antiquaren (Netherlands Assn. of Antiquarian Booksellers), Notendijk 7, 4583 SV Terhole. Tel. 31-0-114-3142-09, fax 31-0-114-e-mail info@nvva.nl, World Wide Web http://www.nvva.nl. *Chair* Gert Jan Bestebreurtje; *Secy.* Peter Everaers.

Nederlandse Boekverkopersbond (Dutch Booksellers Assn.), Arnhemse Bovenweg 100, 3708 AG Zeist. Tel. 088-600-9500, e-mail info@boekbond.nl, World Wide Web http://www.boekbond.nl. *Chair* Rob Haans.

New Zealand

Booksellers New Zealand, P.O. Box 25033, Featherston Street, Wellington 6146. Tel. 4-472-1908, fax 4-472-1912, e-mail info@booksellers.co.nz, World Wide Web http://www.booksellers.co.nz. *Chair* Juliet Blyth. E-mail juliet.blyth@booksellers.co.nz. *CEO* Dan Slevin. E-mail dan.slevin@booksellers.co.nz.

Nigeria

Nigerian Publishers Assn., 1st Floor Premium House, Opp. Evans Brothers (Nig. Publishers) Ltd., Jericho, GPO Box 2541, Dugbe, Ibadan, Oyo States. Tel. 234-803-917-7779, e-mail nigerianpublishers@ymail.com, World Wide Web http://www.nigerianpub lishers.com. *Pres.* Adedapo Gbadega.

Norway

Norske Bokhandlerforening (Norwegian Booksellers Association), Sehesteds gate 6, 0164 Oslo. Tel. 47-22-39-68-00, e-mail firm apost@bokhandlerforeningen.no, World Wide Web http://www.bokhandlerforeningen.no. *Acting Dir.* Elin Øy. E-mail elin@bokhandlerforeningen.no.

Norske Forleggerforening (Norwegian Publishers Assn.), Sehesteds gate 6, 0164 Oslo. Tel. 22-00-75-80, fax 22-33-38-30, e-mail dnf@forleggerforeningen.no, World Wide Web http://www.forleggerforeningen.no. *Chair* Edmund Austigard; *Admin. Dir.* Heidi Austlid.

Peru

Cámara Peruana del Libro (Peruvian Publishers Assn.), Av. Cuba 427, Jesús María, Apdo. 10253, Lima 11. Tel. (511) 265-0735, fax (511) 265-0735, e-mail cp-libro@cpl.org.pe, World Wide Web http://www.cpl.org.pe. *Pres.* José Wilfredo Del Pozo Alarcón.

Philippines

Philippine Educational Publishers Assn., Phoenix Building, 927 Quezon Ave., Quezon City. Tel. (632) 376-4041 local 334, fax (632) 376-4031, e-mail pepasecretariat@gmail.com, World Wide Web http://www.pepa.org.ph. *Pres.* Jose Paolo M. Sibal.

Poland

Władze Stowarzyszenie Księgarzy Polskich (Assn. of Polish Booksellers), ul. Świętokrzyska 14, 00-050 Warsaw. Tel./fax 0-22-827-93-81, e-mail skp@ksiegarze.org.pl, World Wide Web http://www.ksiegarze.org.pl. *Chair* Tadeusz Prześlakiewicz; *Gen. Secy.* Katarzyna Balicka-Więckowska.

Portugal

Associação Portuguesa de Editores e Livreiros (Portuguese Assn. of Publishers and Booksellers), Av. dos Estados Unidas da America 97, 6 Esq., 1700-167 Lisbon.

Tel. 21-843-51-80, e-mail geral@apel.pt, World Wide Web http://www.apel.pt. *Exec. Dir.* João Alvim.

Russia

Assn. of Book Publishers of Russia, 101000, Lubyanka,Luchnikov per., D.4, p. 1, Moscow. Tel. 7-926-900-85-27, e-mail askibook@gmail.com, World Wide Web http://www.aski.ru.

Rossiiskaya Knizhnaya Palata (Russian Book Chamber), Zvezdny boulevard 17, building 1, 129085, Moscow. Tel. 495-688-96-89, fax 495-688 99-91, e-mail info@bookchamber.ru, World Wide Web http://www.book-chamber.ru.

Singapore

Singapore Book Publishers Assn., 9 Jurong Town Hall Road, 02-02 Trade Association Hub, Jurong Town Hall, Singapore 609431 Tel. 65-6957-7093, e-mail info@singapore bookpublishers.sg, World Wide Web http://www.singaporebookpublishers.sg. *President* Max Phua. E-mail schoppert@nus.edu.sg. *Exec. Dir.* Cecilia Woo.

Slovenia

Zdruzenie Zaloznikov in Knjigotrzcev Slovenije Gospodarska Zbornica Slovenije (Assn. of Publishers and Booksellers of Slovenia), Dimičeva 13, SI-1504 Ljubljana. Tel. 386-1-5898-000, fax 386-1-5898-100, e-mail info@gzs.si, World Wide Web https://www.gzs.si/zbornica_knjiznih_zaloznikov_in_knjigotrzcev.

South Africa

Publishers Assn. of South Africa (PASA), P.O. Box 18223, Wynberg 7824. Tel. 21-762-9083, fax 21-762-2763, e-mail pasa@pub lishsa.co.za, World Wide Web http://www.publishsa.co.za. *Chair* Steve Cilliers; *Exec. Dir.* Mpuka Radinku.

South African Booksellers Assn. (formerly Associated Booksellers of Southern Africa), Regus Business Centre, 2 Fir Street, Observatory, 7925, Cape Town. Tel. 27 21 003 8098, e-mail saba@sabooksellers.

com, World Wide Web http://sabooksellers.com. *Pres.* Melvin Kaabwe. E-mail melvin.kaabwe@vanschaik.com.

Spain

Federación de Gremios de Editores de España (Federation of Spanish Publishers Assns.), Calle de Cea Bermúdez 44, 28003 Madrid. Tel. 91-534-51-95, fax 91-535-26-25, e-mail fgee@fge.es, World Wide Web http://www.federacioneditores.org. *Acting Pres.* D. Patrici Tixis; *Secy.* Antonio María Ávila.

Sweden

Svenska Förläggareföreningen (Swedish Publishers Assn.), c/o Svenska Publisher AB, Kungstensgatan 38, 2 tr, 113 59 Stockholm. Tel. 8-736-19-40, e-mail info@forlaggare.se, World Wide Web http://www.forlaggare.se. *Chair* Kristina Ahlinder.

Switzerland

Swiss Booksellers and Publishers Association (SBVV), Limmatstrasse 111, Postfach 8031, Zürich. Tel. 44-421-36-00, fax 44-421-36-18, e-mail info@sbvv.ch, World Wide Web https://www.sbvv.ch. *Pres.* Thomas Kramer. E-mail t.kramer@scheidegger-spiess.ch; *Gen. Mgr.* Tanja Messerli. E-mail tanja.messerli@sbvv.ch.

Thailand

Publishers and Booksellers Assn. of Thailand, 83/159 Soi Ngam Wong Wan 47 (Chinnaket 2), Thung Song Hong, Lak Si, Bangkok 10210. Tel. 2-954-9560-4, fax 02-954-9565-6, e-mail info@pubat.or.th, World Wide Web http://www.pubat.or.th. *Pres.* Chonrungsri Chalermchaikit.

Uganda

Uganda Publishers Assn., P.O. Box 7732, Kampala. Tel. 256-752-707327. World Wide Web https://www.facebook.com/Uganda Publishers/.

United Kingdom

Antiquarian Booksellers Assn., 21 John Street, London WC1N 2BF, England. Tel. 44-0-

20-8004-9512, e-mail admin@aba.org.uk, World Wide Web http://www.aba.org.uk. *Pres.* Pom Harrington; *Secy*: Riley Grant

Assn. of Learned and Professional Society Publishers, Egale 1, 80 St Albans Road, Watford, Hertfordshire WD17 1DL England. Tel. 44 (0)1245 260571, e-mail admin@alpsp.org, World Wide Web http://www.alpsp.org. *Chair* Niamh O'Connor; *Chief Exec.* Wayne Sime.

Booktrust, G8 Battersea Studios, 80 Silverthorne Rd., Battersea, London SW8 3HE, England. Tel. 020 7801 8800, e-mail query@booktrust.org.uk, World Wide Web http://www.booktrust.org.uk. *Pres.* Michael Morpurgo; *Chief Exec.* Diana Gerald.

Publishers Assn., 50 Southwark Street, London SE1 1UN, England. Tel. 44 0 20 7378 0504, e-mail mail@publishers.org.uk, World Wide Web http://www.publishers.org.uk. *Pres.* Stephen Lotinga.

Scottish Book Trust, Sandeman House, Trunk's Close, 55 High St., Edinburgh EH1 1SR, Scotland. Tel. 131-524-0160, e-mail info@scottishbooktrust.com, World Wide Web http://www.scottishbooktrust.com. *CEO* Mark Lambert.

Welsh Books Council (Cyngor Llyfrau Cymru), Castell Brychan, Aberystwyth, Ceredigion SY23 2JB, Wales. Tel. 1970-624-151, fax 1970-625-385, e-mail info@wbc.org.uk, World Wide Web http://www.cllc.org.uk. *Chair* M. Wynn Thomas.

Uruguay

Cámara Uruguaya del Libro (Uruguayan Publishers Assn.), Colón 1476, Apdo. 102, 11000 Montevideo. Tel. 2-916-93-74, fax 2-916-76-28, e-mail gerencia@camaradellibro.com.uy, World Wide Web http://www.camaradellibro.com.uy. *Pres.* Alvaro Risso.

Venezuela

Cámara Venezolana del Libro (Venezuelan Publishers Assn.), Av. Andrés Bello, Centro Andrés Bello, Torre Oeste 11, piso 11, of. 112-0, Caracas 1050. Tel. 212-793-1347, fax 212-793-1368, e-mail cavelibro@gmail.com, World Wide Web https://www.facebook.com/CamaradelLibro/.

Zimbabwe

Zimbabwe Book Publishers Assn., P.O. Box 3041, Harare. Tel. 263-77-706-4272, e-mail danielle.zbpa@gmail.com. World Wide Web https://www.facebook.com/zimbabwebookpublishers/.

National Information Standards Organization (NISO)

NISO, the National Information Standards Organization, a nonprofit association accredited by the American National Standards Institute (ANSI), identifies, develops, maintains, and publishes technical standards to manage information in today's continually changing digital environment. NISO standards apply to both traditional and new technologies and to information across its whole lifecycle, from creation through documentation, use, repurposing, storage, metadata, and preservation. The following listing includes NISO standards of interest to readers of *Library and Book Trade Almanac*.

Content and Collection Management

ANSI/NISO Z39.2-1994 (R2016)	Information Interchange Format ISBN 978-1-937522-70-4
ANSI/NISO Z39.14-1997 (R2015)	Guidelines for Abstracts ISBN 978-1-937522-44-5
ANSI/NISO Z39.18-2005 (R2010)	Scientific and Technical Reports— Preparation, Presentation, and Preservation ISBN 978-1-937522-21-6
ANSI/NISO Z39.19-2005 (R2010)	Guidelines for the Construction, Format, and Management of Monolingual Controlled Vocabularies ISBN 978-1-937522-22-3
ANSI/NISO Z39.23-1997 (S2015)	Standard Technical Report Number Format and Creation ISBN 978-1-937522-45-2
ANSI/NISO Z39.29-2005 (R2010)	Bibliographic References ISBN 978-1-937522-26-1
ANSI/NISO Z39.32-1996 (R2012)	Information on Microfiche Headers ISBN 978-1-937522-29-2
ANSI/NISO Z39.41-1997 (S2015)	Placement Guidelines for Information on Spines ISBN 978-1-937522-46-9

ANSI/NISO Z39.43-1993 (R2017)   Standard Address Number (SAN) for the
Publishing Industry
ISBN 978-1-937522-75-9

ANSI/NISO Z39.48-1992 (R2009)   Permanence of Paper for Publications and
Documents in Libraries and Archives
ISBN 978-1-937522-30-8

ANSI/NISO Z39.71-2006 (R2011)   Holdings Statements for Bibliographic
Items
ISBN 978-1-937522-31-5

ANSI/NISO Z39.73-1994 (R2012)   Single-Tier Steel Bracket Library Shelving
ISBN 978-1-937522-32-2

ANSI/NISO Z39.74-1996 (R2012)   Guides to Accompany Microform Sets
ISBN 978-1-937522-40-7

ANSI/NISO Z39.78-2000 (R2018)   Library Binding
ISBN 978-1-937522-86-5

ANSI/NISO Z39.84-2005 (R2010)   Syntax for the Digital Object Identifier
ISBN 978-1-937522-34-6

ANSI/NISO Z39.85-2012   The Dublin Core Metadata Element Set
ISBN 978-1-937522-14-8

ANSI/NISO Z39.86-2005 (R2012)   Specifications for the Digital Talking Book
ISBN 978-1-937522-35-3

ANSI/NISO Z39.96-2019   JATS: Journal Article Tag Suite, version 1.2
ISBN 978-1-937522-89-6

ANSI/NISO Z39.98-2012   Authoring and Interchange Framework for
Adaptive XML Publishing Specification
ISBN 978-1-937522-07-0

ANSI/NISO Z39.102-2017   STS: Standards Tag Suite
ISBN 978-1-937522-78-0

ANSI/NISO/ISO 12083-1995
(R2009)   Electronic Manuscript Preparation and
Markup
ISBN 978-1-880124-20-8

Standards for Discovery to Delivery

ANSI/NISO Z39.19-2005 (R2010)   Guidelines for the Construction, Format,
and Management of Monolingual
Controlled Vocabularies
ISBN 978-1-937522-22-3

ANSI/NISO Z39.50-2003 (S2014)   Information Retrieval (Z39.50) Application
Service Definition and Protocol
Specification
ISBN 978-1-937522-42-1

ANSI/NISO Z39.83-1-2012   NISO Circulation Interchange Part 1:
Protocol (NCIP), version 2.02
ISBN 978-1-937522-03-2

ANSI/NISO Z39.83-2-2012   NISO Circulation Interchange Protocol
(NCIP) Part 2: Implementation Profile 1,
version 2.02
ISBN 978-1-937522-04-9

ANSI/NISO Z39.85-2012   The Dublin Core Metadata Element Set
ISBN 978-1-937522-14-8

ANSI/NISO Z39.87-2006 (R2017)   Data Dictionary—Technical Metadata for
Digital Still Images
ISBN 978-1-937522-76-6

ANSI/NISO Z39.88-2004 (R2010)   The OpenURL Framework for Context-
Sensitive Services
ISBN 978-1-937522-38-4

ANSI/NISO Z39.89-2003 (S2014)   The U.S. National Z39.50 Profile for
Library Applications
ISBN 978-1-937522-43-8

ANSI/NISO Z39.99-2017   ResourceSync Framework Specification
ISBN 978-1-937522-73-5

Business Information

ANSI/NISO Z39.7-2013   Information Services and Use: Metrics and
Statistics for Libraries and Information
Providers—Data Dictionary
ISBN 978-1-937522-15-5

ANSI/NISO Z39.93-2014   The Standardized Usage Statistics
Harvesting Initiative (SUSHI) Protocol
ISBN 978-1-937522-47-6

Preservation and Storage

ANSI/NISO Z39.32-1996 (R2012)   Information on Microfiche Headers
ISBN 978-1-937522-29-2

ANSI/NISO Z39.48-1992 (R2009)   Permanence of Paper for Publications and
Documents in Libraries and Archives
ISBN 978-1-937522-30-8

ANSI/NISO Z39.73-1994 (R2012)   Single-Tier Steel Bracket Library Shelving
ISBN 978-1-937522-32-2

ANSI/NISO Z39.78-2000 (R2018)   Library Binding
ISBN 978-1-937522-86-5

In Development/NISO Initiatives

NISO develops new standards, reports, and best practices on a continuing basis to support its ongoing standards development program. NISO working groups are currently developing or exploring the following:

- Collection Description Specification (NISO Z39.91-200x)
- Criteria for Indexes (NISO Z39.4-201x)
- Digital Bookmarking and Annotation (NISO Z39.97-201x)
- Information Retrieval Service—Description Specification (NISO Z39.92-200x)
- Information Services and Use Metrics & Statistics for Libraries and Information Providers—Data Dictionary (NISO Z39.7-201x)
- Permanence of Paper for Publications and Documents in Libraries and Archives (ANSI/NISO Z39.48-201x)
- Scientific and Technical Reports—Preparation, Presentation, and Preservation (ANSI/NISO Z39.18-2005 [R201x])
- Standard Interchange Protocol (SIP) (NISO Z39.100-201x)
- Standards-Specific Ontology (SSOS) (NISO Z39.103-201x)

NISO Recommended Practices

A Framework of Guidance for Building Good Digital Collections, 3rd ed., 2007
ISBN 978-1-880124-74-1

NISO RP-2005-01   Ranking of Authentication and Access Methods Available to the Metasearch Environment
ISBN 978-1-880124-89-5

NISO RP-2005-02   Search and Retrieval Results Set Metadata
ISBN 978-1-880124-88-8

NISO RP-2005-03   Search and Retrieval Citation Level Data Elements
ISBN 978-1-880124-87-1

NISO RP-2006-01   Best Practices for Designing Web Services in the Library Context
ISBN 978-1-880124-86-4

NISO RP-2006-02   NISO Metasearch XML Gateway Implementers Guide
ISBN 978-1-880124-85-7

NISO RP-6-2012   RFID in U.S. Libraries
ISBN 978-1-937522-02-5

NISO RP-7-2012   SERU: A Shared Electronic Resource Understanding
ISBN 978-1-937522-08-7

NISO RP-8-2008   Journal Article Versions (JAV)
ISBN 978-1-880124-79-6

NISO RP-9-2014   KBART: Knowledge Bases and Related Tools
ISBN 978-1-937522-41-4

NISO RP-10-2010   Cost of Resource Exchange (CORE) Protocol
ISBN 978-1-880124-84-0

NISO RP-11-2011   ESPReSSO: Establishing Suggested Practices Regarding
Single Sign-On
ISBN 978-1-880124-98-7

NISO RP-12-2012   Physical Delivery of Library Resources
ISBN 978-1-937522-01-8

NISO RP-14-2014   NISO SUSHI Protocol: COUNTER-SUSHI
Implementation Profile
ISBN 978-1-937522-45-2

NISO RP-15-2013   Recommended Practices for Online Supplemental Journal
Article Materials
ISBN 978-1-937522-12-4

NISO RP-16-2013   PIE-J: The Presentation and Identification of E-Journals
ISBN 978-1-937522-05-6

NISO RP-17-2013   Institutional Identification: Identifying Organizations in the
Information Supply Chain
ISBN 978-1-937522-11-7

NISO RP-19-2020   Open Discovery Initiative: Promoting Transparency in
Discovery
ISBN 978-1-950980-08-6

NISO RP-20-2014   Demand Driven Acquisition of Monographs
ISBN 978-1-937522-44-5

NISO RP-21-2013   Improving OpenURLs Through Analytics (IOTA):
Recommendations for Link Resolver Providers
ISBN 978-1-937522-18-6

NISO RP-22-2015   Access License and Indicators
ISBN 978-1-937522-49-0

NISO RP-23-2015   Protocol for Exchanging Serial Content (PESC)
ISBN 978-1-937522-66-7

NISO RP-24-2019   Transfer Code of Practice, version 4.0
ISBN 978-1-937522-90-2

NISO RP-25-2016   Outputs of the NISO Alternative Assessment Project
ISBN 978-1-937522-71-1

NISO RP-26-2019   KBART Automation: Automated Retrieval of Customer
Electronic Holdings
ISBN 978-1-937522-91-9

NISO RP-27-2019   Resource Access in the 21st Century
ISBN 978-1-937522-99-5

NISO RP-30-2020   Manuscript Exchange Common Approach (MECA)
ISBN 978-1-950980-02-4

NISO RP-31-2021   Reproducibility Badging and Definitions
ISBN 978-1-950980-03-1

NISO RP-32-2019   JATS4R Subject & Keyword Guidelines
ISBN 978-1-950980-04-8

NISO RP-33-2020   NISO JATS4R Ethics Statements
ISBN 978-1-950980-05-5

NISO RP-35-2020   JATS4R Preprint Citations
ISBN 978-1-950980-07-9

NISO RP-36-2020   JATS4R Data Citations
ISBN 978-1-950980-09-3

NISO RP-37-2020   JATS4R Funding
ISBN 978-1-950980-10-9

NISO RP-39-2021   JATS4R Peer Review Materials
ISBN: 978-1-950980-12-3

NISO Technical Reports

NISO TR-01-1995   Environmental Guidelines for the Storage of Paper Records
by William K. Wilson
ISBN 978-1-800124-21-5

NISO TR-02-1997   Guidelines for Indexes and Related Information Retrieval
Devices
by James D. Anderson
ISBN 978-1-880124-36-X

NISO TR-03-1999   Guidelines for Alphabetical Arrangement of Letters and
Sorting of Numerals and Other Symbols
by Hans H. Wellisch
ISBN 978-1-880124-41-6

NISO TR-04-2006   Networked Reference Services: Question/Answer
Transaction Protocol
ISBN 978-1-880124-71-0

NISO TR-05-2013   IOTA Working Group Summary of Activities and
Outcomes
ISBN 978-1-937522-17-9

NISO TR-06-2017   Issues in Vocabulary Management
ISBN 978-1-937522-79-7

Other NISO Publications

The Case for New Economic Models to Support Standardization
by Clifford Lynch
ISBN 978-1-880124-90-1

The Exchange of Serials Subscription Information
by Ed Jones
ISBN 978-1-880124-91-8

The Future of Library Resource Discovery
    by Marshall Breeding
    ISBN 978-1-937522-41-4

Information Standards Quarterly (ISQ) [NISO quarterly open access magazine]
    ISSN 1041-0031

Internet, Interoperability and Standards—Filling the Gaps
    by Janifer Gatenby
    ISBN 978-1-880124-92-5

Issues in Crosswalking Content Metadata Standards
    by Margaret St. Pierre and William P. LaPlant
    ISBN 978-1-880124-93-2

Making Good on the Promise of ERM: A Standards and Best Practices
    Discussion Paper
    by the ERM Data Standards and Best Practices Review Steering Committee
    ISBN 978-1-9357522-00-1

Metadata Demystified: A Guide for Publishers
    by Amy Brand, Frank Daly, and Barbara Meyers
    ISBN 978-1-880124-59-8

The Myth of Free Standards: Giving Away the Farm
    by Andrew N. Bank
    ISBN 978-1-880124-94-9

NISO Newsline [free monthly e-newsletter]
    ISSN 1559-2774

NISO Working Group Connection (free quarterly supplement to *Newsline*)
Patents and Open Standards
    by Priscilla Caplan
    ISBN 978-1-880124-95-6

The RFP Writer's Guide to Standards for Library Systems
    by Cynthia Hodgson
    ISBN 978-1-880124-57-4

Streamlining Book Metadata Workflow
    by Judy Luther
    ISBN 978-1-880124-82-6

Understanding Metadata: What Is Metadata, and What Is It For?: A Primer
    by Jenn Riley
    ISBN 978-1-937522-72-8

Up and Running: Implementing Z39.50: Proceedings of a Symposium
    Sponsored by the State Library of Iowa
    edited by Sara L. Randall
    ISBN 978-1-880124-33-8

Z39.50: A Primer on the Protocol
    ISBN 978-1-880124-35-2

Z39.50 Implementation Experiences
    ISBN 978-1-880124-51-2

NISO standards are available at http://www.niso.org/publications/standards.

Recommended Practices, Technical Reports, White Papers, and other publications are available on the NISO website at http://www.niso.org/publications.

For more information, contact NISO, 3600 Clipper Mill Rd., Suite 302, Baltimore, MD 21211. Tel. 301-654-2512, e-mail nisohq@niso.org, World Wide Web http://www.niso.org.

Calendar, 2021–2028

This listing contains information on association meetings and promotional events that are, for the most part, national or international in scope. U.S. state and regional library association meetings are also included.

Due to the COVID-19 pandemic, many conferences scheduled for 2021 and into 2022 have been canceled, rescheduled, or moved to a virtual or hybrid format. The calendar indicates where meetings are scheduled to be held as virtual only; events with cities listed are expected to include an in-person component.

A web URL is included for each event. For meetings scheduled in 2021 and early 2022, the URL will often deliver a dedicated event webpage; for meetings further in the future, the URL may point to event basics including date, venue, and contact information. To confirm the status of a particular conference as well as its start and end dates, please refer to the sponsoring organization's website or contact the association directly.

For information on additional book trade and promotional events, see *Literary Market Place* and *International Literary Market Place*, published by Information Today, Inc., and other library and book trade publications such as *Library Journal*, *School Library Journal*, and *Publishers Weekly*. The American Library Association (ALA) keeps an online calendar at http://www.ala.org/conferencesevents/planning-calendar. An Information Today, Inc. events calendar can be found at http://www.infotoday.com/calendar.shtml.

2021

June

7–10	Assn. of Christian Librarians http://www.acl.org/index.cfm/conference/	Virtual
7–18	Assn. of American University Presses https://aupresses.org/programs-events/ annual-meeting/aupresses-2021/	Virtual
22–23	Assn. of Canadian Publishers Annual Meeting https://publishers.ca/events/	Virtual
22–29	American Library Assn. Annual Conference https://2021.alaannual.org/	Virtual
23–25	Assn. of European Research Libraries https://liberconference.eu/	Virtual
27	Assn. of Jewish Libraries https://jewishlibraries.org/meetinginfo.php	Virtual

| 29–July 1 | London Book Fair | London, UK |
| | https://www.londonbookfair.co.uk/ | |

July

12–16	International Assn. of School Librarianship	Virtual
	https://iasl2021.unt.edu/	
12–20	IEEE International Symposium on Information Theory	Virtual
	https://2021.ieee-isit.org/Virtual Announcement.asp	
14–20	Hong Kong Book Fair	Hong Kong
	https://hkbookfair.hktdc.com/en/ About-Book-Fair/Fair-Details.html	
15–16	Computing Conference	Virtual
	https://saiconference.com/Computing	
19–23	American Assn. of Law Libraries (AALL)	Virtual
	https://www.aallnet.org/conference/	

August

2–6	Society of American Archivists	Virtual
	https://www2.archivists.org/am2021	
11–13	Special Libraries Assn.	Virtual
	https://sla2021.pathable.co/	
14–30	Edinburgh International Book Festival	Edinburgh, UK
	https://www.edbookfest.co.uk/	
17–19	International Federation of Library Assns. (IFLA) General Conf. and Assembly	Virtual
	https://www.ifla.org/wlic2021	
25–28	Beijing International Book Fair	Beijing, China
	https://www.bibf.net/en/	

September

8–12	Moscow International Book Fair	Moscow, Russia
	http://mibf.info/en	
9–11	Colorado Library Assn.	Westminster, CO
	https://cal-webs.org/CALCON_2021	
18–22	North Carolina Library Assn.	Winston-Salem, NC
	https://nclaonline.wildapricot.org/conference	
23–26	Gothenburg Book Fair	Gothenburg, Sweden
	https://goteborg-bookfair.com/	

27–29	Pennsylvania Library Assn. https://www.palibraries.org/page/2021 ConferencePrelim	Virtual
29–30	South Dakota Library Assn. https://www.sdlibraryassociation.org/page/ Conference2021	Virtual
30–Oct. 2	Washington Library Assn. https://www.wla.org/2021-wla-conference	Bellevue, WA

October

6–8	Georgia Libraries Assn. https://gla.georgialibraries.org/glc/	Virtual
6–8	Iowa Library Assn. https://www.iowalibraryassociation.org/index. php/conference	Des Moines, IA
6–8	North Dakota Library Assn. https://ndla.info/index.php#	Grand Forks, ND
12–14	Illinois Library Assn. https://www.ila.org/events/future-ila-annual- conferences	Virtual
12–15	Arkansas Library Assn. https://www.arlib.org/conference	Virtual
13–15	Nebraska Library Assn. https://nebraskalibraries.org/2021_NLA_ Conference_The_World_Turned_Upside_ Down_Reinventing_Libraries_In_Changing_ Times	Omaha, NE
13–15	Ohio Library Council http://olc.org/convention-expo/	Columbus, OH
14–17	Krakow International Book Fair https://www.ksiazka.krakow.pl/gb/	Krakow, Poland
18	New England Library Assn. https://nela.memberclicks.net/2021-annual- conference	Worcester, MA
20–22	New Mexico Library Assn. https://nmla.wildapricot.org/Conferences	Virtual
27–29	Virginia Library Assn. https://www.vla.org/vla-annual-conference	Richmond, VA
20–24	Frankfurt Book Fair https://www.buchmesse.de/en	Frankfurt, Germany
21–23	American Assn. of School Librarians (AASL) National Conference https://national.aasl.org/	Salt Lake City, UT

26–28	Internet Librarian https://www.infotoday.com/conferences.asp	Monterey, CA
27–29	Arizona Library Assn. https://sites.google.com/azla.org/azla2021/ home	Prescott, AZ
28–31	Helsinki Book Fair https://tradefest.io/en/event/helsinki-book-fair	Helsinki, Finland
30–Nov. 2	Assn. for Information Science and Technology (ASIS&T) https://www.asist.org/am21/	Salt Lake City, UT

November

1–5	International Conference on Information and Knowledge Management (CIKM) https://www.cikm2021.org/	Virtual
3–6	New York Library Assn. https://www.nyla.org/4DCGI/cms/review. html?Action= CMS_Document&DocID= 281&MenuKey=conf_info	Syracuse, NY
10–14	Buch Wein International Book Fair https://www.buchwien.at/	Vienna, Austria
15–18	KM World https://www.kmworld.com/Conference/2021	Washington, DC
26–28	Comic-Con Special Edition https://comic-con.org/cci	San Diego, CA
27–Dec. 5	Guadalajara International Book Fair https://www.fil.com.mx/ingles/i_info/i_info_ fil.asp	Guadalajara, Mexico
29–Dec. 1	International Conference of Indigenous Archives, Libraries, and Museums https://www.atalm.org/node/430	Washington, DC

December

| 12–15 | International Conference on Information
Systems (ICIS)
https://icis2021.aisconferences.org/ | Austin, TX |

2022

January

| 4–7 | Hawaii International Conference on System
Sciences
https://hicss.hawaii.edu/#!future-conferences/ctld | Maui, HI |

| 21–24 | American Library Assn. LibLearnX: The Library Learning Experience (LLX) https://alaliblearnx.org/ | San Antonio, TX |

March

| 22–26 | Public Library Assn. http://www.ala.org/pla/education/ conferences | Portland, OR |
| 28–31 | Computers in Libraries http://computersinlibraries.infotoday. com/ 2020/PastEvents.aspx | Arlington, VA |

April

| 25–28 | Texas Library Assn. https://txla.org/annual-conference/general- information/future-dates/ | Fort Worth, TX |

June

| 18–20 | Assn. of American University Presses https://aupresses.org/programs-events/ annual-meeting/save-the-dates/ | Washington, DC |
| 23–28 | American Library Assn. Annual Conference http://www.ala.org/conferencesevents/node/7/ | Washington, DC |

July

| 16–19 | American Assn. of Law Libraries (AALL) https://www.aallnet.org/conference/about/ future-meetings/ | Denver, CO |

September

| 28–30 | South Dakota Library Assn. https://www.sdlibraryassociation.org/page/ FutureConferences | Brookings, SD |

October

| 16–19 | Pennsylvania Library Assn. https://www.palibraries.org/page/More_ Conf | Harrisburg, PA |
| 19–23 | Frankfurt Book Fair https://www.buchmesse.de/en | Frankfurt, Germany |

November

2–5   New York Library Assn.   Saratoga Springs, NY
     https://www.nyla.org/4DCGI/cms/review.
      html?Action= CMS_Document&DocID=
      281&MenuKey=conf_info

December

11–14   International Conference on Information Copenhagen,
     Systems (ICIS)   Denmark
     https://aisnet.org/page/ICISPage

2023

January

27–31   American Library Assn. LibLearnX: The New Orleans, LA
     Library Learning Experience (LLX)
     http://www.ala.org/conferencesevents/node/7/

March

15–18   Assn. of College and Research Libraries Pittsburgh, PA
     http://www.ala.org/acrl/conferences

April

19–22   Texas Library Assn.   Austin, TX
     https://txla.org/annual-conference/general-
      information/future-dates/

June

16–18   Assn. of American University Presses Seattle, WA
     https://aupresses.org/programs-events/annual-
      meeting/save-the-dates/
22–27   American Library Assn. Annual Conference Chicago, IL
     http://www.ala.org/conferencesevents/node/7/

July

15–19   American Assn. of Law Libraries   Boston, MA
     https://www.aallnet.org/conference/about/
      future-meetings/

September

27–29   South Dakota Library Assn.   Rapid City, SD
     https://www.sdlibraryassociation.org/page/
      FutureConferences

October

1–4	Pennsylvania Library Assn. https://www.palibraries.org/page/More_Conf	Pocono Manor, PA
18–22	Frankfurt Book Fair https://www.buchmesse.de/en	Frankfurt, Germany
19–21	American Assn. of School Librarians (AASL) National Conference http://www.ala.org/aasl/conferences/events	Tampa, FL

November

1–4	New York Library Assn. https://www.nyla.org/4DCGI/cms/review. html?Action= CMS_Document&DocID= 281&MenuKey=conf_info	Saratoga Springs, NY

December

10–13	International Conference on Information Systems (ICIS) https://aisnet.org/page/ICISPage	Hyderabad, India

2024

April

3–6	Public Library Assn. http://www.ala.org/pla/education/conferences	Columbus, OH
16–19	Texas Library Assn. https://txla.org/annual-conference/general- information/future-dates/	San Antonio, TX

June

11–13	Assn. of American University Presses https://aupresses.org/programs-events/ annual-meeting/save-the-dates/	Montreal, QC
27–July 2	American Library Assn. Annual Conference http://www.ala.org/conferencesevents/node/7/	San Diego, CA

July

20–23	American Assn. of Law Libraries (AALL) https://www.aallnet.org/conference/about/ future-meetings/	Chicago, IL

September

25–27	South Dakota Library Assn. https://www.sdlibraryassociation.org/page/ FutureConferences	Aberdeen, SD

October

16–20	Frankfurt Book Fair https://www.buchmesse.de/en	Frankfurt, Germany

December

10–13	International Conference on Information Systems (ICIS) https://aisnet.org/page/ICISPage	Bangkok, Thailand

2025

April

1–4	Texas Library Assn. https://txla.org/annual-conference/general- information/future-dates/	Dallas, TX
2–5	Assn. of College and Research Libraries http://www.ala.org/acrl/conferences	Minneapolis, MN

June

26–July 1	American Library Assn. Annual Conference http://www.ala.org/conferencesevents/node/7/	Philadelphia, PA

July

19–22	American Assn. of Law Libraries (AALL) https://www.aallnet.org/conference/about/ future-meetings/	Portland, OR

October

16–18	American Assn. of School Librarians (AASL) National Conference http://www.ala.org/aasl/conferences/events	St. Louis, MO

2026

March

30–Apr. 2	Texas Library Assn. https://txla.org/annual-conference/general- information/future-dates/	Houston, TX

June

25–30   American Library Assn. Annual Conference   Chicago, IL
         http://www.ala.org/conferencesevents/node/7/

2027
March

30–Apr. 2   Texas Library Assn.   Dallas, TX
             https://txla.org/annual-conference/
               general-information/future-dates/

April

7–10   Assn. of College and Research Libraries   Portland, OR
        http://www.ala.org/acrl/conferences

June

24–29   American Library Assn. Annual Conference   New Orleans, LA
         http://www.ala.org/conferencesevents/node/7/

2028
April

24–27   Texas Library Assn.   San Antonio, TX
         https://txla.org/annual-conference/
           general-information/future-dates/

Acronyms

A

AACR2. Anglo-American Cataloging Rules

AAHSL. Association of Academic Health Sciences Libraries

AALL. American Association of Law Libraries

AAP. Association of American Publishers

AASL. American Association of School Librarians

AAU. Association of American Universities

ABA. Acquisitions and Bibliographic Access Directorate

ABA. American Booksellers Association

ABAA. Antiquarian Booksellers' Association of America

ABOS. Association of Bookmobile and Outreach Services

ABPA. American Book Producers Association

ACL. Association of Christian Librarians

ACP. Association of Canadian Publishers

ACRL. Association of College and Research Libraries

ADL. *American Library Directory*

AFSIC. Alternative Farming Systems Information Center

AgLaw. Agricultural Law Information Partnership

AGLINET. Agricultural Libraries Network

AgNIC. Agriculture Network Information Collaborative

AGRICOLA. AGRICultural On-Line Access

AIGA. Professional Association for Design

AIIM. Association for Information and Image Management

AIIP. Association of Independent Information Professionals

AILA. American Indian Library Association

AJL. Association of Jewish Libraries

ALA. American Library Association

ALCTS. Association for Library Collections and Technical Services

ALD. *American Library Directory*

ALIC. Archives Library Information Center

ALISE. Association for Library and Information Science Education

ALS. Academic Libraries Survey

ALSC. Association for Library Service to Children

ALTA. American Literary Translators Association

AM&P. Association Media and Publishing

ANSI. American National Standards Institute

APA. Audio Publishers Association

APALA. Asian/Pacific American Librarians Association

APLU. Association of Public and Land-grant Universities

ARL. Association of Research Libraries

ARLIS/NA. Art Libraries Society of North America

ARMA International (formerly the Association of Records Managers and Administrators)

ARSL. Association for Rural and Small Libraries

ASGCLA. Association of Specialized Government, and Cooperative Library Agencies

ASI. American Society for Indexing

ASIS&T. Association for Information Science and Technology

ASJA. American Society of Journalists and Authors

ATALM. Association of Tribal Archives, Libraries, and Museums

Atla (formerly the American Theological Library Association)

AUPresses. Association of University Presses

AVSL. Association of Vision Science Librarians

AWIC. Animal Welfare Information Center

B

BARD. Braille and Audio Reading Download

BCALA. Black Caucus of the American Library Association

BIBCO. Bibliographic Record Cooperative

BIHIP. Book Industry Health Insurance Partnership

BIPOC. Black, Indigenous, and People of Color

BISAC. Book Industry Systems Advisory Committee

BISG. Book Industry Study Group

BLM. Bureau of Land Management Library

BMI. Book Manufacturers' Institute

BSA. Bibliographical Society of America

BSC-SCB. Bibliographical Society of Canada

C

CAIS. Canadian Association for Information Science

CALA. Chinese American Librarians Association

CALL. Canadian Association of Law Libraries

CARES Act. Coronavirus Aid, Relief, and Economic Security Act

CARL. Canadian Association of Research Libraries

CASE. Copyright Alternative in Small-Claims Enforcement Act

CBC. Children's Book Council

CDO. Collection Development Office

CFUW. Canadian Federation of University Women

CGP. Catalog of U.S. Government Publications

C&I. Cataloging and indexing

CIKM. International Conference on Information and Knowledge Management

CIP. Cataloging in Publication

CLA. Catholic Library Association

CLA. Croatian Library Association

CLIR. Council on Library and Information Resources

CLLE. Center for Learning, Literacy, and Engagement

CMD. Collection Management Division

CMO. Communications and Marketing Office (ALA)

CNI. Coalition for Networked Information

CONSER. Cooperative Online Serials

CONTU. Commission on New Technological Uses of Copyrighted Works

CORD-19. COVID-19 Open Research Dataset

COSLA. Chief Officers of State Library Associations

CRO. Chapter Relations Office (ALA)

CRS. Congressional Research Service

CUI. Controlled unclassified information

D

DAMS. Digital Asset Management System

DDC. Dewey Decimal Classification

DEL. Documenting Endangered Languages

DLF. Digital Library Federation

DLME. Digital Library of the Middle East

DMCA. Digital Millennium Copyright Act

DoD IACs. Department of Defense Information Analysis Centers

DOER. Digital Opportunity Equity Recognition award

DPLA, Digital Public Library of America

DTIC. Defense Technical Information Center

E

ECIP. Electronic Cataloging in Publication Program

ECLS. Early Childhood Longitudinal Study

EDI. Equity, Diversity and Inclusion Assembly

ELS. Education Longitudinal Study

EMIERT. Ethnic and Multicultural Information and Exchange Round Table

ERA. Electronic Records Archives

ERIC. Education Resources Information Center

ERT. Exhibits Round Table

F

FAB. FEDLINK Advisory Board
FDLP. Federal Depository Library Program
FEDLINK. Federal Library and Information Network
FESABID. Federación Española de Sociedades de Archivística, Biblioteconomía, Documentación y Museística
FIAF. International Federation of Film Archives
FMRT. Film and Media Round Table
FNIC. Food and Nutrition Information Center
FOIA. Freedom of Information Act
FRCs. Federal Records Centers
FSRIO. Food Safety Research Information Office
FTRF. Freedom to Read Foundation

G

GameRT. Games and Gaming Round Table
GLBTRT. Gay, Lesbian, Bisexual, and Transgendered Round Table
GNCRT. Graphic Novel and Comics Round Table
GODORT. Government Documents Round Table
GPO. U.S. Government Publishing Office

H

HALO. Help a Library Workout Out
HBCU. Historically Black Colleges and Universities
HRDR. Office for Human Resource Development and Recruitment (ALA)

I

IACs. Information Analysis Centers
IAL. Innovative Approaches to Literacy
IALL. International Association of Law Libraries
IAML. International Association of Music Libraries, Archives and Documentation Centres

IARLA. International Alliance of Research Library Associations
IASL. International Association of School Librarianship
IATUL. International Association of Scientific and Technological University Libraries
IBBY. International Board on Books for Young People
IBPA. Independent Book Publishers Association
ICA. International Council on Archives
ICIS. International Conference on Information Systems
ICOLC. International Coalition of Library Consortia
ICP. International Cataloguing Principles
IFC. Intellectual Freedom Committee (ALA)
IFLA. International Federation of Library Associations and Institutions
IFRT. Intellectual Freedom Round Table
ILA. International Literacy Association
ILAB. International League of Antiquarian Booksellers
ILL. Interlibrary loan
IMLS. Institute of Museum and Library Services
INALJ. Information professionals finding and sharing jobs
IPA. International Publishers Association
IPEDS. Integrated Postsecondary Education Data System
IRO. International Relations Office (ALA)
IRRT. International Relations Round Table
ISBD. International Standard Bibliographical Description
ISBN. International Standard Book Number
ISNs. Canadian International Standard Numbers
ISO. International Organization for Standardization
ISOO. Information Security Oversight Office
ISSN. International Standard Serial Number

J

JCLC. National Joint Conference of Librarians of Color
JELIS. *Journal of Education for Library and Information Science*

K

KHI. Kurdish Heritage Institute

L

LAC. Library and Archives Canada
LAMPHHS. Librarians, Archivists, and
Museum Professionals in the History
of the Health Sciences (formerly
ALHHS/MeMA)
LARC. Library and Research Center (ALA)
LC. Learning and Innovation Office
LC. Library of Congress
LCA Commons. Life Cycle Assessment
Commons
LCA. Library Copyright Alliance
LCI. Leading Change Institute
LearnRT. Learning Round Table (formerly
CLENERT)
LHRT. Library History Round Table
LIBER. Association of European Research
Libraries
LIRT. Library Instruction Round Table
LIS. Library and information science
LITA. Library and Information Technology
Association
LJ. *Library Journal*
LLAMA. Library Leadership and
Management Association
LMPI. Library Materials Price Index
LOC. Library of Congress
LRM. Library Reference Model
LRRT. Library Research Round Table
LRTS. *Library Resources and Technical
Services*
LSCM. Library Services and Content
Management
LSSIRT. Library Support Staff Interests
Round Table
LSTA. Library Services and Technology Act
LTAR. Long-Term Agroecosystem Research
LTC. Libraries Transforming Communities

M

MAGIRT. Map and Geospatial Information
Round Table
MARC. Machine Readable Cataloging
MARS. Material Acquisition Request
Service

METRO. Metropolitan New York Library
Council
MFA. Museums for America
MIPA. Midwest Independent Publishers
Association
MLA. Medical Library Association
MLA. Music Library Association
MLIS. Master of Library and Information
Science
MLSA. Museum and Library Services Act
MMLIS. Master of Management in Library
and Information Science
MPA. Association of Magazine Media

N

NAABPI. North American Academic Books
Price Index
NAC. National Archives Catalog
NACO. Name Authority Cooperative
NAGARA. National Association of
Government Archives and Records
Administrators
NAIBA. New Atlantic Independent
Booksellers Association
NAL. National Agricultural Library
NALDC. National Agricultural Library
Digital Collection
NALT. National Agricultural Library
Thesaurus
NARA. National Archives and Records
Administration
NASIG (formerly North American Serials
Interest Group)
NCAC. National Coalition Against
Censorship
NCES. National Center for Education
Statistics
NCTE. National Council of Teachers of
English
NDC. National Declassification Center
NDNP. National Digital Newspaper Program
NDSA. National Digital Stewardship
Alliance
NEH. National Endowment for the
Humanities
NEIBA. New England Independent
Booksellers Association
NFAIS. National Federation of Advanced
Information Services
NHES. National Household Education
Survey

NHPRC. National Historical Publications and Records Commission
NIH. National Institutes of Health
NISIC. National Invasive Species Information Center
NISO. National Information Standards Organization
NIST. National Institute of Standards and Technology publications
NLE. National Library of Education
NLM. National Library of Medicine
NLS. National Library Service for the Blind and Print Disabled
NLW. National Library Week
NLWD. National Library Workers Day
NMRT. New Members Round Table
NNLM. Network of the National Library of Medicine
NSF. National Science Foundation
NTIS. National Technical Information Service
NTPS. National Teacher and Principal Survey
NTRL. National Technical Reports Library
NYPL. New York Public Library

O

OCIO. Office of the Chief Information Officer (LC)
OCLC. Online Computer Library Center
ODLOS. Office for Diversity, Literacy and Outreach Services (ALA)
OFR. National Archives' Office of the Federal Register
OGIS. Office of Government Information Services
OIB. USSBY Outstanding International Books
OIF. Office for Intellectual Freedom
OLOS. Office for Literacy and Outreach Services
OLS. Office of Library Services

P

PACs. Political action committees
PALA. Polish American Librarians Association
PCC. Program for Cooperative Cataloging
PENS. Public Law Electronic Notification Service

PLA. Public Library Association
PLS. Public Library Survey
PMC. PubMed Central
PPAO. Public Policy and Advocacy Office (ALA)
PPO. Public Programs Office (ALA)
PTRCA. Patent and Trademark Resource Center Association
PW4J. Pub Workers for Justice

R

RBMS. Rare Books and Manuscripts Section
RDA. Resource Description and Access
REALM. REopening Archives, Libraries, and Museums
REFORMA. National Association to Promote Library and Information Services to Latinos and the Spanish-Speaking
RIC. Rural Information Center
RMS. Research Management and Support
RRC. Reading Rooms Committee
RRT. Rainbow Round Table
RtC. Libraries Ready to Code
RUSA. Reference and User Services Association

S

SAA. Society of American Archivists
SACO. Subject Authority Cooperative
SAN. Standard Address Number
SASS. Schools and Staffing Survey
SCBWI. Society of Children's Book Writers and Illustrators
SDGs. Sustainable Development Goals
SI. Society of Illustrators
SIBA (formerly Southern Independent Booksellers Alliance)
SIIA. Software and Information Industry Association
SLA. Special Libraries Association
SLAA. State Library Administrative Agency
SLIDE. School Librarian Investigation— Decline or Evolution?
SPARC. Scholarly Publishing and Academic Resources Coalition
SRA. Sequence Read Archive

SRRT. Social Responsibilities Round Table

SSP. Society for Scholarly Publishing

STEAM. Science, Technology, Engineering, Arts, and Math

STEM. Science, Technology, Engineering, and Mathematics

STM. International Association of Scientific, Technical, and Medical Publishers

T

TOME. Toward an Open Monograph Ecosystem

TPS. Teaching with Primary Sources

TRAIL. Technical Report Archive & Image Library

TRD. Trustworthy Digital Repository certification

U

ULC. Urban Libraries Council

USAIN. United States Agricultural Information Network

USBBY. United States Board on Books for Young People

USPPI. U.S. Periodical Price Index

V

VHP. Veterans History Project

W

WAIC. Water and Agriculture Information Center

WDL. World Digital Library

WIPO. World Intellectual Property Organization

WLIC. World Library and Information Congress

WNBA. Women's National Book Association

Y

YALSA. Young Adult Library Services Association

Index

Note: Page numbers followed by "f" and "t" represent figures and tables respectively. The Directory of Organizations (Part 6) is not included in the index.

A

AALL. *See* American Association of Law Libraries
AASL. *See* American Association of School Librarians
ABA. *See* American Booksellers Association
ABA (Acquisitions and Bibliographic Access Directorate), 37
ABOS (Association of Bookmobile and Outreach Services), 253
Abrams, Stacey, 108
academic book prices
  British, 363–370, 368t–369t
  college books, 350, 351t–353t
  e-books, 342t–343t, 346–347
  North American, 337–350, 340t–341t, 348f, 349f
  textbooks, 344t–345t, 347
academic libraries. *See also* COVID-19 and libraries
  acquisition expenditures, 304t–305t
  buildings, 317t, 318–319
  NCES survey, 93–95
  number in U.S., Canada, 285–287
  2020 Census programs, 26
accessibility, 130–131
acquisition expenditures
  academic libraries, 304t–305t
  government libraries, 308t–309t
  public libraries, 302t–303t
  special libraries, 306t–307t
  table explanations, 301
Acquisitions and Bibliographic Access Directorate (ABA), 37
ACRL. *See* Association of College and Research Libraries
advocacy
  accessibility, 130–131
  children's literature, 171–176

copyright law, 131, 162
higher education, 131–132
information access, 66, 139–143, 162
library funding, 179–181, 213–216
privacy issues, 132
African American museums, 208
AFSIC (Alternative Farming Systems Information Center), 55
Ag Data Commons, 57–58
AGRICOLA, 56–57
Agricultural Law Information Partnership (AgLaw), 60
Agricultural Libraries Network (AGLINET), 60
Agriculture Network Information Collaborative (AgNIC), 59
AJL (Association of Jewish Libraries), 253, 272
ALA. *See* American Library Association
ALA Connect Live, 109
ALA Editions, 118–119
ALA Graphics, 119–120
ALA Neal-Schuman, 118–119
ALCTS (Association for Library Collections and Technical Services), 260–261
Alex Awards, 413
Alexander, Kwame, 126
ALIC (Archives Library Information Center), 89. *See also* National Archives and Records Administration
ALISE (Association for Library and Information Science Education), 153–157, 252–253, 271–272
ALISE Library and Information Science Education Statistical Report, 155
Allen, Danielle, 45
Allen, Woody, 18
ALSC. *See* Association for Library Service to Children

Alternative Farming Systems Information
    Center (AFSIC), 55
Amazon, 6, 19, 20, 124
American Association of Law Libraries
    (AALL)
  awards given, 119, 256–257
  career resources, 222
  job listings, 225
  scholarships, 251
American Association of School Librarians
    (AASL)
  awards given, 259–260
  career resources, 222
  highlights (2020), 115
American Book Trade Directory, 385
American Booksellers Association (ABA),
    121–127
  COVID-19 response, 122–124
  diversity, equity, inclusion actions, 125–126
  governance, 124–125
  leadership, 121–122
  member education and events, 126
  member health care support, 126–127
American Dirt (Cummins), 17
American Library Association (ALA), 105–120
  advocacy, 179–186
  awards given, 107, 110, 257–270
  career resources, 222, 223
  conferences and workshops, 106–108, 116
  COVID-19 and, 3, 114
  discussion lists, 227
  divisions and offices, 105–106, 115–118
  events, celebration, observances, 108–110
  grants, 113–114
  highlights (2020), 110–115
  JobLIST, 225
  leadership, 106
  publishing, 118–120
  scholarships, 251–252
American Libraries magazine, 119–120
American-Scandinavian Foundation, 252
Andujar, Elizabeth Santana, 23
Animal Welfare Information Center (AWIC),
    55
Ankeny Kirkendall Public Library (IA), 311
AnyThink Library (CO), 8
APALA (Asian/Pacific Americans Libraries
    Association), 270
Apropos of Nothing (Allen), 18
Arahova, Antonia, 165
architecture. *See* library buildings
archives. *See* National Archives and Records
    Administration

Archives Gig, 225
Archives Library Information Center
    (ALIC), 89. *See also* National
    Archives and Records
    Administration
ARL. *See* Association of Research Libraries
ARLIS/NA (Art Libraries of North
    America), 225, 270
Arthur, Reagan, 16
ASGCLA (Association of Specialized
    Government and Cooperative Library
    Agencies), 112, 263–264
Asian/Pacific Americans Libraries
    Association (APALA), 270
Association for Information Science &
    Technology (ASIS&T), 225, 270–271
Association for Library and Information
    Science Education (ALISE),
    153–157, 252–253, 271–272
Association for Library Collections and
    Technical Services (ALCTS), 260–261
Association for Library Service to Children
    (ALSC)
  awards given, 261–262
  highlights (2020), 115–116
  notable book and media lists, 418–425
  virtual 2020 Institute, 109
Association of Bookmobile and Outreach
    Services (ABOS), 253
Association of College and Research
    Libraries (ACRL)
  awards given, 262–263
  career resources, 222
  SPARC-ACRL forums, 144
Association of Jewish Libraries (AJL),
    253, 272
Association of Research Libraries (ARL),
    128–138
  advocacy, 130–133
  ARL Academy, 136–137
  awards given, 272
  COVID-19 effects on, 135–136
  data and analytics, 135–136
  diversity, equity, inclusion, 134–135
  highlights (2020), 128–130
  job listings, 225
  mission, 128
  research library promotion, 137–138
Association of Seventh-Day Adventist
    Librarians, 253, 272
Association of Specialized Government
    and Cooperative Library Agencies
    (ASGCLA), 112, 263–264

audiobooks
average prices, 337, 358t–359t
library lending, 6
Listen List, 403
title output, per volume prices, 380t–381t,
384
top ten lists (2020), 427–428
for young adults, 413–416
audiovisual materials
LC collection, 39
public library lending, 324–325
Authenticity Project Fellowship Program,
149–150
awards and honors (by sponsors), 256–281.
See also literary awards and prizes
AALL, 119, 256–257
AJL, 272
ALA, 107, 110, 257–270
ALISE, 156, 271–272
APALA, 270
ARL, 272
ARLIS/NA, 270
ASIS&T, 270–271
Beta Phi Mu, 272–273
BSA, 273–274
CALA, 274
CLA, 274
CLIR, 274–275
CNI, 274
EDUCAUSE, 275–276
FCC, 7, 182
FEDLINK, 48–50
Friends of the NLM, 276
IASL, 276
IBBY, 276
IFLA, 162–163, 276
IMLS, 276
LC, 45–46, 277
LJ, 277
MLA, 277–278
Music Library Association, 278–279
NLS, 279
REFORMA, 279
RUSA, 117
SAA, 279–280
Seventh-Day Adventist Librarians, 272
SLA, 280–281
Theatre Library Association, 281
USBBY, 176, 281
WNBA, 281
AWIC (Animal Welfare Information Center),
55

B

Banned Books Week, 109
Barber, Peggy, 113
Barnard, Henry, 102
BCALA (Black Caucus of the American
Library Association), 223, 225, 264
Beta Phi Mu, 253, 272–273
BIBFRAME, 42
Bibliographical Society of America (BSA),
273–274
Biden, Joe, 186
Biden-Harris administration, 186–187
BIHIP (Book Industry Health Insurance
Partnership), 126–127
Billie Jean King Main Library (CA), 311
BIPOC (Black, Indigenous, and other
People of Color). *See* diversity,
equity, inclusion; social justice and
inequality
Black Caucus of the American Library
Association (BCALA), 223, 225,
264
Black Lives Matter. *See* diversity, equity,
inclusion; social justice and
inequality
BLM (Bureau of Land Management
Library), 49
Blue Shield, 162
book awards. *See* literary awards and prizes
Book Industry Health Insurance Partnership
(BIHIP), 126–127
book prices, price indexes
academic, 337–350, 340t–343t, 348f,
349f
audiobooks, 358t–359t, 380t–381t
average price percent change (2016–2020),
331
British academic books, 363–370,
368t–369t
college books, 350, 351t–353t
e-books, 342t–343t, 360t–361t, 382t–383t
hardcover books, 338t–339t, 373t–376t
overview, 337
paperbacks, 377t–379t
price index use, 370
textbooks, 344t–345t, 347
book production
audiobooks, 380t–381t
by category, 371, 372t, 384
e-books, 382t–383t
hardcover books, 373t–376t
paperbacks, 377t–379t

Bookbird, 172, 174
BookCon, 19
BookExpo, 19
Booklist, 119
books
    adult, 401–402
    audiobooks, 403, 413–416
    children's literature, 171–176, 417–420
    genre fiction, 402
    sales trends, 19–20, 122
    top ten lists (2020), 426–428
    young adult, 404–412
Bookshop.org, 20
bookstores
    COVID-19 effects on, 17, 122–124
    types and number of, 385, 385t–386t
Bosco, Mark, 45
#BoxedOut campaign, 124
Brechner, Kenny, 124
Bridge to Understanding Award (USBBY),
    176, 281
Brody, Stacy, 9
Brown, Wanda Kay, 106, 107, 108
BSA (Bibliographical Society of America),
    273–274
Building Cultural Proficiencies for Racial
    Equity Framework Task Force, 112
Bureau of Labor Statistics, 223
Bureau of Land Management Library
    (BLM), 49

C

CALA (Chinese American Librarians
    Association), 254, 274
Calcasieu Public Library (LA), 112
Call Number with American Libraries
    podcast, 224
Canadian Association of Law Libraries
    (CALL), 253
Canadian Federation of University Women
    (CFUW), 253–254
Canedy, Dana, 18
careers. *See* library employment
CARES Act
    Copyright Office and, 31
    IMLS grants, 202–204
    library funding in, 36, 180
    NEH grants, 114, 193
Catalog of U.S. Government Publications
    (CGP), 76–77
cataloging and indexing programs

Cataloging-in-Publication, 41–42
    "fastest cataloger in the West," 50
    LSCM, 73–74
    PubMed, 65
Catholic Library Association (CLA), 274
Catholic University of America, 26, 46
CDO (Collection Development Office), 38
Cengage, 143
census
    citizenship question, 23
    importance of, 22
    libraries' contributions to, 22–27, 185
    records, 89
Census Data Literacy project, 26–27
Center for Learning, Literacy, and
    Engagement (CLLE), 32–33, 44
Central Arkansas Library System, 7
CFUW (Canadian Federation of University
    Women), 253–254
CGP (Catalog of U.S. Government
    Publications), 76–77
Challenge Grants (NEH), 191, 199
Chief Officers of State Library Associations
    (COSLA), 215
Children in Crisis program, 173
children's literature
    advocacy efforts, 171–176
    digital media, 424–425
    notable books, 418–420
    OIB list, 417–418
    recordings, 421–423
    title output and prices, 384
Chinese American Librarians Association
    (CALA), 254, 274
Chrastka, John, 212, 216
Chronicle of Higher Education Jobs, 226
Chronicling America website, 39
Circulating Ideas podcast, 224
circulation statistics, 289, 322–323
CLA (Catholic Library Association), 274
CLA (Croatian Library Association), 113
CLIR. *See* Council on Library and
    Information Resources
CLIR Issues, 152
CLLE (Center for Learning, Literacy, and
    Engagement), 32–33, 44
CMD (Collection Management Division), 31
Coalition for Networked Information (CNI),
    274
Coffman, Elizabeth, 45
collaboration. *See* partnerships and
    collaboration
Collection Development Office (CDO), 38

Collection Management Division (CMD), 31
collections, collection development
  DTIC, 98
  LC, 33–34, 37–38
  NAL, 53–54
  NLE, 102
  public libraries, 289
Collins, Susan, 181
community engagement
  future trends, 10
  during pandemic, 6–9
  voter engagement, 213–215
Community Library (ID), 311
computer use. See Internet and computer
      access
conferences
  ALA, 106–108, 116
  ALISE, 155–156, 157
  EveryLibrary, 216
  IBBY, 173–174
  IFLA, 159–160
  Open Education, 143
Congressional Relations Office (CRO), 31
Congressional Research Service (CRS), 31,
      35, 74
Consumer Price Index, 331
copyright law
  advocacy efforts, 131, 162
  legislation affecting, 182–184
  virtual programming and, 6
Copyright Office, U.S., 31, 33, 35–36
CORD-19 (COVID-19 Open Research
      Dataset), 64
coronavirus. See COVID-19 and libraries
COSLA (Chief Officers of State Library
      Associations), 215
Council on Library and Information
      Resources (CLIR), 145–152
  awards given, 274–275
  COVID-19 response, 145–148
  fellowships and grants, 145–148, 254
  initiatives and partnerships, 148–152
  publications, 152
COVID (Re)Collections (CLIR blog), 152
COVID-19 and libraries. See also CARES
      Act; trade publishing; specific
      organizations
  closures and restrictions, 3–4
  community needs, 6–9
  FDLP libraries, 72
  FEDLINK survey, 50
  infodemic response, 8–9
  initial virus outbreak, 3

LAC, 167–170
LC, 30–34
  Libraries Build Business, 185–186
  NLM, 62, 63–64, 68
  post-pandemic services, 9–11, 114
  REALM (reopening) project, 5, 204–205
  response to challenges, 4–6
  2020 Census and, 24
  2021 outlook and, 187
COVID-19 Open Research Dataset
      (CORD-19), 64
Cox, Christopher, 10
Craft, Jerry, 126
CRO (Congressional Relations Office), 31
Croatian Library Association (CLA), 113
CRS (Congressional Research Service), 31,
      35, 74
cultural heritage protection, 162
Cummins, Jeanine, 17
Cumsky-Whitlock, Jake, 125
Cyberpunk Librarian podcast, 224

D

Dallanegra-Sanger, Joy, 121–122
David M. Rubenstein Special Response
      Awards, 46
Davis, Gabriele, 49–50
Davis, Marley, 119
D'Azzo Research Library (DRL), 48–49
Defense Technical Information Center
      (DTIC), 97–100
DEL (Documenting Endangered
      Languages), 193
Department of Defense Information Analysis
      Centers (DoD IACs), 99–100
DiAngelo, Robin, 20
digital collections and initiatives
  CLIR grant competition, 145–146
  COVID-19 effects on, 6, 10
  DLME, 150
  ERIC, 103–104
  KHI, 150–151
  LAC, 168–169
  LC, 34
  NAL, 54, 56–59
  NARA, 82, 84, 85
  NEH, 199–200
  newspaper archives, 39, 191
  NTIS, 79–81
  Trustworthy Digital Repository
      certification, 76

Digital Library Federation (DLF),
148–150
Digital Library of the Middle East (DLME),
150
Digital Millennium Copyright Act (DMCA),
131
Digital Opportunity Equity Recognition
(DOER) award, 7, 182
Digital Public Library of America (DPLA),
74
Digitizing Hidden Collections and Archives,
145–146
DigiTop, 57
disabilities in readers
information access and, 130
NLS services, 42
young adult literature, 173, 176
disaster relief, 112, 162
discussion lists, 227
diversity, equity, inclusion. *See also* social
justice and inequality
ABA actions, 125–126
ALA programs, 107, 111–112
ARL advocacy, 131
ARL programs, 134–135
ARL statement, 128
PLA statement, 116
DLF (Digital Library Federation),
148–150
DLME (Digital Library of the Middle East),
150
DMCA (Digital Millennium Copyright Act),
131
DocsTeach, 87
Documenting Endangered Languages
(DEL), 193
DoD IACs (Department of Defense
Information Analysis Centers),
99–100
DOER (Digital Opportunity Equity
Recognition) award, 7, 182
Dollar General Literacy Foundation, 113
Dowling, Michael, 165
DPLA (Digital Public Library of America),
74
DRL (D'Azzo Research Library),
48–49
DTIC (Defense Technical Information
Center), 97–100

E

Early Childhood Longitudinal Study
(ECLS), 95
e-books. *See also* digital collections and
initiatives
academic book prices, 342t–343t, 346–347
average prices, 331, 337, 360t–361t
library lending, 6, 323–324
licensing and library access, 184–185
title output, per volume prices, 382t–383t,
384
titles cataloged, 41–42
top ten lists (2020), 427–428
ECIP (Electronic Cataloging-in-Publication),
41–42, 74
ECLS (Early Childhood Longitudinal
Study), 95
EDSITEment, 193
Education Longitudinal Study of 2002 (ELS),
96
Education Resources Information Center
(ERIC), 103–104
EDUCAUSE, 151, 226, 275–276
election 2020, 186
Electronic Cataloging-in-Publication
(ECIP), 41–42, 74
Electronic Records Archives (ERA), 84
ELS (Education Longitudinal Study of
2002), 96
EMIERT (Ethnic and Multicultural
Information and Exchange Round
Table), 264
Enoch Pratt Free Library (MD), 318
equity initiatives. *See* diversity, equity,
inclusion; social justice and
inequality
ERA (Electronic Records Archives), 84
E-rate program, 182
ERIC (Education Resources Information
Center), 103–104
ERT (Exhibits Round Table), 264
Ethnic and Multicultural Information and
Exchange Round Table (EMIERT),
264
EveryLibrary, 212–217
administration, 212
campaigns, 213–216
conference, 216
COVID-19 response, 213
funding and reporting, 217
history, 212–213
mission, 216

strategic priorities, 217
vision statement, 212
EveryLibrary Institute, 216
Exhibits Round Table (ERT), 264

F

Fairfield Area Library (VA), 318
Farrell, Maggie, 106
Farrow, Dylan, 18
Farrow, Ronan, 18
Federal Communications Commission, 7, 182
Federal Depository Library Program (FDLP)
  Academy, 75
  COVID-19 support, 72
  GPO distribution services, 77–78
  history, 71–72
  LibGuides, 76
  libraries, 72–74, 102
  national collection strategy, 74–75
  Web Archive, 77
Federal Librarian of the Year, 49
Federal Library and Information Network
  (FEDLINK), 46, 48–51
Federal Library Technician of the Year, 49–50
Federal Library / Information Center of the
  Year, 48–49
Federal Records Centers (FRCs), 89
Federal Register, 90–91
Federal-State Partnership, 193
FEDLINK, 46, 48–51
fellowships
  American-Scandinavian Foundation, 252
  CLIR, 146–148, 149–150, 254
  IFLA/OCLC, 162
  NEH, 199
fiction
  notable books, 401–406
  output and pricing, 384
films
  awards, 45
  National Film Registry, 40–41
  preservation programs, 36
  production grants, 192
financial data. *See* library finances
Findley, Erica, 212
Fiocco, Jamie, 121–122, 125
Fitzgerald, Isaac, 126
Five Days (Moore), 106
Flannery (film), 45
Floyd, George, 18, 38, 111
Food and Nutrition Information Center
  (FNIC), 55

Food Safety Research Information Office
  (FSRIO), 55–56
FRCs (Federal Records Centers), 89
Freedom to Read Foundation, 264
Friends of the Library, 110
Friends of the National Library of Medicine,
  276
FSRIO (Food Safety Research Information
  Office), 55–56
funding. *See* library finances

G

Gail Borden Public Library District (IL), 25
Garcia-Febo, Loida, 22
Gay, Lesbian, Bisexual, and Transgender
  Round Table (GLBTRT), 264
genealogy records, 89
Ghikas, Mary W., 110
Glassdoor, 226
global book famine, 130
government agencies. *See specific agencies
  or libraries*
Government Documents Round Table
  (GODORT), 264–265
government information
  DTIC, 98–100
  FDLP Web archive, 77
  GPO, 72–73
  NARA, 82–92
government job listings, 226
government libraries
  acquisition expenditures, 308t–309t
  number in U.S., Canada, 285–287
government regulation. *See* legislation and
  regulations
govinfo.gov, 75–76
GPO. *See* U.S. Government Publishing
  Office
Graham, Bradley, 125
grants
  ALA, 113–114
  ALISE, 156
  CLIR, 145–146
  IFLA, 162–163
  IMLS, 202–204, 206–207, 208–209
  Library Census Equity Grants, 24–25
  NARA, 91–92
  NEH, 114, 190–193, 198–200
  NLM, 68–69
Gray, Freddie, 106
Green Library Award, 163

H

Hachette Book Group (HBG), 17–18
Hall, Tracie D., 3, 106, 108
HALO (Help a Library Worker Out), 213
Handshake website, 226
Hans Christian Andersen Award, 172, 174,
    176, 431
hardcover books
    average prices, 337, 338t–339t
    title output, per volume prices, 371,
        373t–376t, 384
Haverford College library (PA), 318
Hawkeye Community College Library (IA),
    7
Hayden, Carla, 23, 37
Hayden Library (ASU), 318
HBCU Library Alliance, 149, 151
HBG (Hachette Book Group), 17–18
Help a Library Worker Out (HALO), 213
Henderson, Jeff, 106–107
Hicks, Elaine, 9
higher education
    ARL advocacy, 131–132
    job listings, 226
Hill, Allison K., 121, 123, 124
History Hub, 85–86
Holding Space Tour, 106, 108
Houghton Mifflin Harcourt (HMH), 16, 17
How to Be an Antiracist (Kendi), 20
humanities (term), 189–190
humanities councils, 193–197
humanities programming, 198–199

I

I Love Libraries, 111
I Love My Librarian Awards, 107, 281
IAL (Innovative Approaches to Literacy),
    179–180
IASL (International Association of School
    Librarianship), 276
IBBY. See International Board on Books for
    Young People
IBBY Honour List, 173, 174, 176
IBBY-Asahi Reading Promotion Award,
    172–173, 174, 176
IBBY-iRead Reading Promoter Award, 173,
    174, 176
iFederation, 157
IFLA. See International Federation of
    Library Associations and Institutions
IFLA Dynamic Unit and Impact Award, 163

IFLA Journal, 165
IFLA PressReader International Marketing
    Award, 162
IFLA/Systematic Award, 163
IFRT (Intellectual Freedom Round Table), 265
ILL (interlibrary loan), 131, 165
IMLS. See Institute of Museum and Library
    Services
IMLS News, 211
Immigrant Learning Center (MA), 46
INALJ.com, 225
inclusion initiatives. See diversity, equity,
    inclusion
Indeed, 226
Indies First, 124
inequality. See social justice and inequality
infodemic, 8–9, 10–11
information access
    educational materials, 139–143
    government information, 72–73, 77,
        82–92, 98–100
    IFLA advocacy, 162
    LC, 31–32, 41, 42
    Marrakesh Treaty, 130
    NLM, 66
    open scholarship, 132–133
    open science by design, 133
    research data, 104, 140–143
Information Security Oversight Office
    (ISOO), 83
Innovative Approaches to Literacy (IAL),
    179–180
Institute of Museum and Library Services
    (IMLS), 201–211
    awards given, 276
    COVID-19 response, 202–205, 207–208
    funding, 179–180
    Grants to States program, 206–207
    interagency collaboration, 209
    library services, 205, 207–208
    mission and vision, 201
    museum services, 208–209
    policy research, 209–210
    public libraries report (2017), 288–291
    SaveIMLS.org, 215
    SLAA report (2018), 291–294
    strategic goals, 201–202
    surveys, 210, 288–294
    website and publications, 211
Intellectual Freedom Round Table (IFRT), 265
interdisciplinary job listings, 226
interlibrary loan (ILL), 131, 165

International Association of School
    Librarianship (IASL), 276
International Board on Books for Young
    People (IBBY), 171–176
  awards given, 172–173, 174, 276
  Congresses, 173–174
  COVID-19 response, 174–175
  history, 171–172
  mission and programs, 172–173
  U.S. section, 175–176
International Children's Book Day, 173
International Federation of Library
        Associations and Institutions (IFLA),
        159–166
  advocacy, 162
  awards given, 162–163, 276
  conference, 159–160
  core values, 159
  discussion lists, 227
  governance, 160–161
  grants, 162–163
  long-standing projects, 165–166
  membership and finances, 163–165
  personnel and governance, 165
  standards, 161–162
  strategy and global vision, 160
International Standard Book Numbering
        (ISBN), 389–393, 392f
International Standard Serial Number
        (ISSN), 394–396
Internet and computer access
  advocacy and legislation, 181–182
  ALA program, 114
  COVID-19 effects on, 6–7, 9, 111
  in public libraries, 290, 323–324
  2020 Census and, 23–24
Internet Archive, 184
Iraqi-Jewish archives, 150
ISBN (International Standard Book
        Numbering), 389–393, 392f
ISOO (Information Security Oversight
        Office), 83
ISSN (International Standard Serial
        Number), 394–396

J

Jay Jordan IFLA/OCLC fellowships, 162
Jefferson, Julius C., Jr., 4, 106, 108, 109,
    182
JELIS (*Journal of Education for Library and
        Information Science*), 155

job listings, 225–227. *See also* library
    employment
John W. Kluge Prize, 45
Joint Committee on the Library, 35
Joliet Public Library (IL), 7
Joseph W. Lippincott Award, 110
*Journal of Education for Library and
        Information Science* (JELIS), 155

K

Karp, Jonathan, 16
Keefe, Karen Kleckner, 10
Kendi, Ibram X., 20
Khan-Cullors, Patrisse, 126
Kluge Prize, 45
Knight, Melanie, 125
Kossuth, Joanne, 148
Kurdish Heritage Institute (KHI), 150–151

L

LAC (Library and Archives Canada), 167–170
language preservation, 193
Lavine/Ken Burns Prize for Film, 45
law libraries. *See* American Association of
        Law Libraries
Law Library of Congress, 35, 73
LC. *See* Library of Congress
LCA (Library Copyright Alliance), 131
Leading Change Institute (LCI), 151
Learning and Innovation Office (LC), 44
Legal Serials Service Index, 336–337, 336t
legislation and regulations
  ALA statements, 114
  copyright law, 182–184
  diversity, equity, inclusion, 131
  e-book access, 184–185
  election 2020 and, 186
  federal funding, 36–37, 179–181
  Internet access, 181–182
Leicester B. Holland Prize, 46
Leitner, Gerald, 160, 165
Lepman, Jella, 171
Levin, Andy, 180
LHRT (Library History Round Table), 265–266
Librarian Interview Podcast, 224
Librarian Reserve Corps, 9
librarians. *See also* library staff
  awards to, 110, 281
  public, 290–291
  school (*See* school librarians)

Librarian's Guide to Teaching podcast, 224
Librarians of the Year (2020), 9
libraries. *See also* COVID-19 and libraries;
   specific types of libraries or specific
   library names
  disaster relief, 112
  federal depository, 72–74, 102
  IMLS services, 205, 207–208
  number in U.S., Canada, 285–287
  2020 census and, 22–27, 185
Libraries Build Business, 185–186
Libraries Respond, 111
Libraries Transform campaign, 111
Library Advocacy and Funding Conference,
   216
Library and Archives Canada (LAC),
   167–170
library and information science education
  accredited master's programs, 245–250
  experiences and soft skills in, 237
  graduate job search, 239–240
  graduates and job placements, 241t–242t
  internships, 237
  library work experience and, 236–237,
   239t
  scholarship and award recipients,
   256–281
  scholarship sources, 251–255
  second career seekers, 231
  student demographics, 230
Library and Information Technology
   Association (LITA), 265
library buildings
  cost summary, 320t
  COVID-19 adaptations, 10
  current trends, 310
  funding sources, 321t
  new, renovated public, 310–318,
   312t–313t, 314t–316t
  renovated academic, 317t, 318–319
Library Card Sign-up Month, 109
Library Census Equity Grants, 24–25
Library Copyright Alliance (LCA), 131
library employment
  career advice resources, 222–225
  COVID-19 and, 240
  employment rates, 230–231
  gender salary disparity, 221, 228, 233
  job listing sites, 225–227
  job placements, 228t, 229t, 234t–235t, 240
  job satisfaction, 231
  job search, 239
  job settings and duties, 233–236

Library Journal survey highlights, 221,
   228
  library work experience and, 236–237
  salaries, 229t, 230, 232t, 233, 233t, 238t,
   243t–244t, 328–329
  school librarians, 295–300, 296t–297t,
   298t–299t
library finances
  acquisition expenditures, 301, 302t–309t
  ballot measures and political action,
   213–215
  federal funding, 36–37, 179–181
  public libraries, 288–289, 326–329
  SLAAs, 292
Library History Round Table (LHRT),
   265–266
Library Journal (LJ), 221, 228, 277
Library Leadership and Management
   Association (LLAMA), 266
Library Materials Price Index (LMPI)
   Editorial Board, 331, 370
Library of America, 192
Library of Congress (LC), 29–47
  access, 31–32, 41, 42
  awards given, 45–46, 277
  budget and funding, 36–37
  cataloging, 41–42
  collections, 37–38
  contact information, 47
  COVID-19 response, 30–34
  creativity promotion, 44
  educational outreach, 44–45
  highlights (2020), 29–30
  lifelong learning promotion, 44
  preservation programs, 36, 38–41
  reference services, 41
  scholarship promotion, 44
  service units, 35–36
  social media, 43–44
  websites, 42–43
Library of Congress Lavine / Ken Burns
   Prize for Film, 45
Library of Congress Prize for American
   Fiction, 45
library patron visits, 289–290, 322–323
Library Pros podcast, 224
Library Research Round Table (LRRT),
   266
Library Services and Content Management
   (LSCM). *See* U.S. Government
   Publishing Office
Library Services and Technology Act
   (LSTA), 179–180, 215

library staff, 290–291, 293, 325–326
library surveys
   academic libraries, 93–95
   public libraries, 210, 288–291
   school library media centers, 95–96
   SLAAs, 210, 291–294
Library Worklife (ALA), 223
LinkedIn Jobs, 226
Linking our Libraries podcast, 224–225
LIS programs. *See* library and information
   science education
Lison, Barbara, 165
Listen List Council, 403
LITA (Library and Information Technology
   Association), 265
literacy awards, 46
literacy programs, 44, 113
literary awards and prizes, 429–457
   IBBY, 172–173, 174
   LC, 45–46
   YALSA, 413
LJ *(Library Journal)*, 221, 228, 277
LLAMA (Library Leadership and
   Management Association), 266
LMPI (Library Materials Price Index)
   Editorial Board, 331, 370
LOC. *See* Library of Congress
Loree, Sara, 9
Louisville Free Public Library (KY), 310
Lozada, Carlos, 9
LRRT (Library Research Round Table), 266
LSC Communications, 19
LSTA (Library Services and Technology
   Act), 179–180, 215
Lucas, Lisa, 18
Lundén, Inga, 163

M

Mackenzie, Christine, 165
Macmillan Publishers, 16, 17, 184
Manchin, Joe, 181, 182
Mandl, Helen, 165
Map and Geospatial Information Round
   Table (MAGIRT), 266
Marion Public Library (IA), 112
Marlatt, Greta, 49
Marrakesh Treaty, 130
Massachusetts Black Librarians' Network,
   254

master's degree programs, 245–250. *See
   also* library and information science
   education
Material Acquisition Request Service
   (MARS), 38
Material Memory (CLIR podcast), 152
McGraw-Hill, 143
McKinney, L. I., 18
media literacy, 113
Medical Library Association (MLA), 223,
   254, 277–278
MedlinePlus, 66
mega job sites, 226
Mehta, Sonny, 16
Mellon Fellowships for Dissertation
   Research, 147–148
Mendy, Nix, 134
Metropolitan New York Library Council
   (METRO) jobs, 225
Miller, Chanel, 107
MLA (Medical Library Association), 223,
   254, 277–278
MLIS Skills at Work, 223
MLSA (Museum and Library Services Act),
   201
MMLIS. *See* library and information science
   education
Monster job site, 226
Montgomery-Floyd Regional Library (VA),
   8
Moore, Wes, 106
Mountain Plains Library Association,
   254
Museum and Library Services Act (MLSA),
   201
museums
   IMLS CARES grants, 204
   IMLS museum services, 208–209
   National Archives Museum, 86–87
Music Library Association, 278–279

N

NAABPI (North American Academic Books
   Price Index), 346
NAL. *See* National Agricultural Library
NALDC (National Agricultural Library
   Digital Collection), 58
NALT (National Agricultural Library
   Thesaurus), 58–59
NARA. *See* National Archives and Records
   Administration

National Agricultural Library (NAL), 52–61
  collections, 53–54
  digital products, 56–58
  information technology, 60–61
  library services, 55–56
  networks of cooperation, 59–60
  responsibilities, 52
National Agricultural Library Digital
    Collection (NALDC), 58
National Agricultural Library Thesaurus
    (NALT), 58–59
National Archives and Records
    Administration (NARA), 82–92
  administration, 92
  grants, 91–92
  mission and holdings, 82
  publications, 90–91
  records and access, 83–90
  research division and centers, 84–85,
    87–88
  social media use, 86
  strategic goals, 82–83
  website, 85
National Archives Museum, 86–87
National Association to Promote Library and
    Information Services to Latinos and
    the Spanish-Speaking (REFORMA),
    279
National Center for Education Statistics
    (NCES), 93–96
National Center for Families Learning (KY),
    46
National Declassification Center (NDC), 83
National Digital Newspaper Program
    (NDNP), 39, 191
National Digital Stewardship Alliance
    (NDSA), 150
National Emergency Library, 6, 184
National Endowment for the Humanities
    (NEH), 189–200
  Challenge Grants, 191, 199
  divisions and offices, 197–200
  mission, 189
  programs funded by, 114, 190–193
  state humanities councils, 193–197
National Film Preservation Act (1988), 36
National Film Registry, 40–41
National Foundation on the Arts and the
    Humanities, 190
National Friends of Libraries Week, 110
National Historical Publications and Records
    Commission (NHPRC), 91–92

National Invasive Species Information
    Center (NISIC), 56
National Library of Education (NLE),
    101–102
National Library of Medicine (NLM), 62–70
  administration, 70
  COVID-19 response, 62, 63–64, 68
  functions, 62–63
  information access promotion, 66
  information delivery, 65–66
  research and development, 66–68
  research grants, 68–69
  research management and support, 69–70
National Library Service for the Blind and
    Print Disabled (NLS), 42, 279
National Library Week (NLW), 110
National Recording Preservation Act (2000),
    36
National Recording Registry, 39–40
National Teacher and Principal Survey
    (NTPS), 95
National Technical Information Service
    (NTIS), 79–81
National Technical Reports Library (NTRL),
    79–81
Native American/Native Hawaiian CARES
    grants, 203–204
NCES (National Center for Education
    Statistics), 93–96
NDC (National Declassification Center), 83
NDNP (National Digital Newspaper
    Program), 39, 191
NDSA (National Digital Stewardship
    Alliance), 150
NEH. See National Endowment for the
    Humanities
New Members Round Table (NMRT),
    266–267
New York Public Library (NYPL), 4, 24
newspaper archives, 39, 191
NHPRC (National Historical Publications
    and Records Commission), 91–92
Nieto, Nadxieli, 17
NISIC (National Invasive Species
    Information Center), 56
NLE (National Library of Education),
    101–102
NLM. See National Library of Medicine
NLS (National Library Service for the Blind
    and Print Disabled), 42, 279
NLW (National Library Week), 110
NMRT (New Members Round Table),
    266–267

Noble, Safiya, 134
North American Academic Books Price
    Index (NAABPI), 346
Notable Books Council, 401–402
Notable Children's Digital Media, 424–425
NSAIG jobs, 226
NTIS (National Technical Information
    Service), 79–81
NTPS (National Teacher and Principal
    Survey), 95
NTRL (National Technical Reports Library),
    79–81
Nutrition.gov, 56
NYPL (New York Public Library), 4, 24

O

Occupational Outlook Handbook, 223
Office for Diversity, Literacy and Outreach
    Services (ODLOS), 111–112, 267
Office for Information Technology Policy,
    267
Office for Literacy and Outreach Services
    (OLOS), 267
Office of Federal-State Partnership, 193
Office of Government Information Services
    (OGIS), 83–84
Office of the Federal Register, 91
Ohio State Library, 3–4
OIB (Outstanding International Books) list,
    175–176, 417–418
OLOS (Office for Literacy and Outreach
    Services), 267
Onorati, Christine, 125
open access. See information access
Open Access Week, 143
Open Education Conference, 143
Open Education Leadership Program, 143
open scholarship. See information access
Outstanding Books for Young People with
    Disabilities, 173, 176
Outstanding International Books (OIB) list,
    175–176, 417–418
Owens, Victoria, 163

P

PACs (political action committees).
    See EveryLibrary
Pakistan Reading Project, 46
paperback books
    average prices, 337, 354t–357t

title output, per volume prices, 371,
    377t–379t, 384
partnerships and collaboration
    ALISE, 157
    CLIR, 148–152
    GPO, 72–74
    IFLA, 164
    IMLS, 209
    LAC, 169
    NAL, 59–60
    NEH, 193–197
Patterson, James, 123
Peggy Barber Tribute Grant, 113
Penguin Random House (PRH), 16, 18
Pérez-Salmerón, Glòria, 160, 165
periodical and serial prices, price indexes
    average price percent change, 331
    legal serials, 336–337, 336t
    online serials, 366t–367t
    price index use, 370
    price trends, 362–363
    serials, 362, 364t–365t
    USPPI, 332–336, 334t–335t
Perlmutter, Shira, 33, 183
Phoenix Public Library, 25
Pietsch, Michael, 18
Pillar, Arlene, 176
PLA. See Public Library Association
PLS (Public Libraries Survey), 210
podcasts as career resource, 224–225
political action committees (PACs).
    See EveryLibrary
Postdoctoral Fellowship Program, 146–147
PPO (Public Programs Office), 268
Pratham Books, 46
preservation programs
    LC, 36, 38–41
    NAL, 54
    NEH, 192–193, 198
Preservation Week, 110
presidential libraries, 88
presidential papers projects, 191
PRH (Penguin Random House), 16, 18
price indexes. See book prices; periodical
    and serial prices
print books sales, 19–20. See also book
    prices; book production
privacy issues, 132
Prize for American Fiction, 45
professional development, 10, 156
Pub Workers for Justice (PW4J), 18
PubAg, 58
PubDefense, 99

public libraries
    acquisition expenditures, 302t–303t
    buildings, 310–318, 312t–313t, 314t–316t
    IMLS report highlights, 288–291
    number in U.S., Canada, 285–287
    state rankings, 322–329
Public Libraries Podcast, 224
Public Libraries Survey (PLS), 210
Public Library Association (PLA)
    awards given, 267–268
    career advice resources, 223–224
    conference, 108
    highlights (2020), 116–117
Public Programs Office (PPO), 268
publishing. See trade publishing
#PublishingPaidMe, 18
PubMed, 65
PW4J (Pub Workers for Justice), 18

Q

Quad, 19

R

Racial Equity Framework, 134–135
racism. See diversity, equity, inclusion;
    social justice and inequality
rare book collections, 54
Rare Books and Manuscripts Section
    (RBMS), 223
Rather, Dan, 124
reading and discussion programs (NEH),
    191
Reading Rooms Committee (RRC), 32
REALM (REopening Archives, Libraries,
    and Museums) project, 5, 204–205
recordings
    National Recording Preservation Act,
        36
    National Recording Registry, 39–40
    notable for children, 421–423
    Recordings at Risk, 146
Reed, Jack, 180, 181
Reference and User Services Association
    (RUSA), 117, 268–269, 401–403
REFORMA (National Association to
    Promote Library and Information
    Services to Latinos and the Spanish-
    Speaking), 279
Reidy, Carolyn, 16

REopening Archives, Libraries, and
    Museums (REALM) project, 5,
    204–205
research data access
    ERIC role in, 104
    open science by design, 133
    PubDefense, 99
    SPARC advocacy, 139–143
research libraries. See Association of
    Research Libraries
RIC (Rural Information Center), 56
Richland Main Library (SC), 311
Roanoke Public Libraries (VA), 310
Robert B. Downs Intellectual Freedom
    Award, 281
Room to Read, 46
RRC (Reading Rooms Committee), 32
Rural Information Center (RIC), 56
RUSA (Reference and User Services
    Association), 117, 268–269, 401–403

S

SAA (Society of American Archivists), 223,
    254–255, 279–280
Salaam, Yusef, 126
salaries. See library employment
Salary Survey Task Force, 135
SAN (Standard Address Number), 397–399
San José State University (SJSU) School of
    Information, 223
Sargent, John, 16, 184
SASS (Schools and Staffing Survey), 95
SaveIMLS.org, 215
#SaveIndieBookstores, 123
SaveSchoolLibrarians.org, 215
Scholarly Publishing and Academic
    Resources Coalition (SPARC),
    139–144
    activities and outcomes (2020), 142–144
    COVID-19 response, 139
    governance, 144
    mission, 139
    priorities, 140–142
    SPARC-ACRL forums, 144
    strategy, 139–140
scholarships
    ALA, 112
    NEH, 191–192
    recipients (2020), 256–281
    sources for, 251–255
school librarians
    advocacy for, 215–216

employment status, 297–298, 298t–299t
IASL, 276
School Librarians United podcast, 225
state impacts on, 295–296, 296t–297t
school libraries. *See also* COVID-19 and
    libraries
  NCES survey, 95–96
  2020 Census programs, 25
School Library Media Center Survey, 95
Schools and Staffing Survey (SASS), 95
Schwartz, Meredith, 4, 9
SDGs (United Nations 2030 Sustainable
    Development Goals), 110
senior services, 8
serials. *See* periodical and serial prices
Sewell, Rhonda, 23
Sharjah Virtual International Forum, 109
Shibutani, Maia and Alex, 119
Silent Books project, 173, 176
Simon & Schuster (S&S), 16, 18
SimplyHired, 227
SJSU (San José State University) School of
    Information, 223
SLA (Special Libraries Association), 226,
    255, 280–281
SLAA. *See* State Library Administrative
    Agency
SLIDE project, 295–300, 296t–297t,
    298t–299t
social justice and inequality. *See also*
    diversity, equity, inclusion
  in trade publishing, 17–19, 21
  libraries' response to, 7
social media use, 43–44, 86, 154–155
social service assistance, 7
Society of American Archivists (SAA), 223,
    254–255, 279–280
SPARC. *See* Scholarly Publishing and
    Academic Resources Coalition
special collections, 53–54
special libraries
  acquisition expenditures, 306t–307t
  number in U.S., Canada, 286–287
Special Libraries Association (SLA), 226,
    255, 280–281
Spectrum Scholarship Program, 112
S&S (Simon & Schuster), 16, 18
Standard Address Number (SAN),
    397–399
STAR Net STEAM Equity Project, 113
Starks, Geoffrey, 182
state humanities councils, 193–197

State Library Administrative Agency
    (SLAA)
  CARES grants to, 202–203
  grant funding, 206–208
  IMLS report highlights, 291–294
  survey, 210
state rankings, of public libraries, 322–329
STEAM programs, 113
STEM books, 347
Steny H. Hoyer Research Center, 88
STM books, 348–350
Student Exchange Visitor Program,
    132–133
students, in open access initiatives, 142
surveys. *See* library surveys
Sweeney, Patrick "PC," 212, 216

T

T is for Training podcast, 225
teacher programs (NEH), 191, 197–198
Teaching with Primary Sources (TPS), 44
Technical Report Archive & Image Library
    (TRAIL), 74
technology. *See also* Internet and computer
    access
  NAL use, 60–61
  NEH support of, 192
teen/young adult literature
  advocacy of, 171–176
  Alex Awards, 413
  audiobooks, 413–416
  best fiction, 404–406
  for reluctant readers, 407–412
Temple, Karyn, 183
textbooks
  prices, price indexes, 344t–345t, 347
  SPARC advocacy, 142–143
Theatre Library Association, 281
thesauri, 58–59, 99
Tigani, Tegan, 125
Tillis, Tom, 182
Tiny Books to the Rescue project, 174
Toledo Lucas County Public Library,
    311
TPS (Teaching with Primary Sources), 44
trade publishing
  consolidation of, 16
  COVID-19 effects on, 18–20
  future of, 20–21
  social justice demands, 17–19
  year 2020 overview, 16–17

TRAIL (Technical Report Archive & Image Library), 74
Tribal Connect Act, 182
Trump administration budget proposals, 179, 215
Trustworthy Digital Repository (TRD) certification, 76

U

United for Libraries, 117, 269
United Nations 2030 Sustainable Development Goals (SDGs), 110
United States Agricultural Information Network (USAIN), 60
United States Board on Books for Young People (USBBY), 175–176, 281, 417–418
University of California Berkeley Library, 26
U.S. College Books Price Index, 350, 351t–353t
U.S. Copyright Office, 31, 33, 35–36
U.S. Department of Agriculture.
    See National Agricultural Library
U.S. Department of Labor, 223
U.S. Government Publishing Office (GPO), 71–78
  Catalog of U.S. Government Publications, 76–77
  FDLP libraries and services, 71–75, 76, 77–78
  govinfo.gov, 75–76
  history and functions, 71
U.S. Periodical Price Index (USPPI), 332–336, 334t–335t
USAIN (United States Agricultural Information Network), 60
USAJobs.gov, 226
USBBY (United States Board on Books for Young People), 175–176, 281, 417–418

V

Veterans History Project (VHP), 36
virtual programming
  ALA conference, 107–108
  benefits of, 10
  challenges of, 5–6

IBBY, 174–175
LAC, 169
LC, 31, 32–33
volunteers and COVID-19, 8
voter engagement, 186, 213–215
Voucher Scheme, 165
Voyager integrated library management system, 60–61

W

Warner Research Center, 87–88
Water and Agriculture Information Center (WAIC), 56
Waukegan Public Library (IL), 23
Waunakee Public Library (WI), 311
Weisberg, Don, 16
White Fragility (DiAngelo), 20
Whitehead, Colson, 45
Wilburn, Thomas, 6
Witt, Steven W., 165
WLIC (World Library and Information Congress), 159–160
Women's National Book Association (WNBA) Award, 281
Wong, Patricia "Patty" M., 106
Woodberry, Evelyn, 163
World Library and Information Congress (WLIC), 159–160
writings, of prominent Americans, 192

Y

YALSA (Young Adult Library Services Association)
  audiobook list, 413–416
  awards given, 413
  best fiction list, 404–406
  books for reluctant readers, 407–412
  highlights (2020), 117–118, 269–270
young adult literature. See teen/young adult literature
Your Library Career, 224

Z

Zip Recruiter, 227
Zoboi, Ibi, 126